NORD
Compendium
of Rare Diseases
and Disorders

NORD

Compendium

of Rare Diseases and Disorders

The National Organization
for Rare Disorders

Mary Ann Liebert, Inc. publishers

ISBN: 0-913113-41-7

Printed in the United States of America

Contents

Foreword

The publication of the *NORD Compendium of Rare Diseases and Disorders* acknowledges the valuable contribution made by the National Organization for Rare Disorders (NORD) to the rare disease community. Families, patients, physicians, and countless caregivers whose lives have been impacted by one of the approximately 6000 rare diseases (a disease that affects fewer than 200,000 Americans) are all aware; NORD literally *is* the rare disease community.

This amazingly influential coalition evolved from an affiliation of national health agencies and support groups that joined together to form a national foundation, following the success of their unrelenting efforts to establish orphan drug legislation. The collective force of this organization resulted in congressional passage of the *Orphan Drug Act*, and its being signed into law by President Reagan in 1983. NORD's history is a story of the power of patients with rare diseases, who—although individually few in number—were able to use their combined strength and ability to influence the law. The *Orphan Drug Act* constituted a commitment to millions of Americans that they would not be ignored because treatment of their disease is not profitable. In the 10 years prior to passage of the *Orphan Drug Act*, no more than 10 products were developed to treat rare diseases without federal government assistance. The *Orphan Drug Act* amended the 1938 *Federal Food, Drug and Cosmetic Act*, providing incentives for the pharmaceutical industry to develop drugs that otherwise have limited commercial value. It established for the first time in the United States a Federal federal Government government policy to cooperate and assist in a program to facilitate the development of drugs for rare diseases.

Since 1982, NORD and its member organizations have been extraordinarily helpful legislatively for the FDA: in its implementation of the *Orphan Drug Act* through the FDA Office of Orphan Products Development, and its ongoing endeavor to correct the deficiencies and neglect suffered by patients with orphan diseases. More recently, NORD played a key role in generating support for the 2002 *Rare Diseases Act* that authorized the NIH Office of Rare Disease, and increased authorization for funding for the FDA Office of Orphan Products Development Grant Program. The *Orphan Drug Act* has had a significant impact on the treatment of patients with serious rare and life threatening diseases. Although the scarcity of products to treat rare diseases remains a worldwide problem, the passage of the U.S. *Orphan Drug Act* in 1983, has led to the FDA market approval of 288 drug and biological products to treat rare diseases. These products are available to treat a total patient population of more than 14 million. In addition, nearly 1400 products for rare diseases are currently being developed and tested for future FDA approval.

Through its ongoing efforts as a volunteer organization, NORD serves as a vital and effective link between rare disease patient groups, governmental representatives, and the pharmaceutical industry. By providing advocacy on issues such as funding for rare disease research, NORD leadership enables individuals and organizations concerned about specific disorders to work together for the greater good of all. Many of the organization's participating rare disease groups also provide assistance to FDA researchers in locating patients willing to participate in orphan drug clinical trials. NORD's sponsorship of medication assistance programs has helped thousands of patients obtain medications they are not otherwise able to afford, or which are not yet on the market.

The new *NORD Compendium of Rare Diseases and Disorders* lists and briefly describes a large number of rare diseases with and without approved treatment products, and provides information on obtaining additional information from patient organizations focusing on specific disorders. The success of the past 23 years is hailed throughout the world by patients with rare diseases, as well as their families and the health care workers who struggle with them. I am proud and honored to inscribe this printed database that will support their ongoing efforts with evidence of support for all.

Marlene E. Haffner, MD, MPH
Director, Office of Orphan Products Development
U.S. Food and Drug Administration (FDA)

The Need for Reliable and Useful Information About Rare Diseases and Disorders

Physicians and other health care providers are confronted with the need for accurate and timely information on rare diseases to successfully help patients and family members cope with these conditions. This information, on over an estimated 6500 inherited or acquired rare diseases, has become readily available to all in published literature and on the Internet. Patients now are considered active partners with medical professionals in their own health care decisions. The reliable and useful information from various sources contained in the *NORD Compendium of Rare Diseases and Disorders* will lead patients to a better understanding of their rare disease or condition and will bring about changes in their approach to coping on a day-to-day basis until a treatment becomes available.

If progress is to be made in the development of products for the prevention, diagnosis, and treatment of rare diseases, the collaborative efforts of patients and patient advocacy groups, physicians and other health care providers, professional associations, academic research investigators, the pharmaceutical industry, private foundations, government research funding, and regulatory and reimbursement agencies must be encouraged on a global basis. The patient-centered organizations featured in the *NORD Compendium of Rare Diseases and Disorders* are often the only organizations with frequent contact with all of the stakeholders in the rare diseases community.

The roles and responsibilities of rare disease patient advocacy and consumer organizations are rapidly evolving. The availability of useful information about rare disease research and orphan product development activities for the prevention, diagnosis, and treatment purposes continues to grow. This information is assuming a greater role as a source of educational material for patients. Government agencies and the pharmaceutical industry are recognizing the expanding role of patients and advocacy groups as collaborators in research. The continued contributions of patient advocacy groups as developers and disseminators of information assist patients in understanding their disease or disorder, making them key partners in fostering research of rare diseases. Many of the patient advocacy groups have assumed a unique role as a catalyst of research for their disease or disorder.

Continued contributions to publications such as the *NORD Compendium of Rare Diseases and Disorders* are essential to raising public awareness of rare diseases. Information developed by patient advocacy groups, with the assistance of medical and scientific advisory boards, has become widely accepted by both the scientific community and the public as reliable and useful sources of information.

Stephen C. Groft, Pharm.D.
Director, Office of Rare Diseases
National Institutes of Health
Department of Health and Human Services
Bethesda, MD

Introduction

Each month, more than 200,000 people from around the world visit the Web site (www.rarediseases.org) of the National Organization for Rare Disorders (NORD). Additionally, thousands call or write to NORD, seeking information about diseases, referrals to patient organizations, and/or help in addressing specific problems and concerns. For many of these people, there is nowhere else to turn.

What is NORD and how does it help people? NORD is a national charity and a unique federation of voluntary health organizations and individuals dedicated to helping people with rare diseases and assisting the organizations that serve them. It is committed to the identification, treatment, and cure of rare disorders through programs of education, advocacy, research, and services.

It was established in 1983 by patient organizations supporting the *Orphan Drug Act,* an important piece of federal legislation that provides incentives to encourage the development of new treatments for rare disorders. A rare disorder is any disease thought to affect fewer than 200,000 people in the United States. This is the definition used by the U.S. Food and Drug Administration (FDA) to determine whether a treatment may be eligible for "orphan drug" status.

According to the National Institutes of Health (NIH), there are more than 6000 rare disorders affecting more than 25 million Americans. This means that approximately one of every 11 people in the United States has a rare disorder. Even though each disease may affect only a small number of people, rare diseases have a significant impact when considered collectively.

What services does NORD provide?

Information. NORD provides information about rare diseases and patient organizations through its publications, its information center, and its Web site. Originally, this service was focused on patients and families, but today NORD also works to raise awareness of rare diseases among medical professionals, teachers, social workers, and the public. Its free *Physician Guides,* pamphlets about specific diseases, are distributed to doctors throughout the United States and in many other countries.

Medication Assistance. NORD administers various patient assistance programs to help people who are uninsured or underinsured to obtain certain medications they could not otherwise afford. NORD also offers expanded access programs for certain investigational drugs. In addition, it administers premium and co-pay programs that help people with certain diseases pay for health insurance premiums and/or insurance co-pays and deductibles. In 2005, NORD administered the distribution of more than $130 million worth of medications, and $9.8 million worth of co-pay assistance, for needy patients.

Research. NORD encourages the development of new treatments and cures for rare diseases through its Research Program, which includes both grants and fellowships. Donations may be earmarked for research on specific diseases. In 2005, NORD awarded grants and fellowships totaling $486,380 for research on diseases that might not otherwise be studied.

Advocacy. NORD is the voice of the rare-disease community on health-related public policy issues. It works to ensure that people with rare diseases are not forgotten when federal funds are allocated for medical research and social programs. NORD also focuses public attention on policy issues related to consumer safety, access to treatments, and insurance and reimbursement.

Database Subscriptions. Many libraries, universities, and hospitals subscribe to NORD's Rare Disease Database®. Subscriptions provide unlimited access at all times to the full-text versions of reports in understandable language on more than 1170 rare diseases. For information, write to webmaster@ rarediseases.org.

Networking. NORD's Networking Program puts families with the same diagnosis in touch with each other. This helps people find mutual support and encourages the formation of new support groups for specific rare diseases.

Clinical Broadcasts. Although it never endorses particular research projects, NORD increases awareness of opportunities to participate in research through its newsletter, *Orphan Disease Update*, its Web site, and mailings to patients inviting them to contact researchers.

Patient Services. NORD provides assistance to patients and their families in other ways such as helping people find free or low-cost travel options for clinical trials or treatment, and answering questions related to insurance, Medicare, disability rights, and other issues. Patients and family members may contact NORD's registered nurse at RN@rarediseases.org or certified genetic counselor at Genetic_Counselor@rarediseases.org. Patients and their families may also call NORD at (800) 999-NORD with questions or concerns.

4-Star Rating

In 2006, for the third consecutive year, NORD received the top (4-Star) rating from Charity Navigator, an independent charity rating service. The rating recognizes NORD's success in using donated funds effectively to make a difference for patients and families.

NORD Membership

NORD has several categories of membership. Members can include patients, relatives and friends of patients, physicians, genetic counselors, nurses, allied health professionals, teachers, social workers, and others with an interest in rare diseases. In addition, patient organizations that meet certain criteria may become members of NORD. For information about NORD membership, please contact NORD at (203) 744-0100 or go to www.rarediseases.org.

The following organizations are members or associate members of NORD:

2006 National Organization Members

Alagille Syndrome Alliance
Alpha 1 Association
Alpha 1 Foundation
American Brain Tumor Association
American Porphyria Foundation
American Syringomyelia Alliance Project
Aplastic Anemia & MDS International Foundation, Inc.
Association for Glycogen Storage Disease
Association of Gastrointestinal Motility Disorders, Inc. (AGMD)
Batten Disease Support & Research Association
Benign Essential Blepharospasm Research Foundation
Charcot-Marie-Tooth Association
Children's Tumor Foundation
Chromosome 18 Registry Research Society
Cleft Palate Foundation
Cornelia De Lange Syndrome Foundation
Cystinosis Foundation, Inc.
Dysautonomia Foundation, Inc.
Dystonia Medical Research Foundation
DebRA (Dystrophic Epidermolysis Bullosa Research Association of America)
Ehlers-Danlos National Foundation
Erythromelalgia Association
Families of Spinal Muscular Atrophy
Foundation Fighting Blindness
Foundation for Ichthyosis & Related Skin Types
GBS/CIDP Foundation International
Genetic Alliance
Hereditary Color Cancer Association
Hereditary Disease Foundation
HHT Foundation International, Inc.
Histiocytosis Association of America
Huntington's Disease Society of America
Immune Deficiency Foundation
International FOP Association, Inc.
International Rett Syndrome Association
Interstitial Cystitis Association
Kennedy's Disease Association
LAM Foundation
Lowe Syndrome Association, Inc.
Mastocytosis Society, Inc.
Moebius Syndrome Foundation
Mucolipidosis Type IV Foundation, Inc.
Myasthenia Gravis Foundation of America, Inc.
Myositis Association of America, Inc.
Narcolepsy Network, Inc.
National Adrenal Disease Foundation
National Alopecia Areata Foundation
National Ataxia Foundation
National Foundation for Ectodermal Dysplasias
National Fragile X Foundation

National Hemophilia Foundation
National Kidney Foundation
National Marfan Foundation
National MPS Society, Inc.
National Multiple Sclerosis Society
National PKU News
National Spasmodic Torticollis Association
National Tay Sachs & Allied Diseases Association
National Urea Cycle Disorders Foundation
Neurofibromatosis, Inc.
Osteogenesis Imperfecta Foundation
The Oxalosis & Hyperoxaluria Foundation
Paget Foundation for Paget's Disease of Bone and
  Related Disorders
Parkinson's Disease Foundation
Platelet Disorder Support Foundation
Prader Willi Syndrome Association, USA
Pulmonary Hypertension Association
Reflex Sympathetic Dystrophy Syndrome
  Association
Sarcoma Foundation of America
Scleroderma Foundation
Stevens Johnson Syndrome Foundation & Support
  Group
Sturge-Weber Foundation
Tourette Syndrome Association, Inc.
Trigeminal Neuralgia Association
United Leukodystrophy Foundation
United Mitochondrial Disease Foundation
Vasculitis Foundation
Vestibular Disorder Association (VEDA)
VHL Family Alliance
Williams Syndrome Association
Wilson's Disease Association

Associate Organization Members
Acid Maltase Deficiency Association (AMDA)
ALS Association-Greater Philadelphia Chapter
American Autoimmune Related Disease
  Association
American Behcet's Diseases Association
American Self-Help Group Clearinghouse
Association CMTC Cutis Marmorata Telangiectatica
  Children's Project

Canadian Organization for Rare Disorders (CORD)
CDG Family Network Foundation
Children's Cardiomyopathy Foundation
Children's Craniofacial Association
Children's PKU Network
Chromosome Deletion Outreach, Inc.
Chronic Granulomatous Disease Association
CLIMB
Coalition for Pulmonary Fibrosis
Consortium of Multiple Sclerosis Centers
Contact a Family
Cushing Support & Research Foundation, Inc.
Cutis Laxa International
EURORDIS
Family Caregiver Alliance
Family Support Network of North Carolina
Fibromuscular Dysplasia Society of America
Freeman-Sheldon Parent Support Group
GOLD (Global Organization for Lysosomal
  Diseases)
Hereditary Neuropathy Foundation
Hydrocephalus Association
Incontinentia Pigmenti International Foundation
Klippell-Trenaunay Support Group
Les Turner ALS Foundation, Ltd.
Locks of Love
Melorheostosis Association
Mercy Medical Airlift
National Lymphedema Network, Inc.
National Niemann-Pick Disease Foundation
National Organization for Albinism &
  Hypopigmentation (NOAH)
National Spasmodic Dysphonia Association
Organic Acidemia Association
Osteoporosis & Related Bone Diseases National
  Resource Center
Parent to Parent New Zealand, Inc.
Recurrent Respiratory Papillomatosis Foundation
Sarcoid Networking Association
Shwachman-Diamond Syndrome Foundation
Society for Progressive Supranuclear Palsy, Inc.
Sotos Syndrome Support Association
Syncope Trust & Reflex Anoxic Seizures (STARS)
Taiwan Foundation for Rare Disorders
Wisconsin Chronic Fatigue Syndrome Association

Part I

Descriptions

1 5 Oxoprolinuria

Synonyms

Pyroglutamic Aciduria
Pyroglutamicaciduria

5-Oxoprolinuria is a biochemical finding that can arise from two underlying metabolic disorders. It is characterized by excretion of massive amounts of the chemical 5-oxoproline.

The following organizations may provide additional information and support:
The Arc (A National Organization on Mental Retardation)
CLIMB (Children Living with Inherited Metabolic Diseases)
National Institute of Neurological Disorders and Stroke (NINDS)

2 Aarskog Syndrome

Synonyms

Aarskog-Scott Syndrome
AAS
Faciodigitogenital Syndrome
Faciogenital Dysplasia
FGDY

Aarskog syndrome is an extremely rare genetic disorder marked by stunted growth that may not become obvious until the child is about 3 years of age, broad facial abnormalities, musculoskeletal and genital anomalies, and mild mental retardation.

The following organizations may provide additional information and support:
Aarskog Syndrome Parents Support Group
Children's Craniofacial Association
MAGIC Foundation for Children's Growth
March of Dimes Birth Defects Foundation
National Craniofacial Foundation
NIH/National Institute of Arthritis and Musculoskeletal and Skin Diseases

3 Aase Syndrome

Synonyms

Aase-Smith Syndrome II
Congenital Anemia and Triphalangeal Thumbs
Hypoplastic Anemia-Triphalangeal Thumbs, Aase-Smith Type

Aase syndrome is a rare genetic disorder that may be detected during early infancy. The disorder is primarily characterized by the presence of three bones (phalanges) within the thumbs (triphalangeal thumbs) rather than the normal two and abnormally reduced production of red blood cells (hypoplastic anemia). In some instances, additional abnormalities may be present. The exact cause of Aase syndrome is unknown. However, most evidence suggests that the disorder is inherited as an autosomal recessive trait.

The following organizations may provide additional information and support:
Genetic and Rare Diseases (GARD) Information Center
March of Dimes Birth Defects Foundation
NIH/National Heart, Lung and Blood Institute

4 Abetalipoproteinemia

Synonyms

ABL
Bassen-Kornzweig Syndrome
Low Density B-lipoprotein Deficiency
Microsomal Triglyceride Transfer Protein Deficiency
MTP Deficiency

Abetalipoproteinemia is a rare inherited disorder of fat metabolism. Abnormalities in fat metabolism result in malabsorption of dietary fat and various essential vitamins. Affected individuals experience progressive neurological deterioration, muscle weakness, difficulty walking, and blood abnormalities including a condition in which the red blood cells are malformed (acanthocytosis) resulting in low levels of circulating red blood cells (anemia). Affected individuals may also develop degeneration of the retina of the eyes potentially resulting in loss of vision, a condition known as retinitis pigmentosa. Abetalipoproteinemia is inherited as an autosomal recessive trait.

The following organizations may provide additional information and support:
Abetalipoproteinemia Support Group
March of Dimes Birth Defects Foundation
National Lipid Diseases Foundation
NIH/National Heart, Lung and Blood Institute
NIH/National Institute of Diabetes, Digestive & Kidney Diseases
Retinitis Pigmentosa International

5 Ablepharon Macrostomia Syndrome

Synonym

AMS

Ablepharon macrostomia syndrome (AMS) is an extremely rare inherited disorder characterized by various physical abnormalities affecting the head and facial (craniofacial) area, the skin, the fingers, and the genitals. In addition, affected individuals may have malformations of the nipples and the abdominal wall. Infants and children with AMS may also experience delays in language development and, in some cases, mental retardation. In infants with ablepharon macrostomia syndrome, characteristic craniofacial features may include absence or severe underdevelopment of the upper and lower eyelids (ablepharon or microblepharon) as well as absence of eyelashes and eyebrows; an unusually wide, "fish-like" mouth (macrostomia); and/or incompletely developed (rudimentary), low-set ears (pinnae). Abnormalities of the eyes may occur due to, or in association with, ablepharon or microblepharon. Individuals with AMS may also have additional characteristic features including abnormally sparse, thin hair; thin, wrinkled skin with excess (redundant) folds; webbed fingers with limited extension; and/or malformations of the external genitals. In some cases, additional features associated with AMS may include absent or abnormally small (hypoplastic) nipples and/or abdominal wall abnormalities. Although the exact cause of ablepharon macrostomia syndrome is not fully understood, some cases suggest that the disorder may be inherited as an autosomal recessive genetic trait.

The following organizations may provide additional information and support:
Ambiguous Genitalia Support Network
Children's Craniofacial Association
FACES: The National Craniofacial Association
Forward Face, Inc.
NIH/National Eye Institute
NIH/National Institute of Arthritis and Musculoskeletal and Skin Diseases

6 Acanthocheilonemiasis

Synonyms

Acanthocheilonemiasis Perstans
Dipetalonema Perstans
Dipetalonemiasis
Mansonella Perstans

Acanthocheilonemiasis is a rare tropical infectious disease caused by a parasite known as Acanthocheilonema perstans, which belongs to a group of parasitic diseases known as filarial diseases (nematode). This parasite is found, for the most part, in Africa. Symptoms of infection may include red, itchy skin (pruritis), abdominal and chest pain, muscular pain (myalgia), and areas of localized swelling (edema). In addition, the liver and spleen may become abnormally enlarged (hepatosplenomegaly). Laboratory testing may also reveal abnormally elevated levels of certain specialized white blood cells (eosinophilia). The parasite is transmitted through the bite of small flies (*A. coliroides*).

The following organizations may provide additional information and support:
Centers for Disease Control and Prevention
NIH/National Institute of Allergy and Infectious Diseases
World Health Organization (WHO) Regional Office for the Americas (AMRO)

7 Acanthocytosis

Synonyms

Bassen-Kornzweig Syndrome
Low-Density Beta Lipoprotein Deficiency

Acanthocytosis is a digestive disorder that is characterized by the absence of very low density lipoproteins (VLDL) and chylomicrons in the plasma. Chylomicrons are very small fatty droplets that are covered with a beta-lipoprotein and perform an essential function in fat transport in the blood and, thus, in fat metabolism. The absense of VLDL and of chylomicrons interferes with the absorption of fat and leads to excessive fats excretion (steatorrhea). Other symptoms include abnormal red blood cells (acanthocytes), a vision disorder (retinitis pigmentosa), and impaired muscle coordination (ataxia).

The following organizations may provide additional information and support:
CLIMB (Children Living with Inherited Metabolic Diseases)
Foundation Fighting Blindness, Inc.
National Tay-Sachs and Allied Diseases Association, Inc.
NIH/National Institute of Diabetes, Digestive & Kidney Diseases
Retinitis Pigmentosa International

8 Acanthosis Nigricans

Synonym

AN

Disorder Subdivisions

*Acanthosis Nigricans with Insulin Resistance
Type A
Acanthosis Nigricans with Insulin Resistance
Type B
Benign Acanthosis Nigricans
Drug-induced Acanthosis Nigricans
Hereditary Benign Acanthosis Nigricans
Malignant Acanthosis Nigricans
Pseudoacanthosis Nigricans*

Acanthosis nigricans (AN) is a skin disorder characterized by abnormally increased coloration (hyperpigmentation) and "velvety" thickening (hyperkeratosis) of the skin, particularly of skin fold regions, such as of the neck and groin and under the arms (axillae). Various benign (non-cancerous) forms of AN have been identified in which the disorder may be inherited as a primary condition or associated with various underlying syndromes; an excess accumulation of body fat (obesity); or the use of certain medications (i.e., drug-induced AN). In other instances, AN may occur in association with an underlying cancerous tumor (i.e., malignant AN). Experts suggest that AN may be a skin manifestation of insulin resistance, which is a condition characterized by impaired biological responses to insulin. Insulin, a hormone produced by the pancreas, regulates blood glucose levels by promoting the movement of glucose into cells for energy production or into the liver and fat cells for storage. (Glucose is a simple sugar that is the body's primary source of energy for cell metabolism.) Insulin resistance may be associated with various disorders, including obesity and non-insulin-dependent (type II) diabetes mellitus. In individuals with type II diabetes mellitus, the pancreas produces insulin but the body becomes resistant to its effects, leading to insufficient absorption of glucose and abnormally increased glucose levels in the blood (hyperglycemia) and urine. As a result, there may be a gradual onset of certain symptoms, including excessive urination (polyuria) and increased thirst (polydipsia), and the development of particular complications without appropriate treatment.

The following organizations may provide additional information and support:
March of Dimes Birth Defects Foundation
NIH/National Institute of Arthritis and Musculoskeletal and Skin Diseases

9 Achalasia

Synonyms

*Cardiospasm
Dyssynergia Esophagus
Esophageal Aperistalsis
Megaesophagus*

Achalasia is a rare disorder of the esophagus characterized by the abnormal enlargement of the esophagus, impairment of the ability of the esophagus to push food down toward the stomach (peristalsis), and the failure of the ring-shaped muscle (sphincter) at the bottom of the esophagus to relax.

The following organizations may provide additional information and support:
March of Dimes Birth Defects Foundation
NIH/National Digestive Diseases Information Clearinghouse

10 Achard-Thiers Syndrome

Synonym

Diabetic Bearded Woman Syndrome

Achard-Thiers syndrome is a rare disorder that occurs primarily in postmenopausal women and is characterized by type 2 (insulin-resistant) diabetes mellitus and signs of androgen excess. The exact cause of this syndrome is unknown.

The following organizations may provide additional information and support:
American Diabetes Association
National Adrenal Diseases Foundation
NIH/National Institute of Diabetes, Digestive & Kidney Diseases

11 Achondrogenesis

Synonyms

*Chondrogenesis Imperfecta
Hypochondrogenesis
Lethal Neonatal Dwarfism
Lethal Osteochondrodysplasia
Neonatal Dwarfism*

Disorder Subdivisions

*Achondrogenesis, Type III
Achondrogenesis, Type IV
Fraccaro Type, Achondrogenesis (Type IB)
Houston-Harris Type, Achondrogenesis (Type IA)
Langer-Salidino Type, Achondrogenesis (Type II)*

Achondrogenesis is a very rare disorder characterized by extreme short-limbed dwarfism, lack of development of ribs and other major bone formations. The head is usually shaped in a normal way (normocephaly) but may be unusually soft depending on the type of achondrogenesis involved. There are several different types of achondrogenesis, some of which may be life-threatening either in the womb (in utero) or shortly after birth. Achondrogenesis can be inherited as an autosomal or dominant recessive genetic trait.

The following organizations may provide additional information and support:
Human Growth Foundation
Little People of America, Inc.
Little People's Research Fund, Inc.
MAGIC Foundation for Children's Growth
Restricted Growth Association

12 Achondroplasia

Synonyms
ACH
Achondroplastic Dwarfism

Achondroplasia is a rare genetic disorder characterized by an unusually large head (macrocephaly) with a prominent forehead (frontal bossing) and flat (depressed) nasal bridge; short upper arms and legs (rhizomelic dwarfism); unusually prominent abdomen and buttocks; and short hands with fingers that assume a "trident" or three-pronged position during extension. An autosomal dominant genetic trait, achondroplasia occurs as a result of a fresh (new) spontaneous change (mutation) in genetic material in about 90 percent of cases. In achondroplasia, affected individuals have impaired ability to form bone from cartilage (endochondral bone formation).

The following organizations may provide additional information and support:
Human Growth Foundation
Little People of America, Inc.
Little People's Research Fund, Inc.
MAGIC Foundation for Children's Growth
March of Dimes Birth Defects Foundation
NIH/National Arthritis and Musculoskeletal and Skin Diseases Information Clearinghouse
Restricted Growth Association

13 Acidemia, Isovaleric

Synonyms
Isovaleric Acid CoA Dehydrogenase Deficiency
Isovaleric Acidaemia

Isovalericacidemia
Isovaleryl CoA Carboxylase Deficiency
IVA

Isovaleric acidemia is a hereditary metabolic disorder. It is characterized by a deficiency of the enzyme isovaleryl CoA dehydrogenase. The disorder occurs in both an acute and a chronic intermittent form. In the acute form of isovaleric acidemia, vomiting, refusal to eat, and listlessness usually occur. With treatment and low protein diet, the disorder becomes chronically intermittent, and a nearly normal life is possible.

The following organizations may provide additional information and support:
The Arc (A National Organization on Mental Retardation)
CLIMB (Children Living with Inherited Metabolic Diseases)
NIH/National Digestive Diseases Information Clearinghouse
Organic Acidaemias UK
Organic Acidemia Association

14 Acidemia, Methylmalonic

Synonym
Methylmalonic Aciduria

The methylmalonic acidemias are organic acidemias caused by an enzymatic defect in the metabolism of four amino acids (methionine, threonine, isoleucine and valine). This results in an abnormally high level of acid in the blood (acidemia) and body tissues. In the acute form, drowsiness, coma, and seizures may occur. Mental retardation is a long-term consequence. The disorder may be caused by a deficiency of one or more of the enzymes methylmalonyl CoA mutase, methylmalonyl racemase, or adenosylcobalamin synthetic enzymes. Excretion of methylmalonate, a product of amino acid metabolism, in the urine is abnormally high and therefore is a marker of the disorder. All known organic acidemias are inherited as autosomal recessive traits.

The following organizations may provide additional information and support:
The Arc (A National Organization on Mental Retardation)
CLIMB (Children Living with Inherited Metabolic Diseases)
NIH/National Digestive Diseases Information Clearinghouse

Organic Acidaemias UK
Organic Acidemia Association
Taking Action Against Language Disorders for Kids, Inc.

15 Acidemia, Propionic

Synonyms
Hyperglycinemia with Ketoacidosis and Lactic Acidosis, Propionic Type
Ketotic Glycinemia
PCC Deficiency
Propionyl CoA Carboxylase Deficiency

Disorder Subdivisions
Propionic Acidemia, Type I (PCCA Deficiency)
Propionic Acidemia, Type II (PCCB Deficiency)

Propionic acidemia is a rare metabolic disorder characterized by deficiency of propionyl CoA carboxylase, an enzyme involved in the breakdown (catabolism) of the chemical "building blocks" (amino acids) of certain proteins. Symptoms most commonly become apparent during the first weeks of life and may include abnormally diminished muscle tone (hypotonia), poor feeding, vomiting, listlessness (lethargy), excessive loss of fluids from bodily tissues (dehydration), and episodes of uncontrolled electrical activity in the brain (seizures). Without appropriate treatment, coma and potentially life-threatening complications may result. In rare cases, the condition may become apparent later during infancy and may be associated with less severe symptoms and findings. Propionic acidemia is inherited as an autosomal recessive trait.

The following organizations may provide additional information and support:
The Arc (A National Organization on Mental Retardation)
CLIMB (Children Living with Inherited Metabolic Diseases)
NIH/National Digestive Diseases Information Clearinghouse
Organic Acidaemias UK
Organic Acidemia Association
Propionic Acidemia Foundation

16 Acne Rosacea

Synonyms
Acne Erythematosa
Adult Acne
Hypertrophic Rosacea
Rhinophyma
Rosacea

Acne rosacea is a skin disorder limited to the nose, cheeks, chin, and forehead, typically beginning during adulthood. The facial skin becomes oily, reddened, and bumpy. Small red blood vessels are visible. In extreme cases, the nose may appear very red and bulbous.

The following organizations may provide additional information and support:
National Rosacea Society
NIH/National Arthritis and Musculoskeletal and Skin Diseases Information Clearinghouse

17 Acoustic Neuroma

Synonyms
Acoustic Neurilemoma
Bilateral Acoustic Neuroma
Cerebellopontine Angle Tumor
Fibroblastoma, Perineural
Neurinoma of the Acoustic Nerve
Neurofibroma of the Acoustic Nerve
Schwannoma of the Acoustic Nerve

Acoustic neuroma is a benign (non-cancerous) growth that begins at the 8th cranial nerve, which runs from the brain to the inner ear. Any disruption of the signals sent along the 8th cranial nerve will interfere with hearing and with the patient's balance.

The following organizations may provide additional information and support:
Acoustic Neuroma Association
Acoustic Neuroma Association of Canada
Alexander Graham Bell Association for the Deaf, Inc.
American Tinnitus Association
Better Hearing Institute
Children's Tumor Foundation: Ending Neurofibromatosis Through Research
Deafness Research Foundation
NIH/National Institute on Deafness and Other Communication Disorders (Balance)

18 Acquired Aplastic Anemia

Synonym
Idiopathic Aplastic Anemia

Acquired aplastic anemia is a rare disorder caused by profound, almost complete bone marrow failure. Bone marrow is the spongy substance found in the center of the long bones of the body. The bone marrow produces specialized cells (hematopoietic stem cells) that grow and eventually develop into red blood cells (erythrocytes), white blood cells (leukocytes), and platelets. In acquired aplastic anemia, an almost complete absence of hematopoietic stem cells eventually results in low levels of red and white blood cells and platelets (pancytopenia). Specific symptoms associated with acquired aplastic anemia may vary, but include fatigue, chronic infections, dizziness, weakness, headaches, and episodes of excessive bleeding. Although some cases of acquired aplastic anemia occur secondary to other disorders, researchers now believe that most cases result from a disorder of the patient's immune system, in which the immune system mistakenly targets the bone marrow (autoimmunity). This is based on the response of approximately half of patients to immunotherapy, whether it is ATG, cyclosporine, high-dose steroids or cyclophosphamide.

The following organizations may provide additional information and support:
Anemia Institute for Research and Education
Aplastic Anemia & MDS International Foundation, Inc.
Aplastic Anemia & Myelodysplasia Association of Canada
Dubowitz Syndrome Support
Earl J. Goldberg Aplastic Anemia Foundation
NIH/Hematology Branch, National Heart, Lung and Blood Institute (NHLBI)
NIH/National Heart, Lung and Blood Institute

19 Acrocallosal Syndrome, Schinzel Type

Synonyms
Absence of Corpus Callosum, Schinzel Type
ACLS
ACS
Hallux Duplication, Postaxial Polydactyly, and Absence of Corpus Callosum
Schinzel Acrocallosal Syndrome

Acrocallosal syndrome, Schinzel type is a rare genetic disorder that is apparent at birth (congenital). Associated symptoms and findings may be variable, including among affected members of the same family (kindred). However, the disorder is typically characterized by underdevelopment (hypoplasia) or absence (agenesis) of the thick band of nerve fibers joining the two hemispheres of the brain (corpus callosum) and moderate to severe mental retardation. In addition, many affected individuals have malformations of the skull and fa-

cial (craniofacial) region and/or distinctive abnormalities of the fingers and toes (digits). Characteristic craniofacial abnormalities may include an unusually large head (macrocephaly) with a prominent forehead; widely spaced eyes (ocular hypertelorism); downslanting eyelid folds (palpebral fissures); a small nose with a broad nasal bridge; and malformed (dysplastic) ears. Most affected individuals also have distinctive digital malformations, such as the presence of extra (supernumerary) fingers and toes (polydactyly) and webbing or fusion (syndactyly) of certain digits. Additional physical abnormalities may also be present, including growth retardation, resulting in short stature. Although autosomal recessive inheritance has been suggested, acrocallosal syndrome often appears to occur randomly for unknown reasons (sporadically).

The following organizations may provide additional information and support:
AboutFace USA
Agenesis of the Corpus Callosum (ACC) Network
American Heart Association
The Arc (A National Organization on Mental Retardation)
Congenital Heart Anomalies, Support, Education, & Resources
Epilepsy Foundation
FACES: The National Craniofacial Association
Forward Face, Inc.
Guardians of Hydrocephalus Research Foundation
Hydrocephalus Association
Let's Face It (USA)
March of Dimes Birth Defects Foundation
National Hydrocephalus Foundation
National Institute of Neurological Disorders and Stroke (NINDS)
NIH/National Eye Institute

20 Acrodermatitis Enteropathica

Synonyms
AE
Brandt Syndrome
Danbolt-Cross Syndrome
Zinc Deficiency, Congenital

Acrodermatitis enteropathica (AE) is a disorder of zinc metabolism that occurs in one of two forms: an inborn (congenital) form and an acquired form. The inborn form of AE is a rare genetic disorder characterized by intestinal abnormalities that lead to the inability to absorb zinc from the intestine. The lack of zinc presents, characteristically, as: (1)

skin inflammation with pimples (pustular dermatitis) occurring around the mouth and/or anus, (2) diarrhea, and (3) abnormal nails (nail dystrophy). In the acute phase, irritability and emotional disturbances are evident due to wasting (atrophy) of the brain cortex. It is important to recognize and treat this disorder. The acquired form of this disorder generates similar symptoms. Acquired AE sometimes results from special intravenous nutritional programs that are prepared without the appropriate amount of zinc. Supplemental zinc usually eliminates the symptoms.

The following organizations may provide additional information and support:
American Autoimmune Related Diseases Association, Inc.
CLIMB (Children Living with Inherited Metabolic Diseases)
March of Dimes Birth Defects Foundation
NIH/National Digestive Diseases Information Clearinghouse

21   Acrodysostosis

Synonyms
Peripheral Dysostosis-Nasal Hypoplasia-Mental Retardation
PNM

Acrodysostosis is an extremely rare skeletal disorder characterized by abnormally short and malformed bones of the hands and feet (peripheral dysostosis) and underdevelopment of the nose (nasal hypoplasia). Other findings may include progressive growth delays, short stature, and/or unusual head and facial (craniofacial) features. Affected infants may exhibit premature maturation of bones of the hands and feet, malformation and shortening of the forearm bones (radius and ulna) near the wrist, and/or abnormally short fingers and toes (brachydactyly). Characteristic facial features may include a flattened, underdeveloped (hypoplastic) "pug" nose, an underdeveloped upper jaw bone (maxilliary hypoplasia), widely spaced eyes (ocular hypertelorism), and/or an extra fold of skin on either side of the nose that may cover the eyes' inner corners (epicanthal folds). Acrodysostosis is usually accompanied by moderate mental retardation and learning difficulties. It may be inherited as an autosomal dominant trait in some cases, although no gene has yet been identified with this disorder. Acrodysostosis seems to be associated in some cases with advanced parental age.

The following organizations may provide additional information and support:
Little People of America, Inc.
MAGIC Foundation for Children's Growth
Restricted Growth Association

22   Acromegaly

Synonym
Marie Disease

Acromegaly is a rare, slowly progressive chronic disorder that affects adults. The disorder is characterized by an excess of growth hormone. Symptoms include abnormal enlargement in bones of the arms, legs, and head. The bones in the jaws and in the front of the skull are typically the most affected. Acromegaly may also cause thickening of the soft tissues of the body, particularly the heart and accelerated growth leading to tall stature. In most cases, acromegaly is caused by the growth of a benign tumor (adenoma), affecting the pituitary gland.

The following organizations may provide additional information and support:
Canadian Multiple Endocrine Neoplasm Society, Inc.
NIH/National Arthritis and Musculoskeletal and Skin Diseases Information Clearinghouse
Pituitary Network Association (PNA)

23   Acromesomelic Dysplasia

Synonym
Acromesomelic Dwarfism

Acromesomelic dysplasia is an extremely rare inherited progressive disorder characterized by premature fusion of the regions (metaphyses) where the shafts (diaphyses) of certain long bones (i.e., bones of the arms and legs) meet their growing ends (epiphyses). As a result, affected individuals exhibit unusually short forearms, abnormal shortening of bones of the lower (distal) legs, and short stature (short-limbed dwarfism), findings that typically become apparent during the first years of life. Abnormal cartilage and bone development may also affect other bones of the body, particularly those of the hands and feet (i.e., metacarpals, phalanges, metatarsals). At birth, the hands and feet may appear abnormally short and broad. Over time, the apparent disproportion becomes even more obvious, especially during the first years of life. The fingernails and toenails may also appear unusually short and wide. Affected individuals may have additional abnormalities resulting from abnormal cartilage and bone development, including limited extension of the elbows and arms and/or progressive abnormal curvature of the spine. Other characteristic abnormalities include a relatively enlarged head (macrocephaly), slightly flattened midface, and/or small, pug nose. Acromesomelic dysplasia is inherited as an autosomal recessive genetic trait. Relatively recent clinical studies have demonstrated that there are at least two forms that are distinguishable by X-ray and at the molecular level. The Maroteaux type has been traced to chromosome 9 (Gene Map Locus 9p13-p12). The Hunter-Thompson type has been mapped to chromosome 20 (20q11.2).

The following organizations may provide additional information and support:
Little People of America, Inc.
MAGIC Foundation for Children's Growth
NIH/National Arthritis and Musculoskeletal and Skin Diseases Information Clearinghouse
Restricted Growth Association

24 Acromicric Dysplasia

Synonym
Acromicric Skeletal Dysplasia

Acromicric dysplasia is an extremely rare inherited disorder characterized by abnormally short hands and feet, growth retardation and delayed bone maturation leading to short stature, and mild facial abnormalities. Most cases have occurred randomly for no apparent reason (sporadically). However, autosomal dominant inheritance has not been ruled out.

The following organizations may provide additional information and support:
Human Growth Foundation
Little People of America, Inc.
MAGIC Foundation for Children's Growth
Short Stature Foundation

25 ACTH Deficiency

Synonym
Adrenocorticotropic Hormone Deficiency, Isolated

ACTH deficiency arises as a result of decreased or absent production of adrenocorticotropic hormone (ACTH) by the pituitary gland. A decline in the concentration of ACTH in the blood leads to a reduction in the secretion of adrenal hormones, resulting in adrenal insufficiency (hypoadrenalism). Adrenal insufficiency leads to weight loss, lack of appetite (anorexia), weakness, nausea, vomiting, and low blood pressure (hypotension). Because these symptoms are so general, the diagnosis is sometimes delayed or missed entirely. For that reason, some clinicians believe the disorder to be more common than previously thought.

The following organization may provide additional information and support:
NIH/National Institute of Diabetes, Digestive & Kidney Diseases

26 Acute Respiratory Distress Syndrome

Synonyms
Acute Lung Injury
Adult Respiratory Distress Syndrome
ARDS

Acute respiratory distress syndrome (ARDS) is a type of severe, acute lung dysfunction affecting all or most of both lungs that occurs as a result of illness or injury. Although it is sometimes called adult respiratory distress syndrome, it may also affect children. Major symptoms may include breathing difficulties (dyspnea), rapid breathing (tachypnea), excessively deep and rapid breathing (hyperventilation) and insufficient levels of oxygen in the circulating blood (hypoxemia). ARDS may develop in conjunction with widespread infection in the body (sepsis) or as a result of pneumonia, trauma, shock, severe burns, aspiration of food into the lung, multiple blood transfusions, and inhalation of toxic fumes, among other things. It usually develops within 24 to 48 hours after the original illness or injury and is considered a medical emergency. It may progress to involvement of other organs.

The following organizations may provide additional information and support:
American Lung Association
NIH/National Heart, Lung and Blood Institute Information Center

27 Adams-Oliver Syndrome

Synonyms
Absence Defect of Limbs, Scalp, and Skull
Aplasia Cutis Congenita with Terminal Transverse Limb Defects

Congenital Scalp Defects with Distal Limb Reduction Anomalies

Adams-Oliver syndrome (AOS) is an extremely rare inherited disorder characterized by defects of the scalp and abnormalities of the fingers, toes, arms, and/or legs. The physical abnormalities associated with this disorder vary greatly among affected individuals. Some cases may be very mild while others may be severe. In infants with Adams-Oliver syndrome, scalp defects are present at birth (congenital) and may include one or multiple hairless scarred areas that may have abnormally wide (dilated) blood vessels directly under the affected skin. In severe cases, an underlying defect of the bones of the skull may also be present. In addition, infants with this disorder typically have malformations of the hands, arms, feet, and/or legs. These range from abnormally short (hypoplastic) fingers and toes to absent hands and/or lower legs. In some cases, additional abnormalities may also be present. Some cases of Adams-Oliver syndrome occur randomly as the result of a spontaneous genetic change (i.e., new mutation). Inheritance is autosomal dominant.

The following organizations may provide additional information and support:
Adams Oliver Syndrome Support Group
Birth Defect Research for Children, Inc.
NIH/National Arthritis and Musculoskeletal and Skin Diseases Information Clearinghouse

28 Addison's Disease

Synonyms
Adrenal Hypoplasia
Adrenocortical Hypofunction
Adrenocortical Insufficiency
Chronic Adrenocortical Insufficiency
Primary Adrenal Insufficiency
Primary Failure Adrenocortical Insufficiency

Disorder Subdivisions
Congenital Addison's Disease
X-Linked Addison's Disease

Addison's disease is a rare disorder characterized by chronic, usually progressive, inadequate production of the steroid hormones cortisol and aldosterone by the outer layer of cells of the adrenal glands (adrenal cortex). Classical Addison's disease is a consequence of the loss of both of these hormones. Cortisol affects carbohydrate metabolism connective tissue development and the amount of water in the body. Aldosterone affects the sodium and potassium ion equilibrium (electrolyte imbalance) in the body, as well as water levels and, therefore, blood pressure and blood volume. Increased excretion of water and low blood pressure (hypotension) can lead to extremely low concentrations of water in the body (dehydration). Major symptoms of Addison's disease include fatigue, gastrointestinal discomfort, and changes in skin color (pigmentation).

The following organizations may provide additional information and support:
Addison's Disease Self-Help Group (UK)
American Autoimmune Related Diseases Association, Inc.
Autoimmune Information Network, Inc
Congenital Adrenal Hyperplasia Trust (New Zealand)
Medic Alert Foundation International
NIH/National Digestive Diseases Information Clearinghouse
National Adrenal Diseases Foundation

29 Adenoid Cystic Carcinoma

Synonyms
ACC
Adenocystic Carcinoma
Cribriform Carcinoma
Cylindroma

This disease entry was made possible due to the generosity of the Kathleen Keany Memorial Foundation, 8502 East Chapman Avenue, Suite 195, Orange, CA 92869, (714) 538-6920. Adenoid cystic carcinoma (ACC) is a relatively rare form of cancer that most commonly develops in the salivary glands or other regions of the head and neck. In some cases, ACC may arise in other primary sites, such as the skin; the breast; the neck of the uterus (cervix) in females; the prostate gland in males; or other areas. The term "cancer" refers to a group of diseases characterized by abnormal, uncontrolled cellular growth that invades surrounding tissues and may spread (metastasize) to distant bodily tissues or organs via the bloodstream, the lymphatic system, or other means. Different forms of cancer, including adenoid cystic carcinoma, may be classified based upon the cell type involved, the specific nature of the malignancy, the tissues or organs affected, and the disease's clinical course. ACC tumors are characterized by a distinctive pattern in which abnormal "nests" or cords of certain cells (epithelial cells) surround and/or infiltrate ducts or glandular structures within the affected organ. These structures are typically filled with a mucous-like material or contain abnormal fibrous membranes (hyaline membranes). Such characteristics are apparent during microscopic evaluation of the tumor cells. ACC is considered a low-grade malignancy that has a history of slow growth, but tends to be aggressively invasive and to infiltrate nearby lymph nodes as well as the "sheaths" or coatings surrounding nerve fibers (perineural spaces). This form of cancer may have a tendency to recur later at the site where it first developed (local recurrence) and to spread to distant bodily sites, particularly the lungs, potentially resulting in life-threatening complications.

The following organizations may provide additional information and support:
Adenoid Cystic Carcinoma Alliance
Adenoid Cystic Carcinoma Organization International
American Cancer Society, Inc.
Association of Community Cancer Centers
Canadian Cancer Society
Cancer Hope Network
International Cancer Alliance for Research and Education
National Cancer Institute
National Coalition for Cancer Survivorship
OncoLink: The University of Pennsylvania Cancer Center Resource
Rare Cancer Alliance
Support for People with Oral and Head and Neck Cancer, Inc.

30   Adenylosuccinate Lyase Deficiency

Synonyms
Adenylosuccinase Deficiency
Succinylpurinemic Autism

Disorder Subdivisions
Adenylosuccinate Lyase Deficiency Type I
Adenylosuccinate Lyase Deficiency Type II
Adenylosuccinate Lyase Deficiency Type III
Adenylosuccinate Lyase Deficiency Type IV

Adenylosuccinate lyase deficiency (ASLD) is a rare, inherited metabolic disorder due to a lack of the enzyme adenylosuccinate lyase (ASL). The defect is characterized by the appearance of two unusual chemicals, succinylaminoimidazole carboxamide riboside (SAICA riboside) and succinyladenosine, in cerebrospinal fluid, in urine and, to a much smaller extent, in plasma. These compounds, which are never found in healthy individuals, are formed from the two natural compounds acted upon by the enzyme. The symptoms and the physical findings associated with ASLD vary greatly from case to case. As a rule, patients with ASLD present with a mix of neurological symptoms that usually will include some of the following: psychomotor retardation, autistic features, epilepsy, axial hypotonia with peripheral hypertonia, muscle wasting, and secondary feeding problems. Although abnormal physical features (dysmorphism) are not common, when they do occur they may include severe growth failure, small head circumference, brachycephaly, flat occiput, prominent metopic suture, intermittent divergent strabismus, small nose with anteverted nostrils, long and smooth philtrum, thin upper lip, and low set ears. Adenylosuccinate lyase deficiency is categorized as a disorder of the manufacture of purine nucleotides from scratch (biosynthesis) in the body. Purine nucleotides play vital roles in the cells, particularly in the process of building up or breaking down complex body chemicals (intermediary metabolism) and in energy-transforming reactions. Moreover, they serve as building blocks of nucleic acids and thus participate in molecular mechanisms by which genetic information is stored. Just how the genetic and molecular mechanisms interact to generate the symptoms of ASLD is still debated.

31   Adie Syndrome

Synonyms
Adie's Pupil
Adie's Syndrome
Adie's Tonic Pupil
Holmes-Adie Syndrome
Papillotonic Pseudotabes
Tonic Pupil Syndrome

Adie syndrome is a rare neurological disorder affecting the pupil of the eye. In most patients, the pupil is dilated (larger than normal) and slow to react to light on nearby objects. In some patients, however, the pupil may be constricted (smaller than normal) rather than dilated. Absent or poor reflexes are also associated with this disorder. Adie syndrome is neither progressive nor life-threatening, nor is it disabling.

The following organizations may provide additional information and support:
National Institute of Neurological Disorders and Stroke (NINDS)
NIH/National Eye Institute

32 Adrenal Hyperplasia, Congenital (General)

Synonyms

Adrenal Virilism
Adrenogenital Syndrome
CAH
Corticosterone Methyloxidase Deficiency Type I
Hydroxylase Deficiency

Disorder Subdivisions

3-Beta Hydroxysteroid Dehydrogenase
Deficiency
3-Beta-HSD 17-Hydroxylation Deficiency
11-Beta Hydroxylase Deficiency
17 Alpha Hydroxylase Deficiency with 17, 20-
Lyase Deficiency
17-Beta Hydroxysteroid Deficiency
17-Beta-HSD Deficiency
17-Ketosteroid Reductase Deficiency
21-Hydroxylation Deficiency
Cholesterol Desmolase Deficiency
Corticosterone Methyloxidase Deficiency Type II
Lipoid Hyperplasia-Male
Pseudohermaphroditism
Pregnenolone Deficiency

Congenital adrenal hyperplasia (CAH) refers to a group of disorders that result from the impaired ability of the adrenal glands to produce vital steroid hormones (corticosteroids), two of which, glucocorticoids and mineralocorticoids, are normally active in the body. Low blood levels of the hormones cortisol and aldosterone charge the pituitary gland to produce abnormally high amounts of ACTH (adrenocorticotrophic hormone) which, in turn, stimulates the adrenal cortex to produce androgens or male steroid hormones. Fundamentally, CAH is due to genetic defects (mutations) in the genes controlling the manufacture of the enzymes necessary to produce the hormones of the adrenal cortex. The various forms of CAH represent enzyme deficiencies at different stages of the production of the steroid hormones. These include 3-beta hydroxysteroid dehydrogenase (HSD) deficiency, 17-hydroxylase deficiency, 21-hydroxylase deficiency, 17-20 desmolase deficiency, 11-beta hydroxylase deficiency, and 17-alpha hydroxylase deficiency. Almost 95% of cases of CAH are the result of 21-hydroxylase deficiency. The overproduction of male steroid hormones (androgens) at the same time as cortisol and aldosterone are underproduced characterizes the difference between Addison's disease and CAH. One rare form of CAH can result from the overgrowth of fatty-like cells in the adrenal glands (congenital lipoid hyperplasia).

This is also known as male pseudohermaphroditism or 20-22 desmolase deficiency.

The following organizations may provide additional information and support:
Ambiguous Genitalia Support Network
CAH Support Group
CARES Foundation, Inc. (Congenital Adrenal Hyperplasia, Research, Education and Support)
CLIMB (Children Living with Inherited Metabolic Diseases)
Congenital Adrenal Hyperplasia Trust (New Zealand)
CongenitalAdrenalHyperplasia.org
The Hormone Foundation
Intersex Society of North America
MAGIC Foundation for Children's Growth
March of Dimes Birth Defects Foundation
National Adrenal Diseases Foundation
NIH/National Institute of Child Health and Human Development

33 Adrenoleukodystrophy

Synonyms

Addison Disease with Cerebral Sclerosis
Addison-Schilder Disease
Adrenomyeloneuropathy
Adult Onset ALD
ALD
AMN
Bronze Schilder's Disease
Encephalitis Periaxialis Diffusa
Flatau-Schilder Disease
Melanodermic Leukodystrophy
Myelinoclastic Diffuse Sclerosis
Schilder Disease
Schilder Encephalitis
Siewerling-Creutzfeldt Disease
Sudanophilic Leukodystrophy, ADL

Disorder Subdivisions

Childhood Adrenoleukodystrophy
Neonatal Adrenoleukodystrophy

Adrenoleukodystrophy is a rare inherited metabolic disorder characterized by the loss of the fatty covering (myelin sheath) on nerve fibers within the brain (cerebral demyelination) and the progressive degeneration of the adrenal gland (adrenal atrophy). Adrenoleukodystrophy that is inherited as an X-linked genetic trait may begin in childhood or adulthood. However, adrenoleukodystrophy that is inherited as an autosomal recessive genetic trait typically begins during infancy (neonatal period).

The following organizations may provide additional information and support:
ALD Family Support Trust
The Arc (A National Organization on Mental Retardation)
Association Europeene contre les Leucodystrophes
Australian Leukodystrophy Support Group, Inc.
CLIMB (Children Living with Inherited Metabolic Diseases)
Hunter's Hope Foundation, Inc.
Kennedy Krieger Institute
March of Dimes Birth Defects Foundation
National Institute of Neurological Disorders and Stroke (NINDS)
United Leukodystrophy Foundation

34   Afibrinogenemia, Congenital

Synonym
Congenital Afibrinogenemia

Congenital afibrinogenemia is a rare disorder characterized by absence of a certain substance (protein) in the blood that is essential in the blood clotting (coagulation) process. This protein is known as fibrinogen or coagulation factor I. Affected individuals may be susceptible to severe bleeding (hemorrhaging) episodes, particularly during infancy and childhood. Congenital afibrinogenemia is thought to be transmitted as an autosomal recessive trait.

The following organizations may provide additional information and support:
March of Dimes Birth Defects Foundation
National Hemophilia Foundation
NIH/National Heart, Lung and Blood Institute Information Center

35   Agammaglobulinemias, Primary

Synonyms
Antibody Deficiency
Gammaglobulin Deficiency
Immunoglobulin Deficiency

Disorder Subdivisions
Acquired Immunodeficiency Syndrome (AIDS)
Adenosine Deaminase Deficiency, Severe Combined Immunodeficiency with
Anti-Epstein-Barr Virus Nuclear Antigen (EBNA) Antibody Deficiency
Antibody Deficiency with Normal Immunoglobulins, Specific
Antibody Deficiency with Near Normal Immunoglobulins

Autosomal Recessive Agammaglobulinemia
Bruton's Agammaglobulinemia Common
Cellelar Immunodeficiency with Purine Nucleoside Phosphorylase Deficiency
Chronic Mucocutaneous Candidiasis
DiGeorge Syndrome
Duncan's Disease
Dysgammaglobulinemia, Janeway
Hyper IgM Syndrome
Hypogammaglobulinemia
Hypogammaglobulinemia Transient of Infancy
Idiopathic Immunoglobulin Deficiency
IgA Deficiency, Selective
IgG Subclass, Selective Deficiency of
IgM Deficiency, Selective
Immunodeficiency Common, Variable, Unclassifiable
Immunodeficiency with Hyper-IgM
Janeway I
Kappa Light Chain Deficiency
Late-Onset Immunoglobulin Deficiency
Lymphoproliferate X-Linked Syndrome
Secretory Component Deficiency
Secretory IgA Deficiency
Severe Combined Immunodeficiency (SCID)
Thymic Hypoplasia, Agammaglobulinemias, Primary Included
Variable Onset Immunoglobulin Deficiency
Dysgammaglobulinemia
X-Linked Agammaglobulinemia
X-Linked Agammaglobulinemia with Growth Hormone Deficiency
X-Linked Infantile Agammaglobulinemia
X-Linked Recessive Severe Combined Immunodeficiency

Primary agammaglobulinemias are a group of inherited immune deficiencies characterized by insufficient antibodies. Antibodies are composed of certain proteins (immunoglobulins) that are essential to the immune system. They are produced by specialized cells (i.e., B lymphocytes) that circulate in the lymphatic fluid and blood. Antibodies fight off bacteria, viruses, and other foreign substances that threaten the body. Agammaglobulinemias are also characterized by the abnormal function of specialized white blood cells called B lymphocytes. The B lymphocytes are supposed to search out and identify bacteria, viruses, or other foreign substances in the body. T lymphocytes, also known as the "killer cells," assist B lymphocytes to respond to infection and other antigens. However, in some forms of primary agammaglobulinemias, neither the B nor the T lymphocytes function normally. There are three types of primary agammaglobulinemias: X-linked agammaglobulinemia (XLA), X-linked agammaglobulinemia with growth hormone deficiency, and autosomal recessive agammaglobulinemia. All of these disorders are characterized by a weakened immune system that must be enhanced by gammaglobulin in order to fight infections.

The following organizations may provide additional information and support:
American Academy of Allergy Asthma and Immunology
Autoimmune Information Network, Inc.
Centers for Disease Control and Prevention
Immune Deficiency Foundation
International Patient Organization for Primary Immunodeficiencies
Jeffrey Modell Foundation
March of Dimes Birth Defects Foundation
NIH/National Institute of Allergy and Infectious Diseases

36 Agenesis of Corpus Callosum

Synonyms
ACC
Corpus Callosum, Agenesis

Disorder Subdivisions
Acquired Form of ACC
Aicardi Syndrome
Autosomal Recessive Inheritance ACC (e.g., Andermann Syndrome)
X-Linked Dominant Inheritance ACC (e.g., ARX)

Agenesis of corpus callosum (ACC) is a rare disorder that is present at birth (congenital). It is characterized by a partial or complete absence (agenesis) of an area of the brain that connects the two cerebral hemispheres. This part of the brain is normally composed of transverse fibers. The cause of agenesis of corpus callosum is usually not known, but it can be inherited as either an autosomal recessive trait or an X-linked dominant trait. It can also be caused by an infection or injury during the twelfth to the twenty-second week of pregnancy (intrauterine) leading to developmental disturbance of the fetal brain. Intrauterine exposure to alcohol (fetal alcohol syndrome) can also result in ACC. In some cases, mental retardation may result, but intelligence may be only mildly impaired and subtle psychosocial symptoms may be present. ACC is frequently diagnosed

during the first 2 years of life. An epileptic seizure can be the first symptom indicating that a child should be tested for a brain dysfunction. The disorder can also be without apparent symptoms in the mildest cases for many years.

The following organizations may provide additional information and support:
Agenesis of the Corpus Callosum (ACC) Network
The Arc (A National Organization on Mental Retardation)
Birth Defect Research for Children, Inc.
Guardians of Hydrocephalus Research Foundation
Hydrocephalus Association
March of Dimes Birth Defects Foundation
National Hydrocephalus Foundation
National Institute of Neurological Disorders and Stroke (NINDS)
National Organization of Disorders of the Corpus Callosum

37 Agnosia, Primary Visual

Synonyms
Agnosis, Primary
Monomodal Visual Amnesia
Visual Amnesia

Primary visual agnosia is a rare neurological disorder characterized by the total or partial loss of the ability to recognize and identify familiar objects and/or people by sight. This occurs without loss of the ability to actually see the object or person. The symptoms of visual agnosia occur as a result of damage to certain areas of the brain (primary) or in association with other disorders (secondary).

The following organization may provide additional information and support:
National Institute of Neurological Disorders and Stroke (NINDS)

38 Agranulocytosis, Acquired

Synonyms
Agranulocytic Angina
Granulocytopenia, Primary
Neutropenia, Malignant

Acquired agranulocytosis is a rare, drug-induced blood disorder that is characterized by a severe reduction in the number of white blood cells (granulocytes) in the circulating blood. The name granulocyte refers to grain-like bodies within the cell. Granulocytes include basophils, eosinophils, and neutrophils. Acquired agranulocytosis may be caused by a variety of drugs. However, among the drugs to which a patient may be sensitive are several used in the treatment of cancer (cancer chemotherapeutic agents) and others used as antipsychotic medications (e.g., clozapine). The symptoms of this disorder come about as the result of interference in the production of granulocytes in the bone marrow. People with acquired agranulocytosis are susceptible to a variety of bacterial infections, usually caused by otherwise benign bacteria found in the body. Not infrequently, painful ulcers also develop in mucous membranes that line the mouth and/or the gastrointestinal tract.

The following organizations may provide additional information and support:
National Neutropenia Network
Neutropenia Support Association, Inc.
NIH/National Heart, Lung and Blood Institute Information Center

---

39 Ahumada-Del Castillo Syndrome

Synonyms
Amenorrhea-Galactorrhea-FSH Decrease Syndrome
Argonz-Del Castillo Syndrome
Galactorrhea-Amenorrhea without Pregnancy
Nonpuerperal Galactorrhea-Amenorrhea

Ahumada-Del Castillo is a rare endocrine disorder affecting adult females, which is characterized by impairment in the function of the pituitary and hypothalamus glands. Symptoms may include the production of breast milk (lactation) not associated with nursing and the absence of menstrual periods (amenorrhea) due to the lack of monthly ovulation (anovulation).

The following organizations may provide additional information and support:
National Infertility Association
National Infertility Network Exchange
National Women's Health Network
National Women's Health Resource Center

---

40 Aicardi Syndrome

Synonyms
Agenesis of Corpus Callosum-Chorioretinitis Abnormality
Agenesis of Corpus Callosum-Infantile Spasms-Ocular Anomalies
Callosal Agenesis and Ocular Abnormalities
Chorioretinal Anomalies with ACC
Corpus Callosum, Agenesis of and Chorioretinal Abnormality

Aicardi syndrome is an extremely rare congenital disorder in which the structure linking the two cerebral hemispheres of the brain (corpus callosum) fails to develop. The absence of the corpus callosum is associated with frequent seizures, marked abnormalities of the retina and choroid (the thin membrane that covers the retina) of the eyes, and/or mental retardation.

The following organizations may provide additional information and support:
Aicardi Syndrome Awareness and Support Group
Aicardi Syndrome Foundation
Aicardi Syndrome Newsletter, Inc.
The Arc (A National Organization on Mental Retardation)
Blind Children's Fund
March of Dimes Birth Defects Foundation
National Association for Visually Handicapped
National Institute of Neurological Disorders and Stroke (NINDS)

---

41 AIDS (Acquired Immune Deficiency Syndrome)

Synonyms
Acquired Immune Deficiency Syndrome

Disorder Subdivisions
AIDS Prodrome
AIDS Related Complex
AIDS-Related Complex (ARC)
ARC
Mini-AIDS
Wasting/Lymph Node Syndrome

AIDS is an infectious disorder that suppresses the normal function of the immune system. It is caused by the human immunodeficiency virus (HIV), which destroys the body's ability to fight infections. Specific cells of the immune system that are responsible for the proper response to infections (T cells) are destroyed by this virus. Characteristically a person infected with HIV initially experiences no symptoms for a variable period of time. This may be followed by the development of persistent generalized swelling of the lymph nodes (AIDS-related lymphadenopathy). Eventually most patients infected with HIV experience a syndrome of symptoms that includes excessive fatigue, weight loss, and/or skin rashes. The later stages of HIV infection are characterized by the progressive depression of T cells and repeated infections that can even occur during a course of antibiotic therapy for another infection (superinfections). People with AIDS are particularly vulnerable to "opportunistic infections" from bacteria that other people normally fight off. Pneumocystis carinii, which causes severe inflammation of the lungs (pneumonia), is a common infection that affects people with AIDS. Cancers (malignant neoplasms), and a wide variety of neurological abnormalities, most notably the AIDS dementia complex, may also occur. These neurological symptoms occur when HIV infects the nervous system.

The following organizations may provide additional information and support:
AIDSinfo
American Social Health Association
amfAR (American Foundation for AIDS Research)
Anemia Institute for Research and Education
CDC Business Responds to AIDS and Labor Responds to AIDS
Centers for Disease Control and Prevention
Health Information Network
Hemophilia Federation of America
HIV/AIDS Treatment Information Service
Jack Miller Center for Peripheral Neuropathy
National Gay Task Force
NIH/National Institute of Allergy and Infectious Diseases
Sexuality Information and Education Council of the U.S.
Sjældne Diagnoser / Rare Disorders Denmark

42 AIDS Dysmorphic Syndrome

Synonyms
Dysmorphic AIDS
Dysmorphic Acquired Immune Deficiency Syndrome
Fetal AIDS Infection
Fetal Acquired Immune Deficiency Syndrome (AIDS)
Fetal Effects of AIDS
HIV Embryopathy
Perinatal AIDS

The term "AIDS dysmorphic syndrome" or "HIV embryopathy" has been used by some researchers to describe specific facial malformations (i.e., craniofacial dysmorphism), an unusually small head, and growth deficiency in some infants infected with HIV.* Such craniofacial abnormalities have included a prominent, boxlike forehead; large, wide eyes; a flattened nasal bridge; and an unusually pronounced philtrum, which is the vertical groove in the center of the upper lip. However, many investigators have since questioned the significance of these observations. Such researchers indicate that there is lack of evidence for characteristic craniofacial malformations in infants who acquired HIV infection from their mother before, during, or shortly after birth (i.e., perinatally). *HIV is the abbreviation for the human immunodeficiency virus, a retrovirus that infects certain white blood cells called helper T cells (CD4+ cells). HIV infection leads to progressive deterioration of the body's immune system and causes acquired immunodeficiency syndrome (AIDS).

The following organizations may provide additional information and support:
amfAR (American Foundation for AIDS Research)
The Arc (A National Organization on Mental Retardation)
Centers for Disease Control and Prevention
Computerized AIDS Information Network
Jack Miller Center for Peripheral Neuropathy
NIH/National Institute of Allergy and Infectious Diseases

43 Alagille Syndrome

Synonyms
AHD
Arteriohepatic Dysplasia
Cholestasis with Peripheral Pulmonary Stenosis
Syndromatic Hepatic Ductular Hypoplasia

Alagille syndrome is a genetic liver disorder usually present at birth. It is characterized by insufficient passage of bile due to a lower than normal number of bile ducts inside the liver. In some cases, the child may be born with no bile ducts. Major symptoms include prolonged yellow skin discoloration (jaundice), eye and heart structure anomalies, abnormally shaped vertebrae of the spine, compression of nerve space inside the lower spine, an absence of deep tendon reflexes, mental deficiency, facial and kidney (renal) abnormalities, shortened fingers, and pancreatic insufficiency.

The following organizations may provide additional information and support:
Alagille Syndrome Alliance
American Liver Foundation
The Arc (A National Organization on Mental Retardation)
Children's Liver Alliance
Digestive Disease National Coalition
NIH/National Digestive Diseases Information Clearinghouse

44 Albinism

Synonyms

Albinismus
BADS
Congenital Achromia
Hypopigmentation
Oculocutaneous Albinism

Disorder Subdivisions

AIED
Aland Island Eye Disease (X-Linked)
Albinoidism
Autosomal Dominant Albinism
Autosomal Recessive Forms of Ocular Albinism
Black Locks-Albinism-Deafness of Sensoneural Type (BADS)
Brown Albinism
Chediak-Higashi Syndrome
Cross' Syndrome
Forsius-Eriksson Syndrome (X-Linked)
Hermansky-Pudlak Syndrome
Nettleship Falls Syndrome (X-Linked)
Ocular Albinism
Rufous Albinism
Tyrosinase Negative Albinism (Type I)
Tyrosinase Positive Albinism (Type II)
Yellow Mutant Albinism

Albinism is a group of rare inherited disorders characterized by the absence at birth of color (pigmentation) in the skin, hair, and eyes. Albinism is also associated with certain syndromes that produce defects in the eyes (ocular abnormalities). The syndromes of this disorder are categorized as tyrosinase-negative oculocutaneous albinism, tyrosinase-positive oculocutaneous albinism (albinoidism), and ocular albinism.

The following organizations may provide additional information and support:
Albinism Fellowship
March of Dimes Birth Defects Foundation
National Organization for Albinism and Hypopigmentation

NIH/National Institute of Child Health and Human Development
Sjældne Diagnoser / Rare Disorders Denmark

45 Alexander Disease

Synonyms

Dysmyelogenic Leukodystrophy
Dysmyelogenic Leukodystrophy-Megalobare
Fibrinoid Degeneration of Astrocytes
Fibrinoid Leukodystrophy
Hyaline Panneuropathy
Leukodystrophy with Rosenthal Fibers
Megalencephaly with Hyaline Inclusion
Megalencephaly with Hyaline Panneuropathy

Alexander disease is an extremely rare, progressive, neurological disorder that usually becomes apparent during infancy or early childhood. However, less commonly, cases have been described in which symptom onset has occurred in later childhood or adolescence (juvenile onset) or, rarely, during the third to fifth decades of life (adult onset). Alexander disease belongs to a group of rare disorders known as leukodystrophies, which are characterized by degenerative changes of the white matter of the brain. More specifically, in Alexander disease there is a lack of normal amounts of the protective, fatty material (myelin) that forms an insulating wrapping (sheath) around certain nerve fibers (axons). Myelin enables the efficient transmission of nerve impulses and provides the "whitish" appearance of the so-called white matter of the brain. Alexander disease is characterized by deficient myelin formation in infants, and sometimes in juvenile cases, that is most prominent in the front (i.e., frontal) lobes of the brain's two hemispheres (cerebrum). The disorder is also associated with the formation of abnormal, fibrous deposits known as "Rosenthal fibers" throughout certain regions of the brain and spinal cord (central nervous system [CNS]). In infants and young children affected by Alexander disease, associated symptoms and findings include a failure to grow and gain weight at the expected rate (failure to thrive); delays in the development of certain physical, mental, and behavioral skills that are typically acquired at particular stages (psychomotor retardation); and progressive enlargement of the head (macrocephaly). Additional features typically include sudden episodes of uncontrolled electrical activity in the brain (seizures); abnormally increased muscle stiffness and restriction of movement (spasticity); and progressive neurological deterioration. In some cases, there is hydrocephalus. In most cases, Alexander disease appears to occur randomly for unknown reasons (sporadically), with no family history of the disease. In an extremely small number of cases, it is thought that the disorder may have affected more than one family member.

The following organizations may provide additional information and support:
The Arc (A National Organization on Mental Retardation)
Association Europeene contre les Leucodystrophes
Children's Brain Diseases Foundation
Hunter's Hope Foundation, Inc.
Let Them Hear Foundation
March of Dimes Birth Defects Foundation
National Institute of Neurological Disorders and Stroke (NINDS)
United Leukodystrophy Foundation

46 Alkaptonuria

Synonyms
Alcaptonuria (Alternate Spelling for Alkaptonuria)
Alkaptonuric Ochronosis
Hereditary Alkaptonuria
Homogentisic Acid Oxidase Deficiency
Homogentisic Acidura
Ochronosis
Ochronotic Arthritis

Alkaptonuria is a rare hereditary disorder in which homogentisic acid accumulates in the body and destroys connective tissue and bone, creating a condition called ochronosis. Symptoms generally begin during the second or third decade of life, and may progress to incapacitating bone and joint disease by the sixth to eighth decade of life. The condition is characterized by the excretion of large volumes of dark colored urine. The darkened urine is the result of the exposure to the air of homogentisic acid that accumulates in the urine.

The following organizations may provide additional information and support:
Alkaptonuria Society, LTD
CLIMB (Children Living with Inherited Metabolic Diseases)
March of Dimes Birth Defects Foundation
NIH/National Arthritis and Musculoskeletal and Skin Diseases Information Clearinghouse

47 Allan Herndon Syndrome

Synonyms
AHDS
Allan-Herndon-Dudley Mental Retardation
Allan-Herndon-Dudley Syndrome
X-Linked Mental Retardation with Hypotonia

Allan-Herndon syndrome is an extremely rare inherited disorder that may be characterized by severe mental retardation, an impaired ability to form words and speak clearly (dysarthria), diminished muscle tone (hypotonia), and/or movement abnormalities. With the exception of poor muscle tone, most affected infants appear to develop normally during the first months of life. However, by about six months of age, affected infants may seem weak and have an inability to hold up the head. Due to hypotonia, severely reduced motor development, and other abnormalities, affected children may not develop the ability to walk or may walk with difficulty. Associated features often include underdevelopment (hypoplasia) and wasting (atrophy) of muscle tissue; weakness and stiffness of the legs (spastic paraplegia) with exaggerated reflexes (hyperreflexia); relatively slow, involuntary, purposeless, writhing movements (athetoid movements); and/or other movement abnormalities. Affected individuals may also have abnormalities of the skull and facial (craniofacial) region. Allan Herndon syndrome is thought to be inherited as an X-linked recessive trait and therefore is typically fully expressed in males only.

The following organizations may provide additional information and support:
The Arc (A National Organization on Mental Retardation)
NIH/National Institute on Deafness and Other Communication Disorders Information Clearinghouse
WE MOVE (Worldwide Education and Awareness for Movement Disorders)

48 Alopecia Areata

Synonyms
Alopecia Celsi
Alopecia Cicatrisata
Alopecia Circumscripta
Cazenave's Vitiligo
Celsus' Vitiligo
Jonston's Alopecia
Porrigo Decalvans
Vitiligo Capitis

Disorder Subdivisions
Alopecia Seminuniversalis
Alopecia Totalis
Alopecia Universalis

Alopecia areata is a disorder characterized by loss of hair. Sometimes, this means simply a few bare patches on the scalp. In other cases, hair loss is more extensive. Although the exact cause is not known, this is thought to be an autoimmune disorder in which the immune system, the body's own defense system, mistakenly attacks the hair follicles, the tiny structures from which hairs grow. Unpredictable hair loss is the only noticeable symptom of this disorder. Regrowth of hair may or may not occur. Hair loss is usually confined to the head and face, although the entire body may be involved.

The following organizations may provide additional information and support:
American Autoimmune Related Diseases Association, Inc.
Autoimmune Information Network, Inc
Locks of Love
National Alopecia Areata Foundation
National Cancer Institute
NIH/National Arthritis and Musculoskeletal and Skin Diseases Information Clearinghouse

49 Alpers Disease

Synonyms
Alpers Diffuse Degeneration of Cerebral Gray Matter with Hepatic Cirrhosis
Alpers Progressive Infantile Poliodystrophy
Diffuse Cerebral Degeneration in Infancy
Poliodystrophia Cerebri Progressiva
Progressive Cerebral Poliodystrophy

Alpers disease is a progressive neurologic disorder that begins during childhood. Symptoms include increased muscle tone with exaggerated reflexes (spasticity), seizures, loss of cognitive ability (dementia) and, in many cases, liver disease.

The following organizations may provide additional information and support:
Epilepsy Foundation
National Association for Visually Handicapped
National Institute of Neurological Disorders and Stroke (NINDS)
United Mitochondrial Disease Foundation

50 Alpha-1-Antitrypsin Deficiency

Synonyms
A1AD
A1AT Deficiency
AAT
AAT Deficiency
Alpha-1
Antitrypsin Deficiency
Cholestasis, Neonatal
Familial Chronic Obstructive Lung Disease
Familial Emphysema
Hereditary Emphysema
Homozygous Alpha-1-Antitrypsin Deficiency
PI
Protease Inhibitor Deficiency
Serum Protease Inhibitor Deficiency

Alpha-1-antitrypsin deficiency (A1AD) is a hereditary disorder characterized by low levels of a protein called alpha-1-antitrypsin (A1AT) which is found in the blood. This deficiency may predispose an individual to several illnesses but most commonly appears as emphysema, less commonly as liver disease, or more rarely, as a skin condition called panniculitis. A deficiency of A1AT allows substances that break down protein (proteolytic enzymes) to attack various tissues of the body. This results in destructive changes in the lungs (emphysema) and may also affect the liver and joints. Alpha-1-antitrypsin is ordinarily released by specialized, granular white blood cells (neutrophils) in response to infection or inflammation. A deficiency of alpha-1-antitrypsin results in unbalanced (relatively unopposed) rapid breakdown of proteins (protease activity), especially in the supporting elastic structures of the lungs. This destruction over many years leads to emphysema and is accelerated by smoking.

The following organizations may provide additional information and support:
Alpha-1 Association
Alpha-1 Foundation
Alpha-1 Research Registry
American Liver Foundation
American Lung Association
Children's Liver Alliance
Children's Liver Disease Foundation
March of Dimes Birth Defects Foundation
Sjældne Diagnoser / Rare Disorders Denmark

51 Alpha-Mannosidosis

Synonyms

Alpha-Mannosidase B Deficiency
Lysosomal Alpha-D-Mannosidase Deficiency
Mannosidase, Alpha B, Lysosomal
Mannosidosis
Mannosidosis, Alpha B, Lysosomal

Alpha-mannosidosis is one of a group of very rare, inherited, lysosomal storage diseases involving the breakdown (catabolism) of complex molecules composed of a sugar attached to a protein (glycoprotein). These disorders are caused by a deficiency of an enzyme essential to the process of breaking down the complex molecule. As a result, these complex substances accumulate in the cell with profoundly disturbing consequences. The enzyme that is lacking is known as alpha-D-mannosidase and this disorder is one of approximately 50 lysosomal storage diseases. The disorder is inherited as an autosomal recessive trait. The medical community has arranged the symptoms of alpha-mannosidosis into three types: Type 1, the most mild form, generally appears after the age of 10 years; Type 2, the moderate form, may be accompanied by skeletal and muscular defects and is usually slow to progress; Type 3, the most severe form, usually becomes apparent shortly after birth and involves the central nervous system. Progression of Type 3 is very fast.

The following organizations may provide additional information and support:
The Arc (A National Organization on Mental Retardation)
CLIMB (Children Living with Inherited Metabolic Diseases)
International Society for Mannosidosis & Related Diseases, Inc.
NIH/National Digestive Diseases Information Clearinghouse
Vaincre Les Maladies Lysosomales

52 Alport Syndrome

Synonyms

Hematuria-Nephropathy Deafness
Hemorrhagic Familial Nephritis
Hereditary Deafness and Nephropathy
Hereditary Nephritis
Hereditary Nephritis With Sensory Deafness
Nephritis and Nerve Deafness, Hereditary
Nephropathy and Deafness, Hereditary

Disorder Subdivisions

Autosomal Dominant Alport Syndrome (ADAS)
Autosomal Recessive Alport Syndrome (ARAS)
X-Linked Alport Syndrome (XLAS)

Alport syndrome is a group of hereditary disorders characterized by progressive deterioration of parts of the kidney known as basement membranes. This deterioration may lead to chronic kidney (renal) disease. Eventually, severe renal failure (end-stage renal disease or ESRD) may develop. Some types of Alport syndrome may also affect vision and hearing. Most cases of Alport syndrome have an X-linked pattern of inheritance.

The following organizations may provide additional information and support:
American Foundation for Urologic Disease
American Kidney Fund, Inc.
Hereditary Nephritis Foundation
Let Them Hear Foundation
National Kidney Foundation
NIH/National Kidney and Urologic Diseases Information Clearinghouse

53 Alstrom Syndrome

Synonym

ALMS

Alstrom syndrome is a rare genetic disorder most often characterized by vision and hearing abnormalities, childhood obesity, diabetes mellitus, and slowly progressive kidney (renal) dysfunction (chronic nephropathy). Specific features vary from case to case. Additional features sometimes associated with Alstrom syndrome include disease of the heart muscle (cardiomyopathy), skin abnormalities and abnormalities affecting additional organ systems. Intelligence is not affected. Alstrom syndrome is inherited as an autosomal recessive trait.

The following organizations may provide additional information and support:
Alstrom Syndrome International
American Society for Deaf Children
Better Hearing Institute
Blind Children's Center
Blind Children's Fund
Cardiomyopathy Association
Children's Cardiomyopathy Foundation
Foundation Fighting Blindness, Inc.
Little People of America, Inc.

March of Dimes Birth Defects Foundation
Marshall Jan, M.D.
National Association for Parents of Children with Visual Impairments (NAPVI)
National Association for Visually Handicapped
NIH/National Eye Institute
NIH/National Institute on Deafness and Other Communication Disorders (Balance)

54 Alternating Hemiplegia of Childhood

Synonyms
AHC
Alternating Hemiplegia Syndrome

Alternating hemiplegia of childhood (AHC) is a rare neurological disorder characterized by frequent, temporary episodes of paralysis on one side of the body (hemiplegia). Symptoms usually begin before the age of 18 months. This syndrome may be characterized by temporary (transient) hemiplegia of varying degrees; temporary paralysis of the muscles that control eye movement (transient ocular palsies); sudden, involuntary movements of limbs and facial muscles (choreoathetosis); and/or excessive sweating with changes in skin color and body temperature (autonomic nervous system dysfunction). Mental capacity may be affected. The exact cause of AHC is unknown. Some cases of AHC may be inherited as an autosomal dominant trait.

The following organizations may provide additional information and support:
Alternating Hemiplegia of Childhood Foundation (AHC)
National Institute of Neurological Disorders and Stroke (NINDS)

55 Alveolar Capillary Dysplasia

Synonym
ACD

Alveolar capillary dysplasia (ACD) is a rare, likely congenital, disorder of the lungs (pulmonary system) and especially of the blood system serving the lungs. It is a disorder of the newborn. The normal diffusion process of oxygen from the air sacs to the blood in the lungs and, thence, to the heart, fails to develop properly. The disorder is sometimes called misalignment of the pulmonary veins. Rather than misaligned, the pulmonary vein is malpositioned in a site somewhat different from its normal position. Infants with the disorder pres-

ent with the signs of lack of oxygen (hypoxemia) and severely increased pulmonary hypertension. Since treatment is seldom, if ever, effective, life expectancy of the infant is very, very short.

The following organizations may provide additional information and support:
Alveolar Capillary Dysplasia Association
American Lung Association

56 Alveolar Soft Part Sarcoma

Synonyms
Alveolar Sarcoma of Soft Parts
ASP Sarcoma
ASPS

Alveolar soft part sarcoma (ASPS) is a rare sarcoma (malignant tumor of connective tissue) of an unclear cause. It is among the least common sarcomas, representing 0.2-1 percent of large studies of soft tissue sarcomas. Since there are approximately 8000 soft-tissue sarcomas per year that arise in the United States, this means there are on the order of 15 to 80 cases nationwide each year. It is characterized by a painless mass in the leg or buttock, with a particular affinity to travel to the lungs as multiple nodules, presumably while the sarcoma itself is still small. ASPS is very rare, because it involves a specific breaking and joining event between two chromosomes, called an "unbalanced translocation". This finding is observed in essentially all ASPS examined so far. This finding cannot be passed on to children, however, as the finding occurs only in the tumor, not in the normal cells; in addition, there are no families in which multiple family members have ASPS. Treatment is with surgery and radiation for the primary place where the sarcoma arises. For disease that travels to the lungs, sometimes surgery is possible to remove nodules, but more typically chemotherapy is the only option for treatment. This tumor tends to be resistant to standard chemotherapy, so new treatments involving new chemotherapy drugs are also a reasonable option for treatment. Interferon-alfa showed benefit in one person from Japan with ASPS. There is little other data on possible helpful chemotherapy for this tumor.

The following organizations may provide additional information and support:
Alliance Against Alveolar Soft Part Sarcoma
American Cancer Society, Inc.
National Cancer Institute

National Coalition for Cancer Survivorship
Rare Cancer Alliance
Sarcoma Alliance
Sarcoma Foundation of America

NIH/National Institute on Aging
Stem Cell Research Foundation
UCSF Memory and Aging Center
Vasculitis of the Central Nervous System

57 Alveolitis, Extrinsic Allergic

Synonyms
Allergic Interstitial Pneumonitis
Extrinsic Allergic Pneumonia
Hypersensitivity Pneumonitis

Extrinsic allergic alveolitis is a lung disorder resulting from repeated inhalation of organic dust, usually in a specific occupational setting. In the acute form, respiratory symptoms and fever begin several hours after exposure to the dust. The chronic form is characterized by gradual changes in the lung tissue associated with several years of exposure to the irritant.

The following organizations may provide additional information and support:
American Academy of Allergy Asthma and Immunology
American Lung Association
NIH/National Institute of Allergy and Infectious Diseases

58 Alzheimer's Disease

Synonym
Presenile Dementia

Alzheimer's disease is a progressive condition of the brain affecting memory, thought and language. The degenerative changes of Alzheimer's disease lead to patches or plaques in the brain and the entanglement of nerve fibers (neurofibrillary tangles). Memory loss and behavioral changes occur as a result of these changes in brain tissue.

The following organizations may provide additional information and support:
Alzheimer's Association
Alzheimer's Disease Education and Referral Center
Alzheimer's Foundation of America
C-Mac Informational Services, Inc.
John Douglas French Alzheimer's Foundation
March of Dimes Birth Defects Foundation
National Institute of Neurological Disorders and Stroke (NINDS)

59 Ameloblastoma

Synonyms
Adamantinoma
Mandibular Ameloblastoma
Maxillary Ameloblastoma
Odontogenic Tumor

Ameloblastoma is a rare disorder of the jaw involving abnormal tissue growth. The resulting tumors or cysts are usually not malignant (benign) but the tissue growth may be aggressive in the involved area. On occasion, tissue near the jaws, such as around the sinuses and eye sockets, may become involved as well. The tissues involved are most often those that give rise to the teeth so that ameloblastoma may cause facial distortion. Malignancy is uncommon as are metastases, but they do occur.

The following organizations may provide additional information and support:
American Cancer Society, Inc.
NIH/National Oral Health Information Clearinghouse

60 Amelogenesis Imperfecta

Synonyms
Brown Enamel, Hereditary
Hypocalcified (Hypomineralized) Type
Hypomaturation Type (Snow-Capped Teeth)
Hypoplastic (Hypoplastic-Explastic) Type

Amelogenesis imperfecta is a rare inherited disorder characterized by brown discoloration of the teeth, resulting from a lack of calcium (hypocalcification) or underdevelopment (hypoplasia) of the hard outer covering of teeth (enamel). The disorder is divided into numerous forms based on the severity of the enamel defect (e.g., complete absence [agenesis], underdevelopment, etc.). Individuals with amelogenesis imperfecta may be prone to early tooth loss and/or disease of the structures that surround and support the teeth (periodontal disease). Amelogenesis imperfecta may be inherited as an X-linked, autosomal dominant, or autosomal recessive genetic trait, depending on the form present.

The following organizations may provide additional information and support:
National Foundation for Ectodermal Dysplasias
NIH/National Oral Health Information Clearinghouse

61 Amenorrhea, Primary

Synonyms

Absence of Menstruation, Primary
PA

Amenorrhea is the absense of menstrual periods. The term "primary amenorrhea" is used if periods have never started in females aged 16 or older. It is a rare gynecological disorder. Regular menstruation usually begins (menarche) within 2 years of the onset of puberty. Absence of menses by age 16-18 constitutes primary amenorrhea.

The following organizations may provide additional information and support:
American Autoimmune Related Diseases Association, Inc.
National Adrenal Diseases Foundation
National Women's Health Network

62 Amenorrhea-Galactorrhea Syndrome

Synonyms

Amenorrhea-Galactorrhea, Nonpuerperal
Forbes-Albright Syndrome
Galactorrhea-Amenorrhea Syndrome
Nonpuerperal Galactorrhea

Amenorrhea-Galactorrhea syndrome is a rare endocrine disorder characterized by the abnormal production of breast milk (lactation), lack of ovulation (anovulation), and the absence of regular menstrual periods (amenorrhea). This disorder is usually caused by a hormone secreting tumor of the pituitary or hypothalamus gland (adenoma) which produces excessive amounts of prolactin.

The following organizations may provide additional information and support:
National Women's Health Network
National Women's Health Resource Center

63 Amniotic Bands

Synonyms

ABS
Amniotic Band Disruption Complex
Amniotic Band Sequence
Amniotic Band Syndrome
Amniotic Rupture Sequence
Constricting Bands, Congenital
Early Constraint Defects
Oligohydramnios Sequence
Streeter Anomaly

Amniotic bands is an abnormal condition of fetal development in which fibrous bands of tissue that originate from the amniotic sac encircle and constrict certain fetal areas, disrupting fetal growth. The amniotic sac is the thin, membranous sac that contains amniotic fluid and the developing fetus during pregnancy. Amniotic band formation may be associated with early rupture of the amniotic membrane, chronic leakage and abnormally decreased levels of the fluid surrounding the developing fetus (oligohydramnios), and abnormally decreased fetal movements. Associated structural malformations are extremely variable and may depend upon the time of amniotic band formation during fetal development. Such deformities may include abnormalities of the arms and legs (limbs), fingers and toes (digits), spine, lungs, facial area, skull, and/or abdominal and chest region.

The following organizations may provide additional information and support:
Birth Defect Research for Children, Inc.
Genetic and Rare Diseases (GARD) Information Center
NIH/National Institute of Child Health and Human Development

64 Amyloidosis

Disorder Subdivisions

Hereditary Amyloidosis
Localized Amyloidosis
Primary Amyloidosis
Secondary Amyloidosis

Amyloidosis is a group of disorders caused by abnormal folding of proteins leading to fibril formation in one or more body organs, systems or soft tissues. These clumps of protein are called amyloid deposits and the accumulation of amyloid deposits causes the progressive malfunction and eventual failure of the affected organ. Normally, proteins are broken down at about the same rate as they are produced, but these unusually stable amyloid deposits are deposited more rapidly than they can be broken down. The accumulation may be localized in one organ or may be systemic such that several organs are affected. The different types of systemic amyloidosis are sometimes classified as primary, secondary or hereditary. Primary amyloidosis (also called AL) is the most common type of systemic amyloidosis. It is caused by an abnormal plasma cell in the bone marrow and sometimes occurs with multiple myeloma. Secondary amyloidosis (also called AA) occurs in association with another disease such as rheumatoid arthritis, familial Mediterranean fever or other chronic infection or inflammatory disease. Hereditary amyloidosis is a rare type of amyloidosis that is caused by an abnormal gene. There are several abnormal genes that can cause hereditary amyloidosis, but the most common type of hereditary amyloidosis is called ATTR and is caused by a mutation in the TTR gene. Beta2-microglobulin amyloidosis (Aβ2M) is a type of systemic amyloidosis that can occur in patients who have experienced long-term kidney dialysis to remove accumulated impurities or wastes in the blood by mechanical filtration.

The following organizations may provide additional information and support:
Amyloidosis Network International
Amyloidosis Support Groups, Inc
Amyloidosis Support Network, Inc.
Association Fransaise Contre l'amylose
Jack Miller Center for Peripheral Neuropathy
March of Dimes Birth Defects Foundation
NIH/National Arthritis and Musculoskeletal and Skin Diseases Information Clearinghouse

65 Amyotrophic Lateral Sclerosis

Synonyms
ALS
Amyotrophic Lateral Sclerosis-Polyglucosan Bodies
Aran-Duchenne Muscular Atrophy
Gehrig's Disease
Lou Gehrig's Disease
Motor System Disease (Focal and Slow)

Disorder Subdivisions
Benign Focal Amyotrophy of ALS
Infantile Spinal Muscular Atrophy, ALS
Juvenile Spinal Muscular Atrophy, Included
Kugelberg-Welander Disease
Primary Lateral Sclerosis
Progressive Bulbar Palsy, Included
Spinal Muscular Atrophy, Type ALS
Upper Motor Neuron Disease
Werdnig-Hoffman Disease
Wohlfart-Disease

Amyotrophic lateral sclerosis (ALS) is one of a group of disorders known as motor neuron diseases. It is characterized by the progressive degeneration and eventual death of nerve cells (motor neurons) in the brain, brainstem and spinal cord that facilitate communication between the nervous system and voluntary muscles of the body. Ordinarily, motor neurons in the brain (upper motor neurons) send messages to motor neurons in the spinal cord (lower motor neurons) and then to various muscles. ALS affects both the upper and lower motor neurons, so that the transmission of messages is interrupted, and muscles gradually weaken and waste away. As a result, the ability to initiate and control voluntary movement is lost. Ultimately, ALS leads to respiratory failure because affected individuals lose the ability to control muscles in the chest and diaphragm. ALS is often called Lou Gehrig's disease.

The following organizations may provide additional information and support:
ALS Society of Canada
Amyotrophic Lateral Sclerosis Association
Christopher Reeve Paralysis Foundation
Families of Spinal Muscular Atrophy
International Alliance of ALS/MND Associations
Les Turner Amyotrophic Lateral Sclerosis Foundation, Ltd.
Muscular Dystrophy Association
National Institute of Neurological Disorders and Stroke (NINDS)
New Horizons Un-Limited, Inc.
Scottish Motor Neurone Disease Association
Spastic Paraplegia Foundation
Stem Cell Research Foundation
UCSF Memory and Aging Center

66 Anaphylaxis

Synonyms
Allergic Reaction, Severe
Anaphylactic Reaction
Generalized Anaphylaxis

Anaphylaxis is a rare, generalized, potentially life-threatening allergic reaction to a particular substance (allergen) to which individuals have previously developed an extreme sensitivity (hypersensitivity). The reaction typically occurs within seconds or minutes or, more rarely, up to a few hours after exposure to such an allergen. Allergens may include insect venom, certain foods, medications, vaccines, chemicals, or other substances. An anaphylactic reaction may be characterized by development of an itchy, reddish rash (hives); a severe drop in blood pressure; swelling and obstruction of the mouth, nose, and throat; abdominal cramps; nausea and vomiting; diarrhea; and severe difficulties breathing. Without immediate, appropriate treatment, the condition may rapidly lead to a state of unconsciousness (coma) and life-threatening complications.

The following organizations may provide additional information and support:
American Academy of Allergy Asthma and Immunology
Asthma and Allergy Foundation of America, Inc.
NIH/National Institute of Allergy and Infectious Diseases

67 Andersen Disease (GSD IV)

Synonyms
Amylopectinosis
Andersen Glycogenosis
Brancher Deficiency
Branching Enzyme Deficiency
Glycogen Storage Disease IV
Glycogenosis Type IV

Andersen disease belongs to a group of rare genetic disorders of glycogen metabolism, known as "glycogen storage diseases." Glycogen is a complex carbohydrate that is converted into the simple sugar glucose for the body's use as energy. Glycogen storage diseases are characterized by deficiencies of certain enzymes involved in the metabolism of glycogen, leading to an accumulation of abnormal forms or amounts of glycogen in various parts of the body, particularly the liver and muscle. Andersen disease is also known as glycogen storage disease (GSD) type IV. It is caused by deficient activity of the glycogen-branching enzyme, resulting in accumulation of abnormal glycogen in the liver, muscle, and/or other tissues. In most affected individuals, symptoms and findings become evident in the first months of life. Such features typically include failure to grow and gain weight at the expected rate (failure to thrive) and abnormal enlargement of the liver and spleen (hepatosplenomegaly). In such cases, the disease course is typically characterized by progressive liver (hepatic) scarring (cirrhosis) and liver failure, leading to potentially life-threatening complications. In rare cases, however, progressive liver disease may not develop. In addition, several neuromuscular variants of Andersen disease have been described that may be evident at birth, in late childhood,

or adulthood. The disease is inherited as an autosomal recessive trait.

The following organizations may provide additional information and support:
Association for Glycogen Storage Disease
Association for Glycogen Storage Disease (UK)
CLIMB (Children Living with Inherited Metabolic Diseases)
NIH/National Institute of Diabetes, Digestive & Kidney Diseases

68 Androgen Insensitivity Syndrome, Partial

Synonyms
Gilbert-Dreyfus Syndrome
Incomplete Testicular Feminization
Lubs Syndrome
Reifenstein Syndrome
Rosewater Syndrome
Type I Familial Incomplete Male Pseudohermaphroditism

Androgen insensitivity refers to an inability of the body to respond properly to male sex hormones (androgens) produced during pregnancy. This occurs because of a change (mutation) in a gene involved in the production of the protein inside cells that receives the androgen hormone and instructs the cell in how to use it. Partial androgen insensitivity syndrome (PAIS) is part of a spectrum of syndromes that also includes androgen insensitivity syndrome (AIS) and mild androgen insensitivity syndrome (MAIS). In each case, the development of the reproductive and genital organs of the fetus is affected, as a result of the gene mutation. During the first 10 weeks of pregnancy, the external anatomy of male and female embryos appears to be identical. The presence or absence of the male sex hormone testosterone determines whether male or female genitalia develop. In partial androgen insensitivity syndrome, the development of the external genitals will be intermediate between male and female (ambiguous genitalia). Each of these forms of AIS is also a hereditary form of male pseudohermaphroditism, in which the baby is born with testes and possesses both male and female characteristics. The disorder is inherited as an X-linked, recessive trait.

The following organization may provide additional information and support:
Androgen Insensitivity Syndrome Support Group (AISSG)

69 Anemia, Blackfan Diamond

Synonyms
Anemia, Congenital Pure Red Cell
Aplasia, Congenital Pure Red Cell
Chronic Congenital Aregenerative Anemia
Constitutional Erythroid Hypoplasia
DBA
DBS
Diamond-Blackfan Anemia
Erythrogenesis Imperfecta
Estren-Dameshek variant of Fanconi Anemia
Hypoplastic Congenital Anemia

Blackfan-Diamond anemia is a rare blood disorder of unknown cause characterized by deficiency of red blood cells at birth (congenital hypoplastic anemia) and various other symptoms and findings including slow growth, abnormal weakness and fatigue, paleness of the skin, characteristic facial abnormalities, protruding shoulder blades (scapulae), webbing or abnormal shortening of the neck due to fusion of certain bones in the spine (cervical vertebrae), hand deformities, congenital heart defects, and/or other abnormalities. The symptoms and physical findings associated with Blackfan-Diamond anemia vary greatly from case to case. A consistent "pattern" of symptoms and physical findings has not been identified. Blackfan-Diamond anemia may be inherited as either an autosomal dominant or recessive genetic trait.

The following organizations may provide additional information and support:
DBA.UK
Diamond Blackfan Anemia Registry
NIH/National Heart, Lung and Blood Institute

70 Anemia, Fanconi's

Synonyms
Aplastic Anemia with Congenital Anomalies
Congenital Pancytopenia
Constitutional Aplastic Anemia
Fanconi Pancytopenia
Fanconi Panmyelopathy
Fanconi's Anemia, Type I (FA1)
Fanconi's Anemia, Estren-Dameshek Variant

Disorder Subdivisions
Fanconi's Anemia, Complementation Group A (FANCA); FAA
Fanconi's Anemia, Complementation Group B (FANCB); FACB
Fanconi's Anemia, Complementation Group F (FANF); FACF
Fanconi's Anemia, Complementation Group G (FANG); FACG
Fanconi's Anemia, Complementation Group H (FANH); FACH
Fanconi's Anemia, Complementation Group C (FANCC); FAC
Fanconi's Anemia, Complementation Group D (FANCD); FACD
Fanconi's Anemia, Complementation Group E (FANCE); FACE

Fanconi's anemia is a rare genetic disorder that may be apparent at birth or during childhood. The disorder is characterized by deficiency of all bone marrow elements including red blood cells, white blood cells, and platelets (pancytopenia). Fanconi's anemia may also be associated with heart (cardiac), kidney (renal), and/or skeletal abnormalities as well as patchy, brown discolorations (pigmentation changes) of the skin. There are several different subtypes (complementation groups) of Fanconi's anemia, each of which is thought to result from abnormal changes (mutations) of different disease genes. Each subtype appears to share the same characteristic symptoms and findings (phenotype). Fanconi's anemia has autosomal recessive inheritance.

The following organizations may provide additional information and support:
Canadian Fanconi Anemia Research Fund
Fanconi Anaemia Co UK
Fanconi Anemia Research Fund, Inc.
International Fanconi Anemia Registry
Let Them Hear Foundation
March of Dimes Birth Defects Foundation
NIH/Hematology Branch, National Heart, Lung and Blood Institute (NHLBI)
NIH/National Heart, Lung and Blood Institute

71 Anemia, Hemolytic, Acquired Autoimmune

Synonyms
Anemia, Idiopathic Autoimmune Hemolytic
Autoimmune Hemolytic Anemia
Idiopathic Autoimmune Hemolytic Anemia
Immune Hemolytic Anemia

Disorder Subdivisions
Anemia, Cold Antibody Hemolytic
Anemia, Warm Antibody Hemolytic

The autoimmune hemolytic anemias are rare disorders characterized by the premature destruction (hemolysis) of red blood cells at a rate faster than they can be replaced. Acquired hemolytic anemias are non-genetic in origin. Idiopathic acquired autoimmune diseases occur when the body's natural defenses against invading organisms (e.g., lymphocytes, antibodies) destroy its own healthy tissues for no known reason. Normally, the red blood cells (erythrocytes) have a life span of approximately 120 days before being removed by the spleen. The severity of this type of anemia is determined by the life span of the red blood cell and by the rate at which these cells are replaced by the bone marrow. Clinicians are able to determine quite accurately (Coombs test) whether or not red blood cells are carrying with them chemicals that are being incorrectly recognized as an "enemy" and therefore subject to autoimmune destruction. Acquired autoimmune hemolytic anemia is a disorder that occurs in individuals who previously had a normal red blood cell system. The disorder may occur as the result of, or in conjunction with, some other medical condition, in which case it is "secondary" to another disorder. Less commonly, it occurs alone without a precipitating factor. Acquired autoimmune hemolytic anemia occurs in different forms, including warm antibody hemolytic anemia and cold antibody hemolytic anemia. In warm antibody hemolytic anemia, the self-generated antibodies (autoantibodies) attach themselves and cause the destruction of the red blood cells at temperatures above normal body temperature. In contrast, in the cases of cold antibody hemolytic anemia, the self-generated antibodies (autoantibodies) attach themselves and cause the destruction of the red blood cells at temperatures below normal body temperature. (For more information on this disorder, choose Warm Antibody Hemolytic Anemia and/or Cold Antibody Hemolytic Anemia as your search term in the Rare Disease Database.)

The following organizations may provide additional information and support:
American Autoimmune Related Diseases Association, Inc.
Autoimmune Information Network, Inc
March of Dimes Birth Defects Foundation
NIH/National Heart, Lung and Blood Institute Information Center

---

72   Anemia, Hemolytic, Cold Antibody

Synonyms
Anemia, Autoimmune Hemolytic
Cold Agglutinin Disease
Cold Antibody Disease

Cold antibody hemolytic anemia (CAHA) is a rare autoimmune disorder characterized by the pre-mature destruction of red blood cells (RBCs) by the body's natural defenses against invading organisms (antibodies). Normally, the red blood cells have a life span of approximately 120 days before they are destroyed by the spleen. In individuals with CAHA, the red blood cells are destroyed prematurely and the rate of production of new cells in the bone marrow can no longer compensate for their loss. The severity of the anemia is determined by the length of time that the red blood cells survive and by the rate at which the bone marrow continues to create new red blood cell production. The immune hemolytic anemias are classified according to the optimal temperature at which the antibodies act to destroy red blood cells. As their names imply, cold antibody hemolytic anemia occurs at temperatures of approximately 0 to 10 degrees centigrade, while warm antibody hemolytic anemia (WAHA) occurs at temperatures of 37 degrees centigrade or higher. In most cases, CAHA is a primary disorder that typically becomes apparent at 50 to 60 years of age. Symptoms and findings associated with the disorder may include fatigue; low levels of circulating red blood cells (anemia); persistent yellowing of the skin, mucous membranes, and whites of the eyes (jaundice); and/or sweating and coldness of the fingers and/or toes (digits) and uneven bluish or reddish discoloration of the skin of the digits, ankles, and wrists (acrocyanosis or Raynaud's sign). Cold antibody hemolytic anemia may also occur as a secondary disorder in association with a number of different underlying disorders such as certain infectious diseases (e.g., mycoplasma infection, mumps, cytomegalovirus, infectious mononucleosis), immunoproliferative diseases (e.g., non-Hodgkin's lymphoma, chronic lymphocytic leukemia), or connective tissue disorders (e.g., systemic lupus erythematosus). Although CAHA is known to be an autoimmune disorder, its exact underlying cause is not fully understood.

The following organizations may provide additional information and support:
American Autoimmune Related Diseases Association, Inc.
March of Dimes Birth Defects Foundation
NIH/National Heart, Lung and Blood Institute Information Center

---

73   Anemia, Hemolytic, Warm Antibody

Synonyms
Autoimmune Hemolytic Anemia
Warm Reacting Antibody Disease

Warm antibody hemolytic anemia is an autoimmune disorder characterized by the premature destruction of red blood cells by the body's natural defenses against invading organisms (antibodies). Normally, the red blood cells have a life span of approximately 120 days before they are removed by the spleen. In an individual affected with warm antibody hemolytic anemia, the red blood cells are destroyed prematurely and bone marrow production of new cells can no longer compensate for their loss. The severity of the anemia is determined by the time the red blood cells are allowed to survive and by the capacity of the bone marrow to continue new red blood cell production. Immune hemolytic anemias are subdivided by the optimal temperature at which the antibodies destroy red blood cells. As their names imply, warm antibody hemolytic anemia occurs at temperatures of 37 degrees centigrade or higher while cold antibody hemolytic anemia usually occurs at approximately 0 to 10 degrees.

The following organizations may provide additional information and support:
American Autoimmune Related Diseases Association, Inc.
March of Dimes Birth Defects Foundation
NIH/National Heart, Lung and Blood Institute

74 Anemia, Hereditary Nonspherocytic Hemolytic

Synonyms
Congenital Nonspherocytic Hemolytic Anemia
HNHA
NSA
NSHA

Hereditary nonspherocytic hemolytic anemia is a term used to describe a group of rare, genetically transmitted blood disorders characterized by the premature destruction of red blood cells (erythrocytes or RBCs). If the red blood cells cannot be replaced faster than they destroy themselves, anemia is the result. In these disorders, the outside membrane of the cell is weakened, causing it to have an irregular, nonspherical shape and to burst (hemolyze) easily. These disorders are caused by, among other things, defects in the chemical processes involved in the breakdown of sugar molecules (glycolysis). Red blood cells depend on this process for energy and if an enzyme is defective in any one of the stages, the red blood cell cannot function properly and hemolysis, or the breakdown of the membrane that holds the cell together, takes place. The more common of the enzyme de-

ficiencies that lead to HNSHA involve glucose-6-phosphate dehydrogenase (G6PD) deficiency, pyruvate kinase deficiency and hexokinase deficiency. There may be as many as 16 red blood cell enzyme abnormalities that may cause hereditary nonspherocytic hemolytic anemia. In addition, HNSHA may arise as the result of immune disorders, toxic chemicals and drugs, antiviral agents (e.g., ribavirin), physical damage, and infections.

The following organizations may provide additional information and support:
March of Dimes Birth Defects Foundation
NIH/National Heart, Lung and Blood Institute

75 Anemia, Hereditary Spherocytic Hemolytic

Synonyms
Acholuric Jaundice
Chronic Acholuric Jaundice
Congenital Hemolytic Anemia
Congenital Hemolytic Jaundice
Congenital Spherocytic Anemia
Hereditary Spherocytosis
HS
Icterus (Chronic Familial)
Minkowski-Chauffard Syndrome
SPH2
Spherocytic Anemia
Spherocytosis

Hereditary spherocytic hemolytic anemia is a rare blood disorder characterized by defects within red blood cells (intracorpuscular) that result in a shortened survival time for these cells. Red blood cells (erythrocytes) normally circulate for a few months and when they die off are replaced by new erythrocytes. However, in hereditary spherocytic hemolytic anemia, the cells die prematurely. They also have low amounts of fats (lipid) in the cell membranes and an abnormally small amount of surface area. The red blood cells are sphere-shaped (spherocytic) making it difficult for them to pass through the spleen, resulting in the early destruction of these cells (hemolysis). The sphere shape of the red blood cells is the hallmark of hereditary spherocytic hemolytic anemia, and this abnormality may be identified under a microscope. Hereditary spherocytic hemolytic anemia is caused by an inherited metabolic defect.

The following organizations may provide additional information and support:
March of Dimes Birth Defects Foundation
NIH/National Heart, Lung and Blood Institute

76 Anemia, Megaloblastic

Synonyms

Folate Deficiency Anemia
Folic Acid Deficiency Anemia
Hypovitaminosis B12
Megaloblastic Anemia of Pregnancy
Vitamin B12 Deficiency Anemia

An anemia is a condition in which the number of red blood cells (RBCs) or the amount of hemoglobin (the protein in red blood cells that carries oxygen throughout the body) is below normal. Megaloblastic anemias (MGA) are rare blood disorders characterized by the presence of large, structurally and visually abnormal, immature red blood cells (megaloblasts). Decreased numbers and immaturity of white blood cells (leukocytes) and blood platelets (thrombocytes) may also occur. Megaloblastic anemias are usually caused by a deficiency or defective absorption of either vitamin B12 (cobalamin) or folic acid. As a result, they are also known as the vitamin deficiency anemias. In most cases, the fundamental flaws leading to the several forms of MGA caused by vitamin deficiencies are present at the time of birth and exist as a result of a genetic defect. In addition, certain antitumor or immunosuppressive drugs may also cause megaloblastic znemia.

The following organization may provide additional information and support:
NIH/National Heart, Lung and Blood Institute

77 Anemia, Pernicious

Synonyms

Addison's Anemia
Addison-Biermer Anemia
Addisonian Pernicious Anemia
Primary Anemia

Disorder Subdivisions

Adult Onset Pernicious Anemia
Congenital Pernicious Anemia due to Defect of Intrinsic Factor
Enterocyte Cobalamin Malabsorption
Enterocyte Intrinsic Factor Receptor, Defect of
Gastric Intrinsic Factor, Failure of Secretion
Juvenile Intestinal Malabsorption of Vit B12

Pernicious anemia is a rare blood disorder characterized by the inability of the body to properly utilize vitamin B12, which is essential for the development of red blood cells. Most cases result from the lack of the gastric protein known as intrinsic factor, without which vitamin B12 cannot be absorbed. The symptoms of pernicious anemia may include weakness, fatigue, an upset stomach, an abnormally rapid heartbeat (tachycardia), and/or chest pains. Recurring episodes of anemia (megaloblastic) and an abnormal yellow coloration of the skin (jaundice) are also common. Pernicious anemia is thought to be an autoimmune disorder, and certain people may have a genetic predisposition to this disorder. There is a rare congenital form of pernicious anemia in which babies are born lacking the ability to produce effective intrinsic factor. There is also a juvenile form of the disease, but pernicious anemia typically does not appear before the age of 30. The onset of the disease is slow and may span decades. When the disease goes undiagnosed and untreated for a long period of time, it may lead to neurological complications. Nerve cells and blood cells need vitamin B12 to function properly.

The following organizations may provide additional information and support:
American Autoimmune Related Diseases Association, Inc.
The Arc (A National Organization on Mental Retardation)
Autoimmune Information Network, Inc.
NIH/National Heart, Lung and Blood Institute

78 Anemias, Sideroblastic

Disorder Subdivisions

Acquired Sideroblastic Anemia
Hereditary Sideroblastic Anemia
Idiopathic Sideroblastic Anemia

The sideroblastic anemias are a group of blood disorders in which the body has enough iron but is unable to use it to make hemoglobin, which carries oxygen in the blood. As a result, iron accumulates in the mitochondria of red blood cells, giving a ringed appearance to the nucleus (ringed sideroblast). There are three categories of sideroblastic anemias: inherited, acquired, and idiopathic (of unknown origin). The signs and symptoms can range from mild to severe, and include fatigue, breathing difficulties, and weakness. Enlargement of the liver or spleen may also occur. In severe cases, the increased levels of iron in the blood may lead to heart disease, liver damage, and kidney failure.

The following organizations may provide additional information and support:
Iron Disorders Institute
Leukemia & Lymphoma Society
March of Dimes Birth Defects Foundation
NIH/National Heart, Lung and Blood Institute Information Center

79 Anencephaly

Anencephaly is a disorder involving the incomplete development of major parts or all of the brain. Anencephaly is classified as a neural tube defect (NTD), and that term refers to the incomplete development of the brain, spinal cord, and/or their protective coverings. The neural tube is a narrow sheath that is supposed to fold and to close in the third or fourth weeks of pregnancy, in order to form the brain and spinal cord of the embryo. Anencephaly occurs when the anterior or cephalic head-end of this neural tube fails to close, resulting in the failure of major portions of brain, skull and scalp to form. Infants with anencephaly are born without both a forebrain (the front part of the brain) and a cerebrum (the thinking and coordinating part of the brain). Often the remaining brain tissue may be exposed, or without protective covering, either bone or skin. Anencephaly is characterized by the absence of the two hemispheres of the brain. The absent brain tissue is sometimes replaced by a rudimentary brain stem made up of abnormal cystic nerve tissue. Although reflex actions such as breathing and responses to touch or sound may occur, gaining consciousness is almost invariably ruled out.

The following organizations may provide additional information and support:
Birth Defect Research for Children, Inc.
National Institute of Neurological Disorders and Stroke (NINDS)
NIH/National Institute of Child Health and Human Development

80 Angelman Syndrome

Synonyms
AS
Happy Puppet Syndrome (obsolete)

Angelman syndrome is a rare disorder characterized by developmental delay; absence or near absence of speech; unprovoked, prolonged episodes (paroxysms) of inappropriate laughter; characteristic facial abnormalities; and episodes of uncontrolled electrical activity in the brain (seizures). Abnormalities of the head and facial (craniofacial) area may include a small head (microcephaly); deeply set eyes; a large, wide mouth (macrostomia) and a protruding tongue; an underdeveloped upper jaw (maxillary hypoplasia) and protruding lower jaw (mandibular prognathism); and widely spaced teeth. During infancy, feeding difficulties and abnormal sleep patterns are typically present. In addition, by early childhood, individuals with Angelman syndrome have severe developmental delays; impaired control of voluntary movements (ataxia), resulting in a stiff manner of walking (ataxic gait) with jerky arm movements; and characteristic positioning of the arms with flexion of the elbows and wrists. Although affected individuals may be unable to speak, many gradually learn to communicate through other means, such as sign language. In addition, some may have enough receptive language development to understand simple commands. In most affected individuals, Angelman syndrome appears to occur spontaneously (sporadically) for unknown reasons. However, some familial cases have been reported. The disorder is caused by deletion or disruption of a certain gene or genes located on the long arm (q) of chromosome 15 (15q11-q13).

The following organizations may provide additional information and support:
Angelman Syndrome Foundation, Inc.
Angelman Syndrome Support and Education Research Trust
The Arc (A National Organization on Mental Retardation)
Canadian Angelman Syndrome Society
National Institute of Neurological Disorders and Stroke (NINDS)
New Horizons Un-Limited, Inc.
NIH/National Institute of Child Health and Human Development
Sjældne Diagnoser / Rare Disorders Denmark

81 Angioedema, Hereditary

Synonyms
Angioneurotic Edema, Hereditary
C1-INH
C1NH
Complement Component 1 Inhibitor Deficiency
Complement Component C1, Regulatory Component Deficiency
Esterase Inhibitor Deficiency
HAE
HANE

Disorder Subdivisions

C1 Esterase Inhibitor Deficiency, Type I,
Angioedema
C1 Esterase Inhibitor Dysfunction, Type II,
Angioedema

Hereditary angioedema is a rare inherited disorder characterized by recurrent episodes of the accumulation of fluids outside of the blood vessels, blocking the normal flow of blood or lymphatic fluid and causing rapid swelling of tissues in the hands, feet, limbs, face, intestinal tract, or airway. Usually, this swelling is not accompanied by itching, as it might be with an allergic reaction. Swelling of the gastrointestinal tract leads to cramping. Swelling of the airway may lead to obstruction, a potentially very serious complication. These symptoms develop as the result of deficiency or improper functioning of certain proteins that help to maintain the normal flow of fluids through very small blood vessels (capillaries). In some cases, fluid may accumulate in other internal organs. The severity of the disease varies greatly among affected individuals. The most common form of the disorder is hereditary angioedema type I, which is the result of abnormally low levels of certain complex proteins in the blood (C1 esterase inhibitors), known as complements. They help to regulate various body functions (e.g., flow of body fluids in and out of cells). Hereditary angioedema type II, a more uncommon form of the disorder, occurs as the result of the production of abnormal complement proteins.

The following organizations may provide additional information and support:
American Academy of Allergy Asthma and Immunology
Hereditary Angioedema Association, Inc.
Immune Deficiency Foundation
NIH/National Heart, Lung and Blood Institute

82 Aniridia

Synonym
Irideremia

Disorder Subdivisions
AN 1
AN 2
Aniridia Associated with Mental Retardation
Aniridia Type I
Aniridia Type II
WAGR Syndrome
Wilms Tumor Aniridia Gonadoblastoma
Mental Retardation

Aniridia is a rare genetic vision disorder characterized by abnormal development of the eye's iris. The iris is the circular colored membrane in the middle of the eyeball. It is perforated in the center by an opening known as the pupil, which regulates the amount of light that enters the eye. Aniridia is characterized by partial or complete absence of the iris. Various forms of aniridia have been identified. Each can be distinguished by accompanying symptoms.

The following organizations may provide additional information and support:
Aniridia Network
The Arc (A National Organization on Mental Retardation)
Blind Children's Fund
National Association for Parents of Children with Visual Impairments (NAPVI)
National Association for Visually Handicapped
NIH/National Eye Institute

83 Aniridia Cerebellar Ataxia Mental Deficiency

Synonyms
Aniridia, Partial-Cerebellar Ataxia-Mental
Retardation
Aniridia, Partial-Cerebellar Ataxia-
Oligophrenia
Aniridia-Cerebellar Ataxia-Mental Retardation
Gillespie Syndrome

Aniridia, cerebellar ataxia, and mental deficiency, also known as Gillespie syndrome, is an extremely rare inherited disorder that is characterized by the absence, in whole (aniridia) or in part (partial aniridia), of the colored portion (iris) of the eye; impaired coordination of voluntary movements due to underdevelopment (hypoplasia) of the brain's cerebellum (cerebellar ataxia); and mental retardation. The condition usually affects both eyes (bilateral) but a few cases have been reported in which only one eye is affected. Some individuals with this syndrome also exhibit a delay in the acquisition of skills requiring coordination of muscular and mental activity (psychomotor retardation). ACAMD is thought to be inherited as an autosomal recessive genetic trait and is extremely rare, with only 20 to 30 cases reported in the medical literature.

The following organizations may provide additional information and support:
Glaucoma Research Foundation

National Association for Parents of Children with Visual Impairments (NAPVI)
National Association for Visually Handicapped
National Eye Research Foundation
National Institute of Neurological Disorders and Stroke (NINDS)
NIH/National Eye Institute

84 Ankylosing Spondylitis

Synonyms
AS
Bechterew Syndrome
Marie Strumpell Disease
Marie-Strumpell Spondylitis
Spondyloarthritis
Von Bechterew-Strumpell Syndrome

Ankylosing spondylitis is a progressive inflammatory disease that typically becomes evident during early to mid adulthood. The disease is characterized by inflammation (arthritis), stiffness, and pain of various joints of the spine and potential loss of spinal mobility. It may involve joints between the spine and the pelvis, known as the sacroiliac joints; joints within the spinal column of the lower back (lumbar spine), the upper back (thoracic spine), and the neck (cervical spine) to varying degrees; as well as joints of the limbs, particularly the legs. Progression may spontaneously subside at any stage of involvement; however, in some individuals, all regions of the spinal column may eventually become involved. Many affected individuals develop lower back and hip pain that may be more severe at night and after rest. In addition, there is often associated stiffness of affected regions in the morning. In some cases, those with involvement of joints joining the ribs with the spine (costovertebral joints) may have a limited ability to expand the chest to take a deep breath. In addition, in some affected individuals, other associated findings may include recurrent inflammation of the colored region of the eyes (acute iritis), leakage of the aortic valve resulting in a backflow of blood into the lower left chamber (ventricle) of the heart (aortic insufficiency or regurgitation), and/or other abnormalities. The exact cause of ankylosing spondylitis is not known. However, researchers suggest that genetic, immunologic, and/or environmental factors may play some role.

The following organizations may provide additional information and support:
American Juvenile Arthritis Organization
Arthritis Foundation

Autoimmune Information Network, Inc
National Ankylosing Spondylitis Society
NIH/National Arthritis and Musculoskeletal and Skin Diseases Information Clearinghouse

85 Anodontia

Synonym
Anodontia Vera

Disorder Subdivisions
Complete Anodontia
Partial Anodontia (Hypodontia)

Anodontia is a genetic disorder commonly defined as the absence of all teeth, and is extremely rarely encountered in a pure form without any associated abnormalities. Rare but more common than complete anodontia are hypodontia and oligodontia. Hypodontia is genetic in origin and usually involves the absence of from 1 to 6 teeth. Oligodontia is genetic as well and is the term most commonly used to describe conditions in which more than six teeth are missing. These conditions may involve either the primary or permanent sets of teeth, but most cases involve the permanent teeth. These phenomena are associated with a group of non-progressive skin and nerve syndromes called the ectodermal dysplasias. Anodontia, especially, is usually part of a syndrome and seldom occurs as an isolated entity.

The following organizations may provide additional information and support:
National Foundation for Ectodermal Dysplasias
NIH/National Oral Health Information Clearinghouse

86 Anorexia Nervosa

Synonyms
Apepsia Hysterica
Magersucht

Anorexia nervosa is an illness of self-starvation resulting in marked weight loss and characterized by a disturbed sense of body image and anxiety about weight gain. Females with this disorder may also experience absence of menstrual periods.

The following organizations may provide additional information and support:
Anorexia Bulimia Treatment and Education Center
Depression and Related Affective Disorders Association

Eating Disorders Association
National Alliance for the Mentally Ill
National Association of Anorexia Nervosa and Associated Disorders, Inc.
National Eating Disorders Association
National Eating Disorders Organization
National Mental Health Association
National Mental Health Consumers' Self-Help Clearinghouse
NIH/National Institute of Mental Health

87 Anthrax

Synonyms
Black Baine
Malignant Edema
Malignant Pustule
Ragpicker Disease
Siberian Plague
Woolsorter's Disease

Disorder Subdivisions
Cutaneous Anthrax
Gastrointestinal Anthrax
Inhalational Anthrax

Anthrax is an acute infectious disease caused by the spore-forming bacterium Bacillus anthracis. It is usually a disease of wild and domestic animals, including cattle, sheep, and goats. However, human infection, while rare, does occur. Human infection usually results from contact with infected animals or their products. However, anthrax has become of interest because of the possibility that a nation or terrorist group might attempt to use it as a weapon of warfare or terrorism. There are three types of anthrax: cutaneous (through the skin), gastrointestinal, and inhalational.

The following organizations may provide additional information and support:
Centers for Disease Control and Prevention
NIH/National Institute of Allergy and Infectious Diseases
World Health Organization (WHO) Regional Office for the Americas (AMRO)

88 Antiphospholipid Syndrome

Synonyms
Antiphospholipid Antibody Syndrome
APLS
APS

Antiphospholipid syndrome (APLS) is a rare autoimmune disorder characterized by recurring

blood clots that usually appear before 45 years of age. It may also be associated with repeated spontaneous abortions for no apparent reason in young women. There may be a family history of blood clotting disorders in some cases. APS may occur in individuals with lupus or related autoimmune diseases or as a primary syndrome in otherwise healthy individuals.

The following organizations may provide additional information and support:
American Autoimmune Related Diseases Association, Inc.
Antiphospholipid Antibody Support Group
APS Foundation of America, Inc
Autoimmune Information Network, Inc
Lupus Foundation of America, Inc.
National Stroke Association
NIH/National Heart, Lung and Blood Institute Information Center

89 Antisocial Personality Disorder

Synonym
ASP

Antisocial personality disorder is a mental illness that usually becomes apparent before the age of fifteen. Major symptoms may include antisocial behavior in which there is little concern for the rights of others. Excessive drinking, fighting and irresponsibility may also occur.

The following organizations may provide additional information and support:
National Alliance for the Mentally Ill
National Mental Health Association
National Mental Health Consumers' Self-Help Clearinghouse
NIH/National Institute of Mental Health

90 Antithrombin III Deficiency

Synonyms
AT 3
AT III Deficiency
Thrombophilia, Hereditary, Due to AT III

Disorder Subdivisions
Antithrombin III Deficiency, Classical (Type I)
AT III Variant IA
AT III Variant IB

Antithrombin III (AT III) deficiency is a blood disorder characterized by the tendency to form clots in the arteries and/or veins (thrombosis). An inherited tendency to thrombosis is known as thrombophilia. Antithrombin III is a substance in the blood that limits the blood's ability to clot (coagulation). In people with congenital antithrombin III deficiency, there is usually a reduced amount of this substance in the blood due to a genetic abnormality. Antithrombin III deficiency may also be acquired; in such cases, the disorder may be reversible with treatment.

The following organizations may provide additional information and support:
American Liver Foundation
March of Dimes Birth Defects Foundation
NIH/National Heart, Lung and Blood Institute

91 Antley Bixler Syndrome

Synonyms
ABS
Craniosynostosis, Choanal Atresia, Radial Humeral Synostosis
Multisynostotic Osteodysgenesis with Long Bone Fractures
Trapezoidocephaly-Multiple Synostosis Syndrome

Disorder Subdivision
Multisynostotic Osteodysgenesis

Antley-Bixler syndrome is a rare genetic disorder that is primarily characterized by distinctive malformations of the head and facial (craniofacial) area and additional skeletal abnormalities. For example, the disorder is typically associated with premature closure of the fibrous joints (cranial sutures) between particular bones of the skull (craniosynostosis). Many affected infants and children also may have a prominent forehead, underdeveloped midfacial regions (midfacial hypoplasia), protruding eyes (proptosis), and other craniofacial abnormalities. Additional skeletal malformations are usually present, such as fusion of certain adjacent bones of the arms (e.g., radiohumeral or radioulnar synostosis); long, thin fingers and toes (arachnodactyly); and bowing of the thigh bones. In addition, certain joints may become permanently flexed or extended in fixed postures (joint contractures), resulting in restricted movements. Antley-Bixler syndrome often appears to be inherited as an autosomal recessive trait. However, according to researchers, other cases may result from spontaneous (sporadic) genetic changes (mutations) that may be transmitted as an autosomal dominant trait.

The following organizations may provide additional information and support:
Children's Craniofacial Association
FACES: The National Craniofacial Association
March of Dimes Birth Defects Foundation
NIH/National Institute of Child Health & Human Development (Preg & Perinat)

92 APECED Syndrome

Synonyms
Autoimmune Polyglandular Disease Type I
Autoimmune-Polyendocrinopathy-Candidias

Disorder Subdivisions
PGA I
PGA II
PGA III
Polyglandular Autoimmune Syndrome, Type I
Polyglandular Autoimmune Syndrome, Type II
Polyglandular Autoimmune Syndrome, Type III

APECED syndrome is a very rare genetic syndrome involving the autoimmune system. It is a combination of several distinct disorders and is defined as the subnormal functioning of several endocrine glands at the same time (concurrently). The acronym APECED stands for Autoimmune Polyendocrinopathy (APE), Candidiasis (C) and Ectodermal Dysplasia (ED). Autoimmune disease affecting one gland is frequently followed by the impairment of other glands. In this syndrome two major patterns of failure have been described. Type I affects children and adults younger than age 35. It is characterized by below normal secretion of the parathyroid gland (hypoparathyroidism—79%) and the failure of the adrenal cortex to secrete normal volumes of hormones (72%). About 60% of women and about 15% of men fail to mature sexually (hypogonadism). A persistant fungal infection (mucocutaneous candidiasisis) is common and chronic. Type II more frequently strikes adults with peak incidence at about 30 years. Almost invariably it involves the adrenal cortex with thyroid involvement somewhat less frequent. It may also involve the pancreatic islets producing an insulin-dependent diabetes mellitus.

The following organizations may provide additional information and support:
American Lung Association
National Adrenal Diseases Foundation
National Foundation for Ectodermal Dysplasias
NIH/National Digestive Diseases Information Clearinghouse

93   Apert Syndrome

Synonyms

Acrocephalosyndactyly, Type I
ACS I
ACS1
Syndactylic Oxycephaly

Apert syndrome, also known as acrocephalosyndactyly type I (ACS1), is a rare genetic disorder that is apparent at birth (congenital). The disorder is primarily characterized by distinctive malformations of the head and facial (craniofacial) region and defects of the hands and feet. In some instances, mental retardation may also be present. In infants with Apert syndrome, the fibrous joints between certain bones in the skull (cranial sutures) close prematurely (craniosynostosis), causing the head to appear abnormally pointed at the top (acrocephaly). Affected infants also have characteristic facial abnormalities, such as widely spaced eyes (ocular hypertelorism), abnormal protrusion of the eyes (exophthalmos), underdevelopment of midfacial regions (midface hypoplasia), and/or a narrow roof of the mouth (palate). Malformations of the hands and feet may include unusually broad thumbs and great toes, short fingers, and/or partial to complete fusion (syndactyly) of certain fingers and toes (digits). Most commonly, there is complete fusion of bones within the second to the fourth fingers and the presence of a single common nail ("mitten-like" syndactyly). In most instances, Apert syndrome results from new genetic changes (mutations) that appear to occur randomly for unknown reasons (sporadically). In rare cases, the disorder may be inherited as an autosomal dominant trait.

The following organizations may provide additional information and support:
AboutFace International
AboutFace USA
American Heart Association
Apert Support and Information Network
Apert Syndrome Support Group
The Arc (A National Organization on Mental Retardation)
Children's Craniofacial Association
Congenital Heart Anomalies, Support, Education, & Resources
Craniofacial Foundation of America
Danish Apert Syndrome Association (Danmarks Apertforening)
FACES: The National Craniofacial Association
Forward Face, Inc.

Headlines—Craniofacial Support
Let's Face It (USA)
National Craniofacial Foundation
National Foundation for Facial Reconstruction
Sjældne Diagnoser / Rare Disorders Denmark
University of Virginia Craniofacial Anomalies Clinic

94   Aplasia Cutis Congenita

Synonyms

ACC
Congenital Defect of the Skull and Scalp
Scalp Defect Congenital

Aplasia cutis congenita is a rare disorder with a complicated pattern of inheritance. Babies are born with the absence of certain layer(s) of skin, most often on the scalp, but also on the trunk, and/or arms and legs. The affected area is typically covered with a thin, transparent membrane. The skull and/or underlying areas may be visible and be abnormally developed. Aplasia cutis congenita may be the primary disorder or it may occur in association with other underlying disorders.

The following organizations may provide additional information and support:
Genetic and Rare Diseases (GARD) Information Center
March of Dimes Birth Defects Foundation
NIH/National Arthritis and Musculoskeletal and Skin Diseases Information Clearinghouse

95   Apnea, Infantile

Synonym

Infantile Sleep Apnea

Disorder Subdivisions

Central Apnea
Diaphragmatic Apnea
Mixed Apnea
Obstructive Apnea
Upper Airway Apnea

Apnea is a term used to describe the temporary absence of spontaneous breathing. Infantile apnea occurs in children under the age of one year. Apnea may occur because of neurological impairment of the respiratory rhythm or obstruction of air flow through the air passages. The symptoms of infantile apnea include the stoppage of breathing during sleep, an abnormal bluish discoloration to the skin (cyanosis) and sometimes an unusually slow heartbeat (bradycardia). Infantile apnea may be related to some cases of sudden infant death syndrome. Episodes of apnea may decrease with age. However, several forms of adult sleep apnea also exist.

The following organizations may provide additional information and support:
American Sleep Apnea Association
American Sleep Disorders Association
Center for Research in Sleep Disorders
First Candle-SIDS Alliance
National Institute of Neurological Disorders and Stroke (NINDS)
NIH/National Institute of Child Health and Human Development

96 Apnea, Sleep

Synonym
Pediatric Obstructive Sleep Apnea

Disorder Subdivisions
Central Sleep Apnea
Mixed Sleep Apnea
Obstructive Sleep Apnea (Upper Airway Apnea)
Pickwickian Syndrome

Sleep apnea is a sleep disorder characterized by temporary, recurrent interruptions of breathing (respiration) during sleep. Symptoms of this disorder include periodic wakefulness during the night, excessive sleepiness during the day, and loud snoring during sleep. People with this disorder are frequently overweight. Diagnosis and treatment of sleep apnea can avoid serious medical problems that may arise as a consequence of oxygen deprivation in untreated individuals. Sleep apnea occurs in three different forms: obstructive, central, and mixed. An individual's rate of respiration is regulated by a group of nerve cells in the brain that control the rhythm of breathing in response to changing oxygen levels in the blood (respiratory drive). In some apneas, the respiratory drive is abnormal. Obstructive sleep apnea (upper airway apnea), the most common form of sleep apnea, results from the blockage of the respiratory passages during sleep. Affected individuals may struggle to breathe and experience increased respiratory effort. Respiratory drive is unaffected in people with this form of sleep apnea but the blockage prevents them from breathing normally. Obstructive apnea is more likely than central apnea to be associated with snoring and arousal from sleep. In the rare central sleep

apnea, the brain does not send adequate signals to the diaphragm and lungs during sleep, resulting in low respiratory drive. In this form of sleep apnea, breathing stops and does not resume until the oxygen-deprived brain finally sends impulses to the diaphragm and lungs. In infants, central sleep apnea is defined as lasting 20 seconds or more. Mixed sleep apnea is a combination of improper brain signals and obstruction of the respiratory passages. In some cases, sleep apnea is referred to as "Pickwickian syndrome." In these cases, obstructive apnea is combined with obesity and an abnormally short neck. Infantile sleep apnea affects children less than one year old, and its cause is unknown. (For more information on infantile sleep apnea, see the Related Disorders section of this report.)

The following organizations may provide additional information and support:
American Sleep Apnea Association
American Sleep Disorders Association
Center for Research in Sleep Disorders
Narcolepsy Network, Inc.
Narcolepsy and Cataplexy Foundation of America
National Institute of Neurological Disorders and Stroke (NINDS)

97 Apraxia

Disorder Subdivisions
Apraxia, Buccofacial
Apraxia, Classic
Apraxia, Constructional
Apraxia, Ideational
Apraxia, Ideokinetic
Apraxia, Ideomotor
Apraxia, Motor
Apraxia, Oculomotor

Apraxia is a neurological disorder characterized by the inability to perform learned (familiar) movements on command, even though the command is understood and there is a willingness to perform the movement. Both the desire and the capacity to move are present but the person simply cannot execute the act. Patients with apraxia cannot use tools or perform such acts as tying shoelaces or buttoning shirts. The requirements of daily living are difficult to meet. Patients whose ability to speak is interrupted (aphasia) but who are unaffected by apraxia are able to live a relatively normal life; those with significant apraxia are almost invariably dependent. Apraxia comes in several different forms: Limb-kinetic apraxia is the inability to make precise or exact movements with a finger, an arm or a leg. An example is the inability to use a screwdriver notwithstanding that the person affected understands what is to be done and has done it in the past. Ideomotor apraxia is the inability to carry out a command from the brain to mimic limb or head movements performed or suggested by others. Conceptual apraxia is much like ideomotor ataxia but infers a more profound malfunctioning in which the function of tools is no longer understood. Ideational apraxia is the inability to create a plan for a specific movement. Buccofacial apraxia (sometimes called facial-oral apraxia) is the inability to coordinate and carry out facial and lip movements such as whistling, winking, coughing, etc. on command. This form includes verbal or speech developmental apraxia, perhaps the most common form of the disorder. Constructional apraxia affects the person's ability to draw or copy simple diagrams or to construct simple figures. Oculomotor apraxia is a condition in which patients find it difficult to move their eyes. Apraxia is believed to be caused by a lesion in the neural pathways of the brain that contain the learned patterns of movement. It is often a symptom of neurological, metabolic, or other disorders that can involve the brain.

The following organizations may provide additional information and support:
National Aphasia Association
National Institute of Neurological Disorders and Stroke (NINDS)

98 Arachnoid Cysts

Synonym
Cysts, Arachnoid

Disorder Subdivisions
Intracranial Arachnoid Cysts
Spinal Arachnoid Cysts

Arachnoid cysts are fluid-filled sacs that occur on the arachnoid membrane that covers the brain (intracranial) and the spinal cord (spinal). There are three membranes covering these components of the central nervous system: dura mater, arachnoid, and pia mater. Arachnoid cysts appear on the arachnoid membrane, and they may also expand into the space between the pia mater and arachnoid membranes (subarachnoid space). The most common locations for intracranial arachnoid cysts are the middle fossa (near the temporal lobe), the suprasellar region (near the third ventricle) and the posterior fossa, which contains the cerebellum, pons, and medulla oblongata. In many cases,

arachnoid cysts do not cause symptoms (asymptomatic). In cases in which symptoms occur, headaches, seizures and abnormal accumulation of excessive cerebrospinal fluid in the brain (hydrocephalus) are common. The exact cause of arachnoid cysts is unknown. Arachnoid cysts are classified according to location.

The following organization may provide additional information and support:
National Institute of Neurological Disorders and Stroke (NINDS)

99 Arachnoiditis

Synonyms
Arachnitis
Cerebral Arachnoiditis
Chronic Adhesive Arachnoiditis
Serous Circumscribed Meningitis
Spinal Arachnoiditis

Disorder Subdivisions
Adhesive Arachnoiditis
Arachnoiditis Ossificans
Neoplastic Arachnoiditis
Optochiasmatic Arachnoiditis
Postmyelographic Arachnoiditis
Rhinosinusogenic Cerebral Arachnoiditis
Spinal Ossifying Arachnoiditis

Arachnoiditis is a general term for several progressive regional disorders all of which result in the inflammation of parts of the middle membrane surrounding the spinal cord and brain (arachnoid membrane) and the space defined by this membrane (subarachnoid space). Either the spinal cord or the brain may be involved; in some cases, both are affected. This disorder can also be associated with meningitis. The condition may be caused by foreign agents such as anesthesia drugs or testing dyes injected into the spine or arachnoid membrane. Since the subarachnoid space is continuous, it would be expected that a noxious agent introduced in one place would distribute itself throughout the space. However, such is not the case. The lower spinal roots and/or the spinal cord may be affected, while regions close by remain free of inflammation; hence, the term "spinal arachnoiditis." Similarly, the optic nerve and optic chiasm (crossing of nerve fibers) may be affected, giving rise to the term "opticochiasmatic arachnoiditis."

The following organizations may provide additional information and support:

American Paraplegia Society
American Syringomyelia Alliance Project, Inc.
Canadian Syringomyelia Network
National Institute of Neurological Disorders and Stroke (NINDS)
National Spinal Cord Injury Association
Spinal Cord Society

100 Arginase Deficiency

Synonyms
ARG Deficiency
Argininemia
Hyperargininemia

Arginase deficiency is a rare inherited disorder characterized by complete or partial lack of the enzyme arginase. Arginase is one of six enzymes that play a role in the breakdown and removal of nitrogen from the body, a process known as the urea cycle. The lack of the arginase enzyme results in excessive accumulation of nitrogen, in the form of ammonia (hyperammonemia), in the blood and arginine (hyperarginemia) in the blood and cerebrospinal fluid. Affected infants may exhibit mental retardation, seizures, and spasticity. Arginase deficiency is inherited as an autosomal recessive trait. The urea cycle disorders are a group of rare disorders affecting the urea cycle, a series of biochemical processes in which nitrogen is converted into urea and removed from the body through the urine. Nitrogen is a waste product of protein metabolism. Failure to break down nitrogen results in the abnormal accumulation of nitrogen, in the form of ammonia, in the blood.

The following organizations may provide additional information and support:
The Arc (A National Organization on Mental Retardation)
CLIMB (Children Living with Inherited Metabolic Diseases)
National Urea Cycle Disorders Foundation
NIH/National Digestive Diseases Information Clearinghouse

101 Argininosuccinic Aciduria

Synonyms
Arginino Succinase Deficiency
Argininosuccinate Lyase Deficiency
ASA Deficiency
ASL Deficiency

Argininosuccinic aciduria is a rare inherited disorder characterized by deficiency or lack of the enzyme argininosuccinate lyase (ASL). Argininosuccinate lyase is one of six enzymes that play a role in the breakdown and removal of nitrogen from the body, a process known as the urea cycle. The lack of this enzyme results in excessive accumulation of nitrogen, in the form of ammonia (hyperammonemia), in the blood. Affected infants may experience vomiting, refusal to eat, progressive lethargy, and coma. Argininosuccinic aciduria is inherited as an autosomal recessive trait. The urea cycle disorders are a group of rare disorders affecting the urea cycle, a series of biochemical processes in which nitrogen is converted into urea and removed from the body through the urine. Nitrogen is a waste product of protein metabolism. Failure to break down nitrogen results in the abnormal accumulation of nitrogen, in the form of ammonia, in the blood.

The following organizations may provide additional information and support:
American Kidney Fund, Inc.
ASA Kids
CLIMB (Children Living with Inherited Metabolic Diseases)
National Kidney Foundation
National Urea Cycle Disorders Foundation
NIH/National Digestive Diseases Information Clearinghouse

102 Arnold-Chiari Malformation

Synonyms
ACM
Cerebellomedullary Malformation Syndrome

Disorder Subdivisions
Chiari Type I (Chiari Malformation I)
Chiari Type II (Chiari Malformation II)

Arnold-Chiari malformation is a rare malformation of the brain that is sometimes, but not always, apparent at birth. It is characterized by abnormalities in the area where the brain and spinal cord meet that cause part of the cerebellum to protrude through the bottom of the skull (foramen magnum) into the spinal canal. This interferes with the flow of cerebral spinal fluid to and from the brain, leading to accumulation of cerebral spinal fluid in the empty spaces of the spine and brain. The portion of the cerebellum that protrudes into the spinal canal can become elongated and is called the "cerebellar tonsils" because it resembles the tonsils. There are four types of Chiari malformation. Depending on the type, the impact on the affected individual may range from mild to severe.

The following organizations may provide additional information and support:
American Syringomyelia Alliance Project, Inc.
Birth Defect Research for Children, Inc.
Canadian Syringomyelia Network
Hydrocephalus Association
Hydrocephalus Support Group, Inc.
March of Dimes Birth Defects Foundation
National Institute of Neurological Disorders and Stroke (NINDS)
World Arnold Chiari Malformation Association

103   Arteriovenous Malformation

Synonym
AVM

Disorder Subdivisions
Arteriovenous Malformation of the Brain
Spinal Arteriovenous Malformation

Arteriovenous malformation (AVM) is a congenital defect in which arteries and veins are tangled and not connected by capillaries. The lack of capillaries allows blood traveling through the abnormal vessels to flow rapidly and under high pressure and prevents the nutrient rich blood in the arteries from reaching the tissues. AVM can occur in many different parts of the body, but those located in the brain, brainstem and spinal cord (neurological AVM) can affect the entire body.

The following organizations may provide additional information and support:
The BrainPower Project
National Institute of Neurological Disorders and Stroke (NINDS)
Vascular Birthmarks Foundation

104   Arteritis, Giant Cell

Synonyms
Cranial Arteritis
GCA
Granulomatous Arteritis
Temporal Arteritis (Horton's Disease)

Disorder Subdivision
Polymyalgia Rheumatica

Giant cell arteritis is a chronic inflammatory disease characterized by the progressive inflammation of many arteries of the body (panarteritis).

Granular material and abnormally large cells (giant cells) accumulate in the elastic lining of the arteries. Chronic inflammation is sometimes confined to the different branches of the heart's main artery (aorta) and any large arteries can become inflamed. However, the temporal arteries of the head are most frequently affected (temporal arteritis). In rare cases, veins may also be affected by giant cell arteritis. The symptoms of giant cell arteritis may include stiffness, muscle pain, fever, and/or headaches. The exact cause of this disease is not fully understood, although it is thought to be an autoimmune disease that occurs when the body's own immune system attacks healthy tissue. Giant cell arteritis is closely related to polymyalgia rheumatica, another inflammatory disorder. These two disorders have been described in the medical literature as possible variants of the same disease process. Some researchers believe they represent different ends of a disease continuum. The exact nature of the association is not fully understood.

The following organizations may provide additional information and support:
American Autoimmune Related Diseases Association, Inc.
NIH/National Heart, Lung and Blood Institute Information Center

105   Arteritis, Takayasu

Synonyms
Aorta Arch Syndrome
Brachiocephalic Ischemia
Idiopathic Arteritis of Takayasu
Martorell Syndrome
Occlusive Thromboaortopathy
Pulseless Disease
Reverse Coarction
Takayasu Disease
Young Female Arteritis

Takayasu arteritis is a rare disorder characterized by inflammation of the large elastic arteries. The main artery of the heart (aorta) and the pulmonary (lung) artery are affected. This disorder causes progressive inflammation of many arteries in the body (polyarteritis), resulting in the reduction of blood flow. Arteries in the head and arms may be affected, and this can result in the loss of the major pulse points in the body. Some people with Takayasu arteritis have irregular narrowing of portions of the large arteries (segmental stenosis) and abnormal backward flow of blood from the aorta into the left ventricle of the heart (aortic regurgitation).

The following organizations may provide additional information and support:
American Autoimmune Related Diseases Association, Inc.
Autoimmune Information Network, Inc
NIH/National Heart, Lung and Blood Institute Information Center
Takayasu's Arteritis Foundation, International

106 Arthritis, Infectious

Synonyms
Bacterial Arthritis
Purulent Arthritis
Pyarthrosis
Pyogenic Arthritis
Septic Arthritis
Suppurative Arthritis

Infectious arthritis is an inflammation of one or more joints that occurs as a result of infection by bacteria, viruses or, less frequently, fungi or parasites. The symptoms of infectious arthritis depend upon which agent has caused the infection but symptoms often include fever, chills, general weakness, and headaches, followed by inflammation and painful swelling of one or more joints of the body. Most often, the infection begins at some other location in the body and travels via the bloodstream to the joint. Less commonly, the infection starts in the joint in the course of a surgical procedure, injection or other action.

The following organizations may provide additional information and support:
Arthritis Foundation
Arthritis Society
Centers for Disease Control and Prevention
NIH/National Institute of Arthritis and Musculoskeletal and Skin Diseases

107 Arthritis, Juvenile Rheumatoid

Synonyms
JRA
Juvenile Chronic Arthritis

Disorder Subdivisions
Pauciarticular-Onset Disease (Oligoarthritis)
Polyarticular-Onset Disease
Systemic-Onset Disease (Still's Disease)

Juvenile rheumatoid arthritis (JRA) is a rheumatic disease characterized by chronic inflammation (arthritis) of one or more joints in a child age 16 years or younger. Associated symptoms typically include swelling, abnormal warmth, tenderness or pain, and/or stiffness of affected joints that tends to be worse in the mornings. In severe cases, destructive changes may eventually result in limited mobility and possible deformity of affected joints. Some children with JRA may also have generalized symptoms and findings, such as fever, lack of appetite (anorexia), enlargement of the liver and spleen (hepatosplenomegaly), and/or other abnormalities. In addition, some forms of JRA are associated with an increased risk for inflammation of certain regions of the eyes (iridocyclitis). The range and severity of associated symptoms and findings may vary, depending upon the specific form of the disease present. The exact cause of JRA is not known.

The following organizations may provide additional information and support:
American Autoimmune Related Diseases Association, Inc.
American Juvenile Arthritis Organization
Arthritis Foundation
Arthritis Society
Autoimmune Information Network, Inc
NIH/National Arthritis and Musculoskeletal and Skin Diseases Information Clearinghouse
UveitisSupport-MEEI

108 Arthritis, Psoriatic

Synonym
Arthropathic Psoriasis

Disorder Subdivisions
Asymmetric Arthritis
Psoriatic Spondyloarthritis
Symmetric Arthritis

Psoriatic arthritis is a rheumatoid-like arthritic condition characterized by pain and swelling (inflammation) of the joints (arthritis) that occurs in association with gray discoloration or scaly plaques of the skin (psoriasis). Abnormalities of the nails may also be present. In many cases, skin symptoms precede the development of arthritis by several years. The exact cause of the psoriatic arthritis is unknown.

The following organizations may provide additional information and support:
Arthritis Foundation
Arthritis Society
National Psoriasis Foundation
NIH/National Arthritis and Musculoskeletal and Skin Diseases Information Clearinghouse
Psoriatic Arthropathy Alliance

109 Arthrogryposis Multiplex Congenita

Synonyms

AMC
Congenital Multiple Arthrogryposis
Fibrous Ankylosis of Multiple Joints

Disorder Subdivisions

Amyoplasia Congenita
Guerin-Stern Syndrome
Myopathic Arthrogryposis Multiplex Congenita
Neurogenic Arthrogryposis Multiplex Congenita

Arthrogryposis multiplex congenita, a rare disorder that is present at birth (congenital), is characterized by reduced mobility of many joints of the body. Impairment of mobility is due to the overgrowth (proliferation) of fibrous tissue in the joints (fibrous ankylosis). There are many different types of arthrogryposis multiplex congenita and the symptoms vary widely among affected individuals. In the most common form of arthrogryposis multiplex congenita, the range of motion of the joints in the arms and legs (limbs) is limited or fixed. Other findings may include inward rotation of the shoulders, abnormal extension of the elbows, and bending of the wrists and fingers. In addition, the hips may be dislocated and the heels of the feet may be inwardly bent from the midline of the leg while the feet are inwardly bent at the ankle (clubfoot). The cause of arthrogryposis multiplex congenita (AMC) is unknown. Most types of arthrogryposis multiplex congenita are not inherited; however, a rare autosomal recessive form of the disease has been reported in one large inbred Arabic kindred in Israel.

The following organizations may provide additional information and support:
Arthrogryposis Group
AVENUES
Canadian Arthrogryposis Support Team
Human Growth Foundation
MAGIC Foundation for Children's Growth
NIH/National Arthritis and Musculoskeletal and Skin Diseases Information Clearinghouse

110 Asherman's Syndrome

Synonyms

Intrauterine Synechiae
Uterine Synechiae

Asherman's syndrome is an uncommon, acquired, gynecological disorder characterized by changes in the menstrual cycle. Patients experience reduced menstrual flow, increased cramping and abdominal pain, eventual cessation of menstrual cycles (amenorrhea), and, in many instances, infertility. Most often these symptoms are the result of severe inflammation of the lining of the uterus (endometriosis) that is caused by the development of bands of scar tissue that join parts of the walls of the uterus to one another, thus reducing the volume of the uterine cavity (intrauterine adhesions and synechiae). Endometrial scarring and intrauterine adhesions may occur as a result of surgical scraping or cleaning of tissue from the uterine wall (dilatation and curettage [D and C]), infections of the endometrium (e.g., tuberculosis), or other factors.

The following organizations may provide additional information and support:
Asherman's Syndrome Online Community
March of Dimes Birth Defects Foundation
National Women's Health Network

111 Aspartylglycosaminuria

Synonyms

AGA
AGU
Aspartylglucosaminidase Deficiency
Aspartylglucosaminuria
Glycosylasparaginase Deficiency

Aspartylglycosaminuria is a very rare genetic disorder that is concentrated among persons of Finnish descent, but is also found, even more rarely, in other populations around the world. It is an inborn error of metabolism, and one of the lysosomal storage diseases. It becomes apparent after the infant is a few months old. Major symptoms may include coarse facial features, spine and eye deformities, behavior problems and mental retardation. Aspartylglycosaminuria occurs as a result of deficient activity of a particular enzyme, leading to the accumulation of metabolic products in the body.

The following organizations may provide additional information and support:
CLIMB (Children Living with Inherited Metabolic Diseases)
Instituto de Errores Innatos del Metabolismo
International Society for Mannosidosis & Related Diseases, Inc.
National MPS (Mucopolysaccharidoses/Mucolipidoses) Society, Inc.
NIH/National Institute of Diabetes, Digestive & Kidney Diseases

112 Asperger's Syndrome

Synonyms
Asperger's Disorder
Autism, Asperger's Type

Asperger's syndrome is a neuropsychiatric disorder. Children with this disorder experience the inability to understand the feelings of others, abnormal single-mindedness, lack of verbal skills, insensitivity to social cues, withdrawal and obsessive indulgence in special interests. Many clinicians believe that Asperger's syndrome is a subtype of autism that is differentiated by a later onset (i.e., it is usually not recognized before 30 months of age) and by the fact that speech generally is not delayed, as it often is in children with autism. The exact cause of Asperger's syndrome is unknown.

The following organizations may provide additional information and support:
Geneva Centre for Autism
National Autistic Society
National Institute of Neurological Disorders and Stroke (NINDS)
New Horizons Un-Limited, Inc.
Online Asperger Syndrome Information and Support
Organization For Anti-Convulsant Syndrome
R.O.C.K. (Raising Our Celiac Kids)
University Students with Autism and Asperger's Syndrome Web Site

113 Aspergillosis

Synonym
Pulmonary Aspergillosis

Disorder Subdivisions
Aspergilloma
Bronchopulmonary Allergic Aspergillosis
Endocarditis
Invasive Aspergillosis
Madu'ra Foot
Mycetoma
Pulmonary Mycetoma

Aspergillosis is a term used to describe a group of pulmonary infections caused by inhaling the fungus *Aspergillus*. Most people who are exposed to this common fungus are not affected by it, but those with an impaired immune system, or an abnormal immune response, may become ill. Three different infections may be caused by *Aspergillus*: allergic bronchopulmonary aspergillosis, pulmonary mycetoma (aspergilloma) or invasive aspergillosis.

The following organizations may provide additional information and support:
Centers for Disease Control and Prevention
NIH/National Institute of Allergy and Infectious Diseases

114 Astrocytoma

Disorder Subdivisions
Grade I Astrocytoma
Grade II Astrocytoma
Grade III Astrocytoma
Grade IV Astrocytoma

An astrocytoma is a tumor that arises from the star-shaped cells (astrocytes) that form the supportive tissue of the brain. The World Health Organization (WHO) classifies astrocytomas into four grades depending on how fast they are growing and the likelihood that they will spread (infiltrate) to nearby brain tissue. Noninfiltrating astrocytomas usually grow more slowly than the infiltrating forms. Grade I astrocytoma is usually a noninfiltrating tumor. The most common type of grade I astrocytoma is pilocytic astrocytoma which is also known as juvenile pilocytic astrocytoma or JPA. This tumor grows slowly but can become very large. Pilocytic astrocytoma occurs most often in the cerebellum, cerebrum, optic nerve pathway and brainstem. This tumor occurs most often in children and teens and accounts for 2% of all brain tumors. Grade II astrocytoma is also called low-grade astrocytoma or diffuse astrocytoma and is usually an infiltrating tumor. This tumor grows relatively slowly and usually does not have well-defined borders. It occurs most often in adults between the ages of 20 and 60. Grade III astrocytoma is also called anaplastic (malignant) astrocytoma because this tumor grows into surrounding tissue and grows more quickly than a grade II astrocytoma. Anaplastic astrocytoma occurs most often in adults between the ages of 30 and 60, is more common in men and accounts for 4% of all brain tumors. Grade IV astrocytoma is also called glioblastoma multiforme or GBM and is the most invasive type of nervous system tumor. GBM is usually composed of a mix of cell types in addition to astrocytes. This tumor occurs most often in adults between the ages of 50 and 80, is more common in men, and accounts for 23% of all primary brain tumors. (For more information on this condition, choose "glioblastoma" as your search term in the Rare Disease Database".)

The following organizations may provide additional information and support:
American Brain Tumor Association
Brain Tumor Society
Candlelighters Childhood Cancer Foundation
Harvard Brain Tissue Resource Center
National Brain Tumor Foundation
Pediatric Brain Tumor Foundation

115 Astrocytoma, Malignant

Synonyms
Anaplastic Astrocytoma
Astrocytoma, grades 3-4
Giant Cell Glioblastoma, Astrocytoma
Spongioblastoma Multiforme

Malignant astrocytoma is an infiltrating, primary brain tumor, with tentacles that may invade surrounding tissue. This provides a butterfly-like distribution pattern through the white matter of the cerebral hemispheres. The tumor may invade a membrane covering the brain (the dura), or spread via the spinal fluid through the ventricles of the brain. Spread of the tumor (metastasis) outside the brain and spinal cord is rare.

The following organizations may provide additional information and support:
American Brain Tumor Association
American Cancer Society, Inc.
Brain Tumor Society
Candlelighters Childhood Cancer Foundation
Harvard Brain Tissue Resource Center
National Brain Tumor Foundation
National Institute of Neurological Disorders and Stroke (NINDS)

116 Ataxia, Friedreich's

Synonyms
FRDA
Friedreich's Disease
Friedreich's Tabes
Hereditary Ataxia, Friedrich's Type
Spinal Ataxia, Hereditofamilial

Friedreich's ataxia is a genetic, progressive, neurologic movement disorder that typically becomes apparent before adolescence. Initial symptoms may include unsteady posture, frequent falling, and progressive difficulties walking due to an impaired abil-

ity to coordinate voluntary movements (ataxia). Affected individuals may also develop abnormalities of certain reflexes; characteristic foot deformities; increasing incoordination of the arms and hands; slurred speech (dysarthria); and rapid, involuntary eye movements (nystagmus). Friedreich's ataxia may also be associated with cardiomyopathy, a disease of cardiac muscle that may be characterized by shortness of breath upon exertion (dyspnea), chest pain, and irregularities in heart rhythm (cardiac arrythmias). Some affected individuals may also develop diabetes mellitus, a condition in which there is insufficient secretion of the hormone insulin. Primary symptoms may include abnormally increased thirst and urination (polydipsia and polyuria), weight loss, lack of appetite, fatigue, and blurred vision. Friedreich's ataxia may be inherited as an autosomal recessive trait. Cases in which a family history of the disease has not been found may represent new genetic changes (mutations) that occur spontaneously (sporadically). Friedreich's ataxia results from mutations of a gene known as "X25" or "frataxin" located on the long arm (q) of chromosome 9 (9q13). In most affected individuals, the frataxin gene contains errors in the coded "building blocks" (nucleotide bases) that make up the gene's instructions. The symptoms and findings associated with Friedreich's ataxia are thought to result primarily from degenerative changes of nerve fibers of the spinal cord as well as peripheral nerves, which are the motor and sensory nerves and groups of nerve cell bodies (ganglia) outside the brain and spinal cord.

The following organizations may provide additional information and support:
American Diabetes Association
Christopher Reeve Paralysis Foundation
Friedreich's Ataxia Research Alliance
Let Them Hear Foundation
March of Dimes Birth Defects Foundation
Muscular Dystrophy Association
National Ataxia Foundation
National Institute of Neurological Disorders and Stroke (NINDS)
National Scoliosis Foundation

117 Ataxia, Hereditary, Autosomal Dominant

Synonyms
Dentato-Rubro-Pallido-Luysian Atrophy
Episodic Ataxia
Progressive Cerebellar Ataxia, Familial
SCA
Spinocerebellar Ataxia

Disorder Subdivision
Marie's Ataxia

The hereditary ataxias are a group of neurological disorders (ataxias) of varying degrees of rarity that are inherited, in contrast to a related group of neurological disorders that are acquired through accidents, injuries, or other external agents. The hereditary ataxias are characterized by degenerative changes in the brain and spinal cord that lead to an awkward, uncoordinated walk (gait) accompanied often by poor eye-hand coordination and abnormal speech (dysarthria). Hereditary ataxia in one or another of its forms may present at almost any time between infancy and adulthood. The classification of hereditary ataxias is complex with several schools of thought vying for recognition. This report follows the classification presented by Dr. Thomas D. Bird and the University of Washington's GeneReviews. This classification is based on the pattern of inheritance or mode of genetic transmission of the disorder: i.e., autosomal dominant, autosomal recessive and X-linked. The autosomal dominant ataxias, also called the spinocerebellar ataxias, are usually identified as SCA1 through SCA25. Also included are several "episodic ataxias", as well as a very rare disorder known as DRPLA (dentato-rubro-pallido-luysian atrophy). This report deals with the autosomal dominant hereditary ataxias. There are fewer autosomal recessive hereditary ataxias than autosomal dominant hereditary ataxias, and X-linked forms of ataxia are very rare. Until recently, all autosomal dominant ataxias were called Marie's ataxia and all autosomal recessive ataxias were called Friedreich's ataxia.

The following organizations may provide additional information and support:
Ataxia Support Group
National Institute of Neurological Disorders and Stroke (NINDS)
WE MOVE (Worldwide Education and Awareness for Movement Disorders)

118 Ataxia Telangiectasia

Synonyms
AT
Cerebello-Oculocutaneous Telangiectasia
Immunodeficiency with Ataxia Telangiectasia
Louis-Bar Syndrome

Ataxia telangiectasia (AT) is a complex genetic neurodegenerative disorder that may become apparent during infancy or early childhood. The disorder is characterized by progressively impaired coordination of voluntary movements (ataxia); the development of reddish lesions of the skin and mucous membranes due to permanent widening of groups of blood vessels (telangiectasia); and impaired functioning of the immune system (i.e., cellular and humoral immunodeficiency), resulting in increased susceptibility to upper and lower respiratory infections (sinopulmonary infections). Individuals with AT also have an increased risk of developing certain malignancies, particularly of the lymphatic system (lymphomas), the blood-forming organs (e.g., leukemia), and the brain. In those with AT, progressive ataxia typically develops during infancy and may initially be characterized by abnormal swaying of the head and trunk. As the disease progresses, the condition leads to an inability to walk (ambulation) by late childhood or adolescence. Ataxia is often accompanied by difficulty speaking (dysarthria); drooling; and an impaired ability to coordinate certain eye movements (oculomotor apraxia), including the occurrence of involuntary, rapid, rhythmic motions (oscillations) of the eyes while attempting to focus upon certain objects (fixation nystagmus). Affected children may also develop an unusually stooped posture and irregular, rapid, jerky movements that may occur in association with relatively slow, writhing motions (choreoathetosis). In addition, telangiectasias may develop by mid-childhood, often appearing on sun-exposed areas of the skin, such as the bridge of the nose, the ears, and certain regions of the extremities, as well as the mucous membranes of the eyes (conjunctiva). AT is inherited as an autosomal recessive trait. The disorder is caused by changes (mutations) of a gene known as ATM (for "AT mutated") that has been mapped to the long arm (q) of chromosome 11 (11q22.3). The ATM gene controls (encodes for) the production of an enzyme that plays a role in regulating cell division following DNA damage.

The following organizations may provide additional information and support:
American Cancer Society, Inc.
American Diabetes Association
A-T Children's Project (Ataxia Telangiectasia Children's Project)
A-T Medical Research Foundation
March of Dimes Birth Defects Foundation
National Ataxia Foundation
National Institute of Neurological Disorders and Stroke (NINDS)

119   Ataxia with Vitamin E Deficiency

Synonyms
AVED
Familial Isolated Vitamin E Deficiency
Isolated Vitamin E Deficiency

Ataxia with vitamin E deficiency (AVED) is a rare inherited neurodegenerative disorder characterized by impaired ability to coordinate voluntary movements (ataxia) and disease of the peripheral nervous system (peripheral neuropathy). AVED is a progressive disorder that can affect many different systems of the body (multisystem disorder). Specific symptoms vary from case to case. In addition to neurological symptoms, affected individuals may experience eye abnormalities, disorders affecting the heart muscles (cardiomyopathy), and abnormal curvature of the spine (scoliosis). AVED is extremely similar to a more common disorder known as Friedreich's ataxia. AVED is inherited as an autosomal recessive trait. Vitamin E deficiency often occurs secondary to disorders that impair the absorption of vitamin E from fat including liver disorders, disorders of fat metabolism, and disorders of bile secretion. These disorders include cholestasis (a syndrome of various causes characterized by impaired bile secretion); cystic fibrosis (primarily a lung disorder that may also affect bile secretion); primary biliary cirrhosis (a liver disorder that results in cholestasis); and abetalipoproteinemia (a digestive disorder characterized by fat malabsorption). Premature infants may have a low vitamin E reserve because only small amounts of vitamin E cross the placenta, and therefore they may become deficient if fed a formula high in unsaturated fats and low in vitamin E. In rare cases, vitamin E deficiency may be caused by a poor diet. (For more information on the above disorders, choose the specific disorder name for your search term in the Rare Disease Database.)

The following organizations may provide additional information and support:
euro-ATAXIA
Friedreich's Ataxia Research Alliance
March of Dimes Birth Defects Foundation
National Ataxia Foundation
National Institute of Neurological Disorders and Stroke (NINDS)
National Scoliosis Foundation
Retinitis Pigmentosa International

120   Atrial Septal Defects

Synonyms
ASD
Atrioseptal Defects

Disorder Subdivisions
Ostium Primum Defect (endocardial cushion defects included)
Ostium Secundum Defect
Sinus Venosus

Atrial septal defects are a group of rare heart defects that are present at birth (congenital). The normal heart has four chambers with two upper chambers known as atria. They are separated from each other by a fibrous partition known as the atrial septum. The two lower chambers are known as ventricles and are separated from each other by the ventricular septum. Valves connect the atria (left and right) to their respective ventricles. A small opening between the two atria (foramen ovale) is present at birth. Shortly after birth, the atrial septum gradually closes and covers this opening. In infants with atrial septal defects, the atrial septum may not close properly or may be malformed during fetal development. In this disorder, the opening between the atria persists long after it should be closed, resulting in an increase in the workload on the right side of the heart and excessive blood flow to the lungs. Initially the symptoms associated with atrial septal defects may be absent or so mild that they may go unnoticed. Frequently this disorder is not recognized until school age or even adulthood. In adults with undetected atrial septal defects, various respiratory problems and/or heart failure may develop. There are several forms of atrial septal defects, including ostium primum atrial defects, ostium secundum defects, and coronary sinus venosus (sinus venous defect). Most cases of atrial septal defects occur for no apparent reason (sporadic). Other cases are thought to be inherited as autosomal recessive or dominant genetic traits. Atrial septal defects may also occur in association with other disorders such as Down syndrome or Ellis van-Creveld syndrome.

The following organizations may provide additional information and support:
American Heart Association
American Lung Association
Congenital Heart Anomalies, Support, Education, & Resources
Congenital Heart Information Network
Little Hearts, Inc.

March of Dimes Birth Defects Foundation
NIH/National Heart, Lung and Blood Institute Information Center

121 Atrioventricular Septal Defect

Synonyms
Atrioventricular Canal Defects
AVSD
Common Atrioventricular Canal (CAVC) Defect
Endocardial Cushion Defects

Disorder Subdivisions
Complete Atrioventricular Septal Defect
Incomplete Atrioventricular Septal Defect
Partial Atrioventricular Septal Defect
Transitional Atrioventricular Septal Defect

Atrioventricular septal defect (AVSD) is a general term for a group of rare heart defects that are present at birth (congenital). Infants with AVSDs have improperly developed atrial and ventricular septa and adjoining valves. The normal heart has four chambers. The two upper chambers, known as atria, are separated from each other by a fibrous partition called the atrial septum. The two lower chambers, known as ventricles, are separated from each other by the ventricular septum. Valves (e.g., mitral and tricuspid) connect the atria (left and right) to their respective ventricles. The valves allow for blood to be pumped through the chambers. Blood travels from the right ventricle through the pulmonary artery to the lungs where it receives oxygen. The blood returns to the heart through pulmonary veins and enters the left ventricle. The left ventricle sends the now oxygen-filled blood into the main artery of the body (aorta). The aorta sends the blood throughout the body. The parts of the heart described above are formed from an embryonic structure called the endocardial cushions. In individuals with AVSD there is some combination of malformation of these parts of the heart. They may include a hole in the atrial septum, a hole in the ventricular septum, and/or abnormalities of the mitral and triscupid valves. AVSD may be classified as one of three forms: an incomplete (or partial) AVSD (atrial septal defect primum); a transitional form (atrial septal defect and small ventricular septal defect); or a more severe or complete form (large atrial and ventricular defects). The symptoms of AVSD vary greatly and depend on the severity of the malformations (e.g., valve leakage between ventricles and ventricular size). About half the cases of AVSD occur in children with Down syndrome.

The following organizations may provide additional information and support:
American Heart Association
American Lung Association
Congenital Heart Anomalies, Support, Education, & Resources
Congenital Heart Information Network
NIH/National Heart, Lung and Blood Institute Information Center

122 Attention Deficit Hyperactivity Disorder

Synonyms
ADD
ADHD
Attention Deficit Disorder
Hyperkinetic Syndrome

Disorder Subdivisions
ADD, Combined Type
ADHD, Predominantly Hyperactive-Impulsive Type
ADHD, Predominantly Inattentive Type

Attention deficit hyperactivity disorder (ADHD) is a behavioral disorder of childhood characterized by short attention span, excessive impulsiveness, and inappropriate hyperactivity. Symptoms of hyperactivity, impulsivity, and inattentive behavior must have been present before the age of seven years and caused impairment in two or more social, academic, or occupational settings. The exact cause of ADHD is not known.

The following organizations may provide additional information and support:
The Arc (A National Organization on Mental Retardation)
Attention Deficit Disorder Association
CHADD (Children and Adults with Attention-Deficit/Hyperactivity Disorder)
Learning Disabilities Association of America
National Alliance for the Mentally Ill
National Center for Learning Disabilities
National Institute of Neurological Disorders and Stroke (NINDS)
National Mental Health Association
National Mental Health Consumers' Self-Help Clearinghouse
National Network of Learning-Disabled Adults, Inc.
NIH/National Institute of Mental Health
Organization For Anti-Convulsant Syndrome
R.O.C.K. (Raising Our Celiac Kids)

123 Atypical Hemolytic Uremic Syndrome

Synonyms

aHUS
Inherited Hemolytic-Uremic Syndrome

Atypical hemolytic uremic syndrome (aHUS) is an extremely rare group of disorders of the kidneys. It is a distinctly different illness from hemolytic uremic syndrome caused by the bacterium *E. coli* 0157:h7 (Stx HUS). While Stx HUS typically is preceded by a flu-like illness and is associated with that particular strain of *E. coli* bacterium, there is substantial evidence that aHUS is a genetic disorder. Atypical hemolytic uremic syndrome may become a chronic condition, and patients with aHUS may experience repeated attacks of the disorder. When children with Stx HUS recover from the life-threatening initial episode, they are likely to respond well to supportive treatment and to make a good recovery. Children with aHUS are much more likely to develop chronic serious complications such as kidney failure and severe high blood pressure.

The following organizations may provide additional information and support:
American Kidney Fund, Inc.
Foundation for Children with Atypical HUS
National Kidney Foundation

124 Atypical Mole Syndrome

Synonyms

B-K Mole Syndrome
CMM
Cutaneous Malignant Melanoma, Hereditary
DNS, Hereditary
Dysplastic Nevus Syndrome
Familial Atypical Mole-Malignant Melanoma Syndrome
FAMMM
HCMM
Malignant Melanoma, Dysplastic Nevus Type

Atypical mole syndrome, also called dysplastic nevus syndrome, is a disorder of the skin characterized by the presence of many mole-like tumors (nevi). Most people have 10-20 moles over their bodies. People with this syndrome often have more than 100 moles, at least some of which are unusual (atypical) in size and structure. These moles vary in size, location, and coloring. They are usually larger than normal moles (5mm or more in diameter) and have irregular borders. Changes in the appearance of these moles must be taken seriously by patients since such changes may foreshadow the onset of cancerous disease. Individuals with atypical mole syndrome are at greater risk than others for developing cancer of the skin in the form of malignant melanoma. Atypical mole syndrome is thought by some clinicians to be a precursor or forerunner of malignant melanoma. This type of cancer may spread to adjacent parts of the skin or, through the blood and lymph circulation, to other organs.

The following organizations may provide additional information and support:
American Cancer Society, Inc.
Nevus Network
Nevus Outreach, Inc.
Skin Cancer Foundation

125 Autism

Synonyms

Infantile Autism
Kanner Syndrome

Autism is a lifelong, nonprogressive neurologic disorder typically appearing before the age of 30 months. It is characterized by language and communication deficits, withdrawal from social contacts and extreme reactions to changes in the immediate environment. About 75 percent of children with autism have low scores on standardized intelligence tests. The outlook for independent living may be improved with intensive training.

The following organizations may provide additional information and support:
Autism Network International
Autism Research Institute
Autism Services Center
Autism Society of America
Birth Defect Research for Children, Inc.
Federation of Families for Children's Mental Health
Geneva Centre for Autism
MAAP Services for Autism and Asperger Syndrome
March of Dimes Birth Defects Foundation
National Alliance for the Mentally Ill
National Autistic Society
National Institute of Neurological Disorders and Stroke (NINDS)
National Mental Health Association
National Mental Health Consumers' Self-Help Clearinghouse
New Horizons Un-Limited, Inc.
NIH/National Institute of Child Health and Human Development

NIH/National Institute of Mental Health
NIH/National Institute on Deafness and Other Communication Disorders Information Clearinghouse
NIH/National Society for Children and Adults with Autism
Organization For Anti-Convulsant Syndrome
R.O.C.K. (Raising Our Celiac Kids)

126 Autoimmune Polyendocrine Syndrome Type II

Synonyms

Diabetes Mellitus, Addison's Disease, Myxedema
Multiple Endocrine Deficiency Syndrome, Type II
PGA II
Polyglandular Autoimmune Syndrome, Type II
Polyglandular Deficiency Syndrome, Type II
Schmidt Syndrome

Autoimmune polyendocrine syndrome type II, also known as Schmidt syndrome, is a rare autoimmune disorder in which there is a steep drop in production of several essential hormones by the glands that secrete these hormones. When first described, this disorder was thought to involve only adrenal insufficiency (Addison's disease) and thyroid insufficiency (Hashimoto's thyroiditis). However, over time, as more patients were studied, the scope of the disorder was expanded to include disorders of other underperforming endocrine glands. These include the gonads, which secrete sex hormones; the pancreas which secretes insulin and is intimately tied up with diabetes mellitus; and sometimes the parathyroid glands. Failure of the endocrine glands to function is usually accompanied by signs of malnutrition because the ability of the intestinal tract to absorb nutrients is reduced dramatically. Since the combination of affected glands differs from patient to patient, the signs of this disorder are diverse. Most cases of this disorder are sporadic although some clinical researchers believe that there is a familial or hereditary trait associated with AIPS-II. If so, it may involve a complex interaction among many genes.

The following organizations may provide additional information and support:
American Autoimmune Related Diseases Association, Inc.
American Diabetes Association
Celiac Sprue Association/USA, Inc.
Myasthenia Gravis Foundation of America
National Adrenal Diseases Foundation

NIH/National Digestive Diseases Information Clearinghouse
Thyroid Foundation of America, Inc.

127 Autoimmune Thyroiditis

Synonyms

Chronic Thyroiditis
Goitrous Autoimmune Thyroiditis
Hashimoto's Disease
Hashimoto's Syndrome
Hashimoto's Thyroiditis
Lymphadenoid Goiter
Struma Hymphomatosa

Autoimmune thyroiditis (AT), also known as Hashimoto's disease, is a chronic inflammatory disorder of the thyroid gland that is caused by abnormal blood antibodies and white blood cells that mistakenly attack and damage healthy thyroid cells. It is a progressive disease that may destroy the thyroid gland, causing thyroid hormone deficiency (hypothyroidism). Autoimmune thyroiditis presents with various combinations of symptoms, making diagnosis difficult. This disease can occur at any age, but is most often seen in middle-aged women. In rare cases, it may be associated with other autoimmune endocrine disorders.

The following organizations may provide additional information and support:
American Foundation of Thyroid Patients
Autoimmune Information Network, Inc
March of Dimes Birth Defects Foundation
NIH/National Digestive Diseases Information Clearinghouse
Thyroid Foundation of America, Inc.
Thyroid Foundation of Canada
Thyroid Society for Education & Research

128 Babesiosis

Synonyms

Piriplasmosis
Redwater Fever

Babesiosis is a rare infectious disease caused by single-celled microorganisms (protozoa) belonging to the *Babesia* family. It is believed that the *Babesia* protozoa are usually carried and transmitted by ticks (vectors). Babesiosis occurs primarily in animals; however, in rare cases, babesiosis infection may occur in humans. Certain *Babesia* species are known to cause babesiosis infection in humans (e.g., *Babesia microti*), and the deer tick is a known vector. Human babesiosis infection may cause fever, chills, headache, nausea, vomiting, and/or muscle aches (myalgia). Symptoms may be mild in otherwise healthy people; in addition, some infected individuals may exhibit no symptoms (asymptomatic). However, a severe form of babesiosis, which may be life-threatening if untreated, may occur in individuals who have had their spleens removed (splenectomized) or who have an impaired immune system. A different form of babesiosis has been reported in Europe that is associated with a more severe expression of symptoms.

The following organizations may provide additional information and support:
Centers for Disease Control and Prevention
Lyme Disease Foundation
NIH/National Institute of Allergy and Infectious Diseases
World Health Organization (WHO) Regional Office for the Americas (AMRO)

---

129 Balantidiasis

Synonyms
Balantidiosis
Ciliary Dysentery

Balantidiasis is a rare intestinal infection caused by the bacterium, *Balantidium coli*, a single celled parasite (ciliate protozoan) that frequently infects pigs but on occasion (rarely) infects humans. Some infected people may have no symptoms or only mild diarrhea and abdominal discomfort but others may experience more severe symptoms reminiscent of an acute inflammation of the intestines. Symptoms of balantidiasis may be similar to those of other infections that cause intestinal inflammation, for example, amoebic dysentery.

The following organizations may provide additional information and support:
Centers for Disease Control and Prevention
NIH/National Institute of Allergy and Infectious Diseases
World Health Organization (WHO) Regional Office for the Americas (AMRO)

---

130 Baller Gerold Syndrome

Synonyms
Craniosynostosis with Radial Defects
Craniosynostosis-Radial Aplasia Syndrome

Baller-Gerold syndrome is a rare genetic disorder that is apparent at birth (congenital). The disorder is characterized by distinctive malformations of the skull and facial (craniofacial) area and bones of the forearms and hands. In infants with Baller-Gerold syndrome, there is premature fusion of the fibrous joints (cranial sutures) between certain bones in the skull (craniosynostosis). As a result, the head may appear unusually short and wide and/or pointed at the top (turribrachycephaly) or relatively triangular in shape (trigonocephaly). Affected infants may also have a prominent forehead; downslanting eyelid folds (palpebral fissures); small, malformed (dysplastic), low-set ears; and/or other craniofacial abnormalities. Baller-Gerold syndrome is also characterized by under-development (hypoplasia) or absence (aplasia) of the bone on the thumb side of the forearms (radii). In addition, the bone on the "pinky" side of the forearms (ulnae) is unusually short and curved and the thumbs may be underdeveloped or absent. In some cases, additional physical abnormalities and/or mental retardation may also be present. Baller-Gerold syndrome is thought to be inherited as an autosomal recessive trait.

The following organizations may provide additional information and support:
AboutFace USA
Children's Craniofacial Association
FACES: The National Craniofacial Association
Forward Face, Inc.
Let's Face It (USA)
National Craniofacial Foundation

---

131 Balo Disease

Synonyms
Concentric Sclerosis
Encephalitis Periaxialis Concentrica
Leukoencephalitis Periaxialis Concentric

Balo disease is a rare and progressive variant of multiple sclerosis. It usually first appears in adulthood, but childhood cases have also been reported. While multiple sclerosis typically is a disease that waxes and wanes, Balo disease is different in that it tends to be rapidly progressive. Symptoms may include headache, seizures, gradual paralysis, involuntary muscle spasms, and cognitive loss. The alternative names for Balo disease, concentric sclerosis or Balo concentric sclerosis, refer to the fact that Balo disease is characterized by bands of intact myelin (the sheath of fatty substances surrounding nerve fibers) alternating with rings of loss of myelin (demyelination) in various parts of the brain and brain stem. The symptoms of Balo disease vary, according to the areas of the brain that are affected. Symptoms may progress rapidly over several weeks or more slowly over 2 to 3 years.

The following organizations may provide additional information and support:
American Autoimmune Related Diseases Association, Inc.
National Institute of Neurological Disorders and Stroke (NINDS)
United Leukodystrophy Foundation

132 Bannayan-Riley-Ruvalcaba Syndrome

Synonyms

Bannayan-Zonana Syndrome (BZS)
BRRS
Macrocephaly, Multiple Lipomas, and Hemangiomata
Macrocephaly, Pseudopapilledema, and Multiple Hemangiomata
Riley-Smith Syndrome
Ruvalcaba-Myhre-Smith Syndrome (RMSS)

Bannayan-Riley-Ruvalcaba syndrome is a rare inherited disorder characterized by excessive growth before and after birth; an abnormally large head (macrocephaly) that is often long and narrow (scaphocephaly); normal intelligence or mild mental retardation; and/or benign tumor-like growths (hamartomas) that, in most cases, occur below the surface of the skin (subcutaneously). The symptoms of this disorder vary greatly from case to case. In most cases, infants with Bannayan-Riley-Ruvalcaba syndrome exhibit increased birth weight and length. As affected infants age, the growth rate slows and adults with this disorder often attain a height that is within the normal range. Additional findings associated with Bannayan-Riley-Ruvalcaba syndrome may include eye (ocular) abnormalities such as crossed eyes (strabismus), widely spaced eyes (ocular hypertelorism), deviation of one eye away from the other (exotropia), and/or abnormal elevation of the optic disc so that it appears swollen (pseudopapilledema). In addition, affected infants may also have diminished muscle tone (hypotonia); excessive drooling; delayed speech development; and/or a significant delay in the attainment of developmental milestones such as the ability to sit, stand, walk, etc. In some cases, multiple growths (hamartomatous polyps) may develop within the intestines (intestinal polyposis) and, in rare cases, the back wall of the throat (pharynx) and/or tonsils. Additional abnormalities associated with this disorder may include abnor-

mal skin coloration (pigmentation) such as areas of skin that may appear "marbled" (cutis marmorata) and/or the development of freckle-like spots (pigmented macules) on the penis in males or the vulva in females. In some cases, affected individuals may also have skeletal abnormalities and/or abnormalities affecting the muscles (myopathy). Bannayan-Riley-Ruvalcaba syndrome is inherited as an autosomal dominant genetic trait. Bannayan-Riley-Ruvalcaba is the name used to denote the combination of three conditions formerly recognized as separate disorders. These disorders are Bannayan-Zonana syndrome, Riley-Smith syndrome, and Ruvalcaba-Myhre-Smith syndrome.

The following organizations may provide additional information and support:
The Arc (A National Organization on Mental Retardation)
March of Dimes Birth Defects Foundation
National Cancer Institute
National Craniofacial Foundation
NIH/National Arthritis and Musculoskeletal and Skin Diseases Information Clearinghouse

133 Banti Syndrome

Synonyms

Banti's Disease
Hypersplenism

Banti syndrome is a disorder of the spleen, the large, gland-like organ in the upper left side of the abdomen that produces red blood cells before birth and, in newborns, removes and destroys aged red blood cells, and plays a role in fighting infection. In the case of Banti syndrome, the spleen rapidly but prematurely destroys blood cells. This syndrome is characterized by abnormal enlargement of the spleen (splenomegaly) due to obstruction of blood flow in some veins and abnormally increased blood pressure (hypertension) within the veins of the liver (e.g., hepatic or portal veins) or the spleen (splenic veins). The disorder may be due to any number of different factors causing obstruction of portal, hepatic, or splenic veins including abnormalities present at birth (congenital) of such veins, blood clots, or various underlying disorders causing inflammation and obstruction of veins (vascular obstruction) of the liver.

The following organizations may provide additional information and support:
American Liver Foundation
NIH/National Digestive Diseases Information Clearinghouse

134 Bardet-Biedl Syndrome

Synonym

Biedl-Bardet Syndrome

Bardet-Biedl syndrome is a group of rare disorders inherited as autosomal recessive genetic traits. Major features of these disorders may include mental retardation, obesity, delayed sexual development or underdeveloped reproductive organs, progressive pigmentary degeneration of the retinas of the eyes, kidney abnormalities in structure or function, and/or abnormal or extra fingers and/or toes. Confusion exists in the medical literature regarding the difference between Bardet-Biedl syndrome and Laurence-Moon syndrome.

The following organizations may provide additional information and support:
American Council of the Blind, Inc.
American Foundation for the Blind
American Printing House for the Blind
Blind Children's Fund
Foundation Fighting Blindness (Canada)
Foundation Fighting Blindness, Inc.
Laurence Moon Bardet Biedl Syndrome
National Association for Parents of Children with Visual Impairments (NAPVI)
National Association for Visually Handicapped
Prevent Blindness America
Retinitis Pigmentosa International

135 Barrett Esophagus

Synonyms

Barrett Ulcer
BE
Chronic Peptic Ulcer and Esophagitis Syndrome
Columnar-Like Esophagus
Esophagitis-Peptic Ulcer

Barrett esophagus is a rare disorder characterized by chronic inflammation and ulceration of the esophagus (esophagitis). Symptoms develop due to the chronic occurrence of gastroesophageal reflux disease (GERD), which is a condition characterized by backflow of stomach acid into the esophagus and may include episodes of heartburn and recurring pain behind the breastbone (sternum). Late symptoms associated with Barrett esophagus may also include a narrowing (stricture) of the esophagus and difficulty swallowing (dysphagia).

The following organizations may provide additional information and support:
Digestive Disease National Coalition
NIH/National Digestive Diseases Information Clearinghouse

136 Barth Syndrome

Synonyms

3-Methylglutaconic Aciduria, Type II (MGA, Type II)
Cardioskeletal Myopathy, Barth Type
Cardioskeletal Myopathy with Neutropenia and Abnormal Mitochondria
Endocardial Fibroelastosis, Type 2 (EFE2)
X-Linked Cardioskeletal Myopathy and Neutropenia

Barth syndrome is a genetic disorder that appears to occur exclusively in males. Although Barth syndrome typically becomes apparent during infancy or early childhood, the age of onset, associated symptoms and findings, and disease course may vary considerably, even among affected members of the same family (kindred). Primary characteristics of the disorder include abnormalities of heart and skeletal muscle (cardioskeletal myopathy); low levels of certain white blood cells (neutrophils) that help to fight bacterial infections (known as neutropenia); and growth retardation, potentially leading to short stature. The disorder is also associated with increased levels of certain organic acids in the urine and blood, particularly 3-methylglutaconic acid (3-methylglutaconic aciduria/acidemia). In most individuals with Barth syndrome, weakening of the heart muscle (myocardium) leads to enlargement (dilation) of the heart's lower chambers (ventricles). Known as dilated cardiomyopathy, signs of this condition are often present at birth (congenital) or may appear during the first months of life. Dilated cardiomyopathy typically leads to weakening of the heart's pumping action, causing a limited ability to circulate blood to the lungs and the rest of the body (heart failure). Symptoms of heart failure may depend on the child's age and other factors. In young children, for example, heart failure may be manifest as fatigue and shortness of breath (dyspnea) with exertion. Barth syndrome is also associated with abnormally diminished muscle tone (hypotonia) and muscle weakness, often leading to delays in the acquisition of gross motor skills. In addition, affected infants and children may fail to grow and gain weight at the expected rate (failure to thrive); may have mild learning disabilities, (although they usually are of normal intelligence);

and, in many cases, may be prone to recurrent bacterial infections due to low levels of circulating neutrophils in the blood. Without prompt detection and appropriate treatment, heart failure and bacterial infections can be life-threatening complications. Barth syndrome is transmitted as an X-linked recessive trait. A gene responsible for the disorder has been located on the long arm (q) of chromosome X (Xq28).

The following organizations may provide additional information and support:
American Heart Association
American Organ Transplant Association
Barth Syndrome Foundation, Inc.
Cardiac Arrhythmias Research and Education Foundation, Inc.
Cardiomyopathy Association
Children's Cardiomyopathy Foundation
Children's European Mitochondrial Disease Network
CLIMB (Children Living with Inherited Metabolic Diseases)
Lactic Acidosis Support Trust
March of Dimes Birth Defects Foundation
Montgomery Heart Foundation for Cardiomyopathy
National Neutropenia Network
National Transplant Assistance Fund (NTAF)
Neutropenia Support Association, Inc.
NIH/National Heart, Lung and Blood Institute Information Center
Transplant Recipients International Organization, Inc.
TransWeb
United Mitochondrial Disease Foundation

137 Bartonellosis

Synonyms
Bartonella Bacilliformis Infection
Bartonelliasis
Carrion's Disease

Disorder Subdivisions
Oroya Fever
Verruga Peruana (Hemorrhagic Pian; Verruca Peruviana)

Bartonellosis is a rare infectious disease found only in certain regions of South America. It is caused by infection with the bacterium *Bartonella bacilliformis* (*B. bacilliformis*), which is transmitted by sandflies. Bartonellosis is usually

characterized by two distinctive stages: a sudden (acute), potentially life-threatening illness associated with high fever and decreased levels of circulating red blood cells (i.e., hemolytic anemia) and a chronic, benign skin (cutaneous) eruption consisting of raised, reddish-purple nodules.

The following organizations may provide additional information and support:
Centers for Disease Control and Prevention
NIH/National Institute of Allergy and Infectious Diseases
World Health Organization (WHO) Regional Office for the Americas (AMRO)

138 Bartter's Syndrome

Synonyms
Aldosteronism with Normal Blood Pressure
Hyperaldosteronism with Hypokalemic Alkalosis
Hyperaldosteronism without Hypertension
Hypokalemic Alkalosis with Hypercalciuria
Juxtaglomerular Hyperplasia

Bartter's syndrome, also known as hypokalemic alkalosis with hypercalciuria, is a rare inherited disorder characterized by growth deficiency, potentially resulting in short stature; muscle weakness; cramps; and/or loss of potassium from the kidneys (renal potassium wasting). In some cases, affected individuals may exhibit mental retardation. Individuals with Bartter's syndrome have a disturbance in their acid-base ratio (i.e., an accumulation of base or loss of acid) associated with a loss of potassium (hypokalemic alkalosis). Low amounts of potassium may result from overproduction of a certain hormone (aldosterone) that is essential in controlling blood pressure and regulating sodium and potassium levels (hyperaldosteronism). The exact cause of Bartter's syndrome is not known; in some cases, it may be inherited as an autosomal recessive genetic trait.

The following organizations may provide additional information and support:
American Kidney Fund, Inc.
The Arc (A National Organization on Mental Retardation)
March of Dimes Birth Defects Foundation
National Kidney Foundation
NIH/National Institute of Diabetes, Digestive & Kidney Diseases

139 Batten Disease

Synonyms

Batten-Mayou Syndrome
Batten-Spielmeyer-Vogt's Disease
Batten-Vogt Syndrome
Neuronal Ceroid Lipofuscinosis, Juvenile Type
Spielmeyer-Vogt Disease
Spielmeyer-Vogt-Batten Syndrome
Stengel's Syndrome
Stengel-Batten-Mayou-Spielmeyer-Vogt-Stock Disease

Batten disease is the juvenile form of a group of progressive neurological diseases known as neuronal ceroid lipofuscinoses (NCL). It is characterized by accumulation of a fatty substance (lipopigment) in the brain as well as in tissue that does not contain nerve cells. This lipopigment storage disorder is inherited, and is marked by rapidly progressive vision failure (optic atrophy), and neurological disturbances, which may begin before eight years of age. Occurring mostly in families of Northern European Scandinavian ancestry, the disorder affects the brain and may cause both deterioration of intellect and neurological functions.

The following organizations may provide additional information and support:
CLIMB (Children Living with Inherited Metabolic Diseases)
Children's Brain Diseases Foundation
National Batten Disease Registry
National Institute of Neurological Disorders and Stroke (NINDS)
National Pediatric Myoclonus Center
National Tay-Sachs and Allied Diseases Association, Inc.
New York State Institute for Basic Research in Developmental Disabilities

140 Beals Syndrome

Synonyms

Arachnodactyly, Contractural Beals Type
Beals-Hecht Syndrome
CCA
Contractural Arachnodactyly, Congenital
Contractures, Multiple with Arachnodactyly
Ear Anomalies-Contractures-Dysplasia of Bone with Kyphoscoliosis

Beals syndrome is a rare genetic connective tissue disorder inherited as an autosomal dominant trait. The major features of this disorder are long, thin, spiderlike fingers and toes; congenital contractures of the fingers, hips, elbows, knees and ankles; and unusual ears that appear crumpled.

The following organizations may provide additional information and support:
British Coalition of Heritable Disorders of Connective Tissue
Genetic and Rare Diseases (GARD) Information Center
March of Dimes Birth Defects Foundation

141 Beckwith-Wiedemann Syndrome

Synonyms

Beckwith-Syndrome
BWS
EMG Syndrome
Exomphalos-Macroglossia-Gigantism Syndrome
Hypoglycemia with Macroglossia
Macroglossia-Omphalocele-Visceromegaly Syndrome
Omphalocele-Visceromegaly-Macroglossia Syndrome
Visceromegaly-Umbilical Hernia-Macroglossia Syndrome
Wiedmann-Beckwith Syndrome

Beckwith-Wiedemann syndrome (BWS) is a rare genetic disorder. It may be characterized by a wide spectrum of symptoms and findings that vary in range and severity from case to case. However, in many individuals with the syndrome, associated features may include above average weight and length at birth and/or increased growth after birth (postnatally); an unusually large tongue (macroglossia); enlargement of certain abdominal organs (visceromegaly); and/or abdominal wall defects. BWS may also be characterized by low blood sugar levels within the first days of life (neonatal hypoglycemia); advanced bone age, particularly up to age four; the presence of distinctive linear grooves in the ear lobes and/or other abnormalities of the facial area; and/or an increased risk of developing certain childhood cancers. In most instances, BWS results from genetic changes that appear to occur randomly (sporadically). However, in rare cases, the syndrome appears to be familial, suggesting autosomal dominant inheritance. Research indicates that BWS may result from various abnormalities affecting proper expression of a gene or genes within a specific region of chromosome 11 (11p15).

The following organizations may provide additional information and support:
The Arc (A National Organization on Mental Retardation)
Beckwith Wiedemann Support Network
Beckwith-Wiedemann Children's Foundation
Beckwith-Wiedemann Family Forum
Candlelighters Childhood Cancer Foundation
Childhood Cancer Foundation —— Candlelighters Canada
March of Dimes Birth Defects Foundation
National Cancer Institute
National Cancer Institute Physician Data Query (PDQ) Cancer Information Service
National Childhood Cancer Foundation
Neuroblastoma Children's Cancer Society
NIH/National Institute of Child Health and Human Development
OncoLink: The University of Pennsylvania Cancer Center Resource

142 Behcet's Syndrome

Synonyms

Adamantiades-Behcet's Syndrome
BD
Behcet's Disease
Halushi-Behcet's Syndrome
Oculo-Bucco-Genital Syndrome
Touraine's Aphthosis
Triple Symptom Complex of Behcet

Behcet's syndrome is a rare multisystem inflammatory disorder characterized by ulcers affecting the mouth and genitals, various skin lesions, and abnormalities affecting the eyes. Symptoms include areas of abnormal skin changes (lesions) of the mouth and genitals that tend to disappear and recur spontaneously. Inflammation of the outer fibrous layers of tissue (tunic) that surround the eyes (posterior uveitis) also affects individuals with Behcet's syndrome. Additional systems of the body may also be affected including the joints, blood vessels, central nervous system, and/or digestive tract. The exact cause of Behcet's syndrome is unknown.

The following organizations may provide additional information and support:
American Behcet's Disease Association
Arthritis Foundation
Autoimmune Information Network, Inc
Behcet's Organisation Worldwide
CNS Vasculitis Foundation
Erythema Nodosum Yahoo Support Group
National Association for Visually Handicapped

National Institute of Neurological Disorders and Stroke (NINDS)
NIH/National Arthritis and Musculoskeletal and Skin Diseases Information Clearinghouse
NIH/National Eye Institute

143 Bejel

Synonyms

Dichuchwa
Endemic Syphilis
Frenga
Njovera
Nonvenereal Syphilis
Siti
Treponematosis, Bejel Type

Bejel is an infectious disease that is rare in the United States but common in certain parts of the world. The infection is very similar to syphilis but is not sexually transmitted. Most frequently, transmission is by means of non-sexual skin contact or by common use of eating and drinking utensils. The organism that causes bejel belongs to the same family as the bacterium that causes syphilis, pinta and yaws and is known as *treponema*. *Treponemas* are spiral-shaped bacteria (spirochetes). Also known as endemic syphilis, bejel is characterized by lesions of the skin and bones that begin in the mouth and progress in gradual stages. The late stages are the most severe. Bejel is very common in dry, hot climates especially in the countries of the eastern Mediterranean region and in Saharan West Africa.

The following organizations may provide additional information and support:
Centers for Disease Control and Prevention
NIH/National Institute of Allergy and Infectious Diseases
World Health Organization (WHO) Regional Office for the Americas (AMRO)

144 Bell's Palsy

Synonyms

Antoni's Palsy
Facial Nerve Palsy
Facial Paralysis
Idiopathic Facial Palsy
Refrigeration Palsy

Bell's palsy is a nonprogressive neurological disorder of one of the facial nerves (7th cranial nerve). This disorder is characterized by the sudden onset of facial paralysis that may be preceded by a slight fever, pain behind the ear on the affected side, a stiff neck, and weakness and/or stiffness on one side of the face. Paralysis results from decreased blood supply (ischemia) and/or compression of the 7th cranial nerve. The exact cause of Bell's palsy is not known. Viral (e.g., herpes zoster virus) and immune disorders are frequently implicated as a cause for this disorder. There may also be an inherited tendency toward developing Bell's palsy.

The following organizations may provide additional information and support:
Bells Palsy Research Foundation
Jack Miller Center for Peripheral Neuropathy
National Institute of Neurological Disorders and Stroke (NINDS)

---

145 Benign Essential Tremor

Synonyms
Presenile Tremor Syndrome
Tremor, Familial Essential
Tremor, Hereditary Benign

Benign essential tremor is a neurologic movement disorder characterized by involuntary fine rhythmic tremor of a body part or parts, primarily the hands and arms (upper limbs). In many affected individuals, upper limb tremor may occur as an isolated finding. However, in others, tremor may gradually involve other anatomic regions, such as the head, voice, tongue, or roof of the mouth (palate), leading to difficulties articulating speech (dysarthria). Less commonly, tremor may affect muscles of the trunk or legs. In individuals with the condition, tremor tends to occur while voluntarily maintaining a fixed posture against gravity ("postural tremor") or while performing certain goal-directed movements ("kinetic intention tremor"). Although tremor is typically absent with rest—i.e., when the affected muscle is not voluntarily activated—some individuals with advanced disease may develop resting tremors. Although symptom onset may occur during childhood or adolescence, the condition most commonly becomes apparent during adulthood, at an average age of 45 years. Benign essential tremor is generally considered a slowly progressive disorder. Disease progression is characterized by an increase in tremor

amplitude, causing difficulties in performing fine motor skills and varying degrees of functional disability. For example, hand tremor may gradually cause difficulties with manipulating small objects, drinking fluids from a glass, eating, writing, or dressing. (As mentioned above, in some affected individuals, disease progression may also include extension of tremor to other muscle groups.) Benign essential tremor may appear to occur randomly for unknown reasons (sporadically) or be transmitted as an autosomal dominant trait. Researchers suggest that changes (mutations) of different genes may be responsible for the disorder (genetic heterogeneity). For example, during genetic analysis of several affected families (kindreds), investigators located a gene for the disorder, known as "FET1," on the long arm (q) of chromosome 3 (3q13). In another kindred, the disorder was determined to result from mutations of a gene, designated "ETM2," on the short arm (p) of chromosome 2 (2p22-p25).

The following organizations may provide additional information and support:
International Essential Tremor Foundation
March of Dimes Birth Defects Foundation
National Institute of Neurological Disorders and Stroke (NINDS)
WE MOVE (Worldwide Education and Awareness for Movement Disorders)

---

146 Bernard-Soulier Syndrome

Synonyms
BSS
Giant Platelet Syndrome
Hemorrhagiparous Thrombocytic Dystrophy
Macrothrombocytopenia, Familial Bernard-Soulier Type
Platelet Glycoprotein IB Deficiency
Von Willebrand Factor Receptor Deficiency

Bernard-Soulier syndrome (BSS) is a rare inherited disorder of blood clotting (coagulation) characterized by (1) unusually large and irregularly shaped platelets; (2) low platelet count (thrombocytopenia) and (3) prolonged bleeding time (difficulty in clotting). Affected individuals tend to bleed excessively and bruise easily. Most cases of Bernard-Soulier syndrome are inherited as an autosomal recessive genetic trait.

The following organizations may provide additional information and support:
Bernard-Soulier Syndrome Website and Registry
March of Dimes Birth Defects Foundation
NIH/National Heart, Lung and Blood Institute Information Center

147 Berylliosis

Synonyms
Acute Beryllium Disease
Beryllium Granulomatosis
Beryllium Pneumonosis
Beryllium Poisoning

Disorder Subdivisions
Acute Berylliosis (Acute Beryllium Disease)
Chronic Berylliosis (Chronic Beryllium Disease [CBD])

Berylliosis is a form of metal poisoning caused by inhalation of beryllium dusts, vapors, or its compounds or implantation of the substance in the skin. The toxic effects of beryllium most commonly occur due to occupational exposure. Beryllium is a metallic element used in many industries, including electronics, high-technology ceramics, metals extraction, and dental alloy preparation. There are two forms of beryllium-induced lung disease: acute and chronic. Acute berylliosis has a sudden, rapid onset and is characterized by severe inflammation of the lungs (pneumonitis), coughing, increasing breathlessness (dyspnea), and other associated symptoms and findings. In addition, in some individuals, the skin or the eyes may be affected. The more common, chronic form of the disease develops more slowly and, in some cases, may not become apparent for many years after initial beryllium exposure. Chronic berylliosis is characterized by the abnormal formation of inflammatory masses or nodules (granulomas) within certain tissues and organs and widespread scarring and thickening of deep lung tissues (interstitial pulmonary fibrosis). Although granuloma development primarily affects the lungs, it may also occur within other bodily tissues and organs, such as the skin and underlying (subcutaneous) tissues or the liver. In individuals with chronic berylliosis, associated symptoms and findings often include dry coughing, fatigue, weight loss, chest pain, and increasing shortness of breath.

The following organizations may provide additional information and support:
American Lung Association
Centers for Disease Control and Prevention
NIH/National Institute of Allergy and Infectious Diseases

148 Best Vitelliform Macular Dystrophy

Synonyms
Best Macular Dystrophy
Macular Degeneration, Polymorphic Vitelline
Vitelliform Macular Dystrophy, Early-Onset
Vitelliform Macular Dystrophy, Juvenile-Onset
Vitelliform Macular Dystrophy, Type 2

Best vitelliform macular dystrophy is an autosomal dominant genetic form of macular degeneration that usually begins in childhood or adolescence and slowly progresses to affect central vision. The age of onset and severity of vision loss are highly variable. Best vitelliform macular dystrophy is associated with an abnormality in the VMD2 gene.

The following organizations may provide additional information and support:
American Council of the Blind, Inc.
American Foundation for the Blind
Association for Macular Diseases, Inc.
Council of Families with Visual Impairment
Foundation Fighting Blindness, Inc.
Macular Degeneration International
National Association for Parents of Children with Visual Impairments (NAPVI)
National Association for Visually Handicapped
NIH/National Eye Institute

149 Biliary Atresia, Extrahepatic

Synonym
EHBA

Extrahepatic biliary atresia is a rare gastrointestinal disorder characterized by destruction or absence of all or a portion of the bile duct that lies outside the liver (extrahepatic bile duct). The bile duct is a tube that allows the passage of bile from the liver into the gall bladder and, eventually, the small intestine. Bile is a liquid secreted by the liver that plays an essential role in carrying waste products from the liver and breaking down fats in the small intestine. In extrahepatic biliary atresia, absence or destruction of the bile ducts results in the abnormal accumulation of bile in the liver. Affected infants may have yellowing of the skin and whites of the eyes (jaundice) and scarring of the liver (cirrhosis). In some cases, additional abnormalities may be present, including heart defects and kidney and spleen malformations. The exact cause of extrahepatic biliary atresia is unknown.

The following organizations may provide additional information and support:
American Liver Foundation
Canadian Liver Foundation
Children's Liver Alliance
Children's Liver Association for Support Services
Children's Liver Disease Foundation
March of Dimes Birth Defects Foundation
NIH/National Institute of Diabetes, Digestive & Kidney Diseases

150   Binswanger's Disease

Synonyms
Binswanger's Encephalopathy
Multi-infarct Dementia, Binswanger's Type
SAE
Subcortical Dementia
Subcortical Ischemic Vascular Disease
Vascular Dementia, Binswanger's Type

Binswanger's disease is a rare, progressive neurological disorder characterized by injuries (lesions) to the blood vessels supplying the deep white-matter of the brain. Affected individuals usually experience a gradual loss of memory, cognitive, and behavioral abilities, usually over a ten-year period. In some cases, symptoms and physical findings associated with Binswanger's disease may stabilize or improve for a brief time; however, in most cases, progression of the disorder usually returns. Affected individuals experience progressive memory loss and deterioration of intellectual abilities (dementia), strokes, paralysis of one or the other side of the body (hemiparesis), electrical disturbance in the brain (seizures), and/or an abnormally slow, unsteady walk (abnormal gait).

The following organizations may provide additional information and support:
Alzheimer's Association
Alzheimer's Disease Education and Referral Center
National Association for Continence
National Institute of Neurological Disorders and Stroke (NINDS)
NIH/National Institute on Aging

151   Bjornstad Syndrome

Synonyms
Deafness and Pili Torti, Bjornstad Type
Pili Torti and Nerve Deafness
Pili Torti-Sensorineural Hearing Loss

Bjornstad syndrome is an extremely rare inherited disorder characterized by the presence of abnormally flattened, twisted hair shafts (pili torti) and, in most cases, deafness (sensorineural hearing loss). Hearing loss typically affects both ears (bilateral). Individuals with this disorder usually have dry, fragile, lusterless, and/or coarse scalp hair as well as areas of patchy hair loss (alopecia). Both autosomal dominant and recessive inheritance have been reported in the medical literature.

The following organizations may provide additional information and support:
Alexander Graham Bell Association for the Deaf, Inc.
Better Hearing Institute
Birth Defect Research for Children, Inc.
NIH/National Institute of Arthritis and Musculoskeletal and Skin Diseases
NIH/National Institute on Deafness and Other Communication Disorders Information Clearinghouse

152   Bladder Exstrophy-Epispadias-Cloacal Exstrophy Complex

Synonym
Ectopia Vesicae

Bladder exstrophy-epispadias-cloacal exstrophy complex is a spectrum of anomalies involving the urinary tract, genital tract, musculoskeletal system and sometimes the intestinal tract. In classic bladder exstrophy, most anomalies are related to defects of the abdominal wall, bladder, genitalia, pelvic bones, rectum and anus. Bladder exstrophy is a rare developmental abnormality that is present at birth (congenital) in which the bladder and related structures are turned inside out. The rear portion of the bladder wall (posterior vesical wall) turns outward (exstrophy) through an opening in the abdominal wall and urine is excreted through this opening. The extent of the exstrophy depends on how large the opening is. The mildest form is when there is a defect or opening in the tube that carries urine out of the body from the bladder (urethra) and is termed epispadias. The most severe form is when there is a defect in the urethra, bladder and bowel (cloacal exstrophy). Classic bladder exstrophy is when there is a defect in the urethra and bladder and is intermediate in severity. The underlying cause of this complex is not known. The physical characteristics are the result of a developmental abnormality during embryonic growth in which the cloacal membrane is not replaced by tissue that will form the abdominal muscles.

The following organizations may provide additional information and support:
American Foundation for Urologic Disease
Association for Bladder Exstrophy Community
Birth Defect Research for Children, Inc.
National Association for Continence
NIH/National Kidney and Urologic Diseases Information Clearinghouse
Ureterosigmoidostomy Association

153   Blastomycosis

Synonyms
Gilchrist's Disease
North American Blastomycosis

Blastomycosis is a rare infectious multisystem disease that is caused by the fungus *Blastomyces dermatitidis*. The symptoms vary greatly according to the affected organ system. It is characterized by fever, chills, cough, and/or difficulty breathing (dyspnea). In the chronic phase of the disease, the lungs and skin are most frequently affected. The genitourinary tract and bones may also be involved.

The following organizations may provide additional information and support:
Centers for Disease Control and Prevention
NIH/National Institute of Allergy and Infectious Diseases
World Health Organization (WHO) Regional Office for the Americas (AMRO)

154   Blepharophimosis, Ptosis, Epicanthus Inversus Syndrome

Synonyms
Blepharophimosis, Epicanthus Inversus, and Ptosis
BPES

Disorder Subdivisions
Blepharophimosis, Ptosis, Epicanthus Inversus Syndrome, Type I
Blepharophimosis, Ptosis, Epicanthus Inversus Syndrome, Type II

BPES Type I
BPES Type II

Blepharophimosis, ptosis, epicanthus inversus syndrome (BPES) is a rare disorder that is inherited as an autosomal dominant trait. The main findings of this disorder are eyelids that are abnormally narrow horizontally (blepharophimosis), a vertical fold of skin from the lower eyelid up either side of the nose (epicanthus inversus), and drooping of the upper eyelids (ptosis). There are thought to be two types of the syndrome. Type I BPES may involve female infertility and is inherited as an autosomal dominant genetic trait. Both male and female children of a male with type I BPES have a 50% chance of being affected. If females with type I BPES are able to have children, the odds are 50% that each child (male or female) will have type I BPES. Type II BPES is also transmitted as an autosomal dominant genetic trait. Either parent may transmit the disorder and the children have a 50% chance of being affected. Type II is not associated with female infertility.

The following organizations may provide additional information and support:
AboutFace USA
Blepharophimosis, Ptosis, Epicanthus Inversus Family Network
Children's Craniofacial Association
FACES: The National Craniofacial Association
Forward Face, Inc.
National Craniofacial Foundation
Society for the Rehabilitation of the Facially Disfigured, Inc.

155   Blepharospasm, Benign Essential

Synonyms
BEB
Blepharospasm
Secondary Blepharospasm

Benign essential blepharospasm is a rare disorder in which the muscles of the eyelids (orbiculares oculi) do not function properly. There are intermittent and involuntary contractions or spasms of the muscles around the eyes. Although the eyes themselves are unaffected, the patient may eventually become functionally blind because of an inability to open the eyelids. Benign essential blepharospasm is a form of dystonia, which is a group of neuromuscular disorders characterized by muscle spasms.

The following organizations may provide additional information and support:

Benign Essential Blepharospasm Research Foundation, Inc.
Dystonia Medical Research Foundation
Dystonia Society
National Institute of Neurological Disorders and Stroke (NINDS)
WE MOVE (Worldwide Education and Awareness for Movement Disorders)

156   Bloom Syndrome

Synonyms

Bloom-Torre-Mackacek Syndrome
BS
Dwarfism, Levi's Type
Short Stature and Facial Telangiectasis
Short Stature, Telangiectatic Erythema of the Face

Bloom syndrome is a rare genetic disorder characterized by short stature; increased sensitivity to light (photosensitivity); multiple small dilated blood vessels on the face (facial telangiectasia), often resembling a butterfly in shape; immune deficiency leading to increased susceptibility to infections; and, perhaps most importantly, a markedly increased susceptibility to cancer of any organ, but especially to leukemia and lymphoma. Some clinicians classify Bloom syndrome as a chromosomal breakage syndrome; that is, a disorder associated with a high frequency of chromosomal breaks and rearrangements. It is suspected that there is a link between the frequency of chromosomal breaks and the increased propensity toward malignancies. Bloom syndrome is inherited as an autosomal recessive genetic trait. It is often included among the Jewish genetic diseases.

The following organizations may provide additional information and support:
Bloom's Syndrome Registry
Human Growth Foundation
MAGIC Foundation for Children's Growth
March of Dimes Birth Defects Foundation

157   Blue Diaper Syndrome

Synonyms

Drummond's Syndrome
Hypercalcemia, Familial, with Nephrocalcinosis and Indicanuria
Tryptophan Malabsorption

Blue diaper syndrome is a rare, inherited metabolic disorder characterized in infants by bluish urine-stained diapers. The incomplete intestinal breakdown of tryptophan, a dietary nutrient, causes this disorder. Symptoms typically include digestive disturbances, fever, and visual difficulties. Some children with blue diaper syndrome may also develop kidney disease. Blue diaper syndrome is inherited as an autosomal recessive genetic trait.

The following organizations may provide additional information and support:
American Kidney Fund, Inc.
CLIMB (Children Living with Inherited Metabolic Diseases)
March of Dimes Birth Defects Foundation
National Kidney Foundation
NIH/National Digestive Diseases Information Clearinghouse

158   Blue Rubber Bleb Nevus

Synonym

Bean Syndrome

Blue rubber bleb nevus is a very rare congenital blood vessel (vascular) disorder affecting the skin surface as well as the internal organs of the body. Multiple distinctive nodules composed of many blood vessels (hemangiomas) are the primary feature of this disorder. These rubbery skin hemangiomas are blister-like in appearance and vary in color, size, shape, number and site. They may be sensitive to the touch and are usually non-cancerous (benign).

The following organizations may provide additional information and support:
Nevus Network
Nevus Outreach, Inc.
NIH/National Arthritis and Musculoskeletal and Skin Diseases Information Clearinghouse

159   Borjeson Syndrome

Synonyms

BFLS
BORJ
Borjeson-Forssman-Lehmann Syndrome

Borjeson syndrome is a rare genetic disorder primarily characterized by an unusual facial appearance, mental retardation, obesity, seizures, delayed sexual development, and/or poor muscle tone (hypotonia). The disorder is transmitted as an X-linked recessive trait and therefore is usually fully expressed in males only. However, females who carry a single copy of the disease gene (heterozygous carriers) may manifest certain, usually more variable, features of the disorder.

The following organizations may provide additional information and support:
The Arc (A National Organization on Mental Retardation)
Genetic and Rare Diseases (GARD) Information Center
National Institute of Neurological Disorders and Stroke (NINDS)

160   Botulism

Disorder Subdivisions
Foodborne Botulism
Infant Botulism
Wound Botulism

Botulism is a neuromuscular (paralytic) disease caused by a bacterial toxin acting in the intestine (enterotoxin) and causing neuromuscular poisoning (resulting from *Clostridium botulinum* toxin). There are three generally recognized types; foodborne, wound, and infant. Foodborne botulism results when *C. botulinum* toxin, produced in contaminated food, is ingested or the spores are inhaled. Wound botulism is caused by *C. botulinum* toxin in wounds that are contaminated with this bacterium. The most common form of botulism in the United States, infant botulism, is caused by the ingestion or inhaling of *C. botulinum* spores and the subsequent production of botulinum toxin in the intestines of affected infants. (Parenthetically, botulinum toxin has become a therapeutic agent and orphan drug in its own right and is used in the treatment of certain dystonias and other disorders.) Any case of botulism is considered to be a public health emergency because of the potential for toxin-containing foods to injure others who eat them and because of the potential misuse of botulinum toxin as a biological weapon. State and local public health officials by law must be informed immediately whenever botulism is suspected in a human patient.

The following organizations may provide additional information and support:
Centers for Disease Control and Prevention
Food and Drug Administration (FDA) Office of Inquiry & Consumer Information

Infant Botulism Treatment and Prevention Program
NIH/National Institute of Allergy and Infectious Diseases

161   Bowen Hutterite Syndrome

Synonyms
Bowen-Conradi Hutterite Syndrome
Bowen-Conradi Syndrome
Hutterite Syndrome, Bowen-Conradi Type

Bowen Hutterite syndrome is a rare genetic disorder that is apparent at birth (congenital). The disorder is characterized by growth delays before birth (intrauterine growth retardation); failure to grow and gain weight at the expected rate (failure to thrive) during infancy; malformations of the head and facial (craniofacial) area, resulting in a distinctive appearance; and other physical abnormalities. These may include restricted joint movements, abnormal deviation (clinodactyly) or permanent flexion (camptodactyly) of the fifth fingers, foot deformities, and/or undescended testes (cryptorchidism) in affected males. Some affected infants may also have kidney (renal), brain, and/or other malformations. Bowen Hutterite syndrome is inherited as an autosomal recessive trait.

The following organization may provide additional information and support:
Genetic and Rare Diseases (GARD) Information Center

162   Bowenoid Papulosis

Synonym
BP

Bowenoid papulosis is a rare, sexually transmitted disorder thought to be caused by human papillomavirus type 16. This disorder is characterized by lesions that are found on the genitals of males and females. The lesions are reddish brown or violet in color, small, solid, raised and sometimes velvety.

The following organizations may provide additional information and support:
Centers for Disease Control and Prevention
NIH/National Institute of Allergy and Infectious Diseases
Sexuality Information and Education Council of the U.S.

163   Bowen's Disease

Synonyms

Intraepidermal Squamous Cell Carcinoma
Precancerous Dermatosis

Bowen's disease is characterized by a precancerous, slow growing skin malignancy. The major symptom is a red-brown, scaly or crusted patch on the skin which resembles psoriasis or dermatitis. It may occur on any part of the skin or in the mucous membranes.

The following organizations may provide additional information and support:
American Cancer Society, Inc.
National Cancer Institute
NIH/National Arthritis and Musculoskeletal and Skin Diseases Information Clearinghouse
OncoLink: The University of Pennsylvania Cancer Center Resource
Skin Cancer Foundation

164   Brachial Plexus Palsy

Synonyms

Duchenne's Paralysis
Duchenne-Erb Paralysis
Duchenne-Erb Syndrome
Erb's Paralysis
Erb-Duchenne Palsy
Erb-Duchenne Paralysis
Upper Brachial Plexus Palsy, Erb-Duchenne Type
Upper Brachial Plexus Paralysis, Erb-Duchenne Type

Brachial plexus palsy, also known as Erb's palsy, is a paralysis or weakness of the arm caused by an injury to one or more nerves that control and supply the muscles of the shoulder and upper extremities (upper brachial plexus). It is more commonly seen in newborns (neonates) and is often the result of a difficult delivery. When it occurs in adults, the cause typically is an injury that has caused stretching, tearing or other trauma to the brachial plexus network. The brachial plexus is the network of nerves that conducts signals from the spine to the shoulder, arm, and hand. There are four types of brachial plexus injury: avulsion, the most severe type, in which the nerve is ripped from the spine; rupture, in which the nerve is torn but not at the point at which it is attached to the spine; neuroma, in which the nerve is torn and has tried to heal but scar tissue has grown around the site; and neuropraxia (stretch), the most common form of injury, in which the nerve has been damaged but not torn.

The following organizations may provide additional information and support:
Erb's Palsy Group
NIH/National Institute of Arthritis and Musculoskeletal and Skin Diseases
United Brachial Plexus Network (UBPN)

165   Brain Tumors, General

Synonyms

Intracranial Tumors
Primary Tumors of Central Nervous System

Disorder Subdivisions

Brain Tumors, Benign
Brain Tumors, Malignant
Benign Tumors of the Central Nervous System
Malignant Tumors of the Central Nervous System

Brain tumors are abnormal growths in the brain that can be either cancerous (malignant) or noncancerous (benign). The effects on the brain of malignant and benign brain tumors are very similar and can cause the same types of problems depending upon the type of tumor and where it is located in the brain.

The following organizations may provide additional information and support:
American Brain Tumor Association
American Cancer Society, Inc.
Brain Tumor Foundation for Children, Inc.
Brain Tumor Society
Brain Tumour Foundation of Canada
Brain Tumour Foundation, United Kingdom
Cancer Research UK
Candlelighters Childhood Cancer Foundation
Childhood Cancer Foundation—Candlelighters Canada
Children's Brain Tumor Foundation
Harvard Brain Tissue Resource Center
National Brain Tumor Foundation
National Cancer Institute
Pediatric Brain Tumor Foundation
Pituitary Network Association (PNA)
Starting Point: To Connect with Resources Related to Pediatric Neuro-oncology

166 Branchio-Oculo-Facial Syndrome

Synonyms
  BOFS
  Branchiooculofacial Syndrome
  Hemangiomatous Branchial Clefts-Lip
  Pseudocleft Syndrome
  Imperforate Nasolacrimal Duct, and Premature
  Aging Syndrome
  Lip Pseudocleft-hemangiomatous Branchial
  Cyst Syndrome

Branchio-oculo-facial syndrome is a very rare genetic disorder that is apparent at birth (congenital). The disorder may be characterized by low birth weight; presence of an abnormal pit, opening (cleft), or tumor-like skin abnormality (hemangiomatous or atrophic skin lesion) behind both ears (postauricular area); distinctive malformations of the head and facial (craniofacial) area; abnormalities of the eyes; premature graying of the scalp hair during adolescence; and/or other abnormalities. Some individuals with branchio-oculo-facial syndrome may exhibit incomplete closure of the roof of the mouth (cleft palate) and/or an abnormal groove in the upper lip (cleft lip), while others may have an unusually wide, prominent ridge of the upper lip (philtrum) that resembles a surgically repaired cleft lip (pseudocleft). Additional craniofacial abnormalities may include a broad, misshapen (dysplastic) nose and malformed ears. In individuals with the disorder, characteristic eye (ocular) abnormalities may include unusually small eyes (microphthalmia); clouding of the lenses of the eyes (cataracts); crossing of the eyes at birth (congenital strabismus); widely spaced eyes (ocular hypertelorism); and/or absence of tissue (coloboma) from the colored portion of the eyes (iris), giving the iris a "keyhole" appearance. Branchio-oculo-facial syndrome is inherited as an autosomal dominant genetic trait.

The following organizations may provide additional information and support:
FACES: The National Craniofacial Association
Let's Face It (USA)
National Craniofacial Foundation
National Foundation for Facial Reconstruction

167 Branchio-Oto-Renal Syndrome

Synonyms
  BOR Syndrome
  Branchiootic Syndrome
  Branchio-Oto-Renal Dysplasia
  Melnick-Fraser Syndrome

Branchio-oto-renal (BOR) syndrome is a rare disorder inherited as an autosomal dominant genetic trait. This disorder is characterized by pits or ear tags in front of the outer ear, abnormal passages from the throat to the outside surface of the neck (branchial fistulas), branchial cysts, hearing loss and/or kidney (renal) abnormalities.

The following organizations may provide additional information and support:
American Kidney Fund, Inc.
American Society for Deaf Children
Atresia/Microtia Online E-mail Support Group
Let Them Hear Foundation
National Kidney Foundation
NIH/National Institute of Diabetes, Digestive & Kidney Diseases

168 Bronchopulmonary Dysplasia (BPD)

Synonym
  BPD

Bronchopulmonary dysplasia is a chronic bronchial tube and lung disease that affects infants who have been on a ventilator. The disorder usually occurs when an infant is approximately 28 days old, has certain blood-gas and radiographic (x-ray or gamma ray) abnormalities, and has an apparent lung injury causing a respiratory disorder. Pulmonary distress syndrome (lung disease in infants causing difficulty in breathing and collapsed lungs) is often also present.

The following organizations may provide additional information and support:
American Lung Association
NIH/National Heart, Lung and Blood Institute Information Center

169 Brown-Sequard Syndrome

Synonyms
  BSS
  Hemiparaplegic Syndrome
  Hemisection of the Spinal Cord
  Partial Spinal Sensory Syndrome
  Spastic Spinal Monoplegia Syndrome

Brown-Sequard syndrome is a rare spinal disorder that results from an injury to one side of the spinal cord in which the spinal cord is damaged but is not severed completely. It is usually caused by an injury to the spine in the region of the neck or back. In many cases, affected individuals have received some type of puncture wound in the neck or in the back that damages the spine and causes symptoms to appear. Characteristically, the affected person loses the sense of touch, vibrations and/or position in three dimensions below the level of the injury (hemiparalysis or asymmetric paresis). The sensory loss is particularly strong on the same side (ipsilateral) as the injury to the spine. These sensations are accompanied by a loss of the sense of pain and of temperature (hypalgesia) on the side of the body opposite (contralateral) to the side at which the injury was sustained.

The following organizations may provide additional information and support:
American Spinal Injury Association
National Institute of Neurological Disorders and Stroke (NINDS)
National Spinal Cord Injury Association
Spinal Cord Injury Network International
Spinal Cord Society

170   Brown Syndrome

Synonyms
Superior Oblique Tendon Sheath Syndrome
Tendon Sheath Adherence, Superior Oblique

Disorder Subdivisions
Acquired Brown Syndrome
Congenital Brown Syndrome
Primary Brown Syndrome
Secondary Brown Syndrome

Brown syndrome is a rare eye disorder characterized by defects in eye movements. This disorder may be present at birth (congenital) or may occur as the result of another underlying disorder (acquired). Muscles control the movements of the eyes. Some of these muscles turn the eyeball up and down, move the eyeball from side to side, or enable the eyeball to rotate slightly in its socket. The superior oblique tendon sheath of the superior oblique muscle surrounds the eyeball. The symptoms of Brown syndrome are caused by abnormalities of this tendon sheath including shortening, thickening, or inflammation. This results in the inability to move the affected eye upward.

The following organization may provide additional information and support:
NIH/National Eye Institute

171   Brucellosis

Synonyms
Bang Disease
Brucellemia
Brucelliasis
Cyprus Fever
Febris Melitensis
Febris Sudoralis
Febris Undulans
Fievre Caprine
Gibraltar Fever
Goat Fever
Maltese Fever
Mediterranean Fever, Nonfamilial
Melitensis Septicemia
Melitococcosis
Neapolitan Fever
Phthisis

Disorder Subdivisions
Acute Brucellosis
Chronic Brucellosis
Localized Brucellosis
Subacute Brucellosis
Undulant Fever

Brucellosis is an infectious disease that affects livestock and may be transmitted to humans. It is rare in the United States, but occurs more frequently in other parts of the world. The disorder is caused by one of four different species of bacteria that belong to the genus *Brucella*. Initial symptoms of infection may be nonspecific including fevers, muscle pain, headache, loss of appetite, profuse sweating, and physical weakness. In some cases, the symptoms occur suddenly (acute), whereas, in others, symptoms may develop over the course of a few months. If brucellosis is not treated, the disease may take months to resolve once appropriate therapy is begun. Brucellosis may be confined to a certain area of the body (local) or have serious widespread complications that affect various organ systems of the body including the central nervous system. Brucellosis may be prevented if people drink only pasteurized cow and goat's milk. Pasteurization kills the bacteria that cause the disease. However, farmers and people exposed to butchered meat may also be affected by brucellosis.

The following organizations may provide additional information and support:
Centers for Disease Control and Prevention
Food and Drug Administration (FDA) Office of Inquiry & Consumer Information

NIH/National Institute of Allergy and Infectious Diseases
World Health Organization (WHO) Regional Office for the Americas (AMRO)

172 Brugada Syndrome

Brugada syndrome is a rare inherited cardiovascular disorder characterized by disturbances affecting the electrical system of the heart. The main symptom is irregular heartbeats and, without treatment, may potentially result in sudden death. In some cases, no symptoms may precede sudden death. Brugada syndrome may be inherited as an autosomal dominant trait.

The following organizations may provide additional information and support:
American Heart Association
Cardiac Arrhythmias Research and Education Foundation, Inc.
Sudden Arrhythmia Death Syndromes Foundation

173 Bubonic Plague

Synonyms
Black Death
Black Plague
Glandular Plague
Hemorrhagic Plague
Pestis
Pestis Fulminans
Pestis Major
Plague

Disorder Subdivision
Pestis Minor

Bubonic plague is an acute, severe infectious disorder caused by the bacterium (bacillus) *Yersinia pestis.* These bacteria can be carried by small wild rodents, other wild animals or even household pets. The disease can be transmitted to humans through the bites of fleas or through direct contact with infected animal tissues. The disorder is most common in Southeast Asia, but it also occurs in some areas of the United States. Major symptoms include an abrupt onset with chills, fever, and enlarged lymph nodes (buboes). Treatment must start immediately to avoid life-threatening complications. A milder form of bubonic plague, pestis minor, usually resolves in approximately a week with appropriate treatment. Interest in bubonic plague has heightened, in recent years, by the awareness of its potential use as an agent of biological warfare.

The following organizations may provide additional information and support:
Centers for Disease Control and Prevention
NIH/National Institute of Allergy and Infectious Diseases
World Health Organization (WHO) Regional Office for the Americas (AMRO)

174 Budd-Chiari Syndrome

Synonyms
Budd's Syndrome
Chiari-Budd Syndrome
Chiari's Disease
Hepatic Veno-Occlusive Disease
Rokitansky's Disease

Budd-Chiari syndrome is a rare disorder characterized by narrowing and obstruction (occlusion) of the veins of the liver (hepatic veins). Symptoms associated with Budd-Chiari syndrome include pain in the upper right part of the abdomen, an abnormally large liver (hepatomegaly), and/or accumulation of fluid in the space (peritoneal cavity) between the two layers of the membrane that lines the stomach (ascites). Additional findings that may be associated with the disorder include nausea, vomiting, and/or an abnormally large spleen (splenomegaly). The severity of the disorder varies from case to case, depending upon the site and number of affected veins. In some cases, if the major hepatic veins are involved, high blood pressure in the veins carrying blood from the gastrointestinal (GI) tract back to the heart through the liver (portal hypertension) may be present. In most cases, the exact cause of Budd-Chiari syndrome is unknown.

The following organizations may provide additional information and support:
American Liver Foundation
NIH/National Digestive Diseases Information Clearinghouse

175 Buerger's Disease

Synonyms
Inflammatory Occlusive Peripheral Vascular Disease
Occlusive Peripheral Vascular Disease
TAO
Thromboangiitis Obliterans

Buerger's disease is a very rare disorder that, in most cases, affects young or middle-aged male cigarette smokers. It is characterized by narrowing or blockage (occlusion) of the veins and arteries of the extremities, resulting in reduced blood flow to these areas (peripheral vascular disease). The legs are affected more often than the arms. In most cases, the first symptom is extreme pain of the lower arms and legs while at rest. Affected individuals may also experience cramping in the legs when they walk that, in rare cases, may cause limping (claudication). In addition, affected individuals may have sores (ulcers) on the extremities, numbness and tingling and a lack of normal blood flow to the fingers and/or toes when exposed to cold temperatures (Raynaud's phenomenon), and/or inflammation and clotting of certain veins (thrombophlebitis). In severe cases, individuals with Buerger's disease may exhibit tissue death (gangrene) of affected limbs. The exact cause of Buerger's disease is not known; however, most affected individuals are heavy tobacco users.

The following organization may provide additional information and support:
NIH/National Heart, Lung and Blood Institute Information Center

176 Bulimia

Synonym
Eating Disorder, Bulimic Type

Bulimia is a psychiatric disorder consisting of binge eating, often followed by self-induced vomiting or purges by the use of laxatives and diuretics. The majority of affected individuals are female.

The following organizations may provide additional information and support:
Anorexia Bulimia Treatment and Education Center
Eating Disorders Association
National Alliance for the Mentally Ill
National Association of Anorexia Nervosa and Associated Disorders, Inc.
National Eating Disorders Association
National Mental Health Association
National Mental Health Consumers' Self-Help Clearinghouse
NIH/National Institute of Mental Health

177 Bullous Pemphigoid

Synonyms
Benign Pemphigus
Old Age Pemphigus
Parapemphigus
Pemphigoid
Senile Dermatitis Herpetiformis

Bullous pemphigoid is a rare, autoimmune, chronic skin disorder characterized by blistering. This disorder occurs most frequently in elderly people. Generalized blistering occurs in and under the upper layers of the skin and usually subsides spontaneously within several months or years. However, symptoms may recur. In some rare cases of bullous pemphigoid, complications such as pneumonia may develop.

The following organizations may provide additional information and support:
American Autoimmune Related Diseases Association, Inc.
National Cancer Institute
NIH/National Arthritis and Musculoskeletal and Skin Diseases Information Clearinghouse
Pemphigus & Pemphigoid Society

178 Burning Mouth Syndrome

Synonyms
Burning Tongue Syndrome
Glossodynia
Glossopyrosis
Oral Galvanism
Stomatodynia
Stomatopyrosis

Burning mouth syndrome (BMS) is characterized by a burning sensation in the mouth and/or tongue. It is often accompanied by dry mouth and/or a bitter or metallic taste in the mouth. In some cases, this condition may be associated with vitamin B12 deficiency, oral yeast infection (*Candida albicans*), or irritation from dentures (dental prosthetics). The burning sensation may be aggravated by hot, spicy foods but is not caused by them.

The following organizations may provide additional information and support:
NIH/National Institute of Diabetes, Digestive & Kidney Diseases
NIH/National Oral Health Information Clearinghouse

179 C Syndrome

Synonyms

Opitz Trigonocephaly Syndrome
Trigonocephaly "C" Syndrome
Trigonocephaly Syndrome

C syndrome, also known as Opitz trigonocephaly syndrome, is a rare disorder transmitted as a result of "gonadal mosaicism." Mosaicism refers to a condition in which a person has cells that differ from each other in genetic makeup. The difference is usually a variation in the number of chromosomes. Normally, all body cells would have 46 chromosomes, but in mosaicism, some cells may have 45 or 47. Mosaicism occurs as a result of an error in cell division very early in fetal development. Affected individuals are born with a malformation in which the head is a triangular shape due to premature union of the skull bones (trigonocephaly), a narrow pointed forehead, a flat broad nasal bridge with a short nose, vertical folds over the inner corners of the eyes, an abnormal palate that is deeply furrowed, abnormalities of the ear, crossed eyes (strabismus), joints that are bent or in a fixed position, and loose skin. Developmental and learning disabilities are common.

The following organizations may provide additional information and support:
FACES: The National Craniofacial Association
National Craniofacial Foundation

180 Campomelic Syndrome

Synonyms

Acampomelic campomelic "Dysplasia"
CMDI
Campomelic Dwarfism
Campomelic Dysplasia
Campomelic Syndrome, Long-Limb Type
Camptomelic Dwarfism
Camptomelic Syndrome
Camptomelic Syndrome, Long-Limb Type
Dwarfism, Campomelic
SRY-Box 9, SOX9 Mutations Syndrome

Campomelic syndrome is a rare congenital disorder in which multiple anomalies are present. It is characterized by bowing and angular shape of the long bones of the legs, especially the tibia; multiple minor anomalies of the face; cleft palate; other skeletal anomalies such as abnormalities of the shoulder and pelvic area and eleven pairs of ribs instead of the usual twelve; underdevelop-

ment of the trachea; developmental delay in some cases and incomplete development of genitalia in males such that they appear to be females.

The following organizations may provide additional information and support:
Human Growth Foundation
Little People of America, Inc.
NIH/National Arthritis and Musculoskeletal and Skin Diseases Information Clearinghouse

181 Camurati-Engelmann Disease

Synonyms

CED
Diaphyseal Dysplasia Camurati-Engelmann
Engelmann Disease
Progressive Diaphyseal Dysplasia

Camurati-Engelmann disease is a rare genetic disorder characterized by progressive widening and malformation of the shafts of the long bones (diaphyseal dysplasia). Major symptoms may include bone pain, particularly in the legs; skeletal abnormalities; and/or weakness and underdevelopment (hypoplasia) of various muscles. Pain and weakness of the leg muscles may result in an unusual "waddling" walk (gait). Camurati-Engelmann disease is inherited as an autosomal dominant trait.

The following organizations may provide additional information and support:
Genetic and Rare Diseases (GARD) Information Center
NIH/National Arthritis and Musculoskeletal and Skin Diseases Information Clearinghouse

182 Canavan Disease

Synonyms

ACY2 Deficiency
Aminoacylase-2 Deficiency
ASP Deficiency
ASPA Deficiency
Aspartoacylase Deficiency
Canavan's Leukodystrophy
Canavan-Van Bogaert-Bertrand Disease
CD
Spongy Degeneration of the Central Nervous System
Spongy Degeneration of the Neuroaxis
Van Bogaert-Bertrand Syndrome

Canavan disease is a rare inherited neurological disorder characterized by spongy degeneration of the brain and spinal cord (central nervous system). Physical symptoms that appear in early infancy may include progressive mental decline accompanied by the loss of muscle tone, poor head control, an abnormally large head (macrocephaly), and/or irritability. Physical symptoms appear in early infancy and usually progress rapidly. Canavan disease is caused by an abnormality in the ASPA gene that leads to a deficiency of the enzyme aspartoacylase. Canavan disease is inherited as an autosomal recessive genetic disorder.

The following organizations may provide additional information and support:
Association Europeene contre les Leucodystrophes
Canavan Foundation
Canavan Research Illinois
Hunter's Hope Foundation, Inc.
Kennedy Krieger Institute
March of Dimes Birth Defects Foundation
National Institute of Neurological Disorders and Stroke (NINDS)
National Tay-Sachs and Allied Diseases Association, Inc.
United Leukodystrophy Foundation

183 Cancer, Colon

Synonyms
Adenocarcinoma of the Colon
Cancer of the Colon
Cancer of the Large Intestine
Carcinoma of the Colon
Colonic Cancer
Colorectal Cancer

Colon cancer is more commonly called colorectal cancer because the disorder most often affects both parts of the digestive tract, the colon and the rectum. It is one of the most common cancers found in the United States. The cause is unknown. In some people, the tendency to develop colon cancer may be inherited. Cancer is a disease in which the growth of abnormal cells, a tumor, leads to the destruction of healthy cells. If the tumor becomes invasive or aggressive, it may spread into the intestinal wall and to other sites, at which time the tumor is considered malignant. Most malignant colon cancers and/or rectal cancers begin as apparently unthreatening (benign) growths (polyps) inside the colon or rectum. A colorectal polyp is a growth that projects (usually on a stalk) from the lining of the colon or rectum. Such polyps may become ma-

lignant although this is not always the case. The symptoms of colorectal cancer may include changes in bowel habits, blood in the stools, constipation and/or diarrhea, abdominal discomfort and sometimes nausea. Surgery is generally performed to correct this type of cancer. It may be accompanied by radiation therapy and/or chemotherapy.

The following organizations may provide additional information and support:
American Cancer Society, Inc.
Cancer Research UK
Colorectal Cancer Network
Hereditary Colorectal Cancer Registry
Johns Hopkins Hereditary Colorectal Cancer Registry
OncoLink: The University of Pennsylvania Cancer Center Resource

184 Cancer, Prostate

Synonyms
Adenocarcinoma of the Prostate
Cancer of the Prostate Gland
Carcinoma of the Prostate
Prostatic Cancer
Prostatic Carcinoma

Prostate cancer is a prevalent form of cancer affecting only males. Cancer is a disease in which malignant cell development occurs, causing destruction of healthy tissue. The prostate gland, responsible for sperm vitality, is about the size of a walnut and surrounds the part of the male urethra beneath the bladder. Cancer of the prostate gland commonly occurs in older men. Average age of onset is 73 years.

The following organizations may provide additional information and support:
American Cancer Society, Inc.
Cancer Research UK
Dattoli Cancer Foundation, sponsor of Prostate Cancer Resource Network
National Cancer Institute
OncoLink: The University of Pennsylvania Cancer Center Resource
Prostate Cancer Charity (UK)
Prostate Pointers
Robert Mathews Foundation
US TOO International, Inc., Prostate Cancer Survivor Support Groups

185 Cancers, Skin, General

Disorder Subdivisions

Acral Lentiginious Melanoma
Basal Cell Carcinoma
Juvenile Melanoma
Kaposi's Sarcoma
Malignant Lentico Melanoma
Melanoma, Malignant
Skin Cancer, Non-Melanoma
Squamous Cell Carcinomas

There are many different types of skin cancer. Combined together, all types of skin cancer represent the most prevalent type of cancer. Most skin cancers are characterized by changes in the color or texture of the skin, but some types begin under the skin where they can spread to other parts of the body. Malignant melanoma is the most dangerous of this type of skin cancer.

The following organizations may provide additional information and support:
American Cancer Society, Inc.
Cancer Research UK
Candlelighters Childhood Cancer Foundation
National Cancer Institute
OncoLink: The University of Pennsylvania Cancer Center Resource
Skin Cancer Foundation

186 Candidiasis

Synonyms

Candidosis
Moniliasis

Disorder Subdivisions

Candida Granuloma
Candida Infection around the Nails
Candida Paronichia
Candidiasis of the Skin
Cutaneous Candidiasis
Cutaneous Moniliasis
Mucocutaneous Candidiasis, Chronic
Oral Candidiasis
Penis, infected by Candida
Systemic Candidiasis
Thrush
Vaginitis, Caused by Candida
Vulvovaginitis, Caused by Candida
Yeast Infection, Systemic

Candidiasis is an infection caused by a fungus called Candida, most commonly the *Candida al-* *bicans* variety. The Candida, infection (also known as a yeast infection) usually affects the skin and/or the mucous membranes of the mouth, intestines, or the vagina. Candida infections are rarely serious in otherwise healthy people. In rare cases, it may spread through other parts of the body if the patient's immune system is not functioning properly. In the most severe cases, it can affect the blood, the membrane lining the heart muscle (endocardium), or membranes around the brain (meninges).

The following organizations may provide additional information and support:
Centers for Disease Control and Prevention
National Cancer Institute
NIH/National Institute of Allergy and Infectious Diseases
World Health Organization (WHO) Regional Office for the Americas (AMRO)

187 Carbamyl Phosphate Synthetase Deficiency

Synonyms

CPS Deficiency
Hyperammonemia due to Carbamylphosphate Synthetase Deficiency

Carbamyl phosphate synthetase (CPS) deficiency is a rare inherited disorder caused by lack or deficiency of the enzyme carbamyl phosphate synthetase, one of six enzymes that play a role in the breakdown and removal of nitrogen from the body, a process known as the urea cycle. The lack of this enzyme results in excessive accumulation of nitrogen, in the form of ammonia (hyperammonemia), in the blood. Affected infants may experience vomiting, refusal to eat, progressive lethargy, and coma. CPS deficiency is inherited as an autosomal recessive trait. The urea cycle disorders are a group of rare disorders affecting the urea cycle, a series of biochemical processes in which nitrogen is converted into urea and removed from the body through the urine. Nitrogen is a waste product of protein metabolism. Failure to break down nitrogen results in the abnormal accumulation of nitrogen, in the form of ammonia, in the blood.

The following organizations may provide additional information and support:
American Kidney Fund, Inc.

Brusilow, Saul, M.D.
CLIMB (Children Living with Inherited Metabolic Diseases)
National Kidney Foundation
National Urea Cycle Disorders Foundation
NIH/National Digestive Diseases Information Clearinghouse

188 Carbohydrate Deficient Glycoprotein Syndrome Type Ia

Synonyms
CDGIA
CDGS Type Ia
Hypoglycosylation Syndrome Type Ia

Since the publication (1996) and the second update (1998) of the NORD Report on this disorder, the standard name was changed from "carbohydrate-deficient glycoprotein syndrome" to "congenital disorders of glycosylation syndrome (CDGS)". CDGS refers to a group of rare inherited metabolic disorders that share similar but not identical genetic changes (mutations), and similar but not identical biochemical characteristics. These disorders involve the metabolic activity of glycoproteins, complex chemical compounds created by attaching a simple or complex sugar molecule (glycolization) to a specific protein. Such complex glycoproteins play key roles in the development and maintenance of the cell membrane, endocrine glandular function, protein transport, and are active in specific parts of the brain (Golgi apparatus). Attaching the sugar to the protein is a process involving many enzymes and a shortage or lack of any one of these enzymes causes the buildup of intermediate chemical compounds. The accumulation of these compounds is the triggering device of the disorder. Congenital disorders of glycosylation may affect many different parts of the body but it is the most serious when they involve the central and peripheral nervous systems. Recently, medical researchers have agreed to classify the disorder into two major groups. This is based on the chemical pathway in which the defect occurs (mutation leading to an enzyme failure). For the sake of clarity, the disorders that are a result of a faulty enzyme before the sugar molecule is attached to the protein (upstream) are known as Type I disorders. The disorders that arise due to failure in the metabolic process after the sugar molecule has been attached to proteins are known as Type II disorders. There appear to be 12 distinct disorders (subtypes) within Type I and there are 5 distinct disorders (subtypes) within Type II. Of all the CDGS disorders, regardless of type, CDGS Type Ia comprises about 70% of all cases. Glycoproteins have several important functions in the body. They play a role in the complex chemical processes that enable the body to function normally. Examples include, signaling how cells in the body are to interact with one another, participating in the transfer of nutrients from one part of the body to another (transport), playing a role in the proper coagulation of blood, functioning as hormones that regulate certain organs or activities in the body (i.e., endocrine activities that help to regulate the rate of growth, sexual development, and/or metabolism), etc. CDGS Type Ia affects several different organ systems of the body. Especially affected are the central nervous system (i.e., the brain and spinal cord), the peripheral nervous system (i.e., motor and sensory nerves outside the central nervous system), and the liver, in which many of the glycoproteins in the blood are made. Although the severity and range of symptoms may vary from case to case, most affected individuals exhibit severe delays in the acquisition of skills that require the coordination of mental and muscular activity (psychomotor retardation); moderate to severe mental retardation; impaired coordination and balance (cerebellar ataxia) due to underdevelopment (hypoplasia) of certain portions of the brain (cerebellum); impaired nerve transmission to the legs, resulting in progressive, severe muscle thinning and weakness (peripheral neuropathy); skeletal malformations; and/or visual and/or hearing impairment. CDGS Type Ia is inherited as an autosomal recessive genetic trait.

The following organizations may provide additional information and support:
American Speech-Language-Hearing Association
CDG Family Network
CLIMB (Children Living with Inherited Metabolic Diseases)
National Association for Parents of Children with Visual Impairments (NAPVI)
National Association for Visually Handicapped
National Institute of Neurological Disorders and Stroke (NINDS)
NIH/National Arthritis and Musculoskeletal and Skin Diseases Information Clearinghouse
Swedish CDG Society
United Leukodystrophy Foundation
Vaincre Les Maladies Lysosomales

189 Carboxylase Deficiency, Multiple

Synonyms

Biotinidase Deficiency
Carboxylase Deficiency, Multiple
Holocarboxylase Synthetase Deficiency
MCD

Multiple carboxylase deficiency is a genetic metabolic disorder that leads to impaired activity of three enzymes that are dependent on the vitamin biotin: propionyl CoA carboxylase, beta-methylcrotonyl CoA carboxylase, and pyruvate carboxylase. This condition results from a defect in cellular biotin transport or metabolism. Symptoms of the disorder include acidity of the blood and body tissues (acidosis), a widespread red skin rash, baldness, and slowed physical development. The disorder occurs in both a neonatal and a late-onset form and is treatable.

The following organizations may provide additional information and support:
CLIMB (Children Living with Inherited Metabolic Diseases)
Genetic and Rare Diseases (GARD) Information Center
NIH/National Digestive Diseases Information Clearinghouse

190 Carcinoid Syndrome

Synonyms

Carcinoid Apudoma
Carcinoid Cancer
Carcinoid Disease
Functioning Argentaffinoma
Functioning Carcinoid
Malignant Carcinoid Syndrome
Neuroendocrine Tumor Carcinoid Type

Carcinoid syndrome is a disease consisting of a combination of symptoms, physical manifestations, and abnormal laboratory chemical findings caused by a carcinoid tumor. A carcinoid tumor is a tumor that secretes large amounts of the hormone serotonin. These tumors usually arise in the gastrointestinal tract and from there may migrate (metastasize) to the liver. Carcinoid tumors also sometimes develop in the lung. Only about 10% of the people with carcinoid tumors will develop the carcinoid syndrome. Major symptoms of this syndrome include hot, red facial flushing, diarrhea and wheezing. Carcinoid syn-

drome occurs when the tumors produce excessive amounts of serotonin or other substances.

The following organizations may provide additional information and support:
11Q Research and Resource Group
American Cancer Society, Inc.
Carcinoid Cancer Foundation, Inc.
Caring for Carcinoid Foundation

191 Carcinoma, Renal Cell

Synonyms

Grawitz Tumor
Hypernephroma
Nephrocarcinoma
RCC
Renal Adenocarcinoma

Renal cell carcinoma is a form of kidney cancer. Some patients with renal cell carcinoma do not have symptoms (asymptomatic). When symptoms are present, they may include blood in the urine; urine that is brown or rusty-colored; abdominal pain; weight loss; enlargement of one testicle or varicose veins of the testis (varicocele) in a male patient; fever; a thin, malnourished appearance; vision abnormalities; and elevated blood pressure. The most common feature of the syndrome is the passing of blood in the urine (hematuria).

The following organizations may provide additional information and support:
American Cancer Society, Inc.
American Foundation for Urologic Disease
Cancer Research UK
Kidney Cancer Association
National Cancer Institute
National Kidney Foundation
NIH/National Kidney and Urologic Diseases Information Clearinghouse
OncoLink: The University of Pennsylvania Cancer Center Resource
Rare Cancer Alliance

192 Carcinoma, Squamous Cell

Synonyms

Carcinoma, Epidermoid Intradermal
Skin Cancer, Squamous Cell Type

Disorder Subdivision

Bowen's Disease

Squamous cell carcinoma is among the most common types of skin cancer. It usually develops on the tissue of the skin and mucous lining of the body cavities (epithelium) but may occur anywhere on the body. With appropriate treatment, it is usually curable. Squamous cell carcinoma most commonly affects individuals who are exposed to large amounts of sunlight. Susceptibility is related to the amount of melanin pigment in the skin, and light-skinned persons are most vulnerable.

The following organizations may provide additional information and support:
Esophageal Cancer Awareness Association, Inc.
National Cancer Institute
OncoLink: The University of Pennsylvania Cancer Center Resource
Skin Cancer Foundation

193 Cardiofaciocutaneous Syndrome

Synonyms
Cardio-Facial-Cutaneous Syndrome
CFC Syndrome
Facio-Cardio-Cutaneous Syndrome

Cardiofaciocutaneous (CFC) syndrome is a rare genetic disorder first described in 1986, based on the observation of eight unrelated patients with very similar facial appearance characterized by unusually sparse, brittle, curly hair; large head (macrocephaly); a prominent forehead and abnormal narrowing of the sides of the forehead (bitemporal constriction); mental retardation; failure to thrive; heart defects that are present at birth (congenital); short stature and skin abnormalities. CFC syndrome is a dominant genetic disorder caused by a sporadic gene abnormality (mutation) in one of three genes that have been termed BRAF, MEK1 and MEK2. Some affected individuals do not have a mutation in one of these genes, suggesting that other genes are also associated with CFC.

The following organizations may provide additional information and support:
American Heart Association
The Arc (A National Organization on Mental Retardation)
Cardio-Facio-Cutaneous International
Children's Craniofacial Association
Congenital Heart Anomalies, Support, Education, & Resources
Forward Face, Inc.
Foundation for Ichthyosis & Related Skin Types
Hemangioma Support System

March of Dimes Birth Defects Foundation
National Craniofacial Foundation
NIH/National Heart, Lung and Blood Institute Information Center
NIH/National Institute of Arthritis and Musculoskeletal and Skin Diseases
Vascular Birthmarks Foundation

194 Carnitine Deficiency Syndromes

Synonyms
Carnitine Deficiency, Myopathic
Carnitine Deficiency, Primary
Carnitine Deficiency, Secondary
Muscle Carnitine Deficiency
Renal Reabsorption of Carnitine, Defect

Disorder Subdivisions
Myopathic Carnitine Deficiency
Systemic Carnitine Deficiency

Carnitine deficiency syndrome is a rare metabolic disorder that may be inherited in some cases, or occur as a result of other metabolic disorders. Carnitine functions in the body as a carrier of fatty acids to the energy centers in muscles (mitochondria). A deficiency of carnitine, normally produced by the liver and kidneys, can result in extreme muscle weakness and other related symptoms.

The following organizations may provide additional information and support:
CLIMB (Children Living with Inherited Metabolic Diseases)
FOD (Fatty Oxidation Disorders) Family Support Group
March of Dimes Birth Defects Foundation
NIH/National Institute of Diabetes, Digestive & Kidney Diseases
United Mitochondrial Disease Foundation

195 Carnitine Palmitoyltransferase Deficiency

Synonyms
CPT Deficiency
CPTD
Myopathy with Deficiency of Carnitine Palmitoyltransferase
Myopathy-Metabolic, Carnitine Palmitoyltransferase Deficiency

Disorder Subdivisions
Carnitine Palmitoyltransferase Deficiency Type 1

*Carnitine Palmitoyltransferase Deficiency Type 2; Benign Classical
Muscular Form Included; Severe Infantile Form Included*

Carnitine palmitoyltransferase (CPT) deficiency is a very rare metabolic disorder that affects the skeletal muscles and their ability to function properly. CPT deficiency belongs to a group of diseases that involve the defective breakdown (metabolism) of muscle fats (lipids). Prolonged periods of strenuous exercise can trigger an episode of symptoms. These may include muscle aches, stiffness, and weakness. Muscle tissue may break down (rhabdomyolysis) and abnormal levels of myoglobulin may be present in the urine (myoglobinuria). The urine may appear dark reddish-brown after prolonged periods of exercise. Carnitine palmitoyltransferase (CPT) deficiency type 1 typically affects adults and adolescents. Carnitine palmitoyltransferase (CPT) deficiency type 2 may also affect adults; however, a serious form of this type of the disease affects infants.

The following organizations may provide additional information and support:
CLIMB (Children Living with Inherited Metabolic Diseases)
FOD (Fatty Oxidation Disorders) Family Support Group
Muscular Dystrophy Association
NIH/National Institute of Diabetes, Digestive & Kidney Diseases

196 Carnosinemia

Synonyms
*Beta-Alanine-Pyruvate Aminotransferase
Carnosinase Deficiency
Hyper-Beta Carnosinemia
Serum Carnosinase Deficiency*

Carnosinemia is a very rare inherited metabolic disorder characterized by impaired neurological function and developmental delays. Symptoms that begin during infancy may include drowsiness, seizures that may be accompanied by involuntary jerking muscle movements of the arms, legs, or head (myoclonic seizures), and mental retardation.

The following organizations may provide additional information and support:
The Arc (A National Organization on Mental Retardation)

CLIMB (Children Living with Inherited Metabolic Diseases)
March of Dimes Birth Defects Foundation

197 Caroli Disease

Synonym
Congenital Dilatation of Intrahepatic Bile Duct

Caroli disease is a rare inherited disorder characterized by abnormal widening (dilatation) of the ducts that carry bile from the liver (intrahepatic bile ducts). According to the medical literature, there are two forms of Caroli disease. In most cases, the isolated or simple form is characterized by widening of the bile ducts (dilatation or ectasia). A second, more complex form is often called Caroli syndrome. The complex form or syndrome is associated with the presence of bands of fibrous tissue in the liver (congenital hepatic fibrosis) and high blood pressure in the portal artery (portal hypertension). This form of Caroli disease is also often associated, in ways that are not well understood, with polycystic kidney disease, and, in severe cases, liver failure. The genetics of Caroli disease are complex as well. The isolated or simple form is transmitted as an autosomal dominant trait, while the complex form associated with polycystic kidney disease is transmitted as an autosomal recessive trait.

The following organizations may provide additional information and support:
American Liver Foundation
ARPKD/CHF Alliance
NIH/National Digestive Diseases Information Clearinghouse

198 Carpal Tunnel Syndrome

Synonyms
*Constrictive Median Neuropathy
CTS
Median Neuritis
Median Neuropathy
Thenar Amyotrophy of Carpal Origin*

Carpal tunnel syndrome (CTS) is a condition caused by compression of peripheral nerves affecting one or both hands. It is characterized by a sensation of numbness, tingling, burning and/or pain in the hand and wrist. Persons affected by this disorder may be awakened at night with the feeling that the hand has "gone to sleep." Strain or injury involving the hand and wrist or various other disorders may cause CTS. The disorder may appear as a symptom of various other diseases or may occur as a single primary condition.

The following organizations may provide additional information and support:
Eaton's Hand Surgery Links
Jack Miller Center for Peripheral Neuropathy
National Institute of Neurological Disorders and Stroke (NINDS)

---

199 Carpenter Syndrome

Synonyms

ACPS II
Acrocephalopolysyndactyly Type II

Carpenter syndrome belongs to a group of rare genetic disorders known as "acrocephalopolysyndactyly" (ACPS) disorders. All forms of ACPS are characterized by premature closure of the fibrous joints (cranial sutures) between certain bones of the skull (craniosynostosis), causing the top of the head to appear pointed (acrocephaly); webbing or fusion (syndactyly) of certain fingers or toes (digits); and/or more than the normal number of digits (polydactyly). Carpenter syndrome is also known as ACPS type II. Carpenter syndrome is typically evident at or shortly after birth. Due to craniosynostosis, the top of the head may appear unusually conical (acrocephaly) or the head may seem short and broad (brachycephaly). In addition, the cranial sutures often fuse unevenly, causing the head and face to appear dissimilar from one side to the other (craniofacial asymmetry). Additional malformations of the skull and facial (craniofacial) region may include downslanting eyelid folds (palpebral fissures); a flat nasal bridge; malformed (dysplastic), low-set ears; and a small, underdeveloped (hypoplastic) upper and/or lower jaw (maxilla and/or mandible). Individuals with Carpenter syndrome may also have unusually short fingers and toes (brachydactyly); partial fusion of the soft tissues (cutaneous syndactyly) between certain digits; and the presence of extra (supernumerary) toes or, less commonly, additional fingers (polydactyly). In some instances, additional physical abnormalities are present, such as short stature, structural heart malformations (congenital heart defects), mild to moderate obesity, weakening in the abdominal wall near the navel through which the intestine

may protrude (umbilical hernia), or failure of the testes to descend into the scrotum (cryptorchidism) in affected males. In addition, many individuals with the disorder are affected by mild to moderate mental retardation. However, intelligence is normal in some instances. Carpenter syndrome is usually inherited as an autosomal recessive trait.

The following organizations may provide additional information and support:
AboutFace USA
Alexander Graham Bell Association for the Deaf, Inc.
American Heart Association
The Arc (A National Organization on Mental Retardation)
Congenital Heart Anomalies, Support, Education, & Resources
FACES: The National Craniofacial Association
Forward Face, Inc.
Institute of Reconstructive Plastic Surgery (New York University Medical Center New York University School of Medicine)
Let's Face It (USA)
March of Dimes Birth Defects Foundation
National Craniofacial Foundation
NIH/National Institute on Deafness and Other Communication Disorders Information Clearinghouse

---

200 Castleman's Disease

Synonyms

Angiofollicular Lymph Node Hyperplasia
Angiomatous Lymphoid
Castleman Tumor
Giant Benign Lymphoma
Giant Lymph Node Hyperplasia
Hamartoma of the Lymphatics

Castleman's disease is a rare disorder characterized by non-cancerous (benign) growths (tumors) that may develop in the lymph node tissue throughout the body (i.e., systemic disease [plasma cell type]). Most often, they occur in the chest, stomach, and/or neck (i.e., localized disease [hyaline-vascular type]). Less common sites include the armpit (axilla), pelvis, and pancreas. Usually the growths represent abnormal enlargement of the lymph nodes normally found in these areas (lymphoid hamartoma). There are two main types of Castleman's disease: hyaline-vascular type and plasma cell type. The hyaline vascular type accounts for approximately 90 percent of the cases. Most individuals exhibit no symptoms of this form of the disorder (asymptomatic) or they may develop non-cancerous growths in the lymph nodes. The plasma cell type of Castleman's disease may be associated with fever, weight loss, skin rash, early destruction of red blood cells, leading to unusually low levels of circulating red blood cells (hemolytic anemia), and/or abnormally increased amounts of certain immune factors in the blood (hypergammaglobulinemia). A third type of Castleman's disease has been reported in the medical literature. This type may affect more than one area of the body (multicentric or generalized Castleman's disease). Many individuals with multicentric Castleman's disease may exhibit an abnormally large liver and spleen (hepatosplenomegaly). Researchers' opinions in the medical literature differ as to whether multicentric Castleman's disease is a distinct entity or a multicentric form of the plasma cell type of Castleman's disease.

The following organizations may provide additional information and support:
American Autoimmune Related Diseases Association, Inc.
American Cancer Society, Inc.
NIH/National Heart, Lung and Blood Institute Information Center

---

201   Cat Eye Syndrome

Synonyms
CES
Chromosome 22, Inverted Duplication (22pter-22q11)
Chromosome 22, Partial Tetrasomy (22pter-22q11)
Chromosome 22, Partial Trisomy (22pter-22q11)
Schmid-Fraccaro Syndrome

Cat eye syndrome is a rare chromosomal disorder that may be evident at birth. Individuals with a normal chromosomal make-up have two 22nd chromosomes, both of which have a short arm, known as 22p, and a long arm, called 22q. However, in individuals with cat eye syndrome, the short arm and a small region of the long arm of chromosome 22 (i.e., 22pter-22q11) are present three or four times (trisomy or tetrasomy) rather than twice in cells of the body. The name "cat eye syndrome" is derived from a distinctive eye (ocular) abnormality that is present in some af-

fected individuals. This feature consists of partial absence of ocular tissue (coloboma), often affecting both eyes (bilateral). Affected ocular tissues may include the colored region (iris), the middle layer (choroid), and/or the nerve-rich innermost membrane (retina) of the eye. Associated symptoms and findings may vary greatly in range and severity, including among affected members of the same family. While some may have few or mild manifestations that may remain unrecognized, others may have the full spectrum of malformations. However, in many cases, characteristic features of the disorder include mild growth delays before birth; mild mental deficiency; and malformations of the skull and facial (craniofacial) region, the heart, the kidneys, and/or the anal region. More specifically, individuals with cat eye syndrome frequently have coloboma(s), downslanting eyelid folds (palpebral fissures), widely spaced eyes (ocular hypertelorism), and/or other ocular defects; misshapen ears with abnormal outgrowths of skin and small depressions in front of the outer ears (preauricular tags and pits); and/or absence (atresia) of the anal canal, with an abnormal passage (fistula) from the end portion of the large intestine (rectum) into abnormal locations (e.g., the bladder, vagina, or perineum). Additional features may commonly include variable congenital heart (cardiac) defects, kidney (renal) abnormalities, skeletal defects, and/or other physical findings.

The following organizations may provide additional information and support:
American Heart Association
American Liver Foundation
Children's Liver Alliance
Children's Liver Disease Foundation
Chromosome 22 Central
Congenital Heart Anomalies, Support, Education, & Resources
Council of Families with Visual Impairment
IDEAS (IsoDicentric 15 Exchange, Advocacy and Support)
International Foundation for Functional Gastrointestinal Disorders
MAGIC Foundation for Children's Growth
National Association for Parents of Children with Visual Impairments (NAPVI)
National Center for Chromosome Inversions
NIH/National Digestive Diseases Information Clearinghouse
NIH/National Heart, Lung and Blood Institute Information Center

202 Cat-Scratch Disease

Synonyms

Cat-Scratch Adenitis
Cat-Scratch Fever
Cat-Scratch-Oculoglandular Syndrome
Debre's Syndrome
Foshay-Mollaret Cat-Scratch Fever
Lymphadenitis, Regional Nonbacterial
Lymphoreticulosis, Benign Inoculation
Parinaud's Syndrome
Petzetakis' Syndrome

Cat-scratch disease (also commonly known as cat-scratch fever) is a self-limiting infectious disease characterized by swelling and pain in the lymph nodes (regional lymphadenitis). Symptoms can vary from mild to severe, and may include achiness and discomfort (malaise), and/or loss of appetite (anorexia). The disease is caused by the bacterium *Bartonella henselae* and, in most cases, occurs as a result of a scratch, bite, or lick from a cat or kitten. Symptoms may not appear for several days after exposure and may last for several weeks. Although cat-scratch disease usually subsides without treatment, antibiotic and/or antimicrobial therapy may speed recovery. Approximately 22,000 cases are reported in the United States each year, although more mild cases may go unnoticed and resolve without treatment.

The following organizations may provide additional information and support:
Centers for Disease Control and Prevention
NIH/National Institute of Allergy and Infectious Diseases
World Health Organization (WHO) Regional Office for the Americas (AMRO)

203 Cataract Dental Syndrome

Synonyms

Cataract, X-Linked, with Hutchinsonian Teeth
Mesiodens-Cataract Syndrome
Nance-Horan Syndrome
NHS

Cataract-dental syndrome is an extremely rare genetic disorder that may be evident at birth (congenital). It is primarily characterized by abnormalities of the teeth and clouding of the lens of the eyes (congenital cataracts), resulting in poor vision. Additional eye (ocular) abnormalities are also often present, such as unusual smallness of the front, clear portion of the eye through which light passes (microcornea) and involuntary, rapid, rhythmic eye movements (nystagmus). In some cases, the disorder may also be associated with additional physical abnormalities and/or mental retardation. The range and severity of symptoms may vary greatly from case to case, including among affected members of the same family. Cataract-dental syndrome is inherited as an X-linked recessive trait; therefore, it is usually fully expressed in males only. However, females who carry a single copy of the disease gene (heterozygotes) may manifest some of the symptoms and findings associated with the disorder. These may include microcornea and/or clouding of the lens of the eyes (posterior sutural cataract). Symptoms are usually less severe than those of affected males, potentially causing only slightly decreased clearness or clarity of vision (visual acuity). In some cases, abnormalities of the teeth may also be present.

The following organizations may provide additional information and support:
Anophthalmia/Microphthalmia Registry
The Arc (A National Organization on Mental Retardation)
Council of Families with Visual Impairment
Institute for Families
National Association for Parents of Children with Visual Impairments (NAPVI)
National Association for Visually Handicapped
National Federation of the Blind
NIH/National Eye Institute
NIH/National Institute of Dental and Craniofacial Research
Vision World Wide, Inc.

204 Cataracts

Synonyms

Lens Opacities
Opacities of the Lens

Disorder Subdivisions

After-Cataract
Anterior Polar Cataract
Atopic Cataract
Berulean Cataract
Blue Dot Cataract
Complicated Cataract
Congenital Cataract
Coronary Cataract
Diabetic Cataract
Electric Cataract

Heat Ray Cataract
Irradiation Cataract
Lemellar Cataract
Perinuclear Cataract
Punctate Cataract
Secondary Cataract
Toxic Cataract
Traumatic Cataract
Zonular Cataract

Cataracts are abnormalities in the lens of the eye that cause a loss of transparency (opacity). They can occur either in one or in both eyes, and are quite common in the elderly. Congenital cataracts affect infants or young children and are considered to be a rare birth defect. Cataracts tend to cause cloudy vision, and, in many cases, may result in blindness when left untreated.

The following organizations may provide additional information and support:
Blind Children's Fund
National Association for Parents of Children with Visual Impairments (NAPVI)
National Association for Visually Handicapped
NIH/National Eye Institute

205   Catel-Manzke Syndrome

Synonyms
Catel-Manzke Type Palatodigital Syndrome
Hyperphalangy-Clinodactyly of Index Finger with Pierre Robin Syndrome
Index Finger Anomaly with Pierre Robin Syndrome
Pierre Robin Syndrome with Hyperphalangy and Clinodactyly

Catel-Manzke syndrome is a rare genetic disorder characterized by distinctive abnormalities of the index fingers; the classic features of Pierre Robin syndrome; and, in some cases, additional physical findings. Pierre Robin syndrome refers to a sequence of abnormalities that may occur as a distinct syndrome or as part of another underlying disorder. Pierre Robin syndrome is characterized by an unusually small jaw (micrognathia), downward displacement or retraction of the tongue (glossoptosis), and incomplete closure of the roof of the mouth (cleft palate). Infants with Catel-Manzke syndrome have an extra (supernumerary), irregularly shaped bone (i.e., hyperphalangy) located between the first bone of the index finger (proximal phalanx) and the corresponding bone within the body of the hand (second metacarpal).

As a result, the index fingers may be fixed in an abnormally bent position (clinodactyly). In some cases, additional abnormalities of the hands may also be present. Due to the presence of micrognathia, glossoptosis, and cleft palate, affected infants may have feeding and breathing difficulties; growth deficiency; repeated middle ear infections (otitis media); and/or other complications. In addition, some infants with the syndrome may have structural abnormalities of the heart that are present at birth (congenital heart defects). The range and severity of symptoms and findings may vary from case to case. Catel-Manzke syndrome usually appears to occur randomly, for unknown reasons (sporadically).

The following organizations may provide additional information and support:
American Heart Association
Cleft Palate Foundation
Congenital Heart Anomalies, Support, Education, & Resources
March of Dimes Birth Defects Foundation
National Craniofacial Foundation
NIH/National Heart, Lung and Blood Institute Information Center
Pierre Robin Network
Prescription Parents
Wide Smiles

206   Caudal Regression Syndrome

Synonyms
Caudal Dysplasia
Caudal Dysplasia Sequence
Sacral Agenesis, Congenital
Sacral Regression

Caudal regression syndrome is a rare disorder characterized by abnormal development of the lower spine end of the developing fetus. A wide range of abnormalities may occur including partial absence of the tailbone end of the spine causing no apparent symptoms, to extensive abnormalities of the lower vertebrae, pelvis, and spine. Neurological impairment as well as inability to control urination and bowel movements (incontinence) may occur in severe cases.

The following organizations may provide additional information and support:
March of Dimes Birth Defects Foundation
NIH/National Institute of Arthritis and Musculoskeletal and Skin Diseases
Restricted Growth Association

207 Cavernous Malformation

Synonyms

Cavernoma
Cavernous Angioma
Cavernous Hemangioma

Vascular malformations or angiomas are localized collections of blood vessels that are abnormal in structure or number, lead to altered blood flow, and are not cancerous (nonneoplastic). Most vascular malformations are present at birth (congenital) and are suspected to arise between three and eight weeks of gestation, but the specific defect in embryogenesis has not yet been identified for each type of malformation. Some vascular malformations are not congenital, but caused by trauma, radiation, or other injury to the spinal cord. They are typically classified by size, location, and type of change, with the four most common being capillary telangiectasias, cavernous malformations, venous malformations, and arteriovenous malformations. Vascular malformations are sporadic and solitary in the majority of affected persons, however documented cases of autosomal dominant forms exist as well. Cavernous malformations are dilated blood vessels that are characterized by multiple distended "caverns" of blood that flow very slowly. The blood-filled vascular spaces are surrounded by blood vessel walls that do not have enough smooth muscle and stretchable material (elastin), so they are not strong and get distended. Cavernous malformations can be located anywhere in the body, including the liver, rectum, kidney, eyes, nerves, spinal cord and brain. Brain and spinal cord (cerebral) malformations will be focused on here, as they have the potential for serious symptoms. Cerebral cavernous malformations (CCMs) are usually located in the white matter (cortex) of the brain. They are rarely located in the brainstem or hypothalamus, though this may be more common in children than adults. Locations in the spinal cord are more common in the adult population than in children. Cerebral cavernous malformations do not have brain tissue within the malformation like other lesions such as arteriovenous malformations, and they usually do not have defined borders (are not encapsulated). Cerebral cavernous malformations are dynamic, changing in size and number over time. They can range from 0.1 to 9 cm and usually reach a larger size in children than adults (who usually have cavernous malformations only 2-3 cm in size). There is no correlation between size and risk of bleeding or long-term symptoms of brain damage (neurological deficits). Very small amounts of bleeding (microhemorrhages) can cause the development of new vessels, but they usually do not cause physical symptoms. These microhemorrhages show up as black dots on an MRI and contribute to a patient's prognosis and ability to function. According to several studies, cerebral cavernous malfations are present in about 0.5% of the general population, and they account for 8-15% of all brain and spinal vascular malformations. The prevalence of cavernous malformations in children is estimated to be between 0.37 and 0.53% (up to 1 in 200 children have a CCM, whether symptomatic or asymptomatic), and approximately 25% of all diagnosed cavernous malformations are found in children. Before 18 years of age, peak ages of incidence have been found to be 0-2 years (26.8% of children with CCMs) and 13-16 (35.7%). It is unclear why they are distributed in this manner. Other malformations can be present in combination with CCMs, such as small areas where the capillaries or veins do not form correctly (capillary telangiectasias or venous malformations), and this association occurs 8-44% of the time. In fact, some investigators think that some cavernous malformations come from capillary telangiectasias originally. These combinations are more common in children than in adults. When an association of more than one malformation exists (such as a CCM and venous malformation) in the same person, hemorrhage is more common.

The following organizations may provide additional information and support:
The BrainPower Project
Angioma Alliance

208 Cayler Syndrome

Synonyms

ACF with Cardiac Defects
Asymmetric Crying Facies with Cardiac Defects
Cayler Cardiofacial Syndrome
Hypoplasia of the Depressor Anguli Oris Muscle with Cardiac Defects

Cayler syndrome, also known as "asymmetric crying facies with cardiac defects," is an extremely rare disorder characterized by congenital heart defects and the underdevelopment or absence of one of the muscles that control the movements of the lower lip. The disorder is present at birth (congenital) and is usually first noticed when the infant cries or smiles. Half of the lower lip cannot be drawn down and outward because of the incomplete development (hypoplasia) or absence (agenesis) of the depressor anguli oris muscle. Congenital heart defects associated with Cayler syndrome may include ventricular septal defects, atrial septal defects, and/or tetralogy of Fallot. In some rare cases, individuals may have an abnormally small head (microcephaly), unusually small jawbones (micrognathia), small eyes (microphthalmos), and/or mental retardation. Most cases of Cayler syndrome are thought to be inherited as an autosomal dominant trait.

The following organizations may provide additional information and support:
American Heart Association
Congenital Heart Anomalies, Support, Education, & Resources

209 Celiac Disease

Synonyms
CD
Celiac Sprue
GSE
Gluten Enteropathy
Gluten-Sensitive Enteropathy
Nontropical Sprue

Celiac disease is a digestive disorder characterized by intolerance to dietary gluten, which is a protein found in wheat, rye, and barley. Consumption of gluten leads to abnormal changes of the mucous membrane (mucosa) of the small intestine, impairing its ability to properly absorb fats and additional nutrients during digestion (intestinal malabsorption). Symptom onset may occur during childhood or adulthood. In affected children, such symptoms may include diarrhea, vomiting, weight loss or lack of weight gain, painful abdominal bloating, irritability, and/or other abnormalities. Affected adults may have diarrhea or constipation; abdominal cramping and bloating; abnormally bulky, pale, frothy stools that contain increased levels of fat (steatorrhea); weight loss; anemia; muscle cramping; bone pain; exhaustion (lassitude); and/or other symptoms and findings. Although the exact cause of celiac disease is unknown, genetic, immunologic, and environmental factors are thought to play some role.

The following organizations may provide additional information and support:
Autoimmune Information Network, Inc
Celiac Disease Foundation
Celiac Sprue Association/USA, Inc.
Gluten Intolerance Group of North America
Jack Miller Center for Peripheral Neuropathy
NIH/National Digestive Diseases Information Clearinghouse
R.O.C.K. (Raising Our Celiac Kids)

210 Central Core Disease

Synonyms
CCD
CCO
Central Core Disease of Muscle
Muscle Core Disease
Muscular Central Core Disease
Myopathy, Central Core
Myopathy, Central Fibrillar
Shy-Magee Syndrome

Central core disease (CCD) is a relatively rare genetic disorder of infancy and childhood characterized by abnormalities of skeletal (voluntary) muscle (congenital myopathy). Associated symptoms and findings may include abnormally diminished muscle tone (hypotonia), potentially resulting in unusual "floppiness" of muscles; muscle weakness; delays in motor development, such as in walking; and/or, in some cases, associated musculoskeletal problems, such as dislocation of the hips at birth (congenital). CCD may also be associated with susceptibility to malignant hyperthermia, a potentially life-threatening reaction to certain anesthetics or skeletal muscle relaxants. The disorder derives its name from characteristic, abnormal "central cores" within muscle fibers as detected during microscopic examination of small samples of muscle tissue (muscle biopsy). CCD is transmitted as an autosomal dominant trait.

The following organizations may provide additional information and support:
Malignant Hyperthermia Association of the United States (MHAUS)
March of Dimes Birth Defects Foundation
Medic Alert Foundation International
Muscular Dystrophy Association
National Institute of Neurological Disorders and Stroke (NINDS)
North American Malignant Hyperthermia Registry of MHAUS

211 Central Hypoventilation Syndrome, Congenital

Synonym
Autonomic Control, Congenital Failure of
CCHS
CCHS with Hirschsprung Disease, Included
Haddad Syndrome
OHD
Ondine Curse, Congenital
Ondine-Hirschsprung Disease, Included

Congenital central hypoventilation syndrome (CCHS) is a rare neurological disorder present at birth that is characterized by inadequate breathing during sleep and, in more severely affected individuals, also during waking periods. This disorder is associated with a malfunction of the nerves that control involuntary body functions (autonomic nervous system) and abnormal development of early embryonic cells that form the spinal cord (neural crest). The abnormal neural crest development can lead to other abnormalities such as absent or impaired bowel function (Hirschsprung's disease). Most individuals with CCHS have an abnormality in the PHOX2B gene.

The following organizations may provide additional information and support:
American Sleep Disorders Association
Center for Research in Sleep Disorders
Congenital Central Hypoventilation Syndrome (CCHS) Family Support Network
International Foundation for Functional Gastrointestinal Disorders
National Institute of Neurological Disorders and Stroke (NINDS)

212 Cerebellar Agenesis

Synonyms
Cerebellar Aplasia
Cerebellar Hemiagenesis
Cerebellar Hypoplasia

Cerebellar agenesis is a rare disorder thought to be inherited as an autosomal recessive trait. Infants with this disorder are born with partial formation or total absence of the portion of the brain that is located at the base of the skull and known as the cerebellum. Infants with partial formation of the cerebellum may have few or no symptoms of the disorder. When total absence of the cerebellum is present, an affected infant may experience low muscle tone, uncontrollable quivering or movements, involuntary movement of the eyes, and/or an inability to coordinate muscle movements.

The following organizations may provide additional information and support:
March of Dimes Birth Defects Foundation
National Institute of Neurological Disorders and Stroke (NINDS)

213 Cerebellar Degeneration, Subacute

Synonym
Subacute Cerebellar Degeneration

Disorder Subdivisions
Alcoholic Cerebellar Degeneration
Nutritional Cerebellar Degeneration

Subacute cerebellar degeneration (SCD) is characterized by the deterioration of the area of the brain concerned with muscle coordination and balance (the cerebellum). Less frequently, the area involved may include the area connecting the spinal cord to the brain (the medulla oblongata, the cerebral cortex, and the brain stem). There are two types of subacute cerebellar degeneration: paraneoplastic cerebellar degeneration, which sometimes precedes the diagnosis of cancer, and alcoholic or nutritional cerebellar degeneration, caused by a lack of the vitamin B-1 (thiamine). These two types share symptoms but not the same cause.

The following organizations may provide additional information and support:
American Autoimmune Related Diseases Association, Inc.
American Cancer Society, Inc.
March of Dimes Birth Defects Foundation
NIH/National Institute on Aging

214 Cerebral Palsy

Synonyms
Cerebral Diplegia
CP
Infantile Cerebral Paralysis
Little Disease
Palsy

Disorder Subdivisions
Ataxia Cerebral Palsy
Athetoid Cerebral Palsy
Congenital Cerebral Palsy
Diplegia of Cerebral Palsy

Hemiparesis of Cerebral Palsy
Hemiplegia of Cerebral Palsy
Postnatal Cerebral Palsy
Quadriparesis of Cerebral Palsy
Quadriplegia of Cerebral Palsy
Spastic Cerebral Palsy

Cerebral palsy is a neurological movement disorder characterized by the lack of muscle control and impairment in the coordination of movements. This disorder is usually a result of injury to the brain during early development in the uterus, at birth, or in the first 2 years of life. Cerebral palsy is not progressive.

The following organizations may provide additional information and support:
Birth Defect Research for Children, Inc.
Christopher Reeve Paralysis Foundation
Easter Seals National Headquarters
Let Them Hear Foundation
March of Dimes Birth Defects Foundation
National Institute of Neurological Disorders and Stroke (NINDS)
New Horizons Un-Limited, Inc.
NIH/National Institute of Child Health and Human Development
Pathways Awareness Foundation
UCP (United Cerebral Palsy Associations, Inc.)
WE MOVE (Worldwide Education and Awareness for Movement Disorders)

215 Cerebro-Oculo-Facio-Skeletal Syndrome

Synonyms
Cerebrooculofacioskeletal Syndrome
Cockayne Syndrome Type II
COFS Syndrome
Pena Shokeir II Syndrome
Pena Shokeir Syndrome Type II

Cerebro-oculo-facio-skeletal (COFS) syndrome is a genetic degenerative disorder of the brain and spinal cord that begins before birth. The disorder is characterized by growth failure at birth and little or no neurological development, structural abnormalities of the eye and fixed bending of the spine and joints. Abnormalities of the skull, face, limbs and other parts of the body may also occur. COFS syndrome is inherited as an autosomal recessive genetic trait. COFS is now considered to be part of the spectrum of disorders within Cockayne syndrome.

The following organizations may provide additional information and support:
AboutFace USA
Children's Craniofacial Association
FACES: The National Craniofacial Association
Forward Face, Inc.
March of Dimes Birth Defects Foundation
National Craniofacial Foundation
National Institute of Neurological Disorders and Stroke (NINDS)
Society for the Rehabilitation of the Facially Disfigured, Inc.
\

216 Cerebrocostomandibular Syndrome

Synonyms
CCM Syndrome
CCMS
Rib Gap Defects with Micrognathia

Cerebrocostomandibular syndrome is an extremely rare inherited disorder characterized by an abnormally small jaw (micrognathia), malformations of the roof of the mouth (palate), improper positioning of the tongue (glossoptosis), and abnormal development of the ribs (rib dysplasia). In most cases, such abnormalities contribute to respiratory problems (insufficiency) during early infancy. Although some affected individuals have normal intelligence, others exhibit moderate to severe mental retardation. Although research suggests that cerebrocostomandibular syndrome is usually inherited as an autosomal recessive genetic trait, some cases have also been documented in the medical literature that suggest autosomal dominant inheritance.

The following organizations may provide additional information and support:
American Speech-Language-Hearing Association
The Arc (A National Organization on Mental Retardation)
CCMS Support Group
Cleft Palate Foundation
National Craniofacial Foundation
NIH/National Heart, Lung and Blood Institute Information Center
NIH/National Institute on Deafness and Other Communication Disorders Information Clearinghouse
Prescription Parents
Wide Smiles

217 Chagas Disease

Synonyms

American Trypanosomiasis
Brazilian Trypanosomiasis

Chagas disease is a tropical infectious disease caused by the parasite *Trypanosoma cruzi*. It is transmitted by the bite of one of several species of blood-sucking insects or by blood transfusion. Acute Chagas disease usually affects children and typically presents as the mild phase of the disease. However, this is generally followed by a long period of low level, parasitic infection (parasitemia). Many years later, about 10 to 30 percent of people with Chagas disease develop the more severe symptoms associated with "chronic" Chagas disease. The heart and digestive systems are most frequently involved in this phase of the disease. The most common features of late chronic Chagas disease include abnormal enlargement of the esophagus (megaesophagus) and colon (megacolon), and congestive heart failure. Chagas disease occurs primarily in Central and South America.

The following organizations may provide additional information and support:
Centers for Disease Control and Prevention
National Dysautonomia Research Foundation
NIH/National Institute of Allergy and Infectious Diseases
World Health Organization (WHO) Regional Office for the Americas (AMRO)

218 Chalazion

Synonym

Meibomian Cyst
Tarsal Cyst

Chalazion is a round, slowly emerging, localized swelling, in the form of a cyst located on the lower or upper eyelid. (Chalazion is the Greek word for "hailstone" which represents the size of the lump that makes up the cyst.) The usually painless, grainy (granulomatous) mass is due to inflammation, obstruction, and retained secretions of one of the glands that lubricates the edge of the eyelids. These glands secrete sebum, an oily, protective fluid. If one or more of the ducts that drain these glands is blocked, the sebum accumulates under the skin to form a cyst. In rare cases, if the cyst is large, blurred vision may result due to pressure on the cornea, the front, clear portion of the eye through which light passes. In some affected individuals, chalazia may disappear spontaneously. However, in other cases, treatment may be required. Individuals with chronic inflammation of the eyelids (blepharitis) may be prone to recurrences.

The following organizations may provide additional information and support:
NIH/National Eye Institute
Schepens Eye Research Institute

219 Chandler's Syndrome

Synonyms

Dystrophia Endothelialis Cornea
Iris Atrophy with Corneal Edema and Glaucoma

Chandler's syndrome (CS) is a rare eye disorder in which the single layer of cells lining the interior of the cornea proliferates, causing the drying up of the iris, corneal swelling, and unusually high pressure in the eye (glaucoma). CS is one of three syndromes affecting the eyes (progressive iris atrophy and Cogan-Reese syndrome are the other two) that make up the iridocorneal endothelial syndrome. Chandler's syndrome affects females more often than males and usually presents sometime during middle age. Most often the condition affects one eye only but if it is not treated, with time, the second eye may become involved. The combination of high pressure within the eye (glaucoma) and leaking of fluid through the cellular membrane can result in reduced vision with pain.

The following organizations may provide additional information and support:
National Association for Parents of Children with Visual Impairments (NAPVI)
National Association for Visually Handicapped
NIH/National Eye Institute
Prevent Blindness America
Schepens Eye Research Institute

220 Charcot Marie Tooth Disease

Synonyms

CMT
Hereditary Sensory Motor Neuropathy
HSMN
Peroneal Muscular Atrophy

Charcot Marie Tooth hereditary neuropathies are a group of disorders in which the motor and sensory peripheral nerves are affected, resulting in muscle weakness and atrophy, primarily in the legs and sometimes in the hands. CMT hereditary neuropathy affects the nerves that control many muscles in the body. The nerve cells in individuals with this disorder are not able to send electrical signals properly because of abnormalities in the nerve axon or abnormalities in the insulation (myelin) around the axon. Specific gene mutations are responsible for the abnormal function of the peripheral nerves. Charcot Marie Tooth hereditary neuropathy can be inherited in an autosomal dominant, autosomal recessive or X-linked mode of inheritance.

The following organizations may provide additional information and support:
Charcot-Marie-Tooth Association
Hereditary Neuropathy Foundation, Inc.
Jack Miller Center for Peripheral Neuropathy
Let Them Hear Foundation
Muscular Dystrophy Association
National Institute of Neurological Disorders and Stroke (NINDS)

221 CHARGE Syndrome

Synonyms
CHARGE Association
Choanal Atresia, Posterior
Coloboma, Heart, Atresia of the Choanae,
Retardation of Growth and
Development, Genital and Urinary Anomalies,
and Ear Anomalies

CHARGE syndrome is a rare disorder that arises during early fetal development and affects multiple organ systems. The term CHARGE comes from the first letter of some of the more common features seen in these children: (C) = coloboma and cranial nerve abnormalities–defects of the eyeball; (H) = heart defects; (A) = atresia of the choanae (blocked nasal breathing passages); (R) = retardation of growth and development; (G) = genital and urinary abnormalities; (E) = ear abnormalities and hearing loss. Diagnosis is based on a different set of features (see below). In addition to the CHARGE features, most children with CHARGE syndrome have other features, including characteristic facial features, cleft lip or palate, esophageal atresia (blind-ending food pipe) or tracheoesophageal fistula (connection between the wind pipe and the food pipe). The symptoms of CHARGE syndrome vary greatly from one child to another. The exact cause of CHARGE is not known. Most cases occur randomly, for no apparent reason (sporadic). There are a few familial cases.

The following organizations may provide additional information and support:
American Foundation for the Blind
American Speech-Language-Hearing Association
The Arc (A National Organization on Mental Retardation)
Birth Defect Research for Children, Inc.
CHARGE Syndrome Foundation, Inc.
Congenital Heart Anomalies, Support, Education, & Resources
Helen Keller National Center for Deaf-Blind Youths and Adults
Let Them Hear Foundation
National Association for Parents of Children with Visual Impairments (NAPVI)

222 Chediak-Higashi Syndrome

Synonyms
Begnez-Cesar's Syndrome
Chediak-Steinbrinck-Higashi Syndrome
CHS
Leukocytic Anomaly Albinism
Natural Killer Lymphocytes, Defect in
Oculocutaneous Albinism, Chediak-Higashi Type

Chediak-Higashi syndrome (CHS) is a rare, inherited, complex, immune disorder of childhood (usually) characterized by abnormally pale skin and eyes (oculocutaneous albinism). Because the patient's white blood cells (leukocytes) are profoundly affected, especially in their capacity to transport cellular proteins, immune disorders are common, along with an increased susceptibility to infections. In addition, CHS patients tend to bruise and bleed easily. Neurological deficits are also common. CHS is transmitted as an autosomal recessive trait.

The following organizations may provide additional information and support:
International Patient Organization for Primary Immunodeficiencies
Jeffrey Modell Foundation
March of Dimes Birth Defects Foundation
National Organization for Albinism and Hypopigmentation
NIH/National Institute of Allergy and Infectious Diseases

223   Chiari-Frommel Syndrome

Synonyms

Chiari I Syndrome
Frommel-Chiari Syndrome
Lactation-Uterus Atrophy
Postpartum Galactorrhea-Amenorrhea
Syndrome

Chiari-Frommel syndrome is a rare endocrine disorder that affects women who have recently given birth (postpartum) and is characterized by the over-production of breast milk (galactorrhea), lack of ovulation (anovulation), and the absence of regular menstrual periods (amenorrhea). In Chiari-Frommel syndrome, these symptoms persist long (for more than 6 months) after childbirth. The absence of normal hormonal cycles may result in reduced size of the uterus (atrophy). Some cases of Chiari-Frommel syndrome resolve completely without treatment (spontaneously); hormone levels and reproductive function return to normal.

The following organizations may provide additional information and support:
National Infertility Association
Recovery, Inc.

224   Chikungunya

Synonyms

Arbovirus A Chikungunya Type
CHIK
CK

Chikungunya is a rare viral infection transmitted by the bite of an infected mosquito. It is characterized by a rash, fever, and severe joint pain (arthralgias) that usually lasts for 3 to 7 days. Because of its effect on the joints, chikungunya has been classified among the arthritic viruses. It primarily occurs in tropical areas of the world.

The following organizations may provide additional information and support:
Centers for Disease Control and Prevention
NIH/National Institute of Allergy and Infectious Diseases
World Health Organization (WHO) Regional Office for the Americas (AMRO)

225   Chlamydia

Synonym

Chlamydia Trachomatis

Chlamydia is a sexually transmitted bacterial infection with symptoms similar to those of gonorrhea. Until recently, chlamydia was identified primarily when a certain type of eye infection (trachoma) appeared as a symptom. Initially, the symptoms of chlamydia are usually mild and may not be recognized. In rare cases, chlamydia may have serious complications, if left untreated. Individuals who are sexually active and have multiple sex partners are especially at risk for this disease. Since many people with chlamydia do not realize that they have this infection, they may not seek treatment until serious complications occur. Meanwhile, they may have unknowingly spread the disease to others through sexual activity. Treatment with antibiotics is generally successful; however, prevention is the primary course of action.

The following organizations may provide additional information and support:
American Social Health Association
Centers for Disease Control and Prevention
NIH/National Institute of Allergy and Infectious Diseases

226   Cholangitis, Primary Sclerosing

Synonyms

Chronic Obliterative Cholangitis
Fibrosing Cholangitis
Stenosing Cholangitis

Primary sclerosing cholangitis is a rare progressive disorder characterized by inflammation, thickening, and abnormal formation of fibrous tissue (fibrosis) within the passages that carry bile from the liver (bile ducts). This often results in the obstruction or interruption of bile flow from the liver (cholestasis). Symptoms associated with primary sclerosing cholangitis include fatigue and itching (pruritis), followed by yellowing of the skin, mucous membranes, and whites of the eyes (jaundice). In addition, affected individuals may have dark urine, light-colored stools, abdominal pain, and/or nausea. In some cases, the liver may also become abnormally enlarged (hepatomegaly). According to the medical literature, approximately 50 to 75 percent of individuals with primary sclerosing cholangitis may also have ulcerative colitis. The exact cause of primary sclerosing cholangitis is not known.

The following organizations may provide additional information and support:
American Liver Foundation
Autoimmune Information Network, Inc
Canadian Liver Foundation
NIH/National Digestive Diseases Information Clearinghouse

227 Cholecystitis

Disorder Subdivisions
Acalculous Cholecystitis
Gallstone Cholecystitis

Cholecystitis is inflammation of the gallbladder, the pear-shaped muscular sac that lies below the liver. The gallbladder's main function is to store and concentrate bile and to expel the bile through the bile duct during the digestion of fats. (Bile is a greenish-brown liquid produced by the liver that breaks down fats present in the small intestine during digestion.) Cholecystitis may come on suddenly (acute) or may persist over a period of time (chronic). Acute cholecystitis is usually caused by obstruction of the outlet of the gallbladder, which is often due to the development of a stone formed in the biliary tract (gallstone or biliary calculus). Repeated mild episodes of acute cholecystitis may result in chronic cholecystitis, which may be characterized by thickening and shrinking of the gallbladder walls and a resulting inability to store bile. Cholecystitis may cause a variety of symptoms including severe pain in the right side of the abdomen (right upper quadrant) and/or back, nausea, vomiting, indigestion, fever, and persistent yellowing of the skin, mucous membranes, and whites of the eyes (jaundice). In some cases, there may be additional symptoms.

The following organizations may provide additional information and support:
Digestive Disease National Coalition
NIH/National Digestive Diseases Information Clearinghouse

228 Cholera

Synonyms
Asiatic Cholera
Epidemic Cholera

Cholera is an acute infectious disease caused by the bacterium *Vibrio cholerae*, which lives and multiples (colonizes) in the small intestine but does not destroy or invade the intestinal tissue (noninvasive). The major symptom of cholera is massive watery diarrhea that occurs because of a toxin secreted by the bacteria that stimulates the cells of the small intestine to secrete fluid. There are several strains of *V. cholerae* and the severity of the disease is based on the particular infectious strain. Cholera is not a difficult disease to treat and most people recover well with appropriate

oral fluid replacement (hydration). However, if the disease goes untreated, it can rapidly lead to shock, as a result of fluid and electrolyte loss, and to life-threatening complications.

The following organizations may provide additional information and support:
Centers for Disease Control and Prevention
NIH/National Institute of Allergy and Infectious Diseases
World Health Organization (WHO) Regional Office for the Americas (AMRO)

229 Cholestasis

Disorder Subdivisions
Benign Recurrent Intrahepatic Cholestasis
BRIC Syndrome
Cholestasis of Oral Contraceptive Users
Cholestasis of Pregnancy
Estrogen-related Cholestasis
Postoperative Cholestasis
Summerskill Syndrome

Cholestasis is a relatively rare syndrome that results when the flow of bile from the liver is impaired. Bile is a fluid secreted by the liver that passes, via the bile duct, into the intestine where it is essential for the digestion of fats. The many causes of cholestasis produce different symptoms. Common symptoms are dark urine, pale stools, and itchy (pruritic) and yellowed (jaundiced) skin.

The following organizations may provide additional information and support:
American Liver Foundation
Children's Liver Association for Support Services
NIH/National Institute of Diabetes, Digestive & Kidney Diseases

230 Chondrocalcinosis, Familial Articular

Synonyms
Calcium Gout, Familial
Calcium Pyrophosphate Arthropathy, Familial
Calcium Pyrophosphate Dihydrate Deposition Disease
Pseudogout, Familial

Disorder Subdivisions
Chondrocalcinosis-1 (CCAL1)
Chondrocalcinosis-2 (CCAL2)

Familial articular chondrocalcinosis is a rare inherited metabolic disorder characterized by deposits of calcium pyrophosphate dihydrate crystals (CPPD) in one or more joint cartilages resulting in eventual damage to the joints. Symptoms may develop due to decreased activity of the enzyme nucleoside triphosphate pyrophosphohydrolase. The symptoms of familial articular chondrocalcinosis mimic those of classical gout and may include swelling, stiffness, and pain, usually in one joint. The knee is most commonly affected. Chondrocalcinosis occurs in a hereditary form (familial articular chondrocalcinosis), a form associated with metabolic disorders and a sporadic form. The hereditary forms are subdivided into chondrocalcinosis-1 (CCAL1) and chondrocalcinosis-2 (CCAL2).

The following organizations may provide additional information and support:
Genetic and Rare Diseases (GARD) Information Center
March of Dimes Birth Defects Foundation
NIH/National Institute of Arthritis and Musculoskeletal and Skin Diseases

---

231 Chordoma

Synonyms
Clival Chordoma
Familial Chordoma
Intracranial Chordoma
Sacrococcygeal Chordoma
Skull Base Chordoma
Spinal Chordoma

Chordomas are very rare primary bone tumors that can arise at almost any point along the axis of the spine from the base of the skull to the sacrum and coccyx (tailbone). The incidence of chordoma in the general U.S. population is about 8 per 10,000,000 people. They occur somewhat more often in males than females and, for unknown reasons, are rare in African Americans. Under the microscope, chordoma cells appear to be benign, but because of their location, invasive nature, and recurrence rate, the tumors are considered to be malignant. They arise from cellular remnants of the primitive notochord, which is present in the early embryo. In normal mammalian development, the notochord and substances produced by it are involved in forming the tissues that give rise to vertebrae. Normally, the tissues derived from the notochord disappear after the vertebral bodies have begun forming. However, in a small percentage of people, some tissues from the notochord do not disappear. Rarely, these leftover tis-

sues give rise to chordomas. About one-third of chordomas are found in the region around the clivus. The clivus is a bone in the base of the skull. It is located in front of the brainstem and behind the back of the throat (nasopharynx). Chordomas occur with equal frequency in the skull base, the vertebrae and the sacrococcygeal area towards the bottom of the spine. Symptoms of the presence of chordomas vary with their location and size. Most chordomas occur randomly among the population (sporadic). However, some people develop this tumor as a result of a mutation inherited as an autosomal dominant trait.

The following organizations may provide additional information and support:
American Brain Tumor Association
American Cancer Society, Inc.
Brain Tumor Foundation for Children, Inc.
Brain Tumor Society
Brain Tumour Foundation of Canada
Brain Tumour Foundation, United Kingdom
Cancer Research UK
Candlelighters Childhood Cancer Foundation
Childhood Cancer Foundation—Candlelighters Canada
Children's Brain Tumor Foundation
Chordoma Support Group
National Brain Tumor Foundation
National Cancer Institute
Pituitary Network Association (PNA)

---

232 Chorea, Sydenham's

Synonyms
Chorea Minor
Infectious Chorea
Rheumatic Chorea
St. Vitus Dance

Sydenham's chorea is a non-progressive neurological movement disorder characterized by spontaneous movements, lack of coordination of voluntary movements, and muscular weakness. This disorder may occur following a streptococcal infection such as rheumatic fever, meningitis or scarlet fever.

The following organizations may provide additional information and support:
Centers for Disease Control and Prevention
National Institute of Neurological Disorders and Stroke (NINDS)
WE MOVE (Worldwide Education and Awareness for Movement Disorders)

233 Choroideremia

Synonyms

Choroidal Sclerosis
Progressive Choroidal Atrophy
Progressive Tapetochoroidal Dystrophy
TCD

Choroideremia is a genetic disorder of sight that usually affects males. Female carriers may have mild symptoms without loss of vision. Major symptoms include a progressive loss of the peripheral field of vision and night blindness. Night blindness is usually the first noticeable symptom, usually occurring during childhood.

The following organizations may provide additional information and support:
American Council of the Blind, Inc.
American Foundation for the Blind
Blind Children's Fund
Choroideremia Research Foundation, Inc.
Council of Families with Visual Impairment
EyeCare Foundation
Foundation Fighting Blindness (Canada)
Macular Degeneration Support, Inc.
National Association for Parents of Children with Visual Impairments (NAPVI)
National Association for Visually Handicapped
National Federation of the Blind
NIH/National Eye Institute

234 Choroiditis, Serpiginous

Synonyms

Geographic Choroiditis
Geographic Choroidopathy
Geographic Helicoid Peripapillary Choroidopathy (GHPC)
Geographic Serpiginous Choroiditis
Peripapillary Choroidopathy
Serpiginous Choroidopathy

Serpiginous choroiditis is one of the conditions in a group termed the white dot syndromes which all involve inflammation of the retina and choroid and are defined by the appearance of white dots in the posterior inner part of the eye (fundus). Serpiginous choroiditis is a rare recurrent eye disorder characterized by irregularly shaped (serpiginous) lesions involving two layers of the eye surface (the retinal pigment epithelium and the choriocapillaris). No symptoms are apparent unless a specific area of the retina (macula) is damaged. A sudden, painless decrease in vision in one or both eyes may be the first sign of serpiginous choroiditis. Patients may also notice blind gaps in the visual field (scotomata) or a sensation of flashes of light (photopsia). Both eyes are commonly affected, although the second eye may not develop lesions for weeks to years after the first eye. The exact cause of serpiginous choroiditis is not known.

The following organizations may provide additional information and support:
Association for Macular Diseases, Inc.
EyeCare Foundation
National Association for Visually Handicapped
NIH/National Eye Institute

235 Chromosome 3, Monosomy 3p2

Synonyms

Chromosome 3, Deletion of Distal 3p
Chromosome 3, Distal 3p Monosomy
Monosomy 3p2

Chromosome 3, monosomy 3p2 is a rare chromosomal disorder in which the end (distal) portion of the short arm (p) of chromosome 3 is missing (deleted or monosomic). The range and severity of symptoms and findings may be variable. However, associated features often include growth delays before and after birth (prenatal and postnatal growth deficiency); severe to profound mental retardation; distinctive malformations of the skull and facial (craniofacial) region; eyebrows that grow together (synophrys); and/or excessive hair growth (hypertrichosis). Additional physical abnormalities may also be present. In many cases, chromosome 3, monosomy 3p2 appears to occur spontaneously (de novo) for unknown reasons.

The following organizations may provide additional information and support:
AboutFace USA
American Heart Association
The Arc (A National Organization on Mental Retardation)
Children's Craniofacial Association
Chromosome Deletion Outreach, Inc.
Congenital Heart Anomalies, Support, Education, & Resources
Craniofacial Foundation of America
March of Dimes Birth Defects Foundation
NIH/National Eye Institute
NIH/National Institute on Deafness and Other Communication Disorders Information Clearinghouse
NIH/National Kidney and Urologic Diseases Information Clearinghouse
UNIQUE—Rare Chromosome Disorder Support Group

236 Chromosome 3, Trisomy 3q2

Synonyms

Chromosome 3, Distal 3q2 Duplication
Chromosome 3, Distal 3q2 Trisomy
Partial Duplication 3q Syndrome
Partial Trisomy 3q Syndrome

Chromosome 3, trisomy 3q2 is a rare chromosomal disorder in which a portion of the 3rd chromosome appears three times (trisomy) rather than twice in cells of the body. Associated symptoms and findings may be variable, depending upon the specific length and location of the duplicated (trisomic) portion of chromosome 3. However, many affected infants and children have developmental delays, mental retardation, and characteristic abnormalities of the head and facial (craniofacial) area, resulting in a distinctive facial appearance. Such craniofacial abnormalities may include a relatively short head (brachycephaly), widely spaced eyes (ocular hypertelorism), upwardly slanting eyelid folds (palpebral fissures), and a small nose with upturned nostrils (anteverted nares). Affected infants and children also tend to have long eyelashes; arched, bushy, well-defined eyebrows that grow together across the base of the nose (synophrys); an unusually low hairline on the forehead and the back of the neck; and generalized excessive hair growth (hirsutism). Chromosome 3, trisomy 3q2 may also be characterized by eye (ocular) abnormalities, limb defects, structural heart malformations (congenital heart defects), or other physical features.

The following organizations may provide additional information and support:
Support Organization for Trisomy 18, 13, and Related Disorders
UNIQUE—Rare Chromosome Disorder Support Group

237 Chromosome 4, Monosomy 4q

Synonyms

Chromosome 4 Long Arm Deletion
Chromosome 4q-Syndrome

Disorder Subdivisions

Interstitial Deletion of 4q, Included
Proximal Deletion of 4q, Included
Terminal Deletion of 4q, Included

Chromosome 4, monosomy 4q is a chromosomal disorder caused by a partial deletion of the long arm of chromosome 4. The patient may have an extremely prominent forehead (frontal bossing), enlargement of the back part of the head, low placement of ears, short broad hands and feet, unusually small size associated with slow or delayed growth, congenital heart defects, and possible mental retardation.

The following organizations may provide additional information and support:
Chromosome Deletion Outreach, Inc.
UNIQUE—Rare Chromosome Disorder Support Group

238 Chromosome 4, Monosomy Distal 4q

Synonyms

4q Deletion Syndrome, Partial
Chromosome 4, 4q Terminal Deletion Syndrome
Chromosome 4, Partial Monosomy 4q
Del(4q) Syndrome, Partial
Distal 4q Monosomy
Distal 4q-Syndrome

Chromosome 4, monosomy distal 4q is a rare chromosomal disorder in which there is deletion (monosomy) of a portion of the 4th chromosome. Associated symptoms and findings may be variable, depending upon the specific length and location of the deleted portion of chromosome 4. However, characteristic features include growth deficiency after birth (postnatal growth retardation), varying degrees of mental retardation, malformations of the skull and facial (craniofacial) region, structural heart defects, abnormalities of the hands and feet, and/or other physical findings. Chromosome 4, monosomy distal 4q usually appears to result from spontaneous (de novo) errors very early during embryonic development that occur for unknown reasons (sporadically).

The following organizations may provide additional information and support:
AboutFace USA
American Heart Association
The Arc (A National Organization on Mental Retardation)
Children's Craniofacial Association
Chromosome Deletion Outreach, Inc.
Cleft Palate Foundation
Congenital Heart Anomalies, Support, Education, & Resources
Craniofacial Foundation of America

FACES: The National Craniofacial Association
March of Dimes Birth Defects Foundation
National Craniofacial Foundation
Wide Smiles

National Craniofacial Foundation
NIH/National Kidney and Urologic Diseases Information Clearinghouse
Society for the Rehabilitation of the Facially Disfigured, Inc.
Support Organization for Trisomy 18, 13, and Related Disorders
UNIQUE—Rare Chromosome Disorder Support Group

239 Chromosome 4, Partial Trisomy Distal 4q

Synonyms

Chromosome 4, Partial Trisomy 4q (4q2 and 4q3, included)
Chromosome 4, Partial Trisomy 4q (4q21-qter to 4q32-qter, included)
Distal 4q Trisomy
Dup(4q) Syndrome, Partial
Duplication 4q Syndrome, Partial
Partial Trisomy 4q Sayndrome

Chromosome 4, partial trisomy distal 4q is a rare chromosomal disorder in which a portion of the fourth chromosome appears three times (trisomy) rather than twice in cells of the body. Associated symptoms and findings may vary from case to case. However, common features include growth deficiency; mental retardation; distinctive malformations of the skull and facial (craniofacial) region, including an unusually small head (microcephaly), malformed ears, and a prominent nasal bridge; and/or defects of the hands and feet. In some cases, additional physical abnormalities may also be present, such as structural defects of the heart that are present at birth (congenital heart defects); genital abnormalities in affected males; urinary tract defects; and/or other findings. In most cases, the trisomy appears to result from a balanced chromosomal rearrangement in one of the parents; rarely, it is thought to arise from spontaneous (de novo) errors very early in embryonic development that occur for unknown reasons (sporadically).

The following organizations may provide additional information and support:
AboutFace USA
American Heart Association
The Arc (A National Organization on Mental Retardation)
Children's Craniofacial Association
Congenital Heart Anomalies, Support, Education, & Resources
Craniofacial Foundation of America
FACES: The National Craniofacial Association
Forward Face, Inc.
March of Dimes Birth Defects Foundation

240 Chromosome 4 Ring

Synonyms

Ring 4
Ring 4, Chromosome
R4

Chromosome 4 ring is a rare disorder that is typically characterized by loss (deletion) of genetic material from both ends of the 4th chromosome and joining of the chromosomal ends to form a ring. Associated symptoms and findings may vary greatly, depending on the location of lost genetic material and/or other factors. Some affected infants may have a low birth weight; growth retardation; delays in the acquisition of skills requiring the coordination of mental and physical activities (psychomotor retardation); an abnormally small head (microcephaly); a broad, "beaked" nose; and/or various additional physical abnormalities that are present at birth (congenital anomalies). However, cases have also been reported in which chromosome 4 ring is primarily associated with growth retardation, with no major physical anomalies and normal psychomotor development. Chromosome 4 ring is usually caused by spontaneous (de novo) errors very early in the development of the embryo that appear to occur randomly for unknown reasons (sporadically).

The following organizations may provide additional information and support:
AboutFace USA
The Arc (A National Organization on Mental Retardation)
Children's Craniofacial Association
Chromosome Deletion Outreach, Inc.
Craniofacial Foundation of America
March of Dimes Birth Defects Foundation
NIH/National Kidney and Urologic Diseases Information Clearinghouse
UNIQUE—Rare Chromosome Disorder Support Group

241 Chromosome 4, Trisomy 4p

Synonyms

Chromosome 4, Partial Trisomy 4p
Dup(4p) Syndrome
Duplication 4p Syndrome

Chromosome 4, trisomy 4p is a rare chromosomal disorder in which all or a portion of the short arm (p) of chromosome 4 appears three times (trisomy) rather than twice in cells of the body. Associated symptoms and physical findings may vary greatly in range and severity from case to case. Such variability may depend upon the specific length and location of the duplicated (trisomic) portion of chromosome 4p as well as other factors. However, many affected infant have feeding and breathing difficulties, characteristic malformations of the head and facial (craniofacial) area, and abnormalities of the hands and feet. Additional features may include other skeletal defects, genital abnormalities in affected males, or heart (cardiac) defects. Trisomy 4p is also characterized by severe mental retardation.

The following organizations may provide additional information and support:
AboutFace USA
American Heart Association
The Arc (A National Organization on Mental Retardation)
Children's Craniofacial Association
Congenital Heart Anomalies, Support, Education, & Resources
Craniofacial Foundation of America
March of Dimes Birth Defects Foundation
Support Organization for Trisomy 18, 13, and Related Disorders
UNIQUE—Rare Chromosome Disorder Support Group

242 Chromosome 5, Trisomy 5p

Synonyms

Chromosome 5, Trisomy 5p, Complete (5p11-ter), Included
Chromosome 5, Trisomy 5p, Partial, Included
Dup(5p) Syndrome
Duplication 5p Syndrome

Chromosome 5, trisomy 5p is a rare chromosomal disorder in which all or a portion of the short arm (p) of chromosome 5 (5p) appears three times (trisomy) rather than twice in cells of the body. Associated symptoms and findings may be variable, depending upon the specific length and location of the duplicated (trisomic) portion of chromosome 5p. However, in many affected infants and children, such abnormalities may include low muscle tone (hypotonia); an unusually small head (microcephaly) and additional abnormalities of the head and facial (craniofacial) area; unusually long, slender fingers (arachnodactyly); delays in the acquisition of skills requiring the coordination of mental and physical activities (psychomotor retardation); and mental retardation.

The following organizations may provide additional information and support:
The Arc (A National Organization on Mental Retardation)
March of Dimes Birth Defects Foundation
Support Organization for Trisomy 13/18 and Related Disorders, UK
Support Organization for Trisomy 18, 13, and Related Disorders
UNIQUE—Rare Chromosome Disorder Support Group

243 Chromosome 6, Partial Trisomy 6q

Synonyms

6q+ Syndrome, Partial
Chromosome 6, Trisomy 6q2
Distal Duplication 6q
Distal Trisomy 6q
Duplication 6q, Partial
Trisomy 6q Syndrome, Partial
Trisomy 6q, Partial

Chromosome 6, partial trisomy 6q is an extremely rare chromosomal disorder in which a portion of the 6th chromosome (6q) is present three times (trisomy) rather than twice in cells of the body. Associated symptoms and findings may vary in range and severity from case to case. However, many affected infants and children have slow physical development (growth retardation); mental retardation; malformations of the skull and facial (craniofacial) region; an unusually short, webbed neck; abnormal bending (flexion) or extension of certain joints in fixed postures (joint contractures); and/or other physical abnormalities. In most cases, chromosome 6, partial trisomy 6q has been the result of a balanced translocation in one of the parents.

The following organizations may provide additional information and support:
AboutFace USA
The Arc (A National Organization on Mental Retardation)
Children's Craniofacial Association
Craniofacial Foundation of America
March of Dimes Birth Defects Foundation
Spotlight 6
Support Organization for Trisomy 18, 13, and Related Disorders
UNIQUE—Rare Chromosome Disorder Support Group

The following organizations may provide additional information and support:
AboutFace USA
The Arc (A National Organization on Mental Retardation)
Children's Craniofacial Association
Chromosome Deletion Outreach, Inc.
Craniofacial Foundation of America
Let Them Hear Foundation
March of Dimes Birth Defects Foundation
National Association for Parents of Children with Visual Impairments (NAPVI)
National Association for Visually Handicapped
NIH/National Eye Institute
Spotlight 6
UNIQUE—Rare Chromosome Disorder Support Group

244 Chromosome 6 Ring

Synonyms
Ring 6
Ring 6, Chromosome
R6

Chromosome 6 ring is a rare disorder in which there is loss (deletion) of chromosomal material from both ends of the 6th chromosome and joining of the ends to form a ring. Associated symptoms and findings may vary greatly, depending upon the amount and location of lost chromosomal material and other factors. For example, there have been some reported cases in which children with chromosome 6 ring have few physical abnormalities and normal intelligence. However, many with the chromosomal abnormality are affected by growth retardation; varying degrees of mental retardation; mild to severe delays in the acquisition of skills requiring the coordination of mental and physical activities (psychomotor retardation); and/or various abnormalities of the skull and facial (craniofacial) region. Such craniofacial features often include an unusually small head (microcephaly), malformed or low-set ears, and/or a small jaw (micrognathia). Eye (ocular) defects are also relatively common, such as drooping of the upper eyelids (ptosis), unusually small eyes (microphthalmia), abnormal deviation of one eye in relation to the other (strabismus), and/or other findings. Chromosome 6 ring usually appears to result from spontaneous (de novo) errors very early in the development of the embryo that occur for unknown reasons (sporadically).

245 Chromosome 7, Partial Monosomy 7p

Synonyms
Chromosome 7, 7p Deletion Syndrome, Partial
Chromosome 7, Partial Deletion of Short Arm
Del(7p) Syndrome, Partial
Interstitial 7p Monosomy, Included
Partial 7p Monosomy
Terminal 7p Monosomy, Included

Chromosome 7, partial monosomy 7p is a rare chromosomal disorder characterized by deletion (monosomy) of a portion of the short arm (p) of chromosome 7 (7p). Associated symptoms and findings may be variable and may depend on the specific size and location of the deleted segment of 7p. However, in many cases, there is early closure of the fibrous joints (cranial sutures) between certain bones of the skull (craniosynostosis), resulting in an abnormally shaped head. For example, depending on the specific sutures involved, the forehead may appear unusually "triangular shaped" (trigonocephaly) or the head may seem abnormally long and narrow with the top pointed or conical (turricephaly). Affected infants and children may also have additional malformations of the skull and facial (craniofacial) region. Such abnormalities may include an unusually small head (microcephaly), closely or widely set eyes (ocular hypotelorism or hypertelorism), downslanting eyelid folds (palpebral fissures), and/or other findings. Partial monosomy 7p may also be characterized by additional physical features, such as growth deficiency, musculoskeletal abnormalities, genital defects, structural malformations of the heart that are present at birth (congenital heart defects), and/or other abnormalities. In addition, some affected individuals may have varying degrees of mental retardation and delays in the acquisition of skills requiring the coordination of mental and motor activities (psychomotor delays). Normal intelligence has also been reported. In most cases, chromosome 7, partial monosomy 7p appears to result from spontaneous (de novo) errors very early in embryonic development that occur for unknown reasons.

The following organizations may provide additional information and support:
AboutFace USA
American Heart Association
The Arc (A National Organization on Mental Retardation)
Children's Craniofacial Association
Chromosome Deletion Outreach, Inc.
Congenital Heart Anomalies, Support, Education, & Resources
Craniofacial Foundation of America
FACES: The National Craniofacial Association
March of Dimes Birth Defects Foundation
Support Organization for Trisomy 18, 13, and Related Disorders
UNIQUE—Rare Chromosome Disorder Support Group

246   Chromosome 8, Monosomy 8p2

Synonyms
8p-Syndrome, Partial
Chromosome 8, 8p Deletion Syndrome, Partial
Chromosome 8, Partial Deletion of Short Arm
Chromosome 8, Partial Monosomy 8p2
Del(8p) Syndrome, Partial
Distal 8p Monosomy
Partial 8p Monosomy
Terminal 8p-Syndrome (8p21 to 8p23-pter), Included

Chromosome 8, monosomy 8p2 is a rare chromosomal disorder characterized by deletion (monosomy) of a portion of the eighth chromosome. Associated symptoms and findings may vary greatly in range and severity from case to case. However, common features include growth deficiency; mental retardation; malformations of the skull and facial (craniofacial) region, such as a small head (microcephaly) and vertical skin folds that may cover the eyes' inner corners (epicanthal folds); heart (cardiac) abnormalities; and/or genital defects in affected males. Additional craniofacial features may also be present that tend to become less apparent with age, such as a short, broad nose; a low, wide nasal bridge; and/or a small jaw (micrognathia). In most cases, chromosome 8, monosomy 8p2 appears to result from spontaneous (de novo) errors very early in embryonic development that occur for unknown reasons.

The following organizations may provide additional information and support:
American Heart Association
The Arc (A National Organization on Mental Retardation)
Chromosome Deletion Outreach, Inc.
Congenital Heart Anomalies, Support, Education, & Resources
Craniofacial Foundation of America
March of Dimes Birth Defects Foundation
UNIQUE—Rare Chromosome Disorder Support Group

247   Chromosome 9, Partial Monosomy 9p

Synonyms
9p Partial Monosomy
9p-Syndrome, Partial
Chromosome 9, Partial Monosomy 9p22
Chromosome 9, Partial Monosomy 9p22-pter
Del(9p) Syndrome, Partial
Deletion 9p Syndrome, Partial
Distal 9p-Syndrome
Distal Monosomy 9p
Monosomy 9p, Partial
Partial Deletion of Short Arm of Chromosome 9

Chromosome 9, partial monosomy 9p is a rare chromosomal disorder in which there is deletion (monosomy) of a portion of the 9th chromosome. Characteristic symptoms and findings include mental retardation; distinctive malformations of the skull and facial (craniofacial) region, such as an abnormally shaped forehead (i.e., trigonocephaly), upwardly slanting eyelid folds (palpebral fissures), and unusually flat midfacial regions (midfacial hypoplasia); structural malformations of the heart (congenital heart defects); genital defects in affected males and females; and/or additional physical abnormalities. In most cases, chromosome 9, partial monosomy 9p appears to result from spontaneous (de novo) errors very early in embryonic development that occur for unknown reasons (sporadically).

The following organizations may provide additional information and support:
AboutFace USA
American Heart Association
The Arc (A National Organization on Mental Retardation)
Children's Craniofacial Association
Chromosome 9P-Network
Chromosome Deletion Outreach, Inc.
Congenital Heart Anomalies, Support, Education, & Resources
Craniofacial Foundation of America
March of Dimes Birth Defects Foundation
UNIQUE—Rare Chromosome Disorder Support Group

248 Chromosome 9 Ring

Synonyms
R9
Ring 9
Ring 9, Chromosome

Chromosome 9 ring is a rare disorder in which there is loss (deletion) of chromosomal material from both ends of the 9th chromosome and joining of the ends to form a ring. Associated symptoms and findings may vary, depending upon the amount and location of lost chromosomal material and other factors. Some affected individuals may have variable malformations of the skull and facial (craniofacial) region. However, in others with the chromosomal abnormality, such features may not be apparent. Chromosome 9 ring may also be characterized by additional physical features in some cases, including growth retardation, heart defects, genital abnormalities, and/or other findings. In addition, many affected individuals have moderate to severe mental retardation; however, in some instances, intelligence may be in the low normal range. Chromosome 9 ring usually appears to result from spontaneous (de novo) errors very early in the development of the embryo that occur for unknown reasons (sporadically).

The following organizations may provide additional information and support:
AboutFace USA
American Heart Association
The Arc (A National Organization on Mental Retardation)

Children's Craniofacial Association
Chromosome 9P-Network
Chromosome Deletion Outreach, Inc.
Congenital Heart Anomalies, Support, Education, & Resources
Craniofacial Foundation of America
March of Dimes Birth Defects Foundation
UNIQUE—Rare Chromosome Disorder Support Group

249 Chromosome 9, Tetrasomy 9p

Synonyms
Chromosome 9, Tetrasomy 9p Mosaicism
Mosaic Tetrasomy 9p
Tetrasomy 9p
Tetrasomy, Short Arm of Chromosome 9

Chromosome 9, tetrasomy 9p is a very rare chromosomal disorder in which the short arm of the ninth chromosome (9p) appears four times (tetrasomy) rather than twice in all or some cells of the body. Individuals with a normal chromosomal make-up (karyotype) have two 9th chromosomes, both of which have a short arm ("9p") and a long arm ("9q"). However, in individuals with chromosome 9, tetrasomy 9p, four short arms (9ps) are present in cells rather than the normal two. The symptoms of chromosome 9, tetrasomy 9p may vary greatly in range and severity from case to case. Associated abnormalities may include mild growth retardation, moderate to severe delay in the attainment of skills requiring the coordination of muscular and mental activities (psychomotor retardation), and/or moderate to severe mental retardation. In addition, the disorder may be characterized by various physical abnormalities, such as malformations of the skull and facial (craniofacial) region, abnormalities of the hands and fingers, skeletal malformations, and/or heart (cardiac) defects. Chromosome 9, tetrasomy 9p appears to result from spontaneous (de novo) errors very early in embryonic development that occur for unknown reasons (sporadically).

The following organizations may provide additional information and support:
American Heart Association
Support Organization for Trisomy 18, 13, and Related Disorders
Trisomy 9 International Parent Support (9TIPS)
UNIQUE—Rare Chromosome Disorder Support Group

250 Chromosome 9, Trisomy 9p (Multiple Variants)

Synonyms

Chromosome 9, Complete Trisomy 9P
Chromosome 9, Partial Trisomy 9P, Included
Chromosome 9, Trisomy 9pter-q11-13, Included
Chromosome 9, Trisomy 9pter-q22-32, Included
Dup(9p) Syndrome
Duplication 9p Syndrome
Rethore Syndrome (obsolete)
Trisomy 9P Syndrome (Partial), Included

This disease entry was made possible due to the generosity of the Robert Lee and Clara Guthrie Patterson Trust, through grant funds provided for the National Organization for Rare Disorders Pediatric Rare Disease Database Project. Chromosome 9, trisomy 9p is a rare chromosomal syndrome in which a portion of the 9th chromosome appears three times (trisomy) rather than twice in cells of the body. The trisomy may involve a portion of the short arm (9p), the entire short arm, or the short arm and a portion of the long arm (9q) of chromosome 9. (Each chromosome contains a short arm known as "p" and a long arm designated as "q.") Evidence suggests that, in many cases, associated symptoms and findings may be relatively similar among affected infants despite differing lengths of the trisomic (duplicated) segment of 9p. However, in those with larger trisomies (e.g., extending to middle or end [distal] regions of 9q), additional features may also be present that appear to correlate with the extent of the duplication. Virtually all individuals with trisomy 9p are affected by mental retardation and distinctive malformations of the skull and facial (craniofacial) region. In some instances, additional physical abnormalities may also be present, such as other skeletal defects, structural malformations of the heart that are present at birth (congenital heart defects), and/or other findings. In some cases, the trisomy appears to result from a balanced chromosomal rearrangement in one of the parents; in others, it is thought to arise from spontaneous (de novo) errors very early in embryonic development that occur for unknown reasons (sporadically).

The following organizations may provide additional information and support:
AboutFace USA
American Heart Association

The Arc (A National Organization on Mental Retardation)
Congenital Heart Anomalies, Support, Education, & Resources
Craniofacial Foundation of America
March of Dimes Birth Defects Foundation
SOFTWA (Support Organisation for Trisomy and Related Disorders)
Support Organization for Trisomy 13/18 and Related Disorders, UK
Support Organization for Trisomy 18, 13, and Related Disorders
Trisomy 9 International Parent Support (9TIPS)
UNIQUE—Rare Chromosome Disorder Support Group

251 Chromosome 9, Trisomy Mosaic

Synonyms

Trisomy 9 (Complete Trisomy 9 Syndrome), Included
Trisomy 9 Mosaic
Trisomy 9 Mosaicism
Trisomy 9 Mosaicism Syndrome

Chromosome 9, trisomy mosaic, also known as trisomy 9 mosaicism syndrome, is a rare chromosomal disorder in which the entire 9th chromosome appears three times (trisomy) rather than twice in some cells of the body. The term "mosaic" indicates that some cells contain the extra chromosome 9, while others have the normal chromosomal pair. Associated symptoms and findings may vary greatly in range and severity, depending on the percentage of cells with the extra chromosome. However, common features include growth deficiency before birth (intrauterine growth retardation); mental retardation; structural malformations of the heart that are present at birth (congenital heart defects); and/or distinctive abnormalities of the skull and facial (craniofacial) region, such as a sloping forehead, a bulbous nose, short eyelid folds (palpebral fissures), deeply set eyes, and/or low-set, malformed ears. The syndrome may also be characterized by musculoskeletal, genital, kidney (renal), and/or additional physical abnormalities. Chromosome 9, trisomy mosaic may be caused by errors during the division of a parent's reproductive cells (meiosis) or during the division of body tissue cells (somatic cells) early in the development of the embryo (mitosis).

The following organizations may provide additional information and support:
AboutFace USA

American Heart Association
The Arc (A National Organization on Mental Retardation)
Congenital Heart Anomalies, Support, Education, & Resources
Craniofacial Foundation of America
March of Dimes Birth Defects Foundation
SOFTWA (Support Organisation for Trisomy and Related Disorders)
Support Organization for Trisomy 13/18 and Related Disorders, UK
Support Organization for Trisomy 18, 13, and Related Disorders
Trisomy 9 International Parent Support (9TIPS)
UNIQUE—Rare Chromosome Disorder Support Group

252 Chromosome 10, Distal Trisomy 10q

Synonyms

Chromosome 10, Partial Trisomy 10q24-qter
Chromosome 10, Trisomy 10q2
Distal Duplication 10q
Distal Trisomy 10q Syndrome
Dup(10q) Syndrome

Chromosome 10, distal trisomy 10q is an extremely rare chromosomal disorder in which the end (distal) portion of the long arm (q) of one chromosome 10 (10q) appears three times (trisomy) rather than twice in cells of the body. The disorder is characterized by unusually slow growth before and after birth (prenatal and postnatal growth retardation); abnormally diminished muscle tone (hypotonia); severe mental retardation; and severe delays in the acquisition of skills requiring coordination of mental and muscular activities (psychomotor retardation). Affected infants and children may also have distinctive malformations of the head and facial (craniofacial) area; defects of the hands and/or feet; and/or skeletal, heart (cardiac), kidney (renal), and/or respiratory (pulmonary) abnormalities. The range and severity of symptoms and physical findings may vary from case to case, depending upon the exact length and location of the duplicated portion of chromosome 10q. In most cases, chromosome 10, distal trisomy 10q is due to a chromosomal balanced translocation in one of the parents.

The following organizations may provide additional information and support:
Children's Craniofacial Association
Congenital Heart Anomalies, Support, Education, & Resources

Craniofacial Foundation of America
FACES: The National Craniofacial Association
Forward Face, Inc.
National Craniofacial Foundation
NIH/National Heart, Lung and Blood Institute Information Center
NIH/National Kidney and Urologic Diseases Information Clearinghouse
Support Organization for Trisomy 18, 13, and Related Disorders
UNIQUE—Rare Chromosome Disorder Support Group

253 Chromosome 10, Monosomy 10p

Synonyms

10p Deletion Syndrome (Partial)
Chromosome 10, 10p-Partial
Chromosome 10, Partial Deletion (short arm)

Chromosome 10, monosomy 10p is a rare chromosomal disorder in which the end (distal) portion of the short arm (p) of chromosome 10 is missing (deleted or monosomic). The range and severity of symptoms and findings may be variable, depending upon the exact size or location of the deletion on chromosome 10p. However, associated features often include severe mental retardation; growth delays after birth (postnatal growth retardation); distinctive malformations of the skull and facial (craniofacial) region; a short neck; and/or structural defects of the heart that are present at birth (congenital heart defects). Several cases have also been reported in which affected individuals have some features of DiGeorge syndrome (DGS). DGS is a congenital disorder characterized by underdevelopment or absence of the thymus and parathyroid glands, potentially causing abnormalities of the immune system, deficient production of parathyroid hormone (hypoparathyroidism), a heart defect, and associated findings. In many cases, chromosome 10, monosomy 10p appears to occur spontaneously (de novo) for unknown reasons.

The following organizations may provide additional information and support:
AboutFace USA
Alexander Graham Bell Association for the Deaf, Inc.
American Heart Association
The Arc (A National Organization on Mental Retardation)
Children's Craniofacial Association
Chromosome Deletion Outreach, Inc.
Craniofacial Foundation of America

Immune Deficiency Foundation
March of Dimes Birth Defects Foundation
NIH/National Digestive Diseases Information Clearinghouse
NIH/National Institute on Deafness and Other Communication Disorders (Balance)
UNIQUE—Rare Chromosome Disorder Support Group

254   Chromosome 11, Partial Monosomy 11q

Synonyms

11q-Syndrome, Partial
Deletion 11q Syndrome, Partial
Distal 11q Monosomy
Distal 11q-Syndrome
Jacobsen Syndrome
JBS
Monosomy 11q, Partial
Partial Monosomy of Long Arm of Chromosome 11

Chromosome 11, partial monosomy 11q is a rare chromosomal disorder in which a portion of the long arm (q) of chromosome 11 is missing (deleted or monosomic). The range and severity of symptoms may vary, depending upon the exact size and location of the deletion on 11q. Chromosome 11, partial monosomy 11q may be characterized by abnormally slow growth before and after birth (prenatal and postnatal growth retardation), mental retardation, and/or moderate to severe delays in the acquisition of skills requiring the coordination of mental and muscular activity (psychomotor retardation). Characteristic physical abnormalities may include malformations of the head and facial (craniofacial) area, abnormalities of the eyes, malformations of the hands and/or feet, and/or defects of the heart. The exact cause of chromosome 11, partial monosomy 11q is not fully understood.

The following organizations may provide additional information and support:
11Q Research and Resource Group
American Speech-Language-Hearing Association
Children's Craniofacial Association
Chromosome Deletion Outreach, Inc.
Congenital Heart Anomalies, Support, Education, & Resources
Craniofacial Foundation of America
European Chromosome 11q Network
FACES: The National Craniofacial Association
National Craniofacial Foundation
NIH/National Heart, Lung and Blood Institute Information Center

NIH/National Institute on Deafness and Other Communication Disorders Information Clearinghouse
UNIQUE—Rare Chromosome Disorder Support Group

255   Chromosome 11, Partial Trisomy 11q

Synonyms

11q Partial Trisomy
Chromosome 11, Partial Trisomy 11q13-qter
Chromosome 11, Partial Trisomy 11q21-qter
Chromosome 11, Partial Trisomy 11q23-qter
Distal Trisomy 11q
Partial Trisomy 11q
Trisomy 11q, Partial

Chromosome 11, partial trisomy 11q is a rare chromosomal disorder in which the end (distal) portion of the long arm (q) of the 11th chromosome appears three times (trisomy) rather than twice in cells of the body. Although associated symptoms and findings may vary, the disorder is often associated with delayed growth before and after birth (prenatal and postnatal growth retardation); varying degrees of mental retardation; distinctive abnormalities of the skull and facial (craniofacial) region; and/or other features. Chromosomal analysis is necessary for a definite diagnosis.

The following organizations may provide additional information and support:
AboutFace USA
American Heart Association
The Arc (A National Organization on Mental Retardation)
Children's Craniofacial Association
Craniofacial Foundation of America
European Chromosome 11q Network
March of Dimes Birth Defects Foundation
Support Organization for Trisomy 18, 13, and Related Disorders
UNIQUE—Rare Chromosome Disorder Support Group

256   Chromosome 13, Partial Monosomy 13q

Synonyms

13q-Syndrome, Partial
Deletion 13q Syndrome, Partial
Monosomy 13q, Partial
Partial Monosomy of the Long Arm of Chromosome 13

Chromosome 13, partial monosomy 13q is a rare chromosomal disorder in which a portion of the long arm (q) of chromosome 13 is missing (deleted or monosomic). The range and severity of symptoms may vary greatly, depending upon the exact size and location of the deletion on 13q. Chromosome 13, partial monosomy 13q is usually apparent at birth and may be characterized by low birth weight, malformations of the head and facial (craniofacial) area, abnormalities of the eyes, defects of the hands and/or feet, genital malformations in affected males, and/or additional physical abnormalities. Affected infants and children may also exhibit delays in the acquisition of skills requiring the coordination of mental and muscular activity (psychomotor retardation) as well as varying degrees of mental retardation. In the majority of cases, chromosome 13, partial monosomy 13q appears to occur randomly, for no apparent reason (sporadic).

The following organizations may provide additional information and support:
American Heart Association
The Arc (A National Organization on Mental Retardation)
Children's Craniofacial Association
Chromosome Deletion Outreach, Inc.
Congenital Heart Anomalies, Support, Education, & Resources
Craniofacial Foundation of America
FACES: The National Craniofacial Association
Institute for Families
International Foundation for Functional Gastrointestinal Disorders
March of Dimes Birth Defects Foundation
National Cancer Institute
National Craniofacial Foundation
NIH/National Eye Institute
UNIQUE—Rare Chromosome Disorder Support Group

257　Chromosome 14 Ring

Synonyms
Ring 14
Ring Chromosome 14
R14

Chromosome 14 ring is a rare disorder that is characterized by abnormalities of the 14th chromosome. Affected infants and children typically have delays in the acquisition of skills that require the coordination of physical and mental activities (psychomotor delays), mental retardation, growth delays, and episodes of uncontrolled electrical activity in the brain (seizures). The disorder is also characterized by distinctive abnormalities of the head and facial (craniofacial) area. Such abnormalities may include an unusually small head (microcephaly) with a high forehead; an elongated face; widely spaced eyes (ocular hypertelorism); a thin upper lip; a flat nasal bridge with a prominent nasal tip; and large, low-set ears.

The following organizations may provide additional information and support:
Associazione Internazionale Ring 14 (Ring 14 International Support Group)
Chromosome Deletion Outreach, Inc.
Epilepsy Foundation
UNIQUE—Rare Chromosome Disorder Support Group

258　Chromosome 14, Trisomy Mosaic

Synonyms
Trisomy 14 Mosaic
Trisomy 14 Mosaicism Syndrome

Chromosome 14, trisomy mosaic is a rare chromosomal disorder in which chromosome 14 appears three times (trisomy) rather than twice in some cells of the body. The term "mosaic" indicates that some cells contain the extra chromosome 14, whereas others have the normal chromosomal pair. The disorder may be characterized by growth delays before birth (intrauterine growth retardation); failure to grow and gain weight at the expected rate (failure to thrive) during infancy; delays in the acquisition of skills requiring the coordination of mental and physical abilities (psychomotor delays); and mental retardation. Affected infants also have distinctive abnormalities of the head and facial (craniofacial) region, such as a prominent forehead; deeply set, widely spaced eyes; a broad nasal bridge; and low-set, malformed ears. Additional craniofacial abnormalities may include an unusually small lower jaw (micrognathia); a large mouth and thick lips; and incomplete closure or abnormally high arching of the roof of the mouth (palate). Many affected infants also have structural malformations of the heart (e.g., tetralogy of Fallot). In some cases, additional physical abnormalities may also be present.

The following organizations may provide additional information and support:
American Heart Association
The Arc (A National Organization on Mental Retardation)

March of Dimes Birth Defects Foundation
Support Organization for Trisomy 13/18 and Related Disorders, UK
Support Organization for Trisomy 18, 13, and Related Disorders
UNIQUE—Rare Chromosome Disorder Support Group

259   Chromosome 15, Distal Trisomy 15q

Synonyms

Chromosome 15, Trisomy 15q2
Distal Duplication 15q
Partial Duplication 15q Syndrome

Chromosome 15, distal trisomy 15q is an extremely rare chromosomal disorder in which the end (distal) portion of the long arm (q) of the 15th chromosome (15q) appears three times (trisomy) rather than twice in cells of the body. The disorder is characterized by growth delays before and/or after birth (prenatal and/or postnatal growth retardation); mental retardation; and/or distinctive malformations of the head and facial (craniofacial) area. Additional abnormalities typically include an unusually short neck; malformations of the fingers and/or toes; abnormal sideways curvature of the spine (scoliosis) and/or other skeletal malformations; genital abnormalities, particularly in affected males; and/or, in some cases, heart (cardiac) defects. The range and severity of symptoms and physical findings may vary from case to case, depending upon the length and location of the duplicated portion of chromosome 15q. In most cases, chromosome 15, distal trisomy 15q is due to a chromosomal balanced translocation in one of the parents.

The following organizations may provide additional information and support:
American Heart Association
The Arc (A National Organization on Mental Retardation)
Children's Craniofacial Association
Congenital Heart Anomalies, Support, Education, & Resources
March of Dimes Birth Defects Foundation
National Craniofacial Foundation
National Institute of Neurological Disorders and Stroke (NINDS)
Support Organization for Trisomy 18, 13, and Related Disorders
UNIQUE—Rare Chromosome Disorder Support Group

260   Chromosome 15 Ring

Synonyms

Ring 15
Ring 15, Chromosome
Ring 15, Chromosome (mosaic pattern)
R15

Chromosome 15 ring results from loss (deletion) of genetic material from both ends of the 15th chromosome and a joining of the ends to form a ring. Chromosomes are found in the nucleus of all body cells. They carry the genetic characteristics of each individual. Pairs of human chromosomes are numbered from 1 through 22, with an unequal 23rd pair of X and Y chromosomes for males and two X chromosomes for females. Each chromosome has a short arm designated as "p" and a long arm identified by the letter "q." Chromosomes are further subdivided into bands that are numbered. In individuals with chromosome 15 ring, the variability of associated symptoms and findings may depend upon the amount and location of genetic material lost from the 15th chromosome, the stability of the ring chromosome during subsequent cellular divisions, or other factors. Evidence suggests that the clinical features seen in chromosome 15 ring appear to result from deletions of genetic material from the long arm (q) of chromosome 15 (known as "monosomy 15q"), with the ring chromosome typically replacing a normal 15th chromosome. In addition, in some cases, only a certain percentage of an individual's cells may contain chromosome 15 ring, while other cells may have a normal chromosomal makeup (a finding known as "chromosomal mosaicism"), potentially affecting the variability of associated symptoms and findings. In most cases, chromosome 15 ring appears to be caused by spontaneous (de novo) errors very early in embryonic development. In such cases, the parents of the affected child usually have normal chromosomes and a relatively low risk of having another child with the chromosomal abnormality. However, there have been rare cases in which a parent of an affected individual also has chromosome 15 ring. In such instances, the chances are greater of having another child with the chromosomal abnormality. In addition, a few cases have been reported in which chromosome 15 ring has been the result of a "balanced translocation" in one of the parents. Translocations occur when regions of certain chromosomes break off and are rearranged, resulting in shifting of genetic material and an altered set of chromosomes. If a chromosomal rearrangement is balanced, meaning that it consists of an altered but balanced set of chromosomes, it is usually harmless to the carrier. However, such a chromosomal rearrangement may be associated with an increased risk of abnormal chromosomal development in the carrier's offspring. Chromosomal analysis and genetic counseling are typically recommended for parents of an affected child to help confirm or exclude the presence of chromosome 15 ring, potential mosaicism, or a balanced translocation in one of the parents. Many individuals with chromosome 15 ring have some features similar to those associated with Russell-Silver syndrome (RSS), which is a genetic disorder characterized by growth deficiency and short stature, distinctive facial abnormalities, and other features. In some of these cases, genetic analysis has indicated that the prenatal and postnatal growth retardation associated with chromosome 15 ring (and potentially suggestive of RSS) may result from deletion of a gene known as the insulin-like growth factor I receptor (IGF1R) gene, which has been mapped to the long arm of chromosome 15 (15q25-q26).

The following organizations may provide additional information and support:
AboutFace USA
American Heart Association
The Arc (A National Organization on Mental Retardation)
Children's Craniofacial Association
Chromosome Deletion Outreach, Inc.
Craniofacial Foundation of America
Human Growth Foundation
Little People of America, Inc.
March of Dimes Birth Defects Foundation
UNIQUE—Rare Chromosome Disorder Support Group

261 Chromosome 18, Monosomy 18p

Synonyms
18p Deletion Syndrome
18p-Syndrome
Del(18p) Syndrome
Monosomy 18p Syndrome
Short Arm 18 Deletion Syndrome

Chromosome 18, monosomy 18p is a rare chromosomal disorder in which all or part of the short arm (p) of chromosome 18 is deleted

(monosomic). The disorder is typically characterized by short stature, variable degrees of mental retardation, speech delays, malformations of the skull and facial (craniofacial) region, and/or additional physical abnormalities. Associated craniofacial defects may vary greatly in range and severity from case to case. However, such features commonly include an unusually small head (microcephaly); a broad, flat nose; a "carp-shaped" mouth; large, protruding ears; widely spaced eyes (ocular hypertelorism); and/or other abnormalities. Rarely (i.e., in about 10 percent of cases), monosomy 18p may be associated with holoprosencephaly, a condition in which the forebrain (prosencephalon) fails to divide properly during embryonic development. Holoprosencephaly may result in varying degrees of mental retardation, other neurologic findings, and/or extremely variable midline facial defects, such as the presence of a single, central front tooth (maxillary incisor); closely spaced eyes (hypotelorism); an abnormal groove in the upper lip (cleft lip); incomplete closure of the roof of the mouth (cleft palate); and/or, in severe cases, absence of the nose and/or cyclopia. Cyclopia is characterized by fusion of the eye cavities (orbits) into a single cavity containing one eye. In some individuals with monosomy 18p, additional physical abnormalities may be present. Such findings commonly include a short, webbed neck; a broad chest with widely spaced nipples; relatively small hands and feet; and/or an unusually small penis (micropenis) and/or undescended testes (cryptorchidism) in affected males. Monosomy 18p is usually caused by spontaneous (de novo) errors very early in the development of the embryo that appear to occur randomly for unknown reasons (sporadically).

The following organizations may provide additional information and support:
AboutFace USA
American Heart Association
The Arc (A National Organization on Mental Retardation)
Children's Craniofacial Association
Chromosome 18 Registry & Research Society
Chromosome Deletion Outreach, Inc.
Craniofacial Foundation of America
Holoprosencephaly Support Group
Independent Holoprosencephaly Support Site
March of Dimes Birth Defects Foundation
Support Organization for Trisomy 18, 13, and Related Disorders

262   Chromosome 18 Ring

Synonyms

Ring 18

Ring Chromosome 18

R18

Chromosome 18 ring is a rare disorder in which there is loss (deletion) of genetic material from one or both ends of the 18th chromosome and joining of the chromosomal ends to form a ring. Associated symptoms and findings may vary greatly in range and severity from case to case, depending upon the amount and location of lost genetic material and other factors. A ring may also be formed without the loss of any genetic material. However, many individuals with the disorder are affected by mental retardation; low muscle tone (hypotonia); growth retardation; repeated infections during the first years of life; and/or malformations of the skull and facial (craniofacial) region. Such craniofacial features often include an unusually small head (microcephaly), widely spaced eyes (ocular hypertelorism), and/or vertical skin folds that cover the eyes' inner corners (epicanthal folds). Chromosome 18 ring is usually caused by spontaneous (de novo) errors very early in the development of the embryo that appear to occur randomly for unknown reasons (sporadically).

The following organizations may provide additional information and support:
AboutFace USA
The Arc (A National Organization on Mental Retardation)
Children's Craniofacial Association
Chromosome 18 Registry & Research Society
Chromosome Deletion Outreach, Inc.
Craniofacial Foundation of America
Ear Anomalies Reconstructed: Atresia/Microtia Support Group
March of Dimes Birth Defects Foundation
NIH/National Eye Institute
NIH/National Institute on Deafness and Other Communication Disorders Information Clearinghouse
UNIQUE—Rare Chromosome Disorder Support Group

263   Chromosome 18, Tetrasomy 18p

Synonym

Tetrasomy, Short Arm of Chromosome 18

Chromosome 18, tetrasomy 18p is a very rare chromosomal disorder in which the short arm of the 18th chromosome (18p) appears four times (tetrasomy) rather than twice in cells of the body. Individuals with a normal chromosomal make-up (karyotype) have two 18th chromosomes, both of which have a short arm ("18p") and a long arm ("18q"). However, in individuals with chromosome 18, tetrasomy 18p, four short arms (18ps) are present in cells of the body rather than the normal two. The symptoms of chromosome 18, tetrasomy 18p may vary from case to case. Many affected individuals have abnormalities of the head and facial (craniofacial) area; malformations of the spine, hands, and/or feet; neuromuscular abnormalities, such as increased muscle tone (hypertonia), increased reflex reactions (hyperreflexia), and difficulty coordinating movement; kidney (renal) malformations; and/or additional physical abnormalities. In addition, children and adults with chromosome 18, tetrasomy 18p often exhibit moderate to severe mental retardation, limitations in speech, and/or behavioral abnormalities. In most cases, chromosome 18, tetrasomy 18p is the result of a spontaneous (de novo) genetic change (mutation) early in embryonic development that occurs for unknown reasons (sporadic).

The following organizations may provide additional information and support:
AboutFace USA
The Arc (A National Organization on Mental Retardation)
Children's Craniofacial Association
Chromosome 18 Registry & Research Society
Craniofacial Foundation of America
March of Dimes Birth Defects Foundation
National Kidney Foundation
NIH/National Kidney and Urologic Diseases Information Clearinghouse
Support Organization for Trisomy 18, 13, and Related Disorders
UNIQUE—Rare Chromosome Disorder Support Group

264   Chromosome 18q-Syndrome

Synonyms

18q Deletion Syndrome

18q-Syndrome

Chromosome 18 Long Arm Deletion Syndrome

Chromosome 18, Monosomy 18q

Del(18q) Syndrome

Monosomy 18q Syndrome

Chromosome 18q-syndrome (also known as chromosome 18, monosomy 18q) is a rare chromosomal disorder in which there is deletion of part of the long arm (q) of chromosome 18. Associated symptoms and findings may vary greatly in range and severity from case to case. However, characteristic features include short stature; mental retardation; poor muscle tone (hypotonia); malformations of the hands and feet; and abnormalities of the skull and facial (craniofacial) region, such as a small head (microcephaly), a "carp-shaped" mouth, deeply set eyes, prominent ears, and/or unusually flat, underdeveloped midfacial regions (midfacial hypoplasia). Some affected individuals may also have visual abnormalities, hearing impairment, genital malformations, structural heart defects, and/or other physical abnormalities. Chromosome 18q-syndrome usually appears to result from spontaneous (de novo) errors very early during embryonic development that occur for unknown reasons (sporadically).

The following organizations may provide additional information and support:
AboutFace USA
Alexander Graham Bell Association for the Deaf, Inc.
American Heart Association
The Arc (A National Organization on Mental Retardation)
Children's Craniofacial Association
Chromosome 18 Registry & Research Society
Chromosome Deletion Outreach, Inc.
Congenital Heart Anomalies, Support, Education, & Resources
Craniofacial Foundation of America
March of Dimes Birth Defects Foundation
National Association for Parents of Children with Visual Impairments (NAPVI)
National Association for Visually Handicapped
NIH/National Eye Institute
NIH/National Institute on Deafness and Other Communication Disorders Information Clearinghouse
UNIQUE—Rare Chromosome Disorder Support Group

265 Chromosome 21 Ring

Synonyms
Ring 21
Ring 21, Chromosome
R21

Chromosome 21 ring is a rare chromosomal disorder in which the affected infant has a breakage of chromosome 21 at both ends, and the ends of the chromosome join together to form a ring. The amount of genetic material lost at the two ends of the chromosome may vary. As a result, an infant with very little absent genetic material may have no apparent symptoms while an infant with a significant part of the chromosomal ends missing may have many symptoms. When symptoms of the disorder are present, the affected infant may have mental retardation as well as abnormalities of the face, eyes, skeleton, and/or internal organs.

The following organizations may provide additional information and support:
Chromosome Deletion Outreach, Inc.
UNIQUE—Rare Chromosome Disorder Support Group

266 Chromosome 22 Ring

Synonyms
Ring 22
Ring 22, Chromosome
R22

Chromosome 22 ring is a rare disorder characterized by abnormalities of the 22nd chromosome. Associated symptoms and findings may be extremely variable from case to case. However, the disorder is typically associated with moderate to severe mental retardation. Some affected individuals may also have relatively mild, nonspecific physical (i e., dysplastic) features, whereas others may have more distinctive, potentially severe physical abnormalities. According to reports in the medical literature, common findings include diminished muscle tone (hypotonia) and motor incoordination; an unsteady manner of walking (gait); pronounced verbal delays; and/or certain malformations of the skull and facial (craniofacial) region. Such craniofacial abnormalities may include an unusually small head (microcephaly); vertical skin folds that may cover the eyes' inner corners (epicanthal folds); unusually large ears; and/or other malformations. Chromosome 22 ring is usually caused by spontaneous or "de novo" errors very early in the development of the embryo that appear to occur randomly for unknown reasons.

The following organizations may provide additional information and support:
The Arc (A National Organization on Mental Retardation)
Chromosome 22 Central
Chromosome Deletion Outreach, Inc.
March of Dimes Birth Defects Foundation
Ring Chromosome 22 E-Mail Discussion List
UNIQUE—Rare Chromosome Disorder Support Group

267   Chromosome 22, Trisomy Mosaic

Synonyms

Trisomy 22 Mosaic
Trisomy 22 Mosaicism Syndrome

Chromosome 22, trisomy mosaic is a rare chromosomal disorder in which chromosome 22 appears three times (trisomy) rather than twice in some cells of the body. The term "mosaic" indicates that some cells contain the extra chromosome 22, whereas others have the normal chromosomal pair. The range and severity of associated symptoms and findings may vary, depending upon the percentage of cells with the chromosomal abnormality. However, characteristic features typically include growth delays, mental retardation, unequal development of the two sides of the body (hemidystrophy), and webbing of the neck. Affected individuals may also have abnormal outward deviation of the elbows upon extension (cubitus valgus), multiple pigmented moles or birthmarks (nevi), distinctive malformations of the head and facial (craniofacial) area, and other physical abnormalities.

The following organizations may provide additional information and support:
American Heart Association
The Arc (A National Organization on Mental Retardation)
March of Dimes Birth Defects Foundation
Support Organization for Trisomy 13/18 and Related Disorders, UK
Support Organization for Trisomy 18, 13, and Related Disorders
UNIQUE—Rare Chromosome Disorder Support Group

268   Chronic Fatigue Syndrome

Synonyms

CFIDS
CFS
Chronic Fatigue Immune Dysfunction Syndrome

Chronic fatigue syndrome (CFS) is a disorder characterized by profound fatigue and other related symptoms. Standards for the diagnosis of CFS have been defined by researchers at the Centers for Disease Control and Prevention (CDC). These include excessive fatigue that does not respond to bedrest, combined with four or more of the following symptoms: substantial impairment in short-term memory or concentration; sore throat; tender lymph nodes; muscle pain; pain in multiple joints without redness or stiffness; headaches of a new type, pattern or severity; unrefreshing sleep; and a general feeling of ill health (malaise) for up to 24 hours after exertion. The onset of these symptoms is usually sudden, sometimes following a flu-like illness. According to the CDC, the profound fatigue must last for at least 6 months in order for the diagnosis to be confirmed. The syndrome may persist for months or years, and disappear without treatment. The many symptoms of chronic fatigue syndrome do not always occur with the same degree of severity or at the same time. There are usually instances when symptoms may disappear for periods of time. Scientists believe chronic fatigue syndrome is not contagious, and laboratory tests (blood, urine, etc.) are of little value in diagnosing the syndrome.

The following organizations may provide additional information and support:
American Academy of Allergy, Asthma and Immunology
Autoimmune Information Network, Inc
Centers for Disease Control and Prevention
CF Alliance
CFIDS Association of America, Inc.
National CFIDS Foundation, Inc.
National Chronic Fatigue Syndrome & Fibromyalgia Association
New Horizons Un-Limited, Inc.
NIH/National Institute of Allergy and Infectious Diseases

269   Chronic Fatigue Syndrome/Myalgic Encephalomyelitis

Synonyms

Akureyri Disease
Benign Myalgic Encephalomyelitis
CFS
Epidemic Myalgic Encephalomyelitis
Epidemic Neuromyasthenia
Iceland Disease
ME
Raphe Nucleus Encephalopathy
Royal Free Disease
Tapanui Flu

Until the late 1980s, myalgic encephalomyelitis was thought to be a distinct, infectious disorder affecting the central, peripheral and autonomic nervous systems and the muscles. Its major symptom was fatigue to the point of extended periods of exhaustion. A group of experts studying the Epstein-Barr virus first published strict criteria for the symptoms and physical signs of chronic fatigue syndrome in 1988. This case definition was further refined in 1994. The Fact Sheet for CFS published by the National Institutes of Allergy and Infectious Diseases of the National Institutes of Health states that "[T]oday, CFS is also known as myalgic encephalomyelitis, postviral fatigue syndrome, and chronic fatigue and immune dysfunction syndrome." ME/CFS is now recognized as part of a range of illnesses that have fatigue as a major symptom. ME/CFS is not rare. The CDC estimates that there are as many as 500,000 persons in the United States who have CFS-like symptoms. However, the disorder remains debilitating, complex and mysterious in origin, natural history, understanding and treatment.

The following organizations may provide additional information and support:
Centers for Disease Control and Prevention
CF Alliance
CFIDS Association of America, Inc.
MAME, Inc. (Mothers Against Myalgic Encephalomyelitis)
ME Association
Myalgic Encephalopathy Association
National CFIDS Foundation, Inc.
National Chronic Fatigue Syndrome & Fibromyalgia Association
NIH/National Institute of Allergy and Infectious Diseases

270 Chronic Inflammatory Demyelinating Polyneuropathy

Synonyms
Chronic Relapsing Polyneuropathy
CIDP

Chronic inflammatory demyelinating polyneuropathy (CIDP) is a rare neurological disorder in which there is swelling of nerve roots and destruction of the fatty protective covering (myelin sheath) over the nerves. This disorder causes weakness, paralysis and/or impairment in motor function, especially of the arms and legs (limbs). Sensory loss may also be present causing numbness, tingling, or prickling sensations. The motor and sensory impairments usu-

ally affect both sides of the body (symmetrical), and the degree of severity may vary. The course of CIDP may also vary from case to case. Some affected individuals may follow a slow steady pattern of symptoms while others may have symptoms that wax and wane, with the most severe symptoms occurring after many months or a year or more. One feature that distinguishes this disorder from other similar disorders is the lack of a preceding viral infection at least 3 months prior to the appearance of the disorder. In most cases, there is no family history of other similar disorders or disease affecting many nerves (polyneuropathy).

The following organizations may provide additional information and support:
American Autoimmune Related Diseases Association, Inc.
Autoimmune Information Network, Inc
GBS/CIDP Foundation International
Guillain-Barre Syndrome Foundation of Canada, Inc.
Jack Miller Center for Peripheral Neuropathy
National Institute of Neurological Disorders and Stroke (NINDS)

271 Churg Strauss Syndrome

Synonyms
Allergic Angiitis and Granulomatosis
Allergic Granulomatosis
Allergic Granulomatosis and Angiitis
Churg-Strauss Vasculitis
Eosinophilic Granulomatous Vasculitis

Churg-Strauss syndrome is a rare disorder that may affect multiple organ systems, particularly the lungs. The disorder is characterized by the formation and accumulation of an unusually large number of antibodies, abnormal clustering of certain white blood cells (eosinophilia), inflammation of blood vessels (vasculitis), and the development of inflammatory nodular lesions (granulomatosis). Many individuals with Churg-Strauss syndrome have a history of allergy. In addition, asthma and other associated lung (pulmonary) abnormalities (i.e., pulmonary infiltrates) often precede the development of the generalized (systemic) symptoms and findings seen in Churg-Strauss syndrome by one or more years. Asthma, a chronic respiratory disorder, is characterized by inflammation and narrowing of the lungs' airways, causing difficulties breathing (dyspnea), coughing, the production of a high-pitched whistling sound while breathing (wheezing), and/or other symptoms and findings. Nonspecific findings associated with Churg-Strauss syndrome typically include flu-like symptoms, such as fever, a general feeling of weakness and fatigue (malaise), loss of appetite (anorexia), weight loss, and muscle pain (myalgia). Additional symptoms and findings may be variable, depending upon the specific organ systems involved. Without appropriate treatment, serious organ damage and potentially life-threatening complications may result. Although the exact cause of Churg-Strauss syndrome is unknown, many researchers indicate that abnormal immunologic and autoimmune factors play an important role.

The following organizations may provide additional information and support:
American Lung Association
Churg Strauss Syndrome Association
Churg-Strauss Syndrome International Support Group
NIH/National Heart, Lung and Blood Institute Information Center
NIH/National Institute of Allergy and Infectious Diseases
Vasculitis of the Central Nervous System

---

272 Ciguatera Fish Poisoning

Synonyms
Ciguatera Poisoning
Ichthyosarcotoxism

Ciguatera fish poisoning is a rare disorder that occurs because of the ingestion of certain contaminated tropical and subtropical fish. When ingested, the toxin (ciguatoxin), which is present at high levels in these contaminated fish, may affect the digestive, muscular, and/or neurological systems. More than 400 different species of fish have been implicated as a cause of ciguatera fish poisoning, including many that are otherwise considered edible (i.e., sea bass, snapper, and perch). These fish typically inhabit low-lying shore areas or coral reefs in tropical or subtropical areas. In the United States, ciguatera fish poisoning has occurred more frequently in the last decade perhaps as a result of a general increase in fish consumption.

The following organization may provide additional information and support:
Centers for Disease Control and Prevention

---

273 Cirrhosis, Primary Biliary

Synonym
PBC

Primary biliary cirrhosis (PBC) is a chronic progressive liver disorder that primarily affects females and typically becomes apparent during middle age. Obstruction of the small bile ducts is accompanied by yellow discoloration of the skin (jaundice). Excessive amounts of copper accumulate in the liver, and fibrous or granular hardening (induration) of the soft liver tissue develops. The course of primary biliary cirrhosis is divided into four progressive stages. Although the exact cause of primary biliary cirrhosis is unknown, possible immunological, autoimmune, genetic, and/or environmental factors are under investigation as potential causes of the disorder.

The following organizations may provide additional information and support:
American Liver Foundation
Autoimmune Information Network, Inc
NIH/National Digestive Diseases Information Clearinghouse
PBC Patient Support Network
Primary Biliary Cirrhosis Support Group

---

274 Citrullinemia

Synonyms
Argininosuccinic Acid Synthetase Deficiency
ASS Deficiency
Citrullinuria
Inborn Error of Urea Synthesis, Citrullinemia Type
Urea Cycle Disorder, Citrullinemia Type

Citrullinemia is a rare inherited disorder caused by deficiency or lack of the enzyme argininosuccinate synthetase (ASS). Argininosuccinate synthetase is one of six enzymes that play a role in the breakdown and removal of nitrogen from the body, a process known as the urea cycle. The lack of this enzyme results in excessive accumulation of nitrogen, in the form of ammonia (hyperammonemia), in the blood. Affected infants may experience vomiting, refusal to eat, progressive lethargy, and coma. Citrullinemia is inherited as an autosomal recessive trait. The urea cycle disorders are a group of rare disorders affecting the urea cycle, a series of biochemical processes in which nitrogen is converted into urea and removed from the body through the urine. Nitrogen is a waste product of protein metabolism. Failure to break down nitrogen results in the abnormal accumulation of nitrogen, in the form of ammonia, in the blood.

The following organizations may provide additional information and support:
American Kidney Fund, Inc.
CLIMB (Children Living with Inherited Metabolic Diseases)
National Kidney Foundation
National Urea Cycle Disorders Foundation
NIH/National Digestive Diseases Information Clearinghouse

275   Cleft Palate and Cleft Lip

Synonym
Hare Lip

Cleft lip and palate are common malformations that are noticeable at birth (congenital). A cleft is an incomplete closure of the palate or lip or both. This defect is caused when the pair of long bones that form the upper jaw (maxillae) do not fuse properly during the early development. These are congenital (genetic) disorders that occur in the first trimester of pregnancy and may be barely noticeable or severe enough to require surgical and dental care, as well as speech therapy.

The following organizations may provide additional information and support:
AboutFace USA
Birth Defect Research for Children, Inc.
Children's Craniofacial Association
Cleft Palate Foundation
Forward Face, Inc.
Let's Face It (USA)
March of Dimes Birth Defects Foundation
National Craniofacial Foundation
NIH/National Oral Health Information Clearing house
Society for the Rehabilitation of the Facially Disfigured, Inc.
Wide Smiles

276   Cleidocranial Dysplasia

Synonyms
Cleidocranial Dysostosis
Dysplasia, Cleidocranial
Dysplasia, Osteodental
Marie-Sainton Disease

Cleidocranial dysplasia is a rare skeletal dysplasia characterized by short stature, distinctive facial features and narrow, sloping shoulders caused by defective or absent collarbones (clavicles). Major symptoms may include premature closing of the soft spot on the head (coronal), delayed closure of the space between the bones of the skull (fontanels), narrow and abnormally shaped pelvic and pubic bones and deformations in the chest (thoracic region). Delayed eruption of teeth, moderately short stature, a high arched palate, a wide pelvic joint, failure of the lower jaw joints to unite, and fingers that are irregular in length may also be present. Cleidocranial dysplasia is inherited as an autosomal dominant genetic trait.

The following organizations may provide additional information and support:
Children's Craniofacial Association
FACES: The National Craniofacial Association
National Craniofacial Foundation
NIH/National Arthritis and Musculoskeletal and Skin Diseases Information Clearinghouse

277   Clubfoot

Synonyms
Calcaneal Valgus
Calcaneovalgus
Metatarsus Varus
Talipes Calcaneus
Talipes Equinovarus
Talipes Equinus
Talipes Valgus
Talipes Varus
Valgus Calcaneus

Clubfoot is a general term used to describe a group of deformities of the ankles and/or feet that are usually present at birth (congenital). The defect may be mild or severe and may affect one or both of the ankles and/or feet. Different forms of clubfoot may include talipes equinovarus in which the foot is turned inward and downward; calcaneal valgus in which the foot is angled at the heel with the toes pointing upward and outward; and metatarsus varus in which the front of the foot is turned inward. If not corrected, affected individuals may develop an unusual manner of walking (gait) in which weight is placed on the side of the foot (lateral) rather than on the sole. Clubfoot may be caused by a combination of hereditary and other factors (e.g., environment) and may occur as an isolated condition or due to a number of different underlying disorders.

The following organizations may provide additional information and support:
11Q Research and Resource Group
Birth Defect Research for Children, Inc.
March of Dimes Birth Defects Foundation

278   Coats' Disease

Synonyms
Coats Syndrome
Retinal Telangiectasis

Coats' disease is a rare disorder characterized by abnormal development of the blood vessels of the nerve-rich membrane lining the eyes (retina). Affected individuals may experience loss of vision and detachment of the retina. In most cases, only one eye is affected (unilateral). However, in rare cases, both eyes may be affected (bilateral Coats' disease). In these bilateral cases, one eye is affected more than the other (asymmetric Coats' disease). The specific cause of Coats' disease is not known.

The following organizations may provide additional information and support:
American Council of the Blind, Inc.
American Foundation for the Blind
Blind Children's Fund
Council of Families with Visual Impairment
Foundation Fighting Blindness, Inc.
Macular Degeneration Support, Inc.
National Association for Parents of Children with Visual Impairments (NAPVI)
National Association for Visually Handicapped
National Federation of the Blind
NIH/National Eye Institute

279   Cochin Jewish Disorder

Synonyms
Haim-Munk Syndrome
HMS
Kera. Palmoplant. Con., Pes Planus, Ony.,
Periodon., Arach., Acroosteolysis
Keratosis Palmoplantaris with
Periodontopathia and Onychogryposis

Cochin Jewish disorder is a rare genetic disorder characterized by the development of red, scaly thickened patches of skin on the palms of the hands and soles of the feet (palmoplantar hyperkeratosis), frequent pus-producing (pyogenic) skin infections, overgrowth (hypertrophy) of the fingernails and toenails (onychogryposis), and degeneration of the structures that surround and support the teeth (periodontosis). Periodontosis usually results in the premature loss of teeth. Additional features associated with the disorder may include flat feet (pes planus); abnormally long, slender fingers and toes (arachnodactyly); loss of bone tissue at the ends of the fingers and/or toes (acroosteolysis); and/or other physical findings. Cochin Jewish disorder is inherited as an autosomal recessive trait.

The following organizations may provide additional information and support:
NIH/National Institute of Arthritis and Musculoskeletal and Skin Diseases
NIH/National Institute of Dental and Craniofacial Research

280   Cockayne Syndrome

Synonyms
CS
Deafness-Dwarfism-Retinal Atrophy
Dwarfism with Renal Atrophy and Deafness
Neill-Dingwall Syndrome
Progeroid Nanism

Disorder Subdivisions
Classical Form, Cockayne Syndrome Type I (Type A)
Congenital Form, Cockayne Syndrome Type II (Type B)
Late Onset, Cockayne Syndrome Type III (Type C)

Cockayne syndrome (CS) is a rare form of dwarfism. It is an inherited disorder whose diagnosis depends on the presence of three signs (1) growth retardation, i.e., short stature, (2) abnormal sensitivity to light (photosensitivity), and (3) prematurely aged appearance (progeria). In the classical form of Cockayne syndrome (CS type I), the symptoms are progressive and typically become apparent after the age of one year. An early onset or congenital form of Cockayne syndrome (CS type II) is apparent at birth (congenital). There is a third form, known as Cockayne syndrome type III (CS type III), that presents later in the child's development and is generally a milder form of the disease. A fourth form, now recognized as xeroderma pigmentosa-Cockayne syndrome (XP-CS), combines features of both of these disorders.

The following organizations may provide additional information and support:
CLIMB (Children Living with Inherited Metabolic Diseases)
Human Growth Foundation
Let Them Hear Foundation
MAGIC Foundation for Children's Growth
Progeria Research Foundation, Inc.
Share and Care Cockayne Syndrome Network, Inc.

281 Coffin Lowry Syndrome

Synonyms
Coffin Syndrome
Mental Retardation with Osteocartilaginous Abnormalities

Coffin-Lowry syndrome is a rare genetic disorder characterized by mental retardation; abnormalities of the head and facial (craniofacial) area; large, soft hands with short, thin (tapered) fingers; short stature; and/or various skeletal abnormalities. Characteristic facial features may include an underdeveloped upper jawbone (maxillary hypoplasia), an abnormally prominent brow, downslanting eyelid folds (palpebral fissures), widely spaced eyes (hypertelorism), large ears, and/or unusually thick eyebrows. Skeletal abnormalities may include abnormal front-to-back and side-to-side curvature of the spine (kyphoscoliosis) and unusual prominence of the breastbone (sternum) (pectus carinatum). Coffin-Lowry syndrome is caused by mutations in the RSK2 gene and is inherited as an X-linked dominant genetic trait. Males are usually more severely affected than females.

The following organizations may provide additional information and support:
The Arc (A National Organization on Mental Retardation)
Coffin-Lowry Syndrome Foundation
National Institute of Neurological Disorders and Stroke (NINDS)
NIH/National Arthritis and Musculoskeletal and Skin Diseases Information Clearinghouse

282 Coffin Siris Syndrome

Synonyms
Dwarfism-Onychodysplasia
Fifth Digit Syndrome
Mental Retardation with Hypoplastic 5th Fingernails and Toenails
Short Stature-Onychodysplasia

Coffin-Siris syndrome is a rare genetic disorder that may be evident at birth (congenital). The disorder may be characterized by feeding difficulties and frequent respiratory infections during infancy, diminished muscle tone (hypotonia), abnormal looseness (laxity) of the joints, delayed bone age, and mental retardation. In addition, affected infants and children typically have short fifth fingers ("pinkies") and toes with underdeveloped (hypoplastic) or absent nails; other malformations of the fingers and toes; and characteristic abnormalities of the head and facial (craniofacial) area, resulting in a coarse facial appearance. Craniofacial malformations may include an abnormally small head (microcephaly); a wide nose with a low nasal bridge; a wide mouth with thick, prominent lips; thick eyebrows and eyelashes (hypertrichosis); and sparse scalp hair. The underlying cause of Coffin-Siris syndrome is unknown. In most cases, the disorder is thought to result from new genetic changes (mutations) that appear to occur randomly for unknown reasons (sporadically). Familial cases have also been reported that suggest autosomal dominant or autosomal recessive inheritance.

The following organizations may provide additional information and support:
The Arc (A National Organization on Mental Retardation)
Genetic and Rare Diseases (GARD) Information Center
NIH/National Institute of Child Health and Human Development

283 Cogan Reese Syndrome

Synonyms
ICE Syndrome, Cogan-Reese Type
Iridocorneal Endothelial (ICE) Syndrome, Cogan-Resse Type
Iris Naevus Syndrome
Iris Nevus Syndrome

Cogan-Reese syndrome is an extremely rare eye disorder characterized by a matted or smudged appearance to the surface of the iris; the development of small colored lumps on the iris (nodular iris nevi); the attachment of portions of the iris to the cornea (peripheral anterior synechiae); and/or increased pressure in the eye (glaucoma). Secondary glaucoma may lead to vision loss. This disorder most frequently appears in young and middle-aged females, usually affecting only one eye (unilateral) and developing slowly over time.

The following organizations may provide additional information and support:
Glaucoma Research Foundation
National Association for Visually Handicapped
NIH/National Eye Institute
Prevent Blindness America

284   Cohen Syndrome

Synonym
Pepper Syndrome

Cohen syndrome is an extremely variable genetic disorder characterized by diminished muscle tone (hypotonia), abnormalities of the head, face, hands and feet and mental retardation. Affected individuals usually have heads that are smaller than average and a short upper lip through which the incisors are exposed. In many, but not all cases, obesity is present, especially around the torso and is associated with slender arms and legs. A lowered level of white blood cells (neutropenia) is present from birth in some affected individuals. Cohen syndrome is an autosomal recessive genetic disease caused by an abnormal gene located on chromosome 8 at 8q22-q23.

The following organization may provide additional information and support:
Cohen Syndrome Support Group

285   Colitis, Collagenous

Synonym
Microscopic Colitis, Collagenous Type

Collagenous colitis is a rare digestive disorder that primarily affects females and typically becomes apparent during middle age. The disorder is characterized by inflammatory changes of the mucous membranes (mucosa) of the colon (colitis) and abnormal accumulation (excessive deposition) of the protein collagen beneath the surface (epithelial) layer of the mucosa (thickened subepithelial collagenous bands). The colon is the major portion of the large intestine. The medical literature often refers to collagenous colitis as a form of "microscopic colitis," since evidence of inflammation and other abnormalities may only be confirmed through microscopic (i.e., histologic) examination of multiple tissue samples. Individuals with collagenous colitis typically experience episodes of chronic, watery, nonbloody diarrhea. In some instances, episodes may often occur at night (nocturnal diarrhea). Diarrheal episodes may be persistent or may occur at intervals (intermittent) over a period of weeks, months, or years. Other symptoms and findings that may occasionally be associated with such episodes include vague abdominal pain, abdominal swelling (distension), nausea, vomiting, and/or weight loss. The exact cause of collagenous colitis is unknown. Possible immunological, environmental, genetic, and/or other factors are under investigation as potential causes of the disorder.

The following organizations may provide additional information and support:
Crohn's and Colitis Foundation of America
Digestive Disease National Coalition
Gastro-Intestinal Research Foundation
International Foundation for Functional Gastrointestinal Disorders
Intestinal Disease Foundation
NIH/National Digestive Diseases Information Clearinghouse
Pediatric Crohn's & Colitis Association, Inc.
Reach Out for Youth with Ileitis and Colitis, Inc.

286   Colitis, Ulcerative

Synonyms
Chronic Non-Specific Ulcerative Colitis
Colitis Gravis
Idiopathic Non-Specific Ulcerative Colitis
Inflammatory Bowel Disease (IBD), Ulcerative Colitis Type
Proctocolitis, Idiopathic

Ulcerative colitis is an inflammatory bowel disease (IBD) of unknown cause. It is characterized by chronic inflammation and ulceration of the lining of the major portion of the large intestine (colon). In most affected individuals, the lowest region of the large intestine, known as the rectum, is initially affected. As the disease progresses, some or all of the colon may become involved. Although associated symptoms and findings usually become apparent during adolescence or young adulthood, some individuals may experience an initial episode between age 50 to 70. In other cases, symptom onset may occur as early as the first year of life. Ulcerative colitis is usually a chronic disease with repeated episodes of symptoms and remission (relapsing-remitting). However, some affected individuals may have few episodes, whereas others may have severe, continuous symptoms. During an episode, affected individuals may experience attacks of watery diarrhea that may contain pus, blood, and/or mucus; abdominal pain; fever and chills; weight loss; and/or other symptoms and findings. In severe cases, individuals may be at risk for certain serious complications. For example, severe inflammation and ulceration may result in thinning of the wall of the colon, causing tearing (perforation) of the colon and potentially life-threatening complications. In addition, in some cases, individuals with the disorder may eventually develop more generalized (systemic) symptoms, such as certain inflammatory skin or eye conditions; inflammation, pain, and swelling of certain joints (arthritis); chronic inflammation of the liver (chronic active hepatitis); and/or other findings. The specific underlying cause of ulcerative colitis is unknown. However, genetic, immunologic, infectious, and/or psychologic factors are thought to play some causative role.

The following organizations may provide additional information and support:
Autoimmune Information Network, Inc
Crohn's and Colitis Foundation of America
Erythema Nodosum Yahoo Support Group
Gastro-Intestinal Research Foundation
International Foundation for Functional Gastrointestinal Disorders
Intestinal Disease Foundation
NIH/National Digestive Diseases Information Clearinghouse
Pediatric Crohn's & Colitis Association, Inc.
Reach Out for Youth with Ileitis and Colitis, Inc.

287 Colorado Tick Fever

Synonyms
CTF
Mountain Fever
Mountain Tick Fever

Colorado tick fever is a rare viral disease transmitted by ticks that commonly inhabit the western United States. Major symptoms may include fever, headaches, muscle aches, and/or generalized discomfort (myalgia). The symptoms usually last for about a week and resolve on their own.

The following organizations may provide additional information and support:
Centers for Disease Control and Prevention
Lyme Disease Foundation
NIH/National Institute of Allergy and Infectious Diseases
World Health Organization (WHO) Regional Office for the Americas (AMRO)

288 Common Variable Immunodeficiency

Synonyms
Acquired Hypogammaglobulinemia
Common Variable Hypogammaglobulinemia
CVI
CVID
Late-Onset Immunoglobulin Deficiency

Common variable immunodeficiency (CVI) is a group of rare genetic (primary) immunodeficiency disorders in which abnormalities in immune cell development (maturation) result in a decreased ability to appropriately produce antibodies in response to invading microorganisms, toxins, or other foreign substances. The symptoms of CVI usually become apparent during the second to the fourth decade of life. The term "common variable immunodeficiency" is used to designate an immune defect in which there is a substantial reduction of the level of immunizing agents (immunoglobulins) in the fluid portion of the blood (serum). According to the medical literature, most individuals with CVI share common, distinctive symptoms and physical findings (phenotype) due to decreased levels of all major classes of immunoglobulins in blood serum (panhypogammaglobulinemia). Defective production of certain antibodies in response to invading microorganisms (antibody deficiency) and recurrent bacterial infections are also characteristic of CVI. Such infections often affect the upper and lower respiratory tracts and the gastrointestinal (digestive) system. In some cases, individuals with common variable immunodeficiency have an increased tendency to develop certain diseases characterized by abnormal tissue growths (neoplasms) that may be benign or malignant. In addition, some individuals with CVI may have an unusual susceptibility to certain autoimmune diseases. These disorders occur when the body's natural defenses against invading microorganisms mistakenly attack healthy tissue. The range and severity of symptoms and findings associated with CVI may vary from case to case. It is thought that common variable immunodeficiency may result from a combination of genetic defects or from different disease genes (heterogenous). In many cases, there is no clear pattern of inheritance. However, in successive generations of some affected families (kindreds), there is evidence that CVI may be inherited as an autosomal recessive genetic trait. In addition, a rare acquired form of the disorder has been described in the medical literature.

The following organizations may provide additional information and support:
Immune Deficiency Foundation
International Patient Organization for Primary Immunodeficiencies
Jeffrey Modell Foundation
March of Dimes Birth Defects Foundation
NIH/National Heart, Lung and Blood Institute Information Center

289   Condyloma

Synonyms
Condyloma Acuminatum
Genital Wart
Venereal Wart

Condyloma is an infectious disease, usually transmitted by direct sexual contact, that is characterized by the presence of warts caused by the human papilloma virus (HPV). These warts may be found on the genitals, mucous membranes of the mouth, near the anus, or in the rectum.

The following organizations may provide additional information and support:
American Social Health Association
Centers for Disease Control and Prevention
NIH/National Institute of Allergy and Infectious Diseases
Sexuality Information and Education Council of the U.S.

290   Cone Dystrophy

Synonyms
Combined Cone-Rod Degeneration
Cone-Rod Degeneration
Cone-Rod Degeneration, Progressive
Cone-Rod Dystrophy
Retinal Cone Degeneration
Retinal Cone Dystrophy
Retinal Cone-Rod Dystrophy

Cone dystrophy is a rare disorder of the eye that is usually, but not invariably, inherited since the literature contains numerous case reports of this set of symptoms appearing for no apparent reason. The cells that receive light stimuli (cone cells and rod cells) in the retina of the eye deteriorate causing impaired vision. This disorder normally occurs during the first to third decades of life

The following organizations may provide additional information and support:
Association for Macular Diseases, Inc.
Foundation Fighting Blindness (Canada)
Foundation Fighting Blindness, Inc.
Macular Degeneration Support, Inc.
NIH/National Eye Institute
Retinitis Pigmentosa International

291   Congenital Fibrosis of the Extraocular Muscles

Synonyms
Abiotrophic Ophthalmoplegia Externa
Congenital External Ophthalmoplegia
Congenital Ophthalmomyopathy
Congenital Ophthalmoplegia
Congenital Static Familial Ophthalmoplegia
Familial Musculofacial Anomaly
Familial Ophthalmoplegia with Co-Contraction
General Fibrosis Syndrome
Hereditary Congenital Ophthalmoplegia
Ophthalmomyopathia Congenita
Ophthalmoplegia Imperfecta
Strabismus Fixus

Disorder Subdivisions
CFEOM1
CFEOM2
CFEOM3

Congenital fibrosis of the extraocular muscles (CFEOM) describes rare eye movement disorders, present at birth, that result from the dysfunction of all or part of the oculomotor nerve (cranial nerve III) and/or the muscles it serves.

The following organizations may provide additional information and support:
Engle Oculomotility Research Laboratory
March of Dimes Birth Defects Foundation
NIH/National Eye Institute
Prevent Blindness America

292   Congenital Varicella Syndrome

Synonyms
Fetal Effects of Chickenpox
Fetal Effects of Varicella Zoster Virus

Fetal Varicella Infection
Fetal Varicella Zoster Syndrome
Varicella Embryopathy

Congenital varicella syndrome is an extremely rare disorder in which affected infants have distinctive abnormalities at birth (congenital) due to the mother's infection with chickenpox (maternal varicella zoster) early during pregnancy (i.e., up to 20 weeks gestation). Affected newborns may have a low birth weight and characteristic abnormalities of the skin; the arms, legs, hands, and/or feet (extremities); the brain; the eyes; and/or, in rare cases, other areas of the body. The range and severity of associated symptoms and physical findings may vary greatly from case to case depending upon when maternal varicella zoster infection occurred during fetal development. In many cases, newborns with congenital varicella syndrome may be abnormally small and have a low birth weight due to abnormal growth delays during fetal development (intrauterine growth retardation). In addition, distinctive skin abnormalities are often present. Certain areas of the skin may consist of thickened, overgrown (hypertrophic) scar tissue (cicatrix), and surrounding skin may appear abnormally hardened (indurate), red, and inflamed (erythema). Such cicatrix scarring typically occurs on one or more of the arms and/or legs, which may also be malformed, underdeveloped (hypoplastic), and abnormally shortened (reduction deformities). Affected infants may also exhibit incomplete development (hypoplasia) of certain fingers and/or toes (rudimentary digits). In some cases, newborns with congenital varicella syndrome may have abnormalities of the brain such as degeneration of the outer portion of the brain (cortical atrophy) and/or abnormal enlargement of cavities of the brain (dilated ventricles [ventriculomegaly]). There may also be abnormalities of the part of the nervous system that controls involuntary functions (autonomic nervous system) such as damage to, or abnormalities of, certain nerve fibers (sympathetic nerve fibers) that pass from the spinal cord to the neck and/or pelvic area. Some affected infants and children may also exhibit abnormal smallness of the head (microcephaly), delays in the acquisition of skills requiring the coordination of mental and physical activities (psychomotor retardation), varying degrees of mental retardation, and/or learning disabilities. In some cases, characteristic eye (ocular) abnormalities may also be present including loss of transparency of the lenses of the eyes (cataracts); abnormal smallness of one or both eyes

(unilateral or bilateral microphthalmia); involuntary, rapid, side-to-side movements of the eyes (pendular nystagmus); and/or inflammation and scarring of certain membranes of the eyes (chorioretinitis and chorioretinal scarring). Such ocular abnormalities may result in varying degrees of visual impairment. In rare cases, newborns with congenital varicella syndrome may have additional abnormalities associated with the disorder.

The following organizations may provide additional information and support:
Centers for Disease Control and Prevention
HRSA Information Center
National Birth Defects Center
National Institute of Neurological Disorders and Stroke (NINDS)
NIH/National Eye Institute
NIH/National Institute of Allergy and Infectious Diseases
World Health Organization (WHO) Regional Office for the Americas (AMRO)

293   Conjunctivitis, Ligneous

Ligneous conjunctivitis is a rare disorder that is characterized by recurrent lesions of the mucous membranes, especially in the eye. This disorder usually presents itself during childhood and may also be found in the mucous membranes of the larynx, vocal chords, nose, trachea, bronchi, vagina, cervix, and gingiva. The lesions in the mucous membranes have a wood-like (ligneous) consistency to them and are thick, firm, knotty and tough. The cause of this disorder is not known although there have been multiple cases of siblings with this condition suggesting an autosomal recessive inheritance.

The following organizations may provide additional information and support:
American Autoimmune Related Diseases Association, Inc.
NIH/National Eye Institute

294   Conn Syndrome

Synonyms
Aldosteronism, Primary
Hyperaldosteronism, Primary

Conn syndrome is characterized by an increased level of the hormone aldosterone in the blood causing increased sodium levels in the blood. An increase in blood volume (hypervolemia), and a low potassium level (hypokalemic alkalosis) also occur. This disorder is characterized by periods of weakness, unusual sensations such as tingling and warmness, a transient paralysis, and muscle cramps. An increase in blood pressure (hypertension), excessive urination (polyuria), and excessive thirst (polydipsia) can also occur.

The following organizations may provide additional information and support:
National Adrenal Diseases Foundation
National Hypertension Association, Inc.
NIH/National Heart, Lung and Blood Institute Information Center
NIH/National Institute of Diabetes, Digestive & Kidney Diseases

295 Conradi Hunermann Syndrome

Synonyms
Chondrodysplasia Punctata, X-linked Dominant Type
Chondrodystrophia Calcificans Congenita
Conradi Disease
Dysplasia Epiphysialis Punctata

Conradi-Hunermann syndrome is a form of chondrodysplasia punctata, a group of rare, genetic disorders of skeletal development (skeletal dysplasias) characterized by unusual, "dotlike" (punctate) opacities representing abnormal accumulations of calcium salts (calcifications) within the growing ends of long bones (i.e., "stippled" epiphyses) and other regions. Conradi-Hunermann syndrome is commonly associated with mild to moderate growth deficiency; disproportionate shortening of long bones, particularly those of the upper arms (humeri) and the thigh bones (femora); short stature; and/or curvature of the spine. Many affected individuals also have a prominent forehead; unusually flattened midfacial regions (midfacial hypoplasia), with a low nasal bridge; loss of transparency of the lenses of the eyes (cataracts); sparse, coarse scalp hair; and/or abnormal thickening, dryness, and scaling of the skin. In rare cases, mild to moderate mental retardation may also be present. Evidence suggests that Conradi-Hunermann syndrome is usually inherited as an X-linked dominant trait that predominantly occurs in females. However, rare cases have also been reported in which males are affected.

The following organizations may provide additional information and support:
The Arc (A National Organization on Mental Retardation)
Foundation for Ichthyosis & Related Skin Types

Human Growth Foundation
Little People of America, Inc.
Little People's Research Fund, Inc.
MAGIC Foundation for Children's Growth
NIH/National Arthritis and Musculoskeletal and Skin Diseases Information Clearinghouse
NIH/National Eye Institute
Restricted Growth Association

296 Conversion Disorder

Synonyms
Briquet's Syndrome
Hysterical Neurosis, Conversion Type

Conversion disorder is a mental illness characterized by the loss or alteration of physical functioning without any physiological reason. These physical symptoms are the result of emotional conflicts or needs. The symptoms usually appear suddenly and at times of extreme psychological stress. A lack of concern over the debilitating symptoms (la belle indifference), which commonly accompanies this illness, may be a clue to distinguishing it from the physiological disorder it may mimic.

The following organizations may provide additional information and support:
National Alliance for the Mentally Ill
National Mental Health Association
National Mental Health Consumers' Self-Help Clearinghouse
NIH/National Institute of Mental Health

297 Cor Triatriatum

Synonyms
Cor Triatriatum Sinistrum
Triatrial Heart

Cor triatriatum is an extremely rare congenital (present at birth) heart defect. Normally, the human heart has four chambers of which two are the atria. These two are separated from each other by a partition (septum) called the atrial septum. The other two chambers, known as ventricles, are also separated by a septum. In cor triatriatum there is a small extra chamber above the left atrium of the heart. The pulmonary veins, returning blood from the lungs, drain into this extra "third atrium." The passage of blood from the lungs into the heart (left atrium and ventricle) is slowed by this extra chamber. Cor triatriatum may eventually lead to features of congestive heart failure and obstruction over time.

The following organizations may provide additional information and support:
American Heart Association
Congenital Heart Anomalies, Support, Education, & Resources
Congenital Heart Information Network
NIH/National Heart, Lung and Blood Institute

298 Corneal Dystrophies

Synonym
Cornea Dystrophy

Disorder Subdivisions
Anterior Dystrophies
Posterior Dystrophies
Stromal Dystrophies

The corneal dystrophies comprise a group of inherited, usually progressive disorders affecting the cornea (outer clear layer of the eyeball). They are occasionally present at birth but more frequently appear during the teen years and progress throughout life. Most are transmitted as autosomal dominant disorders with the exception of macular corneal dystrophy which is transmitted as an autosomal recessive. The inborn error of metabolism in the tissues in and around the eye that causes the macular form of the disorder has been identified.

The following organizations may provide additional information and support:
Eye Bank Association of America
National Association for Visually Handicapped
National Keratoconus Assistance Foundation
NIH/National Eye Institute

299 Cornelia de Lange Syndrome

Synonyms
BDLS
Brachmann-de Lange Syndrome
CdLS
de Lange Syndrome

Cornelia de Lange syndrome (CdLS) is a rare genetic disorder that is apparent at birth (congenital). Associated symptoms and findings typically include delays in physical development before and after birth (prenatal and postnatal growth retardation); characteristic abnormalities of the head and facial (craniofacial) area, resulting in a distinctive facial appearance; malformations of the hands and arms (upper limbs); and mild to severe mental retardation. Many infants and children with the disorder have an unusually small, short head (microbrachycephaly); an abnormally long vertical groove between the upper lip and nose (philtrum); a depressed nasal bridge; upturned nostrils (anteverted nares); and a protruding upper jaw (maxillary prognathism). Additional characteristic facial abnormalities may include thin, downturned lips; low-set ears; arched, well-defined eyebrows that grow together across the base of the nose (synophrys); an unusually low hairline on the forehead and the back of the neck; and abnormally curly, long eyelashes. Affected individuals may also have distinctive malformations of the limbs, such as unusually small hands and feet, inward deviation (clinodactyly) of the fifth fingers, or webbing (syndactyly) of certain toes. Less commonly, there may be absence of the forearms, hands, and fingers. Infants with Cornelia de Lange syndrome may also have feeding and breathing difficulties; an increased susceptibility to respiratory infections; a low-pitched "growling" cry; heart defects; delayed skeletal maturation; hearing loss; or other physical abnormalities. The range and severity of associated symptoms and findings may be extremely variable from case to case. In most individuals with the disorder, Cornelia de Lange syndrome appears to occur randomly for unknown reasons (sporadic). However, there have been some familial cases, suggesting autosomal dominant inheritance.

The following organizations may provide additional information and support:
The Arc (A National Organization on Mental Retardation)
Children's Craniofacial Association
Congenital Heart Anomalies, Support, Education, & Resources
Cornelia de Lange Syndrome—USA Foundation, Inc.
FACES: The National Craniofacial Association
Forward Face, Inc.
Let Them Hear Foundation
March of Dimes Birth Defects Foundation
NIH/National Institute on Deafness and Other Communication Disorders Information Clearinghouse

300 Corticobasal Degeneration

Synonyms
CBGD
Cortical-Basal Ganglionic Degeneration
Cortico-Basal Ganglionic Degeneration
(CBGD)

Corticobasal degeneration is a rare progressive neurological disorder characterized by cell loss and shrinkage (atrophy) in certain areas of the brain (cerebral cortex and substantia nigra). Affected individuals may have sufficient muscle power for manual tasks but often have difficulty directing their movements appropriately. Initial symptoms typically appear in people during the sixth decade, and may include poor coordination, difficulty accomplishing goal-directed tasks (e.g., buttoning a shirt), and/or difficulty pantomiming actions. Symptoms usually begin on one side of the body (unilateral), but both sides may be affected as the disease progresses. Cognitive impairment (e.g., memory loss) and/or visual-spatial impairments may also occur. The exact cause of corticobasal degeneration is unknown.

The following organizations may provide additional information and support:
National Institute of Neurological Disorders and Stroke (NINDS)
WE MOVE (Worldwide Education and Awareness for Movement Disorders)

301 Costello Syndrome

Synonyms
Faciocutaneoskeletal Syndrome
FCS Syndrome

Costello syndrome is an extremely rare disorder that affects multiple organ systems of the body (multisystem disorder). Costello syndrome is characterized by growth delays after birth (postnatal) leading to short stature; excessive, redundant loose skin on the neck, palms of the hands, fingers, and soles of the feet; development of benign (non-cancerous) growths (papillomata) around the mouth (perioral) and nostrils (nares); mental retardation; and/or characteristic facial appearance. Other physical features may include the development of dry hardened skin on the palms of the hands and the soles of the feet (palmoplantar hyperkeratosis), abnormally deep creases on the palms and soles, and/or abnormally flexible joints of the fingers (hyperextensible). There is an increased incidence of congenital abnormalities of the heart and thickening of the heart muscle called a cardiomyopathy. Characteristic craniofacial features may include an abnormally large head (macrocephaly); low-set ears with large, thick lobes; unusually thick lips; and/or abnormally wide nostrils (nares). Most cases of Costello syndrome are isolated with no other affected family members (sporadic). The exact cause of Costello syndrome is unknown.

The following organizations may provide additional information and support:
American Heart Association
The Arc (A National Organization on Mental Retardation)
Human Growth Foundation
International Costello Syndrome Support Group (UK)
Little People of America, Inc.
MAGIC Foundation for Children's Growth
March of Dimes Birth Defects Foundation
United States Costello Syndrome Family Network

302 Cowpox

Synonyms
Bovine Smallpox
Catpox
Human Cowpox Infection
Vaccinia
Vaccinia Necrosum Progressive Vaccinia

Cowpox is a viral disease that normally affects the udders and teats of cows. On rare occasions, it may be transmitted to humans and produce a characteristic red skin rash and abnormally enlarged lymph nodes (lymphadenopathy). Cowpox is caused by the vaccinia virus and has been known to cause systemic reactions (generalized vaccinia) in some people who have been recently vaccinated against cowpox. Cowpox produces immunity to smallpox and, beginning in the 19th century, the virus for cowpox was used to develop the vaccines used against smallpox. Because of the widespread vaccination, smallpox was wiped out worldwide but has now come under study again because of concern that it might be used as an agent of biological terrorism.

The following organizations may provide additional information and support:
Centers for Disease Control and Prevention
NIH/National Institute of Allergy and Infectious Diseases
World Health Organization (WHO) Regional Office for the Americas (AMRO)

303 Craniofrontonasal Dysplasia

Synonyms
CFND
Craniofrontonasal Dysostosis
Craniofrontonasal Syndrome

Craniofrontonasal dysplasia is a very rare inherited disorder characterized by abnormalities of the head and face (craniofacial area), hands and feet, and certain skeletal bones. Major symptoms of this disorder may include widely spaced eyes (ocular hypertelorism), a groove (cleft) on the tip of the nose, an unusually wide mouth, malformations of the fingers and toes, and/or underdevelopment of portions of the face (midface hypoplasia), such as the forehead, nose, and chin. In addition, the head may have an unusual shape due to premature closure of the fibrous joints (sutures) between certain bones in the skull (coronal synostosis). Craniofrontonasal dysplasia follows X-linked inheritance in most families, but females are more severely affected than males. An autosomal dominant form of the disorder has also been discussed in the medical literature.

The following organizations may provide additional information and support:
AboutFace USA
Children's Craniofacial Association
FACES: The National Craniofacial Association
Forward Face, Inc.
National Craniofacial Foundation

304 Craniometaphyseal Dysplasia

Synonym
Osteochondroplasia

Craniometaphyseal dysplasia is an extremely rare genetic disorder characterized by distinctive abnormalities of the head and facial (craniofacial) area, impairment of certain nerves (cranial nerves) that emerge from the brain, and malformations of the long bones of the arms and legs. In infants and children with craniometaphyseal dysplasia, there may be overgrowth and/or abnormal hardening of certain bones of the skull (cranial hyperostosis and/or sclerosis) and overgrowth (hypertrophy) of craniofacial bones, resulting in widely-spaced eyes (ocular hypetelorism), an abnormally wide nasal bridge, an enlarged lower jaw (mandible), and a "leonine" facial appearance (leontiasis ossea). Compression of certain nerves emerging from the brain (cranial nerves) may result in loss of some motor function (paralysis) in the facial area (cranial nerve palsy) and hearing loss (conductive and/or sensorineural hearing impairment). In addition, in individuals with the disorder, the long bones of the arms and legs may develop abnormally, resulting in unusual "club-like" flaring or broadening of the end portions (metaphyses) of the bones (metaphyseal dysplasia). In some cases, craniometaphyseal dysplasia may be inherited as an autosomal dominant genetic trait; in other cases, the disorder may have an autosomal recessive mode of inheritance.

The following organizations may provide additional information and support:
AboutFace USA
Children's Craniofacial Association
FACES: The National Craniofacial Association
Forward Face, Inc.
National Craniofacial Foundation
National Foundation for Facial Reconstruction

305 Craniosynostosis, Primary

Synonyms
Craniostenosis
CSO

Disorder Subdivisions
Kleeblattschadel Deformity
Plagiocephaly
Scaphocephaly
Trigonocephaly
Turricephaly

Primary craniosynostosis is a rare disorder of the skull that may be inherited as an autosomal dominant or autosomal recessive genetic trait. Premature closure of the bones (sutures) in the skull result in an abnormally shaped head. The severity of symptoms and shape of the skull depend on which skull bones are prematurely closed. This disorder is present at birth.

The following organizations may provide additional information and support:
AboutFace USA
Birth Defect Research for Children, Inc.
Children's Craniofacial Association
FACES: The National Craniofacial Association
Forward Face, Inc.
Guardians of Hydrocephalus Research Foundation
Headlines—Craniofacial Support
Hydrocephalus Association
National Craniofacial Foundation
National Hydrocephalus Foundation

306   Creutzfeldt Jakob Disease

Synonyms

CJD
Jakob's Disease
Jakob-Creutzfeldt Disease
Subacute Spongiform Encephalopathy

Disorder Subdivision

Variant Creutzfeldt-Jakob Disease (V-CJD)

Creutzfeldt-Jakob disease (CJD) is an extremely rare degenerative brain disorder (i.e., "spongiform" encephalopathy) characterized by sudden development of rapidly progressive neurological and neuromuscular symptoms. With symptom onset, affected individuals may develop confusion, depression, behavioral changes, impaired vision, and/or impaired coordination. As the disease progresses, there may be rapidly progressive deterioration of cognitive processes and memory (dementia), resulting in confusion and disorientation, impairment of memory control, personality disintegration, agitation, restlessness, and other symptoms and findings. Affected individuals also develop neuromuscular abnormalities such as muscle weakness and loss of muscle mass (wasting); irregular, rapid, shock-like muscle spasms (myoclonus); and/or relatively slow, involuntary, continual writhing movements (athetosis), particularly of the arms and legs. Later stages of the disease may include further loss of physical and intellectual functions, a state of unconsciousness (coma), and increased susceptibility to repeated infections of the respiratory tract (e.g., pneumonia). In many affected individuals, life-threatening complications may develop less than a year after the disorder becomes apparent. In approximately 90 percent of cases, CJD appears to occur randomly for no apparent reason (sporadically). About 10 percent of affected individuals may have a hereditary predisposition for the disorder. Reports in the medical literature suggest that familial cases of CJD are consistent with an autosomal dominant mode of inheritance. In addition, in some extremely rare cases, CJD may take an infectious form. The disorder is thought to result from changes (mutations) in the gene that regulates the production of the human prion protein or direct contamination (transmission) with abnormal prion protein in infected brain tissue. A variant form of CJD (V-CJD) has been reported in the United Kingdom that affects younger people (median age at onset: 28 years) than does classic CJD. In 1996, experts suggested the possibility that this variant might be associated with consumption of beef from cows with a related infectious brain disorder known as bovine spongiform encephalopathy (BSE) or "mad cow disease." BSE was first identified in the UK in 1986 and the number of reported cases grew rapidly, peaking in the winter of 1992-93 when almost 1,000 new cases were reported each week. Later, BSE also began to appear in some other European countries. Scientific research and debate continue concerning the potential link between BSE and V-CJD. In addition, coordinated national and international efforts are in place concerning the prevention, study, and surveillance of BSE and CJD. In early December 2000, European Union agriculture ministers agreed upon new measures to combat the spread of mad cow disease, including incinerating any cow over 30 months of age that had not tested negative for BSE. (BSE is thought to become detectable and infectious when cattle are approximately 30 months old.)

The following organizations may provide additional information and support:
Alzheimer's Association
Alzheimer's Disease Education and Referral Center
Centers for Disease Control and Prevention
CJD Aware!
CJD Voice
C-Mac Informational Services, Inc.
Creutzfeldt-Jakob Disease Foundation, Inc.
Human BSE Foundation
National Hospice and Palliative Care Organization
National Institute of Neurological Disorders and Stroke (NINDS)
National Prion Disease Pathology Surveillance Center
NIH/National Institute of Allergy and Infectious Diseases
World Health Organization (WHO) Regional Office for the Americas (AMRO)

307   Cri du Chat Syndrome

Synonyms

5p-Syndrome
Cat's Cry Syndrome
Chromosome 5, Monosomy 5p
Chromosome 5p-Syndrome
Le Jeune Syndrome
Partial Deletion of the Short Arm of Chromosome 5 Syndrome

Cri du chat syndrome, a rare chromosomal disorder that is apparent at birth, is characterized by a distinctive high, shrill, mewing, "kitten-like" cry during infancy. This distinctive cry can become less pronounced during late infancy. Other findings and symptoms may include low birth weight and failure to grow at the expected rate (failure to thrive); distinctive abnormalities of the head and face (craniofacial area) including an unusually small head (microcephaly), widely spaced eyes (ocular hypertelorism), and an unusually small jaw (micrognathia); and mental retardation. Cri du chat syndrome is caused by the absence of genetic material (deletion) on the short arm (p) of chromosome 5.

The following organizations may provide additional information and support:
5p-Society
The Arc (A National Organization on Mental Retardation)
Chromosome Deletion Outreach, Inc.
Cri Du Chat Syndrome Support Group
Department of Human Genetics/Cri du Chat
Let Them Hear Foundation
March of Dimes Birth Defects Foundation

308 Crigler Najjar Syndrome Type I

Synonyms
Bilirubin Glucuronosyltransferase Deficiency Type I
Congenital Familial Nonhemolytic Jaundice Type I
Uridine Diphosphate Glucuronosyltransferase, Severe Def. Type I

Crigler-Najjar syndrome type I is a very rare inherited metabolic disorder characterized by the complete absence of the enzyme uridine diphosphate glucuronosyltransferase (UDPGT), which is normally found in the liver. This enzyme is required for the conversion (conjugation) and subsequent excretion of bilirubin from the body. When UDP-glucuronosyltransferase activity is absent, these metabolic processes are hampered and abnormally high levels of bilirubin accumulate in the blood (hyperbilirubinemia). Within the first few days of life, most infants with Crigler-Najjar syndrome type I develop persistent yellowing of the skin, mucous membranes, and whites of the eyes (jaundice). In addition, some affected individuals may develop kernicterus, a potentially life-threatening neurological condition in which toxic levels of bilirubin accumulate in the brain, causing damage to the central nervous system. Early signs of kernicterus may include lack of energy (lethargy), vomiting, fever, and/or unsatisfactory feedings. More serious signs of kernicterus may develop, including abnormal muscle rigidity, resulting in muscle spasms (dystonia) and involuntary movements of the limbs and/or entire body

(athetosis). Crigler-Najjar syndrome type I is inherited as an autosomal recessive genetic trait.

The following organizations may provide additional information and support:
American Liver Foundation
Children's Liver Disease Foundation
CLIMB (Children Living with Inherited Metabolic Diseases)
Crigler-Najjar Association
NIH/National Digestive Diseases Information Clearinghouse
Parents of Infants and Children with Kernicterus

309 Crohn's Disease

Synonyms
CD
Granulomatous Colitis
Ileitis
Regional Enteritis

Disorder Subdivisions
Duodenitis
Enterocolitis
Gastritis
Granulomatous Ileitis
Ileocolitis
Jejunitis
Jejunoileitis

Crohn's disease is an inflammatory bowel disease characterized by severe, chronic inflammation of the intestinal wall or any portion of the gastrointestinal tract. The lower portion of the small intestine (ileum) and the rectum are most commonly affected by this disorder. Symptoms may include watery diarrhea, abdominal pain, fever, and weight loss. The symptoms of Crohn's disease can be difficult to manage and proper diagnosis is often delayed. The exact cause of Crohn's disease is unknown.

The following organizations may provide additional information and support:
Autoimmune Information Network, Inc
Crohn's and Colitis Foundation of America
Erythema Nodosum Yahoo Support Group
Gastro-Intestinal Research Foundation
International Foundation for Functional Gastrointestinal Disorders
Intestinal Disease Foundation
NIH/National Digestive Diseases Information Clearinghouse
NIH/National Institute of Allergy and Infectious Diseases
Pediatric Crohn's & Colitis Association, Inc.

310   Cronkhite-Canada Syndrome

Synonyms

Allergic Granulomatous Angiitis of Cronkhite-Canada
Canada-Cronkhite Disease
CCD
Cronkhite-Canada Syndrome
Gastrointestinal Polyposis and Ectodermal Changes
Polyposis, Skin Pigmentation, Alopecia, and Fingernail Changes

Cronkhite-Canada syndrome (CCS) is a very rare disease with symptoms that include loss of taste, intestinal polyps, hair loss, and nail growth problems. It is difficult to treat because of malabsorption that accompanies the polyps. CCS occurs primarily in older people (the average age is 59) and it is not believed to have a genetic component. There have been fewer than 400 cases reported in the past 50 years, primarily in Japan but also in the U.S. and other countries.

The following organizations may provide additional information and support:
Intestinal Multiple Polyposis and Colorectal Cancer Registry
NIH/National Digestive Diseases Information Clearinghouse

311   Crouzon Syndrome

Synonyms

Craniofacial Dysostosis
Craniostenosis, Crouzon Type
Crouzon Craniofacial Dysostosis

Disorder Subdivisions

Oxycephaly-Acrocephaly
Virchow's Oxycephaly

Crouzon syndrome is a rare genetic disorder that may be evident at birth (congenital) or during infancy. The disorder is characterized by distinctive malformations of the skull and facial (craniofacial) region. Such abnormalities may vary greatly in range and severity from case to case, including among affected family members. However, in most infants with Crouzon syndrome, the fibrous joints between certain bones of the skull (cranial sutures) close prematurely (craniosynostosis). In addition, facial abnormalities typically include unusual bulging or protrusion of the eyeballs (proptosis) due to shal-

low eye cavities (orbits); outward deviation of one of the eyes (divergent strabismus or exotropia); widely spaced eyes (ocular hypertelorism); and a small, underdeveloped upper jaw (hypoplastic maxilla), with protrusion of the lower jaw (relative mandibular prognathism). In some instances, Crouzon syndrome is inherited as an autosomal dominant trait. In other cases, affected individuals have no family history of the disease. In such instances, Crouzon syndrome is thought to result from new genetic changes (mutations) that occur randomly for unknown reasons (sporadically).

The following organizations may provide additional information and support:
AboutFace USA
Alexander Graham Bell Association for the Deaf, Inc.
The Arc (A National Organization on Mental Retardation)
Children's Craniofacial Association
Council of Families with Visual Impairment
Crouzon Support Network
Crouzon's/Meniere's Support Network
FACES: The National Craniofacial Association
Forward Face, Inc.
Headlines—Craniofacial Support
Let Them Hear Foundation
Let's Face It (USA)
March of Dimes Birth Defects Foundation
National Association for Parents of Children with Visual Impairments (NAPVI)
National Craniofacial Foundation
NIH/National Eye Institute
NIH/National Institute on Deafness and Other Communication Disorders Information Clearinghouse
Sjældne Diagnoser / Rare Disorders Denmark
Society for the Rehabilitation of the Facially Disfigured, Inc.

312   Cryoglobulinemia, Essential Mixed

Synonym

EMC

Essential mixed cryoglobulinemia is a rare autoimmune disorder that affects the blood and various other body systems. Major symptoms may include unusual response to cold, skin abnormalities, weakness and blood problems. There may also be joint pain, inflamed blood vessels, and kidney problems.

The following organizations may provide additional information and support:
American Autoimmune Related Diseases Association, Inc.
Autoimmune Information Network, Inc
Jack Miller Center for Peripheral Neuropathy
NIH/National Heart, Lung and Blood Institute Information Center

313 Cryptococcosis

Synonyms
Busse-Buschke Disease
Cryptococcic Meningitis
Cryptococcosis Lung
Cryptococcosis Skin
European Blastomycosis
Torular Meningitis
Torulosis

Cryptococcosis is caused by a fungus known as *Cryptococcosis neoformans*. The infection may be spread to humans through contact with pigeon droppings or unwashed raw fruit. Contact with an infected individual may also spread the infection. Individuals with disorders characterized by lowered immunity (for instance, HIV infection) are at high risk for contracting these infections. Cryptococcosis may appear in various forms depending on how the infection is acquired. In most cases, the infection begins in the lungs (pulmonary form) and may then spread to the brain, urinary tract, skin, and/or bones (disseminated form). When the infection is limited to the lungs, symptoms may be minimal or not apparent at all. Respiratory symptoms may include coughing and chest pain. When the infection spreads, it tends to seek out the central nervous system, especially the brain. In some affected individuals, inflammation of the membranes surrounding the brain and spinal cord (meningitis) may occur as a serious complication. Symptoms associated with meningitis may include dizziness, blurred vision, severe headache, and/or stiffness of the neck. In such cases, immediate treatment is essential to help prevent potentially life-threatening complications.

The following organizations may provide additional information and support:
Centers for Disease Control and Prevention
National Institute of Neurological Disorders and Stroke (NINDS)
NIH/National Institute of Allergy and Infectious Diseases
World Health Organization (WHO) Regional Office for the Americas (AMRO)

314 Cushing's Syndrome

Synonyms
Adrenal Cortex Adenoma
Adrenal Hyperfunction resulting from Pituitary ACTH Excess
Cushing's Disease
Ectopic ACTH Syndrome
Ectopic Adrenocorticotropic Hormone Syndrome

Cushing's syndrome is a rare endocrine disorder characterized by a variety of symptoms and physical abnormalities that occur due to excessive amounts of certain hormones (corticosteroids).

The following organizations may provide additional information and support:
Autoimmune Information Network, Inc
Cushing's Support and Research Foundation, Inc.
National Adrenal Diseases Foundation
NIH/National Digestive Diseases Information Clearinghouse
NIH/National Institute of Child Health and Human Development

315 Cutaneous T-Cell Lymphomas

Synonym
CTCL

Disorder Subdivisions
Granulomatous Slack Skin
Lymphomatoid Papulosis
Mycosis Fungoides
Pagetoid Reticulosis (Woringer-Kolopp Disease)
Primary Cutaneous Anaplastic Large Cell Lymphomas
Sezary Syndrome
Subcutaneous Panniculitic T-Cell Lymphoma

Cutaneous T-cell lymphomas (CTCLs) are a group of disorders characterized by abnormal accumulation of malignant T-cells in the skin potentially resulting in the development of rashes, plaques and tumors. CTCLs belong to a larger group of disorders known as non-Hodgkin's lymphomas (NHLs), which are related malignancies (cancers) that affect the lymphatic system (lymphomas). Functioning as part of the immune system, the lymphatic system helps to protect the body against infection and disease. It consists of a network of tubular channels (lymph vessels) that drain a thin watery fluid known as lymph from different areas of the body into the bloodstream.

Lymph accumulates in the tiny spaces between tissue cells and contains proteins, fats, and certain white blood cells known as lymphocytes. There are two main types of lymphocytes: B-lymphocytes, which may produce specific antibodies to "neutralize" certain invading microorganisms, and T-lymphocytes, which may directly destroy microorganisms or assist in the activities of other lymphocytes. CTCLs result from errors in the production of T-lymphocytes or transformation of T-lymphocytes into malignant cells. In CTCLs abnormal, uncontrolled growth and multiplication (proliferation) of malignant T-lymphocytes result in accumulation of these lymphocytes in the skin. In some cases, malignant lymphocytes may spread to affect the lymph nodes and eventually to other bodily tissues and organs, potentially resulting in life-threatening complications. The specific symptoms and physical findings may vary from case to case, depending upon the extent and region(s) of involvement, the specific type of CTCL present, and various additional factors. Non-Hodgkin's lymphomas, such as CTCLs, may also be categorized based upon certain characteristics of the cancer cells as seen under a microscope and how quickly they may tend to grow and spread. For example, CTCLs may be characterized as "low-grade" (or indolent) lymphomas, which tend to grow slowly and result in few associated symptoms, or "intermediate-grade" or "high-grade" (aggressive) lymphomas, which typically grow rapidly, requiring prompt treatment. Most cases of CTCL, especially the classic form (mycosis fungoides), are slow-growing (indolent) lymphomas.

The following organizations may provide additional information and support:
American Cancer Society, Inc.
Canadian Cancer Society
Cancer Hope Network
Cutaneous Lymphoma Foundation
International Cancer Alliance for Research and Education
Leukemia & Lymphoma Society
Lymphoma Association (UK)
Lymphoma Foundation Canada
Lymphoma Research Foundation
Mycosis Fungoides Network
National Cancer Institute
National Cancer Institute Physician Data Query (PDQ) Cancer Information Service
National Coalition for Cancer Survivorship
OncoLink: The University of Pennsylvania Cancer Center Resource
Rare Cancer Alliance

316 Cutis Laxa

Synonyms
Chalasodermia, Generalized
Chalazodermia, Generalized
Dermatochalasia, Generalized
Dermatolysis, Generalized
Dermatomegaly
Elastorrhexis, Generalized
Occipital Horn Syndrome

Disorder Subdivisions
Acquired Cutis Laxa Syndrome
Congenital Cutis Laxa Syndrome
Cutis Laxa, X-linked (formerly known as Ehlers Danlos IX)

Cutis laxa is rarely encountered and may occur in several inherited (congenital) forms or come about in the course of another disorder (acquired). It is a connective tissue disorder characterized by skin that is loose (lax), hanging, wrinkled, and lacking in elasticity (hyperelasticity). The affected areas of skin may be thickened and dark. In addition, the joints are loose (hypermobility) because of lax ligaments and tendons. The disorder involves a variety of symptoms and signs that result from defects in connective tissue. Defective connective tissue may cause problems in the vocal cords, bones, cartilage, blood vessels, bladder, kidney, digestive system, and lungs. Four separate inherited forms of this disorder have been identified. Most cases are inherited as one or another of two types of autosomal recessive inheritance. However, cases of autosomal dominant inheritance have been reported, as well as a form that is credited to X-linked inheritance.

The following organizations may provide additional information and support:
American Autoimmune Related Diseases Association, Inc.
British Coalition of Heritable Disorders of Connective Tissue
Cutis Laxa Internationale
NIH/National Arthritis and Musculoskeletal and Skin Diseases Information Clearinghouse

317 Cutis Marmorata Telangiectatica Congenita

Synonyms
CMTC
Congenital Generalized Phlebectasia
Congenital Livedo Reticularis
Van Lohuizen Syndrome

Disorder Subdivision

Macrocephaly-CMTC (M-CMTC)

Cutis marmorata telangiectatica congenita (CMTC) is a rare inherited disorder characterized by discolored patches of skin caused by widened (dilated) surface blood vessels (livedo reticularis telangiectases). As a result, the skin has a purple or blue "marbled" or "fishnet" appearance (cutis marmorata). In many affected individuals, large lesions (ulcers) or complete absence of the skin in affected areas may also be present. Approximately 50 percent of affected individuals have additional associated abnormalities including pink or dark red, irregularly shaped patches of skin (nevus flammeus); loss of muscle tissue (wasting) on one side of the body (hemiatrophy); elevated fluid pressure within the eye (glaucoma); and/or undergrowth (hypotrophy) of one leg. A distinct subdivision of CMTC has been identified that is known as macrocephaly-CMTC. In M-CMTC, the skin abnormalities of CMTC occur in association with an abnormally large head (macrocephaly) and the potential development of neurological abnormalities. Most cases of CMTC and M-CMTC occur randomly for no apparent reason (sporadically).

The following organizations may provide additional information and support:
The Arc (A National Organization on Mental Retardation)
Association CMTC
Cobalamin Network
March of Dimes Birth Defects Foundation
Nevus Network
NIH/National Arthritis and Musculoskeletal and Skin Diseases Information Clearinghouse
Vascular Birthmarks Foundation

318 Cyclic Vomiting Syndrome

Synonyms
Abdominal Migraine
Bilious Attacks
Childhood Cyclic Vomiting
Chronic Vomiting in Childhood
Periodic Syndrome
Recurrent Vomiting

Cyclic vomiting syndrome is a rare digestive disorder that affects children and adults. This disorder is characterized by chronic nausea, vomiting, extreme fatigue, motion sickness, abdominal pain and, in some cases, dizziness (vertigo) that may last for hours to days. These episodes of symptoms seem to be similar in onset and duration for each affected individual. The exact cause of cyclic vomiting syndrome is not known.

The following organizations may provide additional information and support:
Cyclic Vomiting Syndrome Association (CVSA)
National Headache Foundation
NIH/National Digestive Diseases Information Clearinghouse

319 Cystic Fibrosis

Synonyms
CF
Fibrocystic Disease of Pancreas
Mucosis
Mucoviscidosis
Pancreatic Fibrosis

Cystic fibrosis is a genetic disease that affects approximately 30,000 children and adults in the United States. Because of a defective gene, mucus-secreting glands within the lining of the lung's airways (bronchi) produce unusually thick, sticky secretions. This clogs the air passages, promotes bacterial growth, and leads to chronic obstruction, inflammation, and infection of the airways. These thick secretions also obstruct the pancreas, keeping digestive enzymes from reaching the intestines to help break down and absorb food. In many cases, this disorder is apparent soon after birth, but 10% of the people with cystic fibrosis do not receive a diagnosis until age 18 or older. There is variation in the severity of symptoms, which may include salty-tasting skin, cough, shortness of breath, excessive appetite but poor weight gain, and greasy, bulky stools. According to the Cystic Fibrosis Foundation, more than 10 million Americans are symptomless carriers of the defective cystic fibrosis gene. An individual must inherit two defective genes, one from each parent, to have cystic fibrosis.

The following organizations may provide additional information and support:
American Lung Association
Canadian Cystic Fibrosis Foundation
Cochrane Cystic Fibrosis and Genetic Disorders Review Group
Cystic Fibrosis Foundation
Cystic Fibrosis Trust
Cystic Fibrosis Worldwide
March of Dimes Birth Defects Foundation
NIH/National Digestive Diseases Information Clearinghouse
Sjældne Diagnoser / Rare Disorders Denmark

320 Cystic Hygroma

Synonyms

Cystic Lymphangioma
Familial Nuchal Bleb
FCH
Fetal Cystic Hygroma
Hygroma Colli

Cystic hygromas are non-malignant malformations of the lymphatic system characterized by single or multiple fluid-filled lesions that occur at sites where the lymphatic system connects to the venous system, most commonly the back of the neck. Typically, this disorder becomes apparent in infancy or early childhood. Ninety percent of cases are symptomatic by the age of 2 years.

The following organizations may provide additional information and support:
American Cancer Society, Inc.
Cystic Hygroma Support Group
National Lymphatic and Venous Diseases Foundation, Inc.

321 Cysticercosis

Cysticercosis is a rare infectious disease caused by the presence and accumulation of the larval cysts of a tapeworm (cestode) within tissues of the body. The scientific name for the tapeworm that causes cysticercosis is *Taenia solium* (*T. solium*), which is also known as the pork tapeworm. T. solium cysts (cysticerci) may affect any area of the body including the brain, a condition known as neurocysticercosis. Symptoms vary from case to case. If cysticerci are located in the brain, central nervous system abnormalities may occur, most often seizures and headaches. Cysticercosis may also affect the eyes, spinal cord, skin and heart.

The following organizations may provide additional information and support:
Centers for Disease Control and Prevention
NIH/National Institute of Allergy and Infectious Diseases
World Health Organization (WHO) Regional Office for the Americas (AMRO)

322 Cystinosis

Synonyms

Cystine Storage Disease
Fanconi II
Lignac-Fanconi Syndrome

Disorder Subdivisions

Abderhalden-Kaufmann-Lignac Syndrome
Adolescent Cystinosis
Adult Cystinosis
Aminoaciduria-Osteomalacia-Hyperphosphaturia Syndrome
Benign Cystinosis
de Toni-Fanconi Syndrome
Dwarfism with Rickets
Infantile Cystinosis
Infantile Fanconi Syndrome with Cystinosis
Intermediate Cystinosis
Juvenile Cystinosis
Lignac-Debre-Fanconi Syndrome
Nephropathic Cystinosis
Nephrotic-Glycosuric-Dwarfism-Rickets-Hypophosphatemic Syndrome

Cystinosis is a rare inherited disorder characterized by the impaired transport of cystine out of parts of cells called lysosomes. Cystine is an amino acid found in many different proteins in the body. Lysosomes, which are membrane bound particles within cells, aid in intracellular digestive function. Cystinosis is characterized by the accumulation of cystine in tissues throughout the body, which can cause certain organs to malfunction. Three distinct forms of cystinosis are recognized. Infantile nephropathic cystinosis is the most severe form of the disease. Symptoms, including abnormal sensitivity to light and loss of color in the retina of the eyes, can appear as early as 6 to 12 months of age. If left untreated, this form of the disease may lead to kidney failure by 10 years of age. In people with intermediate cystinosis or juvenile (adolescent) cystinosis, kidney and eye symptoms typically become apparent during the teenage years or early adulthood. In benign or adult cystinosis, crystalline cystine accumulates primarily in the cornea of the eyes. One of the major complications of cystinosis is renal Fanconi syndrome which is characterized by impaired kidney function including excessive urination (polyuria), excessive thirst (polydipsia), and abnormally low levels of potassium in the blood (hypokalemia).

The following organizations may provide additional information and support:
American Foundation for Urologic Disease
CLIMB (Children Living with Inherited Metabolic Diseases)
Cystinosis Foundation, Inc.
Cystinosis Research Network
Instituto de Errores Innatos del Metabolismo
March of Dimes Birth Defects Foundation

NIH/National Kidney and Urologic Diseases Information Clearinghouse
Vaincre Les Maladies Lysosomales

323   Cystinuria

Synonyms

Cistinuria
Cystine-Lysine-Arginine-Ornithinuria
Cystinuria with Dibasic Aminoaciduria

Disorder Subdivisions

Cystinuria, Type I
Cystinuria, Type II
Cystinuria, Type III
Hypercystinuria

Cystinuria is an inherited metabolic disorder characterized by the abnormal movement (transport) in the intestines and kidneys, of certain organic chemical compounds (amino acids). These include cystine, lysine, arginine, and ornithine. Excessive amounts of undissolved cystine in the urine (cystinuria) cause the formation of stones (calculi) in the kidney, bladder, and/or ureter. Four subtypes of cystinuria are recognized. In type I cystinuria, there is a defect in the active transport of cystine and the amino acids (dibasic) lysine, arginine, and ornithine in the kidneys and small intestine. People who are carriers of the gene for this type of the disorder generally have no symptoms. In type II cystinuria, cystine and lysine transport is severely impaired in the kidneys and only somewhat impaired in the intestines. In type III cystinuria, kidney transport of cystine and lysine is defective; intestinal transport is normal. People who are carriers of the gene for this variety of the disease typically have slightly elevated levels of cystine and lysine in the urine. In hypercystinuria, there is generally a moderate elevation of cystine in the urine; intestinal absorption of cystine and the dibasic amino acids is normal.

The following organizations may provide additional information and support:
American Kidney Fund, Inc.
Cystinuria Support Network
March of Dimes Birth Defects Foundation
National Kidney Foundation

324   Cytochrome C Oxidase Deficiency

Synonyms

Complex IV Deficiency
COX Deficiency
Deficiency of Mitochondrial Respiratory Chain Complex IV

Disorder Subdivisions

COX Def., Infantile Mitochondrial Myopathy, de Toni-Fanconi-Debre Included
COX Deficiency French-Canadian Type
COX Deficiency Type Benign Infantile Mitochondrial Myopathy
Leigh's Syndrome (Subacute Necrotizing Encephalomyelopathy)

Cytochrome C oxidase deficiency is a very rare inherited metabolic disorder characterized by deficiency of the enzyme cytochrome C oxidase (COX), or complex IV, an essential enzyme that is active in the subcellular structures that help to regulate energy production (mitochondria). Deficiency of COX may be limited (localized) to the tissues of the skeletal muscles or may affect several tissues, such as the heart, kidney, liver, brain, and/or connective tissue (fibroblasts); in other cases, the COX deficiency may be generalized (systemic). Four distinct forms of cytochrome C oxidase deficiency have been identfed. The first form of this disorder is known as COX deficiency type benign infantile mitochondrial myopathy. Affected infants exhibit many of the same symptoms as those with the more severe infantile form of the disease; however, because the COX deficiency is limited (localized) to tissues of the skeletal muscles, they typically do not have heart or kidney dysfunction. In the second type of the disease, known as COX deficiency type infantile mitochondrial myopathy, because the COX deficiency affects tissues of the skeletal muscles as well as several other tissues, the disorder may be characterized by a generalized weakness of skeletal muscles (myotonia), abnormalities of the heart and kidneys, and/or abnormally high levels of lactic acid in the blood (lactic acidosis). The third form of COX deficiency, known as Leigh's disease (subacute necrotizing encephalomyelopathy), is thought to be a generalized (systemic) form of COX deficiency. Leigh's disease is characterized by progressive degeneration of the brain and dysfunction of other organs of the body including the heart, kidneys, muscles, and liver. Symptoms may include loss of previously acquired motor skills, loss of appetite, vomiting, irritability, and/or seizure activity. As Leigh's disease progresses, symptoms may also include generalized weakness; loss of muscle tone (hypotonia); and/or episodes of lactic acidosis. In the fourth form of COX deficiency, known as COX deficiency French-Canadian type, the COX deficiency affects tissues of the skeletal muscles, connective tissue, and, in particular, the brain (Leigh's disease) and the liver. Affected infants and children may demonstrate developmental delays, diminished muscle tone (hypotonia), crossing of the eyes (strabismus), Leigh's disease, and/or episodes of lactic acidosis. Many cases of COX deficiency are inherited as an autosomal recessive genetic trait. However, it is possible that other cases may be inherited due to abnormal changes in genetic material (mutation) found within mitochondria (mtDNA).

The following organizations may provide additional information and support:
CLIMB (Children Living with Inherited Metabolic Diseases)
Lactic Acidosis Support Trust
NIH/National Institute of Diabetes, Digestive & Kidney Diseases
United Mitochondrial Disease Foundation

325 Cytomegalovirus Infection

Synonyms
CMV
Cytomegalic Inclusion Disease
Giant Cell Inclusion Disease (CID)
Human Cytomegalovirus Infection
Salivary Gland Disease, CMV Type

Disorder Subdivisions
Acquired Cytomegalovirus Infection
Congenital Cytomegalovirus Infection
Postperfusion Syndrome

Cytomegalovirus infection (CMV) is a viral infection that rarely causes obvious illness. The virus that causes CMV is part of the herpes virus family and, like other herpes viruses, may become dormant for a period of time and then be reactivated. CMV affects young children mainly, but it is estimated that by age 30 in the United States, half of all adults are, or have been, infected. The virus can pass from an infected, pregnant mother to her child through the shared blood supply (umbilical cord). Physicians recognize three clinical forms of CMV. These include: (1) CMV inclusion disease of the newborn, which ranges in severity from being without symptoms to being a severe disease affecting the liver, spleen and central nervous system, with possible developmental disabilities; (2) Acute acquired CMV infection, which is similar to infectious mononucleosis and characterized by fever, a feeling of being not quite right (malaise), skeletal-muscular pain and the absence of a sore throat; (3) CMV in immunocompromised persons (for instance, people who have had organ transplants or who have HIV) with increased risk for difficult eye infections (CMV retinitis), gastrointestinal CMV, and encephalitis.

The following organizations may provide additional information and support:
Centers for Disease Control and Prevention
National Congenital CMV Disease Registry
NIH/National Eye Institute
NIH/National Institute of Allergy and Infectious Diseases

326 Dandy-Walker Malformation

Synonyms
Dandy-Walker Cyst
Dandy-Walker Deformity
Dandy-Walker Syndrome
DWM
Hydrocephalus, Internal, Dandy-Walker Type
Hydrocephalus, Noncommunicating, Dandy-Walker Type
Luschka-Magendie Foramina Atresia

Dandy-Walker malformation is a rare malformation of the brain that is present at birth (congenital). It is characterized by an abnormally enlarged space at the back of the brain (cystic 4th ventricle) that interferes with the normal flow of cerebrospinal fluid through the openings between the ventricle and other parts of the brain (foramina of Magendia and Luschka). Excessive amounts of fluid accumulate around the brain and cause abnormally high pressure within the skull, swelling of the head (congenital hydrocephalus), and neurological impairment. Motor delays and learning problems may also occur. Dandy-Walker malformation is a form of "obstructive" or "internal noncommunicating hydrocephalus," meaning that the normal flow of cerebrospinal fluid is blocked resulting in the widening of the ventricles.

The following organizations may provide additional information and support:
Guardians of Hydrocephalus Research Foundation
Hydrocephalus Association
Hydrocephalus Support Group, Inc.
National Association for Visually Handicapped
National Hydrocephalus Foundation
National Institute of Neurological Disorders and Stroke (NINDS)

327 De Barsy Syndrome

Synonyms
Corneal Clouding-Cutis Laxa-Mental Retardation
Cutis Laxa-Growth Deficiency Syndrome

De Barsy-Moens-Diercks Syndrome
Progeroid Syndrome of De Barsy

De Barsy syndrome is a rare, autosomal recessive genetic disorder, the main characteristics of which are a prematurely aged-looking face (progeria), cloudy corneas, short stature, and mental retardation. The condition is expressed in variable presentations involving complicated patterns of ocular, facial, skeletal, dermatologic and neurological abnormalities.

The following organizations may provide additional information and support:
Genetic and Rare Diseases (GARD) Information Center
March of Dimes Birth Defects Foundation
NIH/National Arthritis and Musculoskeletal and Skin Diseases Information Clearinghouse

328   De Sanctis Cacchione Syndrome

Synonym

Xerodermic Idiocy

De Sanctis-Cacchione syndrome is an extremely rare disorder characterized by the skin and eye symptoms of xeroderma pigmentosum (XP) occurring in association with neurological abnormalities, mental retardation, unusually short stature (dwarfism), and underdevelopment of the testes or ovaries (hypogonadism). Xeroderma pigmentosum is a group of rare inherited skin disorders characterized by a heightened reaction to ultraviolet light (photosensitivity), skin discolorations, and the possible development of several types of eye disorders and skin cancers. The most common neurological abnormalities associated with De Sanctis-Cacchione syndrome are low intelligence, an abnormally small head (microcephaly), the loss of ability to coordinate voluntary movement (ataxia), and/or absent (areflexia) or weakened (hyporeflexia) reflexes. De Sanctis-Cacchione syndrome is inherited as an autosomal recessive trait.

The following organizations may provide additional information and support:
March of Dimes Birth Defects Foundation
NIH/National Arthritis and Musculoskeletal and Skin Diseases Information Clearinghouse
Skin Cancer Foundation
Xeroderma Pigmentosum Registry
XP (Xeroderma Pigmentosum) Society, Inc.

329   Degos Disease

Synonyms

Degos Syndrome
Degos-Kohlmeier Disease
Kohlmeier-Degos Disease
Malignant Atrophic Papulosis

Degos disease is a rare systemic disorder that affects small and medium sized arteries, causing them to become blocked (occlusive arteriopathy). Degos disease usually progresses through two stages. During the first stage, characteristic skin lesions appear that may last for a period of time ranging from weeks to years. The second stage of Degos disease is most frequently characterized by lesions in the small intestine, but other organs may also be affected. Major symptoms may include abdominal pain, diarrhea, and/or weight loss. Intestinal lesions may break through the wall of the bowel (perforation), a potentially life-threatening complication. The exact cause of Degos disease is unknown.

The following organizations may provide additional information and support:
Degos Patients' Support Network
Digestive Disease National Coalition
NIH/National Digestive Diseases Information Clearinghouse

330   Dejerine Sottas Disease

Synonyms

Hereditary Motor Sensory Neuropathy Type III,
HSMN Type III
Hypertrophic Interstitial Neuritis
Hypertrophic Interstitial Neuropathy
Hypertrophic Interstitial Radiculoneuropathy
Onion-Bulb Neuropathy

Dejerine-Sottas disease is an inherited neurological disorder that progressively affects mobility. Peripheral nerves become enlarged or thickened leading to muscle weakness. Progress of the disorder is irregular and often accompanied by pain, weakness, numbness, and a tingling, prickling or burning sensation in the legs. Many people with Dejerine-Sottas disease continue to lead active lives. Most neurologists now consider this disorder to be one of 5 types of hereditary motor sensory neuropathy (HMSN) which simply means genetically transmitted disorder of the nerves associated with movement. Dejerine-Sottas disease is one of several that comprise type III and in which the protective sheath around the long nerves breaks down (demyelination) for unknown reasons exposing and endangering the nerve. The nerves are enlarged due to an accumulation of connective tissue that may present in the form of "onion-bulbs."

The following organizations may provide additional information and support:
Jack Miller Center for Peripheral Neuropathy
March of Dimes Birth Defects Foundation
Muscular Dystrophy Association
National Institute of Neurological Disorders and Stroke (NINDS)

331 Dengue Fever

Synonyms
Breakbone Fever
Dandy Fever
Dengue Hemorrhagic Fever
Dengue Shock Syndrome
Duengero
Seven Day Fever, Dengue Type

Dengue fever is an acute viral infection characterized by fever. It is caused by a bite from mosquitoes carrying dengue virus. The primary form of Dengue fever is characterized by a skin rash and a high fever with severe pain in the head and muscles. Other symptoms may include shaking chills, diarrhea, and vomiting. Bouts of extreme exhaustion may last for months after the initial symptoms. The secondary forms of this disorder are called Dengue hemorrhagic fever and Dengue shock syndrome. These usually are caused by a secondary infection with a different type of Dengue virus (type 2), but may also be caused by the same virus that causes Dengue fever. Several days after onset other symptoms may include fever, bleeding under the skin, red spots on the legs, and bleeding into the intestines. A marked fall in blood pressure (shock) occurs in very severe cases.

The following organizations may provide additional information and support:
Centers for Disease Control and Prevention
NIH/National Institute of Allergy and Infectious Diseases
World Health Organization (WHO) Regional Office for the Americas (AMRO)

332 Dentin Dysplasia, Coronal

Synonyms
Anomalous Dysplasia of Dentin
Coronal Dentin Dysplasia

Dentin Dysplasia, Type II
Pulp Stones
Pulpal Dysplasia

Coronal dentin dysplasia is a rare inherited dental defect that is also known as dentin dysplasia, type II. It is characterized by abnormal development (dysplasia) of the hard tissue (i.e., dentin) that is beneath the enamel, surrounds the pulp, and forms the major part of the teeth. In those with coronal dentin dysplasia, the baby teeth (primary or deciduous teeth) are brownish blue with a translucent "opalescence." (Opalescence refers to a milky, opal-like display of colors in reflected light [iridescence].) However, the permanent teeth appear normal in color. As seen on dental x-ray imaging, the pulp chambers of the primary teeth—or the natural cavities that contain living pulp in the exposed portion of the teeth (crowns)—are obliterated by abnormal dentin. In addition, the pulp-containing canals within the roots of the teeth (root canals) are smaller than normal. The permanent teeth also have distinctive abnormalities of the pulp chambers. Coronal dentin dysplasia is transmitted as an autosomal dominant trait.

The following organizations may provide additional information and support:
Genetic and Rare Diseases (GARD) Information Center
NIH/National Oral Health Information Clearinghouse

333 Dentin Dysplasia, Type I

Synonyms
Dentin Dysplasia, Radicular
Opalescent Dentin
Pulpless Teeth
Radicular Dentin Dysplasia
Rootless Teeth
Thistle Tube Teeth

Dentin dysplasia type I is an inherited disorder characterized by atypical development of the "dentin" of a person's teeth. Dentin makes up most of the tooth and is the bone-like material under the enamel. It serves to contain the pulp of the tooth. The pulp is a soft tissue that is well supplied with blood vessels and nerves. This disorder is also known as radicular dentin dysplasia because the underdeveloped, abnormal pulp tissue is predominately in the roots of the teeth. The teeth lack pulp chambers or have half-moon shaped pulp chambers in short or abnormally shaped roots. The condition may affect juvenile as well as adult teeth and, since the roots are abnormally short, usually leads to the premature loss of teeth. The color of the teeth is usually normal.

The following organizations may provide additional information and support:
National Foundation for Ectodermal Dysplasias
NIH/National Oral Health Information Clearinghouse

---

334 Dentinogenesis Imperfecta Type III

Synonyms
Brandywine Type Dentinogenesis Imperfecta
Dentinogenesis Imperfecta, Shields Type

Dentinogenesis imperfecta type III (DGI-III) is one of five distinct, hereditary disorders of dentin development affecting the teeth. Dentin is the hard, bone-like material that makes up most of a tooth and lies under the enamel serving to protect the soft, pulp tissue. These heritable dentin disorders may affect only the teeth or may be associated with the condition known as osteogenesis imperfecta. Whether this association is present is a major criterion in the classification of dentinogenesis imperfecta into three types. The teeth of people who have inherited one of the DGIs are usually pale-colored and lustrous (opalescent). They are awkwardly formed and situated in the gums; they wear away readily and break easily. Patients with DGI type I also are affected by osteogenesis imperfecta, and the whites of their eyes (sclera) are blue in color. Patients with DGI type II are NOT affected by osteogenesis imperfecta, but show the other clinical signs. Patients with DGI type III appear to be limited, in large measure, to a population in the region around Brandywine in southern Maryland.

The following organizations may provide additional information and support:
National Foundation for Ectodermal Dysplasias
NIH/National Oral Health Information Clearinghouse

---

335 Depersonalization Disorder

Synonym
Depersonalization Neurosis

Depersonalization disorder is a psychiatric disorder affecting emotions and behavior. It is characterized by an alteration in how an affected individual perceives or experiences his or her unique sense of self. The usual sense of one's own reality is temporarily lost or changed. A feeling of detachment from, or being an outside observer of, one's mental processes or body occurs such as the sensation of being in a dream.

The following organizations may provide additional information and support:
National Alliance for the Mentally Ill
National Mental Health Association
National Mental Health Consumers' Self-Help Clearinghouse
NIH/National Institute of Mental Health

---

336 Dercum Disease

Synonyms
Adiposis Dolorosa
Juxta-Articular Adiposis Dolorosa

Dercum disease is a rare disorder characterized by multiple, painful fatty deposits (lipomas), primarily on the trunk, forearms, and lower legs. It is associated with pain that may be caused by these deposits pressing on nearby nerves. This disorder usually occurs in obese females between the ages of 45 and 60. Various areas of the body may swell for no apparent reason. The swelling may disappear without treatment, leaving hardened tissue or pendulous skin folds. In some cases, affected individuals may also experience depression, lethargy, and/or confusion.

The following organizations may provide additional information and support:
American Chronic Pain Association
Dercum's Support
NIH/National Institute of Diabetes, Digestive & Kidney Diseases

---

337 Dermatitis, Atopic

Synonyms
Atopic Eczema
Besnier Prurigo
Constitutional Eczema
Disseminated Neurodermatitis
Eczema

Atopic dermatitis is a common chronic inherited form of eczema. Eczema is a skin condition characterized by redness, swelling (edema), oozing, crusting, scaling, burning pain, and itching (pruritus). Scratching or rubbing eczema may lead to thickening and marking of the skin (lichenification). The causes of eczema fall into two classifications: 1) constitutional eczema (atopic dermatitis), and 2) external eczema which is caused by allergies, irritations, or chemical reactions such as in contact dermatitis.

The following organizations may provide additional information and support:
Allergy Information Association
American Academy of Allergy, Asthma and Immunology
American Academy of Dermatology
Autoimmune Information Network, Inc
NIH/National Institute of Arthritis and Musculoskeletal and Skin Diseases

338 Dermatitis, Contact

Synonyms
Delayed Hypersensitivity
Dermatitis Medicamentosa
Dermatitis Venenata
Drug Hypersensitivity

Disorder Subdivisions
Allergic Contact Dermatitis
Irritant Contact Dermatitis
Photoallergic Contact Dermatitis
Phototoxic Contact Dermatitis

Contact dermatitis is an acute or chronic skin inflammation triggered by substances that come in contact with the skin. Affected individuals may have abnormal redness of the skin (erythema) and/or itching (pruritis). Symptoms and physical findings associated with contact dermatitis vary greatly depending upon the cause of the disorder. Causes of contact dermatitis include an allergic reaction or response to a substance or a direct toxic effect of a substance (e.g., chemical irritants, medications, certain plants).

The following organizations may provide additional information and support:
Allergy Information Association
American Academy of Allergy Asthma and Immunology
Autoimmune Information Network, Inc
National Eczema Association for Science and Education
NIH/National Arthritis and Musculoskeletal and Skin Diseases Information Clearinghouse

339 Dermatitis Herpetiformis

Synonyms
Brocq-Duhring Disease
Dermatitis Multiformis
DH
Duhring Disease

Dermatitis herpetiformis, also known as Duhring disease, is a rare, chronic, skin disorder characterized by the presence of groups of severely itchy (pruritic) blisters and raised skin lesions (papules). These are more common on the knees, elbows, buttocks and shoulder blades. The exact cause of this disease is not known although it is frequently associated with the inability to digest gluten (gluten sensitive enteropathy [GSE] or celiac sprue).

The following organizations may provide additional information and support:
Gluten Intolerance Group of North America
NIH/National Arthritis and Musculoskeletal and Skin Diseases Information Clearinghouse

340 Dermatomyositis

Disorder Subdivisions
Adult Dermatomyositis
Dermatomyositis Sine Myositis
Juvenile (Childhood) Dermatomyositis (JDMS)

Dermatomyositis is a progressive connective tissue disorder characterized by inflammatory and degenerative changes of the muscles and skin. Associated symptoms and physical findings may vary widely from case to case. Muscle abnormalities may begin with aches and weakness of the muscles of the trunk, upper arms, hips, and thighs (proximal muscles). Muscles may be stiff, sore, and tender and, eventually, show signs of degeneration (atrophy). Affected individuals may experience difficulty in performing certain functions, such as raising their arms and/or climbing stairs. In addition, affected individuals may experience speech and swallowing difficulties. Skin abnormalities associated with dermatomyositis often include a distinctive reddish-purple rash (heliotrope rash) on the upper eyelids, across the cheeks and bridge of the nose in a "butterfly" distribution, the forehead, or additional skin regions; scaling and degenerative (atrophic) changes of affected skin on the extending surfaces of the knuckles, elbows, knees, and/or other regions (Gottron's sign); an abnormal accumulation of fluid (edema) in body tissues surrounding the eyes; and/or other features. The symptoms of childhood dermatomyositis are similar to those associated with the adult form of the disorder. However, onset is usually more sudden. In addition, abnormal accumulations of calcium deposits (calcifications) in muscle and skin tissues as well as involvement of the digestive (gastrointestinal [GI]) tract are more common in the childhood form of dermatomyositis. Although the exact cause of dermatomyositis is not known, it is thought to be an autoimmune disorder.

The following organizations may provide additional information and support:
American Autoimmune Related Diseases Association, Inc.
Arthritis Foundation
Autoimmune Information Network, Inc
British Coalition of Heritable Disorders of Connective Tissue
Muscular Dystrophy Association
Myositis Association
Myositis Support Group
NIH/National Institute of Arthritis and Musculoskeletal and Skin Diseases

341 Devic Disease

Synonyms
Devic Syndrome
Neuromyelitis Optica
Ophthalmoneuromyelitis
Optic Neuroencephalomyelopathy
Optic Neuromyelitis
Opticomyelitis
Retrobulbar Neuropathy

Devic disease, also known as neuromyelitis optica, is a rare nerve disorder characterized by optic neuritis occurring in conjunction with transverse myelitis. Optic neuritis is characterized by inflammation and swelling of the nerves in the eyes that transmit impulses from the retinas to the brain (optic nerves). Transverse myelitis is characterized by inflammation and swelling of the nerves in the spinal cord. Most individuals with Devic disease have an initial phase of the disorder consisting of a slight fever, sore throat and/or head cold. Affected individuals may also experience loss of clear vision (acuity), mild paralysis (usually of the lower limbs), and loss of bladder and bowel control. Devic disease may occur spontaneously, or in conjunction with multiple sclerosis or systemic lupus erythematosus.

The following organizations may provide additional information and support:
American Autoimmune Related Diseases Association, Inc.
National Institute of Neurological Disorders and Stroke (NINDS)
NIH/National Eye Institute
Transverse Myelitis Association

342 Dextrocardia with Situs Inversus

Synonym
Mirror-Image Dextrocardia

Dextrocardia with situs inversus is a rare heart condition characterized by abnormal positioning of the heart. In this condition, the tip of the heart (apex) is positioned on the right side of the chest. Additionally, the position of the heart chambers as well as the visceral organs such as the liver and spleen is reversed (situs inversus). However, most affected individuals can live a normal life without associated symptoms or disability.

The following organizations may provide additional information and support:
Adult Congenital Heart Association
American Heart Association
Congenital Heart Anomalies, Support, Education, & Resources
March of Dimes Birth Defects Foundation
NIH/National Heart, Lung and Blood Institute Information Center

343 Diabetes Insipidus

Synonyms
CDI
Central Diabetes Insipidus
Diabetes Insipidus, Neurohypophyseal
NDI
Nephrogenic Diabetes Insipidus
Vasopressin-Resistant Diabetes Insipidus
Vasopressin-Sensitive Diabetes Insipidus

Diabetes insipidus is a rare metabolic disease that is not related to diabetes mellitus. It is characterized by a deficiency of the hormone vasopressin (anti-diuretic hormone [ADH]), which is produced in the posterior lobe of the pituitary gland. The lack of effect of this hormone on the kidney causes excretion of excessive quantities of very dilute (but otherwise normal) urine. Excessive thirst and urination are the major symptoms of this disorder.

The following organizations may provide additional information and support:
Diabetes Insipidus Foundation, Inc.
The Hormone Foundation
Nephrogenic Diabetes Insipidus Foundation
NIH/National Diabetes Information Clearinghouse
Pituitary Network Association (PNA)

.

344 Diabetes, Insulin Dependent

Synonyms

Diabetes Mellitus, Type I
IDDM
Juvenile Diabetes
Type I Diabetes

Insulin-dependent diabetes is a disorder in which the body does not produce enough insulin and is, therefore, unable to convert nutrients into the energy necessary for daily activity. Insulin, a hormone produced by the pancreas, regulates blood glucose levels by promoting the movement of glucose into cells for energy production or into the liver and fat cells for storage. (Glucose is a simple sugar that is the body's primary source of energy for cell metabolism.) The disorder affects females and males in equal numbers. Although the exact causes of insulin-dependent diabetes are not known, autoimmune, genetic and environmental (i.e., viral) factors seem to play a role.

The following organizations may provide additional information and support:
American Diabetes Association
Autoimmune Information Network, Inc.
The Hormone Foundation
JDF-Juvenile Diabetes Research Foundation Canada
Juvenile Diabetes Research Foundation International
New Horizons Un-Limited, Inc.
NIH/National Diabetes Information Clearinghouse

345 Diastrophic Dysplasia

Synonyms

DD
Diastrophic Dwarfism
Diastrophic Nanism Syndrome
DTD

Diastrophic dysplasia, which is also known as disastrophic dwarfism, is a rare disorder that is present at birth (congenital). The range and severity of associated symptoms and physical findings may vary greatly from case to case. However, the disorder is often characterized by short stature and unusually short arms and legs (short-limbed dwarfism); abnormal development of bones (skeletal dysplasia) and joints (joint dysplasia) in many areas of the body; progressive abnormal curvature of the spine (scoliosis and/or kyphosis); abnormal tissue changes of the outer, visible portions of the ears (pinnae); and/or, in some cases, malformations of the head and facial (craniofacial) area. In most infants with diastrophic dysplasia, the first bone within the body of each hand (first metacarpals) may be unusually small and "oval shaped," causing the thumbs to deviate away (abduction) from the body ("hitchhiker thumbs"). Other fingers may also be abnormally short (brachydactyly) and joints between certain bones of the fingers (proximal interphalangeal joints) may become fused (symphalangism), causing limited flexion and restricted movement of the finger joints. Affected infants also typically have severe foot deformities (talipes or "clubfeet") due to abnormal deviation and fusion of certain bones within the body of each foot (metatarsals). In addition, many children with the disorder experience limited extension, partial (subluxation) or complete dislocation, and/or permanent flexion and immobilization (contractures) of certain joints. In most infants with diastrophic dysplasia, there is also incomplete closure of bones of the spinal column (spina bifida occulta) within the neck area and the upper portion of the back (lower cervical and upper thoracic vertebrae). In addition, during the first year of life, some affected children may begin to develop progressive abnormal sideways curvature of the spine (scoliosis). During adolescence, individuals with the disorder may also develop abnormal front-to-back curvature of the spine (kyphosis), particularly affecting vertebrae within the neck area (cervical vertebrae). In severe cases, progressive kyphosis may lead to difficulties breathing (respiratory distress). Some individuals may also be prone to experiencing partial dislocation (subluxation) of joints between the central areas (bodies) of cervical vertebrae, potentially resulting in spinal cord injury. Such injury may cause muscle weakness (paresis) or paralysis and/or life-threatening complications. In addition, most newborns with diastrophic dysplasia have or develop abnormal fluid-filled sacs (cysts) within the outer, visible portions of the ears (pinnae).

Within the first weeks of life, the pinnae become swollen and inflamed and unusually firm, thick, and abnormal in shape. Over time, the abnormal areas of tissue (lesions) may accumulate deposits of calcium salts (calcification) and eventually develop into bone (ossification). Some affected infants may also have abnormalities of the head and facial (craniofacial) area including incomplete closure of the roof of the mouth (cleft palate) and/or abnormal smallness of the jaws (micrognathia). In addition, in some affected infants, abnormalities of supportive connective tissue (cartilage) within the windpipe (trachea), voice box (larynx), and certain air passages in the lungs (bronchi) may result in collapse of these airways, causing life-threatening complications such as respiratory obstruction and difficulties breathing. In some individuals with the disorder, additional symptoms and physical findings may also be present. Diastrophic dysplasia is inherited as an autosomal recessive trait.

The following organizations may provide additional information and support:
AboutFace USA
Cleft Palate Foundation
Human Growth Foundation
Little People of America, Inc.
MAGIC Foundation for Children's Growth
March of Dimes Birth Defects Foundation
National Craniofacial Foundation
National Spinal Cord Injury Association
NIH/National Institute of Arthritis and Musculoskeletal and Skin Diseases
NIH/National Institute of Child Health & Human Development (Preg & Perinat)
NIH/National Institute on Deafness and Other Communication Disorders (Balance)
Prescription Parents
Spinal Cord Injury Network International
Wide Smiles

346 Diencephalic Syndrome

Synonyms
Diencephalic Syndrome of Childhood
Diencephalic Syndrome of Emaciation
Paramedian Diencephalic Syndrome
Russell's Diencephalic Cachexia
Russell's Syndrome

The diencephalic syndrome is a very rare neurological disorder characterized by failure to thrive, abnormal thinness (emaciation), amnesia, intense sleepiness, unusual eye position and sometimes blindness. It is normally seen in infancy or early childhood but some cases have been reported in older children and even adults. Diencephalic syndrome is usually caused by a brain tumor such as a low-grade glioma or astrocytoma.

The following organizations may provide additional information and support:
American Cancer Society, Inc.
Children's Brain Tumor Foundation
Guardians of Hydrocephalus Research Foundation
Hydrocephalus Association
National Hydrocephalus Foundation
Pediatric Brain Tumor Foundation

347 Diffuse Idiopathic Skeletal Hyperostosis

Synonyms
Diffuse Idiopathic Skeletal Hyperostosis
DISH
Forestier's Disease
Spinal Diffuse Idiopathic Skeletal Hyperostosis
Spinal DISH
Vertebral Ankylosing Hyperostosis

Diffuse idiopathic skeletal hyperostosis (DISH), also known as Forestier's disease, affects the ligaments around the spine. Sections of the ligaments turn into bone in this disorder, which is considered to be a form of degenerative arthritis. The conversion of ligamental tissue to bone usually extends along the sides of the vertebrae of the spine. (This may be called flowing calcification.) Also, DISH is associated with inflammation (tendinitis) and calcification of the tendons, especially at the points at which the tendon attaches to the bones. When this happens, the patient is said to have developed bone spurs, especially in the heel and ankles (heel spurs). DISH affects three or more vertebrae that are most often located in the chest or in the spine between the chest and pelvis. It is a disorder of older patients, more often affecting men than women ages 50-60. The disorder is often found in association with diabetes, high blood pressure, heart disease and obesity.

The following organization may provide additional information and support:
NIH/National Arthritis and Musculoskeletal and Skin Diseases Information Clearinghouse

348 DiGeorge Syndrome

Synonyms

Chromosome 22q11 Deletion Syndrome
Congenital Absence of the Thymus and
Parathyroids
DGS
Harrington Syndrome
Pharyngeal Pouch Syndrome
Third and Fourth Pharyngeal Pouch
Syndrome
Thymic Agenesis
Thymic Aplasia, DiGeorge Type
Thymic Hypoplasia, DiGeorge Type
Thymus, Congenital, Aplasia

DiGeorge syndrome is a rare immunodeficiency disorder characterized by various congenital abnormalities that develop because of defects that occur during early fetal development. These defects occur in areas known as the 3rd and 4th pharyngeal pouches, which later develop into the thymus and parathyroid glands. Developmental abnormalities may also occur in the 4th branchial arch. Normally the thymus gland is located below the thyroid gland in the neck and front of the chest and is the primary gland of the lymphatic system, which is necessary for the normal functioning of the immune system. The parathyroid glands, located on the sides of the thyroid gland, are responsible for the maintenance of normal levels of calcium in the blood. The thymus and parathyroid glands are missing or underdeveloped in children with DiGeorge syndrome. The symptoms of this disorder vary greatly, depending upon the extent of the missing thymus and parathyroid tissue. The primary problem caused by DiGeorge syndrome is the repeated occurrence of various infections due to a diminished immune system.

The following organizations may provide additional information and support:
The Arc (A National Organization on Mental Retardation)
Chromosome 22 Central
Immune Deficiency Foundation
International Patient Organization for Primary Immunodeficiencies
March of Dimes Birth Defects Foundation
NIH/National Institute of Child Health and Human Development
NIH/National Institute on Deafness and Other Communication Disorders (Balance)

349 Dilatation of the Pulmonary Artery, Idiopathic

Synonym

IDPA

Idiopathic dilatation of the pulmonary artery (IDPA) is a rare congenital defect characterized by a wider than normal main pulmonary artery in the absence of any apparent anatomical or physiological cause.

The following organizations may provide additional information and support:
American Lung Association
NIH/National Heart, Lung and Blood Institute

350 Disaccharide Intolerance I

Synonyms

Congenital Sucrose Isomaltose Malabsorption
CSID
SI Deficiency
Sucrase-Isomaltase Deficiency, Congenital
Sucrose Intolerance, Congenital

Disaccharide intolerance I is a rare inherited metabolic disorder characterized by the deficiency or absence of the enzymes sucrase and isomaltase. This enzyme complex (sucrase-isomaltase) assists in the breakdown of certain sugars (i.e., sucrose) and certain products of starch digestion (dextrins). The sucrase-isomaltase enzyme complex is normally found within the tiny, finger-like projections (microvilli or brush border) lining the small intestine. When this enzyme complex is deficient, nutrients based on ingested sucrose and starch cannot be absorbed properly from the gut. Symptoms of this disorder become evident soon after sucrose or starches, as found in modified milk formulas with sucrose or polycose, are ingested by an affected infant. Breast-fed infants or those on lactose-only formula manifest no symptoms until such time as sucrose (found in fruit juices, solid foods, and/or some medications) is introduced into the diet. Symptoms are variable among affected individuals but usually include watery diarrhea, abdominal swelling (distension) and/or discomfort, among others. Intolerance to starch often disappears within the first few years of life and the symptoms of sucrose intolerance usually improve as the affected child ages. Disaccharide intolerance I is inherited as an autosomal recessive genetic trait.

The following organizations may provide additional information and support:
CLIMB (Children Living with Inherited Metabolic Diseases)
CSID Parent Support Group
March of Dimes Birth Defects Foundation

351 Diverticulitis

Synonym

Colon, Diverticulitis

Diverticulitis is a common digestive disorder and a frequent complication of diverticulosis. Diverticulosis is a condition characterized by the presense of small sac-like protrusions or outpouchings of mucosal layer of tissue through the muscular wall of the large intestine (colon). These protrusions are known as diverticula and may occur in any part of the colon, but most often in a lower part (sigmoid colon). The inflammation of one or more of these sacs is called diverticulitis. Symptoms may include abdominal pain, tenderness, fever, digestive problems, and/or bleeding from part of the large intestine (rectum).

The following organizations may provide additional information and support:
Digestive Disease National Coalition
Intestinal Disease Foundation
NIH/National Digestive Diseases Information Clearinghouse

352 Diverticulosis

Synonyms

Colon, Diverticulosis
Diverticulosis of the Colon

Diverticulosis is characterized by small sac-like protrusions (hernias) of inner intestinal tissue through the muscular wall of the large intestine (colon). These protrusions are called diverticula and may occur in any part of the colon, but most frequently are found in the lowest part (sigmoid).

The following organizations may provide additional information and support:
Digestive Disease National Coalition
Intestinal Disease Foundation
NIH/National Digestive Diseases Information Clearinghouse

353 DOOR Syndrome

Synonyms

Deafness, Onychodystrophy, Osteodystrophy, and Mental Retardation
DOOR(S) Syndrome

DOOR syndrome is a rare genetic disorder that may be recognized shortly after birth. "DOOR," an acronym for characteristic abnormalities associated with the syndrome, stands for (D)eafness due to a defect of the inner ear or auditory nerve (sensorineural hearing loss); (O)nychodystrophy or malformation of the nails; (O)steodystrophy, meaning malformation of certain bones; and mild to profound mental (R)etardation. In addition, in some cases, affected infants may have sudden episodes of uncontrolled electrical activity in the brain (seizures). Distinctive nail abnormalities may include underdeveloped, misshapen, or absent fingernails and/or toenails, while characteristic bone malformations may consist of an extra small bone in the thumbs and/or great toes (triphalangy) and/or underdevelopment (hypoplasia) of bones in other fingers and/or toes. DOOR syndrome is inherited as an autosomal recessive trait.

The following organizations may provide additional information and support:
American Society for Deaf Children
Better Hearing Institute
Epilepsy Foundation
National Institute of Neurological Disorders and Stroke (NINDS)
NIH/National Institute of Arthritis and Musculoskeletal and Skin Diseases

354 Down Syndrome

Synonyms

Chromosome 21, Mosaic 21 Syndrome
Chromosome 21, Translocation 21 Syndrome
Trisomy 21 Syndrome
Trisomy G Syndrome

Down syndrome is a chromosomal disorder in which all or a portion of chromosome 21 appears three times (trisomy) rather than twice in cells of the body. In some affected individuals, only a percentage of cells may contain the chromosomal abnormality (mosaicism). Symptoms and findings may vary greatly in range and severity, depending on the specific length and location of the duplicated (trisomic) portion of chromosome 21 as well as the percentage of cells containing the abnormality. However, in many affected individuals, such abnormalities may include low muscle tone (hypotonia); a tendency to keep the mouth open with protrusion of the tongue; and distinctive malformations of the head and facial (craniofacial) area, such as a short, small head (microbrachycephaly), upwardly slanting eyelid folds (palpebral fissures), a depressed nasal bridge, a small nose, and a relatively flat facial profile. Individuals with Down syndrome may also have unusually small, misshapen (dysplastic) ears; a narrow roof of the mouth (palate); vertical skin folds covering the inner corners of the eyes (epicanthal folds); dental abnormalities; and excessive skin on the back of the neck. Abnormalities of the extremities are also often present, such as unusually short arms and legs; short fingers; and unusual skin ridge patterns (dermatoglyphics) on the fingers, palms, and toes. Affected individuals may also have short stature, poor coordination, mild to severe mental retardation, and hearing impairment. In some cases, Down syndrome may also be characterized by structural malformations of the heart at birth (congenital heart defects). In addition, those with the disorder may have an increased susceptibility to respiratory disease (e.g., pneumonia), other infectious diseases, and malignancies in which there is an increased proliferation of certain white blood cells (leukemia). Such abnormalities may lead to potentially life-threatening complications in some cases.

The following organizations may provide additional information and support:
ANDO (Apoyo al Nino Down)
The Arc (A National Organization on Mental Retardation)
Association for Children with Down Syndrome, Inc.
Birth Defect Research for Children, Inc.
International Mosaic Down Syndrome Association
March of Dimes Birth Defects Foundation
National Center for Down's Syndrome
National Down Syndrome Congress
National Down Syndrome Society
National Institute of Mental Retardation
New Horizons Un-Limited, Inc.
NIH/National Institute of Child Health and Human Development
R.O.C.K. (Raising Our Celiac Kids)

355 Dracunculosis

Synonyms
Dracontiasis
Dracunculiasis
Fiery Serpent Infection
Guinea Worm Infection

Dracunculosis is an infection caused by a parasitic worm known as *Dracunculus medinensis,* the guinea worm. Infected water fleas release the larvae of the worm into drinking water. Ingestion of contaminated water causes the larvae to migrate from the intestines via the abdominal cavity to the tissue under the skin. The larvae mature and release a toxic substance that makes the overlying skin ulcerate. After treatment, symptoms disappear and the worms can be safely removed from the skin.

The following organizations may provide additional information and support:
Centers for Disease Control and Prevention
NIH/National Institute of Allergy and Infectious Diseases
World Health Organization (WHO) Regional Office for the Americas (AMRO)

356 Drash Syndrome

Synonyms
Denys-Drash Syndrome
Nephropathy-Pseudohermaphroditism-Wilms Tumor
Pseudohermaphroditism-Nephron Disorder-Wilm's Tumor
Wilms Tumor and Pseudohermaphroditism
Wilms Tumor-Pseuodohermaphroditism-Glomerulopathy
Wilms Tumor-Pseudohermaphroditism-Nephropathy

Drash syndrome is a very rare disorder that typically appears for no apparent reason (sporadically). In rare cases, it may be inherited as an autosomal dominant genetic trait. This disorder usually appears early in life. In its complete form, it is characterized by the combination of abnormal kidney function, genital abnormalities (pseudohermaphroditism), and a cancerous tumor of the kidney called a Wilms' tumor. Some affected individuals may have the incomplete form of Drash syndrome, which consists of abnormal kidney function with either genital abnormalities (pseudohermaphroditism) or Wilms' tumor. This disorder predominantly affects males but a few female cases have been reported.

The following organizations may provide additional information and support:
American Cancer Society, Inc.
American Kidney Fund, Inc.
Candlelighters Childhood Cancer Foundation
National Kidney Foundation

357 Duane Syndrome

Synonyms
DR Syndrome
Duane's Retraction Syndrome
Eye Retraction Syndrome
Retraction Syndrome
Stilling-Turk-Duane Syndrome

Disorder Subdivisions
Duane Syndrome Type 1A, 1B, 1C
Duane Syndrome Type 2A, 2B, 2C
Duane Syndrome Type 3A, 3B, 3C

Duane syndrome (DS) is an eye movement disorder present at birth (congenital) characterized by a limited ability to move the eye inward toward the nose (adduction), outward toward the ear (abduction), or in both directions. In addition, when the affected eye(s) moves inward toward the nose, the eyeball retracts (pulls in) and the eye opening (palpebral fissure) narrows. In some cases, when the eye attempts to look inward, it moves upward (upshoot) or downward (downshoot). Duane syndrome falls under the larger heading of strabismus (misalignment of the eyes) under the subclassification of incomitant strabismus (misalignment of the eyes that varies with gaze directions) and subheading of extraocular fibrosis syndromes (conditions associated with fibrosis of the muscles that move the eyes). Although the "muscle fibrosis" association suggests that syndromes under this heading are primary disorders of muscle, evidence suggests that DS (and other syndromes under this heading) may be primary disorders of nerve "innervation" (the distribution or supply of nerves). Duane syndrome has been subdivided clinically into three types: type 1, type 2, and type 3.

The following organizations may provide additional information and support:
Let Them Hear Foundation

March of Dimes Birth Defects Foundation
NIH/National Eye Institute
NIH/Office of Rare Diseases
Schepens Eye Research Institute

358 Dubin Johnson Syndrome

Synonyms
Chronic Idiopathic Jaundice
Conjugated Hyperbilirubinemia
DJS
Hyperbilirubinemia II

Dubin Johnson syndrome is a rare genetic liver disorder that tends to affect people of Middle Eastern Jewish heritage disproportionately to other groups. It appears to be associated with clotting factor VII in this population. Symptoms may include a yellowish color to the skin (jaundice), and a liver that is sometimes enlarged and tender.

The following organizations may provide additional information and support:
American Liver Foundation
NIH/National Digestive Diseases Information Clearinghouse

359 Dubowitz Syndrome

Synonym
Intrauterine Dwarfism

Dubowitz syndrome is a very rare genetic and developmental disorder involving multiple congenital (inherited) anomalies including but not limited to: (1) growth failure/short stature; (2) unusual but characteristic facial features; (3) a small head (microencephaly); (4) mild (usually) mental retardation; and (5), in at least 50% of the cases, eczema. Multiple organ systems are affected and the disorder is unpredictable and extremely variable in its expression. Symptoms may be detected while the fetus is still in the uterus (intrauterine) as well as immediately after birth (neonatal). Facial appearance is a key to the diagnosis, with characteristic high or sloping forehead; sparse hair; flat, undeveloped (hypoplastic) bones above the eyes (supraorbital ridges); increased distance between the eyes (ocular hypertelorism); drooping eyelids (ptosis); sparse (hypoplastic) lateral eyebrows; very small lower jaw (micrognathia) and receding chin (retrognathia). Affected children are often hyperactive, stubborn and shy.

The following organizations may provide additional information and support:
The Arc (A National Organization on Mental Retardation)
Genetic and Rare Diseases (GARD) Information Center
Learning Disabilities Association of America

---

360   Duodenal Atresia or Stenosis

Synonyms
Duodenal Atresia
Duodenal Stenosis

Duodenal atresia or stenosis is a rare congenital digestive disorder that usually occurs for no apparent reason (sporadically). However, a few cases of duodenal atresia have been inherited as an autosomal recessive genetic trait. Duodenal atresia is a disease of newborn infants. Absence or complete closure (atresia) of a portion of the channel (lumen) within the first part of the small intestine (duodenum), or partial obstruction due to narrowing (stenosis) of the duodenum, is present. Other associated abnormalities may be found in over half of those affected with duodenal atresia or duodenal stenosis.

The following organizations may provide additional information and support:
American Society of Parenteral and Enteral Nutrition
Digestive Disease National Coalition
NIH/National Digestive Diseases Information Clearinghouse

---

361   Dupuytren's Contracture

Synonyms
Palmar Fibromas
Palmar Fibromatosis, Familial
Plantar Fibromas
Plantar Fibromatosis, Familial

Dupuytren's contracture is a rare connective tissue disorder characterized by fixation of the joints (e.g., proximal interphalangeal joints and metacarpophalangeal joints) of certain fingers in a permanently flexed position (joint contractures). Due to abnormal thickening and shortening of the bands of fibrous tissue beneath the skin of the palm (palmar fascia), a hardened nodule may develop, eventually forming an abnormal band of hardened (fibrotic) tissue. As a result, the fingers of the affected area begin to be drawn in toward the palm over several months or years and cannot be pulled back (contracture). In addition, the skin of the affected area may pucker. In most cases, the ring and pinky (fourth and fifth) fingers are most affected. In addition, the disorder usually affects both hands (bilateral). Although the exact cause of Dupuytren's contracture is unknown, risk for the disorder appears to be increased by alcoholic liver disease (cirrhosis) and the presence of certain other diseases, including diabetes, thyroid problems, and epilepsy. In addition, it is thought that genetic predisposition may be a factor.

The following organizations may provide additional information and support:
Eaton's Hand Surgery Links
March of Dimes Birth Defects Foundation
NIH/National Arthritis and Musculoskeletal and Skin Diseases Information Clearinghouse

---

362   Dyggve-Melchior-Clausen Syndrome

Synonyms
DMC Disease
DMC Syndrome
Smith-McCort Dysplasia

Disorder Subdivision
Smith-McCort Syndrome

Dyggve-Melchior-Clausen (DMC) syndrome is a rare genetic disorder characterized by abnormal skeletal development and mental retardation. Symptoms may include growth deficiency resulting in short stature, various skeletal abnormalities, and mental retardation. DMC is inherited as an autosomal recessive trait. A variant of DMC syndrome, known as Smith McCort dysplasia, is characterized by similar abnormal skeletal development, but without mental deficiencies. Smith-McCort syndrome has an X-linked recessive inheritance pattern.

The following organizations may provide additional information and support:
The Arc (A National Organization on Mental Retardation)
Human Growth Foundation
Little People of America, Inc.
MAGIC Foundation for Children's Growth
March of Dimes Birth Defects Foundation
NIH/National Institute of Child Health & Human Development (Preg & Perinat)

363 Dysautonomia, Familial

Synonyms
FD
HSAN-III
HSN-III
Hereditary Sensory and Autonomic Neuropathy, Type III (HSAN, Type III)
Hereditary Sensory Neuropathy Type III
Riley-Day Syndrome

Familial dysautonomia is a rare genetic disorder of the autonomic nervous system (ANS) that primarily affects people of Eastern European Jewish heritage. It is characterized by diminished sensitivity to pain, lack of overflow tearing in the eyes, a decrease in the number of knob-like projections that cover the tongue (fungiform papillae), unusual fluctuations of body temperature, and unstable blood pressure. Symptoms of this disorder are apparent at birth. The autonomic nervous system controls vital involuntary body functions.

The following organizations may provide additional information and support:
Dysautonomia Foundation, Inc.
Dysautonomia Foundation, Inc., Toronto Chapter
Familial Dysautonomia Hope Foundation
March of Dimes Birth Defects Foundation
National Dysautonomia Research Foundation
National Institute of Neurological Disorders and Stroke (NINDS)

364 Dyschondrosteosis

Synonyms
Dwarfism, Deformity with Mesomelic
Leri-Weil Dyschondrosteosis
Leri-Weil Syndrome
Leri-Weill Disease
Mesomelic Dwarfism-Madelung Deformity

Dyschondrosteosis is a very rare inherited disorder characterized by unusually shortened, bowed bones in the forearms (radius and ulna), abnormal deviation of the wrist toward the thumb side of the hand due to shortening of the radius and dislocation of the end portion of the ulna (Madelung deformity), unusually short lower legs, and associated short stature (mesomelic dwarfism). Affected individuals may also exhibit abnormalities of the large bone of the upper arm (humerus); abnormal bony growths projecting outward from the surface of the shin bones (exostoses of the tibia); unusually short, broad bones in the fingers and toes; and/or abnormalities of the hipbone (i.e., coxa valga). Dyschondrosteosis appears to affect females more severely than males. The disorder is inherited as an autosomal dominant or "pseudoautosomal" trait.

The following organizations may provide additional information and support:
Human Growth Foundation
Little People of America, Inc.
Little People's Research Fund, Inc.
MAGIC Foundation for Children's Growth

365 Dyskeratosis Congenita

Synonyms
DKC
Dyschromatosis Universalis Hereditaria
Dyskeratosis Congenita Syndrome
Dyskeratosis Congenita, Autosomal Recessive
Dyskeratosis Congenita, Scoggins Type
Zinsser-Cole-Engman Syndrome

Dyskeratosis congenita is a rare disorder in which three groups of symptoms occur: darkening and/or unusual absence of skin color (hyper/hypopigmentation); progressive nail dystrophy; and slowly changing characteristics of mucous membranes (leukoplakia) in the anus, urethra, lips, mouth and/or eye. Other symptoms found in some patients with this syndrome may be reduction in red and white blood cells and platelets (pancytopenia), overgrowth of skin on the palms of the hands and soles of the feet, excessive sweating of the palms and soles, sparse or absent hair, fragile bones, underdeveloped testes, and dental abnormalities. Dyskeratosis congenita is more prevalent among males than females and an X-linked recessive inheritance is the most common form although cases of autosomal recessive and autosomal dominant inheritance have been recorded. This disorder has also occurred sporadically (no known cause) in a significant number of cases.

The following organizations may provide additional information and support:
March of Dimes Birth Defects Foundation
National Foundation for Ectodermal Dysplasias
NIH/National Heart, Lung and Blood Institute Information Center

366 Dyslexia

Synonyms
Congenital Word Blindness
Developmental Reading Disorder
Primary Reading Disability
Specific Reading Disability

Dyslexia is a condition in which an individual with normal vision is unable to interpret written language, and therefore is unable to read or may read slowly with great difficulty. Onset is during childhood, and males are affected most often.

The following organizations may provide additional information and support:
George Washington University HEATH Resource Center
International Dyslexia Association
Learning Disabilities Association of America
Learning Disabilities Worldwide
National Center for Learning Disabilities
National Institute of Neurological Disorders and Stroke (NINDS)
National Network of Learning-Disabled Adults, Inc.

367 Dysplasia, Epiphysealis Hemimelica

Synonyms
Aclasis, Tarsoepiphyseal
Chondrodystrophy, Epiphyseal
DEH
Dysplasia Epiphyseal Hemimelica
Epiphyseal Osteochondroma, Benign
Tarsomegaly
Trevor Disease

Epiphysealis hemimelica dysplasia is a disorder that affects bone joints. It is characterized by overgrowth of the cartilage on the end (epiphysis) of one or more of the long bones (carpal or tarsal bones) in the hand or foot. Less often, the cartilage on other bones such as those in the ankle, knee or hip joint can be affected. Usually only one limb is involved. The limbs may be unequal in length.

The following organizations may provide additional information and support:
Genetic and Rare Diseases (GARD) Information Center
NIH/National Arthritis and Musculoskeletal and Skin Diseases Information Clearinghouse
Restricted Growth Association

368 Dysplasia, Fibrous

Disorder Subdivisions
Monostotic Fibrous Dysplasia; Jaffe-Lichtenstein Disease
Polyostotic Fibrous Dysplasia

Fibrous dysplasia is a term that refers to either a group of chronic conditions featuring cystic bone growth that may arise from abnormal bone development or to a disease of bone marrow (medullary bone) characterized by benign cysts. Fibrous dysplasia is characterized by uneven growth, pain, brittleness, and deformity of the affected bones. This disorder may involve a single bone (monostotic fibrous dysplasia or Jaffe-Lichtenstein disease) or may affect multiple bones (polyostotic fibrous dysplasia). Fibrous dysplasia is usually evident during childhood, and the bone lesions usually stop developing at puberty. These lesions may be painful, deforming and widespread. The bones most often affected are the ribs, skull, facial bones, thigh bone (femur), shin bone (tibia), upper arm (humerus), and pelvis. Occasionally, the bones in the spine (vertebrae) are affected. Some, but not all, affected individuals experience repeated bone fractures. The exact cause of fibrous dysplasia is not known.

The following organizations may provide additional information and support:
International Center for Skeletal Dysplasia
MAGIC Foundation for Children's Growth
NIH Osteoporosis and Related Bone Diseases National Resource Center
NIH/National Institute of Arthritis and Musculoskeletal and Skin Diseases
Paget Foundation for Paget's Disease of Bone and Related Disorders

369 Dysthymia

Synonyms
Depression, Mild
Depressive Neurosis

Dysthymia is a common psychological disorder characterized by a chronic but mild depressive state that has been present in an individual for more than 2 years. When the depressive state has lasted for several years, it may be difficult to distinguish between a person's usual functioning and the mood disturbance. Dysthymia is a chronic mood disturbance that is classified as a form of neurosis. It must be distinguished from major depression disorders.

The following organizations may provide additional information and support:
NIH/National Institute of Mental Health
NIH/National Institute of Mental Health (Depression Hotline)
National Alliance for the Mentally Ill
National Mental Health Association
National Mental Health Consumers' Self-Help Clearinghouse

370   Dystonia

Synonym
Torsion Dystonia

Disorder Subdivisions
Blepharospasm (Benign Essential
Blepharospasm [BEB])
Cervical Dystonia (Spasmodic Torticollis [ST])
Childhood-onset Dystonia
Dopa-responsive Dystonia (DRD)
Early-onset Dystonia
Focal Dystonia
Generalized Dystonia
Late-onset Dystonia
Myoclonic Dystonia
Oromandibular Dystonia
Paroxysmal Dystonia
Paroxysmal Dystonia Choreathetosis
Paroxysmal Kinesigenic Dystonia (PKD)
Primary Dystonia
Rapid-onset Dystonia-Parkinsonism (RDP)
Secondary Dystonia
Segmental Dystonia
Spasmodic Dysphonia (SD)
Spasmodic Torticollis (Cervical Dystonia)
Tardive Dyskinesia
Tardive Dystonia
Writer's Cramp
X-Linked Dystonia-Parkinsonism

Dystonia is a group of movement disorders that vary in their symptoms, causes, progression, and treatments. This group of neurological conditions is generally characterized by involuntary muscle contractions that force the body into abnormal, sometimes painful, movements and positions (postures). Dystonia may be focal (affecting an isolated body part), segmental (affecting adjacent body areas, or generalized (affecting many major muscle groups simultaneously). There are many different causes for dystonia. Genetic as well as non-genetic factors contribute to all forms of dystonia. The most characteristic finding associated with dystonia is twisting, repetitive movements that affect the neck, torso, limbs, eyes, face, vocal chords, and/or a combination of these muscle groups.

The following organizations may provide additional information and support:
Dystonia Medical Research Foundation
Dystonia Society
National Institute of Neurological Disorders and Stroke (NINDS)
National Spasmodic Dysphonia Association
Organization for Anti-Convulsant Syndrome
Spasmodic Torticollis Dystonia, Inc
WE MOVE (Worldwide Education and Awareness for Movement Disorders)

371   Dystrophy, Asphyxiating Thoracic

Synonyms
Asphyxiating Thoracic Dysplasia
ATD
Jeune Syndrome
Thoracic-Pelvic-Phalangeal Dystrophy

Asphyxiating thoracic dystrophy is a very rare form of congenital dwarfism affecting the development of the bone structure, particularly of the chest (thorax) but also of the legs and arms. Typical, major characteristics include failure of the rib cage to develop correctly, kidney problems (renal failure due to polycystitis), and shortened bones of the arms and legs.

The following organizations may provide additional information and support:
Human Growth Foundation
International Center for Skeletal Dysplasia
MAGIC Foundation for Children's Growth
NIH/National Arthritis and Musculoskeletal and Skin Diseases Information Clearinghouse
Restricted Growth Association

372   Dystrophy, Myotonic

Synonyms
Curschmann-Batten-Steinert Syndrome
DM
Dystrophia Myotonia
Myotonia Atrophica
Steinert Disease

Disorder Subdivisions
Myotonic Dystrophy Type 1 (DM1)
Myotonic Dystrophy Type 2 (DM2)

Myotonic dystrophy type 1 (DM1) is an autosomal dominant, multi-system disorder that affects both smooth and skeletal muscles and may affect the central nervous system, heart, eyes, and/or endocrine systems. There are three types of DM1 that are distinguished by the severity of disease and age of onset. Mild DM1 is characterized by cataracts and sustained muscle contractions (myotonia). Classic DM1 is characterized by muscle weakness and wasting (atrophy), cataracts, myotonia and abnormalities in the heart's conduction of electrical impulses. Congenital DM1 is characterized by muscle weakness (hypotonia), difficulty breathing, mental retardation and early death. DM1 is caused by an abnormality in the DMPK gene. Affected individuals have an increased number of copies of a portion of this gene called CTG. The greater the number of repeated copies of CTG, the more severe the disorder. Myotonic dystrophy type 2 (DM2), formerly called proximal myotonic myopathy (PROMM) is an autosomal dominant disorder with symptoms that are similar to DM1, but tend to be milder and more variable than DM1. DM2 is an autosomal dominant genetic disorder caused by an abnormality in the ZNF9 gene on chromosome 3q. Affected individuals have an increased number of copies of a portion of this gene.

The following organizations may provide additional information and support:
International Myotonic Dystrophy Organization
Muscular Dystrophy Association
Myotonic Dystrophy Support Group
National Institute of Neurological Disorders and Stroke (NINDS)
NIH/National Institute of Arthritis and Musculoskeletal and Skin Diseases

373 Eales Disease

Synonyms
Eales Retinopathy
Idiopathic Peripheral Periphlebitis

Eales disease is a rare disorder of sight that appears as an inflammation and white haze around the outercoat of the veins in the retina. The disorder is most prevalent among young males and normally affects both eyes. Usually, vision is suddenly blurred because the clear jelly that fills the eyeball behind the lens of the eye seeps out (vitreous hemorrhaging).

The following organizations may provide additional information and support:
NIH/National Eye Institute
Schepens Eye Research Institute

374 Ear, Patella, Short Stature Syndrome

Synonyms
EPS
Meier-Gorlin Syndrome
Microtia, Absent Patellae, Micrognathia Syndrome

Ear, patella, short stature syndrome (EPS) is a very rare genetic disorder characterized by small ears (microtia), absent or small knee caps (patellae), and short stature. Other findings include various skeletal abnormalities, early feeding difficulties, and poor weight gain. In addition, characteristic features of the head and face may be present including a small mouth (microstomia), with full lips, small circumference of the head (microcephaly), and/or underdevelopment (hypoplasia) of the upper (maxillary) and/or lower (mandibular) jaw bones (micrognathia). EPS is thought to be inherited as an autosomal recessive genetic disorder.

The following organizations may provide additional information and support:
Better Hearing Institute
Birth Defect Research for Children, Inc.
Ear Anomalies Reconstructed: Atresia/Microtia Support Group
Human Growth Foundation
Little People of America, Inc.
NIH/National Institute of Arthritis and Musculoskeletal and Skin Diseases
NIH/National Institute on Deafness and Other Communication Disorders Information Clearinghouse

375 Ectodermal Dysplasias

Disorder Subdivisions
Anhidrotic X-Linked Ectodermal Dysplasias
Anodontia
Book Syndrome
Chaund's Ectodermal Dysplasias
Chondroectodermal Dysplasias
Christ-Siemans-Touraine Syndrome
Cloustons Syndrome
Curly Hair-Ankyloblephanon-Nail Dysplasia
Dentooculocutaneous Syndrome
Ectrodactyly Ectodermal Dysplasias Clefting Syndrome
Ellis-van Creveld Syndrome

Facial Ectodermal Dysplasias
Freire-Maia Syndrome
Gorlin's Syndrome
Hidrotic Ectodermal Dysplasias
Hypohidrotic Ectodermal Dysplasias,
Autorecessive
Hypoplastic Enamel-Onycholysis-
Hypohidrosis
Incontinentia Pigmenti
Marshall's Ectodermal Dysplasias With Ocular
and Hearing Defects
Monilethrix
Naegeli Ectodermal Dysplasias
Nail Dystrophy-Deafness Syndrome
Oculodentodigital Syndrome
Odontotrichomelic Syndrome
Onychotrichodysplasia with Neutropenia
Oral-Facial-Digital Syndrome (Type I)
Otodental Dysplasia
Pachyonychia Congenita
Palmoplantar Hyperkeratosis and Alopecia
Rapp-Hodgkin Hypohidrotic Ectodermal
Dysplasias
Robertson's Ectodermal Dysplasias
Rosselli-Gulienatti Syndrome
Schopf-Schultz-Passarge Syndrome
Stevanovic's Ectodermal Dysplasias
Tooth and Nail Syndrome
Trichodento Osseous Syndrome
Trichorhinophalangeal Syndrome
Triphalangeal Thumbs-Hypoplastic Distal
Phalanges-Onychodystrophy
Witkop Ectodermal Dysplasias
Xeroderma, Talipes, and Enamel Defect

The ectodermal dysplasias are a group of hereditary, non-progressive syndromes in which the affected tissue derives primarily from the ectodermal germ layer. The skin, its derivatives, and some other organs are involved. A predisposition to respiratory infections, due to a somewhat depressed immune system and to defective mucous glands in parts of the respiratory tract, is the most life-threatening characteristic of this group of disorders.

The following organizations may provide additional information and support:
Let Them Hear Foundation
Locks of Love
March of Dimes Birth Defects Foundation
National Foundation for Ectodermal Dysplasias
NIH/National Oral Health Information Clearinghouse
PC Project

376 Ectrodactyly Ectodermal Dysplasia Cleft Lip/Palate

Synonyms
Ectrodactyly-Ectodermal Dysplasia-Clefting
Syndrome
EEC Syndrome

Ectrodactyly-ectodermal dysplasia-cleft lip/palate (EEC syndrome) is a rare form of ectodermal dysplasia inherited as an autosomal dominant genetic trait the symptoms of which can vary from mild to severe. The most common symptoms found in patients with EEC syndrome are: missing or irregular fingers and/or toes (ectrodactyly), abnormalities of the hair and glands, cleft lip and/or palate, or unusual facial features, as well as abnormalities of the eyes and urinary tract.

The following organizations may provide additional information and support:
National Foundation for Ectodermal Dysplasias
NIH/National Arthritis and Musculoskeletal and Skin Diseases Information Clearinghouse

377 Edema, Idiopathic

Synonyms
Cyclic Edema
Periodic Edema

Idiopathic edema is a common disorder that occurs almost exclusively in women. It is characterized by salt retention in the absence of heart, kidney, or liver disease. The swelling (edema) may be episodic or persistent. Swelling of the face, hands, and feet develops rapidly, frequently accompanied by headache, irritability, and depression. Weight gain also occurs.

The following organizations may provide additional information and support:
NIH/National Digestive Diseases Information Clearinghouse
NIH/National Heart, Lung and Blood Institute

378 Ehlers-Danlos Syndrome

Synonyms
E-D Syndrome
EDS

Disorder Subdivisions
Arthrochalasis Multiplex Congenita (Type VII)
Benign Hypermobility Syndrome (Type III)

Dermatosparaxis (Type VII)
Dermatosparaxis Type (Formerly EDS VII, Autosomal Recessive)
EDS Arterial-Ecchymotic Type (Type IV)
EDS Arthrochalasia Type (formerly EDS VII, Autosomal Dominant)
EDS, Autosomal Dominant, Unspecified Type
EDS, Autosomal Recessive, Unspecified Type
EDS Classic Severe Form (Type I)
EDS Classical Type (Formerly EDS I and EDS II)
EDS Dysfibronectinemic Type (Type X)
EDS Gravis Type (Type I)
EDS Hypermobility Type (formerly EDS III)
EDS Kyphoscoliosis Type (formerly EDS VI)
EDS Kyphoscoliotic Type (Type VI)
EDS Mitis Type (Type II)
EDS Ocular-Scoliotic Type (Type VI)
EDS Periodontosis Type (formerly EDS Type VIII)
EDS Progeroid Form
EDS Types VIIA and VIIB
EDS Type VIIC
EDS Vascular Type (formerly EDS IV)
EDS, X-linked (formerly EDS Type V)
Ehlers-Danlos Syndrome Type I
Ehlers-Danlos Syndrome Type II
Ehlers-Danlos Syndrome Type III
Ehlers-Danlos Syndrome Type IV
Ehlers-Danlos Syndrome Type V
Ehlers-Danlos Syndrome Type VI
Ehlers-Danlos Syndrome Type VII, Autosomal Dominant
Ehlers-Danlos Syndrome Type VII, Autosomal Recessive
Ehlers-Danlos Syndrome Type VIII
Ehlers-Danlos Syndrome Type IX (obsolete)
Ehlers-Danlos Syndrome Type X
Ehlers-Danlos Syndrome Type XI (obsolete)

Ehlers-Danlos syndrome (EDS) is a group of hereditary connective tissue disorders characterized by defects of the major structural protein in the body (collagen). Collagen, a tough, fibrous protein, plays an essential role in holding together, strengthening, and providing elasticity to bodily cells and tissues. Due to defects of collagen, primary EDS symptoms and findings include abnormally flexible, loose joints (articular hypermobility) that may easily become dislocated; unusually loose, thin, stretchy (elastic) skin; and excessive fragility of the skin, blood vessels, and other bodily tissues and membranes. The different types of EDS were originally categorized in a classification system that used Roman numerals (e.g., EDS I to EDS XI), based upon each form's associated symptoms and findings (clinical evidence) and underlying cause. A revised, simplified classification system (revised nosology) has since been described in the medical literature that categorizes EDS into six major subtypes, based upon clinical evidence, underlying biochemical defects, and mode of inheritance. Each subtype of EDS is a distinct hereditary disorder that may affect individuals within certain families (kindreds). In other words, parents with one subtype of EDS will not have children with another EDS subtype. Depending upon the specific subtype present, Ehlers-Danlos syndrome is usually transmitted as an autosomal dominant or autosomal recessive trait.

The following organizations may provide additional information and support:
British Coalition of Heritable Disorders of Connective Tissue
EDS Today
Ehlers Danlos Foundation of New Zealand
Ehlers-Danlos National Foundation (EDNF)
Ehlers-Danlos Syndrome Support Group UK
Ehlers-Danlos Syndrome UK Support Group
NIH/National Institute of Arthritis and Musculoskeletal and Skin Diseases
Sjældne Diagnoser / Rare Disorders Denmark

---

379   Eisenmenger Syndrome

Synonyms
Eisenmenger Complex
Eisenmenger Disease
Eisenmenger Reaction

Eisenmenger syndrome is a progressive heart condition that develops as a complication of certain structural heart malformations present at birth (congenital heart defects). Due to such defects, there may be abnormal blood flow between certain heart regions (e.g., from the left to the right lower chamber [ventricle] of the heart [left-to-right shunt]) or between major blood vessels (aorta and pulmonary artery) and a gradual rise in blood pressure within the pulmonary artery, which carries oxygen-poor (deoxygenated) blood to the lungs (i.e., pulmonary hypertension). Without early surgical correction of the underlying defect, such changes may cause progressive damage to and increased resistance to blood flow within small blood vessels in lung tissue (pulmonary vascular disease) and associated complications (e.g., reversed [right-to-left] ventricular shunt, etc.). The symptoms and signs of Eisenmenger syndrome often do not occur until about the second or third decade of life; however, they may develop more rapidly in some cases. Such findings may include bluish discoloration of the skin and mucous membranes (cyanosis), increasing difficulties breathing (dyspnea) with exertion, fainting episodes (syncope), and other abnormalities due to insufficient oxygen supply to body cells (hypoxia), leading to potentially life-threatening complications. Eisenmenger syndrome most frequently occurs as a complication of ventricular septal defects (VSDs). A VSD is characterized by an abnormal opening in the fibrous partition (septum) that normally separates the two lower heart chambers (ventricles), allowing abnormal blood flow between the two ventricles. Changes associated with Eisenmenger syndrome may also occur due to other septal defects of the heart, abnormal persistence of the fetal opening between the pulmonary artery and aorta (patent ductus arteriosus), or other congenital defects in which there is abnormal communication between the aorta and pulmonary artery.

The following organizations may provide additional information and support:
American Heart Association
American Organ Transplant Association
Children's Heart Association for Support and Education
Congenital Heart Anomalies, Support, Education, & Resources
Little Hearts, Inc.
March of Dimes Birth Defects Foundation
National Foundation For Transplants
National Transplant Assistance Fund (NTAF)
NIH/National Heart, Lung and Blood Institute Information Center
Second Wind Lung Transplant Association, Inc.

---

380   Elephantiasis

Synonym
Elephantitis

Elephantiasis is a rare disorder of the lymphatic system. Inflammation of the lymphatic vessels causes extreme enlargement of the affected area, most commonly a limb or parts of the head and torso. It occurs most commonly in tropical regions and particularly in parts of Africa.

The following organizations may provide additional information and support:
Centers for Disease Control and Prevention
NIH/National Institute of Allergy and Infectious Diseases

381   Ellis Van Creveld Syndrome

Synonyms
Chondroectodermal Dysplasia
Mesoectodermal Dysplasia

Ellis-Van Creveld syndrome is a rare genetic disorder characterized by short limb dwarfism, additional fingers and/or toes (polydactyly), abnormal development of fingernails and, in over half of the cases, congenital heart defects. This disorder is inherited through an autosomal recessive trait.

The following organizations may provide additional information and support:
Ellis Van Creveld Support Group
Ellis Van-Creveld Syndrome Support Group
Ellis-van Creveld Syndrome Web Site
Human Growth Foundation
MAGIC Foundation for Children's Growth
Restricted Growth Association

---

382   Emphysema, Congenital Lobar

Synonyms
CLE
Congenital Pulmonary Emphysema
Emphysema, Localized Congenital
Lobar Emphysema, Infantile
Lobar Tension Emphysema in Infancy

Congenital lobar emphysema is a rare respiratory disorder in which air can enter the lungs but cannot escape, causing overinflation (hyperinflation) of the lobes of the lung. It is most often detected in newborns or young infants, but some cases do not become apparent until adulthood. This disorder may be severe enough to cause associated heart problems (15% of cases) or so mild as to never become apparent. Some cases of congenital lobar emphysema may be caused by autosomal dominant inheritance while others occur for no apparent reason (sporadic).

The following organizations may provide additional information and support:
American Lung Association
March of Dimes Birth Defects Foundation
NIH/National Heart, Lung and Blood Institute Information Center

383 Empty Sella Syndrome

Synonym

Empty Sella Turcica

The primary form of empty sella syndrome is a rare inherited disorder of the brain that is transmitted as an autosomal dominant trait. The disorder is characterized by an empty space filled with cerebrospinal fluid in the sella turcica area of the brain. The area fills with fluid as a result of a defect in the sella diaphragm. Symptoms and findings may include unusual facial features, a highly-arched palate, moderate short stature, increased bone density (osteosclerosis), and normal pituitary function. The secondary form of this disorder is caused by another underlying disorder or defect (e.g., surgery, radiation therapy, etc.). In the idiopathic form of the disease, the exact cause is not known. This form of the disorder affects mostly obese, middle-aged women.

The following organizations may provide additional information and support:
March of Dimes Birth Defects Foundation
National Institute of Neurological Disorders and Stroke (NINDS)

384 Encephalitis, Herpes Simplex

Synonyms

Herpes Encephalitis
Herpetic Brainstem Encephalitis
Herpetic Meningoencephalitis
HSE

Herpes simplex encephalitis (HSE) is a rare neurological disorder characterized by inflammation of the brain (encephalitis). Common symptoms include headaches, fevers, drowsiness, hyperactivity, and/or general weakness. The disorder may have some symptoms similar to those associated with meningitis, such as a stiff neck, altered reflexes, confusion, and/or speech abnormalities. Skin lesions usually are not found in association with herpes simplex encephalitis. Herpes simplex encephalitis is caused by a virus known as herpes simplex virus (HSV).

The following organizations may provide additional information and support:
Centers for Disease Control and Prevention
Encephalitis Society
National Institute of Neurological Disorders and Stroke (NINDS)
NIH/National Institute of Allergy and Infectious Diseases

385 Encephalitis, Japanese

Synonyms

Japanese B Encephalitis
JE
Russian Autumnal Encephalitis
Summer Encephalitis

Japanese encephalitis is a severe inflammation of the brain caused by the Japanese B encephalitis virus that is transmitted by the bite of infected mosquitoes in certain areas of the world, particularly Asia. This disorder most commonly affects children and tends to be more actively spread during the summer. Symptoms include high fever, headaches, weakness, nausea, vomiting, paralysis, personality changes, and coma, possibly leading to neurological damage or death.

The following organizations may provide additional information and support:
Centers for Disease Control and Prevention
Encephalitis Society
NIH/National Institute of Allergy and Infectious Diseases
World Health Organization (WHO) Regional Office for the Americas (AMRO)

386 Encephalitis, Rasmussen's

Synonyms

Chronic Encephalitis and Epilepsy
Chronic Localized (Focal) Encephalitis
Epilepsy, Hemiplegia and Mental Retardation
Rasmussen's Syndrome

Rasmussen's encephalitis is a rare central nervous system disorder characterized by chronic inflammation of the brain (encephalitis) and episodes of uncontrolled electrical disturbances in the brain that cause convulsive seizures (epilepsy). Progressive symptoms including paralysis of one side of the body (hemiparesis) and mental retardation may also occur. Although the exact cause of this disorder is not known, it is thought to result from an unidentified viral infection.

The following organizations may provide additional information and support:
The Arc (A National Organization on Mental Retardation)
Centers for Disease Control and Prevention
Encephalitis Society
National Institute of Neurological Disorders and Stroke (NINDS)
Rasmussen's Syndrome and Hemispherectomy Support Network

387 Encephalocele

Synonyms
Bifid Cranium
Cephalocele
Cranial Meningoencephalocele
Craniocele
Cranium Bifidum

Encephalocele is a rare disorder in which an infant is born with a gap in the skull; that is, a part of one or more of the plates that form the skull does not seal. The membranes that cover the brain (meninges), and brain tissue, protrude through this gap. It is likely that this disorder is caused by the failure of the neural tube to close during development of the fetus.

The following organizations may provide additional information and support:
AboutFace USA
Birth Defect Research for Children, Inc.
Children's Craniofacial Association
FACES: The National Craniofacial Association
Forward Face, Inc.
Guardians of Hydrocephalus Research Foundation
Hydrocephalus Association
National Craniofacial Foundation
National Hydrocephalus Foundation
National Institute of Neurological Disorders and Stroke (NINDS)

388 Endocardial Fibroelastosis

Synonyms
EFE
Endocardial Dysplasia
Fetal Endomyocardial Fibrosis
Subendocardial Sclerosis

Endocardial fibroelastosis (EFE) is a rare heart disorder that affects infants and children. It is characterized by a thickening within the muscular lining of the heart chambers due to an increase in the amount of supporting connective tissue (inelastic collagen) and elastic fibers. The normal heart has four chambers. Two chambers, known as atria, are separated from each other by a partition called the atrial septum. The other two chambers, known as ventricles, are also separated by a septum. Valves connect the atria (left and right) to their respective ventricles. The symptoms of endocardial fibroelastosis are related to the overgrowth of fibrous tissues causing abnormal enlargement of the heart (cardiac hypertrophy),

especially the left ventricle. Impaired heart and lung function eventually lead to congestive heart failure. Endocardial fibroelastosis may occur for no apparent reason (sporadic) or may be inherited as an X-linked (EFE2) or autosomal recessive (EFE1) genetic trait.

The following organizations may provide additional information and support:
American Heart Association
Congenital Heart Anomalies, Support, Education, & Resources
March of Dimes Birth Defects Foundation
NIH/National Heart, Lung and Blood Institute

389 Endocarditis, Infective

Synonyms
Endocarditis, Bacterial
IE

Disorder Subdivisions
Endocarditis, Bacterial Acute
Endocarditis, Bacterial Subacute
Endocarditis, Prosthetic Valvular (PVE)

Infective endocarditis is a bacterial infection of the inner lining of the heart muscle (endocardium). This inner lining also covers the heart valves, and it is these valves which are primarily affected by infective endocarditis. If the infection remains untreated, multiplying bacteria may eventually destroy the valves and result in heart failure. Bacteria may also form small clots (emboli) which move through the blood and block small arteries. These clots may lodge in various parts of the body including the brain and cause serious damage. There are several forms of infective endocarditis. Two types that have similar symptoms but are caused by different bacteria are acute bacterial endocarditis and subacute bacterial endocarditis. Acute bacterial endocarditis may affect normal heart valves, while subacute bacterial endocarditis more commonly affects heart valves which have been previously damaged by disease. A third type of infective endocarditis, prosthetic valvular endocarditis (PVE), may develop in patients who have previously had artificial (prosthetic) valve replacement or tissue valve replacement.

The following organizations may provide additional information and support:
American Heart Association
Centers for Disease Control and Prevention
NIH/National Heart, Lung and Blood Institute Information Center

390 Endometriosis

Synonyms

Endometrial Growths
Endometrial Implants

Endometriosis is a prevalent gynecological condition that affects women. It is characterized by an inability to shed the build-up of tissue that normally forms in the uterus (endometrium) before menstruation. As a result the built-up tissue escapes from the uterus and spreads to other parts of the pelvic area, sometimes spreading as far as the lungs. Major symptoms may include lower back pain, pain in the thighs or excessive pain during the menstrual cycle, repeated miscarriages, and infertility. Bleeding from the rectum or bladder may also occur.

The following organizations may provide additional information and support:
Endometriosis Association
National Women's Health Network
NIH/National Institute of Child Health and Human Development
OBGYN.net: The Obstetrics & Gynecology Network

391 Endomyocardial Fibrosis

Synonyms

Davies' Disease
EMF
Fibroelastic Endocarditis
Loeffler Endomyocardial Fibrosis with Eosinophilia
Loeffler Fibroplastic Parietal Endocarditis
Loeffler's Disease

Disorder Subdivisions

Biventricular Fibrosis
Left Ventricular Fibrosis
Right Ventricular Fibrosis

Endomyocardial fibrosis (EMF) is a progressive disease of unknown origin (idiopathic) that may seriously affect the heart. Its most obvious feature is a gross change in the makeup of the lining of the heart cavities (the endocardium) of one or both of the lower chambers of the heart (the ventricles) leading to the replacement of normal cells with fibrous tissue (fibrosis). This process is progressive and leads to the narrowing (constriction) of the right or left ventricular cavities. It may involve the valves between the chambers of the heart as well as the tendon-like cords that fix the valves to the ventricles (chordae tendineae). Loeffler's disease is a disease of the heart much like endomyocardial fibrosis. Some clinicians regard it as an early stage of EMF, although this idea remains controversial. Loeffler's disease is a rare disorder of unknown origin, characterized by abnormal increases in the number of particular white blood cells (eosinophilia), and like EMF, gross fibrosis of the endocardium, and inflammation of small blood vessels (arteritis).

The following organizations may provide additional information and support:
American Heart Association
Centers for Disease Control and Prevention
Congenital Heart Anomalies, Support, Education, & Resources
NIH/Developmental Endocrinology Branch

392 Enterobiasis

Synonyms

Oxyuriasis
Pinworm Infection
Seatworm Infection

Enterobiasis or pinworm infection is a common, contagious, parasitic infestation found mainly in children. The disorder is spread by swallowing or inhaling the tiny eggs of the pinworm. Enterobiasis rarely causes any serious physical problems except for the main symptom, which is severe rectal itching.

The following organizations may provide additional information and support:
Centers for Disease Control and Prevention
NIH/National Institute of Allergy and Infectious Diseases

393 Eosinophilia Myalgia

Synonyms

Eosinophilic Myalgia
L-Tryptophan Disease
Tryptophan Disease
Tryptophan Syndrome

Eosinophilia myalgia syndrome is associated with the ingestion of large amounts of contaminated L-tryptophan, a dietary supplement often sold in health food stores. The contaminant remains unknown. It is a disease of abrupt onset causing severe, disabling, chronic muscle pain, skin symptoms and other neurotoxic reactions. Diagnosis is not easy and depends on finding unusually high levels of eosinophils (circulating white blood cells) over a period of at least 6 months.

The following organizations may provide additional information and support:
Centers for Disease Control and Prevention
National Eosinophilia Myalgia Syndrome Network
NIH/National Institute of Arthritis and Musculoskeletal and Skin Diseases

394   Eosinophilic Fasciitis

Synonyms
Eosinophilia Syndrome
Eosinophilic Syndrome
Shulman Syndrome

Eosinophilic fasciitis is a disorder of unknown cause characterized by symmetric and painful inflammation and loss of elasticity in the tissues of the arms and legs. The disorder has recently been recognized as a variant of scleroderma, a disease in which connective tissue in the body shrinks and hardens. Eosinophilic fasciitis most commonly affects middle-aged men. It has also been related to ingestion of L-tryptophan, a food supplement sold in health food stores as a sleeping aid.

The following organizations may provide additional information and support:
American Autoimmune Related Diseases Association, Inc.
Centers for Disease Control and Prevention
NIH/National Institute of Allergy and Infectious Diseases

395   Epidermal Nevus Syndrome

Synonyms
Ichthyosis Hystrix Gravior
Inflammatory Linear Nevus Sebaceous Syndrome
Lambert Type Ichthyosis
Linear Nevus Sebaceous Syndrome
Linear Sebaceous Nevus Sequence
Linear Sebaceous Nevus Syndrome
Nevus Sebaceous of Jadassohn
Porcupine Man
Sebaceous Nevus Syndrome

Epidermal nevus syndrome is a rare disorder characterized by distinctive birth marks (nevus) on the skin. Neurological and skeletal abnormalities may also occur. This disorder is usually apparent at birth (due to the skin lesions which are most often seen in the midface from the forehead down into the nasal area) and is often associated with seizures, mental deficiency, eye problems, bone malformations and atrophy of the brain. The exact cause of epidermal nevus syndrome is not known although an autosomal dominant trait of inheritance seems to occur in approximately two thirds of the cases.

The following organizations may provide additional information and support:
Foundation for Ichthyosis & Related Skin Types
Nevus Network
NIH/National Arthritis and Musculoskeletal and Skin Diseases Information Clearinghouse

396   Epidermolysis Bullosa

Synonyms
Acantholysis Bullosa
Acanthosis Bullosa
Bullosa Hereditaria
Dowling-Meara Syndrome
EB
Epidermolysis Bullosa Acquisita
Epidermolysis Bullosa Hereditaria
Epidermolysis Bullosa Letalias
Epidermolysis Hereditaria Tarda
Goldscheider's Disease
Hallopeau-Siemens Disease
Heinrichsbauer Syndrome
Herlitz Syndrome
Hyperplastic Epidermolysis Bullosa
Keratolysis
Kobner's Disease
Localized Epidermolysis Bullosa
Non-Scarring Epidermolysis Bullosa
Polydysplastic Epidermolysis Bullosa
Scarring Bullosa
Simplex Epidermolysis Bullosa
Weber-Cockayne Disease

Disorder Subdivisions
Dystrophic Epidermolysis Bullosa
Epidermolysis Bullosa Simplex
Junctional Epidermolysis Bullosa

Epidermolysis bullosa (EB) refers to a group of rare, inherited skin diseases characterized by recurring painful blisters and open sores, often in response to minor trauma, as a result of the unusually fragile nature of the skin. Some severe forms may involve the eyes, tongue, and esophagus, and some may produce scarring and disabling musculoskeletal deformities. There are three major forms: epidermolysis bullosa simplex (EB simplex), the most common; dystrophic epidermolysis bullosa (DEB), and junctional epidermolysis bullosa (JEB).

The following organizations may provide additional information and support:
Cardio-Facio-Cutaneous Family Network (CFC)
DebRA-United Kingdom
Dystrophic Epidermolysis Bullosa Research Association of America, Inc. (DEBRA)
EB Medical Research Foundation
Macular Degeneration International
March of Dimes Birth Defects Foundation
National Cancer Institute

397   Epidermolytic Hyperkeratosis

Synonyms
BCIE
Bullous Congenital CIE
EHK

Epidermolytic hyperkeratosis is a hereditary skin disorder that is characterized by a thick, blistering, warty hardening of the skin over most of the body, particularly in the skin creases over the joints. The skin may be fragile and may blister easily following injury.

The following organizations may provide additional information and support:
Foundation for Ichthyosis & Related Skin Types
March of Dimes Birth Defects Foundation
NIH/National Arthritis and Musculoskeletal and Skin Diseases Information Clearinghouse
Northwestern University Medical School

398   Epididymitis

Disorder Subdivisions
Epididymitis, Nonspecific Bacterial
Epididymitis, Sexually-Transmitted

Epididymitis is inflammation of the long, tightly coiled tube behind each testicle (epididymis) that carries sperm from the testicle to the spermatic duct. Affected individuals usually have painful swelling of the one epididymis and the associated testicle. In some cases, the second testicle may also be tender. In addition, affected individuals have fever, painful swelling and redness (erythema) of the scrotum, and/or inflammation of the tube from which urine is carried from the bladder (urethritis). The two main forms of epididymitis are the sexually-transmitted form and the nonspecific bacterial form.

The following organizations may provide additional information and support:
American Social Health Association
Centers for Disease Control and Prevention
NIH/National Institute of Child Health and Human Development

399   Epilepsy

Synonyms
Convulsions
Seizures

Disorder Subdivisions
Abdominal Epilepsy
Akinetic Seizure
Epilepsia Procursiva
Febrile Seizures
Focal Epilepsy
Grand Mal Epilepsy
Jacksonian Epilepsy
Lundborg-Unverricht Disease
Major Epilepsy
Minor Epilepsy
Myoclonic Astatic Petit Mal Epilepsy
Myoclonic Progressive Familial Epilepsy
Myoclonic Seizure
Petit Mal Epilepsy
Petit Mal Variant
Psychomotor Convulsion
Psychomotor Epilepsy
Psychomotor Equivalent Epilepsy
Pyknoepilepsy
Status Epilepticus
Temporal Lobe Epilepsy
Unverricht Syndrome
Unverricht-Lundborg-Laf Disease

Epilepsy is a group of disorders of the central nervous system characterized by repeated convulsive (paroxysomal) electrical disturbances in the brain. The major symptoms may include loss of consciousness, convulsions, spasms, sensory confusion and disturbances in the nerves that control involuntary body functions (autonomic nervous system). Episodes of these symptoms are frequently preceded by an "aura." An aura is described as a feeling of uneasiness or sensory discomfort that precedes the onset of a seizure. Epilepsy may take several different forms including: grand mal epilepsy (major epilepsy, status epilepticus); Jacksonian epilepsy (focal epilepsy); myoclonic progressive familial epilepsy (Unverricht syndrome, Lundborg-Unverricht disease, Unverricht-Lundborg-Laf disease); petit mal epilepsy (minor epilepsy, pyknoepilepsy, akinetic seizure, myoclonic seizure); myoclonic astatic petit mal epilepsy (Lennox-Gastaut syndrome, petit mal variant); febrile seizures; and psychomotor epilepsy (temporal lobe epilepsy, psychomotor equivalent, psychomotor convulsion with epilepsia procursiva, abdominal epilepsy).

The following organizations may provide additional information and support:
AED Pregnancy Registry
American Epilepsy Society
Epilepsy Canada
Epilepsy Foundation
March of Dimes Birth Defects Foundation
National Institute of Neurological Disorders and Stroke (NINDS)
New Horizons Un-Limited, Inc.
Organization for Anti-Convulsant Syndrome

400   Epitheliopathy, Acute Posterior Multifocal Placoid Pigment

Synonyms
Acute Multifocal Placoid Pigment Epitheliopathy
Acute Placoid Pigment Epitheliopathy
AMPPE
APMPPE
Multifocal Placoid Pigment Epitheliopathy

Acute posterior multifocal placoid pigment epitheliopathy (APMPPE) is a rare eye disorder of unknown (idiopathic) cause. The disorder is characterized by the impairment of central vision in one eye (unilateral) but, within a few days, the second eye may also become affected (bilateral). In most cases, the disorder resolves within a few weeks without loss of clearness of vision (acuity). However, in some cases, visual acuity does not improve. This disorder occurs predominantly in young adults, with a mean age of onset of 27 years. It is reported that, in approximately one-third of the cases, an influenza-like illness preceded the development of the disorder.

The following organizations may provide additional information and support:
National Association for Visually Handicapped
NIH/National Eye Institute

401   Erdheim Chester Disease

Synonyms
ECD
Lipoid Granulomatosis

Erdheim-Chester disease (ECD) is a rare multisystem disorder of adulthood. It is characterized by excessive production and accumulation of histiocytes within multiple tissues and organs. Histiocytes are large phagocytic cells (macrophages) that normally play a role in responding to infection and injury. (A phagocytic cell is any "scavenger cell" that engulfs and destroys invading microorganisms or cellular debris.) In those with ECD, sites of involvement may include the long bones, skin, tissues behind the eyeballs, lungs, brain, pituitary gland, and/or additional tissues and organs. Associated symptoms and findings and disease course depend on the specific location and extent of such involvement. The specific underlying cause of ECD is unknown.

The following organizations may provide additional information and support:
National Institute of Neurological Disorders and Stroke (NINDS)
NIH/National Arthritis and Musculoskeletal and Skin Diseases Information Clearinghouse
NIH/National Heart, Lung and Blood Institute Information Center

402   Erysipelas

Synonyms
Cellulitis
Saint Anthony's Fire

Erysipelas is an infection of the upper layers of the skin (superficial). The most common cause is group A streptococcal bacteria, especially *Streptococcus pyogenes*. Erysipelas results in a fiery red rash with raised edges that can easily be distinguished from the skin around it. The affected skin may be warm to the touch. At one time, erysipelas was thought to affect mostly the face, but recent studies suggest that the distribution of the inflammation is changing since at the present time the legs are involved in almost 80% of cases. The rash may also appear on the arms or trunk. Erysipelas begins with minor trauma, such as a bruise, burn, wound, or incision. When the rash appears on the trunk, arms, or legs, it is usually at the site of a surgical incision or a wound.

The following organizations may provide additional information and support:
American Academy of Allergy Asthma and Immunology
Centers for Disease Control and Prevention
NIH/National Institute of Allergy and Infectious Diseases

403   Erythema Multiforme

Synonyms
Dermatostomatitis, Erythema Multiforme Type
Erythema Multiforme Bullosum
Erythema Polymorphe, Erythema Multiforme Type
Febrile Mucocutaneous Syndrome
Herpes Iris, Erythema Multiforme Type

Erythema multiforme (EM) is the name applied to a group of hypersensitivity disorders, affecting mostly children and young adults, and characterized by symmetric red, patchy lesions, primarily on the arms and legs. The cause is unknown, but EM frequently occurs in association with herpes simplex virus, suggesting an immunologic process initiated by the virus. In half of the cases, the triggering agents appear to be medications, including anticonvulsants, sulfonamides, nonsteroidal anti-inflammatory drugs, and other antibiotics. In addition, some cases appear to be associated with infectious organisms such as *Mycoplasma pneumoniae* and many viral agents. Erythema multiforme is the mildest of three skin disorders that are often discussed in relation to each other. More severe is Stevens-Johnson syndrome. The most severe of the three is toxic epidermal necrolysis (TEN).

The following organizations may provide additional information and support:
NIH/National Institute of Arthritis and Musculoskeletal and Skin Diseases
Stevens Johnson Syndrome Foundation and Support Group

404   Erythroderma Desquamativa of Leiner

Synonyms
Erythroderma Desquamativum of Infancy
Leiner Disease
Leiner-Moussous Desquamative Erythroderma

Erythroderma desquamativa of Leiner is a rare skin disorder that usually first appears during the end of the first month of life or the beginning of the second month. The disorder is characterized by the appearance of a reddish, thickened rash on various parts of an infant's body. Additional symptoms include chronic diarrhea and the failure to gain weight at the expected rate (failure to thrive). The exact cause of erythroderma desquamativa of Leiner is unknown.

The following organizations may provide additional information and support:
March of Dimes Birth Defects Foundation
NIH/National Arthritis and Musculoskeletal and Skin Diseases Information Clearinghouse

405   Erythrokeratodermia with Ataxia

Synonym
Giroux Barbeau Syndrome

Erythrokeratodermia with ataxia (EKDA) is a hereditary disorder of the skin and nervous system (neurocutaneous syndrome) characterized by groups of hard, red plaques that develop during infancy and childhood. When these skin lesions heal, the disorder seems to become dormant for several years, after which the neurological symptoms and signs emerge in the form of a typically awkward gait (ataxia) when the affected individual is around 40 years of age or older. Many researchers active in the study of the family of diseases known as the ichthyoses consider EKDA to be a variant of an ichthyotic disorder, erythrokeratodermia variabilis (EKDV). However, there is no general consensus on this at this time.

The following organizations may provide additional information and support:
Foundation for Ichthyosis & Related Skin Types
National Registry for Ichthyosis and Related Disorders
NIH/National Arthritis and Musculoskeletal and Skin Diseases Information Clearinghouse

406   Erythromelalgia

Synonyms
Erythermalgia
Gerhardt Disease
Mitchell Disease
Weir-Mitchell Disease

Disorder Subdivisions
Primary Erythromelalgia, Familial
Secondary Erythromelalgia

Erythromelalgia is a rare condition that primarily affects the feet and, less commonly, the hands (extremities). It is characterized by intense, burning pain of affected extremities, severe redness (erythema), and increased skin temperature that may be episodic or almost continuous in nature. (The prefix "erythro-" denotes redness, "mel-" is a combining form meaning limb or limbs, and the suffix "-algia" indicates pain.) Although erythromelalgia typically affects both sides of the body (bilateral), it may sometimes involve only one side (unilateral). In addition, the disease course may be extremely variable from case to case. For example, in some individuals, symptom onset may be gradual (insidious), with the condition potentially remaining relatively mild for years. However, in others, it may have a sudden (acute) onset, possibly spreading and becoming severe over weeks. The specific underlying cause of erythromelalgia remains unknown. However, the condition is thought to result from vasomotor abnormalities or dysfunction in the normal narrowing (constriction) and widening (dilation) of the diameter (caliber) of certain blood vessels, leading to abnormalities of blood flow to the extremities. Erythromelalgia may be an isolated, primary condition or occur secondary to various underlying disorders. Primary erythromelalgia may appear to occur randomly for unknown reasons (sporadically) or may be familial, suggesting autosomal dominant inheritance.

The following organizations may provide additional information and support:
Erythromelalgia Association
NIH/National Institute of Arthritis and Musculoskeletal and Skin Diseases

407   Erythropoietic Protoporphyria

Synonyms
EPP
Erythrohepatic Protoporphyria
Protoporphyria

Erythropoietic protoporphyria (EPP) is a rare inherited metabolic disorder characterized by a deficiency of the enzyme ferrochelatase (FECH). Due to abnormally low levels of this enzyme, excessive amounts of protoporphyrin accumulate in the bone marrow, blood plasma, and red blood cells. The major symptom of this disorder is hypersensitivity of the skin to sunlight and some types of artificial light, such as fluorescent lights (photosensitivity). After exposure to light, the skin may become itchy and red. Affected individuals may also experience a burning sensation on their skin. The hands, arms, and face are the most commonly affected areas. Some people with erythropoietic protoporphyria may also have complications related to liver and gallbladder function. Erythropoietic protoporphyria is inherited as an autosomal dominant genetic trait with poor penetrance. Erythropoietic protoporphyria is one of a group of disorders known as the porphyrias. The porphyrias are all characterized by abnormally high levels of particular chemicals (porphyrins) in the body due to deficiencies of certain enzymes essential to the synthesis of hemoglobin. There are at least seven types of porphyria. The symptoms associated with the various types of porphyria differ, depending upon the specific enzyme that is deficient. It is important to note that people who have one type of porphyria do not develop any of the other types.

The following organizations may provide additional information and support:
American Porphyria Foundation
CLIMB (Children Living with Inherited Metabolic Diseases)
Canadian Porphyria Foundation, Inc.
Erythropoietic Protoporphyria Research and Education Fund
Medic Alert Foundation International
NIH/National Digestive Diseases Information Clearinghouse

408   Esophageal Atresia and/or Tracheoesophageal Fistula

Synonyms
Atresia of Esophagus with or without Tracheoesophageal Fistula
Esophageal Atresia
Tracheoesophageal Fistula
Tracheoesophageal Fistula with or without Esophageal Atresia

Esophageal atresia and tracheoesophageal fistula are disorders of the esophagus that may be inherited as an autosomal recessive genetic trait, or may result from developmental problems in a fetus. Esophageal atresia is a condition in which the patient is born with an abnormality in the part of the digestive tube that runs from below the tongue to the stomach (esophagus). This disorder is commonly associated with tracheoesophageal fistula which is an abnormal tubelike passage between the windpipe and esophagus. Symptoms of these disorders may be excessive salivation, choking, the return of swallowed food into the mouth, and/or a swollen abdomen when a tracheo-esophageal fistula is present.

The following organizations may provide additional information and support:
EA/TEF Child and Family Support Connection, Inc.
NIH/National Digestive Diseases Information Clearinghouse
TEF/VATER/VACTRL National Support Network

409 Essential Iris Atrophy

Synonyms
ICE Syndrome, Essential Iris Atrophy Type
Iridocorneal Endothelial (ICE) Syndrome,
Essential Iris Atrophy
Progressive Essential Iris Atrophy

Essential iris atrophy is a very rare, progressive disorder of the eye characterized by a pupil that is out of place and/or distorted, areas of degeneration on the iris (atrophy), and/or holes in the iris. This disorder most frequently affects only one eye (unilateral) and develops slowly over time. Attachment of portions of the iris to the cornea (peripheral anterior synechiae) and/or abnormalities in the cornea may lead to secondary glaucoma and vision loss. Essential iris atrophy is one of three iridocorneal endothelial (ICE) syndromes, each of which usually affects one eye of young to middle-aged men and women. The ICE syndromes (essential iris atrophy, Chandler syndrome, and Cogan-Reese syndrome) are distinct from one another. However, these disorders all affect the eye. Some of their symptoms overlap, making it difficult to distinguish between them.

The following organizations may provide additional information and support:
Glaucoma Research Foundation
National Association for Parents of Children with Visual Impairments (NAPVI)
National Association for Visually Handicapped
NIH/National Eye Institute
Prevent Blindness America

410 Ewing's Sarcoma

Synonyms
EFT
Ewing Family of Tumors
Ewing Tumor
TEF
Tumor of the Ewing Family (TEF)

Disorder Subdivisions
Askin's Tumor
Ewing's Sarcoma of Bone
Extraosseous Ewing's (EOE) Sarcoma
Primitive Neuroectodermal Tumor (PNET)

Ewing's sarcoma is a rare bone tumor that occurs most often in adolescents. It may also arise outside of the bone in soft tissue (extraosseous Ewing's sarcoma). Ewing's sarcoma is related to another type of tumor known as primitive neuroectodermal tumor (PNET). Researchers have learned that both of these tumors arise from the same primitive cell and now refer to these tumors as the Ewing family of tumors (EFT). This general term encompasses Ewing's sarcoma of bone, extraosseous Ewing's sarcoma, primitive neuroectodermal tumor, and Askin's tumor (a tumor of the chest wall). Ewing's sarcoma of bone accounts for approximately 87 percent of the tumors in this family. Ewing's sarcoma of bone most often affects the long bone of the legs (femur) and flat bones such as those found in the pelvis and chest wall. Ewing's sarcoma is an aggressive cancer that may spread (metastasize) to the lungs, other bones, and bone marrow potentially causing life-threatening complications. The exact cause of these tumors is unknown.

The following organizations may provide additional information and support:
American Cancer Society, Inc.
March of Dimes Birth Defects Foundation
National Cancer Institute
National Coalition for Cancer Survivorship
OncoLink: The University of Pennsylvania Cancer Center Resource
Rare Cancer Alliance
Sarcoma Alliance
Sarcoma Foundation of America

411 Exostoses, Multiple

Synonyms
Diaphyseal Aclasis
EXT
External Chondromatosis Syndrome
Multiple Cartilaginous Exostoses
Multiple Exostoses
Multiple Exostoses Syndrome
Multiple Osteochondromatosis

Hereditary multiple exostoses (HME) is a rare skeletal disorder that is inherited in an autosomal dominant fashion. As the name suggests, this disorder is characterized by multiple bony growths or tumors (exostoses), often on the growing end (epiphysis) of the long bones of the legs, arms, and digits. These bony growths are covered by cartilage and usually continue to grow until shortly after puberty. They may cause deformities, especially of the ankle, knee, and wrist.

The following organizations may provide additional information and support:
MHE (Multiple Hereditary Exostoses) Family Support Group
MHE and Me—A Support Group for Kids with Multiple Hereditary Exostoses
NIH/National Arthritis and Musculoskeletal and Skin Diseases Information Clearinghouse

CLIMB (Children Living with Inherited Metabolic Diseases)
Canadian Society for Mucopolysaccharide and Related Diseases, Inc.
Fabry Support & Information Group
Instituto de Errores Innatos del Metabolismo
International Center for Fabry Disease
March of Dimes Birth Defects Foundation
Morbus Fabry Homepage Germany
National Institute of Neurological Disorders and Stroke (NINDS)
National MPS (Mucopolysaccharidoses/Mucolipidoses) Society, Inc.
National Tay-Sachs and Allied Diseases Association, Inc.

412 Fabry Disease

Synonyms
Alpha-Galactosidase A Deficiency
Anderson-Fabry Disease
Angiokeratoma Corporis Diffusum
Angiokeratoma Diffuse
Ceramide Trihexosidase Deficiency
GLA Deficiency
Hereditary Dystopic Lipidosis

Fabry disease is a rare genetic disorder of lipid metabolism characterized by a deficiency of the enzyme alpha-galactosidase A, also known as ceramidetrihexosidase. The disorder belongs to a group of diseases known as lysosomal storage disorders. Lysosomes function as the primary digestive units within cells. Enzymes within lysosomes break down or digest particular nutrients, such as certain fats and carbohydrates. Low levels or inactivity of the alpha-galactosidase A enzyme leads to the abnormal accumulation of a substance consisting of fatty material and carbohydrates (i.e., glycolipids such as glycosphingolipid) in various organs of the body, particularly blood vessels and the eyes. Symptoms of Fabry disease may include the appearance of clusters of wart-like discolorations on the skin (angiokeratomas), abdominal pain, and/or visual impairment. Later in the course of the disease, kidney failure, heart irregularities, and/or progressive neurological abnormalities may cause serious complications. Fabry disease, which is inherited as an X-linked recessive trait, primarily affects males. A milder form of the disease has been identified in females.

The following organizations may provide additional information and support:

413 Facioscapulohumeral Muscular Dystrophy

Synonyms
FMD
FSH
FSHD
Facio-Scapulo-Humeral Dystrophy
Muscular Dystrophy, Facioscapulohumeral
Muscular Dystrophy, Landouzy Dejerine

Disorder Subdivisions
Infantile Facioscapulohumeral Muscular Dystrophy

Facioscapulohumeral muscular dystrophy (FSHD), also known as Landouzy-Dejerine muscular dystrophy, is a neuromuscular disorder. Symptom onset usually occurs in adolescence or early adulthood; however, less commonly, symptoms may become apparent as early as infancy or early childhood. The disorder is typically initially characterized by weakness of facial, shoulder, and/or upper arm muscles. Associated abnormalities may include an impaired ability to completely close the eyes, limited movements of the lips, and difficulties raising the arms over the head. Affected individuals may also eventually develop weakness and associated wasting (atrophy) of muscles of the hips and thighs and/or involvement of lower leg muscles. Although the disease course may be variable, FSHD is most typically characterized by relatively slow disease progression. Specific symptoms and findings may also vary in range and severity, including among affected members of the same family (kindred). FSHD is usually inherited as an autosomal dominant trait. However, in up to approximately 30 percent of affected individuals, there is no apparent family history of the disorder. In some of these cases, FSHD may be due to new genetic changes (mutations) that appear to occur spontaneously for unknown reasons (sporadically).

The following organizations may provide additional information and support:
European Alliance of Neuromuscular Disorders Associations
FSH Society, Inc.
March of Dimes Birth Defects Foundation
Muscular Dystrophy Association
Muscular Dystrophy Association (Australia)
Muscular Dystrophy Association of Canada
Muscular Dystrophy Association of New Zealand, Inc.
Muscular Dystrophy Campaign
Muscular Dystrophy Ireland
National Institute of Neurological Disorders and Stroke (NINDS)
Society for Muscular Dystrophy Information International
Spina Bifida Hydrocephalus Queensland

414   Factor IX Deficiency

Synonyms
Christmas Disease
Hemophilia B, Factor IX
PTC Deficiency
Plasma Thromboplastin Component Deficiency

Factor IX deficiency is a severe genetic bleeding disorder that resembles classic hemophilia A, although it occurs only one-fifth as often as hemophilia A. Factor IX is a component of the blood clotting substance thromboplastin. It is deficient at birth in patients with this disorder. Factor IX deficiency varies in severity between families and occurs most often among males. In rare instances, female carriers have been known to exhibit this deficiency in a mild form. Symptoms include prolonged bleeding episodes, and in very severe cases, joint pain and bone deformities.

The following organizations may provide additional information and support:
Canadian Hemophilia Society
National Hemophilia Foundation
NIH/National Heart, Lung and Blood Institute Information Center
World Federation of Hemophilia

415   Factor XIII Deficiency

Synonyms
Fibrin Stabilizing Factor Deficiency
Fibrinase Deficiency
Fibrinoligase Deficiency
Laki-Lorand Factor Deficiency
Plasma Transglutaminase Deficiency

Disorder Subdivisions
Acquired Factor XIII Deficiency
Congenital Factor XIII Deficiency

Factor XIII deficiency is an extremely rare inherited blood disorder characterized by abnormal blood clotting that may result in abnormal bleeding. Associated symptoms and findings occur as the result of a deficiency in the blood clotting factor F13A1 (factor XIII). In affected individuals, the blood fails to clot appropriately, resulting in poor wound healing. Blood may seep into surrounding soft tissues, resulting in local pain and swelling. Internal bleeding may occur; approximately 25 percent of affected individuals experience bleeding in the brain (intracranial hemorrhage). Factor XIII deficiency may be inherited as an autosomal dominant genetic trait. The disease may also be acquired in association with other disorders such as sickle cell disease or Henoch-Schonlein purpura.

The following organizations may provide additional information and support:
National Hemophilia Foundation
NIH/National Heart, Lung and Blood Institute
World Federation of Hemophilia

416   Fahr's Disease

Synonyms
Cerebrovascular Ferrocalcinosis
Fahr Disease
Idiopathic Basal Ganglia Calcification (IBGC)
Nonarteriosclerotic Cerebral Calcifications
SPD Calcinosis
Striopallidodentate Calcinosis

Fahr's disease is a rare degenerative neurological disorder characterized by the presence of abnormal calcium deposits (calcifications) and associated cell loss in certain areas of the brain (e.g., basal ganglia). The condition is often referred to as idiopathic basal ganglia calcification or IBGC because there is no apparent explanation for such calcification in these brain regions (idiopathic). Associated symptoms include progressive deterioration of cognitive abilities (dementia) and loss of acquired motor skills. As the condition progresses, paralysis may develop that is associated with increased muscle stiffness (rigidity) and restricted movements (spastic paralysis). Additional abnormalities may include relatively slow, involuntary, continual writhing movements (athetosis) or chorea, a related condition characterized by irregular, rapid, jerky movements. In some affected individuals, there may also be gradual deterioration of the nerve fibers that transmit impulses from the retinas to the brain (optic atrophy), a condition associated with partial or near complete visual impairment. According to reports in the medical literature, Fahr's disease is often familial. Familial Fahr's disease may be transmitted as an autosomal recessive trait or, in other affected families (kindreds), may have autosomal dominant inheritance. In other instances, the condition appears to occur randomly for unknown reasons (sporadically). Some experts suggest that the condition may sometimes result from an unidentified infection during pregnancy affecting the developing fetus (intrauterine infection).

The following organizations may provide additional information and support:
C-Mac Informational Services, Inc.
National Institute of Neurological Disorders and Stroke (NINDS)
Parkinson's Disease—Movement Disorders Group

417   Familial Adenomatous Polyposis

Synonyms
Adenomatous Polyposis of the Colon (APC)
FAP
Familial Multiple Polyposis
Hereditary Polyposis Coli
Multiple Polyposis of the Colon

Disorder Subdivisions
ACR (Adenomatosis of the Colon and Rectum)
Adenomatous Polyposis, Familial
Attenuated Adenomatous Polyposis Coli (Flat Adenoma Syndrome)
Familial Adenomatous Colon Polyposis
Familial Polyposis Coli
Gardner Syndrome
Intestinal Polyposis I
Multiple Familial Polyposis
Turcot Syndrome

Familial adenomatous polyposis is a group of rare inherited disorders of the gastrointestinal system. Initially it is characterized by benign growths (adenomatous polyps) in the mucous lining of the gastrointestinal tract. Symptoms may include diarrhea, bleeding from the end portion of the large intestine (rectum), fatigue, abdominal pain, and weight loss. If left untreated, affected individuals usually develop cancer of the colon and/or rectum. Familial adenomatous polyposis is inherited as an autosomal dominant trait.

The following organizations may provide additional information and support:
American Cancer Society, Inc.
Delaware Cancer Registry
Familial GI Cancer Registry
Familial Polyposis Registry
Ferguson Hospital
Hereditary Colon Cancer Association (HCCA)
Hereditary Colorectal Cancer Registry
Intestinal Multiple Polyposis and Colorectal Cancer Registry
M. D. Anderson Cancer Center Hereditary Colorectal Cancer Registry
March of Dimes Birth Defects Foundation
National Cancer Institute
NIH/National Digestive Diseases Information Clearinghouse
Northwestern University Medical School
OncoLink: The University of Pennsylvania Cancer Center Resource
Roswell Park Family Cancer Registry
Southeastern Hereditary Colorectal Cancer Registry
Strang-Cornell Hereditary Colon Cancer Program

418   Familial Eosinophilic Cellulitis

Synonyms
Eosinophilic Cellulitis
Granulomatous Dermatitis with Eosinophilia
Wells' Syndrome

Familial eosinophilic cellulitis is a rare skin disorder. It is characterized by raised, red, swollen, and warm areas of skin, in a flame-shaped pattern with associated pain. The exact cause of the disease is unknown. However, bites of spiders, bees, mites, fleas, or ticks (arthropods) are often associated with this skin condition.

The following organizations may provide additional information and support:
American Academy of Allergy Asthma and Immunology
American Autoimmune Related Diseases Association, Inc.
Centers for Disease Control and Prevention
NIH/National Institute of Allergy and Infectious Diseases

419 Familial Juvenile Hyperuricemic Nephropathy

Synonyms
FGN
Familial Gouty Nephropathy
Familial Juvenile Gouty Nephropathy
Familial Nephropathy Associated with Hyperuricemia
Familial Nephropathy with Gout
Juvenile Gouty Nephropathy
Uromodulin Associated Kidney Disease

Familial juvenile hyperuricemic nephropathy is a rare, inherited disease of the kidneys, often characterized by early onset (teenage years), gout in both males and females, kidney failure, reduced concentrations of uric acid in the urine (hypouricuria) and increased concentrations of uric acid in the blood (hyperuricemia).

The following organizations may provide additional information and support:
American Association of Kidney Patients
American Kidney Fund, Inc.
March of Dimes Birth Defects Foundation
National Kidney Foundation
NIH/National Institute of Arthritis and Musculoskeletal and Skin Diseases
NIH/National Kidney and Urologic Diseases Information Clearinghouse

420 Familial Lipoprotein Lipase Deficiency

Synonyms
LIPD Deficiency
LPL Deficiency
Chylomicronemia, Familial
Hyperchylomicronemia, Familial
Hyperlipemia, Essential Familial
Hyperlipemia, Idiopathic, Burger-Grutz Type
Hyperlipoproteinemia, Type 1A
Lipase D Deficiency

Lipoprotein Lipase Deficiency
Lipoprotein Lipase, Included; LPL, Included

Familial lipoprotein lipase deficiency is a rare hereditary enzyme deficiency that results in abnormal breakdown of fats in the body. It is characterized by a massive accumulation of fatty droplets (chylomicrons) in blood plasma and a corresponding increase of the blood plasma concentration of fatty substances called triglycerides. The disorder is caused by a mutation in the LPL gene leading to very low or absent activity of the lipoprotein lipase enzyme. Symptoms of familial LPL deficiency usually begin in childhood and include abdominal pain, acute and recurrent inflammation of the pancreas (pancreatitis), skin lesions called eruptive cutaneous xanthoma and an enlargement of the liver and spleen (hepatosplenomegaly).

The following organizations may provide additional information and support:
CLIMB (Children Living with Inherited Metabolic Diseases)
Genetic and Rare Diseases (GARD) Information Center
NIH/National Digestive Diseases Information Clearinghouse

421 Farber's Disease

Synonyms
Acid Ceramidase Deficiency
Farber's Lipogranulomatosis

Farber's disease is a rare inherited metabolic disorder. It is one of the diseases known as lysosomal storage diseases. These are inherited errors of metabolism that happen as the result of the lack or malfunction of a particular enzyme needed to break down complex chemical compounds in the structures within cells known as lysosomes. In this case, the enzyme that is missing is acid ceramidase. The deficiency of this enzyme leads to the accumulation of a substance known as ceramide and is associated with characteristic symptoms and progressive tissue damage, particularly in the joints, liver, lung, and nervous system. Farber's disease is usually recognized by the presence of three symptoms: painful and progressively deformed joints, nodules under the skin, and progressive hoarseness. Other organ systems may also be involved. Farber's disease is inherited as an autosomal recessive genetic trait.

The following organizations may provide additional information and support:
CLIMB (Children Living with Inherited Metabolic Diseases)
NIH/National Arthritis and Musculoskeletal and Skin Diseases Information Clearinghouse
Vaincre Les Maladies Lysosomales

422 Fascioliasis

Synonyms
Fasciolosis
Liver Fluke Disease

Disorder Subdivision
Halzoun Syndrome

Fascioliasis is a rare infectious disorder caused by parasites. These parasites are liver flukes that live in plant-eating animals. Liver flukes can be found on water plants in certain parts of the world. When the parasite invades the liver, bile passages may be blocked. A subdivision of fascioliasis called Halzoun syndrome affects the throat (pharynx). This infection can usually be controlled and/or cured with timely treatment.

The following organizations may provide additional information and support:
American Liver Foundation
Centers for Disease Control and Prevention
NIH/National Institute of Allergy and Infectious Diseases

423 Felty Syndrome

Synonyms
Splenomegaly with Rheumatoid Arthritis

Felty syndrome is a rare form of rheumatoid arthritis, a disorder characterized by painful, stiff, and swollen joints. Major symptoms and physical findings of Felty syndrome include an unusually large spleen (splenomegaly) and abnormally low levels of certain white blood cells (neutrophils [neutropenia]). As a result of neutropenia, affected individuals may have an increased susceptibility to certain infections. Other symptoms associated with Felty syndrome may include fatigue, fever, weight loss, and/or discoloration of patches of skin (brown pigmentation). The exact cause of Felty syndrome is unknown. It is believed to be an autoimmune disorder.

The following organization may provide additional information and support:
NIH/National Arthritis and Musculoskeletal and Skin Diseases Information Clearinghouse

424 Femoral Facial Syndrome

Synonyms
Femoral Dysgenesis, Bilateral
Femoral Dysgenesis, Bilateral-Robin Anomaly
Femoral Hypoplasia-Unusual Facies Syndrome

Femoral-facial syndrome is a rare disorder that occurs randomly (sporadically) in the population. There have been, however, a few cases reported in which the disorder appeared to be inherited as an autosomal dominant genetic trait. The major symptoms of this disorder are underdeveloped thigh bones (femurs) and unusual facial features.

The following organizations may provide additional information and support:
Genetic and Rare Diseases (GARD) Information Center
NIH/National Arthritis and Musculoskeletal and Skin Diseases Information Clearinghouse

425 Fetal Alcohol Syndrome

Synonyms
Alcohol, Fetal Effects of
Alcohol-Related Birth Defects
Alcoholic Embryopathy
FAS

Fetal alcohol syndrome (FAS) is a characteristic pattern of mental and physical birth defects that results from maternal use of alcohol during pregnancy. The range and severity of associated abnormalities may vary greatly from case to case. However, characteristic features may include growth delays before and after birth (prenatal and postnatal growth retardation); malformations of the skull and facial (craniofacial) region; brain abnormalities; and/or additional physical findings. FAS may also be associated with varying degrees of mental retardation, learning abnormalities, and/or behavioral problems that, in some cases, may occur in the absence of obvious physical abnormalities.

The following organizations may provide additional information and support:
The Arc (A National Organization on Mental Retardation)

Centers for Disease Control and Prevention
Family Empowerment Network: Supporting Families Affected by FAS/FAE
National Alliance for the Mentally Ill
National Mental Health Association
National Mental Health Consumers' Self-Help Clearinghouse
National Organization on Fetal Alcohol Syndrome
NIH/Institute on Alcohol Abuse and Alcoholism
NIH/National Institute of Mental Health

426 Fetal Hydantoin Syndrome

Synonyms

Dilantin Embryopathy
Phenytoin Embryopathy

Fetal hydantoin syndrome is a rare disorder that is caused by exposure of a fetus to the anticonvulsant drug phenytoin (Dilantin). The symptoms of this disorder may include abnormalities of the skull and facial features, growth deficiencies, underdeveloped nails of the fingers and toes, and/or mild developmental delays. Other findings occasionally associated with this syndrome include cleft lip and palate, having an unusually small head (microcephaly) and brain malformations with more significant developmental delays.

The following organizations may provide additional information and support:
The Arc (A National Organization on Mental Retardation)
Cleft Palate Foundation
March of Dimes Birth Defects Foundation
National Fetal Anticonvulsant Syndrome Association

427 Fetal Retinoid Syndrome

Synonyms

Accutane Embryopathy
Accutane, Fetal Effects of
Isotretinoin Embryopathy
Isotretinoin Teratogen Syndrome
Isotretinoin, Fetal Effects of
Retinoic Acid Embryopathy

Fetal retinoid syndrome is a characteristic pattern of mental and physical birth defects that results from maternal use of retinoids, the synthetic derivatives of vitamin A, during pregnancy. The most well known retinoid is isotretinoin (Accutane), a drug used to treat severe cystic acne. The range and severity of associated abnormalities will vary greatly from case to case. However, characteristic features may include growth delays before and after birth (prenatal and postnatal growth retardation); malformations of the skull and facial (craniofacial) region; central nervous system abnormalities; heart abnormalities; and/or additional physical findings.

428 Fetal Valproate Syndrome

Synonyms

Dalpro, Fetal Effects From
Depakene, Fetal Effects From
Depakote Sprinkle, Fetal Effects From
Depakote, Fetal Effects From
Divalproex, Fetal Effects From
Epival, Fetal Effects From
Fetal Anti-Convulsive Syndrome
Myproic Acid, Fetal Effects From
Valproic Acid, Fetal Effects From

Fetal valproate syndrome is a rare congenital disorder caused by exposure of the fetus to valproic acid (Dalpro, Depakene, Depakote, Depakote sprinkle, divalproex, Epival, myproic acid) during the first 3 months of pregnancy. Valproic acid is an anticonvulsant drug used to control certain types of seizures in the treatment of epilepsy. A small percentage of pregnant women who take this medication can have a child with fetal valproate syndrome. The exact prevalence of this condition remains to be established. Symptoms of this disorder may include spina bifida, distinctive facial features, and other musculoskeletal abnormalities.

The following organizations may provide additional information and support:
International Federation for Spina Bifida and Hydrocephalus
National Fetal Anticonvulsant Syndrome Association
Organization for Anti-Convulsant Syndrome
Spina Bifida Association of America
Spina Bifida and Hydrocephalus Association of Canada

429 FG Syndrome

Synonym

Opitz-Kaveggia Syndrome

FG syndrome is an uncommon hereditary disorder that affects males. The presence and severity of symptoms vary from patient to patient. Some females may have certain physical characteristics related to FG syndrome because they are "carriers" of the trait, but they are not affected by the disorder itself. Males with FG syndrome may have mental retardation, an absence of an anal opening (imperforate anus) or an abnormally placed anus, constipation, diminished muscle tone (hypotonia), a large head and certain other physical characteristics. Deafness may be present in some patients. Individuals with FG syndrome seem to have a specific personality type and are often friendly, outgoing, and hyperactive with a short attention span.

The following organizations may provide additional information and support:
FG Syndrome Family Alliance
FG Syndrome Support Group

430 Fiber Type Disproportion, Congenital

Synonyms
Atrophy of Type I Fibers
CFTD
CFTDM
Myopathy of Congenital Fiber Type Disproportion
Myopathy, Congenital, With Fiber-Type Disproportion

Congenital fiber type disproportion (CFTD) is a rare genetic muscle disease that is apparent at birth. Major symptoms may include loss of muscle tone (hypotonia) and weakness, scoliosis, a drawing up of the muscles, high arched palate, dislocated hips, short stature, and deformities of the feet.

The following organizations may provide additional information and support:
March of Dimes Birth Defects Foundation
National Institute of Neurological Disorders and Stroke (NINDS)
NIH/National Institute of Arthritis and Musculoskeletal and Skin Diseases

431 Fibrodysplasia Ossificans Progressiva (FOP)

Synonyms
FOP
Myositis Ossificans Progressiva
Stone Man (Obsolete)

Fibrodysplasia Ossificans Progressiva (FOP) is a very rare inherited connective tissue disorder characterized by the abnormal development of bone in areas of the body where bone is not normally present (heterotopic ossification), such as the ligaments, tendons, and muscles. Major symptoms may include skeletal malformations and/or abnormally short and malformed toes and fingers. The abnormal development of bone may lead to stiffness in affected areas and may also limit movement in affected joints (e.g., knees, wrists, shoulders, spine, and/or neck). Fibrodysplasia ossificans progressiva usually begins during early childhood and progresses throughout life. Most cases of FOP occur randomly (sporadic). The genetic mutation that results in this disorder has been identified. This disease entry was made possible due to the generosity of the Robert Lee and Clara Guthrie Patterson Trust, through grant funds provided for the National Organization for Rare Disorders' "Pediatric Rare Disease Database Project."

The following organizations may provide additional information and support:
British Coalition of Heritable Disorders of Connective Tissue
International Fibrodysplasia Ossificans Progressiva Association
March of Dimes Birth Defects Foundation
NIH/National Arthritis and Musculoskeletal and Skin Diseases Information Clearinghouse

432 Fibromatosis, Congenital Generalized

Synonyms
CGF
Infantile Myofibromatosis (IM)

Disorder Subdivision
Congenital Multiple Fibromatosis

Congenital generalized fibromatosis (CGF) is a pediatric condition that is often now referred to as "infantile myofibromatosis" (IM). It is characterized by the formation of single or multiple noncancerous (benign) tumors that appear to be derived from cells forming certain supporting and binding tissues of the body and involuntary (smooth) muscle. These firm, nodular, potentially locally invasive tumors may involve the skin and underlying (subcutaneous) tissues, muscle tissue, bones, and/or certain internal organs (viscera). In many cases, the tumors are present at birth (congenital), develop within the first few weeks of life, or may initially become apparent before the age of 2 years. Following initial growth and multiplication (proliferation) of tumor cells, the tumors usually eventually recede and disappear on their own (spontaneously). Those with solitary or multiple lesions without visceral involvement typically have a benign disease course. However, in infants with severe or widespread involvement of vital internal organs (i.e., multicentric, visceral involvement), potentially life-threatening complications may occur.

The following organizations may provide additional information and support:
American Cancer Society, Inc.
March of Dimes Birth Defects Foundation
National Cancer Institute
National Cancer Institute Physician Data Query (PDQ) Cancer Information Service
OncoLink: The University of Pennsylvania Cancer Center Resource

433 Fibromyalgia

Synonyms
Fibromyositis
Fibrositis
Muscular Rheumatism
Musculoskeletal Pain Syndrome
Nonarticular Rheumatism
Periarticular Fibrositis
Rheumatoid Myositis
Tension Myalgia

Fibromyalgia is a chronic disorder characterized by pain throughout much of the body. The pain may begin gradually or have a sudden onset. Other symptoms are muscle spasms, fatigue, muscle tissue stiffness and non-restorative (unrefreshing) sleep. The exact cause of this disorder is unknown.The terms fibrositis, fibromyositis, periarticular fibrositis, and rheumatoid myositis are still being used by many to describe this condition. The ending of "itis" on each of these terms is actually incorrect. "Itis" means inflammation, and there is no inflammation in fibromyalgia. The term fibromyalgia has now become the accepted term, but many people continue to be diagnosed with the other synonyms. Tension myalgia is another synonym that is currently being used.

The following organizations may provide additional information and support:
American Chronic Pain Association
Arthritis Foundation
Autoimmune Information Network, Inc
CF Alliance
Eastern Paralyzed Veterans Association

Erythema Nodosum Yahoo Support Group
Fibromyalgia Educational Systems
Irish Chronic Pain Association
Myositis Association
National CFIDS Foundation, Inc.
National Chronic Fatigue Syndrome & Fibromyalgia Association
NIH/National Institute of Arthritis and Musculoskeletal and Skin Diseases

434 Filariasis

Synonyms
Bancroftian Filariasis
Filarial Elephantiasis
Filariasis Malayi
Malayi Tropical Eosinophilia
Wuchereriasis

Filariasis is an infectious tropical disease caused by any one of several thread-like parasitic round worms. The two species of worms most often associated with this disease are Wuchereria bancrofti and Brugia malayi. The larval form of the parasite transmits the disease to humans by the bite of a mosquito. In the early stages of the infection, the patient characteristically complains of fever, chills, headache, and skin lesions. Any one of several antiparasitic agents may be effective in eliminating the worm. However, if the disease is left untreated, obstruction of the lymph flow will cause particular areas of the body especially the legs and external genitals, to swell profoundly. Symptoms are primarily a response to adult worms that cause inflammation. Chronic inflammation may progress to hardening of the lymphatic vessels (fibrosis) and obstruction of the lymph flow.

The following organizations may provide additional information and support:
Centers for Disease Control and Prevention
International Filariasis Association
NIH/National Institute of Allergy and Infectious Diseases
World Health Organization (WHO) Regional Office for the Americas (AMRO)

435 Filippi Syndrome

Synonym
Syndactyly Type I with Microcephaly and Mental Retardation

Filippi syndrome is a rare genetic disorder that may be apparent at birth (congenital). The disorder is characterized by an unusual facial appearance, abnormalities of the fingers and toes, and mild to severe mental retardation. Primary physical findings include growth delays, an abnormally small head (microcephaly), webbing or fusion (syndactyly) of certain fingers and toes, and inward deviation or bending (clinodactyly) of the fifth fingers ("pinkies"). Filippi syndrome is transmitted as an autosomal recessive trait.

The following organization may provide additional information and support:
Genetic and Rare Diseases (GARD) Information Center

436 Fitz Hugh Curtis Syndrome

Synonyms
Gonococcal Perihepatitis
Perihepatitis Syndrome

Fitz-Hugh-Curtis syndrome is a rare disorder that develops in females as a result of complications of pelvic inflammatory disease. The disorder is characterized by string-like scar tissue (adhesions) that attaches between the liver and other sites in the abdominal lining (peritoneum). Symptoms can mimic those of hepatitis. Severe pain in the upper right area of the abdomen is usually present. Infection occurs, caused by the Chlamydia trachomatis bacteria.

The following organizations may provide additional information and support:
Centers for Disease Control and Prevention
Council on Sex Information and Education
NIH/National Institute of Allergy and Infectious Diseases
Sexuality Information and Education Council of the U.S.

437 Floating Harbor Syndrome

Synonyms
FHS
Pelletier-Leisti Syndrome

Floating-Harbor syndrome (FHS) is an extremely rare disorder characterized by short stature, delayed language skills, and a triangular shaped face. A broad nose, deep-set eyes and a wide mouth with thin lips give an affected individual a distinct appearance. FHS was named after the hospitals at which the first two cases were seen: the Boston Floating Hospital and Harbor General Hospital in California. The cause of this disorder is not known.

The following organizations may provide additional information and support:

Floating Harbor Syndrome Support Group
Human Growth Foundation
NIH/National Arthritis and Musculoskeletal and Skin Diseases Information Clearinghouse
Restricted Growth Association

438 Focal Dermal Hypoplasia

Synonyms
Combined Mesoectodermal Dysplasia
DHOF
Ectodermal and Mesodermal Dysplasia with Osseous Involvement
Ectodermal and Mesodermal Dysplasia, Congenital
FDH
Focal Dermal Dysplasia Syndrome
Focal Dermato-Phalangeal Dysplasia
FODH
Goltz Syndrome
Goltz-Gorlin Syndrome

Focal dermal hypoplasia is a rare form of ectodermal dysplasia that is thought to be inherited as an X-linked dominant genetic trait with lethality in males. It is found primarily in females. This disorder is characterized by skin abnormalities in which there are underdeveloped areas of skin that form streaks or lines and tumor-like herniations of fat on the skin. Skeletal, facial, dental, ocular and soft tissue defects are also present.

The following organizations may provide additional information and support:
Anophthalmia/Microphthalmia Registry
National Foundation for Ectodermal Dysplasias
NIH/National Arthritis and Musculoskeletal and Skin Diseases Information Clearinghouse
NIH/National Oral Health Information Clearinghouse

439 Forbes Disease

Synonyms
Amylo-1,6-Glucosidase Deficiency
Cori Disease
Debrancher Deficiency
Glycogen Storage Disease III
Glycogenosis Type III
Limit Dextrinosis

Forbes disease (GSD-III) is one of several glycogen storage disorders (GSD) that are inherited as autosomal recessive traits. Symptoms are caused by a lack of the enzyme amylo-1,6 glucosidase (debrancher enzyme). This enzyme deficiency causes excess amounts of an abnormal glycogen (the stored form of energy that comes from carbohydrates) to be deposited in the liver, muscles and, in some cases, the heart. There are two forms of this disorder. GSD-IIIA affects about 85% of patients with Forbes disease and involves both the liver and the muscles. GSD-IIIB affects only the liver.

The following organizations may provide additional information and support:
Association for Glycogen Storage Disease
Association for Glycogen Storage Disease (UK)
CLIMB (Children Living with Inherited Metabolic Diseases)
Muscular Dystrophy Association
NIH/National Digestive Diseases Information Clearinghouse

440   Formaldehyde Poisoning

Synonyms
Formaldehyde Exposure
Formaldehyde Toxicity
Formalin Intoxication
Formalin Toxicity

Formaldehyde poisoning is a disorder brought about by breathing the fumes of formaldehyde. This can occur while working directly with formaldehyde, or using equipment cleaned with formaldehyde. Major symptoms may include eye, nose, and throat irritation; headaches; and/or skin rashes.

The following organizations may provide additional information and support:
Centers for Disease Control and Prevention
National Center for Environmental Health Strategies, Inc.
National Institute for Occupational Safety and Health

441   Fountain Syndrome

Synonym
Mental Retardation-Deafness-Skeletal Abnormalit.-Coarse Face with Full Lips

Fountain syndrome is an extremely rare inherited disorder that is characterized by mental retardation; abnormal swelling of the cheeks and lips due to the excessive accumulation of body fluids under the skin (subcutaneous) of the face (edema); skeletal abnormalities; and/or deafness due to malformation of a structure (cochlea) within the inner ear. Fountain syndrome is inherited as an autosomal recessive trait.

The following organizations may provide additional information and support:
American Speech-Language-Hearing Association
Epilepsy Foundation
NIH/National Arthritis and Musculoskeletal and Skin Diseases Information Clearinghouse
NIH/National Institute on Deafness and Other Communication Disorders Information Clearinghouse

442   Fournier Gangrene

Synonyms
Fournier Disease
Fournier Gangrenes
Necrotizing Fasciitis of the Perineum and Genitalia
Synergistic Necrotizing Fasciitis of the Perineum and Genitalia

Fournier gangrene is a serious, rapidly progressive infective gangrene involving the scrotum, penis, and/or perineum caused by a broad array of microorganisms, acting in mutual support of one another (synergistically) and usually resulting from local trauma, operative procedures, or urinary tract disease. Since 1950, more than 1,800 cases for study have been reported in English language medical literature. This disease occurs worldwide and, although it is recognized more frequently among male adults, has been identified also among women and children. Treatment usually consists of the surgical removal (debridement) of extensive areas of dead tissue (necrosis, necrotic) and the administration of broad-spectrum intravenous antibiotics. Surgical reconstruction may follow where necessary.

The following organizations may provide additional information and support:
NIH/National Institute of Arthritis and Musculoskeletal and Skin Diseases
NIH/National Institute of General Medical Sciences

443   Fox Fordyce Disease

Synonyms
Apocrine Duct Occlusion
Sweat Retention Disease

Fox-Fordyce disease is a rare disorder that occurs almost solely in women. It is characterized by the development of intense itching usually in the underarm area, the pubic area, and around the nipple of the breast. Perspiration becomes trapped in the sweat gland and in the surrounding area causing intense itching, inflammation, and enlargement of the glands. Skin in the area may become darkened and dry; raised patches develop. Hair follicles in the area dry out resulting in loss or breakage of hair.

The following organization may provide additional information and support:
NIH/National Arthritis and Musculoskeletal and Skin Diseases Information Clearinghouse

444 Fragile X Syndrome

Synonyms
FRAXA
Marker X Syndrome
Martin-Bell Syndrome
X-linked Mental Retardation and Macroorchidism

Fragile X syndrome is a defect of the X chromosome which causes mild mental retardation. The disorder occurs more frequently and severely among males than females. This condition is the leading known familial cause of mental retardation in the United States. Language delays, behavioral problems, autism or autistic-like behavior (including poor eye contact and hand-flapping), enlarged external genitalia (macroorchidism), large or prominent ears, hyperactivity, delayed motor development and/or poor sensory skills are among the wide range of symptoms associated with this disorder.

The following organizations may provide additional information and support:
The Arc (A National Organization on Mental Retardation)
Fragile X Society
FRAXA Research Foundation
Let Them Hear Foundation
National Fragile X Foundation
New Horizons Un-Limited, Inc.
New York State Institute for Basic Research in Developmental Disabilities
NIH/National Institute of Child Health and Human Development
NIH/National Institute on Aging

445 Fraser Syndrome

Synonym
Cryptophthalmos-Syndactyly Syndrome

Fraser syndrome is a rare genetic disorder characterized by partial webbing of the fingers and/or toes (partial syndactyly), kidney (renal) abnormalities, genital malformations, and/or, in some cases, complete fusion of the eyelids (cryptophthalmos) that may be associated with malformation of the eyes, causing blindness. In infants with Fraser syndrome, renal malformations may include improper development (dysplasia), underdevelopment (hypoplasia), or absence of one or both kidneys (unilateral or bilateral renal agenesis). In affected males, one or both testes may fail to descend into the scrotum (cryptorchidism), the urinary opening (meatus) may be abnormally placed on the underside of the penis (hypospadias), and/or the penis may be abnormally small (micropenis). Affected females may have malformed fallopian tubes, an abnormally enlarged clitoris (clitoromegaly), and/or an abnormally shaped uterus (bicornate uterus). In addition, the folds of skin on either side of the vaginal opening (labia) may be abnormally fused. Infants and children with Fraser syndrome may also have additional abnormalities including malformations of the middle and outer ear that may result in hearing impairment. Fraser syndrome is inherited as an autosomal recessive genetic trait.

The following organizations may provide additional information and support:
AboutFace USA
American Kidney Fund, Inc.
Children's Craniofacial Association
FACES: The National Craniofacial Association
Forward Face, Inc.
National Craniofacial Foundation
National Foundation for Facial Reconstruction
National Kidney Foundation

446 Freeman Sheldon Syndrome

Synonyms
Craniocarpotarsal Dystrophy (Dysplasia)
Distal Arthrogryposis Type 2A
FSS
Whistling Face Syndrome
Whistling Face-Windmill Vane Hand Syndrome

Freeman-Sheldon syndrome is a rare inherited disorder characterized by multiple contractures (i.e., restricted movement around two or more body areas) at birth (congenital), abnormalities of the head and face (craniofacial) area, defects of the hands and feet, and skeletal malformations. Craniofacial abnormalities may consist of characteristic facial features that cause the individual to appear to be whistling. These features include an extremely small puckered mouth (microstomia); a "full" forehead appearance; unusually prominent cheeks; and thin, pursed lips. Affected infants may also have an unusually flat middle portion of the face, a high roof of the mouth (palate), an unusually small jaw (micrognathia), an abnormally small tongue (microglossia), and/or a raised, scar-like mark in the shape of an "H" or a "V" extending from the lower lip to the chin. Affected infants often have abnormalities affecting the eyes including widely-spaced deep-set eyes, crossed eyes (strabismus), and/or downslanting eyelid folds (palpebral fissures). Malformations of the hands and feet are also characteristic of Freeman-Sheldon syndrome. Children with Freeman-Sheldon syndrome may also exhibit speech impairment; swallowing and eating difficulties; vomiting; failure to grow and gain weight at the expected rate (failure to thrive); and/or respiratory problems that may result in life-threatening complications. Freeman-Sheldon syndrome can be inherited as an autosomal dominant genetic trait. However, most cases occur randomly with no apparent cause (sporadically).

The following organizations may provide additional information and support:
AboutFace USA
Association for Spina Bifida and Hydrocephalus
Craniofacial Foundation of America
FACES: The National Craniofacial Association
Freeman-Sheldon Parent Support Group
Malignant Hyperthermia Association of the United States (MHAUS)
March of Dimes Birth Defects Foundation
National Craniofacial Foundation
NIH/National Arthritis and Musculoskeletal and Skin Diseases Information Clearinghouse

447   Frey's Syndrome

Synonyms
Auriculotemporal Syndrome
Baillarger's Syndrome
Dupuy's Syndrome
Salivosudoriparous Syndrome
Sweating Gustatory Syndrome
von Frey's Syndrome

Frey's syndrome is a rare neurological disorder that results from injury or surgery near the parotid glands (which manufacture saliva), damaging the facial nerve. The parotid glands are the largest salivary glands and are located on the side of the face below and in front of the ear. This syndrome is characterized by flushing or sweating on one side of the face when certain foods are consumed. The symptoms usually are mild and well tolerated by most individuals. Relief from symptoms may require treatment in some cases.

The following organization may provide additional information and support:
National Institute of Neurological Disorders and Stroke (NINDS)

448   Froehlich's Syndrome

Synonyms
Adiposogenital Dystrophy
Babinski-Froelich Syndrome
Dystrophia Adiposogenitalis
Frolich's Syndrome
Hypothalamic Infantilism-Obesity
Launois-Cleret Syndrome
Sexual Infantilism

Froehlich syndrome is a constellation of endocrine abnormalities believed to result from damage to the hypothalamus, a part of the brain where certain functions such as sleep cycles and body temperature are regulated. Froehlich syndrome appears to be acquired while certain other disorders that resemble it, such as Prader-Willi syndrome, are genetic. This syndrome appears to affect males mostly. The more obvious and frequently encountered characteristics are delayed puberty, small testes, and obesity. Teen-age boys with this disorder must be distinguished from those who have inherited growth delay disorders or Prader Willi syndrome.

The following organizations may provide additional information and support:
The Arc (A National Organization on Mental Retardation)
Human Growth Foundation
MAGIC Foundation for Children's Growth
National Institute of Neurological Disorders and Stroke (NINDS)

449 Frontofacionasal Dysplasia

Synonyms

Cleft Lip-Palate, Blepharophimosis, Lagophthalmos, and Hypertelorism
Facio-Fronto-Nasal Dysplasia
Frontofacionasal Dysostosis
Nasal-Fronto-Faciodysplasia

Frontofacionasal dysplasia is a rare genetic disorder that is apparent at birth (congenital). The disorder is primarily characterized by malformations of the head and facial (craniofacial) area and eye (ocular) defects. Craniofacial malformations may include an unusually short, broad head (brachycephaly); incomplete closure of the roof of the mouth (cleft palate); an abnormal groove in the upper lip (cleft lip); and underdevelopment (hypoplasia) of the nose with malformation of the nostrils. Affected infants may also have abnormal narrowing of the folds (palpebral fissures) between the upper and lower eyelids (blepharophimosis) and an unusually increased distance between the eyes (ocular hypertelorism). Additional eye abnormalities may include partial absence of tissue (coloboma) from the upper eyelids or the colored regions of the eyes (irides) and an inability to completely close the eyes (lagophthalmos). Frontofacionasal dysplasia appears to be inherited as an autosomal recessive trait.

The following organizations may provide additional information and support:
AboutFace USA
Children's Craniofacial Association
Cleft Palate Foundation
FACES: The National Craniofacial Association
Forward Face, Inc.
National Craniofacial Foundation
Prescription Parents
Society for the Rehabilitation of the Facially Disfigured, Inc.
Wide Smiles

450 Frontonasal Dysplasia

Synonyms

FND
Median Cleft Face Syndrome

Frontonasal dysplasia, also known as median cleft face syndrome, is a very rare disorder characterized by abnormalities affecting the head and facial (craniofacial) region. Major physical characteristics may include widely spaced eyes (ocular hypertelorism); a flat broad nose; and/or a vertical groove down the middle of the face. The depth and width of the vertical groove may vary greatly. In some cases, the tip of the nose may be missing; in more severe cases, the nose may separate vertically into two parts. In addition, an abnormal skin-covered gap in the front of the head (anterior cranium occultum) may also be present in some cases. The exact cause of frontonasal dysplasia is not known. Most cases occur randomly, for no apparent reason (sporadically). However, some cases are thought to run in families.

The following organizations may provide additional information and support:
AboutFace USA
Children's Craniofacial Association
FACES: The National Craniofacial Association
Forward Face, Inc.
National Craniofacial Foundation

451 Fructose Intolerance, Hereditary

Synonyms

Fructose-1-Phosphate Aldolase Deficiency
Fructosemia

There are three inherited disorders of fructose metabolism that are recognized and characterized. Essential fructosuria is a mild disorder not requiring treatment, while hereditary fructose intolerance (HFI) and hereditary fructose-1,6-biphosphatase deficiency (HFBP) are treatable and controllable but must be taken seriously. Hereditary fructose intolerance (HFI) is an inherited inability to digest fructose (fruit sugar) or its precursors (sugar, sorbitol and brown sugar). This is due to a deficiency of activity of the enzyme fructose-1-phosphate aldolase, resulting in an accumulation of fructose-1-phosphate in the liver, kidney, and small intestine. Fructose is a naturally occurring sugar that is used as a sweetener in many foods, including many baby foods. This disorder can be life threatening in infants and ranges from mild to severe in older children and adults. People who have HFI usually develop a strong dislike for sweets and fruit. After eating foods containing fructose, they may experience such symptoms as severe abdominal pain, vomiting, and low blood sugar (hypoglycemia). Early diagnosis is important because most people who have HFI can lead normal lives if they adopt a fructose-free diet. If left untreated however, the condition can lead to permanent physical harm, including especially, serious liver and kidney damage.

The following organizations may provide additional information and support:
Genetic and Rare Diseases (GARD) Information Center
NIH/National Digestive Diseases Information Clearinghouse

452   Fructosuria

Synonyms
Essential Fructosuria
Hepatic Fructokinase Deficiency
Ketohexokinase Deficiency
Levulosuria

Fructosuria is a rare but benign inherited metabolic disorder. It is characterized by the excretion of fruit sugar (fructose) in the urine. Normally, no fructose is excreted in the urine. This condition is caused by a deficiency of the enzyme fructokinase in the liver. This enzyme is needed for the synthesis of glycogen (the body's form of stored energy) from fructose. The presence of fructose in the blood and urine may lead to an incorrect diagnosis of diabetes mellitus.

The following organizations may provide additional information and support:
CLIMB (Children Living with Inherited Metabolic Diseases)
NIH/National Institute of Diabetes, Digestive & Kidney Diseases

453   Fryns Syndrome

Synonym
FRNS

Fryns syndrome is an extremely rare inherited disorder characterized by multiple abnormalities that are present at birth (congenital). Characteristic symptoms and physical findings include protrusion of part of the stomach and/or small intestines into the chest cavity (diaphragmatic hernia), abnormalities of the head and face area (craniofacial region), and underdevelopment of the ends of the fingers and toes (distal digit hypoplasia). Additional symptoms include underdevelopment (hypoplasia) of the lungs, incomplete closure of the roof of the mouth (cleft palate), cardiac defects, and varying degrees of mental retardation. Fryns syndrome is inherited as an autosomal recessive trait.

The following organizations may provide additional information and support:
AboutFace USA
Children's Craniofacial Association
Craniofacial Foundation of America
FACES: The National Craniofacial Association
Forward Face, Inc.
March of Dimes Birth Defects Foundation
NIH/National Institute of Child Health & Human Development (Preg & Perinat)

454   Fucosidosis

Synonym
Alpha-L-Fucosidase Deficiency

Disorder Subdivisions
Fucosidosis Type 1
Fucosidosis Type 2
Fucosidosis Type 3 (proposed)

Fucosidosis is an extremely rare inherited lysosomal storage disease characterized by a deficiency of the enzyme alpha-L-fucosidase. This disorder belongs to a group of diseases known as lysosomal storage disorders. Lysosomes are particles bound in membranes within cells that break down certain fats and carbohydrates. Low levels of the alpha-L-fucosidase enzyme lead to the abnormal accumulation of certain fucose-containing complex compounds (i.e., glycosphingolipids, glycolipids, and glycoproteins) in many tissues of the body. Many researchers believe there are two types of fucosidosis (i.e., type 1 and type 2), determined mainly by the severity of the symptoms. Other scientists theorize there are three types, with the age of onset and the disease severity being the determining factors. The symptoms of fucosidosis type 1, the most severe form of the disease, may become apparent as early as 6 months of age. Symptoms may include progressive deterioration of the brain and spinal cord (central nervous system), mental retardation, loss of previously acquired intellectual skills, and growth retardation leading to short stature. Other physical findings and features become apparent over time including multiple deformities of the bones (dysostosis multiplex), coarse facial features, enlargement of the heart (cardiomegaly), enlargement of the liver and spleen (hepatosplenomegaly), and/or episodes of uncontrolled electrical activity in the brain (seizures). Additional symptoms may include increased or decreased perspiration and/or malfunction of the gallbladder and/or salivary glands. In fucosidosis type 2, deterioration of the central nervous system becomes apparent in the first few years of life; symptoms progress more slowly than in type 1. Other symptoms may be similar to but milder than those of type 1. The most noticeable feature distinguishing fucosidosis type 1 from type 2 is the appearance of horny or warty growths (angiokeratomas) on the skin in those individuals with type 2. Fucosidosis types 1 and 2 may be found in the same family. Many researchers believe that there is no clear distinction between the three proposed types of fucosidosis and that they actually represent varying clinical expressions of the disorder rather than distinct subtypes. Fucosidosis is inherited as an autosomal recessive genetic trait.

The following organizations may provide additional information and support:
International Society for Mannosidosis & Related Diseases, Inc.
National Institute of Neurological Disorders and Stroke (NINDS)
National Tay-Sachs and Allied Diseases Association, Inc.
Vaincre Les Maladies Lysosomales

455 Fukuyama Type Congenital Muscular Dystrophy

Synonyms
Cerebromuscular Dystrophy, Fukuyama Type
Congenital Muscular Dystrophy, Fukuyama Type
FCMD
Micropolygyria With Muscular Dystrophy
Muscular Dystrophy, Congenital Progressive with Mental Retardation
Muscular Dystrophy, Congenital With Central Nervous System Involvement
Muscular Dystrophy, Congenital, Fukuyama Type
Muscular Dystrophy, Fukuyama Type

Fukuyama type congenital muscular dystrophy (FCMD) is one of several forms of a rare type of muscular dystrophy known as congenital muscular dystrophy. It is inherited as an autosomal recessive trait. Symptoms of this disorder are apparent at birth and progress slowly. In addition to general muscle weakness and deformities of the joints (contractures), FCMD is often accompanied by seizures, mental retardation and speech prob-

lems. This disorder is predominantly found in Japan.

The following organizations may provide additional information and support:
Muscular Dystrophy Association
National Institute of Neurological Disorders and Stroke (NINDS)
New Horizons Un-Limited, Inc.
Society for Muscular Dystrophy Information International

456 Galactosemia

Synonyms
Classic Galactosemia
GALT Deficiency
Galactose-1-Phosphate Uridyl Transferase Deficiency

Galactosemia is a rare, hereditary disorder of carbohydrate metabolism that affects the body's ability to convert galactose (a sugar contained in milk, including human mother's milk) to glucose (a different type of sugar). Galactose is converted to glucose by a series of three enzyme reactions. The disorder is caused by a deficiency of an enzyme known as "galactose-1-phosphate uridyl transferase" which is vital to this process. Galactosemia may also be referred to as classic galactosemia because a few variants of the gene for galactosemia have been identified. One variant causes a milder form of the disorder known as Duarte galactosemia. Classic galactosemia is the most severe form. Because milk is the staple of an infant's diet, early diagnosis and treatment of this disorder is absolutely essential to avoid serious lifelong disability.

The following organizations may provide additional information and support:
CLIMB (Children Living with Inherited Metabolic Diseases)
Children's Liver Alliance
Cochrane Cystic Fibrosis and Genetic Disorders Review Group
Galactosaemia Support Group
NIH/National Digestive Diseases Information Clearinghouse
Parents of Galactosemic Children, Inc.
Sjëldne Diagnoser / Rare Disorders Denmark

457 Galloway-Mowat Syndrome

Synonyms

Galloway Syndrome
Hiatal Hernia-Microcephaly-Nephrosis,
Galloway Type
Microcephaly-Hiatal Hernia-Nephrosis,
Galloway Type
Microcephaly-Hiatal Hernia-Nephrotic
Syndrome
Nephrosis-Microcephaly Syndrome
Nephrosis-Neuronal Dysmigration Syndrome

Galloway-Mowat syndrome, which is also known as microcephaly-hiatal hernia-nephrotic syndrome, is an extremely rare genetic disorder that is characterized by a variety of physical and developmental abnormalities. Physical features may include an unusually small head (microcephaly) and additional abnormalities of the head and facial (craniofacial) area; damage to clusters of capillaries in the kidneys (focal glomerulosclerosis and/or diffuse mesangial sclerosis), resulting in abnormal kidney function (nephrotic syndrome); and, in many cases, protrusion of part of the stomach through an abnormal opening (esophageal hiatus) in the diaphragm (hiatal hernia). Additional physical abnormalities are often present. These may include various malformations of the brain, seizures, diminished muscle tone throughout the body (generalized hypotonia), and/or increased reflex reactions (hyperreflexia). Infants and children with Galloway-Mowat syndrome may also exhibit developmental abnormalities including an inability to perform certain movement (motor) skills normal for their age and a profound delay in the attainment of skills requiring the coordination of muscular and mental activity (psychomotor retardation). Mental retardation may also be present. Galloway-Mowat syndrome is inherited as an autosomal recessive trait.

The following organizations may provide additional information and support:
Epilepsy Foundation
National Institute of Neurological Disorders and Stroke (NINDS)
National Kidney Foundation
NIH/National Kidney and Urologic Diseases Information Clearinghouse

458 Gardner Syndrome

Synonyms

Bone Tumor-Epidermoid Cyst-Polyposis
Familial Adenomatous Polyposis with
Extraintestinal Manifestations
FAPG
GRS
Intestinal Polyposis III
Oldfield Syndrome
Polyposis, Gardner Type
Polyposis-Osteomatosis-Epidermoid Cyst
Syndrome

Gardner syndrome is a rare, inherited disorder characterized by multiple growths (polyps) in the colon (often 1,000 or more), extra teeth (supernumerary), bony tumors of the skull (osteomas), and fatty cysts and/or fibrous tumors in the skin (fibromas or epithelial cysts). Gardner syndrome is a variant of familial adenomatous polyposis, a rare group of disorders characterized by the growth of multiple polyps in the colon. Gardner syndrome is inherited as an autosomal dominant trait.

The following organizations may provide additional information and support:
American Cancer Society, Inc.
Familial Polyposis Registry
Hereditary Colon Cancer Association (HCCA)
Intestinal Multiple Polyposis and Colorectal Cancer Registry
NIH/National Institute of Diabetes, Digestive & Kidney Diseases

459 Gastritis, Chronic, Erosive

Synonyms

Idiopathic Chronic, Erosive Gastritis
Varioliform Gastritis

Chronic, erosive gastritis is characterized by many inflamed lesions in the mucous lining of the stomach. It may be a transitory or a chronic condition lasting for years.

The following organizations may provide additional information and support:
Crohn's and Colitis Foundation of America
Digestive Disease National Coalition
NIH/National Institute of Diabetes, Digestive & Kidney Diseases

460 Gastritis, Giant Hypertrophic

Synonyms
Gastroenteropathy, Protein Losing
Giant Hypertrophy of the Gastric Mucosa
Hypertrophic Gastropathy
Menetrier Disease

Giant hypertrophic gastritis (GHG) is a general term for inflammation of the stomach due to the accumulation of inflammatory cells in the inner wall (mucosa) of the stomach resulting in abnormally large, coiled ridges or folds that resemble polyps in the inner wall of the stomach (hypertrophic gastric folds). GHG encompasses a collection of disorders. The symptoms of GHG may vary from case to case. The exact cause of GHG is unknown. There is considerable confusion and contradiction in the medical literature regarding disorders involving large gastric folds. GHG is often used as a synonym for Menetrier disease. However, Menetrier disease is not a true form of gastritis. A diagnosis of Menetrier disease should indicate massive overgrowth of mucous cells (foveola) in the gastric mucosa (foveolar hyperplasia) and minimal inflammation. Foveolar hyperplasia results in large gastric folds. Because inflammation is minimal, Menetrier disease is classified as a form of hyperplastic gastropathy and not a form of gastritis. Some researchers believe that GHG and Menetrier disease may be variants of the same disorder or different parts of one disease spectrum.

The following organization may provide additional information and support:
NIH/National Digestive Diseases Information Clearinghouse

461 Gastroenteritis, Eosinophilic

Synonym
EG

Eosinophilic gastroenteritis is a rare digestive disease characterized by the presence of a particular type of white blood cell (eosinophils) in one or more of the three layers that make up the lining of the gastrointestinal (GI) tract. This includes the stomach, small intestines, and large intestines.

The following organizations may provide additional information and support:
Digestive Disease National Coalition

NIH/National Digestive Diseases Information Clearinghouse

462 Gastroesophageal Reflux

Synonyms
GER
GERD
Pediatric Gastroesophageal Reflux
Reflux Esophagitis

Gastroesophageal reflux (GERD) is a digestive disorder characterized by the passage or flowing back (reflux) of the contents of the stomach or small intestines (duodenum) into the esophagus. The esophagus is the tube that carries food from the mouth to the stomach (esophagus). Symptoms of gastroesophageal reflux may include a sensation of warmth or burning rising up to the neck area (heartburn or pyrosis), swallowing difficulties (dysphagia), and chest pain. This condition is a common problem and may be a symptom of other gastrointestinal disorders.

The following organizations may provide additional information and support:
Digestive Disease National Coalition
NIH/National Digestive Diseases Information Clearinghouse
Pediatric/Adolescent Gastroesophageal Reflux Association, Inc.
Tracheo Oesophageal Fistula Support Group (TOFS)

463 Gastrointestinal Stromal Tumors

Synonym
GIST

Gastrointestinal stromal tumors (GIST) belong to a group of cancers known as soft tissue sarcomas. The number of new cases in the United States annually has been estimated to be 5,000-6,000. Tumors usually arise from the intestinal tract with the most common site being the stomach, followed by the small intestine, and the colon/rectum with rare cases arising in the esophagus. There are also tumors that appear to arise in the membranous tissue lining the wall of the stomach (peritoneum) or in a fold of such membranous tissue (the omentum). There are also case reports of tumors arising in the appendix and/or pancreas. These tumors most commonly present with abdominal pain, bleeding or signs of intestinal obstruction. They spread most commonly to sites within the abdominal cavity and to the liver, although there are rare cases of spread to the lungs and bone. GIST results from a change in one of two genes, KIT or PDGFR, which leads to continued growth and division of tumor cells. There are a few reported cases of families in which a gene mutation is inherited; however, the majority of tumors are sporadic and not inherited. Treatment is with surgery. Patients who have disease that has spread are treated with surgery when possible and with imatinib mesylate (Gleevec, Glivec), a tyrosine kinase inhibitor that inhibits the KIT or PDGFR responsible for tumor growth. Ongoing studies are testing to see if imatinib mesylate can delay or prevent recurrence of GIST after the tumor has been removed (resection). Standard chemotherapy is not effective for this type of sarcoma, with a less than 5% response rate. The role of imatinib mesylate in pediatric GIST is being studied at this time.

The following organizations may provide additional information and support:
American Cancer Society, Inc.
GIST Cancer Research Fund
GIST Support International
Life Raft Group
National Cancer Institute
National Coalition for Cancer Survivorship
OncoLink: The University of Pennsylvania Cancer Center Resource
Rare Cancer Alliance
Sarcoma Alliance
Sarcoma Foundation of America

464   Gastroschisis

Synonyms
Abdominal Wall Defect
Aparoschisis

Gastroschisis is a rare congenital disorder in which a defect is present in the wall of the abdomen. Typically there is a small abdominal cavity with herniated abdominal organs that usually appear on the right side of the abdomen. There is no membranous sac covering the organs and the intestines may be swollen and look shortened due to exposure to the liquid that surrounds the fetus during pregnancy (amniotic fluid).

The following organizations may provide additional information and support:
Birth Defect Research for Children, Inc.

Digestive Disease National Coalition
NIH/National Digestive Diseases Information Clearinghouse

465   Gaucher Disease

Synonym
Sphingolipidosis 1

Disorder Subdivisions
Norrbottnian Gaucher Disease
Type I Gaucher Disease
Type II Gaucher Disease
Type III Gaucher Disease

Gaucher disease is a rare, inherited metabolic disorder in which deficiency of the enzyme glucocerebrosidase results in the accumulation of harmful quantities of certain fats (lipids), specifically the glycolipid glucocerebroside, throughout the body especially within the bone marrow, spleen and liver. The symptoms and physical findings associated with Gaucher disease vary greatly from case to case. Some individuals will develop few or no symptoms (asymptomatic); others may have serious complications. Common symptoms associated with Gaucher disease include an abnormally enlarged liver and/or spleen (hepatosplenomegaly), low levels of circulating red blood cells (anemia), low levels of platelets (thrombocytopenia), and skeletal abnormalities. Platelets are blood cells that promote clotting and patients with thrombocytopenia may develop bleeding problems. Three separate forms of Gaucher disease have been identified and are distinguished by the absence of, or the presence and extent of, neurological complications. All three forms of Gaucher disease are inherited as autosomal recessive traits. Gaucher disease is categorized as a lysosomal storage disorder. Lysosomes are the major digestive units in cells. Enzymes within lysosomes break down or "digest" nutrients, including certain complex carbohydrates and fats. In Gaucher disease certain fats, known as glycolipids, abnormally accumulate in the body because of the lack of the enzyme, glucocerebrosidase. This accumulation or "storage" of lipids leads to the various symptoms or physical findings associated with a lysosomal storage disease. Gaucher disease is the most common type of lysosomal storage disorder.

The following organizations may provide additional information and support:
The Arc (A National Organization on Mental Retardation)

Cochrane Cystic Fibrosis and Genetic Disorders Review Group
Gauchers Association (UK)
Instituto de Errores Innatos del Metabolismo
March of Dimes Birth Defects Foundation
National Gaucher Foundation, Inc.
National Institute of Neurological Disorders and Stroke (NINDS)
National Tay-Sachs and Allied Diseases Association, Inc.
Sjëldne Diagnoser / Rare Disorders Denmark
Vaincre Les Maladies Lysosomales

466   Gerstmann Syndrome

Synonyms
Developmental Gerstmann Syndrome
GS
Gerstmann Tetrad

Gerstmann syndrome is a rare neurological disorder that can occur as the result of a brain injury or as a developmental disorder. The syndrome is characterized by the loss or absence of four sensory abilities. These include the loss of the ability to express thoughts in writing (agraphia, dysgraphia), to perform simple arithmetic problems (acalculia), to recognize or indicate one's own or another's fingers (finger agnosia), and to distinguish between right and left. The disorder has not been found to run in families. Children who are bright and functioning intellectually at a high level may be affected by the disorder as well as those with brain damage.

The following organizations may provide additional information and support:
CJD Voice
Learning Disabilities Association of America

467   Gianotti Crosti Syndrome

Synonyms
Acrodermatitis, Infantile Lichenoid
Acrodermatitis, Papular Infantile
Crosti-Gianotti Syndrome
GCS
Papular Acrodermatitis of Childhood

Gianotti-Crosti syndrome is a rare skin disease affecting children between the ages of 9 months and 9 years. Major symptoms may include blisters on the skin of the legs, buttocks and arms. The disorder is usually preceded by a viral infection.

The following organizations may provide additional information and support:
Centers for Disease Control and Prevention
NIH/National Arthritis and Musculoskeletal and Skin Diseases Information Clearinghouse
NIH/National Institute of Allergy and Infectious Diseases

468   Giant Cell Myocarditis

Synonyms
GCM
Idiopathic Giant Cell Myocarditis

Giant cell myocarditis is a rare cardiovascular disorder that occurs for unknown reasons (idiopathic). It is characterized by inflammation of the heart muscle (myocardium), a condition referred to as myocarditis. Inflammation is caused by widespread infiltration of giant cells associated with other inflammatory cells and heart muscle cell destruction. Giant cells are abnormal masses produced by the fusion of inflammatory cells called macrophages. Individuals with giant cell myocarditis may develop abnormal heartbeats, chest pain and, eventually, heart failure. Many individuals eventually require a heart transplant. The disorder most often occurs in young adults.

The following organizations may provide additional information and support:
American Autoimmune Related Diseases Association, Inc.
American Heart Association
Children's Cardiomyopathy Foundation
Myocarditis Program at Mayo Clinic
NIH/National Heart, Lung and Blood Institute Information Center

469   Giardiasis

Synonyms
Beaver Fever
Lambliasis

Giardiasis is an infectious disease that is caused by single-celled parasites (microorganisms) known as protozoa that belong to the Giardia lamblia family. Some individuals with giardiasis will not have any symptoms (asymptomatic). Others will have a variety of symptoms affecting the gastrointestinal tract including acute or chronic diarrhea, abdominal cramps, bloating, and a general feeling of ill health (malaise). The parasites live in the small intestines of humans and other mammals.

The Giardia lamblia parasite has caused epidemics in certain parts of the United States where animals such as beavers contaminated drinking water by excreting the parasite through their feces. The Giardia lamblia cysts can survive in cold water for several months.

The following organizations may provide additional information and support:
Centers for Disease Control and Prevention
NIH/National Institute of Allergy and Infectious Diseases
World Health Organization (WHO) Regional Office for the Americas (AMRO)

---

470 Gilbert Syndrome

Synonyms
Constitutional Liver Dysfunction
Familial Jaundice
Gilbert's Disease
Gilbert-Lereboullet Syndrome
Hyperbilirubinemia I
Icterus Intermittens Juvenalis
Meulengracht's Disease
Unconjugated Benign Bilirubinemia

One of a benign (harmless) group of metabolic abnormalities, Gilbert syndrome is a hereditary disorder leading to a defect in the clearance (removal) of bile pigment (bilirubin) from the liver. This syndrome is common but innocuous and easily controllable.

The following organizations may provide additional information and support:
American Liver Foundation
Children's Liver Alliance
Children's Liver Disease Foundation
March of Dimes Birth Defects Foundation
NIH/National Digestive Diseases Information Clearinghouse
Parents of Infants and Children with Kernicterus

---

471 Glanzmann Thrombasthenia

Synonyms
Diacyclothrombopathia IIb-IIIa
GP IIb-IIIa Complex, Deficiency of
GTA
Glanzmann Disease
Glanzmann Thrombasthenia, Type A
Glanzmann-Naegeli Syndrome
Glycoprotein Complex IIb/IIIa, Deficiency of

Platelet Fibrinogen Receptor Deficiency
Thrombasthenia
Thrombasthenia of Glanzmann and Naegeli

Glanzmann thrombasthenia (GT) is a rare inherited blood clotting (coagulation) disorder characterized by the impaired function of specialized red blood cells (platelets) that are essential for proper blood clotting. Symptoms of this disorder may include abnormal bleeding and/or hemorrhage. The symptoms are not progressive, however, prolonged untreated or unsuccessfully treated hemorrhaging associated with Glanzmann thrombasthenia may be life threatening.

The following organizations may provide additional information and support:
March of Dimes Birth Defects Foundation
NIH/National Heart, Lung and Blood Institute Information Center

---

472 Glioblastoma Multiforme

Synonyms
Giant Cell Glioblastoma, Multiforme
Spongioblastoma Multiforme, Glioblastoma

Glioblastoma multiforme is a highly malignant, rapidly infiltrating, primary brain tumor, with tentacles that may invade surrounding tissue. This provides a butterfly-like distribution pattern through the white matter of the cerebral hemispheres. The tumor may invade a membrane covering the brain (the dura), or spread via the spinal fluid through the ventricles of the brain. Spread of the tumor (metastasis) outside the brain and spinal cord is rare.

The following organizations may provide additional information and support:
American Brain Tumor Association
American Cancer Society, Inc.
Brain Tumor Society
Candlelighters Childhood Cancer Foundation
Harvard Brain Tissue Resource Center
National Brain Tumor Foundation
National Cancer Institute
Pediatric Brain Tumor Foundation

---

473 Glucose-Galactose Malabsorption

Synonyms
Carbohydrate Intolerance of Glucose Galactose
Complex Carbohydrate Intolerance

Glucose-galactose malabsorption (carbohydrate intolerance) is a genetic disorder characterized by the small intestine's inability to transport and absorb glucose and galactose (sugars which can be broken down no further, or monosaccharides). Glucose and galactose have almost identical chemical structures, and normally the same transport enzyme provides them with entry into specialized cells in the small intestine where they are absorbed and transferred to other cells. Glucose-galactose malabsorption is inherited as an recessive genetic trait. The defective gene responsible for this disorder (the sodium-glucose cotransporter [SGLT1]) is located on the long arm of chromosome 22 (22q13.1). The glucose and galactose which have not been absorbed through the specialized cells of the small intestine are then poorly absorbed much further along in the intestine. This abnormal absorption may interfere with other intestinal absorption processes.

The following organizations may provide additional information and support:
Genetic and Rare Diseases (GARD) Information Center
March of Dimes Birth Defects Foundation
NIH/National Digestive Diseases Information Clearinghouse

---

474 Glucose-6-Phosphate Dehydrogenase Deficiency

Synonym
G6PD Deficiency

Glucose-6-phosphate dehydrogenase (G6PD) deficiency (G6PDD) is an inherited, sex-linked, metabolic disorder characterized by an enzyme defect that leads to the breakdown of red blood cells (hemolysis) upon exposure to stresses associated with some bacterial infections or certain drugs. A deficiency of this enzyme may result in the premature destruction of red blood cells (an acute hemolytic anemia or a chronic spherocytic type) when an affected individual is exposed to certain medications or chemicals, experiences certain viral or bacterial infections, and/or inhales the pollen of, or consumes, fava beans (favism). Glucose-6-phosphate dehydrogenase deficiency is inherited as an X-linked genetic trait. It is a common inborn error of metabolism among humans. More than 300 variants of the disorder have been identified, resulting from mutations of the glucose-6-phosphate dehydrogenase gene. The severity of symptoms associated with G6PD deficiency may

vary greatly among affected individuals, depending upon the specific form of the disorder that is present. Neonatal G6PDD is particularly dangerous to an infant. It is manageable if caught early, and screening for the disorder is common. The role of the enzyme G6PD is to maintain the pathway to generate a chemical called glutathione, which in a particular form is an antioxidant. The antioxidant is necessary to protect the cell's hemoglobin and its cell wall (red cell membrane). If the level of antioxidant is too low, then the cell's hemoglobin will not bind oxygen (its main purpose); the cell wall will break allowing the cell contents, including the modified hemoglobin, to spill out.

The following organizations may provide additional information and support:
CLIMB (Children Living with Inherited Metabolic Diseases)
NIH/National Institute of Diabetes, Digestive & Kidney Diseases
Parents of Infants and Children with Kernicterus

---

475 Glutaricaciduria I

Synonyms
Dicarboxylic Aminoaciduria
GA I
Glutaric Acidemia I
Glutaric Aciduria I
Glutaricacidemia I
Glutaryl-CoA Dehydrogenase Deficiency
Glutaurate-Aspartate Transport Defect

Glutaricaciduria I (GA-I) is a rare hereditary metabolic disorder, caused by a deficiency of the enzyme glutaryl-CoA dehydrogenase. One of a group of disorders known as "organic acidemias," it is characterized by an enlarged head (macrocephaly), decreased muscle tone (hypotonia), vomiting, and excess acid in the blood. Affected individuals may also have involuntary movements of the trunk and limbs (dystonia or athetosis) and mental retardation may also occur. Babies with glutaricaciduria I are sometimes mistakenly thought by medical professionals to be abused babies because they present with subdural and/or retinal hemorrhages.

The following organizations may provide additional information and support:
The Arc (A National Organization on Mental Retardation)

CLIMB (Children Living with Inherited Metabolic Diseases)
International Organization of Glutaric Acidemia
Lactic Acidosis Support Trust
Organic Acidaemias UK
Organic Acidemia Association

476 Glutaricaciduria II

Synonyms
Electron Transfer Flavoprotein, Deficiency of
Electron Transfer Flavoprotein: Ubiquinone Oxidoreductase, Deficiency of
GA II
Glutaric Acidemia II
Glutaric Aciduria II
Glutaricacidemia II
MADD
Multiple Acyl-Co-A Dehydrogenation Deficiency

Glutaricaciduria II is one of the conditions termed organic acidemias. Individuals with these conditions have a deficiency or absence of an enzyme that prevents them from breaking down certain chemicals in the body, resulting in the accumulation of several organic acids in the blood and urine. Two enzymes that may be deficient in glutaricaciduria II are electron transfer flavoprotein (ETF) and ETF-ubiquinone oxidoreductase (ETF:QO). A complete enzyme deficiency causes a severe form of the disorder termed neonatal glutaricaciduria ll that is associated with a short life span and, sometimes, with specific physical birth defects. The less severe form of the disorder is termed late onset glutaricaciduria ll and has an extremely variable age of onset. Symptoms include nausea, vomiting, weakness and low blood sugar (hypoglycemia). Glutaricaciduria II is inherited as an autosomal recessive genetic disorder.

The following organizations may provide additional information and support:
CLIMB (Children Living with Inherited Metabolic Diseases)
FOD (Fatty Oxidation Disorders) Family Support Group
International Organization of Glutaric Acidemia
Lactic Acidosis Support Trust
Organic Acidaemias UK
Organic Acidemia Association

477 Glycogen Storage Disease VIII

Synonyms
Glycogenosis Type VIII
Hepatic Phosphorylase Kinase Deficiency
PYKL
Phosphorylase Kinase Deficiency of Liver

Glycogen storage disease VIII is one of a group of hereditary disorders caused by a lack of one or more enzymes involved in glycogen synthesis or breakdown and characterized by deposition of abnormal amounts or types of glycogen in tissues. Excessive amounts of glycogen (which acts to store energy for later use) are deposited in the liver, causing it to become enlarged (hepatomegaly).

The following organizations may provide additional information and support:
Association for Glycogen Storage Disease (UK)
CLIMB (Children Living with Inherited Metabolic Diseases)
Children's Liver Alliance
March of Dimes Birth Defects Foundation
NIH/National Institute of Diabetes, Digestive & Kidney Diseases

478 Glycogen Storage Disease Type V

Synonyms
GSD V
Glycogen Storage Disease
Glycogen Storage Disease Type V
Glycogenosis Type V
McArdle Disease
Myophosphorylase Deficiency

Glycogen storage disease type V (McArdle disease or GSD-V) is one of several inherited glycogen storage diseases all of which are caused by failures of specific enzymes required for the storage of energy-supplying glycogen. In the case of GSD-V, symptoms are caused by the lack of the crucial enzyme muscle phosphorylase (myophosphorylase). This enzyme is needed for the breakdown of glycogen (the body's form of stored energy) into sugar (glucose) in muscle tissues. All of the glycogen storage diseases are characterized by the inability to break down glycogen, but in each case this occurs for a different reason. Unlike most of the other GSDs, type V has two autosomal recessive forms, a childhood-onset form and an adult-onset form. In addition, there is a much more rare autosomal dominant form of GSD-V. The clinical features of GSD-V are exercise intolerance, muscle cramping, and dark, burgundy-colored urine due to the presence of myoglobin (myoglobinuria).

The following organizations may provide additional information and support:
Association for Glycogen Storage Disease
Association for Glycogen Storage Disease (UK)
CLIMB (Children Living with Inherited Metabolic Diseases)
Muscular Dystrophy Association
NIH/National Digestive Diseases Information Clearinghouse
Vaincre Les Maladies Lysosomales

479 Goldenhar Syndrome (Oculo Auriculo Vertebral Spectrum)

Synonyms
Facio-Auriculo-Vertebral Spectrum
FAV
First and Second Branchial Arch Syndrome
Goldenhar-Gorlin Syndrome
OAV Spectrum
Oculo-Auriculo-Vertebral Dysplasia

Disorder Subdivision
Hemifacial Microsomia (HFM)

Goldenhar syndrome, a term that is often used synonymously with "oculo-auriculo-vertebral (OAV) spectrum," is a rare disorder that is apparent at birth (congenital). The disorder is characterized by a wide spectrum of symptoms and physical features that may vary greatly in range and severity from case to case. However, such abnormalities tend to involve the cheekbones, jaw, mouth, ears, eyes, and/or bones of the spinal column (vertebrae). Although, in most cases, such malformations affect one side of the body (unilateral), approximately 10 to 33 percent of affected individuals have such malformations on both sides of the body (bilateral), with one side typically more affected than the other (asymmetry). In the majority of such cases, the right side is more severely affected than the left. Again, although Goldenhar syndrome (OAV spectrum) is an extremely variable disorder, abnormalities typically affect certain portions of the head and facial (craniofacial) area and/or bones of the spinal column (vertebrae). Due to craniofacial malformations, an affected in-

dividual's face may appear smaller on one side than the other (hemifacial microsomia); in addition, if both sides are affected (bilateral), the face may appear dissimilar from one side to the other (facial asymmetry). Craniofacial abnormalities may include underdevelopment of the cheekbones (malar hypoplasia), bones of the upper and lower jaws (maxillary and mandibular hypoplasia), and the bones forming a portion of the lower skull (temporal hypoplasia); incomplete development of certain muscles of the face; an abnormally wide mouth (macrostomia); incomplete closure of the roof of the mouth (cleft palate); an abnormal groove in the upper lip (cleft lip); and/or abnormalities of the teeth. Affected individuals may also exhibit absence (anotia) and/or malformation (microtia) of the outer ears (auricles or pinnae); narrow, blind ending, or absent external ear canals (atresia); abnormal outgrowths of skin and cartilage on or in front of the ears (preauricular tags); and/or abnormalities affecting the middle and/or inner ears, contributing to or resulting in hearing impairment (i.e., conductive and/or sensorineural hearing loss). Eye abnormalities may also be present including the formation of cysts on the eyeballs (epibulbar dermoids and lipodermoids), partial absence of tissue (coloboma) from the upper eyelids, abnormal smallness of the eyes (microphthalmia), narrowing of the eyelid folds (palpebral fissures) between the upper and lower eyelids (blepharophimosis), crossing of the eyes (strabismus), and/or other eye abnormalities. Vertebral malformations associated with Goldenhar syndrome (OAV spectrum) may include incomplete development (hypoplasia), fusion, and/or absence of certain vertebrae. In addition, many affected individuals may have additional skeletal, neurological, heart (cardiac), lung (pulmonary), kidney (renal), and/or gastrointestinal abnormalities. In approximately five to 15 percent of affected individuals, mild mental retardation may also be present. A variety of terms has been used to describe this extremely variable disorder. According to the medical literature, when malformations primarily involve the jaw, mouth, and ears and, in most cases, affect one side of the body (unilateral), the disorder is often referred to as "hemifacial microsomia." If abnormalities of the vertebrae and the eyes are also present, the disorder is often called "Goldenhar syndrome." Within the medical literature, the term "oculo-auriculo-vertebral (OAV) spectrum" is often used synonymously with Goldenhar syndrome and hemifacial microsomia. However, due to the complexity and varying severity and expression of the OAV spectrum, some researchers suggest that hemifacial microsomia and Goldenhar syndrome actually represent different aspects or levels of severity of OAV spectrum. In most cases, Goldenhar syndrome (OAV spectrum) appears to occur randomly, with no apparent cause (sporadic). However, in some cases, positive family histories have been present that have suggested autosomal dominant or recessive inheritance. In addition, some researchers suggest that the disorder may be caused by the interaction of many genes, possibly in combination with environmental factors (multifactorial inheritance).

The following organizations may provide additional information and support:
American Speech-Language-Hearing Association
Anophthalmia/Microphthalmia Registry
The Arc (A National Organization on Mental Retardation)
Atresia/Microtia Online E-mail Support Group
Birth Defect Research for Children, Inc.
Children's Craniofacial Association
Congenital Heart Anomalies, Support, Education, & Resources
Ear Anomalies Reconstructed: Atresia/Microtia Support Group
EA/TEF Child and Family Support Connection, Inc.
Goldenhar Syndrome Support Network Society
International Children's Anophthalmia Network (ican)
Let Them Hear Foundation
March of Dimes Birth Defects Foundation
National Association for Parents of Children with Visual Impairments (NAPVI)
National Kidney Foundation
NIH/National Eye Institute
NIH/National Heart, Lung and Blood Institute Information Center

480 Goodman Syndrome

Synonyms
ACPS IV
Acrocephalopolysyndactyly Type IV

Goodman syndrome (acrocephalopolysyndactyly type IV) is an extremely rare genetic disorder characterized by marked malformations of the head and face, abnormalities of the hands and feet, and congenital heart disease. The syndrome is inherited as an autosomal recessive trait. Some researchers feel that Goodman syndrome is a variant of Carpenter syndrome (acrocephalopolysyndactyly type II).

The following organizations may provide additional information and support:
AboutFace USA
American Heart Association
Children's Craniofacial Association
Congenital Heart Anomalies, Support, Education, & Resources
FACES: The National Craniofacial Association
Forward Face, Inc.
Let's Face It (USA)
National Craniofacial Foundation
National Foundation for Facial Reconstruction
NIH/National Heart, Lung and Blood Institute Information Center

481 Goodpasture Syndrome

Synonym
Pneumorenal Syndrome

Goodpasture syndrome is a rare autoimmune disorder characterized by inflammation of the filtering structures (glomeruli) of the kidneys (glomerulonephritis) and excessive bleeding into the lungs (pulmonary hemorrhaging). Autoimmune syndromes occur when the body's natural defenses (antibodies) against invading or "foreign" organisms begin to attack the body's own tissue, often for unknown reasons. Symptoms of Goodpasture syndrome include recurrent episodes of coughing up of blood (hemoptysis), difficulty breathing (dyspnea), fatigue, chest pain, and/or abnormally low levels of circulating red blood cells (anemia). In many cases, Goodpasture syndrome may result in an inability of the kidneys to process waste products from the blood and excrete them in the urine (acute renal failure). In some cases of Goodpasture syndrome, affected individuals have had an upper respiratory tract infection before the development of the disorder. The exact cause of Goodpasture syndrome is not known.

The following organizations may provide additional information and support:
American Autoimmune Related Diseases Association, Inc.
American Lung Association
Autoimmune Information Network, Inc
National Kidney Foundation
NIH/National Kidney and Urologic Diseases Information Clearinghouse

482 Gordon Syndrome

Synonyms

Arthrogryposis Multiplex Congenita, Distal, Type IIA
Camptodactyly-Cleft Palate-Clubfoot
Distal Arthrogryposis, Type IIA

Gordon syndrome is an extremely rare disorder that belongs to a group of genetic disorders known as the distal arthrogryposes. These disorders typically involve stiffness and impaired mobility of certain joints of the lower arms and legs (distal extremities) including the knees, elbows, wrists, and/or ankles. These joints tend to be permanently fixed in a bent or flexed position (contractures). Gordon syndrome is characterized by the permanent fixation of several fingers in a flexed position (camptodactyly), abnormal bending inward of the foot (clubfoot or talipes), and, less frequently, incomplete closure of the roof of the mouth (cleft palate). In some cases, additional abnormalities may also be present. The range and severity of symptoms may vary from case to case. Gordon syndrome is inherited as an autosomal dominant trait.

The following organizations may provide additional information and support:
AVENUES
Canadian Arthrogryposis Support Team
NIH/National Arthritis and Musculoskeletal and Skin Diseases Information Clearinghouse

483 Gorham's Disease

Synonyms

Disappearing Bone Disease
Essential Osteolysis
Gorham's Syndrome
Gorham-Stout Syndrome
Idiopathic Massive Osteolysis
Massive Gorham Osteolysis
Massive Osteolysis
Morbus Gorham-Stout Disease
Progressive Massive Osteolysis
Vanishing Bone Disease

Gorham's disease (GD) is an extremely rare bone disorder; fewer than 200 cases are reported in the medical literature. It is characterized by bone loss (osteolysis) often associated with swelling or abnormal blood vessel growth (angiomatous proliferation). Bone loss can occur in just one bone or spread to soft tissue and adjacent bones. Although the disease may strike any of the bones of the body, it is more often recognized earlier when the bones at the top of the head (calvarium) and/or the mandibles are involved. Because of its rarity, the disorder often goes unrecognized. As a result of that, coupled with a lack of agreement on how best to treat Gorham's disease once it is recognized, treatment may often be delayed. The cause of Gorham's disease is unknown.

The following organization may provide additional information and support:
NIH/National Institute of Arthritis and Musculoskeletal and Skin Diseases

484 Gorlin-Chaudhry-Moss Syndrome

Synonyms

Craniofacial Dysostosis-PD Arteriosus-Hypertrichosis-Hypoplasia of Labia
Craniosynostosis-Hypertrichosis-Facial and Other Anomalies
GCM Syndrome

Gorlin-Chaudhry-Moss syndrome is an extremely rare inherited disorder characterized by premature closure of the fibrous joints (sutures) between certain bones in the skull (craniosynostosis), unusually small eyes (microphthalmia), absence of some teeth (hypodontia), and/or excessive amounts of hair (hypertrichosis) on most areas of the body. Affected individuals may also exhibit a mild delay in physical development (growth retardation); short fingers and/or toes; and/or underdevelopment (hypoplasia) of the two long folds of skin on either side of the vaginal opening (labia majora) in females. In addition, there may be an abnormal opening between the two large blood vessels that carry blood away from the heart (pulmonary artery and aorta), causing inappropriate recirculation of some blood through the lungs, rather than throughout the rest of the body (patent ductus arteriosus). In some cases, mild mental retardation may also be present. It is believed that Gorlin-Chaudhry-Moss syndrome may be inherited as an autosomal recessive trait.

The following organizations may provide additional information and support:
American Heart Association
Children's Craniofacial Association
FACES: The National Craniofacial Association
Forward Face, Inc.
National Craniofacial Foundation
NIH/National Institute of Dental and Craniofacial Research

485 Gottron Syndrome

Synonyms
Acrogeria, Gottron type
Familial Acrogeria
Familial Acromicria
H. Gottron's syndrome

Gottron syndrome (GS) is an extremely rare inherited disorder characterized by the appearance of premature aging (progeria), especially in the form of unusually fragile, thin skin on the hands and feet (distal extremities). GS is described as a mild, nonprogressive, congenital form of skin atrophy due to the loss of the fatty tissue directly under the skin (subcutaneous atrophy). Other findings may include abnormally small hands and feet with unusually prominent veins on the chest; small stature; and/or abnormally small jaw (micrognathia). Other characteristics that develop later in life may include premature senility, endocrine disturbances and cataracts. Gottron syndrome is thought to be inherited as an autosomal recessive genetic trait. Only about 40 cases have been reported in the medical literature. There is some debate in the literature regarding a possible relationship between Gottron syndrome and Ehlers-Danlos syndrome, type IV. Some clinicians believe the terms are synonymous. Others disagree.

The following organizations may provide additional information and support:
March of Dimes Birth Defects Foundation
Progeria Research Foundation, Inc.

486 Graft versus Host Disease

Synonym
GVHD

Disorder Subdivisions
Acute GVHD
Chronic GVHD

Graft versus host disease (GVHD) is a rare disorder that can strike persons whose immune system is suppressed and have either received a blood transfusion or a bone marrow transplant. Symptoms may include skin rash, intestinal problems similar to colitis, and liver dysfunction.

The following organizations may provide additional information and support:
Autoimmune Information Network, Inc.
Caitlin Raymond International Registry

Locks of Love
NIH/National Heart, Lung and Blood Institute Information Center

487 Granuloma Annulare

Synonym
Lichen Annularis

Disorder Subdivisions
Generalized (Disseminated) Granuloma Annulare
Linear Granuloma Annulare
Localized Granuloma Annulare
Perforating Granuloma Annulare
Subcutaneous Granuloma Annulare

Granuloma annulare is a chronic degenerative skin disorder. The most common form is localized granuloma annulare, which is characterized by the presence of small, firm red or yellow colored bumps (nodules or papules) that appear arranged in a ring on the skin. In most cases, the sizes of the lesions range from one to five centimeters. The most commonly affected sites include the feet, hands, and fingers. In addition to the localized form, there are four less common forms: generalized or disseminated, linear, perforating, and subcutaneous. The lesions associated with granuloma annulare usually disappear without treatment (spontaneous remission). However, the lesions often reappear. The exact cause of granuloma annulare is unknown.

The following organization may provide additional information and support:
NIH/National Arthritis and Musculoskeletal and Skin Diseases Information Clearinghouse

488 Granulomatous Disease, Chronic

Synonyms
CGD
Chronic Dysphagocytosis
Congenital Dysphagocytosis
Fatal Granulomatous Disease of Childhood
Granulomatosis, Chronic, Familial
Granulomatosis, Septic, Progressive
Impotent Neutrophil Syndrome

Chronic granulomatous disease (CGD) is a rare inherited primary immune deficiency disorder that affects certain white blood corpuscles (lymphocytes). The disorder is characterized by widespread granulomatous tumor-like lesions, and an inability to resist repeated infectious diseases. Life-threatening recurrent fungal and bacterial infections affecting the skin, lungs, and bones may occur along with swollen areas of inflamed tissues known as granulomas. Symptoms usually begin in infancy or childhood. Individuals with mild forms of the disorder may not develop symptoms until the teens or adulthood. The exact cause of chronic granulomatous disease is unknown.

The following organizations may provide additional information and support:
Chronic Granulomatous Disease Association, Inc.
Chronic Granulomatous Disease Registry
Chronic Granulomatous Disorder Research Trust (CGD)
Immune Deficiency Foundation
International Patient Organization for Primary Immunodeficiencies
Jeffrey Modell Foundation
NIH/National Institute of Allergy and Infectious Diseases

489 Granulomatosis, Lymphomatoid

Synonyms
Benign Lymph Angiitis and Granulomatosis
Malignant Lymph Angiitis and Granulomatosis
Pulmonary Angiitis
Pulmonary Wegener's Granulomatosis

Lymphomatoid granulomatosis is a rare, progressive, disease of the lymph nodes and blood vessels characterized by infiltration and destruction of the veins and arteries by nodular lesions created by accumulations of atypical cells of various kinds. These lesions can affect various parts of the body, especially the lungs. However, the condition may start by affecting the small arteries and eventually the lungs, skin, kidneys and nervous system. In 10% to 15% of the cases the benign condition becomes malignant in the form of a cancerous growth in the lymph nodes (lymphoma).

The following organizations may provide additional information and support:
American Autoimmune Related Diseases Association, Inc.
American Cancer Society, Inc.
American Lung Association
Rare Cancer Alliance

490 Graves' Disease

Synonyms
Basedow Disease
Exophthalmic Goiter
Graves' Hyperthyroidism
Parry Disease

Graves' disease is a rare disease affecting the thyroid gland and often the skin and eyes. This disorder is characterized by abnormal enlargement of the thyroid gland (goiter) and increased secretion of thyroid hormone (hyperthyroidism). Symptoms of Graves' disease may include fatigue, weight loss, an abnormal intolerance of heat, muscle weakness, and protrusion or bulging of the eyeballs from their sockets. The exact cause of Graves' disease is not known, although an imbalance in the immune system is thought to play a role.

The following organizations may provide additional information and support:
American Foundation of Thyroid Patients
Autoimmune Information Network, Inc
National Graves' Disease Foundation
NIH/National Digestive Diseases Information Clearinghouse
Thyroid Foundation of America, Inc.
Thyroid Foundation of Canada
Thyroid Society for Education & Research

491 Greig Cephalopolysyndactyly Syndrome

Synonyms
Frontodigital Syndrome (obsolete)
GCPS
Hootnick-Holmes Syndrome (obsolete)
Polysyndactyly with Peculiar Skull Shape
Polysyndactyly-Dysmorphic Craniofacies, Greig Type

Greig cephalopolysyndactyly syndrome (GCPS) is a rare genetic disorder characterized by physical abnormalities affecting the fingers and toes (digits) and the head and facial (craniofacial) area. Characteristic digital features may include extra (supernumerary) fingers and/or toes (polydactyly), webbing and/or fusion of the fingers and/or toes (syndactyly), and/or additional abnormalities. Craniofacial malformations associated with this disorder may include a large and/or unusually shaped skull; a high, prominent forehead (frontal bossing); an abnormally broad nasal bridge; widely spaced eyes (ocular hypertelorism); and/or other physical abnormalities. The range and severity of symptoms may vary greatly from case to case. In most cases, GCPS is inherited as an autosomal dominant trait.

The following organizations may provide additional information and support:
AboutFace USA
Children's Craniofacial Association
FACES: The National Craniofacial Association
Forward Face, Inc.
National Craniofacial Foundation
Society for the Rehabilitation of the Facially Disfigured, Inc.

492 Grover's Disease

Synonyms
TAD
Transient Acantholytic Dermatosis

Grover's disease is a rare temporary skin disorder that consists of small, firm, raised red lesions on the skin. Under a microscope one finds separation of closely connected cells in the skin's outer layers (acantholysis) that can be identified by a dermatologist. Small blisters containing a watery liquid are present. These blisters tend to group and have a swollen red border around them. Grover's disease is mainly seen in males over the age of forty. Its cause is unknown but it is thought to be related to trauma to sun damaged skin.

The following organization may provide additional information and support:
NIH/National Arthritis and Musculoskeletal and Skin Diseases Information Clearinghouse

493 Growth Delay, Constitutional

Synonyms
CDGP
CGD
Constitutional Delay in Growth and Adolescence
Constitutional Delay in Growth and Puberty
Constitutional Short Stature
Idiopathic Growth Delay
Physiologic Delayed Puberty
Sporadic Short Stature

Constitutional growth delay (CGD) is a term describing a temporary delay in the skeletal growth and height of a child with no other physical abnormalities causing the delay. Short stature may be the result of a growth pattern inherited from a parent (familial) or occur for no apparent reason (idiopathic). Typically at some point during childhood growth slows down, eventually resuming at a normal rate. CGD is the most common cause of short stature and delayed puberty. The exact cause of CGD is unknown.

The following organizations may provide additional information and support:
Human Growth Foundation
Little People of America, Inc.
Little People's Research Fund, Inc.
MAGIC Foundation for Children's Growth

494 Growth Hormone Deficiency

Synonym
GHD

Growth hormone is manufactured in the pituitary gland. If it is missing or reduced in quantity during infancy or childhood, it results in growth retardation, short stature and other maturation delays. Growth hormone deficiency (GHD) causes an absence or delay of lengthening and widening of the skeletal bones inappropriate to the chronological age of the child. A sufficient quantity of growth hormone is required during childhood to maintain growth and normalize sexual maturity. In some cases the onset of the disorder occurs prenatally (before birth), and in others the condition occurs months or years later. Laboratory testing is necessary before a diagnosis of growth hormone deficiency is made because growth and maturity delays can be caused by a wide variety of other factors, including normal genetic influences.

The following organizations may provide additional information and support:
Human Growth Foundation
Little People of America, Inc.
Little People's Research Fund, Inc.
MAGIC Foundation for Children's Growth
NIH/National Institute of Child Health and Human Development

495 Guillain Barre Syndrome

Synonyms
Acute Autoimmune Peripheral Neuropathy
Acute Immune-Mediated Polyneuropathy
Acute Inflammatory Demyelinating Polyneuropathy
Acute Inflammatory Demyelinating Polyradiculoneuropathy
Acute Inflammatory Neuropathy
Acute Inflammatory Polyneuropathy
GBS
Landry's Ascending Paralysis
Landry-Guillain-Barre-Strohl Syndrome
Post-Infective Polyneuritis

Disorder Subdivisions
Acute Motor Axonal Neuropathy
Acute Motor Neuropathy with Conduction Block
Acute Motor-Sensory Axonal Neuropathy
Chronic Inflammatory Demyelinating Polyneuropathy (CIDP)
Miller-Fisher Syndrome
Multifocal Motor Neuropathy
Multifocal Motor Sensory Demyelinating Neuropathy

Guillain-Barré syndrome (GBS) is a very rare, rapidly progressive disorder that consists of inflammation of the nerves (polyneuritis) and, usually, muscle weakness, often progressing to frank paralysis. Although the precise cause of GBS is unknown, a viral or respiratory infection precedes the onset of the syndrome in about half of the cases. This has led to the theory that GBS may be an autoimmune disease (caused by the body's own immune system). Damage to the covering of nerve cells (myelin) and nerve axons (the extension of the nerve cell that conducts impulses away from the nerve cell body) results in delayed nerve signal transmission. There is a corresponding weakness in the muscles that are supplied or innervated by the damaged nerves. The following variants of GBS (acute inflammatory neuropathy or acute inflammatory demyelinating polyradiculoneuropathy) are recognized: Miller Fisher syndrome, acute motor-sensory axonal polyneuropathy, acute motor axonal polyneuropathy, chronic inflammatory polyneuropathy (chronic inflammatory demyelinating polyradiculoneuropathy; also called chronic relapsing or recurring inflammatory polyneuropathy), and chronic polyneuropathy with conduction block.

The following organizations may provide additional information and support:
Autoimmune Information Network, Inc
Christopher Reeve Paralysis Foundation
GBS/CIDP Foundation International
Guillain-Barre Syndrome Foundation of Canada, Inc.
Guillain-Barre Syndrome Support Group
Jack Miller Center for Peripheral Neuropathy
National Institute of Neurological Disorders and Stroke (NINDS)

496 Hageman Factor Deficiency

Synonyms
Factor XII Deficiency
HAF Deficiency
Hageman Trait

Hageman factor deficiency is a rare inherited blood disorder that causes prolonged clotting (coagulation) of blood in a test tube without the presence of prolonged clinical bleeding tendencies. It is caused by a deficiency of the Hageman factor (factor XII), a plasma protein (glycoprotein). Although it is thought that factor XII is needed for blood clotting, when it is deficient, other blood clotting factors tend to compensate for its absence. This disorder is thought to be benign and usually presents no symptoms (asymptomatic); it is usually only accidentally discovered through pre-operative blood tests that are required by hospitals. Of substantial recent interest is the role of antibodies to factor XII in recurrent pregnancy losses.

The following organizations may provide additional information and support:
National Hemophilia Foundation
NIH/National Heart, Lung and Blood Institute Information Center

497 Hajdu Cheney Syndrome

Synonyms
Acro-Dento-Osteo-Dysplasia
Acroosteolysis Dominant Type
Acroosteolysis with Osteoporosis and Changes in Skull and Mandible
Arthrodentoosteodysplasia
Cheney syndrome
HCS

Hajdu-Cheney syndrome (HCS) is a rare, heritable disorder of connective tissue; only about 50 cases have been reported in the medical literature. The breakdown of bone (osteolysis), especially the outermost bones of the fingers and toes (acroosteolysis), is a major characteristic of HCS. In addition, patients with HCS frequently have skull deformities, short stature, joint laxity, reduction of bone mass (osteoporosis) and other signs. Most affected individuals have normal mental development but a small proportion show mild mental retardation. Although the majority of cases are of unknown cause, the presence of multiple cases in one family suggests that autosomal dominant genetic transmission may be possible.

The following organizations may provide additional information and support:
March of Dimes Birth Defects Foundation
NIH/National Institute of Arthritis and Musculoskeletal and Skin Diseases

498 Hallermann Streiff Syndrome

Synonyms
Francois Dyscephaly Syndrome
Hallermann-Streiff-Francois Syndrome
HSS
Oculomandibulodyscephaly with Hypotrichosis
Oculomandibulofacial Syndrome

Hallermann-Streiff syndrome is a rare genetic disorder that is primarily characterized by distinctive malformations of the skull and facial (craniofacial) region; sparse hair (hypotrichosis); eye (ocular) abnormalities; dental defects; degenerative skin changes (atrophy), particularly in the scalp and nasal regions; and/or short stature (i.e., dwarfism). Characteristic craniofacial features include a short, broad head (brachycephaly) with an unusually prominent forehead and/or sides of the skull (frontal and/or parietal bossing); a small, underdeveloped lower jaw (hypoplastic mandible); a narrow, highly arched roof of the mouth (palate); and a thin, pinched, tapering nose. Many affected individuals also have clouding of the lenses of the eyes at birth (congenital cataracts); unusually small eyes (microphthalmia); and/or other ocular abnormalities. Dental defects may include the presence of certain teeth at birth (natal teeth) and absence (hypodontia or partial adontia), malformation, and/or improper alignment of teeth. In almost all cases, Hallermann-Streiff syndrome has appeared to occur randomly for unknown reasons (sporadically) and may be the result of a new change to genetic material (mutation).

The following organizations may provide additional information and support:
Children's Craniofacial Association
Craniofacial Foundation of America
FACES: The National Craniofacial Association
Hallerman-Streiff Syndrome Support Group
Institute for Families
Little People of America, Inc.
March of Dimes Birth Defects Foundation
National Association for Parents of Children with Visual Impairments (NAPVI)
National Craniofacial Foundation
NIH/National Eye Institute

499 Hand-Foot-Mouth Syndrome

Synonyms
Hand, Foot and Mouth Disease
HFMS
Vesicular Stomatitis with Exanthem

Hand-foot-mouth syndrome is an infectious disease that, in most cases, is caused by the coxsackie virus A16. The disease most often occurs in young children and is characterized by a rash of small blister-like sores (lesions). The rash usually occurs on the palms of the hands, soles of the feet, and in the mouth.

The following organizations may provide additional information and support:
Centers for Disease Control and Prevention
NIH/National Institute of Allergy and Infectious Diseases

500 Hanhart Syndrome

Synonyms
Aglossia-Adactylia
Hypoglossia-Hypodactylia Syndrome
Peromelia with Micrognathia

Hanhart syndrome is a rare birth defect in which the most obvious signs are a short, incompletely developed tongue (hypoglossia); absent or partially missing fingers and/or toes (hypodactylia); malformed arms and/or legs (peromelia); and an extremely small jaw (micrognathia). A more complete list of other signs frequently encountered may be found below. The severity of these physical abnormalities varies greatly from case to case. Children with this disorder often have some, but not all, of the symptoms. The cause of Hanhart syndrome is not fully understood.

The following organizations may provide additional information and support:
FACES: The National Craniofacial Association
Forward Face, Inc.
National Craniofacial Foundation

501 Hantavirus Pulmonary Syndrome

Synonyms

Four Corners Hantavirus (FCV)
Hantavirus-Associated Respiratory Distress Syndrome (HARDS)
HPS

Hantavirus pulmonary syndrome is an infectious disease caused by the Muerto Canyon hantavirus. Transmission occurs when direct or indirect (airborne) contact is made with the saliva or waste products of rodents that carry the virus, most commonly the deer mouse (Peromyscus maniculatus). Initial symptoms may include fever, muscle aches (myalgias), headache, cough, and/or difficulty breathing. Symptoms progress rapidly, and abnormally low blood pressure (hypotension), shock, and/or respiratory failure may occur.

The following organizations may provide additional information and support:
Centers for Disease Control and Prevention
NIH/National Institute of Allergy and Infectious Diseases
World Health Organization (WHO) Regional Office for the Americas (AMRO)

502 Hartnup Disease

Synonyms

H Disease
Hart Syndrome
Hartnup Disorder
Hartnup Syndrome
Pellagra-Cerebellar Ataxia-Renal Aminoaciduria Syndrome
Tryptophan Pyrrolase Deficiency

Hartnup disease is a rare metabolic disorder inherited as an autosomal recessive trait. It involves an inborn error of amino acid metabolism as well as niacin deficiency. Factors that may precipitate acute attacks of this disorder may include poor nutrition, exposure to sunlight, sulphonamide medications and/or psychological stress. Hartnup disease may be marked by skin problems, coordination impairment, vision problems, mild mental retardation, gastrointestinal problems, and central nervous system abnormalities. Frequency of attacks usually diminishes with age.

The following organizations may provide additional information and support:
The Arc (National Organization on Mental Retardation)
CLIMB (Children Living with Inherited Metabolic Diseases)
March of Dimes Birth Defects Foundation
NIH/National Institute of Diabetes, Digestive & Kidney Diseases

503 Hay-Wells Syndrome

Synonyms

AEC Syndrome
Ankyloblepharon-Ectodermal Defects-Cleft Lip/Palate
Hay-Wells Syndrome of Ectodermal Dysplasia

Hay-Wells syndrome, also known as ankyloblepharon-ectodermal dysplasia-clefting (AEC) syndrome, is a rare inherited disorder that belongs to a group of disorders known as the ectodermal dysplasias. Major characteristics of Hay-Wells syndrome include sparse, coarse, wiry hair; small, sparse eyelashes; excess bands of fibrous tissue that cause the edges (margins) of the upper and lower eyelids to fuse together (ankyloblepharon filiforme adnatum); cleft palate; and less often cleft lip. Hay-Wells syndrome is inherited as an autosomal dominant trait. The ectodermal dysplasias are a group of more than 150 related disorders that result from abnormalities during early embryonic development. Ectodermal dysplasias typically affect the hair, teeth, nails, and/or skin. The ectodermal dysplasias are inherited disorders, but the pattern of inheritance is varied.

The following organizations may provide additional information and support:
Cleft Palate Foundation
Craniofacial Foundation of America
March of Dimes Birth Defects Foundation
National Craniofacial Foundation
National Foundation for Ectodermal Dysplasias
NIH/National Institute of Arthritis and Musculoskeletal and Skin Diseases
NIH/National Oral Health Information Clearinghouse

504 Headache, Cluster

Synonyms
Chronic Paroxysmal Hemicrania (Sjaastad Syndrome)
Cluster Headaches
Episodic Paroxysmal Hemicrania
Familial Cluster Headaches
Histamine Cephalalgia
Vasogenic Facial Pain

Disorder Subdivisions
Chronic Cluster Headache
Cyclic Cluster Headache

Cluster headaches are a rare form of severe disabling headache. The headaches are deep, non-throbbing, extremely painful ones that tend to recur in the same area of the head or face with each occurrence. They usually come on during sleep and may awaken an affected individual. In some cases, cluster headaches occur during the day as well. Cluster headaches tend to occur on and off daily for several weeks only to disappear for months or, in some cases, years. They typically last somewhere between 30 minutes and 2 hours. Cluster headaches are often associated with watering of the eyes and nose. Chronic paroxysmal hemicrania and episodic paroxysmal hemicrania are variants of cluster headaches. Both forms closely resemble cluster headaches except for a few distinctive features, particularly their response to different treatment options.

The following organizations may provide additional information and support:
American Council for Headache Education
JAMA Migraine Information Center
National Headache Foundation
National Institute of Neurological Disorders and Stroke (NINDS)
Organization for Understanding Cluster Headaches (O.U.C.H.)
Vasculitis of the Central Nervous System

505 Heart Block, Congenital

Synonym
Atrioventricular (AV) Block

Disorder Subdivisions
First Degree Congenital Heart Block
Second Degree Con. Heart Block (Wenckebach [Mobitz I]; Mobitz II; Included)
Third Degree Congenital (Complete) Heart Block

Congenital heart block is characterized by interference with the transfer of electrical nerve impulses (conduction) that regulate the normal rhythmic pumping activity of the heart muscle (heart block). The severity of such conduction abnormalities may vary among affected individuals. The normal heart has four chambers. The two upper chambers are known as the atria and the two lower chambers are known as the ventricles. In the mild form of heart block (first degree), the two upper chambers of the heart (atria) beat normally, but the contractions of the two lower chambers (ventricles) slightly lag behind. In the more severe forms (second degree), only a half to a quarter of the atrial beats are conducted to the ventricles. In complete heart block (third degree), the atria and ventricles beat independently. In most cases, infants with first or second degree experience no symptoms (asymptomatic). However, infants with complete heart block may experience episodes of unconsciousness (syncope), breathlessness, and/or fatigue.

The following organizations may provide additional information and support:
American Heart Association
Congenital Heart Anomalies, Support, Education, & Resources
Congenital Heart Information Network
International Bundle Branch Block Association
NIH/National Heart, Lung and Blood Institute

506 Heavy Metal Poisoning

Synonym
Heavy Metal Toxicity

Disorder Subdivisions
Aluminum Poisoning
Antimony Poisoning
Arsenic Poisoning
Barium Poisoning
Bismuth Poisoning
Cadmium Poisoning
Chromium Poisoning
Cobalt Poisoning
Copper Poisoning
Gold Poisoning
Iron Poisoning
Lead Poisoning
Lithium Poisoning
Manganese Poisoning
Mercury Poisoning
Nickel Poisoning
Phosphorous Poisoning

Platinum Poisoning
Selenium Poisoning
Silver Poisoning
Thallium Poisoning
Tin Poisoning
Zinc Poisoning

Heavy metal poisoning is the accumulation of heavy metals, in toxic amounts, in the soft tissues of the body. Symptoms and physical findings associated with heavy metal poisoning vary according to the metal accumulated. Many of the heavy metals, such as zinc, copper, chromium, iron and manganese, are essential to body function in very small amounts. But, if these metals accumulate in the body in concentrations sufficient to cause poisoning, then serious damage may occur. The heavy metals most commonly associated with poisoning of humans are lead, mercury, arsenic and cadmium. Heavy metal poisoning may occur as a result of industrial exposure, air or water pollution, foods, medicines, improperly coated food containers, or the ingestion of lead-based paints.

The following organizations may provide additional information and support:
Food and Drug Administration (FDA) Office of Inquiry & Consumer Information
National Safety Council/Environmental Health Center

507 Hemangioma Thrombocytopenia Syndrome

Synonyms
Kasabach-Merritt Syndrome
Thrombocytopenia-Hemangioma Syndrome

Hemangioma-thrombocytopenia syndrome (also known as Kasabach-Merritt syndrome) is a rare disorder characterized by an abnormal blood condition in which the low number of blood platelets causes bleeding (thrombocytopenia). The thrombocytopenia is found in association with a benign tumor consisting of large, blood-filled spaces (cavernous hemangioma). The exact cause of this disorder is not known.

The following organizations may provide additional information and support:
Hemangioma Support System
National Organization of Vascular Anomalies—NOVA
NIH/National Heart, Lung and Blood Institute

508 Hematuria, Benign, Familial

Synonyms
Hematuria, Benign, Recurrent
Hematuria, Essential
Nephropathy, Thin Glomerular Basement Membrane Disease
Nephropathy, Thin-Basement-Membrane

Benign familial hematuria, also known as thin-basement-membrane nephropathy, is a kidney disease that usually begins during childhood. The disorder is characterized by the presence of red blood cells in the urine (hematuria). The blood in the urine may be present in microscopic amounts (microscopic hematuria) and not visible to the eye, present in small amounts that give the urine a "cloudy" or "smoky" appearance, or easily visible. Many individuals with the disorder have abnormalities of the kidney's glomeruli, the clusters of small blood vessels (capillaries) that normally filter the blood passing through the kidneys (glomeruli filtration). In such cases, the membrane (basement membrane) supporting the loops of capillaries that make up the renal glomeruli may be abnormally thin. Benign familial hematuria may be inherited as an autosomal dominant genetic trait.

The following organizations may provide additional information and support:
American Foundation for Urologic Disease
American Kidney Fund, Inc.
March of Dimes Birth Defects Foundation
National Kidney Foundation
NIH/National Kidney and Urologic Diseases Information Clearinghouse

509 Hemochromatosis, Hereditary

Synonyms
Bronze Diabetes
Cirrhosis, Congenital Pigmentary
Familial Hemochromatosis
HH
Hemochromatosis Syndrome
Hemosiderosis
Iron Overload Disease
Primary Hemochromatosis

Hereditary hemochromatosis (HH) is a genetic disorder of iron storage characterized by excessive intestinal absorption of dietary iron. Increased iron absorption leads to excessive accumulation of iron deposits within cells of the liver, heart, pituitary gland, pancreas, and other organs, gradually causing tissue damage and impaired functioning of affected organs. Hereditary hemochromatosis is considered one of the most common genetic disorders in Caucasians. However, many investigators indicate that the condition often remains undetected and therefore is underdiagnosed. Hereditary hemochromatosis is transmitted as an autosomal recessive trait. It is caused by changes (mutations) of a gene known as HFE located on the short arm (p) of chromosome 6 (6p21.3). Several different mutations of this gene have been identified that may contribute to the development of hereditary hemochromatosis. Associated symptoms and findings may become apparent in individuals who inherit two mutated copies of the HFE gene (homozygous). However, in other cases, individuals with two mutated HFE genes may not manifest symptoms (variable penetrance and expressivity). In contrast, some who inherit only one mutated copy of the HFE gene (heterozygous carriers) may have symptoms and findings associated with hereditary hemochromatosis. In such cases, the disease may be "triggered" in genetically predisposed individuals due to a number of precipitating factors, such as inflammation of the liver (hepatitis) or alcoholism. In addition, investigators suggest that mutations of other genes may have some role in causing the disorder or modifying its expression (genetic heterogeneity).

The following organizations may provide additional information and support:
American Hemochromatosis Society (AHS)
Hemochromatosis Foundation, Inc.
Iron Disorders Institute
Iron Overload Diseases Association, Inc.
March of Dimes Birth Defects Foundation
NIH/National Institute of Diabetes, Digestive & Kidney Diseases

510 Hemoglobinuria, Paroxysmal Cold

Synonyms
Donath-Landsteiner Hemolytic Anemia
Donath-Landsteiner Syndrome
Dressler Syndrome
Harley Syndrome
Immune Hemolytic Anemia, Paroxysmal Cold
PCH

Paroxysmal cold hemoglobinuria is a very rare autoimmune hemolytic disorder characterized by the premature destruction of healthy red blood cells minutes to hours after exposure to cold. Autoim-

mune diseases occur when the body's natural defenses against invading organisms (e.g., lymphocytes, antibodies) destroy healthy tissue for unknown reasons. Normally, red blood cells have a life span of approximately 120 days before they are removed by the spleen. In an individual affected with paroxysmal cold hemoglobinuria, the red blood cells are destroyed prematurely and suddenly (paroxysmally) upon exposure to temperatures of 10 to 15 degrees Centigrade and below.

The following organizations may provide additional information and support:
American Autoimmune Related Diseases Association, Inc.
NIH/National Institute of Allergy and Infectious Diseases

511 Hemoglobinuria, Paroxysmal Nocturnal

Synonyms
Marchiafava-Micheli Syndrome
PNH

Paroxysmal nocturnal hemoglobinuria (PNH) is a rare, acquired stem cell disorder. The classic finding is the premature destruction of red blood cells (hemolysis), resulting in repeated episodes of hemoglobin in the urine (hemoglobinuria). Hemoglobin is the red, iron-rich pigment of blood. Individuals with hemoglobinuria may exhibit dark-colored or bloody urine. In addition to hemolysis, individuals with PNH are also susceptible to developing repeated, potentially life-threatening blood clots (thromboses). Affected individuals also have some degree of underlying bone marrow dysfunction or insufficiency. Bone marrow, the spongy center of the large bones of the body, produces hematopoietic stem cells, which grow and eventually develop into red blood cells (erythrocytes), white blood cells (leukocytes), and platelets. Severe bone marrow dysfunction potentially results in low levels of red and white blood cells and platelets (pancytopenia). The specific symptoms of PNH vary greatly and affected individuals usually do not exhibit all of the symptoms potentially associated with the disorder. Researchers believe that two factors are necessary for the development of PNH: an acquired somatic mutation of the PIG-A gene, which affects hematopoietic stem cells; and a predisposition to the multiplication and expansion of these defective stem cells.

The following organizations may provide additional information and support:
Aplastic Anemia & MDS International Foundation, Inc.
NIH/Hematology Branch, National Heart, Lung and Blood Institute (NHLBI)
NIH/National Institute of Allergy and Infectious Diseases
PNH Support Group

512 Hemolytic Uremic Syndrome

Synonyms

Gasser Syndrome
HUS

Hemolytic-uremic syndrome (HUS) is a very rare disorder that primarily affects young children between the ages of one and 10 years, particularly those under the age of 4 years. In many cases, the onset of HUS is preceded by a flu-like illness (gastroenteritis) characterized by vomiting, abdominal pain, fever, and diarrhea, which, in some cases, may be bloody. Symptoms of hemolytic-uremic syndrome usually become apparent three to 10 days after the development of gastroenteritis and may include sudden paleness (pallor), irritability, weakness, lack of energy (lethargy), and/or excretion of abnormally diminished amounts of urine (oliguria). The disease typically progresses to include inability of the kidneys to process waste products from the blood and excrete them into the urine (acute renal failure); a decrease in circulating red blood cells (microangiopathic hemolytic anemia); a decrease in circulating blood platelets, which assist in blood clotting functions (thrombocytopenia); and the abnormal accumulation of platelets within certain blood vessels (microthrombi), reducing the blood flow to several organs (e.g., kidneys, pancreas, brain) potentially leading to multiple organ dysfunction or failure. In some cases, neurological problems may be present at the onset of hemolytic-uremic syndrome or may occur at any time during the disorder's progression. Neurological symptoms may include dizziness, seizures (partial or generalized), disorientation or confusion, and/or loss of consciousness (coma). The onset of hemolytic-uremic syndrome is most frequently associated with infection by a particular strain (O157:H7) of Escherichia coli (E. coli) bacterium. Occasionally, adults may be affected by hemolytic-uremic syndrome.

The following organizations may provide additional information and support:
American Kidney Fund, Inc.

National Institute of Neurological Disorders and Stroke (NINDS)
National Kidney Foundation
NIH/National Institute of Allergy and Infectious Diseases
NIH/National Institute of Diabetes, Digestive & Kidney Diseases
World Health Organization (WHO) Regional Office for the Americas (AMRO)

513 Hemophilia

Synonyms

AHF Deficiency
AHG Deficiency
Antihemophilic Factor Deficiency
Antihemophilic Globulin Deficiency
Christmas Disease
Classical Hemophilia

Disorder Subdivisions

Hemophilia A (Factor VIII Deficiency)
Hemophilia B (Factor IX Deficiency)
Hemophilia C (Factor XI Deficiency)

Hemophilia is a rare inherited blood clotting (coagulation) disorder caused by inactive or deficient blood proteins (usually factor VIII). Factor VIII is one of several proteins that enable the blood to clot. Hemophilia may be classified as mild, moderate, or severe. The level of severity is determined by the percentage of active clotting factor in the blood (normal percentage ranges from 50 to 150 percent). People who have severe hemophilia have less than one percent of active clotting factor in their blood. There are three major types of hemophilia: hemophilia A (also known as classical hemophilia, factor VIII deficiency or antihemophilic globulin [AHG] deficiency); hemophilia B (Christmas disease or factor IX deficiency); and hemophilia C (factor XI deficiency). Hemophilia A and B are inherited as X-linked recessive genetic traits, while hemophilia C is inherited as an autosomal recessive genetic trait. Therefore, while hemophilia A and B are fully expressed in males only, hemophilia C affects males and females in equal numbers.

The following organizations may provide additional information and support:
Canadian Hemophilia Society
Cochrane Cystic Fibrosis and Genetic Disorders Review Group
Hemophilia Federation of America
Irish Haemophilia Society

March of Dimes Birth Defects Foundation
National Hemophilia Foundation
NIH/National Heart, Lung and Blood Institute Information Center
Sjëldne Diagnoser / Rare Disorders Denmark
World Federation of Hemophilia

514   Hemorrhagic Telangiectasia, Hereditary

Synonyms
HHT
Osler-Weber-Rendu Syndrome
Rendu-Osler-Weber Syndrome

Disorder Subdivisions
Hereditary Hemorrhagic Telangiectasia Type I
Hereditary Hemorrhagic Telangiectasia Type II
Hereditary Hemorrhagic Telangiectasia Type III

Hereditary hemorrhagic telangiectasia (HHT or Osler-Weber-Rendu syndrome) is a rare inherited disorder characterized by malformations of various blood vessels (vascular dysplasia), usually resulting in excessive bleeding (hemorrhaging). Chronic nosebleeds are often the first apparent symptom associated with hereditary hemorrhagic telangiectasia. Malformation of various blood vessels may result in abnormalities affecting various organ systems of the body including the lungs, brain, and liver. Hereditary hemorrhagic telangiectasia is inherited as an autosomal dominant trait.

The following organizations may provide additional information and support:
HHT Foundation International, Inc.
March of Dimes Birth Defects Foundation
NIH/National Heart, Lung and Blood Institute

515   Hepatic Fibrosis, Congenital

Synonym
CHF

Congenital hepatic fibrosis (CHF) is a rare disease that affects both the liver and kidneys. The patient is born with this disorder (congenital), and it is inherited as an autosomal recessive trait. The typical liver abnormalities are an enlarged liver (hepatomegaly), increased pressure in the venous system that carries blood from different organs to the liver (portal hypertension), and fiber-like connective tissue that spreads over and through the liver (hepatic fibrosis), often referred to as hepatic lesions. Gastrointestinal (stomach and intestines)

bleeding is frequently an early sign of this condition. Affected individuals also have impaired renal function, usually caused, in children and teenagers, by an autosomal recessive polycystic kidney disease (ARPKD). Impaired renal function associated with CHF in adults is caused by an autosomal dominant polycystic kidney disease (ADPKD). The relationship of ARPKD to CHF is the subject of substantial controversy. Some clinicians suggest that the two conditions represent one disorder with a range of clinical/pathological presentations.

The following organizations may provide additional information and support:
American Kidney Fund, Inc.
American Liver Foundation
ARPKD/CHF Alliance
International Patient Advocacy Association
National Kidney Foundation
NIH/National Kidney and Urologic Diseases Information Clearinghouse

516   Hepatitis B

Synonyms
Diffuse Hepatocellular Inflammatory Disease
HBV

Hepatitis B is a contagious liver disease caused by the hepatitis B virus (HBV), one of three viral agents that cause inflammation of the liver known as "hepatitis" or "diffuse hepatocellular inflammatory disease." Hepatitis B is characterized by fever, nausea, vomiting, and yellow discoloration of the skin, eyes and mucous membranes (jaundice). In its most serious form, if left untreated, hepatitis B can become a chronic infection leading to chronic liver disease and potentially increasing the risk of developing liver cancer. The hepatitis B virus can be passed from mother to unborn child, and is highly contagious through bodily fluids such as blood, semen and possibly saliva. It is often spread from person to person through intravenous drug use or sexual contact.

The following organizations may provide additional information and support:
American Liver Foundation
American Social Health Association
Centers for Disease Control and Prevention
Hepatitis B Foundation
Hepatitis Foundation International
Immunization Action Coalition/Hepatitis B Coalition
Jack Miller Center for Peripheral Neuropathy
NIH/National Institute of Allergy and Infectious Diseases

517   Hepatitis C

Synonyms
NANB Hepatitis
Non-A, Non-B Hepatitis

Hepatitis C is an infectious liver disease caused by hepatitis C virus (HCV) infection. The main causes of the spread of this disease are transfusion with contaminated blood or the sharing of contaminated intravenous needles. More rarely, transmission may occur due to sexual contact with an infected individual or occupational exposure to contaminated blood. Associated symptoms, which may range from mild to severe, may include fever, fatigue, weakness, abdominal pain, nausea, vomiting, and yellowish discoloration of the skin, mucous membranes, and whites of the eyes (jaundice). In some cases, affected individuals may develop chronic liver disease, such as scarring (fibrosis) and impaired functioning of the liver (cirrhosis) or liver cancer (e.g., hepatocellular carcinoma).

The following organizations may provide additional information and support:
American Liver Foundation
Anemia Institute for Research and Education
Centers for Disease Control and Prevention
Hepatitis C Society of Canada
Hepatitis Foundation International
Jack Miller Center for Peripheral Neuropathy
NIH/National Institute of Allergy and Infectious Diseases

518   Hepatitis, Neonatal

Synonyms
Cirrhosis, Congenital Liver
Cirrhosis, Giant Cell of Newborns
Giant Cell Disease of the Liver
Giant Cell Hepatitis
Idiopathic Neonatal Hepatitis

Neonatal hepatitis refers to a group of liver disorders that affect newborns between the ages of about 1 and 2 months, and produce a typical yellow color to the infant's skin (jaundice). In contrast to infants with biliary atresia, those with neonatal hepatitis have normal, intact, bile ducts (biliary tracts). Most, but by no means all, cases of neonatal hepatitis can be traced to rare, inherited errors of metabolism or to prenatal infection by one or another of the hepatitis viruses. Many cases, however, seem to occur for no apparent reason (sporadic) and, in rare instances, neonatal hepatitis may be inherited as an autosomal recessive genetic trait.

The following organizations may provide additional information and support:
American Liver Foundation
Children's Liver Alliance
Hepatitis Foundation International
NIH/National Digestive Diseases Information Clearinghouse

519   Hepatorenal Syndrome

Synonyms
Hepato-Renal Syndrome
HRS

Hepatorenal syndrome includes two types of progressive, kidney (renal) failure which are the result of severe LIVER disease: NOT of primary KIDNEY dysfunction. In each case, symptoms such as yellowing of the skin (jaundice) and urination problems occur in the two types of this liver disease. The blood circulation of hepatorenal syndrome patients has unique features. The volume of blood circulated by the heart (cardiac output), is above normal. The arteries that circulate oxygenated blood from the lungs to the rest of the body (systemic circulation) widen in contrast to the arteries of the kidney, which narrow causing a decrease in the blood flow through the kidney.

The following organizations may provide additional information and support:
American Association of Kidney Patients
American Foundation for Urologic Disease
American Kidney Fund, Inc.
American Liver Foundation
NIH/National Kidney and Urologic Diseases Information Clearinghouse

520   Hermansky Pudlak Syndrome

Synonyms
Albinism with Hemorrhagic Diathesis and
Pigmented Reticuloendothelial Cells
Delta Storage Pool Disease
HPS

Hermansky-Pudlak syndrome is a rare, hereditary disorder that consists of four characteristics: lack of skin pigmentation (albinism), blood platelet dysfunction with prolonged bleeding, visual impairment, and abnormal storage of a fatty-like substance (ceroid lipofuscin) in various tissues of the body.

The following organizations may provide additional information and support:
Blind Children's Fund
Gahl, William A., M.D.
Hermansky-Pudlak Syndrome Network, Inc.
National Association for Parents of Children with Visual Impairments (NAPVI)
National Association for Visually Handicapped
NIH/National Institute of Arthritis and Musculoskeletal and Skin Diseases
NIH/National Institute of Child Health and Human Development

521   Hermaphroditism, True

Synonyms
Hermaphrodism
Hermaphroditism

True hermaphroditism is a very rare genetic disorder in which an infant is born with the internal reproductive organs (gonads) of both sexes (i.e., female ovaries and male testes). The external sex organs of an affected individual are usually a combination of male and female.

The following organizations may provide additional information and support:
Genetic and Rare Diseases (GARD) Information Center
Intersex Society of North America
March of Dimes Birth Defects Foundation

522   Herpes, Neonatal

Synonyms
Herpes Simplex Infection of Newborn
Herpesvirus Hominis Infection of Newborn

Neonatal herpes is a rare disorder affecting newborn infants infected with the herpes simplex virus (HSV), also called herpesvirus hominis. In most instances, a parent with oral or genital herpes transfers the disorder to an offspring before, during, or shortly after birth. Symptoms vary from mild to severe depending on which of two types of herpes simplex virus is involved. Type 1 HSV is responsible for the more severe cases of the disorder while patients with Type 2 HSV usually present with milder symptoms. Another way of classifying this disorder depends on probable outcomes (prognosis). Using prognosis as the classi-

fying principal yields three forms: 1. disseminated neonatal herpes infection, 2. central nervous sytem herpes in the neonate, and 3. mucocutaneous and ocular herpes.

The following organizations may provide additional information and support:
Centers for Disease Control and Prevention
NIH/National Institute of Allergy and Infectious Diseases

523   Hers Disease

Synonyms
Glycogen Storage Disease VI
Glycogenosis Type VI
Hepatophosphorylase Deficiency Glycogenosis
Liver Phosphorylase Deficiency
Phosphorylase Deficiency Glycogen Storage Disease

Hers disease is a hereditary glycogen storage disease (GSD) that usually has milder symptoms than most other types and is caused by a deficiency of the enzyme, liver phosphorylase. Hers disease is characterized by enlargement of the liver (hepatomegaly), moderately low blood sugar (hypoglycemia), elevated levels of acetone and other ketone bodies in the blood (ketosis), and moderate growth retardation. Symptoms are not always evident during childhood, and children are usually able to lead normal lives. However, in some instances, symptoms may be severe.

The following organizations may provide additional information and support:
Association for Glycogen Storage Disease
Association for Glycogen Storage Disease (UK)
CLIMB (Children Living with Inherited Metabolic Diseases)
NIH/National Institute of Diabetes, Digestive & Kidney Diseases

524   Hiccups, Chronic

Synonyms
Hiccough, Chronic
Hiccups, Persistent
Intractable Hiccups
Singultus, Intractable

A hiccup is an involuntary spasmodic contraction of the muscle at the base of the lungs (diaphragm) followed by the rapid closure of the vocal cords. Usually, hiccups last for a few hours or, occasionally, a day or two. However, chronic hiccups are ones that continue for an extended period of time. Episodes that last for more than 2 days and less than a month are sometimes called persistent hiccups. On rare occasions, hiccups persist even longer than a month or recur frequently over an extended period of time. The longest recorded episode of these chronic hiccups lasted 60 years. Sometimes, although not always, hiccups that persist may indicate the presence of another medical problem. Some illnesses for which continuing hiccups may be a symptom include: pleurisy of the diaphragm, pneumonia, uremia, alcoholism, disorders of the stomach or esophagus, and bowel diseases. Hiccups may also be associated with pancreatitis, pregnancy, bladder irritation, liver cancer or hepatitis. Surgery, tumors, and lesions may also cause persistent hiccups.

The following organization may provide additional information and support:
NIH/National Heart, Lung and Blood Institute Information Center

525 Hidradenitis Suppurativa

Synonyms
Hidradenitis Axillaris
HS

Hidradenitis suppurativa is a chronic, pus-producing (suppurative), scarring (cicatricial) disease process that occurs due to obstruction of hair follicles and secondary infection and inflammation of certain sweat glands (apocrine glands), particularly those under the arms (axillae) or within the anal/genital (anogenital) region. The disease is characterized by the development of recurrent, boil-like nodular lesions and deep pus-containing pockets of infection (abscesses) that may eventually rupture through the skin. Healing of affected areas is typically associated with progressive scarring (fibrosis). The specific underlying cause of hidradenitis suppurativa is unknown.

The following organizations may provide additional information and support:
Hidradenitis Suppurativa Foundation, Inc
HS-USA, Inc.
NIH/National Institute of Allergy and Infectious Diseases
NIH/National Institute of Arthritis and Musculoskeletal and Skin Diseases

526 Hirschsprung's Disease

Synonyms
Colonic Aganglionosis
Congenital Megacolon
HSCR
Intestinal Aganglionosis
Megacolon, Aganglionic

Hirschsprung's disease (HSCR) is characterized by the absence of particular nerve cells (ganglions) in a segment of the bowel. The absence of ganglion cells causes the muscles to lose their ability to move the stool through the intestine (peristalsis). Constipation occurs and obstruction of the colon becomes more obvious and perhaps painful. HSCR can occur as an isolated problem or as part of disorder that affects multiple organ systems.

The following organizations may provide additional information and support:
Bowel Group for Kids Incorporated
International Foundation for Functional Gastrointestinal Disorders
NIH/National Digestive Diseases Information Clearinghouse
Pull-thru Network
Stem Cell Research Foundation

527 Histidinemia

Synonyms
HAL Deficiency
HIS Deficiency
Histidase Deficiency
Histidine Ammonia-Lyase (HAL) Deficiency
Hyperhistidinemia

Histidinemia is a rare hereditary metabolic disorder characterized by a deficiency of the enzyme histidase, which is necessary for the metabolism of the amino acid histidine. The concentration of histidine is elevated in the blood. Excessive amounts of histidine, imidazole pyruvic acid, and other imidazole metabolism products are excreted in the urine. The majority of individuals with histidinemia have no obvious symptoms that would indicate that a person has this disorder (asymptomatic). Histidinemia is inherited as an autosomal recessive trait.

The following organizations may provide additional information and support:
CLIMB (Children Living with Inherited Metabolic Diseases)

Genetic and Rare Diseases (GARD) Information Center
NIH/National Institute of Diabetes, Digestive & Kidney Diseases

528 Hodgkin's Disease

Synonyms
Hodgkin Disease
Hodgkin's Lymphoma

Hodgkin's disease is one of a group of cancers known as a lymphoma. Lymphoma is a general term used to describe cancers that affect the lymphatic system, especially the lymph nodes. Tumors often form in the lymph nodes (places where lymphatic vessels unite) and/or the area around the nodes. Fever, night sweats, and weight loss may occur along with swollen lymph nodes. The exact cause of Hodgkin's disease is unknown.

The following organizations may provide additional information and support:
American Cancer Society, Inc.
Cancer Research UK
Center for International Blood and Marrow Transplant Research
Leukemia & Lymphoma Society
Lymphoma Association (UK)
Lymphoma Foundation Canada
Lymphoma Research Foundation
National Cancer Institute
OncoLink: The University of Pennsylvania Cancer Center Resource
Rare Cancer Alliance

529 Holoprosencephaly

Synonyms
Alobar Holoprosencephaly
Arhinencephaly
Familial Alobar Holoprosencephaly
Holoprosencephaly Malformation Complex
Holoprosencephaly Sequence
HS
Lobar Holoprosencephaly
Semilobar Holoprosencephaly

Holoprosencephaly is the failure of the prosencephalon section of the forebrain (the part of the brain in the fetus that evolves into parts of the adult brain) to develop. This causes defects in the development of the middle of the face and in brain structure and function. Closely set eyes (hypotelorism), missing front teeth (incisors), and an abnormally small head (microcephaly) may occur. Rarely, severely affected infants are born with cyclopia (the eyes fused into one) and a deformed or absent nose.

The following organizations may provide additional information and support:
Birth Defect Research for Children, Inc.
Carter Centers for Brain Research in Holoprosencephaly and Related Malformations
Independent Holoprosencephaly Support Site
Society for the Rehabilitation of the Facially Disfigured, Inc.

530 Holt Oram Syndrome

Synonyms
Atriodigital Dysplasia
Heart-Hand Syndrome
HOS1

Holt-Oram syndrome is a disorder that is characterized by abnormalities in the bones of the upper limb and a family or personal history of a congenital heart malformation or an abnormality in the electrical impulses that coordinate the muscle contraction of the heart (cardiac conduction defect). In some affected individuals, an abnormal wrist (carpal) bone is the only evidence of the disease. Seventy-five percent of those affected have a congenital heart malformation. Holt-Oram syndrome is an autosomal dominant genetic condition that is associated with an abnormality in the TBX5 gene.

The following organizations may provide additional information and support:
American Heart Association
Congenital Heart Anomalies, Support, Education, & Resources
Congenital Heart Information Network
NIH/National Arthritis and Musculoskeletal and Skin Diseases Information Clearinghouse
NIH/National Heart, Lung and Blood Institute Information Center
Reach: The Association for Children with Hand or Arm Deficiency

531 Homocystinuria

Homocystinuria is a rare metabolic condition characterized by an excess of the compound homocystine in the urine. The condition may result from deficiency of any of several enzymes involved in the conversion of the essential amino acid methionine to another amino acid (cysteine)—or, less commonly, impaired conversion of the compound homocysteine to methionine. Enzymes are proteins that accelerate the rate of chemical reactions in the body. Certain amino acids, which are the chemical building blocks of proteins, are essential for proper growth and development. In most cases, homocystinuria is caused by reduced activity of an enzyme known as cystathionine beta-synthase (CBS). Due to deficiency of the CBS enzyme, infants with homocystinuria may fail to grow and gain weight at the expected rate (failure to thrive) and have developmental delays. By approximately age three, additional, more specific symptoms and findings may become apparent. These may include partial dislocation (subluxation) of the lens of the eyes (ectopia lentis), associated "quivering" (iridodonesis) of the colored region of the eyes (iris), severe nearsightedness (myopia), and other eye (ocular) abnormalities. Although intelligence may be normal in some cases, many children may be affected by progressive mental retardation. In addition, some may develop psychiatric disturbances and/or episodes of uncontrolled electrical activity in the brain (seizures). Affected individuals also tend to be thin with unusually tall stature; long, slender fingers and toes (arachnodactyly); and elongated arms and legs ("marfanoid" features). Additional skeletal abnormalities may include progressive sideways curvature of the spine (scoliosis), abnormal protrusion or depression of the breastbone (pectus carinatum or excavatum), and generalized loss of bone density (osteoporosis). In addition, in those with the disorder, blood clots may tend to develop or become lodged within certain large and small blood vessels (thromboembolisms), potentially leading to life-threatening complications. Homocystinuria due to deficiency of cystathionine synthase is inherited as an autosomal recessive trait. The disorder results from changes (mutations) of a gene on the long arm (q) of chromosome 21 (21q22.3) that regulates the production of the CBS enzyme.

The following organizations may provide additional information and support:
The Arc (A National Organization on Mental Retardation)
Belgian Association for Metabolic Diseases (BOKS)
CLIMB (Children Living with Inherited Metabolic Diseases)
March of Dimes Birth Defects Foundation
NIH/National Digestive Diseases Information Clearinghouse

532 Horner's Syndrome

Synonyms
Bernard-Horner Syndrome
Oculosympathetic Palsy

Horner syndrome is a relatively rare disorder characterized by a constricted pupil (miosis), drooping of the upper eyelid (ptosis), absence of sweating of the face (anhidrosis), and sinking of the eyeball into the bony cavity that protects the eye (enophthalmos). These are the four classic signs of the disorder. The congenital, and more rare, form of Horner syndrome is present at birth but the cause is not known. Most often, Horner syndrome is acquired as a result of some kind of interference with the sympathetic nerves serving the eyes. The underlying causes can vary enormously, from a snake or insect bite to a neck trauma made by a blunt instrument.

The following organizations may provide additional information and support:
Genetic and Rare Diseases (GARD) Information Center
NIH/National Eye Institute

533 Human Granulocytic Ehrlichiosis (HGE)

Synonyms
HGE
Human Ehrlichial Infection, Human Granulocytic Type

Human granulocytic ehrlichiosis (HGE) is a rare infectious disease that belongs to a group of diseases known as the human ehrlichioses. The ehrlichioses are infectious diseases caused by bacteria in the "Ehrlichia" family. Several forms of human ehrlichial infection have been identified including human granulocytic ehrlichiosis (HGE), Sennetsu fever, and human monocytic ehrlichiosis (HME). Though caused by different strains of Ehrlichia bacteria, the disorders are all characterized by similar symptoms. The symptoms of human granulocytic ehrlichiosis (HGE) may include a sudden high fever, headache, muscle aches (myalgia), chills, and a general feeling of weakness and fatigue (malaise) within a week or so after initial infection. In most cases, abnormal laboratory findings may occur including an abnormally low number of circulating blood platelets (thrombocytopenia), a decrease in white blood cells (leukopenia), and an abnormal increase in the level of certain liver enzymes (hepatic transaminases). In some cases, symptoms may progress to include nausea, vomiting, cough, diarrhea, loss of appetite (anorexia), and/or confusion. If human granulocytic ehrlichiosis is left untreated, life-threatening symptoms, such as kidney failure and/or respiratory problems, may develop in some cases. Human granulocytic ehrlichiosis is caused by a bacterium of the ehrlichiosis family that has not yet been named. The Ehrlichial bacterium is carried and transmitted by certain ticks (vectors), such as the deer tick (Ixodes dammini) and the American dog tick (Dermacentor variabilis).

The following organizations may provide additional information and support:
American Lyme Disease Foundation, Inc.
Centers for Disease Control and Prevention
Lyme Disease Foundation
NIH/National Institute of Allergy and Infectious Diseases
World Health Organization (WHO) Regional Office for the Americas (AMRO)

534 Human Monocytic Ehrlichiosis (HME)

Synonym
Human Ehrlichial Infection, Human Monocytic Type

Human monocytic ehrlichiosis (HME) is a rare infectious disease belonging to a group of diseases known as the human ehrlichioses. These diseases are caused by bacteria belonging to the "ehrlichia" family. Several forms of human ehrlichioses have been identified, including human monocytic ehrlichiosis, sennetsu fever, and human granulocytic ehrlichiosis. Though caused by different strains of Ehrlichia bacteria, the disorders are characterized by similar symptoms. The symptoms of human monocytic ehrlichiosis may include a sudden high fever, headache, muscle aches (myalgia), chills, and a general feeling of weakness and fatigue (malaise) within a few weeks after initial infection. In addition, in many cases, laboratory findings may indicate an abnormally low number of circulating blood platelets (thrombocytopenia), a decrease in white blood cells (leukopenia), and an abnormal increase in the level of certain liver enzymes (hepatic transaminases). In some individuals, symptoms may progress to include nausea, vomiting, diarrhea, weight loss, and/or confusion. If HME is left untreated, life-threatening symptoms, such as kidney failure and respiratory

insufficiency, may develop in some cases. Human monocytic ehrlichiosis is caused by the bacteria Ehrlichia chaffeensis (or E. chaffeensis). E. chaffeensis is carried and transmitted by certain ticks (vectors), such as the lone star tick (Amblyomma americanum) and the American dog tick (Dermacentor variabilis).

The following organizations may provide additional information and support:
Centers for Disease Control and Prevention
Lyme Disease Foundation
NIH/National Institute of Allergy and Infectious Diseases
World Health Organization (WHO) Regional Office for the Americas (AMRO)

535 Hunter Syndrome

Synonyms
MPS II
MPS Disorder II
Mucopolysaccharidosis Type II

Disorder Subdivisions
MPS IIA
MPS IIB

Hunter syndrome, also known as mucopolysaccharidosis II, is a rare inborn error of metabolism characterized by deficiency of an enzyme known as iduronate sulfatase. The mucopolysaccharidoses (MPS) are a group of hereditary metabolic diseases known as lysosomal storage disorders. Lysosomes function as the primary digestive units within cells. Enzymes within lysosomes break down or digest particular nutrients, such as certain carbohydrates and fats. In individuals with MPS disorders, including Hunter syndrome, deficiency or improper functioning of lysosomal enzymes leads to an abnormal accumulation of certain complex carbohydrates (glycosaminoglycans [mucopolysaccharides]) in cells within various bodily tissues, such as the skeleton, joints, brain, spinal cord, heart, spleen, or liver. Initial symptoms and findings associated with Hunter syndrome usually become apparent between age 2 to 4 years. Such abnormalities may include progressive growth delays, resulting in short stature; joint stiffness, with associated restriction of movements; and coarsening of facial features, including thickening of the lips, tongue, and nostrils. Affected children may also have an abnormally large head (macrocephaly), a short neck and broad chest, delayed tooth eruption, progressive hearing loss, and enlargement of the liver and spleen (hepatosplenomegaly). Two relatively distinct clinical forms of Hunter syndrome have been recognized. In the mild form of the disease (MPS IIB), intelligence may be normal or only slightly impaired. However, in the more severe form (MPS IIA), profound mental retardation may be apparent by late childhood. In addition, slower disease progression tends to occur in those with the mild form of the disorder. Hunter syndrome is inherited as an X-linked recessive trait. Mild and severe forms of the disorder result from changes (mutations) of a gene (i.e., IDS gene) that regulates production of the iduronate sulfatase enzyme. The IDS gene is located on the long arm (q) of chromosome X (Xq28).

The following organizations may provide additional information and support:
The Arc (A National Organization on Mental Retardation)
Canadian Society for Mucopolysaccharide and Related Diseases, Inc.
CLIMB (Children Living with Inherited Metabolic Diseases)
Let Them Hear Foundation
March of Dimes Birth Defects Foundation
National MPS (Mucopolysaccharidoses/Mucolipidoses) Society, Inc.
NIH/National Institute of Diabetes, Digestive & Kidney Diseases
Society for Mucopolysaccharide Diseases
Vaincre Les Maladies Lysosomales

536 Huntington's Disease

Synonyms
Chronic Progressive Chorea
Degenerative Chorea
HD
Hereditary Chorea
Hereditary Chronic Progressive Chorea
Huntington's Chorea
VEOHD
Very Early Onset Huntington's Disease
Woody Guthrie's Disease

Huntington's disease is a genetic, progressive, neurodegenerative disorder characterized by the gradual development of involuntary muscle movements affecting the hands, feet, face, and trunk and progressive deterioration of cognitive processes and memory (dementia). Neurologic movement abnormalities may include uncontrolled, irregular, rapid, jerky movements (chorea) and athetosis, a condition characterized by relatively slow, writhing involuntary movements. Dementia is typically associated with progressive disorientation and confusion, personality disintegration, impairment of memory control, restlessness, agitation, and other symptoms and findings. In individuals with the disorder, disease duration may range from approximately 10 years up to 25 years or more. Life-threatening complications may result from pneumonia or other infections, injuries related to falls, or other associated developments. Huntington's disease is transmitted as an autosomal dominant trait. The disease results from changes (mutations) of a gene known as "huntingtin" located on the short arm (p) of chromosome 4 (4p16.3). In those with the disorder, the huntingtin gene contains errors in the coded "building blocks" (nucleotide bases) that make up the gene's instructions. The gene contains abnormally long repeats of coded instructions consisting of the basic chemicals cytosine, adenine, and guanine (CAG trinucleotide repeat expansion). The length of the expanded repeats may affect the age at symptom onset. The specific symptoms and physical features associated with Huntington's disease result from degeneration of nerve cells (neurons) within certain areas of the brain (e.g., basal ganglia, cerebral cortex).

The following organizations may provide additional information and support:
Alzheimer's Foundation of America
Hereditary Disease Foundation
Huntington Society of Canada
Huntington's Disease Society of America
March of Dimes Birth Defects Foundation
National Institute of Neurological Disorders and Stroke (NINDS)
New Horizons Un-Limited, Inc.
Sjëldne Diagnoser / Rare Disorders Denmark
UCSF Memory and Aging Center
WE MOVE (Worldwide Education and Awareness for Movement Disorders)

537 Hydranencephaly

Synonym
Hydroanencephaly

Hydranencephaly is a central nervous system disorder characterized by an enlarged head and neurological deficits. The exact cause of hydranencephaly is not known. This extremely rare form of hydrocephalus involves the absence of portions of the brain. Results of neurologic examination in newborns may be normal or abnormal. The head usually appears enlarged at birth. Vision impairment, lack of growth and intellectual deficits are symptomatic of this disorder.

The following organizations may provide additional information and support:
The Arc (A National Organization on Mental Retardation)
Children's Brain Diseases Foundation
Guardians of Hydrocephalus Research Foundation
Hydrocephalus Association
March of Dimes Birth Defects Foundation
National Hydrocephalus Foundation
National Institute of Neurological Disorders and Stroke (NINDS)

538 Hydrocephalus

Synonyms
Hydrocephaly
Water on the Brain

Disorder Subdivisions
Benign Hydrocephalus
Communicating Hydrocephalus
Internal Hydrocephalus
Non-Communicating Hydrocephalus
Normal Pressure Hydrocephalus
Obstructive Hydrocephalus

Hydrocephalus is a condition in which abnormally widened (dilated) cerebral spaces in the brain (ventricles) inhibit the normal flow of cerebrospinal fluid (CSF). The cerebrospinal fluid accumulates in the skull and puts pressure on the brain tissue. An enlarged head in infants and increased cerebrospinal fluid pressure are frequent findings but are not necessary for the diagnosis of hydrocephalus. There are several different forms of hydrocephalus: communicating hydrocephalus, non-communicating hydrocephalus or obstructive hydrocephalus, internal hydrocephalus, normal pressure hydrocephalus, and benign hydrocephalus.

The following organizations may provide additional information and support:
The Arc (A National Organization on Mental Retardation)
Association for Spina Bifida and Hydrocephalus
Birth Defect Research for Children, Inc.
Guardians of Hydrocephalus Research Foundation
Hydrocephalus Association
Hydrocephalus Foundation, Inc.

Hydrocephalus Support Group, Inc.
International Federation for Spina Bifida and Hydrocephalus
March of Dimes Birth Defects Foundation
National Hydrocephalus Foundation
National Institute of Neurological Disorders and Stroke (NINDS)
Sjëldne Diagnoser / Rare Disorders Denmark
Spina Bifida and Hydrocephalus Association of Ontario
Spina Bifida Hydrocephalus Queensland

539 Hyper IgM Syndrome

Synonyms
Dysgammaglobulinemia Type I
HIM
IHIS
IMD3
Immunodeficiency with Increased IgM
Immunodeficiency-3

Hyper-IgM syndrome (HIM) is a rare genetic (primary) immunodeficiency disorder that is typically inherited as an X-linked recessive genetic trait. Symptoms and physical findings associated with the disorder usually become apparent in the first or second year of life. Hyper-IgM syndrome may be characterized by recurrent pus-producing (pyogenic) bacterial infections of the upper and lower respiratory tract including the sinuses (sinusitis) and/or the lungs (pneumonitis or pneumonia); the middle ear (otitis media); the membrane that lines the eyelids and the white portions (sclera) of the eyes (conjunctivitis); the skin (pyoderma); and/or, in some cases, other areas. Individuals with hyper-IgM syndrome are also susceptible to "opportunistic" infections, i.e., infections caused by microorganisms that usually do not cause disease in individuals with fully functioning immune systems (non-immunocompromised) or widespread (systemic) overwhelming disease by microorganisms that typically cause only localized, mild infections. In individuals with hyper-IgM syndrome, such opportunistic infections may include those caused by Pneumocystis carinii, a microorganism that causes a form of pneumonia, or Cryptosporidium, a single-celled parasite (protozoa) that can cause infections of the intestinal tract. In addition, individuals with hyper-IgM syndrome are prone to certain autoimmune disorders affecting particular elements of the blood, such as neutropenia, a condition in which there is an abnormal decrease of certain white blood cells (neutrophils). Additional physical findings often associated with the disorder may include enlargement (hypertrophy) of the tonsils, enlargement of the liver and spleen (hepatosplenomegaly), chronic diarrhea and impaired absorption of nutrients by the intestinal tract (malabsorption), and/or other symptoms. The range and severity of symptoms and physical features associated with this disorder may vary from case to case. Because approximately 70 percent of reported cases of hyper-IgM syndrome are inherited as an X-linked recessive genetic trait, the vast majority of affected individuals are male. However, some cases of autosomal recessive and autosomal dominant genetic inheritance have been reported. In addition, a rare acquired form of the disorder has been described in the medical literature.

The following organizations may provide additional information and support:
American Academy of Allergy Asthma and Immunology
American Autoimmune Related Diseases Association, Inc.
Center for International Blood and Marrow Transplant Research
Immune Deficiency Foundation
International Patient Organization for Primary Immunodeficiencies
Jeffrey Modell Foundation
March of Dimes Birth Defects Foundation
National Bone Marrow Transplant Link
National Neutropenia Network
Neutropenia Support Association, Inc.
NIH/National Arthritis and Musculoskeletal and Skin Diseases Information Clearinghouse
NIH/National Heart, Lung and Blood Institute Information Center

540 Hypercholesterolemia

Disorder Subdivisions
High Blood Cholesterol, Familial
High Cholesterol, Familial
High Serum Cholesterol, Familial
Hyperlipidema, Familial

Hypercholesterolemia means unusually high cholesterol. It is a common disorder characterized by a high accumulation of fats in the blood. It is one of the leading causes of atherosclerosis (fatty obstruction of the blood vessels), heart attack and stroke. High cholesterol is the leading health problem in the United States and other Western countries accounting for 50 percent of all deaths. This disorder appears to get worse with advancing age,

although in rare cases children can also be affected.

The following organizations may provide additional information and support:
American Heart Association
Inherited High Cholesterol Foundation
NIH/National Heart, Lung and Blood Institute Information Center

541 Hyperemesis Gravidarum

Hyperemesis gravidarum (HG) is a rare disorder characterized by severe and persistent nausea and vomiting during pregnancy that may necessitate hospitalization. As a result of frequent nausea and vomiting, affected women experience dehydration, vitamin and mineral deficit, and the loss of greater than five percent of their original body weight. Nausea and vomiting of pregnancy (NVP), more widely known as morning sickness, is a common condition of pregnancy. Many researchers believe that NVP should be regarded as a continuum of symptoms that may impact an affected woman's physical, mental and social well-being to varying degrees. Hyperemesis gravidarum represents the severe end of the continuum. No specific line exists that separates hyperemesis gravidarum from NVP; in most cases, affected individuals progress from mild or moderate nausea and vomiting to hyperemesis gravidarum. The exact cause of hyperemesis gravidarum is not known.

The following organizations may provide additional information and support:
National Healthy Mothers, Healthy Babies Coalition
National Women's Health Network
National Women's Health Resource Center
NIH/National Institute of Child Health and Human Development
NIH/Office of Research on Women's Health

542 Hyperexplexia

Synonyms
Exaggerated Startle Reaction
Familial Startle Disease
Hyperekplexia
Kok Disease
Startle Disease

Hyperexplexia is a rare autosomal dominant, hereditary, neurological disorder that may affect infants as newborns (neonatal) or prior to birth (in utero). It may also affect children and adults. Individuals with this disorder have an excessive startle reaction to sudden unexpected noise, movement, or touch. Symptoms include extreme muscle tension (stiffness or hypertonia) that can cause the affected person to fall stiffly, like a log, without loss of consciousness. Exaggeration of reflexes (hyperreflexia), and an unstable way of walking (gait) may also occur. The treatment of hyperexplexia is relatively uncomplicated and involves the use of anti-anxiety and anti-spastic medicines. However, the disorder is frequently misdiagnosed as a form of epilepsy so that the process of getting an accurate diagnosis may be prolonged.

The following organization may provide additional information and support:
National Institute of Neurological Disorders and Stroke (NINDS)

543 Hyperhidrosis, Primary

Disorder Subdivision
Generalized Hyperhidrosis

Primary hyperhidrosis is a rare disorder characterized by excessive sweating without known cause on the palms of the hands, the soles of the feet, in the armpits (axillary), in the groin area, and/or under the breasts. The exact cause of primary hyperhidrosis is not known. When excessive sweating occurs as part of some other disorder, it is said to be secondary hyperhidrosis, which is a more commonly encountered condition than is primary hyperhidrosis.

The following organization may provide additional information and support:
NIH/National Institute of Arthritis and Musculoskeletal and Skin Diseases

544 Hyperkalemia

Synonyms
High Potassium
Hyperpotassemia

Hyperkalemia is a condition caused by an abnormally high concentration of potassium in the blood. Potassium is a key element in contraction of muscles (including the heart) and for the functioning of many complicated proteins (enzymes). Potassium is found primarily in the skeletal mus-

cle and bone, and participates with sodium to contribute to the normal flow between the body fluids and the cells of the body (homeostasis). The concentration of potassium in the body is regulated by the kidneys, and balance is maintained through excretion in urine. When the kidneys are functioning normally, the amount of potassium in the diet is usually sufficient for use by the body and the excess is excreted. Chemical and hormonal influences also help regulate the internal potassium balance. When hyperkalemia occurs, there is an imbalance resulting from a dysfunction of these normal processes. Normally, 98% of the potassium in the body is found in the cells of various tissues, while only about 2% is circulating in the blood. When hyperkalemia occurs, it may come about because of an increase in total body potassium or as a result of increased release of potassium from the cells to the blood. Abnormally high levels of potassium in the blood or urine suggest the presence of another underlying medical condition. Because potassium helps to regulate muscle activity, including the activity of heart (cardiac) muscle, hyperkalemia needs to be taken seriously.

The following organizations may provide additional information and support:
Digestive Disease National Coalition
NIH/National Digestive Diseases Information Clearinghouse

545 Hyperlipoproteinemia Type III

Synonyms
Broad Beta Disease
Dysbetalipoproteinemia
Familial Dysbetalipoproteinemia
Remnant Removal Disease

Hyperlipoproteinemia type III, also known as dysbetalipoproteinemia or broad beta disease, is a rare genetic disorder characterized by improper breakdown (metabolism) of certain fatty materials known as lipids, specifically cholesterol and triglycerides. This results in the abnormal accumulation of lipids in the body (hyperlipidemia). Affected individuals may develop multiple yellowish, lipid-filled bumps (papules) or plaques on the skin (xanthomas). Affected individuals may also develop the buildup of fatty materials in the blood vessels (artherosclerosis) potentially obstructing blood flow and resulting in coronary heart disease or peripheral vascular disease. Most cases of hyperlipoproteinemia type III are inherited as an autosomal recessive trait.

The following organizations may provide additional information and support:
American Heart Association
March of Dimes Birth Defects Foundation
NIH/National Heart, Lung and Blood Institute Information Center

546 Hyperlipoproteinemia Type IV

Synonyms
Carbohydrate-Induced Hyperlipemia
Hypercholesterolemia, Type IV
Hyperlipidemia IV
Hyperprebeta-Lipoproteinemia
Hypertriglyceridemia, Endogenous

Hyperlipoproteinemia type IV is a not uncommon inherited metabolic disorder that is characterized by increased blood levels of the triglyceride form of fat that makes up very low-density lipids (VLDL). Abnormally high blood levels of triglycerides or cholesterol (another form of blood plasma fat) may be the result of poor dietary habits, genetic causes, or other metabolic disorders or a side effect of certain drugs. Hyperlipoproteinemia type IV is one of a family of five types of hyperlipoproteinemia, which is an indicator of a risk of heart disease. Each of types I through IV presents a different profile of blood fat and a different set of associated risks of heart disease. Hyperlipoproteinemia and hyperlipidemia are synonymous. Both refer to an excess of fatty substances (lipids) in the blood. The condition may also be called hyperlipoproteinemia because the fats are transported through the blood as attachments to specialized proteins. These fat-protein complex molecules are called lipoproteins, among which the better known are HDL (high density lipoprotein, LDL (low density lipoprotein), and VLDL (very low density lipoprotein). Studies have shown that the risk of heart disease is directly proportional to the blood level of a complex chemical called LDL-cholesterol and inversely proportional to the blood level of HDL-cholesterol. If the blood level of LDL is high, then the risk of heart disease is also high. However, if the blood level of HDL is high, the risk of heart disease is correspondingly low. Hyperlipoproteinemia type IV is common and frequently runs in families; i.e. it is genetic in origin. It is characterized by high blood triglyceride levels and obesity, usually with mild diabetes.

The following organizations may provide additional information and support:
American Heart Association
NIH/National Heart, Lung and Blood Institute Information Center

547 Hyperostosis Frontalis Interna

Synonyms
Endostosis Crani
Hyperostosis Calvariae Interna
Morgagni-Stewart-Morel Syndrome

Hyperostosis frontalis interna is characterized by the thickening of the frontal bone of the skull. It is not clear that this disorder is actually rare. Some clinicians believe that it may be a common abnormality found in as many as 12 percent of the female population. The disorder may be found associated with a variety of conditions such as seizures, headaches, obesity, diabetes insipidus, excessive hair growth and sex gland disturbances. Increased serum alkaline phosphatase and elevated serum calcium may occur.

The following organizations may provide additional information and support:
Children's Craniofacial Association
FACES: The National Craniofacial Association
National Craniofacial Foundation
NIH/National Arthritis and Musculoskeletal and Skin Diseases Information Clearinghouse

548 Hyperoxaluria, Primary (Type I)

Synonyms
Oxalosis
PH Type I

Primary hyperoxaluria (type I) is a hereditary disorder characterized by an inborn error of glyoxylate. Excessive formation of oxalate occurs in the liver, resulting in excessive levels of oxalate in the blood and urine. Calcium oxalate does not dissolve and consequently stones are formed in the urinary tract.

The following organizations may provide additional information and support:
Children's Liver Alliance
CLIMB (Children Living with Inherited Metabolic Diseases)
NIH/National Digestive Diseases Information Clearinghouse
Oxalosis and Hyperoxaluria Foundation

549 Hyperprolinemia Type I

Synonym

Proline Oxidase Deficiency

Two types of hyperprolinemia are recognized by physicians and clinical researchers. Each represents an inherited inborn error of metabolism involving the amino acid, proline. Proline is abundant in nature and readily found in a variety of foods. Hyperprolinemia type I (HP-I) is characterized by abnormally high levels of proline in the blood. The high level of blood proline is the result of a deficiency of the enzyme proline oxidase, which is essential to the normal breakdown (metabolism) of proline. There are often no clinical manifestations of HP-I. Hyperprolinemia II (HP-II) results from the deficiency of another enzyme and also results in high blood proline levels, as well as other more severe clinical manifestations than are seen in HP-I. Mild mental retardation and convulsions are commonly associated with HP-II.

The following organizations may provide additional information and support:
CLIMB (Children Living with Inherited Metabolic Diseases)
Genetic and Rare Diseases (GARD) Information Center
NIH/National Institute of Diabetes, Digestive & Kidney Diseases

550 Hyperprolinemia Type II

Synonym

Pyrroline Carboxylate Dehydrogenase Deficiency

Two types of hyperprolinemia are recognized by physicians and clinical researchers. Each represents an inherited inborn error of metabolism involving the amino acid, proline. Hyperprolinemia type I (HP-I) is characterized by high levels of proline in the blood resulting from a deficiency of the enzyme proline oxidase, which is key to the breakdown (metabolism) of proline. There are often no clinical manifestations of HP-I. Hyperprolinemia II (HP-II) is a rare metabolic disorder that results from the deficiency of the enzyme known as delta-pyrroline-5-carboxylate (P-5-C) dehydrogenase. This disorder results in more severe clinical manifestations than are seen in HP-I, and may be associated with mild mental retardation and seizures.

The following organizations may provide additional information and support:
The Arc (A National Organization on Mental Retardation)
CLIMB (Children Living with Inherited Metabolic Diseases)
Genetic and Rare Diseases (GARD) Information Center
NIH/National Institute of Diabetes, Digestive & Kidney Diseases

551 Hyperthermia

Synonyms

Heat Stress
Heat-Related Illness

Hyperthermia occurs when a person's body temperature rises and remains above the normal; 98.6°F. Most frequently, this occurs during the heat of summer and among the elderly. However, it may also be triggered by other medical conditions or certain medications. Hyperthermia is sometimes induced as a palliative measure in the treatment of certain cancerous conditions.

The following organization may provide additional information and support:
NIH/National Institute on Aging

552 Hypochondroplasia

Synonym

HCH

Hypochrondroplasia is a genetic disorder characterized by small stature and disproportionately short arms, legs, hands, and feet (short-limbed dwarfism). Short stature often is not recognized until early to mid childhood or, in some cases, as late as adulthood. In those with the disorder, bowing of the legs typically develops during early childhood but often improves spontaneously with age. Some affected individuals may also have an abnormally large head (macrocephaly), a relatively prominent forehead, and/or other physical abnormalities associated with the disorder. In addition, in about 10 percent of cases, mild mental retardation may be present. In some cases, hypochondroplasia appears to occur randomly for unknown reasons (sporadically) with no apparent family history. In other instances, the disorder is familial with autosomal dominant inheritance.

The following organizations may provide additional information and support:
Human Growth Foundation
Little People of America, Inc.
Little People's Research Fund, Inc.
MAGIC Foundation for Children's Growth
NIH/National Institute of Arthritis and Musculoskeletal and Skin Diseases
Restricted Growth Association

553 Hypoglycemia

Synonyms

Exogenous Hypoglycemia
Factitious Hypoglycemia
Fasting Hypoglycemia
Iatrogenic Hypoglycemia
Infantile Hypoglycemia
Low Blood Sugar
Neonatal Hypoglycemia
Reactive Functional Hypoglycemia
Reactive Hypoglycemia, Secondary to Mild Diabetes
Spontaneous Hypoglycemia
Tachyalimentation Hypoglycemia

Hypoglycemia is a common condition characterized by an abnormally low blood sugar (glucose) level. Glucose is an important fuel for the body. A low level of glucose in the blood (hypoglycemia) produces symptoms such as tiredness, weakness, shakiness, paleness, confusion and dizziness. In many cases, hypoglycemia occurs as a complication of diabetes treatment. As a result, it is important for people with diabetes to learn to recognize the symptoms of hypoglycemia and know what to do when those symptoms occur. Insulin is the hormone produced in the pancreas that regulates the metabolism of sugar. Since hypoglycemia may be an indication that there is too much insulin in the blood, the condition is sometimes called an insulin reaction. Occasionally, hypoglycemia may indicate the presence of underlying disease, including inherited metabolic dis-orders. It may also occur as a result of taking certain medications, including some that are not for diabetes.

The following organizations may provide additional information and support:
NIH/National Digestive Diseases Information Clearinghouse
NIH/National Institute of Diabetes, Digestive & Kidney Diseases

554 Hypohidrotic Ectodermal Dysplasia

Synonyms

Anhidrotic Ectodermal Dysplasia
Christ-Siemens-Touraine Syndrome
CST Syndrome
EDA
HED

Hypohidrotic ectodermal dysplasia (HED) is a rare inherited multisystem disorder that belongs to the group of diseases known as ectodermal dysplasias. Ectodermal dysplasias typically affect the hair, teeth, nails, and/or skin. HED is primarily characterized by partial or complete absence of certain sweat glands (eccrine glands), causing lack of or diminished sweating (anhidrosis or hypohidrosis), heat intolerance, and fever; abnormally sparse hair (hypotrichosis); and absence (hypodontia) and/or malformation of certain teeth. Many individuals with HED also have characteristic facial abnormalities including a prominent forehead, a sunken nasal bridge (so-called "saddle nose"), unusually thick lips, and/or a large chin. The skin on most of the body may be abnormally thin, dry, and soft with an abnormal lack of pigmentation (hypopigmentation). However, the skin around the eyes (periorbital) may be darkly pigmented (hyperpigmentation) and finely wrinkled, appearing prematurely aged. In many cases, affected infants and children may also exhibit underdevelopment (hypoplasia) or absence (aplasia) of mucous glands within the respiratory and gastrointestinal (GI) tracts and, in some cases, decreased function of certain components of the immune system (e.g., depressed lymphocyte function, cellular immune hypofunction), potentially causing an increased susceptibility to certain infections and/or allergic conditions. Many affected infants and children experience recurrent attacks of wheezing and breathlessness (asthma); respiratory infections; chronic inflammation of the nasal passages (atrophic rhinitis); scaling, itchy (pruritic) skin rashes (eczema); and/or other findings. HED is usually inherited as an X-linked recessive genetic trait; in such cases, the disorder is fully expressed in males only. However, females who carry a single copy of the disease gene (heterozygote carriers) may exhibit some of the symptoms and findings associated with the disorder. These may include absence and/or malformation of certain teeth, sparse hair, and/or reduced sweating. Researchers also have reported cases in which HED appears to be inherited as an autosomal recessive genetic trait. In such cases, the disorder is fully expressed in both males and females.

The following organizations may provide additional information and support:
March of Dimes Birth Defects Foundation
National Foundation for Ectodermal Dysplasias
NIH/National Institute of Arthritis and Musculoskeletal and Skin Diseases
NIH/National Oral Health Information Clearinghouse

555   Hypokalemia

Synonyms

Hypokalemic Syndrome
Hypopotassemia Syndrome
Low Potassium Syndrome
Nephritis, Potassium-Losing
Potassium Loss Syndrome

Hypokalemia is a metabolic imbalance characterized by extremely low potassium levels in the blood. It is a symptom of another disease or condition, or a side effect of diuretic drugs. The body needs potassium for the contraction of muscles (including the heart), and for the functioning of many complicated proteins (enzymes). Potassium is found primarily in the skeletal muscle and bone, and participates with sodium to contribute to the normal flow of body fluids between the cells in the body. The normal concentration of potassium in the body is regulated by the kidneys through the excretion of urine. When the kidneys are functioning normally, the amount of potassium in the diet is sufficient for use by the body and the excess is usually excreted through urine and sweat. Body chemicals and hormones such as aldosterone also regulate potassium balance. Secretion of the hormone insulin, which is normally stimulated by food, prevents a temporary diet-induced hypokalemia by increasing cell absorption of potassium. When hypokalemia occurs, there is an imbalance resulting from a dysfunction in this normal process, or the rapid loss of urine or sweat without replacement of sufficient potassium.

The following organizations may provide additional information and support:
CLIMB (Children Living with Inherited Metabolic Diseases)
Digestive Disease National Coalition
NIH/National Institute of Diabetes, Digestive & Kidney Diseases

556   Hypomelanosis of Ito

Synonyms

HMI
Incontinenti Pigmenti Achromians
IPA
ITO
ITO Hypomelanosis

Hypomelanosis of Ito (HI) is a rare disorder that is distinguished by a lack of skin color (hypopigmentation) affecting many areas of the body. The defect in skin color is likely to appear as streaks, patches, or whorls. It is often associated with other symptoms such as intellectual and developmental retardation, seizures (neurological anomalies), ocular, skeletal and dental problems and/or a small head. The diagnosis is sometimes difficult due to the number and variety of other conditions that may be present and confuse the situation. Most cases of HI are not the result of an inherited defect, although some cases are inherited as an autosomal dominant trait.

The following organizations may provide additional information and support:
HITS (UK) (Family Support Network)
March of Dimes Birth Defects Foundation
NIH/National Institute of Arthritis and Musculoskeletal and Skin Diseases

557   Hypoparathyroidism

Synonyms

Parathyroid, Underactivity of
Tetany

Hypoparathyroidism is a condition characterized by insufficient production of parathyroid hormones by the parathyroid glands, the small, oval glands located near the thyroid gland in the neck. Parathyroid hormones (along with vitamin D and the hormone calcitonin, which is produced by the thyroid gland) play a role in regulating levels of calcium in the blood. Due to deficiency of parathyroid hormones, affected individuals exhibit abnormally low levels of calcium in the blood (hypocalcemia). Symptoms and findings associated with hypoparathyroidism may include weakness, muscle cramps, excessive nervousness, headaches, and/or increased excitability (hyperexcitability) of nerves resulting in uncontrollable twitching and cramping spasms of certain muscles such as those of the hands, feet, arms, and/or face (tetany). Hypoparathyroidism may result from absence of the parathyroid glands at birth, occur due to or in association with a number of different underlying disorders, or result from removal of or damage to the parathyroid glands. In rare cases, hypoparathyroidism may be inherited as an autosomal recessive genetic trait.

The following organizations may provide additional information and support:
The Hormone Foundation
Hypoparathyroidism Association, Inc.
NIH/National Digestive Diseases Information Clearinghouse
NIH/National Institute of Child Health and Human Development
Thyroid Foundation of America, Inc.
Thyroid Foundation of Canada

558 Hypophosphatasia

Synonyms
HHRH
Hypercalciuric Rickets
Hypophosphatemic Rickets with Hypercalcemia

Disorder Subdivisions
Hypophosphatasia, Adult
Hypophosphatasia, Childhood
Hypophosphatasia, Infantile
Pseudohypophosphatasia

Hypophosphatasia is an inborn metabolic disorder of the bones characterized by skeletal defects resembling those of rickets. The symptoms result from a failure of bone mineral to be deposited in young, uncalcified bone (osteoid), and in the cartilage at the end of the long bones (epiphyses) during early years. The activity of the enzyme alkaline phosphatase in blood serum and bone cells is lower than normal. Urinary excretion and blood plasma concentrations of phosphoethanolamine and inorganic pyrophosphate are abnormally high. Unlike other forms of rickets, hypophosphatasia does not respond to treatment with vitamin D.

The following organizations may provide additional information and support:
CLIMB (Children Living with Inherited Metabolic Diseases)
MAGIC Foundation for Children's Growth
March of Dimes Birth Defects Foundation
NIH/National Arthritis and Musculoskeletal and Skin Diseases Information Clearinghouse
Williams Syndrome Foundation
XLH Network Inc.

559 Hypophosphatemia, Familial

Synonyms
Hereditary Type I Hypophosphatemia (HPDR I)
Hereditary Type II Hypophosphatemia (HPDR II)
Hypophosphatemic D-Resistant Rickets I
Hypophosphatemic D-Resistant Rickets II
Phosphate Diabetes
X-Linked Hypophosphatemia (XLH)
X-Linked Vitamin D-Resistant Rickets

Disorder Subdivisions
Autosomal Dominant Hypophosphatemic Rickets (ADHR)
Autosomal Recessive Hypophosphatemic Rickets
X-Linked Hypophosphatemic Rickets

Familial hypophosphatemia is a rare inherited disorder characterized by impaired transport of phosphate and altered vitamin-D metabolism in the kidneys. In addition, calcium and phosphate are not absorbed properly in the intestines, which can lead to softening of bones. Familial hypophosphatemia results in rickets, a childhood bone disease with characteristic growth plate abnormalities and progressive softening of the bone structure. In adults, the growth plate is not present so that the rickets primarily affects bone, a process generally called osteomalacia. Major symptoms of familial hypophosphatemia include skeletal malformations, bone pain, and abnormally bowed legs. Affected infants often fail to grow at the expected rate, potentially resulting in short stature. Familial hypophosphatemia is most often inherited as an X-linked trait. However, autosomal dominant and recessive forms of familial hypophosphatemia have been reported in the medical literature.

The following organizations may provide additional information and support:
March of Dimes Birth Defects Foundation
NIH/National Digestive Diseases Information Clearinghouse
XLH Network Inc.

560 Hypoplastic Left Heart Syndrome

Synonyms
Aortic and Mitral Atresia with Hypoplasic Left Heart Syndrome
HLHS

Hypoplastic left heart syndrome is a term used to describe a group of closely related rare heart defects that are present at birth (congenital). The normal heart has four chambers. The two upper chambers, known as atria, are separated from each other by a fibrous partition known as the atrial septum. The two lower chambers are known as ventricles and are separated from each other by the ventricular septum. Valves connect the atria (left and right) to their respective ventricles. The valves allow for blood to be pumped through the chambers. Blood travels from the right ventricle through the pulmonary artery to the lungs where it receives oxygen. The blood returns to the heart through pulmonary veins and enters the left ventricle. The left ventricle sends the now oxygen-filled blood into the main artery of the body (aorta). The aorta sends the blood throughout the body. Hypoplastic left heart syndrome is characterized by the underdevelopment (hypoplasia) of the chambers on the left side of the heart (i.e., left atrium and ventricle). In addition, the mitral valve, which connects these chambers to each other, is usually abnormally narrow (stenosis) or closed (atresia) and the aortic valve, which connects the heart to the major vessels that lead from the lungs (ascending aorta), may also be narrow or closed. Infants with hypoplastic left heart syndrome also have an abnormally narrow ascending aorta.

The following organizations may provide additional information and support:
American Heart Association
Birth Defect Research for Children, Inc.
Congenital Heart Anomalies, Support, Education, & Resources
Congenital Heart Information Network
Little Hearts, Inc.
NIH/National Heart, Lung and Blood Institute

561 Hypotension, Orthostatic

Synonym
Postural Hypotension

Orthostatic hypotension (OH) describes an extreme drop in blood pressure that may occur when a person stands up suddenly and the blood pools in the blood vessels of the legs. Because of this pooling, the amount of blood carried back to the heart by the veins is decreased. Subsequently, less blood is pumped out from the heart, resulting in a sudden drop in blood pressure. By definition, the drop in blood pressure must be greater than 20 mm of mercury during contraction of the heart muscles (systole) and more than 10 mm of mercury during expansion of the heart muscles (diastole). Among children and teenagers, short-lived episodes of OH are normal and not uncommon. Episodes among the elderly are always to be taken seriously. Normally, specialized cells in the body (baroreceptors) quickly respond to changes in blood pressure. These baroreceptors then activate the autonomic nervous system to increase, via reflex action, levels of catecholamines (e.g., epinephrine, norepinephrine) in the body. Increased catecholamine levels rapidly restore the blood pressure. A defect in this spontaneous response (reflex), prevents the heart rate and blood pressure from rising adequately and orthostatic hypotension results. Fainting and falling are the usual consequences. Some clinical neurologists prefer to focus on three primary syndromes of the failure or breakdown of the autonomic nervous system. These are: Acute or subacute idiopathic pandysautonomia (ASIP) refers to the breakdown of the autonomic nervous system (control of breathing, blood circulation, pain, taste, etc.) from unknown causes. Pure autonomic failure (PAF) is sometimes defined as the presence of orthostatic hypotension (without an identifiable cause such as medically prescribed drugs) without evidence of any other neurological problem(s). This term, according to an international consensus committee, replaces Bradbury-Egglestone syndrome, idiopathic orthostatic hypotension, and progressive autonomic failure. Multiple system atrophy (MSA) a neurodegenerative disease marked by a combination of symptoms affecting movement, blood pressure, and other autonomic body functions; hence, the label multiple system atrophy. This term embraces three forms of MSA: Shy-Drager syndrome (MSA-A), olivopontocerebellar atrophy (MSA-C), and striatonigral degeneration (MSA-P). For the purposes of this report, Shy-Drager syndrome (MSA-A) is of greater interest since the autonomic nervous system is most acutely affected. (Note that in the MSA terms above, A = Autonomous; C = Cerebellar; and P = Parkinsonism) .

The following organizations may provide additional information and support:
Autonomic Dysfunction Center
National Dysautonomia Research Foundation
National Institute of Neurological Disorders and Stroke (NINDS)

562 **Hypothyroidism**

Synonym
Myxedema

Hypothyroidism is a condition characterized by abnormally decreased activity of the thyroid gland and deficient production of thyroid hormones. The thyroid gland secretes hormones that play an essential role in regulating growth, maturation, and the rate of metabolism. Specific symptoms and findings associated with hypothyroidism may be variable, depending upon the age at symptom onset, the degree of thyroid hormone deficiency, and/or other factors. In many adults with hypothyroidism, the condition may be characterized by generalized fatigue and lack of energy (lethargy), muscle weakness and cramping, dryness of the skin and hair, incomplete or infrequent passing of stools (constipation), sensitivity to cold, and other symptoms. If the condition is present at birth (congenital hypothyroidism), associated symptoms and findings may become apparent during early infancy. These may include respiratory and feeding difficulties, listlessness, protrusion of the abdomen, constipation, dry skin, coarse hair, progressive accumulation of fluid within bodily tissues, and other associated abnormalities. Some affected infants may have progressive retardation of physical and mental development that becomes increasingly severe (cretinism) without early recognition of the condition and prompt treatment. There are several different causes of hypothyroidism. The condition may result from an underlying defect that is present at birth (congenital), such as improper development (dysplasia) or absence (aplasia) of the thyroid gland or biochemical (enzymatic) abnormalities. The condition may also develop later during childhood or adulthood (acquired) due to certain underlying disorders, the use of particular medications, or surgical removal of the thyroid gland. Although hypothyroidism most frequently affects adult females, the condition occurs in both genders and may become apparent at any age.

The following organizations may provide additional information and support:
American Foundation of Thyroid Patients
The Hormone Foundation
NIH/National Digestive Diseases Information Clearinghouse
Thyroid Foundation of America, Inc.
Thyroid Society for Education & Research

563 **Hypotonia, Benign Congenital**

Synonym
BCH

Benign congenital hypotonia (BCH) has been an outdated term since 1956, when the first congenital muscle disease, central core disease, was described. Now specific diagnoses can be made in most patients. As clinicians and researchers have gained greater understanding of neuromuscular diseases, the phrase has been dropped and replaced by names of specific neuromuscular disorders. Symptoms and findings associated with the group of neuromuscular disorders formerly known as benign congenital hypotonia include low muscle tone (hypotonia) at birth or in the first few months and general "floppiness" of muscles. Some of the disorders are non-progressive, which means that they do not increase in severity. Most improve over time but mild weakness persists into adulthood. Some of the disorders do progress in the adult years and may have associated problems.

The following organizations may provide additional information and support:
March of Dimes Birth Defects Foundation
National Institute of Neurological Disorders and Stroke (NINDS)
Pathways Awareness Foundation

564 **I Cell Disease**

Synonyms
GNPTA
Inclusion Cell Disease
Leroy Disease
ML II
ML Disorder, Type II
Mucolipidosis II
N-Acetylglucosamine-1-Phosphotransferase Deficiency

I-cell disease (mucolipidosis II) is a rare inherited metabolic disorder characterized by coarse facial features, skeletal abnormalities and mental retardation. The symptoms of I-cell disease are similar to, but more severe than, those of Hurler syndrome. The symptoms associated with this disorder typically become obvious during infancy and may include multiple abnormalities of the skull and face and growth delays. This disorder belongs to a group of diseases known as lysosomal storage disorders. Lysosomes are particles bound in membranes within cells that break down certain fats and carbohydrates. Multiple enzyme deficiencies associated with I-cell disease lead to the accumulation of certain fatty substances (mucolipids) and certain complex carbohydrates (mucopolysaccharides) within the cells of many tissues of the body. I-cell disease is caused by a mutation in the GNPTA gene that leads to a deficiency in the enzyme UDP-N-acetylglucoseamine-1-phosphotransferase. I-cell disease is inherited as an autosomal recessive genetic trait.

The following organizations may provide additional information and support:
The Arc (A National Organization on Mental Retardation)
Canadian Society for Mucopolysaccharide and Related Diseases, Inc.
CLIMB (Children Living with Inherited Metabolic Diseases)
International Society for Mannosidosis & Related Diseases, Inc.
National MPS (Mucopolysaccharidoses/Mucolipidoses) Society, Inc.
NIH/National Digestive Diseases Information Clearinghouse
Society for Mucopolysaccharide Diseases
Vaincre Les Maladies Lysosomales

---

565 Ichthyosis

Synonym
Disorders of Cornification

Disorder Subdivisions
Chanarin-Dorfman Syndrome (Neutral Lipid Storage Disease)
CHILD Syndrome (Unilateral Hemidysplasia)
Conradi-Hunermann Syndrome (X-Linked Dominant Chondrodysplasia Punctata)
Darier Disease
Giroux-Barbeau Syndrome
Hailey-Hailey Disease (Benign Familial Pemphigus)
KID Syndrome (Keratitis, Ichthyosis, Deafness)
Netherton Syndrome (Ichthyosis Linearis Circumflexa)
Refsum's Disease (Phytanic Acid Storage Disease)
Rud's Syndrome
Sjogren-Larsson Syndrome
Tay's Syndrome (Trichothiodystrophy, IBIDS Syndrome)
X-linked Ichthyosis
Congenital Ichthyosiform Erythroderma (CIE)
Epidermal Nevi (Ichthyosis Hystrix, Linear Epidermal Nevus)
Epidermolytic Hyperkeratosis (EHK)
Erythrokeratodermia Variabilis (EKV)
Harlequin Ichthyosis (Harlequin Fetus)
Ichthyosis Hystrix Curth-Macklin Type
Ichthyosis Vulgaris (Ichthyosis Simplex)
Keratosis Follicularis Spinulosa Decalvans
Lamellar Ichthyosis
Multiple Sulfatase Deficiency
Pachyonychia Congenita
Palmoplantar Keratodermas (PPK)
Peeling Skin Syndrome
Pityriasis Rubra Pilaris (PRP)

Ichthyosis is a general term for a family of rare genetic skin diseases characterized by dry, thickened, scaling skin. The various forms are distinguished from one another by: (1) extent of the scaling and how widely and where the scaling is scattered over the body; (2) the presence or absence and intensity of reddening of the skin (erythroderma); (3) the mode of inheritance; and (4) the character of associated abnormalities.

The following organizations may provide additional information and support:
Foundation for Ichthyosis & Related Skin Types
NIH/National Arthritis and Musculoskeletal and Skin Diseases Information Clearinghouse
National Registry for Ichthyosis and Related Disorders

---

566 Ichthyosis, Chanarin Dorfman Syndrome

Synonyms
Chanarin Dorfman Disease
Disorder of Cornification 12 (Neutral Lipid Storage Type)
DOC 12 (Neutral Lipid Storage Type)
Dorfman Chanarin Syndrome
Ichthyosiform Erythroderma with Leukocyte Vacuolation
Ichthyotic Neutral Lipid Storage Disease
Neutral Lipid Storage Disease
Triglyceride Storage Disease Impaired Long-Chain Fatty Acid Oxidation

Chanarin Dorfman syndrome is a rare hereditary disorder of fat (lipid) metabolism. It is characterized by scaly skin (ichthyosis), degeneration of the muscles (myopathy), and abnormal white blood cells with small spaces (vacuoles) filled with fat (lipids).

The following organizations may provide additional information and support:
Foundation for Ichthyosis & Related Skin Types
NIH/National Institute of Allergy and Infectious Diseases

567   Ichthyosis, CHILD Syndrome

Synonyms

CHILD Naevus
CHILD Nevus
Congenital Hemidysplasia with Ichthyosis Erythroderma and Limb Defects
Disorders of Cornification 16
DOC 16, Unilateral Hemidysplasia Type
Unilateral Hemidysplasia Type
Unilateral Ichthyosiform Erythroderma with Ipsilateral Malformations, Limb

CHILD syndrome (an acronym for congenital hemidysplasia with ichthyosiform erythroderma and limb defects) is an inherited disorder, affecting primarily women, that is characterized by ichthyosis-like skin abnormalities and limb defects on one side of the body. Other abnormalities may be present, as well. If defects of other body organs are present, they are usually on the same side of the body as the skin and limb abnormalities.

The following organizations may provide additional information and support:
Foundation for Ichthyosis & Related Skin Types
NIH/National Institute of Allergy and Infectious Diseases

568   Ichthyosis, Erythrokeratodermia Progressiva Symmetrica

Synonyms

Disorder of Cornification 20
DOC 20
ECPSG
Erythrokeratodermia Congenitalis Progressiva Symmetrica, Gottron
Gottron's Erythrokeratodermia Congenitalis Progressiva Symmetrica

Erythrokeratodermia progressiva symmetrica is a rare hereditary skin disorder characterized by red hardened (keratotic) plaques with clear limits. These plaques are distributed symmetrically on the surface of both sides of the body, as well as on the head, buttocks, and extremities. The lesions first appear during infancy. This disorder is a form

of ichthyosis, a group of rare hereditary disorders characterized by scaly skin.

The following organizations may provide additional information and support:
Foundation for Ichthyosis & Related Skin Types
National Registry for Ichthyosis and Related Disorders
NIH/National Arthritis and Musculoskeletal and Skin Diseases Information Clearinghouse

569   Ichthyosis, Erythrokeratodermia Variabilis

Synonyms

EKV
Keratosis Rubra Figurata
Mendes Da Costa Syndrome

Erythrokeratodermia variabilis is an inherited skin disorder characterized by two features: short-lasting red patches in various sizes and shapes that may involve any part of the body; and thickening of the skin (hyperkeratosis). The hyperkeratosis can either be generalized, or localized as fixed, sharply defined, thickened plaques. The hyperkeratosis may also involve the skin of the palms and soles. Skin lesions are made worse by sudden changes in temperature and friction. The red patches may be accompanied by a burning sensation.

The following organizations may provide additional information and support:
Foundation for Ichthyosis & Related Skin Types
NIH/National Arthritis and Musculoskeletal and Skin Diseases Information Clearinghouse

570   Ichthyosis, Erythrokeratolysis Hiemalis

Synonyms

Disorder of Cornification 19 (Erythrokeratolysis Hiemalis)
DOC 19
Erythrokeratolysis Hiemalis
Keratolytic Winter Erythema
Oudtshoorn Skin

Erythrokeratolysis hiemalis is a form of ichthyosis, which is a group of hereditary skin disorders. This condition is characterized by periodic attacks of red (erythematous) plaques that are distributed equally on both sides of the body. A layer of skin can be peeled from these plaques. Symptoms usually improve with age.

The following organizations may provide additional information and support:
Foundation for Ichthyosis & Related Skin Types
NIH/National Arthritis and Musculoskeletal and Skin Diseases Information Clearinghouse

571 Ichthyosis, Harlequin Type

Synonyms
Harlequin Fetus
Ichthyosis Fetalis

Harlequin ichthyosis is a rare genetic skin disorder. The newborn infant is covered with plates of thick skin that crack and split apart. The thick plates can pull at and distort facial features and can restrict breathing and eating. Harlequin infants need to be cared for in the neonatal intensive care unit immediately.

The following organizations may provide additional information and support:
Foundation for Ichthyosis & Related Skin Types
National Registry for Ichthyosis and Related Disorders
NIH/National Institute of Allergy and Infectious Diseases

572 Ichthyosis Hystrix, Curth Macklin Type

Synonyms
Disorder of Cornification 8, Curth-Macklin Type
DOC 8, Curth-Macklin Type

Ichthyosis hystrix, Curth-Macklin type is a rare inherited skin disorder. It is characterized by scaling skin (ichthyosis) ranging from mild to severe. Thick, horny skin (keratoderma) on the palms of the hands and the soles of the feet may occur with no other symptoms, or the whole body surface may be covered with scales.

The following organizations may provide additional information and support:
Foundation for Ichthyosis & Related Skin Types
National Registry for Ichthyosis and Related Disorders
NIH/National Institute of Allergy and Infectious Diseases

573 Ichthyosis, Keratosis Follicularis Spinulosa Decalvans

Synonyms
Disorder of Cornification 24
DOC 24
Siemens Syndrome

Keratosis follicularis spinulosa decalvans (KFSD) is a rare, inherited, skin disorder that affects men predominately and is characterized by hardening of the skin (keratosis) in several parts of the body. Most frequently, the face, neck, and forearms are involved. The thickening of the skin is accompanied by the loss of eyebrows, eyelashes and beard. Baldness (alopecia) usually occurs.

The following organizations may provide additional information and support:
Foundation for Ichthyosis & Related Skin Types
National Registry for Ichthyosis and Related Disorders
NIH/National Arthritis and Musculoskeletal and Skin Diseases Information Clearinghouse

574 Ichthyosis, Lamellar

Synonyms
Collodion Baby
Ichthyosis Congenita
Lamellar Ichthyosis, Type 1 and Type 2
Non-Bullous Congenital Ichthyosiform Erythroderma (Non-Bullous CIE)

Lamellar ichthyosis is a rare genetic skin disorder. In lamellar ichthyosis, the skin cells are produced at a normal rate, but they do not separate normally at the surface of the outermost layer of skin (stratum corneum) and are not shed as quickly as they should be. The result of this retention is the formation of scale.

The following organizations may provide additional information and support:
Foundation for Ichthyosis & Related Skin Types
National Registry for Ichthyosis and Related Disorders
NIH/National Arthritis and Musculoskeletal and Skin Diseases Information Clearinghouse

575 Ichthyosis, Netherton Syndrome

Synonyms
Comel-Netherton Syndrome
Ichthyosis Linearis Circumflexa

Netherton syndrome is a rare hereditary disorder characterized by scaling skin, hair anomalies, increased susceptibility to atopic eczema (a skin condition that can result in dry, red and flaky skin), elevated IgE levels, and other related symptoms. Netherton syndrome is inherited as an autosomal recessive trait.

The following organizations may provide additional information and support:
Foundation for Ichthyosis & Related Skin Types
National Registry for Ichthyosis and Related Disorders
NIH/National Arthritis and Musculoskeletal and Skin Diseases Information Clearinghouse

576 Ichthyosis, Sjogren Larsson Syndrome

Synonyms
Ichthyosis, Spastic Neurologic Disorder, Mental Retardation
SLS

Sjögren-Larsson syndrome is an inherited disorder characterized by scaling skin (ichthyosis), mental retardation, speech abnormalities, and spasticity. Affected infants develop various degrees of reddened skin with fine scales soon after birth. After infancy, the skin loses its redness and dark scales often appear on the neck and under the arms. Additionally, larger plate-like thick scales may develop on the lower legs. Developmental delay, speech abnormalities and seizures may accompany skin symptoms. Spasticity in the legs typically impairs motor ability and walking. Many children with this disorder have glistening white dots or degeneration of the pigment in the retina of the eye.

The following organizations may provide additional information and support:
The Arc (A National Organization on Mental Retardation)
Foundation for Ichthyosis & Related Skin Types
NIH/National Arthritis and Musculoskeletal and Skin Diseases Information Clearinghouse

577 Ichthyosis, Trichothiodystrophy

Synonyms
IBIDS Syndrome
PIBIDS Syndrome
Tay Syndrome
TTD

Trichothiodystrophy is a hereditary disorder characterized by brittle hair, which may be accompanied by a variety of other manifestations. It is sometimes called PIBIDS, a term that refers to the association of photosensitivity ichthyosis, brittle hair, intellectual impairment, decreased fertility, and short stature. Without photosensitivity the condition has been termed IBIDS, and without ichthyosis, BIDS. Many patients have recurrent infections, and abnormalities of the bone and teeth may also occur. The defining feature of trichothiodystrophy is brittle hair, which is sulfur deficient and, when examined with a microscope and polarized light, demonstrates a characteristic light and dark (tiger tail) banding.

The following organizations may provide additional information and support:
Foundation for Ichthyosis & Related Skin Types
National Registry for Ichthyosis and Related Disorders
NIH/National Arthritis and Musculoskeletal Skin Diseases Information Clearinghouse

578 Ichthyosis Vulgaris

Synonym
Ichthyosis Simplex

In ichthyosis vulgaris, the skin cells are produced at a normal rate, but they do not shed normally at the surface of the outermost layer of skin (stratum corneum) and are not shed as quickly as they should be. The result is a build-up of scale. Fine scales usually develop on the back and over muscles near the joints, such as an elbow or knee (extensor muscles). Ichthyosis is usually most common and severe over the lower legs.

The following organizations may provide additional information and support:
Foundation for Ichthyosis & Related Skin Types
National Registry for Ichthyosis and Related Disorders
NIH/National Arthritis and Musculoskeletal and Skin Diseases Information Clearinghouse

579 Ichthyosis, X Linked

Synonyms

Placental Steroid Sulfatase Deficiency; STS
Recessive X-linked Ichthyosis
Steroid Sulfatase Deficiency
Steroid Sulfatase Deficiency Disease; SSDD

X-linked ichthyosis is a genetic skin disorder that affects males. It is an inborn error of metabolism characterized by a deficiency of the enzyme steroid sulfatase. Under normal conditions, this enzyme breaks down (metabolizes) cholesterol sulfate, a member of the chemical family of steroids. Cholesterol sulfate plays a role in maintaining the integrity of the skin. If steroid metabolism is interrupted and cholesterol sulfate accumulates in the skin cells, the skin cells stick together more strongly than usual. The normal shedding of dead skin cells is inhibited and the skin cells build up and clump into scales.

The following organizations may provide additional information and support:
Foundation for Ichthyosis & Related Skin Types
National Registry for Ichthyosis and Related Disorders
NIH/National Institute of Arthritis and Musculoskeletal and Skin Diseases

580 Idiopathic Pulmonary Fibrosis

Synonyms

Alveolocapillary block
Cryptogenic Fibrosing Alveolitis
Diffuse Fibrosing Alveolitis
Fibrosing Alveolitis
Hamman-Rich Syndrome
Interstitial Diffuse Pulmonary Fibrosis

Idiopathic pulmonary fibrosis is an inflammatory lung disorder of unknown origin (idiopathic) characterized by abnormal formation of fibrous tissue (fibrosis) between the tiny air sacs (alveoli) or ducts of the lungs. Coughing and rapid, shallow breathing occur with moderate exercise. The skin may appear slightly bluish (cyanotic) due to lack of circulating oxygen. Complications such as infection, emphysema or heart problems may develop.

The following organizations may provide additional information and support:
American Autoimmune Related Diseases Association, Inc.
American Lung Association

Autoimmune Information Network, Inc
Coalition for Pulmonary Fibrosis
NIH/National Heart, Lung and Blood Institute
Pulmonary Fibrosis Foundation

581 IgA Nephropathy

Synonyms

Berger's Disease
Idiopathic Renal Hematuria
Mesangial IgA Nephropathy

IgA nephropathy is a chronic kidney disease that usually first appears during adolescence and young adulthood and often progresses to kidney failure. It usually follows a viral infection of the upper respiratory or gastrointestinal tracts. The major symptom is the passing of blood in the urine (hematuria). There may be associated pain in the loin area.

The following organizations may provide additional information and support:
American Foundation for Urologic Disease
American Kidney Fund, Inc.
Autoimmune Information Network, Inc
IgA Nephropathy Support Network
National Kidney Foundation
NIH/National Kidney and Urologic Diseases Information Clearinghouse

582 Imperforate Anus

Synonyms

Anal Atresia
Anal Membrane
Anal Stenosis
Anorectal Malformations
Ectopic Anus
High Imperforate Anus
Low Imperforate Anus
Perineal Anus
Rectoperineal Fistula

Imperforate anus is a rare inborn abnormality characterized by the absence or abnormal localization of the anus. The rectum or the colon may be connected to the vagina or the bladder by a tunnel (fistula). With surgical correction, normal elimination can become possible.

The following organizations may provide additional information and support:
Birth Defect Research for Children, Inc.
Bowel Group for Kids Incorporated

National Advisory Service to Parents of Children with a Stoma (NASPCS)—The Charity for Incontinent and Stoma Children
NIH/National Digestive Diseases Information Clearinghouse
Pull-thru Network

583 Incontinentia Pigmenti

Synonyms

Bloch-Siemens Incontinentia Pigmenti
Melanoblastosis Cutis Linearis
Bloch-Siemens-Sulzberger Syndrome
Bloch-Sulzberger Syndrome
IP
Pigmented Dermatosis, Siemens-Bloch Type

Incontinentia pigmenti (IP) is a rare genetic dermatological disorder affecting the skin, hair, teeth, and central nervous system. Progressive skin changes occur in four stages, the first of which appears in early infancy or is present at birth. IP is inherited as an X-linked dominant trait.

The following organizations may provide additional information and support:
Incontinentia Pigmenti International Foundation
March of Dimes Birth Defects Foundation
NIH/National Institute of Arthritis and Musculoskeletal and Skin Diseases

584 Interstitial Cystitis

Synonyms

Hunner's Patch
Hunner's Ulcer
IC
Pelvic Pain Syndrome
Trigonitis
Urethral Syndrome

Interstitial cystitis is a chronic, painful inflammatory condition of the bladder wall characterized by pressure and pain above the pubic area along with increased frequency and urgency of urination. This occurs because of chronic inflammation of the lining of the bladder and swelling of the interior walls of the bladder. Affected individuals urinate frequently with pain even though there is no diagnosed bladder infection. In a small percentage of cases, people with interstitial cystitis also have scarring and ulcerations on the membranes that line the bladder. Interstitial cystitis typically affects young and middle-aged women, although men can also have this disorder. The exact cause of interstitial cystitis is not known.

The following organizations may provide additional information and support:
American Foundation for Urologic Disease
Interstitial Cystitis Association
NIH/National Kidney and Urologic Diseases Information Clearinghouse

585 Intestinal Pseudoobstruction

Synonyms

Chronic Idiopathic Intestinal Pseudoobstruction
CIIP
Congenital Short Bowel Syndrome
Hypomotility Disorder
Pseudointestinal Obstruction Syndrome
Pseudoobstructive Syndrome

Intestinal pseudoobstruction is a digestive disorder that may be present at birth. The intestinal walls are unable to contract normally (hypomotility) to generate wave-like (peristaltic) motion. This condition resembles a true obstruction, but no such blockage exists. Abdominal pain, vomiting, diarrhea, constipation, malabsorption of nutrients leading to weight loss and/or failure to thrive, are signal signs. Enlargement of various parts of the small intestine or bowel also occur. There are two kinds of intestinal pseudoobstruction, depending on the source of the failure of the gastrointestinal tract. If the problem is abnormal functioning of the nerves of the abdominal wall leading to nonsynchronized contractions, then the episode is classified as neurogenic and the disorder is known as neuropathic pseudoobstruction. If the functional failure can be traced to weak or absent contractions of the muscle itself, then it is classified as myogenic and the disorder is known as myopathic pseudoobstruction.

The following organizations may provide additional information and support:
Association of Gastrointestinal Motility Disorders, Inc. (AGMD)
Bowel Group for Kids Incorporated
International Foundation for Functional Gastrointestinal Disorders
NIH/National Institute of Diabetes, Digestive & Kidney Diseases

586   IRF6-Related Disorders

Synonyms

Popliteal Pterygium Syndrome
Van der Woude Syndrome

IRF6-related disorders include a spectrum of disorders caused by abnormalities in the interferon regulatory factor 6 (IRF6) gene. Van der Woude syndrome (VWS) is at the mild end of the spectrum and popliteal pterygium syndrome (PPS) is at the severe end of the spectrum. Individuals with VWS can have lip pits alone, cleft lip or cleft palate alone, or a combination of these anomalies. The physical features associated with popliteal pterygium syndrome include cleft lip and/or cleft palate, lower lip pits, webbed skin (pterygium) on the backs of both legs (popliteal) and between the legs (intercrural), malformation and/or under-development of the genitals, webbing or fusion of the fingers and/or toes (syndactyly), adhesion of upper and lower jaw and adhesion of upper and lower eyelids. A cone-shaped fold of skin on the nail of the big toe is a very distinctive finding in this condition.

The following organizations may provide additional information and support:
AboutFace USA
American Cleft Palate/Craniofacial Association (Physians Only)
Children's Craniofacial Association
Cleft Palate Foundation
Forward Face, Inc.
National Craniofacial Foundation
NIH/National Arthritis and Musculoskeletal and Skin Diseases Information Clearinghouse
Wide Smiles

587   Irritable Bowel Syndrome

Synonyms

Adaptive Colitis
Colonic Neurosis
IBS
Irritable Colon Syndrome
Mucous Colitis
Spastic Colon
Unstable Colon

Irritable bowel syndrome, also known as spastic colon or mucous colitis, is a digestive disorder characterized by an abnormal increase in the mobility of the intestines (small and large). Symptoms may include abdominal pain, constipation, and di-arrhea. This disorder is common; about 50 percent of all gastrointestinal problems are associated with irritable bowel syndrome. There is no organic disease present, only the function of the intestines is affected. However, based on the symptoms, this disease can be confused with other organic bowel diseases.

The following organizations may provide additional information and support:
CF Alliance
Crohn's and Colitis Foundation of America
Digestive Disease National Coalition
Eastern Paralyzed Veterans Association
Erythema Nodosum Yahoo Support Group
International Foundation for Functional Gastrointestinal Disorders
Intestinal Disease Foundation
NIH/National Digestive Diseases Information Clearinghouse

588   Ivemark Syndrome

Synonyms

Asplenia Syndrome
Bilateral Right-Sidedness Sequence
Splenic Agenesis Syndrome

Ivemark syndrome is a rare progressive disorder usually evident at birth. It is characterized by the absence of a spleen, malformations of the cardiovascular system and abnormal displacement of internal organs.

The following organization may provide additional information and support:
Ivemark Syndrome Association

589   Jackson-Weiss Syndrome

Synonyms

Craniosynostosis, Midfacial Hypoplasia, and Foot Abnormalities
Jackson-Weiss Craniosynostosis

Jackson-Weiss syndrome (JWS) is a rare genetic disorder characterized by distinctive malformations of the head and facial (craniofacial) area and abnormalities of the feet. The range and severity of symptoms and findings may be extremely variable, including among affected members of the same family (kindred). However, primary findings may include premature closure of the fibrous joints (cranial sutures) between certain bones of the skull (craniosynostosis); unusually flat, underdeveloped midfacial regions (midfacial hypoplasia); abnormally broad great toes; and/or malformation or fusion of certain bones within the feet. In some cases, Jackson-Weiss syndrome may result from new genetic changes (mutations) that appear to occur randomly for unknown reasons (sporadically). In other affected individuals, the disorder may be inherited as an autosomal dominant trait.

The following organizations may provide additional information and support:
AboutFace USA
Children's Craniofacial Association
FACES: The National Craniofacial Association
Forward Face, Inc.
National Craniofacial Foundation

590   Jansen Type Metaphyseal Chondrodysplasia

Synonyms
Jansen Disease
Jansen Metaphyseal Dysostosis
Murk Jansen Type Metaphyseal Chondrodysplasia

Jansen type metaphyseal chondrodysplasia is an extremely rare progressive disorder in which portions of the bones of the arms and legs develop abnormally with unusual cartilage formations and subsequent abnormal bone formation at the large (bulbous) end portions (metaphyses) of these long bones (metaphyseal chondrodysplasia). As a result, affected individuals exhibit unusually short arms and legs and short stature (short-limbed dwarfism), findings that typically become apparent during early childhood. Abnormal cartilage and bone development may also affect other bones of the body, particularly those of the hands and feet (i.e., metacarpals and metatarsals). Infants with Jansen type metaphyseal chondrodysplasia may also have characteristic facial abnormalities and additional skeletal malformations. During childhood, affected individuals may begin to exhibit progressive stiffening and swelling of many joints and/or an unusual "waddling gait" and squatting stance. In addition, affected adults may eventually develop abnormally hardened (sclerotic) bones especially in the back of the head (cranial bones), which, in some cases, may lead to blindness and/or deafness. In addition, in some cases, affected individuals have abnormally high levels of calcium in the blood (hypercalcemia). The range and severity of symptoms may vary from case to case. Most cases of Jansen type meta-

physeal chondrodysplasia occur randomly as the result of a spontaneous genetic change (i.e., new genetic mutation)

The following organizations may provide additional information and support:
Craniofacial Foundation of America
Human Growth Foundation
Little People of America, Inc.
MAGIC Foundation for Children's Growth
National Craniofacial Foundation
NIH/National Arthritis and Musculoskeletal and Skin Diseases Information Clearinghouse
NIH/National Institute on Deafness and Other Communication Disorders Information Clearinghouse

591   Jarcho-Levin Syndrome

Synonyms
Costovertebral Segmentation Anomalies
Spondylocostal Dysostosis
Spondylocostal Dysplasia
Spondylothoracic Dysostosis
Spondylothoracic Dysplasia

Disorder Subdivisions
SCDO1
SCDO2

Jarcho-Levin syndrome is a rare genetic disorder characterized by distinctive malformations of bones of the spinal column (vertebrae) and the ribs, respiratory insufficiency, and/or other abnormalities. Infants born with Jarcho-Levin syndrome have short necks, limited neck motion due to abnormalities of the cervical vertebrae and short stature. In most cases, infants with Jarcho-Levin syndrome experience respiratory insufficiency and are prone to repeated respiratory infections (pneumonia) that result in life-threatening complications. The vertebrae are fused and the ribs fail to develop properly; therefore, the chest cavity is too small to accommodate the growing lungs. There are apparently two forms of Jarcho-Levin syndrome that are inherited as autosomal recessive genetic traits and termed spondylocostal dysostosis type 1 (SCDO1) and spondylocostal dysostosis type 2 (SCDO2).

The following organizations may provide additional information and support:
Genetic and Rare Diseases (GARD) Information Center
Restricted Growth Association

592 Jejunal Atresia

Synonyms
Apple Peel Syndrome
Christmas Tree Syndrome

Jejunal atresia is a rare genetic disorder. Patients with this disorder are born with a partial absence of the fold of the stomach membrane that connects the small intestine to the back wall of the abdomen. As a result, one of the three portions of the small intestine (the jejunal) twists around one of the arteries of the colon called the marginal artery and causes a blockage (atresia). Symptoms in individuals with this disorder include vomiting, a swollen abdomen, and constipation.

The following organizations may provide additional information and support:
NIH/National Digestive Diseases Information Clearinghouse
Parent Education Network

593 Jervell and Lange-Nielsen Syndrome

Synonyms
Autosomal Recessive Long QT Syndrome
Cardioauditory Syndrome
Cardioauditory Syndrome of Jervell and Lange-Nielsen
Deafness, Congenital, and Functional Heart Disease
Surdocardiac Syndrome

Jervell and Lange-Nielsen syndrome is a rare inherited disorder characterized by deafness present at birth (congenital) occurring in association with abnormalities affecting the electrical system of the heart. The severity of cardiac symptoms associated with Jervell and Lange-Nielsen syndrome varies from case to case. Some individuals may have no apparent symptoms (asymptomatic); others may develop abnormally increased heartbeats (tachyarrhythmias) resulting in episodes of unconsciousness (syncope), cardiac arrest, and potentially sudden death. Physical activity, excitement or stress may trigger the onset of these symptoms. Jervell and Lange-Nielsen syndrome is usually detected during early childhood and is inherited as an autosomal recessive trait.

The following organizations may provide additional information and support:
American Heart Association
Cardiac Arrhythmias Research and Education Foundation, Inc.

Deaf Communications Institute
Deafness Research Foundation
EAR (Education and Auditory Research) Foundation
European Long QT Syndrome Information Center
International Long QT Syndrome Registry
NIH/National Heart, Lung and Blood Institute Information Center
Sudden Arrhythmia Death Syndromes Foundation

594 Job Syndrome

Synonyms
HIE Syndrome
Hyper-IgE Syndrome
Hyperimmunoglobulin E Syndrome
Hyperimmunoglobulin E-Recurrent Infection Syndrome
Hyperimmunoglobulinemia E-Staphylococcal
Job-Buckley Syndrome

Job syndrome is an immunodeficiency syndrome characterized by recurrent bacterial (staphylococcal) infections, particularly of the skin, and markedly elevated IgE [Immunoglobulin E] levels. Some patients have an autosomal dominant inheritance. The staphylococcal infection may involve the skin, lungs, joints and other sites. Some patients have coarse features; some are fair and redheaded. Decreased bone density and frequent fractures are common. Some present with neutrophils (a particular white blood cell) that don't function normally. Signs of allergy, e.g., eczema, asthma and/or runny noses, are sometimes present as well. Treatment consists of intermittent or continuous antibiotics.

The following organizations may provide additional information and support:
Immune Deficiency Foundation
International Patient Organization for Primary Immunodeficiencies
March of Dimes Birth Defects Foundation
NIH/National Institute of Allergy and Infectious Diseases

595 Johanson-Blizzard Syndrome

Synonyms
Ectodermal Dysplasia-Exocrine Pancreatic Insufficiency
JBS
Malabsorption-Ectodermal Dysplasia-Nasal Alar Hypoplasia
Nasal Alar Hypoplasia, Hypothyroidism, Pancreatic Achylia, Cong. Deafness

Johanson-Blizzard syndrome (JBS) is an extremely rare inherited disorder characterized by an unusually small nose that appears "beak shaped" due to absence (aplasia) or underdevelopment (hypoplasia) of the nostrils (nasal alae); abnormally small, malformed primary (deciduous) teeth and misshapen or absent secondary (permanent) teeth; and/or unusually sparse, dry, coarse scalp hair that tends to have a distinctive "upsweep" in the forehead area. In addition, affected infants may have a low birth weight, demonstrate signs of insufficient intestinal absorption (malabsorption) of fats and other nutrients due to abnormal development of the pancreas (exocrine pancreatic insufficiency), and fail to grow and gain weight at the expected rate (failure to thrive) during the first years of life, contributing to short stature. Approximately one third of infants with Johanson-Blizzard syndrome also demonstrate abnormally decreased activity of the thyroid gland and underproduction of thyroid hormones (hypothyroidism), causing generalized weakness and contributing to growth retardation as well as abnormal delays in the acquisition of skills requiring the coordination of mental and physicial activity (psychomotor retardation). In many cases, affected infants may also exhibit hearing impairment of both ears at birth due to abnormalities of the inner ear (congenital bilateral sensorineural hearing loss) and may experience associated, severe speech impairment. In addition, approximately 60 percent of affected children have moderate mental retardation; however, others may have normal intelligence or mild retardation. In many cases, additional abnormalities may also be present. The range and severity of symptoms may vary greatly from case to case. Johanson-Blizzard syndrome has autosomal recessive inheritance.

The following organizations may provide additional information and support:
Congenital Heart Anomalies, Support, Education, & Resources
FACES: The National Craniofacial Association
MAGIC Foundation for Children's Growth
National Advisory Service to Parents of Children with a Stoma (NASPCS)—The Charity for Incontinent and Stoma Children
National Craniofacial Foundation
NIH/National Digestive Diseases Information Clearinghouse
NIH/National Institute of Dental and Craniofacial Research
Pull-thru Network
Restricted Growth Association

596 Joubert Syndrome

Synonyms
Cerebellar Vermis Agenesis, Hyperpnea, Episodic-Eye Moves-Ataxia-Retardation
Cerebellar Vermis Aplasia
Cerebellarparenchymal Disorder IV
Cerebelloparenchymal Disorder IV Familial
Choriretinal Coloboma-Joubert Syndrome
Hyperpnea, Episodic-Abnormal Eye Movement
Joubert-Bolthauser Syndrome
Kidneys, Cystic-Retinal Aplasia Joubert Syndrome
Polydactyly-Joubert Syndrome
Retinal Aplastic-Cystic Kidneys-Joubert Syndrome
Vermis Aplasia
Vermis Cerebellar Agenesis

Joubert syndrome is a very rare neurological disorder involving a malformation of the area of the brain that controls balance and coordination. Generally motor activity is slowed (psychomotor retardation) and there are abnormal eye movements. Respiratory irregularities, including rapid panting, may occur during infancy.

The following organizations may provide additional information and support:
The Arc (A National Organization on Mental Retardation)
Joubert Syndrome Foundation and Related Cerebellar Disorders
National Institute of Neurological Disorders and Stroke (NINDS)

597 Juberg-Marsidi Syndrome

Synonyms
JMS
Juberg-Marsidi Mental Retardation Syndrome
Mental Retardation, X-linked with Growth Delay, Deafness, Microgenitalism

Juberg-Marsidi syndrome is an extremely rare X-linked inherited disorder that is fully expressed in males only, and is apparent at birth (congenital) or during the first few weeks of life (neonatal period). Affected children exhibit severe mental retardation; delays in reaching developmental milestones (e.g., crawling, walking, etc.); muscle weakness; diminished muscle tone (hypotonia); and/or delayed bone growth as well as growth retardation, resulting in short stature. Affected infants also exhibit hearing loss; underdevelopment of the genitals (microgenitalism); and/or abnormalities of the head and facial (craniofacial) area such as an abnormally small head (microcephaly), a flat (depressed) nasal bridge, eye (ocular) abnormalities, and/or, in some cases, additional physical abnormalities. The range and severity of symptoms may vary from case to case. Juberg-Marsidi syndrome is inherited as an X-linked recessive genetic trait.

The following organization may provide additional information and support:
NIH/National Eye Institute

598 Jumping Frenchmen of Maine

Synonyms
Jumping Frenchmen
Latah (Observed in Malaysia)
Myriachit (Observed in Siberia)

"Jumping Frenchmen" is a disorder characterized by an unusually extreme startle reaction. The startle reaction is a natural response to an unexpected noise or sight. This disorder was first identified during the late nineteenth century in Maine and the Canadian province of Quebec. Lumberjacks of French Canadian descent were originally associated with this phenomenon but it has since been observed in other societies in many parts of the world as well. "Jumping Frenchmen" is suspected to be a genetic disorder and/or an extreme conditioned response to a particular situation possibly influenced by cultural factors. Symptoms tend to improve with age.

The following organization may provide additional information and support:
National Institute of Neurological Disorders and Stroke (NINDS)

599 Kabuki Make-up Syndrome

Synonyms
KMS
Niikawakuroki Syndrome

Kabuki make-up syndrome is a rare disorder characterized by mental retardation, short stature, unusual facial features, abnormalities of the skeleton and unusual skin ridge patterns on the fingers, toes, palms of the hands and soles of the feet. The majority of the reported cases of this disor-

der have occurred for no apparent reason (sporadic). However, several cases have been reported to be inherited as an autosomal dominant trait.

The following organization may provide additional information and support:
National Institute of Neurological Disorders and Stroke (NINDS)

600 Kallmann Syndrome

Synonyms
Hypogonadism with Anosmia
Hypogonadotropic Hypogonadism and Anosmia

Kallmann syndrome is a rare inherited disorder in which the organ that produces sex cells does not function properly (hypogonadism) and there is a loss of the sense of smell (anosmia). The impaired production of hormones as well as sperm and egg cells often causes delayed puberty, growth and infertility. This disorder affects both males and females, although it is more common in males.

The following organizations may provide additional information and support:
March of Dimes Birth Defects Foundation
NIH/National Institute of Child Health and Human Development

601 Kartagener Syndrome

Synonyms
Chronic Sinobronchial Disease and Dextrocardia
Dextrocardia, Bronchiectasis and Sinusitis
Kartagener Triad
Primary Ciliary Dyskinesia, Kartagener Type
Siewert Syndrome
Situs Inversus, Bronchiectasis and Sinusitis

Kartagener syndrome is a genetic disorder combining three major symptoms. These include chronic enlargement of the bronchial tubes (bronchiectasis), chronic inflammation of the lining of the sinuses (sinusitis), and abnormal cross-positioning of body organs during prenatal development (situs inversus).

The following organizations may provide additional information and support:
American Lung Association
PCD Foundation

602 Kawasaki Disease

Synonyms

Kawasaki Syndrome
MLNS
Mucocutaneous Lymph Node Syndrome

Kawasaki disease is an acute multisystem inflammatory disease of blood vessels (vasculitis) that most commonly affects infants and young children. The disease may be characterized by a high fever, inflammation of the mucous membranes of the mouth and throat, a reddish skin rash, and swelling of lymph nodes (lymphadenopathy). In addition, individuals with Kawasaki disease may develop inflammation of arteries that transport blood to heart muscle (coronary arteritis), associated widening or bulging (aneurysms) of the walls of affected coronary arteries, inflammation of heart muscle (myocarditis), and/or other symptoms and findings. Kawasaki disease is the primary cause of acquired heart disease in children in the United States. Although the cause of the disease is unknown, it is widely thought to be due to infection or an abnormal immune response to infection.

The following organizations may provide additional information and support:
Autoimmune Information Network, Inc
Centers for Disease Control and Prevention
Congenital Heart Information Network
Kawasaki Families' Network
NIH/National Institute of Allergy and Infectious Diseases

603 KBG Syndrome

Synonym

Short Stature, Facial/Skeletal Anomalies-Retardation-Macrodontia

KBG syndrome is a very rare genetic disorder characterized by short stature, moderate to severe degrees of mental retardation, developmental abnormalities of the limbs, bones of the spine (vertebrae), extremities, and/or underdevelopment of the bones of the skeleton. Abnormalities of the head and face (craniofacial dysmorphism) and malformations of the teeth and jaws (dento-skeletal dysplasia) may also be present. The exact cause of KBG syndrome is unknown, but most cases are believed to be autosomal dominant traits with variable degree of penetrance.

The following organizations may provide additional information and support:
The Arc (A National Organization on Mental Retardation)
Children's Craniofacial Association
FACES: The National Craniofacial Association
New York State Institute for Basic Research in Developmental Disabilities
NIH/National Institute of Child Health and Human Development
NIH/National Institute of Dental and Craniofacial Research

604 Kearns-Sayre Syndrome

Synonyms

CPEO with Myopathy
CPEO with Ragged-Red Fibers
Chronic Progressive External Ophthalmoplegia and Myopathy
Chronic Progressive External Ophthalmoplegia with Ragged Red Fibers
KSS
Kearns-Sayre Disease
Mitochondrial Cytopathy, Kearn-Sayre Type
Oculocraniosomatic Syndrome (obsolete)
Ophthalmoplegia, Pigmentary Degeneration of the Retina and Cadiomyopathy
Ophthalmoplegia Plus Syndrome

Kearns-Sayre syndrome is a rare neuromuscular disorder characterized by three primary findings: progressive paralysis of certain eye muscles (chronic progressive external ophthalmoplegia [CPEO]); abnormal accumulation of colored (pigmented) material on the nerve-rich membrane lining the eyes (atypical retinitis pigmentosa), leading to chronic inflammation, progressive degeneration, and wearing away of certain eye structures (pigmentary degeneration of the retina); and heart disease (cardiomyopathy) such as heart block. Other findings may include muscle weakness, short stature, hearing loss, and/or the loss of ability to coordinate voluntary movements (ataxia) due to problems affecting part of the brain (cerebellum). In some cases, Kearns-Sayre syndrome may be associated with other disorders and/or conditions. Kearns-Sayre syndrome belongs (in part) to a group of rare neuromuscular disorders known as mitochondrial encephalomyopathies. Mitochondrial encephalomyopathies are disorders in which a defect in genetic material arises from a part of the cell structure that releases energy (mitochondria), causing the brain and muscles to function improperly (encephalomyopathies). In these disorders, abnormally high numbers of defective mitochondria are present. In approximately 80 percent of cases of Kearns-Sayre syndrome, tests will reveal missing genetic material (deletion) involving the unique DNA in mitochondria (mtDNA). This disease entry was made possible due to the generosity of the Robert Lee and Clara Guthrie Patterson Trust, through grant funds provided for the National Organization for Rare Disorders' "Pediatric Rare Disease Database Project."

The following organizations may provide additional information and support:
American Heart Association
Foundation Fighting Blindness, Inc.
March of Dimes Birth Defects Foundation
National Association for Visually Handicapped
National Institute of Neurological Disorders and Stroke (NINDS)
NIH/National Arthritis and Musculoskeletal and Skin Diseases Information Clearinghouse
NIH/National Eye Institute
United Mitochondrial Disease Foundation

605 Kennedy Disease

Synonyms
KD
SBMA
Spinal and Bulbar Muscular Atrophy
X-linked Spinal and Bulbar Muscular Atrophy

Kennedy disease is a rare, slowly progressive muscular disorder that affects males only and is inherited as an X-linked genetic trait. Uncontrollable twitching (fasciculations) followed by weakness and wasting of the muscles becomes apparent sometime after the age of fifteen. The muscles of the face, lips, tongue, mouth, throat, vocal chords, trunk and limbs may be affected. Very large calves may also be found in some patients with this disorder. Kennedy disease is caused by a mutation in the androgen receptor (AR) gene. Androgen insensitivity leads to abnormal swelling of the breasts (gynecomastia), small testes and infertility.

The following organizations may provide additional information and support:
Families of Spinal Muscular Atrophy
Kennedy's Disease Association
Muscular Dystrophy Association
National Ataxia Foundation
National Institute of Neurological Disorders and Stroke (NINDS)

606 Kenny-Caffey Syndrome

Synonyms
Dwarfism, Cortical Thickening of the Tubular Bones & Transient Hypocalcemia
Kenny Disease
Kenny Syndrome
Medullary Stenosis, Congenital
Tubular Stenosis, Kenny Type

Disorder Subdivisions
KCS2
Kenny-Caffey Syndrome, Dominant Type
Kenny-Caffey Syndrome, Recessive Type

Kenny-Caffey syndrome is an extremely rare hereditary skeletal disorder characterized by thickening of the long bones, thin marrow cavities in the bones (medullary stenosis), and abnormalities affecting the head and eyes. Most cases are obvious at birth (congenital). The primary outcome of Kenny-Caffey syndrome is short stature. Mental abilities are rarely affected. Individuals with Kenny-Caffey syndrome may also have recurrent episodes of low levels of calcium in the blood stream (hypocalcemia) that is caused by insufficient production of parathyroid hormones (hypoparathyroidism). In most cases, Kenny-Caffey syndrome is inherited as an autosomal dominant trait. Other cases are inherited as an autosomal recessive trait. X-linked autosomal recessive inheritance has not been ruled out.

The following organizations may provide additional information and support:
Children's Craniofacial Association
FACES: The National Craniofacial Association
Human Growth Foundation
Hypoparathyroidism Association, Inc.
Little People of America, Inc.
Little People's Research Fund, Inc.

607 Keratitis Ichthyosis Deafness Syndrome

Synonyms
Ichthyosiform Erythroderma, Corneal Involvement, and Deafness Syndrome
KID Syndrome

Keratitis, ichthyosis, deafness (KID) syndrome is a rare, genetic, multi-system disorder. It is characterized by defects of the surface of the corneas (keratitis), red, rough thickened plaques of skin (erythrokeratoderma) and sensorineural deafness or severe hearing impairment. The skin on the palms of the hands and soles of the feet and the nails may be affected.

The following organizations may provide additional information and support:
Foundation for Ichthyosis & Related Skin Types
NIH/National Arthritis and Musculoskeletal and Skin Diseases Information Clearinghouse
NIH/National Eye Institute

608   Keratoconjunctivitis, Vernal

Synonyms
Seasonal Conjunctivitis
Spring Ophthalmia
VKC

Vernal keratoconjunctivitis is a non-contagious, seasonal allergic disorder usually appearing during the spring or warm weather. Major symptoms include hard, cobblestone-like bumps (papillae) on the upper eyelid, stringy or mucous discharge, inflammation of the mucous membrane lining the inside of the eyelid (conjunctiva) and the tough, white, outer coat of the eyeball (sclera), sensitivity to light and intense itching.

The following organizations may provide additional information and support:
NIH/National Eye Institute
NIH/National Institute of Allergy and Infectious Diseases

609   Keratoconus

Synonyms
Conical Cornea
KC

Keratoconus is a non-inflammatory eye (ocular) condition characterized by progressive changes of the shape of the cornea. The cornea is the thin-walled, "dome-shaped" transparent region forming the front of the eyeball; it serves as a protective covering and helps to focus or bend (refract) light waves onto the retina at the back of the eye. In those with keratoconus, slowly progressive thinning of the cornea causes it to protrude forward in a conical shape, leading to blurry vision and other vision problems. Keratoconus often begins at puberty. Although the specific underlying cause of the condition is unknown, investigators indicate that genetic factors may play some role. In addition, in some cases,

keratoconus may occur in association with a variety of other disorders.

The following organizations may provide additional information and support:
Eye Bank Association of America
National Association for Visually Handicapped
National Keratoconus Assistance Foundation
National Keratoconus Foundation
NIH/National Eye Institute

610   Keratomalacia

Keratomalacia is an eye (ocular) condition, usually affecting both eyes (bilateral), that results from severe deficiency of vitamin A. That deficiency may be dietary (i.e., intake) or metabolic (i.e., absorption). Vitamin A is essential for normal vision as well as proper bone growth, healthy skin, and protection of the mucous membranes of the digestive, respiratory, and urinary tracts against infection. Early symptoms may include poor vision at night or in dim light (night blindness) and extreme dryness of the eyes (i.e., xerophthalmia), followed by wrinkling, progressive cloudiness, and increasing softening of the corneas (i.e., keratomalacia). With advancing vitamin A deficiency, dry, "foamy," silver-gray deposits (Bitot spots) may appear on the delicate membranes covering the whites of the eyes. Without adequate treatment, increasing softening of the corneas may lead to corneal infection, rupture (perforation), and degenerative tissue changes, resulting in blindness. In addition, in some cases, vitamin A deficiency may have additional effects, particularly during infancy and childhood. In some developing countries, vitamin A deficiency in the diet and associated keratomalacia are a major cause of childhood blindness. In such regions, vitamin A deficiency often occurs as part of nonselective general malnutrition in infants and young children. Although rare in developed countries, vitamin A deficiency and keratomalacia may occur secondary to conditions associated with impaired absorption, storage, or transport of vitamin A, such as celiac disease, ulcerative colitis, cystic fibrosis, liver disease, or intestinal bypass surgery and any condition that affects absorption of fat-soluble vitamins.

The following organizations may provide additional information and support:
Blind Children's Center
National Association for Visually Handicapped
National Eye Research Foundation

NIH/National Digestive Diseases Information Clearinghouse
NIH/National Eye Institute
Prevent Blindness America
World Health Organization (WHO) Regional Office for the Americas (AMRO)

611 Keratosis Follicularis

Synonyms
Darier Disease
Darier-White Disease
Dyskeratosis Follicularis Vegetans
Psorospermosis Follicularis
White-Darier Disease

Keratosis follicularis (KF) is a rare, gradually progressive, hereditary skin disorder. It is characterized by wart-like spots and/or broader, rough areas (papules, plaques) on the scalp, forehead, face, neck, area behind the ears, and the central torso, back and front. In addition, thickening and discoloration of the nails in association with the skin changes is a reliable sign. Some mild neurological and psychiatric symptoms are sometimes associated with KF. Keratosis follicularis is inherited as an autosomal dominant genetic trait.

The following organizations may provide additional information and support:
Foundation for Ichthyosis & Related Skin Types
March of Dimes Birth Defects Foundation
NIH/National Arthritis and Musculoskeletal and Skin Diseases Information Clearinghouse

612 Keratosis, Seborrheic

Synonyms
Acanthotic Nevus
Keratosis Seborrheica
Seborrheic Warts
Senile Warts
Verruca

Seborrheic keratosis is a skin disorder usually characterized by discolored lesions that appear to be "stuck on" the skin surface. Warts may appear and skin is often oily or greasy. These skin lesions are sometimes mistaken for cancerous growths and tend to appear predominately during middle age. Itching, irritation, inflammations or unsightliness of lesions may require surgical removal of affected skin areas.

The following organization may provide additional information and support:
NIH/National Arthritis and Musculoskeletal and Skin Diseases Information Clearinghouse

613 Kernicterus

Synonym
Bilirubin Encephalopathy

Kernicterus is a rare neurological disorder characterized by excessive levels of bilirubin in the blood (hyperbilirubinemia) during infancy. Bilirubin is an orange-yellow bile pigment that is a by-product of the natural breakdown of hemoglobin in red blood cells (hemolysis). Toxic levels of bilirubin may accumulate in the brain, potentially resulting in a variety of symptoms and physical findings. These symptoms may include lack of energy (lethargy), poor feeding habits, fever, and vomiting. Affected infants may also experience the absence of certain reflexes (e.g., Moro reflex, etc.); mild to severe muscle spasms including those in which the head and heels are bent backward and the body bows forward (opisthotonus); and/or uncontrolled involuntary muscle movements (spasticity). In some cases, infants with kernicterus may develop life-threatening complications.

The following organizations may provide additional information and support:
American Liver Foundation
March of Dimes Birth Defects Foundation
NIH/National Institute of Diabetes, Digestive & Kidney Diseases
Parents of Infants and Children with Kernicterus

614 Kienbock Disease

Synonyms
Lunatomalacia
Osteochondrosis of the Lunate Bone

Kienbock disease is an acquired bone disorder. Abnormalities of the lunate bone in the wrist develops following an injury or inflammation. Recurrent pain and stiffness occur in conjunction with thickening, swelling and tenderness in soft tissue overlying the lunate bone. The range of motion in the wrist may become limited.

The following organization may provide additional information and support:
NIH/National Arthritis and Musculoskeletal and Skin Diseases Information Clearinghouse

615 Kikuchi's Disease

Synonyms

Histiocytic Necrotizing Lymphadenitis
HNL
Kikuchi-Fujimoto Disease
Kikuchi's Histiocytic Necrotizing Lymphadenitis
Necrotizing Lymphadenitis

Kikuchi's disease, also known as histiocytic necrotizing lymphadenopathy, is a rare, benign (non-cancerous, nonmalignant) disorder of the lymph nodes of young adults, predominantly of young women. This disorder is often mistaken for malignant lymphoma, especially cervical adenopathy because the symptoms are very similar. The lesions, or tissue anomalies of this disorder cause the lymph nodes to become enlarged, inflamed and painful. The exact cause of Kikuchi's disease is not known. Perhaps the primary threat is a misdiagnosis of a malignant lymphoma.

The following organization may provide additional information and support:
NIH/National Institute of Allergy and Infectious Diseases

616 Kleine-Levin Syndrome

Synonyms

Familial Hibernation Syndrome
Kleine-Levin Hibernation Syndrome
Periodic Somnolence and Morbid Hunger

Kleine-Levin syndrome is a rare disorder characterized by the need for excessive amounts of sleep (hypersomnolence), (i.e., up to 20 hours a day); excessive food intake (compulsive hyperphagia); and an abnormally uninhibited sexual drive. The disorder primarily affects adolescent males. When awake, affected individuals may exhibit irritability, lack of energy (lethargy), and/or lack of emotions (apathy). They may also appear confused (disoriented) and experience hallucinations. Symptoms of Kleine-Levin syndrome are cyclical. An affected individual may go for weeks or months without experiencing symptoms. When present, symptoms may persist for days to weeks. In some cases, the symptoms associated with Kleine-Levin syndrome eventually disappear with advancing age. However, episodes may recur later during life.The exact cause of Kleine-Levin syndrome is not known. However, researchers believe that in some cases, hereditary factors may cause some individuals to have a genetic predis-

position to developing the disorder. It is thought that symptoms of Kleine-Levin syndrome may be related to malfunction of the portion of the brain that helps to regulate functions such as sleep, appetite, and body temperature (hypothalamus). Some researchers speculate that Kleine-Levin syndrome may be an autoimmune disorder.

The following organizations may provide additional information and support:
American Sleep Disorders Association
Kleine-Levin Syndrome Foundation
National Institute of Neurological Disorders and Stroke (NINDS)
National Mental Health Association
National Mental Health Consumers' Self-Help Clearinghouse
National Sleep Foundation
NIH/National Institute of Mental Health

617 Klinefelter Syndrome

Synonyms

Chromosome 46, XY/47,XXY (Mosiac)
Chromosome 48 XXXY
Chromosome 48 XXYY
Chromosome XXY
Hypergonadotropic Hypogonadism
Primary Hypogonadism
Seminiferous Tubule Dysgenesis

The classic form of Klinefelter syndrome causes impaired function of the testes (primary hypogonadism) in males. This rare disorder is characterized by the presence of an extra X chromosome. Klinefelter syndrome may not be diagnosed until puberty because the symptoms may be very subtle until that age and secondary sex characteristics are not apparent before puberty.

The following organizations may provide additional information and support:
49XXXXY
American Association for Klinefelter Syndrome Information and Support
Intersex Society of North America
Klinefelter Syndrome & Associates
Klinefelter Syndrome Association of Canada
Klinefelter's Syndrome Support Group of Australia (K.S.S.G)
March of Dimes Birth Defects Foundation
NIH/National Institute of Child Health and Human Development
XXYY Project

618 Klippel-Trenaunay Syndrome

Synonyms
Angio-Osteohypertrophy Syndrome
Congenital Dysplastic Angiectasia
Elephantiasis Congenita Angiomatosa
Hemangiectatic Hypertrophy
Klippel-Trenaunay-Weber Syndrome
KTS
KTW Syndrome
Osteohypertrophic Nevus Flammeus

Disorder Subdivision
Parkes-Weber Syndrome

Klippel-Trenaunay syndrome, a rare disorder that is present at birth (congenital), is characterized by abnormal benign growths on the skin (cutaneous) consisting of masses of blood vessels (hemangiomas), excessive growth (hypertrophy) of the soft tissue and bone of a leg and/or arm (limb), and varicose veins. (In individuals with the disorder, such hypertrophy typically affects one side of the body [hemihypertrophy].) In many cases, hemangiomas may consist of distinctive purplish-reddish birthmarks ("port wine stain" or nevus flammeus) on certain areas of the skin. The symptoms and findings associated with the disorder may vary in range and severity from case to case.

The following organizations may provide additional information and support:
Klippel-Trenaunay Support Group
Lymphovenous Canada
March of Dimes Birth Defects Foundation
National Institute of Neurological Disorders and Stroke (NINDS)
Nevus Network
The Sturge-Weber Foundation

619 Klippel-Feil Syndrome

Synonyms
Cervical Vertebral Fusion
Congenital Cervical Synostosis
KFS

Disorder Subdivisions
Klippel-Feil Syndrome, Type I
Klippel-Feil Syndrome, Type II
Klippel-Feil Syndrome, Type III

Klippel-Feil syndrome (KFS) is a rare condition that is evident at birth (congenital). KFS is primarily characterized by abnormal union or fusion of two or more bones of the spinal column (vertebrae) within the neck (cervical vertebrae). Some affected individuals may also have an abnormally short neck, restricted movement of the head and neck, and a low hairline at the back of the head (posterior hairline). In some individuals with KFS, the condition may be associated with additional physical abnormalities. These may include abnormal curvature of the spine (scoliosis), rib defects, or other skeletal abnormalities; hearing impairment; certain malformations of the head and facial (craniofacial) area; or structural abnormalities of the heart (congenital heart defects). In addition, in some cases, neurological complications may result due to associated spinal cord injury. In most individuals with KFS, the condition appears to occur randomly for unknown reasons (sporadically). However, in other cases, KFS may be inherited as an autosomal dominant or autosomal recessive trait.

The following organizations may provide additional information and support:
KFS (Klippel-Feil Syndrome) Network Online
Klippel-Feil Syndrome Support Line
Let Them Hear Foundation
NIH/National Arthritis and Musculoskeletal and Skin Diseases Information Clearinghouse

620 Kluver-Bucy Syndrome

Synonym
Bilateral Temporal Lobe Disorder

Kluver-Bucy syndrome is a very rare cerebral neurological disorder. Major symptoms may include an urge to put all kinds of objects into the mouth, memory loss, extreme sexual behavior, placidity, and visual distractibility.

The following organizations may provide additional information and support:
Alzheimer's Association
Alzheimer's Disease Education and Referral Center
National Institute of Neurological Disorders and Stroke (NINDS)
NIH/National Institute on Deafness and Other Communication Disorders (Balance)

621 Kniest Dysplasia

Synonyms
Kniest Syndrome
Kniest Chondrodystrophy
Metatropic Dwarfism, Type II
Metatropic Dysplasia, Type II
Swiss Cheese Cartilage Syndrome

Kniest dysplasia is one of several forms of dwarfism that is caused by a change (mutation) in a gene known as COL2A1. This gene is involved in the production of a particular protein that forms type 2 collagen, which is essential for the normal development of bones and other connective tissue. Changes in the composition of type 2 collagen lead to abnormal skeletal growth and, thus, to a variety of dwarfing conditions known as skeletal dysplasias. Some of the signs and symptoms of Kniest dysplasia, such as short stature, enlarged knees, and cleft palate, are usually present at birth. Other characteristics may not appear for 2 or 3 years.

The following organizations may provide additional information and support:
Human Growth Foundation
Kniest SED Group
Little People of America, Inc.
Little People's Research Fund, Inc.
MAGIC Foundation for Children's Growth
Restricted Growth Association

622   Kohler Disease

Synonyms
Kohler's Disease (of the Tarsal Navicular)
Kohler's Osteochondrosis of the Tarsal Navicular
Navicular Osteochondrosis

Kohler disease is a rare bone disorder of the foot in children that may be the result of stress-related compression at a critical time during the period of growth. It is characterized by limping caused by pain and swelling in the foot. It most often occurs in children between the ages of three and seven, and it affects males five times more often than it does females. Typically, just one foot is affected. Children appear to grow out of the disorder, and the affected bones regain their size, density and structure within a year. For some, however, symptoms may last as long as 2 years.

The following organization may provide additional information and support:
NIH/National Institute of Arthritis and Musculoskeletal and Skin Diseases

623   Kufs Disease

Synonyms
Adult-Onset Ceroidosis
Amaurotic Familial Idiocy, Adult
Ceroid-Lipofuscinosis, Adult Form
Generalized Lipofuscinosis
Neuronal Ceroid Lipofuscinosis, Adult Type

Kufs disease is characterized by neurologic symptoms that may mimic mental illness, movement malfunction, and problems with sight. Kufs disease is linked to excess accumulations of pigments (lipofuscins) dissolved in fat tissues that are found throughout the central nervous system. Kufs disease, Batten disease, Bielchowsky disease, and Santavuori-Haltia disease are different forms of the same family of disorders (neuronal ceroid lipofuscinoses [NCL]) that are differentiated by the age of onset. The various forms of this disorder are often extremely difficult to differentiate from other progressive degenerative diseases of the central nervous system.

The following organizations may provide additional information and support:
The Arc (A National Organization on Mental Retardation)
Children's Brain Diseases Foundation
National Institute of Neurological Disorders and Stroke (NINDS)
National Tay-Sachs and Allied Diseases Association, Inc.

624   Kugelberg Welander Syndrome

Synonyms
Juvenile Spinal Muscular Atrophy
KWS
SMA3
Spinal Muscular Atrophy Type 3

Kugelberg Welander syndrome is a type of spinal muscular atrophy. It is a rare inherited neuromuscular disorder characterized by wasting and weakness in the muscles of the arms and legs, twitching, clumsiness in walking, and eventual loss of reflexes. Symptoms of Kugelberg Welander syndrome occur after 12 months of age. Patients learn to walk but fall frequently and have trouble walking up and down stairs at 2-3 years of age. The legs are more severely affected than the arms. The long-term prognosis depends on the degree of motor function attained as a child. Kugelberg Welander syndrome is inherited as an autosomal recessive trait. Molecular genetic testing has revealed that all types of autosomal recessive SMA are caused by mutations in the SMN (survival motor neuron) gene on chromosome 5. Deletion of the NAIP (neuronal apoptosis inhibitory protein) gene that is close to the SMN gene is also associated with SMA. More patients with Werdnig Hoffman disease (SMA1) than other types of SMA have NAIP deletions. The relationship between specific mutations in the SMN gene and nearby genes and the severity of SMA is still being investigated so classification of SMA subdivisions is based on age of onset of symptoms as opposed to the genetic profile.

The following organizations may provide additional information and support:
Families of Spinal Muscular Atrophy
Jennifer Trust for Spinal Muscular Atrophy
March of Dimes Birth Defects Foundation
Muscular Dystrophy Association
National Institute of Neurological Disorders and Stroke (NINDS)

625 L1 Syndrome

Synonyms
Adducted Thumbs-Mental Retardation
Congenital Clasped Thumb with Mental Retardation
Garies-Mason Syndrome
Mental Retardation, Aphasia, Shuffling Gait, Adducted Thumbs (MASA)
X-linked Mental Retardation-Clasped Thumb Syndrome

L1 syndrome is a genetic condition occurring in males that usually includes hydrocephalus, mental retardation, spasticity of legs and clasped (adducted) thumbs. L1 syndrome is caused by an abnormality (mutation) in the L1CAM gene. Different types of mutations result in different disease characteristics, but disease severity is variable, even in affected members of the same family.

The following organizations may provide additional information and support:
Guardians of Hydrocephalus Research Foundation
Hydrocephalus Association
National Aphasia Association
National Hydrocephalus Foundation
National Institute of Neurological Disorders and Stroke (NINDS)
NIH/National Institute on Deafness and Other Communication Disorders Information Clearinghouse

626 Laband Syndrome

Synonyms
Gingival Fibromatosis, Abnormal Fingers, Nails, Nose, Ear, Splenomegaly
Zimmermann-Laband Syndrome
ZLS

Laband syndrome is an extremely rare inherited disorder characterized by abnormalities of the head and facial (craniofacial) area and the hands and feet. Most children with this disorder have abnormally large gums (gingival fibromatosis). Overgrown gums may affect the ability to chew, swallow, and/or speak. In addition, affected infants may exhibit abnormally long, thin fingers and toes and/or deformed (dysplastic) or absent nails at birth. In some cases, mental retardation may also be present. Laband syndrome is inherited as an autosomal dominant trait.

The following organizations may provide additional information and support:
NIH/National Institute of Arthritis and Musculoskeletal and Skin Diseases
NIH/National Institute of Dental and Craniofacial Research

627 Lactose Intolerance

Synonyms
Alactasia
Disaccharidase Deficiency
Glucose-Galactose Malabsorption
Hypolactasia
Lactase Deficiency
Lactase Isolated Intolerance

Disorder Subdivisions
Congenital Lactose Intolerance
Lactose Intolerance of Adulthood
Lactose Intolerance of Childhood
Neonatal Lactose Intolerance

Lactose is the predominant sugar found in milk and milk products. People with lactose intolerance (LI) cannot properly digest lactose because they lack or are deficient in the enzyme, lactase, which is key to the digestion of lactose. Lactose is a complex sugar made up of two different sugar molecules (disaccharide), galactose and glucose, each of which is a simple (monosaccharide) sugar and more readily absorbed in the body's stomach and intestine and processed in other organs. LI is common among adults in the United States and elsewhere. It is worrisome and uncomfortable but not at all dangerous. This disorder is an inborn error of carbohydrate metabolism characterized by the impaired ability to absorb nutrients from the small intestine (malabsorption syndrome).

The following organizations may provide additional information and support:
March of Dimes Birth Defects Foundation
NIH/National Institute of Diabetes, Digestive & Kidney Diseases

628 LADD Syndrome

Synonyms

Lacrimo-Auriculo-Dento-Digital Syndrome
LADD
Levy-Hollister Syndrome
Limb Malformations-Dento-Digital Syndrome

LADD syndrome is a rare genetic disorder characterized primarily by malformations of the upper limbs and inherited through an autosomal dominant trait. Other symptoms of the disorder may include: malformations in the structures and ducts that secrete tears and drain them from the surface of the eyeball (the lacrimal apparatus); abnormalities of the teeth; small cupped ears; absent or underdeveloped salivary glands; hearing loss; abnormalities of the sexual and urinary system of the body (genitourinary) and/or unusual skin ridge patterns.

The following organizations may provide additional information and support:
Genetic and Rare Diseases (GARD) Information Center
NIH/National Arthritis and Musculoskeletal and Skin Diseases Information Clearinghouse

629 Lambert-Eaton Myasthenic Syndrome

Synonyms

Eaton-Lambert Syndrome
Lambert-Eaton Syndrome
Myasthenic Syndrome of Lambert-Eaton

Lambert-Eaton myasthenic syndrome (LEMS) is a rare autoimmune disorder characterized by the gradual onset of muscle weakness, especially of the pelvic and thigh muscles. Approximately 60 percent of LEMS cases are associated with a small cell lung cancer, and the onset of LEMS symptoms often precedes the detection of the cancer. The LEMS patients with cancer tend to be older and nearly always have a long history of smoking. In cases in which there is no associated cancer, disease onset can be at any age.

The following organizations may provide additional information and support:
American Autoimmune Related Diseases Association, Inc.
Autoimmune Information Network, Inc
March of Dimes Birth Defects Foundation
Muscular Dystrophy Association
Myasthenia Gravis Foundation of America
National Institute of Neurological Disorders and Stroke (NINDS)

630 Landau Kleffner Syndrome

Synonyms

Acquired Aphasia with Convulsive Disorder
Acquired Epileptic Aphasia
Infantile Acquired Aphasia
LKS

Landau-Kleffner syndrome is a rare neurological disorder of childhood that is characterized by the loss of the ability to understand speech and deterioration of previously acquired speech and language skills (aphasia). Most children with Landau-Kleffner syndrome also experience episodes of uncontrolled electrical disturbances in the brain (convulsive epileptic seizures). Some affected children also lose the ability to identify environmental sounds and show a general lack of attention to sounds (auditory agnosia). The exact cause of this disorder is not known. Symptoms, which develop due to brain dysfunction, vary greatly among affected individuals.

The following organizations may provide additional information and support:
American Speech-Language-Hearing Association
Epilepsy Canada
Epilepsy Foundation
FOLKS: Friends of Landau Kleffner Syndrome
National Aphasia Association
National Institute of Neurological Disorders and Stroke (NINDS)
NIH/National Institute on Deafness and Other Communication Disorders (Balance)

631 Langerhans Cell Histiocytosis

Synonyms

Histiocytosis X
Langerhans-Cell Granulomatosis
LCH
Non-Lipid Reticuloendotheliosis
Systemic Aleukemic Reticuloendotheliosis
Type II Histiocytosis

Disorder Subdivisions

Abt-Letterer-Siwe Disease
Eosinophilic Granuloma
Hand-Schueller-Christian Syndrome
Hashimoto-Pritzker Syndrome
Letterer-Siwe Disease
Pure Cutaneous Histiocytosis
Self-Healing Histiocytosis

Langerhans cell histiocytosis (LCH) is a rare spectrum of disorders characterized by overproduction (proliferation) and accumulation of a specific type of white blood cell (histiocyte) in the various tissues and organs of the body (lesions). The lesions may include certain distinctive granule-containing cells (Langerhans cells) involved in certain immune responses, as well as other white blood cells (e.g., monocytes, eosinophils). Associated symptoms and findings may vary from case to case, depending upon the specific tissues and organs affected and the extent of involvement. Most affected individuals have single or multiple bone lesions characterized by degenerative changes and loss of the calcium of bone (osteolysis). Although the skull is most commonly affected, there may also be involvement of other bones, such as those of the spine (vertebrae) and the long bones of the arms and legs. Affected individuals may have no apparent symptoms (asymptomatic), and may experience associated pain and swelling, and/or develop certain complications, such as fractures or secondary compression of the spinal cord. In some cases, other tissues and organs may also be affected, including the skin, lungs, or other areas. In some individuals, LCH may be associated with involvement of the pituitary gland leading to diabetes insipidus. The exact cause of Langerhans cell histiocytosis is unknown. Langerhans cell histiocytosis was selected by the Histiocyte Society to replace the older, less specific term histiocytosis X. Histiocytosis X encompassed three entities known as eosinophilic granuloma, Hand-Schuller-Christian disease, and Letterer-Siwe disease that were characterized by the accumulation of histiocytes. The "X" denoted that the cause and development of the disorder was not understood. Langerhans cell histiocytosis was chosen because it is now known that Langerhans cells play the central role in the development of these disorders.

The following organizations may provide additional information and support:
American Lung Association
Diabetes Insipidus Foundation, Inc.
Histiocytosis Association of America
Histiocytosis Association of Canada
March of Dimes Birth Defects Foundation
NIH/National Heart, Lung and Blood Institute Information Center

632 Laron Syndrome

Synonyms
GHBP
GHR
Growth Hormone Binding Protein Deficiency or Dysfunction
Growth Hormone Receptor Deficiency or Dysfunction
Laron Dwarfism
Laron Type Pituitary Dwarfism I
LTD1
Pituitary Dwarfism II

Laron syndrome type I (LTD1), a rare genetic disorder, is caused by the body's inability to use the growth hormone (GH) that it produces. The problem lies not in the production of growth hormone but rather in a defective GH-receptor gene. This defect prevents the proper binding of the GH molecule, leaving high levels of unbound growth hormone in the plasma. Laron syndrome is characterized by short stature and delayed bone age, as well as high levels of circulating growth hormone. A second form of the disorder known as Laron syndrome type II (LTD2) shows typical clinical features of the Laron syndrome but is due to a defect in the biochemical processing of growth hormone after the hormone has been bound on the cell surface.

The following organizations may provide additional information and support:
Human Growth Foundation
Little People of America, Inc.
Little People's Research Fund, Inc.
MAGIC Foundation for Children's Growth

633 Larsen Syndrome

Synonyms
Desbuquois Syndrome
Joint Dislocations/Unusual Facies/Skeletal Abnormalities
Multiple Joint Dislocations, Larson-like Skeletal Abnormalities/Joint Dislocations/Unusual Facies

Larsen syndrome is a rare genetic disorder in which associated features may vary greatly in range and severity from case to case. However, primary features may include multiple joint dislocations; foot deformities; non-tapering, cylindrically shaped fingers; and/or an unusual facial appearance. In some cases, additional features may be present, such as short stature, additional skeletal abnormalities, incomplete closure of the roof of the mouth (cleft palate), heart defects, hearing impairment, mental retardation, and/or other abnormalities.

The following organizations may provide additional information and support:

The Arc (A National Organization on Mental Retardation)
Children's Craniofacial Association
Congenital Heart Anomalies, Support, Education, & Resources
FACES: The National Craniofacial Association
Little People of America, Inc.
March of Dimes Birth Defects Foundation
NIH/National Arthritis and Musculoskeletal and Skin Diseases Information Clearinghouse

634 Laurence Moon Syndrome

Synonyms

Adipogenital-Retinitis Pigmentosa Syndrome
Laurence Syndrome
LM Syndrome

Laurence-Moon syndrome is a rare inherited disorder characterized by diminished hormone production by the testes or ovaries (hypogonadism), progressive loss of vision (retinitis pigmentosa), mental retardation, and paralysis of the legs and lower part of the body accompanied by involuntary muscle contractions (spastic paraplegia). Confusion exists in the medical literature regarding the difference between Laurence-Moon syndrome and Bardet-Biedl syndrome. Some researchers believe that Bardet-Biedl syndrome is a subdivision of Laurence-Moon syndrome, which they term "Laurence-Moon-Biedl syndrome."

The following organizations may provide additional information and support:
American Council of the Blind, Inc.
American Foundation for the Blind
The Arc (A National Organization on Mental Retardation)
Blind Children's Fund
Council of Families with Visual Impairment
Laurence Moon Bardet Biedl Syndrome
March of Dimes Birth Defects Foundation
National Association for Parents of Children with Visual Impairments (NAPVI)
National Association for Visually Handicapped
National Institute of Neurological Disorders and Stroke (NINDS)
Prevent Blindness America

635 Leber Hereditary Optic Neuropathy

Synonyms

Hereditary Optic Neuroretinopathy
Leber's Disease
Leber's Optic Atrophy
Leber's Optic Neuropathy (LHON)

Leber hereditary optic neuropathy (LHON) is a rare inherited disorder of the eye that is characterized by the relatively slow, painless, progressive loss of vision. This disorder can initially affect one eye or both, but both eyes are usually affected within 6 months. In most cases, visual loss is permanent. LHON is a genetic disorder that occurs as the result of a mutation in the mitochondrial DNA that is inherited from the mother or arises as a new sporadic mitochondrial DNA mutation.

The following organizations may provide additional information and support:
American Council of the Blind, Inc.
American Foundation for the Blind
Blind Children's Center
Council of Families with Visual Impairment
Guiding Eyes for the Blind, Inc.
International Foundation for Optic Nerve Disease (IFOND)
Macular Degeneration Support, Inc.
National Association for Parents of Children with Visual Impairments (NAPVI)
National Association for Visually Handicapped
National Federation of the Blind
NIH/National Eye Institute
United Mitochondrial Disease Foundation

636 Leber's Congenital Amaurosis

Synonyms

Congenital Absence of the Rods and Cones
Congenital Retinal Blindness
Congenital Retinitis Pigmentosa
LCA
Leber's Amaurosis
Leber's Congenital Tapetoretinal Degeneration
Leber's Congenital Tapetoretinal Dysplasia

Leber's congenital amaurosis (LCA) is a rare genetic eye disorder. Affected infants are often blind at birth or lose their sight within the first few of years of life. Other symptoms may include crossed eyes (strabismus); rapid, involuntary eye movements (nystagmus); unusual sensitivity to light (photophobia); clouding of the lenses of the eyes (cataracts); and/or abnormal protrusion of the front (anterior), clear portion of the eye through which light passes (cornea) (keratoconus). In addition, some infants may exhibit hearing loss, mental retardation, and/or a delay in the acquisition of skills that require the coordination of mental and muscular activity (psychomotor retardation).

Leber's congenital amaurosis is inherited as an autosomal recessive genetic trait.

The following organizations may provide additional information and support:
American Council of the Blind, Inc.
American Foundation for the Blind
Blind Children's Fund
Foundation Fighting Blindness (Canada)
Foundation Fighting Blindness, Inc.
Leber's Links: Leber's Congenital Amaurosis, Blindness, and Visual Impairment
National Association for Parents of Children with Visual Impairments (NAPVI)
National Association for Visually Handicapped
NIH/National Eye Institute
Retinitis Pigmentosa International

637 Legg-Calve-Perthes Disease

Synonyms
LCPD
Perthes Disease

Legg-Calve-Perthes disease (LCPD) is one of a group of disorders known as the osteochondroses. The osteochondroses typically are characterized by degeneration (avascular necrosis) and subsequent regeneration of the growing end of a bone (epiphyses). In Legg-Calve-Perthes disease, the growing end (epiphysis) of the upper portion (capital) of the thigh bone (femur) is affected. Researchers believe that an unexplained interruption of the blood supply (ischemia) to the capital femoral epiphysis results in degeneration (avascular necrosis) and deformity of the thigh bone in this area. Symptoms may include a limp with or without pain in the hip, knee, thigh, and/or groin; muscle spasms; delayed maturation of the femur (delayed bone age); mild short stature; and/or limited movements of the affected hip. The disease process seems to be self-limiting as new blood supplies are established (revascularization) and new healthy bone forms (reossifies) in the affected area. Most cases of Legg-Calve-Perthes disease occur randomly for no apparent reason (sporadically).

The following organizations may provide additional information and support:
March of Dimes Birth Defects Foundation
NIH/National Institute of Arthritis and Musculoskeletal and Skin Diseases

638 Legionnaires' Disease

Synonyms
Legionellosis
Pontiac Fever

Legionnaires' disease is recognized as an acute respiratory pneumonia caused by the aerobic gram-negative microorganism, Legionella pneumophila, and other species. This microorganism may also affect other body systems. Afflicted patients may have pulmonary (lung and bronchi), gastrointestinal tract, and central nervous system complications. Renal insufficiency may occur occasionally and can be severe enough to require dialysis.

The following organizations may provide additional information and support:
Centers for Disease Control and Prevention
NIH/National Institute of Allergy and Infectious Diseases
World Health Organization (WHO) Regional Office for the Americas (AMRO)

639 Leigh's Disease

Synonyms
Leigh Necrotizing Encephalopathy
Leigh's Syndrome
Necrotizing Encephalomyelopathy of Leigh's
SNE
Subacute Necrotizing Encephalopathy

Disorder Subdivisions
Adult-Onset Subacute Necrotizing Encephalomyelopathy
Classical Leigh's Disease
Infantile Necrotizing Encephalopathy
X-Linked Infantile Nectrotizing Encephalopathy

Leigh's disease is a rare inherited neurometabolic disorder. It is characterized by the degeneration of the central nervous system (i.e., brain, spinal cord, and optic nerve). The symptoms of Leigh's disease usually begin between the ages of 3 months and 2 years. Symptoms are associated with progressive neurological deterioration and may include loss of previously acquired motor skills, loss of appetite, vomiting, irritability, and/or seizure activity. As Leigh's disease progresses, symptoms may also include generalized weakness, lack of muscle tone, and episodes of lactic acidosis, which may lead to impairment of respiratory and kidney function. In most cases, Leigh's disease is inherited as an autosomal recessive genetic trait. However, autosomal dominant, X-linked recessive, and mitochondrial inheritance have also been noted. There appear to be several different types of genetically determined enzyme defects that can cause Leigh's disease.

The following organizations may provide additional information and support:
The Arc (A National Organization on Mental Retardation)
CLIMB (Children Living with Inherited Metabolic Diseases)
Children's Brain Diseases Foundation
Lactic Acidosis Support Trust
March of Dimes Birth Defects Foundation
National Institute of Neurological Disorders and Stroke (NINDS)
United Mitochondrial Disease Foundation

640 Lennox-Gastaut Syndrome

Synonym
LGS

Lennox-Gastaut syndrome (LGS) is a rare disorder that typically becomes apparent during infancy or early childhood. The disorder is characterized by frequent episodes of uncontrolled electrical disturbances in the brain (seizures) and, in many cases, abnormal delays in the acquisition of skills that require the coordination of mental and muscular activity (psychomotor retardation). Individuals with the disorder may experience several different types of seizures. Lennox-Gastaut syndrome may be due to or occur in association with a number of different underlying disorders or conditions.

The following organizations may provide additional information and support:
Epilepsy Foundation
National Institute of Neurological Disorders and Stroke (NINDS)

641 Lenz Microphthalmia Syndrome

Synonyms
Lenz Dysmorphogenetic Syndrome
Lenz Dysplasia
Lenz Syndrome
MAA
Microphthalmia or Anophthalmos with Associated Anomalies (obsolete)

Lenz microphthalmia syndrome is an extremely rare inherited disorder characterized by abnormal smallness of one or both eyes (unilateral or bilateral microphthalmos) and/or droopy eyelids (blepharoptosis), resulting in visual impairment. In rare cases, affected infants may exhibit complete absence of the eyes (anophthalmia). Most affected infants also exhibit developmental delay and mental retardation, ranging from mild to severe. Additional physical abnormalities are often associated with this disorder such as an unusually small head (microcephaly) and/or malformations of the teeth, ears, and/or fingers and/or toes (digits). The range and severity of findings may vary from case to case. Lenz microphthalmia syndrome, which is inherited as an X-linked recessive genetic trait, is fully expressed in males only. However, females who carry one copy of the disease gene (heterozygotes) may exhibit some of the symptoms associated with the disorder, such as an abnormally small head (microcephaly), short stature, and/or malformations of the fingers and/or toes.

The following organizations may provide additional information and support:
Council of Families with Visual Impairment
International Children's Anophthalmia Network (ICAN)
National Association for Parents of Children with Visual Impairments (NAPVI)
National Association for Visually Handicapped
National Federation of the Blind
NIH/National Eye Institute

642 LEOPARD Syndrome

Synonyms
Cardiocutaneous Syndrome
Cardiomyopathic Lentiginosis
Multiple Lentigines Syndrome
Progressive Cardiomyopathic Lentiginosis

LEOPARD syndrome is an extremely rare inherited disorder characterized by abnormalities of the skin, the structure and function of the heart, the inner ear, the head and facial (craniofacial) area, and/or the genitals. In individuals with the disorder, the range and severity of symptoms and physical characteristics may vary from case to case. "LEOPARD," an acronym for the characteristic abnormalities associated with the disorder, stands for (L)entigines, multiple black or dark brown "freckle-like" spots on the skin; (E)lectrocardiographic conduction defects, abnormalities of the electrical activity—and the coordination of proper contractions—of the heart; (O)cular hypertelorism, widely-spaced eyes; (P)ulmonary stenosis, obstruction of the normal outflow of blood from the lower right chamber (ventricle) of the heart; (A)bnormalities of the genitals; (R)etarded growth resulting in short stature; and (D)eafness or hearing loss due to malfunction of the inner ear (sensorineural deafness). Some individuals with LEOPARD syndrome may also exhibit mild mental retardation, speech difficulties, and/or, in some cases, additional physical abnormalities. In most cases, LEOPARD syndrome appears to occur randomly for unknown reasons (sporadically). However, in other cases, the disorder is thought to be inherited as an autosomal dominant genetic trait.

The following organizations may provide additional information and support:
American Heart Association
Congenital Heart Anomalies, Support, Education, & Resources
Human Growth Foundation
MAGIC Foundation for Children's Growth
NIH/National Heart, Lung and Blood Institute Information Center
Restricted Growth Association

643   Leprechaunism

Synonym
Donohue Syndrome

Leprechaunism is an extremely rare disorder characterized by abnormal resistance to insulin that results in a variety of distinguishing characteristics, including growth delays and abnormalities affecting the endocrine system (i.e., the system of glands that secrete hormones into the blood system). Affected infants may also have distinctive characteristics of the head and face (craniofacial region), low birth weight, skin abnormalities, and enlargement of the breast and clitoris in females and the penis in males. Leprechaunism is inherited as an autosomal recessive genetic trait.

The following organizations may provide additional information and support:
The Arc (A National Organization on Mental Retardation)
Children's Craniofacial Association
CLIMB (Children Living with Inherited Metabolic Diseases)
Human Growth Foundation
March of Dimes Birth Defects Foundation
NIH/National Institute of Child Health and Human Development

644   Leprosy

Synonym
Hansen's Disease

Disorder Subdivisions
Borderline Lepromatous Leprosy
Borderline Tuberculoid Leprosy
Indeterminate Leprosy
Lepromatous Leprosy
Midborderline Leprosy
Tuberculoid Leprosy

Leprosy is a chronic infectious disease of humans caused by the bacteria Mycobacterium leprae. For many years, it was considered a mysterious disorder associated with some type of curse, and persons with the disease were isolated and ostracized. Today, there is effective treatment and the disease can be cured. There is no longer any justification for isolating persons with leprosy. The disease can affect the skin, mucous membranes, and eyes and some of the nerves that are located outside the central nervous system (peripheral nerves). These are primarily the nerves of the hands, feet, and eyes, and some of the nerves in the skin. In severe, untreated cases, loss of sensation, muscle paralysis of hands and feet, disfigurement, and blindness may occur. Leprosy has traditionally been classified into two major types, tuberculoid and lepromatous. Patients with tuberculoid leprosy have limited disease and relatively few bacteria in the skin and nerves, while lepromatous patients have widespread disease and large numbers of bacteria. Tuberculoid leprosy is characterized by a few flat or slightly raised skin lesions of various sizes that are typically pale or slightly red, dry, hairless, and numb to touch (anesthetic). Lepromatous leprosy is at the other end of the spectrum, with a much more generalized disease, diffuse involvement of the skin, thickening of many peripheral nerves, and at times involvement of other organs, such as eyes, nose, testicles, and bone. There are also intermediate subtypes between these two extremes that are commonly known as borderline leprosy. The intermediate subtypes are borderline tuberculoid, midborderline, and borderline lepromatous leprosy. Borderline leprosy and the subtypes are characterized by more extensive disease than polar tuberculoid, with more numerous skin lesions and more nerve involvement, but not as widespread disease as in lepromatous leprosy. Indeterminate leprosy refers to a very early form of leprosy that consists of a single skin lesion with slightly diminished sensation to touch. It will usually progress to one of the major types of leprosy. In 1982, the World Health Organization proposed a simplified classification that has only two classifications, Paucibacillary (PB) and Multibacillary (MB), leprosy. This classification is now used worldwide for treatment purposes. The older and somewhat more complex classification is still used in some programs, especially for clinical research studies. The Paucibacillary classification encompasses indeterminate, tuberculoid and borderline tuberculoid leprosy. The Multibacillary classification includes midborderline, borderline lepromatous and lepromatous leprosy. **REMINDER** The information contained in the Rare Disease Database is provided for educational purposes only. It should not be used for diagnostic or treatment purposes. If you wish to obtain more detailed information about this disorder, please contact your personal physician and/or the agencies listed in the "Resources" section of this report.

The following organizations may provide additional information and support:
American Leprosy Missions
Centers for Disease Control and Prevention
Jack Miller Center for Peripheral Neuropathy
National Hansen's Disease Programs
NIH/National Institute of Allergy and Infectious Diseases

645 Leptospirosis

Synonyms
Canefield Fever
Canicola Fever
Field Fever
Mud Fever
Seven Day Fever, Leptospirosis
Spirochetosis
Swineherd Disease

Leptospirosis is an infectious disease that affects humans and animals. It results in a wide range of symptoms, and some people may have no symptoms at all. It is caused by a spiral-shaped bacterium (spirochete). Symptoms include high fever, chills, muscle aches, headache, vomiting, diarrhea, and jaundice (yellow skin and eyes). A definitive diagnosis requires laboratory testing of a blood or urine sample. Early detection is important because the disease can cause serious complications if not treated early in its course. These include kidney damage (nephrosis), meningitis (inflammation of the tissue around the brain or spinal cord), respiratory distress and/or liver failure.

The following organizations may provide additional information and support:
Centers for Disease Control and Prevention
NIH/National Institute of Allergy and Infectious Diseases

World Health Organization (WHO) Regional Office for the Americas (AMRO)

646 Leri Pleonosteosis

Synonym
Pleonosteosis, Leri Type

Leri pleonosteosis is an extremely rare inherited disorder characterized by unusual, flattened facial features, abnormalities of the hands and feet, skeletal malformations, short stature, and/or limitation of joint movements. Characteristic abnormalities of the hands and feet may include unusually broad and/or short thumbs and great toes (brachydactyly) that may be bent outward from the body (valgus position); as a result, the hands may have a "spade-shaped" appearance. Skeletal malformations may include knees that are bent backward (genu recurvitum) and abnormal enlargement of the cartilaginous structures that surround the upper portion of the spinal cord (posterior neural arches of the cervical vertebrae). In addition, affected individuals may develop thickened tissue on the palms (palmar) and forearms. Symptoms may vary from case to case. Leri pleonosteosis is inherited as an autosomal dominant genetic trait.

The following organizations may provide additional information and support:
Human Growth Foundation
Little People of America, Inc.
Little People's Research Fund, Inc.
NIH/National Institute of Arthritis and Musculoskeletal and Skin Diseases
Restricted Growth Association

647 Lesch-Nyhan Syndrome

Synonyms
Hereditary Hyperuricemia and Choreoathetosis Syndrome
HGPRT, Absence of
HPRT, Absence of
Hyperuricemia, Choreoathetosis, Self-multilation Syndrome
Hyperuricemia-Oligophrenia
Hypoxanthine-Guanine Phosphoribosyltranferase Defec. (Complete Absense of)
Juvenile Gout, Choreoathetosis, and Mental Retardation Syndrome
Nyhan Syndrome

Lesch-Nyhan syndrome is a rare inborn error of purine metabolism characterized by the absence or deficiency of the enzyme hypoxanthine-guanine phosphoribosyltransferase (HPRT). Purine, a nitrogen-containing compound found in many foods (e.g., organ meats, poultry, and legumes) is not broken down properly due to the absence of HPRT. Uric acid levels are abnormally high in people with Lesch-Nyhan syndrome and sodium urate crystals may abnormally accumulate in the joints, kidneys, central nervous system, and other tissues of the body. Lesch-Nyhan syndrome is inherited as an X-linked recessive genetic disorder that most often affects males. The symptoms of Lesch-Nyhan syndrome include impaired kidney function, joint pain, and self-mutilating behaviors such as lip and finger biting and/or head banging. Additional symptoms may include muscle weakness (hypotonia), uncontrolled spastic muscle movements, and neurological impairment.

The following organizations may provide additional information and support:
The Arc (A National Organization on Mental Retardation)
CLIMB (Children Living with Inherited Metabolic Diseases)
Information Center on Disabled and Gifted Education
International Lesch-Nyhan Disease Association
Lesch-Nyhan Syndrome Children's Research Foundation
Lesch-Nyhan Syndrome Registry
National Institute of Neurological Disorders and Stroke (NINDS)
Purine Research Society

648   Leukemia, Chronic Lymphocytic

Synonym
CLL

Chronic lymphocytic leukemia is a malignant blood disorder in which there is an increased number of white blood cells formed in the lymphoid tissue. This uncontrolled buildup and enlargement of lymphoid tissue can occur in various sites of the body such as the lymph nodes, spleen, bone marrow, and lungs. There are many different forms of leukemia, which are all characterized by an overabundance of white blood cells. In chronic lymphocytic leukemia the disease occurs in the lymphoid tissue.The lymph vessels, which return fluids to the circulatory system, and the lymph nodes, which are a mass of tissue separated into compartments by connective tissue, make up the

immune system. The lymph nodes serve as filters, removing foreign particles, tissue debris, and bacterial cells from the circulation. When this system is not working properly, the body's defenses cannot fight off foreign particles. In the majority of cases, chronic lymphocytic leukemia is the result of a rapid production of B lymphocyte cells (a short-lived type of white blood cell that is responsible for the production of vertebrate serum proteins that include antibodies). A small percentage of chronic lymphocytic leukemia cases stem from the overproduction of T lymphocyte cells (a type of white blood cell that have a long life and are important in the resistance of disease).

The following organizations may provide additional information and support:
American Cancer Society, Inc.
Cancer Research UK
Children's Leukemia Research Association
Leukemia & Lymphoma Society
National Cancer Institute
OncoLink: The University of Pennsylvania Cancer Center Resource
Rare Cancer Alliance

649   Leukemia, Chronic Myelogenous

Synonyms
CGL
Chronic Granulocytic Leukemia
Chronic Myelocytic Leukemia
Chronic Myeloid Leukemia
GML

Chronic myelogenous leukemia is a rare myeloproliferative disorder characterized by the excessive development of white blood cells in the spongy tissue found inside large bones of the body (bone marrow), spleen, liver and blood. As the disease progresses, the leukemic cells invade other areas of the body including the intestinal tract, kidneys, lungs, gonads and lymph nodes. There are two phases to chronic myelogenous leukemia. The first phase, or chronic phase, is characterized by a slow, progressive overproduction of white blood cells. An advanced phase is called the acute phase or blast crisis. At this point, over 50 percent of the cells in the bone marrow are immature malignant cells (blast cells or promelocytes). In the acute phase, the leukemia is very aggressive and does not respond well to therapy. Approximately 85 percent of all individuals with chronic myelogenous leukemia enter the acute phase.

The following organizations may provide additional information and support:
American Cancer Society, Inc.
Cancer Research UK
Center for International Blood and Marrow Transplant Research
Children's Leukemia Research Association
Leukemia & Lymphoma Society
Myeloproliferative Mailing List (MPD-SUPPORT-L)
National Cancer Institute
OncoLink: The University of Pennsylvania Cancer Center Resource
Rare Cancer Alliance

650 Leukemia, Hairy Cell

Synonyms
HCL
Leukemic Reticuloendotheliosis

Hairy cell leukemia is a rare type of blood cancer characterized by the presence of abnormal mononuclear blood cells called "hairy cells," and by a deficiency of other blood cell elements (pancytopenia), including an abnormal decrease of certain white blood cells (neutrophils [neutropenia]) and certain red blood cells (platelets [thrombocytopenia]). Affected individuals usually exhibit fatigue, weakness, fever, weight loss, and/or abdominal discomfort due to an abnormally enlarged spleen (splenomegaly). In addition, affected individuals may have a slightly enlarged liver (hepatomegaly) and may be unusually susceptible to bruising and/or severe infection. The exact cause of hairy cell leukemia is not known.

The following organizations may provide additional information and support:
American Cancer Society, Inc.
Children's Leukemia Research Association
Hairy Cell Leukemia Research Foundation
Leukemia & Lymphoma Society
National Cancer Institute
OncoLink: The University of Pennsylvania Cancer Center Resource
Rare Cancer Alliance

651 Leukodystrophy

Disorder Subdivisions
Adrenoleukodystrophy
Alexanders Disease
Canavan's Disease, Included
Cerebrotendinous Xanthomatosis
Globoid Leukodystrophy
Krabbe's Disease, Included
Metachromatic Leukodystrophy
Pelizaeus-Merzbacher Brain Sclerosis
Refsum's Disease
Schilder's Disease
Sudanophilic Leukodystrophy, Included

Leukodystrophy is the name given to a group of very rare, progressive, metabolic, genetic diseases that affect the brain, spinal cord and often the peripheral nerves. Each of the leukodystrophies will affect one of the chemicals that make up the myelin sheath or white matter of the brain, causing the various types of leukodystrophy. The myelin sheath, which acts as insulation of the nervous system, is composed of different lipids (fatty substances). Thus defects in production and degradation of these lipids can lead to the many ways in which these diseases can manifest themselves.

The following organizations may provide additional information and support:
Australian Leukodystrophy Support Group, Inc.
Hunter's Hope Foundation, Inc.
Kennedy Krieger Institute
National Institute of Neurological Disorders and Stroke (NINDS)
National Tay-Sachs and Allied Diseases Association, Inc.
United Leukodystrophy Foundation

652 Leukodystrophy, Krabbe's

Synonyms
Galactocerebrosidase (GALC) Deficiency
Galactocerebroside Beta-Galactosidase Deficiency
Galactosylceramidase Deficiency
Galactosylceramide Lipidosis
Globoid Cell Leukoencephalopathy
Krabbe's Disease
Leukodystrophy, Globoid Cell
Sphingolipidosis, Krabbe's Type

Krabbe's leukodystrophy is a rare inherited lipid storage disorder caused by a deficiency of the enzyme galactocerebrosidase (GALC), which is necessary for the breakdown (metabolism) of the sphingolipids galactosylceremide and psychosine. Failure to break down these sphingolipids results in degeneration of the myelin sheath surrounding nerves in the brain (demyelination). Characteristic globoid cells appear in affected areas of the brain. This metabolic disorder is characterized by progressive neurological dysfunction such as mental retardation, paralysis, blindness, deafness and paralysis of certain facial muscles (pseudobulbar palsy). Krabbe's leukodystrophy is inherited as an autosomal recessive trait.

The following organizations may provide additional information and support:
The Arc (A National Organization on Mental Retardation)
Association Europeene Contre les Leucodystrophes
Australian Leukodystrophy Support Group, Inc.
CLIMB (Children Living with Inherited Metabolic Diseases)
Hunter's Hope Foundation, Inc.
Kennedy Krieger Institute
National Institute of Neurological Disorders and Stroke (NINDS)
United Leukodystrophy Foundation

653   Leukodystrophy, Metachromatic

Synonyms
ARSA
Arylsulfatase A Deficiency
Cerebroside Sulfatase Deficiency
Diffuse Cerebral Sclerosis
Greenfield Disease
Late-Onset Metachromatic Leukodystrophy
Metachromatic Form of Diffuse Cerebral
Metachromatic Leukoencephalopathy
MLD
Sulfatide Lipidosis
Sulfatidosis

Disorder Subdivisions
Adult Metachromatic Leukodystrophy
Juvenile Metachromatic Leukodystrophy
Late Infantile Metachromatic Leukodystrophy

Metachromatic leukodystrophy, the most common form of leukodystrophy, is a rare inherited neurometabolic disorder affecting the white matter of the brain (leukoencephalopathy). It is characterized by the accumulation of a fatty substance known as sulfatide (a sphingolipid) in the brain and other areas of the body (i.e., liver, gallbladder, kidneys, and/or spleen). The fatty protective covering on the nerve fibers (myelin) is lost from areas of the central nervous system (CNS) due to the buildup of sulfatide. Symptoms of metachromatic leukodystrophy may include convulsions, seizures, personality changes, spasticity, progressive dementia, motor disturbances progressing to

paralysis, and/or visual impairment leading to blindness. Metachromatic leukodystrophy is inherited as an autosomal recessive trait. There are three forms of the disease that have similar symptoms. However, they are distinguished by the age of onset: infantile, juvenile, and adult forms of metachromatic leukodystrophy.

The following organizations may provide additional information and support:
Association Europeene Contre les Leucodystrophes
Australian Leukodystrophy Support Group, Inc.
Hunter's Hope Foundation, Inc.
Instituto de Errores Innatos del Metabolismo
Kennedy Krieger Institute
National Institute of Neurological Disorders and Stroke (NINDS)
National Tay-Sachs and Allied Diseases Association, Inc.
United Leukodystrophy Foundation

654   Lichen Planus

Synonyms
Csillag's Disease, Planus Type
Guttate Morphea, Planus Type
Guttate Scleroderma
Hallopeau's Disease, Type I
Lichen Planus Sclerosus Atrophicus
Lichen Ruber Planus
Von Zambusch's Disease
White Spot Disease
Zambusch's Disease

Lichen planus is a rare, recurrent, itchy rash or area of inflammatory eruptions (lesions) of unknown origin characterized by shiny reddish-purple spots on the skin and gray-white ones in the mouth. The disorder may present as itchy spots on the wrist, legs, torso, genitals, mouth, or lips. The eruptions may appear as small separate, angular spots that may coalesce into rough scaly patches. This disorder is frequently accompanied by oral lesions of the mucous membranes that line the mouth. The disorder affects women more frequently than men.

The following organizations may provide additional information and support:
Autoimmune Information Network, Inc
International Oral Lichen Planus Support Group
NIH/National Institute of Arthritis and Musculoskeletal and Skin Diseases

655 Lichen Sclerosus

Synonyms

Csillag's Disease (Sclerosus)
Guttate Morphea (Sclerosus)
Guttate Scleroderma, Lichen Sclerosus Type
Hallopeau I Disease
Lichen Sclerosus et Atrophicus
Von Zambusch Disease
White-Spot Disease

Lichen sclerosus is a chronic skin disorder that most commonly affects post-menopausal women. However, it is sometimes identified among pre-menopausal women, and, even more rarely, among males. When found in males, the disease is known as balanitis xerotica obliterans. Lichen sclerosus is characterized by skin changes of the external genitalia (i.e., vulva, head of the penis), although other parts of the body may also be affected. Intense itching often accompanies attacks of lichen sclerosus. The disorder is not contagious nor is it a sexually transmitted disease. In the recent past, a genetic component for lichen sclerosus has been recognized. In addition, many clinical researchers believe that it is a disorder of the immunological system. The understanding of the causes of this disorder is still incomplete. Lichen sclerosus can develop concurrently with other conditions.

The following organizations may provide additional information and support:
American Autoimmune Related Diseases Association, Inc.
National Vulvodynia Association
National Women's Health Network
National Women's Health Resource Center
NIH/National Institute of Arthritis and Musculoskeletal and Skin Diseases

656 Lipodystrophy

Disorder Subdivisions

Acquired Lipodystrophy
Acquired Partial Lipodystrophy
Barraquer-Simons Disease
Berardinelli-Seip Syndrome
Centrifugal Lipodystrophy
Cephalothoracic Lipodystrophy
Congenital Lipodystrophy
Hollaender-Simons Disease
Insulin Lipodystrophy
Koebberling-Dunnigan Syndrome
Lawrence-Seip Syndrome

Leprechaunism
Lipoatrophic Diabetes Mellitus
Localized Lipodystrophy
Membranous Lipodystrophy
Mesenteric Lipodystrophy
Nasu Lipodystrophy
Partial Lipodystrophy
Progressive Lipodystrophy
Seip Syndrome
Simons Syndrome
Smith Disease
Total Lipodystrophy
Unilateral Partial Lipodystrophy
Whipple Disease

Lipodystrophies are a group of rare metabolic disorders which can be either inherited or acquired. They are characterized by abnormalities in fatty (adipose) tissue associated with total or partial loss of body fat, abnormalities of carbohydrate and lipid metabolism, severe resistance to naturally occurring and synthetic insulin, and immune system dysfunction. These disorders are differentiated by degrees of severity, and by areas or systems of the body affected. Lipodystrophies can also be associated with other disorders and various developmental abnormalities.

The following organizations may provide additional information and support:
American Diabetes Association
The Arc (A National Organization on Mental Retardation)
CLIMB (Children Living with Inherited Metabolic Diseases)
March of Dimes Birth Defects Foundation
NIH/National Digestive Diseases Information Clearinghouse

657 Lissencephaly

Synonyms

Agyria
Lissencephaly, Type I

Disorder Subdivisions

Isolated Lissencephaly Sequence (ILS)
Lissencephaly 1 (LIS1)
Miller-Dieker Syndrome
Norman-Roberts Syndrome
X-linked Lissencephaly

Classical lissencephaly, also known as lissencephaly type I, is a brain malformation that may occur as an isolated abnormality (isolated lissencephaly sequence [ILS]) or in association with certain underlying syndromes (e.g., Miller-Dieker syndrome, Norman-Roberts syndrome). The condition is characterized by absence (agyria) or incomplete development (pachygyria) of the ridges or convolutions (gyri) of the outer region of the brain (cerebral cortex), causing the brain's surface to appear unusually smooth. In infants with classical lissencephaly, the head circumference may be smaller than would otherwise be expected (microcephaly). Additional abnormalities may include sudden episodes of uncontrolled electrical activity in the brain (seizures), severe or profound mental retardation, feeding difficulties, growth retardation, and impaired motor abilities. If an underlying syndrome is present, there may be additional symptoms and physical findings. Researchers indicate that there may be various possible causes of isolated lissencephaly, including viral infections or insufficient blood flow to the brain during fetal development or certain genetic factors. Changes (mutations) of at least two different genes have been implicated in isolated lissencephaly: a gene located on chromosome 17 (known as LIS1) and a gene located on the X-chromosome (known as XLIS or Doublecortin).

The following organizations may provide additional information and support:
Lissencephaly Contact Group
Lissencephaly Network, Inc.
National Institute of Neurological Disorders and Stroke (NINDS)
Support Network for Pachygyria, Agyria, Lissencephaly

658 Listeriosis

Synonym
Listeria Infection

Disorder Subdivisions
Granulomatosis Infantiseptica
Listeriosis of Pregnancy
Neonatal Listeriosis

Listeriosis is a rare infectious disorder caused by the bacterium Listeria monocytogenes, which is usually transmitted to humans through contaminated food products, often improperly pasteurized milk or cheese. Some cases have been transmitted through contact with other infected persons or animals. Cases range in severity from a transient carrier state with no apparent symptoms, to acute suddenly occurring (fulminant) spread of bacteria throughout the blood stream (bac-

teremia). Many factors may contribute to development of symptoms. Listeriosis most often affects newborns, the elderly, pregnant women, and individuals with weakened immune systems. Prompt recognition and treatment of the disease is necessary to avoid several serious complications.

The following organizations may provide additional information and support:
Centers for Disease Control and Prevention
Food and Drug Administration (FDA) Office of Inquiry & Consumer Information
NIH/National Institute of Allergy and Infectious Diseases
World Health Organization (WHO) Regional Office for the Americas (AMRO)

659 Locked-In Syndrome

Synonyms
Cerebromedullospinal Disconnection
De-Efferented State
Pseudocoma

Locked-in syndrome is characterized by complete paralysis except for voluntary eye movements. It is usually caused by lesions in the nerve centers that control muscle contractions, or a blood clot that blocks circulation of oxygen to the brain stem.

The following organizations may provide additional information and support:
Genetic and Rare Diseases (GARD) Information Center
National Institute of Neurological Disorders and Stroke (NINDS)

660 Loken-Senior Syndrome

Synonyms
Juvenile Nephronophthisis with Leber Amaurosis
Renal Dysplasia and Retinal Aplasia
Renal Dysplasia-Blindness, Hereditary
Renal-Retinal Dysplasia
Renal-Retinal Syndrome
Senior-Loken Syndrome

Loken-Senior syndrome is a rare disorder inherited as an autosomal recessive genetic trait. This disorder is characterized by progressive wasting of the filtering unit of the kidney (nephronophthisis), with or without medullary cystic renal disease, and progressive eye disease. Typically this disorder becomes apparent during the first year of life.

The following organizations may provide additional information and support:
American Foundation for Urologic Disease
American Kidney Fund, Inc.
Blind Children's Center
Blind Children's Fund
Foundation Fighting Blindness, Inc.
National Association for Parents of Children with Visual Impairments (NAPVI)
National Association for Visually Handicapped
National Kidney Foundation
NIH/National Eye Institute
NIH/National Kidney and Urologic Diseases Information Clearinghouse
Retinitis Pigmentosa International

661 Lowe Syndrome

Synonyms
Cerebro-Oculorenal Dystrophy
Lowe-Bickel Syndrome
Lowe's Disease
Lowe-Terry-MacLachlan Syndrome
LS
OCRL
Oculocerebrorenal Dystrophy
Oculocerebrorenal Syndrome
Renal-Oculocerebrodystrophy

Lowe syndrome, also known as oculo-cerebro-renal syndrome, is a rare inherited metabolic disease that affects males. This disorder is characterized by lack of muscle tone (hypotonia), multiple abnormalities of the eyes and bones, the presence at birth of clouding of the lenses of the eyes (cataracts), mental retardation, short stature, and kidney problems. Other findings may include protrusion of the eyeball from the eye socket (enophthalmos); failure to gain weight and grow at the expected rate; weak or absent deep tendon reflexes; and multiple kidney problems (e.g., renal tubular dysfunction, renal hyperaminoaciduria, etc.). Lowe syndrome is inherited as an X-linked genetic trait and symptoms develop due to lack of the enzyme phosphatidylinositol 4,5-biphosphate 5 phosphatase.

The following organizations may provide additional information and support:
The Arc (A National Organization on Mental Retardation)
Lowe Syndrome Association
March of Dimes Birth Defects Foundation
NIH/National Human Genome Research Institute

662 Lupus

Synonyms
Disseminated Lupus Erythematosus
Lupus Erythematosus

Disorder Subdivisions
Discoid Lupus Erythematosus (DLE)
Drug-Induced Lupus Erythematosus
Systemic Lupus Erythematosus (SLE)

Lupus is a chronic, inflammatory autoimmune disorder affecting the connective tissue. In autoimmune disorders, the body's own immune system attacks healthy cells and tissues causing inflammation and malfunction of various organ systems. In lupus, the organ systems most often involved include the skin, kidneys, blood and joints. Many different symptoms are associated with lupus, and most affected individuals do not experience all of the symptoms. In some cases, lupus may be a mild disorder affecting only a few organ systems. In other cases, it may result in serious complications. There are at least three forms of lupus: the classic form, systemic lupus erythematosus; a form that only affects the skin, discoid lupus erythematosus; and drug-induced lupus erythematosus. The term lupus is most often used to denote systemic lupus erythematosus.

The following organizations may provide additional information and support:
American Juvenile Arthritis Organization
APS Foundation of America, Inc
Arthritis Foundation
Autoimmune Information Network, Inc
CNS Vasculitis Foundation
Eastern Paralyzed Veterans Association
Erythema Nodosum Yahoo Support Group
Jack Miller Center for Peripheral Neuropathy
Lupus Canada
Lupus Foundation of America, Inc.
Lupus Society of Alberta
NIH/National Arthritis and Musculoskeletal and Skin Diseases Information Clearinghouse
Vasculitis of the Central Nervous System

663 Lyme Disease

Synonyms
LD
Lyme Arthritis
Lyme Borreliosis

Lyme disease is an infectious disease caused by the spirochete bacterium Borrelia burgdorferi.

The bacterium is carried and transmitted by deer ticks (Ixodes dammini). In most cases, Lyme disease is first characterized by the appearance of a red skin lesion (erythema chronicum migrans), which begins as a small elevated round spot (papule) that expands to at least five centimeters in diameter. Symptoms may then progress to include low-grade fever, chills, muscle aches (myalgia), headaches, a general feeling of weakness and fatigue (malaise), and/or pain and stiffness of the large joints (infectious arthritis), especially in the knees. Such symptoms may tend to occur in recurrent cycles. In severe cases, heart muscle (myocardial) and/or neurological abnormalities may occur.

The following organizations may provide additional information and support:
American Lyme Disease Foundation, Inc.
Arthritis Foundation
California Lyme Disease Association
Centers for Disease Control and Prevention
Jack Miller Center for Peripheral Neuropathy
Lyme Disease Foundation
NIH/National Arthritis and Musculoskeletal and Skin Diseases Information Clearinghouse

---

664 Lymphadenopathy, Angioimmunoblastic with Dysproteinemia

Synonyms
AILD
Immunoblastic Lymphadenopathy

Angioimmunoblastic lymphadenopathy with dysproteinemia (AILD) is a progressive immune system disorder possibly caused by viral infections, chronic stimulation of immune responses or drug treatments prescribed for other conditions. This disorder occurs mostly among persons over 50 years of age. Fever, chills, sweating, a general feeling of discomfort, weight loss, and/or skin rashes are the major symptoms. In some cases, AILD may evolve into a severe form of lymphoma (a type of cancer).

The following organizations may provide additional information and support:
Immune Deficiency Foundation
International Patient Organization for Primary Immunodeficiencies
NIH/National Institute of Allergy and Infectious Diseases

---

665 Lymphangioleiomyomatosis

Synonyms
LAM
Lymphangioleimyomatosis
Lymphangioleiomatosis
Pulmonary Lymphangiomyomatosis
Sporadic Lymphangioleiomyomatosis

Lymphangioleiomyomatosis (LAM) is a rare progressive multisystem disorder that predominantly affects women of childbearing age. It occurs in women who have tuberous sclerosis, and also in women who do not have a heritable genetic disorder. LAM is characterized by the spread and uncontrolled growth (proliferation) of specialized cells (smooth muscle cells) in certain organs of the body, especially the lungs. Common symptoms associated with LAM include coughing and/or difficulty breathing (dyspnea), especially following periods of exercise or exertion. Affected individuals may also experience complications including collapse of a lung or fluid accumulation around the lungs (pleural effusion). The disorder is progressive and, in some cases, may result in chronic respiratory failure.

The following organizations may provide additional information and support:
American Lung Association
British Lung Foundation
LAM Foundation
NIH/National Heart, Lung and Blood Institute Information Center
Second Wind Lung Transplant Association, Inc.

---

666 Lymphatic Malformations

Synonyms
Cystic Hygromas, Included
LMs
Lymphangiomas

Lymphatic malformations (LMs) are abnormalities of lymphatic vessels that have sometimes been referred to as lymphangiomas. They arise due to defects during embryonic development, resulting in abnormal, localized or generalized lesions that may vary in size, extent, and severity. LMs typically appear early in life, with most apparent at birth or during infancy or early childhood. Although LMs may develop in many different regions, common locations include the face and neck, the torso, under the arms (axillae), or the extremities.

The following organizations may provide additional information and support:
Cystic Hygroma Support Group
Lymphovenous Canada
March of Dimes Birth Defects Foundation
National Lymphatic and Venous Diseases Foundation, Inc.

667   Lymphedema, Hereditary

Disorder Subdivisions

Congenital Hereditary Lymphedema
Familial Lymphedema Praecox
Hereditary Lymphedema Tarda
Hereditary Lymphedema, Type I
Hereditary Lymphedema, Type II
Meige's Lymphedema
Milroy Disease
Nonne-Milroy-Meige Syndrome

Hereditary lymphedema is an inherited disorder of the lymphatic system that is characterized by abnormal swelling of certain parts of the body. The lymphatic system is a circulatory network of vessels, ducts, and nodes that filter and distribute certain fluid (lymph) and blood cells throughout the body. Lymphatic fluid collects in the soft tissues in and under the skin (subcutaneous) due to the obstruction, malformation, or underdevelopment (hypoplasia) of various lymphatic vessels. There are three forms of hereditary lymphedema: congenital hereditary lymphedema or Milroy disease, lymphedema praecox or Meige disease, and lymphedema tarda. In most cases, hereditary lymphedema is inherited as an autosomal dominant genetic trait.

The following organizations may provide additional information and support:
Lymphatic Research Foundation
Lymphovenous Canada
National Lipedema Association, Inc.
National Lymphatic and Venous Diseases Foundation, Inc.
National Lymphedema Network
NIH/National Heart, Lung and Blood Institute

668   Lymphocytic Infiltrate of Jessner

Synonyms

Benign Lymphocytic Infiltrate of the Skin
Jessner-Kanof Lymphocytic Infiltration

Jessner lymphocytic infiltrate of the skin is an uncommon disorder that is characterized by benign accumulations of lymph cells in the skin. These small lesions are solid, pink or red in color, and appear on the face, neck, and/or back. Skin surrounding these lesions may be itchy and turn red. The lesions may remain unchanged for several years and then spontaneously disappear, leaving no scars. Not much is known about this disorder. In fact, there is some difference of opinion as to whether it is distinguishable as a separate condition or represents a stage of some other disorder. Some scientists believe that Jessner lymphocytic infiltrate may be a type of lupus erythematosus tumidus (LET) or discoid lupus erythematosus (DLE).

The following organization may provide additional information and support:
NIH/National Institute of Arthritis and Musculoskeletal and Skin Diseases

669   Lymphoma, Gastric, Non Hodgkins Type

Synonyms

Non-Hodgkins Gastric Lymphoma
Stomach Lymphoma, Non-Hodgkins Type

Non-Hodgkins type gastric lymphoma is a rare form of stomach cancer characterized by unrestrained growth of certain lymphoid cells of the stomach. This form of cancer is thought to arise from certain white blood cells (lymphocytes) within lymphoid tissue of the stomach's mucous membrane (mucosa). Non-Hodgkins type gastric lymphoma may be a primary disease process (primary lymphoma) or may develop due to another underlying lymphoma. Symptoms and findings associated with non-Hodgkins type gastric lymphoma may include pain, bleeding, obstruction of, and/or the development of a hole in the wall of the stomach (perforation). In many affected individuals, an abnormal mass may be felt (palpable) in the upper middle (epigastric) region of the abdomen. Non-Hodgkins type gastric lymphoma affects males more often than females and usually appears to occur during middle age. According to the medical literature, non-Hodgkins type gastric lymphoma tends to occur an average of approximately 10 years earlier than gastric adenocarcinoma, a more common form of stomach cancer.

The following organizations may provide additional information and support:
American Cancer Society, Inc.
Cancer Research UK

Leukemia & Lymphoma Society
Lymphoma Association (UK)
Lymphoma Foundation Canada
Lymphoma Research Foundation
National Cancer Institute
OncoLink: The University of Pennsylvania Cancer Center Resource
Rare Cancer Alliance

670   Lynch Syndromes

Synonyms

Hereditary Nonpolyposis Colorectal Cancer (Lynch Syndrome I and II)
Hereditary Nonpolyposis Colorectal Carcinoma

Disorder Subdivisions

Cancer Family Syndrome, Lynch Type
Hereditary Site Specific Cancer
Lynch Syndrome I
Lynch Syndrome II

The Lynch syndromes are rare hereditary disorders that usually cause cancer to develop either in the colorectal area or in other sites. Primary cancers may develop in the female genital tract, stomach, brain, breasts, or urological system. The cancers of the colorectal area associated with the Lynch syndromes usually develop at a younger age than is normally found in other persons with colorectal cancer.

The following organizations may provide additional information and support:
American Cancer Society, Inc.
National Cancer Institute
OncoLink: The University of Pennsylvania Cancer Center Resource

671   Lysosomal Storage Disorders

Lysosomal storage diseases are inherited metabolic diseases that are characterized by an abnormal build-up of various toxic materials in the body's cells as a result of enzyme deficiencies. There are nearly 50 of these disorders altogether, and they may affect different parts of the body, including the skeleton, brain, skin, heart, and central nervous system. New lysosomal storage disorders continue to be identified. While clinical trials are in progress on possible treatments for some of these diseases, there is currently no approved treatment for many lysosomal storage diseases.

The following organizations may provide additional information and support:
The Arc (A National Organization on Mental Retardation)
CLIMB (Children Living with Inherited Metabolic Diseases)
Instituto de Errores Innatos del Metabolismo
Lysosomal Diseases New Zealand
March of Dimes Birth Defects Foundation
National Institute of Neurological Disorders and Stroke (NINDS)
A National Organization on Mental Retardation-Vaincre Les Maladies Lysosomales
NIH/National Institute of Child Health and Human Development
NIH/National Institute of Diabetes, Digestive & Kidney Diseases

672   Machado-Joseph Disease

Synonyms

Autosomal Dominant Spinocerebellar Degeneration
Azorean Neurologic Disease
Joseph Disease
Machado Disease
MJD
Nigrospinodentatal Degeneration
Spinocerebellar Ataxia Type III (SCA 3)
Striatonigral Degeneration, Autosomal Dominant Type

Disorder Subdivisions

Machado-Joseph Disease Type I (MJD-I)
Machado-Joseph Disease Type II (MJD-II)
Machado-Joseph Disease Type III (MJD-III)

Machado-Joseph disease (MJD-III), also called spinocerebellar ataxia type III, is a rare, inherited, ataxia (lack of muscular control) affecting the central nervous system and characterized by the slow degeneration of particular areas of the brain called the hindbrain. Patients with MJD may eventually become crippled and/or paralyzed but their intellect remains intact. The onset of symptoms of MJD varies from early teens to late adulthood. Three forms of Machado-Joseph disease are recognized: types MJD-I, MJD-II, and MJD-III. The differences in the types of MJD relate to the age of onset and severity. Earlier onset usually produces more severe symptoms.

The following organizations may provide additional information and support:
International Joseph Disease Foundation, Inc.

March of Dimes Birth Defects Foundation
National Institute of Neurological Disorders and Stroke (NINDS)

673   Macroglossia

Synonyms
Enlarged Tongue
Giant Tongue

Disorder Subdivision
Congenital Macroglossia

Macroglossia is the abnormal enlargement of the tongue. In rare cases, macroglossia occurs as an isolated finding that is present at birth (congenital). In many cases, macroglossia may occur secondary to a primary disorder that may be either congenital (e.g., Down syndrome or Beckwith-Wiedemann syndrome) or acquired (e.g., as a result of trauma or malignancy). Symptoms and physical findings associated with macroglossia may include noisy, high-pitched breathing (stridor), snoring, and/or feeding difficulties. In some cases, the tongue may protrude from the mouth. When inherited, macroglossia is transmitted as an autosomal dominant genetic trait.

The following organizations may provide additional information and support:
NIH/National Oral Health Information Clearinghouse
Smell and Taste Center

674   Macular Degeneration

Synonyms
Foveal Dystrophy, Progressive
Macula Lutea, Degeneration
Macular Dystrophy
Tapetoretinal Degeneration

Disorder Subdivisions
Adult Macula Lutea Retinae Degeneration
Behr 1
Behr 2
Juvenile Macular Degeneration
Macular Degeneration, Disciform
Macular Degeneration, Senile
Presenile Macula Lutea Retinae Degeneration
Stargardt's Disease (STGD)

Macular degeneration is a degenerative disease affecting the macula or center of the retina of the eye. It results in progressive loss of central vision.

Occurring most often among older people, it is the most common cause of vision loss in people over age 55. It is believed that both genetic and environmental factors influence this disease.

The following organizations may provide additional information and support:
American Council of the Blind, Inc.
American Foundation for the Blind
Association for Macular Diseases, Inc.
Council of Families with Visual Impairment
EyeCare Foundation
Foundation Fighting Blindness (Canada)
Macular Degeneration International
Macular Degeneration Support, Inc.
Macular Disease Society
National Association for Visually Handicapped
NIH/National Eye Institute
Vision World Wide, Inc.

675   Madelung's Disease

Synonyms
Benign Symmetrical Lipomatosis
Launois-Bensaude
MSL
Multiple Symmetric Lipomatosis

Madelung's disease is a disorder of fat metabolism (lipid storage) that results in an unusual accumulation of fat deposits around the neck and shoulder areas. Adult alcoholic males are most often affected, although women and those who do not drink alcohol can also get Madelung's disease.

The following organizations may provide additional information and support:
About Madelung's
NIH/National Institute of Diabetes, Digestive & Kidney Diseases

676   Maffucci Syndrome

Synonyms
Dyschondrodysplasia with Hemangiomas
Enchondromatosis with Multiple Cavernous Hemangiomas
Hemangiomatosis Chondrodystrophica
Kast Syndrome
Multiple Angiomas and Endochondromas

Maffucci syndrome is a rare genetic disorder characterized by benign overgrowths of cartilage (enchondromas), skeletal deformities, and dark red irregularly shaped patches of skin (hemangiomas).

Enchondromas are most often found in certain bones (phalanges) of the hands and feet. Skeletal malformations may include legs that are disproportionate in length and/or abnormal side-to-side curvature of the spine (scoliosis). In many cases, bones may tend to fracture easily. In most cases, hemangiomas appear at birth or during early childhood and may be progressive. Maffucci syndrome is inherited as an autosomal dominant genetic trait.

The following organizations may provide additional information and support:
American Cancer Society, Inc.
Birth Defect Research for Children, Inc.
NIH/National Arthritis and Musculoskeletal and Skin Diseases Information Clearinghouse
NIH/National Heart, Lung and Blood Institute

677 Mal de Debarquement

Synonym
MdDS

Mal de debarquement syndrome (MdDS) is a rare and little understood disorder of the body's balance system (vestibular system) and refers to the rocking sensation and/or sense of imbalance that persists for an excessive length of time after an ocean cruise, plane flight or other motion experience. Most people after exposure to an ocean trip or long airplane ride will experience "motion" after the event is over and for a short period of time. But for persons with MdDS, these sensations may last for 6 months or a year or even many years. Symptoms may diminish in time or periodically disappear and reappear after days, months, or years, sometimes after another motion experience or sometimes spontaneously. This syndrome is probably more common than the literature might lead us to believe, as the level of awareness in the general population as well as among health personnel is very low. The disproportionate length of time over which the discomfort persists is normally unaccompanied by nausea, nor is it responsive to motion-sickness drugs. For reasons that are not understood, women are overwhelmingly more likely to come down with MdDS than are men. However, most studies so far have disavowed hormones as a cause.

The following organizations may provide additional information and support:
EAR (Education and Auditory Research) Foundation
MdDS Balance Disorder Foundation, A National Heritage Foundation

National Institute of Neurological Disorders and Stroke (NINDS)
Vestibular Disorders Association (VEDA)

678 Malaria

Synonyms
Acute Malaria
Ague
Autochthonous Malaria
Chronic Malaria
Imported Malaria
Induced Malaria
Intermittent Malaria
Jungle Fever
Paludism
Relapsing Malaria
Swamp Fever
Therapeutic Malaria

Disorder Subdivisions
Aesthetivoautumnal Fever
Algid Malaria
Benign Tertian Malaria
Bilious Remittent Malaria
Blackwater Fever
Cerebral Malaria
Double Tertian Malaria
Dysentric Algid Malaria
Falciparum Fever
Gastric Malaria
Hemorrhagic Malaria
Malaria Comatosa
Malignant Tertian Fever
Malignant Tertian Malaria
Nonan Malaria
Ovale Tertian Malaria
Pernicious Malaria
Plasmodium Falciparum Malaria
Plasmodium Malariae Malaria
Plasmodium Ovale Malaria
Plasmodium Vivax Malaria
Quartan Fever
Quartan Malaria
Quotidian Fever
Quotidian Malaria
Remittent Malaria
Tertian Fever
Tertian Malaria
Vivax Fever

Malaria is a communicable parasitic disorder spread through the bite of the Anopheles mosquito. Major symptoms may vary depending on which species of parasite causes the infection and the stage of development of the parasite. Chills and fever commonly occur, although not every case follows the same pattern. Although the disorder was once thought to be under control throughout the world, malaria is a widespread infection especially in the tropics where certain types of mosquitos are becoming resistant to pesticides. The annual number of cases reported in the United States has increased in recent years.

The following organizations may provide additional information and support:
Centers for Disease Control and Prevention
NIH/National Institute of Allergy and Infectious Diseases
World Health Organization (WHO) Regional Office for the Americas (AMRO)

679 Malignant Hyperthermia

Synonyms
Hyperthermia of Anesthesia
Malignant Hyperpyrexia

Malignant hyperthermia (MH) is an autosomal dominant genetic disorder in which affected individuals are susceptible to adverse reactions to certain anesthetic drugs. The drugs that trigger malignant hyperthermia are the volatile inhalation gases including sevoflurane, desflurane, isoflurane, halothane, enflurane, methoxyflurane and depolarizing muscle relaxants such a succinylcholine. The characteristics of a malignant hyperthermia episode are variable and include muscle rigidity, high blood pressure (hypertension) increased levels of carbon monoxide in blood or exhaled gas, rapid irregular heart rate, rapid deep breathing, blue skin, acidity of the blood and muscle damage. Body temperature can rise rapidly (hyperthermia), but sometimes only occurs late in an episode. When an episode is not recognized and treated, internal bleeding, brain damage, skeletal muscle degeneration (rhabdomyolysis), and kidney and heart failure can result.

The following organizations may provide additional information and support:
Malignant Hyperthermia Association of the United States (MHAUS)
Malignant Hyperthermia Hotline
Malignant Hyperthermia Investigation Unit
NIH/National Institute of General Medical Sciences
North American Malignant Hyperthermia Registry of MHAUS

680 Mallory-Weiss Syndrome

Synonyms
Gastroesophageal Laceration-Hemorrhage
Mallory-Weiss Laceration
Mallory-Weiss Tear

Mallory-Weiss syndrome refers to a tear or laceration of the mucous membrane, most commonly at the point where the esophagus and the stomach meet (gastroesophageal junction). Such a tear may result in severe bleeding from the gastrointestinal tract. The immediate cause of the lesion is usually a protracted period of vomiting.

The following organizations may provide additional information and support:
Digestive Disease National Coalition
NIH/National Digestive Diseases Information Clearinghouse

681 Manic Depression, Bipolar

Synonyms
Bipolar Disorder, Depressed
Bipolar Disorder, Manic
Bipolar Disorder, Manic Depression
Bipolar Disorder, Mixed
BMD
Manic Depression
Manic Depressive Disorder
Manic Depressive Illness
Manic Depressive Psychosis

Bipolar manic depression is a mental illness in which intense mood swings occur, usually with remissions and recurrences. Depressive symptoms may be most common and can last at least a full day and perhaps several weeks or longer. Manic symptoms may involve hyperactivity and feelings of invincibility, happiness and restlessness.

The following organizations may provide additional information and support:
Bipolar Disorders Information Center
Child and Adolescent Bipolar Foundation (CABF)
Depression and Bipolar Support Alliance (DBSA)
Depression and Related Affective Disorders Association
National Alliance for the Mentally Ill
National Mental Health Association
National Mental Health Consumers' Self-Help Clearinghouse
New Horizons Un-Limited, Inc.
NIH/National Institute of Mental Health

NIH/National Institute of Mental Health (Depression Hotline)

682 Mantle Cell Lymphoma

Mantle cell lymphoma (MCL) belongs to a group of diseases known as non-Hodgkin's lymphomas, which are related malignancies (cancers) that affect the lymphatic system (lymphomas). Functioning as part of the immune system, the lymphatic system helps to protect the body against infection and disease. It consists of a network of tubular channels (lymph vessels) that drain a thin watery fluid known as lymph from different areas of the body into the bloodstream. Lymph accumulates in the tiny spaces between tissue cells and contains proteins, fats, and certain white blood cells known as lymphocytes. As lymph moves through the lymphatic system, it is filtered by a network of small structures known as lymph nodes that help to remove microorganisms (e.g., viruses, bacteria, etc.) and other foreign bodies. Groups of lymph nodes are located throughout the body, including in the neck, under the arms (axillae), at the elbows, and in the chest, abdomen, and groin. Lymphocytes are stored within lymph nodes and may also be found in other lymphatic tissues. In addition to the lymph nodes, the lymphatic system includes the spleen, which filters worn-out red blood cells and produces lymphocytes, and the tonsils, which are masses of lymphoid tissue in the throat region that help to fight infection. Lymphatic tissues also include the thymus, a relatively small organ behind the breastbone that is thought to play an important role in the immune system until puberty, as well as the bone marrow, which is the spongy tissue inside the cavities of bones that manufactures blood cells. Lymphatic tissue or circulating lymphocytes may also be located in other regions of the body, such as the skin, small intestine, liver, and other organs. There are two main types of lymphocytes: B-lymphocytes, which may produce specific antibodies to "neutralize" certain invading microorganisms, and T-lymphocytes, which may directly destroy microorganisms or assist in the activities of other lymphocytes. Mantle cell lymphoma and other cancers of the lymphatic system (lymphomas) result from errors in the production of a lymphocyte or transformation of a lymphocyte into a malignant cell. Abnormal, uncontrolled growth and multiplication (proliferation) of malignant lymphocytes may lead to enlargement of a specific lymph node region or regions; involvement of other lymphatic tissues, such as the spleen and bone marrow; and spread to other bodily tissues and organs, potentially resulting in life-threatening complications. The specific symptoms and physical findings may vary from case to case, depending upon the extent and region(s) of involvement and other factors. Non-Hodgkin's lymphomas (NHLs) may be broadly classified into lymphomas that arise from abnormal B-lymphocytes (B-cell lymphomas) and those derived from abnormal T-lymphocytes (T-cell lymphomas). Mantle cell lymphoma (MCL) is a B-cell lymphoma that develops from malignant B-lymphocytes within a region of the lymph node known as the mantle zone. NHLs may also be categorized based upon certain characteristics of the cancer cells as seen under a microscope and how quickly they may tend to grow and spread. For example, NHLs may be characterized as "low-grade" (or indolent) lymphomas, which tend to grow slowly and result in few associated symptoms, or "intermediate-" or "high-grade" (aggressive) lymphomas, which typically grow rapidly, requiring prompt treatment. There is some debate concerning whether MCL should be categorized as a slow-growing (indolent) or rapidly-growing (aggressive) lymphoma. Although experts have classified MCL as an aggressive lymphoma, it has been shown to have certain characteristics of indolent lymphoma. According to various estimates, MCL represents approximately 2 to 7 percent of adult NHLs in the United States and Europe. It primarily affects men over the age of 50 years. Many affected individuals have widespread disease at diagnosis, with involved regions often including multiple lymph nodes, the spleen, and, potentially, the bone marrow, the liver, and/or regions of the digestive (gastrointestinal) tract.

The following organizations may provide additional information and support:
American Cancer Society, Inc.
Association of Community Cancer Centers
Canadian Cancer Society
Cancer Hope Network
International Cancer Alliance for Research and Education
Leukemia & Lymphoma Society
Lymphoma Association (UK)
Lymphoma Foundation Canada
Lymphoma Research Foundation
National Cancer Institute
National Cancer Institute Physician Data Query (PDQ) Cancer Information Service
National Coalition for Cancer Survivorship
OncoLink: The University of Pennsylvania Cancer Center Resource
Rare Cancer Alliance

683   Maple Syrup Urine Disease

Synonyms
BCKD Deficiency
Branched Chain Alpha-Ketoacid
Dehydrogenase Deficiency
Branched Chain Ketonuria I
Classical Maple Syrup Urine Disease
MSUD

Disorder Subdivisions
Classic Maple Syrup Urine Disease
Intermediate Maple Syrup Urine Disease
Intermittent Maple Syrup Urine Disease
Thiamine-Responsive Maple Syrup Urine Disease

Maple syrup urine disease (MSUD) is an extremely rare inherited metabolic disorder characterized by a distinctive sweet odor of the urine and sweat. It is a serious disorder that, unless treated promptly and correctly, can be life-threatening. Therapy must be started at the earliest possible age to achieve the best results. MSUD is manageable, just as diabetes is manageable, but care and attention must be given to diet and to the treatment of even minor illnesses. Symptoms develop because the body is unable to break down (metabolize) three of the essential amino acids, leucine, isoleucine, and valine. They are essential because they are used by the body to build proteins, and they are three of 11 amino acids that must be obtained as part of the daily diet since the body cannot synthesize them. These three amino aids share a common characteristic of chemical structure and are thus known as the branched chain amino acids (BCAAs). An affected newborn will present with abnormally high concentrations of acidic metabolic by-products of the BCAAs in the blood and other tissues (metabolic acidosis) that, if left untreated, may lead to seizures or coma, and may be life-threatening. Genetically, there appear to be three forms of the disorder: IA, IB, and II. Clinically, at least four forms are described, to which some clinicians add a fifth.

The following organizations may provide additional information and support:
The Arc (A National Organization on Mental Retardation)
Belgian Association for Metabolic Diseases (BOKS)
CLIMB (Children Living with Inherited Metabolic Diseases)
Maple Syrup Urine Disease Family Support Group
March of Dimes Birth Defects Foundation
NIH/National Digestive Diseases Information Clearinghouse

684   Marcus Gunn Phenomenon

Synonyms
Marcus Gunn (Jaw-Winking) Syndrome
Marcus Gunn Ptosis (with Jaw-Winking)
Maxillopalpebral Synkinesis

Marcus Gunn phenomenon is a rare genetic disorder that is usually present at birth. It is characterized by the movement of one upper eyelid in a rapid rising motion each time the jaw moves. Other eye abnormalities and vision difficulties may also occur. The exact cause of this phenomenon is not known.

The following organizations may provide additional information and support:
March of Dimes Birth Defects Foundation
NIH/National Eye Institute

685   Marden-Walker Syndrome

Synonyms
Connective Tissue Disorder, Marden-Walker Type
MWS

Marden-Walker syndrome is a rare connective tissue disorder that is inherited as an autosomal recessive trait. Patients with this disorder typically have a distinct facial expression, a cleft or high-arched palate, small or receding jaw (micrognathia), bone joints in a fixed position, growth delay and limited control of muscle movement. Marden-Walker syndrome affects males more often than females.

The following organizations may provide additional information and support:
British Coalition of Heritable Disorders of Connective Tissue
National Home of Your Own Alliance

686   Marfan Syndrome

Synonyms
Arachnodactyly
Contractural Arachnodactyly
Dolichostenomelia
Marfanoid Hypermobility Syndrome

Marfan syndrome is an inherited disorder that affects the connective tissue of the heart and blood vessels (cardiovascular system). The musculoskeletal system (ligaments and muscles) and ocular system (eyes) are also affected. Major symptoms also include unusual height, large hands and feet, and involvement of the lungs. Symptoms vary greatly among affected individuals. Marfan syndrome is inherited as an autosomal dominant trait.

The following organizations may provide additional information and support:
British Coalition of Heritable Disorders of Connective Tissue
Canadian Marfan Association
Let Them Hear Foundation
March of Dimes Birth Defects Foundation
Marfan Association UK
National Marfan Foundation
NIH/National Arthritis and Musculoskeletal and Skin Diseases Information Clearinghouse
Sjëldne Diagnoser / Rare Disorders Denmark

687 Marinesco-Sjogren Syndrome

Synonyms
Marinesco-Garland Syndrome
Marinesco-Sjogren Syndrome-
Hypergonadotrophic Hypogonadism
Marinesco-Sjogren Syndrome-Myopathy
Marinesco-Sjogren Syndrome-Neuropathy
Marinesco-Sjogren-Garland Syndrome
Moravcsik-Marinesco-Sjogren Syndrome
Myopathy-Marinesco-Sjogren Syndrome

Marinesco-Sjogren syndrome (MSS) is a rare disorder that is inherited as an autosomal recessive genetic condition. The major features of this disorder are a loss of muscle coordination as a result of an affect on the cerebellum (cerebellar ataxia), cloudiness of the eyes' lenses (cataracts), increased muscle tension (spasticity), progressive muscle weakness, short stature, and mental deficits.

The following organizations may provide additional information and support:
Marinesco-Sjogren Syndrome Support Group
National Institute of Neurological Disorders and Stroke (NINDS)
National Scoliosis Foundation
NIH/National Arthritis and Musculoskeletal and Skin Diseases Information Clearinghouse

688 Maroteaux-Lamy Syndrome

Synonyms
Arylsulfatase-B Deficiency
MPS VI
MPS Disorder VI
Mucopolysaccharidosis VI
Polydystrophic Dwarfism

Maroteaux-Lamy syndrome is a rare genetic metabolic disorder that belongs to a group of disorders known as the mucopolysaccharidoses. The disorder is also known as mucopolysaccharidosis (MPS) type VI. Maroteaux-Lamy syndrome occurs in three types: a classic severe type, an intermediate type, and a mild type. The syndrome is characterized by a deficiency in the enzyme arylsulfatase B (also called N-acetylgalactosamine-4-sulfatase), which leads to an excess of dermatan sulfate in the urine. In general, growth retardation occurs from 2 to 3 years of age, with coarsening of facial features and abnormalities in the bones of hands and spine. Joint stiffness also occurs. The intellect is usually normal. The mucopolysaccharidoses (MPS) are a group of inherited lysosomal storage disorders. Lysosomes function as the primary digestive units within cells. Enzymes within lysosomes break down or digest particular nutrients, such as certain carbohydrates and fats. In individuals with MPS disorders, deficiency or malfunction of specific lysosomal enzymes leads to an abnormal accumulation of certain complex carbohydrates (mucopolysaccharides or glycosaminoglycans) in the arteries, skeleton, eyes, joints, ears, skin, and/or teeth. These accumulations may also be found in the respiratory system, liver, spleen, central nervous system, blood, and bone marrow. This accumulation eventually causes progressive damage to cells, tissues, and various organ systems of the body. There are several different types and subtypes of mucopolysaccharidosis. These disorders, with one exception, are inherited as autosomal recessive traits.

The following organizations may provide additional information and support:
Blind Children's Fund
Canadian Society for Mucopolysaccharide and Related Diseases, Inc.
CLIMB (Children Living with Inherited Metabolic Diseases)
National Association for Visually Handicapped
National MPS (Mucopolysaccharidoses/Mucolipidoses) Society, Inc.
NIH/National Digestive Diseases Information Clearinghouse

Society for Mucopolysaccharide Diseases
Vaincre Les Maladies Lysosomales

689 Marshall-Smith Syndrome

Synonym

 MSS

Marshall-Smith syndrome is characterized by un-usually quick physical growth and bone develop-ment (maturation), usually starting before birth. Other symptoms can include respiratory difficul-ties, mental retardation, and certain physical char-acteristics. (Note: Marshall-Smith syndrome is not to be confused with "Marshall" syndrome, which is very different from "Marshall-Smith" syndrome.)

The following organizations may provide addi-tional information and support:
Human Growth Foundation
Little People of America, Inc.
Little People's Research Fund, Inc.
MAGIC Foundation for Children's Growth

690 Marshall Syndrome

Synonym

 Deafness-Myopia-Cataract-Saddle Nose, Marshall Type

Marshall syndrome is a rare genetic disorder. Ma-jor symptoms may include a distinctive face with a flattened nasal bridge and nostrils that are tilted upward, widely spaced eyes, nearsightedness, cat-aracts and hearing loss. Marshall syndrome is in-herited as an autosomal dominant trait.

The following organizations may provide addi-tional information and support:
American Society for Deaf Children
Children's Craniofacial Association
Let's Face It (USA)
National Foundation for Facial Reconstruction
NIH/National Eye Institute

691 Mastocytosis

Synonyms

 Systemic Mast Cell Disease
 Systemic Mastocytosis
 Urticaria Pigmentosa

Disorder Subdivisions

 Aggressive Systemic Mastocytosis
 Cutaneous Mastocytosis

 Indolent Systemic Mastocytosis
 Mast Cell Leukemia
 Mast Cell Sarcoma/Extracutaneous Mastocytoma
 Mastocytosis with an Associated Hematological Disorder

Mastocytosis is a rare disorder characterized by abnormal accumulations of mast cells in skin, bone marrow, and internal organs such as the liver, spleen and lymph nodes. Cases beginning during adulthood tend to involve the inner organs in addition to the skin whereas, during childhood, the condition is often marked by skin manifesta-tions with minimal or no organ involvement. When there is evidence of bone marrow or in-ternal organ involvement, the disease is referred to as "systemic mastocytosis." Although the ma-jority of cases follow an indolent course, some pa-tients may have evidence of a blood disorder such as a myelodysplastic or myeloproliferative disor-der at the time of diagnosis. The course and prog-nosis of mastocytosis in these patients are deter-mined by this associated hematologic disorder. More aggressive forms of mastocytosis and mast cell leukemias are very rarely encountered.

The following organizations may provide addi-tional information and support:
CMPD Education Foundation
Mastocytosis Society, Inc.
NIH/National Arthritis and Musculoskeletal and Skin Diseases Information Clearinghouse

692 Maxillofacial Dysostosis

Synonym

 Hypoplasia of the Maxilla, Primary Familial

Maxillofacial dysostosis is a rare disorder inherited as an autosomal dominant trait. Major character-istics include an underdeveloped upper jaw, de-layed speech as well as poor articulation, down-slanting of the eyelids, and malformations of the external ear.

The following organizations may provide addi-tional information and support:
AboutFace USA
Children's Craniofacial Association
FACES: The National Craniofacial Association
Forward Face, Inc.
Let's Face It (USA)
National Craniofacial Foundation

693 Maxillonasal Dysplasia, Binder Type

Synonyms

Binder Syndrome
Maxillonasal Dysplasia
Nasomaxillary Hypoplasia

Binder type maxillonasal dysplasia is a rare condition characterized by abnormal development (dysplasia) of the nasal and upper jaw (nasomaxillary) regions. Affected individuals typically have an unusually flat, underdeveloped midface (midfacial hypoplasia), with an abnormally short nose and flat nasal bridge; underdeveloped upper jaw; relatively protruding lower jaw (mandible); and/or a "reverse overbite" (class III malocclusion). In some reported cases, various additional abnormalities have also been present, particularly of the spinal column of the neck (cervical vertebral anomalies). Many researchers suggest that Binder type maxillonasal dysplasia does not represent a distinct disease entity or syndrome, but, rather, is a nonspecific abnormality of the nasomaxillary regions. In most cases, the condition appears to occur randomly for unknown reasons (sporadically); rare familial cases have also been reported.

The following organizations may provide additional information and support:
AboutFace USA
Children's Craniofacial Association
FACES: The National Craniofacial Association
National Craniofacial Foundation
National Foundation for Facial Reconstruction
NIH/National Institute of Arthritis and Musculoskeletal and Skin Diseases

694 May-Hegglin Anomaly

Synonyms

Dohle Leukocyte Inclusions with Giant Platelets
Dohle's Bodies-Myelopathy
Hegglin's Disease
Leukocytic Inclusions with Platelet Abnormality
Macrothrombocytopenia with Leukocyte Inclusions
MHA

May-Hegglin Anomaly is a rare, inherited, blood platelet disorder characterized by abnormally large and misshapen platelets (giant platelets) and defects of the white blood cells known as leukocytes. The defect of the white blood cells consists of the presence of very small (2-5 micrometers)

rods, known as Dohle bodies, in the fluid portion of the cell (cytoplasm). Some people with this disorder may have no symptoms while others may have various bleeding abnormalities. In mild cases, treatment for May-Hegglin anomaly is not usually necessary. In more severe cases, transfusions of blood platelets may be necessary. In the past couple of years, it has become clear to physicians studying this disorder that May-Hegglin anomaly is one of a family of five autosomal dominant, giant platelet disorders, each of which involves slight variants (alleles) of the same gene in the same location. The other giant platelet disorders related to May-Hegglin anomaly are Sebastian syndrome, Fechtner syndrome, Epstein syndrome, and the Alport-like syndrome with macrothrombocytopenia. Advances in the understanding of one of these syndromes may help in understanding the others.

The following organizations may provide additional information and support:
March of Dimes Birth Defects Foundation
NIH/National Heart, Lung and Blood Institute Information Center

695 McCune-Albright Syndrome

Synonyms

Albright Syndrome
MAS
Osteitis Fibrosa Disseminata
PFD
POFD
Polyostotic, Fibrous Dysplasia
Precocious Puberty with Polyostotic Fibrosis and Abnormal Pigmentation

McCune-Albright syndrome (MAS) is a rare multisystem disorder characterized by (1) replacement of normal bone tissue with areas of abnormal fibrous growth (fibrous dysplasia); (2) patches of abnormal skin pigmentation (i.e., areas of light-brown skin [cafe-au-lait spots] with jagged borders); abnormalities in the glands that regulate the body's rate of growth, its sexual development, and certain other metabolic functions (multiple endocrine dysfunction). Depending on the number and location of the skeletal abnormalities, mobility may be impaired, as well as vision and/or hearing, and the individual may experience substantial pain. Malfunctioning endocrine glands can result in the development of secondary sexual characteristics at an age younger than normal (precocious puberty). McCune-Albright syndrome is the result of a genetic change (mutation) that occurs randomly, for no apparent reason (sporadic). In individuals with the disorder, this sporadic genetic mutation is present in only some of the body's cells (mosaic pattern). The symptoms and physical characteristics associated with the disorder vary greatly from case to case, depending upon the specific body cells and tissues that are affected by the genetic mutation. This mutation occurs after fertilization (postzygotic somatic mutation). It is not inherited from the parents. The range of severity of the disorder is very broad: some children are diagnosed in early infancy with obvious anomalies of bone and increased hormone production by one or more of the endocrine glands; others show no evidence of bone, skin or endocrine malfunction in childhood and may enter puberty at an appropriate age.

The following organizations may provide additional information and support:
MAGIC Foundation for Children's Growth
NIH/National Arthritis and Musculoskeletal and Skin Diseases Information Clearinghouse
NIH/National Institute of Child Health and Human Development
Paget Foundation for Paget's Disease of Bone and Related Disorders

696   McKusick Type Metaphyseal Chondrodysplasia

Synonyms
Cartilage-Hair Hypoplasia
CHH

McKusick type metaphyseal chondrodysplasia, also known as cartilage-hair hypoplasia, is a rare progressive inherited disorder characterized by unusually fine, sparse hair and short stature with abnormally short arms and legs (short-limbed dwarfism). Portions of the long bones of the arms and legs develop abnormally with unusual cartilage formations and subsequent abnormal bone formation at the large (bulbous) end portions (metaphyses) of these long bones (metaphyseal chondrodysplasia). In addition, most individuals with McKusick type metaphyseal chondrodysplasia may exhibit impairment of specialized cells (T-cells) that play an important role in helping the body's immune system to fight infection (cellular immunodeficiency). Affected individuals may also have abnormally low levels of certain white blood cells (neutropenia and lymphopenia); low levels

of circulating red blood cells (anemia); and/or increased susceptibility to certain infections, such as chickenpox. In some cases, affected infants may also exhibit improper intestinal absorption of certain necessary nutrients (malabsorption) and/or dental abnormalities such as unusually small teeth (microdontia). Some individuals with the disorder may also have additional physical abnormalities. The range and severity of symptoms vary widely from case to case. McKusick type metaphyseal chondrodysplasia is inherited as an autosomal recessive trait.

The following organizations may provide additional information and support:
Human Growth Foundation
Immune Deficiency Foundation
Little People of America, Inc.
MAGIC Foundation for Children's Growth
NIH/National Heart, Lung and Blood Institute Information Center

697   Measles

Synonyms
Morbilli
Nine Day Measles
Rubeola

Measles is a highly contagious viral disease occurring primarily in children. This disease is characterized by fever, cough, acute nasal mucous membrane discharge (coryza), inflammation of the lining of the eyelids (conjunctivitis), a spreading rash, and eruption of small, irregular, bright red spots (Koplik's spots) on the inner cheeks in the mouth with a minute bluish or white speck in the center of each. It is often difficult to avoid exposure to measles because it can be contracted from someone whose symptoms have not yet appeared. Measles is not contagious four days after appearance of the rash. As a result of vaccination to prevent measles, all cases that now occur in the United States have been brought from other countries. Measles continues to be a significant public health problem in developing countries, with 30-40 million cases per year. Most reported cases are from Africa.

The following organizations may provide additional information and support:
Centers for Disease Control and Prevention
NIH/National Institute of Allergy and Infectious Diseases

698 Meckel Syndrome

Synonyms
Dysencephalia Splanchnocystica
Gruber Syndrome
Meckel-Gruber Syndrome
MES
MKS

Disorder Subdivisions
Meckel Syndrome Type 1
Meckel Syndrome Type 2
Meckel Syndrome Type 3

Meckel syndrome is a rare inherited disorder characterized by abnormalities affecting several organ systems of the body (multisystem). Three classic symptoms are normally associated with Meckel syndrome: protrusion of a portion of the brain and its surrounding membranes (meninges) through a defect in the back or front of the skull (occipital encephalocele), multiple cysts on the kidneys (polycystic kidneys), and extra fingers and/or toes (polydactyly). Affected children may also have abnormalities affecting the head and face (craniofacial area), liver, lungs, and genitourinary tract. Meckel syndrome is inherited as an autosomal recessive trait.

The following organizations may provide additional information and support:
Genetic and Rare Diseases (GARD) Information Center
NIH/National Institute of Child Health and Human Development

699 Mediterranean Fever, Familial

Synonyms
Armenian Syndrome
Benign Paroxysmal Peritonitis
Familial Paroxysmal Polyserositis
FMF
MEF
Periodic Amyloid Syndrome
Periodic Peritonitis Syndrome
Polyserositis, Recurrent
Reimann Periodic Disease
Reimann's Syndrome
Siegel-Cattan-Mamou Syndrome

Familial Mediterranean fever (FMF) is a rare, inherited, inflammatory disease characterized by recurrent attacks of fever and acute inflammation of the membranes that line the abdominal cavity (peritonitis) and/or the lungs (pleuritis); pain and swelling of the joints (arthritis); and/or the heart (pericarditis) and, in some cases, skin rashes. In addition, some affected individuals may experience a serious complication known as amyloidosis, which is characterized by abnormal accumulation of a fatty-like substance (amyloid) in various parts of the body. If amyloid accumulates in the kidneys (renal amyloidosis), kidney function may be impaired and life-threatening complications may occur. In most instances, but not exclusively, FMF affects persons of Mediterranean origin such as Sephardic Jews, Arabs, Armenians, and Turks. FMF is inherited as an autosomal recessive trait. The causative gene on the short arm of chromosome 16 has been cloned.

The following organizations may provide additional information and support:
March of Dimes Birth Defects Foundation
NIH/National Digestive Diseases Information Clearinghouse
NIH/National Institute of Arthritis and Musculoskeletal and Skin Diseases

700 Medium Chain Acyl-CoA Dehydrogenase Deficiency

Synonyms
ACADM Deficiency
Carnitine Deficiency Secondary to MCAD Deficiency
Dicarboxylicaciduria due to Defect in Beta-Oxidation of Fatty Acids
Dicarboxylicaciduria due to MCADH Deficiency
MCAD Deficiency
Nonketotic Hypoglycemia and Carnitine Deficiency due to MCAD Deficiency

Medium chain acyl-CoA dehydrogenase (MCAD) deficiency is a rare genetic metabolic disorder characterized by a deficiency of the enzyme medium chain acyl-CoA dehydrogenase. This enzyme is found to be most active in the liver, certain white blood cells (leukocytes), and certain connective tissue cells (fibroblasts) and is necessary for the breakdown (oxidation) of certain fats (medium chain fatty acids). Failure to break down these fats can lead to the abnormal accumulation of fatty acids in the liver and the brain. Abnormally low levels of the MCAD enzyme may also hamper or interrupt other processes associated with the metabolism of fatty acids. In infants with MCAD deficiency, symptoms may include recurrent episodes of unusually low levels of a certain sugar (glucose) in the blood (hypoglycemia), lack of energy (lethargy), vomiting, and/or liver malfunction. These symptoms are most frequently triggered when an affected infant does not eat for an extended period of time (fasting). In some cases, a viral illness (e.g., upper respiratory infection) that limits food intake may cause the symptoms to occur. MCAD deficiency is the most common disease in a group of disorders that involve abnormalities of fatty acid metabolism (fatty acid oxidation disorders [FODs]). MCAD deficiency is inherited as an autosomal recessive trait. This disease entry was made possible due to the generosity of the Robert Lee and Clara Guthrie Patterson Trust, through grant funds provided for the National Organization for Rare Disorders' "Pediatric Rare Disease Database Project."

The following organizations may provide additional information and support:
CLIMB (Children Living with Inherited Metabolic Diseases)
FOD (Fatty Oxidation Disorders) Family Support Group
Lactic Acidosis Support Trust
NIH/National Institute of Diabetes, Digestive & Kidney Diseases
Organic Acidaemias UK
Organic Acidemia Association
United Mitochondrial Disease Foundation

701 Medullary Cystic Kidney Disease/Nephronophthisis

Synonyms
Cystic Disease of the Renal Medulla
Cysts of the Renal Medulla, Congenital
Familial Juvenile Hyperuricemic Nephropathy
Loken-Senior Syndrome
Polycystic Kidney Disease, Medullary Type
Renal-Retinal Dysplasia with Medullary Cystic Disease
Uromodulin Associated Kidney Disease

Disorder Subdivisions
Medullary Cystic Kidney Disease
Nephronophthisis

Medullary cystic kidney disease/nephronophthisis describes a number of different conditions that have the following features in common: (1) They are inherited. (2) Kidney disease develops, and dialysis or kidney transplant is required for treatment at some point. (3) Affected individuals some-

times, but not always, produce very large amounts of urine over the course of the day and may suffer from bed-wetting. (4) CAT scans or ultrasounds identify cysts in the middle (medulla) of the kidney in some, but not all, patients. (5) Gout develops in some types of this disease. These diseases can be divided into two groups or subtypes. The first group, termed nephronophthisis, is characterized by an autosomal recessive inheritance. This means that affected children must inherit two genes for the disease that have a mistake (mutation) in them. There are at least four types of nephronophthisis. All four types are associated with the production of large amounts of urine early in life and bed-wetting. In type 1, kidney failure develops at about age 13. In type 2, kidney failure usually develops from 1 to 3 years of age. In type 3, kidney failure develops at about age 19, and in type 4, kidney failure develops in the teenage years. In addition, about 15 percent of people with nephronophthisis also experience visual impairment caused by degeneration of the retina of the eyes (renal-retinal dysplasia). The second group, termed medullary cystic kidney disease, is characterized by autosomal dominant inheritance. There are at least two types of medullary cystic kidney disease, and kidney failure develops between ages 30 and 70. Gout is frequently present in medullary cystic kidney disease type 2. [For more information on this disorder, see the section on familial juvenile hyperuricemic nephropathy, which is the same disease.]

The following organizations may provide additional information and support:
American Foundation for Urologic Disease
American Kidney Fund, Inc.
March of Dimes Birth Defects Foundation
National Kidney Foundation
NIH/National Kidney and Urologic Diseases Information Clearinghouse

702 Medullary Sponge Kidney

Synonyms
Cacchi-Ricci Disease
Cystic Dilatation of Renal Collecting Tubes
Precalyceal Canalicular Ectasia
Sponge Kidney
Tubular Ectasia

Medullary sponge kidney is a rare disorder characterized by the formation of cystic malformations in the collecting ducts and the tubular structures within the kidneys (tubules) that collect urine. One or both kidneys may be affected. The initial symptoms of this disorder may include blood in the urine (hematuria), calcium stone formation in the kidneys (nephrolithiasis) or infection. The exact cause of medullary sponge kidney is not known.

The following organizations may provide additional information and support:
American Foundation for Urologic Disease
American Kidney Fund, Inc.
March of Dimes Birth Defects Foundation
National Kidney Foundation
NIH/National Kidney and Urologic Diseases Information Clearinghouse

703 Medulloblastoma

Medulloblastoma is a cancerous (malignant) tumor of the lower part of the brain (infratentorial [posterior fossa] tumor) that is derived from immature nerve cells known as neuroblasts (i.e., primitive neuroectodermal tumor [PNET]). It is considered the most common malignant brain tumor in children yet is extremely rare in adults. Medulloblastomas generally arise in the back (posterior), mid region (i.e., vermis) of the cerebellum, which is the part of the brain behind the brain stem involved in coordinating voluntary movements and regulating balance and posture. They typically infiltrate the roof or side wall of the fluid-filled fourth cavity (ventricle) of the brain, extending into the cavity. (There are four ventricles within the brain that are filled with cerebrospinal fluid [CSF] and joined by ducts, through which the fluid circulates.) Medulloblastomas may invade the protective membranes (meninges) surrounding the brain and spread (metastasize) via the CSF to the spinal cord, to the surface of the hemispheres of the brain (cerebrum), and, less commonly, to sites outside the brain and spinal cord (i.e., central nervous system), particularly to bone.

The following organizations may provide additional information and support:
American Brain Tumor Association
American Cancer Society, Inc.
Brain Tumor Society
Candlelighters Childhood Cancer Foundation
Harvard Brain Tissue Resource Center
National Brain Tumor Foundation
National Cancer Institute

National Cancer Institute Physician Data Query (PDQ) Cancer Information Service
OncoLink: The University of Pennsylvania Cancer Center Resource
Pediatric Brain Tumor Foundation

704 Megalocornea-Mental Retardation Syndrome

Synonyms
MMR Syndrome
Neuhauser Syndrome

Megalocornea-mental retardation syndrome is an extremely rare genetic disorder characterized by distinctive abnormalities of the eyes, diminished muscle tone that is apparent at birth (congenital hypotonia), and varying degrees of mental retardation. In some cases, additional abnormalities may also be present. The range and severity of symptoms and physical findings may vary from case to case. In most infants with megalocornea-mental retardation syndrome, the front, clear portion of the eyes through which light passes may be abnormally large (megalocornea). Both eyes are usually affected (bilateral involvement). Many affected infants also have additional eye (ocular) abnormalities including underdevelopment of the colored portion of the eyes (iris hypoplasia), abnormal "unsteadiness" of the irises during eye movements (iridodonesis), and/or other ocular abnormalities, potentially leading to varying degrees of visual impairment. In addition to abnormally diminished muscle tone (hypotonia), most affected infants also have additional neuromuscular abnormalities including abnormal delays in the acquisition of skills requiring the coordination of mental and muscular activities (psychomotor retardation) and/or an impaired ability to coordinate voluntary movements (ataxia). In most cases, affected infants and children also have moderate to severe mental retardation. In some cases, infants and children with megalocornea-mental retardation syndrome may have additional abnormalities including short stature; episodes of uncontrolled electrical disturbances in the brain (seizures); and/or certain distinctive abnormalities of the head and facial (craniofacial) area. Such craniofacial malformations may include an unusually prominent forehead (frontal bossing), widely spaced eyes (ocular hypertelorism), a long upper lip, an abnormally small lower jaw (hypoplastic mandible), and/or unusually large and/or "cup-shaped" ears. In most cases, megalocornea-mental retardation syndrome appears to occur randomly for unknown reasons (sporadically). In other cases, the disorder is thought to be inherited as an autosomal recessive genetic trait.

The following organizations may provide additional information and support:
Children's Craniofacial Association
Council of Families with Visual Impairment
Craniofacial Foundation of America
Glaucoma Research Foundation
Human Growth Foundation
National Association for Parents of Children with Visual Impairments (NAPVI)
National Association for Visually Handicapped
National Institute of Neurological Disorders and Stroke (NINDS)
NIH/National Eye Institute

705   Meige Syndrome

Synonyms
Brueghel Syndrome
Idiopathic Blepharospasm-Oromandibular Dystonia Syndrome
Segmental Cranial Dystonia

Meige syndrome is a rare neurological movement disorder (dyskinesia) characterized by spasms of the muscles of the eyelids and associated loss of tone in these eyelid muscles. Symptoms may include excessive blinking (blepharospasm) or involuntary eyelid closure. On occasion, the muscles of the face may also be involved. The exact cause of Meige syndrome is not known. This disorder generally affects people during late middle age.

The following organizations may provide additional information and support:
Benign Essential Blepharospasm Research Foundation, Inc.
Dystonia Medical Research Foundation
National Institute of Neurological Disorders and Stroke (NINDS)

706   Melanoma, Malignant

Synonyms
Melanoblastoma
Melanocarcinoma
Melanoepithelioma
Melanoma
Melanosarcoma
Melanoscirrhus
Melanotic Carcinoma
Nevus Pigmentosa

Disorder Subdivisions
Acral Lentiginous Melanoma
Juvenile Melanoma, Malignant
Malignant Lentigo (Melanoma)

Malignant melanoma is a common skin cancer that arises from the melanin cells within the upper layer of the skin (epidermis) or from similar cells that may be found in moles (nevi). This type of skin cancer may send down roots into deeper layers of the skin. Some of these microscopic roots may spread (metastasize) causing new tumor growths in vital organs of the body.

The following organizations may provide additional information and support:
American Cancer Society, Inc.
Cancer Research UK
Rare Cancer Alliance
Skin Cancer Foundation

707   MELAS Syndrome

Synonyms
Mitochondrial Myopathy, Encephalopathy, Lactic Acidosis, Stroke-Like Episode
Myopathy, Mitochondrial-Encephalopathy-Lactic Acidosis-Stroke

MELAS syndrome is one of a group of rare muscular disorders that are called mitochondrial encephalomyopathies. Mitochondrial encephalomyopathies are disorders in which a defect in genetic material arises from a part of the cell structure that releases energy (mitochondria) resulting in disease of the brain and muscles (encephalomyopathies). This mitochondrial defect and a condition known as "ragged red fibers" (an abnormality of muscle tissue when viewed under a microscope) are typically present. The most characteristic symptom of MELAS syndrome is recurring, stroke-like episodes in which sudden headaches are followed by vomiting and seizures. Short stature, an accumulation of lactic acid in the blood (lactic acidosis), and muscular weakness on one side of the body (hemiparesis) are typically present. Visual symptoms may include impaired vision or blindness in one half of the visual field (hemianopsia) and/or blindness due to lesions in the area of the brain concerned with vision (cortical blindness). Although the exact cause of MELAS syndrome is not fully understood, it has been found to run in families (familial).

The following organizations may provide additional information and support:
CLIMB (Children Living with Inherited Metabolic Diseases)
Children's European Mitochondrial Disease Network
Epilepsy Foundation
Lactic Acidosis Support Trust
Mitochondrial Support Group
Muscular Dystrophy Association
National Institute of Neurological Disorders and Stroke (NINDS)
United Mitochondrial Disease Foundation
Vereniging voor Kinder met Stofwisselingsziekten

708 Meleda Disease

Synonyms
Keratosis Palmoplantaris Transgradiens of Siemens
Mal de Meleda

Meleda disease is an extremely rare inherited skin disorder characterized by the slowly progressive development of dry, thick patches of skin on the palms of the hands and soles of the feet (palmoplantar hyperkeratosis). Affected skin may be unusually red (erythema) and become abnormally thick and scaly (symmetrical cornification). Affected children may also exhibit various abnormalities of the nails; excessive sweating (hyperhidrosis) associated with an unpleasant odor; and/or, in some cases, development of small, firm raised lesions (lichenoid plaques). The range and severity of symptoms may vary from case to case. Meleda disease is inherited as an autosomal recessive trait.

The following organizations may provide additional information and support:
March of Dimes Birth Defects Foundation
NIH/National Arthritis and Musculoskeletal and Skin Diseases Information Clearinghouse

709 Melkersson-Rosenthal Syndrome

Synonyms
Cheilitis Granulomatosa
MRS
Melkersson Syndrome

Melkersson-Rosenthal syndrome is a rare neurological disorder. Recurrent swelling (edema) of the face, especially the lip, is accompanied by intermittent paralysis and a fissured tongue (lingua plicata). This disorder usually begins during childhood.

The following organizations may provide additional information and support:
American Autoimmune Related Diseases Association, Inc.
March of Dimes Birth Defects Foundation
National Institute of Neurological Disorders and Stroke (NINDS)

710 Melnick-Needles Syndrome

Synonyms
Melnick-Needles Osteodysplasty
MNS
Osteodysplasty of Melnick and Needles

Melnick-Needles syndrome (MNS) is a genetic disorder of bone characterized by skeletal abnormalities and a specific facial appearance. The skeletal abnormalities include bowing of long bones, s-curved leg bones, ribbon-like ribs and a hardening of the skull base. The typical facial features include prominent, protruding eyes, full cheeks, an extremely small lower jaw and a hairy forehead. The condition may affect many bones of the body causing deformity and in some cases short stature. Melnick-Needles syndrome is thought to be inherited as an X-linked dominant genetic disorder.

The following organization may provide additional information and support:
Melnick-Needles Syndrome Support Group

711 Membranoproliferative Glomerulonephritis Type II

Synonyms
Dense Deposit Disease
MPGN Type II

Membranoproliferative glomerulonephritis type II (MPGN2) is one of three related types of a disease of the tiny filtering mechanism (glomeruli) of the kidney. The disease is probably autoimmune, although just what triggers the immune system to generate an autoimmune response is not known. The glomeruli are the part of the internal kidney structures where the blood flows through very small capillaries and is filtered through membranes to form urine. When this disease is present, deposits of immune materials spread through the membranes leading to a thickening of the capillary walls, and therefore disrupting the kidney function. Levels of some blood proteins related to the immune system (blood "complements") are altered in membranoproliferative glomerulonephritis. In particular, levels of some specific complement proteins are very low in the blood. This condition is referred to as "hypocomplementemia." In addition, blood may be found in the urine (hematuria), as well as proteins not normally found in urine samples (proteinuria). Damage to the glomeruli is progressive, leading in most cases to kidney failure and to long-term kidney dialysis or to kidney transplantation.

The following organizations may provide additional information and support:
Kidneeds Greater Cedar Rapids Foundation
National Kidney Foundation

712 Meniere Disease

Synonyms
Endolymphatic Hydrops
Labyrinthine Hydrops
Labyrinthine Syndrome
Lermoyez Syndrome

Meniere's disease is a disorder characterized by recurrent prostrating dizziness (vertigo), possible hearing loss and ringing sounds (tinnitus). It is associated with dilation of the membranous labyrinth (endolymphatic hydrops) in the ear.

The following organizations may provide additional information and support:
American Tinnitus Association
Autoimmune Information Network, Inc
Better Hearing Institute
Crouzon's/Meniere's Support Network
EAR (Education and Auditory Research) Foundation
Meniere's Australia, Inc.
Meniere's Disease and Dizziness Support Group
Meniere's Network
National Meniere's Disease Foundation, Inc.
NIH/National Institute on Deafness and Other Communication Disorders (Balance)
Vestibular Disorders Association (VEDA)

713 Meningioma

Synonyms
Arachnoidal Fibroblastoma
Dural Endothelioma
Leptomeningioma
Meningeal Fibroblastoma

Disorder Subdivisions
Frontal Tumor, Meningioma
Parietal Tumor, Meningioma
Temporal Tumor, Meningioma

Meningiomas are benign, slow-growing tumors, classified as brain tumors, but actually growing in the three protective membranes that surround the brain (meninges). Sometimes they cause thickening or thinning of adjoining skull bones. Meningiomas do not spread to other areas of the body.

The following organizations may provide additional information and support:
American Brain Tumor Association
American Cancer Society, Inc.
Brain Tumor Society
Harvard Brain Tissue Resource Center
National Brain Tumor Foundation

714 Meningitis

Disorder Subdivisions
Adult Meningitis
Infantile Meningitis
Neonatal Meningitis
Waterhouse-Friderichsen Syndrome, Meningitis

Meningitis is characterized by inflammation of the membranes (meninges) around the brain or spinal cord. The disorder can occur in three different forms: adult, infantile, and neonatal. This inflammation may be caused by different types of bacteria, viruses, fungi, or malignant tumors. Chemical reactions to certain injections into the spinal canal can also cause meningitis. This inflammation can begin suddenly (acute) or develop gradually (subacute). Adult forms of meningitis are characterized by fever, headache, and a stiff neck, sometimes with aching muscles. Nausea, vomiting and other symptoms may occur. Treatment with antibiotics is usually effective against the infection.

The following organizations may provide additional information and support:
The Arc (A National Organization on Mental Retardation)
Centers for Disease Control and Prevention
Child Brain Injury Trust
National Meningitis Association
NIH/National Institute of Allergy and Infectious Diseases
World Health Organization (WHO) Regional Office for the Americas (AMRO)

715 Meningitis, Bacterial

Synonyms
Bacterial Meningitis
Pyogenic Meningitis

Bacterial meningitis is a central nervous system disease caused by certain types of bacteria. Meningitis is characterized by inflammation of the membranes (meninges) around the brain or spinal cord. Inflammation can begin suddenly (acute) or develop gradually (subacute). Major symptoms may include fever, headache, and a stiff neck, sometimes with aching muscles. Nausea, vomiting and other symptoms may occur.

The following organizations may provide additional information and support:
Centers for Disease Control and Prevention
Child Brain Injury Trust
National Meningitis Association
NIH/National Institute of Allergy and Infectious Diseases
World Health Organization (WHO) Regional Office for the Americas (AMRO)

716 Meningitis, Meningococcal

Synonyms
Bacterial Meningococcal Meningitis
Epidemic Cerebrospinal Meningitis
Meningococcal Meningitis

Meningococcal meningitis is a form of meningitis caused by a specific bacterium known as *Neisseria meningitidis*. Meningitis is characterized by inflammation of the membranes (meninges) around the brain or spinal cord. This inflammation can begin suddenly (acute) or develop gradually (subacute). Symptoms may include fever, headache, and a stiff neck, sometimes with aching muscles. Nausea, vomiting and other symptoms may also occur. Skin rashes occur in about half of all individuals with meningococcal meningitis. Treatment with antibiotics and other drugs is usually effective against this infection.

The following organizations may provide additional information and support:
Centers for Disease Control and Prevention
Child Brain Injury Trust
National Meningitis Association
NIH/National Institute of Allergy and Infectious Diseases

World Health Organization (WHO) Regional Office for the Americas (AMRO)

717 Meningitis, Tuberculous

Synonyms
TBM
Tuberculous Meningitis

Tuberculous meningitis (TBM) is a form of meningitis characterized by inflammation of the membranes (meninges) around the brain or spinal cord and caused by a specific bacterium known as Mycobacterium tuberculosis. In TBM, the disorder develops gradually. Treatment with antibiotics and other drugs is usually effective against the infection.

The following organizations may provide additional information and support:
Centers for Disease Control and Prevention
Child Brain Injury Trust
NIH/National Institute of Allergy and Infectious Diseases

718 Meningococcemia

Synonyms
Meningococcal Disease
Meningococcemia-Meningitis

Disorder Subdivisions
Chronic Meningococcemia
Fulminant Meningococcemia (Waterhouse-Friderichsen Syndrome)

Meningococcemia is a rare infectious disease characterized by upper respiratory tract infection, fever, skin rash and lesions, eye and ear problems, and possibly a sudden state of extreme physical depression (shock) which may be life-threatening without appropriate medical care. There are two forms of meningococcemia. Fluminant meningococcemia develops very rapidly and is more severe than chronic meningococcemia, which has a waxing and waning course.

The following organizations may provide additional information and support:
Centers for Disease Control and Prevention
National Meningitis Association
NIH/National Institute of Allergy and Infectious Diseases

719 Menkes Disease

Synonyms
Copper Transport Disease
Kinky Hair Disease
Steely Hair Disease
Trichopoliodystrophy
X-linked Copper Deficiency

Disorder Subdivision
X-linked Copper Malabsorption

Menkes disease is a genetic disorder of copper metabolism that is detectable before birth (prenatally) and which follows a progressively degenerative path involving several organs of the body but especially the brain. It is characterized by seizures, mental retardation, stunted growth, failure to thrive, unstable body temperature, and very unusual color and texture of hair. It is the failure of the copper transport systems within the cell and then across the cell membrane that are responsible for the symptoms of the disorder. Because of the failure of this transport system, copper is unavailable to various cells where it is essential for the structure and function of various enzymes that control the development of hair, brain, bones, liver and arteries. Menkes disease is inherited as an X-linked recessive trait and is found disproportionately in male children.

The following organizations may provide additional information and support:
Justin Gordon and Menkes Syndrome Network
National Institute of Neurological Disorders and Stroke (NINDS)

720 MERRF Syndrome

Synonyms
Fukuhara Syndrome
MERRF
Myoclonus Epilepsy Associated with Ragged Red Fibers
Myoencephalopathy Ragged-Red Fiber Disease

MERRF syndrome (myoclonus epilepsy associated with ragged-red fibers) is one of a group of rare muscular disorders that are called mitochondrial encephalomyopathies. Mitochondrial encephalomyopathies are disorders in which a defect in the genetic material arises from a part of the cell structure that releases energy (mitochondria). This can cause a dysfunction of the brain and muscles (encephalomyopathies). The mitochondrial defect as well as "ragged-red fibers" (an abnormality of tissue when viewed under a microscope) are always present. The most characteristic symptom of MERRF syndrome is myoclonic seizures that are usually sudden, brief, jerking, spasms that can affect the limbs or the entire body. Impairment of the ability to coordinate movements (ataxia), as well as an abnormal accumulation of lactic acid in the blood (lactic acidosis) may also be present in affected individuals. Difficulty speaking (dysarthria), optic atrophy, short stature, hearing loss, dementia, and involuntary jerking of the eyes (nystagmus) may also occur.

The following organizations may provide additional information and support:
CLIMB (Children Living with Inherited Metabolic Diseases)
Children's European Mitochondrial Disease Network
Epilepsy Foundation
Lactic Acidosis Support Trust
Mitochondrial Support Group
Muscular Dystrophy Association
National Institute of Neurological Disorders and Stroke (NINDS)
United Mitochondrial Disease Foundation
Vereniging voor Kinder met Stofwisselingsziekten

721 Mesenteritis, Retractile

Synonyms
Mesenteric Panniculitis
Nodular Mesenteritis
Non-specific Sclerosing Mesenteritis
Sclerosing Panniculitis

Retractile mesenteritis, also known as mesenteric panniculitis, is a disorder that affects the digestive tract membranes. It is characterized by infection, inflammation and intestinal obstructions. Major symptoms include abdominal pain, nausea, vomiting, weight loss, and fever.

The following organizations may provide additional information and support:
Digestive Disease National Coalition
NIH/National Digestive Diseases Information Clearinghouse
Panniculitis Support Group

722   Mesothelioma

Synonym

Malignant Mesothelioma

Mesothelioma is a rare form of cancer that affects the membrane that covers and protects various internal organs of the body (mesothelium). The mesothelium is composed of two layers of specialized cells known as mesothelial cells. One layer directly surrounds an organ; the other forms a protective sac around the organ. The most common form of mesothelioma affects the membrane or sac that lines the lungs (pleura). Other common sites include the membrane lining the stomach (peritoneum) and the membrane lining the heart (pericardium).The term "cancer" refers to a group of diseases characterized by abnormal, uncontrolled cellular growth (e.g., mesothelial cells) that invades surrounding tissues and may spread (metastasize) to distant bodily tissues or organs via the bloodstream, the lymphatic system, or other means. Different forms of cancer, including mesothelioma, may be classified based upon the cell type involved, the specific nature of the malignancy, the tissues or organs affected, and the disease's clinical course. Symptoms of mesothelioma vary depending upon the location, type and stage of the cancer. Approximately 70 to 80 percent of cases of mesothelioma result from exposure to asbestos. Symptoms of mesothelioma may not appear until up to 50 years after initial exposure to asbestos. However, after symptoms become apparent, mesothelioma may rapidly progress to cause life-threatening complications.

The following organizations may provide additional information and support:
American Cancer Society, Inc.
American Lung Association
Asbestos Disease Awareness Organization
Canadian Cancer Society
Cancer Care, Inc.
Mesothelioma Applied Research Foundation, Inc.
National Cancer Information Center
National Cancer Institute
Rare Cancer Alliance

723   Metaphyseal Chondrodysplasia, Schmid Type

Synonyms

Japanese Type Spondylometaphyseal Dysplasia
MCDS
Schmid Metaphyseal Dysostosis

Metaphyseal chondrodysplasia, Schmid type (MCDS), is a very rare inherited disorder characterized by short stature with abnormally short arms and legs (short-limbed dwarfism) and bowed legs (genu varum). Other physical characteristics may include outward "flaring" of the bones of the lower rib cage, lumbar lordosis, pain in the legs, and/or hip deformities in which the thigh bone is angled toward the center of the body (coxa vara). Such abnormalities of the legs and hips typically result in an unusual "waddling" walk (gait). MCDS is transmitted as an autosomal dominant trait.

The following organization may provide additional information and support:
NIH/National Institute of Child Health and Human Development

724   Metatropic Dysplasia I

Synonyms

Chondrodystrophy, Hyperplastic Form
Dwarfism, Metatropic
Metatropic Dwarfism
Metatropic Dwarfism Syndrome
Metatropic Dysplasia

Metatropic dysplasia I is a rare genetic disorder characterized by extremely small stature, with short arms and legs. Other characteristics of this disorder are a narrow thorax, short ribs, and kyphoscoliosis (backward and sideways curvature of the spinal column) which develops into short trunk dwarfism.

The following organizations may provide additional information and support:
Human Growth Foundation
Little People of America, Inc.
Little People's Research Fund, Inc.
MAGIC Foundation for Children's Growth
Metatropic Dysplasia Dwarf Registry

725   Microvillus Inclusion Disease

Synonyms

Congenital Familial Protracted Diarrhea
Congenital Microvillus Atrophy
Davidson's Disease
Familial Enteropathy, Microvillus

Microvillus inclusion disease is an extremely rare inherited intestinal disorder (enteropathy) that is typically apparent within hours or days after birth. The disorder is characterized by chronic, severe, watery diarrhea and insufficient absorption (malabsorption) of necessary nutrients due to incomplete development (hypoplasia) and/or degeneration (atrophy) of certain cells of the wall of the small intestine (e.g., hypoplastic villus atrophy, defective brush-border assembly and differentiation). In infants with microvillus inclusion disease, chronic diarrhea and malabsorption may result in severe dehydration, deficiency of necessary nutrients (malnutrition), a failure to grow and gain weight at the expected rate (failure to thrive), and/or disturbance of the body's balance of acids and bases, which is essential in regulating the body's composition of bodily fluids (acidosis). Microvillus inclusion disease is inherited as an autosomal recessive genetic trait.

The following organizations may provide additional information and support:
March of Dimes Birth Defects Foundation
NIH/National Institute of Diabetes, Digestive & Kidney Diseases

726   Mikulicz Syndrome

Synonyms
Dacryosialoadenopathia
Dacryosialoadenopathy
Mikulicz-Radecki Syndrome
Mikulicz-Sjogren Syndrome
von Mikulicz Syndrome

Mikulicz syndrome is a chronic condition characterized by the abnormal enlargement of glands in the head and neck, including those near the ears (parotids) and those around the eyes (lacrimal) and mouth (salivary). The tonsils and other glands in the soft tissue of the face and neck may also be involved. Although the disorder is almost always described as benign, it always occurs in association with another underlying disorder such as tuberculosis, leukemia, syphilis, Hodgkin's disease, lymphosarcoma, Sjogren syndrome, or lupus (SLE). People who have Mikulicz syndrome are at heightened risk for developing lymphomas. Some people with Mikulicz syndrome may experience recurring fevers. The fever may be accompanied by dry eyes, diminished tear production (lacrimation), and inflammation of various parts of the eyes (uveitis). Lacrimal gland enlargement, parotid gland enlargement, dry mouth and dry eyes are the classic signs. The exact cause of Mikulicz syndrome is not known. Some scientists believe that Mikulicz syndrome should be considered a form of Sjogren syndrome.

The following organizations may provide additional information and support:
American Autoimmune Related Diseases Association, Inc.
NIH/National Oral Health Information Clearinghouse
Sjogren's Syndrome Foundation, Inc.

727   Miller Syndrome

Synonym
POADS

Disorder Subdivisions
Acrofacial Dysostosis, Postaxial Type
Acrofacial Dysostosis, Type Genee-Wiedep
Genee-Wiedemann Syndrome
Postaxial Acrofacial Dysostosis

Miller syndrome, also known as postaxial acrofacial dysostosis, is an extremely rare genetic disorder that is apparent at birth (congenital). The disorder is characterized by distinctive craniofacial malformations occurring in association with abnormalities of the outer aspects of the forearms and lower legs (postaxial limb deficiency). Craniofacial malformations may include underdevelopment of the cheekbones (malar hypoplasia); an abnormally small jaw (micrognathia); incomplete closure of the roof of the mouth (cleft palate); small, protruding, "cup-shaped" ears; and/or absence of tissue from (colobomas) and/or drooping of the lower eyelids, exposing the conjunctivae, the thin, delicate mucous membranes that line the eyelids as well as a portion of the eyeballs (ectropion). In infants and children with Miller syndrome, limb abnormalities may include incomplete development (hypoplasia), webbing (syndactyly), and/or absence of certain fingers and/or toes (e.g., the fifth digits and, in some cases, the fourth and third digits) and/or underdevelopment (hypoplasia) of the bones on the "pinky" side (ulna) and, in some cases, the thumb side of the forearms (radius), causing the forearms to appear unusually short. Additional physical abnormalities may be present in some cases. Miller syndrome is thought to be inherited as an autosomal recessive genetic trait.

The following organizations may provide additional information and support:
American Society for Deaf Children

Aniridia Network
Children's Craniofacial Association
FACES: The National Craniofacial Association
Foundation for Nager and Miller Syndromes
National Craniofacial Foundation

728   Mitral Valve Prolapse Syndrome

Synonyms
Barlow Syndrome
Billowing Mitral Leaflet Syndrome
Click-Murmur Syndrome
Floppy Valve Syndrome
Mitral Click-Murmur Syndrome
Mitral Leaflet Syndrome
MVP
MVPS
Systolic Click-Murmur Syndrome

The mitral valve is the valve between the left upper and left lower chambers (left atrium and left ventricle) of the heart. Mitral valve prolapse syndrome (MVP) is a common condition in which one or both of the flaps (cusps) of the mitral valve bulge or collapse backward (prolapse) into the left atrium during ventricular contraction (systole). In some cases, this may allow leakage or the backward flow of blood from the left ventricle back into the left atrium (mitral regurgitation). The exact underlying mechanism responsible for MVP remains unknown. In many affected individuals, the condition appears to occur in the absence of an associated disorder or syndrome (idiopathic). Evidence indicates that the condition is sometimes familial, suggesting autosomal dominant inheritance. In other cases, MVP occurs in association with certain inherited connective tissue diseases, other heart abnormalities, or other underlying conditions, disorders, or syndromes. In many individuals with MVP, no associated symptoms are apparent (asymptomatic). However, in other cases, the condition may result in chest pain, abnormal heart rhythms (arrhythmias), fatigue, dizziness, and/or other symptoms and signs. MVP is often associated with a characteristic click and/or a subsequent delayed murmur that may be detected through use of a stethoscope during physical examination.

The following organizations may provide additional information and support:
American Heart Association
Cardiac Arrhythmias Research and Education Foundation, Inc.

Congenital Heart Anomalies, Support, Education, & Resources
March of Dimes Birth Defects Foundation
NIH/National Heart, Lung and Blood Institute Information Center

729   Mixed Connective Tissue Disease (MCTD)

Synonyms
Connective Tissue Disease
MCTD

Mixed connective tissue disease (MCTD) is a rare connective tissue disorder. MCTD is used to describe what may be an overlapping group of connective tissue disorders that cannot be diagnosed in more specific terms. These disorders include systemic lupus erythematosus, polymyositis, and scleroderma. Individuals with MCTD have symptoms of each of these disorders including arthritic, cardiac, pulmonary and skin manifestations; kidney disease; muscle weakness; and dysfunction of the esophagus. The exact cause of mixed connective tissue disease is unknown.

The following organizations may provide additional information and support:
American Autoimmune Related Diseases Association, Inc.
Arthritis Foundation
Autoimmune Information Network, Inc
British Coalition of Heritable Disorders of Connective Tissue
Lupus Foundation of America, Inc.
National Marfan Foundation
NIH/National Institute of Arthritis and Musculoskeletal and Skin Diseases
Scleroderma Foundation
Scleroderma Research Foundation
Sjogren's Syndrome Foundation, Inc.

730   Moebius Syndrome

Synonyms
Congenital Facial Diplegia Syndrome
Congenital Oculofacial Paralysis
Mobius Syndrome
Moebius Sequence

Moebius syndrome is a rare developmental disorder present at birth (congenital) that is characterized by facial paralysis. Affected individuals are not able to smile or frown because two important nerves, the sixth (abducens) and seventh (facialis) cranial nerves are absent or not fully developed. In some instances, this syndrome may also be associated with physical problems in other parts of the body.

The following organizations may provide additional information and support:
AboutFace USA
Birth Defect Research for Children, Inc.
Children's Craniofacial Association
Cleft Palate Foundation
FACES: The National Craniofacial Association
Forward Face, Inc.
Let Them Hear Foundation
Let's Face It (USA)
Moebius Syndrome Foundation
Moebius Syndrome Support Network (UK)
National Institute of Neurological Disorders and Stroke (NINDS)
Society for the Rehabilitation of the Facially Disfigured, Inc.

731 Monilethrix

Monilethrix is a rare inherited disorder characterized by sparse, dry, and/or brittle hair that often breaks before reaching more than a few inches in length. The hair may lack luster, and there may be patchy areas of hair loss (alopecia). Another common symptom may be the appearance of elevated spots (papules) surrounding the hair follicles that may be covered with gray or brown crusts or scales (perifollicular hyperkeratosis). When viewed under a microscope, the hair shaft resembles a string of evenly-spaced beads. In most cases, monilethrix is inherited as an autosomal dominant trait.

The following organizations may provide additional information and support:
Genetic and Rare Diseases (GARD) Information Center
Locks of Love

732 Morquio Syndrome

Synonyms
Morquio Disease
MPS IV
Mucopolysaccharidosis IV

Disorder Subdivisions
Morquio Syndrome A
Morquio Syndrome B

Morquio syndrome (mucopolysaccharidosis type IV; MPS IV) is a mucopolysaccharide storage disease that exists in two forms (Morquio syndromes A and B) and occurs because of a deficiency of the enzymes N-acetyl-galactosamine-6-sulfatase and beta-galactosidase, respectively. A deficiency of either enzyme leads to the accumulation of mucopolysaccharides in the body, abnormal skeletal development, and additional symptoms. In most cases, individuals with Morquio syndrome have normal intelligence. The clinical features of MPS IV-B are usually fewer and milder than those associated with MPS IV-A. Symptoms may include growth retardation, a prominent lower face, an abnormally short neck, knees that are abnormally close together (knock knees or genu valgum), flat feet, abnormal sideways and front-to-back or side-to-side curvature of the spine (kyphoscoliosis), abnormal development of the growing ends of the long bones (epiphyses), and/or a prominent breast bone (pectus carinatum). Hearing loss, weakness of the legs, and/or additional abnormalities may also occur. The mucopolysaccharidoses (MPS) are a group of inherited lysosomal storage disorders. Lysosomes function as the primary digestive units within cells. Enzymes within lysosomes break down or digest particular nutrients, such as certain carbohydrates and fats. In individuals with MPS disorders, deficiency or malfunction of specific lysosomal enzymes leads to an abnormal accumulation of certain complex carbohydrates (mucopolysaccharides or glycosaminoglycans) in the arteries, skeleton, eyes, joints, ears, skin, and/or teeth. These accumulations may also be found in the respiratory system, liver, spleen, central nervous system, blood, and bone marrow. This accumulation eventually causes progressive damage to cells, tissues, and various organ systems of the body. There are several different types and subtypes of mucopolysaccharidosis. These disorders, with one exception, are inherited as autosomal recessive traits.

The following organizations may provide additional information and support:
Canadian Society for Mucopolysaccharide and Related Diseases, Inc.
CLIMB (Children Living with Inherited Metabolic Diseases)
Instituto de Errores Innatos del Metabolismo
National MPS (Mucopolysaccharidoses/Mucolipidoses) Society, Inc.
NIH/National Digestive Diseases Information Clearinghouse
Society for Mucopolysaccharide Diseases
Vaincre Les Maladies Lysosomales

733 Motor Neuron Disease

Synonyms
Motoneuron Disease
Motoneurone Disease
Motor Neuron Syndrome
Motor Neurone Disease

Disorder Subdivisions
ALS Included
Amyotrophic Lateral Sclerosis
Benign Focal Amyotrophy
Duchenne's Paralysis
Infantile Spinal Muscular Atrophy (All Types)
Juvenile Spinal Muscular Atrophy
Kugelberg-Welander Syndrome
Lou Gehrig's Disease, Included
Progressive Bulbar Palsy
Spinal Muscular Atrophy, All Types
Werdnig-Hoffmann Disease

Motor neuron disease comprises a group of severe disorders of the nervous system characterized by progressive degeneration of motor neurons (neurons are the basic nerve cells that combine to form nerves). Motor neurons control the behavior of muscles. Motor neuron diseases may affect the upper motor neurons, nerves that lead from the brain to the medulla (a part of the brain stem) or to the spinal cord, or the lower motor neurons, nerves that lead from the spinal cord to the muscles of the body, or both. Spasms and exaggerated reflexes indicate damage to the upper motor neurons. A progressive wasting (atrophy) and weakness of muscles that have lost their nerve supply indicate damage to the lower motor neurons.

The following organizations may provide additional information and support:
Amyotrophic Lateral Sclerosis Association
Families of Spinal Muscular Atrophy
International Alliance of ALS/MND Associations
Motor Neurone Disease Association
Muscular Dystrophy Association
National Institute of Neurological Disorders and Stroke (NINDS)
Scottish Motor Neurone Disease Association

734 Mountain Sickness, Acute

Synonyms
Acosta's Disease
Acute High Altitude Sickness
AMS
High Altitude Illness
Hypoxia, Mountain Sickness (Acute)
Mareo
Puna
Soroche

Disorder Subdivisions
HACE
HAPE
High Altitude Cerebral Edema (HACE)
High Altitude Pulmonary Edema (HAPE)

Acute mountain sickness is a group of symptoms that may occur in some people who ascend rapidly to altitudes higher than 8200 ft. (2500 m). Major symptoms may include headaches, nausea, vomiting, and insomnia.

735 Mowat-Wilson Syndrome

Synonyms
Hirschsprung Disease-Mental Retardation Syndrome
MWS

Mowat-Wilson syndrome (MWS) is a rare genetic disorder that may be apparent at birth or in the first year of life. MWS is characterized by mental retardation, distinctive facial features and seizures. Other congenital anomalies occur in some individuals and can include a gastrointestinal disease known as Hirschsprung disease in which a narrowing of a portion of the colon is present, heart (cardiac) defects, kidney (renal) abnormalities, male genital abnormalities and short stature. Some affected individuals may not be recognized until childhood or adulthood, especially when Hirschsprung disease is not present. Mowat-Wilson syndrome is caused by an abnormality in ZFHX1B gene that is usually the result of a new genetic change (mutation) in the affected person.

The following organizations may provide additional information and support:
Association of Genetic Support of Australasia, Inc.
Congenital Heart Anomalies, Support, Education, & Resources
International Foundation for Functional Gastrointestinal Disorders
NIH/National Institute of Child Health & Human Development (Preg & Perinat)
Pull-thru Network

736 Moyamoya Syndrome

Synonym

Moya-moya Disease

Moyamoya syndrome is a progressive disorder that affects the blood vessels in the brain (cerebrovascular). It is characterized by the narrowing (stenosis) and/or closing (occlusion) of the carotid artery, the major artery that delivers blood to the brain. Inadequate blood supply leads to reduced oxygen to the brain, and it is this oxygen deprivation that causes the signs of Moyamoya. Those signs most typically include paralysis of the feet, legs or the upper extremities. Headaches, various vision problems, mental retardation, and psychiatric problems may also occur. Approximately 10% of cases of Moyamoya syndrome are due to a genetic cause and are termed primary Moyamoya syndrome. Secondary Moyamoya syndrome refers to cases in which the syndrome is a consequence or result of another underlying disorder. In secondary Moyamoya syndrome, when it is not a result of a genetic cause, it is important for the physician to determine the root underlying cause.

The following organizations may provide additional information and support:
Moyamoya.com
National Institute of Neurological Disorders and Stroke (NINDS)

737 Mucha Habermann Disease

Synonyms

Pityriasis Lichenoides et Varioliformis Acuta
PLEVA

Mucha-Habermann disease is a rare skin disorder of uncertain origin characterized by recurrent red, round and elevated lesions (papules), hemorrhages under the skin (purpura), and blister-like lesions (vesicles). It occurs most often in young adults and children. Historically, Mucha-Habermann referred only to the acute form of this disease. Now the term applies both to the acute and the chronic, less florid form.

The following organizations may provide additional information and support:
American Autoimmune Related Diseases Association, Inc.
NIH/National Arthritis and Musculoskeletal and Skin Diseases Information Clearinghouse

738 Mucolipidosis IV

Synonyms

Berman Syndrome
Ganglioside Neuraminidase Deficiency
Ganglioside Sialidase Deficiency
ML IV
ML Disorder IV
Neuraminidase Deficiency
Sialolipidosis

Mucolipidosis IV is a rare inherited metabolic disorder believed to be characterized by a deficiency of transport channel receptor protein, based upon the discovery of the mucolipidosis IV gene. This deficiency may lead to the accumulation of certain fatty substances (mucolipids) and certain complex carbohydrates (mucopolysaccharides) within the cells of many tissues of the body. Mucolipidosis IV is characterized by mental retardation; severe impairment in the acquisition of skills requiring the coordination of muscular and mental activities (psychomotor retardation); diminished muscle tone (hypotonia); clouding (opacity) of the clear portion of the eyes through which light passes (cornea); and/or degeneration of the nerve-rich membrane lining the eyes (retinal degeneration). Mucolipidosis IV is thought to be inherited as an autosomal recessive genetic trait.

The following organizations may provide additional information and support:
ML 4 (Mucolipidosis Type IV Foundation)
NIH/National Digestive Diseases Information Clearinghouse

739 Mucopolysaccharidoses

Synonyms

MPS
MPS Disorder

Disorder Subdivisions

MPS I H (Hurler Disease)
MPS I H/S (Hurler/Scheie Syndrome)
MPS I S (Scheie Syndrome)
MPS II-(Hunter Syndrome)
MPS III A, B, C, and D (Sanfilippo Syndrome)
MPS IV A and B (Morquio Syndrome)
MPS V (obsolete)
MPS VI (Maroteaux-Lamy Syndrome)
MPS VII (Sly Syndrome)
MPS VIII (obsolete)
MPS IX (Hyaluronidase Deficiency)

The mucopolysaccharidoses (MPS) are a group of inherited lysosomal storage disorders. Lysosomes function as the primary digestive units within cells. Enzymes within lysosomes break down or digest particular nutrients, such as certain carbohydrates and fats. In individuals with MPS disorders, deficiency or malfunction of specific lysosomal enzymes leads to an abnormal accumulation of certain complex carbohydrates (mucopolysaccharides or glycosaminoglycans) in the arteries, skeleton, eyes, joints, ears, skin, and/or teeth. These accumulations may also be found in the respiratory system, liver, spleen, central nervous system, blood, and bone marrow. This accumulation eventually causes progressive damage to cells, tissues, and various organ systems of the body. There are several different types and subtypes of mucopolysaccharidosis. These disorders, with one exception, are inherited as autosomal recessive traits.

The following organizations may provide additional information and support:
Belgian Association for Metabolic Diseases (BOKS)
Canadian Society for Mucopolysaccharide and Related Diseases, Inc.
Gesellschaft fur Mukopolysaccharidosen und ahuliche Erkrankungen
Instituto de Errores Innatos del Metabolismo
Let Them Hear Foundation
March of Dimes Birth Defects Foundation
National Institute of Neurological Disorders and Stroke (NINDS)
National MPS (Mucopolysaccharidoses/Mucolipidoses) Society, Inc.
NIH/National Institute of Diabetes, Digestive & Kidney Diseases
Society for Mucopolysaccharide Diseases
Vaincre Les Maladies Lysosomales

740   Mucopolysaccharidosis Type I

Synonyms
Gargoylism
Hurler Disease
MPS I
MPS Disorder I

Disorder Subdivisions
Hurler Syndrome (MPS IH)
Hurler-Scheie Syndrome (MPS IH/S)
Scheie Syndrome (MPS IS)

Mucopolysaccharidoses (MPS disorders) are a group of rare genetic disorders caused by the deficiency of one of ten specific lysosomal enzymes, resulting in an inability to metabolize complex carbohydrates (mucopolysaccharides) into simpler

molecules. The accumulation of these large, undegraded mucopolysaccharides in the cells of the body causes a number of physical symptoms and abnormalities. Mucopolysaccharidosis type I (MPS I) is a form of MPS caused by a deficiency of the enzyme alpha-L-iduronidase. The most severe form of MPS I is often called Hurler syndrome (or MPS IH). It is named for the physician, Gertrud Hurler, who first described the disorder in 1919. A milder form of MPS I is called Scheie syndrome (or MPS IS), and the name Hurler-Scheie (MPS IH/S) is sometimes applied to an intermediate form that does not fit clearly in either the milder or more severe category.

The following organizations may provide additional information and support:
The Arc (A National Organization on Mental Retardation)
CLIMB (Children Living with Inherited Metabolic Diseases)
Canadian Society for Mucopolysaccharide and Related Diseases, Inc.
Let Them Hear Foundation
National MPS (Mucopolysaccharidoses/Mucolipidoses) Society, Inc.
Society for Mucopolysaccharide Diseases

741   Mucopolysaccharidosis Type III

Synonyms
MPS III
MPS Disorder III
Mucopolysaccharide Storage Disease Type III
Oligophrenic Polydystrophy
Polydystrophia Oligophrenia

Disorder Subdivisions
Sanfilippo Disease (Types A, B, C, and D)
Sanfilippo Syndrome (Types A, B, C, and D)

The mucopolysaccharidoses (MPS disorders) are a group of rare genetic disorders caused by the deficiency of one of the lysosomal enzymes, resulting in an inability to metabolize complex carbohydrates (mucopolysaccharides) into simpler molecules. High concentrations of mucopolysaccharides in the cells of the central nervous system, including the brain, cause the neurological and developmental deficits that accompany these disorders. Mucopolysaccharides are rather thick jelly-like ("muco") compounds made of long chains ("poly") of sugar-like (saccharides) molecules used to make connective tissues in the body. Lysosomal enzymes are found in the lysosome, a very small membrane-contained body (organelle) found in the cytoplasm of most cells. The lysosome is often called the "waste disposal plant" of the cell. The accumulation of these large, undegraded mucopolysaccharides in the cells of the body is the cause of a number of physical symptoms and abnormalities. MPS-III (Sanfilippo syndrome) is one of seven MPS disorders. It is an inborn error of metabolism that is transmitted as an autosomal recessive genetic disorder. MPS-lll has been subdivided into four types: MPS-III type A, MPS-III type B, MPS-III type C, and MPS-III type D. All types are associated with some degree of mental deterioration, but the severity depends on the particular type of MPS-III. Several physical defects may be present, and the severity of these defects varies with the type of MPS-III. In the case of each type of MPS-III, abnormal amounts of a specific, chemically complex molecule is excreted in the urine. The excreted chemical is the same for each of the four types of MPS-III, since the defective gene involves a different step, and thus a different enzyme, in the deconstruction of the same mucopolysaccharide. By testing for one or another of these enzymes, the variant type may be readily identified.

The following organizations may provide additional information and support:
The Arc (A National Organization on Mental Retardation)
CLIMB (Children Living with Inherited Metabolic Diseases)
Canadian Society for Mucopolysaccharide and Related Diseases, Inc.
National MPS (Mucopolysaccharidoses/Mucolipidoses) Society, Inc.
NIH/National Digestive Diseases Information Clearinghouse
Society for Mucopolysaccharide Diseases
Vaincre Les Maladies Lysosomales

742 Mucous Membrane Pemphigoid

Synonyms
Cicatricial Pemphigoid
CP
MMP
Mucous Membrane Pemphigoid

Disorder Subdivisions
Brunsting-Perry Syndrome
Localized Cicatricial Pemphigoid
Vegetating Cicatricial Pemphigoid

Mucous membrane pemphigoid (MMP) is a rare group of chronic autoimmune disorders characterized by blistering lesions that primarily affect the various mucous membranes of the body. The mucous membranes of the mouth and eyes are most often affected. The mucous membranes of the nose, throat, genitalia, and anus may also be affected. The symptoms of MMP vary among affected individuals depending upon the specific site(s) involved and the progression of the disease. Blistering lesions eventually heal, sometimes with scarring. Progressive scarring may potentially lead to serious complications affecting the eyes and throat. In some cases, blistering lesions also form on the skin, especially in the head and neck area. The exact cause of MMP is unknown. Mucous membrane pemphigoid has been known by many different names within the medical literature including benign mucous membrane pemphigoid, cicatricial (scarring) pemphigoid, and ocular cicatricial pemphigoid. In March of 2002, a consensus group of researchers determined that mucous membrane pemphigoid was the best designation for this group of disorders. The term "benign" mucous membrane pemphigoid was deemed inappropriate because of the potential for serious complications in some cases. The term "cicatricial" pemphigoid excluded affected individuals who do not develop scarring. Site-specific terms such as "ocular" cicatricial pemphigoid excluded individuals with multiple site involvement.

The following organizations may provide additional information and support:
American Autoimmune Related Diseases Association, Inc.
Autoimmune Information Network, Inc
International Pemphigus Foundation
NIH/National Arthritis and Musculoskeletal and Skin Diseases Information Clearinghouse

743 MULIBREY Nanism Syndrome (Perheentupa Syndrome)

Synonyms
Constrictive Pericarditis with Dwarfism
Dwarfism-Pericarditis
Mulibrey Dwarfism
Perheentupa Syndrome
Pericardial Constriction with Growth Failure

MULIBREY nanism syndrome (Perheentupa syndrome) is an extremely rare inherited disorder characterized by profound growth delays (dwarfism) and distinctive abnormalities of the muscles, liver, brain, and eyes. The acronym MULI-BREY stands for (MU)scle, (LI)ver, (BR)ain, and (EY)e. "Nanism" is another word for "dwarfism." Characteristic symptoms may include low birth weight, short stature, and severe progressive growth delays. Muscles are usually underdeveloped and lack normal tone (hypotonia). Some infants with this disorder may have an abnormally large liver (hepatomegaly). Other findings may include abnormal widening (dilation) of the spaces surrounding the brain (cerebral ventricles) and the excessive accumulation of fluid (cerebrospinal) around the brain (hydrocephalus). Infants with MULIBREY nanism typically have yellow discolorations in their eyes. In addition, a portion of the inner layer of the eyes may be underdeveloped (choriocapillaris hypoplasia). Vision may also be impaired (amblyopia). Infants with MULIBREY nanism syndrome may also experience symptoms related to overgrowth of the fibrous sac that surrounds the heart (constrictive pericarditis). Symptoms may include excessive fluid in the lungs (pulmonary effusion) and abnormal fluid accumulation in the abdomen (ascites). Other related symptoms may include unusual swelling of the arms and/or legs (peripheral edema) and/or enlargement of the heart. MULIBREY nanism syndrome is inherited as an autosomal recessive genetic trait.

The following organizations may provide additional information and support:
American Heart Association
Human Growth Foundation
Hydrocephalus Association
Hydrocephalus Support Group, Inc.
Little People of America, Inc.
Little People's Research Fund, Inc.
NIH/National Eye Institute

744   Mullerian Aplasia

Synonyms
Mullerian Duct Aplasia
Mullerian Duct Failure

Mullerian aplasia is a rare disorder that affects only females. It is characterized by the absence of the uterus, the cervix, and the upper part of the vagina in a female who has normal ovarian function and normal external genitalia. Although females with this disorder develop normal secondary sexual characteristics during puberty (e.g., breast development and pubic hair), the failure of menstrual cycles to begin (primary amenorrhea) is usually the initial symptom. The exact cause of mullerian

aplasia is not known. The unusual physical characteristics associated with this disorder seem to result from developmental abnormalities during embryonic or fetal growth.

The following organizations may provide additional information and support:
American Kidney Fund, Inc.
National Kidney Foundation
NIH/National Kidney and Urologic Diseases Information Clearinghouse

745   Multiple Epiphyseal Dysplasia

Synonym
MED

Disorder Subdivisions
Multiple Epiphyseal Dysplasia, Fairbank Type
Multiple Epiphyseal Dysplasia, Ribbing Type

Multiple epiphyseal dysplasia (MED) is a rare inherited spectrum of disorders characterized by malformation (dysplasia) of the "growing portion" or head of the long bones (epiphyses). Affected individuals may have an abnormally short thighbone (femur), unusually short hands and fingers, mild short stature, a waddling gait, and/or pain in the hips and knees. In some cases, painful swelling and inflammation of certain joints (arthritis) may be present as early as 5 years of age. Most cases of multiple epiphyseal dysplasia are inherited as autosomal dominant traits; rare cases are inherited as autosomal recessive traits.

The following organizations may provide additional information and support:
Human Growth Foundation
International Center for Skeletal Dysplasia
MAGIC Foundation for Children's Growth
NIH/National Institute of Child Health and Human Development
Restricted Growth Association

746   Multiple Sclerosis

Synonyms
Demyelinating Disease
Disseminated Sclerosis
MS
Primary Progressive Multiple Sclerosis
Relapsing-Remitting Multiple Sclerosis

Multiple sclerosis is a chronic neuroimmunologic (both the nervous system and the immunological system are involved) disorder of the central nervous system involving the brain, spinal cord and optic nerves. By means of a mechanism not clearly understood, the protective fatty, insulating substance called myelin sheath that covers the nerve is destroyed. The inflammatory attacks that produce the characteristic scarring (plaques or patches) of the myelin sheath occur randomly, vary in intensity, and at multiple sites. The course of the disease may advance, relapse, remit, or stabilize. The randomness of the location of plaques or patches affects the nerve's ability to transmit information (neurotransmission) and causes a wide range of neurological symptoms, which may vary from person to person. Recently it has been learned that the nerve fibers themselves (axons), in addition to the myelin sheaths, are affected by the neuroimmunologic attacks. Damage to the nerve cells may be irreversible. As a result, clinicians recommend early intervention with one of the disease-modifying agents.

The following organizations may provide additional information and support:
Autoimmune Information Network, Inc
Christopher Reeve Paralysis Foundation
Consortium of Multiple Sclerosis Centers
Multiple Sclerosis International Federation
National Institute of Neurological Disorders and Stroke (NINDS)
National Multiple Sclerosis Society
New Horizons Un-Limited, Inc.
Spastic Paraplegia Foundation
Stem Cell Research Foundation
Vasculitis of the Central Nervous System
WE MOVE (Worldwide Education and Awareness for Movement Disorders)

747 Multiple Sulfatase Deficiency

Synonyms
Disorder of Conification 13
DOC 13 (Multiple Sulfatase Deficiency)
Mucosulfatidosis
Multiple Sulfatase Deficiency (DOC 13)
Multiple Sulfatase Deficiency Syndrome

Multiple sulfatase deficiency is a very rare hereditary metabolic disorder in which all of the known sulfatase enzymes (thought to be seven in number) are deficient or inoperative. Major symptoms include mildly coarsened facial features, deafness, and an enlarged liver and spleen (hepatosplenomegaly). Abnormalities of the skeleton may occur, such as curvature of the spine (lumbar

kyphosis) and the breast bone. The skin is usually dry and scaly (ichthyosis). Before symptoms are noticeable, children with this disorder usually develop more slowly than normal. They may not learn to walk or speak as quickly as other children.

The following organizations may provide additional information and support:
Association Europeene contre les Leucodystrophes
CLIMB (Children Living with Inherited Metabolic Diseases)
Foundation for Ichthyosis & Related Skin Types
National Institute of Neurological Disorders and Stroke (NINDS)
National Tay-Sachs and Allied Diseases Association, Inc.
Vaincre Les Maladies Lysosomales

748 Multiple System Atrophy

Synonym
MSA

Disorder Subdivisions
Progressive Autonomic Failure with Multiple System Atrophy
Shy-Drager Syndrome (SDS)
Sporadic OPCA
Sporadic Olivopontocerebellar Atrophy
Striatonigral Degeneration (SND)

Multiple system atrophy (MSA) is a rare progressive neurological disorder characterized by a varying combination of symptoms. Affected individuals may experience symptoms similar to those found in Parkinson's disease (parkinsonism); cerebellar signs such as progressive impairment of the ability to coordinate voluntary movements (cerebellar ataxia); and impaired functioning of the portion of the nervous system (autonomic nervous system) that regulates certain involuntary body functions (autonomic failure) such as heart rate, blood pressure, sweating, and bowel and bladder control. The exact cause of multiple system atrophy is unknown.The term multiple system atrophy has generated significant controversy and confusion in the medical literature. The term now encompasses three conditions once thought to be separate disorders, specifically Shy-Drager syndrome, striatonigral degeneration, and sporadic olivopontocerebellar atrophy. Additionally, there is a hereditary form of olivopontocerebellar atrophy that is not part of the multiple system atrophy spectrum.

The following organizations may provide additional information and support:
Autonomic Dysfunction Center
National Dysautonomia Research Foundation
National Institute of Neurological Disorders and Stroke (NINDS)
National Parkinson Foundation, Inc.
Parkinson's Disease Foundation, Inc.
Shy-Drager Syndrome/Multiple System Atrophy Support Group
WE MOVE (Worldwide Education and Awareness for Movement Disorders)

749   Mulvihill-Smith Syndrome

Synonym
Progeriod Short Stature with Pigmented Nevi

Mulvihill-Smith syndrome is an extremely rare disorder characterized by low birth weight; growth delays leading to short stature (dwarfism); and/or a prematurely aged facial appearance. Other findings may include additional abnormalities of the head and facial (craniofacial) areas, multiple deeply-colored skin lesions (pigmented nevi), hearing impairment, and/or mental retardation. Eventually, some affected individuals may develop diminished capabilities to resist and fight off repeated infections (primary immunodeficiency). The range and severity of symptoms varies from case to case. All reported cases of Mulvihill-Smith syndrome have occurred as isolated cases. It is possible that this condition is due to a new dominant gene mutation.

The following organizations may provide additional information and support:
NIH/National Arthritis and Musculoskeletal and Skin Diseases Information Clearinghouse
NIH/National Eye Institute

750   Mumps

Synonyms
Infective Parotitis
Parotitis

Mumps is an acute viral illness that causes a painful inflammation and swelling of the saliva glands. These glands include the parotid, submaxillary, sublingual and buccal salivary glands. Mumps used to be a common infectious disease of childhood until a vaccine was developed in 1967 to immunize children against the virus that causes the disorder. However, recent outbreaks of mumps among adolescents and young adults have

raised questions about lifetime immunity from the vaccine.

The following organizations may provide additional information and support:
Centers for Disease Control and Prevention
NIH/National Institute of Allergy and Infectious Diseases

751   MURCS Association

Synonyms
Mullerian Duct and Renal Agenesis with Upper Limb and Rib Anomalies
Mullerian Duct Aplasia-Renal Aplasia-Cervicothoracic Somite Dysplasia
Mullerian Duct-Renal-Cervicothoracic-Upper Limb Defects
Mullerian-Renal-Cervicothoracic Somite Abnormalities

MURCS association is a very rare developmental disorder that affects only females. The acronym MURCS stands for (MU)llerian, (R)enal, (C)ervicothoracic (S)omite abnormalities. This rare disorder is characterized by the absence of the uterus, cervix, and upper part of the vagina (mullerian aplasia); kidney (renal) abnormalities, including absent (agenic) and/or improperly positioned (ectopic) kidneys; and/or malformations of the spinal column, ribs, and/or arms. Some affected females may exhibit additional physical abnormalities, such as malformations of the head and facial (craniofacial) area. In individuals with MURCS association, symptoms vary from case to case. MURCS association appears to occur randomly, with no apparent cause (sporadic). Some researchers suggest that the malformations associated with this disorder may result from abnormal changes in cellular material (blastema) in portions of the embryo that later develop into the arms, certain bones (vertebrae) in the spinal column, the kidneys, and adjacent structures (e.g., fallopian tubes).

The following organizations may provide additional information and support:
National Kidney Foundation
NIH/National Kidney and Urologic Diseases Information Clearinghouse

752   Muscular Dystrophy, Becker

Synonyms
Benign Juvenile Muscular Dystrophy
BMD
Progressive Tardive Muscular Dystrophy

Becker muscular dystrophy is in the category of inherited muscle wasting diseases caused by a gene abnormality (mutation) that results in deficient or abnormal production of the dystrophin protein (dystrophinopathies). The abnormal gene is called DMD and is located on the X chromosome. Becker muscular dystrophy follows X-linked recessive inheritance so it mostly affects males, but some females are affected. Becker muscular dystrophy usually begins in the teens or early twenties and symptoms vary greatly between affected individuals. Muscle deterioration progresses slowly but usually results in the need for a wheelchair. Muscles of the heart deteriorate (cardiomyopathy) in some affected individuals, and this process can become life-threatening. Learning disabilities involving visual abilities may be present.

The following organizations may provide additional information and support:
Let Them Hear Foundation
Muscular Dystrophy Association
Muscular Dystrophy Campaign
National Institute of Neurological Disorders and Stroke (NINDS)
New Horizons Un-Limited, Inc.
Parent Project Muscular Dystrophy
Society for Muscular Dystrophy Information International

753 Muscular Dystrophy, Duchenne

Synonyms
Childhood Muscular Dystrophy
DMD
Muscular Dystrophy, Classic X-linked Recessive
Progressive Muscular Dystrophy of Childhood
Pseudohypertrophic Muscular Dystrophy

Duchenne muscular dystrophy, a hereditary degenerative disease of skeletal (voluntary) muscles, is considered the most prevalent form of childhood muscular dystrophy. The disorder typically is recognized from approximately age 3 to 6 years and has a relatively rapid, progressive disease course. Duchenne muscular dystrophy is initially characterized by muscle weakness and wasting (atrophy) within the pelvic area that may be followed by involvement of the shoulder muscles. With disease progression, muscle weakness and atrophy affect the trunk and forearms and gradually progress to involve most major muscles of the body. In individuals with the disorder, initial findings may include an unusual, waddling manner of walking (gait); difficulty climbing stairs or rising from a sitting position; and repeated falling. With disease progression, additional abnormalities may develop, such as progressive curvature of the spine; wasting of thigh muscles and abnormal enlargement of the calves due to degenerative changes of muscle fibers (pseudohypertrophy); and abnormal fixation of certain joints (joint contractures) due to muscle weakness, prolonged immobility, and shortening of muscle fibers. By approximately age 10 to 12, most affected individuals require the use of a wheelchair. Duchenne muscular dystrophy is also typically characterized by additional abnormalities, including involvement of heart muscle (cardiomyopathy) and varying degrees of intellectual impairment. Affected individuals may develop an increased susceptibility to respiratory infections (e.g., pneumonia), respiratory failure, impaired ability of the heart to pump blood effectively (heart failure), or other serious findings, leading to potentially life-threatening complications by late adolescence or early adulthood. Duchenne muscular dystrophy is caused by changes (mutations) of a gene on the short arm (p) of chromosome X (Xp21.2). The gene regulates the production of a protein that is found in skeletal and cardiac muscle. Known as dystrophin, the protein is thought to play an important role in maintaining the structure of these muscle cells. In most affected individuals, Duchenne muscular dystrophy is inherited as an X-linked recessive trait. Therefore, the disorder is usually fully expressed in males only. However, in rare instances, females who carry a copy of the mutated gene (heterozygous carriers) may develop certain, typically milder symptoms associated with the disorder. In addition, for some individuals with Duchenne muscular dystrophy, there is no family history of the disease. In such cases, the disorder may be caused by new (sporadic) genetic mutations that occur for unknown reasons.

The following organizations may provide additional information and support:
Let Them Hear Foundation
March of Dimes Birth Defects Foundation
Muscular Dystrophy Association
Muscular Dystrophy Association of Canada
Muscular Dystrophy Campaign
National Institute of Neurological Disorders and Stroke (NINDS)
New Horizons Un-Limited, Inc.
Parent Project Muscular Dystrophy
Society for Muscular Dystrophy Information International

754 Muscular Dystrophy, Emery-Dreifuss

Synonyms

Autosomal Dominant Emery-Dreifuss Muscular Dystrophy
Autosomal Recessive Emery-Dreifuss Muscular Dystrophy
Dreifuss-Emery Type Muscular Dystrophy with Contractures
EDMD
Emery-Dreifuss Syndrome
Tardive Muscular Dystrophy

Disorder Subdivision

X-Linked Recessive Emery-Dreifuss Muscular Dystrophy

Emery-Dreifuss muscular dystrophy is a rare, often slowly progressive form of muscular dystrophy affecting the muscles of the arms, legs, face, neck, spine and heart. The disorder consists of the clinical triad of weakness and degeneration (atrophy) of certain muscles, joints that are fixed in a flexed or extended position (contractures), and abnormalities affecting the heart (cardiomyopathy). Major symptoms may include muscle wasting and weakness particularly in the upper legs and arms (humeroperoneal regions) and contractures of the elbows, Achilles tendons, and upper back muscles. In some cases, additional abnormalities may be present. Emery-Dreifuss muscular dystrophy is inherited as an X-linked, autosomal dominant or autosomal recessive trait.

The following organizations may provide additional information and support:
Let Them Hear Foundation
Muscular Dystrophy Association
Muscular Dystrophy Campaign
National Institute of Neurological Disorders and Stroke (NINDS)
New Horizons Un-Limited, Inc.
Society for Muscular Dystrophy Information International

755 Muscular Dystrophy, Limb Girdle

Synonyms

Erb Muscular Dystrophy
Leyden-Moebius Muscular Dystrophy
LGMD
Pelvofemoral Muscular Dystrophy
Proximal Muscular Dystrophy

Limb-girdle muscular dystrophy is a group of inherited, progressive disorders that are characterized by weakness and wasting (atrophy) of muscles of the hip and shoulder areas. Several different forms of the disorder have been identified that are caused by abnormal changes (mutations) of certain genes. Of these disease subtypes, at least eight have autosomal recessive inheritance and at least three are transmitted as an autosomal dominant trait. In most individuals with limb-girdle muscular dystrophy, associated symptoms and findings become apparent during childhood. However, less commonly, symptom onset may begin during adolescence or adulthood. Muscle weakness may spread from the lower limbs to the upper limbs or vice versa. Although the disorder typically progresses slowly, some affected individuals experience rapid disease progression.

The following organizations may provide additional information and support:
Let Them Hear Foundation
Muscular Dystrophy Association
Muscular Dystrophy Campaign
National Institute of Neurological Disorders and Stroke (NINDS)
New Horizons Un-Limited, Inc.
Society for Muscular Dystrophy Information International

756 Muscular Dystrophy, Oculo-Gastrointestinal

Disorder Subdivisions

Intestinal Pseudoobstruction with External Ophthalmoplegia
Oculogastrointestinal Muscular Dystrophy
Ophthalmoplegia-Intestinal Pseudoobstruction
Visceral Myopathy-External Ophthalmoplegia

Oculo-gastrointestinal muscular dystrophy is a very rare form of muscular dystrophy that affects females more often than males. It is inherited as an autosomal recessive trait and its major characteristics are droopy eyelids (ptosis), loss of movement of the external muscles of the eye (external ophthalmoplegia), and a progressive condition in which the intestinal walls are unable to contract normally causing abdominal pain, diarrhea, constipation, and malabsorption of nutrients (progressive intestinal pseudo-obstruction).

The following organizations may provide additional information and support:
Association of Gastrointestinal Motility Disorders, Inc. (AGMD)

International Foundation for Functional Gastrointestinal Disorders
Let Them Hear Foundation
Muscular Dystrophy Campaign
National Institute of Neurological Disorders and Stroke (NINDS)
New Horizons Un-Limited, Inc.
Parent Education Network
Society for Muscular Dystrophy Information International

757   Mutism, Selective

Synonym

Mutism, Elective (Obsolete)

Selective mutism is a rare psychiatric condition primarily occurring during childhood. It is characterized by the failure to speak in social situations. Ability to understand spoken language and to speak is usually not impaired. Symptoms include excessive shyness, and social anxiety.

The following organizations may provide additional information and support:
National Alliance for the Mentally Ill
National Mental Health Association
National Mental Health Consumers' Self-Help Clearinghouse
NIH/National Institute of Mental Health
Selective Mutism Foundation, Inc.

758   Myasthenia Gravis

Synonyms

Erb-Goldflam Syndrome
MG
Myasthenia Gravis Pseudoparalytica

Disorder Subdivisions

Congenital Myasthenia Gravis
Familial Infantile (Congenital) Myasthenia Gravis
Generalized Myasthenia Gravis
Ocular Myasthenia Gravis
Transitory Neonatal Myasthenia Gravis

Myasthenia gravis is a neuromuscular disorder primarily characterized by muscle weakness and muscle fatigue. Although the disorder usually becomes apparent during adulthood, symptom onset may occur at any age. The condition may be restricted to certain muscle groups, particularly those of the eyes (ocular myasthenia gravis), or may become more generalized (generalized myas-

thenia gravis), involving multiple muscle groups. Most individuals with myasthenia gravis develop weakness and drooping of the eyelids (ptosis); weakness of eye muscles, resulting in double vision (diplopia); and excessive muscle fatigue following activity. Additional features commonly include weakness of facial muscles; impaired articulation of speech (dysarthria); difficulties chewing and swallowing (dysphagia); and weakness of the upper arms and legs (proximal limb weakness). In addition, in about 10 percent of cases, affected individuals may develop potentially life-threatening complications due to severe involvement of muscles used during breathing (myasthenic crisis). Myasthenia gravis results from an abnormal immune reaction in which the body's natural immune defenses (i.e., antibodies) inappropriately attack and gradually destroy certain receptors in muscles that receive nerve impulses (antibody-mediated autoimmune response).

The following organizations may provide additional information and support:
Autoimmune Information Network, Inc
Muscular Dystrophy Association
Myasthenia Gravis Foundation of America
Myasthenia Gravis Links
National Institute of Neurological Disorders and Stroke (NINDS)
New Horizons Un-Limited, Inc.

759   Mycosis Fungoides

Synonym

Granuloma Fungoides

Disorder Subdivision

Vidal-Brocq Mycosis Fungoides

Mycosis fungoides is a rare form of T-cell lymphoma of the skin (cutaneous); the disease is typically slowly progressive and chronic. In individuals with mycosis fungoides, the skin becomes infiltrated with plaques and nodules that are composed of lymphocytes. In advanced cases, ulcerated tumors and infiltration of lymph nodes by diseased cells may occur. The disorder may spread to other parts of the body including the gastrointestinal system, liver, spleen, or brain.

The following organizations may provide additional information and support:
American Cancer Society, Inc.
Cutaneous Lymphoma Foundation
Cutaneous Lymphoma Network

Mycosis Fungoides Network
Skin Cancer Foundation

760   Myelodysplastic Syndromes

Synonyms
Myelodysplasia
Pre-leukemia

Myelodysplastic syndromes (MDS) are a rare group of blood disorders that occur as a result of improper development of blood cells within the bone marrow. The three main types of blood cells (i.e., red blood cells, white blood cells and platelets) are affected. Red blood cells deliver oxygen to the body, white blood cells help fight infections, and platelets assist in clotting to stop blood loss. These improperly developed blood cells fail to develop normally and enter the bloodstream. As a result, individuals with MDS have abnormally low blood cell levels (low blood counts). General symptoms associated with MDS include fatigue, dizziness, weakness, bruising and bleeding, frequent infections, and headaches. In some cases, MDS may progress to life-threatening failure of the bone marrow or develop into an acute leukemia. The exact cause of MDS is unknown. There are no certain environmental risk factors.

The following organizations may provide additional information and support:
American Cancer Society, Inc.
Anemia Institute for Research and Education
Aplastic Anemia & MDS International Foundation, Inc.
Aplastic Anemia & Myelodysplasia Association of Canada
Leukemia & Lymphoma Society
National Bone Marrow Transplant Link
National Cancer Institute
National Marrow Donor Program
NIH/National Heart, Lung and Blood Institute Information Center
World Health Organization (WHO) Regional Office for the Americas (AMRO)

761   Myelofibrosis, Idiopathic

Synonyms
Agnogenic Myeloid Metaplasia (AMM)
Myelofibrosis and Myeloid Metaplasia
Myelofibrosis-Osteosclerosis (MOS)
Myelosclerosis
Osteosclerosis
Primary Myelofibrosis (PMF)

Myelofibrosis is a condition characterized by formation of fibrous tissue (fibrosis) within the bone marrow. Bone marrow is sponge-like tissue found within the bones of the body and is responsible for the production of all blood cells (i.e., red and white blood cells and platelets). Myelofibrosis may occur as a secondary characteristic to other disorders such as polycythemia vera, certain metabolic disorders, and/or chronic myeloid leukemia. In many cases, the cause of myelofibrosis is unknown (idiopathic). In idiopathic myelofibrosis, the ability of the bone marrow to produce red blood cells may be impaired. Symptoms of idiopathic myelofibrosis may include abnormally low levels of circulating red blood cells (anemia), an abnormally large spleen (splenomegaly), an abnormally large liver (hepatomegaly), weight loss, weakness and fatigue due to replacement of normal bone marrow cells, and/or episodes of severe pain in the abdomen, bones, and joints. In many cases, myelofibrosis occurs in association with increased bone density and the formation of small sharp pieces of bone (spicules) within the marrow cavity and increased bone density (osteosclerosis).

The following organizations may provide additional information and support:
American Cancer Society, Inc.
Center for International Blood and Marrow Transplant Research
CMPD Education Foundation
Italian Registry of Myelofibrosis with Myeloid Metaplasia
Myeloproliferative Mailing List (MPD-SUPPORT-L)
National Bone Marrow Transplant Link
NIH/National Heart, Lung and Blood Institute Information Center

762   Myeloma, Multiple

Synonyms
Kahler Disease
Myelomatosis
Plasma Cell Myeloma

Disorder Subdivisions
Extramedullary Plasmacytoma
Nonsecretory Myeloma
Osteosclerotic Myeloma
Plasma Cell Leukemia
Smoldering Myeloma
Solitary Plasmacytoma of Bone

Multiple myeloma is a rare form of cancer characterized by excessive production (proliferation) and improper function of certain cells (plasma cells) found in the bone marrow. Plasma cells, which are a type of white blood cell, are produced in the bone marrow and eventually enter the bloodstream. Excessive plasma cells may eventually mass together to form a tumor or tumors in various sites of the body, especially the bone marrow. If only a single tumor is present, the term solitary plasmocytoma is used. When multiple tumors are present, the term multiple myeloma is used. Plasma cells are a key component of the immune system and secrete a substance known as myeloma proteins (M-proteins), a type of antibody. Antibodies are special proteins that the body produces to combat invading microorganisms, toxins, or other foreign substances. Overproduction of plasma cells in affected individuals results in abnormally high levels of these proteins within the body. Major symptoms of multiple myeloma may include bone pain, especially in the back and the ribs; low levels of circulating red blood cells (anemia) resulting in weakness, fatigue, and lack of color (pallor); and kidney (renal) abnormalities. In most cases, affected individuals are more susceptible to bacterial infections such as pneumonia. The exact cause of multiple myeloma is unknown.

The following organizations may provide additional information and support:
American Cancer Society, Inc.
Cancer Research UK
International Myeloma Foundation
Leukemia & Lymphoma Society
Multiple Myeloma Research Foundation
National Cancer Institute
NIH/Hematology Branch, National Heart, Lung and Blood Institute (NHLBI)

763 Myhre Syndrome

Synonym
Growth-Mental Deficiency Syndrome of Myhre

Myhre syndrome is an extremely rare inherited disorder characterized by mental retardation, short stature, unusual facial features, and various bone (skeletal) abnormalities. Characteristic facial features may include abnormally narrow skin folds (palpebral fissures) between the upper and lower eyelids (blepharophimosis), underdevelopment of the upper jaw bone (maxillary hypoplasia), and an unusually prominent jaw (prognathism). Other findings may include hearing impairment, abnormal enlargement of the muscles (muscular hyper-

trophy), and/or joint stiffness. Myhre syndrome is thought to be inherited as an autosomal dominant genetic trait.

The following organization may provide additional information and support:
Little People of America, Inc.

764 Myoclonus, General

Disorder Subdivisions
Action Myoclonus
Arrhythmic Myoclonus
Dyssynergia Cerebellaris Myoclonica
Familial Arrhythmic Myoclonus
Hereditary Essential Myoclonus
Infantile Myoclonic Encephalopathy and Polymyoclonia
Intention Myoclonus
Nocturnal Myoclonus
Opsoclonus
Palatal Myoclonus
Paramyoclonus Multiple
Pathological Myoclonus
Postanoxic Intention Myoclonus
Postencephalitic Intention Myoclonus
Progressive Myoclonic Epilepsy
Respiratory Myoclonus
Rhythmical Myoclonus
Segmental Myoclonus
Stimulus-Sensitive Myoclonus

Myoclonus is a neurological movement disorder characterized by sudden, involuntary contractions of skeletal muscles. Based on the various symptoms, there are three types of myoclonus: intention myoclonus, rhythmical myoclonus, and arrhythmic myoclonus. Intention myoclonus (action myoclonus) includes postanoxic myoclonus and postencephalitic myoclonus. Arrhythmic myoclonus (stimulus-sensitive myoclonus) includes: hereditary essential myoclonus (paramyoclonus multiplex), hyperexplexia (essential startle disease), opsoclonus (infantile myoclonic encephalopathy, polymyoclonia familial arrhythmic myoclonus), progressive myoclonic epilepsy, and Ramsay Hunt syndrome (dyssynergia cerebellaris myoclonia). Rhythmical myoclonus includes (segmental myoclonus), nocturnal myoclonus, palatal myoclonus, and respiratory myoclonus.

The following organizations may provide additional information and support:
Epilepsy Canada
Epilepsy Foundation

March of Dimes Birth Defects Foundation
Moving Forward
National Institute of Neurological Disorders and
Stroke (NINDS)
National Pediatric Myoclonus Center
Opsoclonus-Myoclonus Support Network, Inc.
WE MOVE (Worldwide Education and Awareness
for Movement Disorders)

765   Myopathy, Congenital, Batten Turner Type

Synonyms
  Batten Turner Congenital Myopathy
  Batten Turner Syndrome

Batten Turner type congenital myopathy is an extremely rare, inherited muscle disease (myopathy) and is characterized by the lack of muscle tone or floppiness at birth (congenital hypotonia). The symptoms of Batten Turner type congenital myopathy are slowly progressive during infancy and childhood. However, this disorder is not progressive in adulthood.

The following organizations may provide additional information and support:
March of Dimes Birth Defects Foundation
National Institute of Neurological Disorders and
Stroke (NINDS)

766   Myopathy, Desmin Storage

Synonyms
  Cardiomyopathy Due to Desmin Defect
  Desmin Storage Myopathy
  *Myopathy with Sarcoplasmic Bodies and
  Intermediate Filaments*

Disorder Subdivisions
  *Autosomal Dominant Desmin Distal Myopathy
  with Late Onset*
  *Cardiomyopathy Associated with Desmin
  Storage Myopathy*
  *Congenital Proximal Myopathy Associated with
  Desmin Storage Myopathy*

Desmin storage myopathy (DSM) is a rare inherited muscle disorder that may be apparent at birth (congenital) or may not appear until as late as age 40. Three forms of this disorder have been described in the medical literature. The symptoms and age of onset depend upon which form affects the individual. Symptoms of late onset desmin storage myopathy (autosomal dominant DSM) may

include weakness of the muscles at the base of the thumb and/or weakness of the muscles used to flex the hand. Muscle weakness in the face, shoulder, and/or pelvic area, a spine that curves backward and to one side, and/or heart disease may occur in the congenital form of the disorder. The third form of desmin storage myopathy is characterized by heart disease (cardiomyopathy associated with DSM) that appears at variable ages and may lead to life-threatening complications.

The following organizations may provide additional information and support:
American Heart Association
March of Dimes Birth Defects Foundation
NIH/National Heart, Lung and Blood Institute Information Center

767   Myopathy, Scapuloperoneal

Synonyms
  Scapuloperoneal Muscular Dystrophy
  Scapuloperoneal Syndrome, Myopathic Type

Scapuloperoneal myopathy is a rare genetic disorder characterized by weakness and wasting of certain muscles. Symptoms are usually limited to the shoulder blade area (scapula) and the smaller of the two leg muscle groups below the knee (peroneal). Facial muscles may be affected in a few cases. The leg symptoms often appear before the shoulder muscles become weakened. The rate of progression of the disorder varies from case to case. This condition can also occur in combination with other disorders. Scapuloperoneal myopathy is inherited as an autosomal dominant trait.

The following organizations may provide additional information and support:
Muscular Dystrophy Association
NIH/National Institute of Arthritis and Musculoskeletal and Skin Diseases
Scapuloperoneal Disease Association

768   Myositis, Inclusion Body

Synonym
  IBM

Disorder Subdivision
  Inflammatory Myopathy

Inclusion body myositis (IBM) is a rare inflammatory muscular disorder that usually becomes apparent during adulthood. The disorder presents as slow progressive weakness and withering away (atrophy) of the muscles (myositis), especially of the arms and legs. Inclusion body myositis frequently is diagnosed when a patient is unresponsive to therapy prescribed for polymyositis. IBM is characterized by the gradual onset (over months or years) of muscle fatigue and weakness; a clear tendency to strike men more frequently than women; and affecting both the muscles closest to the body's trunk (proximal) and those farthest from the trunk (distal). Onset is usually after age 50, although it may occur earlier.

The following organizations may provide additional information and support:
Muscular Dystrophy Association
Myositis Association
NIH/National Arthritis and Musculoskeletal and Skin Diseases Information Clearinghouse

769   Myotonia Congenita

Disorder Subdivisions

Becker Disease
Myotonia Congenita, Autosomal Recessive (MCR)
Generalized Thomsen Disease (THD) Myotonia Congenita, Autosomal Dominant

Myotonia congenita is a rare genetic disorder in which an abnormality of voluntary (skeletal) muscle fiber membranes causes an unusually exaggerated response to stimulation (hyperexcitability). As a result, affected individuals have difficulty relaxing certain muscles after contracting them (myotonia), muscle stiffness (rigidity), and associated symptoms. Such symptoms tend to occur when attempting to move certain muscles after rest. In many cases, individuals with myotonia congenita also have abnormal enlargement of the muscles (hypertrophy), resulting in a "herculean" or "body-builder like" appearance. Two main forms of myotonia congenita have been described: Thomsen disease and Becker disease. In individuals with Thomsen disease, symptoms and findings such as myotonia, associated muscle rigidity, and abnormal muscle enlargement may become apparent from infancy to approximately 2 to 3 years of age. In many cases, muscles of the eyelids, hands, and legs may be most affected. Thomsen disease is transmitted as an autosomal dominant trait. In those with Becker disease, symptoms most commonly become apparent between the ages of 4 and 12 years. As in Thomsen type myotonia congenita, affected individuals develop myo-

tonia, associated muscle rigidity, and abnormal muscle enlargement (hypertrophy). However, in contrast to Thomsen type, such symptoms are progressive and tend to be more severe. In addition, muscle hypertrophy may be particularly striking, and muscle weakness may be present. Becker disease is inherited as an autosomal recessive trait.

The following organizations may provide additional information and support:
Malignant Hyperthermia Association of the United States (MHAUS)
Muscular Dystrophy Association
National Institute of Neurological Disorders and Stroke (NINDS)
NIH/National Arthritis and Musculoskeletal and Skin Diseases Information Clearinghouse

770   Myotubular Myopathy

Synonyms

Autosomal Dominant Centronuclear Myopathy
Autosomal Recessive Centronuclear Myopathy
Centronuclear Myopathy
Myopathy, Myotubular
Myotubular Myopathy Type 1 (MTM1)
Myotubular Myopathy, X-linked
X-linked Congenital Recessive Muscle Hypotrophy with Central Nuclei
X-linked Myotubular Myopathy
X-linked Recessive Centronuclear Myopathy
X-linked Recessive Myotubular Myopathy

Disorder Subdivisions

Autosomal Dominant Centronuclear Myopathy
Autosomal Recessive Centronuclear Myopathy
X-Linked Centronuclear Myopathy

Myotubular myopathy is a rare muscle-wasting disorder that occurs in three forms based on severity, inheritance, and symptoms. X-linked myotubular myopathy, the most severe form, is generally present at birth or occurs in infancy. Autosomal recessive myotubular myopathy is a less severe form that usually occurs during infancy or childhood. The least severe form, autosomal dominant myotubular myopathy, usually presents between the first and third decades of life and is slowly progressive.

The following organizations may provide additional information and support:
Muscular Dystrophy Association
Myotubular Myopathy Resource Group
National Institute of Neurological Disorders and Stroke (NINDS)

771 N-Acetyl Glutamate Synthetase Deficiency

Synonyms

*Hyperammonemia Due to N-Acetylglutamate
Synthetase Deficiency*
NAGS Deficiency

N-acetylglutamate synthetase (NAGS) deficiency is a rare genetic disorder characterized by complete or partial lack of the enzyme N-acetylglutamate synthetase (NAGS). NAGS is one of six enzymes that play a role in the breakdown and removal of nitrogen from the body, a process known as the urea cycle. The lack of the NAGS enzyme results in excessive accumulation of nitrogen, in the form of ammonia (hyperammonemia), in the blood. Excess ammonia, which is a neurotoxin, travels to the central nervous system through the blood, resulting in the symptoms and physical findings associated with NAGS deficiency. Symptoms include vomiting, refusal to eat, progressive lethargy, and coma. NAGS deficiency is inherited as an autosomal recessive trait. The urea cycle disorders are a group of rare disorders affecting the urea cycle, a series of biochemical processes in which nitrogen is converted into urea and removed from the body through the urine. Nitrogen is a waste product of protein metabolism. Failure to break down nitrogen results in the abnormal accumulation of nitrogen, in the form of ammonia, in the blood.

The following organizations may provide additional information and support:
American Kidney Fund, Inc.
Brusilow, Saul, M.D.
CLIMB (Children Living with Inherited Metabolic Diseases)
National Kidney Foundation
National Urea Cycle Disorders Foundation
NIH/National Digestive Diseases Information Clearinghouse

772 Nager Syndrome

Synonyms

Acrofacial Dysostosis, Nager Type
AFD
Nager Acrofacial Dysostosis Syndrome
Split Hand Deformity-Mandibulofacial Dysostosis

Nager syndrome is a rare disorder that may or may not be genetically derived. Major symptoms may include underdevelopment of the cheek and jaw area of the face. Down-sloping of the opening of the eyes, a smaller than normal jaw, lack or absence of the lower eyelashes, lack of development of the internal and external ear with related hearing problems and cleft palate may also occur. There may be underdevelopment or absence of the thumb, shortened forearms and poor movement in the elbow. Breathing and feeding problems may be present in infants with this syndrome.

The following organizations may provide additional information and support:
American Society for Deaf Children
Children's Craniofacial Association
FACES: The National Craniofacial Association
Forward Face, Inc.
Foundation for Nager and Miller Syndromes
Let's Face It (USA)
National Craniofacial Foundation

773 Nail-Patella Syndrome

Synonyms

Fong Disease
Hereditary Onychoosteodysplasia (HOOD)
NPS
Onychoosteodysplasia
Turner-Kieser Syndrome

Nail-patella syndrome (NPS) is a rare genetic disorder that is usually apparent at birth or during early childhood. Although the symptoms and physical characteristics associated with NPS may vary, characteristic abnormalities tend to include improper development (dysplasia) of the fingernails and toenails; absence (aplasia) and/or underdevelopment (hypoplasia) of the knee caps (patellae); underdevelopment of certain bones and/or webbing of skin at the bend of the elbow(s); and/or abnormal projections of bone from the upper (superior) portion of both sides of the hipbone (bilateral iliac horns). In addition, some individuals within certain families (kindreds) may have abnormally increased fluid pressure of the eyes (glaucoma). The condition results due to progressive blockage of the outflow of fluid (aqueous humor) from the front chamber of the eyes (open-angle glaucoma). Without appropriate treatment, the gradual increase in fluid pressure may cause increased narrowing of visual fields and eventual blindness. Other eye (ocular) abnormalities may also be associated with NPS. For example, in some affected individuals, the inner margin (pupillary margin) of the colored portion of the eyes (irides) may appear abnormally dark (hyperpigmentation) and "cloverleaf shaped" (Lester iris). Approximately 30 to 40 percent of individuals with NPS may also develop abnormalities in kidney function (nephropathy) that may be apparent during childhood or later in life. Nail-patella syndrome is inherited as an autosomal dominant trait.

The following organizations may provide additional information and support:
American Association of Kidney Patients
American Foundation for Urologic Disease
American Kidney Fund, Inc.
Nail Patella Syndrome Networking/Support Group
Nail Patella Syndrome Worldwide
Nail-Patella Syndrome (NPS) Web Site
National Kidney Foundation
NIH/National Arthritis and Musculoskeletal and Skin Diseases Information Clearinghouse
NIH/National Kidney and Urologic Diseases Information Clearinghouse

774 Narcolepsy

Synonyms
Gelineau's Syndrome
Narcoleptic Syndrome
Paroxysmal Sleep
Sleep Epilepsy

Narcolepsy is a rare disorder characterized by chronic, excessive attacks of drowsiness during the day, sudden extreme muscle weakness (cataplexy), hallucinations, paralysis while sleeping, and disrupted sleep during the night. Attacks of drowsiness may persist only a few minutes or last for hours, and may vary in frequency from a few incidents to several during a single day. Although the exact cause of narcolepsy is not known, many researchers suspect that genetic factors play a role in the development of the disorder.

The following organizations may provide additional information and support:
American Sleep Disorders Association
Center for Narcolepsy Research
Center for Research in Sleep Disorders
Medic Alert Foundation International
Narcolepsy and Cataplexy Foundation of America
Narcolepsy Institute
Narcolepsy Network, Inc.

National Institute of Neurological Disorders and Stroke (NINDS)
National Narcolepsy Registry

775 Nelson Syndrome

Synonym
Pituitary Tumor after Adrenalectomy

Nelson syndrome is a disorder characterized by abnormal hormone secretion, enlargement of the pituitary gland (hypophysis), and the development of large and invasive growths known as adenomas. It occurs in an estimated 15 to 25 percent of people who undergo surgical removal of the adrenal glands for Cushing disease. Symptoms associated with Nelson syndrome include intense skin discoloration (hyperpigmentation), headaches, vision impairment, and the cessation of menstrual periods in women.

The following organization may provide additional information and support:
National Institute of Neurological Disorders and Stroke (NINDS)

776 Nemaline Myopathy

Synonyms
Congenital Rod Disease
NM
Rod Myopathy

Nemaline myopathy is a rare inherited neuromuscular disease that is usually apparent at birth (congenital) and characterized by extreme muscle weakness (hypotonia). Laboratory examination of muscle tissue samples from people with nemaline myopathy reveal the presence of fine fibrous threads known as nemaline rods that interfere with the muscle function.

The following organizations may provide additional information and support:
March of Dimes Birth Defects Foundation
Muscular Dystrophy Association
National Institute of Neurological Disorders and Stroke (NINDS)
Nemaline Myopathy Website

777 Neonatal Lupus

Synonyms
Congenital Lupus
Congenital Lupus Erythematosus
Neonatal Lupus Erythematosus
Neonatal Lupus Syndrome

Neonatal lupus is a rare autoimmune disorder that is present at birth (congenital). Affected infants often develop a characteristic red rash or skin eruption. In addition, infants with neonatal lupus may develop liver disease, a heart condition known as congenital heart block, and/or low numbers of circulating blood platelets that assist in blood clotting functions (thrombocytopenia). The symptoms associated with neonatal lupus, with the exception of congenital heart block, usually resolve within the first several months of life. The exact cause of neonatal lupus is unknown, although researchers speculate that specific antibodies that travel from a pregnant woman to her developing fetus via the placenta play a significant role. Neonatal lupus is not the infant form of lupus (systemic lupus erythematosus) although the skin rash resembles the one associated with lupus. Neonatal lupus is a separate disorder.

The following organizations may provide additional information and support:
American Autoimmune Related Diseases Association, Inc.
Lupus Canada
Lupus Foundation of America, Inc.
March of Dimes Birth Defects Foundation
NIH/National Institute of Child Health and Human Development

778 Neu-Laxova Syndrome

Synonym
NLS

Neu-Laxova syndrome (NLS) is a rare genetic disorder that is inherited as an autosomal recessive trait. The syndrome is characterized by severe growth delays before birth (intrauterine growth retardation); low birth weight and length; and distinctive abnormalities of the head and facial (craniofacial) region. These may include marked smallness of the head (microcephaly), sloping of the forehead, widely spaced eyes (ocular hypertelorism), and other malformations, resulting in a distinctive facial appearance. NLS is also typically characterized by abnormal accumulations of fluid

in tissues throughout the body (generalized edema); permanent flexion and immobilization of multiple joints (flexion contractures); other limb malformations; and/or abnormalities of the brain, skin, genitals, kidneys, and/or heart.

The following organizations may provide additional information and support:
March of Dimes Birth Defects Foundation
National Institute of Neurological Disorders and Stroke (NINDS)

779 Neurasthenia

Synonyms
Cardiac Neurosis
Chronic Asthenia
Da Costa's Syndrome
Effort Syndrome
Functional Cardiovascular Disease
Primary Neurasthenia
Soldier's Heart
Subacute Asthenia

Disorder Subdivisions
Angioparalytic Neurasthenia
Angiopathic Neurasthemia
Gastric Neurasthenia
Neurasthenia Gravis
Neurasthenia Precox
Neurocirculatory Asthenia
Pulsating Neurasthenia

The word "neurasthenia" is a term that has fallen into disuse among psychiatrists in the United States and Australia. It remains in use in the United Kingdom. Where it is used, it covers a wide spectrum of symptoms including the sensation of pain or of numbness in various parts of the body, chronic fatigue, weakness, anxiety, and fainting. Additional findings associated with this term may include rapid intense heartbeat that may be irregular (palpitations, tachycardia); cold, clammy hands and feet; abnormally rapid breathing (hyperventilating); dizziness or faintness; periodic sighing; and/or sweating for no apparent reason.

The following organizations may provide additional information and support:
National Alliance for the Mentally Ill
National Mental Health Association
National Mental Health Consumers' Self-Help Clearinghouse
NIH/National Institute of Mental Health

780   Neuroacanthocytosis

Synonyms

Acanthocytosis-Neurologic Disorder
Amyotrophic Chorea with Acanthocytosis,
Familial
Choreoacanthocytosis
Levine-Critchley Syndrome

Neuroacanthocytosis is a very rare disorder inherited as an autosomal recessive or possibly an autosomal dominant genetic trait. Onset of neuroacanthocytosis usually occurs during adolescence or early adulthood. Major symptoms of this disorder are wasting of muscles with uncontrolled rapid muscular movements (amyotropic chorea) and abnormal red blood cells (acanthocytosis).

The following organizations may provide additional information and support:
March of Dimes Birth Defects Foundation
National Institute of Neurological Disorders and Stroke (NINDS)

781   Neurodegeneration with Brain Iron Accumulation Type 1

Synonyms

Hallervorden-Spatz Syndrome
HSS
NBIA1
Pantothenate Kinase Associated
Neurodegeneration (PKAN)
Pigmentary Degeneration of Globus Pallidus,
Substantia Nigra, Red Nucleus

Neurodegeneration with brain iron accumulation type 1 (Hallervorden-Spatz syndrome) is a rare, inherited, neurological movement disorder characterized by the progressive degeneration of the nervous system (neurodegenerative disorder). Recently, one of the genetic causes was identified; however, there are probably other causative genes that exist that have not yet been found. Approximately 50% of individuals with a clinical diagnosis of NBIA1 have gene mutations in PANK2, which helps to metabolize vitamin B5. The common feature among all individuals with NBIA1 is iron accumulation in the brain, along with a progressive movement disorder. Individuals can plateau for long periods of time and then undergo intervals of rapid deterioration. Symptoms may vary greatly from case to case, partly because the genetic cause may differ between families. There are likely different genes that cause NBIA1 and furthermore different mutations within a gene that could lead to a more or less severe presentation. The factors that influence disease severity and the rate of progression are still unknown. Common features include dystonia (an abnormality in muscle tone), muscular rigidity, and sudden involuntary muscle spasms (spasticity). These features can result in clumsiness, gait (walking) problems, difficulty controlling movement, and speech problems. Another common feature is degeneration of the retina, resulting in progressive night blindness and loss of peripheral (side) vision. In general, symptoms are progressive and become worse over time.This disorder was formerly known as Hallervorden-Spatz syndrome, but because of concerns about the unethical activities of Dr. Hallervorden (and perhaps also Dr. Spatz) involving euthanasia of mentally ill patients during World War II, the name has been changed. Neurodegeneration with brain iron accumulation type 1 reflects the continuing discoveries about the underlying cause of the disorder. This name is increasingly used in the scientific literature. The term NBIA1 is general enough to cover all conditions previously categorized as Hallervorden-Spatz syndrome. The largest subgroup of NBIA observed so far is PKAN (pantothenate kinase associated neurodegeneration). It is a defect of the gene PANK2, which causes a deficiency of the enzyme pantothenate kinase. As the terminology changes, one may notice the terms NBIA and PKAN being used interchangeably with HSS.

The following organizations may provide additional information and support:
The Arc (A National Organization on Mental Retardation)
CLIMB (Children Living with Inherited Metabolic Diseases)
Dystonia Clinical Research Center
Dystonia Medical Research Foundation
National Institute of Neurological Disorders and Stroke (NINDS)
NBIA Disorders Association
A National Organization on Mental Retardation

782　Neurofibromatosis Type 1 (NF-1)

Synonyms

NF-1
Recklinghausen's Phakomatosis
Von Recklinghausen's Disease
Von Recklinghausen's Neurofibromatosis
Neurofibroma, Multiple
Neurofibromatosis-Pheochromocytoma-
Duodenal Carcinoid Syndrome
Peripheral Neurofibromatosis

Disorder Subdivision

Segmental Neurofibromatosis

Neurofibromatosis type 1 (NF-1), also called von Recklinghausen's disease, is a rare genetic disorder characterized by the development of multiple noncancerous (benign) tumors of nerves and skin (neurofibromas) and areas of abnormally decreased or increased coloration (hypo- or hyperpigmentation) of the skin. Areas of abnormal pigmentation typically include pale tan or light brown discolorations (cafe-au-lait spots) on the skin of the trunk and other regions as well as freckling, particularly under the arms (axillary) and in the groin (inguinal) area. Such abnormalities of skin pigmentation are often evident by one year of age and tend to increase in size and number over time. At birth or early childhood, affected individuals may have relatively large benign tumors that consist of bundles of nerves (plexiform neurofibromas). Individuals with NF-1 may also develop benign tumor-like nodules of the colored regions of the eyes (Lisch nodules) or tumors of the optic nerves (second cranial nerves), which transmit nerve impulses from the innermost, nerve-rich membrane of the eyes (retinas) to the brain. More rarely, affected individuals may develop certain malignant (cancerous) tumors. NF-1 may also be characterized by unusual largeness of the head (macrocephaly) and relatively short stature. Additional abnormalities may also be present, such as episodes of uncontrolled electrical activity in the brain (seizures); learning disabilities; speech difficulties; abnormally increased activity (hyperactivity); and skeletal malformations, including progressive curvature of the spine (scoliosis), bowing of the lower legs, and improper development of certain bones. In individuals with NF-1, associated symptoms and findings may vary greatly in range and severity from case to case. Most people with NF-1 have normal intelligence but learning disabilities appear in about 50% of children with

NF-1. NF-1 is caused by changes (mutations) of a relatively large gene on the long arm (q) of chromosome 17 (17q11.2). The gene regulates the production of a protein known as neurofibromin, which is thought to function as a tumor suppressor. In about 50% of individuals with NF-1, the disorder results from spontaneous (sporadic) mutations of the gene that occur for unknown reasons. In others with the disorder, NF-1 is inherited as an autosomal dominant trait.The name "neurofibromatosis" is sometimes used generally to describe NF-1 as well as a second, distinct form of NF known as neurofibromatosis type II (NF-2). Also an autosomal dominant disorder, NF-2 is primarily characterized by benign tumors of both acoustic nerves, leading to progressive hearing loss. The auditory nerves (eight cranial nerves) transmit nerve impulses from the inner ear to the brain.

The following organizations may provide additional information and support:
Baylor College of Medicine Neurofibromatosis Clinic
BC Neurofibromatosis Foundation
Boston Children's Hospital
Cedars-Sinai Medical Genetics-Birth Defects Center
Children's Hospital (Philadelphia) Fibromatosis Clinic
Children's National Medical Center
Children's Tumor Foundation: Ending Neurofibromatosis Through Research
Let Them Hear Foundation
March of Dimes Birth Defects Foundation
Massachusetts General Hospital Neurofibromatosis Clinic
National Institute of Neurological Disorders and Stroke (NINDS)
Neurofibromatosis, Inc.
Sjëldne Diagnoser / Rare Disorders Denmark
University of Chicago Neurofibromatosis Clinic

783　Neurofibromatosis Type 2 (NF-2)

Synonyms

Bilateral Acoustic Neurofibromatosis
Central Form, Neurofibromatosis
NF-2
Vestibular Schwannoma Neurofibromatosis

Neurofibromatosis type 2 (NF-2) is a rare genetic disorder that is primarily characterized by benign (noncancerous) tumors of the nerves that transmit sound impulses from the inner ears to the brain (bilateral acoustic neuromas vestibular schwannomas). Associated symptoms and findings may become evident during childhood, adolescence, or early adulthood. Depending on the exact location and size of the acoustic neuromas/vestibular schwannomas, such findings may include disturbances of balance and walking (gait); dizziness; headache; facial weakness, numbness, or pain; ringing in the ears (tinnitus); and/or progressive hearing loss. In some individuals with NF-2, additional abnormalities may also be present. These may include loss of transparency of the lenses of the eyes (juvenile posterior subcapsular opacities), progressive visual impairment, or an increased risk of developing certain tumors of the brain and spinal cord (central nervous system). NF-2 results from changes (mutations) of a gene on the long arm (q) of chromosome 22 (22q12.2). The NF-2 gene regulates the production of a protein that functions as a tumor suppressor. In some individuals with NF-2, the disorder is caused by new (sporadic) mutations of the gene that occur for unknown reasons. In other affected individuals, NF-2 is inherited as an autosomal dominant trait. The term "neurofibromatosis" is sometimes also used to describe a second, distinct form of NF known as neurofibromatosis type I (NF-1). More common than NF-2, NF-1 is primarily characterized by the development of multiple noncancerous (benign) tumors of nerves and skin (neurofibromas) and areas of abnormally decreased or increased coloration (hypo- or hyperpigmentation) of the skin, such as pale tan or light brown discolorations (cafe-au-lait spots) on the skin of the trunk or other regions. In contrast, in individuals with NF-2, benign fibrous tumors of the skin (cutaneous neurofibromas) and areas of abnormal pigmentation are considered relatively rare. As with NF-2, NF-1 may be inherited as an autosomal dominant trait or appear to occur randomly due to new (sporadic) genetic changes.

The following organizations may provide additional information and support:
Acoustic Neuroma Association of Canada
BC Neurofibromatosis Foundation
Better Hearing Institute
Cedars-Sinai Medical Genetics-Birth Defects Center
Children's National Medical Center
Children's Tumor Foundation: Ending Neurofibromatosis Through Research
Let Them Hear Foundation

Massachusetts General Hospital Neurofibromatosis Clinic
National Association of the Deaf
National Institute of Neurological Disorders and Stroke (NINDS)
Neurofibromatosis, Inc.
NF-2 Sharing Network
NIH/National Institute on Deafness and Other Communication Disorders (Balance)
Sjëldne Diagnoser / Rare Disorders Denmark
University of Chicago Neurofibromatosis Clinic

---

784   Neuroleptic Malignant Syndrome

Synonyms
Drug-Induced Movement Disorder
Hyperthermia
Neuroleptic-Induced Acute Dystonia

Neuroleptic malignant syndrome is a rare but potentially life-threatening reaction to the use of almost any of a group of antipsychotic drugs or major tranquilizers (neuroleptics). These drugs are commonly prescribed for the treatment of schizophrenia and other neurological, mental, or emotional disorders. Several of the more commonly prescribed neuroleptics include thioridazine, haloperidol, chlorpromazine, fluphenazine and perphenazine. The syndrome is characterized by high fever, stiffness of the muscles, altered mental status (paranoid behavior), and autonomic dysfunction. Autonomic dysfunction alludes to defective operations of the components of the involuntary (autonomic) nervous system, leading to wide swings of blood pressure, excessive sweating and excessive secretion of saliva. A genetic basis for the disorder is suspected but not proven. It does appear to be clear that a defect in the receptors to dopamine (dopamine D2 receptor antagonism) is an important contributor to the cause of neuroleptic malignant syndrome.

The following organizations may provide additional information and support:
Malignant Hyperthermia Association of the United States (MHAUS)
Medic Alert Foundation International
National Alliance for the Mentally Ill
National Mental Health Association
National Mental Health Consumers' Self-Help Clearinghouse
NIH/National Institute of Mental Health
North American Malignant Hyperthermia Registry of MHAUS

785 Neuromyotonia

Synonyms
Continuous Muscle Fiber Activity Syndrome
Isaacs' Syndrome
Isaacs-Merten Syndrome
Quantal Squander

Neuromyotonia is a rare neuromuscular disorder characterized by abnormal nerve impulses from the peripheral nerves. These impulses cause continuous muscle fiber activity that may continue, even during sleep. The disorder, which has both inherited and acquired forms, is characterized by muscular stiffness and cramping, particularly in the limbs. Continuous fine vibrating muscle movements (myokymia) can be seen. Muscle weakness may also be present. Muscle relaxation may be difficult especially after physical activity involving the particular muscle(s).

The following organizations may provide additional information and support:
Genetic and Rare Diseases (GARD) Information Center
NIH/National Arthritis and Musculoskeletal and Skin Diseases Information Clearinghouse

786 Neuropathy, Ataxia and Retinitis Pigmentosa

Neuropathy, ataxia and retinitis pigmentosa (NARP) syndrome is a rare genetic disorder. It is characterized by nerve disease affecting the nerves outside of the central nervous system (peripheral neuropathy), an impaired ability to coordinate voluntary movements (ataxia), an eye condition known as retinitis pigmentosa (RP), and a variety of additional abnormalities. RP is a general term for a group of vision disorders that cause progressive degeneration of the membrane lining the eyes (retina) resulting in visual impairment. The specific symptoms of NARP syndrome in each individual vary greatly from case to case. The disorder is a maternally inherited mitochondrial disease. NARP syndrome belongs to a group of disorders known as mitochondrial disorders. These disorders are characterized by mutations affecting the parts of the cell that release energy (mitochondria). Mitochondrial diseases often hamper the ability of affected cells to break down food and oxygen and produce energy. In most mitochondrial disorders, abnormally high numbers of defective mitochondria are present in the cells of the body. Mitochondrial diseases often affect more than one organ system of the body. NARP syndrome is caused by a specific mutation affecting the mitochondrial gene known as the ATPase 6 gene. This mutation can also cause a specific subtype of Leigh's syndrome known as maternally inherited Leigh's syndrome (MILS). In fact, when individuals have more than 90 percent of mutated mitochondrial DNA (mtDNA) in their cells, they are classified as having MILS and not NARP syndrome. Most individuals with NARP syndrome have 70-80 percent of mutated mtDNA.

787 Neuropathy, Congenital Hypomyelination

Synonyms
Charcot-Marie-Tooth Type 4E
CHN
CMT4E
Congenital Dysmyelinating Neuropathy
Congenital Hypomyelinating Polyneuropathy
Congenital Hypomyelination
Congenital Hypomyelination (Onion Bulb),
Polyneuropathy
Congenital Hypomyelination Neuropathy
Congenital Neuropathy caused by
Hypomyelination
Hypomyelination Neuropathy

Congenital hypomyelination neuropathy (CHN) is a neurological disorder present at birth. Major symptoms may include respiratory difficulty, muscle weakness and incoordination, poor muscle tone (neonatal hypotonia), absence of reflexes (areflexia), difficulty in walking (ataxia), and/or impaired abilities to feel or move part of the body.

The following organizations may provide additional information and support:
American Autoimmune Related Diseases Association, Inc.
March of Dimes Birth Defects Foundation
National Institute of Neurological Disorders and Stroke (NINDS)

788 Neuropathy, Giant Axonal

Synonym
GAN

Giant axonal neuropathy is a rare hereditary motor and sensory neuropathy (HSMN) that severely affects the central nervous system. The first symptoms appear in early childhood. This disorder is characterized by abnormalities in the peripheral and central nervous systems including low muscle tone (hypotonia), muscle weakness, decreased reflexes, impaired muscle coordination (ataxia), seizures and mental retardation. Pale, tightly curled hair is frequently seen in those affected. Giant axonal neuropathy follows autosomal recessive genetic inheritance.

The following organizations may provide additional information and support:
March of Dimes Birth Defects Foundation
Muscular Dystrophy Association of Canada
National Institute of Neurological Disorders and Stroke (NINDS)

789 Neuropathy, Hereditary Sensory, Type I

Synonyms
HSAN1
Neuropathy, Hereditary Sensory Radicular, Autosomal Dominant
Neuropathy, Hereditary Sensory and Autonomic, Type I HSAN1

The hereditary sensory neuropathies (HSN) include 4-6 similar but distinct inherited, degenerative disorders of the nervous system (neurodegenerative) that frequently progress to loss of feeling, especially in the hands and feet. The classification of the hereditary sensory neuropathies is complicated, and the experts do not always agree. This report deals with HSN type I. There is a separate report in NORD's Rare Disease Database dealing with HSN type II. One other type of hereditary sensory neuropathy, HSN-III, is related to, or identical with, familial dysautonomia (Riley-Day syndrome). Another type, HSN-IV, is related to, or identical with, a form of Charcot-Marie-Tooth disorder. Hereditary sensory neuropathy type I (HSN1) is a rare genetic disorder characterized by the loss of sensation (sensory loss), especially in the feet and legs and, less severely, in the hands and forearms. The sensory loss is due to abnormal functioning of the sensory nerves that control responses to pain and temperature and may also affect the autonomic nervous system that controls other involuntary or automatic body processes. The disorder is inherited as an autosomal dominant trait, and the mutated gene has been identified and tracked to a site on chromosome 9. HSNs of various types may attack a single nerve (mononeuropathy) or many nerves simultaneously (polyneuropathy). The resulting symptoms may involve sensory, motor, reflex, or blood vessel (vasomotor) functions.

The following organizations may provide additional information and support:
Jack Miller Center for Peripheral Neuropathy
March of Dimes Birth Defects Foundation
National Institute of Neurological Disorders and Stroke (NINDS)

790 Neuropathy, Hereditary Sensory, Type II

Synonyms
Acroosteolysis, Giaccai Type
Acroosteolysis, Neurogenic
Congenital Sensory Neuropathy
Hereditary Sensory and Autonomic Neuropathy, Type II (HSAN Type II)
Hereditary Sensory Radicular Neuropathy, Autosomal Recessive
HSAN II
Morvan Disease
Neuropathy, Progressive Sensory, of Children
Radicular Neuropathy, Sensory, Recessive
Sensory Radicular Neuropathy, Recessive

The hereditary sensory neuropathies (HSN) include 4-6 similar but distinct inherited degenerative disorders of the nervous system (neurodegenerative) that frequently progress to loss of feeling, especially in the hands and feet. Some types of HSN are related to or identical with some forms of Charcot-Marie-Tooth disorder, and others are related to or identical with familial dysautonomia (Riley-Day syndrome). The classification of the HSNs is complicated, and the experts do not always agree on it. Hereditary sensory neuropathy type II (HSN2) is a rare genetic disorder that usually begins in childhood by affecting the nerves that serve the lower arms and hands and the lower legs and feet (the peripheral nerves). Symptoms start with inflamed fingers or toes especially around the nails. Infection is common and worsens as ulcers (open sores) form on the fingers and on the soles of the feet. The loss of sensation in both hands and feet often leads to neglect of the wounds. This can become serious, even leading to amputation in extreme cases, so it is important to care for any such wounds. The disorder affects many of the body's systems, is characterized by early onset (infancy or early childhood) and is transmitted genetically as an autosomal recessive trait.

The following organizations may provide additional information and support:
Jack Miller Center for Peripheral Neuropathy
March of Dimes Birth Defects Foundation
National Institute of Neurological Disorders and Stroke (NINDS)

---

791 Neuropathy, Hereditary Sensory, Type IV

Synonyms
Familial Dysautonomia, Type II
Hereditary Sensory and Autonomic Neuropathy IV
HSAN IV
HSN IV
Insensitivity to Pain, Congenital, with Anhydrosis; CIPA
Neuropathy, Congenital Sensory, with Anhydrosis

The hereditary sensory neuropathies (HSN) include 4-6 similar but distinct inherited degenerative disorders of the nervous system (neurodegenerative) that frequently progress to loss of feeling, especially in the hands and feet. The classification of these diseases is complicated, and sometimes a source of disagreement among the experts. Hereditary sensory neuropathy type IV (HSN4) is a rare genetic disorder characterized by the loss of sensation (sensory loss), especially in the feet and legs and, less severely, in the hands and forearms. The sensory loss is due to abnormal functioning of small, unmyelinated nerve fibers and portions of the spinal cord that control responses to pain and temperature as well as other involuntary or automatic body processes. Sweating is almost completely absent with this disorder. Mental retardation is usually present. The disorder is inherited as an autosomal recessive trait. The gene involved is located on chromosome 1. HSNs of various types may attack a single nerve (mononeuropathy) or many nerves simultaneously (polyneuropathy). The resulting symptoms may involve sensory, motor, reflex, or blood vessel (vasomotor) functions.

The following organization may provide additional information and support:
Jack Miller Center for Peripheral Neuropathy

---

792 Neuropathy, Peripheral

Synonyms
Mononeuritis Multiplex
Mononeuritis, Peripheral
Mononeuropathym Peripheral
Multiple Peripheral Neuritis
Peripheral Neuritis
Polyneuritis, Peripheral
Polyneuropathy, Peripheral

Disorder Subdivisions
Peroneal Nerve Palsy
Radial Nerve Palsy
Saturday Night Palsy
Tardy Ulnar Palsy
Ulnar Nerve Palsy

Peripheral neuropathy is an umbrella term that denotes a disorder of, or damage to, the peripheral nervous system. The peripheral nervous system consists of all the motor and sensory nerves that connect the brain and spinal cord to the rest of the body (i.e., the nerves outside the central nervous system). The symptoms and physical findings associated with peripheral neuropathies vary greatly from case to case and may be extremely complex. More than 100 different peripheral neuropathies are recognized, each with a distinguishing set of symptoms, development path, and prognosis. Disorders affecting only one nerve are described as a mononeuropathies while disorders affecting more than one nerve are called polyneuropathies. If two nerves affecting different parts of the body are involved, the disorder is described as a mononeuritis multiplex. In some cases, symptoms emerge abruptly, progress rapidly, and are slow to subside. Some chronic forms emerge only gradually and progress slowly. Some chronic forms appear to be resolved but are subject to relapses. Most often, symptoms such as pain, tingling, and/or muscle weakness start in both of the feet (bilateral) and progress up the legs. This is usually followed by symptoms in the hands that progress up the arms.

The following organizations may provide additional information and support:
Jack Miller Center for Peripheral Neuropathy
National Institute of Neurological Disorders and Stroke (NINDS)
Neuropathy Association

793 Neutropenia, Cyclic

Synonyms

CN
Cyclic Hematopoiesis
Human Cyclic Neutropenia
Periodic Neutropenia

Cyclic neutropenia is a rare blood disorder characterized by recurrent episodes of abnormally low levels of certain white blood cells (neutrophils) in the body. Neutrophils are instrumental in fighting off infection by surrounding and destroying bacteria that enter the body. Symptoms associated with cyclic neutropenia may include fever, a general feeling of ill health (malaise), and/or sores (ulcers) of the mucous membranes of the mouth. In most cases, individuals with low levels of neutrophils (neutropenia) are abnormally susceptible to recurrent infections.

The following organizations may provide additional information and support:
National Neutropenia Network
Neutropenia Support Association, Inc.
NIH/National Heart, Lung and Blood Institute Information Center
Severe Chronic Neutropenia International Registry
Severe Chronic Neutropenia International Registry Australia

794 Neutropenia, Severe Chronic

Disorder Subdivisions

Neutropenia, Chronic Congenital
Neutropenia, Chronic Idiopathic
Neutropenia, Cyclic

Severe chronic neutropenia is a rare blood disorder characterized by abnormally low levels of certain white blood cells (neutrophils) in the body (neutropenia). Neutrophils play an essential role in fighting bacterial infections by surrounding and destroying invading bacteria (phagocytosis). Symptoms associated with severe chronic neutropenia include recurring fevers, mouth sores (ulcers), and/or inflammation of the tissues that surround and support the teeth (periodontitis). Due to low levels of neutrophils, affected individuals may be more susceptible to recurring infections that, in some cases, may result in life-threatening complications. Severe chronic neutropenia may last for months or years and can affect both children and adults. There are three main forms of the disorder: congenital, idiopathic, and cyclic neutropenia. Severe chronic neutropenia may be inherited or acquired or may occur for unknown reasons (idiopathic).

The following organizations may provide additional information and support:
National Neutropenia Network
Neutropenia Support Association, Inc.
NIH/National Heart, Lung and Blood Institute Information Center
Severe Chronic Neutropenia International Registry
Severe Chronic Neutropenia International Registry Australia

795 Nevoid Basal Cell Carcinoma Syndrome

Synonyms

Basal Cell Nevus Syndrome
Gorlin Syndrome
Gorlin-Goltz Syndrome
Hermans-Herzberg Phakomatosis
NBCCS
Nevus, Epitheliomatosis Multiplex with

Nevoid basal cell carcinoma syndrome (NBCCS), also known as Gorlin or Gorlin-Goltz syndrome, is an inherited disorder characterized by a tendency to develop multiple cancerous cysts, lesions (nevi) of the skin and lining of the mouth, and other developmental and systemic defects. Almost any of the body's organ systems may be affected. The lesions (nevus, nevi) are usually found in the outer layer of the skin (epidermis) or in the mucous membranes of the mouth. The connective tissues and the nervous and vascular (blood vessel) systems of the body may also be affected. The skin lesions are limited in size, but not in number, and are not usually due to any external causes.

The following organizations may provide additional information and support:
American Cancer Society, Inc.
Basal Cell Carcinoma Nevus Syndrome Life Support Network
Gorlin Syndrome Group
National Cancer Institute
OncoLink: The University of Pennsylvania Cancer Center Resource
Rare Cancer Alliance
Skin Cancer Foundation

796 Nezelof's Syndrome

Synonyms

Alymphocytosis, Pure
Combined Immunodeficiency with
Immunoglobulins
Immune Defect due to Absence of Thymus
Immunodeficiency Cellular, with Abnormal
Immunoglobulin Synthesis
Severe Combined Immunodeficiency, Nezelof
Type
Thymic Aplasia, Nezelof's
Thymic Dysplasia with Normal
Immunoglobulins
T-Lymphocyte Deficiency

Disorder Subdivisions

PNP Deficiency
Purine Nucleoside Phosphorylase Deficiency

Nezelof's syndrome is an extremely rare immune deficiency disorder characterized by the impairment of cellular immunity against infections, especially by those agents that do not normally cause serious illness (opportunistic infections). In cell-mediated immune responses, specialized white blood cells known as T lymphocytes or "killer cells" help B lymphocytes respond to infectious foreign agents that invade the body. Nezelof's syndrome may also include some abnormalities in humoral immunity. In this form of immune response, antibodies that are produced by specialized cells (i.e., B lymphocytes) circulate in the lymphatic fluid and blood. Antibodies fight off bacteria, viruses, and other foreign substances that threaten the body. B lymphocytes enable the body to produce and maintain circulating antibodies. In a subgroup of people with Nezelof's syndrome, immune deficiency may be caused by a lack of the enzyme purine nucleoside phosphorylase (PNP).

The following organizations may provide additional information and support:
American Academy of Allergy Asthma and Immunology
Immune Deficiency Foundation
International Patient Organization for Primary Immunodeficiencies
Jeffrey Modell Foundation
March of Dimes Birth Defects Foundation
NIH/National Institute of Allergy and Infectious Diseases

797 Niemann Pick Disease

Synonyms

DAF Syndrome
Juvenile Dystonic Lipidosis
Lipid Histiocytosis
Lipidosis, Sphingomyelin
NPD
Sphingomyelinase Deficiency

Disorder Subdivisions

Nieman Pick Disease Type A (Acute
Neuronopathic Form)
Nieman Pick Disease Type B
Nieman Pick Disease Type C (Chronic
Neuronopathic Form)
Nieman Pick Disease Type D (Nova Scotia
Variant)
Nieman Pick Disease Type E
Nieman Pick Disease Type F (Sea-Blue
Histiocyte Disease)

Niemann-Pick disease (NPD) is a group of rare inherited disorders of fat metabolism. At least five types of Niemann-Pick disease have been identified (NPD types A, B, C, D, and E). Symptoms of types A and B occur as a result of a deficiency of the enzyme acid sphingomyelinase (ASM), which is needed to break down sphingomyelin, a fatty substance found mostly in the brain and nervous system. This deficiency results in abnormal accumulation of excessive amounts of sphingomyelin in many organs of the body such as the liver, spleen, and brain. Symptoms of type C occur because of impaired trafficking of large molecules within cells, which results in the accumulation of excessive amounts of cholesterol and other lipids (glycosphingolipids) in tissues throughout the body. The metabolic defect in type C can lead to a secondary reduction in ASM activity in some cells. The division of Niemann Pick disease into groups A, B, C and D was proposed by Allan Crocker in 1961 after he and Sidney Farber had expanded the category of Niemann-Pick disease by applying the diagnosis to all patients with "foam cells" and lipid storage in the tissues. This had led to the inclusion of older and less severely affected people than those originally described by Niemann and Pick. Symptoms common to all types of Niemann-Pick disease include yellow discoloration of the skin, eyes, and/or mucous membranes (jaundice), progressive loss of motor skills, feeding difficulties, learning disabilities, and an abnormally enlarged liver and/or spleen (hepatosplenomegaly). The different types of Niemann-Pick disease are inherited as autosomal recessive traits.

The following organizations may provide additional information and support:
Ara Parseghian Medical Research Foundation
CLIMB (Children Living with Inherited Metabolic Diseases)
Instituto de Errores Innatos del Metabolismo
National Institute of Neurological Disorders and Stroke (NINDS)
National Niemann-Pick Disease Foundation, Inc.
National Tay-Sachs and Allied Diseases Association, Inc.

798 Nocardiosis

Synonym
Lung Nocardiosis

Nocardiosis is an infectious pulmonary disease characterized by abscesses in the lungs. These abscesses may extend through the chest wall. The infection is spread through the body via the bloodstream by a microorganism called Nocardia asteroides.

The following organizations may provide additional information and support:
Centers for Disease Control and Prevention
NIH/National Institute of Allergy and Infectious Diseases

799 Nonketotic Hyperglycinemia

Synonyms
Glycinemia, Nonketotic
Hyperglycinemia, Nonketotic

Nonketotic hyperglycinemia is an inborn error of metabolism characterized by the accumulation of large amounts of the amino acid glycine in blood, urine and, particularly, the cerebrospinal fluid (CSF). The metabolic block occurs in the conversion of glycine into smaller molecules. There are four forms of this disorder: a relatively common neonatal form, an infantile form, a mild-episodic form, and a late-onset form.

The following organizations may provide additional information and support:
The Arc (A National Organization on Mental Retardation)

CLIMB (Children Living with Inherited Metabolic Diseases)
NIH/National Digestive Diseases Information Clearinghouse
Non-Ketotic Hyperglycinemia (NKH) International Family Network
Organic Acidaemias UK
Vaincre Les Maladies Lysosomales

800 Noonan Syndrome

Synonyms
Female Pseudo-Turner Syndrome
Male Turner Syndrome
NS
Turner Phenotype with Normal Chromosomes (Karyotype)

Noonan syndrome is a rare genetic disorder that is typically evident at birth (congenital). The disorder may be characterized by a wide spectrum of symptoms and physical features that vary greatly in range and severity. In many affected individuals, associated abnormalities include a distinctive facial appearance; a broad or webbed neck; a low hairline in the back of the head; and short stature. Characteristic abnormalities of the head and facial (craniofacial) area may include widely set eyes (ocular hypertelorism); vertical skin folds that may cover the eyes' inner corners (epicanthal folds); drooping of the upper eyelids (ptosis); a small jaw (micrognathia); a low nasal bridge; and low-set, prominent, abnormally rotated ears (pinnae). Distinctive skeletal malformations are also typically present, such as abnormalities of the breastbone (sternum), curvature of the spine (kyphosis and/or scoliosis), and outward deviation of the elbows (cubitus valgus). Many infants with Noonan syndrome also have heart (cardiac) defects, such as obstruction of proper blood flow from the lower right chamber of the heart to the lungs (pulmonary valvular stenosis). Additional abnormalities may include malformations of certain blood and lymph vessels, blood clotting and platelet deficiencies, mild mental retardation, failure of the testes to descend into the scrotum (cryptorchidism) by the first year of life in affected males, and/or other symptoms and findings. In some affected individuals, Noonan syndrome appears to result from spontaneous (sporadic) genetic changes (mutations). In others, the disorder may be transmitted as an autosomal dominant trait. Genetic analysis of one affected multigenerational family (kindred) suggests that the disorder may result from mutations of a gene located on the long arm (q) of chromosome 12 (12q24). However, many investigators indicate that Noonan syndrome may be caused by mutations of different genes (genetic heterogeneity).

The following organizations may provide additional information and support:
American Heart Association
The Arc (A National Organization on Mental Retardation)
Children's Cardiomyopathy Foundation
Congenital Heart Anomalies, Support, Education, & Resources
Human Growth Foundation
MAGIC Foundation for Children's Growth
March of Dimes Birth Defects Foundation
NIH/National Heart, Lung and Blood Institute Information Center
Restricted Growth Association
The Noonan Syndrome Support Group, Inc.

801 Norrie Disease

Synonyms
Anderson-Warburg Syndrome
Atrophia Bulborum Hereditaria
Episkopi Blindness
Fetal Iritis Syndrome
ND
NDP
Norrie Syndrome
Whitnall-Norman Syndrome

Norrie disease is a rare inherited neurodevelopmental disorder characterized by blindness in both eyes (bilateral) at birth (congenital). In some cases, children with this disorder may also experience varying degrees of mental retardation. Additional symptoms associated with Norrie disease may include mild to profound hearing loss and additional eye abnormalities. The lenses of the eyes may become cloudy (cataracts) during early infancy and the eyeballs may shrink (phthisis bulbi). Norrie disease is inherited as an X-linked recessive trait.

The following organizations may provide additional information and support:
American Council of the Blind, Inc.
American Foundation for the Blind
American Society for Deaf Children
The Arc (A National Organization on Mental Retardation)
Blind Children's Center
Blind Children's Fund
Council of Families with Visual Impairment

Deafness Research Foundation
Foundation Fighting Blindness, Inc.
Let Them Hear Foundation
National Association for Parents of Children with Visual Impairments (NAPVI)
National Association for Visually Handicapped
National Association of the Deaf
National Federation of the Blind
NIH/National Eye Institute
Norrie Disease Association
Retinitis Pigmentosa International

802 Nystagmus, Benign Paroxysmal Positional

Synonyms
BPPN
Cupulolithiasis
Labyrinthine Positional Nystagmus
Paroxysmal Positional Nystagmus

Benign paroxysmal positional nystagmus is a disorder of the vestibular system in the middle ear that causes dizziness due to altered function of the semicircular canals, usually involving the posterior canal but sometimes involving the horizontal canal. The dizziness, which is accompanied by abnormal eye movements or nystagmus, occurs suddenly and without warning; thus, it is "paroxysmal." It is also "positional" because the symptoms increase with certain movements of the head or body. It is the position of the head, rather than the movement, that causes the symptoms.

The following organizations may provide additional information and support:
American Nystagmus Network, Inc.
EAR (Education and Auditory Research) Foundation
National Institute of Neurological Disorders and Stroke (NINDS)
Vestibular Disorders Association (VEDA)

803 Obsessive Compulsive Disorder

Synonyms
Obsessive Compulsive Neurosis
OCD

Obsessive compulsive disorder is characterized by recurrent habitual obsessive or compulsive thoughts or actions. These obsessions and compulsions may become very distressing and time-consuming. In severe cases they can significantly interfere with a person's normal routine, occupational functioning, usual social activities or relationships with others.

The following organizations may provide additional information and support:
National Mental Health Association
NIH/National Institute of Mental Health
Obsessive Compulsive Anonymous
Obsessive-Compulsive Foundation, Inc.
Tourette Syndrome Association, Inc.

804 Ochoa Syndrome

Synonyms
Hydronephrosis with Peculiar Facial Expression
Inverted Smile and Occult Neuropathic Bladder
Partial Facial Palsy with Urinary Abnormalities
Urofacial Syndrome

Ochoa (urofacial) syndrome, also known as hydronephrosis with peculiar facial expression, is an extremely rare inherited disorder characterized by an abnormal facial expression and obstructive disease of the urinary tract (uropathy) that are present at birth (congenital). When affected infants smile, their facial musculature turns upside down or "inverts" so that they appear to be grimacing or crying. The urinary abnormality is an obstructive uropathy in which failure of nerve signals between the bladder and the spinal cord results in incomplete emptying of the bladder (neurogenic or neuropathic bladder). In addition, neurogenic bladder may result in involuntary discharge of urine (enuresis), urinary tract infections, and/or abnormal accumulation of urine in the kidneys (hydronephrosis). Additional abnormalities may include inflammation of the kidneys and pelvis (pyelonephritis), backflow of urine into the tubes that carry urine from the kidney to the bladder (vesicoureteral reflex), and/or involuntary spasms of the ring of muscle around the anus (external sphincter). In some cases, affected individuals may develop renal failure during adolescence or the early 20s, potentially leading to life-threatening complications. Ochoa syndrome occurs due to disruption or changes (mutations) of a gene on the long arm (q) of chromosome 10 (10q23-q24). Ochoa syndrome has been identified as an autosomal recessive trait.

The following organizations may provide additional information and support:

American Association of Kidney Patients
American Kidney Fund, Inc.
National Kidney Foundation
NIH/National Kidney and Urologic Diseases Information Clearinghouse

805 Ocular Motor Apraxia, Cogan Type

Synonyms
COMA
Congenital Oculomotor Apraxia
Oculomotor Apraxia, Cogan Type
Saccade Initiation Failure, Congenital

Cogan type ocular motor apraxia is a rare inherited eye disorder that is present at birth (congenital). The disorder is characterized by a defect in side-to-side (horizontal) eye movements, both voluntary and responsive. When affected infants rotate their heads to the side to look at an object, their eyes will lag and then move in the opposite direction. In order to compensate for this, the infants will sharply jerk their heads past the desired object in an effort to bring the eyes to a position where they can view the object. The disorder can also be associated with mild developmental delay and speech difficulties. Symptoms of this disorder usually improve throughout the first and second decades of life. Cogan type ocular motor apraxia is a genetic condition for which the inheritance pattern has not been well established. It is not clear if it is inherited as an autosomal recessive genetic trait or an autosomal dominant genetic trait.

The following organizations may provide additional information and support:
National Eye Research Foundation
NIH/National Eye Institute
Ocular Motor Apraxia Home Page

806 Oculocerebral Syndrome with Hypopigmentation

Synonyms
Cross Syndrome
Cross-McKusick-Breen Syndrome
Depigmentation-Gingival Fibromatosis-Microphthalmia
Kramer Syndrome

Oculocerebral syndrome with hypopigmentation is an extremely rare inherited disorder characterized by the lack of normal color (hypopigmentation) of the skin and hair and abnormalities of the central nervous system that affect the eyes and certain parts of the brain (oculocerebral). Physical findings at birth include unusually light skin color and silvery-gray hair. Abnormal findings associated with the central nervous system may include abnormal smallness of one or both eyes (microphthalmia); clouding (opacities) of the front, clear portion of the eye through which light passes (cornea); and/or rapid, involuntary eye movements (nystagmus). Additional symptoms that may develop during infancy include involuntary muscle contractions, associated loss of muscle function (spastic paraplegia), developmental delays, and/or mental retardation. Oculocerebral syndrome with hypopigmentation is believed to be inherited as an autosomal recessive genetic trait.

The following organizations may provide additional information and support:
National Association for Parents of Children with Visual Impairments (NAPVI)
National Association for Visually Handicapped
NIH/National Arthritis and Musculoskeletal and Skin Diseases Information Clearinghouse
NIH/National Eye Institute

807 Oculocerebrocutaneous Syndrome

Synonyms
Delleman Syndrome
Delleman-Oorthuys Syndrome
OCC Syndrome
OCCS
Orbital Cyst with Cerebral and Focal Dermal Malformations

Oculocerebrocutaneous (OCC) syndrome, a rare genetic disorder, is apparent at birth (congenital). The disorder is characterized primarily by eye (ocular), brain (e.g., cerebral), and skin (cutaneous) malformations. For example, many affected infants have semisolid or fluid-filled swellings (cysts) within the cavities of the skull (orbits) that accommodate the eyeballs and associated structures. In most cases, the eye on the affected side or sides is also abnormally small (microphthalmos). Brain abnormalities associated with OCC syndrome may include malformations of the ventricular system in the middle of the brain, multiple fluid-filled spaces within the outer region of the cerebral hemispheres (cerebral cortex), and absence of the band of nerve fibers that joins the brain's hemispheres (agenesis of the corpus callosum). Affected infants and children may also have mental retardation and episodes of uncontrolled electrical activity in the

brain (seizures). In addition, OCC syndrome is characterized by underdevelopment or absence of skin in certain localized regions (focal dermal hypoplasia or aplasia) and most have protruding, flesh-colored or brownish outgrowths of skin (cutaneous tags) within certain facial areas, including around the eyelids, on the cheeks, or near the ears. In all individuals with OCC syndrome, the disorder appears to occur randomly for unknown reasons (isolated, with no family history of similar disorders).

The following organizations may provide additional information and support:
Agenesis of the Corpus Callosum (ACC) Network
Anophthalmia/Microphthalmia Registry
Epilepsy Foundation
International Children's Anophthalmia Network (ican)
March of Dimes Birth Defects Foundation
Micro & Anophthalmic Children's Society
National Institute of Neurological Disorders and Stroke (NINDS)

808 Oculo-Dento-Digital Dysplasia

Synonyms
Dento-Oculo-Osseous Dysplasia
Oculo Dento Digital Dysplasia
Oculodentodigital Dysplasia
Oculo-Dento-Osseous Dysplasia
ODD Syndrome
ODDD
ODOD
Osseous-Oculo-Dento Dysplasia

Oculo-dento-digital dysplasia is a rare disorder that may be inherited as an autosomal dominant trait or be caused by a new change in the genes that occurs for no apparent reason (mutation). There also have been a few instances in which it is thought to have been inherited as an autosomal recessive trait. Major symptoms of cculo-dento-digital dysplasia are webbing of the fourth and fifth fingers, an abnormally small transparent part of the eye (microcornea), a slender nose with narrow nostrils, underdevelopment of the outer flaring wall of each nostril (alae), defective enamel and dry hair that grows slowly.

The following organizations may provide additional information and support:
National Foundation for Ectodermal Dysplasias
NIH/National Arthritis and Musculoskeletal and Skin Diseases Information Clearinghouse

NIH/National Oral Health Information Clearinghouse
Oculo-Dento-Digital Dysplasia Support Group

809 Olivopontocerebellar Atrophy, Hereditary

Synonym
Hereditary OPCA

Disorder Subdivisions
OPCA, Fickler-Winkler Type
OPCA, Holguin Type
OPCA, Menzel Type
OPCA, Schut-Haymaker Type
OPCA with Dementia and Extrapyramidal Signs
OPCA with Retinal Degeneration
OPCA1
OPCA2
OPCA3
OPCA4
OPCA5
SCA, Cuban Type
SCA1
SCA2
SCA7
Spinocerebellar Ataxia 1
Spinocerebellar Ataxia 2
Spinocerebellar Ataxia 7

Hereditary olivopontocerebellar atrophy (OPCA) is a rare group of disorders characterized by progressive balance problems (disequilibrium), progressive impairment of the ability to coordinate voluntary movements (cerebellar ataxia), and difficulty speaking or slurred speech (dysarthria). There are at least five distinct forms of hereditary OPCA. All forms of hereditary OPCA, except one, are inherited as autosomal dominant traits.The term olivopontocerebellar atrophy has generated significant controversy and confusion in the medical literature because of its association with two distinct groups of disorders, specifically multiple system atrophy (MSA) and spinocerebellar ataxia (SCA). OPCA may refer to a specific form of MSA or one of several types of SCA. Hereditary OPCA refers to the group of disorders that overlaps with SCA. Both forms of OPCA are characterized by progressive degeneration of certain structures of the brain, especially the cerebellum, pons, and inferior olives. The cerebellum is the part of the brain that plays a role in maintaining balance and posture as well as coordinating voluntary movement. The pons is part of the brainstem and con-tains important neuronal pathways between the cerebrum, spinal cord, and cerebellum. The pons serves as a relay point for messages between these structures. The inferior olives are two round structures that contain nuclei that are involved with balance, coordination and motor activity.

The following organizations may provide additional information and support:
March of Dimes Birth Defects Foundation
National Ataxia Foundation
National Institute of Neurological Disorders and Stroke (NINDS)
National Parkinson Foundation, Inc.
WE MOVE (Worldwide Education and Awareness for Movement Disorders)

810 Ollier Disease

Synonyms
Dyschondroplasia
Enchondromatosis
Multiple Cartilaginous Enchondroses
Multiple Enchondromatosis

Ollier disease is a rare skeletal disorder characterized by abnormal bone development (skeletal dysplasia). While this disorder may be present at birth (congenital); it may not become apparent until early childhood when symptoms, such as deformities or improper limb growth, are more obvious. Ollier disease primarily affects the long bones and cartilage of the joints of the arms and legs, specifically the area where the shaft and head of a long bone meet (metaphyses). The pelvis is often involved; and even more rarely, the ribs, breast bone (sternum), and/or skull may also be affected. Ollier disease manifests as greater than normal growth of the cartilage in the long bones of the legs and arms so that growth is abnormal and the outer layer (cortical bone) of the bone becomes thin and more fragile. These masses of cartilage are benign (non-cancerous) tumors known as enchondromas. Enchondromas may occur at anytime. After puberty these growths stabilize as cartilage is replaced by bone. In rare cases, the enchondromas may undergo malignant changes (e.g., chondrosarcomas). The exact cause of Ollier disease is not known, although in some cases it may be inherited as an autosomal dominant genetic trait.When the enchondromas of Ollier disease are accompanied by substantial, most often benign, proliferation of blood vessels (hemangiomas), the array of symptoms is known as Maffucci syndrome.

The following organization may provide additional information and support:
NIH/National Institute of Arthritis and Musculoskeletal and Skin Diseases

811 Opitz G/BBB Syndrome

Synonyms

BBBG Syndrome
Hypertelorism with Esophageal Abnormalities and Hypospadias
Hypertelorism-Hypospadias Syndrome
Hypospadias-Dysphagia Syndrome
Opitz BBB Syndrome
Opitz BBB/G Compound Syndrome
Opitz BBBG Syndrome
Opitz G Syndrome
Opitz Hypertelorism-Hypospadias Syndrome
Opitz Oculogenitolaryngeal Syndrome
Opitz Syndrome
Opitz-Frias Syndrome
Telecanthus-Hypospadias Syndrome

Disorder Subdivisions

BBB Syndrome (Opitz)
G Syndrome

Opitz G/BBB syndrome or Opitz syndrome is a genetic disorder that may be evident at birth. The syndrome may be characterized by distinctive malformations of the head and facial (craniofacial) area, including widely set eyes (ocular hypertelorism); an abnormal groove in the upper lip (cleft lip); incomplete closure of the roof of the mouth (cleft palate); upwardly or downwardly slanting eyelid folds (palpebral fissures); vertical skin folds that may cover the eyes' inner corners (epicanthal folds); or a wide, flat nasal bridge. In addition, in affected males, abnormalities typically include failure of the testes to descend into the scrotum (cryptorchidism), clefting of the scrotum (bifid scrotum), or abnormal placement of the urinary opening (meatus) on the underside of the penis (hypospadias). Affected individuals may also have malformations of the windpipe (trachea) and the larynx, which connects the trachea and the throat (pharynx); underdevelopment of the lungs (pulmonary hypoplasia); and associated swallowing and breathing difficulties. Opitz syndrome may also be characterized by additional abnormalities, including partial or complete closure of the anal opening (imperforate anus); underdevelopment or absence of the thick band of nerve fibers that joins the two hemispheres of the brain (hypoplasia or

agenesis of the corpus callosum); kidney (renal) abnormalities; heart (cardiac) defects; or mental retardation.Opitz syndrome was originally categorized as two distinct disorders: i.e., Opitz G and Opitz BBB syndromes. Yet many investigators have since determined that the disorders represent the same clinical entity with different modes of genetic transmission. The form of the disorder previously designated as Opitz BBB syndrome is transmitted as an X-linked trait. This X-linked disorder appears to be caused by changes (mutations) of a gene, known as MID1 (for "midline-1"), that is located on the short arm (p) of chromosome X (Xp22). The form originally classified as Opitz G syndrome is inherited as an autosomal dominant trait. It is thought to result from deletions of genetic material from the long arm (q) of chromosome 22 (22q11.2).

The following organizations may provide additional information and support:
22q and You Center
Opitz G/BBB Family Network, Inc.

812 Opportunistic Infections

Opportunistic infections are mild to severe infectious diseases in a compromised host. The infections are caused by microorganisms that normally do not cause serious disease in healthy people. These infections may occur in individuals whose immune system or other physiological defenses are impaired or compromised in some way. The inability to resist such opportunistic infections is usually caused by an underlying disease or trauma, or from procedures and/or drugs that are used to treat another medical condition. Opportunistic infections may be caused by bacteria, fungi, viruses, or parasites. Symptoms vary according to the microorganism involved and the extent of involvement. Treatment or medical management of opportunistic infections may be difficult because some of these microorganisms may be resistant to standard antibiotic therapy. In some cases an affected individual may have a dysfunctional immune system (compromised) that is not able to fight the infection.

The following organizations may provide additional information and support:
Centers for Disease Control and Prevention
NIH/National Institute of Allergy and Infectious Diseases

813 Opsoclonus-Myoclonus Syndrome

Synonyms
Dancing Eyes-Dancing Feet
Kinsbourne Syndrome
Myoclonic Encephalopathy, Kinsbourne Type
Opsoclonic Encephalopathy

Opsoclonus-myoclonus syndrome is a rare neurological disorder that usually affects infants and young children. It is characterized by the sudden onset of brief, repeated, shock-like spasms of muscles within the arms, legs, or entire body (myoclonus), an impaired ability to control voluntary movements (ataxia), and continual, involuntary, rapid eye movements in both horizontal and vertical directions (opsoclonus). In approximately 50 percent of affected individuals, a malignant tumor, usually a tumor of embryonic nerve cells (neuroblastoma), is responsible for the symptoms associated with opsoclonus myoclonus. In most other cases, the disorder may be due to a viral infection such as Coxsackievirus B3, poliovirus, or St. Louis encephalitis virus. Rarely, it may result from other underlying causes such as a tumor within the skull (intracranial tumors) or hydrocephalus, a condition in which inhibition of the normal flow of cerebrospinal fluid (CSF) and abnormal widening (dilatation) of the cerebral spaces of the brain (ventricles) causes accumulation of CSF in the skull and potentially increased pressure on brain tissue.

The following organizations may provide additional information and support:
Dancing Eye Syndrome Support Trust
National Institute of Neurological Disorders and Stroke (NINDS)
National Pediatric Myoclonus Center
Opsoclonus-Myoclonus Support Network, Inc.

814 Oral Facial Digital Syndrome

Synonyms
Mohr Syndrome
OFD Syndrome
Oral-Facial-Digital Syndrome
Orofaciodigital Syndrome

Disorder Subdivisions
Oral-Facial-Digital Syndrome I
Oral-Facial-Digital Syndrome II
Oral-Facial-Digital Syndrome III
Oral-Facial-Digital Syndrome IV

Oral-facial-digital syndrome (OFD) is an umbrella term for several apparently distinctive genetic modifications. Symptoms include frequent episodic neuromuscular disturbances, congenital malformations such as cleft palate, other facial deformities, malformation of the hands and feet, shortened limbs and differing degrees of mental retardation.

The following organizations may provide additional information and support:
AboutFace USA
The Arc (A National Organization on Mental Retardation)
Children's Craniofacial Association
FACES: The National Craniofacial Association
Forward Face, Inc.
Let's Face It (USA)
National Foundation for Facial Reconstruction
National Foundation of Dentistry For the Handicapped
NIH/National Oral Health Information Clearinghouse

815 Organic Personality Syndrome

Synonym
Personality Syndrome, Organic

Organic personality syndrome or organic mental syndrome is a mental disorder characterized by a short-term or long-term personality disturbance largely due to brain dysfunction. The ability to reason, remember, imagine, and learn may not be affected, but the individual's judgement may be so poor that continual supervision may be necessary. Left unattended, he or she may behave in ways that could cause difficult or dangerous problems.

The following organizations may provide additional information and support:
National Alliance for the Mentally Ill
National Mental Health Association
National Mental Health Consumers' Self-Help Clearinghouse
NIH/National Institute of Mental Health

816 Ornithine Transcarbamylase Deficiency

Synonyms
Hyperammonemia due to Ornithine Transcarbamylase Deficiency
Hyperammonemia Type II
Ornithine Carbamyl Transferase Deficiency
OTC Deficiency

Ornithine transcarbamylase (OTC) deficiency is a rare genetic disorder characterized by complete or partial lack of the enzyme ornithine transcarbamylase (OTC). OTC is one of six enzymes that play a role in the breakdown and removal of nitrogen from the body, a process known as the urea cycle. The lack of the OTC enzyme results in excessive accumulation of nitrogen, in the form of ammonia (hyperammonemia), in the blood. Excess ammonia, which is a neurotoxin, travels to the central nervous system through the blood, resulting in the symptoms and physical findings associated with OTC deficiency. Symptoms include vomiting, refusal to eat, progressive lethargy, and coma. OTC deficiency is inherited as an X-linked recessive trait. The urea cycle disorders are a group of rare disorders affecting the urea cycle, a series of biochemical processes in which nitrogen is converted into urea and removed from the body through the urine. Nitrogen is a waste product of protein metabolism. Failure to break down nitrogen results in the abnormal accumulation of nitrogen, in the form of ammonia, in the blood.

The following organizations may provide additional information and support:
Belgian Association for Metabolic Diseases (BOKS)
CLIMB (Children Living with Inherited Metabolic Diseases)
National Kidney Foundation
National Urea Cycle Disorders Foundation
NIH/National Digestive Diseases Information Clearinghouse
Organic Acidaemias UK

---

817 Orocraniodigital Syndrome

Synonyms
Cleft Lip/Palate with Abnormal Thumbs and Microcephaly
Cranio-Oro-Digital Syndrome
Digital-Oro-Cranio Syndrome
Juberg Hayward Syndrome

Orocraniodigital syndrome is an extremely rare inherited disorder characterized by multiple malformations of the head and face (craniofacial area) and the fingers and toes (digits). Major characteristics may include a vertical groove in the upper lip (cleft lip) and/or the inside, upper portion of the mouth (cleft palate), an abnormally small head (microcephaly), widely spaced eyes (ocular hypertelorism), improper development (hypoplasia) of the thumbs and/or toes, and/or webbing (syndactyly) of the toes. In some cases, malformations of certain skeletal bones may also be present.

Mental retardation has occurred in the majority of cases. Orocraniodigital syndrome may be inherited as an autosomal recessive genetic trait.

The following organizations may provide additional information and support:
AboutFace USA
Children's Craniofacial Association
Cleft Palate Foundation
FACES: The National Craniofacial Association
Forward Face, Inc.
National Craniofacial Foundation
Wide Smiles

---

818 Osgood Schlatter Condition

Synonyms
Osgood-Schlatter's Disease
Osteochondrosis, Tibial Tubercle
Schlatter Disease

Osgood-Schlatter condition (formerly known as Osgood-Schlatter's disease) is a painful condition characterized by tiny, microfractures of the bony bump in the lower leg bone (tibia) where the ligament from the kneecap (patella) is inserted into the tibia. The bump is known as the tibial tubercle. It is a disorder of the early teens, especially during a growth spurt, more likely to affect young men than young women, especially athletes of either sex who are active in games requiring substantial running and/or jumping. It is a common, transient, short-term disorder, also called an overuse condition, that usually requires only rest and restraint from further strenuous activity for a relatively short period of time before it heals itself.

The following organization may provide additional information and support:
NIH/National Arthritis and Musculoskeletal and Skin Diseases Information Clearinghouse

---

819 Osteogenesis Imperfecta

Synonyms
Brittle Bone Disease
Ekman-Lobstein Disease
Lobstein Disease (Type I)
OI
Vrolik Disease (Type II)

Disorder Subdivisions
Osteogenesis Imperfecta Type I
Osteogenesis Imperfecta Type II

Osteogenesis Imperfecta Type III
Osteogenesis Imperfecta Type IV

Osteogenesis imperfecta (OI) is a group of rare disorders affecting the connective tissue and characterized by extremely fragile bones that break or fracture easily (brittle bones), often without apparent cause. The specific symptoms and physical findings associated with OI vary greatly from case to case. The severity of OI also varies greatly, even among individuals of the same family. OI may be a mild disorder or may result in severe complications. Four main types of OI have been identified. OI type I is the most common and the mildest form of the disorder. OI type II is the most severe. In most cases, the various forms of osteogenesis imperfecta are inherited as autosomal dominant traits.

The following organizations may provide additional information and support:
Canadian Osteogenesis Imperfecta Society
Children's Brittle Bone Foundation
Let Them Hear Foundation
March of Dimes Birth Defects Foundation
NIH/National Institute of Arthritis and Musculoskeletal and Skin Diseases
NIH/National Institute of Child Health and Human Development
Osteogenesis Imperfecta Foundation, Inc.
Sjældne Diagnoser / Rare Disorders Denmark

820 Osteomyelitis

Synonym
Hematogenous Osteomyelitis

Disorder Subdivisions
Anaerobic Osteomyelitis
Osteomyelitis due to Vascular Insufficiency
Osteomyelitis, Pyogenic, Acute
Osteomyelitis, Pyogenic, Chronic
Vertebral Osteomyelitis

Osteomyelitis is a bone infection, usually caused by bacteria, that can be either acute or chronic. This disorder usually occurs as a result of an infection in one part of the body that is transported through the bloodstream to a bone in a distant location. Among children and teens, the long bones of the legs and arms are most frequently affected. In adults, osteomyelitis most often affects the vertebrae of the spine and/or the hips.

The following organization may provide additional information and support:
NIH/National Arthritis and Musculoskeletal and Skin Diseases Information Clearinghouse

821 Osteonecrosis

Synonyms
Aseptic Necrosis
Avascular Necrosis of Bone
Ischemic Necrosis of Bone

Osteonecrosis is the destruction (necrosis) of bone tissue, often due to an interference with the supply of blood to the bone. It most commonly affects the joints and bones of the hips, knees and/or shoulders. It may occur as a result of bone injuries (trauma-related osteonecrosis) or in conjunction with other diseases or risk factors (nontraumatic osteonecrosis). Risk factors include excessive alcohol intake, some blood coagulation disorders, inflammatory conditions such as rheumatoid arthritis and systemic lupus erythematosus, and reactions to some medications such as steroids.

The following organizations may provide additional information and support:
Arthritis Foundation
National Osteonecrosis Foundation
NIH/National Arthritis and Musculoskeletal and Skin Diseases Information Clearinghouse

822 Osteopetrosis

Synonyms
Albers-Schonberg Disease
Marble Bones
Osteosclerosis Fragilis Generalisata

Disorder Subdivisions
Osteopetrosis, Autosomal Dominant; Adult Type
Osteopetrosis, Autosomal Recessive; Malignant Infantile Type
Osteopetrosis, Mild Autosomal Recessive; Intermediate Type

Osteopetrosis may be inherited as either a dominant or recessive trait and is marked by increased bone density, brittle bones, and, in some cases, skeletal abnormalities. Although symptoms may not initially be apparent in people with mild forms of this disorder, trivial injuries may cause bone fractures due to abnormalities of the bone. There are three major types of osteopetrosis: the malignant infantile form, the intermediate form, and the adult form. The adult form is milder than the other forms, and may not be diagnosed until adolescence or adulthood when symptoms first appear. The intermediate form, found in children younger than 10 years old, is more severe than the adult form but less severe than the malignant infantile form. The malignant infantile form is apparent from birth and frequently shortens life expectancy.

The following organizations may provide additional information and support:
CLIMB (Children Living with Inherited Metabolic Diseases)
Let Them Hear Foundation
NIH Osteoporosis and Related Bone Diseases National Resource Center
NIH/National Arthritis and Musculoskeletal and Skin Diseases Information Clearinghouse
Osteopetrosis Support Trust (UK)
Paget Foundation for Paget's Disease of Bone and Related Disorders

---

823   Otopalatodigital Syndrome Type I and II

Synonyms
Cranioorodigital Syndrome
Faciopalatoosseous Syndrome
FPO
OPD Syndrome

Disorder Subdivisions
OPD Syndrome, Type I
OPD Syndrome, Type II

Otopalatodigital syndrome type I and type II are rare X-linked genetic disorders in which complete expression of the disease occurs only in males. Females may be mildly affected with some of the symptoms. OPD type I is the milder form of the disease and is characterized by cleft palate, hearing loss and skeletal abnormalities in the skull and limbs. OPD type II includes these abnormalities as well as growth deficiency and abnormalities of the brain and is frequently not compatible with life.

The following organizations may provide additional information and support:
Children's Craniofacial Association
FACES: The National Craniofacial Association
Let Them Hear Foundation
Let's Face It (USA)

National Craniofacial Foundation
National Foundation for Facial Reconstruction
Oto Palatal Digital Syndrome Family Resource Network

---

824   Pachydermoperiostosis

Synonyms
Pachydermoperiostosis Syndrome
Rosenfeld-Kloepfer Syndrome
Touraine-Solente-Gole Syndrome

Pachydermoperiostosis is a rare disorder characterized by clubbing of the fingers, thickening of the skin of the face (pachyderma), and excessive sweating (hyperhidrosis). It typically appears during childhood or adolescence, often around the time of puberty, and progresses slowly for about ten years. Specific symptoms include enlargement of the fingers and toes (clubbing), a condition in which there is a fibrous covering on the ends of the long bones (periostosis), coarse facial features, increased bulk of the skin on the scalp forming folds, depressions or furrows of the scalp (cutis verticis gyrata), and/or excessive sweating of the hands and feet. Pachydermoperiostosis is the complete or primary form of a more common disorder known as idiopathic primary hypertrophic osteoarthropathy (HOA).

The following organizations may provide additional information and support:
March of Dimes Birth Defects Foundation
NIH/National Arthritis and Musculoskeletal and Skin Diseases Information Clearinghouse

---

825   Pachyonychia Congenita

Disorder Subdivisions
Pachyonychia Congenita Type 1 (PC-1)
Pachyonychia Congenita Type 2 (PC-2)

Pachyonychia congenita is a rare disorder inherited in an autosomal dominant fashion. It can be divided into two main forms, PC type 1 and PC type 2. The predominant features common to both types are thick nails (hypertrophic nail dystrophy), thick skin on the palms and soles (focal palmoplantar keratoderma) and a white outer layer on the tongue and cheek (oral leukokeratosis). PC-2 is distinguished from PC-1 by the presence of widespread pilosebaceous (associated with hair and related glands) cysts, or cysts that normally develop during puberty; in PC-1 there may be a limited distribution of cysts. Teeth that are present at birth (natal teeth) are a specific feature of PC-2 but they are not always present (not fully penetrant).

The following organization may provide additional information and support:
PC Project

826 Paget's Disease

Synonyms
Osteitis Deformans
Paget's Disease of Bone

Paget's disease of bone is a chronic, slowly progressive skeletal condition of abnormally rapid bone destruction (osteolytic) and reformation (osteoblastic). The new bone may occur in one or more regions of the body and is structurally abnormal, dense and fragile. This abnormal development may cause bone pain, arthritis, deformities and fractures. The bones most frequently affected are in the spine, skull, pelvis and lower legs. The exact cause of Paget's disease is not known.

The following organizations may provide additional information and support:
Let Them Hear Foundation
NIH Osteoporosis and Related Bone Diseases National Resource Center
Paget Foundation for Paget's Disease of Bone and Related Disorders

827 Paget's Disease of the Breast

Synonyms
Mammary Paget's Disease
Paget's Disease of the Nipple
Paget's Disease of the Nipple and Areola

Paget's disease of the breast is a rare form of breast cancer that almost exclusively occurs in women. However, rare cases have been recorded in which men have been affected. The condition was originally reported in 1874 by Sir James Paget, an English surgeon, who also described an unrelated skeletal condition known as Paget's disease of the bone. It is essential to note that these disorders are distinct disease entities that are medically unrelated. Paget's disease of the breast is characterized by inflammatory, "eczema-like" changes of the nipple that may extend to involve the areola, which is the circular, darkened (pigmented) region of skin surrounding the nipple. Initial find-

ings often include itching (pruritus), scaling, and crusting of and/or discharge from the nipple. In those with Paget's disease of the breast, distinctive tumor cells (known as Paget cells) are present within the outermost layer of skin (epidermis) of the nipple. In addition, the condition is often associated with an underlying malignancy (i.e., cancer) of the milk ducts (ductal carcinoma). The malignancy may be confined to cells lining the milk ducts (carcinoma in situ) or may have invaded surrounding tissue (infiltrating carcinoma). (The milk ducts [lactiferous ducts] are the channels that carry milk secreted by lobes of the breast to the nipple.) Paget's disease of the breast is thought to represent approximately two to four percent of breast cancers.

The following organizations may provide additional information and support:
American Cancer Society, Inc.
Breast Cancer Advisory Center
Breast Cancer Society of Canada
Canadian Breast Cancer Network
National Alliance of Breast Cancer Organizations
National Breast Cancer Coalition
National Cancer Institute
National Cancer Institute Physician Data Query (PDQ) Cancer Information Service
National Women's Health Network
OncoLink: The University of Pennsylvania Cancer Center Resource
SHARE—Self-Help For Women With Breast or Ovarian Cancer
Skin Cancer Foundation
Y-ME National Breast Cancer Organization

828 Pallister-Hall Syndrome

Synonyms
CAVE (Cerebro-Acro-Visceral Early Lethality) Complex
Congenital Hypothalamic Hamartoblastoma Syndrome
Hall-Pallister Syndrome
PHS

Pallister-Hall syndrome (PHS) is an extremely rare genetic disorder that may be apparent at birth (congenital). The symptoms and findings associated with the disorder may vary greatly in range and severity from case to case. However, in many individuals with Pallister-Hall syndrome, associated abnormalities may include a malformation of the hypothalamus (hypothalamic hamartomablastoma), a portion of the brain that coordinates the function of the pituitary gland and has several other functions; decreased pituitary function (hypopituitarism); the presence of extra (supernumerary) fingers and/or toes (central or postaxial polydactyly); an abnormal division of the epiglottis (bifid epiglottis); and/or a condition in which a thin covering blocks the anal opening or the passage that normally connects the anus and the lowest part of the large intestine (rectum) fails to develop (imperforate anus). Additional symptoms and findings may include characteristic malformations of the head and facial (craniofacial) area and/or other abnormalities. Pallister-Hall syndrome has autosomal dominant inheritance. Cases in which a positive family history has not been found are thought to represent new genetic changes (mutations) that occur randomly, with no apparent cause (sporadic).

The following organizations may provide additional information and support:
American Brain Tumor Association
Hydrocephalus Association
Hydrocephalus Support Group, Inc.
Pallister-Hall Foundation (Aust.)
Pallister-Hall Syndrome Family Support Network

829 Pallister-Killian Mosaic Syndrome

Synonyms
Chromosome 12, Isochromosome 12p Mosaic
Killian Syndrome
Killian/Teschler-Nicola Syndrome
Pallister Mosaic Syndrome
Pallister Mosaic Syndrome Tetrasomy 12p
Teschler-Nicola/Killian Syndrome

Pallister-Killian mosaic syndrome is a rare chromosomal disorder caused by the presence of four copies of the short arm of chromosome 12 instead of the normal two. Major symptoms may include a coarse face with a high forehead, sparse hair on the scalp, an abnormally wide space between the eyes, a fold of the skin over the inner corner of the eyes, and a broad nasal bridge with a highly arched palate. Mental retardation, loss of muscle tone, and streaks of skin lacking color are often present.

The following organizations may provide additional information and support:
The Arc (A National Organization on Mental Retardation)
Chromosome Deletion Outreach, Inc.
UNIQUE—Rare Chromosome Disorder Support Group

830 Pallister W Syndrome

Synonym
W Syndrome

Pallister W syndrome is a rare genetic disorder characterized by unusual facial features such as clefting of the palate and the upper lip, a broad flat nose, widely spaced slanted eyes, and/or downslanting eyelid folds (palpebral fissures). Other symptoms may include mental retardation, speech problems, bone deformities of the arms and legs, and/or seizures. The exact cause of Pallister W syndrome is not known.

The following organizations may provide additional information and support:
AboutFace USA
Children's Craniofacial Association
FACES: The National Craniofacial Association
Forward Face, Inc.
Let's Face It (USA)
National Craniofacial Foundation
National Foundation for Facial Reconstruction

831 Pancreatic Islet Cell Tumor

Synonyms
Encephalopathy, Hypoglycemic
Multiple Endocrine Adenomatosis

Pancreatic-islet cell tumors appear in one of two forms. They may be nonfunctioning or functioning tumors. Nonfunctioning tumors may cause obstruction in the shortest part of the small intestine (duodenum) or in the biliary tract, which connects the liver to the duodenum and includes the gallbladder. These nonfunctioning tumors may erode and bleed into the stomach and/or the intestines, or they may cause an abdominal mass. Functioning tumors secrete excessive amounts of hormones, which may lead to various syndromes including low blood sugar (hypoglycemia), multiple bleeding ulcers (Zollinger-Ellison syndrome), pancreatic cholera (Verner-Morrison syndrome), carcinoid syndrome or diabetes. Islet cells are small, isolated masses of cells that make up the Islet of Langerhans in the pancreas. When functioning normally, they secrete the protein hormones insulin and glucagon. Tumors composed of irregular islet cells may occur alone or in a group of many tumors. Approximately 90% of islet-cell tumors are noncancerous (benign). They usually range in size from 0.5 to 2 cm in diameter.

The following organizations may provide additional information and support:
American Cancer Society, Inc.
NIH/National Digestive Diseases Information Clearinghouse

832   Panic Anxiety Syndrome

Synonyms
Anxiety Neurosis
Anxiety State
Panic Disorder

Panic anxiety syndrome is a psychiatric disorder characterized by recurrent and unpredictable anxiety attacks with no apparent cause for the symptoms, such as threat of danger or attack. Panic-anxiety syndrome is believed to be caused by biochemical factors, though the specific cause of the disorder is not yet known.

The following organizations may provide additional information and support:
Anxiety Disorders Association of America
Depression and Related Affective Disorders Association
National Alliance for the Mentally Ill
National Mental Health Association
National Mental Health Consumers' Self-Help Clearinghouse
NIH/National Institute of Mental Health

833   Panniculitis, Idiopathic Nodular

Synonyms
Nodular Nonsuppurative Panniculitis
Pfeiffer-Weber-Christian Syndrome
Relapsing Febrile Nodular Nonsuppurative Panniculitis
Weber Christian Disease (so-called)

Idiopathic nodular panniculitis is a rare spectrum of skin disorders characterized by single or multiple, tender or painful bumps below the surface of the skin (subcutaneous nodules) that usually lead to inflammation of the subcutaneous layer of fat (panniculitis). These nodules tend to be 1-2 centimeters large and most often affect the legs and feet (lower extremities). In most cases, idiopathic nodular panniculitis is associated with fever, a general feeling of ill health (malaise), muscle pain (myalgia), and/or abdominal pain. These symptoms may subside after a few days or weeks and may recur weeks, months, or years later. The exact cause of idiopathic nodular panniculitis is not known (idiopathic).

The following organizations may provide additional information and support:
Erythema Nodosum Yahoo Support Group
NIH/National Arthritis and Musculoskeletal and Skin Diseases Information Clearinghouse
NIH/National Institute of Allergy and Infectious Diseases
Panniculitis Support Group

834   Papillitis

Synonym
Optic Nerve Papillitis

Papillitis, also known as optic neuritis, is characterized by inflammation and deterioration of the portion of the optic nerve known as the optic disk. Also referred to as the "blind spot," the optic disk (optic papilla) is that portion of the optic nerve that enters the eye and joins with the nerve-rich membrane lining the eye (retina). The optic nerves are the pair of nerves (second cranial nerves) that transmit impulses from the retina to the brain. Individuals with papillitis experience loss of vision in one eye that may occur within several hours of onset. The severity of visual impairment may vary from case to case, ranging from slight visual deficiency to complete loss of light perception. In addition, affected individuals experience a reduction in color perception. In some cases, spontaneous recovery may occur. However, in other cases, permanent visual impairment may result if the underlying cause is not detected or treated. Papillitis may occur for unknown reasons, after a viral illness, or due to or in association with a number of different underlying disorders or other factors.

The following organizations may provide additional information and support:
National Association for Visually Handicapped
NIH/National Eye Institute

835   Papillon-Lefevre Syndrome

Synonyms
Hyperkeratosis Palmoplantaris with Periodontosis
Keratoris Palmoplantaris with Periodontopathia
Palmar-Plantar Hyperkeratosis and Concomitant Periodontal Destruction
Palmoplantar Keratoderma with Periodontosis

Papillon-Lefevre syndrome (PLS) is an extremely rare genetic disorder that typically becomes apparent from approximately one to 5 years of age. PLS is characterized by the development of dry scaly patches on the skin of the palms and the soles (palmar-plantar hyperkeratosis) in association with severe inflammation and degeneration of the structures surrounding and supporting the teeth (periodontium). The primary (deciduous) teeth frequently become loose and fall out by about age five. Without treatment, most of the secondary (permanent) teeth may also be lost by approximately age 17. Additional symptoms and findings associated with PLS may include frequent pus-producing (pyogenic) skin infections, abnormalities of the nails (nail dystrophy), and excessive perspiration (hyperhidrosis). Papillon-Lefevre syndrome is transmitted as an autosomal recessive trait. Genetic analysis of several affected families (kindreds) suggests that the disorder may result from changes (mutations) of a gene that regulates production of an enzyme known as cathespin C. The gene is located on the long arm (q) of chromosome 11 (11q14).

The following organizations may provide additional information and support:
NIH/National Arthritis and Musculoskeletal and Skin Diseases Information Clearinghouse
NIH/National Institute of Dental and Craniofacial Research

---

836   Paracoccidioidomycosis

Synonyms
Lobo Disease
Lutz-Splendore-Almeida Disease
PCM
Paracoccidioidal Granuloma
South American Blastomycosis

Paracoccidioidomycosis (PCM) is a chronic infectious tropical disease caused by the fungus *Paracoccidioides brasiliensis*. The initial infection usually occurs in the lungs, but may also spread to the skin, mucous membranes, and other parts of the body. Specialized cells that line the walls of blood and lymphatic vessels and dispose of cellular waste (reticuloendothelial system) may also be affected by paracoccidioidomycosis. If the patient does not receive treatment, life-threatening complications can occur. Most cases of this disease occur in South and Central America.

The following organizations may provide additional information and support:
Centers for Disease Control and Prevention
NIH/National Institute of Allergy and Infectious Diseases

World Health Organization (WHO) Regional Office for the Americas (AMRO)

---

837   Paramyotonia Congenita

Synonyms
Eulenburg Disease
Myotonia Congenita Intermittens
Paralysis Periodica Paramyotonica
Paramyotonia Congenita of Von Eulenburg
Von Eulenburg Paramyotonia Congenita

Paramyotonia congenita is a rare muscular disorder inherited as an autosomal dominant trait. This nonprogressive disorder is characterized by a condition in which the muscles do not relax after contracting (myotonia). Symptoms can be triggered by exposure to the cold. There are also intermittent periods of a type of paralysis in which there is no muscle tone (flaccid paresis). This condition does not necessarily coincide with exposure to cold temperatures or myotonia. There is no wasting (atrophy) or increase in bulk (hypertrophy) of muscles with this disorder.

The following organizations may provide additional information and support:
Muscular Dystrophy Association
NIH/National Arthritis and Musculoskeletal and Skin Diseases Information Clearinghouse

---

838   Paraplegia, Hereditary Spastic

Synonyms
Familial Spastic Paraplegia
FSP
HSP
Spastic Spinal Familial Paralysis
Strumpell Disease
Strumpell-Lorrain Familial Spasmodic Paraplegia
Strumpell-Lorraine Syndrome
Strumpell's Familial Paraplegia

Disorder Subdivisions
Hereditary Spastic Paraplegia, Complicated
Hereditary Spastic Paraplegia, Uncomplicated ("Pure")

Hereditary spastic paraplegia (HSP) is a group of inherited neurological disorders characterized by progressive weakness (paraplegia) and increased muscle tone and stiffness (spasticity) of leg muscles. HSP is also sometimes referred to as familial spastic paraplegia (FSP) or Strumpell-Lorraine syndrome. The age at symptom onset and the degree of muscle weakness and spasticity may be extremely variable from case to case, including among individuals within the same family (kindred). According to reports in the medical literature, symptom onset may occur as early as infancy or as late as the eighth or ninth decade of life; however, symptoms may most often develop during early to mid-adulthood. Initial findings typically include stiffness and relatively mild weakness of leg muscles, balance difficulties, unexplained tripping and falls, and an unusually "clumsy" manner of walking (gait). As the disorder progresses, walking may become increasingly difficult. However, complete loss of the ability to walk is relatively rare. HSP may be classified into two major subtypes: "uncomplicated" or "complicated" HSP. In individuals with uncomplicated (or "pure") HSP, progressive spastic paraplegia occurs as an isolated, primary finding. In those with complicated HSP, additional neurologic abnormalities are present. Some individuals with uncomplicated HSP may develop muscle spasms and difficulties with bladder control. In those with complicated HSP, associated symptoms and findings may include visual and/or hearing impairment, mental retardation, impaired control of voluntary movements (ataxia), and/or other abnormalities. According to researchers, changes (mutations) of many different genes may cause HSP. In most cases, such mutations appear to be transmitted as an autosomal dominant trait. More rarely, mutations for HSP may be inherited as an autosomal recessive or X-linked recessive trait. The basic underlying defect or defects in HSP are unknown. However, associated symptoms appear to result from progressive degenerative changes of regions of the spinal cord (corticospinal tracts) that convey motor impulses from the brain to muscles involved in controlling certain voluntary movements.

The following organizations may provide additional information and support:
National Institute of Neurological Disorders and Stroke (NINDS)
Spastic Paraplegia Foundation
Tom Wahlig Foundation— JENA
WE MOVE (Worldwide Education and Awareness for Movement Disorders)

839   Parkinson's Disease

Synonyms
Drug-Induced Parkinsonism
Paralysis Agitans
Parkinsonism
Postencephalitic Parkinsonism
Secondary Parkinsonism
Shaking Palsy
Symptomatic Parkinsonism

Parkinson's disease is a slowly progressive neurologic condition characterized by involuntary trembling (tremor), muscular stiffness or inflexibility (rigidity), slowness of movement and difficulty carrying out voluntary movements. Degenerative changes occur in areas deep within the brain (substantia nigra and other pigmented regions of the brain), causing a decrease in dopamine levels in the brain. Dopamine is a neurotransmitter, which is a chemical that sends a signal in the brain. Parkinsonian symptoms can also develop secondary to hydrocephalus (a condition in which the head is enlarged and areas of the brain accumulate excessive fluids, resulting in an increase in pressure on the brain), head trauma, inflammation of the brain (encephalitis), obstructions (infarcts) or tumors deep within the cerebral hemispheres and the upper brain stem (basal ganglia), or exposure to certain drugs and toxins. Parkinson's disease is slowly progressive and may not become incapacitating for many years.

The following organizations may provide additional information and support:
Alzheimer's Foundation of America
Awakenings (Parkinson's Disease Information and News)
National Institute of Neurological Disorders and Stroke (NINDS)
National Parkinson Foundation, Inc.
New Horizons Un-Limited, Inc.
NIH/National Institute of Allergy and Infectious Diseases
Parkinson's Disease Foundation, Inc.
Stem Cell Research Foundation
Vasculitis of the Central Nervous System
WE MOVE (Worldwide Education and Awareness for Movement Disorders)

840   Parry-Romberg Syndrome

Synonyms
HFA
Progressive Facial Hemiatrophy
Progressive Hemifacial Atrophy
PRS
Romberg Syndrome

Parry-Romberg syndrome is a rare disorder characterized by slowly progressive degeneration (atrophy) of the soft tissues of half of the face (hemifacial atrophy). Some individuals may experience distinctive changes of the eyes and hair; and neurological abnormalities including episodes of uncontrolled electrical disturbances in the brain (seizures) and episodes of severe pain in tissues supplied by the fifth cranial nerve (trigeminal nerve) including the mouth, cheek, nose, and/or other facial tissues (trigeminal neuralgia). Symptoms and physical findings associated with Parry-Romberg syndrome usually become apparent during the first or early during the second decade of life. In rare cases, the disorder is apparent at birth. The majority of individuals with Parry-Romberg syndrome experience symptoms before the age of 20 years. In individuals with the disorder, initial facial changes usually involve the tissues above the upper jaw (maxilla) or between the nose and the upper corner of the lip (nasolabial fold) and progress to involve the angle of the mouth, the areas around the eye, the brow, the ear, and/or the neck. Progressive tissue wasting can be on either side of the face. In some rare cases, the atrophy may be bilateral. Affected areas may demonstrate shrinkage and atrophy of tissues beneath the skin (subcutaneous tissue), the layer of fat under the skin (subcutaneous fat), and underlying cartilage, muscle, and bone. In addition, the skin overlying affected areas may become darkly pigmented (hyperpigmentation) with, in some cases, areas of hyperpigmentation and patches of unpigmented skin (vitiligo). Many individuals also experience atrophy of half of the upper lip and tongue as well as abnormal exposure, delayed eruption, or wasting of the roots of certain teeth on the affected side. Symptoms of Parry-Romberg syndrome may begin at any age. Facial atrophy may cease abruptly, or progress slowly and then become stationary. If the atrophy becomes stationary, it may reactivate later in life. In other cases, the atrophy may progress indefinitely. In some cases, hair abnormalities may also appear on the affected side, including whitening (blanching) of the hair as well as abnormal bald patches on the scalp and loss of eyelashes and the middle (median) portion of the eyebrows (alopecia). In addition, some individuals with Parry-Romberg syndrome may also experience associated neurological abnormalities. These may include severe headaches that last for extended periods of time and may be accompanied by visual abnormalities, nausea, and vomiting (migraines); facial pain (trigeminal neuralgia); and/or periods of uncontrolled electrical disturbances in the brain (seizures) that usually are characterized by rapid spasms of a muscle group that spread to adjacent muscles (contralateral Jacksonian epilepsy). The

range and severity of associated symptoms and findings may vary from case to case. In most cases, Parry-Romberg syndrome appears to occur randomly for unknown reasons (sporadically).

The following organizations may provide additional information and support:
Epilepsy Foundation
March of Dimes Birth Defects Foundation
National Craniofacial Foundation
National Institute of Neurological Disorders and Stroke (NINDS)
NIH/National Oral Health Information Clearinghouse
Romberg's Connection
Society for the Rehabilitation of the Facially Disfigured, Inc.
Trigeminal Neuralgia Association (TNA)

841 Pars Planitis

Synonyms
Intermediate Uveitis (UI)
Peripheral Retinal Inflammation
PP
Vitritis

Although pars planitis is generally benign, there can be significant vision loss in extreme cases. It is an immunological disorder of the eye characterized by inflammation of a part of the uvea, the layer of tissue between the sclera and the retina, the membranes protecting the eyeball. The uvea, in turn, is made up of three portions: the iris, the ciliary body, and the choroid. In addition, the uvea contains many of the blood vessels that supply the eye. The pars plana is a narrow section of the ciliary body, inflammation of which is known as pars planitis. In association with the inflammation or immunological response, fluid and cells infiltrate the clear gelatin-like substance (vitreous humor) of the eyeball, near the retina and/or pars plana. As a result, swelling of the eye or eyes can also occur. The inflammation occurs in the intermediate zone of the eye; that is, between the anterior part(s) of the eye (iris) and the posterior part(s), the retina and/or choroid. It has therefore been designated as one of the diseases of a family of intermediate uveitis. In some cases, the disturbance of vision may be slightly progressive.

The following organizations may provide additional information and support:
American Autoimmune Related Diseases Association, Inc.

Association for Macular Diseases, Inc.
NIH/National Eye Institute
UveitisSupport-MEEI

842 Parsonage-Turner Syndrome

Synonyms
Brachial Neuritis
Brachial Plexus Neuritis
Idiopathic Brachial Plexus Neuropathy
Neuralgic Amyotrophy

Parsonage-Turner syndrome is a relatively common condition characterized by inflammation of the network of nerves that control and supply (innervate) the muscles of the chest, shoulders, and arms (brachial plexus). Individuals with the condition first experience a sudden onset of severe pain across the shoulder and upper arm. The muscles of the affected shoulder show weakness, wasting (atrophy), and paralysis (atrophic paralysis) within a few hours or days of the onset of the disorder. Although individuals with the condition may experience paralysis of the affected areas that lasts for months or years in some cases, recovery is usually complete. The exact cause of Parsonage-Turner syndrome is not known.

The following organizations may provide additional information and support:
American Autoimmune Related Diseases Association, Inc.
NIH/National Arthritis and Musculoskeletal and Skin Diseases Information Clearinghouse

843 Patulous Eustachian Tube

Synonyms
P.E.T.
pET

In patulous eustachian tube (pET) dysfunction, the eustachian tube stays open most of the time. The eustachian tube is a passageway from the back of the nose to the middle ear that may be opened or closed by action of a valve-like device. Under normal circumstances, it remains closed for most of the day, opening only on occasion to equalize air pressure in the middle ear and the exterior environment. If the tube remains open, the patient complains of hearing one's own voice or one's breathing as too loud (autophony), hearing echoes of one's own voice, or hearing ocean waves much like the sound produced by holding a shell over one's ear. The condition is benign but may generate, over time, serious and even extreme responses to the abnormal sounds.

The following organizations may provide additional information and support:
Better Hearing Institute
EAR (Education and Auditory Research) Foundation
NIH/National Institute on Deafness and Other Communication Disorders (Balance)

844 Pediatric Cardiomyopathy

Synonyms
Arrhythmogenic Right Ventricular Cardiomyopathy (ARVC)
Asymmetrical Septal Hypertrophy
Familial Congestive Cardiomyopathy
Familial Dilated Cardiomyopathy (FDC)
Hypertrophic Obstructive Cardiomyopathy (HOCM)
Idiopathic Dilated Cardiomyopathy
Idiopathic Hypertrophic Subaortic Stenosis
Non-obstructive Hypertrophic Cardiomyopathy

Disorder Subdivisions
Arrhythmogenic Right Ventricular Dysplasia (ARVD)
Dilated Cardiomyopathy
Hypertrophic Cardiomyopathy (HCM)
Restrictive Cardiomyopathy

Pediatric cardiomyopathy is a rare heart condition that affects infants and children. Specifically, cardiomyopathy means disease of the heart muscle (myocardium). Several different types of cardiomyopathy exist and the specific symptoms vary from case to case. In some cases, no symptoms may be present (asymptomatic); in many cases, cardiomyopathy is a progressive condition that may result in an impaired ability of the heart to pump blood; fatigue; heart block; irregular heartbeats (tachycardia); and, potentially, heart failure and sudden cardiac death. Cardiomyopathy may be termed ischemic or nonischemic. Ischemic cardiomyopathy refers to cases that occur due to a lack of blood flow and oxygen (ischemia) to the heart. Such cases often result from hardening of the arteries (coronary artery disease). Nonischemic cardiomyopathy refers to cases that occur due to structural damage or malfunction of the heart muscle. Nearly all cases of pediatric cardiomyopathy are nonischemic. This report deals with nonischemic pediatric cardiomyopathy. Cardiomyopathy may also be termed primary or secondary.

Primary cardiomyopathy refers to cases where cardiomyopathy occurs by itself or for unknown reasons (idiopathic). Secondary cardiomyopathy refers to cases where the disease occurs secondary to a known cause such as heart muscle inflammation (myocarditis) caused by viral or bacterial infections; exposure to certain toxins such as heavy metals or excessive alcohol use; or certain disorders that affect the heart and/or additional organ systems. According to the Pediatric Cardiomyopathy Registry, approximately 79 percent of pediatric cardiomyopathy cases occur for unknown reasons (idiopathic). Nonischemic cardiomyopathy may be further divided into four subtypes based upon the specific changes within the heart. These subtypes are: dilated, hypertrophic, restrictive and arrhythmogenic right ventricular dysplasia.

The following organizations may provide additional information and support:
American Heart Association
Cardiac Arrhythmias Research and Education Foundation, Inc.
Cardiomyopathy Association
Children's Cardiomyopathy Foundation
Congenital Heart Information Network
HOPE (The Heart of Pediatric Electrophysiology)
Hypertrophic Cardiomyopathy Association of America
Irish Heart Foundation
Montgomery Heart Foundation for Cardiomyopathy
NIH/National Heart, Lung and Blood Institute Information Center

---

845 Peeling Skin Syndrome

Synonyms
Deciduous Skin
Familial Continuous Skin Peeling
Keratolysis Exfoliativa Congenita
Skin Peeling Syndrome

Peeling skin syndrome is an extremely rare inherited disorder characterized by continual, spontaneous skin peeling (exfoliation). Other findings may include reddening of the skin (erythema) and itching (pruritus). At least one group working on this disorder distinguishes between a non-inflammatory form called type A and an inflammatory form known as type B. Type B is associated with congenital erythroderma, a condition in which the skin has an intense red color. There is mounting evidence that the inflammatory type B is a variant of Netherton syndrome. Based on its occurrence in families in which husband and wife are close relatives, peeling skin

syndrome is likely to be transmitted as an autosomal recessive genetic trait.

The following organizations may provide additional information and support:
Foundation for Ichthyosis & Related Skin Types
NIH/National Arthritis and Musculoskeletal and Skin Diseases Information Clearinghouse

---

846 Pelizaeus-Merzbacher Brain Sclerosis

Synonyms
Pelizaeus-Merzbacher Disease
PMD
Sclerosis, Diffuse Familial Brain
Sudanophilic Leukodystrophy, Pelizaeus-Merzbacher Type

Disorder Subdivisions
Acute Infantile Pelizaeus-Merzbacher Brain Sclerosis
Autosomal Dominant Pelizaeus-Merzbacher Brain Sclerosis
Classical X-Linked Pelizaeus-Merzbacher Brain Sclerosis
Late Onset Pelizaeus-Merzbacher Brain Sclerosis

Pelizaeus-Merzbacher brain sclerosis is a rare inherited disorder affecting the central nervous system that is associated with abnormalities of the white matter of the brain. Symptoms develop due to lack of the fatty covering of nerve cells (myelin sheath). Many areas of the central nervous system may be affected, including the deep portions of the cerebrum (subcortical), cerebellum, and/or brain stem. Symptoms may include the impaired ability to coordinate movement (ataxia), involuntary muscle spasms (spasticity) that result in slow, stiff movements of the legs, delays in reaching developmental milestones, loss of motor abilities, and the progressive deterioration of intellectual function. The symptoms of Pelizaeus-Merzbacher brain sclerosis are usually slowly progressive. Several forms of the disorder have been identified, including classical X-linked Pelizaeus-Merzbacher brain sclerosis; acute infantile (or connatal) Pelizaeus-Merzbacher brain sclerosis; and autosomal dominant, adult-onset (or late-onset) Pelizaeus-Merzbacher brain sclerosis.

The following organizations may provide additional information and support:
Association Europeene contre les Leucodystrophes
CLIMB (Children Living with Inherited Metabolic Diseases)

Hunter's Hope Foundation, Inc.
March of Dimes Birth Defects Foundation
National Institute of Neurological Disorders and Stroke (NINDS)
Pelizaeus Merzbacher Disease Support Group
United Leukodystrophy Foundation

847 Pemphigus

Synonyms

Benign Chronic Familial Pemphigus
Benign Familial Pemphigus
Brazilian Pemphigus Foliaceus
Fogo Selvagem
Hailey-Hailey Disease

Disorder Subdivisions

Drug-Induced Pemphigus
Exfoliative Dermatitis
Pemphigus Erythematosus
Pemphigus Foliaceus
Pemphigus Herpetiformis
Pemphigus Vegetans
Pemphigus Vulgaris

Pemphigus is a group of rare autoimmune skin disorders characterized by the development of blisters in the outer layer of the skin (epidermis) and mucous membranes (thin moist layers that line the body's internal surfaces). The location and type of blisters vary according to the type of pemphigus. If left untreated, pemphigus can be a serious illness.

The following organizations may provide additional information and support:
American Autoimmune Related Diseases Association, Inc.
Autoimmune Information Network, Inc
International Pemphigus Foundation
National Cancer Institute
NIH/National Arthritis and Musculoskeletal and Skin Diseases Information Clearinghouse
Pemphigus & Pemphigoid Society

848 Penta X Syndrome

Synonyms

49, XXXXX Chromosome Constitution
49, XXXXX Karyotype
49,XXXXX Syndrome
Pentasomy X
XXXXX Syndrome

Penta X syndrome is a rare chromosomal disorder that affects females. Females normally have two X chromosomes. However, in those with penta X syndrome, there are three additional (or a total of five) X chromosomes in the nuclei of body cells (pentasomy X). The condition is typically characterized by moderate to severe mental retardation, short stature, malformations of the skull and facial (craniofacial) region, and/or other physical abnormalities. Characteristic craniofacial malformations may include upslanting eyelid folds (palpebral fissures), a flat nasal bridge, malformed ears, a short neck with a low hairline, and/or other findings. Penta X syndrome may also be characterized by abnormal deviation (clinodactyly) or permanent flexion (camptodactyly) of the "pinkies" or fifth fingers; heart and/or kidney defects; deficient development of the ovaries and uterus; and/or other physical findings. The disorder results from errors during the division of reproductive cells in one of the parents.

The following organizations may provide additional information and support:
AboutFace USA
American Heart Association
The Arc (A National Organization on Mental Retardation)
Children's Craniofacial Association
Craniofacial Foundation of America
March of Dimes Birth Defects Foundation
National Dissemination Center for Children with Disabilities
Support Organization for Trisomy 18, 13, and Related Disorders
UNIQUE—Rare Chromosome Disorder Support Group

849 Pentalogy of Cantrell

Synonyms

Cantrell Pentalogy
Cantrell Syndrome
Cantrell-Haller-Ravich Syndrome
Pentalogy Syndrome
Peritoneopericardial Diaphragmatic Hernia
TAS Midline Defect
TAS, Midline Defects, Included
Thoracoabdominal Ectopia Cordis
Thoracoabdominal Syndrome

Pentalogy of Cantrell is a very rare disorder characterized by a combination of severe defects of the middle of the chest including the sternum, diaphragm, heart, and abdominal wall. This defect can affect males or females and is apparent at birth or shortly after.

The following organizations may provide additional information and support:
CHERUBS—The Association of Congenital Diaphragmatic Hernia Research, Advocacy and Support
Real Hope for CDH (Congenital Diaphragmatic Hernia) Foundation

---

850 PEPCK Deficiency, Mitochondrial

Synonym
Phosphoenolpyruvate Carboxykinase Deficiency

Mitochondrial PEPCK deficiency is an extremely rare disorder of carbohydrate metabolism inherited as an autosomal recessive trait. A deficiency of the enzyme phosphoenolpyruvate carboxykinase, which is a key enzyme in the conversion of proteins and fat to glucose (gluconeogenesis), causes an excess of acid in the circulating blood (acidemia). Characteristics of this disorder are low blood sugar (hypoglycemia), loss of muscle tone, an abnormal enlargement of the liver and failure to gain weight and grow normally.

The following organizations may provide additional information and support:
CLIMB (Children Living with Inherited Metabolic Diseases)
Lactic Acidosis Support Trust
NIH/National Digestive Diseases Information Clearinghouse
United Mitochondrial Disease Foundation

---

851 Perisylvian Syndrome, Congenital Bilateral

Synonym
CBPS

Congenital bilateral perisylvian syndrome (CBPS) is an extremely rare neurological disorder that may be apparent at birth (congenital), infancy, or later during childhood. It is characterized by partial paralysis of muscles on both sides (diplegia) of the face, tongue, jaws, and throat (pseudobulbar palsy); difficulties in speaking (dysarthria), chewing (mastication), and swallowing (dysphagia); and/or sudden episodes of uncontrolled electrical activity in the brain (epilepsy). In most cases, mild to severe mental retardation is also present. Associated symptoms and findings are thought to be due to improper development of the outer surface of the brain (cerebral cortex) during embryonic growth (neuronal dysmigration). In most

cases, the disorder appears to occur randomly for unknown reasons (sporadically).

The following organizations may provide additional information and support:
Epilepsy Canada
Epilepsy Foundation
Lissencephaly Network, Inc.
National Institute of Neurological Disorders and Stroke (NINDS)
Support Network for Pachygyria, Agyria, Lissencephaly

---

852 Perniosis

Synonyms
Chilblains
Cold Induced Vascular Disease
Erythema, Pernio
Pernio

Perniosis is an inflammatory disorder that is triggered by prolonged exposure to cold and damp (humid) conditions. It is a form of inflammation of the small blood vessels (vasculitis) and is characterized by painful, itchy, tender, skin lesions on the lower legs, hands, toes, feet, ears and face. The lesions usually last for 2 to 3 weeks. One form of the disorder affects the blood vessels of the thighs.

The following organization may provide additional information and support:
NIH/National Heart, Lung and Blood Institute

---

853 Pertussis

Synonym
Whooping Cough

Pertussis is a highly contagious acute respiratory disease caused by the bacteria *Bordetella pertussis*. This disease has three stages: catarrhal, paroxysmal, and convalescent. The symptoms of the catarrhal stage are mild and may go unnoticed. The paroxysmal stage of pertussis is characterized by episodes of coughing with a distinctive "whooping" sound when breathing in (inspiration). This characteristic cough gives the disease its common name, whooping cough. During the convalescent stage, episodes of coughing are less frequent and symptoms improve. The incidence of pertussis has diminished greatly with widespread use of the DPT vaccine (diphtheria, pertussis, tetanus), but in certain areas of the United States outbreaks have occurred periodically in recent years.

The following organizations may provide additional information and support:
Centers for Disease Control and Prevention
NIH/National Institute of Allergy and Infectious Diseases
NIH/National Institute of Child Health and Human Development
World Health Organization (WHO) Regional Office for the Americas (AMRO)

854   Peutz-Jeghers Syndrome

Synonyms
Hutchinson-Weber-Peutz Syndrome
Intestinal Polyposis II
Intestinal Polyposis-Cutaneous Pigmentation Syndrome
Jegher's Syndrome
Lentigio-Polypose-Digestive Syndrome
Melanoplakia-Intestinal Polyposis
Peutz-Touraine Syndrome
PJS
Polyposis, Hamartomatous Intestinal
Polyps and Spots Syndrome

Peutz-Jeghers syndrome is a rare inherited disorder characterized by multiple benign nodular growths (hamartomas) on the mucous lining of the intestinal wall. Affected individuals also have dark skin discolorations, especially around the lips and mucous membranes of the mouth.

The following organizations may provide additional information and support:
American Cancer Society, Inc.
Hereditary Colon Cancer Association (HCCA)
International Peutz-Jeghers Support Group
March of Dimes Birth Defects Foundation
NIH/National Digestive Diseases Information Clearinghouse
OncoLink: The University of Pennsylvania Cancer Center Resource
Peutz Jeghers Syndrome Online Support Group

855   Peyronie Disease

Synonyms
Chronic Cavernositis
Fibrous Cavernositis
Fibrous Plaques of the Penis
Fibrous Sclerosis of the Penis
Penile Fibromatosis
Penile Fibrosis
Penile Induration
Plastic Induration Corpora Cavernosa
Plastic Induration of the Penis
Van Buren's Disease

Peyronie disease is a rare connective tissue disorder characterized by the development of fibrous plaques in the soft tissue of the penis of adult males. Affected individuals may experience pain, have cord-like lesions on the penis, and/or exhibit abnormal curvature of the penis when erect. In some cases, these conditions may make it impossible for many affected individuals to have normal sexual intercourse unless treated. Symptoms may be chronic, or may spontaneously resolve in some cases. The exact cause of Peyronie disease is not known.

The following organizations may provide additional information and support:
American Foundation for Urologic Disease
NIH/National Kidney and Urologic Diseases Information Clearinghouse

856   Pfeiffer Syndrome Type I

Synonyms
Acrocephalosyndactyly Type I, Subtype I
Acrocephalosyndactyly V (ACS5 or ACS V), Subtype I
Classic Type Pfeiffer Syndrome
Noack Syndrome, Type I

Pfeiffer syndrome is a very rare genetic disorder characterized by abnormalities of the head and facial (craniofacial) area, distinctive malformations of the fingers and toes (digits), and/or additional physical abnormalities. This disorder, which is also known as acrocephalosyndactyly type V, is generally accepted to be the same disorder as Noack syndrome (acrocephalopolysyndactyly type I). The acrocephalosyndactyly (ACS) disorders are a group of very rare genetic disorders characterized by premature closure of the fibrous joints (cranial sutures) between certain bones of the skull (craniosynostosis), causing the top of the head to appear abnormally pointed (acrocephaly), and webbing or fusion of certain fingers and/or toes (syndactyly). According to the medical literature, researchers have recognized three subtypes of Pfeiffer syndrome: namely, Pfeiffer syndrome types I, II, and III. Major findings that may be associated with all forms of the disorder include premature fusion of certain cranial sutures (craniosynostosis), abnormally broad thumbs and great toes that may bend outward (varus deformity), and syndactyly of certain fingers and toes. The range and severity of associated symptoms and findings may vary greatly from case to case. In most infants with type I, or classic type Pfeiffer syndrome, craniosynostosis causes the head to appear short and unusually pointed at the top (turribrachycephaly). Affected infants and children typically have craniofacial abnormalities including an unusually high, full forehead; a flattened middle portion of the face (midface hypoplasia); a small nose with a flattened bridge; widely spaced eyes (ocular hypertelorism); an underdeveloped upper jaw (hypoplastic maxilla), causing the lower jaw to appear unusually prominent (relative mandibular prognathism); and/or dental abnormalities. Individuals with Pfeiffer syndrome type I also have digital abnormalities including the malformations mentioned above (i.e., abnormally broad thumbs and great toes that may bend outward [varus deformity] and syndactyly). Intelligence is usually normal. In some cases, Pfeiffer syndrome type I may be due to new genetic changes (mutations) that occur randomly, with no apparent cause (sporadic). In other cases, the disorder may be inherited as an autosomal dominant genetic trait.

The following organizations may provide additional information and support:
AboutFace USA
Children's Craniofacial Association
FACES: The National Craniofacial Association
Headlines—Craniofacial Support
Let's Face It (USA)
March of Dimes Birth Defects Foundation
National Craniofacial Foundation
National Hydrocephalus Foundation
NIH/National Institute on Deafness and Other Communication Disorders Information Clearinghouse

857 Phelan-McDermid Syndrome

Synonym

Deletion 22q13 Syndrome

Phelan-McDermid syndrome is a rare chromosomal disorder in which a portion of the long arm (q) of chromosome 22 is missing (deleted or monosomic). Although the range and severity of symptoms may vary, Phelan-McDermid syndrome is generally thought to be characterized by low muscle tone, normal to accelerated growth, absent to severely delayed speech, moderate to profound mental retardation, and minor dysmorphic features. A rare number of cases with much smaller (submicroscopic) deletions of 22q13 are reported to result in mild developmental delay. Current research indicates that the inability of the gene involved to produce sufficient protein for normal functioning (haploinsufficiency) may be responsible for most of the neurologic symptoms (developmental delay and absent speech) associated with this disorder.

The following organizations may provide additional information and support:
22q13 Deletion Syndrome Foundation/Phelan-McDermid Syndrome
Chromosome 22 Central
Chromosome Deletion Outreach, Inc.
UNIQUE—Rare Chromosome Disorder Support Group

858 Phenylketonuria

Synonyms

Classical Phenylketonuria
Hyperphenylalanemia
PKU
Phenylalanine Hydroxylase Deficiency
Phenylalaninemia

Phenylketonuria (PKU) is an inborn error of metabolism that is detectable during the first days of life with appropriate blood testing (e.g., during routine neonatal screening). PKU is characterized by absence or deficiency of an enzyme (phenylalanine hydroxylase) that is responsible for processing the essential amino acid phenylalanine. (Amino acids, the chemical building blocks of proteins, are essential for proper growth and development.) With normal enzymatic activity, phenylalanine is converted to another amino acid (tyrosine), which is then utilized by the body. However, when the phenylalanine hydroxylase enzyme is absent or deficient, phenylalanine abnormally accumulates in the blood and is toxic to brain tissue. Symptoms associated with PKU are typically absent in newborns. Affected infants may be abnormally drowsy and listless (lethargic) and have difficulties feeding. In addition, untreated infants with PKU tend to have unusually light eyes, skin, and hair (light pigmentation) and may develop a rash that appears similar to eczema, an inflammatory skin condition that may be characterized by itching, redness, and blistering in affected areas. Without treatment, most infants with PKU develop mental retardation that is typically severe. Those with untreated PKU may also develop additional neurologic symptoms, such as episodes of uncontrolled electrical activity in the brain (seizures), abnormally increased activity (hyperactivity), poor coordination and a clumsy manner of walking (gait), abnormal posturing, aggressive behavior, or psychiatric disturbances. Additional symptoms and findings may include nausea, vomiting, and a musty or "mousy" body odor due to the presence of a by-product of phenylalanine (phenylacetic acid) in the urine and sweat. To prevent mental retardation, treatment consists of a carefully controlled, phenylalanine-restricted diet beginning during the first days or weeks of life. Most experts suggest that a phenylalanine-restricted diet should be lifelong in persons with classical PKU. Classical PKU refers to persons with 2 severe mutations of the phenylalanine hydroxylase gene.

The following organizations may provide additional information and support:
Belgian Association for Metabolic Diseases (BOKS)
Children's PKU Network
Cochrane Cystic Fibrosis and Genetic Disorders Review Group
March of Dimes Birth Defects Foundation
Mid-Atlantic Connection for PKU and Allied Disorders, Inc.
National Institute of Mental Retardation
National PKU News
NIH/National Institute of Child Health and Human Development
Phenylalanine Hydroxylase Locus Knowledgebase (PAHdb)

859 Pheochromocytoma

Synonym
Chromaffin Cell Tumor

Disorder Subdivisions
Extra-adrenal Pheochromocytoma
Malignant Pheochromocytoma
Paraganglioma

Pheochromocytoma is a rare type of tumor that arises from certain cells known as chromaffin cells, which produce hormones necessary for the body to function properly. Most pheochromocytomas originate in one of the two adrenal glands located above the kidneys in the back of the upper ab-

domen. Most chromaffin cells are found in the adrenal gland's inner layer, which is known as the adrenal medulla. Approximately 90 percent of pheochromocytomas occur in the adrenal medulla. Approximately 10 percent occur outside of this area. These cases are referred to as extra-adrenal pheochromocytomas or paragangliomas. Paragangliomas may be found in the chest, heart, bladder, and/or neck or base of the skull. Symptoms associated with pheochromocytomas include high blood pressure (hypertension), headaches, excessive sweating, and/or heart palpitations. In most cases, pheochromocytomas occur randomly, for unknown reasons (sporadically). In approximately 10 to 20 percent of cases, pheochromocytomas may be inherited as an autosomal dominant trait. Some inherited cases may occur as part of a larger disorder such as multiple endocrine neoplasia types 2a and 2b, von Hippel-Lindau syndrome, or neurofibromatosis or familial paraganglioma syndromes.

The following organizations may provide additional information and support:
American Cancer Society, Inc.
March of Dimes Birth Defects Foundation
National Adrenal Diseases Foundation
National Cancer Institute
National Dysautonomia Research Foundation
Rare Cancer Alliance

860 Phocomelia Syndrome

Synonyms
Roberts SC-Phocomelia Syndrome
Roberts Tetraphocomelia Syndrome
SC Phocomelia Syndrome

Disorder Subdivision
Fetal Effects of Thalidomide

Phocomelia syndrome is a birth defect that may occur sporadically or be genetically transmitted in some cases. In other cases it may be caused by toxins (such as certain drugs) taken by a pregnant woman. Major symptoms may include growth and mental deficiencies, defects in the eyes, ears, and nose, and characteristic deficient limb development affecting the arms and possibly the legs.

The following organization may provide additional information and support:
National Rehabilitation Information Center

861 Phosphoglycerate Kinase Deficiency

Synonyms

Anemia, Hemolytic with PGK Deficiency
Erythrocyte Phosphoglycerate Kinase Deficiency
PGK
Phosphoglycerokinase

Phosphoglycerate kinase deficiency is an extremely rare inherited metabolic disorder characterized by deficiency of the enzyme phosphoglycerate kinase. This enzyme is essential for the breakdown of glycogen, resulting in the release of energy. Symptoms and findings associated with the disorder may include low levels of circulating red blood cells (hemolytic anemia); varying degrees of mental retardation; rapidly changing emotions (emotional lability); an impaired ability to communicate through and/or to comprehend speech or writing (aphasia); exercise-induced pain, stiffness, or cramps; enlargement of the spleen (splenomegaly); and/or paralysis of one side of the body (hemiplegia). In most cases, phosphoglycerate kinase deficiency is inherited as an X-linked genetic trait. In such cases, the disorder is fully expressed in males only; however, some females who carry one copy of the disease gene (heterozygotes) may have hemolytic anemia.

The following organizations may provide additional information and support:
CLIMB (Children Living with Inherited Metabolic Diseases)
Muscular Dystrophy Association
NIH/National Institute of Diabetes, Digestive & Kidney Diseases

862 Pica

Synonyms

Eating Disorder, Pica Type
Pica Eating Disorder

Pica is an eating disorder that is characterized by the repeated eating of non-nutritive substances over a period of one month or longer. Patients may eat non-edible objects such as paint, plaster, dirt, ice, or laundry starch. Pica generally affects small children, pregnant women, and people whose cultural environment is most compatible with the eating of non-food items.

The following organizations may provide additional information and support:
Centers for Disease Control and Prevention
Federation of Families for Children's Mental Health

National Alliance for the Mentally Ill
National Mental Health Association
National Mental Health Consumers' Self-Help Clearinghouse
NIH/National Institute of Diabetes, Digestive & Kidney Diseases
NIH/National Institute of Mental Health

863 Pick's Disease

Synonyms

Dementia with Lobar Atrophy and Neuronal Cytoplasmic Inclusions
Diffuse Degenerative Cerebral Disease
Lobar Atrophy of the Brain
Pick Disease of the Brain

Pick's disease is a very rare progressive disease that affects certain areas of the brain (i.e., temporal and frontal lobes). Symptoms of this disorder may include loss of intellectual abilities and changes in behavior (e.g., lack of inhibition) and personality. Affected individuals may exhibit confusion and a general lack of concern about their surroundings. Other symptoms may include unusual speech patterns and the repetition of another's words (echolalia). In the majority of cases, the exact cause of Pick's disease is not known; however, about 10 to 20 percent of cases are thought to be inherited as an autosomal dominant genetic trait.

The following organizations may provide additional information and support:
Alzheimer's Association
Alzheimer's Disease Education and Referral Center
C-Mac Informational Services, Inc.
National Institute of Neurological Disorders and Stroke (NINDS)
NIH/National Institute on Aging

864 Pierre Robin Sequence

Synonyms

Glossoptosis, Micrognathia, and Cleft Palate
Pierre Robin
Pierre Robin Anomalad
Pierre Robin Complex
Pierre Robin Deformity
Pierre Robin Malformation Sequence
Pierre Robin Syndrome
Pierre Robin Triad
Robin Anomalad
Robin Complex
Robin Syndrome

Pierre Robin sequence is characterized by an unusually small lower jaw (micrognathia) and downward displacement of the tongue (glossoptosis). Some infants also have an abnormal opening in the roof of the mouth (cleft palate); both the soft and hard palate can be affected.

The following organizations may provide additional information and support:
Birth Defect Research for Children, Inc.
Children's Craniofacial Association
Congenital Heart Anomalies, Support, Education, & Resources
FACES: The National Craniofacial Association
Let Them Hear Foundation
Pierre Robin Network
Prescription Parents
Wide Smiles

865 Pineal Cysts, Symptomatic

Synonym

Nonneoplastic Large Pineal Cysts

Pineal cysts are benign (non-cancerous) fluid-filled sacs located in the region of the brain that contains the pineal gland. Small pineal cysts (.5 cm or smaller) are common occurrences, often found incidentally on routine neurological exams. Small pineal cysts rarely cause symptoms (asymptomatic). Larger pineal cysts are rare findings that may cause a variety of symptoms (symptomatic). Symptoms may include headaches, increased pressure on the brain because of accumulation of excessive cerebrospinal fluid (hydrocephalus), and vision abnormalities. Large symptomatic pineal cysts may potentially cause serious conditions such as seizures and loss of consciousness. The exact cause of symptomatic pineal cysts is unknown.

866 Pinta

Synonyms

Azul
Carate
Empeines
Lota
Mal del Pinto
Tina

Pinta is a rare infectious tropical disease affecting the skin that is caused by the bacterium *Treponema carateum,* which is transmitted by direct, nonsexual contact. Pinta progresses through three distinct stages, which are characterized by various skin lesions and discoloration. Other organ systems are not affected. Exposed areas of the skin such as the face and extremities are most often affected. Pinta is classified as a treponematosis, which is an infectious disease caused by a treponema. Treponemas are a genus of spiral-shaped bacteria (spirochetes). Treponemas cause several infectious diseases including pinta, yaws, and syphilis.

The following organizations may provide additional information and support:
Centers for Disease Control and Prevention
NIH/National Institute of Allergy and Infectious Diseases
World Health Organization (WHO) Regional Office for the Americas (AMRO)

867 Pityriasis Rubra Pilaris

Synonyms

Devergie Disease
Lichen Acuminatus
Lichen Psoriasis
Lichen Ruber Acuminatus
Pityriasis Pilaris
PRP

Pityriasis rubra pilaris is a mildly itchy chronic skin disorder that is possibly caused by an inherited metabolic defect. Initially, the disorder is characterized by elevated spots (papules) on the skin. These spots grow and become connected, producing red plaques over large areas.

The following organizations may provide additional information and support:
Foundation for Ichthyosis & Related Skin Types
NIH/National Institute of Arthritis and Musculoskeletal and Skin Diseases
Pityriasis Rubra Pilaris (PRP) Support Group (online)

868 Pleuropulmonary Blastoma

Synonyms

Cystic Mesenchymal Hamartoma
Mesenchymal Cystic Hamartoma
Pneumoblastoma
PPB
Pulmonary Rhabdomyosarcoma
Rhabdomyosarcoma in Lung Cyst

Pleuropulmonary blastoma (PPB) is a rare childhood cancer occurring in the chest, specifically in the lungs or in the coverings of the lungs called "pleura." PPB occurs almost exclusively in children under the age of approximately 7–8 years and rarely in older children, in teenagers and more rarely in adults. Three subtypes of PPB exist and are called type I, type II, and type III PPB. Type I PPB takes the form of cysts in the lungs (air-filled pockets) and occurs in the youngest children with PPB (from birth to about 2 years of age). Type II PPB has cysts and solid tumor. Type III PPB is entirely solid tumor. Types II and III PPB tend to occur after age 2 years. Children with type I PPB can have the disease come back. If type I PPB comes back, it usually happens within about 4 years of the original diagnosis, and it is usually type II or III when it recurs. Children with type I PPB have a better outlook ("prognosis") than children with types II and III PPB; most type I PPB patients are cured (more than 80%). Treatment for type I consists of surgery and possibly chemotherapy; for types II and III PPB surgery, chemotherapy and possibly radiation therapy is recommended. At present, about 50-60% of types II and III children are cured.What kind of cancer is PPB? PPB is a childhood cancer in the family of cancers called "soft tissue cancers," which are scientifically called "sarcomas." PPB is, therefore, a "soft tissue sarcoma." PPB is related to, or in the broad family of, cancers such as cancers of muscle, cartilage, and connective tissues. Physicians classify diseases this way in order to compare features and to compare treatments. Often treatments that are effective for one member of a family of cancers are effective for other members of that family. PPB occurs in the lungs so PPB can be called a "lung cancer." But PPB has no connection whatsoever with lung cancers in adults that are often related to tobacco use. Can PPB spread to other parts of the body? Like many cancers, PPB can spread through the blood to other areas of the body. When a cancer spreads to another part of the body it is called a "metastasis" of the cancer. Types II and III PPB can metastasize. The most common location for a PPB metastasis is the brain. It can also spread to the bones, the liver, and remaining parts of the lung. It is not known why PPB has this pattern of spread to brain, liver, or bones. PPB can also spread by growing directly into tissues next to the lung like the diaphragm. PPB family cancer syndrome: In about 25% of children with PPB, there are other childhood cancers or abnormalities in the PPB patient or in their families. This is called the PPB family cancer syndrome. This can include lung cysts, kidney cysts, thyroid tumors (sometimes malignant), and various other cancers. It is not known what causes the abnormalities in these children and families, but research is underway to discover the presumed genetic basis for this tendency to childhood cancers or other abnormalities. It should be emphasized that many children and adults in these families have no medical problems.

The following organizations may provide additional information and support:
International Pleuropulmonary Blastoma Registry
Rare Cancer Alliance

---

869 Pneumonia, Eosinophilic

Synonym
Pulmonary Infiltrates with Eosinophilia

Eosinophilic pneumonia is a disorder characterized by an inflammation of the lungs and an abnormal increase in the number of certain white blood cells (eosinophils) in the lymph nodes, lungs and blood. This disorder is usually associated with allergic conditions and various parasitic infections.

The following organizations may provide additional information and support:
Centers for Disease Control and Prevention
NIH/National Institute of Allergy and Infectious Diseases

---

870 Pneumonia, Interstitial

Synonyms
Bronchiolitis Obliterans Organizing Pneumonia (Boop)
Chronic Fibrous Pneumonia
Diffuse Alveolar Damage
Fibrous Interstitial Pneumonia
Giant Cell Interstitial Pneumonia
Idiopathic Interstitial Pneumonia
Usual Interstitial Pneumonia (UIP)

Disorder Subdivisions
Acute Interstitial Pneumonia (AIP)
Cryptogenic Organizing Pneumonia (COP)
Desquamative Interstitial Pneumonia (DIP)
Idiopathic Pulmonary Fibrosis (IPF)
Lymphoid Interstitial Pneumonia (LIP)
Nonspecific Interstitial Pneumonia (NSIP)
Respiratory Bronchiolitis-Associated Interstitial Lung Disease (RB-ILD)

The abnormal accumulation of inflammatory cells in lung tissue may lead to any one of several disorders with similar signs and symptoms. As white blood cells and protein-rich plasma build up in the air sacs of the lungs (alveoli), inflammation is generated. The inflammatory process, if it lasts long enough, may harden the fluid and the resultant firm, fibrous substance (scarring) may replace the lung tissue. If the scarring is extensive, the air sacs may be destroyed over time and the resultant space replaced by cysts. The American Thoracic Society and the European Respiratory Society jointly studied the interstitial pneumonias during 2001 and issued a Multidisciplinary Consensus Classification of the Idiopathic Interstitial Pneumonias. This consensus statement was intended to replace several older classification schemes that had led to a confusion of names and syndromes. Participants agreed that the idiopathic interstitial pneumonias (IIPs) comprise a number of clinical entities that are each rare and sufficiently different from one another to be considered as distinct disorders. This report follows the joint ARS/ERS classification.

The following organizations may provide additional information and support:
American Lung Association
NIH/National Heart, Lung and Blood Institute Information Center

871 POEMS Syndrome

Synonyms
Crow-Fukase Syndrome
PEP Syndrome
Polyneuropathy-Organomegaly-Endocrinopathy-M Protein-Skin Lesions
Shimpo Syndrome
Takatsuki Syndrome

POEMS syndrome is an extremely rare multisystem disorder. POEMS is an acronym that stands for (P)olyneuropathy, disease affecting many nerves; (O)rganomegaly, abnormal enlargement of an organ; (E)ndocrinopathy, disease affecting certain hormone-producing glands that help to regulate the rate of growth, sexual development, and certain metabolic functions (endocrine system); (M)onoclonal gammopathy or M proteins; and (S)kin defects. Common symptoms include progressive weakness of the nerves in the arms and legs, an abnormally enlarged liver and/or spleen (hepatosplenomegaly), abnormally darkening of the skin (hyperpigmentation) and excessive hair growth (hypertrichosis). Endocrine abnormalities such as failure of the ovaries and testes (gonads)

to function properly (primary gonadal failure) and diabetes mellitus type I may be present. Specific endocrine abnormalities associated with POEMS syndrome vary from case to case. POEMS syndrome is associated with a group of disorders known as monoclonal gammopathies or plasma cell dyscrasias. These disorders are characterized by the uncontrolled growth of a single clone (monoclonal) of plasma cells, which results in the abnormal accumulation of M-proteins (also known as immunoglobulin M or IgM) in the blood. M-proteins are supposed to fight foreign substances in the body such as viruses and bacteria, but researchers suspect that they play a role in the development of POEMS syndrome. However, the specific role M-proteins play and the exact cause of POEMS syndrome is unknown.

The following organizations may provide additional information and support:
American Autoimmune Related Diseases Association, Inc.
Jack Miller Center for Peripheral Neuropathy
National Institute of Neurological Disorders and Stroke (NINDS)
Neuropathy Association
NIH/Developmental Endocrinology Branch
NIH/National Arthritis and Musculoskeletal and Skin Diseases Information Clearinghouse

872 Poland Syndrome

Synonyms
Poland Anomaly
Poland Sequence
Poland Syndactyly
Unilateral Defect of Pectoralis Muscle and Syndactyly of the Hand

Poland syndrome is a rare condition that is evident at birth (congenital). Associated features may be extremely variable from case to case. However, it is classically characterized by absence (aplasia) of chest wall muscles on one side of the body (unilateral) and abnormally short, webbed fingers (symbrachydactyly) of the hand on the same side (ipsilateral). In those with the condition, there is typically unilateral absence of the pectoralis minor and the sternal or breastbone portion of the pectoralis major. The pectoralis minor is a thin, triangular muscle of the upper chest wall; the pectoralis major is a large, fanlike muscle that covers most of the upper, front part of the chest. Affected individuals may have variable associated features, such as underdevelopment or absence of one nipple (including the darkened area around the nipple [areola]) and/or patchy absence of hair under the arm (axilla). In females, there may be underdevelopment or absence (aplasia) of one breast and underlying (subcutaneous) tissues. In some cases, associated skeletal abnormalities may also be present, such as underdevelopment or absence of upper ribs; elevation of the shoulder blade (Sprengel deformity); and/or shortening of the arm, with underdevelopment of the forearm bones (i.e., ulna and radius). Poland syndrome affects males more commonly than females and most frequently involves the right side of the body. The exact cause of the condition is unknown.

The following organizations may provide additional information and support:
Birth Defect Research for Children, Inc.
NIH/National Arthritis and Musculoskeletal and Skin Diseases Information Clearinghouse

873   Polyarteritis Nodosa

Synonyms
PAN
Periarteritis
Polyarteritis

Polyarteritis nodosa is a rare multisystem disorder characterized by widespread inflammation, weakening, and damage to small and medium-sized arteries. Blood vessels in any organ or organ system may be affected, including those supplying the kidneys, heart, intestine, nervous system, and/or skeletal muscles. Damage to affected arteries may result in abnormally increased blood pressure (hypertension), "ballooning" (aneurysm) of an arterial wall, the formation of blood clots (thrombosis), obstruction of blood supply to certain tissues, and/or tissue damage and loss (necrosis) in certain affected areas. The disorder is more common among men, and is more likely to present during early middle age, between 40 and 50 years. Although the exact cause of polyarteritis nodosa is not known, it is clear that an attack may be triggered by any of several drugs or vaccines or by a reaction to infections (either bacterial or viral) such as strep or staph infections or hepatitis B virus. Many researchers suspect that the disorder is due to disturbances of the body's immune system.

The following organizations may provide additional information and support:
American Autoimmune Related Diseases Association, Inc.

Autoimmune Information Network, Inc
CNS Vasculitis Foundation
Jack Miller Center for Peripheral Neuropathy
NIH/National Institute of Allergy and Infectious Diseases

874   Polychondritis

Synonyms
Chronic Atrophic Polychondritis
Generalized or Systemic Chondromalacia
Meyenburg-Altherr-Uehlinger Syndrome
Relapsing Perichondritis
Relapsing Polychondritis
von Meyenburg Disease

Polychondritis is a rare degenerative disease characterized by recurrent inflammation of the cartilage in the body. Deterioration of the cartilage may affect any site of the body where cartilage is present. Ears, larynx and trachea may become "floppy," and the bridge of the nose can collapse into a "saddlenose" shape. The aortic heart valve may also be affected.

The following organizations may provide additional information and support:
Arthritis Foundation
Autoimmune Information Network, Inc
NIH/National Arthritis and Musculoskeletal and Skin Diseases Information Clearinghouse
Polychondritis Educational Society, Ltd.
Polychondritis/Rheumatoid Arthritis Clinic

875   Polycystic Kidney Diseases

Synonyms
PKD
Polycystic Renal Diseases

Disorder Subdivisions
ADPKD
Adult Polycystic Kidney Disease
ARPKD
Autosomal Dominant Polycystic Kidney Disease
Autosomal Recessive Polycystic Kidney Disease
Infantile Autosomal Recessive Polycystic Kidney Disease
Juvenile Autosomal Recessive Polycystic Kidney Disease
Neonatal Autosomal Recessive Polycystic Kidney Disease
Perinatal Polycystic Kidney Diseases

PKD1
PKD2
PKD3
*Potter Type I Infantile Polycystic Kidney
Diseases*
Potter Type III Polycystic Kidney Disease

Polycystic kidney diseases are inherited renal disorders characterized by the presence of multiple cysts in both kidneys (bilateral renal cysts). Normal kidney tissue is replaced by fluid-filled sacs or cysts of varying sizes that become larger as the disease progresses. Findings associated with polycystic kidney diseases include abnormally high blood pressure (hypertension) and the progressive loss of kidney function, leading to end-stage renal failure. Symptoms may include abdominal distention, vomiting, and/or failure to thrive. Some infants with autosomal recessive polycystic kidney disease (ARPKD) have unusual facial features. This occurs when there is a severe reduction in the amount of amniotic fluid surrounding the developing fetus (oligohydramnios), resulting in what is known as the Potter deformation sequence. There are two major subdivisions of polycystic kidney disease (PKD): autosomal recessive polycystic kidney disease (ARPKD) and autosomal dominant polycystic kidney disease (ADPKD). ARPKD was previously subdivided into perinatal, neonatal, infantile, and juvenile forms. The different forms of the disease were based on the age at onset, which frequently correlates with the rate of progression and severity of the symptoms. This classification is archaic and is no longer valid nor should it be used. ADPKD typically affects adults although increasing numbers of children are identified because of the increased use of ultrasound. ADPKD typically progresses more slowly than ARPKD.

The following organizations may provide additional information and support:
American Foundation for Urologic Disease
American Kidney Fund, Inc.
ARPKD/CHF Alliance
Birth Defect Research for Children, Inc.
Guay-Woodford, Lisa M., M.D.
International Patient Advocacy Association
March of Dimes Birth Defects Foundation
National Hypertension Association, Inc.
National Kidney Foundation
NIH/National Kidney and Urologic Diseases Information Clearinghouse
PKD Foundation

876 Polycystic Liver Disease

Synonyms
PCLD
PLD

Polycystic liver disease is an inherited disorder characterized by many cysts of various sizes scattered throughout the liver. Abdominal discomfort from swelling of the liver may occur; however, most affected individuals do not have any symptoms. In some cases, polycystic liver disease appears to occur randomly, with no apparent cause (sporadically). Most cases are inherited as an autosomal dominant genetic trait. Sometimes, cysts are found in the liver in association with the presence of autosomal dominant polycystic kidney disease (AD-PKD). In fact, about half of the people who have AD-PKD experience liver cysts. However, kidney cysts are uncommon in those affected by polycystic liver disease.

The following organizations may provide additional information and support:
American Liver Foundation
NIH/National Institute of Diabetes, Digestive & Kidney Diseases

877 Polycystic Ovary Syndrome

Synonyms
Anovulation with Hyperandrogenism
Bilateral Polycystic Ovarian Syndrome
Ovarian Hyperthecosis
Ovarian Syndrome
PCOS
Polycystic Bilateral Ovarian Syndrome
POS
Sclerocystic Ovarian Disease
Stein-Leventhal Syndrome

Polycystic ovary syndrome (PCOS) affects women and is a complex of symptoms that are not necessarily all present in all cases. Some, but not all, affected women have multiple cysts on the ovaries (polycystic ovaries). Other characteristics include the absence of menstruation (amenorrhea) or irregular menstruation, failure of the ovary to release eggs (anovulation), elevated levels of the male hormones known as androgens (hyperandrogenism), excessive amounts of body hair (hirsutism), a high rate of miscarriage, and infertility. Three criteria often used for a diagnosis are menstrual irregularity, hyperandrogenism, and exclusion of other disease. There is some evidence that PCOS is an inherited condition.

The following organizations may provide additional information and support:
Congenital Adrenal Hyperplasia Trust (New Zealand)
The Hormone Foundation
National Women's Health Network
NIH/National Institute of Child Health and Human Development
OBGYN.net: The Obstetrics & Gynecology Network
Polycystic Ovarian Syndrome Association

878 Polycythemia Vera

Synonyms
Erythremia
Osler-Vaquez Disease
Polycythemia Rubra Vera
Primary Polycythemia
Splenomegalic Polycythemia
Vaquez-Osler Disease

Polycythemia vera is a rare, chronic disorder involving an overproduction of blood cells in the bone marrow (myeloproliferative). The overproduction of red blood cells is most dramatic, but production of white blood cells and platelets is also elevated in most cases. Red blood cells carry oxygen to the body. White blood cells fight infection. Platelets are involved in clotting of the blood. In most cases, affected individuals may experience headaches, weakness, dizziness (vertigo), and/or a ringing noise in the ear (tinnitus). In some cases, individuals with polycythemia vera experience itching (pruritis), especially after a hot bath. Affected individuals often have an abnormally enlarged spleen (splenomegaly) and/or liver (hepatomegaly). In some cases, affected individuals may have associated conditions including high blood pressure (hypertension), the formation of blood clots (thrombosis), rupturing of and loss of blood (hemorrhaging) from certain blood vessels, and/or Budd-Chiari syndrome, a rare disorder characterized by obstruction (occlusion) of veins of the liver (hepatic veins). The exact cause of polycythemia vera is not known.

The following organizations may provide additional information and support:
CMPD Education Foundation
Myeloproliferative Mailing List (MPD-SUPPORT-L)

NIH/National Heart, Lung and Blood Institute
Sjældne Diagnoser / Rare Disorders Denmark

879 Polyglucosan Body Disease, Adult

Synonyms
APBD
Polyglucosan Body Disease, Adult Form

Adult polyglucosan body disease (APBD) is a rare, chronically progressive, metabolic disorder with severe neurological expression. It is caused by the abnormal accumulation of microscopic material (polyglucosan bodies), predominantly within the myelinated nerve fibers (motor neurons). The polyglucosan bodies are spherical and composed of large, complex, sugar-based molecules (branched polysaccharides).The disorder typically affects both upper and lower motor neurons, resulting from nerve damage within the brain and spinal cord (central nervous system) respectively. Symptoms usually begin during middle age or later and usually include muscle weakness, loss of sensation, and/or wasting of muscles (atrophy) in the arms and/or legs. Impaired bladder control (neurogenic bladder) and/or mental confusion (dementia) also occur.

The following organizations may provide additional information and support:
Amyotrophic Lateral Sclerosis Association
National Institute of Neurological Disorders and Stroke (NINDS)

880 Polymorphous Low-Grade Adenocarcinoma

Synonyms
Lobular Carcinoma of the Minor Salivary Glands
Low-Grade Papillary Carcinoma of the Palate
PLGA
Pleomorphic Adenoma
Terminal Duct Carcinoma

Polymorphous low-grade adenocarcinoma (PLGA) is a rare tumor of the salivary glands that is limited, to a great extent, to the minor salivary glands and commonly, but not exclusively, localized in the palate of the mouth. The major salivary glands are the parotid glands (at the side of the face, below the ears), the sublingual glands (below the tongue), and the submandibular glands (below the lower jaw). As the name suggests, each of the major salivary glands is of substantial size and visible to the naked eye. There are about 600 to 1,000 minor salivary glands that are microscopic in size. These minor salivary glands are found in the lining (mucosa) of the lips, tongue, and hard and soft palate, as well as inside the nose, cheeks, and sinuses. Less than one (1%) percent of all cancers reported in the USA are salivary cancers and, of these, 80% begin in the parotid glands, and about 15% begin in the submandibular glands, leaving only 5% that begin in the sublingual and minor salivary glands. Most of the tumors that start in the major salivary glands turn out to be benign, while most, but not all, of the cancers that start in the minor salivary glands turn out to be malignant.

The following organizations may provide additional information and support:
Let's Face It (USA)
National Cancer Information Center
National Cancer Institute
Support for People with Oral and Head and Neck Cancer, Inc.

881   Polymyalgia Rheumatica

Synonyms
Anarthritic Syndrome
Arthritic Rheumatoid Disease
PMR

Polymyalgia rheumatica is a rare inflammatory disease characterized by muscle pain (myalgia), stiffness, and additional generalized systemic symptoms such as fatigue, low-grade fever, and/or a general feeling of ill health (malaise). Polymyalgia rheumatica can be a relatively benign condition that is extremely responsive to treatment. In some rare cases, permanent muscle weakness, degeneration and loss (atrophy) of muscle mass, and disability may occur. The exact cause of polymyalgia rheumatica is unknown, although immunological factors and familial tendencies (genetic predisposition) have been mentioned in the medical literature.Polymyalgia rheumatica is closely related to giant cell arteritis, another inflammatory disorder. Giant cell arteritis is characterized by progressive inflammation of many arteries of the body. These two disorders have been described in the medical literature as possible variants of the same disease process. Some researchers believe they represent different ends of a disease continuum. The exact nature of the association is not fully understood.

The following organizations may provide additional information and support:
Arthritis Foundation
Autoimmune Information Network, Inc
NIH/National Institute of Arthritis and Musculoskeletal and Skin Diseases

882   Polymyositis

Disorder Subdivisions
Childhood Polymyositis
Polymyositis Associated with Malignant Tumors
Polymyositis Associated with Mixed Connective Tissue Disease (Overlap Syn)
Polymyositis Associated with Sclerodermatomyositis
Primary Idiopathic Polymyositis

Polymyositis is a systemic connective tissue disorder characterized by inflammatory and degenerative changes in the muscles, leading to symmetric weakness and some degree of muscle atrophy. The areas principally affected are the hip, shoulders, arms, pharynx and neck.

The following organizations may provide additional information and support:
Arthritis Foundation
Autoimmune Information Network, Inc
British Coalition of Heritable Disorders of Connective Tissue
Muscular Dystrophy Association
Myositis Association
Myositis Support Group
Poltz, Paul

883   Pompe Disease

Synonyms
Acid Maltase Deficiency
Alpha-1,4 Glucosidase Deficiency
Cardiomegalia Glycogenica Diffusa
Generalized Glycogenosis
Glycogenosis Type II
Lysosomal Glucosidase Deficiency

Disorder Subdivision
Glycogen Storage Disease Type II

Pompe disease is a hereditary metabolic disorder caused by the complete or partial deficiency of the enzyme acid alpha-glucosidase (also known as lysosomal alpha-glucosidase or acid maltase). This enzyme deficiency causes excess amounts of glycogen to accumulate in the lysosomes of many cell types but predominantly in muscle cells. The resulting cellular damage manifests as muscle weakness and/or respiratory difficulty. There are 49 rare genetic disorders known as lysosomal storage diseases, and Pompe disease is one of them. It is also classified as glycogen storage disease type II (GSD II).

The following organizations may provide additional information and support:
Acid Maltase Deficiency Association, Inc.
Association for Glycogen Storage Disease
Association for Glycogen Storage Disease (UK)
Belgian Association for Metabolic Diseases (BOKS)
CLIMB (Children Living with Inherited Metabolic Diseases)
Children's Cardiomyopathy Foundation
Instituto de Errores Innatos del Metabolismo
Muscular Dystrophy Association
NIH/National Institute of Diabetes, Digestive & Kidney Diseases
Vaincre Les Maladies Lysosomales

884 Porphyria

Disorder Subdivisions
Acute Intermittent Porphyria
ALA-D Porphyria
Congenital Erythropoietic Porphyria
Hereditary Coproporphyria
Porphyria Cutanea Tarda
Protoporphyria
Variegate Porphyria

Porphyria is a group of at least eight metabolic disorders that arise as a result of a malfunction in one of the eight steps in the body's synthesis of a complex molecule called heme. Heme is essential for the transport of oxygen to cells in the body. If any step in the synthesis of heme is blocked, an intermediate chemical accumulates in the cell, resulting in oxygen depletion. Those intermediate chemicals, known as porphyrins or porphyrin precursors, are the substances of which heme is composed. There are two general categories of porphyrias, those that affect the skin and those that affect the nervous system. The former are called cutaneous porphyrias. The latter are called acute porphyrias. Because the symptoms of the various porphyrias may resemble symptoms of other disorders, diagnosis may be difficult. Each type of porphyria represents a deficiency of a specific enzyme needed for the synthesis of heme. Treatment is specific to the type of porphyria. The

porphyrias are inherited conditions, but do not all follow the same mode of inheritance.

The following organizations may provide additional information and support:
American Porphyria Foundation
Belgian Association for Metabolic Diseases (BOKS)
Canadian Porphyria Foundation, Inc.
NIH/National Digestive Diseases Information Clearinghouse
.

885 Porphyria, Acute Intermittent

Synonyms
AIP
Porphyria, Swedish Type
Porphyria Acute Intermittent
Pyrroloporphyria

Acute intermittent porphyria (AIP) is a rare metabolic disorder that is characterized by deficiency of the enzyme porphobilinogen deaminase (PBG-D), also known as uroporphyrinogen I-synthase. This enzyme deficiency results in the accumulation of porphyrins or porphyrin precursors in the body. These are natural chemicals that normally do not accumulate in the body. This enzyme deficiency by itself is not sufficient to produce symptoms of the disease (latent). Additional factors must also be present such as hormones, drugs and dietary changes that trigger the appearance of symptoms. Symptoms of AIP may include abdominal pain, constipation, and muscle weakness. AIP is one of a group of disorders known as the porphyrias. The common feature in all porphyrias is the excess accumulation in the body of porphyrins or porphyrin precursors. Different types of porphyias are characterized by the accumulation of different types of porphyrin chemicals. Porphyrias can also be classified into two groups: the "hepatic" and "erythropoietic" types. In the hepatic types of porphyria, porphyrins and related substances originate in excess amounts from the liver; in the erythropoietic types, they originate mostly from the bone marrow.The porphyrias with skin manifestations are sometimes called "cutaneous porphyrias." The "acute porphyrias" are characterized by sudden attacks of pain and other neurological symptoms. These acute symptoms may be severe and often rapidly appear. An individual may be considered latent if he or she has the characteristic enzyme deficiency but has never developed symptoms. There can be a wide spectrum of severity between the latent and active cases of any particular type of porphyria. The symptoms and treatments of the different types of porphyrias are not the same.

The following organizations may provide additional information and support:
American Porphyria Foundation
CLIMB (Children Living with Inherited Metabolic Diseases)
Canadian Porphyria Foundation, Inc.
Medic Alert Foundation International
NIH/National Digestive Diseases Information Clearinghouse

886 Porphyria, ALA-D

Synonym
Porphyria, ALA-D Type

ALA-D porphyria, a recently described form of acute porphyria, is inherited as an autosomal recessive trait and seems to be extremely rare. This form of porphyria is one of the "hepatic" porphyrias. The porphyrias are a group of at least seven disorders. The common feature in all porphyrias is the excess accumulation in the body of "porphyrins" or "porphyrin precursors." These are natural chemicals that normally do not accumulate in the body. Precisely which one of these porphyrin chemicals builds up depends upon the type of porphyria that a patient has. Porphyrias can also be classified into two groups: the "hepatic" and "erythropoietic" types. Porphyrins and related substances originate in excess amounts from the liver in the hepatic types, and mostly from the bone marrow in the erythropoietic types. The porphyrias with skin manifestations are sometimes called "cutaneous porphyrias." The "acute porphyrias" are characterized by sudden attacks of pain and other neurological manifestations. These acute symptoms can be both rapidly-appearing and severe. An individual may be considered in a "latent" condition if he or she has the characteristic enzyme deficiency, but has never developed symptoms. There can be a wide spectrum of severity between the "latent" and "active" cases of any particular type of this disorder. The symptoms and treatments of the different types of porphyrias are not the same.

The following organizations may provide additional information and support:
American Porphyria Foundation
CLIMB (Children Living with Inherited Metabolic Diseases)
Canadian Porphyria Foundation, Inc.

Medic Alert Foundation International
NIH/National Digestive Diseases Information Clearinghouse

887 Porphyria, Congenital Erythropoietic

Synonyms
CEP
Congenital Porphyria
Guenther Porphyria
Gunther Disease

Congenital erythropoietic porphyria (CEP) is extremely rare and is inherited through an autosomal recessive trait. It is also known as Guenther porphyria. The deficient enzyme is uroporphyrinogen III cosynthase. As is characteristic of the erythropoietic porphyrias, symptoms usually begin during infancy. CEP is manifested by markedly increased levels of porphyrins in bone marrow, red blood cells, plasma, urine and feces. Porphyrins are also deposited in the teeth and bones. The porphyrias are a group of at least seven disorders. The common feature in all porphyrias is the excess accumulation in the body of "porphyrins" or "porphyrin precursors." These are natural chemicals that normally do not accumulate in the body. Precisely which one of these porphyrin chemicals builds up depends upon the type of porphyria that a patient has. Porphyrias can also be classified into two groups: the "hepatic" and "erythropoietic" types. Porphyrins and related substances originate in excess amounts from the liver in the hepatic types, and mostly from the bone marrow in the erythropoietic types. The porphyrias with skin manifestations are sometimes called "cutaneous porphyrias." The "acute porphyrias" are those characterized by sudden attacks of pain and other neurological manifestations. These acute symptoms can be both rapidly-appearing and severe. An individual may be considered in a "latent" condition if he or she has the characteristic enzyme deficiency, but has never developed symptoms. There can be a wide spectrum of severity between the "latent" and "active" cases of any particular type of this disorder. The symptoms and treatments of the different types of porphyrias are not the same.

The following organizations may provide additional information and support:
American Porphyria Foundation
Canadian Porphyria Foundation, Inc.
CLIMB (Children Living with Inherited Metabolic Diseases)

NIH/National Digestive Diseases Information Clearinghouse

888   Porphyria Cutanea Tarda

Synonyms
PCT
PCT, Type II
Porphyria Cutanea Tarda, Type II
Porphyria, Hepatocutaneous Type
Porphyria, Hepatoerythropoietic
Symptomatic Porphyria
UROD Deficiency
Uroporphyrinogen Decarboxylase
Uroporphyrinogen Decarboxylase Deficiency

Porphyria cutanea tarda (PCT) is a type of porphyria in which affected individuals are sensitive to sunlight. Exposed skin shows abnormalities that range from slight fragility of the skin to persistent scarring and disfiguration. Due to fragility of the skin, minor trauma may induce blister formation. Areas of increased and decreased pigment content may be noted on the skin. Blistering of light exposed skin and increased hair growth are also characteristic. PCT is caused by a deficiency of the uroporphyrinogen decarboxylase (URO-D) enzyme in the liver. The disorder can be acquired or can be caused by an inherited gene mutation in the UROD gene. The inherited form of PCT is also called familial PCT and follows autosomal dominant inheritance. Many individuals with a UROD gene mutation never experience symptoms of the disease.PCT becomes active and causes symptoms when triggered by an environmental factor that affects liver cells (hepatocytes). These environmental factors include alcohol, estrogens, hepatitis C, and human immunodeficiency viruses (HIV). Individuals who have disorders that lead to excess iron in tissues such as hemochromatosis also have an increased risk of developing PCT. It is usually necessary for an environmental trigger to be present to cause symptoms of either the acquired or inherited type of PCT.

The following organizations may provide additional information and support:
American Porphyria Foundation
Canadian Porphyria Foundation, Inc.
CLIMB (Children Living with Inherited Metabolic Diseases)
Medic Alert Foundation International
NIH/National Digestive Diseases Information Clearinghouse

889   Porphyria, Hereditary Coproporphyria

Synonyms
HCP
Porphyria Hepatica, Coproporphyria

Hereditary coproporphyria is an autosomal dominant form of hepatic porphyria that is very similar to acute intermittent porphyria, although it is usually a less severe disease. It is caused by an enzyme deficiency. Some patients develop skin photosensitivity, and must avoid sunlight. The diagnosis is established by finding excess coproporphyrin in urine and stool (other types of porphyrins show little or no increase). Urinary ALA and PBG are increased during acute attacks, but may become normal on recovery. The porphyrias are a group of at least seven disorders. The common feature in all porphyrias is the excess accumulation in the body of "porphyrins" or "porphyrin precursors." These are natural chemicals that normally do not accumulate in the body. Precisely which one of these porphyrin chemicals builds up depends upon the type of porphyria that a patient has. Porphyrias can also be classified into two groups: the "hepatic" and "erythropoietic" types. Porphyrins and related substances originate in excess amounts from the liver in the hepatic types, and mostly from the bone marrow in the erythropoietic types. The porphyrias with skin manifestations are sometimes called "cutaneous porphyrias." The "acute porphyrias" are characterized by sudden attacks of pain and other neurological manifestations. These acute symptoms can be both rapidly-appearing and severe. An individual may be considered in a "latent" condition if he or she has the characteristic enzyme deficiency, but has never developed symptoms. There can be a wide spectrum of severity between the "latent" and "active" cases of any particular type of this disorder. The symptoms and treatments of the different types of porphyrias are not the same.

The following organizations may provide additional information and support:
American Porphyria Foundation
Canadian Porphyria Foundation, Inc.
CLIMB (Children Living with Inherited Metabolic Diseases)
Medic Alert Foundation International
NIH/National Digestive Diseases Information Clearinghouse

890 Porphyria, Variegate

Synonyms

Mixed Hepatic Porphyria
Porphyria Cutanea Tarda Hereditaria
Porphyria Hepatica, Variegate
South African Genetic Porphyria
VP

Variegate porphyria (VP), a form of hepatic porphyria, is most common in the South African white population and is much less frequent elsewhere. It is an autosomal dominant disorder and may produce acute attacks (as in acute intermittent porphyria) as well as skin photosensitivity. This form of porphyria is also due to an enzyme deficiency.The diagnosis may be made by finding excess coproporphyrin in urine and both coproporphyrin and protoporphyrin in feces. In patients with photosensitive skin changes alone, it is important to distinguish varigate porphyria or hereditary coproporphyria (HCP) from porphyria cutanea tarda (PCT), because treatment by phlebotomy or low-dose chloroquine is not successful in VP and HCP. Acute attacks are managed and may be prevented as in AIP.The porphyrias are a group of at least seven disorders. The common feature in all porphyrias is the excess accumulation in the body of "porphyrins" or "porphyrin precursors." These are natural chemicals that normally do not accumulate in the body. Precisely which one of these porphyrin chemicals builds up depends upon the type of porphyria that a patient has. Porphyrias can also be classified into two groups: the "hepatic" and "erythropoietic" types. Porphyrins and related substances originate in excess amounts from the liver in the hepatic types, and mostly from the bone marrow in the erythropoietic types.The porphyrias with skin manifestations are sometimes called "cutaneous porphyrias." The "acute porphyrias" are characterized by sudden attacks of pain and other neurological manifestations. These acute symptoms can be both rapidly-appearing and severe. An individual may be considered in a "latent" condition if he or she has the characteristic enzyme deficiency, but has never developed symptoms. There can be a wide spectrum of severity between the "latent" and "active" cases of any particular type of this disorder. The symptoms and treatments of the different types of porphyrias are not the same.

The following organizations may provide additional information and support:

American Porphyria Foundation
Canadian Porphyria Foundation, Inc.
CLIMB (Children Living with Inherited Metabolic Diseases)
Medic Alert Foundation International
NIH/National Digestive Diseases Information Clearinghouse

891 Post-Polio Syndrome

Synonyms

Polio, Late Effects
Post-Polio Muscular Atrophy
Post-Polio Sequelae
Postpoliomyelitis Syndrome

Post-polio syndrome (PPS) is a syndrome that affects some people who have had polio (poliomyelitis) and occurs many years (typically from 10 to 40 years) after recovery from the initial infection. It is characterized by the development of progressive weakness in muscles that were affected by the original polio infection. In addition, those affected may experience extreme fatigue and joint pain. Skeletal deformities, such as scoliosis, may occur as a result of this syndrome. There is variation in the severity of symptoms. In severe cases, symptoms may mimic those of the rare disorder known as Lou Gehrig's disease (amyotrophic lateral sclerosis). The degree of muscle atrophy during the post-polio period appears to reflect the severity of the impact of the initial polio infection. People who were significantly affected by polio are more likely to experience severe symptoms from post-polio syndrome. The cause of this syndrome is not known. Although exact numbers are not available, it has been estimated that there are 300,000 polio survivors in the United States and that from one-fourth to one-half of them may ultimately develop some degree of post-polio syndrome.

The following organizations may provide additional information and support:
British Polio Fellowship
Centers for Disease Control and Prevention
New Horizons Un-Limited, Inc.
Polio Society
Post-Polio Health International

892 Posterior Uveitis

Synonym

Choroiditis

Uveitis is a general term that refers to inflammation of the part of the eye known as the uvea.

The uvea is a relatively thick, strong layer of fibrous tissue that encloses and protects the eyeball. It consists of three parts: the iris, the ciliary body, and the choroid. There are three types of uveitis, classified according to the part of the uvea that is affected. Anterior uveitis, which affects the front part of the eye, is also sometimes called iritis since the iris is part of the front of the eye. Intermediate uveitis, also known as pars planitis or cyclitis, refers to inflammation of tissues in the area just behind the iris and lens of the eye. Posterior uveitis, also known as choroiditis, refers to inflammation of the choroid, the back part of the uvea. Posterior uveitis may affect the retina and/or the optic nerve, and may lead to permanent loss of vision. Posterior uveitis is the rare form of the disorder and is the type of uveitis most associated with loss of vision. The other two forms are more common, and more frequently result in acute symptoms, but only rarely cause vision loss.

The following organizations may provide additional information and support:
American Autoimmune Related Diseases Association, Inc.
NIH/National Eye Institute
NIH/National Institute of Allergy and Infectious Diseases
UveitisSupport-MEEI

893 Prader-Willi Syndrome

Synonyms
Cryptorchidism-Dwarfism-Subnormal Mentality
HHHO
Hypogenital Dystrophy with Diabetic Tendency
Hypotonia-Hypomentia-Hypogonadism-Obesity Syndrome
Labhart-Willi Syndrome
Prader-Labhart-Willi Fancone Syndrome
Willi-Prader Syndrome

Prader-Willi syndrome is a genetic disorder characterized in infancy by diminished muscle tone (hypotonia), feeding difficulties, and failure to grow and gain weight (failure to thrive). In childhood, features of the disorder include short stature, genital abnormalities and an excessive appetite. Progressive obesity results because of a lack of feeling satisfied after completing a meal (satiety) that leads to overeating. Without appropriate treatment, individuals with severe progressive obesity may have an increased risk of cardiac insufficiency, diabetes or other serious conditions

that may lead to potentially life-threatening complications. All individuals with Prader-Willi syndrome have some cognitive impairment that ranges from borderline normal with learning disabilities to mild mental retardation. Behavior problems are common and can include temper tantrums, obsessive/compulsive behavior, and skin picking. Prader-Willi syndrome occurs when the genes in a specific region of chromosome 15 do not function. The abnormal genes usually result from random errors in development, but are sometimes inherited.

The following organizations may provide additional information and support:
March of Dimes Birth Defects Foundation
NIH/National Institute of Child Health and Human Development
Prader-Willi France
Prader-Willi Syndrome Association (UK)
Prader-Willi Syndrome Association (USA)
Sjældne Diagnoser / Rare Disorders Denmark

894 Precocious Puberty

Synonyms
Familial Testotoxicosis
Gonadotropin-Independent Familial Sexual Precocity
Pubertas Praecox

Disorder Subdivisions
Central Precocious Puberty
Gonadotropin-Dependent Precocious Puberty
Gonadotropin-Independent Precocious Puberty
Heterosexual Precocious Puberty
Idiopathic Precocious Puberty
Isosexual Precocious Puberty
Male-Limited Precocious Puberty
Peripheral Precocious Puberty
True Precocious Puberty

Precocious puberty means an abnormally early onset of puberty. A sequence of events occurs during which a child develops into a young adult beginning at an unexpectedly early age. Glands that secrete growth and sex hormones begin to function abnormally early in life resulting in this condition. The exact cause of precocious puberty is not known.

The following organizations may provide additional information and support:
Congenital Adrenal Hyperplasia Trust (New Zealand)
March of Dimes Birth Defects Foundation

National Adrenal Diseases Foundation
NIH/National Institute of Child Health and Human Development

895 Primary Lateral Sclerosis

Synonyms
Central Motor Neuron Disease
PLS

Primary lateral sclerosis (PLS) is a rare, neuromuscular disorder that affects the central motor neurons and is characterized by painless but progressive weakness and stiffness of the muscles of the legs. Such weakness may progress to affect the arms and the muscles at the base of the brain (bulbar muscles). Less frequently, the muscles of the face are affected. In most cases, the disorder affects adults during midlife. The exact cause of primary lateral sclerosis is unknown.

The following organizations may provide additional information and support:
Amyotrophic Lateral Sclerosis Association
Connecticut Connection
International Alliance of ALS/MND Associations
Les Turner Amyotrophic Lateral Sclerosis Foundation, Ltd.
Motor Neurone Disease Association
National Institute of Neurological Disorders and Stroke (NINDS)
Spastic Paraplegia Foundation

896 Primary Orthostatic Tremor

Primary orthostatic tremor is a rare movement disorder characterized by a rapid tremor in the legs that occurs when standing. The tremor disappears partially or completely when an affected person is walking or sitting. Individuals with primary orthostatic tremor experience feelings of unsteadiness or imbalance. In many cases, the tremors become more severe over time. The exact cause of primary orthostatic tremor is unknown.

The following organizations may provide additional information and support:
International Essential Tremor Foundation
National Institute of Neurological Disorders and Stroke (NINDS)
OT Resources
WE MOVE (Worldwide Education and Awareness for Movement Disorders)

897 Proctitis

Synonyms
Antibiotic-Induced Proctitis
Gonorrheal Proctitis
Herpetic Proctitis
Ischemic Proctitis
Radiation Proctitis
Syphilitic Proctitis

Proctitis is a chronic inflammatory disease arising in the rectum and characterized by bloody diarrhea. There are two types of proctitis, ulcerative and gonorrheal, which are differentiated by the means in which they are contracted. Gonorrheal proctitis is transmitted through sexual contact.

The following organizations may provide additional information and support:
NIH/National Digestive Diseases Information Clearinghouse
Sexuality Information and Education Council of the U.S.

898 Progeria, Hutchinson-Gilford

Synonyms
HGPS
Hutchinson-Gilford Progeria Syndrome
Hutchinson-Gilford Syndrome
Premature Aging Syndrome
Progeria
Progeria of Childhood

Progeria, or Hutchinson-Gilford progeria syndrome, is a rare, fatal, genetic condition of childhood with striking features resembling premature aging. Children with progeria usually have a normal appearance in early infancy. At approximately nine to 24 months of age, affected children begin to experience profound growth delays, resulting in short stature and low weight. They also develop a distinctive facial appearance characterized by a disproportionately small face in comparison to the head; an underdeveloped jaw (micrognathia); malformation and crowding of the teeth; abnormally prominent eyes; a small, nose; prominent eyes and a subtle blueness around the mouth. In addition, by the second year of life, the scalp hair, eyebrows, and eyelashes are lost (alopecia), and the scalp hair may be replaced by small, downy, white or blond hairs. Additional characteristic features include generalized atherosclerosis, cardiovascular disease and stroke, hip dislocations, unusually prominent veins of the scalp, loss of the layer of fat beneath the skin (subcutaneous adipose tissue), defects of the nails, joint stiffness, skeletal defects, and/or other abnormalities. According to reports in the medical literature, individuals with Hutchinson-Gilford progeria syndrome develop premature, widespread thickening and loss of elasticity of artery walls (arteriosclerosis), which result in life-threatening complications during childhood, adolescence, or early adulthood. Children with progeria die of heart disease (atherosclerosis) at an average age of 13 years, with a range of about eight to 21 years. Progeria is caused by a mutation of the gene LMNA, or lamin A. The lamin A protein is the scaffolding that holds the nucleus of a cell together. Researchers now believe that the defective lamin A protein makes the nucleus unstable. That cellular instability appears to lead to the process of premature aging in progeria. Because neither parent carries or expresses the mutation, each case is believed to represent a sporadic, new mutation that happens most notably in a single sperm or egg immediately prior to conception.

The following organizations may provide additional information and support:
Progeria Research Foundation
Progeria Research Foundation, Inc.

---

899 Progressive Myoclonus Epilepsy

Synonyms
Epilepsy, Myoclonic Progressive Familial
Myoclonic Epilepsy
Myoclonic Progressive Familial Epilepsy
Myoclonus Epilepsy
Progressive Familial Myoclonic Epilepsy

Disorder Subdivisions
Baltic Myoclonus Epilepsy
Lafora Body Disease
Lafora Disease, Included
Lundborg-Unverricht Disease, Included
Myoclonic Epilepsy, Hartung Type
Unverricht Disease
Unverricht-Lundborg Disease

Progressive myoclonus epilepsy (PME) is a syndrome involving the central nervous system and representing more than a dozen different diseases. These diseases share certain features, including a worsening of symptoms over time and the presence of both muscle contractions (myoclonus) and seizures (epilepsy). Patients may have more than

one type of seizure, such as petit mal or grand mal. PME is progressive, but the rate of progression may be quick or slow, depending on the underlying disease. Progressive myoclonus epilepsy (PME) is different from myoclonic epilepsy. In myoclonic epilepsy, the myoclonic jerking motions occur as part of the seizure. In PME, myoclonus occurs separately from seizures, the two respond differently to the same drugs, they evolve differently during the natural history of the disease, and they cause different problems for the patient. Some drugs that are good for seizures, e.g. phenytoin and carbamazepine, may tend to make the myoclonus worse.

The following organizations may provide additional information and support:
Epilepsy Canada
Epilepsy Foundation
National Institute of Neurological Disorders and Stroke (NINDS)
National Pediatric Myoclonus Center

---

900 Progressive Osseous Heteroplasia (POH)

Synonym
POH

Progressive osseous heteroplasia (POH) is an extremely rare disorder characterized by abnormal development of bone in areas of the body where bone is not normally present (heterotopic ossification). The disorder first appears as areas of patchy bone formation (ossification) on the skin during infancy; heterotopic ossification progresses to involve superficial and deep connective tissues, areas of fat beneath the skin (subcutaneous fat), muscles, tendons, ligaments, and the bands of fibrous tissues that support muscle (fascia). This abnormal formation of bone may restrict the movement of affected joints and/or hinder the growth of affected limbs. The course of the disease is unpredictable; some areas of the body may become severely affected while others may remain unaffected. The exact cause of progressive osseous heteroplasia is not known.

The following organizations may provide additional information and support:
NIH/National Arthritis and Musculoskeletal and Skin Diseases Information Clearinghouse
Progressive Osseous Heteroplasia Association

901 Progressive Supranuclear Palsy

Synonyms

Nuchal Dystonia Dementia Syndrome
PSP
Steele-Richardson-Olszewski Syndrome

Progressive supranuclear palsy (PSP) is a rare degenerative neurological disorder characterized by loss of balance when walking; loss of control of voluntary eye movement, especially in the downward direction, and other voluntary muscle activity (akinesia); abnormal rigidity (spasticity); postural instability; speech difficulties (dysarthria); and problems related to swallowing and eating (dysphagia). Affected individuals frequently experience personality changes and cognitive impairment. For example, the ability to recognize, judge, and perceive may be affected. Symptoms typically begin in one's 60s, but can start as early as the 40s. The exact cause of progressive supranuclear palsy is unknown. PSP is often misdiagnosed as Parkinson's disease, Alzheimer's disease, or other neurodegenerative disorders.

The following organizations may provide additional information and support:
National Institute of Neurological Disorders and Stroke (NINDS)
National Parkinson Foundation, Inc.
Progressive Supranuclear Palsy (PSP Europe) Association
Society for Progressive Supranuclear Palsy
UCSF Memory and Aging Center
WE MOVE (Worldwide Education and Awareness for Movement Disorders)

902 Prostatitis

Synonym

Prostate Infection (Inflammatory)

Disorder Subdivisions

Prostatitis, Acute Bacterial
Prostatitis, Chronic Bacterial
Prostatitis, Nonbacterial
Prostatodynia

Prostatitis is a common infection of the prostate gland, the gland near the penis that is situated at the base of the male urethra. The prostate secretes an alkaline fluid that is the major ingredient of ejaculatory fluid. Prostatitis is classified into four subcategories: acute bacterial, chronic bacterial, nonbacterial and prostatodynia.

The following organizations may provide additional information and support:
American Foundation for Urologic Disease
NIH/National Kidney and Urologic Diseases Information Clearinghouse

903 Proteus Syndrome

Synonyms

Encephalocraniocutaneous Lipomatosis
Hemihypertrophy, Macrocephaly
Partial Gigantism of Hands and Feet, Nevi, Hemihypertrophy, Macrocephaly

Proteus syndrome is an overgrowth condition that affects the body in a patchy or mosaic manner. It causes overgrowth of bones, fatty tissues, and skin.

The following organizations may provide additional information and support:
NIH/National Arthritis and Musculoskeletal and Skin Diseases Information Clearinghouse
Proteus Syndrome Foundation

904 Prune-Belly Syndrome

Synonyms

Abdominal Muscle Deficiency Syndrome
Congenital Absence of the Abdominal Muscles
Eagle-Barrett Syndrome
Obrinsky Syndrome

Prune-Belly syndrome, also known as Eagle-Barrett syndrome, is a rare disorder characterized by partial or complete absence of the stomach (abdominal) muscles, failure of both testes to descend into the scrotum (bilateral cryptorchidism), and/or urinary tract malformations. The urinary malformations may include abnormal widening (dilation) of the tubes that bring urine to the bladder (ureters), accumulation of urine in the ureters (hydroureter) and the kidneys (hydronephrosis), and/or backflow of urine from the bladder into the ureters (vesicoureteral reflux). Complications associated with Prune-Belly syndrome may include underdevelopment of the lungs (pulmonary hypoplasia) and/or chronic renal failure. The exact cause of Prune-Belly syndrome is not known.

The following organizations may provide additional information and support:
Digestive Disease National Coalition
National Prune Belly Syndrome Network
NIH/National Arthritis and Musculoskeletal and Skin Diseases Information Clearinghouse

NIH/National Digestive Diseases Information Clearinghouse
Prune Belly Syndrome Network, Inc.

905   Pseudo-Hurler Polydystrophy

Synonyms

Gangliosidosis GM1 Type 1
GLB1
ML III
ML Disorder III
Mucolipidosis III
Mucopolysaccharidosis VII
Pseudopolydystrophy
Pseudo-Polydystrophy

Pseudo-Hurler polydystrophy (mucolipidosis type III) is a rare genetic metabolic disorder characterized by a defective enzyme known as UPD-N-acetylglucosamine-1-phosphotransferase. This defective enzyme ultimately results in the accumulation of certain complex carbohydrates (mucopolysaccharides) and fatty substances (mucolipids) in various tissues of the body. The symptoms of this disorder are similar, but less severe than those of I-cell disease (mucolipidosis type II) and may include progressive joint stiffness, curvature of the spine (scoliosis), and/or skeletal deformities of the hands (e.g., claw-hands). Growth delays accompanied by deterioration of the hip joints typically develop in children with pseudo-Hurler polydystrophy. Additional symptoms may include clouding of the corneas of the eyes, mild to moderate coarseness of facial features, mild mental retardation, easy fatigability, and/or heart disease. Pseudo-Hurler polydystrophy is inherited as an autosomal recessive trait. This disorder belongs to a group of diseases known as lysosomal storage disorders. Lysosomes are particles bound in membranes within cells that break down certain fats and carbohydrates. Defective lysosomal enzymes associated with pseudo-Hurler polydystrophy leads to the accumulation of certain fatty substances (mucolipids) and certain complex carbohydrates (mucopolysaccharides) within the cells of many tissues of the body.

The following organizations may provide additional information and support:
The Arc (A National Organization on Mental Retardation)
Canadian Society for Mucopolysaccharide and Related Diseases, Inc.
CLIMB (Children Living with Inherited Metabolic Diseases)
International Society for Mannosidosis & Related Diseases, Inc.
National MPS (Mucopolysaccharidoses/Mucolipidoses) Society, Inc.
NIH/National Digestive Diseases Information Clearinghouse
Society for Mucopolysaccharide Diseases
Vaincre Les Maladies Lysosomales

906   Pseudoachondroplastic Dysplasia

Pseudoachondroplastic dysplasia is a rare inherited disorder characterized by skeletal malformations resulting in short legs and mild to moderate short stature (short-limbed dwarfism). Affected individuals may have short, stubby fingers (brachydactyly), abnormally bowed legs (genu varum), and/or a malformation in which the knees are abnormally close together and the ankles are unusually far apart (genu valgum). In addition, affected individuals may have spinal abnormalities including abnormally increased curvature of the bones of the lower spine (lumbar lordosis) and front-to-back curvature of the spine (kyphosis). Cases of pseudoachondroplastic dysplasia are due to mutations of the COMP gene. Most cases of pseudoachondroplastic dysplasia are inherited as an autosomal dominant trait. However, a recessive form of the disorder may also exist.

The following organizations may provide additional information and support:
Little People of America, Inc.
MAGIC Foundation for Children's Growth
March of Dimes Birth Defects Foundation
NIH/National Arthritis and Musculoskeletal and Skin Diseases Information Clearinghouse

907   Pseudocholinesterase Deficiency

Synonyms

Apnea, Postanesthetic
Butyrylcholinesterase
Cholinesterase II Deficiency
Pseudocholinesterase E1
Succinylcholine Sensitivity
Suxamethonium Sensitivity

Pseudocholinesterase deficiency is an uncommon genetic disorder that makes an affected person very sensitive to any of several anesthetic agents, especially those derived from the drug known as

choline. When anesthetic drugs such as succinylcholine or mivacurium are administered to a susceptible person, the muscles that work the lungs
may become paralyzed. Mechanical ventilation is
essential until the excess anesthetic agent is me-
tabolized and normal breathing is resumed.

*The following organizations may provide addi-
tional information and support:*
Genetic and Rare Diseases (GARD) Information
Center
NIH/National Institute of General Medical Sciences

---

908 Pseudohypoparathyroidism

Synonym
Martin-Albright Syndrome

Pseudohypoparathyroidism is a hereditary disorder characterized by an inadequate response to
the parathyroid hormone, although the hormone
is present in normal amounts. This inadequate response affects bone growth in individuals with
pseudohypoparathyroidism. Affected individuals
may also experience headaches, unusual sensations, weakness, easy fatigue, lack of energy,
blurred vision, and/or abnormal sensitivity (hypersensitivity) to light. Additional symptoms and
findings may include stiffness or cramps in the
arms and/or legs, palpitations, and/or abdominal
pain. In addition, individuals with pseudohypoparathyroidism may have an abnormally round
face, thick short stature, unusually short fourth fingers, and mental retardation. Hormonal and calcium replacement therapy is often helpful, but the
lack of growth may persist.

*The following organizations may provide addi-
tional information and support:*
The Hormone Foundation
NIH/National Digestive Diseases Information Clearinghouse

---

909 Pseudomyxoma Peritonei

Synonyms
Colloid Carcinoma
Disseminated Peritoneal Adenocarcinoma
Malignant Appendical Tumor
Malignant Large Bowel Cystadenocarcinoma
*Malignant Large Bowel Peritoneal
Carcinomatosis*
Malignant Large Bowel Tumor
Mucinous Cyst Adenocarcinoma
Mucinous Cystadenoma
Peritoneal Mucinous Carcinomatosis
Pseudomyxoma Ovarii

Pseudomyxoma peritonei is a rare malignant
growth characterized by the progressive accumulation of mucus-secreting (mucinous) tumor cells
within the abdomen and pelvis. The disorder develops after a small growth (polyp) located within
the appendix bursts through the wall of the appendix, and spreads mucus-producing tumor cells
throughout the surrounding surfaces (e.g., the
membrane that lines the abdominal cavity [peri-
toneum]). As mucinous tumor cells accumulate,
the abdominal area becomes swollen and digestive (gastrointestinal) function becomes impaired.
Pseudomyxoma peritonei develops at a variable
rate, but may grow at a slower rate (indolent) than
other malignancies within the abdomen.

*The following organizations may provide addi-
tional information and support:*
American Cancer Society, Inc.
National Cancer Institute
PMP Pals Network

---

910 Pseudotumor Cerebri

Synonyms
Benign Intracranial Hypertension
*Idiopathic Intracranial Hypertension (Primary
Intracranial Hypertension)*
Secondary Intracranial Hypertension

Intracranial hypertension (pseudotumor cerebri)
is characterized by increased pressure inside the
skull. Intracranial means inside the skull and hypertension means high fluid pressure. Basically,
the pressure of the fluid that surrounds the brain
(cerebrospinal fluid or CSF) is too high. Elevated
CSF pressure produces severe headache and often visual difficulties, which, if left untreated can
result in loss of vision or blindness. Pseudotumor cerebri and benign intracranial hypertension
are both former names for intracranial hypertension (IH) which are now considered inaccu-
rate. These names do not adequately describe
the disorder and downplay the seriousness of
IH. There are two categories of IH: primary intracranial hypertension and secondary intracranial hypertension. Primary intracranial hypertension, also known as idiopathic intracranial
hypertension (IIH), occurs without known cause.
This form most often occurs in young, overweight, females in their reproductive years (ages
20–45). Secondary intracranial hypertension has

an identifiable, causative agent, including drugs (such as tetracycline, lithium, vitamin A-derived oral acne medications, and steroids, especially during withdrawal), growth hormone treatments, excessive ingestion of vitamin A, sleep apnea and certain systemic diseases such as lupus, leukemia, kidney failure (uremia), meningitis and dural venous sinus thrombosis. Many other causes have been suggested in the medical literature but have not yet been confirmed as true causes. Although many factors are known to trigger the disease, the mechanism by which IH occurs, in either primary or secondary forms, is not known. In many cases, either type of IH may be chronic.

The following organizations may provide additional information and support:
Intracranial Hypertension Research Foundation (IHRF)
National Institute of Neurological Disorders and Stroke (NINDS)
Pseudotumor Cerebri Support Network

---

911   Pseudoxanthoma Elasticum (PXE)

Synonyms
Elastosis Dystrophica Syndrome (Obsolete)
Gronblad-Strandberg Syndrome
Systemic Elastorrhexis (Obsolete)

Disorder Subdivisions
PXE, Dominant Type
PXE, Recessive Type

Pseudoxanthoma elasticum, PXE, is an inherited disorder that affects selected connective tissue in some parts of the body. Elastic tissue in the body becomes mineralized; that is, calcium and other minerals are deposited in the tissue. This can result in changes in the skin, eyes, cardiovascular system, and gastrointestinal system. Clinicians first recognized PXE more than 100 years ago. Researchers have made a number of significant advances in the past few years.

The following organizations may provide additional information and support:
British Coalition of Heritable Disorders of Connective Tissue
Macular Degeneration Support, Inc.
National Association for Pseudoxanthoma Elasticum (NAPE)
NIH/National Eye Institute

NIH/National Heart, Lung and Blood Institute Information Center
NIH/National Institute of Arthritis and Musculoskeletal and Skin Diseases
PXE International, Inc.

---

912   Psittacosis

Synonyms
Ornithosis
Parrot Fever

Psittacosis is an uncommon infectious disorder among humans. It is transmitted from infected birds by inhaling dried secretions and droppings. It is rare among humans, with fewer than 50 confirmed cases per year between 1996 and 2002.

The following organizations may provide additional information and support:
Centers for Disease Control and Prevention
NIH/National Institute of Allergy and Infectious Diseases

---

913   Psoriasis

Psoriasis is a chronic, inflammatory skin disease characterized by dry, reddish (erythematous), thickened patches of skin that are covered with silvery-gray scales. These patches may be referred to as papules or plaques and most often affect the scalp, elbows, knees, hands, feet and/or lower back. The plaques may be intensely itchy (pruritis) or sore. In some cases, individuals with psoriasis may experience abnormalities affecting the fingernails, toenails, and the soft tissues inside the mouth. The severity of psoriasis varies from case to case. Psoriasis may be classified as mild, moderate or severe depending upon the amount of skin involved and the effect on an individual's quality of life. In approximately one-third of cases a family history of psoriasis is present.

The following organizations may provide additional information and support:
Autoimmune Information Network, Inc.
National Psoriasis Foundation
NIH/National Arthritis and Musculoskeletal and Skin Diseases Information Clearinghouse
Psoriatic Arthropathy Alliance

914 Pterygium Syndrome, Multiple

Synonyms

Escobar Syndrome
Multiple Pterygium Syndrome
Pterygium Colli Syndrome
Pterygium Universale

Multiple pterygium syndrome is a very rare genetic disorder characterized by minor facial anomalies, short stature, vertebral defects, multiple joints in a fixed position (contractures) and webbing (pterygia) of the neck, inside bend of the elbows, back of the knees, armpits and fingers. Multiple pterygium syndrome usually follows autosomal recessive inheritance but can also follow autosomal dominant inheritance.

The following organizations may provide additional information and support:
Genetic and Rare Diseases (GARD) Information Center
NIH/National Arthritis and Musculoskeletal and Skin Diseases Information Clearinghouse

915 Pulmonary Alveolar Proteinosis

Synonyms

Alveolar Lipoproteinosis
PAP
Phospholipidosis

Disorder Subdivisions

Congenital Pulmonary Alveolar Proteinosis
Idiopathic Pulmonary Alveolar Proteinosis
Secondary Pulmonary Alveolar Proteinosis

Pulmonary alveolar proteinosis (PAP) is a rare lung disorder characterized by the accumulation of grainy material consisting mostly of protein and fat (lipoproteinaceous material) in the air sacs of the lungs (alveoli). Breathing often becomes progressively difficult. The disorder occurs in different forms, ranging from mild to severe, and can affect individuals of any age. PAP may occur secondary to many environmental exposures or underlying diseases. However, most cases of PAP occur for no known reason (idiopathic or primary PAP). An extremely rare form of PAP occurs in newborns (congenital PAP).

The following organizations may provide additional information and support:
American Lung Association

NIH/National Heart, Lung and Blood Institute Information Center

916 Pulmonary Hypertension, Primary

Synonyms

Familial Primary Pulmonary Hypertension
PPH
Primary Obliterative Pulmonary Vascular Disease
Primary Pulmonary Hypertension
Pulmonary Arterial Hypertension

Primary pulmonary hypertension is a rare, progressive disorder characterized by high blood pressure (hypertension) of the main artery of the lungs (pulmonary artery). The pulmonary artery is the blood vessel that carries blood from the heart through the lungs. Symptoms of primary pulmonary hypertension include shortness of breath (dyspnea) especially during exercise, chest pain, and fainting episodes. The exact cause of primary pulmonary hypertension is unknown.

The following organizations may provide additional information and support:
American Heart Association
American Lung Association
Foundation for Pulmonary Hypertension, Inc.
Newman, John H., M.D.
NIH/National Heart, Lung and Blood Institute Information Center
Pulmonary Hypertension Association

917 Pulmonary Hypertension, Secondary

Synonym

Pulmonary Arterial Hypertension, Secondary

Secondary pulmonary hypertension is a disorder of the blood vessels in the lungs. It usually is the result of other lung diseases or related diseases in other organs. Affected individuals have high blood pressure (hypertension) of the main artery of the lungs (pulmonary artery). The disorder is characterized by breathing difficulties, especially after exertion.

The following organizations may provide additional information and support:
American Heart Association
American Lung Association
Foundation for Pulmonary Hypertension, Inc.
NIH/National Heart, Lung and Blood Institute Information Center
Pulmonary Hypertension Association

918   Pure Red Cell Aplasia, Acquired

Synonyms
PRCA
Pure Red Blood Cell Aplasia

Acquired pure red cell aplasia is a rare bone marrow disorder characterized by an isolated decline of red blood cells (erythrocytes) produced by the bone marrow. Affected individuals may experience fatigue, lethargy, and/or abnormal paleness of the skin (pallor). Acquired pure red cell aplasia may occur for unknown reasons (idiopathic) or as a primary autoimmune disorder. It is also believed that acquired pure red cell aplasia may occur secondary to a tumor of the thymus gland (thyoma), viral infections, or certain drugs.

The following organizations may provide additional information and support:
American Autoimmune Related Diseases Association, Inc.
Aplastic Anemia & MDS International Foundation, Inc.
NIH/National Heart, Lung and Blood Institute

919   Purpura, Henoch-Schonlein

Synonyms
Allergic Purpura
Allergic Vasculitis
Anaphylactoid Purpura
Hemorrhagic Capillary Toxicosis
Henoch-Schonlein Purpura
HSP
Leukocytoclastic Vasculitis
Nonthrombocytopenic Idiopathic Purpura
Peliosis Rheumatica
Rheumatic Purpura
Schonlein-Henoch Purpura

Disorder Subdivisions
Henoch's Purpura
Schonlein's Purpura

Henoch-Schonlein purpura is a rare inflammatory disease of the small blood vessels (capillaries) and is usually a self-limited disease. It is the most common form of childhood vascular inflammation (vasculitis) and results in inflammatory changes in the small blood vessels. The symptoms of Henoch-Schonlein purpura usually begin suddenly and may include headache, fever, loss of appetite, cramping abdominal pain, and joint pain. Red or purple spots typically appear on the skin (pe-

techial purpura). Inflammatory changes associated with Henoch-Schonlein purpura can also develop in the joints, kidneys, digestive system, and, in rare cases, the brain and spinal cord (central nervous system). In one form of the disorder, termed Schonlein's purpura, the skin and joints are affected but the gastrointestinal tract is not. In another form, known as Henoch's purpura, affected individuals have purplish spots on the skin and acute abdominal problems. People with Henoch's purpura are not affected by joint disease. The exact cause of Henoh-Schonlein purpura is not fully understood, although research suggests that it may be an autoimmune disease or, in some rare cases, an extreme allergic reaction to certain offending substances (e.g., foods or drugs).

The following organizations may provide additional information and support:
American Autoimmune Related Diseases Association, Inc.
American Kidney Fund, Inc.
National Kidney Foundation
NIH/National Heart, Lung and Blood Institute Information Center
NIH/National Institute of Allergy and Infectious Diseases
Platelet Disorder Support Association

920   Purpura, Idiopathic Thrombocytopenic

Synonyms
ITP
Purpura Hemorrhagica ITP
Werlhof Disease

Idiopathic thrombocytopenic purpura (ITP) is a rare autoimmune bleeding disorder characterized by the abnormally low levels of certain blood cells called platelets, creating a condition known as thrombocytopenia. Platelets are specialized blood cells that help prevent and stop bleeding by inducing clotting. In ITP, there is no readily apparent cause or underlying disease (idiopathic). The cells of the immune system, lymphocytes, produce anti-platelet antibodies that attach to the platelets. The presence of antibodies on platelets leads to their destruction in the spleen. The disorder is characterized by abnormal bleeding into the skin resulting in bruising, which is what the term purpura means. Bleeding from mucous membranes also occurs, and may subsequently result in low levels of circulating red blood cells (anemia). ITP presents as a brief, self-limiting form of the disorder (acute ITP) or a longer-term form (chronic ITP). Acute ITP accounts for about 90% of cases, and chronic ITP accounts for the remainder. Eighty percent (80%) of the children with ITP have the acute form while the chronic form affects mostly adults. The acute form usually resolves without treatment (spontaneously) within 3 to 6 months. When thrombocytopenia lasts for more than six to 12 months, ITP is classified as the chronic form. Onset of acute ITP is often rapid, while the onset of the chronic form may be gradual.

The following organizations may provide additional information and support:
American Autoimmune Related Diseases Association, Inc.
Autoimmune Information Network, Inc
ITP Association
ITP Foundation
ITP People Place
ITP Society of the Children's Blood Foundation
ITP Support Association
NIH/Hematology Branch, National Heart, Lung and Blood Institute (NHLBI)
NIH/National Heart, Lung and Blood Institute Information Center
Platelet Disorder Support Association

921 Purpura, Thrombotic Thrombocytopenic

Synonyms
Microangiopathic Hemolytic Anemia
Moschowitz Disease
TTP

Thrombotic thrombocytopenia purpura (TTP) is a rare, serious blood disease. Major symptoms may include a severe decrease in the number of blood platelets (thrombocytopenia), abnormal destruction of red blood cells (hemolytic anemia), and disturbances in the nervous system. Kidney dysfunction and fever are also common. The exact cause of thrombotic thrombocytopenia purpura is unknown.

The following organizations may provide additional information and support:
Genetic and Rare Diseases (GARD) Information Center
March of Dimes Birth Defects Foundation
NIH/National Heart, Lung and Blood Institute Information Center

922 Pyknodysostosis

Synonyms
PKND
PYCD
Pycnodysostosis

Pyknodysostosis is a rare disorder that is inherited as an autosomal recessive genetic trait. This disorder is characterized by short stature, increased bone density (osteosclerosis/osteopetrosis), underdevelopment of the tips of fingers with absent or small nails, fragile bones that may fracture easily, abnormal or absent collarbone (clavicle), and skull abnormalities with a protruding forehead and bulge on the back of the skull caused by delayed suture closure.

The following organizations may provide additional information and support:
AboutFace USA
Children's Craniofacial Association
NIH/National Arthritis and Musculoskeletal and Skin Diseases Information Clearinghouse

923 Pyoderma Gangrenosum

Pyoderma gangrenosum is a rare skin disorder of unknown origin. The disorder may first appear as a red bump, blister, or small pus-filled growth (pustule) on the skin. These small growths eventually enlarge into swollen open sores (ulcerations). Any area of the body may become affected. In many cases, the exact cause of pyoderma gangrenosum is unknown (idiopathic). In fewer than 50 percent of cases, pyoderma gangrenosum occurs as a secondary characteristic to another disorder such as inflammatory bowel disease, hepatitis, or myeloproliferative disorders. Although the exact cause of pyoderma gangrenosum is unknown, it is thought to be an autoimmune disorder.

The following organizations may provide additional information and support:
American Autoimmune Related Diseases Association, Inc.
Crohn's and Colitis Foundation of America
Erythema Nodosum Yahoo Support Group
NIH/National Arthritis and Musculoskeletal and Skin Diseases Information Clearinghouse

924 Pyridoxine-Dependent Seizures

Pyridoxine-dependent seizures (PDS) is a rare cause of stubborn, difficult to control, (intractable) neonatal seizures, of which more than 100 cases have now been reported in the medical literature. PDS presents in a variety of forms with variable signs and symptoms (phenotypically heterogeneous). The one clinical feature characteristic of all patients with PDS is intractable seizures that are not controlled with anticonvulsants but which do respond both clinically and on EEG (electroencephalographically) to large daily supplements of pyridoxine. These patients are not pyridoxine-deficient. They are metabolically dependent on the vitamin. In other words, without supplemental pyridoxine, the patient's blood level of pyridoxine is normal but the patient will experience seizures. With supplemental pyridoxine, the patient's pyridoxine blood is normal or elevated, but the patient will not experience seizures. Pyridoxine therapy will be required for life.

The following organizations may provide additional information and support:
American Epilepsy Society
Epilepsy Foundation
Pyridoxine-Dependent Seizures Patient Registry

925 Pyruvate Carboxylase Deficiency

Synonyms
Ataxia with Lactic Acidosis, Type II
PC Deficiency

Disorder Subdivisions
PC Deficiency, Group A
PC Deficiency, Group B
Pyruvate Carboxylase Deficiency, Group A
Pyruvate Carboxylase Deficiency, Group B

Pyruvate carboxylase deficiency is a rare genetic metabolic disorder that is present at birth. It is classified as a lactic acidemia in which the conversion of pyruvate to oxaloacetate is blocked, impairing gluconeogenesis and resulting in an overabundance of lactic acid in the blood. Major symptoms may include delayed development, muscle weakness (hypotonia), impaired ability to control voluntary movements (ataxia), seizures, and vomiting.

The following organizations may provide additional information and support:
Brusilow, Saul, M.D.

CLIMB (Children Living with Inherited Metabolic Diseases)
Lactic Acidosis Support Trust
National Institute of Neurological Disorders and Stroke (NINDS)
NIH/National Institute of Diabetes, Digestive & Kidney Diseases
United Mitochondrial Disease Foundation

926 Pyruvate Dehydrogenase Deficiency

Synonyms
PDCD
PDH deficiency
Intermittent Ataxia with Pyruvate Dehydrogenase Deficiency
Lactic and Pyruvate Acidemia with Carbohydrate Sensitivity
Lactic and Pyruvate Acidemia with Episodic Ataxia and Weakness

Pyruvate dehydrogenase complex deficiency (PDCD) is a rare disorder of carbohydrate metabolism caused by a deficiency of one or more enzymes in the pyruvate dehydrogenase complex. The age of onset and severity of disease depends on the activity level of the PDC enzymes. Individuals with PDCD beginning prenatally or in infancy usually die in early childhood. Those who develop PDCD later in childhood may have mental retardation and other neurological symptoms and usually survive into adulthood. Approximately 25% of individuals with PDCD have an abnormality in the PHE1A gene located on the X chromosome. Approximately 75% of affected individuals have a form of the disorder that follows autosomal recessive inheritance.

The following organizations may provide additional information and support:
The Arc (A National Organization on Mental Retardation)
CLIMB (Children Living with Inherited Metabolic Diseases)
Lactic Acidosis Support Trust
National Institute of Neurological Disorders and Stroke (NINDS)
Organic Acidaemias UK
United Mitochondrial Disease Foundation

927 **Pyruvate Kinase Deficiency**

Synonym

Nonspherocytic Hemolytic Anemia, Congenital with Low PK Kinetics

Red cell pyruvate kinase deficiency is a hereditary blood disorder characterized by a deficiency of the enzyme pyruvate kinase. Physical findings associated with the disorder may include reduced levels of oxygen-carrying hemoglobulin in the blood due to premature destruction of red blood cells (hemolytic anemia); abnormally increased levels of bilirubin in the blood (hyperbilirubinemia); abnormal enlargement of the spleen (splenomegaly); and/or other abnormalities. Pyruvate kinase deficiency is inherited as an autosomal recessive genetic trait. It is one of a group of diseases known as hereditary nonspherocytic hemolytic anemias. (Nonspherocytic refers to the fact that the red blood cells do not assume a spherical shape, as they do with some blood disorders.)

The following organizations may provide additional information and support:
Genetic and Rare Diseases (GARD) Information Center
Lactic Acidosis Support Trust
NIH/National Heart, Lung and Blood Institute

928 **Q Fever**

Synonym

Q Fever Pneumonia

Q fever is an infectious disease that is spread by the inhalation or ingestion of bacteria of the family *Rickettsia* and, more specifically, the species known as *Coxiella burnetii*. Most other rickettsial diseases are spread by the transmission of the bacterium via a tick bite. This disease is spread by breathing contaminated air or eating or drinking a contaminated substance. Farm workers, especially those who work with animals, people who work in slaughterhouses, and veterinarians are especially vulnerable to this disease. Because infection can occur as a result of airborne transmission, this is one of the diseases that has been studied as a possible bacteriological weapon. Most cases are mild but some (about 2-3% of cases) may be acute and show signs of liver damage (hepatitis), and inflammation of heart muscle (myocarditis) or the heart lining (pericarditis).

The following organizations may provide additional information and support:
Centers for Disease Control and Prevention
NIH/National Institute of Allergy and Infectious Diseases
World Health Organization (WHO) Regional Office for the Americas (AMRO)

929 **Rabies**

Synonyms

Hydrophobia
Lyssa

Rabies is an infectious disease that can affect all species of warmblooded animals, including man. This disorder is transmitted by the saliva of an infected animal and is caused by a virus (*Neurotropic lyssavirus*) that affects the salivary glands and the central nervous system. The symptoms may lead to serious complications if the virus is not treated immediately.

The following organizations may provide additional information and support:
Centers for Disease Control and Prevention
NIH/National Institute of Allergy and Infectious Diseases
World Health Organization (WHO) Regional Office for the Americas (AMRO)

930 **Rabson-Mendenhall Syndrome**

Rabson-Mendenhall syndrome is an extremely rare genetic disorder characterized by severe insulin resistance. Insulin, a hormone produced by the pancreas, regulates blood sugar levels by promoting the movement of glucose (a simple sugar) into cells for energy production or into the liver and fat cells for storage. Initial symptoms of Rabson-Mendenhall syndrome include abnormalities of the head and face (craniofacial region), abnormalities of the teeth and nails, and skin abnormalities such as acanthosis nigricans, a skin disorder characterized by abnormally increased coloration (hyperpigmentation) and "velvety" thickening (hyperkeratosis) of the skin, particularly of skin fold regions, such as of the neck, groin, and under the arms. In most cases, additional symptoms are present. Rabson-Mendenhall syndrome is inherited as an autosomal recessive trait.

The following organizations may provide additional information and support:
American Diabetes Association
March of Dimes Birth Defects Foundation
NIH/Developmental Endocrinology Branch
NIH/National Institute of Child Health and Human Development
NIH/National Institute of Diabetes, Digestive & Kidney Diseases

931 Radiation Syndromes

Synonyms
Radiation Disease
Radiation Effects
Radiation Illness
Radiation Injuries
Radiation Reaction
Radiation Sickness

Radiation syndromes describe the harmful effects—acute, delayed, or chronic—produced by exposure to ionizing radiations. Tissues vary in response to immediate radiation injury according to the following descending order of sensitivity: (1) lymph cells (2) reproductive organs (3) proliferating cells of the bone marrow (4) epithelial cells of the bowel (5) top layer (epidermis) of the skin (6) liver cells (7) epithelium of the little lung sacs (alveoli) and bile passages (8) kidney epithelial cells (9) endothelial cells of the membranes around the lungs, lining the chest cavity (pleura) and the abdominal cavity (peritoneum) (10) nerve cells (11) bone cells (12) muscle and connective tissue. Generally, the more rapid the turnover of the cell, the greater the radiation sensitivity.

The following organizations may provide additional information and support:
American Cancer Society, Inc.
Leukemia & Lymphoma Society
National Association of Radiation Survivors
National Council on Radiation Protection and Measurements

932 Ramsay-Hunt Syndrome

Ramsay-Hunt syndrome (RHS) is a rare neurological disorder characterized by paralysis of certain facial nerves (facial palsy) and a rash affecting the ear or mouth. Ear abnormalities such as ringing in the ears (tinnitus) and hearing loss may be present. Ramsay-Hunt syndrome is caused by the varicella zoster virus (VZV), the same virus that causes chickenpox in children and shingles (herpes zoster) in adults. In cases of Ramsay-Hunt syndrome, previously inactive varicella-zoster virus is reactivated and spreads to affect the facial nerves. The disorder is named after James Ramsay Hunt, a physician.

The following organizations may provide additional information and support:
American Pain Society
Bell's Palsy Research Foundation
Bell's Palsy Web Site and Online Support Group
Jack Miller Center for Peripheral Neuropathy
VZV Research Foundation

933 Rapp-Hodgkin Syndrome

Synonyms
Ectodermal Dysplasia, Anhidrotic, with Cleft Lip and Cleft Palate
Ectodermal Dysplasia, Rapp-Hodgkin Type
Rapp-Hodgkin (Hypohidrotic) Ectodermal Dysplasia Syndrome
RHS

Rapp-Hodgkin syndrome, an extremely rare inherited multisystem disorder that is apparent at birth (congenital) or during infancy, belongs to a group of diseases known as ectodermal dysplasias. Ectodermal dysplasias typically affect the skin, teeth, hair, and/or nails. Rapp-Hodgkin syndrome is characterized by a reduced ability to sweat (hypohidrosis); an incomplete closure of the roof of the mouth (cleft palate) and/or an abnormal groove in the upper lip (cleft lip); partial or complete absence (hypodontia or partial anodontia) and/or abnormal smallness (microdontia) of primary and secondary (permanent) teeth. Infants and children with the disorder also have abnormally sparse, coarse, wiry scalp hair that is often lost prematurely during adulthood (alopecia); unusually slow-growing, improperly developed nails (dysplastic); and, in some cases, additional physical abnormalities. In most cases, Rapp-Hodgkin syndrome is inherited as an autosomal dominant trait.

The following organizations may provide additional information and support:
Cleft Palate Foundation
Craniofacial Foundation of America
March of Dimes Birth Defects Foundation
National Craniofacial Foundation
National Foundation for Ectodermal Dysplasias

NIH/National Arthritis and Musculoskeletal and Skin Diseases Information Clearinghouse
NIH/National Institute of Dental and Craniofacial Research
NIH/National Oral Health Information Clearinghouse

934   Raynaud's Disease and Phenomenon

Synonyms
Primary Raynaud's Disease
PRP
Symmetric Asphyxia

Raynaud's disease is a common vascular disorder characterized by episodes of constriction of very small arteries (arteriole vasospasm) in the fingers and skin. Symptoms in the fingers include unusual paleness, absence of color (pallor), and/or a red or bluish color to the skin (cyanosis) usually occurring with exposure to cold temperatures or stress. Occasionally other parts of the body are affected including the nose, ears, and/or tongue. Raynaud's disease is a common benign condition and does not usually occur in association with any other underlying disorder. A secondary form of the disease, known as Raynaud's phenomenon, affects a small number of individuals. This form of the disorder is usually found in association with another underlying systemic disorder.

The following organizations may provide additional information and support:
American Heart Association
Autoimmune Information Network, Inc
CF Alliance
NIH/National Heart, Lung and Blood Institute Information Center
Raynaud's & Scleroderma Association (UK)

935   Recurrent Respiratory Papillomatosis

Synonyms
Juvenile Laryngeal Papilloma
Laryngeal Papilloma
Respiratory Papillomatosis

Disorder Subdivisions
Adult-Onset Respiratory Papillomatosis
Juvenile Respiratory Papillomatosis

Recurrent respiratory papillomatosis is a rare viral disease characterized by multiple benign growths (papillomas) in the middle and lower respiratory tract. Symptoms usually begin with hoarseness and/or a change in voice. The growths may be surgically removed, but frequently recur and may require additional surgery. Affected individuals may experience long periods without recurrence (remission), and/or the disease may disappear completely. Children under 5 years of age are most commonly affected, although adults represent about one-third of all documented cases. People with recurrent respiratory papillomatosis may have difficulty breathing (dyspnea) and/or experience other life-threatening complications if the papillomas block the airway.

The following organizations may provide additional information and support:
NIH/National Heart, Lung and Blood Institute Information Center
NIH/National Institute of Allergy and Infectious Diseases
Recurrent Respiratory Papillomatosis Foundation

936   Reflex Sympathetic Dystrophy Syndrome

Synonyms
Algodystrophy
Algoneurodystrophy
Causalgia Syndrome (Major)
Complex Regional Pain Syndrome
Reflex Neurovascular Dystrophy
RSDS
Sudeck's Atrophy

Reflex sympathetic dystrophy syndrome (RSDS), also known as complex regional pain syndrome, is a rare disorder of the sympathetic nervous system that is characterized by chronic, severe pain. The sympathetic nervous system is that part of the autonomic nervous system that regulates involuntary functions of the body such as increasing heart rate, constricting blood vessels, and increasing blood pressure. Excessive or abnormal responses of portions of the sympathetic nervous system are thought to be responsible for the pain associated with reflex sympathetic dystrophy syndrome. The symptoms of reflex sympathetic dystrophy syndrome typically begin with burning pain, especially in an arm, finger(s), palm of the hand(s), and/or shoulder(s). In some individuals, RSDS may occur in one or both legs or it may be localized to one knee or hip. Frequently, RSDS may be misdiagnosed as a painful nerve injury. The skin over the affected area(s) may become swollen (edema) and inflamed. Affected skin may be extremely sensitive to touch and to hot or cold temperatures (cutaneous hypersensitivity). The affected limb(s) may perspire excessively and be warm to the touch (vasomotor instability). The exact cause of RSDS is not fully understood, although it may be associated with injury to the nerves, trauma, surgery, atherosclerotic cardiovascular disease, infection, or radiation therapy.

The following organizations may provide additional information and support:
American Chronic Pain Association
American Pain Foundation
American Pain Society
American RSDHope
Arthritis Foundation
International Association for the Study of Pain (IASP)
Irish Chronic Pain Association
National Institute of Neurological Disorders and Stroke (NINDS)
PARC: Promoting Awareness of RSD/CRPS in Canada
Reflex Sympathetic Dystrophy Network
Reflex Sympathetic Dystrophy Syndrome Association of America
Vasculitis of the Central Nervous System
Worldwide Congress on Pain

937 Refsum Disease

Synonyms

Disorder of Cornification 11 (Phytanic Acid Type)
DOC 11 (Phytanic Acid Type)
Heredopathia Atactica Polyneuritiformis
Hypertrophic Neuropathy of Refsum
Phytanic Acid Storage Disease
Refsum Disease

Refsum disease is one of a family of genetic disorders known as the leukodystrophies in which, as a consequence of the disruption of lipid metabolism, the myelin sheath that insulates and protects the nerves of the brain fails to grow. It is inherited as an autosomal recessive trait. It is characterized by progressive loss of vision (retinitis pigmentosa); degenerative nerve disease (peripheral neuropathy); failure of muscle coordination (ataxia); and dry, rough, scaly skin (ichthyosis). The disorder is caused by the accumulation of a particular fatty acid (phytanic acid) in blood plasma and tissues. This occurs because of a malfunction of the gene that makes the enzyme that breaks down (metabolizes) this acid. The essential enzyme is absent. Treatment with a diet low in foods that contain phytanic acid can be bene-

ficial. Our bodies cannot make phytanic acid. Instead, it is introduced to the body in certain foods, including dairy products, beef, lamb and some seafood.

The following organizations may provide additional information and support:
Association Europeene contre les Leucodystrophes
Blind Children's Fund
CLIMB (Children Living with Inherited Metabolic Diseases)
Foundation Fighting Blindness, Inc.
Foundation for Ichthyosis & Related Skin Types
Hunter's Hope Foundation, Inc.
Let Them Hear Foundation
National Association for Visually Handicapped
National Institute of Neurological Disorders and Stroke (NINDS)
National Registry for Ichthyosis and Related Disorders
Retinitis Pigmentosa International
United Leukodystrophy Foundation

938 Reiter Syndrome

Synonyms

Arthritis Urethritica
Blennorrheal Idiopathic Arthritis
Conjunctivo-Urethro-Synovial Syndrome
Feissinger-Leroy-Reiter Syndrome
Polyarthritis Enterica
Ruhr's Syndrome
Urethro-Oculo-Articular Syndrome
Venereal Arthritis
Waelsch's Syndrome

Reiter syndrome is a rare disorder characterized by arthritis, inflammation of the urinary tract (nongonococcal urethritis), and inflammation of the mucous membranes that line the eyes (conjunctivitis). Painful and swollen joints occur because of an underlying infection (reactive arthritis). Sores (lesions) may also occur on the skin and the mucous membranes of the mouth. In most cases, Reiter syndrome is transmitted through sexual contact (venereal). However, occasionally there is an underlying infection of the small bowel (enteric) that may contribute to the onset of Reiter syndrome. All the symptoms of the disease may not appear at once, and they may also disappear and then recur.

The following organizations may provide additional information and support:
Autoimmune Information Network, Inc
Centers for Disease Control and Prevention

NIH/National Arthritis and Musculoskeletal and Skin Diseases Information Clearinghouse
Sexuality Information and Education Council of the U.S.

939 Renal Agenesis, Bilateral

Synonyms
Kidney Agenesis
Renal Agenesis

Bilateral renal agenesis is the absence of both kidneys at birth. It is a genetic disorder characterized by a failure of the kidneys to develop in a fetus. This absence of kidneys causes a deficiency of amniotic fluid (oligohydramnios) in a pregnant woman. Normally, the amniotic fluid acts as a cushion for the developing fetus. When there is an insufficient amount of this fluid, compression of the fetus may occur resulting in further malformations of the baby. This disorder is more common in infants born of a parent who has a kidney malformation, particularly the absence of one kidney (unilateral renal agenesis). Studies have proven that unilateral renal agenesis and bilateral renal agenesis are genetically related.

The following organizations may provide additional information and support:
American Association of Kidney Patients
American Foundation for Urologic Disease
American Kidney Fund, Inc.
Birth Defect Research for Children, Inc.
National Kidney Foundation
NIH/National Institute of Diabetes, Digestive & Kidney Diseases

940 Renal Glycosuria

Synonyms
Benign Glycosuria
Familial Renal Glycosuria
Nondiabetic Glycosuria
Primary Renal Glycosuria
Renal Glucosuria

Disorder Subdivisions
Renal Glycosuria, Type A
Renal Glycosuria, Type B
Renal Glycosuria, Type O

Renal glycosuria, also known as renal glucosuria, is a rare condition in which the simple sugar glucose is eliminated (excreted) in the urine despite normal or low blood glucose levels. With normal kidney (renal) function, glucose is excreted in the urine only when there are abnormally elevated levels of glucose in the blood. However, in those with renal glycosuria, glucose is abnormally eliminated in the urine due to improper functioning of the renal tubules, which are primary components of the filtering units of the kidneys (nephrons). In most affected individuals, the condition causes no apparent symptoms (asymptomatic) or serious effects. When renal glycosuria occurs as an isolated finding with otherwise normal kidney function, the condition is thought to be inherited as an autosomal recessive trait.

The following organizations may provide additional information and support:
American Association of Kidney Patients
American Foundation for Urologic Disease
American Kidney Fund, Inc.
National Kidney Foundation
NIH/National Digestive Diseases Information Clearinghouse

941 Respiratory Distress Syndrome, Infant

Synonyms
Hyaline Membrane Disease
Infantile Respiratory Distress Syndrome
IRDS

Disorder Subdivision
Surfactant Protein-B Deficiency

Infant respiratory distress syndrome is a lung disorder that tends to affect premature infants. Major symptoms include difficulty in breathing and collapsed lungs, potentially requiring mechanical ventilation or positive end-expiratory pressure (PEEP).

The following organizations may provide additional information and support:
American Lung Association
NIH/National Heart, Lung and Blood Institute Information Center

942 Restless Legs Syndrome

Synonym
Ekbom Syndrome

Restless legs syndrome (RLS) is a neurologic movement disorder characterized by abnormal, uncomfortable sensations in the legs that typically occur or worsen at rest. Such sensations, known as paresthesias or dysesthesias, are often likened to crawling, cramping, aching, burning, itching, or prickling deep within the affected areas. Although the legs are usually involved, paresthesias or dysesthesias may also sometimes affect the arms or other areas of the body. Affected individuals feel an irresistible urge to move in an effort to alleviate such sensations. As a result, those with RLS may vigorously move the affected area, engage in pacing, or perform other, often repetitive movements, such as stretching, bending, or rocking. Symptoms typically worsen in the evening or at night, often resulting in sleep disturbances. Some individuals with RLS may also develop symptoms during other extended periods of inactivity, such as while sitting in a movie theater or traveling in a car. RLS may occur as a primary condition or due to another underlying disorder, certain medications, or other factors (secondary or symptomatic RLS). In primary RLS, the disorder occurs for unknown reasons (idiopathic) in the absence of other underlying disorders. Secondary RLS may occur in association with certain conditions, such as iron deficiency, low levels of the oxygen-carrying component of red blood cells (anemia), kidney failure, or pregnancy.

The following organizations may provide additional information and support:
March of Dimes Birth Defects Foundation
National Institute of Neurological Disorders and Stroke (NINDS)
Restless Legs Syndrome Foundation, Inc.
WE MOVE (Worldwide Education and Awareness for Movement Disorders)

943   Retinitis Pigmentosa

Synonyms
Progressive Pigmentary Retinopathy
RP

Retinitis pigmentosa (RP) is one name for a large group of inherited vision disorders that causes progressive degeneration of the retina of the eyes. Peripheral (or side) vision gradually decreases and eventually is lost. Central vision is usually preserved until late in these conditions. Some forms of retinitis pgmentosa can be associated with deafness, kidney disease, and other malfunctions, central nervous system and metabolic disorders, and chromosomal abnormalities.

The following organizations may provide additional information and support:
American Council of the Blind, Inc.
American Foundation for the Blind

American Printing House for the Blind
Blind Children's Center
Council of Families with Visual Impairment
Foundation Fighting Blindness (Canada)
Foundation Fighting Blindness, Inc.
National Association for Parents of Children with Visual Impairments (NAPVI)
National Association for Visually Handicapped
National Federation of the Blind
NIH/National Eye Institute
Recording for the Blind, Inc.
Retinitis Pigmentosa International
ROPARD:The Association for Retinopathy of Prematurity and Related Diseases
Vision World Wide, Inc.

944   Retinoblastoma

Retinoblastoma is an extremely rare malignant tumor that develops in the nerve-rich layers that line the back of the eyes (retina). It occurs most commonly in children under the age of three. The most typical finding associated with retinoblastoma is the reflection of light off a tumor behind the lens of the eye, which causes the pupil to appear white, the so called "cat's eye reflex" (leukokoria). In addition, the eyes may be crossed (strabismus). In some affected children, the eye(s) may become red and/or painful. The presence of a retinoblastoma may cause a rise in the pressure in the eyeball (glaucoma). Retinoblastomas may affect one eye (unilateral) or both eyes (bilateral). In most cases, retinoblastomas occur spontaneously for no apparent reason (sporadic).

The following organizations may provide additional information and support:
American Cancer Society, Inc.
Candlelighters Childhood Cancer Foundation
Eye Cancer Network
EyeCare Foundation
Institute for Families
National Cancer Institute
National Childhood Cancer Foundation
NIH/National Eye Institute

945   Retinopathy, Arteriosclerotic

Synonym
Arteriosclerosis, Retina

Arteriosclerotic retinopathy is a series of changes in the retina that are caused by arteriosclerosis. It is characterized by bleeding in the retina, thick fluid oozing from the retina, impaired oxygenation of the retina, an abrupt reduction of blood flow to the heart muscle that may cause dying off of tissue (myocardial infarction), and hardening of the walls of the little arteries (arterioles) in the eye. These degenerative changes can cause vision impairment.

The following organizations may provide additional information and support:
American Council of the Blind, Inc.
American Foundation for the Blind
American Heart Association
Council of Families with Visual Impairment
National Association for Visually Handicapped
National Eye Research Foundation
NIH/National Eye Institute
Schepens Eye Research Institute

946 Retinopathy, Diabetic

Synonyms
Insulin-Dependent Diabetes Retinopathy
Non-Insulin Dependent Diabetes Mellitus Retinopathy

Diabetic retinopathy is a complication of diabetes and a disorder of the light sensitive tissue of the eye (the retina). This condition is characterized by destructive changes in the blood vessels of the retina, which, if left unchecked, may lead to visual impairment or blindness. The severity of the damage to the retina is highly correlated with the length of time the patient has had diabetes. For reasons that are not well understood, the blood vessels of the retina lack their normal oxygen load. Capillaries tend to close off, further depleting the oxygen supply. The diabetes process also weakens the walls of these blood vessels, which tend to become enlarged and form micro-aneurysms. Not infrequently, the small blood vessels break causing hemorrhage and contributing to the patient's clouded vision.

The following organizations may provide additional information and support:
American Diabetes Association
American Foundation for the Blind
Juvenile Diabetes Research Foundation International
National Association for Visually Handicapped
NIH/National Eye Institute
ROPARD: The Association for Retinopathy of Prematurity and Related Diseases

947 Retinopathy, Hypertensive

Hypertensive retinopathy is characterized by high blood pressure (hypertension) that results in abnormalities affecting the nerve-rich membrane that lines the eyes (retina). The most common manifestation of hypertensive retinopathy is narrowing (occlusion) of the tiny arteries (arterioles) of the eye. In some cases, hypertensive retinopathy may result in loss of clarity of vision (visual acuity).

The following organizations may provide additional information and support:
American Council of the Blind, Inc.
American Foundation for the Blind
American Heart Association
Council of Families with Visual Impairment
National Association for Visually Handicapped
National Eye Research Foundation
NIH/National Eye Institute
Schepens Eye Research Institute

948 Retinopathy of Prematurity

Synonyms
Retrolental Fibroplasia (Obsolete)
ROP

Retinopathy of prematurity (ROP) is a potentially blinding disease affecting the retinas in premature infants. The retinas are the light-sensitive linings of the insides of the eyes. In infants born prematurely, the blood vessels that supply the retinas are not yet completely developed. Although blood vessel growth continues after birth, these vessels may develop in an abnormal, disorganized pattern, known as ROP. In some affected infants, the changes associated with ROP spontaneously subside. However, in others, ROP may lead to bleeding, scarring of the retina, retinal detachment and visual loss. Even in cases in which ROP changes cease or regress spontaneously, affected children may have an increased risk of certain eye (ocular) abnormalities, including nearsightedness, misalignment of the eyes (strabismus), and/or future retinal detachment. The two major risk factors for ROP are a low birth weight and premature delivery.

The following organizations may provide additional information and support:
The Arc (A National Organization on Mental Retardation)
Eye Care

National Association for Parents of Children with Visual Impairments (NAPVI)
National Association for Visually Handicapped
NIH/National Eye Institute
ROPARD:The Association for Retinopathy of Prematurity and Related Diseases
Schepens Eye Research Institute

949 Retinoschisis

Synonyms

Congenital Retinal Cyst
Congenital Vascular Veils in the Retina
Giant Cyst of the Retina
Vitreoretinal Dystrophy

Disorder Subdivisions

Blessig Cysts
Congenital Retinoschisis
Familial Foveal Retinoschisis
Iwanoff Cysts
Peripheral Cystoid Degeneration of the Retina
Retinoschisis, Juvenile
Retinoschisis, Senile
Retinoschisis, Typical

Retinoschisis means splitting of the eye's retina into two layers. There are two forms of this disorder. The most common is an acquired form that affects both men and women. It usually occurs in middle age or beyond, although it can occur earlier, and it is sometimes known as senile retinoschisis. The other form is present at birth (congenital) and affects mostly boys and young men. It is known as juvenile, X-linked retinoschisis. The disorder is characterized by a slow, progressive loss of parts of the field of vision corresponding to the areas of the retina that have become split. Either form may be associated with the development of saclike blisters (cysts) in the retina.

The following organizations may provide additional information and support:
American Council of the Blind, Inc.
American Foundation for the Blind
Association for Macular Diseases, Inc.
Blind Children's Fund
Council of Families with Visual Impairment
Foundation Fighting Blindness, Inc.
Macular Degeneration Support, Inc.
National Association for Parents of Children with Visual Impairments (NAPVI)
National Association for Visually Handicapped
NIH/National Eye Institute

Retinitis Pigmentosa International
ROPARD: The Association for Retinopathy of Prematurity and Related Diseases

950 Retroperitoneal Fibrosis

Synonyms

Idiopathic Retroperitoneal Fibrosis
Ormond's Disease

Retroperitoneal fibrosis is a rare inflammatory disorder in which abnormal formation of fiber-like tissue (fibrosis) occurs behind the membrane that lines the cavity of the abdomen (peritoneum). This abnormal tissue growth often spreads to affect the tubes that carry urine from the kidney to the bladder (ureters). Often these tubes become blocked by the excess tissue. Specific symptoms may vary depending upon the exact location of tissue growth and how far it spreads. In most cases the cause of this disorder is unknown (idiopathic).

The following organizations may provide additional information and support:
National Kidney Foundation
NIH/National Digestive Diseases Information Clearinghouse

951 Rett Syndrome

Synonyms

Autism, Ataxia, and Loss of Purposeful Hand Use
RS
RTS

Rett syndrome is a rare neurodevelopmental disorder that appears to occur almost exclusively in females but can occur rarely in males. Infants and children with the disorder typically develop normally until about 7 to 18 months of age, when they may begin to lose previously acquired skills (developmental regression), such as purposeful hand movements and the ability to communicate. Additional abnormalities typically include slowing of head growth (acquired microcephaly); development of distinctive, uncontrolled (stereotypic) hand movements, such as hand clapping, rubbing, or "wringing"; and impaired control of voluntary movements required for coordination of walking (gait apraxia). Affected children also typically develop autistic-like behaviors, breathing irregularities, feeding and swallowing difficulties, growth retardation, and episodes of uncontrolled electrical activity in the brain (seizures). Rett syndrome results from a mutation (change) on the X chromosome that is transmitted as an X-linked trait. However, most cases are thought to represent new mutations that appear to occur spontaneously (sporadically) for unknown reasons. In some affected females, the disorder may result from mutations of a gene known as MECP2 that is located on the long arm (q) of chromosome X (Xq28). The MECP2 gene is thought to play an essential role in brain development.

The following organizations may provide additional information and support:
The Arc (A National Organization on Mental Retardation)
International Rett Syndrome Association
March of Dimes Birth Defects Foundation
National Institute of Neurological Disorders and Stroke (NINDS)
New Horizons Un-Limited, Inc.
Rett Syndrome Research Foundation (RSRF)
Sjældne Diagnoser / Rare Disorders Denmark
WE MOVE (Worldwide Education and Awareness for Movement Disorders)

952 Reye Syndrome

Synonyms
Fatty Liver with Encephalopathy
Reye's Syndrome
RS

Reye syndrome is a rare disorder of childhood and adolescence. It primarily affects individuals under 18 years of age, particularly children from approximately age four to 12 years. In rare cases, infants or young adults may be affected. The disorder's cause is unknown. However, there appears to be an association between the onset of Reye syndrome and the use of aspirin-containing medications (salicylates) in children or adolescents with certain viral illnesses, particularly upper respiratory tract infections (e.g., influenza B) or, in some cases, chickenpox (varicella). Although any organ system may be involved, Reye syndrome is primarily characterized by distinctive, fatty changes of the liver and sudden (acute) swelling of the brain (cerebral edema). Associated symptoms and findings may include the sudden onset of severe, persistent vomiting; elevated levels of certain liver enzymes in the blood (hepatic transaminases); unusually high amounts of am-

monia in the blood (hyperammonemia); disturbances of consciousness; sudden episodes of uncontrolled electrical activity in the brain (seizures); and/or other abnormalities, leading to potentially life-threatening complications in some cases. Due to the potential association between the use of aspirin-containing agents and the development of Reye syndrome, it is advised that such medications be avoided for individuals under age 18 years who are affected by viral infections such as influenza or chickenpox.

The following organizations may provide additional information and support:
Centers for Disease Control and Prevention
National Institute of Neurological Disorders and Stroke (NINDS)
National Reye's Syndrome Foundation, Inc.

953 Rh Disease

Synonyms
Congenital Anemia of Newborn
Erythroblastosis Fetalis
Erythroblastosis Neonatorum
Hemolytic Anemia of Newborn
Hemolytic Disease of Newborn
Icterus Gravis Neonatorum
Rh Factor Incompatibility
Rh Incompatibility
Rhesus Incompatibility

Rh disease or Rh incompatibility (also known as erythroblastosis fetalis) occurs when a woman with Rh-negative blood conceives a child with Rh-positive blood. Red blood cells are destroyed (hemolysis) because of this incompatibility, leading to anemia and other symptoms in the infant. Symptoms vary in severity among affected infants and may include an unusual yellowish coloration of the skin (jaundice); swelling of the chest and abdomen due to the accumulation of fluid (edema); and/or a pale appearance of the skin. In more severe cases, affected infants may experience life-threatening complications. Rh disease occurs only when a mother's blood is Rh-negative and her baby's blood is Rh-positive.

The following organization may provide additional information and support:
NIH/National Heart, Lung and Blood Institute Information Center

954 Rheumatic Fever

Synonyms
Acute Rheumatic Fever
Inflammatory Rheumatism
Rheumatic Arthritis

Rheumatic fever is an inflammatory disease that is rare in the United States but common in some other parts of the world. It primarily affects children between the ages of 6 and 16, and develops after an infection with streptococcal bacteria, such as strep throat or scarlet fever. About 3% of those with untreated strep infection will develop rheumatic fever. Rheumatic fever may affect the heart, joints, nervous system and/or skin. In more than half of all cases, it leads to serious inflammatory disease of the valves of the heart. Joint disease is the second most common consequence of rheumatic fever.

The following organizations may provide additional information and support:
Autoimmune Information Network, Inc
Centers for Disease Control and Prevention
NIH/National Institute of Allergy and Infectious Diseases
World Health Organization (WHO) Regional Office for the Americas (AMRO)

955 Rickets, Vitamin D Deficiency

Synonyms
Nutritional Rickets
Rickets
Vitamin-D Deficiency Rickets

Vitamin-D deficiency rickets, a disorder that becomes apparent during infancy or childhood, is the result of insufficient amounts of vitamin D in the body. The vitamin deficiency may be caused by poor nutrition, a lack of exposure to the sun, or malabsorption syndromes in which the intestines do not adequately absorb nutrients from foods. Vitamin D is needed for the metabolism of calcium and phosphorus in the body, which, in turn affects how calcium is deposited in the bones; thus it is considered essential for proper bone development and growth. Major symptoms of vitamin D deficiency rickets include bone disease, restlessness, and slow growth. This disorder is rare in the United States but is not uncommon in certain areas of the world.

The following organizations may provide additional information and support:
NIH/National Digestive Diseases Information Clearinghouse
XLH Network (UK)
XLH Network Inc.

956 Rieger Syndrome

Synonyms
Goniodysgenesis-Hypodontia
Iridogoniodysgenesis with Somatic Anomalies
RGS

Rieger syndrome is a rare genetic disorder characterized by absent or underdeveloped (hypodontia or partial adontia) teeth, mild craniofacial abnormalities, and various abnormalities of the eye, especially glaucoma. If unaccompanied by other signs and symptoms, the eye abnormalities are referred to as Rieger eye anomalies. Specialists recognize two genetic forms of Rieger syndrome. Type I occurs as a result of mutations on chromosome 4 and type II results from mutations on chromosome 13.

The following organizations may provide additional information and support:
Blind Children's Fund
National Association for Parents of Children with Visual Impairments (NAPVI)
National Association for Visually Handicapped
National Foundation for Ectodermal Dysplasias
NIH/National Eye Institute

957 Roberts Syndrome

Synonyms
Hypomelia-Hypotrichosis-Facial Hemangioma Syndrome
Pseudothalidomide Syndrome
SC Syndrome

Disorder Subdivision
Phocomelia

Roberts syndrome is a rare genetic disorder characterized by growth delays before and after birth (pre- and postnatal growth deficiency); malformations of the arms and legs (limbs); distinctive abnormalities of the skull and facial (craniofacial) region. Mental retardation occurs in some cases; normal intelligence has also been reported. In infants with Roberts syndrome, the arms and legs may be incompletely developed (limb reduction abnormalities). Such abnormalities may range from absence of all four limbs (tetraphocomelia) to less severe degrees of limb reduction, such as underdevelopment and/or absence of certain bones of the upper arms (humeri), forearms (radii and/or ulnae), thighs (femurs), shins (tibiae), and/or outside of the lower legs (fibulae). Characteristic craniofacial abnormalities may include an unusually small, broad head (microbrachycephaly); abnormal grooves on either side of the upper lip (bilateral cleft lip); incomplete development of the roof of the mouth (cleft palate); thin, small wings of the nose (hypoplastic nasal alae); and/or low-set, malformed (dysplastic) ears. Additional abnormalities are often present. Roberts syndrome is probably genetically heterogeneous. While it is inherited as an autosomal recessive trait in most families, the possibility of new mutation in an autosomal dominant gene cannot be excluded. For many years, some researchers believed that Roberts syndrome and SC phocomelia syndrome were separate disorders. However, researchers now believe that the two disorders are different expressions of one distinct disorder.

The following organizations may provide additional information and support:
AboutFace USA
Children's Craniofacial Association
FACES: The National Craniofacial Association
Forward Face, Inc.
Francke, Uta, M.D.
March of Dimes Birth Defects Foundation
National Craniofacial Foundation
NIH/National Institute of Child Health and Human Development

---

958 Robinow Syndrome

Synonyms
Acral Dysostosis with Facial and Genital Abnormalities
Fetal Face Syndrome
Robinow Dwarfism

Disorder Subdivisions
Robinow Syndrome Dominant Form
Robinow Syndrome Recessive Form
(COVESDEM Syndrome)

Robinow syndrome is an extremely rare inherited disorder characterized by mild to moderate short stature due to growth delays after birth (postnatal growth retardation); distinctive abnormalities of the head and facial (craniofacial) area; additional skeletal malformations; and/or genital abnormalities. The facial features of infants with Robinow syndrome resemble those of an eight-week-old fetus; within the medical literature, this condition is often referred to as "fetal face." Characteristic craniofacial features may include an abnormally large head (macrocephaly) with a bulging forehead (frontal bossing); widely spaced eyes (ocular hypertelorism) that are abnormally prominent; a small, upturned nose with nostrils that are flared forward (anteverted); and/or a sunken (depressed) nasal bridge. Skeletal malformations may include forearm bones (radius and ulna) that are unusually short (forearm brachymelia), abnormally short fingers and toes, permanent fixation of the fifth fingers in a bent position (clinodactyly), unusually small hands with broad thumbs, malformation of the ribs, abnormal side-to-side curvature of the spine (scoliosis), and/or underdevelopment of one side of the bones in the middle (thoracic) portion of the spinal column (hemivertebrae). Genital abnormalities associated with Robinow syndrome may include an abnormally small penis (micropenis) and failure of the testes to descend into the scrotum (cryptorchidism) in affected males and underdevelopment (hypoplasia) of the clitoris and the outer, elongated folds of skin on either side of the vaginal opening (labia majora) in affected females. The range and severity of symptoms vary from case to case. In some cases, Robinow syndrome has autosomal dominant inheritance; in other cases, the disorder may have an autosomal recessive mode of inheritance. According to the medical literature, individuals with the recessive form of Robinow syndrome may have more numerous abnormalities of the ribs and the bones of the spinal column (vertebrae) than in the dominant form of the disorder. In addition, the symptoms and physical findings associated with the recessive form tend to be more severe.

The following organizations may provide additional information and support:
Children's Craniofacial Association
Congenital Heart Anomalies, Support, Education, & Resources
Craniofacial Foundation of America
Human Growth Foundation
Little People of America, Inc.
MAGIC Foundation for Children's Growth
National Craniofacial Foundation
NIH/National Arthritis and Musculoskeletal and Skin Diseases Information Clearinghouse
Restricted Growth Association
Robinow Syndrome Foundation

959 Rocky Mountain Spotted Fever

Synonyms

RMSF
Sao Paulo Typhus
Tickborne Typhus Fever

Disorder Subdivision

Fulminant Rocky Mountain Spotted Fever

Rocky Mountain spotted fever (RMSF) is an infectious disease that belongs to a group of diseases known as the spotted fever group rickettsioses. It is caused by infection with the bacterium *Rickettsia rickettsii* (*R. rickettsii*), which is usually transmitted by a tick bite. When introduced into the body, the bacterium spreads by the bloodstream or lymphatic vessels and multiplies within and damages certain cells lining the inside of small blood (vascular) vessels (i.e., endothelial cells) as well as vascular smooth muscle cells. Such damage leads to inflammatory changes of affected blood vessels (vasculitis), leakage of fluid from the blood vessels, an abnormal accumulation of fluid in body tissues (edema), and additional abnormalities, resulting in the symptoms and findings associated with the disease. Approximately two to 14 days after initial infection, early symptoms may include a high fever, severe headaches, muscle pain (myalgia), nausea, vomiting, loss of appetite (anorexia), abdominal pain, and/or features. In addition, in most individuals with RMSF, a distinctive rash develops about three to 5 days after fever onset. The rash often initially appears on the skin of the wrists and ankles and spreads to involve the palms of the hands, the soles of the feet, the forearms, the trunk, the buttocks, and the neck and facial areas. The rash typically initially consists of small, flat pinkish spots (macules) that eventually become raised (papules) and darker. The lesions usually develop "pinpoint" reddish spots (petechia) due to localized bleeding (hemorrhaging) and may merge to form larger hemorrhagic patches. In some severe cases, insufficient oxygenated blood supply to certain tissues may lead to areas of tissue loss (necrosis). R. rickettsii infection may affect blood vessels, tissues, and organs throughout the body, including the lungs, brain and spinal cord (central nervous system), heart, liver, and kidneys. Associated symptoms and findings may vary, depending upon the specific tissues and organs affected. Without timely, appropriate treatment, individuals with severe disease may develop potentially life-threatening complications due to tissue and organ injury and dysfunction. As its name indicates, the disease was originally recognized in the Rocky Mountain states. It has since been reported throughout the continental United States as well as Mexico, Canada, Central America, and South America. As noted above, in most cases, infection with the R. rickettsii bacterium results from tick bites. Several different types of ticks serve as "vectors" for the disease, transmitting the R. rickettsii bacterium to humans.

The following organizations may provide additional information and support:
Centers for Disease Control and Prevention
Lyme Disease Foundation
NIH/National Institute of Allergy and Infectious Diseases
World Health Organization (WHO) Regional Office for the Americas (AMRO)

960 Romano-Ward Syndrome

Synonyms

Autosomal Dominant Long QT Syndrome
Long QT Syndrome Type 1
Long QT Syndrome without Deafness
LQTS1
Romano-Ward Long QT Syndrome
RWS
Ward-Romano Syndrome

Romano-Ward syndrome is an inherited heart (cardiac) disorder characterized by abnormalities affecting the electrical system of the heart. The severity of Romano-Ward syndrome varies greatly from case to case. Some individuals may have no apparent symptoms (asymptomatic); others may develop abnormally increased heartbeats (tachyarrhythmias) resulting in episodes of unconsciousness (syncope), cardiac arrest, and potentially sudden death. Romano-Ward syndrome is inherited as an autosomal dominant trait.

The following organizations may provide additional information and support:
American Heart Association
European Long QT Syndrome Information Center
Genetic and Rare Diseases (GARD) Information Center
HOPE (The Heart of Pediatric Electrophysiology)
International Long QT Syndrome Registry
NIH/National Heart, Lung and Blood Institute Information Center
Sudden Arrhythmia Death Syndromes Foundation

961 Rosai-Dorfman Disease

Synonyms

RDD

SHML

Sinus Histiocytosis with Massive Lymphadenopathy

Rosai-Dorfman disease is a rare disorder characterized by over-production (proliferation) and accumulation of a specific type of white blood cell (histiocyte) in the lymph nodes of the body (lymphadenopathy), most often those of the neck (cervical lymphadenopathy). In some cases, abnormal accumulation of histiocytes may occur in other areas of the body besides the lymph nodes (extranodal). These areas include the skin, central nervous system, kidney, and digestive tract. The symptoms and physical findings associated with Rosai-Dorfman disease vary depending upon the specific areas of the body that are affected. The exact cause of Rosai-Dorfman disease is unknown.

The following organizations may provide additional information and support:

Histiocytosis Association of America

NIH/National Heart, Lung and Blood Institute

962 Rosenberg-Chutorian Syndrome

Synonyms

Optic Atrophy, Polyneuropathy, and Deafness

Polyneuropathy-Deafness-Optic Atrophy

Rosenberg-Chutorian syndrome is an extremely rare genetic disorder characterized by the triad of hearing loss, degeneration of the optic nerve (optic atrophy) and neurological abnormalities, specifically disease of the nerves outside of the central nervous system (peripheral neuropathy). The arms and legs are most often affected by peripheral neuropathy. Rosenberg-Chutorian syndrome is inherited as an X-linked, possibly semidominant, disorder. At least two other disorders are characterized by optic atrophy, hearing loss and peripheral neuropathy: Iwashita syndrome and Hagemoser syndrome. Most researchers consider these two disorders and Rosenberg-Chutorian syndrome separate disorders.

The following organizations may provide additional information and support:

Better Hearing Institute

Genetic and Rare Diseases (GARD) Information Center

March of Dimes Birth Defects Foundation

National Association for Visually Handicapped

National Institute of Neurological Disorders and Stroke (NINDS)

NIH/National Institute of Child Health and Human Development

963 Roseola Infantum

Synonyms

Exanthem Subitum

Pseudorubella

Sixth Disease

Roseola infantum is an acute infectious disorder of infants or very young children. Characterized by high fever and the appearance of a red skin rash, this disorder may resemble rubella after the fever has disappeared. Seizures may also occur.

The following organizations may provide additional information and support:

American Academy of Allergy Asthma and Immunology

Centers for Disease Control and Prevention

NIH/National Institute of Allergy and Infectious Diseases

964 Rothmund-Thomson Syndrome

Synonyms

Poikiloderma Atrophicans and Cataract

Poikiloderma Congenitale

RTS

Rothmund-Thomson syndrome is an extremely rare inherited multisystem disorder that is usually apparent during early infancy. The disorder is typically characterized by distinctive abnormalities of the skin, defects of the hair, clouding of the lenses of the eyes (juvenile cataracts), short stature and other skeletal abnormalities, malformations of the head and facial (craniofacial) area, and other physical abnormalities. In rare cases, mental retardation may be present. The range and severity of symptoms may vary from case to case. During early infancy, individuals with Rothmund-Thomson syndrome develop abnormally red, inflamed patches (plaques) on the skin (erythema) accompanied by abnormal accumulations of fluid between layers of tissue under the skin (edema). Such plaques typically first appear on the cheeks. In most cases, additional areas of the skin may then become involved to a lesser degree (e.g., the skin of the ears, forehead, chin, hands, forearms, lower legs, etc.). Inflammation eventually tends to recede and the skin of affected areas develops a condition known as poikiloderma, characterized by abnormal widening (dilation) of groups of small blood vessels (telangiectasia); skin tissue degeneration (atrophy); and patchy areas of abnormally decreased and/or unusually increased pigmentation (depigmentation and hyperpigmentation). In many cases, additional skin abnormalities may also occur. Many infants and children with Rothmund-Thomson syndrome also have additional physical abnormalities including hair that is gray and abnormally sparse; the development of abnormal clouding of the lenses of the eyes (juvenile cataracts); growth delays leading to mild to severe short stature (dwarfism); and/or additional skeletal abnormalities such as unusually small, short hands and feet, underdeveloped (hypoplastic) or absent thumbs, and/or underdeveloped (hypoplastic) or missing forearm bones (ulna and radii). Affected infants and children may also have characteristic abnormalities of the craniofacial area including a prominent forehead (frontal bossing), a sunken nasal bridge (saddle nose), a protruding lower jaw (prognathism), and/or dental abnormalities. In some cases, affected individuals may have additional physical abnormalities including deficient activity of the ovaries in females or testes in males (hypogonadism), resulting in irregular menstruation in affected females and delayed sexual development in affected males and females. Rothmund-Thomson syndrome is inherited as an autosomal recessive genetic trait.

The following organizations may provide additional information and support:
Human Growth Foundation
Little People of America, Inc.
MAGIC Foundation for Children's Growth
National Association for Parents of Children with Visual Impairments (NAPVI)
National Association for Visually Handicapped
NIH/National Arthritis and Musculoskeletal and Skin Diseases Information Clearinghouse
NIH/National Eye Institute
NIH/National Institute of Dental and Craniofacial Research

965 **Roussy-Levy Syndrome**

Synonyms
Charcot-Marie-Tooth Disease (Variant)
Charcot-Marie-Tooth-Roussy-Levy Disease
Hereditary Areflexic Dystasia
Hereditary Motor Sensory Neuropathy
Hereditary Motor Sensory Neuropathy I
HMSN I

Roussy-Levy syndrome, also known as hereditary

areflexic dystasia, is a rare genetic neuromuscular disorder that typically becomes apparent during early childhood. The disorder is characterized by incoordination, poor judgment of movements (sensory ataxia), and absence of reflexes (areflexia) of the lower legs and, eventually, the hands; weakness and degeneration (atrophy) of muscles of the lower legs; abnormally high arches of the feet with increased extension of the toes (pes cavus or "clawfoot"); and tremors of the hands. Many affected individuals also have an abnormal front-to-back and sideways curvature of the spine (kyphoscoliosis). In individuals with Roussy-Levy syndrome, there is a failed communication of certain nerve signals to muscles of the lower legs (denervation). Roussy-Levy syndrome is inherited as an autosomal dominant genetic trait.

The following organizations may provide additional information and support:
Charcot-Marie-Tooth Association
National Institute of Neurological Disorders and Stroke (NINDS)

966 **Rubella**

Synonyms
German Measles
Three-Day Measles

Rubella is a viral infection characterized by fever, headache, swollen lymph nodes, aching joints, and a distinctive red rash. Although it is sometimes called German measles or three-day measles, it is not caused by the same virus that causes measles. Rubella is generally mild in children and more severe but not life-threatening in adults. However, if a pregnant woman is infected with rubella, it can cause serious problems for the unborn child. In the United States, most children receive the measles-mumps-rubella (MMR) vaccine, and therefore the disease has become uncommon. In March 2005, health officials announced that rubella had been eliminated from the United States. However, it is still important for Americans to vaccinate their children, and women who are pregnant or might get pregnant still need to be sure they are immune, because the disease exists elsewhere. According to the Centers for Disease Control and Prevention (CDC), nine rubella cases were reported in the United States in 2004, and all of them originated in other countries.

The following organizations may provide additional information and support:
Centers for Disease Control and Prevention

NIH/National Institute of Allergy and Infectious Diseases

967 Rubella, Congenital

Synonyms
Congenital German Measles
Congenital Rubella Syndrome
Expanded Rubella Syndrome

Congenital rubella is a syndrome that occurs when a fetus has been infected with the rubella virus while in the uterus. It is primarily characterized by abnormalities of the heart and nervous system, the eyes and the ears. The fetus is most vulnerable to the virus during the first 3 months of pregnancy, although pregnant women are advised to avoid exposure to rubella virus at all times. Women who contract rubella during pregnancy have a high risk of having a baby with congenital rubella.

The following organizations may provide additional information and support:
The Arc (A National Organization on Mental Retardation)
Helen Keller National Center for Deaf-Blind Youths and Adults
March of Dimes Birth Defects Foundation

968 Rubinstein-Taybi Syndrome

Synonyms
Broad Thumbs and Great Toes, Characteristic Facies, and Mental Retardation
Michail-Matsoukas-Theodorou-Rubinstein-Taybi Syndrome
RSTS
Rubinstein Syndrome
Rubinstein Taybi (RTS) Broad Thumb-Hallux Syndrome

Rubinstein-Taybi syndrome is a rare genetic multisystem disorder that affects many organ systems of the body. The group of findings (constellation) associated with this syndrome include growth retardation and delayed bone age; mental retardation; distinctive abnormalities of the head and face (craniofacial dysmorphism), including widely spaced eyes (hypertelorism), a broad nasal bridge, and an abnormally large or "beak-shaped" nose; abnormally broad thumbs and great toes (halluces); and/or breathing and swallowing difficulties. In addition, most affected children experience delays in attaining developmental milestones (e.g., sitting, crawling, walking, talking, etc.) and/or de-

lays in the acquisition of skills requiring coordination of muscular and mental activity (psychomotor retardation). Additional craniofacial abnormalities may include an abnormally small head (microcephaly); a highly-arched roof of the mouth (palate); an unusually small (hypoplastic) lower jaw (micrognathia); crossed eyes (strabismus); droopy eyelids (ptosis); downwardly slanting eyelid folds (palpebral fissures); and/or an extra fold of skin on either side of the nose that may cover the eyes' inner corners (epicanthal folds). In addition, many individuals with Rubinstein-Taybi syndrome may have malformations of the heart, kidneys, urogenital system, and/or skeletal system. In most cases, the skin is also affected. The range and severity of symptoms and physical findings may vary widely from case to case. Most cases of Rubinstein-Taybi syndrome occur randomly, for no apparent reason (sporadic).

The following organizations may provide additional information and support:
The Arc (A National Organization on Mental Retardation)
Children's Craniofacial Association
Congenital Heart Anomalies, Support, Education, & Resources
FACES: The National Craniofacial Association
National Craniofacial Foundation
NIH/National Institute of Arthritis and Musculoskeletal and Skin Diseases
Rubinstein, Jack H.
Rubinstein-Taybi Parent Group USA
Rubinstein-Taybi Syndrome UK Support Group

969 Russell-Silver Syndrome (RSS)

Synonyms
RSS
Russell Syndrome
Russell-Silver Dwarfism
Silver Syndrome
Silver-Russell Dwarfism
Silver-Russell Syndrome
SRS

Disorder Subdivision
Russell-Silver Syndrome, X-linked (Partington Syndrome)

Russell-Silver syndrome is a very rare genetic disorder characterized by growth delays before birth (prenatal or intrauterine growth retardation); overgrowth of one side of the body (hemihypertrophy or asymmetry); unusual characteristic facial features; and other physical abnormalities. Growth delays before birth affect both weight and linear growth. As a result, although carried to full term (normal gestational age), affected infants may be abnormally small and have low birth weight. In addition, growth delays and immature bone development (growth retardation and delayed bone age) continue after birth (postnatally). As a result, affected children may exhibit short stature and may be unusually small and thin for their age. In most cases (65 to 80 percent), asymmetry or overgrowth of one side of the body is obvious at birth. Asymmetry may affect the head, trunk, arms, and/or legs. The extent and severity of asymmetry vary greatly among affected children. Characteristic facial features may include a triangular-shaped face with a small, pointed chin; an abnormally prominent forehead (frontal bossing); bluish discoloration of the tough, outer membranes covering the eyeballs (blue sclera); an unusually small, wide mouth; downturned corners of the mouth; and/or an abnormally small jaw (micrognathia). The range and severity of symptoms associated with Russell-Silver syndrome vary greatly from case to case. Other physical findings associated with this disorder may include permanent fixation of the fifth fingers in a bent position (clinodactyly); webbing of the second and third toes (syndactyly); underdevelopment (hypoplasia) of certain bones of the fingers (phalanges); development of smooth, coffee-colored patches on the skin (cafe-au-lait spots); and/or abnormalities of the kidney and urinary tract. Most cases of Russell-Silver syndrome are the result of new genetic changes (mutations) that occur randomly for no apparent reason (sporadic). If this mutation were to be inherited, it would do so as an autosomal dominant genetic trait. In rare cases, it is thought that the disorder may be inherited as an autosomal recessive genetic trait. In addition, a rare form of Russell-Silver syndrome is thought to be inherited as an X-linked dominant genetic trait.

The following organizations may provide additional information and support:
The Arc (A National Organization on Mental Retardation)
Human Growth Foundation
Little People of America, Inc.
MAGIC Foundation for Children's Growth
NIH/National Institute of Arthritis and Musculoskeletal and Skin Diseases
Restricted Growth Association

970 Ruvalcaba Syndrome

Synonym
Osseous Dysplasia with Mental Retardation, Ruvalcaba Type

Ruvalcaba syndrome is a rare inherited disorder characterized by short stature, abnormalities affecting the head and facial (craniofacial) area, mental retardation, skeletal malformations, and/or underdeveloped (hypoplastic) genitalia. Characteristic craniofacial features include an abnormally small head (microcephaly); an abnormally small, narrow nose; and downslanting eyelid folds (palpebral fissures). Skeletal malformations may include fifth fingers that are permanently fixed in a bent position (clinodactyly) and/or abnormally short bones between the wrists and the fingers (metacarpals) and the ankles and toes (metatarsals), resulting in unusually small hands and feet. In addition, affected children may have abnormal side-to-side curvature of the spine (scoliosis) and/or unusual prominence of the breast bone (pectus carinatum). Ruvalcaba syndrome is thought to be inherited as an autosomal dominant genetic trait.

The following organizations may provide additional information and support:
The Arc (A National Organization on Mental Retardation)
FACES: The National Craniofacial Association
Human Growth Foundation

971 Saethre-Chotzen Syndrome

Synonyms
Acrocephalosyndactyly Type III
Acrocephaly, Skull Asymmetry, and Mild Syndactyly
ACS Type III
ACS3
Chotzen Syndrome
SCS

Disorder Subdivision
Acrocephaly, Skull Asymmetry, and Mild Retardation

Saethre-Chotzen syndrome belongs to a group of rare genetic disorders known as "acrocephalosyndactyly" disorders. All are characterized by premature closure of the fibrous joints (cranial sutures) between certain bones of the skull (craniosynostosis), causing the top of the head to appear pointed (acrocephaly), and/or webbing or fusion (syndactyly) of certain fingers or toes (digits). Saethre-Chotzen syndrome is also known as acrocephalosyndactyly type III. In many infants with Saethre-Chotzen syndrome, cranial sutures may fuse unevenly, causing the head and face to appear somewhat dissimilar from one side to the other (craniofacial asymmetry). Additional malformations of the skull and facial (craniofacial) region may also be present, such as widely spaced eyes (ocular hypertelorism) with unusually shallow eye cavities (orbits); drooping of the upper eyelids (ptosis); and abnormal deviation of one eye in relation to the other (strabismus). Some affected individuals may also have a "beaked" nose; deviation of the partition that separates the nostrils (deviated nasal septum); small, low-set, malformed ears; and an underdeveloped upper jaw (hypoplastic maxilla). The disorder is also associated with malformations of the hands and feet, such as partial fusion of soft tissues (cutaneous syndactyly) of certain fingers and toes (digits); unusually short digits (brachydactyly); and broad great toes. Although intelligence is usually normal, some affected individuals may have mild to moderate mental retardation. Saethre-Chotzen syndrome is usually inherited as an autosomal dominant trait.

The following organizations may provide additional information and support:
AboutFace USA
The Arc (A National Organization on Mental Retardation)
Children's Craniofacial Association
FACES: The National Craniofacial Association
Forward Face, Inc.
Headlines—Craniofacial Support
Let's Face It (USA)
March of Dimes Birth Defects Foundation
National Craniofacial Foundation
Society for the Rehabilitation of the Facially Disfigured, Inc.

---

972 Sakati Syndrome

Synonyms
ACPS III
ACPS with Leg Hypoplasia
Acrocephalopolysyndactyly Type III
Sakati-Nyhan Syndrome

Sakati syndrome belongs to a group of rare genetic disorders known as "acrocephalopolysyndactyly" (ACPS). All forms of ACPS are characterized by premature closure of the fibrous joints (cranial sutures) between certain bones of the skull (craniosynostosis), causing the top of the head to appear pointed (acrocephaly); webbing or fusion (syndactyly) of certain fingers or toes (digits); and/or more than the normal number of digits (polydactyly). In addition, Sakati syndrome, which is also known as ACPS type III, is associated with abnormalities of bones of the legs, structural heart malformations that are present at birth (congenital heart defects), and/or other findings. Sakati syndrome is thought to be caused by a new genetic change (mutation) that occurs randomly for unknown reasons (sporadically).

The following organizations may provide additional information and support:
AboutFace USA
American Heart Association
Children's Craniofacial Association
Congenital Heart Anomalies, Support, Education, & Resources
FACES: The National Craniofacial Association
Forward Face, Inc.
Let's Face It (USA)
National Craniofacial Foundation
National Foundation for Facial Reconstruction

---

973 Sandhoff Disease

Synonyms
Gangliosidosis Beta Hexosaminidase B Deficiency
Gangliosidosis GM2 Type 2

Sandhoff disease is a rare inherited lipid storage disorder resulting in the progressive deterioration of the central nervous system. A deficiency of the enzyme hexosaminidase (beta-subunit) results in the accumulation of certain fats (lipids or fatty acids) in the brain and other organs of the body. Sandhoff disease is a severe form of Tay-Sachs disease and is not limited to any particular ethnic group.

The following organizations may provide additional information and support:
Blind Children's Fund
March of Dimes Birth Defects Foundation
National Association for Visually Handicapped
National Institute of Neurological Disorders and Stroke (NINDS)
National Tay-Sachs and Allied Diseases Association, Inc.

974 Santavuori Disease

Synonyms

CLN1

INCL

Infantile Finnish Type Neuronal Ceroid Lipofuscinosis (Balkan Disease)

Infantile Neuronal Ceroid Lipofuscinosis

Infantile Type Neuronal Ceroid Lipofuscinosis

Neuronal Ceroid Lipofuscinosis Type 1

Santavuori-Haltia Disease

Santavuori disease, an extremely rare inherited disorder, belongs to a group of progressive degenerative neurometabolic diseases known as the neuronal ceroid lipofuscinoses (NCL). These diseases share certain similar symptoms and are distinguished in part by the age at which such symptoms appear. Santavuori disease is considered the infantile form of the neuronal ceroid lipofuscinoses. In most cases, infants with Santavuori disease appear to develop normally until approximately nine to 19 months of age. They may then begin to exhibit a delay in the acquisition of skills that require the coordination of mental and muscular activity (psychomotor retardation). In addition, affected infants begin to lose previously acquired physical and mental abilities (developmental regression). Affected infants may then experience a variety of symptoms including episodes of uncontrolled electrical disturbances in the brain (seizures), impaired ability to coordinate voluntary movements (cerebellar ataxia), abnormally diminished muscle tone (hypotonia), and repeated, brief, shock-like muscle spasms of the arms, legs, or entire body (myoclonic seizures). Affected infants also experience progressive visual impairment due to deterioration of the nerves of the eyes (optic nerves) that transmit impulses from the nerve-rich membranes lining the eyes (retina) to the brain (optic atrophy). Neurological impairment continues to progress and may be characterized by an inability to move voluntarily (immobility); sudden involuntary muscle spasms (spasticity); and lack of response to stimuli in the environment. Life-threatening complications may develop by the end of the first decade. The symptoms and physical characteristics of Santavuori disease are due to abnormal accumulation of certain fatty, granular substances (i.e., pigmented lipids [lipopigments] ceroid and lipofuscin) within nerve cells (neurons) of the brain as well as other tissues of the body. Santavuori disease is inherited as an autosomal recessive genetic trait.

The following organizations may provide additional information and support:

Batten Disease Support and Research Association

Children's Brain Diseases Foundation

Epilepsy Foundation

National Institute of Neurological Disorders and Stroke (NINDS)

National Tay-Sachs and Allied Diseases Association, Inc.

NIH/National Eye Institute

Vaincre Les Maladies Lysosomales

975 Sarcoidosis

Synonyms

Sarcoid of Boeck

Schaumann's Disease

Disorder Subdivisions

Acute Sarcoidosis; Heerferdt-Waldenstrom and Lofgren's Syndromes (Included)

Chronic Sarcoidosis

Subacute Sarcoidosis

Sarcoidosis is a multisystem disorder that most often affects individuals between 20 and 40 years of age. Females appear to be affected more frequently than males. Sarcoidosis is characterized by the abnormal formation of inflammatory masses or nodules (granulomas) consisting of certain granular white blood cells (modified macrophages or epithelioid cells) in certain organs of the body. The granulomas that are formed are thought to alter the normal structure of and, potentially, the normal functions of, the affected organ(s), causing symptoms associated with the particular body system(s) in question. In individuals with sarcoidosis, such granuloma formation most commonly affects the lungs. However, in many cases, the upper respiratory system, lymph nodes, skin, and/or eyes may be involved. In addition, in some cases, other organs may be affected, including the liver, bone marrow, spleen, musculoskeletal system, heart, salivary glands, and/or nervous system (i.e., central or peripheral nervous system). The range and severity of symptoms associated with sarcoidosis vary greatly, depending upon the specific organ(s) involved and the degree of such involvement. In some cases, the symptoms of sarcoidosis may begin suddenly (acute), sometimes severely, and subside in a relatively short period of time (self limited). Acute sarcoidosis is often characterized by fatigue, fever, generalized muscle aches, difficulty breathing (dyspnea), joint pain, swollen glands, skin eruptions, eye irregularities, and/or other symptoms. In the subacute form, affected individuals may experience no symptoms (asymptomatic), even with organ involvement. In the chronic form of sarcoidosis, symptoms may appear slowly and subtly, and may persist or recur over a long time span. Initial symptoms of the chronic form of the disorder may include difficulty breathing (dyspnea), dry cough, limited airflow, and other respiratory abnormalities. Symptoms associated with other organ involvement may follow. The exact cause of sarcoidosis is not known. However, possible infectious, environmental, genetic, and immunological factors are under investigation as potential causes of the disorder.

The following organizations may provide additional information and support:
American Lung Association
Autoimmune Information Network, Inc
Erythema Nodosum Yahoo Support Group
Foundation for Sarcoidosis Research
Jack Miller Center for Peripheral Neuropathy
National Sarcoidosis Resource Center
NIH/National Eye Institute
NIH/National Heart, Lung and Blood Institute Information Center
NIH/National Institute of Arthritis and Musculoskeletal and Skin Diseases
Sarcoid Networking Association
Sarcoidosis Center
Sarcoidosis Network Foundation, Inc.
Sarcoidosis Online Sites: A Comprehensive Source for Sarcoidosis Information on the Internet
Sarcoidosis Research Institute
UveitisSupport-MEEI

---

976 Schindler Disease

Synonyms
Alpha-Galactosidase B Deficiency
Alpha-GalNAc Deficiency, Schindler Type
Alpha-N-Acetylgalactosaminidase Deficiency, Schindler Type
Alpha-NAGA Deficiency, Schindler Type
GALB Deficiency
Lysosomal Alpha-N-Acetylgalactosaminidase Deficiency, Schindler Type
Neuroaxonal Dystrophy, Schindler Type
Neuronal Axonal Dystrophy, Schindler Type

Disorder Subdivisions
Adult Onset Schindler Disease
Angiokeratoma Corporis Diffusum-Glycopeptiduria
Classic Schindler Disease
Infantile Onset Schindler Disease
Kanzaki Disease
Lysosomal Glycoaminoacid Storage Disease-Angiokeratoma Corporis Diffusum
Schindler Disease, Infantile Onset
Schindler Disease, Type I (Infantile Onset)
Schindler Disease, Type II (Adult Onset)

Schindler disease is a rare inherited metabolic disorder characterized by a deficiency of the lysosomal enzyme alpha-N-acetylgalactosaminidase (alpha-NAGA). The disorder belongs to a group of diseases known as lysosomal storage disorders. Lysosomes function as the primary digestive units within cells. Enzymes within lysosomes break down or digest particular nutrients, such as certain fats and carbohydrates. In individuals with Schindler disease, deficiency of the alpha-NAGA enzyme leads to an abnormal accumulation of certain complex compounds (glycosphingolipids) in many tissues of the body. There are two forms of Schindler disease. The classical form of the disorder, known as Schindler disease, type I, has an infantile onset. Affected individuals appear to develop normally until approximately 1 year of age, when they begin to lose previously acquired skills that require the coordination of physical and mental activities (developmental regression). Additional neurological and neuromuscular symptoms may become apparent, including diminished muscle tone (hypotonia) and weakness; involuntary, rapid eye movements (nystagmus); visual impairment; and episodes of uncontrolled electrical activity in the brain (seizures). With continuing disease progression, affected children typically develop restricted movements of certain muscles due to progressively increased muscle rigidity, severe mental retardation, hearing and visual impairment, and a lack of response to stimuli in the environment. Schindler disease, type II, which is also known as Kanzaki disease, is the adult-onset form of the disorder. Associated symptoms may not become apparent until the second or third decade of life. In this milder form of the disease, symptoms may include the development of clusters of wart-like discolorations on the skin (angiokeratomas); permanent widening of groups of blood vessels (telangiectasia), causing redness of the skin in affected areas; relative coarsening of facial features; and mild intellectual impairment. The progressive neurological degeneration characteristically seen in the infantile form of the disease has not occurred in association with Schindler disease, type II. Both forms of Schindler disease are inherited as autosomal recessive traits. According to investigators, different changes (mutations) of the same gene are responsible for the infantile- and adult-onset forms of the disease. The gene has been mapped to the long arm (q) of chromosome 22 (22q11).

The following organizations may provide additional information and support:
CLIMB (Children Living with Inherited Metabolic Diseases)
International Society for Mannosidosis & Related Diseases, Inc.
National Institute of Neurological Disorders and Stroke (NINDS)
National Tay-Sachs and Allied Diseases Association, Inc.
Vaincre Les Maladies Lysosomales

977 Schinzel-Giedion Syndrome

Synonym
Schinzel-Giedion Midface-Retraction Syndrome

Schinzel-Giedion syndrome is a very rare disorder with characteristic facial features, skeletal abnormalities, and obstruction of the tube that carries urine from the kidney to the bladder (ureter). This obstruction may lead to enlarged and damaged kidneys (hydronephrosis). Symptoms characteristic of Schinzel-Giedion syndrome also include excessive hair-growth (hypertrichosis), a flat midface (midface retraction), seizures, clubfeet, broad ribs, mental retardation, and short arms and legs.

The following organizations may provide additional information and support:
The Arc (A National Organization on Mental Retardation)
Genetic and Rare Diseases (GARD) Information Center

978 Schinzel Syndrome

Synonyms
Pallister Syndrome
Ulnar-Mammary Syndrome
Ulnar-Mammary Syndrome of Pallister
UMS

Schinzel syndrome, also known as ulnar-mammary syndrome, is a rare inherited disorder characterized by abnormalities of the bones of the hands and forearms in association with underdevelopment (hypoplasia) and dysfunction of certain sweat (apocrine) glands and/or the breasts (mammary glands). Abnormalities affecting the hands and/or forearms range from underdevelopment of the bone in the tip of the fifth finger (hypoplastic terminal phalanx) to underdevelopment or complete absence of the bone on the outer aspect of the forearm (ulna). In addition, certain sweat glands such as those located under the arms may be underdeveloped or absent, resulting in diminished ability or inability to sweat (perspire). In some cases, the breasts (mammary glands) may also be underdeveloped or absent; as a result, affected females exhibit a diminished ability or an inability to produce milk (lactate). The range and severity of physical abnormalities associated with Schinzel syndrome varies greatly among affected individuals; some cases may be very mild, while others may be more severe.

The following organizations may provide additional information and support:
NIH/National Institute of Arthritis and Musculoskeletal and Skin Diseases

979 Schwartz-Jampel Syndrome

Synonyms
Chondrodystrophic Myotonia
Myotonic Myopathy, Dwarfism,
Chondrodystrophy, Ocular and Facial
Anomalies
Schwartz-Jampel-Aberfeld Syndrome
SJA Syndrome
SJS

Disorder Subdivisions
Schwartz-Jampel Syndrome, Type 2
Schwartz-Jampel Syndrome, Types 1A and 1B

Schwartz-Jampel syndrome (SJS) is a rare genetic disorder characterized by abnormalities of the skeletal muscles, including muscle weakness and stiffness (myotonic myopathy); abnormal bone development (bone dysplasia); permanent bending or extension of certain joints in a fixed position (joint contractures); and/or growth delays resulting in abnormally short stature (dwarfism). Affected individuals may also have small, fixed facial features and various abnormalities of the eyes, some of which may cause impaired vision. The range and severity of symptoms may vary from case to case. Two types of the disorder have been identified that may be differentiated by age of onset and other factors. Schwartz-Jampel syndrome type 1, which is considered the classical form of the disorder, may become apparent during early to late infancy or childhood. Schwartz-Jampel syndrome type 2, a more rare form of the disorder, is typically recognized at birth (congenital). Most researchers now believe that SJS type 2 is actually the same disorder as Stuve-Wiedemann syndrome and not a form of Schwartz-Jampel syndrome. Schwartz-Jampel syndrome is thought to be inherited as an autosomal recessive trait. However, some cases reported in the medical literature suggest an autosomal dominant inheritance pattern.

The following organizations may provide additional information and support:
Anophthalmia/Microphthalmia Registry
International Children's Anophthalmia Network (ican)
Malignant Hyperthermia Association of the United States (MHAUS)
National Association for Parents of Children with Visual Impairments (NAPVI)
National Association for Visually Handicapped
NIH/National Arthritis and Musculoskeletal and Skin Diseases Information Clearinghouse
NIH/National Eye Institute

980 Scleroderma

Synonyms
Progressive Systemic Sclerosis
PSS
Sclerosis, Familial Progressive Systemic
Systemic Sclerosis

Disorder Subdivisions
CREST Syndrome
Linear Scleroderma
Morphea

Scleroderma is a rare connective tissue disorder characterized by abnormal thickening of the skin. Connective tissue is composed of collagen, which supports and binds other body tissues. There are several types of scleroderma. Some types affect certain, specific parts of the body, while other types can affect the whole body and internal organs (systemic).

The following organizations may provide additional information and support:
Autoimmune Information Network, Inc
British Coalition of Heritable Disorders of Connective Tissue

Juvenile Scleroderma Network, Inc.
Lupus Society of Alberta
National Registry for Childhood Onset Scleroderma
NIH/National Arthritis and Musculoskeletal and Skin Diseases Information Clearinghouse
Scleroderma Foundation
Scleroderma Research Foundation

981 Scott Craniodigital Syndrome

Synonyms
Craniodigital Syndrome of Scott
Craniodigital Syndrome-Mental Retardation, Scott Type
Scott Syndrome

Scott craniodigital syndrome is a condition that has only been found in two families. The manifestations include unusual head shape, growth and developmental delay, and mild webbing between the fingers and toes (syndactyly)

The following organizations may provide additional information and support:
Children's Craniofacial Association
Craniofacial Foundation of America
FACES: The National Craniofacial Association
Forward Face, Inc.

982 Seckel Syndrome

Synonyms
Bird-Headed Dwarfism, Seckel Type
Microcephalic Primordial Dwarfism I
Nanocephalic Dwarfism
Seckel Type Dwarfism

Seckel syndrome is an extremely rare inherited disorder characterized by growth delays prior to birth (intrauterine growth retardation) resulting in low birth weight. Growth delays continue after birth (postnatal) resulting in short stature (dwarfism). Other symptoms and physical features associated with Seckel syndrome include an abnormally small head (microcephaly); varying degrees of mental retardation; and/or unusual characteristic facial features including "beak-like" protrusion of the nose. Other facial features may include abnormally large eyes, a narrow face, malformed ears, and/or an unusually small jaw (micrognathia). In addition, some affected infants may exhibit permanent fixation of the fifth fingers in a bent position (clinodactyly), malformation (dysplasia) of the hips, dislocation of a bone in the forearm (radial dislocation), and/or other physical abnormalities. Seckel syndrome is thought to be inherited as an autosomal recessive genetic trait.

The following organizations may provide additional information and support:
AboutFace USA
The Arc (A National Organization on Mental Retardation)
Children's Craniofacial Association
Craniofacial Foundation of America
Forward Face, Inc.
Human Growth Foundation
Little People of America, Inc.
National Craniofacial Foundation
Restricted Growth Association

983 Seitelberger Disease (Infantile Neuroaxonal Dystrophy)

Synonym
INAD

Disorder Subdivision
Prenatal or Connatal Neuroaxonal Dystrophy

Seitelberger disease, also known as infantile neuroaxonal dystrophy, is an extremely rare inherited degenerative disorder of the nervous system characterized by abnormalities of nerve endings (axons) within the brain and spinal cord (central nervous system) and outside the central nervous system (peripheral nerves). In most cases, infants and children with Seitelberger disease appear to develop normally until approximately 14 to 18 months of age, when they may begin to experience progressively increased difficulties in walking. In other cases, symptoms may begin at approximately 6 to 8 months of age, at which time infants may experience delays or an arrest in the acquisition of skills requiring the coordination of mental and physical activities (delayed psychomotor development). Affected infants and children may then begin to lose previously acquired skills (psychomotor regression) including sitting and standing and may demonstrate progressive neuromuscular impairment characterized by generalized muscle weakness, severely diminished muscle tone (hypotonia), abnormally exaggerated reflex responses (hyperreflexia), and/or unusually weak, depressed, or absent reflexes. In some cases, as the disorder progresses, affected children may also experience involuntary movements of

the face and hands, sudden involuntary muscle spasms (spasticity) of the lower arms and legs (limbs), and progressive paralysis of the legs and lower part of the body (paraplegia). Progressive mental retardation occurs in association with gradual motor impairment. Children with Seitelberger disease also experience progressive neurological impairment including involuntary, rapid, side-to-side movements of the eyes (pendular nystagmus); crossing of the eyes (strabismus); gradual deterioration of the nerves of the eyes (optic atrophy), progressing to blindness; and/or hearing impairment. As neurological impairment progresses, affected children may experience disorientation and loss of intellectual function (dementia); impaired response to touch (tactile stimulation); uncontrolled, rigid extensions and rotations of the arms, legs, fingers, and toes due to progressively degenerative brain abnormalities (decerebrate rigidity); and increased susceptibility to repeated infections of the respiratory tract. Life-threatening complications may develop by the end of the first decade. The symptoms and physical characteristics associated with Seitelberger disease occur due to swelling and degeneration of nerve endings (dystrophic axonal swellings or "spheroids") in certain areas of the brain and spinal cord (central nervous system or neuroaxis) and outside the central nervous system (peripheral nerves). In most cases, Seitelberger disease is inherited as an autosomal recessive genetic trait.

The following organizations may provide additional information and support:
March of Dimes Birth Defects Foundation
National Institute of Neurological Disorders and Stroke (NINDS)
NIH/National Eye Institute
United Leukodystrophy Foundation

984 Sennetsu Fever

Synonym
Human Ehrlichial Infection, Sennetsu Type

Sennetsu fever is a rare infectious disease belonging to a group of diseases known as the human ehrlichioses. These diseases are caused by bacteria belonging to the *Ehrlichia* family. Several forms of human ehrlichial infection have been identified including Sennetsu fever, human monocytic ehrlichiosis (HME), and human granulocytic ehrlichiosis (HGE). Though caused by different strains of ehrlichia bacteria, the disorders are all characterized by similar symptoms.The symptoms of Sennetsu fever may include a sudden high fever, headache, and muscle aches (myalgia) within a few weeks after initial infection. In some cases, affected individuals may also experience nausea, vomiting, and/or loss of appetite (anorexia). In addition, in many cases, abnormal laboratory findings may include a decrease in white blood cells (leukopenia) and/or an abnormal increase in the level of certain liver enzymes (hepatic transaminases). Sennetsu fever is caused by the bacterium Ehrlichia sennetsu. The vector (or carrier) for this bacterium has not yet been determined; however, some researchers believe that infection may result from the ingestion of raw fish.

The following organizations may provide additional information and support:
Centers for Disease Control and Prevention
NIH/National Institute of Allergy and Infectious Diseases
World Health Organization (WHO) Regional Office for the Americas (AMRO)

985 Septooptic Dysplasia

Synonyms
DeMorsier Syndrome
SOD

Septooptic dysplasia is a disorder that results from incomplete development of the forebrain and pituitary gland. This condition is characterized by underdevelopment (hypoplasia) of the optic nerves that transmit impulses from the nerve-rich membranes lining the retina of the eye to the brain; abnormalities of midline structures of the brain such as the septum pellucidum and corpus callosum; and diminished activity of the pituitary gland, the hormone-producing gland at the base of the brain. Most people with septooptic dysplasia have abnormal eye movements (nystagmus) and some affected individuals have partial or complete blindness in one or both eyes. Some affected children have normal intelligence and others have learning disabilities and mental retardation. Deficiencies of certain hormones result in growth retardation and short stature. The cause of septooptic dysplasia is not fully understood. Most cases are thought to occur randomly for unknown reasons (sporadic), but some families have been reported with more than one affected child, suggesting autosomal recessive inheritance.

The following organizations may provide additional information and support:
American Foundation for the Blind
The Arc (A National Organization on Mental Retardation)
Blind Children's Center
Blind Children's Fund
Council of Families with Visual Impairment
Diabetes Insipidus Foundation, Inc.
FOCUS Families—For Our Children's Unique Sight
Foundation Fighting Blindness, Inc.
Human Growth Foundation
MAGIC Foundation for Children's Growth
National Association for Parents of Children with Visual Impairments (NAPVI)
National Federation of the Blind
NIH/National Digestive Diseases Information Clearinghouse

986 Setleis Syndrome

Synonyms
Bitemporal Forceps Marks Syndrome
Facial Ectodermal Dysplasia
FFDD Type II
Focal Facial Dermal Dysplasia Type II

Setleis syndrome is an extremely rare inherited disorder that belongs to a group of diseases known as ectodermal dysplasias. Ectodermal dysplasias typically affect the hair, teeth, nails, and/or skin. Setleis syndrome is characterized by distinctive abnormalities of the facial area that may be apparent at birth (congenital). Most affected infants have multiple, scar-like, circular depressions on both temples (bitemporal). These marks closely resemble those made when forceps are used to assist delivery. In addition, affected infants may have puffy, wrinkled skin around the eyes (periorbital) and/or abnormalities of the eyelashes, eyebrows, and eyelids. Infants with Setleis syndrome may be missing eyelashes on both the upper and lower lids, or they may have multiple rows of lashes on the upper lids but none on the lower lids. In addition, in some cases, the bridge of the nose may appear flat, while the tip may appear unusually rounded (bulbous). Affected infants often have loose, excessive (redundant) skin, particularly in the area of the nose and the chin. Due to such facial abnormalities, infants with Setleis syndrome may have an aged and/or "leonine" (lion-like) appearance. The range and severity of symptoms may vary from case to case. Most cases of Setleis syndrome are thought to be inherited as an autosomal recessive genetic trait.

The following organizations may provide additional information and support:
Children's Craniofacial Association
Craniofacial Foundation of America
Forward Face, Inc.
National Craniofacial Foundation
National Foundation for Ectodermal Dysplasias
NIH/National Institute of Arthritis and Musculoskeletal and Skin Diseases

987 Severe Combined Immunodeficiency

Synonym
SCID

Disorder Subdivisions
ADA Deficiency
Adenosine Deaminase Deficiency
Autosomal Recessive Severe Combined Immunodeficiency
Bare Lymphocyte Syndrome
Reticular Dysgenesis
X-Linked Recessive Severe Combined Immunodeficiency with Leukopenia

Severe combined immunodeficiency (SCID) is a group of rare congenital syndromes characterized by little if any immune responses. This results in frequent recurring infections. Cellular immune responses involve specialized white blood cells known as T lymphocytes or "killer cells." These cells assist other white blood cells (B lymphocytes) to respond to infectious, foreign agents that invade the body (i.e., bacteria or viruses). The B lymphocytes maintain immunity by enabling the body to produce and preserve circulating antibodies. People with severe combined immunodeficiency are unusually susceptible to recurrent infections with bacteria, viruses, fungi, and other infectious agents that can be life-threatening. There are several types of severe combined immunodeficiencies. These include: autosomal recessive severe combined immunodeficiency, X-linked recessive severe combined immunodeficiency, adenosine deaminase deficiency (ADA), bare lymphocyte syndrome, severe combined immunodeficiency with leukopenia (reticular dysgenesis), and Swiss-type agammaglobulinemia. Each type of severe combined immune deficiency is caused by a different genetic defect, but the primary symptom is reduced or absent immune functions, and all types are hereditary.

The following organizations may provide additional information and support:
American Academy of Allergy Asthma and Immunology

Immune Deficiency Foundation
International Patient Organization for Primary Immunodeficiencies
March of Dimes Birth Defects Foundation
NIH/National Institute of Allergy and Infectious Diseases

988 Sheehan Syndrome

Synonyms
Postpartum Hypopituitarism
Postpartum Panhypopituitarism
Postpartum Panhypopituitary Syndrome
Postpartum Pituitary Necrosis
Simmond's Disease

Sheehan syndrome (SS) arises, subsequent to the birth of a baby, because of damage to the pituitary gland that results in a reduced output of the hormones and other products produced by that endocrine gland (hypopituitarism). The pituitary gland is made up of anterior and posterior portions, and the anterior part is particularly vulnerable to the shock that may result from the loss of blood during delivery. The pituitary is a small gland, located deep in the brain, that produces many of the hormones that control essential bodily processes. During pregnancy, the pituitary gland grows to about double its normal size and is susceptible to postpartum complications. If tissue in the anterior pituitary dies because of postpartum hemorrhaging, the hormonal balance of the body is thrown completely out of equilibrium with consequences that show up as symptoms of Sheehan syndrome. The chronic form presents months to years later, while the even more rare acute form shows up shortly after delivery.

The following organizations may provide additional information and support:
NIH/National Digestive Diseases Information Clearinghouse
Thyroid Foundation of America, Inc.

989 Short Chain Acyl CoA Dehydrogenase Deficiency (SCAD)

Synonyms
Acyl-CoA Dehydrogenase Deficiency, Short-Chain
Lipid-Storage Myopathy Associated with SCAD Deficiency
SCAD Deficiency
SCAD Deficiency, Adult-Onset (Localized)
SCAD Deficiency, Congenital (Generalized)
SCADH Deficiency

Short-chain acyl-CoA dehydrogenase deficiency is an extremely rare inherited disorder of fat metabolism belonging to a group of diseases known as fatty acid oxidation disorders (FOD). It occurs because of a deficiency of an enzyme. The enzyme, known as short-chain acyl-CoA dehydrogenase enzyme, is involved in the breakdown of complex fatty acids into more simple substances. This takes place in the cell's mitochondria, small, well-defined bodies found in all cells in which energy is generated from the breakdown of complex substances into simpler ones (mitochondrial oxidation). When this enzyme is deficient, excessive amounts of fatty acids accumulate in the liver and muscle tissues, and ammonia and other products accumulate in the blood and body tissues. Although SCAD was initially thought to produce severe problems including progressive muscle weakness, hypotonia, acidemia, developmental delay, and even early death, it is now believed that this disorder is both more common and less severe in many cases than originally thought at the time of its discovery 20 years ago. Since the advent of expanded newborn screening programs using tandem mass spectrometry technology, many more SCAD infants are being detected, many of whom are well and asymptomatic. When symptoms are present, they tend to appear soon (days to weeks) after birth and include lack of weight gain, general failure to thrive, vomiting, and poor feeding.

The following organizations may provide additional information and support:
CLIMB (Children Living with Inherited Metabolic Diseases)
FOD (Fatty Oxidation Disorders) Family Support Group
NIH/National Institute of Diabetes, Digestive & Kidney Diseases
Organic Acidaemias UK
Organic Acidemia Association
United Mitochondrial Disease Foundation

990 SHORT Syndrome

Synonyms
Growth Retardation-Rieger Anomaly
Lipodystrophy, Partial, with Rieger Anomaly and Short Stature
Reiger Anomaly-Growth Retardation
Short Stature-Hyperextensibility-Rieger Anomaly-Teething Delay

SHORT syndrome is a condition in which affected individuals have multiple birth defects in different organ systems. The term SHORT is an acronym with each letter representing one of the common findings in affected persons: (S) = short stature (H) = hyperextensibility of joints and/or hernia (inguinal) (O) = ocular depression (R) = Rieger anomaly (T) = teething delay. Other characteristics common in SHORT syndrome are a triangular face, small chin with a dimple, a loss of fat under the skin (lipodystrophy), abnormal position of the ears, hearing loss and delayed speech.

The following organizations may provide additional information and support:
Human Growth Foundation
Little People of America, Inc.
Little People's Research Fund, Inc.
MAGIC Foundation for Children's Growth
NIH/National Arthritis and Musculoskeletal and Skin Diseases Information Clearinghouse
NIH/National Eye Institute
Restricted Growth Association

991 Shwachman Syndrome

Synonyms
Lipomatosis of Pancreas, Congenital Pancreatic Insufficiency and Bone Marrow Dysfunction
Shwachman-Bodian Syndrome
Shwachman-Diamond Syndrome
Shwachman-Diamond-Oski Syndrome

Shwachman syndrome is a rare genetic disorder with multiple and varied manifestations. The disorder is typically characterized by signs of insufficient absorption (malabsorption) of fats and other nutrients due to abnormal development of the pancreas (pancreatic insufficiency) and improper functioning of the bone marrow (bone marrow dysfunction), resulting in low levels of circulating blood cells (hematologic abnormalities). Additional characteristic findings may include short stature; abnormal bone development affecting the rib cage and/or bones in the arms and/or legs (metaphyseal dysostosis); and/or liver abnormalities. Due to abnormal skeletal changes, individuals with Shwachman syndrome may have abnormal thickening of the ribs and their supporting connective tissue (costochondral thickening), resulting in unusually short, flared ribs. In addition, improper bone development (abnormal ossification) within the arms and/or legs (limbs) may cause growth delay in particular bones. Many children with Shwachman syndrome may also be smaller than expected for their ages, with below average height (short stature) and weight. Although malabsorption due to pancreatic insufficiency may itself cause problems with growth and nutrition, short stature appears to be one of the many primary manifestations of Shwachman syndrome. In addition, as a result of bone marrow dysfunction, individuals with Shwachman syndrome may have a decrease in any or all types of blood cells. Therefore, they may have low levels of certain white blood cells (neutropenia), platelets (thrombocytopenia), red blood cells (anemia), and/or all types of blood cells (pancytopenia). Neutropenia is the most common blood abnormality associated with Shwachman syndrome. Because neutrophils, a type of white blood cell, play an essential role in fighting bacterial infections, many affected individuals are prone to repeated bacterial infections (e.g., recurrent respiratory infections [pneumonia] and infections of the middle ear [otitis media]); in some cases, infections may be severe. Some affected individuals may also have abnormal enlargement of the liver (hepatomegaly), increased levels of certain liver enzymes in the blood, and/or other findings in association with the disorder. Shwachman syndrome is believed to be inherited as an autosomal recessive trait.

The following organizations may provide additional information and support:
National Neutropenia Network
Neutropenia Support Association, Inc.
NIH/National Arthritis and Musculoskeletal and Skin Diseases Information Clearinghouse
NIH/National Digestive Diseases Information Clearinghouse
NIH/National Heart, Lung and Blood Institute Information Center
Shwachman-Diamond Syndrome Foundation

---

992 Sialadenitis

Synonym
Salivary Gland Infection

Sialadenitis is a condition characterized by inflammation and enlargement of one or more of the salivary glands, the glands that secrete saliva into the mouth. There are both acute and chronic forms. Sialadenitis is often associated with pain, tenderness, redness, and gradual, localized swelling of the affected area. The exact cause of sialadenitis is not known.

The following organizations may provide additional information and support:
NIH/National Oral Health Information Clearinghouse

993 Sialidosis

Synonyms
Alpha-Neuraminidase Deficiency
Cherry Red Spot and Myoclonus Syndrome
Glycoprotein Neuraminidase, Deficiency of
Lipomucopolysaccharidosis Type I
ML I
Mucolipidosis I
Sialidase Deficiency

Disorder Subdivisions
Sialidosis Type I (Juvenile)
Sialidosis Type II (Infantile)

Sialidosis is a very rare inherited metabolic disorder characterized by a deficiency of the enzyme alpha-neuraminidase. This disorder belongs to a group of diseases known as lysosomal disorders. Lysosomes are particles bound in membranes within cells that break down certain fats and carbohydrates. The deficiency of alpha-neuraminidase that characterizes sialidosis leads to the abnormal accumulation of certain complex carbohydrates (mucopolysaccharides) and certain fatty substances (mucolipids) in many tissues of the body. Previously known as mucolipidosis I, sialidosis belongs to a subgroup of lysosomal diseases known as mucolipidoses. The symptoms of sialidosis type I, which typically begin during the 2nd decade of life, may include sudden involuntary muscle contractions (myoclonus), the appearance of red spots (cherry-red macules) in the eyes, and/or other neurological findings. Sialidosis type II may begin during infancy or later. It is characterized by the same visual characteristics as sialidosis type I, as well as other symptoms such as mildly coarse facial features, skeletal malformations, and/or mild mental retardation. Sialidosis is inherited as an autosomal recessive genetic trait.

The following organizations may provide additional information and support:
The Arc (A National Organization on Mental Retardation)
Canadian Society for Mucopolysaccharide and Related Diseases, Inc.
CLIMB (Children Living with Inherited Metabolic Diseases)
International Society for Mannosidosis & Related Diseases, Inc.
NIH/National Digestive Diseases Information Clearinghouse
Society for Mucopolysaccharide Diseases
Vaincre Les Maladies Lysosomales

994 Sickle Cell Disease

Synonyms

Sickle Cell Anemia
Sickle Cell Trait

Disorder Subdivisions

Sickle Cell-Hemoglobin C Disease
Sickle Cell-Hemoglobin D Disease
Sickle Cell-Thalassemia Disease

Sickle cell disease is a rare inherited blood disorder. It is characterized by the presence of sickle or crescent shaped red blood cells (erythrocytes) in the bloodstream. These abnormally shaped cells become rigid and lodge themselves in the very tiny blood vessels (capillaries) of the peripheral blood system (blood vessels at a distance from the heart). The capillaries become clogged, preventing the normal flow of oxygen to tissues. Sickle cell disease has several recognized forms including sickle cell anemia, sickle cell hemoglobin C disease and sickle cell thalassemia disease.

The following organizations may provide additional information and support:
Anemia Institute for Research and Education
Cochrane Cystic Fibrosis and Genetic Disorders Review Group
Cooley's Anemia Foundation, Inc.
March of Dimes Birth Defects Foundation
NIH/National Heart, Lung and Blood Institute Information Center
Sickle Cell Disease Association of America, Inc.
Sickle Cell Disease Association of Piedmont

995 Simian B Virus Infection

Synonyms

H Simiae Encephalomyelitis
Herpesvirus Simiae, B Virus
Monkey B Virus

Simian B virus infection is caused by a type of herpesvirus. It is an infectious disorder contracted chiefly by laboratory workers exposed to infected monkeys and/or simian tissue cultures. It is characterized by a viral invasion of the brain (encephalitis) and the membranes (meninges) surrounding the brain. Occasionally, the infection affects the spinal cord structures as well (encephalomyelitis). Neurological damage may result from this infection. Without treatment, some cases of Simian B virus may be life-threatening.

The following organizations may provide additional information and support:
Centers for Disease Control and Prevention
NIH/National Institute of Allergy and Infectious Diseases
World Health Organization (WHO) Regional Office for the Americas (AMRO)

996 Simpson Dysmorphia Syndrome

Synonyms

Bulldog Syndrome
DGSX Golabi-Rosen Syndrome, Included
Dysplasia Gigantism Syndrome, X-Linked
SDYS
SGB Syndrome
Simpson-Golabi-Behmel Syndrome

Disorder Subdivisions

Simpson Dysmorphia Syndrome Type 1 (SDYS1)
Simpson Dysmorphia Syndrome Type 2 (SDYS2)

Simpson dysmorphia syndrome types 1 and 2 are two forms of a rare, X-linked recessive, inherited disorder characterized by unusually large fetuses (prenatal overgrowth) and unusually large babies (postnatal overgrowth). In addition, affected individuals have characteristic facial features, more than two nipples (supernumerary nipples), and multisystemic malformations that may vary from child to child. Chief among these are cardiac malformations, mild to moderate mental retardation, cleft palate, and more than the five fingers and/or toes (polydactyly). Symptoms associated with the more common form, Simpson dysmorphia syndrome type 1 (SDYS1), are less severe than those presented in SDYS2. Individuals usually reach an above-average height. The general distinguishing features typically become less apparent in adulthood.

The following organizations may provide additional information and support:
Beckwith Wiedemann Support Network
Children's Craniofacial Association
FACES: The National Craniofacial Association
NIH/National Arthritis and Musculoskeletal and Skin Diseases Information Clearinghouse

997 Singleton-Merten Syndrome

Synonym

Merten-Singleton Syndrome

Singleton-Merten syndrome is an extremely rare, multisystem disorder the major characteristics of which are tooth abnormalities (dental dysplasia), calcifications in the aorta, the major artery of the body, and certain valves of the heart (i.e., aortic and mitral valves), as well as progressive thinning and loss of protein of the bones (osteoporosis), especially the upper and back portions of the skull (cranium). Other physical findings usually associated with Singleton-Merten syndrome may include generalized muscle weakness; progressive loss or wasting away of muscle tissue (atrophy); growth retardation, possibly resulting in short stature; delays in motor development; a skin condition characterized by thickened patches of red, scaly skin, particularly on the fingers; and/or malformation of the hips and/or feet. It appears that, in some cases, Singleton-Merten syndrome is present as a result of a random (sporadic) mutation that occurs for no apparent reason. In other cases, an autosomal dominant pattern of inheritance has been suggested.

The following organizations may provide additional information and support:
Congenital Heart Anomalies, Support, Education, & Resources
NIH Osteoporosis and Related Bone Diseases National Resource Center
NIH/National Heart, Lung and Blood Institute Information Center
NIH/National Institute of Arthritis and Musculoskeletal and Skin Diseases

998 Sinonasal Undifferentiated Carcinoma

Sinonasal undifferentiated carcinoma (SNUC) is a rare cancer of the nasal cavity and/or paranasal sinuses. Initial symptoms range from bloody nose, runny nose, double vision, and bulging eye to chronic infections and nasal obstruction. It has been associated with several types of papilloma in the nasal cavity, which are benign, but can give rise to malignancy. Prior irradiation for other cancers has been associated with the development of SNUC in a number of cases, and has been associated with a genetic mutation known to be associated with cancer development. Most patients have not had prior irradiation, and no other causes have demonstrated to be significant, though some studies have found that woodworkers and nickel factory workers are generally more susceptible to sinonasal malignancy of all types.

The following organizations may provide additional information and support:
American Cancer Society, Inc.
National Cancer Institute
Support for People with Oral and Head and Neck Cancer, Inc.

999 Sirenomelia Sequence

Synonyms
Mermaid Syndrome
Sirenomelus

Sirenomelia sequence is a birth defect in which affected infants are born with a single lower extremity or with two legs that are fused together. Due to the wide range of possible physical deformities that may occur, the symptoms and physical findings associated with sirenomelia sequence vary greatly from case to case.

The following organizations may provide additional information and support:
Genetic and Rare Diseases (GARD) Information Center
NIH/National Institute of Child Health and Human Development

1000 Sjogren Syndrome

Synonyms
Dacryosialoadenopathia atrophicans
Gougerot-Houwer-Sjogren
Gougerot-Sjogren
Keratoconjunctivitis Sicca
Keratoconjunctivitis Sicca-Xerostomia
Secreto-Inhibitor-Xerodermostenosis
Sicca Syndrome

Sjogren syndrome is an autoimmune disorder characterized by degeneration of the mucus-secreting glands, particularly the tear ducts of the eyes (lacrimal) and saliva glands of the mouth. Autoimmune disorders are caused when the body's natural defenses (antibodies, lymphocytes, etc.) against invading organisms suddenly begin to attack healthy tissue. Sjogren syndrome is also associated with inflammatory disorders such as arthritis or lupus.

The following organizations may provide additional information and support:
Arthritis Foundation
Autoimmune Information Network, Inc
CNS Vasculitis Foundation

Jack Miller Center for Peripheral Neuropathy
Lupus Society of Alberta
NIH/National Arthritis and Musculoskeletal and Skin Diseases Information Clearinghouse
NIH/National Eye Institute
NIH/National Oral Health Information Clearinghouse
Sjogren's Syndrome Foundation, Inc.
Swedish Sjogren's Syndrome Association

1001 Sly Syndrome

Synonyms
Beta-Glucuronidase Deficiency
GUSB Deficiency
MPS VII
MPS Disorder, Type VII
Mucopolysaccharidosis Type VII

Mucopolysaccharidoses, which are also known as mucopolysaccharide storage (MPS) diseases, are a group of rare genetic disorders caused by the deficiency of one of ten specific lysosomal enzymes. The lysosomes are particles bound in membranes within cells that break down certain fats and carbohydrates (mucopolysaccharides) into simpler molecules. The accumulation of these large, undegraded mucopolysaccharides in the cells of the body causes a number of physical symptoms and abnormalities. Sly syndrome (MPS-VII) is an MPS storage disease caused by a deficiency of the enzyme beta-glucuronidase that leads to an accumulation of dermatan sulfate (DS), heparan sulfate (HS) and chondroitin sulfate (CS) in many tissues and organs of the body including the central nervous system. The clinical features of Sly syndrome vary from patient to patient, but all have short stature due to growth retardation, changes in bones visible on X-rays and some degree of mental retardation. Survival into adulthood is common with milder cases and osteoarthritis is a common complication.The symptoms of Sly syndrome are similar to those of Hurler syndrome (MPS I) and the other mucopolysaccharidoses. Symptoms may include mental retardation, short stature with an unusually short trunk, and/or abnormalities of the intestines, corneas of the eyes, and/or the skeletal system. Sly syndrome is inherited as an autosomal recessive genetic trait.

The following organizations may provide additional information and support:
The Arc (A National Organization on Mental Retardation)

Canadian Society for Mucopolysaccharide and Related Diseases, Inc.
CLIMB (Children Living with Inherited Metabolic Diseases)
National MPS (Mucopolysaccharidoses/Mucolipidoses) Society, Inc.
NIH/National Digestive Diseases Information Clearinghouse
Society for Mucopolysaccharide Diseases
Vaincre Les Maladies Lysosomales

1002 Smallpox

Disorder Subdivisions
Variola Major (Smallpox)
Variola Minor (Alastrim)

Smallpox is an infectious disease caused by the variola virus. It is characterized by fever, a general feeling of ill health (malaise), headaches and back pain. These initial symptoms are followed by a rash and small, raised bumps or lesions (pocks) within 2 or 3 days. Smallpox was a highly contagious disease, but was declared eradicated in 1980. However, recently smallpox has become of interest because of the possibility of its use as a weapon of warfare or of terrorism. There were two strains of smallpox, variola major and variola minor.

The following organizations may provide additional information and support:
Centers for Disease Control and Prevention
NIH/National Institute of Allergy and Infectious Diseases
World Health Organization (WHO) Regional Office for the Americas (AMRO)

1003 Smith-Lemli-Opitz Syndrome

Synonyms
DHCR7 Abnormality
RSH Syndrome
SLO Syndrome
SLOS

Smith-Lemli-Opitz syndrome (SLOS) is a variable genetic disorder that is characterized by slow growth before and after birth, small head (microcephaly), mild to moderate mental retardation and multiple birth defects including particular facial features, cleft palate, heart defects, fused second and third toes, extra fingers and toes and underdeveloped external genitals in males. The severity of SLOS varies greatly in affected individuals, even in the same family, and some have normal development and only minor birth defects. SLOS is caused by a deficiency in the enzyme 7-dehydrocholesterol reductase that results in an abnormality in cholesterol metabolism. SLOS is inherited as an autosomal recessive genetic disorder.

The following organizations may provide additional information and support:
The Arc (A National Organization on Mental Retardation)
Smith-Lemli-Opitz/RSH Advocacy and Exchange

1004   Smith-Magenis Syndrome

Synonyms
Chromosome 17, Interstitial Deletion 17p
SMCR
Smith-Magenis Chromosome Region
SMS

Smith-Magenis syndrome is characterized by particular facial features, developmental delays, mental retardation and behavioral abnormalities. The facial features include a broad square-shaped face, an abnormally short, broad head (brachycephaly); an abnormally broad, flat midface; a broad nasal bridge; an unusually prominent jaw (prognathism); eyebrows growing across the base of the nose (synophrys); a short full tipped nose and fleshy upper lip with a tented appearance. Developmental delays and intelligence are variable but most affected individuals have mild to moderate mental retardation. Behavioral abnormalities include sleep disturbances, repetitive movements (stereotypies) and a tendency to inflict harm on oneself. Smith-Magenis syndrome occurs when there is a missing piece of chromosome on the short arm of chromosome 17 (17p11.2).

The following organizations may provide additional information and support:
American Society for Deaf Children
Chromosome Deletion Outreach, Inc.
PRISMS (Parents & Researchers Interested in Smith-Magenis Syndrome)
Smith-Magenis Syndrome Foundation

1005   Sneddon Syndrome

Synonyms
Livedo Reticularis and Cerebrovascular Accidents
Sneddon's Syndrome

Sneddon syndrome is a rare progressive disorder affecting the blood vessels characterized by the association of a skin condition and neurological abnormalities. Characteristics include multiple episodes of reduced blood flow to the brain (cerebral ischemia) and bluish net-like patterns of discoloration on the skin surrounding normal-appearing skin (livedo reticularis). Major symptoms may include headache, dizziness, abnormally high blood pressure (hypertension), heart disease, mini-strokes, and/or stroke. Lesions (infarcts) may develop within the central nervous system as a result of reduced blood flow to the brain and may cause reduced mental capacity, memory loss, and/or other neurological symptoms. The exact cause of Sneddon syndrome is unknown.

The following organizations may provide additional information and support:
National Institute of Neurological Disorders and Stroke (NINDS)
National Stroke Association
NIH/National Heart, Lung and Blood Institute Information Center
Sneddon Foundation (Stichting Sneddon)

1006   Sotos Syndrome

Synonym
Cerebral Gigantism

Sotos syndrome is a variable genetic disorder characterized by excessive growth before and after birth. One of the major features of Sotos syndrome is a particular facial appearance that includes facial flushing, an abnormally prominent forehead (frontal bossing), down-slanting eyelid folds (palpebral fissures), prominent, narrow jaw, a long narrow face and a head shape that is similar to an inverted pear. Height and head circumference are measured to be greater than average for most affected children. Developmental delays are present in most children with Sotos syndrome and can include motor and language delays as well as mental retardation ranging from mild to severe. Other problems associated with Sotos syndrome include jaundice in newborns, curved spine (scoliosis), seizures, crossed eyes (strabismus), conductive hearing loss, congenital heart defects, kidney abnormalities and behavioral problems. Affected individuals also have a slightly increased risk to develop specific types of tumors. Sotos syndrome is caused by an abnormality (mutation) in the NSD1 gene.

The following organizations may provide additional information and support:
The Arc (A National Organization on Mental Retardation)
March of Dimes Birth Defects Foundation
Restricted Growth Association
Sjældne Diagnoser / Rare Disorders Denmark
Sotos Syndrome Support Association
Sotos Syndrome Support Association of Canada/ Association Canadienne d'entraide du Syndrome de Sotos
Sotos Syndrome Support Group of Great Britain
Sotos, Juan, M.D.

1007 Spasmodic Dysphonia

Synonyms
CSD (Chronic Spasmodic Dysphonia)
Dysphonia Spastica
Laryngeal Dystonia
SD
Spastic Dysphonia

Disorder Subdivisions
Abductor Spasmodic Dysphonia
Adductor Spasmodic Dysphonia

Spasmodic dysphonia is a voice disorder characterized by momentary periods of uncontrolled vocal spasms, tightness in the throat, and/or recurrent hoarseness. At certain times, affected individuals must make a conscious effort to speak. The most frequent sign of this disorder is a sudden, momentary lapse or interruption of the voice. Spasmodic dysphonia is a form of dystonia, a group of neurological movement disorders characterized by involuntary muscle spasms.There are two types of spasmodic dysphonia: Abductor spasmodic dysphonia and the more common adductor spasmodic dysphonia. The cause of spasmodic dysphonia is not known.

The following organizations may provide additional information and support:
Dystonia Medical Research Foundation
Dystonia Society
National Spasmodic Dysphonia Association
NIH/National Institute on Deafness and Other Communication Disorders (Balance)
Spasmodic Dysphonia Support Group
WE MOVE (Worldwide Education and Awareness for Movement Disorders)

1008 Spasmodic Torticollis

Synonyms
Cervical Dystonia
ICD
Idiopathic Cervical Dystonia
Spasmodic Wryneck
Torticollis

Disorder Subdivisions
Clonic Spasmodic Torticollis
Mixed Tonic and Clonic Torticollis
Tonic Spasmodic Torticollis

Spasmodic torticollis, also known as cervical dystonia, is a form of dystonia characterized by intermittent spasms of the neck muscles resulting in involuntary rotation and tilting of the head. These movements are frequently painful. There are three different varieties of the disorder: tonic, causing sustained turning of the head to one side; clonic, causing shaking movements of the head; and mixed tonic and clonic, involving both kinds of movements. The exact cause of this disorder is usually unknown, and it tends to appear in adults.

The following organizations may provide additional information and support:
Dystonia Medical Research Foundation
National Institute of Neurological Disorders and Stroke (NINDS)
National Spasmodic Torticollis Association
Spasmodic Torticollis Dystonia, Inc
WE MOVE (Worldwide Education and Awareness for Movement Disorders)

1009 Spina Bifida

Synonyms
Neural Tube Defect
SB

Disorder Subdivisions
Spina Bifida Cystica
Spina Bifida Occulta

Spina bifida is characterized by incomplete closure of certain bones of the spinal column (vertebrae), leaving a portion of the spinal cord exposed. Part of the contents of the spinal canal may protrude through this opening. In the most severe form, rachischisis, the opening is extensive. Spina bifida may cause difficulties with bladder control and walking and/or other abnormalities, depending on the severity of associated symptoms.

The following organizations may provide additional information and support:
Association for Spina Bifida and Hydrocephalus
Birth Defect Research for Children, Inc.
Christopher Reeve Paralysis Foundation
Easter Seals National Headquarters
International Federation for Spina Bifida and Hydrocephalus
March of Dimes Birth Defects Foundation
National Institute of Neurological Disorders and Stroke (NINDS)
New Horizons Un-Limited, Inc.
Pathways Awareness Foundation
Sjældne Diagnoser / Rare Disorders Denmark
Spina Bifida and Hydrocephalus Association of Canada
Spina Bifida and Hydrocephalus Association of Ontario
Spina Bifida Association of America
Spina Bifida Hydrocephalus Queensland

1010   Spinal Muscular Atrophy

Synonym
SMA

Disorder Subdivisions
Kugelberg-Welander Disease or Juvenile SMA (SMA3)
Prenatal Onset SMA or Arthrogryposis Multiplex Congenita-SMA
SMA, Mild Child and Adolescent Form (SMA2)
Spinal Muscular Atrophy Type 4 (SMA4)
Werdnig-Hoffman Disease or Infantile Muscular Atrophy (SMA1)

Spinal muscular atrophy (SMA) that is caused by a deletion of the SMN gene on chromosome 5 is an inherited progressive neuromuscular disorder characterized by degeneration of groups of nerve cells (motor nuclei) within the lowest region of the brain (lower brainstem) and certain motor neurons in the spinal cord (anterior horn cells). Motor neurons are nerve cells that transmit nerve impulses from the spinal cord or brain (central nervous system) to muscle or glandular tissue. Typical symptoms are a slowly progressive muscle weakness and muscle wasting (atrophy). Affected individuals have poor muscle tone, muscle weakness on both sides of the body without, or with minimal, involvement of the face muscles, twitching tongue and a lack of deep tendon reflexes. SMA is divided into subtypes based on age of onset of symptoms and maximum function achieved. Spinal muscular atrophy is inherited as an autosomal recessive trait. Molecular genetic

testing has revealed that all types of autosomal recessive SMA are caused by mutations in the SMN (survival motor neuron) gene on chromosome 5. Deletion of the NAIP (neuronal apoptosis inhibitory protein) gene that is close to the SMN gene is also associated with SMA. More patients with Werdnig Hoffman disease (SMA1) than other types of SMA have NAIP deletions. The relationship between specific mutations in the SMN gene and nearby genes and the severity of SMA is still being investigated so classification of SMA subdivisions is based on age of onset of symptoms and maximum function achieved, as opposed to the genetic profile. Other types of SMA exist with different prognoses.

The following organizations may provide additional information and support:
Families of Spinal Muscular Atrophy
Jennifer Trust for Spinal Muscular Atrophy
March of Dimes Birth Defects Foundation
Muscular Dystrophy Association
National Institute of Neurological Disorders and Stroke (NINDS)
New Horizons Un-Limited, Inc.

1011   Split Hand/Split Foot Malformation

Synonyms
Ectrodactilia of the Hand
Ectrodactyly
Ektrodactyly of the Hand
Karsch-Neugebauer Syndrome
Lobster Claw Deformity
Split Hand Malformation
Split-Hand/Foot Deformity
Split-Hand/Foot Malformation

Split hand/split foot malformation (SHFM) is a genetic disorder characterized by the complete or partial absence of some fingers or toes, often combined with clefts in the hands or feet. There may also be the appearance of webbing between fingers or toes (syndactyly). This may give the hands and/or feet a claw-like appearance. There are many types and combinations of deformities that appear in split hand/split foot malformation. They range widely in severity, even in members of the same family. The malformation may occur alone, or it may occur as a component of a syndrome with other characteristics.

The following organizations may provide additional information and support:
Genetic and Rare Diseases (GARD) Information Center

NIH/National Arthritis and Musculoskeletal and Skin Diseases Information Clearinghouse
.

1012 Spondyloepiphyseal Dysplasia, Congenital

Synonyms
Pseudoachondroplasia
SED Congenital
SEDC

Congenital spondyloepiphyseal dysplasia is a rare genetic disorder characterized by growth deficiency before birth (prenatally), spinal malformations, and/or abnormalities affecting the eyes. As affected individuals age, growth deficiency eventually results in short stature (dwarfism) due, in part, to a disproportionately short neck and trunk, and a hip deformity in which the thigh bone is angled toward the center of the body (coxa vara). In most cases, affected individuals may have diminished muscle tone (hypotonia), abnormal front-to-back and side-to-side curvature of the spine (kyphoscoliosis), abnormal inward curvature of the spine (lumbar lordosis), and/or unusual protrusion of the breast bone (sternum), a condition known as pectus carinatum. Affected individuals also have abnormalities affecting the eyes including nearsightedness (myopia) and, in approximately 50 percent of cases, detachment of the nerve-rich membrane lining the eye (retina). Congenital spondyloepiphyseal dysplasia is inherited as an autosomal dominant trait.

The following organizations may provide additional information and support:
Human Growth Foundation
Kniest SED Group
Little People of America, Inc.
Little People's Research Fund, Inc.
MAGIC Foundation for Children's Growth

1013 Spondyloepiphyseal Dysplasia Tarda

Synonyms
SED Tarda
X-linked Spondyloepiphyseal Dysplasia

Spondyloepiphyseal dysplasia tarda (SEDT) is a rare, hereditary, skeletal disorder that affects males only. Physical characteristics include moderate short-stature (dwarfism), moderate to severe spinal deformities, barrel-chest, disproportionately short trunk, and premature osteoarthritis. An extremely rare form of SEDT, the Toledo type, differs from typical SEDT by its autosomal recessive mode of genetic transmission and by the presence of a metabolic abnormality in the urine.

The following organizations may provide additional information and support:
Human Growth Foundation
Kniest SED Group
Little People of America, Inc.
Little People's Research Fund, Inc.
MAGIC Foundation for Children's Growth

1014 Sprengel Deformity

Synonyms
High Scapula
Scapula Elevata

Sprengel deformity is a rare congenital disorder in which the shoulder blade is displaced upward. The elevated shoulder blade causes a lump in the back of the base of the neck and may limit movement of the arm on the affected side. This disorder typically appears at birth for no apparent reason although there have been cases in which the disorder was inherited as an autosomal dominant trait. Other skeletal and muscular abnormalities have been found in association with Sprengel deformity.

The following organizations may provide additional information and support:
Genetic and Rare Diseases (GARD) Information Center
NIH/National Arthritis and Musculoskeletal and Skin Diseases Information Clearinghouse

1015 Stenosis, Spinal

Synonyms
Cervical Spinal Stenosis
Degenerative Lumbar Spinal Stenosis
Familial Lumbar Stenosis
Lumbar Canal Stenosis
Lumbar Spinal Stenosis
Lumbosacral Spinal Stenosis
Spondylotic Caudal Radiculopathy
Stenosis of the Lumbar Vertebral Canal
Tandem Spinal Stenosis
Thoracic Spinal Canal Stenosis

Spinal stenosis is a rare condition characterized by abnormal narrowing (stenosis) of the spaces within the spinal canal, spinal nerve root canals, or the bones of the spinal column (vertebrae). Affected individuals may experience pain in the lower back and/or the legs. In some cases, affected individuals may have difficulty walking. Spinal stenosis may occur as a result of spinal injury, surgery, abnormal bone growth, or deterioration. In some cases, spinal stenosis may be inherited as an autosomal dominant genetic trait.

The following organizations may provide additional information and support:
March of Dimes Birth Defects Foundation
National Scoliosis Foundation
NIH/National Institute of Arthritis and Musculoskeletal and Skin Diseases

---

1016 Stevens-Johnson Syndrome

Synonyms
Dermatostomatitis, Stevens Johnson Type
Ectodermosis Erosiva Pluriorificialis
Erythema Multiforme Exudativum
Erythema Polymorphe, Stevens Johnson Type
Febrile Mucocutaneous Syndrome, Stevens Johnson Type
Herpes Iris, Stevens-Johnson Type
Johnson-Stevens Disease

Until recently the relationship of Stevens-Johnson syndrome to other severe blistering disorders was a matter of some debate. Now a consensus seems to be evolving that describes SJS as a rare disorder involving lesions of the mucous membranes along with small blisters on the reddish or purplish, flat, thickened patches of skin. As a result, SJS is now distinguished as a separate disorder from erythema multiforme major (EMM). SJS is now considered to be a less severe variant of toxic epidermal necrolysis (TEN). SJS and TEN appear to be characterized by identical clinical signs and symptoms, identical treatment approach and identical prognosis. Patients diagnosed with TEN can present with symptoms ranging from 10% skin involvement and severe threat to the patient's sight to a presentation involving 90% of the skin but only a modest threat to the patient's sight. SJS (and TEN) is an inflammatory disorder of the skin triggered by an allergic reaction to certain drugs including antibiotics, such as some sulfonamides, tetracycline, amoxicillin, and ampicillin. In some cases, nonsteroidal anti-inflammatory medications and anticonvulsants, such as Tegretol and phenobarbital have also been implicated. Over-the-counter medications may act as triggers as well. In some cases, it is also possible that the disorder

may be traced to a reaction to an infection. One report suggests that the term SJS be limited to cases in which less than 10% of the total body surface area is involved. The authors suggest that the term TEN be limited to cases in which 30% or more of the total body surface area is involved. The term SJS/TEN Overlap is used to describe patients in whom between 10-30% of the total body surface area involved.

The following organizations may provide additional information and support:
NIH/National Eye Institute
NIH/National Institute of Allergy and Infectious Diseases
NIH/National Institute of Arthritis and Musculoskeletal and Skin Diseases
Stevens Johnson Syndrome Foundation and Support Group

1017 Stickler Syndrome

Synonyms
Arthro-Ophthalmopathy
Epiphyseal Changes and High Myopia
Ophthalmoarthropathy
Weissenbacher-Zweymuller Syndrome

Stickler syndrome refers to a group of disorders of the connective tissue that involves several of the body's organ systems such as the eye, skeleton, inner ear, and/or the head and face. Connective tissue is made up of a protein known as collagen that develops into the several varieties found in the body. It is the tissue that physically supports many organs in the body and may act like a glue or an elastic band that allows muscles to stretch and contract. Stickler syndrome often affects the connective tissue of the eye, especially in the interior of the eyeball (vitreous humor), and the ends of the bones that make up the joints of the body (epiphysis). Most authorities agree that there are four types of Stickler syndrome, of which three are reasonably well differentiated and a fourth remains not well understood. Stickler syndrome type I; (STL1): This form is responsible for about 75% of reported cases and presents with a full array of symptoms (eye, ear, jaw and cleft, joints). Stickler syndrome type II; (STL2): Patients with this form also present with a full array of symptoms. Stickler syndrome type III; (STL3): Patients with this form present with a "Stickler-like" syndrome that affects the joints and hearing without involving the eyes. This form is also known as oto-spondylo-megaepiphyseal dysplasia (OSMED).

The following organizations may provide additional information and support:
Let Them Hear Foundation
NIH/National Eye Institute
Stickler Involved People
Stickler Syndrome Support Group

1018 Stiff-Person Syndrome

Synonyms
Moersch-Woltmann Syndrome
Muscular Rigidity—Progressive Spasm
SMS
Stiff Man Syndrome

Stiff-person syndrome is an extremely rare neurological disorder characterized by progressive muscle stiffness (rigidity) and spasms. It usually begins in young adults, first involving muscles of the trunk and progressing to affect muscles of the legs. This syndrome may begin as recurring (intermittent) episodes of stiffness and spasms, often precipitated by surprise or minor physical contact. Those affected have a characteristic stiff-legged way of walking (gait) and increase in the curvature of the spine (lordotic posture). The exact cause of stiff person syndrome is not known.

The following organizations may provide additional information and support:
American Autoimmune Related Diseases Association, Inc.
Autoimmune Information Network, Inc
National Institute of Neurological Disorders and Stroke (NINDS)

1019 Streptococcus, Group B

Synonyms
GBS
Group B Strep
Group B Streptococcal Septicemia of the Newborn
Lancefield Group B Streptococcus
Sepsis of the Newborn
Streptococcus Agalactiae

Disorder Subdivisions
Adult Onset Streptococcus, Group B
Infant Early-Onset Streptococcus, Group B
Infant Late-Onset Streptococcus, Group B

Group B streptococcus (group B strep) is a type of bacteria that causes infection among newborns, pregnant women or women after childbirth, females after gynecologic surgery, and older male and female patients with other serious diseases. Group B strep remains the most common cause among newborns (neonates) of infection of the blood (septicemia) and of the brain (meningitis). The responsible bacterium, usually S. agalactiae, may be found most often in the vagina and rectum of females and may be transmitted sexually, as well as to a fetus as the infant passes through the birth canal. Group B strep infection of newborns may be prevented by giving pregnant women who are carriers antibiotics through the vein (intravenously) during labor. The U.S. Centers for Disease Control and Prevention (CDC) recommend that any pregnant woman who has had a baby with group B strep disease in the past, who has a bladder (urinary tract) infection caused by group B strep, or who tests positive for group B strep during pregnancy should receive antibiotics during labor. Prevention and prompt treatment are important because group B strep infections may become life-threatening among newborns. GBS disease is said to be early onset if it is obvious within the first week of life. It is said to be late onset if the disease is evident after the first week of life and before the end of the first 3 months. Those at greatest risk of GBS disease are newborn children of infected mothers, women after childbirth, females after gynecologic surgery and older male and female patients with other serious diseases.

The following organizations may provide additional information and support:
Centers for Disease Control and Prevention
Group B Strep Association
NIH/National Institute of Allergy and Infectious Diseases

1020 Sturge-Weber Syndrome

Synonyms
Dimitri Disease
Encephalofacial Angiomatosis
Encephalotrigeminal Angiomatosis
Leptomeningeal Angiomatosis
Meningeal Capillary Angiomatosis
SWS
Sturge-Kalischer-Weber Syndrome
Sturge-Weber Phakomatosis

Sturge-Weber syndrome is composed of three major symptoms. Excessive blood vessel growths (leptomeningeal angiomas) are accompanied by accumulations of calcium inside the brain, and seizures. Facial birth marks (nevus flammeus) appear usually on one side of the face. Angiomas similar to those found in the brain can develop inside the eye, often with secondary glaucoma.

The following organizations may provide additional information and support:
The Arc (A National Organization on Mental Retardation)
Chugani, Diane M.D.
Comi, Anne M.D.
Enjolras, Odile, M.D.
National Institute of Neurological Disorders and Stroke (NINDS)
The Sturge-Weber Foundation
Vascular Birthmarks Foundation

1021   Stuve-Wiedemann Syndrome

Stuve-Wiedemann syndrome is a rare skeletal disorder present at birth (congenital). It is characterized by short stature, bowing of the long bones of the arms and legs (campomelia), and fingers or toes that are permanently flexed (camptodactyly) outward away from the thumb (ulnar deviation). Affected infants may develop life-threatening complications such as episodes where there is a sudden rise in body temperature (hyperthermia) or respiratory distress. Stuve-Wiedemann syndrome is inherited as an autosomal recessive trait. Some researchers believe that Stuve-Wiedemann syndrome and Schwartz-Jampel syndrome (SJS) type II are the same disorder. SJS was previously believed to be the newborn (neonatal) form of SJS. However, the clinical and radiographic pictures of Stuve-Wiedemann and SJS type II are nearly identical leading many researchers to believe the two disorders are a single entity. Radiographic pictures are records of internal structures of the body made from the use of x-rays or gamma rays.In the past, Stuve-Wiedemann syndrome was thought to be a lethal condition in all cases. Today, there are reports in the literature describing patients who survive.

1022   Subacute Sclerosing Panencephalitis

Synonyms
Dawson's Disease
Dawson's Encephalitis
Panencephalitis, Subacute Sclerosing
SSPE

Subacute sclerosing panencephalitis (SSPE) is a progressive neurological disorder characterized by inflammation of the brain (encephalitis). The dis-

ease may develop due to reactivation of the measles virus or an inappropriate immune response to the measles virus. SSPE usually develops 2 to 10 years after the original viral attack. Initial symptoms may include memory loss, irritability, seizures, involuntary muscle movements, and/or behavioral changes, leading to neurological deterioration.

The following organization may provide additional information and support:
NIH/National Institute of Allergy and Infectious Diseases

1023   Succinic Semialdehyde Dehydrogenase Deficiency

Synonyms
4-Hydroxybutyric Aciduria
SSADH Deficiency

Succinic semialdehyde dehydrogenase (SSADH) deficiency is a rare inborn error of metabolism that is inherited as an autosomal recessive trait. In individuals with the disorder, deficient activity of the SSADH enzyme disrupts the metabolism of gamma-aminobutyric acid (GABA). GABA is a natural chemical known as a "neurotransmitter" that serves to inhibit the electrical activities of nerve cells (inhibitory neurotransmitter). SSADH deficiency leads to abnormal accumulation of the compound succinic semialdehyde, which is reduced or converted to 4-hydroxybutyric acid, also known as GHB (gamma-hydroxybutyric acid). GHB is a natural compound that has a wide range of effects within the nervous system. The "hallmark" laboratory finding associated with SSADH deficiency is elevated levels of GHB in the urine (i.e., 4-hydroxybutyric or gamma-hydroxybutyric aciduria), the liquid portion of the blood (plasma), and the fluid that flows through the brain and spinal canal (cerebrospinal fluid [CSF]). SSADH deficiency leads to various neurological and neuromuscular symptoms and findings. These abnormalities may be extremely variable from case to case, including among affected members of the same families (kindreds). However, most individuals with SSADH deficiency are affected by mild to severe mental retardation, delays in the acquisition of skills requiring the coordination of mental and physical activities (psychomotor retardation), and delays in language and speech development. In addition, in some cases, initial findings may include diminished muscle tone (hypotonia), an impaired ability to coordinate voluntary movements (ataxia), and/or episodes of uncontrolled electrical activity in the brain (seizures). Some affected individuals may also have additional abnormalities, such as decreased reflex reactions (hyporeflexia); involuntary, rapid, rhythmic eye movements (nystagmus); increased muscular activity (hyperkinesis); and/or behavioral abnormalities.

The following organizations may provide additional information and support:
The Arc (A National Organization on Mental Retardation)
CLIMB (Children Living with Inherited Metabolic Diseases)
Epilepsy Foundation
March of Dimes Birth Defects Foundation
National Institute of Neurological Disorders and Stroke (NINDS)
NIH/National Institute of Child Health & Human Development (Preg & Perinat)
NIH/National Institute of Diabetes, Digestive & Kidney Diseases
Pediatric Neurotransmitter Disease Association (PND Association)

1024 Sudden Infant Death Syndrome

Synonyms
Cot Death
Crib Death
SIDS

Sudden infant death syndrome (SIDS) is the sudden death of any infant that is unexpected by history and in which no adequate cause for death can be found. The disorder occurs in infants under the age of one year.

The following organizations may provide additional information and support:
American Sudden Infant Death Syndrome Institute
First Candle-SIDS Alliance
National Institute of Neurological Disorders and Stroke (NINDS)
National SIDS and Infant Death Resource Center
NIH/National Institute of Child Health and Human Development
SIDS Educational Services, Inc.

1025 Summitt Syndrome

Synonym
Summitt's Acrocephalosyndactyly

Summitt syndrome is an extremely rare genetic disorder characterized by malformations of the head, abnormalities of the hands and/or feet, and obesity. The syndrome is inherited as an autosomal recessive genetic trait. Some researchers believe that Summitt syndrome is one of seven closely related forms of a disorder characterized by characteristic malformations of the head and webbing between several toes and/or fingers (acrocephalopolysyndactyly). The malformations of the head are the result of the premature closings of the seams (cranial sutures) between the bony plates that make up the skull. Of the various forms of this disorder, many geneticists believe that Summitt syndrome is closely related to Carpenter syndrome (acrocephalopolysyndactyly type II).

The following organizations may provide additional information and support:
AboutFace USA
Children's Craniofacial Association
FACES: The National Craniofacial Association
Forward Face, Inc.
Let's Face It (USA)
National Craniofacial Foundation
National Foundation for Facial Reconstruction

1026 Susac Syndrome

Synonyms
Microangiopathy of the Retina, Cochlea, and Brain
Retinocochleocerebral Vasculopathy
Sicret Syndrome

Susac syndrome is an extremely rare neurological disorder characterized by symptoms and signs involving a combination of three systems: disturbances of motion involving the brain, vision loss, and hearing loss. These problems arise as a result of damage to the very small blood vessels (microangiopathy) serving the brain, the retina of the eye, and the snail-like tube that forms part of the inner ear (cochlea). The syndrome, which is sometimes misdiagnosed as multiple sclerosis, usually occurs in young women but men may also be affected. It appears to be autoimmune in nature although the cause remains unknown at this time. The symptoms appear to remain stable (monophasic) with little or no progression. The syndrome is thought self-limiting; that is, improvement is spontaneous although in some cases there may be residual dysfunction. The extent to which Susac syndrome may respond to treatment is not clear.

1027 Sutton Disease II

Synonyms

Aphthous Stomatitis, Recurrent
Aphthous Ulcer, Recurrent
Major Aphthous Ulcer
Major Canker Sore
Major Ulcerative Stomatitis
Periadenitis Mucosa Necrotica, Recurrent Type II
RAU
Recurrent Scarring Aphthae
von Mikulicz's Aphthae
Von Zahorsky's Disease

Sutton disease II is characterized by the recurring eruption of painful inflamed ulcers in the mouth (stomatitis). There may be multiple ulcers of varying sizes. These ulcers in the mouth are commonly called canker sores. Sutton disease II is also known as recurrent aphthous stomatitis. The exact cause of this disease is not fully understood, although it may be due to an abnormal immune response to the bacteria that are normally in the mouth.

The following organization may provide additional information and support:
NIH/National Oral Health Information Clearinghouse

1028 Sweet Syndrome

Synonym

Febrile Neutrophilic Dermatosis, Acute

Sweet syndrome is a rare skin disorder characterized by fever, inflammation of the joints (arthritis), and the sudden onset of a rash. The rash consists of bluish-red, tender papules that usually occur on the arms, legs, face or neck, most often on one side of the body (asymmetric). In approximately 80 percent of cases, Sweet syndrome occurs by itself for no known reason (idiopathic). In 10 to 20 percent of cases, the disorder is associated with an underlying malignancy, usually a hematologic malignancy such as certain types of leukemia. The exact cause of Sweet syndrome is unknown.

The following organization may provide additional information and support:
NIH/National Arthritis and Musculoskeletal and Skin Diseases Information Clearinghouse

1029 Syphilis, Acquired

Synonyms

Lues, Acquired
Venereal Disease

Disorder Subdivision

Neurosyphilis

Syphilis is a chronic infectious disease caused by a spirochete (microorganism) called *Treponema pallidum*. It is transmitted by direct contact with an infected lesion, usually through sexual intercourse. When untreated, syphilis progresses through primary, secondary and latent stages. The early stages of syphilis may not have any detectable symptoms. In some cases, symptoms can remain dormant for years. Eventually any tissue or vascular organ in the body may be affected. Syphilis may also be acquired by the fetus in the uterus (congenital syphilis). Syphilis, especially when detected early, may be cured with appropriate treatment.

The following organizations may provide additional information and support:
Centers for Disease Control and Prevention
NIH/National Institute of Allergy and Infectious Diseases
Sexuality Information and Education Council of the U.S.

1030 Syphilis, Congenital

Synonym

Lues, Congenital

Congenital syphilis is a chronic infectious disease caused by a spirochete (Treponema pallidum) acquired by the fetus in the uterus before birth. Symptoms of this disease may not become apparent until several weeks or months after birth and, in some cases, may take years to appear. Congenital syphilis is passed on to the child from the mother who acquired the disease prior to or during pregnancy. The infant is more likely to have congenital syphilis when the mother has been infected during pregnancy although it is not uncommon for an infant to acquire congenital syphilis from a mother who was infected prior to pregnancy. Symptoms of early congenital syphilis include fever, skin problems and low birth weight. In late congenital syphilis, the symptoms of the disease do not usually become apparent until 2 to 5 years of age. In rare cases, the disease may remain latent for years with symptoms not being diagnosed until well into adulthood.

The following organizations may provide additional information and support:
Centers for Disease Control and Prevention
NIH/National Institute of Allergy and Infectious Diseases

1031 Syringobulbia

Syringobulbia is a neurological disorder characterized by a fluid-filled cavity (syrinx) within the spinal cord that extends to involve the brain stem. It usually occurs as a slitlike gap within the lower brain stem that may affect the lower cranial nerves including sensory and motor nerve pathways by disruption or compression.

The following organizations may provide additional information and support:
American Spinal Injury Association
American Syringomyelia Alliance Project, Inc.
National Institute of Neurological Disorders and Stroke (NINDS)
National Spinal Cord Injury Association

1032 Syringomyelia

Synonym
Morvan Disease

Syringomyelia is a neurological disorder characterized by a fluid-filled cavity (syrinx) within the spinal cord. The cavity, for unknown reasons, often expands during adolescence or the young adult years. The syrinx is situated near the middle of the spine. It may extend across the spinal cord or along almost all of its length.

The following organizations may provide additional information and support:
American Syringomyelia Alliance Project, Inc.
Canadian Syringomyelia Network
Christopher Reeve Paralysis Foundation
World Arnold Chiari Malformation Association

1033 Tangier Disease

Synonyms
Alpha High-Density Lipoprotein Deficieny
Alphalipoproteinemia
Analphalipoproteinemia
Familial Alpha-Lipoprotein Deficiency
Familial High-Density Lipoprotein Deficiency

Tangier disease is an inherited blood disorder involving decreased concentrations of fat compounds in the blood called high density lipoproteins. Large amounts of these compounds may accumulate in certain organs of the body causing tissue discoloration. In later stages, these accumulations may cause organ enlargement and/or blood circulation problems.

The following organizations may provide additional information and support:
National Institute of Neurological Disorders and Stroke (NINDS)
National Tay-Sachs and Allied Diseases Association, Inc.

1034 Tardive Dyskinesia

Synonyms
Linguofacial Dyskinesia
Oral-facial Dyskinesia
Tardive Dystonia
Tardive Oral Dyskinesia
TD

Tardive dyskinesia (TD) is an involuntary neurological movement disorder caused by the use of neuroleptic drugs that are prescribed to treat certain psychiatric or gastrointestinal conditions. Long-term use of these drugs may produce biochemical abnormalities in the area of the brain known as the striatum. The reasons that some people who take these drugs may get tardive dyskinesia, and some people do not, is unknown. Tardive dystonia is believed to be the more severe form of tardive dyskinesia.

The following organizations may provide additional information and support:
National Alliance for the Mentally Ill
National Institute of Neurological Disorders and Stroke (NINDS)
National Mental Health Association
NIH/National Institute of Mental Health
WE MOVE (Worldwide Education and Awareness for Movement Disorders)

1035 Tarsal Tunnel Syndrome

Synonym
Posterior Tibial Nerve Neuralgia

Tarsal tunnel syndrome involves pressure on nerves to the foot causing pain. Persons with this disorder may notice a painful burning or tingling sensation in and around the ankles, sometimes extending to the toes. The disorder usually affects people who stand on their feet for long periods of time.

The following organizations may provide additional information and support:
NIH/National Arthritis and Musculoskeletal and Skin Diseases Information Clearinghouse

---

1036 Tarui Disease

Synonyms
Glycogen Disease of Muscle, Type VII
Glycogen Storage Disease VII
Glycogenosis Type VII
Muscle Phosphofructokinase Deficiency
Phosphofructokinase Deficiency

Tarui disease is a glycogen storage disease. Symptoms of this hereditary metabolic disorder are caused by a lack of the enzyme phosphofructokinase in muscle and a partial deficiency of the enzyme in red blood cells. The enzyme deficiency prevents the breakdown of glucose into energy. Tarui disease is characterized by pain and cramps in muscles during heavy exercise.

The following organizations may provide additional information and support:
Association for Glycogen Storage Disease
Association for Glycogen Storage Disease (UK)
CLIMB (Children Living with Inherited Metabolic Diseases)
Muscular Dystrophy Association
NIH/National Digestive Diseases Information Clearinghouse
Vaincre Les Maladies Lysosomales

1037 Tay-Sachs Disease

Synonyms
Amaurotic Familial Idiocy
Amaurotic Familial Infantile Idiocy
Cerebromacular Degeneration
GM2 Gangliosidosis, Type 1
Hexoaminidase Alpha-Subunit Deficiency (Variant B)
Infantile Cerebral Ganglioside
Infantile Sipoidosis GM-2 Gangliosideosis (Type S)
Lipidosis, Ganglioside, Infantile
Sphingolipidosis, Tay-Sachs

Tay-Sachs disease is a rare, neurodegenerative disorder in which deficiency of an enzyme (hex-

osaminidase A) results in excessive accumulation of certain fats (lipids) known as gangliosides in the brain and nerve cells. This abnormal accumulation of gangliosides leads to progressive dysfunction of the central nervous system. This disorder is categorized as a lysosomal storage disease. Lysosomes are the major digestive units in cells. Enzymes within lysosomes break down or "digest" nutrients, including certain complex carbohydrates and fats. Symptoms associated with Tay-Sachs disease may include an exaggerated startle response to sudden noises, listlessness, loss of previously acquired skills (i.e., psychomotor regression), and severely diminished muscle tone (hypotonia). With disease progression, affected infants and children may develop cherry-red spots within the middle layer of the eyes, gradual loss of vision, and deafness, increasing muscle stiffness and restricted movements (spasticity), eventual paralysis, uncontrolled electrical disturbances in the brain (seizures), and deterioration of cognitive processes (dementia). The classical form of Tay-Sachs disease occurs during infancy; an adult form (late-onset Tay-Sachs disease) may occur anytime from adolescence to the mid 30s. Tay-Sachs disease is inherited as an autosomal recessive trait. The disorder results from changes (mutations) of a gene known as the HEXA gene, which regulates production of the hexosaminidase A enzyme. The HEXA gene has been mapped to the long arm (q) of chromosome 15 (15q23-q24).

The following organizations may provide additional information and support:
Canadian Society for Mucopolysaccharide and Related Diseases, Inc.
CLIMB (Children Living with Inherited Metabolic Diseases)
Instituto de Errores Innatos del Metabolismo
Let Them Hear Foundation
March of Dimes Birth Defects Foundation
National Institute of Neurological Disorders and Stroke (NINDS)
National Tay-Sachs and Allied Diseases Association, Inc.
NIH/National Institute of Child Health and Human Development

1038 Telecanthus with Associated Abnormalities

Synonyms
BBB Syndrome
Dystopia Canthorum
G Syndrome

Hypertelorism with Esophageal Abnormality and Hypospadias
Opitz BBBG Syndrome
Opitz-Frias Syndrome
Opitz-G Syndrome

Telecanthus with associated abnormalities (TCAA) is a very rare genetic disorder affecting the eyes and other parts of the body. Major symptoms include very widely spaced eyes (hypertelorism), urinary tract anomalies, and abnormalities in the development of the mouth and the lips. The G syndrome and the BBB syndrome, both of which were first described by Dr. John M. Opitz, are now believed to be one and the same disorder and identical to TCAA as well. Males and females seem to be almost equally liable to present with this disorder but the effect is usually more severe on males than on females. The disorder is compatible with normal intelligence and life expectancy.

The following organizations may provide additional information and support:
AboutFace USA
The Arc (A National Organization on Mental Retardation)
Children's Craniofacial Association
FACES: The National Craniofacial Association
Forward Face, Inc.
National Craniofacial Foundation
Society for the Rehabilitation of the Facially Disfigured, Inc.

1039 Temporomandibular Joint Dysfunction (TMJ)

Synonyms
Costes Syndrome
Impostor Disease
Myofascial Pain-Dysfunction Syndrome
Pain-Dysfunction Syndrome
Temporomandibular Joint Syndrome
TMJ

Temporomandibular joint (TMJ) dysfunction is a general term for a group of conditions that affect the temporomandibular joint. The TMJs are small joints that connect the lower jaw (mandible) to the temporal bone of the skull. TMJ dysfunction is characterized by pain of the jaw joint that is made worse during or after eating or yawning. It can cause limited jaw movement and clicks and pops during chewing. In severe cases, pain can radiate into the neck, shoulders and back.

The following organizations may provide additional information and support:
American Chronic Pain Association
American Pain Society
NIH/National Institute of Dental and Craniofacial Research
NIH/National Oral Health Information Clearinghouse
TMJ Association, Ltd.

1040 Tethered Spinal Cord Syndrome

Synonyms
Congenital Tethered Cervical Spinal Cord Syndrome
Occult Spinal Dysraphism Sequence
Tethered Cervical Spinal Cord Syndrome
Tethered Cord Malformation Sequence
Tethered Cord Syndrome

Tethered spinal cord syndrome is a disorder characterized by progressive neurological deterioration that results from compression of the lowermost bundle of nerves of the spinal cord (cauda equina). It is most commonly associated with a defective closing of the neural tube (precursor of the spinal column) during embryonic development (spina bifida).

The following organizations may provide additional information and support:
Birth Defect Research for Children, Inc.
International Federation for Spina Bifida and Hydrocephalus
National Institute of Neurological Disorders and Stroke (NINDS)
Spina Bifida and Hydrocephalus Association of Canada
Spina Bifida Association of America

1041 Tetrahydrobiopterin Deficiency

Synonyms
Atypical Hyperphenylalaninemia
Atypical PKU
BH4 Deficiency
Malignant Hyperphenylalaninemia
Malignant PKU

Disorder Subdivisions
Tetrahydrobiopterin Regeneration
Tetrahydrobiopterin Synthesis

Tetrahydrobiopterin deficiency is a rare genetic, neurological disorder present at birth. It is caused by an inherited inborn error of metabolism. Tetrahydrobiopterin is a natural substance (coenzyme) that enhances the action of other enzymes. When tetrahydrobiopterin is deficient, an abnormally high blood level of the amino acid phenylalanine, along with low levels of certain neurotransmitters, usually occurs. To avoid irreversible neurological damage, diagnosis and treatment of this progressive disorder is essential as early as possible in life. The subdivisions of tetrahydrobiopterin deficiency are as follows: (1) tetrahydrobiopterin synthesis, (2) GTP cyclohydrolase I (GTPCH), (3) deficiency 6-pyruvoyl tetrahydropterin synthase (PTPS), (4) deficiency tetrahydrobiopterin regeneration pterin-4-alpha-carbinolamine dehydratase (PCD), (5) deficiency dihydropteridine reductase (DHPR) deficiency.

The following organizations may provide additional information and support:
The Arc (A National Organization on Mental Retardation)
CLIMB (Children Living with Inherited Metabolic Diseases)
National Institute of Mental Retardation
National Institute of Neurological Disorders and Stroke (NINDS)
Syncope Trust & Reflex Anoxic Seizures

1042 Tetralogy of Fallot

Synonyms
Fallot's Tetralogy
Pulmonic Stenosis-Ventricular Septal Defect

Tetralogy of Fallot is the most common form of cyanotic congenital heart disease. Cyanosis is the abnormal bluish discoloration of the skin that occurs because of low levels of circulating oxygen in the blood. Tetralogy of Fallot consists of the combination of four different heart defects: a ventricular septal defect (VSD); obstructed outflow of blood from the right ventricle to the lungs (pulmonary stenosis); a displaced aorta, which causes blood to flow into the aorta from both the right and left ventricles (dextroposition or overriding aorta); and abnormal enlargement of the right ventricle (right ventricular hypertrophy). The severity of the symptoms is related to the degree of blood flow obstruction from the right ventricle. The normal heart has four chambers. The two upper chambers, known as atria, are separated from each other by a fibrous partition known as the atrial septum. The two lower chambers are known as

ventricles and are separated from each other by the ventricular septum. Valves connect the atria (left and right) to their respective ventricles. The valves allow for blood to be pumped through the chambers. Blood travels from the right ventricle through the pulmonary artery to the lungs where it receives oxygen. The blood returns to the heart through pulmonary veins and enters the left ventricle. The left ventricle sends the now oxygen-filled blood into the main artery of the body (aorta). The aorta sends the blood throughout the body. If infants with tetralogy of Fallot are not treated, the symptoms usually become progressively more severe. Blood flow to the lungs may be further decreased and severe cyanosis may cause life-threatening complications. The exact cause of tetralogy of Fallot is not known.

The following organizations may provide additional information and support:
Adult Congenital Heart Association
American Heart Association
Congenital Heart Anomalies, Support, Education, & Resources
Little Hearts, Inc.
NIH/National Heart, Lung and Blood Institute Information Center

1043 Thalamic Syndrome (Dejerine-Roussy)

Synonyms
Central Pain Syndrome
Central Post-Stroke Syndrome
Dejerine-Roussy Syndrome
Posterior Thalamic Syndrome
Retrolenticular Syndrome
Thalamic Hyperesthetic Anesthesia
Thalamic Pain Syndrome

Thalamic syndrome (Dejerine-Roussy) is a rare neurological disorder in which the body becomes hypersensitive to pain as a result of damage to the thalamus, a part of the brain that affects sensation. The thalamus has been described as the brain's sensory relay station. Primary symptoms are pain and loss of sensation, usually in the face, arms, and/or legs. Pain or discomfort may be felt after being mildly touched or even in the absence of a stimulus. The pain associated with thalamic syndrome may be made worse by exposure to heat or cold and by emotional distress. Sometimes, this may include even such emotions as those brought on by listening to music.

The following organization may provide additional information and support:
National Institute of Neurological Disorders and Stroke (NINDS)

1044 Thalassemia Major

Synonyms
Beta Thalassemia Major
Cooley's Anemia
Erythroblastotic Anemia of Childhood
Hemoglobin Lepore Syndromes
Hereditary Leptocytosis, Major
Mediterranean Anemia
Microcythemia
Target Cell Anemia
Thalassemia, Major

Thalassemia major is a rare blood disorder characterized by a marked increase in F hemoglobin and a decrease in the production of certain oxygen carrying proteins in red blood cells (beta polypeptide chains in the hemoglobin molecule). Thalassemia major is the most severe form of chronic familial anemias that result from the premature destruction of red blood cells (hemolytisis). This disease was originally found in people living near the Mediterranean Sea. People with this disorder also have a reduced number of circulating red blood cells (erythrocytes). Thalassemia major is inherited as an autosomal recessive trait.

The following organizations may provide additional information and support:
Anemia Institute for Research and Education
Children's Blood Foundation
Cochrane Cystic Fibrosis and Genetic Disorders Review Group
Cooley's Anemia Foundation, Inc.
March of Dimes Birth Defects Foundation
NIH/National Heart, Lung and Blood Institute Information Center
Sickle Cell Disease Association of America, Inc.
Sickle Cell Disease Foundation of California
Sjældne Diagnoser / Rare Disorders Denmark

1045 Thalassemia Minor

Synonyms
Beta Thalassemia Minor
Hereditary Leptocytosis, Minor
Heterozygous Beta Thalassemia

Thalassemia minor is a rare blood disorder characterized by a moderately low level of hemoglobin in red blood cells (anemia). This disorder is inherited. People with thalassemia minor have one of a pair (heterozygous) of the thalassemia gene. If a person has two copies of the gene, they will have thalassemia major, which is a more serious disease.

The following organizations may provide additional information and support:
Anemia Institute for Research and Education
Cooley's Anemia Foundation, Inc.
March of Dimes Birth Defects Foundation
NIH/National Heart, Lung and Blood Institute
Sickle Cell Disease Association of America, Inc.
Sjældne Diagnoser / Rare Disorders Denmark

1046 Three M Syndrome

Synonyms
3@M Syndrome
Dolichospondylic Dysplasia
Three-M Slender-Boned Nanism (3-MSBN)

Three M syndrome is an extremely rare inherited disorder characterized by low birth weight, short stature (dwarfism), characteristic abnormalities of the head and facial (craniofacial) area, distinctive skeletal malformations, and/or other physical abnormalities. The name "three M" refers to the last initials of three researchers (J.D. Miller, V.A. McKusick, P. Malvaux) who were among the first to identify the disorder. Characteristic craniofacial malformations typically include a long, narrow head (dolichocephaly), an unusually prominent forehead (frontal bossing), and a triangular-shaped face with a prominent, pointed chin, large ears, and/or abnormally flat cheeks. In addition, in some affected children, the teeth may be abnormally crowded together; as a result, the upper and lower teeth may not meet properly (malocclusion). Skeletal abnormalities associated with the disorder include unusually thin bones, particularly the shafts of the long bones of the arms and legs (diaphyses); abnormally long, thin bones of the spinal column (vertebrae); and/or distinctive malformations of the ribs and shoulder blades (scapulae). Affected individuals may also have additional abnormalities including permanent fixation of certain fingers in a bent position (clinodactyly), unusually short fifth fingers, and/or increased flexibility (hyperextensibility) of the joints. The range and severity of symptoms and physicial features may vary from case to case. Three M syndrome is thought to be inherited as an autosomal recessive genetic trait.

The following organizations may provide additional information and support:
Children's Craniofacial Association
Craniofacial Foundation of America
Little People of America, Inc.
MAGIC Foundation for Children's Growth
March of Dimes Birth Defects Foundation
NIH/National Arthritis and Musculoskeletal and Skin Diseases Information Clearinghouse
Restricted Growth Association

1047   Thrombocythemia, Essential

Synonyms

Essential Hemorrhagic Thrombocythemia
Essential Thrombocytosis
ET
Idiopathic Thrombocythemia
Primary Thrombocythemia

Essential thrombocythemia (ET) is one of four rare, myeloproliferative disorders (MPDs). Myeloproliferative means uncontrolled production of cells by the bone marrow. Each of the four myeloproliferative disorders is characterized by overproduction of a different, but essential, type of blood cell resulting in a high concentration of these cells in the blood. Essential thrombocythemia is characterized by overproduction of the precursor cells to blood platelets (megakaryocytes) which, in turn, leads to a vastly increased number of platelets in the blood. Platelets are specialized cells in blood essential for the normal process of clotting. In addition to overproduction of platelets, other symptoms and signs of ET may include an enlarged spleen (splenomegaly); bleeding from the gut, gums and/or nose (hemorrhaging); and constricted or blocked arteries (thrombosis). As many as two-thirds of patients are without symptoms (asymptomatic) upon initial examination. Most patients present with symptoms related to small or large vessel thrombosis or minor bleeding. Presentation with a major bleeding episode is very unusual. Clots may occur in the small arteries of the toes and fingers, leading to pain, warmth, tissue death (gangrene) and/or classic erythromelalgia. Erythromelalgia refers to a syndrome of redness and burning pain in the extremities. The incidence of the thrombotic and bleeding episodes is minimized, but not eliminated, with reduction of the platelet count to normal. In some instances, this chronic disorder may be progressive, evolving in relatively rare cases into acute leukemia or myelofibrosis. The three other myeloproliferative disorders are: Poly-

cythemia vera, in which blood contains abnormally high concentrations of red blood cells (erythrocytes). Chronic myelogenous leukemia, which is characterized by abnormally high concentrations of white blood cells (neutrophils) or their precursor cells, granulocytes. Agnogenic myeloid metaplasia, in which red blood cells have the shape of a teardrop rather than a disc. In this disorder, something goes wrong with the marrow microenvironment that affects the structure of the red blood cell. These blood cells all arise from a common "ancestor," the stem cell, which in its undifferentiated form can become a red blood cell, a white blood cell, or a platelet. The term secondary thrombocythemia is used to describe the problems involving persistent, high blood platelet counts associated with some underlying condition such as malignancy, infection, inflammatory disease, or iron deficiency.

The following organizations may provide additional information and support:
CMPD Education Foundation
Myeloproliferative Mailing List (MPD-SUPPORT-L)
NIH/National Heart, Lung and Blood Institute Information Center

---

1048   Thrombocytopenia-Absent Radius Syndrome

Synonyms

Radial Aplasia-Amegakaryocytic Thrombocytopenia
Radial Aplasia-Thrombocytopenia Syndrome
TAR Syndrome
Thrombocytopenia-Absent Radii Syndrome

Disorder Subdivision

Tetraphocomelia-Thrombocytopenia Syndrome

Thrombocytopenia-absent radius (TAR) syndrome is a rare genetic disorder that is apparent at birth (congenital). The disorder is characterized by low levels of platelets in the blood (thrombocytopenia), resulting in potentially severe bleeding episodes (hemorrhaging) primarily during infancy. Other characteristic findings include absence (aplasia) of the bone on the thumb side of the forearms (radii) and underdevelopment (hypoplasia) or absence of the bone on the "pinky" side of the forearms (ulnae). Other abnormalities may also be present, such as structural malformations of the heart (congenital heart defects), kidney (renal) defects, and/or mental retardation that may be secondary to bleeding episodes in the skull (intracranial hemorrhages) during infancy. TAR syndrome is inherited as an autosomal recessive trait.

The following organizations may provide additional information and support:
American Heart Association
Congenital Heart Anomalies, Support, Education, & Resources
March of Dimes Birth Defects Foundation
NIH/National Heart, Lung and Blood Institute Information Center
Reach: The Association for Children with Hand or Arm Deficiency
Thrombocytopenia Absent Radius Syndrome Association

1049 Thrombocytopenia, Essential

Synonym
TTP

Disorder Subdivisions
Hemolytic-Uremic Syndrome
HUS
Idiopathic Thrombocytopenic Purpura
ITP
Moschowitz Disease, Essential
Purpura Hemorrhagica
Thrombotic Thrombocytopenic Purpura
Werlhof's Disease

Essential thrombocytopenia is a rare blood disease characterized by reduced levels of platelets in the circulating blood. Platelets are essential to blood-clotting and, if they are in short supply, bleeding may occur that can become life-threatening. The platelets are produced in the bone marrow and may be in reduced supply because of (1) impaired or reduced platelet production in the marrow, (2) increased destruction of platelets faster than they can be replaced by the marrow, or (3) the presence of one of several genetic disorders. There are also false thrombocytopenias. Major symptoms include a tendency to bleed excessively into the skin or mucous membranes, especially during menstruation, nosebleeds and bleeding gums.

The following organizations may provide additional information and support:
NIH/National Heart, Lung and Blood Institute Information Center
Thrombocytopenia Absent Radius Syndrome Association

1050 Tietze Syndrome

Synonyms
Chondropathia Tuberosa
Costochondral Junction Syndrome

Disorder Subdivision
Costosternal Chondrodynia

Tietze syndrome is a rare, inflammatory disorder characterized by chest pain and swelling of the cartilage of one or more of the upper ribs (costochondral junction). Onset of pain may be gradual or sudden and may spread to affect the arms and/or shoulders. Tietze syndrome is considered a benign syndrome and, in some cases, may resolve itself without treatment. The exact cause of Tietze syndrome is not known.

The following organization may provide additional information and support:
NIH/National Arthritis and Musculoskeletal and Skin Diseases Information Clearinghouse

1051 Timothy Syndrome

Timothy syndrome (TS) is a rare genetic disorder characterized by a spectrum of problems that include an abnormally prolonged cardiac "repolarization" time (long QT interval). This refers to the process of returning heart cells to a resting state in preparation for the next heartbeat. The prolonged repolarization time predisposes individuals to abnormal heart rhythms (arrhythmias), cardiac arrest and sudden death. Other problems included in the TS spectrum are webbing of fingers and/or toes (syndactyly); structural heart abnormalities present at birth (congenital); a weakened immune system; developmental delays and autism. Timothy syndrome was identified in 2004 by researchers at Children's Hospital Boston, Howard Hughes Medical Institute, University of Utah and University of Pavia, Pavia, Italy. Despite the complexity of health concerns, this syndrome arises from a single, spontaneous mutation in the Ca(v)1.2 Calcium Channel gene called CACNA1C. Multiple body systems are affected by this mutation due to impairment of a very fundamental cell ion channel, found in most tissues and organs, which controls the amount of calcium entering a cell. As a result of this mutation, the ion channel gating closure is affected and cells are overwhelmed by a continuous influx of calcium. The affected gene is active (expressed) in cardiac muscle cells as well as tissues of the gastrointestinal system, lungs, immune system, smooth muscle, testes, and brain, including regions of the brain that are associated with abnormalities observed in autism.

The following organizations may provide additional information and support:
American Heart Association
HOPE (The Heart of Pediatric Electrophysiology)
NIH/National Heart, Lung and Blood Institute Information Center
Sudden Arrhythmia Death Syndromes Foundation

1052 Tinnitus

Synonym
Subjective Tinnitus

Tinnitus is a common condition characterized by the sensation of sound for which there is no external source outside the individual. In other words, people with tinnitus perceive sound when no environmental or external sounds are present. These sounds have been described as clicking, buzzing, and/or ringing. Tinnitus commonly occurs as a side effect of certain drugs and because of other underlying disorders (secondary), especially those of the middle and inner ear (i.e., cochlea). In rare cases, no underlying cause can be found and the condition is termed "idiopathic" tinnitus. Infection, obstruction of blood vessels near the ear, and/or environmental factors have also been implicated as a cause of tinnitus.

The following organizations may provide additional information and support:
American Hearing Research Foundation
American Tinnitus Association
Better Hearing Institute
Meniere's Network
NIH/National Institute on Deafness and Other Communication Disorders (Balance)
Vestibular Disorders Association (VEDA)

1053 Tolosa Hunt Syndrome

Synonyms
Ophthalmoplegia Syndrome
Ophthalmoplegia, Painful
Ophthalmoplegia, Recurrent

Tolosa-Hunt syndrome is a rare disorder characterized by severe headaches and pain around the sides and back of the eye, along with weakness and paralysis (ophthalmoplegia) of certain eye muscles. Symptoms usually affect only one side of the head (unilateral). In most cases, affected individuals experience intense sharp pain and paralysis of muscles around the eye. Symptoms subside without intervention (spontaneous remission) and recur without a distinct pattern (randomly). In addition, affected individuals may exhibit paralysis (palsy) of certain facial nerves and drooping of the upper eyelid (ptosis). Other symptoms may include double vision, fever, chronic fatigue, headaches, a feeling that one's surroundings are spinning (vertigo), pain in the joints (arthralgia), and/or abnormal protrusion of one or both eyeballs (exophthalmos). The exact cause of Tolosa-Hunt syndrome is not known, but the disorder is thought to be associated with inflammation of the areas behind the eyes (cavernous sinus and superior orbital fissure).

The following organizations may provide additional information and support:
American Autoimmune Related Diseases Association, Inc.
National Association for Visually Handicapped
National Headache Foundation
National Institute of Neurological Disorders and Stroke (NINDS)

1054 Tongue Carcinoma

Synonyms
Cancer of the Tongue
Carcinoma of the Tongue

Tongue carcinoma is an oral cancer that is characterized by an ulcerating malignant tumor, usually on the side of the tongue, consisting of scaly (squamous) cells. The tumor may spread to the lymph nodes on the same side of the neck.

The following organizations may provide additional information and support:
American Cancer Society, Inc.
National Cancer Institute
OncoLink: The University of Pennsylvania Cancer Center Resource
Rare Cancer Alliance
Support for People with Oral and Head and Neck Cancer, Inc.

1055 Tongue, Fissured

Synonyms
Cerebriform Tongue
Furrowed Tongue
Grooved Tongue
Lingua Fissurata
Lingua Plicata
Lingua Scrotalis

Plicated Tongue
Scrotal Tongue

Fissured tongue is a benign condition that is sometimes referred to as scrotal or plicated tongue. It is characterized by numerous shallow or deep grooves or furrows (fissures) on the back (dorsal) surface of the tongue. The surface furrows may differ in size and depth, radiate outward, and cause the tongue to have a wrinkled appearance. The condition may be evident at birth (congenital) or become apparent during childhood or later. Reports suggest that the frequency and severity of fissured tongue appear to increase with age. In some cases, fissured tongue may develop in association with infection or malnutrition. In other affected individuals, it may occur with certain underlying syndromes or may be a familial condition, suggesting autosomal dominant inheritance.

The following organizations may provide additional information and support:
NIH/National Oral Health Information Clearinghouse
University of Pennsylvania Smell and Taste Center

1056 Tongue, Geographic

Synonyms
Benign Migratory Glossitis
BMG
Glossitis Areata Migrans
Wandering Rash Tongue

Geographic tongue is a benign, most often asymptomatic, inflammation of the tongue (glossitis) that may come and go and recur over time. The term alludes to the 'map-like' appearance of the irregular, denuded patches on the tongue's surface that may feel slightly sore, 'hot' and itchy. The patches, and the patterns they form, result from the loss of the tiny finger-like projections (papillae) from the tongue's surface.

The following organizations may provide additional information and support:
NIH/National Oral Health Information Clearinghouse
University of Pennsylvania Smell and Taste Center

1057 Tongue, Hairy

Synonyms
Black Hairy Tongue
Black Tongue

Lingua Nigra
Lingua Villosa Nigra

Hairy tongue is an uncommon, benign condition that is also known as black hairy tongue or lingua nigra. It is characterized by abnormal elongation and blackish or dark brownish discoloration or "staining" of the thread-like elevations (filiform papillae) that cover most of the tongue's surface (dorsum linguae). Such changes often begin at the back (posterior) region of the top of the tongue and extend toward the front (anterior) of the tongue's surface but never involve the undersurface. The specific underlying cause of hairy tongue is unknown. However, possible predisposing factors may include poor oral hygiene and overgrowth of pigment-producing bacteria or fungi in the mouth, treatment with certain antibiotic medications, smoking, chewing tobacco, and/or mouthwash use.

The following organizations may provide additional information and support:
NIH/National Oral Health Information Clearinghouse
University of Pennsylvania Smell and Taste Center

1058 Tooth and Nail Syndrome

Synonyms
Dysplasia of Nails with Hypodontia
Nail Dysgenesis and Hypodontia

Tooth and nail syndrome is a rare genetic disorder that belongs to a group of diseases known as ectodermal dysplasia. Ectodermal dysplasia typically affects the teeth, nails, hair, and/or skin. Tooth and nail syndrome is characterized by absence (hypodontia) and/or malformation of certain primary (deciduous) and secondary (permanent) teeth occurring in association with improper development (dysplasia) of the nails, particularly the toenails. In individuals with tooth and nail syndrome, certain primary teeth and/or several secondary teeth may either be absent or widely spaced and/or conical in shape (coniform). In addition, in infants with the disorder, certain nails may be absent at birth and may grow extremely slowly, particularly during the first two to three years of life. The nails may be unusually small and underdeveloped (hypoplastic), with distinctive, abnormal hollowing that causes them to appear spoon shaped. The toenails are usually more severely affected than the fingernails. In rare cases, additional symptoms and findings are present. Tooth and nail syndrome is inherited as an autosomal dominant genetic trait.

The following organizations may provide additional information and support:
National Foundation for Ectodermal Dysplasias
NIH/National Institute of Dental and Craniofacial Research
NIH/National Oral Health Information Clearinghouse

1059 TORCH Syndrome

Synonyms

Torch Infection
Toxoplasmosis, Other Agents, Rubella,
Cytomegalovirus, Herpes Simplex

TORCH syndrome refers to infection of a developing fetus or newborn by any of a group of infectious agents. "TORCH" is an acronym meaning (T)oxoplasmosis, (O)ther Agents, (R)ubella (also known as German Measles), (C)ytomegalovirus, and (H)erpes Simplex. Infection with any of these agents (i.e., Toxoplasma gondii, rubella virus, cytomegalovirus, herpes simplex viruses) may cause a constellation of similar symptoms in affected newborns. These may include fever; difficulties feeding; small areas of bleeding under the skin, causing the appearance of small reddish or purplish spots; enlargement of the liver and spleen (hepatosplenomegaly); yellowish discoloration of the skin, whites of the eyes, and mucous membranes (jaundice); hearing impairment; abnormalities of the eyes; and/or other symptoms and findings. Each infectious agent may also result in additional abnormalities that may be variable, depending upon a number of factors (e.g., stage of fetal development).

The following organizations may provide additional information and support:
Centers for Disease Control and Prevention
Genetic and Rare Diseases (GARD) Information Center
March of Dimes Birth Defects Foundation
National Institute of Neurological Disorders and Stroke (NINDS)
NIH/National Institute of Allergy and Infectious Diseases
NIH/National Institute of Child Health and Human Development

1060 Tourette Syndrome

Synonyms

Chronic Motor Tic
Chronic Multiple Tics
Gilles de la Tourette's disease
Gilles de la Tourette's syndrome
GTS
Habit Spasms
Maladie de Tics
Paulitis
Tics
Tourette's Disorder
TS

Tourette syndrome is a hereditary neurological movement disorder that is characterized by repetitive motor and vocal tics. Symptoms may include involuntary movements of the extremities, shoulders, and face accompanied by uncontrollable sounds and, in some cases, inappropriate words. Tourette syndrome is neither a progressive nor degenerative disorder; rather, symptoms tend to be variable and follow a chronic waxing and waning course throughout an otherwise normal life span. The specific symptoms associated with Tourette syndrome often vary greatly from case to case. The exact cause of Tourette syndrome is unknown.

The following organizations may provide additional information and support:
National Institute of Neurological Disorders and Stroke (NINDS)
New Horizons Un-Limited, Inc.
Sjældne Diagnoser / Rare Disorders Denmark
Tourette Syndrome Association, Inc.
Tourette Syndrome Foundation of Canada
WE MOVE (Worldwide Education and Awareness for Movement Disorders)

1061 Townes-Brocks Syndrome

Synonyms

Deafness, Sensorineural, with Imperforate Anus
and Hypoplastic Thumbs
Imperforate Anus with Hand, Foot and Ear
Anomalies
Townes Syndrome

Townes-Brocks syndrome is a rare genetic disorder present at birth. Symptoms of the disorder and the severity of these symptoms vary from person to person. Major characteristics may include an absence of an anal opening in association with hand, foot and ear abnormalities. Hearing loss or deafness due to lesions or dysfunctions of part of the internal ear or its nerve tracts and centers (sensorineural hearing loss or deafness) is present in some patients.

The following organizations may provide additional information and support:
Genetic and Rare Diseases (GARD) Information Center
Let Them Hear Foundation

1062 Toxic Epidermal Necrolysis

Synonyms

Acute Toxic Epidermolysis
Dermatitis Exfoliativa
Lyell Syndrome
Lyelles Syndrome
Ritter Disease
Ritter-Lyell Syndrome
Scalded Skin Syndrome
Staphyloccal Scalded Skin Syndrome
TEN
Toxic Epidermal Necrolysis

Toxic epidermal necrolysis (TEN) is a rare, sometimes life-threatening unless properly treated, immunological disorder of the skin. It is characterized by blisters that meld into one another to cover a substantial portion of the body (30% and more), and extensive peeling or sloughing off of skin (exfoliation and denudation). The exposed under layer of skin (dermis) is red and suggests severe scalding. Often, the mucous membranes become involved, especially around the eyes (conjunctivitis), but also the mouth, throat, and bronchial tree. Onset can occur at any age. The infantile form frequently follows an infection. In adults the disorder is usually caused by a reaction to taking a pharmaceutical drug, especially anticonvulsants, non-steroid anti-inflammatories, and/or some antibiotics. TEN is thought to be an immunological disorder and to be one of a family of three skin disorders. TEN is considered to be the more serious, followed by Stevens-Johnson syndrome and erythema multiforme, in order of severity of disease.

The following organizations may provide additional information and support:
Dystrophic Epidermolysis Bullosa Research Association of America, Inc. (DEBRA)
NIH/National Arthritis and Musculoskeletal and Skin Diseases Information Clearinghouse
Stevens Johnson Syndrome Foundation and Support Group
University of Pennsylvania Dermatology Clinic

1063 Toxic Shock Syndrome

Synonym

TSS

Toxic shock syndrome is a rare multisystem disease with many widespread symptoms. It is caused by a toxin that is produced and secreted by the bacterium Staphylococcus aureus. The symptoms of toxic shock syndrome may include a sudden high fever, nausea, vomiting, diarrhea, abnormally low blood pressure (hypotension), and a characteristic skin rash that resembles a bad sunburn. Most cases of toxic shock syndrome occur in menstruating females in association with the use of tampons. Other cases may occur in association with postoperative wound infections, nasal packing, or other factors.

The following organizations may provide additional information and support:
Centers for Disease Control and Prevention
NIH/National Institute of Allergy and Infectious Diseases
World Health Organization (WHO) Regional Office for the Americas (AMRO)

1064 Toxocariasis

Synonym

Toxocaral Larva Migrans

Disorder Subdivisions

Covert Toxocariasis; Asymptomatic Toxocariasis
Ocular Larva Migrans (OLM); Ocular Toxocariasis
Visceral Larva Migrans (VLM); Visceral Toxocariasis

Toxocariasis is an infectious disease caused by the parasite *toxocara*, a worm of dogs and cats. Toxocariasis is not limited to pet owners. The eggs of the parasite are passed in the stool and lie dormant in the soil. For unknown reasons, humans become infected when exposed to the eggs passed only by dogs. Infection occurs when there is purposeful or incidental ingestion of soil from hand to mouth through such activities as biting finger nails or inserting recently contaminated objects such as toys into the mouth. (Consequently, the disorder is found disproportionately among children.) Once ingested, the eggs hatch into larvae and burrow into body tissue of all types. The symptoms experienced depend on the number of eggs ingested and the person's immune status, yet a single egg has the potential of causing blindness. Everywhere the larvae travel, they cause inflammation and tissue death.

The following organizations may provide additional information and support:
Centers for Disease Control and Prevention
NIH/National Institute of Allergy and Infectious Diseases

1065 Toxoplasmosis

Toxoplasmosis is an infectious disease that can be caused by contact with a microscopic parasitic organism called *toxoplasma gondii*. This parasitic infection, found worldwide, can either be acquired or be present at birth (congenital). The congenital type is a result of a maternal infection during pregnancy that is transmitted to the fetus and involves lesions of the central nervous system. These lesions may lead to blindness, brain defects and more serious conditions. The disorder may be most severe when it is transmitted to the fetus during the second through sixth month of pregnancy. Millions of people are infected with the Toxoplasma parasite, but very few exhibit symptoms because a healthy person's immune system usually keeps the parasite from causing illness. For people with a compromised immune system, such as those with HIV-AIDs, toxoplasmosis can be a serious disorder. The most common ways in which the acquired form is spread include cleaning a cat's litter box, eating contaminated meat that is raw or undercooked, and drinking contaminated water.

The following organizations may provide additional information and support:
The Arc (A National Organization on Mental Retardation)
Centers for Disease Control and Prevention
NIH/National Institute of Allergy and Infectious Diseases

1066 Transverse Myelitis

Disorder Subdivisions
Ascending Myelitis
Brown-Sequard Syndrome
Concussion Myelitis
Foix-Alajouanine Myelitis
Funicular Myelitis
Subacute Necrotizing Myelitis
Systemic Myelitis

Transverse myelitis is a neurological disorder of the spine caused by inflammation across the spinal cord. It is sometimes associated with the term myelopathy, which refers to any disorder of the spinal cord. However, transverse myelitis is a more specific term for inflammation (myelitis) across the width of the spinal cord (transverse) that results in changed function below this level while function remains normal above. Symptoms are related to movement and sensory functions. This disorder occurs in both adults and children, and typically begins with a rather rapid development of symptoms over the course of several hours, days, or weeks. Symptoms may include lower back pain, weakness in the legs and arms, sensory disturbance, spasms leading to gradual paralysis, and bowel or bladder disfunction. In most cases, this is a disorder that occurs on a single occasion, although a small number of individuals may experience recurrence. The initial occurrence may be followed, over a period of several weeks or months, by a period of recovery, although this does not happen in all cases. There is considerable variability in the degree of recovery achieved. Transverse myelitis is sometimes associated with other diseases, including systemic autoimmune diseases like systemic lupus erythematosus and sarcoidosis. It may be occur following viral or bacterial infections, especially those associated with a rash, spinal cord injuries, or immune reactions.

The following organizations may provide additional information and support:
American Paraplegia Society
Christopher Reeve Paralysis Foundation
National Institute of Neurological Disorders and Stroke (NINDS)
National Spinal Cord Injury Association
Spinal Cord Society
Transverse Myelitis Association

1067 Treacher-Collins Syndrome

Synonyms
Franceschetti-Zwalen-Klein Syndrome
Mandibulofacial Dysostosis
MFD1
TCOF1
TCS
Treacher Collins-Franceschetti Syndrome 1

Treacher-Collins syndrome is a rare inherited disorder characterized by distinctive abnormalities of the head and facial (craniofacial) area due to underdevelopment (hypoplasia) of certain portions of the skull (e.g., supraorbital rims and zygomatic arches). Although the symptoms and physical characteristics associated with Treacher Collins syndrome can vary greatly in severity from patient to patient, craniofacial abnormalities tend to involve the cheekbones, jaws, mouth, ears, and/or eyes. Craniofacial malformations associated with Treacher-Collins syndrome include underdeveloped (hypoplastic) or absent cheek (malar) bones; an incompletely developed, abnormally small lower jaw (mandibular hypoplasia and micrognathia); an unusually large mouth (macrostomia); malformations of the roof of the mouth (palate); and/or dental abnormalities such as misaligned teeth (malocclusion). Affected infants may also have underdeveloped (hypoplastic) and/or malformed (dysplastic) ears (pinnae) with blind ending or absent external ear canals (microtia), resulting in hearing impairment (conductive hearing loss). In addition, infants with Treacher-Collins syndrome may exhibit abnormally downwardly slanted upper and lower eyelids (palpebral fissures), a notching (colobomas) from the outer third of the lower eyelids, and/or additional eye (ocular) abnormalities, resulting in varying degrees of visual impairment in some cases. Some individuals with the disorder have additional physical abnormalities. In approximately 40 percent of cases, Treacher-Collins syndrome is inherited as an autosomal dominant genetic trait, passed on by an affected parent. However, in about 60 percent of cases, a positive family history is not found. Such cases represent new genetic changes (mutations) that occur randomly, with no apparent cause (sporadic).

The following organizations may provide additional information and support:
AboutFace USA
American Society for Deaf Children
Atresia/Microtia Online E-mail Support Group
Children's Craniofacial Association
Council of Families with Visual Impairment
Craniofacial Foundation of America
Ear Anomalies Reconstructed: Atresia/Microtia Support Group
FACES: The National Craniofacial Association
Forward Face, Inc.
Let Them Hear Foundation
Let's Face It (USA)
NIH/National Institute on Deafness and Other Communication Disorders Information Clearinghouse
Treacher Collins Foundation

1068 Tricho Dento Osseous Syndrome

Synonym
TDO Syndrome

Disorder Subdivisions
TDO-I
TDO-II
TDO-III

Tricho-dento-osseous (TDO) syndrome is a rare inherited multisystem disorder that belongs to a group of diseases known as ectodermal dysplasias. Ectodermal dysplasias typically affect the hair, teeth, nails, and/or skin. TDO syndrome is characterized by kinky or curly hair; poorly developed tooth enamel; and unusual thickness and/or denseness (sclerosis) of the top portion of the skull (calvaria) and/or the long bones (i.e., bones in the arms and legs). In some cases, affected individuals also exhibit abnormally thin, brittle nails or premature closure (fusion) of the fibrous joints between certain bones in the skull (craniosynostosis), causing the head to appear abnormally long and narrow (dolicocephaly). There may be three distinct types of TDO syndrome. Some researchers suggest that these variants may be differentiated mainly by whether the calvaria and/or long bones exhibit abnormal hardening (sclerosis), thickening, and/or density. Other symptoms also vary among the three disorder types. TDO syndrome is inherited as an autosomal dominant genetic trait.

The following organizations may provide additional information and support:
AboutFace USA
Children's Craniofacial Association
Craniofacial Foundation of America
FACES: The National Craniofacial Association
National Craniofacial Foundation
National Foundation for Ectodermal Dysplasias
NIH/National Institute of Arthritis and Musculoskeletal and Skin Diseases
NIH/National Oral Health Information Clearinghouse

1069 Trichorhinophalangeal Syndrome Type I

Synonyms
TRP Syndrome
TRPS1

Trichorhinophalangeal syndrome type I (TRPS1) is an extremely rare inherited multisystem disorder. TRPS1 is characterized by thin, sparse scalp hair, unusual facial features, abnormalities of the fingers and/or toes, and multiple abnormalities of the "growing ends" (epiphyses) of the bones (skeletal dysplasia), especially in the hands and feet. Characteristic facial features may include a rounded (bulbous) "pear-shaped" nose, an abnormally small jaw (micrognathia), dental anomalies, and/or unusually large (prominent) ears. In most cases, the fingers and/or toes may be abnormally short (brachydactyly) and curved. In addition, affected individuals may exhibit short stature. The range and severity of symptoms may vary from case to case. In most cases, trichorhinophalangeal syndrome type I has autosomal dominant inheritance.

The following organizations may provide additional information and support:
Human Growth Foundation
Langer-Giedion Syndrome Association
Little People of America, Inc.
National Foundation for Ectodermal Dysplasias
NIH/National Institute of Arthritis and Musculoskeletal and Skin Diseases

---

1070   Trichorhinophalangeal Syndrome Type II

Synonyms
Langer Giedion Syndrome
TRPS2

Trichorhinophalangeal syndrome type II (TRPS2), also known as Langer-Giedion syndrome, is an extremely rare inherited multisystem disorder. TRPS2 is characterized by fine, thin hair; unusual facial features; progressive growth retardation resulting in short stature (dwarfism); abnormally short fingers and toes (brachydactyly); "cone-shaped" formation of the "growing ends" of certain bones (epiphyseal coning); and/or development of multiple bony growths (exostoses) projecting outward from the surfaces of various bones of the body. In addition, affected individuals may exhibit unusually flexible (hyperextensible) joints, diminished muscle tone (hypotonia), excess folds of skin (redundant skin), and/or discolored elevated spots on the skin (maculopapular nevi). Affected individuals may also exhibit mild to severe mental retardation, hearing loss (sensorineural deafness), and/or delayed speech development. The range and severity of symptoms varies greatly from case to case. TRPS2 is due to the absence of genetic material (chromosomal

deletions) on chromosome 8. The size of the deletion varies from case to case.

The following organizations may provide additional information and support:
Langer-Giedion Syndrome Association
Little People of America, Inc.
March of Dimes Birth Defects Foundation
National Foundation for Ectodermal Dysplasias
NIH/National Institute of Arthritis and Musculoskeletal and Skin Diseases
NIH/National Institute on Deafness and Other Communication Disorders Information Clearinghouse

---

1071   Trichorhinophalangeal Syndrome Type III

Synonyms
Sugio-Kajii Syndrome
TRPS3

Trichorhinophalangeal syndrome type III (TRPS3), also known as Sugio-Kajii syndrome, is an extremely rare inherited multisystem disorder. TRPS3 is characterized by fine, thin light-colored hair; unusual facial features; abnormalities of the fingers and/or toes; and multiple abnormalities of the "growing ends" (epiphyses) of the bones (skeletal dysplasia), especially in the hands and feet. Characteristic facial features may include a pear-shaped or rounded (bulbous) nose; an abnormally long prominent groove (philtrum) in the upper lip; and/or abnormalities such as delayed eruption of teeth. In addition, affected individuals also exhibit severe shortening of the fingers and toes (brachydactyly) due to improper development of bones in the hands and feet (metacarpophalangeal shortening). Additional features often include short stature (dwarfism) and/or additional skeletal abnormalities. The range and severity of symptoms may vary from case to case. TRPS3 is thought to have autosomal dominant inheritance.

The following organizations may provide additional information and support:
Human Growth Foundation
Langer-Giedion Syndrome Association
Little People of America, Inc.
March of Dimes Birth Defects Foundation
National Foundation for Ectodermal Dysplasias
NIH/National Institute of Arthritis and Musculoskeletal and Skin Diseases

1072 Trichotillomania

Synonym

Hair-Pulling Syndrome

Trichotillomania is an impulse control disorder characterized by an overwhelming urge to pull out one's own hair, often resulting in patches of baldness. The hair on the scalp is most often affected. The eyelashes, eyebrows, and beard are also affected often. In some cases, affected individuals chew and/or swallow (ingest) the hair they have pulled out (trichophagy). The exact cause of trichotillomania is unknown.

The following organizations may provide additional information and support:
Federation of Families for Children's Mental Health
Locks of Love
National Alliance for the Mentally Ill
National Mental Health Association
National Mental Health Consumers' Self-Help Clearinghouse
NIH/National Institute of Mental Health
Obsessive-Compulsive Foundation, Inc.
Trichotillomania Learning Center

1073 Trigeminal Neuralgia (Tic Douloureux)

Synonyms

Fothergill Disease
Tic Douloureux
Trifacial Neuralgia

Trigeminal neuralgia, also known as tic douloureux, is a disorder of the fifth cranial nerve (trigeminal nerve) characterized by attacks of intense, stabbing pain affecting the mouth, cheek, nose, and/or other areas on one side of the face. The exact cause of trigeminal neuralgia is not fully understood.

The following organizations may provide additional information and support:
American Chronic Pain Association
American Pain Society
National Institute of Neurological Disorders and Stroke (NINDS)
NIH/National Oral Health Information Clearinghouse
Trigeminal Neuralgia Association (TNA)

1074 Trimethylaminuria

Synonyms

Fish Odor Syndrome
Flavin Containing Monooxygenase 2
FMO, Adult Liver Form
FMO2
Stale Fish Syndrome

Trimethylaminuria is a rare disorder in which the body's metabolic processes fail to alter the chemical trimethylamine. Trimethylamine is notable for its unpleasant smell. It is the chemical that gives rotten fish a bad smell. When the normal metabolic process fails, trimethylamine accumulates in the body, and its odor is detected in the person's sweat, urine and breath. The consequences of emitting a foul odor can be socially and psychologically damaging among adolescents and adults. The genetic or primary form of this disorder is transmitted as an autosomal recessive trait. A secondary form of trimethylaminuria may result from the side effects of treatment with large doses of the amino acid derivative L-carnitine (levocarnitine). The metabolic deficiency occurs as a result of a failure in the cell to make a specific protein, in this case, the enzyme flavin-containing monooxygenase 3. Enzymes are nature's catalysts and act to speed up biochemical activities. Without this enzyme, foods containing carnitine, choline and/or trimethylamine-N-oxide are processed to trimethylamine and no further, causing a strong fishy odor. This secondary form of the disorder is a result of an overload of trimethylamine. In this case, there is not enough of the enzyme to get rid of the excess trimethylamine.

The following organizations may provide additional information and support:
CLIMB (Children Living with Inherited Metabolic Diseases)
Genetic and Rare Diseases (GARD) Information Center
Trimethylaminuria Foundation
Trimethylaminuria Midwest Region Foundation

1075 Triplo-X Syndrome

Synonyms

47,XXX Chromosome Constitution
47,XXX Karyotype
47,XXX Syndrome
Triple X Syndrome
Trisomy X

Triplo-X syndrome is a chromosomal abnormality that affects females. Females normally have two

X chromosomes; however, those with triplo-X syndrome carry three X chromosomes (trisomy X) in the nuclei of body cells. No specific pattern of symptoms and malformations (phenotype) has been found to be associated with this abnormal chromosomal make-up (i.e., 47,XXX karyotype). Many affected females appear to have no or very few associated symptoms, while others may have various abnormalities. However, investigators indicate that triplo-X syndrome is a relatively common cause of learning difficulties, particularly language-based disabilities (e.g., dyslexia), in females. Evidence suggests that affected females typically have normal intelligence with IQs that tend to be lower than that of their brothers and sisters (siblings). Mental retardation rarely occurs. Infants and children with triplo-X syndrome may tend to have delayed acquisition of certain motor skills and delayed language and speech development. Affected females often are of tall stature. According to researchers, although sexual development and fertility are usually normal, some may have delayed puberty and/or fertility problems. In addition, in some cases, certain physical abnormalities have been reported, such as a relatively small head, vertical skin folds that may cover the eyes' inner corners (epicanthal folds), and/or other findings. Triplo-X syndrome results from errors during the division of reproductive cells in one of the parents.

The following organizations may provide additional information and support:
International Dyslexia Association
Learning Disabilities Association of America
March of Dimes Birth Defects Foundation
National Center for Learning Disabilities
National Dissemination Center for Children with Disabilities
UNIQUE—Rare Chromosome Disorder Support Group

1076 Triploid Syndrome

Synonyms

2n/3n Mixoploidy
3n Syndrome
Chromosome Triploidy Syndrome
Diploid/Triploid Mixoploidy
Triploidy
Triploidy Syndrome

Triploid syndrome is an extremely rare chromosomal disorder. Individuals with triploid syndrome have three of every chromosome for a total of sixty-nine rather than the normal forty-six chromosomes. Babies with triploid syndrome usually are lost through early miscarriage. However, some infants have been born and survived as long as 5 months. Affected infants are usually small and have multiple birth defects. Those that survive are usually mosaic, meaning that some cells have the normal number of 46 chromosomes and some cells have a complete extra set of chromosomes.

The following organization may provide additional information and support:
UNIQUE—Rare Chromosome Disorder Support Group

1077 Trismus Pseudocamptodactyly Syndrome

Synonyms

Camptodactyly-Limited Jaw Excursion
Dutch-Kennedy Syndrome
Hecht Syndrome
Mouth, Inability to Open Completely, and Short Finger-Flexor Tendons

Trismus-pseudocamptodactyly syndrome is a very rare inherited disorder characterized by the inability to completely open the mouth (trismus), causing difficulty with chewing (mastication) and/or the presence of abnormally short muscle-tendon units in the fingers, causing the fingers to curve or bend (camptodactyly) when the hand is bent back at the wrist (dorsiflexion). Because the fingers are not permanently bent or curved, this particular finding is termed "pseudocamptodactyly" (pseudo meaning false). In addition, the muscle-tendon units of the forearms and/or the legs may also be abnormally short, resulting in limited movements and various deformities of the feet. Individuals with this disorder are slightly shorter than would otherwise be expected (mild short stature). The severity of these physical findings varies from individual to individual. Trismus-pseudocamptodactyly syndrome is thought to be inherited as an autosomal dominant trait.

The following organizations may provide additional information and support:
Genetic and Rare Diseases (GARD) Information Center
NIH/National Arthritis and Musculoskeletal and Skin Diseases Information Clearinghouse

1078 Trisomy

Synonym
Chromosomal Triplication

Trisomies are very rare genetic disorders characterized by a chromosome aberration. Chromosomes are found in the nucleus of all body cells. They carry the genetic characteristics of each individual. Pairs of human chromosomes are numbered from 1 through 22, with an unequal 23rd pair of X and Y chromosomes for males, and two X chromosomes for females. People with a trisomy have an extra chromosome added to one of the normal pairs. Each chromosome has a short arm that is designated "p" and a long arm identified by the letter "q." The triplication of the chromosome may be partial; i.e., with only a portion of the chromosome duplicated. Defects are classified by the name of the abnormal chromosome pair and which portion of the chromosome is affected. For example, 22p+ means that there is an extra short arm added to the 22nd pair of chromosomes. In general, the most common symptom of the trisomies is mental retardation.

The following organizations may provide additional information and support:
The Arc (A National Organization on Mental Retardation)
National Down Syndrome Congress
Support Organization for Trisomy 18, 13, and Related Disorders

1079 Trisomy 13 Syndrome

Synonyms
Chromosome 13, Trisomy 13 Complete
Complete Trisomy 13 Syndrome
D Trisomy Syndrome
Patau Syndrome

Trisomy 13 syndrome is a rare chromosomal disorder in which all or a portion of chromosome 13 appears three times (trisomy) rather than twice in cells of the body. In some affected individuals, only a percentage of cells may contain the extra 13th chromosome (mosaicism), whereas other cells contain the normal chromosomal pair. In individuals with trisomy 13 syndrome, the range and severity of associated symptoms and findings may depend on the specific location of the duplicated (trisomic) portion of chromosome 13, as well as the percentage of cells containing the abnormality. However, in many affected infants and children, such abnormalities may

include developmental delays, profound mental retardation, unusually small eyes (microphthalmia), an abnormal groove in the upper lip (cleft lip), incomplete closure of the roof of the mouth (cleft palate), undescended testes (cryptorchidism) in affected males, and extra (supernumerary) fingers and toes (polydactyly). Additional malformations of the head and facial (craniofacial) area may also be present, such as a relatively small head (microcephaly) with a sloping forehead; a broad, flat nose; widely set eyes (ocular hypertelorism); vertical skin folds covering the eyes; inner corners (epicanthal folds); scalp defects; and malformed, low-set ears. Affected infants may also have incomplete development of certain regions of the brain (e.g., the forebrain); kidney (renal) malformations; and structural heart (cardiac) defects at birth (congenital). For example, characteristic heart defects may include an abnormal opening in the partition dividing the upper or lower chambers of the heart (atrial or ventricular septal defects) or persistence of the fetal opening between the two major arteries (aorta, pulmonary artery) emerging from the heart (patent ductus arteriosus). Many infants with trisomy 13 syndrome fail to grow and gain weight at the expected rate (failure to thrive) and have severe feeding difficulties, diminished muscle tone (hypotonia), and episodes in which there is temporary cessation of spontaneous breathing (apnea). Life-threatening complications may develop during infancy or early childhood.

The following organizations may provide additional information and support:
The Arc (A National Organization on Mental Retardation)
Let Them Hear Foundation
Living with Trisomy 13
March of Dimes Birth Defects Foundation
Support Organization for Trisomy 13/18 and Related Disorders, UK
Support Organization for Trisomy 18, 13, and Related Disorders
UNIQUE—Rare Chromosome Disorder Support Group

1080 Trisomy 18 Syndrome

Synonyms
Chromosome 18, Trisomy 18 Complete
Complete Trisomy 18 Syndrome
Edward's Syndrome
Trisomy E Syndrome

Trisomy 18 syndrome is a rare chromosomal disorder in which all or a critical region of chromosome 18 appears three times (trisomy) rather than twice in cells of the body. In some cases, the chromosomal abnormality may be present in only a percentage of cells, whereas other cells contain the normal chromosomal pair (mosaicism). Depending on the specific location of the duplicated (trisomic) portion of chromosome 18—as well as the percentage of cells containing the abnormality—symptoms and findings may be extremely variable from case to case. However, in many affected infants, such abnormalities may include growth deficiency, feeding and breathing difficulties, developmental delays, mental retardation, and, in affected males, undescended testes (cryptorchidism). Individuals with trisomy 18 syndrome may also have distinctive malformations of the head and facial (craniofacial) area, such as a prominent back portion of the head; low-set, malformed ears; an abnormally small jaw (micrognathia); a small mouth with an unusually narrow roof (palate); and an upturned nose. Affected infants may also have narrow eyelid folds (palpebral fissures), widely spaced eyes (ocular hypertelorism), and drooping of the upper eyelids (ptosis). Malformations of the hands and feet are also often present, including overlapped, flexed fingers; webbing of the second and third toes; and a deformity in which the heels are turned inward and the soles are flexed (clubfeet [talipes equinovarus]). Infants with trisomy 18 syndrome may also have a small pelvis with limited movements of the hips, a short breastbone (sternum), kidney malformations, and structural heart (cardiac) defects at birth (congenital). Such cardiac defects may include an abnormal opening in the partition dividing the lower chambers of the heart (ventricular septal defect) or persistence of the fetal opening between the two major arteries (aorta, pulmonary artery) emerging from the heart (patent ductus arteriosus). Congenital heart defects and respiratory difficulties may lead to potentially life-threatening complications during infancy or childhood.

The following organizations may provide additional information and support:
The Arc (A National Organization on Mental Retardation)
Birth Defect Research for Children, Inc.
Let Them Hear Foundation
Support Organization for Trisomy 13/18 and Related Disorders, UK
Support Organization for Trisomy 18, 13, and Related Disorders
UNIQUE—Rare Chromosome Disorder Support Group

1081 Tropical Sprue

Synonyms
Hill Diarrhea
Tropical Diarrhea

Tropical sprue is a rare digestive disease in which the small intestine's ability to absorb nutrients is impaired (malabsorption). Consequently, nutritional deficiencies and abnormalities in the mucous lining of the small intestine may be present. The exact cause of this disorder is not known, however it may be related to environmental and nutritional conditions in the tropical regions where it is most prevalent.

The following organizations may provide additional information and support:
Centers for Disease Control and Prevention
NIH/National Digestive Diseases Information Clearinghouse

1082 Truncus Arteriosus

Synonym
Buchanan's Syndrome

Truncus arteriosus is a rare type of heart disease that is present at birth (congenital) in which there is a single main blood vessel, rather than the normal two, carrying blood away from the heart. Instead of having a separate pulmonary artery, to carry blood to the lungs, and aorta, to carry blood to the rest of the body, a baby with truncus arteriosus has just one blood vessel leaving the heart which then branches into other blood vessels. Blood from both ventricles of the heart is mixed, resulting in a situation in which some oxygen-rich blood travels needlessly back to the lungs and some oxygen-poor blood travels to the rest of the body. Babies with this condition may have a bluish tint (cyanosis) to their skin, lips, and fingernails. In most cases, truncus arteriosus occurs in conjunction with a missing upper portion of the wall between the ventricles of the heart (ventricular septal defect).

The following organizations may provide additional information and support:
Adult Congenital Heart Association
American Heart Association
Congenital Heart Anomalies, Support, Education, & Resources
NIH/National Heart, Lung and Blood Institute Information Center

1083 Tuberculosis

Synonyms

Consumption
TB

Tuberculosis (TB) is an acute or chronic bacterial infection found most commonly in the lungs. The infection is spread like a cold, mainly through airborne droplets breathed into the air by a person infected with TB. The bacteria causes formation of small tissue masses called tubercles. In the lungs these tubercles produce breathing impairment, coughing and release of sputum. TB may recur after long periods of inactivity (latency) if not treated adequately. Many variations of TB exist and are distinguished by the area of the body affected, degree of severity and affected population. This disease today is considered curable and preventable. It is very rare in the United States but is on an upsurge.

The following organizations may provide additional information and support:
American Lung Association
Centers for Disease Control and Prevention
NIH/National Institute of Allergy and Infectious Diseases
World Health Organization (WHO) Regional Office for the Americas (AMRO)

1084 Tuberous Sclerosis

Synonyms

Bourneville Pringle Syndrome
Epiloia
Phakomatosis TS
TSC1
TSC2
Tuberose Sclerosis
Tuberous Sclerosis Complex
Tuberous Sclerosis-1

Tuberous sclerosis is a rare genetic multisystem disorder that is typically apparent shortly after birth. The disorder may be characterized by episodes of uncontrolled electrical activity in the brain (seizures); mental retardation; distinctive skin abnormalities (lesions); and benign (noncancerous), tumor-like nodules (hamartomas) of the brain, certain regions of the eyes (e.g., retinas), the heart, the kidneys, the lungs, or other tissues or organs. In addition, many affected individuals may have cyst-like areas within certain skeletal regions, particularly bones of the fingers and toes (phalanges). Characteristic skin lesions include sharply defined areas of decreased skin coloration (hypopigmentation) that may develop during infancy and relatively small reddish nodules that may appear on the cheeks and nose beginning at approximately age four. These reddish lesions eventually enlarge, blend together (coalesce), and develop a wart-like appearance (sebaceous adenomas). Additional skin lesions may also develop, including flat, "coffee-colored" areas of increased skin pigmentation (café-au-lait spots); benign, fibrous nodules (fibromas) arising around or beneath the nails; or rough, elevated, "knobby" lesions (shagreen patches) on the lower back. Tuberous sclerosis results from changes (mutations) in a gene or genes that may occur spontaneously (sporadically) for unknown reasons or be inherited as an autosomal dominant trait. Most cases represent new (sporadic) gene mutations, with no family history of the disease. Mutations of at least two different genes are known to cause tuberous sclerosis. One gene (TSC1) has been mapped to the long arm (q) of chromosome 9 (9q34). A second gene for the disease (TSC2) is located on the short arm (p) of chromosome 16 (16p13.3). It remains unclear whether some sporadic and familial cases of the disease may be caused by mutations of other, currently unidentified genes (genetic heterogeneity).

The following organizations may provide additional information and support:
The Arc (A National Organization on Mental Retardation)
Epilepsy Foundation
March of Dimes Birth Defects Foundation
National Institute of Neurological Disorders and Stroke (NINDS)
Rothberg Institute, Inc
Sjældne Diagnoser / Rare Disorders Denmark
Tuberous Sclerosis Alliance
Tuberous Sclerosis Association (UK)
Tuberous Sclerosis Canada (Sclerose Tubereuse)

1085 Tularemia

Synonyms

Deerfly Fever
Rabbit Fever

Tularemia is a rare infectious disease that most often affects small mammals such as rabbits, rodents and hares. It is highly infectious and is most often transmitted to humans by handling an infected animal or being bit by an infected tick or fly. People have not been known to transmit the infection to others. The disease is caused by the bacterium *Francisella tularensis*. The severity of tularemia varies greatly. Some cases are mild and self-limiting; others may have serious complications, and a small percentage (about 2 percent) even become life-threatening.

The following organizations may provide additional information and support:
Centers for Disease Control and Prevention
NIH/National Institute of Allergy and Infectious Diseases
World Health Organization (WHO) Regional Office for the Americas (AMRO)

1086 Turcot Syndrome

Synonyms
Brain Tumor-Polyposis Syndrome
Glioma-Polyposis Syndrome

Turcot syndrome is a rare inherited disorder characterized by the association of benign growths (adenomatous polyps) in the mucous lining of the gastrointestinal tract with tumors of the central nervous system. Symptoms associated with polyp formation may include diarrhea, bleeding from the end portion of the large intestine (rectum), fatigue, abdominal pain, and weight loss. Affected individuals may also experience neurological symptoms, depending upon the type, size and location of the associated brain tumor. Some researchers believe that Turcot syndrome is a variant of familial adenomatous polyposis. Others believe that it is a separate disorder. The exact cause of Turcot syndrome is not known.

The following organizations may provide additional information and support:
American Brain Tumor Association
Brain Tumor Foundation for Children, Inc.
Brain Tumor Society
Brain Tumour Foundation of Canada
Brain Tumour Foundation, United Kingdom
Children's Brain Tumor Foundation
Familial GI Cancer Registry
Familial Polyposis Registry
Hereditary Colon Cancer Association (HCCA)
Hereditary Colorectal Cancer Registry
Intestinal Multiple Polyposis and Colorectal Cancer Registry
March of Dimes Birth Defects Foundation
National Brain Tumor Foundation
National Cancer Institute

NIH/National Digestive Diseases Information Clearinghouse
OncoLink: The University of Pennsylvania Cancer Center Resource
Southeastern Hereditary Colorectal Cancer Registry
Strang-Cornell Hereditary Colon Cancer Program

1087 Turner Syndrome

Synonyms
45, X Syndrome
Bonnevie-Ulrich Syndrome
Chromosome X, Monosomy X
Gonadal Dysgenesis (45,X)
Gonadal Dysgenesis (XO)
Monosomy X
Morgagni-Turner-Albright Syndrome
Ovarian Dwarfism, Turner Type
Ovary Aplasia, Turner Type
Pterygolymphangiectasia
Schereshevkii-Turner Syndrome
Turner-Varny Syndrome
XO Syndrome

Turner syndrome is a rare chromosomal disorder of females characterized by short stature and the lack of sexual development at puberty. Other physical features may include a short neck with a webbed appearance, heart defects, kidney abnormalities, and/or various other malformations. Among affected females, there is also a heightened incidence of osteoporosis, type II diabetes, and hypothyroidism. There appears to be great variability in the degree to which girls with Turner syndrome are affected by any of its manifestations. Turner syndrome occurs when one of the two X chromosomes normally found in women is missing or incomplete. Although the exact cause of Turner syndrome is not known, it appears to occur as a result of a random error during the division (meiosis) of sex cells.

The following organizations may provide additional information and support:
Birth Defect Research for Children, Inc.
Human Growth Foundation
Let Them Hear Foundation
March of Dimes Birth Defects Foundation
New Horizons Un-Limited, Inc.
NIH/National Institute of Child Health and Human Development
Turner Syndrome Society of the United States
Turner Syndrome Support Society (UK)
Turner's Syndrome Society

1088 Twin-Twin Transfusion Syndrome

Synonyms

Fetal Transfusion Syndrome
Fetofetal Transfusion Syndrome
TTTS
Twin-to-Twin Transfusion Syndrome

Twin-twin transfusion syndrome (TTTS) is a rare disorder that sometimes occurs when women are pregnant with identical (monozygotic) twins. It is a rare disease of the placenta, the organ that joins the mother to her offspring and provides nourishment to the developing fetuses. During the development of identical twins, there are often blood vessels in the fetuses' shared placenta that connect their blood circulations (placental anastomoses). In most cases, the blood flows properly through these vessels. However, in twin-twin transfusion syndrome, the blood begins to flow unevenly, with one fetal twin receiving too much blood (recipient) and one receiving too little (donor). The recipient twin may experience heart failure due to continual strain on its heart and blood vessels (cardiovascular system). The donor twin, on the other hand, may experience life-threatening anemia due to its inadequate supply of blood. Such an imbalance in blood flow (i.e., twin-twin transfusion) can occur at any time during the pregnancy, including during delivery. The effects of twin-twin transfusion syndrome can vary in severity from case to case, depending upon when during pregnancy the syndrome occurs, when it is diagnosed, and any treatment that may be given. The cause of twin-twin transfusion syndrome is not fully understood, although it is known that placental characteristics play an important role.

The following organizations may provide additional information and support:
Twin Hope (Twin-Twin Transfusion Syndrome)
Twin to Twin Transfusion Syndrome Foundation

1089 Typhoid

Synonyms

Enteric Fever
Salmonella Typhi Infection
Typhoid Fever

Typhoid fever is a bacterial infection that is rare in the United States. However, it is not rare in many other countries. Major symptoms may include unusually high fever, headache, loss of appetite, fatigue, abdominal pain and diarrhea.

The following organizations may provide additional information and support:
Centers for Disease Control and Prevention
NIH/National Institute of Allergy and Infectious Diseases
World Health Organization (WHO) Regional Office for the Americas (AMRO)

1090 Tyrosinemia, Hereditary

Synonyms

Congenital Tyrosinosis
Fumarylacetoacetase Deficiency
Hepatorenal Tyrosinemia
Hereditary Tyrosinemia Type 1

Disorder Subdivisions

Tyrosinemia Type 1, Acute Form
Tyrosinemia Type 1, Chronic Form

Tyrosinemia type I is a rare genetic metabolic disorder characterized by lack of the enzyme fumarylacetoacetate hydrolase (FAH), which is needed to break down the amino acid tyrosine. Failure to properly break down tyrosine leads to abnormal accumulation of tyrosine and its metabolites in the liver, potentially resulting in severe liver disease. Tyrosine may also accumulate in the kidneys and central nervous system. Symptoms and physical findings associated with tyrosinemia type I include failure to gain weight and grow at the expected rate (failure to thrive), fever, diarrhea, vomiting, an abnormally enlarged liver (hepatomegaly), and yellowing of the skin and the whites of the eyes (jaundice). Tyrosinemia type I may progress to more serious complications such as severe liver disease. Tyrosinemia type one is inherited as an autosomal recessive trait.

The following organizations may provide additional information and support:
American Liver Foundation
Belgian Association for Metabolic Diseases (BOKS)
CLIMB (Children Living with Inherited Metabolic Diseases)
Children's Liver Alliance
Hereditary Tyrosinemia Group (Groupe Aide Aux Enfants Tyrosinemiques Du Quebec)
March of Dimes Birth Defects Foundation
NIH/National Institute of Diabetes, Digestive & Kidney Diseases

1091   Urticaria, Cholinergic

Synonym

Physical Urticaria, Cholinergic Type

Cholinergic urticaria is a relatively common disorder of the immune system characterized by an immediate skin reaction (hypersensitivity) to heat, emotional stress, and/or exercise. Symptoms of the disorder include the appearance of distinctive small skin eruptions (hives) with well-defined borders and pale centers, surrounded by patches of red skin (wheal-and-flare reaction). These red areas are typically intensely itchy (pruritus). Occasionally, cholinergic urticaria may be associated with systemic symptoms such as fever and/or difficulty breathing. The symptoms of cholinergic urticaria may develop due to the reaction of specific immune system antibodies (IgE) to certain antigens, leading to a hypersensitivity response (type I) and the wheal-and-flare reaction that is typical of cholinergic urticaria.

The following organizations may provide additional information and support:
Allergy Information Association
American Academy of Allergy Asthma and Immunology
NIH/National Institute of Allergy and Infectious Diseases

1092   Urticaria, Cold

Disorder Subdivisions

Primary Idiopathic Cold Urticaria
Urticaria Idiopathic Cold (Familial or Acquired)

Cold urticaria is a chronic, reactive skin disorder. It is probably the most common form of physical urticaria (hives). Major symptoms may include abnormal reddening of the skin (erythema), hives and itching after exposure of the skin to cold temperatures. There are two forms of the disorder: essential (acquired) cold urticaria, and familial (hereditary) cold urticaria. The symptoms of the acquired form become obvious in two to 5 minutes after exposure to the triggering substance or situation, while it takes 24 to 48 hours for symptoms of familial cold urticaria to appear. Also, symptoms tend to last longer with the familial form, typically about 24 hours although they may remain for as long as 48 hours. With the acquired form, symptoms tend to last for 1 to 2 hours.

The following organizations may provide additional information and support:
American Academy of Allergy Asthma and Immunology
American Autoimmune Related Diseases Association, Inc.
Asthma and Allergy Foundation of America, Inc.
NIH/National Institute of Allergy and Infectious Diseases

1093   Urticaria, Papular

Synonyms

Angioedema and Urticaria
Giant Urticaria
Hives, Giant
Lichen Urticatus
Quincke Syndrome
Urticaria, Papular

Papular urticaria, more commonly known as "hives," is characterized by local elevated ridges (wheals) and redness (erythema) of the skin. This condition is usually triggered by allergic reactions to insect bites, sensitivity to drugs, or other environmental causes. The first symptom of papular urticaria is usually itching (pruritus), followed by the appearance of small or large wheals. In some cases, swelling of the soft tissues of the face, neck, and hands (angioedema) may also occur. Papular urticaria may be caused by drug allergies, insect stings or bites, desensitization injections (allergy shots), or ingestion of certain foods (particularly eggs, shellfish, nuts, or fruits) by individuals who are allergic to these substances.

The following organizations may provide additional information and support:
Allergy Information Association
American Academy of Allergy Asthma and Immunology
NIH/National Institute of Allergy and Infectious Diseases

1094   Urticaria, Physical

Synonyms

Autographism
Physical Allergy Urticaria

Disorder Subdivisions

Aquagenic Urticaria
Cold Urticaria
Dermatographia
Dermographism

Physical urticaria is a condition in which red (erythematous) allergic skin lesions and itching (pruritus) are produced by exposure to cold temperatures, water, or mild trauma. The disorder occurs most commonly in infants.

The following organizations may provide additional information and support:
Allergy Information Association
American Academy of Allergy Asthma and Immunology
NIH/National Institute of Allergy and Infectious Diseases

1095   Urticaria Pigmentosa

Synonyms
Localized Infantile Mastocytosis
Mastocytosis, Infantile
Nettleship's, E. Disease Type I
Urticaria, Perstans Hemorrhagica
Xanthelasmoidea

Urticaria pigmentosa is a rare skin disorder that is a localized (cutaneous) form of mastocytosis. Some clinicians suggest that urticaria pigmentosa is the childhood form of mastocytosis. Mast cells are specialized cells of connective tissue that release substances such as histamine (a chemical important in the inflammatory process) and heparin (an anti-clotting agent) when the body's alarm mechanism is set off. When mast cells cluster and multiply excessively (proliferate), histamine and heparin are released into the skin (mastocytosis). The characteristic skin lesions of urticaria pigmentosa appear in these areas. Urticaria pigmentosa is generally benign and is usually self-limited. The exact cause of the disease is not known, although some cases may be inherited.

The following organizations may provide additional information and support:
American Academy of Allergy Asthma and Immunology
NIH/National Institute of Allergy and Infectious Diseases

1096   Usher Syndrome

Synonyms
Hereditary Deafness-Retinitis Pigmentosa
Retinitis Pigmentosa and Congenital Deafness

Disorder Subdivisions
Usher Type I
Usher Type II
Usher Type III
Usher Type IV

Usher syndrome is a rare inherited disorder primarily characterized by deafness due to an impaired ability of the auditory nerves to transmit sensory input to the brain (sensorineual hearing loss) accompanied by retinitis pigmentosa, a disorder that causes progressive loss of vision. Researchers have identified three types of Usher syndrome and debated the existence of a fourth type. The age at which the disorder appears along with the severity of symptoms distinguishes the different types of Usher syndrome. Usher syndrome is inherited as an autosomal recessive genetic trait. The possible fourth type of Usher syndrome may be inherited as an X-linked genetic trait.

The following organizations may provide additional information and support:
Alexander Graham Bell Association for the Deaf, Inc.
American Council of the Blind, Inc.
American Foundation for the Blind
American Society for Deaf Children
Blind Children's Center
Blind Children's Fund
Council of Families with Visual Impairment
Deafness Research Foundation
Foundation Fighting Blindness (Canada)
Foundation Fighting Blindness, Inc.
Let Them Hear Foundation
National Association for Parents of Children with Visual Impairments (NAPVI)
National Association for Visually Handicapped
National Federation of the Blind
NIH/National Eye Institute
NIH/National Institute on Deafness and Other Communication Disorders (Balance)
Retinitis Pigmentosa International

1097   VACTERL Association

Synonyms
VACTERLS Association
VATER Association
VATERS Association

VACTERL association is a nonrandom association of birth defects that affects multiple organ systems. The term VACTERL is an acronym with each letter representing the first letter of one of the more common findings seen in affected children: (V) = vertebral abnormalities (A) = anal atresia (C) = cardiac (heart) defects (T) = tracheoesophageal fistula (E) = esophageal atresia (R) = renal (kidney) abnormalities (L) = limb abnormalities. In addition, to the above mentioned features, affected children may also exhibit less frequent abnormalities including growth deficiencies and failure to gain weight and grow at the expected rate (failure to thrive). In some cases, the acronym VATER association is used. Some researchers have added an (S) to the VACTERL or VATER acronym to represent a single umbilical artery instead of the normal two. Mental functioning and intelligence is usually unaffected. The exact cause of VACTERL association is unknown. Most cases occur randomly, for no apparent reason (sporadic).

The following organizations may provide additional information and support:
Birth Defect Research for Children, Inc.
Congenital Heart Anomalies, Support, Education, & Resources
EA/TEF Child and Family Support Connection, Inc.
March of Dimes Birth Defects Foundation
Pull-thru Network
TEF/VATER/VACTRL National Support Network
Tracheo Oesophageal Fistula Support Group (TOFS)
VATER Connection, Inc.

1098   VACTERL with Hydrocephalus

Synonyms
VACTERL Association with Hydrocephalus
VACTERL-H Association
VATER Association with Hydrocephalus

VACTERL with hydrocephalus is an extremely rare genetic disorder in which the multisystem features of VACTERL association occur in addition to hydrocephalus. The term VACTERL is an acronym with each letter representing the first letter of the more common findings seen in affected children: (V) = vertebral abnormalities (A) = anal atresia (C) = cardiac (heart) defects (T) = tracheo-esophageal fistula (E) = esophageal atresia (R) = renal (kidney) abnormalities (L) = limb abnormalities. Hydrocephalus is a condition in which accumulation of excessive cerebrospinal fluid (CSF) in the skull causes pressure on the tissues of the brain, resulting in a variety of symptoms. VACTERL with hydrocephalus is inherited as an autosomal recessive or X-linked recessive trait. VACTERL with hydrocephalus is a distinct genetic disorder separate from VACTERL association, a nonrandom association of birth defects.

The following organizations may provide additional information and support:
Birth Defect Research for Children, Inc.
Congenital Heart Anomalies, Support, Education, & Resources
EA/TEF Child and Family Support Connection, Inc.
Hydrocephalus Association
March of Dimes Birth Defects Foundation
National Hydrocephalus Foundation
Pull-thru Network
TEF/VATER/VACTRL National Support Network
Tracheo Oesophageal Fistula Support Group (TOFS)
VATER Connection, Inc.

1099   Valinemia

Synonyms
Hypervalinemia
Valine Transaminase Deficiency

Valinemia is a very rare metabolic disorder. It is characterized by elevated levels of the amino acid valine in the blood and urine caused by a deficiency of the enzyme valine transaminase. This enzyme is needed in the breakdown (metabolism) of valine. Infants with valinemia usually have a lack of appetite, vomit frequently, and fail to thrive. Low muscle tone (hypotonia) and hyperactivity also occur. The breakdown of valine involves at least seven stages and a deficiency of the appropriate enzyme at any of these stages leads to a disorder of varying severity and rarity.

The following organizations may provide additional information and support:
CLIMB (Children Living with Inherited Metabolic Diseases)
NIH/National Institute of Diabetes, Digestive & Kidney Diseases

1100   Varicella Zoster

Synonyms
Chickenpox
Herpes Zoster
Shingles

Disorder Subdivisions
Herpes Zoster Ophthalmicus
Postherpetic Neuralgia
Zoster Sine Herpete

Varicella zoster is an infectious disease caused by a common virus known as herpes virus, also known as the varicella zoster virus (VZV). During childhood, the virus causes chickenpox (varicella), while, during adulthood, it causes shingles (herpes zoster). Chickenpox is a highly contagious disease characterized by an itchy skin rash and fever. Chickenpox usually begins with mild constitutional symptoms such as a mild headache, moderate fever and discomfort followed by an eruption appearing in itchy groups of flat or elevated spots and blisters, which form crusts. The virus lies dormant in individuals who have had chickenpox as children. Shingles is a painful localized recurrence of the skin rash during adulthood. Shingles occur because the virus is reactivated.

The following organizations may provide additional information and support:
American Pain Society
Centers for Disease Control and Prevention
Jack Miller Center for Peripheral Neuropathy
NIH/National Institute of Allergy and Infectious Diseases
VZV Research Foundation
World Health Organization (WHO) Regional Office for the Americas (AMRO)

1101 Vascular Malformations of the Brain

Synonyms
Cerebral Malformations, Vascular
Intracranial Vascular Malformations
Occult Intracranial Vascular Malformations

Disorder Subdivisions
Arteriovenous Malformation
Cavernous Malformations
Mixed Malformations
Telangiectasis
Vein of Galen Malformation
Venous Malformations

As the name suggests, vascular malformations of the brain is an umbrella term for at least six conditions in which blood vessels of the brain are affected. Such malformations are classified into several types in which the symptoms, severity, and causes vary. These types of VMB are: (1) arteriovenous malformations (AVM), abnormal arteries and veins; (2) cavernous malformations (CM), enlarged blood-filled spaces; (3) venous angiomas (VA), abnormal veins; (4) telangiectasias (TA), enlarged capillary-sized vessels; (5) vein of Galen malformations (VGM); and (6) mixed malformations (MM).

The following organizations may provide additional information and support:
The BrainPower Project
National Institute of Neurological Disorders and Stroke (NINDS)

1102 Vasculitis

Synonym
Angiitis

Vasculitis is inflammation of blood vessels. In individuals with vasculitis, inflammation damages the lining of affected blood vessels, causing narrowing, the formation of blood clots (thrombosis), and/or blockage. As a result, there may be restriction of oxygenated blood supply to certain tissues (ischemia), potentially resulting in pain, tissue damage, and, in some cases, malfunction of certain affected organs. Vasculitis may affect veins and arteries of any type or size; may involve a single organ or many organs and tissues of the body; and may be a primary disease process or occur due to or in association with a number of different underlying disorders. Therefore, the range and severity of symptoms and findings associated with vasculitis may vary greatly. The specific underlying cause of vasculitis is not fully understood. However, in most cases, it is thought to be due to disturbances of the body's immune system.

The following organizations may provide additional information and support:
American Autoimmune Related Diseases Association, Inc.
Autoimmune Information Network, Inc
Central Nervous System Vasculitis Foundation, Inc.
Churg Strauss Syndrome Association
CNSV Network
Jack Miller Center for Peripheral Neuropathy
NIH/National Heart, Lung and Blood Institute Information Center

1103 Vasculitis, Cutaneous Necrotizing

Synonyms
Cutaneous Leukocytoclastic Angiitis
Dermal Necrotizing Angiitis
Hypersensitivity Vasculitis

Cutaneous necrotizing vasculitis (CNV) is characterized by inflammation and tissue damage (necrosis) of blood vessel walls (lumen) and associated skin (cutaneous) lesions. CNV may be a primary disease process or occur as a result of, or in association with, a number of different underlying disorders (e.g., certain infections, certain autoimmune disorders) or other factors (e.g., allergic reaction or hypersensitivity to certain medications, toxins, or inhaled environmental irritants). It is important to determine whether there is an underlying disorder that leads to the CNV before treatment is started. CNV is one of a larger group of disorders involving inflammation and blood vessels known as the vasculitides or the vasculitic syndromes. These syndromes range from modest disorders limited to the skin to more serious ones that may involve various organ systems.

The following organizations may provide additional information and support:
American Autoimmune Related Diseases Association, Inc.
NIH/National Heart, Lung and Blood Institute Information Center

1104 Velocardiofacial Syndrome

Synonyms
Conotruncal Anomaly Face Syndrome
Craniofacial Syndrome
Shprintzen Syndrome

Velocardiofacial syndrome (VCFS), a rare genetic disorder, is characterized by abnormalities of the head and facial (craniofacial) area, heart defects that are present at birth (congenital heart defects), diminished muscle tone (hypotonia), mild small stature, slight delays in the acquisition of skills requiring the coordination of mental and muscular activities (psychomotor retardation), and learning disabilities. Some of those affected also develop psychiatric problems. The syndrome is associated with many different features, and not all will be present in every case. Cleft palate (an opening in the roof of the mouth) and characteristic facial features are among the most common features found with this syndrome. The heart defect most often associated with velocardiofacial syndrome is an abnormal opening in the fibrous partition (septum) that separates the heart's two lower chambers (ventricular septal defect). Additional symptoms and findings often associated with the disorder may include eye (ocular) defects such as clouding of the lenses of the eyes (cataracts) and/or abnormalities of blood vessels in the nerve-rich membranes lining the eyes (tortuous retinal vessels). Psychiatric problems may vary as well, from moderate behav-

ioral change to severe bipolar mood swings or schizophrenia. The range and severity of symptoms vary greatly from case to case. Velocardiofacial syndrome is inherited as an autosomal dominant genetic trait and is sometimes known as chromosome 22q11 deletion spectrum because it is associated with multiple identifying features known to occur as a result of a deletion of genetic material on chromosome 22. This syndrome is also associated with other names (see synonyms).

The following organizations may provide additional information and support:
22q and You Center
American Heart Association
Chromosome 22 Central
FACES: The National Craniofacial Association
National Foundation for Facial Reconstruction
NIH/National Institute on Deafness and Other Communication Disorders Information Clearinghouse
NIH/National Oral Health Information Clearinghouse
Velo-Cardio-Facial Syndrome Educational Foundation

1105 Ventricular Septal Defects

Synonyms
Congenital Ventricular Defects
Hole in the Heart
VSD

Disorder Subdivisions
Common Ventricle
Cor Triloculare Biatriatum
Eisenmenger Syndrome
Maladie de Roger
Roger Disease

Ventricular septal defects are heart defects that are present at birth (congenital). The normal heart has four chambers. The two upper chambers, known as atria, are separated from each other by a fibrous partition known as the atrial septum. The two lower chambers are known as ventricles and are separated from each other by the ventricular septum. Valves connect the atria (left and right) to their respective ventricles. The aorta, the main vessel of arterial circulation, carries blood from the left ventricle and away from the heart. Ventricular septal defects can occur in any portion of the ventricular septum. The size and location of the defect determine the severity of the symptoms. Small ventricular septal defects can close on their own (spontaneously) or become less significant as the child matures and grows. Moderately-sized defects can cause congestive heart failure, which is characterized by an abnormally rapid rate of breathing (tachypnea), wheezing, unusually fast heartbeat (tachycardia), enlarged liver (hepatomegaly), and/or failure to thrive. Large ventricular septal defects can cause life-threatening complications during infancy. Persistent elevation of the pressure within the artery that carries blood away from the heart and to the lungs (pulmonary artery) can cause permanent damage to the lungs. The exact cause of ventricular septal defects is not fully understood.

The following organizations may provide additional information and support:
Adult Congenital Heart Association
American Heart Association
Congenital Heart Anomalies, Support, Education, & Resources
Little Hearts, Inc.
NIH/National Heart, Lung and Blood Institute Information Center

1106 Very Long Chain Acyl CoA Dehydrogenase Deficiency (LCAD)

Synonyms
ACADL
LCAD Deficiency
Long Chain Acyl-CoA Dehydrogenase Deficiency
Nonketotic Hypoglycemia Caused by Deficiency of Acyl-CoA Dehydrogenase
VLCAD

Very long-chain acyl-CoA dehydrogenase deficiency (VLCAD) is a rare genetic disorder of fatty acid metabolism that is transmitted as an autosomal recessive trait. It occurs when an enzyme needed to break down certain very long-chain fatty acids is missing or not working properly. VLCAD is one of the metabolic diseases known as fatty acid oxidation (FOD) diseases. In the past, the name long-chain acyl-CoA dehydrogenase deficiency (LCAD) was applied to one such disease, but today it is believed that all cases once thought to be LCAD are actually VLCAD. The breakdown of fatty acids takes place in the mitochondria found in each cell. The mitochondria are small, well-defined bodies that are found in the cytoplasm of cells and in which the body generates energy from the breakdown of complex substances into simpler ones (mitochondrial oxidation). There appear to be two forms of VLCAD: an early-onset, severe form which, if unrecognized and undiag-

nosed, may lead to extreme weakness of the heart muscles (cardiomyopathy) and may be life-threatening (VLCAD-C), and a later-onset, milder form, sometimes referred to as VLCAD-H, that is characterized by repeated bouts of low blood sugar (hypoglycemia). Since the advent of expanded newborn screening programs using tandem mass spectrometry technology, more VLCAD infants are being detected earlier in the course of the disorder than in the past.

The following organizations may provide additional information and support:
CLIMB (Children Living with Inherited Metabolic Diseases)
FOD (Fatty Oxidation Disorders) Family Support Group
NIH/National Digestive Diseases Information Clearinghouse
Organic Acidaemias UK
Organic Acidemia Association
United Mitochondrial Disease Foundation

1107 Vitamin B12 Deficiency

Synonym
Cobalamin Deficiency

Vitamin B12 deficiency is characterized by an abnormally low blood level of this vitamin. The disorder can be caused by a poor diet, inadequate absorption or utilization of B12 that may follow stomach and intestinal surgery or an increase in certain intestinal organisms. The deficiency causes changes in the blood and the central nervous system. Injection of this vitamin usually cures the disorder if the underlying cause can be corrected.

The following organizations may provide additional information and support:
American Autoimmune Related Diseases Association, Inc.
Cobalamin Network
Jack Miller Center for Peripheral Neuropathy
NIH/National Digestive Diseases Information Clearinghouse
NIH/National Heart, Lung and Blood Institute

1108 Vitiligo

Synonym
Leukoderma

Vitiligo is a dermatological condition characterized by the appearance of white patches of skin on different parts of the body as a result of the destruction of the cells that make pigment (melanocytes). This may vary from one or two white spots on the skin to large areas of depigmentation. Vitiligo is not contagious. It seems to occur more often among people who have certain autoimmune diseases. For some people, although not for everyone, the depigmentation is progressive.

The following organizations may provide additional information and support:
American Vitiligo Research Foundation, Inc.
Autoimmune Information Network, Inc
National Vitiligo Foundation
NIH/National Institute of Arthritis and Musculoskeletal and Skin Diseases

---

1109 Vogt-Koyanagi-Harada Syndrome

Synonyms
> *Alopecia-Poliosis-Uveitis-Vitiligo-Deafness-Cutaneous-Uveo-Oto Syndrome*
> *Harada Syndrome*
> *Uveomeningitis Syndrome*
> *VKH Syndrome*

Vogt-Koyanagi-Harada syndrome is a rare disease of unknown origin that affects many body systems, including the eyes, ears, skin, and the covering of the brain and spinal cord (the meninges). The most noticeable symptom is a rapid loss of vision. There may also be neurological signs such as severe headache, vertigo, nausea, and drowsiness. Loss of hearing, and loss of hair (alopecia) and skin color may occur along, with whitening (loss of pigmentation) of the hair and eyelashes (poliosis).

The following organizations may provide additional information and support:
American Autoimmune Related Diseases Association, Inc.
National Association for Visually Handicapped
National Institute of Neurological Disorders and Stroke (NINDS)
NIH/National Eye Institute

1110 Von Gierke Disease

Synonyms
> *Glycogen Storage Disease I*
> *Glycogenosis Type I*
> *Hepatorenal Glycogenosis*

Disorder Subdivisions
> *Glycogenosis Type IA*
> *Glycogenosis Type IB*
> *Glucose-6-Phospate Translocase Deficiency*
> *Glucose-6-Phosphate Transport Defect*
> *Glucose-6-Phosphatase Deficiency*

Von Gierke disease is a glycogen storage disease. This hereditary metabolic disorder is caused by an inborn lack of the enzyme glucose-6-phosphatase. This enzyme is needed to convert the main carbohydrate storage material (glycogen) into sugar (glucose), which the body uses for its energy needs. A deficiency causes deposits of excess glycogen in the liver and kidney cells.

The following organizations may provide additional information and support:
Association for Glycogen Storage Disease
Association for Glycogen Storage Disease (UK)
CLIMB (Children Living with Inherited Metabolic Diseases)
Children's Fund for Glycogen Storage Disease Research, Inc.
NIH/National Institute of Diabetes, Digestive & Kidney Diseases

---

1111 Von Hippel-Lindau Disease

Synonyms
> *Angiomatosis Retinae*
> *Angiophakomatosis Retinae et Cerebelli*
> *Cerebelloretinal Hemangioblastomatosis*
> *Hippel Disease*
> *Hippel-Lindau Syndrome*
> *HLS*
> *Lindau Disease*
> *Retinocerebellar Angiomatosis*
> *VHL*

Von Hippel-Lindau disease is a rare inherited multisystem disorder characterized by the abnormal growth of blood vessels in certain parts of the body (angiomatosis). Very small blood vessels (capillaries) "knot" together to form benign growths known as angiomas. These may develop in the retinas of the eyes (retinoangioma) or in the brain (cerebellar hemangioblastoma). Benign growths may also occur in other parts of the brain, spinal cord, the adrenal glands (pheochromocytoma), and other parts of the body. The symptoms of von Hippel-Lindau disease vary greatly and depend on the size and location of the growths. People with von Hippel-Lindau disease are also genetically predisposed to certain types of malignant tumors (i.e., renal cell carcinoma).

The following organizations may provide additional information and support:
Genetic and Rare Diseases (GARD) Information Center
National Institute of Neurological Disorders and Stroke (NINDS)
NIH/National Eye Institute
Sjældne Diagnoser / Rare Disorders Denmark
VHL Family Alliance
VHL Family Alliance, UK

1112 von Willebrand Disease

Synonyms

Angiohemophilia
Constitutional Thrombopathy
Minot-von Willebrand Disease
Pseudohemophilia
Vascular Hemophilia
Willebrand-Juergens Disease

von Willebrand disease is a hereditary blood clotting disorder characterized by prolonged bleeding. Blood clotting is slowed due to a deficiency of the von Willebrand factor protein and factor VIII protein (the factor VIII complex). Also, platelets do not stick normally causing excessively slow clotting time. Increased risk of excessive bleeding following surgery, dental procedures or injury occurs in individuals with this disorder. The tendency to prolonged bleeding usually decreases with age.

The following organizations may provide additional information and support:
Canadian Hemophilia Society
Hemophilia Federation of America
Irish Haemophilia Society
National Hemophilia Foundation
NIH/National Heart, Lung and Blood Institute Information Center
World Federation of Hemophilia

1113 Vulvovaginitis

Synonyms

Bacterial Vaginitis
Genital Candidiasis
Nonspecific Vaginitis
Trichomoniasis
Vaginitis
Vaginitis, Gardnerella Vaginalis
Vaginitis, Haemophilus Vaginalis
Yeast Infection, Vaginal

Vulvovaginitis is a common bacterial infection characterized by the simultaneous inflammation of the external parts of the female genital organs (vulva) and the canal that leads from the uterus to the external opening (vagina). It is one of the most frequent causes of genital symptoms in women. When only the vagina is inflamed, the disorder is called vaginitis. The symptoms and treatments of vulvovaginitis depend on the specific bacteria that caused the disorder. The most common types of vulvovaginitis are genital candidiasis (also called yeast infection), trichomoniasis, and nonspecific vaginitis (also called haemophilus vaginalis vaginitis, bacterial vaginitis or gardnerella vaginalis vaginitis). Some types of vulvovaginitis are rarer than others. Vulvovaginitis occurs when the normal acid/alkaline balance of the vagina is disturbed. Yeast, fungi and other harmful organisms that are normally present may grow in excessive amounts causing infection of the vaginal walls.

The following organizations may provide additional information and support:
Centers for Disease Control and Prevention
National Vulvodynia Association
NIH/National Institute of Allergy and Infectious Diseases

1114 Waardenburg Syndrome

Synonym
WS

Disorder Subdivisions

Waardenburg Syndrome Type I (WS1)
Waardenburg Syndrome Type II (WS2)
Waardenburg Syndrome Type IIA (WS2A)
Waardenburg Syndrome Type IIB (WS2B)
Waardenburg Syndrome Type III (WS3)
Waardenburg Syndrome Type IV (WS4)

Waardenburg syndrome is a genetic disorder that may be evident at birth (congenital). The range and severity of associated symptoms and findings may vary greatly from case to case. However, primary features often include distinctive facial abnormalities; unusually diminished coloration (pigmentation) of the hair, the skin, and/or the iris of both eyes (irides); and/or congenital deafness. More specifically, some affected individuals may have an unusually wide nasal bridge due to sideways (lateral) displacement of the inner angles (canthi) of the eyes (dystopia canthorum). In addition, pigmentary abnormalities may include a white lock of hair growing above the forehead (white forelock); premature graying or whitening of the hair; differences in the coloration of the two irides or in different regions of the same iris (heterochromia irides); and/or patchy, abnormally light (depigmented) regions of skin (leukoderma). Some affected individuals may also have hearing impairment due to abnormalities of the inner ear (sensorineural deafness). Researchers have described different types of Waardenburg syndrome (WS), based upon associated symptoms and specific genetic findings. For example, Waardenburg syndrome type I (WS1) is characteristically associated with sideways displacement of the inner angles of the eyes (i.e., dystopia canthorum), yet type II (WS2) is not associated with this feature. In addition, WS1 and WS2 are known to be caused by alterations (mutations) of different genes. Another form, known as type III (WS3), has been described in which characteristic facial, eye (ocular), and hearing (auditory) abnormalities may be associated with distinctive malformations of the arms and hands (upper limbs). A fourth form, known as WS4 or Waardenburg-Hirschsprung disease, may be characterized by primary features of WS in association with Hirschsprung disease. The latter is a digestive (gastrointestinal) disorder in which there is absence of groups of specialized nerve cell bodies within a region of the smooth (involuntary) muscle wall of the large intestine. In most cases, Waardenburg syndrome is transmitted as an autosomal dominant trait. A number of different disease genes have been identified that may cause Waardenburg syndrome in certain individuals or families (kindreds).

The following organizations may provide additional information and support:
Alexander Graham Bell Association for the Deaf, Inc.
American Foundation for the Blind
Council of Families with Visual Impairment
FACES: The National Craniofacial Association
Let Them Hear Foundation
March of Dimes Birth Defects Foundation
National Association for Visually Handicapped
National Association of the Deaf
National Craniofacial Foundation
National Crisis Center for the Deaf
National Organization for Albinism and Hypopigmentation
National Vitiligo Foundation
NIH/National Eye Institute

1115 WAGR Syndrome

Synonyms
WAGR Complex
Wilms' Tumor-Aniridia-Genitourinary Anomalies-Mental Retardation Syndrome
Wilms' Tumor-Aniridia-Gonadoblastoma-Mental Retardation Syndrome

Disorder Subdivisions
AGR Triad
Aniridia-Ambiguous Genitalia-Mental Retardation
Aniridia-Wilms' Tumor Association
Aniridia-Wilms' Tumor-Gonadoblastoma
AWTA

WAGR syndrome is a rare genetic syndrome in which there is a predisposition to several conditions, including certain malignancies, distinctive eye abnormalities, and/or mental retardation. "WAGR" is an acronym for the characteristic abnormalities associated with the syndrome. The acronym stands for (W)ilms' Tumor, the most common form of kidney cancer in children; (A)niridia, partial or complete absence of the colored region of the eye(s) (iris or irides); (G)onadoblastoma, cancer of the cells that form the testes in males or the ovaries in females (gonads); and Mental (R)etardation. A combination of two or more of these conditions must be present for an individual to be diagnosed with WAGR syndrome. The clinical picture varies, depending upon the combination of associated abnormalities. The only feature that has been present in all documented cases of WAGR syndrome, with only one known exception, is aniridia. WAGR syndrome is caused by defects (mutations) of adjacent genes on a region of chromosome 11 (11p13). In most cases, such genetic changes (e.g., deletions at band 11p13) occur spontaneously during early embryonic development (de novo) for unknown reasons (sporadic).

The following organizations may provide additional information and support:
Ambiguous Genitalia Support Network
American Cancer Society, Inc.
American Kidney Fund, Inc.
Aniridia Network
Candlelighters Childhood Cancer Foundation
Glaucoma Research Foundation
International WAGR Syndrome Association
March of Dimes Birth Defects Foundation

National Eye Research Foundation
National Kidney Foundation
NIH/National Eye Institute

1116 Waldenstrom Macroglobulinemia

Synonyms

Hyperglobulinemic Purpura
Macroglobulinemia
Waldenstroem's Macroglobulinemia
Waldenstrom's Purpura
Waldenstrom's Syndrome

Waldenstrom macroglobulinemia (WMG) is a malignant disorder of the blood and lymph, characterized by the excess production of large antibodies (macroglobulins) by plasma cells and/or abnormal lymphocytes. Large numbers of these lymphocytes, combined with abnormal immunoglobulin-M (Ig-M), grow in the bone marrow cavity. In its early stages, it is termed a monoclonal gammopathy of undetermined significance (MGUS). These disorders, monoclonal gammopathies or plasma cell dyscrasias, are characterized as the uncontrolled growth of a single clone (monoclonal) of plasma cells, which results in the abnormal accumulation of M-proteins (also known as immunoglobulin M or lgM) in the blood. M-proteins are supposed to fight foreign substances in the body such as viruses and bacteria. MGUS means that the synthesis of normal immunoglobulins by a particular line of cells is disrupted, resulting in the production of abnormal proteins. This condition, at least at the outset, usually requires no treatment until symptoms appear, sometimes years after diagnosis.

The following organizations may provide additional information and support:
American Cancer Society, Inc.
International Waldenstrom's Macroglobulinemia Foundation
NIH/National Heart, Lung and Blood Institute

1117 Waldmann Disease

Synonyms

Dysproteinemia, Familial
Enteropathy, Hypercatabolic Protein-Losing
Familial Hypoproteinemia with Lymphangiectatic Enteropathy
Hypoproteinemia, Idiopathic
Intestinal Lymphangiectasia
Intestinal Lymphangiectasis
Lymphangiectasia, Primary Intestinal
Lymphangiectasis, Primary Intestinal
Lymphangiectatic Protein-Losing Enteropathy
Lymphedema, Neonatal due to Exudative Enteropathy
Protein-Losing Enteropathy Secondary to Congestive Heart Failure

Waldmann disease is a rare digestive disorder characterized by abnormally enlarged (dilatation) lymph vessels supplying the lining (lamina propria) of the small intestine. The main symptoms are abdominal discomfort and swelling of the limbs. The disorder may be present at birth (congenital) or acquired.

The following organizations may provide additional information and support:
Genetic and Rare Diseases (GARD) Information Center
March of Dimes Birth Defects Foundation
National Lymphatic and Venous Diseases Foundation, Inc.
NIH/National Digestive Diseases Information Clearinghouse

1118 Walker-Warburg Syndrome

Synonyms

Cerebroocular Dysgenesis
Cerebroocular Dysplasia-Muscular Dystrophy Syndrome
Chemke Syndrome
COD
COD-MD Syndrome
HARD +/-E Syndrome
HARD Syndrome
Hydrocephalus, Agyria, and Retinal Dysplasia
Pagon Syndrome
Warburg Syndrome

Walker-Warburg syndrome is a rare disorder that is inherited as an autosomal recessive genetic trait. Walker-Warburg syndrome is also known as HARD +/-E syndrome, which is an acronym for (H)ydrocephalus, (A)gyria, (R)etinal (D)ysplasia and, in some cases, (E)ncephalocele. The most consistent features of this disorder are a lack of normal folds of the brain (lissencephaly), malformations of the back portion of the brain (cerebellum), abnormalities of the retina of the eye, and progressive degeneration and weakness of the voluntary muscles (congenital muscular dystrophy).

The following organizations may provide additional information and support:
Guardians of Hydrocephalus Research Foundation
Hydrocephalus Association
Lissencephaly Network, Inc.
National Hydrocephalus Foundation
National Institute of Neurological Disorders and Stroke (NINDS)

1119 Wandering Spleen

Synonyms
Displaced Spleen
Drifting Spleen
Floating Spleen
Pelvic Spleen
Splenic Ptosis
Splenoptosis
Systopic Spleen
WS

Congenital wandering spleen is a very rare, randomly distributed, birth defect characterized by the absence or weakness of one or more of the ligaments that hold the spleen in its normal position in the upper left abdomen. The disorder is not genetic in origin. Instead of ligaments, the spleen is attached by a stalk-like tissue supplied with blood vessels (vascular pedicle). If the pedicle is twisted in the course of the movement of the spleen, the blood supply may be interrupted or blocked (ischemia) to the point of severe damage to the blood vessels (infarction). Because there is little or nothing to hold it in place the spleen "wanders" in the lower abdomen or pelvis where it may be mistaken for an unidentified abdominal mass. Symptoms of wandering spleen are typically those associated with an abnormally large size of the spleen (splenomegaly) or the unusual position of the spleen in the abdomen. Enlargement is most often the result of twisting (torsion) of the splenic arteries and veins or, in some cases, the formation of a blood clot (infarct) in the spleen. "Acquired" wandering spleen may occur during adulthood due to injuries or other underlying conditions that may weaken the ligaments that hold the spleen in its normal position (e.g., connective tissue disease or pregnancy).

1120 Weaver Syndrome

Synonyms
Weaver-Smith Syndrome
WSS

Weaver syndrome is characterized by rapid growth. Usually starting before birth (prenatal onset), physical growth and bone development (maturation) can occur more quickly than average. Other symptoms can include increased muscle tone (hypertonia) with exaggerated reflexes (spasticity), slow development of voluntary movements (psychomotor retardation), specific physical characteristics, and/or foot deformities. Babies with this syndrome have a hoarse low-pitched cry.

The following organizations may provide additional information and support:
Human Growth Foundation
Little People of America, Inc.
Little People's Research Fund, Inc.
MAGIC Foundation for Children's Growth
Weaver Syndrome Network

1121 Wegener's Granulomatosis

Synonyms
Necrotizing Respiratory Granulomatosis
Pathergic Granulomatosis

Wegener's granulomatosis is an uncommon disorder characterized by inflammation of blood vessels (vasculitis) that results in damage to various organ systems of the body, most often the respiratory tract and kidneys. Symptoms may include ulcerations of the mucous membranes in the nose with secondary bacterial infection, a persistent runny nose, sinus pain, and chronic middle ear infection (otitis media) potentially resulting in hearing loss. In some cases, kidney abnormalities may progress to kidney failure, a serious complication. If the lungs are affected, a cough, expectoration of blood (hemoptysis), and inflammation of the thin membrane lining the outside of the lungs and the inside of the lung may be present. The exact cause of Wegener's granulomatosis is not known.

The following organizations may provide additional information and support:
American Kidney Fund, Inc.
American Lung Association
Autoimmune Information Network, Inc
National Kidney Foundation
NIH/National Heart, Lung and Blood Institute Information Center
Wegener's Granulomatosis Association

1122 Weil Syndrome

Synonyms

Fiedler Disease
Icteric Leptospirosis
Icterohemorrhagic Leptospirosis
Infectious Jaundice
Lancereaux-Mathieu-Weil Spirochetosis
Leptospiral Jaundice
Spirochetal Jaundice
Weil Disease

Weil syndrome, a rare infectious disorder, is a severe form of the bacterial infection caused by *Leptospira* bacteria known as leptospirosis. Weil syndrome is characterized by dysfunction of the kidneys and liver, abnormal enlargement of the liver (hepatomegaly), persistent yellowing of the skin, mucous membranes, and whites of the eyes (jaundice), and/or alterations in consciousness. In most cases, Weil syndrome occurs among individuals who are exposed to affected animals.

The following organizations may provide additional information and support:
Centers for Disease Control and Prevention
NIH/National Institute of Allergy and Infectious Diseases
World Health Organization (WHO) Regional Office for the Americas (AMRO)

1123 Weill-Marchesani Syndrome

Synonyms

Congenital Mesodermal Dysmorphodystrophy
Mesodermal Dysmorphodystrophy,
Brachymorphic Type, Congenital
Spherophakia-Brachymorphia Syndrome
WM Syndrome
WMS

Weill-Marchesani syndrome is a rare, genetic disorder characterized by short stature; an unusually short, broad head (brachycephaly) and other facial abnormalities; hand defects, including unusually short fingers (brachydactyly); and distinctive eye (ocular) abnormalities. These typically include unusually small, round lenses of the eyes (spherophakia) that may be prone to dislocating (ectopia lentis) as well as other ocular defects. Due to such abnormalities, affected individuals may have varying degrees of visual impairment, ranging from nearsightedness (myopia) to blindness. Researchers suggest that Weill-Marchesani syndrome may have autosomal recessive or autosomal dominant inheritance.

The following organizations may provide additional information and support:
Glaucoma Research Foundation
Human Growth Foundation
International Glaucoma Association
Little People of America, Inc.
Little People's Research Fund, Inc.
MAGIC Foundation for Children's Growth
March of Dimes Birth Defects Foundation
National Association for Visually Handicapped
NIH/National Eye Institute

1124 Weismann Netter Stuhl Syndrome

Synonyms

Anterior Bowing of the Legs with Dwarfism
Skeletal Dysplasia, Weismann Netter Stuhl Type
Toxopachyosteose
Toxopachyosteose Diaphysaire Tibio-Peroniere
Weismann-Netter Syndrome

Weismann-Netter-Stuhl syndrome is an extremely rare inherited skeletal disorder characterized by the abnormal development of bone (osseous dysplasia). Affected individuals exhibit bowing of the long portions (shafts) of the shinbone (tibia) and the outer, smaller bone of the leg below the knee (fibula). In some individuals, other bones may also be affected, such as the ribs, pelvis, spinal column, and/or bones in the arms. The primary characteristic of Weismann-Netter-Stuhl syndrome is short stature (dwarfism). In most cases, this disorder is thought to be inherited as an autosomal dominant trait.

The following organizations may provide additional information and support:
Human Growth Foundation
Little People of America, Inc.
Little People's Research Fund, Inc.
NIH/National Institute of Child Health and Human Development

1125 Werdnig-Hoffman Disease

Synonyms

Infantile Spinal Muscular Atrophy
SMA 1
SMA, Infantile Acute Form
Spinal Muscular Atrophy Type 1
Werdnig-Hoffman Paralysis

Werdnig-Hoffmann disease is a type of spinal muscular atrophy. It is a rare, inherited progressive neuromuscular disorder of infancy, characterized by degeneration of groups of nerve cells (motor nuclei) within the lowest region of the brain (lower brain stem) and certain motor neurons in the spinal cord (anterior horn cells). Motor neurons are nerve cells that transmit nerve impulses from the spinal cord or brain (central nervous system) to muscle or glandular tissue. Approximately 80% of SMA falls into the severe category (SMA1). Infants with SMA1 experience severe weakness before 6 months of age, and the patient never achieves the ability to sit independently when placed. Muscle weakness, lack of motor development and poor muscle tone are the major clinical manifestations of SMA1. Infants with the gravest prognosis have problems sucking or swallowing. Some show abdominal breathing in the first few months of life. Muscle weakness occurs on both sides of the body and the ocular muscles are not affected. A twitching of the tongue is often seen. Intelligence is normal. Most affected children die before 2 years of age but survival may be dependent on the degree of respiratory function. For infants who appear to develop normally during the first months of life, muscles of the pelvic, trunk, and shoulder areas may initially appear to be disproportionately affected. With disease progression, diminished muscle tone and weakness may gradually spread to affect almost all voluntary muscles, with the exception of certain muscles controlling movements of the eyes. Infants with Werdnig Hoffmann disease may lack head control, may be unable to roll over or support their weight, and tend to lie relatively still, with little or no movement (flaccid paralysis). In addition, they may develop difficulties sucking, swallowing, and breathing; have an increased susceptibility to respiratory infections; or develop other complications that may lead to potentially life-threatening abnormalities within the first months or years of life. For infants who appear to have normal development for several months prior to the onset of muscle weakness, the disorder may tend to have a more slowly progressive course. Werdnig Hoffmann disease is inherited as an autosomal recessive trait. Molecular genetic testing has revealed that all types of autosomal recessive SMA are caused by mutations in the SMN (survival motor neuron) gene on chromosome 5. Deletion of the NAIP (neuronal apoptosis inhibitory protein) gene that is close to the SMN gene is also associated with SMA. More patients with Werdnig Hoffman disease (SMA1) than other types of SMA have NAIP deletions. The relationship between specific mutations in the SMN gene and nearby genes and the severity of SMA is still being investigated so classification of SMA subdivisions is based on age of onset of symptoms as opposed to the genetic profile.

The following organizations may provide additional information and support:
Families of Spinal Muscular Atrophy
Jennifer Trust for Spinal Muscular Atrophy
March of Dimes Birth Defects Foundation
Muscular Dystrophy Association
Muscular Dystrophy Campaign
National Institute of Neurological Disorders and Stroke (NINDS)

1126 Werner Syndrome

Synonyms
Progeria of Adulthood
WNS
WS

Werner syndrome is a rare progressive disorder that is characterized by the appearance of unusually accelerated aging (progeria). Although the disorder is typically recognized by the third or fourth decades of life, certain characteristic findings are present beginning during childhood, adolescence, and early adulthood. Children with Werner syndrome have an abnormally slow growth rate, and there is cessation of growth at puberty. As a result, affected individuals have unusually short stature and low weight even relative to height. By age 25, those with the disorder typically experience early graying (canities) and premature loss of scalp hair (alopecia). As the disease progresses, additional abnormalities include loss of the layer of fat beneath the skin (subcutaneous adipose tissue); severe wasting (atrophy) of muscle tissue in certain areas of the body; and degenerative skin changes, particularly in the facial area, the upper arms and hands, and the lower legs and feet (distal extremities). Due to degenerative changes affecting the facial area, individuals with Werner syndrome may have unusually prominent eyes, a beaked or pinched nose, and/or other characteristic facial abnormalities. Werner syndrome may also be characterized by development of a distinctive high-pitched voice; eye abnormalities, including premature clouding of the lenses of the eyes due to aging (bilateral senile cataracts); and certain endocrine defects, such as impaired functioning of the ovaries in females or testes in males (hypogonadism) or abnormal production of the hormone insulin by the pancreas and resistance to the effects of insulin (non-insulin-dependent diabetes mellitus). In addition, individuals with

Werner syndrome develop progressive thickening and loss of elasticity of artery walls (arteriosclerosis). Affected blood vessels typically include the arteries that transport oxygen-rich (oxygenated) blood to heart muscle (coronary arteries). Some affected individuals may also be susceptible to developing certain benign (noncancerous) or malignant tumors. Progressive arteriosclerosis, malignancies, and/or associated abnormalities may result in potentially life-threatening complications by approximately the fourth or fifth decade of life. Werner syndrome is inherited as an autosomal recessive trait.

The following organizations may provide additional information and support:
Genetic and Rare Diseases (GARD) Information Center
International Registry of Werner Syndrome
March of Dimes Birth Defects Foundation
NIH/National Institute of Allergy and Infectious Diseases
NIH/National Institute on Aging
Progeria Research Foundation, Inc.

1127 Wernicke-Korsakoff Syndrome

Synonym
Gayet-Wernicke Syndrome

Disorder Subdivisions
Korsakoff Amnesic Syndrome
Korsakoff Psychosis
Korsakoff Syndrome
Psychosis Polyneurotica
Wernicke Disease
Wernicke Encephalopathy
Wernicke Syndrome

Wernicke syndrome and Korsakoff syndrome are related disorders that often occur due to a deficiency of thiamine (vitamin B1). Wernicke's syndrome, also known as Wernicke encephalopathy, is a neurological disease characterized by the clinical triad of confusion, the inability to coordinate voluntary movement (ataxia), and eye (ocular) abnormalities. Korsakoff's syndrome is a mental disorder characterized by disproportionate memory loss in relation to other mental aspects. When these two disorders occur together, the term Wernicke-Korsakoff syndrome is used. In the United States, most cases occur in alcoholics. Some researchers believe Wernicke and Korsakoff syndromes are separate yet related disorders; others believe them to be different stages of the same disorder or disease spectrum.

Wernicke syndrome is considered the acute phase with a shorter duration and more serious symptoms. Korsakoff syndrome is considered the chronic phase and is a long-lasting condition.

The following organizations may provide additional information and support:
National Clearinghouse for Alcohol and Drug Information
National Mental Health Association
NIH/Institute on Alcohol Abuse and Alcoholism
NIH/National Digestive Diseases Information Clearinghouse
NIH/National Institute of Mental Health

1128 West Nile Encephalitis

Synonyms
Kunjin Fever
West Nile Fever

West Nile encephalitis is an inflammation of the brain caused by the West Nile virus, which was first identified in Uganda in the 1930s and first found in the United States in 1999. The disease is spread to humans through the bite of mosquitoes who have fed upon infected birds. It is not spread from person to person, nor is it spread directly from other animals to people, although horses and some other animals are known to become ill from infection with West Nile virus. In humans, most cases are mild with flu-like symptoms, but the disease may occasionally be severe and may even be life-threatening.

The following organizations may provide additional information and support:
Centers for Disease Control and Prevention
National Institute of Neurological Disorders and Stroke (NINDS)
NIH/National Institute of Allergy and Infectious Diseases

1129 West Syndrome

Synonyms
Generalized Flexion Epilepsy
Infantile Epileptic Encephalopathy
Infantile Myoclonic Encephalopathy
Infantile Spasms
Jackknife Convulsion
Massive Myoclonia
Salaam Spasms

West syndrome is a rare form of infantile spasm that occurs very early in the development of an infant. Unusual brain wave patterns occur (hypsarrhythmia) and possibly mental retardation. The spasms that occur may range from violent jack-knife or "salaam" movements where the whole body bends in half, or they may be no more than a mild twitching of the nose or mouth. These spasms usually begin in the early months after birth and can often be helped with medication. There may be many different causes for the spasms. Neurological testing will be helpful in determining the cause.

The following organizations may provide additional information and support:
Epilepsy Foundation
National Institute of Neurological Disorders and Stroke (NINDS)

1130 Whipple Disease

Synonyms
Intestinal Lipodystrophy
Intestinal Lipophagic Granulomatosis
Malabsorption Syndrome
Secondary Non-tropical Sprue

Whipple disease is a rare disease resulting from bacterial infection that leads to inadequate absorption of nutrients (malabsorption) from the intestine. It is believed to result from infection with bacteria known as *Tropheryma whippelii*. The infection usually involves the small intestine, but over time, the disease may affect various parts of the body, including the heart, lungs, brain, and eyes.

The following organizations may provide additional information and support:
Centers for Disease Control and Prevention
NIH/National Digestive Diseases Information Clearinghouse

1131 Wieacker Syndrome

Synonyms
Apraxia, Oculomotor, with Congenital Contractures and Muscle Atrophy
Contractures of Feet, Muscle Atrophy, and Oculomotor Apraxia
Wieacker-Wolff Syndrome
WWS

Wieacker syndrome is a rare, slowly progressive, genetic disorder characterized by deformities of the joints of the feet (contracture), muscle atrophy, mild mental retardation and an impaired ability to move certain muscles of the eyes, face and tongue. Wieacker syndrome is inherited as an X-linked recessive trait.

The following organizations may provide additional information and support:
Genetic and Rare Diseases (GARD) Information Center
March of Dimes Birth Defects Foundation
National Institute of Neurological Disorders and Stroke (NINDS)
NIH/National Institute of Arthritis and Musculoskeletal and Skin Diseases

---

1132 Wiedemann Rautenstrauch Syndrome

Synonyms
Neonatal Progeroid Syndrome
Neonatal Pseudo-Hydrocephalic Progeroid Syndrome of Wiedemann-Rautenstrauch
Rautenstrauch-Wiedemann Syndrome
Rautenstrauch-Wiedemann Type Neonatal Progeria

Wiedemann-Rautenstrauch syndrome (also known as neonatal progeroid syndrome) is an extremely rare genetic disorder characterized by an aged appearance at birth (neonatal progeroid appearance); growth delays before and after birth (prenatal and postnatal growth retardation); and deficiency or absence of the layer of fat under the skin (subcutaneous lipoatrophy), causing the skin to appear abnormally thin, fragile, and wrinkled. In addition, for reasons that are not understood, abnormal deposits of fat may accumulate around the buttocks, the areas around the genitals and the anus (anogenital area), and the area between the ribs and the hips (flanks). Affected infants and children also have distinctive malformations of the head and facial (craniofacial) area including an unusually prominent forehead (frontal bossing) and sides of the skull (parietal bossing), causing the head to appear abnormally large (pseudohydrocephalus); unusually small, underdeveloped (hypoplastic) bones of the face and abnormally small facial features; a small "beak-shaped" nose that becomes more pronounced with advancing age; and/or sparse scalp hair, eyebrows, and/or eyelashes. Most infants and children with Wiedemann-Rautenstrauch syndrome also have unusually thin arms and legs; abnormally large hands and feet; progressive neurological and neuromuscular abnormalities; varying degrees of mental retardation; and severe delays in the acquisition of skills requiring the coordination of mental and muscular activities (psychomotor retardation). In addition, in many cases, affected infants and children are prone to repeated respiratory infections that may result in life-threatening complications. Wiedemann-Rautenstrauch syndrome is inherited as an autosomal recessive trait.

The following organizations may provide additional information and support:
National Institute of Neurological Disorders and Stroke (NINDS)
Progeria Research Foundation, Inc.

1133 Wildervanck Syndrome

Synonyms
Cervico-Oculo-Acoustic Syndrome
COA Syndrome

Wildervanck syndrome, also known as cervicooculoacoustic syndrome, is a rare genetic disorder that primarily affects females. The disorder is characterized by a skeletal condition known as Klippel-Feil syndrome (KFS); abnormalities of certain eye (ocular) movements (i.e., Duane syndrome); and/or hearing impairment at birth (congenital). In individuals with KFS, there is abnormal union or fusion of two or more bones of the spinal column (vertebrae) within the neck (cervical vertebrae). Duane syndrome is characterized by limitation or absence of certain horizontal eye movements; retraction or "drawing back" of the eyeball into the eye cavity (orbit) upon attempting to look inward; and, in some cases, abnormal deviation of one eye in relation to the other (strabismus). In some affected individuals, additional physical abnormalities may also be present. In most cases, Wildervanck syndrome appears to occur randomly for unknown reasons (sporadically).

The following organizations may provide additional information and support:
Alexander Graham Bell Association for the Deaf, Inc.
American Society for Deaf Children
Deafness Research Foundation
Let Them Hear Foundation
NIH/National Arthritis and Musculoskeletal and Skin Diseases Information Clearinghouse
NIH/National Eye Institute

1134 Williams Syndrome

Synonyms
Beuren Syndrome
Early Hypercalcemia Syndrome with Elfin Facies
Elfin Facies with Hypercalcemia
Hypercalcemia-Supravalvar Aortic Stenosis
WBS
Williams-Beuren Syndrome
WMS

Williams syndrome, also known as Williams-Beuren syndrome, is a rare genetic disorder characterized by growth delays before and after birth (prenatal and postnatal growth retardation), short stature, varying levels of mental deficiency, and distinctive facial abnormalities that typically become more pronounced with age. Characteristic facial features may include a round face, full cheeks, thick lips, a large mouth that is usually held open, and a broad nasal bridge with nostrils that flare forward (anteverted nares). Affected individuals may also have unusually short eyelid folds (palpebral fissures), flared eyebrows, a small lower jaw (mandible), and prominent ears. Dental abnormalities may also be present including abnormally small, underdeveloped teeth (hypodontia) with small, slender roots. Williams syndrome may also be associated with heart (cardiac) defects, abnormally increased levels of calcium in the blood during infancy (infantile hypercalcemia), musculoskeletal defects, and/or other abnormalities. Cardiac defects may include obstruction of proper blood flow from the lower right chamber (ventricle) of the heart to the lungs (pulmonary stenosis) or abnormal narrowing above the valve in the heart between the left ventricle and the main artery of the body (supravalvular aortic stenosis). Musculoskeletal abnormalities associated with Williams syndrome may include depression of the breastbone (pectus excavatum), abnormal curvature of the spine (scoliosis or kyphosis), or an awkward gait. In addition, most affected individuals have mild to moderate mental retardation; poor visual-motor integration skills; a friendly, outgoing, talkative manner of speech; and a short attention span with easy distractability. In most individuals with Williams syndrome, the disorder appears to occur spontaneously for unknown reasons (sporadically). However, familial cases have also been reported. Sporadic and familial cases are thought to result from deletion of genetic material from adjacent genes (contiguous genes) within a specific region of chromosome 7 (7q11.23).

The following organizations may provide additional information and support:
The Arc (National Organization on Mental Retardation)
Canadian Association for Williams Syndrome
New Horizons Un-Limited, Inc.
NIH/National Institute of Child Health and Human Development
Williams Syndrome Association
Williams Syndrome Foundation

1135 Wilms' Tumor

Synonyms
Embryoma Kidney
Embryonal Adenomyosarcoma Kidney
Embryonal Carcinosarcoma Kidney
Embryonal Mixed Tumor Kidney
Nephroblastoma

Wilms' tumor is the most common form of kidney cancer in children, accounting for 6 to 8 percent of all childhood cancers. About 500 new cases are diagnosed in the USA per year. The exact cause is not known, although it is thought that in 10-15% of affected individuals, one or more mutated genes create a predisposition to Wilms' tumor. Typically, this disease first appears when the affected child is about 3 years old. Wilms' tumor can often be treated successfully, depending on the stage of the tumor at detection and the age and general health of the child.

The following organizations may provide additional information and support:
American Cancer Society, Inc.
American Kidney Fund, Inc.
Aniridia Network
The Arc (A National Organization on Mental Retardation)
Candlelighters Childhood Cancer Foundation
Childhood Cancer Foundation—Candlelighters Canada
National Kidney Foundation

1136 Wilson's Disease

Synonyms
Hepatolenticular Degeneration
Lenticular Degeneration, Progressive

Wilson's disease is a rare genetic disorder characterized by excess copper stored in various body tissues, particularly the liver, brain, and corneas of the eyes. The disease is progressive and, if left untreated, it may cause liver (hepatic) disease, central nervous system dysfunction, and death. Early diagnosis and treatment may prevent serious long-term disability and life threatening complications. Treatment is aimed at reducing the amount of copper that has accumulated in the body and maintaining normal copper levels thereafter.

The following organizations may provide additional information and support:
American Liver Foundation
March of Dimes Birth Defects Foundation
National Institute of Neurological Disorders and Stroke (NINDS)
Sjældne Diagnoser / Rare Disorders Denmark
WE MOVE (Worldwide Education and Awareness for Movement Disorders)
Wilson's Disease Association International

1137 Winchester Syndrome

Synonym
Winchester-Grossman Syndrome

Winchester syndrome is an extremely rare connective tissue disorder believed by some scientists to be closely related to the mucopolysaccharidoses, which is a group of hereditary metabolic diseases caused by the absence or malfunction of certain enzymes, leading to the accumulation in cells and tissues of molecules that would normally be broken down into smaller units. This syndrome is characterized by short stature, arthritis-like symptoms, nodules under the skin (subcutaneous), coarse facial features, and eye and teeth abnormalities. Winchester syndrome is believed to be inherited as an autosomal recessive trait.

The following organizations may provide additional information and support:
Genetic and Rare Diseases (GARD) Information Center
NIH/National Arthritis and Musculoskeletal and Skin Diseases Information Clearinghouse

1138 Wiskott-Aldrich Syndrome

Synonyms
Aldrich Syndrome
Eczema-Thrombocytopenia-Immunodeficiency Syndrome

IMD2
Immunodeficiency, Wiskott-Aldrich Type
Immunodeficiency-2
WAS

Wiskott-Aldrich syndrome (WAS) is a rare inherited disorder that may be characterized by recurrent infections due to defects in the immune system (i.e., partial defects in T lymphocyte and B lymphocyte systems [combined immunodeficiency]); abnormal bleeding caused by a deficiency in circulating blood platelets (thrombocytopenia); a high incidence of "autoimmune-like" symptoms; and the presence of scaling, itchy skin rashes (eczema) that may be mild in some affected individuals and severe in others. The range and severity of symptoms and physical features associated with the disorder may vary greatly from case to case. Because Wiskott-Aldrich syndrome is inherited as an X-linked recessive genetic trait, the disorder is usually fully expressed in males only.

The following organizations may provide additional information and support:
American Academy of Allergy Asthma and Immunology
Center for International Blood and Marrow Transplant Research
Immune Deficiency Foundation
International Patient Organization for Primary Immunodeficiencies
Jeffrey Modell Foundation
March of Dimes Birth Defects Foundation
National Bone Marrow Transplant Link
NIH/National Arthritis and Musculoskeletal and Skin Diseases Information Clearinghouse
NIH/National Heart, Lung and Blood Institute Information Center
NIH/National Institute of Allergy and Infectious Diseases

1139 Wolf-Hirschhorn Syndrome

Synonyms

4p-Syndrome, Partial
Chromosome 4, Partial Deletion 4p
Chromosome 4, Partial Monosomy 4p
Partial Deletion of the Short Arm of Chromosome 4
WHCR
WHS
Wolf Syndrome
Wolf-Hirschhorn Chromosome Region (WHCR)

Wolf-Hirschhorn syndrome is an extremely rare chromosomal disorder caused by a partial deletion (monosomy) of the short arm ("p") of chromosome 4. Major symptoms may include extremely wide-set eyes (ocular hypertelorism) with a broad or beaked nose, a small head (microcephaly), low-set malformed ears, mental and growth deficiency, heart (cardiac) defects, and seizures. Because the amount of genetic material deleted varies, the symptoms of this syndrome vary from case to case.

The following organizations may provide additional information and support:
4P-Support Group
Chromosome Deletion Outreach, Inc.
Wolf-Hirschhorn Syndrome Support Group
World Health Organization (WHO) Regional Office for the Americas (AMRO)

1140 Wolff-Parkinson White Syndrome

Synonyms

Accessory Atrioventricular Pathways
Preexcitation Syndrome
WPW Syndrome

Wolff-Parkinson-White syndrome is a rare disorder involving irregularities in the heartbeat (cardiac arrhythmia). Patients have an extra circuit or pathway, called the Bundle of Kent, through which electrical signals are conducted to the heart, allowing excessive stimulation. Palpitations (sensation of rapid or irregular beating of the heart), weakness, and shortness of breath may occur.

The following organizations may provide additional information and support:
American Heart Association
Cardiomyopathy Association
Congenital Heart Anomalies, Support, Education, & Resources
HOPE (The Heart of Pediatric Electrophysiology)
NIH/National Heart, Lung and Blood Institute Information Center

1141 Wolfram Syndrome

Synonyms

Diabetes Insipidus, Diabetes Mellitus, Optic Atrophy and Deafness
DIDMOAD

Wolfram syndrome is the inherited association of childhood-onset diabetes mellitus and progressive-onset optic atrophy. All people affected by Wolfram syndrome have juvenile-onset diabetes mellitus and degeneration of the optic nerve (optic atrophy). In addition, about 70 to 75% of those affected develop diabetes insipidus and about two-thirds develop auditory nerve deafness. Another name for the syndrome is DIDMOAD, which refers to diabetes insipidus, diabetes mellitus, optic atrophy, and deafness.

The following organizations may provide additional information and support:
Diabetes Insipidus Foundation, Inc.
March of Dimes Birth Defects Foundation
National Association for Parents of Children with Visual Impairments (NAPVI)
National Association for Visually Handicapped
NIH/National Diabetes Information Clearinghouse
NIH/National Eye Institute
NIH/National Heart, Lung and Blood Institute Information Center
United Mitochondrial Disease Foundation

1142 Wyburn-Mason Syndrome

Synonym
Cerebroretinal Arteriovenous Aneurysm

Wyburn-Mason syndrome is a rare hereditary disorder characterized by blood vessel (vascular) malformations (i.e., arteriovenous aneurysms) of the brain and the nerve-rich, innermost membranes of the eyes (retinas); "birthmarks" or pigmented, facial skin blemishes (facial nevi); and, in some cases, mental changes. An arteriovenous aneurysm is a vascular abnormality in which there is widening (dilation) of the walls of an artery and a vein, with abnormal blood flow (communication) between the blood vessels (i.e., between the arterial and venous systems). (Arteries typically carry oxygen-rich blood from the heart to body cells, while veins transport oxygen-deficient blood to the heart and lungs for the exchange of oxygen and carbon dioxide.)

The following organizations may provide additional information and support:
National Aphasia Association
National Institute of Neurological Disorders and Stroke (NINDS)
NIH/National Eye Institute

1143 X-Linked Juvenile Retinoschisis

Synonyms
Juvenile Retinoschisis
RS, X-Linked
X-Linked Retinoschisis

X-linked juvenile retinoschisis (RS) is a genetic disorder affecting males. Major symptoms include poor eyesight and degeneration of the retina. The retina consists of membrane layers in the eye that receive visual images. It is composed of supportive and protective structures, nervous system components and layers including "rods" and "cones." RS is due to splitting of the retina, which, in turn, causes slow, progressive loss of parts of the fields of vision corresponding to the areas of the retina that have become split. Often, RS is associated with the development of cysts (sac-like blisters) in the retina.

The following organizations may provide additional information and support:
Association for Macular Diseases, Inc.
National Association for Visually Handicapped
NIH/National Eye Institute
ROPARD: The Association for Retinopathy of Prematurity and Related Diseases
Sieving, Paul, M.D., Ph.D.

1144 X-Linked Lymphoproliferative Syndrome

Synonyms
Duncan Disease
EBV Susceptibility (EBVS)
Epstein-Barr Virus-Induced Lymphoproliferative Disease in Males
Immunodeficiency-5 (IMD5)
Purtilo Syndrome
X-Linked Progressive Combined Variable Immunodeficiency
XLP

X-linked lymphoproliferative syndrome (XLP) is an extremely rare inherited (primary) immunodeficiency disorder characterized by a defective immune system response to infection with the Epstein-Barr virus (EBV). This herpes virus is common among the general population and causes infectious mononucleosis (IM), usually with no long-lasting effects. However, in individuals with X-linked lymphoproliferative syndrome, exposure to EBV may result in severe, life-threatening infectious mononucleosis; abnormally low levels of antibodies in the blood and body secretions (hypogammaglobulinemia), resulting in increased susceptibility to various infections; malignancies of certain types of lymphoid tissue (B-cell lymphomas); and/or other abnormalities. The range of symptoms and findings associated with XLP may vary from case to case. In addition, the range of effects may change in an affected individual over time. In most cases, individuals with XLP experience an onset of symptoms anytime from approximately 6 months to 10 years of age. Approximately half of individuals with X-linked lymphoproliferative syndrome experience severe, life-threatening mononucleosis characterized by fever, inflammation and soreness of the throat (pharyngitis), swollen lymph glands, enlargement of the spleen (splenomegaly), enlargement of the liver (hepatomegaly), and/or abnormal functioning of the liver, resulting in yellowing of the skin, mucous membranes, and whites of the eyes (jaundice or icterus). In some cases, individuals who experience life-threatening mononucleosis infection may subsequently have an abnormal increase (i.e., proliferation) of certain white blood cells (lymphocytes and histiocytes) in particular organs, severe liver damage and/or failure, damage to the blood-cell generating bone marrow (hematopoietic marrow cells) that may result in aplastic anemia, and/or other symptoms that may result in life-threatening complications in affected children or adults. Aplastic anemia is characterized by a marked deficiency of all types of blood cells (pancytopenia) including low levels of red blood cells, certain white blood cells, and platelets, specialized red blood cells that function to assist appropriate blood clotting. In individuals with XLP, a decrease in platelets (thrombocytopenia) results in increased susceptibility to bruising and excessive bleeding (hemorrhaging). Because X-linked lymphoproliferative syndrome is inherited as an X-linked recessive genetic trait, the disorder is usually fully expressed in males only.

The following organizations may provide additional information and support:
Center for International Blood and Marrow Transplant Research
Immune Deficiency Foundation
International Patient Organization for Primary Immunodeficiencies
Jeffrey Modell Foundation
March of Dimes Birth Defects Foundation
National Bone Marrow Transplant Link
National Cancer Institute

NIH/Hematology Branch, National Heart, Lung and Blood Institute (NHLBI)
NIH/National Institute of Allergy and Infectious Diseases
OncoLink: The University of Pennsylvania Cancer Center Resource
UNIQUE—Rare Chromosome Disorder Support Group

1145 Xeroderma Pigmentosum

Synonyms

Kaposi Disease (not Kaposi Sarcoma)
Xeroderma Pigmentosum, Variant Type, XP-V
XP

Disorder Subdivisions

Xeroderma Pigmentosum, Dominant Type
Xeroderma Pigmentosum, Type A, I, XPA, Classical Form
Xeroderma Pigmentosum, Type B, II, XPB
Xeroderma Pigmentosum, Type C, III, XPC
Xeroderma Pigmentosum, Type D, IV, XPD
Xeroderma Pigmentosum, Type E, V, XPE
Xeroderma Pigmentosum, Type F, VI, XPF
Xeroderma Pigmentosum, Type G, VII, XPG

Xeroderma pigmentosum (XP) is a group of rare inherited skin disorders characterized by a heightened reaction to sunlight (photosensitivity) with skin blistering occurring after exposure to the sun. In some cases, pain and blistering may occur immediately after contact with sunlight. Acute sunburn and persistent redness or inflammation of the skin (erythema) are also early symptoms of XP. In most cases, these symptoms may be apparent immediately after birth or occur within the next 3 years. In other cases, symptoms may not develop until later in childhood or, more rarely, may not be recognized until adulthood. Other symptoms of XP may include discolorations, weakness and fragility, and/or scarring of the skin. Xeroderma pigmentosum affects the eyes as well as the skin, has been associated with several forms of skin cancer, and, in some cases, may occur along with dwarfism, mental retardation, and/or delayed development. Several subtypes of XP (i.e., XP complementation groups) have been identified, based upon different defects in the body's ability to repair DNA damaged by ultraviolet light (UV). According to the medical literature, the symptoms and findings associated with the classic form of xeroderma pigmentosum, known as XP, type A (XPA), may also occur in association with the other XP subtypes. These include: XP, type B (XPB);

XP, type C (XPC); XP, type D (XPD); XP, type E (XPE); XP, type F (XPF); and XP, type G (XPG). These XP subtypes are transmitted as an autosomal recessive trait. In addition, another subtype of the disorder, known as XP, dominant type, has autosomal dominant inheritance. In addition to the XP subtypes discussed above, researchers have identified another form of the disorder known as XP, variant type (XP-V). As with the other XP subtypes, symptoms and findings associated with the classic form of XP may also be seen in individuals with XP-V. XP-V cells have a normal or near normal ability to repair UV-induced DNA damage (nucleotide excisional repair); however, they are defective in replicating UV-damaged DNA during the division and reproduction of cells. Although the disorder's mode of inheritance is unknown, most researchers suspect that XP-V is transmitted as an autosomal recessive trait.

The following organizations may provide additional information and support:
The Arc (A National Organization on Mental Retardation)
NIH/National Arthritis and Musculoskeletal and Skin Diseases Information Clearinghouse
Skin Cancer Foundation
Xeroderma Pigmentosum Registry
XP (Xeroderma Pigmentosum) Society, Inc.

1146 XYY Syndrome

Synonyms
47,XYY Karyotype
47,XYY Syndrome
Diplo-Y Syndrome
Polysomy Y
XYY Chromosome Pattern
YY Syndrome

XYY syndrome is a rare chromosomal disorder that affects males. It is caused by the presence of an extra Y chromosome. Males normally have one X and one Y chromosome. However, individuals with this syndrome have one X and two Y chromosome. Affected individuals are usually very tall and thin. Many experience severe acne during adolescence. Additional symptoms may include antisocial or behavioral problems and learning disabilities. Intelligence is usually normal, although IQ, on average, is 10 to 15 points lower than siblings.

The following organizations may provide additional information and support:
March of Dimes Birth Defects Foundation
National Alliance for the Mentally Ill
National Mental Health Association
National Mental Health Consumers' Self-Help Clearinghouse
NIH/National Institute of Mental Health

1147 Yaws

Yaws is an infectious tropical disease caused by the spirochete (spiral shaped) bacterium known as *Treponema pertenue*. The disease presents in three stages of which the first and second are easily treated. The third, however, may involve complex changes to the bones in many parts of the body. The first stage is characterized by the appearance of small, painless bumps on the skin that group together and grow until they resemble a strawberry. The skin may break open, forming an ulcer. The second stage (usually starting several weeks or months after the first) presents with a crispy, crunchy rash that may cover arms, legs, buttocks and/or face. If the bottoms of the feet are involved, walking is painful and the stage is known as "crab yaws." Stage 3 yaws involves the long bones, joints, and/or skin. Yaws is very common in tropical areas of the world but rare in the United States. It is not a sexually transmitted disease.

The following organizations may provide additional information and support:
Centers for Disease Control and Prevention
NIH/National Institute of Allergy and Infectious Diseases
World Health Organization (WHO) Regional Office for the Americas (AMRO)

1148 Yellow Fever

Synonym
Bunyavirus Infection

Yellow fever is a viral infection that causes damage to the liver, kidney, heart and gastrointestinal tract. Major symptoms may include sudden onset of fever, yellowing of the skin (jaundice) and hemorrhage. It occurs predominately in South America, the Caribbean Islands and Africa. The disease is spread through bites of infected mosquitos. Incidence of the disease tends to increase in the summer as the mosquito population increases, and it occurs year round in tropical climates. Yellow fever has two cycles: the sylvan cycle in which mosquitos primarily spread the disease among forest-dwelling primates, and the urban cycle in which the infection is spread from human to human.

The following organizations may provide additional information and support:
Centers for Disease Control and Prevention
NIH/National Institute of Allergy and Infectious Diseases
World Health Organization (WHO) Regional Office for the Americas (AMRO)

1149 Yellow Nail Syndrome

Yellow nail syndrome is a very rare disorder involving a combination of lymphedema (swelling) of the lower extremities, recurrent pneumonia, bronchiectasis, and yellowed nails. Most patients have disease of the lower lobe of the lung which may be due to obstruction and/or infection. Bronchiectasis is an irreversible enlargement of one or more of the bronchi due to the destruction of the muscular and elastic supporting tissues.

The following organizations may provide additional information and support:
American Lung Association
NIH/National Arthritis and Musculoskeletal and Skin Diseases Information Clearinghouse
NIH/National Heart, Lung and Blood Institute Information Center

1150 Yunis-Varon Syndrome

Synonym
Cleidocranial Dysplasia w/ Micrognathia, Absent Thumbs, & Distal Aphalangia

Yunis-Varon syndrome is an extremely rare genetic multisystem disorder with defects affecting the skeletal; ectodermal tissue (i.e., nails, hair, and teeth); and cardiorespiratory (i.e., heart and lungs) systems. It is characterized by growth retardation prior to and after birth; defective growth of the bones of the skull along with complete or partial absence of the shoulder blades (cleidocranial dysplasia); characteristic facial features; and/or abnormalities of the fingers and/or toes. Characteristic facial features may include an extremely small jaw (micrognathia), thin lips, sparse or absent eyebrows and/or eyelashes, and/or an unusually short

vertical groove (philtrum) in the upper lip. Abnormalities of the fingers and toes may include absence (aplasia) or underdevelopment (hypoplasia) of the thumbs and/or the bones at the ends of the fingers and the great toes (distal phalanges). In most cases, infants with this disorder experience severe feeding problems and respiratory difficulties. In addition, affected infants may have heart defects (e.g., abnormal enlargement of the heart muscle [hypertrophic cardiomyopathy]). In some cases, feeding problems, respiratory difficulties, and/or heart defects may result in life-threatening complications during infancy. Yunis-Varon syndrome is inherited as an autosomal recessive trait.

The following organizations may provide additional information and support:
National Craniofacial Foundation
NIH/National Heart, Lung and Blood Institute Information Center

1151 Zellweger Syndrome

Synonyms
Bowen Syndrome
Cerebrohepatorenal Syndrome

Zellweger syndrome is a rare, hereditary disorder characterized by a deficiency or absence of peroxisomes in the cells of the liver, kidneys, and brain. Peroxisomes are very small, membrane-bound structures within the cytoplasm of cells that function as part of the body's waste disposal system. In the absence of the enzymes normally found in peroxisomes, waste products, especially very long chain fatty acids (VLCFA), accumulate in the cells of the affected organ. The accumulation of these waste products has profound affects on the development of the fetus. Zellweger syndrome is one of a group of genetic disorders known as leukodystrophies that affect growth of the myelin sheath, which lines nerve fibers in the brain and speeds the conduction of nerve impulses.

The following organizations may provide additional information and support:
The Arc (A National Organization on Mental Retardation)
Association Europeene contre les Leucodystrophes
Hunter's Hope Foundation, Inc.
National Institute of Neurological Disorders and Stroke (NINDS)
United Leukodystrophy Foundation

1152 Zollinger Ellison Syndrome

Synonyms

Gastrinoma
Pancreatic Ulcerogenic Tumor Syndrome
Z-E Syndrome
ZES

Zollinger-Ellison syndrome (ZES) is characterized by the development of a tumor (gastrinoma) or tumors that secrete excessive levels of gastrin, a hormone that stimulates production of acid by the stomach. Many affected individuals develop multiple gastrinomas, approximately half to two-thirds of which may be cancerous (malignant). In most cases, the tumors arise within the pancreas and/or the upper region of the small intestine (duodenum). Due to excessive acid production (gastric acid hypersecretion), individuals with ZES may develop peptic ulcers of the stomach, the duodenum, and/or other regions of the digestive tract. Peptic ulcers are sores or raw areas within the digestive tract where the lining has been eroded by stomach acid and digestive juices. Symptoms and findings associated with ZES may include mild to severe abdominal pain; diarrhea; increased amounts of fat in the stools (steatorrhea); and/or other abnormalities. In most affected individuals, ZES appears to develop randomly (sporadically) for unknown reasons. In approximately 25 percent of cases, ZES occurs in association with a genetic syndrome known as multiple endocrine neoplasia type 1 (MEN-1).

The following organizations may provide additional information and support:
Canadian Multiple Endocrine Neoplasm Society, Inc.
NIH/National Institute of Diabetes, Digestive & Kidney Diseases

Part II

Organizations

1153 4P- Support Group

P.O. Box 1676
Gresham, OR 97030

Phone: (503) 661-7546
E-mail: fourthchromosome@aol.com
http://www.4p-supportgroup.org

4P- Support Group is a voluntary, not-for-profit organization that supports parents whose children have 4th chromosome conditions. It provides a newsletter and a listserv, and they are both available to parents, friends, relatives and healthcare professionals.

President: Wendy Trout (2004-2006)
Executive Director: Larry Bentley (Contact Person)
Year Established: 1985

Keywords
4P Support Group; 4P- Support Group; Chromosomal Abnormalities; Chromosome 4p Minus Syndrome; WHS; Wolf Hirschhorn Syndrome; Wolf Syndrome; Wolf-Hirschhorn (4P-) Parent Contact Group

1154 5p- Society

PO Box 268
Lakewood, CA 90714-0268

Phone: (562) 804-4506
Fax: (562) 920-5240
Toll Free: (888) 970-0777
E-mail: director@fivepminus.org
http://www.fivepminus.org

The 5p- Society is a voluntary, not-for-profit organization dedicated to providing information and support to individuals with a deletion of the short arm (p) of chromosome 5 and their families. The 5p- Society promotes patient advocacy, engages in-patient and professional education, and provides a variety of educational and support materials including a regular newsletter and brochures.

President: Greg Abbruzzuse
Executive Director: Laura Castillo
Year Established: 1985

Keywords
5p- Society; Chromosomal Abnormalities; Chromosome 5p Minus; Chromosome 5P Minus Syndrome; Cri du Chat Syndrome; Deletion 5p; Deletion Short Arm Chromosome 5; Monosomy 5p

1155 8p Duplication Support Group

The Genetics Center
1 Children's Plaza
The Children's Medical Center
Dayton, OH 45404

Phone: (937) 641-5645
Fax: (937) 641-5325
E-mail: genE-mail@aol.com

The 8p Duplication Support Group is a support organization based at The Genetics Center, Children' s Medical Center, Dayton, Ohio. Established in 1994, the support group is dedicated to matching families of children with chromosome 8p duplication disorders to promote the exchange of information, resources, and mutual support. Chromosome 8p duplication disorders are extremely rare chromosomal disorders in which all or a portion of the short arm ("p") of chromosome 8 appears three times rather than twice in cells of the body. These rare chromosomal disorders, known as 8p "duplications" or "trisomies" (or "inverted duplications," if the chromosomal material is also inverted) may be characterized by a variety of symptoms and physical features depending upon the exact length and location of the duplicated material on chromosome 8p. Such symptoms and physical features may include abnormally decreased muscle tone, growth delays during childhood, mental retardation, distinctive malformations of the head and facial area, abnormalities of the fingers and/or nails, cardiac defects, and/or other physical abnormalities. In addition to providing networking services, the 8p Duplication Support Group engages in patient education and provides referrals including to genetic counseling.

Executive Director: Faith Callif-Daley, M.S., C.G.C. (Contact Person)
Year Established: 1994

Keywords
8p Duplication Support Group; Chromosome 8p Duplication; Chromosome 8p Trisomy; Inversion Duplication of Chromosome 8p; Inverted Duplication Chromosome 8p

1156 11Q Research and Resource Group

83 Lantern Hill Road
Mystic, CT 06355

Phone: (860) 599-4015
Fax: (860) 441-6159
E-mail: david_m_george@groton.pfizer.com
http://web.ukonline.co.uk/c.jones/11q/contents.htm

The 11q Research and Resource Group is a not-for-profit organization dedicated to providing information, assistance, and support to parents, other family members, and healthcare professionals caring for children with structural abnormalities of chromosome 11, particularly abnormalities of 11q (the "long arm" of chromosome 11). The group primarily provides information and support concerning Jacobsen syndrome, a rare chromosomal disorder also known as "partial deletion" or "partial monosomy" of chromosome 11q. This rare chromosomal disorder may be characterized by a variety of symptoms and physical features including abnormally slow growth before and after birth, delayed psychomotor development, mental retardation, distinctive malformations of the head and facial area, abnormalities of the eyes, malformations of the hands and/or feet, defects of the heart, and/or other physical abnormalities. Established in 1996 and consisting of about 150 members, the 11q Research and Resource Group engages in patient advocacy, promotes research, and offers a variety of services including networking opportunities.

President: David George
Year Established: 1996
Acronym: 11Q R+R

Keywords
11Q Research and Resource Group; 11Q R+R; Advocacy; Amyloidosis; Carcinoid Syndrome; Chromosome 11 Partial 11q Syndrome; Chromosome 11 Partial Deletion 11q Syndrome; Chromosome 11 Partial Monosomy 11q; Chromosome 11q Deletion; Chromosome 11q Translocation; Chromosome 11q Trisomy; Clubfoot; Distal 11q Monosomy; Distal 11q Syndrome; Jacobsen Syndrome; Networking

1157 22q and You Center
The Department of Clinical Genetics
The Children's Hospital of Philadelphia
One Children's Center
34th Street and Civic Center Boulevard
Philadelphia, PA 19104

Phone: (215) 590-2920
Fax: (215) 590-3298
E-mail: lunny@E-mail.chop.edu
http://www.cbil.upenn.edu/VCFS/22qandyou/

The 22q and You Center, located within the Children's Hospital of Philadelphia, is a national nonprofit voluntary health organization dedicated to providing information and support to individuals, families, and medical professionals interested in the chromosome 22q11.2 deletion. This chromosomal disorder is also known as DiGeorge anomaly and ve-

locardiofacial syndrome (VCFS). Opitz G/BBB syndrome, asymmetric crying face syndrome, CATCH 22, and conotruncal cardiac anomaly are also included in this group of disorders. Established in 1996 and consisting of 2,500 members, the 22q and You Center publishes a quarterly newsletter titled, "22q and You."

Executive Director: Donna McDonald-McGinn, M.S., C.G.C.
Year Established: 1996

Keywords
22q and You; 22q and You Center; Asymmetric Crying Face Syndrome; Chromosome 22q; Chromosome 22q11.2 Deletion; Conotruncal Anomaly Face Syndrome; Conotruncal Cardiac Anomalies; DiGeorge Syndrome; Opitz G/BBB Syndrome; VCFS

1158 22q13 Deletion Syndrome Foundation/Phelan-McDermid Syndrome
c/o Greenwood Genetic Center
2 Doctor Way
Greenville, SC 29605

Phone: (864) 250-7944
Fax: (864) 250-9582
E-mail: sam22q13@aol.com
http://www.22q13.com

The 22q13 Deletion Syndrome Foundation/Phelan-McDermid Syndrome is a voluntary, not-for-profit organization that raises money and organizes support-group meetings for patients and families affected by Phelan-McDermid syndrome. Phelan-McDermid syndrome is a rare chromosomal disorder in which a portion of the long arm (q) of chromosome 22 is missing (deleted or monosomic). The fund-raising arm of the support group is achieving the foundation's mission to build a support alliance for individuals with the chromosome 22q13 deletion by providing families and professionals with scientific education and information exchange.

President: Sue Lomas (2002-2006)
Executive Director: Dr. Curtis Rogers
Year Established: 2002

Keywords
22q13 Deletion Syndrome Foundation/Phelan-McDermid Syndrome; 22q13 Deletion Syndrome; Networking; Phelan McDermid Syndrome; Support Groups

1159 49XXXXY

870 Miranda Green
Palo Alto, CA 94306

Phone: (360) 892-7547
E-mail: epwatzka@iname.com

49XXXXY is a not-for-profit, self-help organization dedicated to providing mutual support to families of those affected by 49XXXXY syndrome. This is a rare chromosomal disorder that affects males and may be characterized by growth retardation, hypogonadism, craniofacial and other bone abnormalities, cardiac malformations, varying degrees of mental retardation, delayed language development, and/or behavioral problems. While males normally have one X and one Y chromosome, males with 49XXXXY syndrome have four X chromosomes and one Y chromosome. 49XXXXY syndrome is considered an extremely rare variant of Klinefelter syndrome. Established in 1990, 49XXXXY enables affected families to exchange information, support, and resources through its networking program. The organization supports a pen pal program, makes appropriate referrals, and offers phone support to affected families. 49XXXXY also provides a variety of educational and support materials including a regular newsletter and brochures.

President: Elise Watzka
Year Established: 1990

Keywords
49XXXXY; 49XXXXY Syndrome; Klinefelter Syndrome Variant

1160 Aarskog Syndrome Parents Support Group

62 Robin Hill Lane
Levittown, PA 19055-1411

Phone: (215) 943-7131
E-mail: shannonfaith49@msn.com

The Aarskog Syndrome Parents Support Group is a not-for-profit, self-help organization dedicated to providing information and support to parents of children with Aarskog syndrome. This is a rare genetic disorder characterized by distinctive facial abnormalities, unusually small hands, genital abnormalities, short stature, mild mental retardation, speech and language delays, and orthopedic problems. Established in 1993, the Aarskog Syndrome Parents Support Group offers phone and letter support; enables parents to exchange information, support, and resources through its parent-

to-parent matching program; engages in patient advocacy; and supports and promotes ongoing medical research. The Aarskog Syndrome Parents Support Group also offers a variety of educational and support materials, including fact sheets, article reprints, case study information, and a regular newsletter.

Executive Director: Shannon Caranci
Year Established: 1993

Keywords
Aarskog Syndrome; Aarskog Syndrome Parents Support Group

1161 Abetalipoproteinemia Support Group

Phone: (480) 659-0540
Fax: cell (480) 688-9027
http://www.yahoogroups.com

Abetalipoproteinemia is an online support group that disseminates information about the care and treatment of people with abetalipoproteinemia, a rare, incurable, genetic disorder characterized by the body's inability to properly absorb and transport fats. The group provides information to health professionals and the general public, as well as to affected families. It also supports parents in their quest for treatment for their children, and provides opportunities for sharing information related to the diagnosis and treatment of this very rare disorder. The only meetings are online, although members of the group may also share their telephone numbers with each other. To access this group, go to www.yahoogroups.com, register and then choose Abetalipoproteinemia Support Group.

President: Ruth Gold

Keywords
Abetalipoproteinemia; Abetalipoproteinemia Support Group; Networking; Referrals; Support Groups

1162 Abiding Hearts

705 14th Street
Butte, MT 59701

Phone: (406) 782-4894
Fax: (406) 587-7197
TDD: (800) 223-3131
E-mail: abidinghearts@yahoo.com

Abiding Hearts is a not-for-profit organization dedicated to providing support and information to parents continuing their pregnancies after prenatal testing has revealed the presence of birth defects, some of which may be life threatening. Established in 1993, Abiding Hearts provides a network of contact parents in a growing number of areas across the United States, enabling the exchange of support, information, and resources between new members and parents who have already experienced similar circumstances. Abiding Hearts also promotes patient advocacy; provides referrals to support groups and other services; and offers a variety of educational and support materials to parents and other affected family members, healthcare professionals, and the general public through its directory, brochures, reports, and its regular newsletter.

President: Maria LaFond (1993-Present)
Executive Director: Kathleen Johnson
Year Established: 1993

Keywords
Abiding Hearts; Birth Defects

1163 ABIL Inc. (Agoraphobics Building Independent Lives)

400 West 32nd Street
Richmond, VA 23225

Phone: (804) 353-3964
Fax: (804) 353-3687
E-mail: abil1996@aol.com
http://www.anxietysupport.org

Agoraphobics Building Independent Lives (ABIL, Inc.) is a nonprofit "grassroots volunteer organization" dedicated to providing hope, support, and advocacy to people affected by panic attacks, phobias, and/or agoraphobia. By establishing nationwide self-help groups and providing public education, ABIL has worked since 1986 to improve treatment and awareness, both medical and social, of people with panic disorders. ABIL publishes a quarterly newsletter and brochures, establishes telephone and pen pal connections, conducts lectures, makes appropriate referrals, and maintains a database of information for the general public. If there is no local ABIL support group available, ABIL also offers guidelines, materials, and support for those interested in creating support groups in their communities. Memberships are available at a yearly rate.

President: Brandi Cummings, PharmaD, BCPS
Executive Director: Yolande A. Long, M.S.W. (Administrator)
Year Established: 1986
Acronym: ABIL, Inc.

Keywords
ABIL Inc. (Agoraphobics Building Independent Lives); Agoraphobia; Panic Attacks; Phobias

1164 About Madelung's

7251 Brentwood Boulevad
Apt 163
Brentwood, CA 94513

Phone: (925) 516-6744
E-mail: madelungs@yahoo.com
http://www.geocities.com/madelungs/madelungs-home.html

About Madelung's was established in 2003 as a connecting point for anyone dealing with this extremely rare condition. It was once thought there were only 600 cases in the conditions over 2500 year history, but we know that those numbers can't have been right, there are about 50 known US cases today, and many more cases of related conditions such as HIV lipodystrophy, Dercum's disease, and multiple familial lipomatosis. The mission of About Madelung's is the same as it has always been, a point of contact and a source of recent information for anyone dealing with this baffling and complicated condition. About Madelung's has already accomplished three goals 1) Debunking the almost mythical stereotypes about this condition, 2) Identifying more cases in patients who were previously undiagnosed or incorrectly diagnosed, and 3) Making sure that no one has to deal with this condition alone.

President: Jennifer Mandell
Year Established: 2003

Keywords
About Madelung's; Angiolipomas; Dercum's Disease; HIV Lipodystrophy; Lipodystrophy; Madelung's Disease; Unencapsulated

1165 AboutFace International

123 Edward Street
Suite 1003
Toronto
Ontario, M5G 1E2, Canada

Phone: (416) 597-2229
Fax: (416) 597-8494
Toll Free: (800) 665-3223
E-mail: info@aboutfaceinternational.org
http://www.aboutfaceinternational.org

AboutFace International (AFI) is an international, nonprofit organization that provides information, emotional support, and educational programs for and on behalf of individuals with facial differences and their families. The organization seeks to increase public awareness and understanding of the challenges and abilities of people with facial differences. Founded in 1985, AboutFace memberships consist of individuals, parents, families, and friends touched by facial differences as well as healthcare and social service providers, educators and other professionals. The vision of About Face is to assist all persons with facial differences to have a positive self-image and self-esteem so that they can participate fully in their communities.

President: Robert Pielsticker
Executive Director: Anna Pileggi
Year Established: 1985

Keywords
AboutFace International; Apert Syndrome; Burns; Cancer; Cleft Lip; Cleft Palate; Craniofacial Anomalies; Craniosynostosis; Crouzon Disease; Cystic Hygroma; Educational Resources; Frontonasal Dysplasia; Goldenhar Syndrome; Hemangioma; Hemifacial Microsomia; Hypertelorism; Lymphangioma; Moebius Syndrome; Nager Syndrome; Neurofibromatosis; Oral Facial Digital Syndrome; Pierre Robin Sequence; Port Wine Stain; School Programs; Sturge Weber Syndrome; Treacher Collins Syndrome; Vascular Malformations

1166 AboutFace USA
P.O. Box 158
South Beloit, IL 61080

Toll Free: (888) 486-1209
E-mail: info@AboutFaceUSA.org
http://www.aboutfaceusa.org

AboutFace USA provides information and emotional support to individuals with facial differences. Families are also included as part of its support network. AboutFace USA works to increase public understanding through awareness programs and education on behalf of those it serves. AboutFace USA welcomes individuals whose facial differences are present at birth, such as cleft lip and palate, Apert, Crouzon, Treacher Collin, microtia, hemangiomas, and Moebius syndrome, as well as other conditions. Others served are those who have differences as a result of illness, disease or trauma, stroke, cancer, accident and fire.

President: David Reisberg
Executive Director: Rickie Gill

Year Established: 1987
Acronym: AboutFace

Keywords
AboutFace USA; Apert Syndrome; Baller Gerold Syndrome; Carpenter Syndrome; Cerebro Oculo Facio Skeletal Syndrome; Cleft Advocate; Cleft Palate and Cleft Lip; Craniofacial Conditions; Craniofrontonasal Dysplasia; Craniometaphyseal Dysplasia; Craniosynostosis; Craniosynostosis, Primary; Crouzon Disease; Cystic Hygroma; Encephalocele; Facial Anomalies; Facial Difference; Fraser Syndrome; Frontofacionasal Dysplasia; Frontonasal Dysplasia; Goldenhar Syndrome; Goodman Syndrome; Greig Cephalopolysyndactyly Syndrome; Hemangioma; Jackson Weiss Syndrome; Maxillofacial Dysostosis; Maxillonasal Dysplasia, Binder Type; Moebius Syndrome; Oral Facial Digital Syndrome; Orocraniodigital Syndrome; Pallister W Syndrome; Pathfinder Group; Pfeiffer Syndrome; Rapp Hodgkin Ectodermal Dysplasia; Saethre Chotzen Syndrome; Sakati Syndrome; Summitt Syndrome; Support Network; Treacher Collins Syndrome

1167 Achromatopsia Network
P.O. Box 214
Berkeley, CA 94701-0214

Phone: (510) 540-4700
Fax: (510) 540-4767
E-mail: editor@achromat.org
http://www.achromat.org

The Achromatopsia Network is a nonprofit organization for individuals and families affected by congenital, inherited achromatopsia, a very rare vision disorder. Most members of the network are affected by the form of achromatopsia known as rod monochromacy. Some are affected by a rare form known as blue cone monochromacy. Begun in 1994, the network provides information about this disorder and helps individuals and families affected by achromatopsia to connect with one another. Publications available include three books: "Understanding and Coping with Achromatopsia," "Living with Achromatopsia," and "Handbook of Information for Members of the Achromatopsia Network." There are over 500 members in this network, most of who are in the United States.

President: Frances Futterman (Facilitator)
Year Established: 1993

Keywords
Achromatopsia; Achromatopsia Network; Achromatopsia, Rod Monochromatism, Congenital; Color

Vision Deficiency; Colorblindness, Total; Cone Dystrophy; Eye Disorders; Light Hypersensitivity; Monochromatism, Blue Cone; Monochromatism, Rod; Photodysphoria; Photosensitivity; Visual Impairments

1168 Acid Maltase Deficiency Association, Inc.

P.O. Box 700248
San Antonio, TX 78270-0248

Phone: (210) 494-6144
Fax: (210) 490-7161
E-mail: tianrama@aol.com
http://www.amda-pompe.org

The Acid Maltase Deficiency Association, Inc., is a nonprofit organization directed toward the advancement of research in acid maltase deficiency (also known as Pompe's disease). Pompe's disease, a glycogen storage disease with onset during infancy, childhood, or adulthood, is inherited as an autosomal recessive genetic trait. Symptoms develop due to deficiency of the enzyme, alpha-1, 4 glucosidase. Founded in 1995 and consisting of over 500 members, the association publishes brochures and informational literature; sponsors an annual conference for the scientific community to discuss crucial issues related to Pompe's disease; and maintains a patient/family registry. This registry is used to disseminate information to affected families about current scientific breakthroughs, dietary information, and other issues vital to daily living. In addition the AMDA sends out a newsletter and sponsors patient informational teleconference calls.

President: Randall House (1995 - Present)
Executive Director: Marylyn House (Patient Coordinator)
Year Established: 1995
Acronym: AMDA

Keywords
Acid Maltase Deficiency Association, Inc.; Acid Maltase Deficiency; Alpha 1,4 Glucosidase Deficiency; AMD; AMDA; Glycogen Storage Disease Type II; Glycogenosis Type II; Lysosomal Glucosidase Deficiency; Pompe Disease

1169 Acoustic Neuroma Association

600 Peachtree Parkway
Suite 108
Cumming, GA 30041

Phone: (770) 205-8211
Fax: (770) 205-0239

E-mail: info@ANAUSA.org
http://www.ANAUSA.org

The Acoustic Neuroma Association (ANA) is a nonprofit organization dedicated to providing information and support to individuals with an acoustic neuroma. An acoustic neuroma is a benign tumor of the eighth (auditory) cranial nerve. Established in 1981, the association seeks to educate the public regarding symptoms suggestive of acoustic neuroma in order to promote early diagnosis and successful treatment. In addition, the Acoustic Neuroma Association provides referrals to support groups and offers a variety of educational and support materials through its database, quarterly newsletter, brochures, and audiovisual aids.

President: John Zipprich (2003)
Executive Director: Judy B. Vitucci
Year Established: 1981
Acronym: ANA

Keywords
Acoustic Neuroma Association; Acoustic Neuroma; ANA; Cranial Nerve Disorders; Tumor (Benign), Cranial Nerve

1170 Acoustic Neuroma Association of Canada

Box 369
Edmonton
Alberta, T5J 2J6, Canada

Phone: (780) 428-3384
Fax: (780) 428-3909
Toll Free: (800) 561-2622
E-mail: info@anac.ca
http://www.anac.ca

The Acoustic Neuroma Association of Canada (ANAC) is a not-for-profit, self-help organization dedicated to providing a comfortable environment for people who have or are facing the removal of acoustic neuromas and other tumors involving the cranial nerves. Acoustic neuromas are benign (noncancerous) tumors affecting the eighth cranial nerve, which is located in the auditory canal of the ear. Established in 1984, ANAC provides support; furnishes information on patient rehabilitation to physicians and healthcare personnel interested in the treatment of benign tumors and the alleviation of post-surgical problems; and promotes and supports research on the cause, development, and treatment of acoustic neuromas. ANAC consists of 500 members and produces educational materials including a quarterly newsletter titled, "The Connection," a pamphlet on acoustic neuroma, and a brochure titled, "The Hope is Recognition and Treatment." Program activities include regular support group meetings, patient advocacy, patient networking, and patient education.

Executive Director: Cheryl Bauer (National Coordinator)
Year Established: 1984
Acronym: ANAC

Keywords
Acoustic Neurilemoma; Acoustic Neuroma Association of Canada; Cerebellopontine Angle Tumor; Fibroblastoma, Perineural; Neurofibroma; Neuroma; Neuroma, Bilateral Acoustic; Schwannoma

1171 Adams-Oliver Syndrome Support Group

14 College View
Connah's Quay
Deeside, CH5 4BY, United Kingdom

Phone: +44 (0) 1244-81-6209
E-mail: sandy.ivins@btinternet.com

Founded in 1993, the Adams-Oliver Syndrome Support Group is an organization that works to create and enhance public awareness about Adams-Oliver syndrome, a rare genetic disorder characterized by distinctive malformations of the scalp and abnormalities of the fingers, toes, arms, and/or legs. The group provides an information packet on this inherited disorder and is working to build a network of people who can discuss common problems and concerns that arise for affected individuals, families, friends, and caregivers.

President: Sandra Ivins
Year Established: 1993

Keywords
Adams-Oliver Syndrome; Adams Oliver Syndrome Support Group

1172 Addison and Cushing International Federation

P.O. Box 52137
The Hague, 2505 CC, The Netherlands

Phone: +31 (0) 15-369-9339
Fax: +31 (0) 15-369-9339
E-mail: info@nvacp.nl
http://www.nvacp.nl

The Addison and Cushing International Federation (ACIF), established in 1996, is a platform of organizations involved in the support of those affected with Addison's disease, Cushing's syndrome (or disease) and related adrenal or pituitary-related diseases (e.g., acromegaly, CAH and other disorders). ACIF maintains a listing of organizations, support groups and individuals who want to start support groups interested in the field of adrenal and pituitary disorders. The ACIF web site remains a part of the web site of the Dutch Addison and Cushing Society (NVACP). Whenever possible, messages will be diverted to existing patient support groups already known to ACIF. Addison's disease is a rare disorder characterized by deficiency of certain hormones (i.e., hydrocortisone and aldosterone) produced by the outer region (cortex) of the adrenal glands. Cushing's syndrome is a hormonal disorder characterized by abnormally increased levels of certain hormones (i.e., corticosteroid hormones) produced by the adrenal glands.

Executive Director: Laurens V. Mijnders
Year Established: 1996
Acronym: ACIF

Keywords
ACIF; Addison and Cushing International Federation; Addison's Disease; Adrenal Diseases; CAH; Congenital Adrenal Hyperplasia

1173 Addison's Disease Self-Help Group (UK)

21 George Road
Guildford, Surrey, GU1 4NP, United Kingdom

Phone: +44 (0) 1483-083-0672
Fax: +44 (0) 1483-083-0673
E-mail: feedback@adshg.org.uk
http://www.adshg.org.uk

The Addison's Disease Self-Help Group (UK) is a not-for-profit organization located in the United Kingdom. It helps people, mainly in the UK, who have been affected by Addison's disease, a rare disorder characterized by chronic, usually progressive, inadequate production of the steroid hormones cortisol and aldosterone by the outer layer of cells of the adrenal glands. ADSHG (UK) works to support people with adrenal failure, and promotes better medical understanding of this rare condition. The services of ADSHG (UK) for its members include a newsletter, emergency treatment instructions, educational materials, and access to an e-mail discussion/support group.

President: Katherine G. White (Chair)
Executive Director: Nick Willson (Trustee)
Year Established: 1984
Acronym: ADSHG (UK)

Keywords
ADSHG (UK); Addison's Disease; Addison's Disease Self Help Group (UK); Adrenal Failure; Adrenal Insufficiency; Networking; Support Groups; United Kingdom

1174 Adenoid Cystic Carcinoma Alliance

Adenoid Cystic Carcinoma Alliance
P.O. Box 82
1649 N. Pacana Way
Green Valley, AZ 85614

Phone: (520) 625-5495
Fax: (951) 609-3982
E-mail: sharon.lane@rare-cancer.org
http://www.rare-cancer.org/adenoid-cystic-carcinoma/

The Adenoid Cystic Carcinoma Alliance was formed to raise awareness and disseminate information about this rare form of cancer. Our web site offers extensive disease information, personal stories, a support forum, patient database, and support funding for research projects. Adenoid cystic carcinoma is a rare form of cancer that usually begins in the head, neck or breast areas, but has been diagnosed in a variety of body sites.

Executive Director: Sharon Lane
Year Established: 1997
Acronym: ACCA

Keywords
ACC; ACCA; Adenoid Cystic Carcinoma Alliance; Adenoid Cystic Carcinoma; Carcinoma, Adenocystic

1175 Adenoid Cystic Carcinoma Organization International

PO Box 15482
San Diego, CA 92175
E-mail: accoi_info@yahoo.com
http://www.orgsites.com/ca/acco

The Adenoid Cystic Carcinoma Organization International provides education about adenoid cystic carcinoma, information on treatment and treatment facilities, current research updates. It helps to fund ACC research and provides an online support group for ACC patients and caregivers. Adenoid cystic carcinoma is a relatively rare form of cancer that most commonly develops in the salivary glands or other regions of the head and neck, but can occur in other parts of the body as well. Services of this not-for-profit organization include patient networking, support groups, and patient/physician education.

President: Prudence Jackson
Year Established: 2000
Acronym: ACCOI

Keywords
ACC; ACCOI; Adenoid Cystic Carcinoma; Adenoid Cystic Carcinoma Organization International; Networking; Support Groups

1176 Adult Congenital Heart Association

6757 Greene Street
Philadelphia, PA 19119

Phone: (215) 849-1260
Fax: (215) 849-1261
E-mail: info@achaheart.org
http://www.achaheart.org/

The Adult Congenital Heart Association (ACHA) is a nonprofit organization that seeks to improve the quality of life and extend the lives of adults with congenital heart defects. Through education, outreach, advocacy, and promotion of research, ACHA serves and supports the more than one million adults with congenital heart defects, their families, and the medical community. ACHA publishes a quarterly newsletter entitled "Heart Matters," hosts a very active message board for peer support, and periodically holds regional and national conferences at locations across the United States.

President: Amy Verstappen (2002-Present)
Executive Director: Amy Verstappen
Year Established: 1998
Acronym: ACHA

Keywords
ACHA; Adult Congenital Heart AssociationAortic Stenosis; Atrial Septal Defect; Coarctation of the Aorta; Congenital Heart Defects; Dextrocardia with Situs Inversus; Double Outlet Right Ventricle; Ebstein's Anomaly; Eisenmenger Syndrome; Patent Ductus Arteriosus; Pulmonary Stenosis; Tetralogy of Fallot; Transposition of the Great Arteries; Tricuspid Atresia; Truncus Arteriosus; Ventricular Septal Defects

1177 AED Pregnancy Registry

149 CNY-MGH East
Room 10010
Charlestown, MA 02129-2000

Phone: (617) 726-7739
Fax: (617) 724-1911
Toll Free: (888) 233-2334
E-mail: aedregistry@helix.mgh.harvard.edu
http://www.aedpregnancyregistry.org

The AED (Antiepileptic Drug) Pregnancy Registry enrolls any pregnant woman who is taking any antiepileptic drug for any reason. The list of drugs includes Ativan, Mysoline, Carbatrol, Neurontin, Depakene, Phenobarbital, Depatoe, Phenytek, Diamox, Tegretol, Dilantin, Topamax, Felbatol, Tranxene, Gabitril, Trileptal, Keppra, Valium, Klonopin, Zarontin, Lamictal, and Zonegran.

President: Lewis B. Holmes, M.D. (Director)
Executive Director: Elizabeth J. Baldwin (Coordinator)
Year Established: 1996
Acronym: AED Pregnancy Registry

Keywords
AED Pregnancy Registry; Anticonvulsant; Antiepileptic Drug Pregnancy Registry; Anxiety; Birth Defects; Depression; Epilepsy; Malformations; Migraines; Psychiatric Disorders; Seizure Disorders; Seizures

1178   Agenesis of the Corpus Callosum (ACC) Network

5749 Merrill Hall
Room 18
University of Maine
Orono, ME 04469-5749

Phone: (207) 581-3119
Fax: (207) 581-3120
E-mail: um-acc@maine.edu

The Agenesis of the Corpus Callosum (ACC) Network is a not-for-profit, self-help organization dedicated to providing information and support to individuals with agenesis of the corpus callosum, their families, and professionals. This condition is characterized by the complete or partial absence of the thick band of nerve fibers (corpus callosum) that connects the two cerebral hemispheres. Established in 1990, the Agenesis of the Corpus Callosum Network also provides support to individuals with other callosal disorders, including dysgenesis (malformation) and hypoplasia (thin) of the corpus callosum. The Agenesis of the Corpus Callosum Network facilitates the exchange of information, support, and resources through its networking programs.

Executive Director: Kathy Schilmoeller
Year Established: 1990
Acronym: ACC Network

Keywords
Acallosal; ACC; Agenesis of the Corpus Callosum (ACC) NetworkAcrocallosal Syndrome, Schinzel Type; Agenesis of the Corpus Callosum; Callosal; Corpus Callosum; Corpus Callosum Abnormalities; Corpus Callosum, Underdevelopment of; Dysgenesis of the Corpus Callosum; Hypoplasia of the Corpus Callosum; Oculocerebrocutaneous Syndrome

1179   Aicardi Syndrome Awareness and Support Group

29 Delavan Avenue
Toronto
Ontario, M5P 1T2, Canada

Phone: (416) 481-4095
E-mail: asasn@sympatico.ca
http://www.aicardisyndrome.org/

The Aicardi Syndrome Awareness and Support Group (ASASG) is a national self-help organization dedicated to providing information and support to Canadian families affected by Aicardi syndrome. It also acts as an information gathering and sharing resource for healthcare professionals. Aicardi syndrome, an extremely rare genetic disorder that affects only females, is characterized by absence of the thick band of nerve fibers that connects the left and right hemispheres of the brain (agenesis of the corpus callosum), seizures and spasms, characteristic retinal lesions, mental retardation, and/or other abnormalities. ASASG was established in the late 1980s in coordination with the Aicardi Syndrome Newsletter, Inc. (see below). ASASG is committed to providing a network of information, communication, and support to families of children with Aicardi syndrome; strengthening and empowering families in becoming advocates for their affected children; gathering current research articles and findings regarding Aicardi syndrome and other related topics for distribution to member families; providing information about Aicardi syndrome to the public; and serving as a reference and resource contact for medical, educational, and professional organizations.

President: Nancy Hately
Executive Director: Same as above.
Year Established: 1987
Acronym: ASASG

Keywords
Aicardi Syndrome; Aicardi Syndrome Awareness and Support Group; Agenesis of Corpus Callosum (Chorioretinitis Abnormality); ASASG; Callosal Agenesis and Ocular Abnormalities; Choriorentinal Anomalies with ACC; Corpus Callosum, Agenesis of and Chorioretinal Abnormality

1180 Aicardi Syndrome Foundation

P.O. Box 3202
St. Charles, IL 60174

Toll Free: (800) 374-8518
E-mail: foundation@aicardisyndrome.org
http://www.aicardisyndrome.org

The Aicardi Syndrome Foundation (ASF) is a voluntary rare disorder organization founded in 1993 to provide a network and financial support for families who have children afflicted by Aicardi syndrome, a congenital disorder in which the structure linking the two cerebral hemispheres of the brain (corpus callosum) fails to develop. ASF also provides grants for medical research on the disorder. In addition to patient networking, ASF also offers education and support groups to those affected.

President: Al Meo
Year Established: 1993
Acronym: ASF

Keywords
Aicardi Syndrome; Aicardi Syndrome Foundation; ASF; Networking; Research; Support Groups

1181 Aicardi Syndrome Newsletter, Inc.

1510 Polo Fields Court
Louisville, KY 40245

Phone: (502) 244-9152
E-mail: AICNews@aol.com
http://www.aicardisyndrome.org

Aicardi Syndrome Newsletter, Inc., is a voluntary, not-for-profit organization dedicated to providing a network of information and support to families with children who have Aicardi syndrome and strengthening and empowering families in becoming advocates for their children. Aicardi syndrome, an extremely rare genetic disorder that affects only females, is characterized by absence of the thick band of nerve fibers that connects the left and right hemispheres of the brain (agenesis of the corpus callosum), seizures and spasms, characteristic retinal lesions, mental retardation, and/or other abnormalities. The newsletter provides current research, articles, and findings regarding Aicardi syndrome for member families. In addition, it distributes information about Aicardi syndrome to the public and serves as a reference and resource contact for medical, education, and professional organizations. Aicardi Syndrome Newsletter, Inc., provides several educational materials including reports, brochures, and a bibliography of published journal articles. Biennial international conferences are held in the U.S. every other (even) year.

President: Denise Park Parsons
Executive Director: Ande Glasmacher
Year Established: 1991
Acronym: ASN

Keywords
Absence of Corpus Callosum; Aicardi Syndrome; Aicardi Syndrome Newsletter, Inc.; Dutch; French; German; Greek; Italian; Networking; Portuguese; Research; Retinal Lacunae; Seizures; Support Groups

1182 Alagille Syndrome Alliance

10500 SW Starr Drive
Tualatin, OR 97062

Phone: (503) 885-0455
Fax: (503) 885-0455
E-mail: alagille@earthlink.net
http://www.alagille.org

The Alagille Syndrome Alliance is a not-for-profit voluntary organization that functions as a support network for people affected by Alagille syndrome, a rare genetic disorder. Established in 1993, the Alagille Syndrome Alliance is dedicated to providing support to children with this disorder, their family members, and healthcare professionals who care for people with Alagille syndrome. The Alliance advocates for continuing medical research into the cause, prevention, and treatment of Alagille syndrome, and serves as a central location for resources related to the diagnosis and treatment of this rare disorder. The Alagille Syndrome Alliance offers a matching service to interested families as well as advice and consultation through specialists on its Medical Advisory Board.

President: Cindy L. Hahn (1993–Present)
Year Established: 1993

Keywords
AHD; Alagille Syndrome; Alagille Syndrome Alliance; Cholestasis with Peripheral Pulmonary Stenosis; Dysplasia, Arteriohepatic; Intrahepatic Biliary

Atresia; Intrahepatic Biliary Dysgenesis; Syndromic Bile Duct Paucity; Syndromic Hepatic Ductular Hypoplasia; Watson Alagille Syndrome

1183 Albinism Fellowship

P.O. Box 77
Burnley
Lancashire, BB11 5GN, United Kingdom

Phone: +44 (0) 1282-77-1900
E-mail: info@albinism.org.uk
http://www.albinism.org.uk

The Albinism Fellowship is a voluntary organization that aims to provide information, advice, and support for people with albinism, parents, families, teachers, physicians, ophthalmologists, and other people with an interest in the condition. The fellowship has charitable status in Scotland. Its membership extends around the world and is networked with similar organizations in the US and Australia. The fellowship was founded in 1979 by a retired ophthalmologist.

President: Mark Sanderson
Year Established: 1979

Keywords
Achromia, Congenital; Albinism; Albinism Fellowship; Albinsim, Oculocutaneous; Albinismus; BADS; Hypopigmentation

1184 ALD Family Support Trust

4 Morley House
320 Regent Street
London, W1B 3BB, United Kingdom

Phone: +44 (0) 207-631-3336
Fax: +44 (0) 207-631-3336
E-mail: info@aldfst.org.uk
http://www.aldfst.org.uk

The ALD Family Support Trust (ALDFST) is a not-for-profit organization dedicated to furthering medical research into adrenoleukodystrophy (ALD); providing grants and allowances for the purposes of medical treatment and care of children with ALD; and educating the public about ALD. Adrenoleukodystrophy is a rare inherited metabolic disorder characterized by the loss of the protective fatty sheath around nerve fibers within the brain (cerebral demyelination) and progressive degeneration of the adrenal gland (adrenal atrophy), causing progressive mental deterioration, neuromuscular abnormalities and loss of the ability to speak, blindness, and life-threatening complications.

Established in 1993 and consisting of approximately 57 members, the trust also has a support group and provides networking opportunities to parents. Educational materials include pamphlets and a regular newsletter.

President: Attia G. Attia
Year Established: 1993
Acronym: ALDFST

Keywords
ALD; ALDFST; Addison Disease with Cerebral Sclerosis; Addison Schilder Disease; Adrenoleukodystrophy; Adrenomyeloneuropathy; ALD Family Support Trust; AMN; Attia Research Trust into ALD; Bronze Schilder's Disease; Encephalitis, Periaxialis Diffusa; Encephalitis, Schilder; Flatau Schilder Disease; Leukodystrophy, Sudanophilic; Onset ALD, Adult; Schilder's Disease; Sclerosis, Myeloclastic Diffuse; Siewerling Creutzfeldt Disease

1185 Alexander Graham Bell Association for the Deaf, Inc.

3417 Volta Place, NW
Washington, D.C. 20007-2778

Phone: (202) 337-5220
Fax: (202) 337-8314
Toll Free: (866) 337-5220
E-mail: info@agbell.org
http://www.agbell.org

The Alexander Graham Bell Association for the Deaf, Inc., is a not-for-profit organization dedicated to helping hearing-impaired individuals by developing maximal use of residual hearing, speech reading, and speech and language skills. It strives to promote better public understanding of hearing loss. The association advocates the detection of hearing loss in early infancy as well as appropriate hearing aid use. It also collaborates on research relating to auditory or verbal communication. Established in 1890 by Alexander Graham Bell, the organization is also committed to working for better educational opportunities for affected children; providing in-service training for teachers; and offering scholarships. In addition, the association disseminates information on the causes of hearing impairment and options for remedial treatment. It collaborates with physicians, audiologists, speech/language specialists, and educators to promote educational, vocational, and social opportunities for affected individuals. The organization also supports legislation beneficial to affected individuals, conducts international conferences, and has one of the world's largest historical collections of information on deafness.

President: Inez Janger
Executive Director: Todd Houston
Year Established: 1890

Keywords
Acoustic Neuroma; Alexander Graham Bell Association for the Deaf, Inc.; Bjornstad Syndrome; Carpenter Syndrome; Chromosome 10, Monosomy 10p; Chromosome 18q Syndrome; Crouzon Syndrome; Deafness; Hearing Impairment; Hearing Loss; Usher's Syndrome; Waardenburg Syndrome; Wildervanck Syndrome

1186 Alkaptonuria Society, LTD

12 High Beeches
Court Hey
Roby Road
Childwall, Liverpool, L16 39A, United Kingdom

Phone: +44 (0) 151-737-1862
Fax: +44 (0) 151-737-1862
E-mail: aku.aps@tiscali.co.uk
http://www.alkaptonuria.info

The aim of the Alkaptonuria Society is to create an information and support network for people diagnosed with alkaptonuria. This is an inborn error of metabolism due to a deficiency of an enzyme that results in urine that turns dark upon standing, progressive joint destruction, and pigment deposition in connective tissues. The Alkaptonuria Society provides news and information on its web site, and raises funds for research on this rare disorder.

Executive Director: Mr. Robert Charles Gregory
Year Established: 2003

Keywords
Advocacy; Alcaptonuria; Alkaptonuria Society, LTD; H.O.A.D.; Networking; Ocranosis; Research

1187 Alliance Against Alveolar Soft Part Sarcoma

141-08 Coolidge Avenue
Briarwood, NY 11435

Phone: (718) 523-7752
Fax: (718) 657-0516
E-mail: info@alveolarspsarcoma.net
http://www.alveolarspsarcoma.net/

The Alliance Against Alveolar Soft Part Sarcoma (TAAASPS) is solely dedicated to the eradication of alveolar soft part sarcoma, a rare type of cancer involving a tumor typically in the leg or buttocks that may later spread to the lungs. The Alliance works to raise awareness of this disease and to raise funds for research to support the development of more effective therapies. TAAASPS is currently working with several institutions to develop a vaccine against the disease. It also offers programs such as support groups for patients and family members, patient networking, and patient education.

President: Rose Britley (2003-present)
Executive Director: Dr. Mark Thornton, MD (Vice President)
Year Established: 2000
Acronym: TAAASPS

Keywords
Alliance Against Alveolar Soft Part Sarcoma; Alveolar Soft Part Sarcoma; Networking; Support Groups; TAAASPS

1188 Alpha-1 Association

275 West Street
Suite 210
Annapolis, MD 21401

Fax: (410) 216-6983
Toll Free: (800) 521-3025
E-mail: info@alpha1.org
http://www.alpha1.org

The Alpha-1 Association is a not-for-profit, voluntary health organization that was formed to provide information and support to individuals and families affected by alpha-1-antitrypsin deficiency. Alpha-1-antitrypsin deficiency is a rare hereditary metabolic disease characterized by low levels of the enzyme alpha-1-antitrypsin and progressive degenerative and destructive changes in the lungs. Founded in 1991, the organization functions as a clearinghouse for information to assist healthcare professionals and affected individuals. In addition, it engages in patient advocacy and aids in the support of medical research into the control and cure of alpha-1-antitrypsin deficiency. Educational materials produced by the association include brochures, newsletters, and videos.

President: Jan Petersen, Esq.
Executive Director: Miriam O'Day, Senior Director of Public Policy
Year Established: 1991
Acronym: A1A

Keywords
A1AT Deficiency; Alpha-1 Antitrypsin Deficiency; Alpha-1-Antitrypsin Deficiency National Association; Alpha-1 Association; Emphysema, Familial; Emphysema, Genetic

1189 Alpha-1 Foundation

2937 SW 27th Avenue
Suite 302
Miami, FL 33133

Phone: (305) 567-9888
Fax: (305) 567-1317
Toll Free: (877) 228-7321
E-mail: jhall@alphaone.org
http://www.Alphaone.org

The Alpha-1 Foundation is a not-for-profit voluntary organization dedicated to providing the leadership and resources that will result in increased research, improved health, worldwide detection, and a cure for alpha-1. Alpha-1-antitrypsin deficiency (A1AD) is a hereditary disorder characterized by low levels of a protein called alpha-1-antitrypsin (A1AT), which is found in the blood.

President: John W. Walsh
Year Established: 1995
Acronym: A1F

Keywords
A1F; AAT Deficiency; Alpha-1 Antitrypsin Deficiency; Alpha-1 Foundation

1190 Alpha-1 Research Registry

c/o Medical University of South Carolina
96 Jonathan Lucus Street
Suite 812-CSB
PO Box 250630
Charleston, SC 29425

Phone: (843) 792-0260
Fax: (843) 792-0260
Toll Free: (877) 866-2383
E-mail: alphaone@musc.edu
http://www.alphaoneregistry.org

The Alpha-1 Research Registry is a confidential database of individuals diagnosed with, or identified as carriers of, alpha-1 antitrypsin deficiency. Low levels of a protein called alpha-1-antitrypsin which is found in the blood and protects the lungs so that they can work normally characterize this hereditary disorder. When the level of this protein is deficient, the lungs may be damaged, and breathing may be affected. The registry was established in 1997 by the Alpha-1 Foundation to facilitate research toward improved treatment and, ultimately, a cure for this disorder. It is located at the Medical University of South Carolina in Charleston.

President: Charlie Strange, MD
Executive Director: Yonge Jones / Laura Schwarz
Year Established: 1997

Keywords
Alpha 1 Research Registry; Alpha-1 Antitrypsin Deficiency; Alpha-1 Research Registry

1191 ALS Society of Canada

265 Yorkland Boulevard
Suite 300
Toronto
Ontario, M2J 1S5, Canada

Phone: (416) 49-7 22
Fax: (416) 49-1 12
Toll Free: (800) 26-7 42
E-mail: susan@alsont.ca
http://www.alsont.ca

The ALS Society of Canada is a national, not-for-profit organization dedicated to providing information and support to individuals and family members affected by ALS and to promoting research to find a cure for the disorder. Amyotrophic lateral sclerosis (ALS), also known as "Lou Gehrig's disease," is a rapidly progressive neuromuscular disease characterized by degeneration of the motor neurons responsible for transmitting electrical impulses from the brain to the voluntary muscles throughout the body. Established in 1977, the ALS Society, which operates in many locations across Canada, provides support and counseling for people with ALS, their families, and caregivers; raises funds to support research into the cause of and a potential cure for ALS; engages in patient advocacy; offers networking services; and provides equipment such as wheelchairs.

President: Sharon Weir
Executive Director: Suzanne Graham Walker
Year Established: 1977
Acronym: ALS Society of Canada

Keywords
ALS; ALS Society of Canada; Amyotrophic Lateral Sclerosis; Amyotrophic Lateral Sclerosis Society of Canada; Amyotrophic Lateral Sclerosis with Polyglu-

cosan Bodies; Aran Duchenne Muscular Atrophy; Gehrig's Disease; Lou Gehrig's Disease; Motor System Disease (Focal and Slow)

1192 Alstrom Syndrome International

14 Whitney Farm Road
Mt. Desert, ME 04660

Phone: (802) 228-8358
Fax: (207) 288-6078
Toll Free: (800) 371-3628
E-mail: jdm@jax.org OR robin@acadia.net
http://www.jax.org/alstrom

Alstrom Syndrome International (ASI) is a not-for-profit organization for individuals with Alstrom syndrome, their families and friends, healthcare professionals, researchers, and all individuals whose lives have been touched by this rare disorder. Alstrom syndrome is a genetic disorder that is slowly progressive, affecting multiple organ systems. Affected individuals experience progressive degeneration of the retina, resulting in childhood blindness; mild to moderate hearing impairment; glucose intolerance (non-insulin dependent diabetes mellitus) that develops in early adulthood; childhood obesity that often moderates to high-normal weight in adulthood; progressive kidney failure; congestive heart failure that becomes apparent during infancy, adolescence, or adulthood; and/or other symptoms and findings. Alstrom Syndrome International was established by six affected families in 1995 (as the Society for Alstrom Syndrome Families, SASF) and currently consists of approximately 200 members. ASI's mission is "to provide support, information, and coordination world-wide to families and professionals in order to treat and cure Alstrom syndrome." The organization is committed to providing information, support, resources, and networking opportunities to affected individuals and family members; and promoting and encouraging genetic and clinical research with the ultimate hope of developing a therapy for Alstrom syndrome and related disorders.

President: Anne D. Nordstrom, Chair Board of Directors
Executive Director: Robert P. Marshall
Year Established: 1995
Acronym: ASI

Keywords
Alstroem's Syndrome; Alstrom's Disease; Alstrom Syndrome International; ASI; Dilated Cardiomyopathy; Hearing Loss; Insulin Resistance; Obesity; Renal Failure; Retinitis Pigmentosa; Type 2 Diabetes

1193 Alstrom Syndrome UK

49 Southfield Avenue
Paignton
South Devon, TQ3 1LH, United Kingdom

Phone: +44 (0) 1803-52-4238
Fax: +44 (0) 1803-52-4238
E-mail: info@alstrom.org.uk
http://www.alstrom.org.uk

Alstrom Syndrome UK is an international voluntary health organization dedicated to providing information, resources, and support to individuals affected by Alstrom syndrome, family members, and healthcare professionals. Alstrom syndrome is a rare genetic disorder characterized by progressive degeneration of the nerve-rich membrane lining the eyes (retinitis pigmentosa), resulting in early visual loss; mild to moderate deafness; glucose intolerance (non-insulin dependent diabetes mellitus) that develops in early adulthood; moderate obesity; progressive kidney failure; and/or other symptoms and findings. Alstrom Syndrome UK was established in 1998 by the parents of two children with the disorder. The organization, which is affiliated with the Society of Alstrom Syndrome Families (SASF International Research Group), is committed to raising public and professional awareness of Alstrom syndrome, promoting research into the cause of the disorder, and engaging in patient advocacy. In addition, Alstrom Syndrome UK conducts family conferences and offers other networking opportunities that enable affected families to exchange information, support, and resources. The organization's educational materials include an information packet, a bibliography of medical journal articles, and a regular newsletter.

President: Kay Parkinson, L.L.B.
Executive Director: John Parkinson
Year Established: 1998
Acronym: AS UK

Keywords
Alstrom Syndrome UK; Alstrom's Disease; AS UK; Cardiomyopathy, Dilated; Diabetes Type II; Dutch; French; German; Russian; Scoliosis

1194 Alternating Hemiplegia of Childhood Foundation (AHC)

11700 Merriman Road
Livonia, MI 48150

Phone: (650) 365-5798
Fax: (650) 365-5798

Toll Free: (888) 225-3353
E-mail: laegan6@sbcglobal.net
http://www.ahckids.org

The Alternating Hemiplegia of Childhood Foundation (formally known as IFAHC) is a voluntary, not-for-profit organization dedicated to providing current information to affected individuals and their families. AHC is a rare neurological disorder characterized by frequent, temporary episodes of paralysis on one side of the body (hemiplegia); temporary paralysis of the muscles that control eye movement (transient ocular palsies); sudden, involuntary movements of limbs and facial muscles (choreoathetosis); and/or excessive sweating with changes in skin color and body temperature (autonomic nervous system dysfunction). Symptoms usually become apparent before the age of 18 months. High stress activities have been known to cause the attacks, as well as the presence of a cold or upper respiratory problem. Bright lights, temperature changes, and exposure to water may also affect children with AHC. Fewer than 100 children in the United States, and fewer than 250 worldwide, have been diagnosed with AHC. It is only within relatively recent years that AHC has been recognized as a distinct disorder. Many children are initially diagnosed with epilepsy or other seizure disorders. Founded in 1993 by two families who have children affected by this disorder, the organization supports ongoing medical research into the cause, treatment, and potential cure of AHC. It also disseminates information to promote proper diagnosis; maintains a registry of families, affected children, and physicians who are familiar with AHC; has a medical advisory board; and produces brochures and a regular newsletter.

President: Richard George
Executive Director: Lynn Egan (Contact Person)
Year Established: 1993
Acronym: AHCF

Keywords
AHC; AHCF; Alternating Hemiplegia of Childhood; Alternating Hemiplegia of Childhood Foundation (AHC); International Foundation for Alternating Hemiplegia of Childhood

1195 Alveolar Capillary Dysplasia Association
5902 Marcie Court
Garland, TX 75044-4958

Phone: (972) 414-4422
E-mail: sdesj@verizon.net
http://www.acd-association.com

The Alveolar Capillary Dysplasia Association is a not-for-profit organization dedicated to providing information, support, and resources to parents of children born with alveolar capillary dysplasia (ACD). ACD is a condition characterized by abnormal development (dysplasia) of the tiny air sacs in the lungs (alveoli). In all reported cases, ACD has occurred in association with primary pulmonary hypertension of the newborn (PPHN), which is characterized by abnormally increased blood pressure in the arteries supplying the lungs. Affected infants also typically have misalignment of pulmonary veins, poor development of certain capillaries, and/or other findings. In most cases, during the first days of life, affected newborns develop a bluish discoloration of the skin and mucous membranes (cyanosis) due to abnormally low levels of circulating oxygen (hypoxia), and experience difficulty breathing. In many cases, life-threatening complications may result within three to four weeks. The condition usually appears to occur randomly, for no apparent reason (sporadic). However, a few familial cases have been reported. The Alveolar Capillary Dysplasia Association was established in 1997 by the parents of a child born with ACD. The association is committed to providing mutual support to affected families through networking services; offering information concerning current research; educating the medical community and the general public about alveolar capillary dysplasia; and working with affected families and the medical community to expand the current knowledge of ACD.

President: Steve and Donna Hanson
Year Established: 1997
Acronym: ACDA

Keywords
ACD; ACDA; Alveolar Capillary Dysplasia; Alveolar Capillary Dysplasia Association; Networking

1196 Alzheimer Society of Canada
20 Eglinton Avenue West
Suite 1200
Toronto
Ontario, M4R 1K8, Canada

Phone: (416) 488-8772
Fax: (416) 488-3778
Toll Free: (800) 616-8816
E-mail: info@alzheimer.ca
http://www.alzheimer.ca

The Alzheimer Society of Canada is a not-for-profit Canadian health organization that is dedicated to providing a nationwide network of services to help Canadians affected by Alzheimer's disease, a degenerative neurological disease characterized by progressive deterioration of cognitive processes and memory (dementia). Affected individuals experience progressive memory failure; confusion and disorientation; changes in mood, behavior, and personality; speech difficulties; and other symptoms and findings. The Alzheimer Society of Canada was founded in 1978 and has 10 provincial societies across Canada. The society's objectives include alleviating the personal and social consequences of Alzheimer's disease, supporting those who are caring for people with the disease, promoting public understanding and awareness, and funding biomedical, social, and psychological research. The society offers a variety of programs and services including conducting an annual national awareness program, providing care guidelines for caregivers, and running Safely Home TM.

President: Carl Parsons
Executive Director: Steve Rudin
Year Established: 1978

Keywords
Aging; Alzheimer Society of Canada; Alzeimer's Disease; Caregiving; Cognitive Decline; Dementia; Geriatrics

---

1197 Alzheimer's Association
225 North Michigan Avenue
Suite 1700
Chicago, IL 60601-7633

Phone: (312) 335-8700
Fax: (312) 335-1110
Toll Free: (800) 272-3900
E-mail: info@alz.org
http://www.alz.org

The Alzheimer's Association is a national, not-for-profit voluntary organization dedicated to promoting and supporting research into the causes, cure, and prevention of Alzheimer's disease and providing education and support services to people with Alzheimer's Disease, their families, and caregivers. Established in 1980, the association works through a network of more than 220 local chapters, more than 2,000 support groups, and 35,000 volunteers nationwide. The goals of the Alzheimer's Association include education, chapter formation, advocacy for improved public policy and needed legislation, and patient and family services to aid present and future patients and caregivers. Activities of the association include the promotion of

fund-raising for research through its Medical and Scientific Advisory Board; publication of the quarterly "Alzheimer's Association Newsletter"; and promotion of public awareness by publicizing such national annual events as Memory Walk and the national education conference. In addition, the association operates a 24-hour telephone hotline to assist people with Alzheimer's disease and their families.

President: Sheldon Goldberg
Year Established: 1980
Acronym: ADRDA

Keywords
ADRDA; Alzheimer's Association; Alzheimer's Disease; Creutzfeldt-Jakob Disease; Dementia, Senile; Kluver Bucy Syndrome; Pick's Disease

---

1198 Alzheimer's Disease Education and Referral Center
P.O. Box 8250
Silver Spring, MD 20907-8250

Phone: (301) 495-3311
Fax: (301) 495-3334
Toll Free: (800) 438-4380
E-mail: adear@alzheimers.org
http://www.alzheimers.org

The Alzheimer's Disease Education and Referral (ADEAR) Center is a service of the National Institute on Aging (NIA) and National Institutes of Health, dedicated to providing information about Alzheimer's disease and related disorders to the general public, patients and their families, and health professionals. Established in 1990, ADEAR seeks to investigate the basic mechanisms of Alzheimer's disease, manage the symptoms, and help families cope with the effects of the disease. The organization maintains an online bibliographic database of materials and resources. This database is available to the public as the "Alzheimer's Disease Sub file" of the Combined Health Information Database (CHID) and is a valuable resource for health professionals, administrators, social service workers, and caregivers. CHID contains information on patient brochures, fact sheets, books, journals, audiovisuals, directories, and posters.

Executive Director: Jennifer Watson (Project Director)
Year Established: 1990
Acronym: ADEAR

Keywords
AD; Alzheimer's Disease; Alzheimer's Disease Education and Referral Center; Binswanger's Disease; Creutzfeldt-Jakob Disease; Degenerative Brain Disorders; Dementia, Irreversible; Kluver Bucy Syndrome; Pick's Disease

1199 Alzheimer's Disease International

64 Great Suffolk Street
London, SE1 OBL, United Kingdom

Phone: +44 (0) 207-7981-0880
Fax: +44 (0) 207-7928-2357
E-mail: info@alz.co.uk
http://www.alz.co.uk

Alzheimer's Disease International is a not-for-profit umbrella organization consisting of 69 Alzheimer's disease organizations around the world that offer information, support, and resources to affected individuals, family members, and other caregivers. Alzheimer's disease is a degenerative neurological disease that affects memory, cognition, behavior, and emotion. Affected individuals experience progressive deterioration of cognitive processes and memory (dementia), resulting in confusion and disorientation, personality disintegration, memory failure, speech difficulties, agitation and restlessness. Alzheimer's Disease International (ADI) was established in 1984 and is in official relations with the World Health Organization. ADI is committed to collaborating with other international organizations with similar interests, stimulating public and political awareness at the national and international levels, and encouraging research. ADI's member organizations provide practical and emotional support to affected individuals and family members; information to affected families, healthcare professionals, and the public; advocacy services on behalf of people with dementia and their families; training for caregivers; and direct services, such as daycare and respite care.

Year Established: 1984
Acronym: ADI

Keywords
Alzheimer's Disease; Alzheimer's Disease International

1200 Alzheimer's Foundation of America

322 8th Avenue
6th Floor
New York, NY 10001

Phone: (866) 232-8484
Fax: (646) 638-1546
Toll Free: (866) 232-8484
E-mail: info@alzfdn.org
http://www.alzfdn.org

The Alzheimer's Foundation of America (AFA) is a national voluntary, not-for-profit charitable organization. Founded in 2002, AFA is dedicated to meeting the educational, social, and emotional needs of individuals and families affected by Alzheimer's disease and related disorders. AFA unites member organizations throughout the country to collaborate on program design and implementation, education and advocacy, and programs and resources. Additionally, AFA works to raise public awareness about Alzheimer's and related disorders.

President: Eric J Hall, CEO
Year Established: 2002
Acronym: AFA

Keywords
AFA; Alzheimer's Disease; Alzheimer's Foundation of America; Caregivers; Caregiving; Dementia; Huntington's Disease; Memory Screening; Parkinson's Disease

1201 Alzheimer's Society (UK)

Gordon House
10 Greencoat Place
London, SW1P 1PH, United Kingdom

Phone: +44 (0) 207-306-0606
Fax: +44 (0) 207-306-0808
E-mail: enquiries@alzheimers.org.uk
http://www.alzheimers.org.uk/

The Alzheimer's Society is a voluntary organization in the United Kingdom dedicated to providing information and support to individuals caring for those with Alzheimer's disease; ensuring quality day and home care for affected individuals; and funding medical and scientific research and campaigns for improved health and social services. Alzheimer's disease is a neurological disease characterized by progressive deterioration of cognitive processes and memory (dementia), resulting in confusion, disorientation, personality disintegration, memory failure, speech difficulties, restlessness, agitation, and other symptoms and findings. The Alzheimer's Disease Society, which includes 22,000 members and approximately 300 branches and support groups, brings together caregivers, family members, health and social care professionals, researchers and scientists, and policy makers through shared concern for people with dementia and those who care for them. The society is committed to providing comprehensive, current information on all forms of dementia, legal and financial matters, social and health services, and benefits; offering a network of branches, caregiver groups, caregiver contacts, befriending projects, and telephone help lines; providing quality day care and home care through its Care Consortium of local branches; and supporting affected families in financial need.

Executive Director: Harry Cayton

Keywords
Alzheimer's Disease; Alzheimer's Society (UK)

1202 Ambiguous Genitalia Support Network

P.O. Box 313
Clements, CA 95227-0313

E-mail: agsn@inreach.com

The Ambiguous Genitalia Support Network is a voluntary health organization consisting of affected individuals, parents, other family members, and professionals. Established in 1994, the Ambiguous Genitalia Support Network is dedicated to providing information, assistance, and support to families of children diagnosed with ambiguous genitalia. Ambiguous genitalia are those in which it is difficult to classify the infant as male or female. The group/network is made up of parents, families, and professionals, all with the common goal of making educated and informed decisions about children's health, medical care, and well-being related to intersex conditions.

President: Cherie Sintes (1994-Present)
Executive Director: Same as above.
Year Established: 1994
Acronym: AGSN

Keywords
Ablepharon Macrostomia Syndrome; Adrenal Hyperplasia, Congenital; Ambiguous Genitalia; Ambiguous Genitalia Support Network; WAGR Syndrome

1203 American Alliance of Cancer Pain Initiatives (AACPI)

1300 University Avenue
Suite 4720
Madison, WI 53706

Phone: (605) 265-4013
Fax: (605) 265-4014
E-mail: lmlindn1@wisc.edu
http://www.aacpi.wisc.edu

The American Alliance of Cancer Pain Initiatives (AACPI) is dedicated to promoting cancer pain relief nationwide by supporting the efforts of State Cancer Pain Initiatives. Cancer Pain Initiatives are voluntary, grassroots organizations composed of nurses, physicians, pharmacists, social workers, psychologists, and representatives of clergy, higher education, and government. Initiatives and their participants provide education and advocacy to healthcare providers, cancer patients, and patients' families. The AACPI provides national leadership and advocacy for the Initiative movement, recommends program direction, supports Initiative growth and development, facilitates regular communication among Initiatives, fosters collaborations with other organizations, and organizes an annual national meeting for Initiatives. As part of a broader movement to promote high quality healthcare for all, the AACPI is working to create a nation in which no one suffers needlessly from cancer pain.

President: Dr. June Dahl (Director)
Executive Director: Mary Bennett (Out-Reach Director)
Year Established: 1998
Acronym: AACPI

Keywords
AACPI; Advocacy; American Alliance of Cancer Pain Initatives (AACPI); Cancer Pain Management

1204 American Association for Cancer Research

615 Chestnut Street
17th Floor
Philadelphia, PA 19106-4404

Phone: (215) 440-9300
Fax: (215) 440-9313
E-mail: webmaster@aacr.org
http://www.aacr.org/

The American Association for Cancer Research (AACR), a scientific society of over 13,000 laboratory and clinical cancer researchers, was founded in 1907 to facilitate communication and dissemination of knowledge among scientists and others dedicated to cancer issues; foster research in cancer and related biomedical sciences; encourage presentation and discussion of new and important observations in the field; foster public education, science education, and training; and advance the understanding of cancer etiology, prevention, diagnosis, and treatment throughout the world. The AACR publishes four journals; convenes an annual meeting attended by more than 7,500 scientists from around the world; organizes several scientific conferences each year on new and significant developments in research; offers educational workshops and grants to young investigators; maintains an active public education program; and interacts frequently with cancer survivors, lay advocates, and the general public in support of its mission.

President: Susan Band Horwitz, PhD
Executive Director: Margaret Foti
Year Established: 1907
Acronym: AACR

Keywords
American Association for Cancer Research

1205 American Association for Klinefelter Syndrome Information and Support
2945 West Farwell Avenue
Chicago, IL 60645-2925

Phone: (773) 761-5298
Fax: (773) 761-5298
Toll Free: (888) 466-5747
E-mail: KSinfo@aaksis.org
http://www.aaksis.org

AAKSIS is a 501(c)(3) not-for-profit organization incorporated in Illinois. AAKSIS (pronounced "access") is a national voluntary organization with the mission of education, support, research and understanding of XXY and its variants, collectively known as Klinefelter syndrome. This disorder, characterized by the presence of an extra X chromosome, causes impaired function of the testes in males. AAKSIS supports greater awareness and understanding among the general public, medical profession, and affected men and their families through education and sharing of information about this medical condition and its effects. Established in 2000, the organization sponsors national and regional meetings, maintains a 24-hour hotline and web site, and publishes a newsletter and other informational materials.

President: Roberta Rappaport
Year Established: 2000
Acronym: AAKSIS

Keywords
AAKSIS; American Association for Klinefelter Syndrome Information and Support; Chromosome XXY; Klinefelter Syndrome

---

1206 American Association of Kidney Patients
3505 East Frontage Road
Suite 315
Tampa, FL 33607

Phone: (813) 636-8100
Fax: (813) 636-8122
Toll Free: (800) 749-2257
E-mail: info@aakp.org
http://www.aakp.org

The American Association of Kidney Patients (AAKP) is a not-for-profit organization committed to serving the needs of people with kidney disorders and their families. The association's programs include support for people dealing with the physical, emotional, and social impacts of kidney diseases. The association assists affected individuals to adjust to their own particular circumstances and challenges. It offers a variety of educational materials including bi-monthly and quarterly patient magazines.

President: Brenda Dyson (2001-Present)
Executive Director: Kris Robinson
Year Established: 1969
Acronym: AAKP

Keywords
AAKP; American Association of Kidney Patients; Bilateral Renal Agenesis; Familial Juvenile Hyperuricemic Nephropathy; Glycosuria, Renal; Hepatorenal Syndrome; Kidney Disease; Kidney Disorders; Nail Patella Syndrome; Ochoa Syndrome; Renal Disease; Renal Glycosuria

---

1207 American Association of the Deaf-Blind
8630 Fenton Street
Suite 121
Silver Spring, MD 20910

Phone: (301) 495-4403
Fax: (301) 495-4404
TDD: (301) 495-4402
E-mail: info@aadb.org
http://www.aadb.org

The American Association of the Deaf-Blind is a national consumer organization of, by, and for deaf-blind Americans and their supporters. Its members represent all walks of life with diverse social, educational, communication, and vocational backgrounds. AADB's mission is to ensure that deaf-blind people achieve their maximum potential through increased independence, productivity and integration into the community. The association provides a national conference; a membership drive; a magazine, The Deaf-Blind American; information; referral; technical assistance; and advocacy.

Executive Director: Jamie McNamara Pope
Year Established: 1984
Acronym: AADB

Keywords
AADB; Advocacy; American Association of the Deaf-Blind; Deaf-Blind; Hearing and Vision Impairments; Hearing and Vision Losses

---

1208 American Autoimmune Related Diseases Association, Inc.

22100 Gratiot Avenue
Eastpointe, MI 48021

Phone: (586) 776-3900
Fax: (586) 776-3903
Toll Free: (800) 598-4668
E-mail: aarda@aarda.org
http://www.aarda.org/

The American Autoimmune Related Diseases Association, Inc. (AARDA) is a national, not-for-profit, voluntary health agency dedicated to bringing a national focus to autoimmunity, a major cause of serious chronic diseases. The association was founded for the purposes of supporting research to find a cure for autoimmune diseases and providing services to affected individuals. Its goals include increasing the public's awareness that autoimmunity is the cause of more than 80 serious chronic diseases; bringing national focus and collaborative effort among state and national voluntary health groups that represent autoimmune diseases; and serving as a national advocate for individuals and families affected by the physical, emotional, and financial effects of autoimmune disease. The American Autoimmune Related Diseases Association produces educational and support materials including fact sheets, brochures, pamphlets, and a newsletter entitled "In Focus."

President: Virginia T. Ladd
Year Established: 1991
Acronym: AARDA

Keywords
AARDA; Acrodermatitis Enteropathica; Addison's Disease; Alopecia Areata; Alveolitis, Fibrosing; Amenorrhea, Primary; American Autoimmune Related Diseases Association, Inc.; Anemia, Hemolytic, Acquired Autoimmune; Anemia, Hemolytic, Cold Antibody; Anemia, Hemolytic, Warm Antibody; Anemia, Pernicious; Ankylosing Spondylitis; Antiphospholipid Syndrome; APL; Arteritis, Giant Cell; Arteritis, Takayasu; Arteritis, Temporal; Arthritis, Juvenile Rheumatoid; Arthritis, Psoriatic; Arthritis, Rheumatoid; Autoimmune Diseases; Autoimmune Thyroid Disease; Behcet's Syndrome; Cardiomyopathy; Chronic Fatigue Syndrome; Chronic Inflammatory Demyelinating Polyneuropathy; Cirrho-sis, Primary Biliary; Colitis, Ulcerative; Crohn's Disease; Diabetes, Insulin Dependent; Diabetes, Juvenile; Fibromyalgia; Graves' Disease; Guillain Barre Syndrome; Hashimoto's Syndrome; Hemolytic Anemia; Hepatitis, Chronic Active; Herpes Gestationis; Idiopathic Thrombocytopenic Purpura; Interstitial Cystitis; Lupus; Melkersson Rosenthal Syndrome; Mixed Connective Tissue Disease (MCTD); Multiple Sclerosis; Myasthenia Gravis; Myocarditis, Autoimmune; Myositis; Necrotizing Hemorrhagic Leukoencephalitis, Acute; Nephritis, Anti GMB; Nephritis, Anti TBM; Neutropenia; Pemphigus Vulgaris; Polyarteritis Nodosa; Polyglandular Syndrome Type I Autoimmune; Polyglandular Syndrome Type II Autoimmune; Polymyalgia Rheumatica; Polymyositis; Psoriasis; Raynaud's Disease and Phenomenon; Rheumatic Fever; Sarcoidosis; Scleroderma; Silicon Adjuvant Immunologic Disease; Sjogren Syndrome; Vasculitis; Vitiligo

---

1209 American Behçet's Disease Association

PO Box 19952
Amarillo, TX 79114-9952

Fax: (806) 622-2257
Toll Free: (800) 723-4238
E-mail: cfornabaio@behcets.com
http://www.behcets.com

The American Behçet's Disease Association is a voluntary, not-for-profit, self-help organization dedicated to providing support and informational materials to people with Behçet's disease and involved physicians. Behçet's syndrome is a rare chronic relapsing inflammatory disorder characterized by recurrent mouth ulcers, inflammation of the eyes, genital ulcers, rashes, and/or other symptoms. The American Behçet's Disease Association produces a quarterly newsletter and conducts patient conferences and family counseling sessions. In addition, it distributes informational literature, makes physician referrals, and encourages patient-to-patient networking. Translations of some materials are available. The American Behçet's Disease Association serves the entire United States. Regional support groups are located in Sacramento CA, San Francisco CA, Phoenix AZ, Oklahoma City OK, St. Louis MO, Huntsville AL, Atlanta GA, Virginia, New York City and upstate New York, New Jersey, New England and other locations. The American Behçet's Disease Association also maintains a database of scientific research into Behçet's disease.

President: Cathy Fornabaio
Executive Director: Belinda Rivas
Year Established: 1985
Acronym: ABDA

Keywords
ABDA; American Behcet's Disease Association; Bechet's Syndrome; Dutch; Italian; Networking; Support Groups

1210 American Brain Tumor Association

2720 River Road
Suite 146
Des Plaines, IL 60018

Phone: (847) 827-9910
Fax: (847) 827-9918
Toll Free: (800) 886-2282
E-mail: info@abta.org
http://www.abta.org

The American Brain Tumor Association (ABTA) is an independent, not-for-profit organization founded in 1973. Services include more than 40 publications that address brain tumors, their treatment, and coping with the disease. These publications are written in easy-to-understand language. The materials address brain tumors in all age groups. The association provides free social service consultations by telephone; a mentorship program for new brain tumor support group leaders; a nationwide database of established support groups; a resource listing of physicians participating in clinical trials; "Connections" pen pal program; regional patient/family meetings held in communities across the country; and ABTA Kids - a web site just for children interested in brain tumors.

President: John Hipchen (2004-Present)
Executive Director: Naomi Berkowitz
Year Established: 1973
Acronym: ABTA

Keywords
ABTA; American Brain Tumor Association; Astrocytoma; Astrocytoma, Benign; Astrocytoma, Malignant; Benign Brain Tumor; Brain Cancer; Brain Tumor; Chordoma; Ependymoma; Glioblastoma; Glioblastoma Multiforme; Malignant Brain Tumor; Medulloblastoma; Meningioma; Oligodendroglioma; Pallister Hall Syndrome; Support Groups; Tumor, Pituitary; Tumors, Brain; Tumors, Childhood Brain; Turcot Syndrome

1211 American Cancer Society, Inc.

1599 Clifton Road NE
Atlanta, GA 30329

Phone: (404) 320-3333
Toll Free: (800) 227-2345
http://www.cancer.org

The American Cancer Society (ACS) is a nationwide, community-based, voluntary health organization dedicated to eliminating cancer as a major health problem by preventing cancer and diminishing problems associated with a diagnosis of cancer through programs of research, education, advocacy, and service. Founded in 1913 and consisting of two million volunteers, the society funds ongoing medical research by scientists who are studying cancer. In addition, the media and public rely on the society for statistical research and epidemiological data. Through the "Resources, Information, and Guidance Program," the ACS provides callers with information about cancer, ACS services, and other resources in the community that meet the practical, social, psychological, and other needs of individuals and families affected by cancer. The society also publishes guidelines that assist physicians in establishing appropriate recommendations for the prevention and early treatment of the disease. In addition, the ACS actively seeks to educate policy makers at all levels of government about the history of cancer and the impact of health related legislation on the lives of people with cancer.

President: Mary A. Simmonds, MD
Executive Director: John Seffrin, Ph.D.
Year Established: 1913
Acronym: ACS

Keywords
ACS; Adenoid Cystic Carcinoma; Alveolar Soft Part Sarcoma; Ameloblastoma; American Cancer Society, Inc.; Astrocytoma, Malignant; Ataxia Telangiectasia; Atypical Mole Syndrome; Bowen's Disease; Brain Tumors; Cancer; Carcinoid Syndrome; Carcinoma; Castleman's Disease; Cerebellar Degeneration, Subacute; Chordoma; Colon Cancer; Cutaneous T Cell Lymphomas; Cystic Hygroma; Diencephalic Syndrome; Drash Syndrome; Ewing's Sarcoma; Familial Adenomatous Polyposis; Fibromatosis; Gardner Syndrome; Gastrointestinal Stromal Tumors; Glioblastoma Multiforme; Granulomatosis, Lymphomatoid; Hodgkin's Disease; Leukemia, Chronic Lymphocytic; Leukemia, Chronic Myelogenous; Leukemia, Hairy Cell; Lymphoma, Gastric, Non Hodgkins Type; Lynch Syndromes; Maffucci Syndrome; Mantle Cell Lymphoma; Medulloblastoma; Melanoma, Malignant; Meningioma; Mesothelioma; Mycosis Fungoides; Myelodysplastic Syndromes; Myelofibrosis, Idiopathic; Myeloma, Multiple; Nevoid Basal Cell Carcinoma Syndrome; Paget's Disease of the Breast; Pancreatic Islet Cell Tumor; Peutz Jeghers Syndrome; Pheochromocytoma; Prostrate Cancer; Pseudomyxoma Peritonei; Radiation Syndromes; Renal Cell Carcinoma; Retinoblastoma; Sinonasal Undifferentiated

Carcinoma; Skin Cancer; Tongue Carcinoma; Tumors, Malignant; WAGR Syndrome; Waldenstrom's Macroglobulinemia; Wilms' Tumor

1212 American Celiac Society-Dietary Support Coalition

P.O. Box 23455
New Orleans, LA 70183

Phone: (504) 737-3293
E-mail: americanceliacsociety@yahoo.com

The American Celiac Society-Dietary Support Coalition is a nonprofit, self-help organization that provides support, education, and encouragement for people with celiac sprue and other dietary disorders and food allergies, including dermatitis herpetiformis, Crohn's disease, lactose intolerance, and wheat intolerance. Through patient and general education, nationwide support groups, networking, referrals, and research, ACS/DCS works to increase the awareness of dietary disorders and to identify food products that may contain gluten-gliaden, lactose, corn or soya. ACS/DCS also publishes a newsletter, patient packets, brochures, and offers audio-visual aids for its members. The society offers some Spanish language materials, and has limited Spanish and Italian speaking resources.

President: Annette Bentley
Acronym: ACS/DSC

Keywords
ACS/DSC; Allergies, Food; American Celiac Society-Dietary Support Coalition; Celiac Disease; Celiac Sprue; Crohn's Disease; Dermatitis, Herpetiformis; Glucose Intolerance; Italian; Wheat Intolerance

1213 American Chronic Pain Association

P.O. Box 850
Rocklin, CA 95677

Phone: (916) 632-0922
Fax: (916) 632-3208
Toll Free: (800) 533-3231
E-mail: ACPA@Pacbell.net
http://www.theacpa.org

The American Chronic Pain Association is a nonprofit, self-help organization that provides assistance and hope to individuals with chronic pain. Established in 1980, the American Chronic Pain Association operates support groups throughout the United States and offers its members positive and constructive methods for dealing with chronic pain. Groups usually consist

of approximately 10 members who learn useful techniques for pain management through discussion, mutual support, and informational exchanges. Educational materials produced by the American Chronic Pain Association include "Help & Hope" pamphlets and brochures, guidelines for the selection of a pain unit, the "American Chronic Pain Association Member Workbook," tapes, and the "American Chronic Pain Association Chronicle."

President: Nicole Kelly
Executive Director: Penney Cowan
Year Established: 1980
Acronym: ACPA

Keywords
ACPA; American Chronic Pain Association; Chronic Pain; Dercum Disease; Fibromyalgia; Reflex Sympathetic Dystrophy Syndrome; Russian; Temporomandibular Joint Dysfunction; Tic Douloureux; TMJ; Trigeminal Neuralgia

1214 American Council for Headache Education

19 Mantua Road
Mt. Royal, NJ 08061

Phone: (609) 423-0258
Fax: (856) 423-0082
Toll Free: (800) 255-2243
E-mail: achehq@talley.com
http://www.achenet.org

The American Council for Headache Education (ACHE) is a national, voluntary, nonprofit organization dedicated to advancing the treatment and management of headache and to raising the public awareness of headache as a valid, biologically based illness. Its educational mission reaches out to health career policy makers, employers, and opinion leaders as well as to affected individuals and their families. ACHE's goal is to help affected individuals gain more control over all aspects of their lives-medical, social, and economical. The organization offers a national network of Headache Support Groups; online networking opportunities and information; referrals; advocacy services; and a variety of materials including local support group listings, brochures, booklets, and a regular newsletter.

President: Jan Lewis Brandes, MD
Executive Director: Linda McGillicuddy
Year Established: 1990
Acronym: ACHE

Keywords
ACHE; Advocacy; American Council for Headache Education; Cluster Headache; Facial Pain; Headache, Chronic Daily; Headaches; Migraine; Networking; Support Groups; Tension Headache

1215 American Council of the Blind, Inc.

1155 15th Street
Suite 1004
Washington, DC 20005

Phone: (202) 467-5081
Fax: (202) 467-5085
Toll Free: (800) 424-8666
http://www.acb.org

The American Council of the Blind is a national, not-for-profit, advocacy organization for people who are blind or visually impaired. Established in 1961, the council is dedicated to improving the well being of all blind and visually impaired people. To this end, it seeks to improve the social, economic, and cultural levels of affected individuals. The council is dedicated to improving educational and rehabilitation opportunities, and cooperating with public and private institutions and organizations concerned with services for people who are blind. It produces a variety of publications, including the "Braille Forum." Produced in Braille, large print, four-track cassette, and on computer disk, this magazine contains articles on employment, legislation, sports and leisure activities, and new products and services. The council also supports a national toll-free information and referral service.

President: Christopher Gray
Executive Director: Melony Brunson
Year Established: 1961
Acronym: ACB

Keywords
ACB; American Council of the Blind, Inc.; Bardet-Biedl Syndrome; Blindness; Choroideremia; Coats' Disease; Laurence Moon Syndrome; Leber's Congenital Amaurosis; Leber's Optic Atrophy; Macular Degeneration; Norrie Disease; Retinitis Pigmentosa; Retinopathy, Arteriosclerotic; Retinopathy, Hypertensive; Retinoschisis; Usher's Syndrome; Visual Impairments; Waardenburg Syndrome

1216 American Diabetes Association

National Call Center
1701 N. Beauregard Street
Alexandria, VA 22311

Phone: (703) 549-1500
Fax: (703) 549-6995
Toll Free: (800) 342-2383
E-mail: askADA@diabetes.org
http://www.diabetes.org

The American Diabetes Association is a nonprofit health organization providing diabetes research, information, and advocacy. Founded in 1940, it conducts programs in all 50 states and the District of Columbia.

Year Established: 1940

Keywords
Achard-Thiers Syndrome; American Diabetes Association; Ataxia, Friedreich's; Ataxia Telangiectasia; Autoimmune Polyendocrine Syndrome Type II; Diabetes; Diabetes Insipidus; Diabetes, Insulin Dependent; Diabetes Mellitus; Lipodystrophy; Rabson-Mendenhall Syndrome; Retinopathy, Diabetic; Schmidt Syndrome; Wolfram Syndrome

1217 American Foundation for the Blind

11 Penn Plaza
Suite 300
New York, NY 10001

Phone: (212) 502-7600
Fax: (212) 502-7777
Toll Free: (800) 232-5463
TDD: (212) 502-7662
E-mail: afbinfo@afb.org
http://www.afb.org

The American Foundation for the Blind (AFB) is a national, not-for-profit, voluntary organization established in 1921 and recognized as Helen Keller's cause in the United States. AFB is a national resource for people who are blind or visually impaired, the organizations that serve them, and the general public. The mission of AFB is to enable people who are blind or visually impaired to achieve equality of access and opportunity that will ensure freedom of choice in their lives. AFB fulfills this mission through four primary areas of activity. These include: the development, collection and dissemination of information on blindness and visual impairment; identification, analysis, and resolution of critical issues related to blindness and visual impairment; education of the public and policy makers as to the needs and capabilities of people who are blind or visually impaired; and the production and distribution of talking books and other audio materials. AFB records and duplicates talking books under contract to the Library of Congress and publishes books, pamphlets, videos, and periodicals about blindness for professionals and health care consumers.

President: Carl R. Augusto
Executive Director: Unknown
Year Established: 1921
Acronym: AFB

Keywords
AFB; American Foundation for the Blind; Bardet-Biedl Syndrome; Blindness; Coats' Disease; Laurence Moon Syndrome; Leber's Congenital Amaurosis; Leber's Optic Atrophy; Macular Degeneration; Norrie Disease; Retinitis Pigmentosa; Retinopathy, Diabetic; Retinopathy, Hypertensive; Retinoschisis; Usher's Syndrome; Visual Impairments; Waardenburg Syndrome

1218 American Foundation of Thyroid Patients

4322 Douglas Avenue
Midland, TX 79703

E-mail: thyroid@flash.net
http://www.thyroidfoundation.org

The American Foundation of Thyroid Patients, which is headquartered in Texas, is a voluntary, not-for-profit, self-help organization. With its newsletter, brochures, audio-visual aids and other materials, it provides information on thyroid disease to patients and their families, as well as to health professionals and the general public. The foundation provides information through its newsletter, which is called Thyroid USA, and other materials on the various thyroid diseases. A low-cost screening program is available for thyroid disease as well as other disorders. Physician referrals are also available, as is assistance to persons interested in developing local chapters.

President: Kelly Hale
Year Established: 1993
Acronym: AFTP

Keywords
AFTP; American Foundation of Thyroid Patients; Autoimmune Thyroiditis; Graves' Disease; Hashimoto's Syndrome; Hyperthyroidism; Hypothyroidism; Thyroiditis, Hashimoto's

1219 American Health Assistance Foundation

22512 Gateway Center Drive
Clarksburg, MD 20871

Phone: (301) 948-3244
Fax: (301) 258-9454

Toll Free: (800) 437-2423
E-mail: eberger@ahaf.org
http://www.ahaf.org

The American Health Assistance Foundation (AHAF) is a national, nonprofit, health organization dedicated to raising funds for scientific research on age-related and degenerative diseases, educating the public about these diseases, and providing financial assistance to Alzheimer's disease patients and their caregivers. Some of the age-related and degenerative diseases with which AHAF is concerned include Alzheimer's disease, macular degeneration, glaucoma, heart disease, and stroke.

President: Brian K. Regan, Ph.D.
Executive Director: Kathleen Honaker
Year Established: 1973
Acronym: AHAF

Keywords
AHAF; Alzheimer's Disease; American Health Assistance Foundation; Glaucoma; Heart Disease; Stroke

1220 American Hearing Research Foundation

8 South Michigan Avenue
Suite 814
Chicago, IL 60603-4539

Phone: (312) 726-9670
Fax: (312) 726-9695
E-mail: blederer@american-hearing.org
http://www.american-hearing.org

The American Hearing Research Foundation is a voluntary organization dedicated to providing support for medical research into the causes, prevention, and cure of deafness, impaired hearing, and balance disorders and to promoting hearing health education. Established in 1966, the American Hearing Foundation provides referrals and produces educational materials including a regular newsletter and pamphlets entitled "Facts and Fancies About Hearing Aids," "Care of the Ears and Hearing for Health," and "So You Have Had An Ear Operation...What Next?"

President: Alan G. Micco, MD
Executive Director: William L. Lederer
Year Established: 1966

Keywords
American Hearing Research Foundation; Balance Disorders; Deafness; Hearing Impairment; Tinnitus

1221 American Heart Association

National Center
7272 Greenville Avenue
Dallas, TX 75231-4596

Phone: (214) 373-6300
Fax: (214) 373-0268
Toll Free: (800) 242-8721
E-mail: inquire@heart.org
http://www.americanheart.org

The American Heart Association (AHA), a national, not-for-profit, voluntary health agency funded by private contributions, is dedicated to the reduction of death and disability from cardiovascular diseases including heart diseases and stroke. The association consists of approximately 2,000 community organizations in all states, the District of Columbia, and Puerto Rico. More than 4 million people volunteer with the association to fight cardiovascular diseases, the nation's number one cause of death and leading cause of disability. Preventing heart disease and stroke is the first priority of the American Heart Association. In support of this goal, the association has contributed more than one billion dollars to cardiovascular research since 1949. The association also distributes a variety of educational materials and sponsors continuing medical education (CME) seminars and meetings.

President: Robert O. Bonow, M.D.
Executive Director: M. Cass Wheeler (Chief Executive Officer)
Year Established: 1949
Acronym: AHA

Keywords
AHA; American Heart Association; Atrial Septal Defects; Atrioventricular Septal Defects; Cardiovascular Disease; Cardiovascular Disorders; Congenital Heart Defects; Cor Triatriatum; Endocarditis, Infective; Heart Block, Congenital; Heart Disease; Heart Disorders; Holt Oram Syndrome; Hypercholesterolemia; Hyperlipoproteinemia Type IV; Hypoplastic Left Heart Syndrome; Kearns Sayre Disease; Mitral Valve Prolapse Syndrome; Myopathy, Desmin Storage; Pulmonary Hypertension, Primary; Pulmonary Hypertension, Secondary; Retinopathy, Hypertensive; Romano Ward Syndrome; Shprintzen VCF Syndrome; Stroke; Tetralogy of Fallot; Truncus Arteriosus, Persistent; Ventricular Septal Defects; Wolff Parkinson White Syndrome

1222 American Hemochromatosis Society (AHS)

4044 W. Lake Mary Boulevard
Suite 104 PMB 416
Lake Mary, FL 32746-2012

Phone: (407) 829-4488
Fax: (407) 333-1284
Toll Free: (888) 655-4766
E-mail: mail@americanhs.org
http://www.americanhs.org

The American Hemochromatosis Society (AHS) is a not-for-profit voluntary organization dedicated to educating the public, medical community and media by distributing the most current information available on hereditary hemochromatosis (HH). This is a metabolic disorder characterized by excessive absorption of iron, which eventually damages numerous organs. The objectives of AHS include promoting population and newborn screening with genetic testing for HH, banning genetic discrimination and providing compassionate support of all patients with hereditary hemochromatosis. Educational materials include "What Every Senior Should Know About Hereditary Hemochromatosis" and "The ABC's of Pediatric Hereditary Hemochromatosis."

President: Sandra Thomas (1998-Present)
Executive Director: David Geise Snyder
Year Established: 1998
Acronym: AHS

Keywords
AHS; American Hemochromatosis Society; American Hemochromatosis Society (AHS); Hereditary Hemochromatosis; Iron Overload Disease

1223 American Institute of Stress

124 Park Avenue
Yonkers, NY 10703

Phone: (914) 963-1200
Fax: (914) 965-6267
E-mail: stress125@optonline.net
http://www.stress.org

The American Institute of Stress (AIS), established in 1978, is a nonprofit organization dedicated to advancing knowledge of mind-body relationships and the role of stress in health and illness. Its Board of Trustees consists of physicians, healthcare professionals and lay individuals with expertise in various stress-related areas as well as interest in the role of stress in disease and promoting health. Eligibility for fellowships is granted to those who can demonstrate expertise by virtue of training, publications or practical experience. Updated files are maintained on all stress-related topics from which informational packets can be ordered. A monthly newsletter is available to subscribers, members and fellows. AIS also organize and participate in conferences dealing with relevant issues.

President: Paul J. Rosch, M.D., F.A.C.P.
Executive Director: Anna Huzil
Year Established: 1978
Acronym: AIS

Keywords
AIS; American Institute of Stress; Anxiety; Depression; Stress Related Disorders

1224 American Juvenile Arthritis Organization
Arthritis Foundation, National Office
1330 West Peachtree Street
Atlanta, GA 30309

Phone: (404) 872-7100
Fax: (404) 872-9559
Toll Free: (800) 568-4045
E-mail: help@arthritis.org
http://www.arthritis.org

The American Juvenile Arthritis Organization (AJAO), a not-for-profit organization, is devoted to serving the needs of children, teens, and young adults with childhood rheumatic diseases, and those of their families. These diseases include juvenile rheumatoid arthritis, lupus (systemic lupus erythematosus), ankylosing spondylitis and other related conditions. Juvenile arthritis is medically different from the adult form of arthritis and may be far more severe in some cases. The American Juvenile Arthritis Organization was founded in 1981 to help serve the special needs of affected individuals and families, friends, and healthcare professionals. The organization enables members to exchange ideas and support, and serves as a clearinghouse of information. It sponsors an annual conference; monitors and promotes legislation that benefits individuals with juvenile arthritis; provides appropriate referrals; and sponsors research concerning potential causes, improved treatments, preventive measures, and possible cures.

President: John H. Klippel, MD
Executive Director: Katie Bitner
Year Established: 1981
Acronym: AJAO

Keywords
AJAO; American Juvenile Arthritis Organization; Ankylosing Spondylitis; Arthritis; Arthritis, Juvenile; Arthritis, Rheumatoid; Dermatomyositis; Lupus; Pseudoxanthoma Elasticum; PXE; Rheumatic Diseases of Childhood; Winchester Syndrome

1225 American Kidney Fund, Inc.
6110 Executive Boulevard
Suite 1010
Rockville, MD 20852

Phone: (301) 881-3052
Fax: (301) 881-0898
Toll Free: (800) 638-8299
E-mail: helpline@kindeyfund.org
http://www.kidneyfund.org

The American Kidney Fund, Inc., (AKF) is a national, not-for-profit health organization dedicated to providing direct financial aid to dialysis patients, transplant recipients, and donors to help cover the cost of treatment-related expenses. Grants are available to help patients afford the costs of medication, transportation, transient dialysis, and special dietary needs. Established in 1971, the American Kidney Fund promotes and supports research for kidney diseases, kidney donor development, and public and professional education. The American Kidney Fund publishes a newsletter as well as several brochures on kidney diseases, other related disorders, treatments, nutrition, and organ donation. Some selections are written specifically for children. Several brochures are also available in Spanish.

Executive Director: Karen M. Sendelback
Year Established: 1971
Acronym: AKF

Keywords
AKF; Alport Syndrome; American Kidney Fund, Inc.; Argininosuccinic Aciduria; Atypical Hemolytic Uremic Syndrome; Bartter's Syndrome; Blue Diaper Syndrome; Branchio Oto Renal Syndrome; Carbamyl Phosphate Synthetase Deficiency; Citrullinemia; Cystinuria; Drash Syndrome; Familial Juvenile Hyperuricemic Nephropathy; Financial Aid; Fraser Syndrome; German; Hematuria, Benign, Familial; Hemolytic Uremic Syndrome; Hepatic Fibrosis, Congenital; Hepatorenal Syndrome; IgA Nephropathy; Kidney Disease; Kidney Disorders; Loken Senior Syndrome; Medullary Cystic Kidney Disease/Nephronophthisis; Medullary Sponge Kidney; Mullerian Aplasia; N Acetyl Glutamate Synthetase Defi-

ciency; Nail Patella Syndrome; Ochoa Syndrome; Polycystic Kidney Diseases; Purpura, Henoch Schonlein; Renal Agenesis, Bilateral; Renal Disease; Renal Glycosuria; Transplantation, Renal; WAGR Syndrome; Wegener's Granulomatosis; Wilms' Tumor

1226 American Latex Allergy Association (A.L.E.R.T., Inc.)

PO Box 198
Slinger, WI 53213-0930

Toll Free: (888) 972-5378
TDD: (888) 972-5378
E-mail: alert@latexallergyresources.org
http://www.latexallergyresources.org

American Latex Allergy Association (A.L.E.R.T., Inc.) is a voluntary, nonprofit organization dedicated to creating awareness of latex allergy and providing support to affected individuals and family members. Latex is a natural rubber used in certain medical devices such as catheters and surgical gloves, as well as many products such as adhesives and paints. It has been estimated that approximately one percent of the general population, and about five to 15 percent of healthcare workers and others regularly exposed to latex in their work environments, are allergic to latex. Upon latex exposure, affected individuals may experience symptoms that range from mild to severe and include one or more of the following: hives or welts, swelling of affected areas, sneezing, headache, reddened, teary, and/or itchy eyes, hoarseness of the voice and/or soreness of the throat, abdominal cramps, and/or tightness of the chest, wheezing, and/or shortness of breath. Continued exposure to latex may cause a severe, potentially life-threatening allergic reaction (anaphylactic shock). The organization is committed to providing information and emotional support to affected individuals and their families and educating the public about latex allergy. A.L.E.R.T., Inc. is also dedicated to promoting the establishment of policies concerning the care of individuals with latex allergy; minimization of latex exposure for employees in all healthcare facilities and industrial settings; and research into the treatment and prevention of latex allergy.

President: Marsha Smith
Executive Director: Sue Lockwood
Year Established: 1993
Acronym: ALERT, Inc.

Keywords
ALERT, Inc.; American Latex Allergy Association; American Latex Allergy Association (A.L.E.R.T., Inc.); Latex Allergy; NRLA

1227 American Leprosy Missions

1 ALM Way
Greenville, SC 29601

Phone: (864) 271-7040
Fax: (864) 271-7062
Toll Free: (800) 543-3135
E-mail: amlep@leprosy.org
http://www.leprosy.org

The American Leprosy Missions (ALM) is a not-for-profit service organization devoted to the care of people with leprosy and to the eventual cure of this disorder. Leprosy, also known as Hansen's disease, is a progressive, chronic infectious disease caused by the bacterium, *Mycobacterium leprae*. The disorder affects nerves outside the central nervous system (peripheral nerves), particularly in the facial area and the limbs. In severe cases, loss of sensation, disfigurement, and/or blindness may occur. ALM also aids Buruli ulcer programs in Ghana, Ivory Coast, and the Democratic Republic of the Congo. Buruli is a flesh-destroying disease that affects mainly children under 15. ALM is working with the Infectious Disease Research Institute (IDRI) in Seattle to develop a vaccine against leprosy.

President: Christopher J. Doyle
Year Established: 1906

Keywords
ALM; American Leprosy Missions; Buruli Ulcer; Hansen's Disease; Leprosy

1228 American Liver Foundation

75 Maiden Lane
Suite 603
New York, NY 10038

Phone: (212) 668-1000
Fax: (212) 483-8179
Toll Free: (800) 465-4837
E-mail: info@liverfoundation.org
http://www.liverfoundation.org

The American Liver Foundation (ALF) is a national, voluntary, non-profit organization dedicated to the prevention, treatment, and cure of hepatitis and other liver diseases through research, education and advocacy. Established in 1976, ALF provides a national help line, educational information and programs, physician referrals, extensive scientific research grants, and a nationwide network of chapters and support groups.

President: Alan P. Brownstein, MPH
Year Established: 1976
Acronym: ALF

Keywords
Alagille Syndrome; ALF; Alpha-1 Antitrypsin Deficiency; American Liver Foundation; Biliary Atresia; Cancer, Liver; Cholangitis, Sclerosing; Cirrhosis; Cirrhosis, Primary Biliary;; Drug-induced Liver Injury; Fatty Liver; Galactosemia; Gallstones; Gilbert Syndrome; Glycogen Storage Disease; Hemochromatosis, Hereditary; Hepatitis C; Hepatitis, Autoimmune; Hepatitis, Chronic Active; Hepatitis, Neonatal; Liver Disease; Liver, Cystic Disease of the; Porphyria; Reye Syndrome; Sarcoidosis; Transplantation, Liver; Tyrosinemia; Wilson's Disease

1229 American Lung Association

61 Broadway, 6th Floor
New York, NY 10006

Phone: (212) 315-8700
Fax: (212) 315-8870
Toll Free: (800) 586-4872
http://www.lungusa.org

The American Lung Association (ALA) is a national, not-for-profit, voluntary health organization dedicated to the prevention, cure, and control of all types of lung disease such as asthma, emphysema, tuberculosis, and lung cancer. This is accomplished through programs of community service, public health education, advocacy, and research. The ALA was established in 1904 as the National Association for the Study and Prevention of Tuberculosis. As the number of tuberculosis cases declined over the years, the association widened its focus to include other forms of lung disease and, in 1973, changed its name to the American Lung Association. The association offers assistance through support groups, genetic counseling, patient networking, referrals, and the development and dissemination of educational materials. Such materials include reports, brochures, audiovisual aids, and Spanish language materials.

President: John L. Kirkwood
Year Established: 1904
Acronym: ALA

Keywords
Acute Respiratory Distress Syndrome; Advocacy; ALA; Alpha-1 Antitrypsin Deficiency; Alveolar Capillary Dysplasia; Alveolitis, Extrinsic Allergic; American Lung Association; APECED Syndrome; Asthma; Atrial Septal Defects; Atrioventricular Septal Defect;

Berylliosis; Bronchopulmonary Dysplasia (BPD); Cancer, Lung; Chronic Obstructive Pulmonary Disease; Churg Strauss Syndrome; Cystic Fibrosis; Dilatation of the Pulmonary Artery, Idiopathic; Emphysema; Emphysema, Congenital Lobar; COPD; Goodpasture Syndrome; Granulomatosis, Lymphomatoid; Idiopathic Pulmonary Fibrosis; Kartagener Syndrome; Langerhans Cell Histiocytosis; Lung Diseases; Lymphangioleiomyomatosis; Mesothelioma; Networking; Pneumonia, Interstitial; Pulmonary Alveolar Proteinosis; Pulmonary Disease; Pulmonary Hypertension; Research; Respiratory Distress Syndrome, Infant; Sarcoidosis; Smoking Cessation; Support Groups; Tuberculosis; Wegener's Granulomatosis; Yellow Nail Syndrome

1230 American Lyme Disease Foundation, Inc.

PO Box 684
Somers, NY 10589

E-mail: inquire@aldf.com
http://www.aldf.com

The American Lyme Disease Foundation, Inc., (ALDF) is a nonprofit organization that is dedicated to advancing treatment, research, prevention, and public awareness of Lyme disease and other tick borne illnesses. Lyme disease is an infectious tick-transmitted disease characterized by an early skin lesion and, subsequently, a growing red area on the skin (i.e., "bull's eye" rash). In some cases, later symptoms may include joint, neurological, and/or heart problems. Established in 1990, the foundation focuses on public and professional education and support of research. It provides a toll-free number and a national physician referral service. The ALDF also supports peer-reviewed research into the prevention and control of tick-borne infections.

Year Established: 1990
Acronym: ALDF

Keywords
ALDF; American Lyme Disease Foundation, Inc.; HGE; Human Granulocytic Ehrlichiosis; Lyme Arthritis; Lyme Borreliosis; Lyme Disease

1231 American Nystagmus Network, Inc.

303-D Beltine Place SW
Suite 321
Decatur, AL 35603

E-mail: webmaster@nystagmus.org
http://www.nystagmus.org

The mission of the American Nystagmus Network is to improve the quality of life for all persons and families affected by nystagmus through an organized support network, education, research, and public awareness. Nystagmus is characterized by involuntary, oscillating eye movement, which often affects visual acuity. It is not a specific medical condition, but rather a symptom of an underlying sensory or neuromuscular disorder. ANN serves an international audience, with listserve members in India, the United Kingdom, the Netherlands, and New Zealand. It grew out of a nystagmus Internet E-mail list introduced in 1997.

President: Jeffrey D. Lowry
Year Established: 1999
Acronym: ANN

Keywords
American Nystagmus Network, Inc.; ANN; Networking; Nystagmus

1232 American Pain Foundation

201 North Charles Street
Suite 710
Baltimore, MD 21201

Phone: (410) 783-7292
Fax: (410) 385-1832
Toll Free: (888) 615-7246
E-mail: info@painfoundation.org
http://www.painfoundation.org

The American Pain Foundation (APF) is a nonprofit education, research, and advocacy organization working to eliminate the national epidemic of undertreated pain in America. APF has been working with consumers, healthcare professionals, regulators, families, and others since 1997 to broaden the understanding of pain, increase access to available treatments, and support research. It serves as a clearinghouse and resource center for people in pain, their families, healthcare professionals, policy makers, and the media. APF promotes the recognition of pain as a critical healthcare issue. It advocates for changes in professional training, regulatory processes , and healthcare delivery systems to ensure that people with pain have high quality care.

President: Barbara Friedman (Development Specialist)
Executive Director: Tamara Sloan-Anderson (Program Development Diretor
Year Established: 1997
Acronym: APF

Keywords
Advocacy; American Pain Foundation; APF; Chinese; Chronic Pain; Networking; Pain Management; Reflex Sympathetic Dystrophy Syndrome; Research; Support Groups

1233 American Paraplegia Society

75-20 Astoria Boulevard
Jackson Heights, NY 11370-1177

Phone: (718) 803-3782
Fax: (718) 803-0414
E-mail: aps@UnitedSpinal.ORG
http://www.apssci.org

Founded in 1954 and incorporated in 1977, the American Paraplegia Society (APS) is dedicated to improving the quality of medical care delivered to persons with spinal cord impairment. Spinal cord medicine is recognized as a discipline that encompasses many components of specialized care. In view of this diversity, one of the major functions of APS is to foster the interchange of ideas in clinical and basic science.

Year Established: 1954
Acronym: APS

Keywords
American Paraplegia Society; Paraplegia; Spinal Cord Injury

1234 American Porphyria Foundation

PO Box 22712
Houston, TX 77227

Phone: (713) 266-9617
Fax: (713) 840-9552
E-mail: porphyrus@aol.com
http://www.porphyriafoundation.com

The American Porphyria Foundation is a national voluntary health organization established in 1981 to enhance public awareness of the porphyrias and to aid in advancing treatments of these disorders. Porphyria is a group of rare genetic disorders characterized by disturbances of porphyrin metabolism. The foundation assists people with porphyria and physicians by serving as an information source and exchange. It also provides individuals with the opportunity to participate in research, support groups, political action programs, seminars, and fund-raising projects. The foundation produces a variety of publications including a general brochure and several disease specific brochures.

President: James Young
Executive Director: Desiree Lyon
Year Established: 1981
Acronym: APF

Keywords
ADP; AIP; American Porphyria Foundation; APF; Coproporphyria; EPP; Erythropoietic Protoporphyria; HCP; Hereditary Coproporphyria; Porphyria; Porphyria, ALA-D; Porphyria, Acute Intermittent; Porphyria, Congenital Erythropoietic; Porphyria, Cutanea Tarda; Porphyria, Hereditary Coproporphyria; Porphyria, Variegate

1235   American Printing House for the Blind

1839 Frankfort Avenue
P.O. Box 6085
Louisville, KY 40206-0085

Phone: (502) 895-2405
Fax: (502) 899-2274
Toll Free: (800) 223-1839
E-mail: info@aph.org
http://www.aph.org

The American Printing House for the Blind (APH) is a national, not-for-profit, voluntary self-help organization dedicated to assisting blind individuals and their families. Established in 1858, the American Printing House for the Blind offers books, magazines, and other publications in braille or large print or in recorded versions. APH also produces a large number of educational and self-help materials, and offers referrals to other organizations for further support and assistance.

President: Tuck Tinsley, III
Year Established: 1858
Acronym: APH

Keywords
American Printing House for the Blind; Blindness; Visually Impaired

1236   American RSDHope

P.O. Box 875
Harrison, ME 04040-0875

Phone: (207) 583-4589
Fax: (207) 583-4978
E-mail: rsdhope@adelphia.net
http://www.rsdhope.org

The American RSDHope Group is a national not-for-profit organization dedicated to increasing awareness of reflex sympathetic dystrophy syndrome (RSDS) among affected individuals, their family members, health professionals, and the general public. RSDS is a rare disorder of the sympathetic nervous system that is characterized by chronic, severe pain following a simple trauma, break or fracture, sharp force injury, or surgery. The sympathetic nervous system is that part of the autonomic nervous system which regulates involuntary bodily functions such as increasing heart rate, constricting blood vessels, and increasing blood pressure. Excessive or abnormal responses of portions of the sympathetic nervous system are thought to be responsible for the pain associated with reflex sympathetic dystrophy syndrome. Established in 1995, the American RSDHope Group produces educational materials including newsletters, national seminars, videotapes, information packets, and one on one assistance when needed. It makes information available to patients, their families, and their healthcare professionals. RSDHope has established the Hope For Tomorrow Research Fund, which has no administrative costs.

Executive Director: Keith R. Orsini
Year Established: 1995
Acronym: American RSDHope

Keywords
American RSDHope; Reflex Sympathetic Dystrophy Syndrome; RSDS

1237   American Self-Help Group Clearinghouse (National Office)

Saint Clare's Hospital
25 Pocono Road
Denville, NJ 07834-2995

Phone: (973) 326-6789
Fax: (973) 326-9467
TDD: (973) 625-9053
E-mail: ASHC@cybernex.net
http://www.selfhelpgroups.org

The American Self-Help Clearinghouse is a not-for-profit service organization that increases the awareness, utilization, and development of self-help support groups and networks across the country. Established in 1990, the clearinghouse provides free consultation assistance to those individuals interested in starting needed new member-run national/international rare disorder support and information-sharing networks. The clearinghouse also provides information on existing national/international self-help groups for a wide range of illnesses, disabilities, addictions, and stressful life situations such as bereavement. It places people in contact with local self-help clearinghouses in many states. In addition, the American Self-Help Clearinghouse provides a variety of educational and support materials including a hand-out on "Ideas for Starting a Self-Help Group," a brochure on "Developing a Self-Help Support Network for Persons with a Rare Illness," the latest paperback edition of "The Self-Help Sourcebook," and a free listing of phone contacts for self-help clearinghouses across the country.

Executive Director: Edward Madara
Year Established: 1990

Keywords
American Self Help Group Clearinghouse; American Self-Help Clearinghouse; American Self-Help Group Clearinghouse (National Office); Bereavement

1238 American Skin Association

346 Park Avenue South
4th Floor
New York, NY 10010

Phone: (212) 889-4858
Fax: (212) 689-4959
E-mail: info@americanskin.org
http://www.americanskin.org

The American Skin Association (ASA), founded in 1987, is a volunteer-led health organization dedicated, through research, education, and advocacy, to saving lives and alleviating human suffering caused by the full spectrum of skin disease.

President: Howard P. Milstein (Chairman)
Executive Director: Joyce Weidler (Managing Director)
Year Established: 1987
Acronym: ASA

Keywords
American Skin Association; ASA; Contact Dermatitis; Eczema; Melanoma; Psoriasis; Research Grants; Skin Cancer; Skin Disorders; Sun Damage; Vitiligo

1239 American Sleep Apnea Association

1424 K Street NW
Suite 302
Washington, DC 20005

Phone: (202) 293-3650
Fax: (202) 293-3656
E-mail: asaa@sleepapnea.org
http://www.sleepapnea.org

The American Sleep Apnea Association (ASAA) is a not-for-profit, health service organization dedicated to reducing injuries, disabilities, and potentially life-threatening complications that may be caused by sleep apnea, a condition characterized by breathing difficulties while sleeping. Sleep apnea may occur during childhood or adulthood, may be genetic, and may occur due to, or in association with, a number of different underlying disorders. Established in 1990, the Association works to improve the well being of affected individuals and family members; promotes early diagnosis and appropriate treatment; and supports basic research into the causes and treatments of the disorder. It also fosters a nationwide ASAA A.W.A.K.E. Network, a network of self-help groups that provide additional information and support to individuals affected by sleep apnea. The American Sleep Apnea Association provides educational materials including videotape, brochures, a regular newsletter, and guidelines to help individuals start local support groups.

President: Rochelle Goldberg, MD
Executive Director: Edward Grandi
Year Established: 1990
Acronym: ASAA

Keywords
American Sleep Apnea Association; Apnea, Central; Apnea, Infantile; Apnea, Obstructive; Apnea, Sleep

1240 American Social Health Association

P.O. Box 13827
Research Triangle Park, NC 27709

Phone: (919) 361-8400
Fax: (919) 361-8425
E-mail: info@ashastd.org
http://www.ashastd.org

The American Social Health Association (ASHA) is a not-for-profit voluntary organization dedicated to stopping sexually transmitted diseases (STDs) and their harmful consequences to individuals, families, and communities. Established in 1914, ASHA provides direct patient support through the Herpes Resource Center/National Herpes Hotline and the HPV Support Group, which coordinate a network of over 100 local support groups and publish quarterly journals. ASHA also operates the National AIDS Hotline and the National STD Hotline, both under contract with the Centers for Disease Control and Prevention (CDC), as well as the FIRST STEP Hotline and Health Check Hotline, components of North Carolina's effort to improve the health and development of children in the state. In addition, ASHA advocates for increased funding for STD programs and public policies on STD control, working through its office in Washington D.C.; provides leadership for the National Coalition to Fight Sexually Transmitted Diseases; and operates the Women's Health Matters program. The organization also administers the ASHA Research Fund for STD research. ASHA's materials include an annual report, quarterly catalog, and pamphlets.

President: Linda L. Alexander, Ph.D., FAAN (CEO)
Executive Director: Allison Wright Kalloo, M.P.H. (Director of PR)
Year Established: 1914
Acronym: ASHA

Keywords
Acquired Immune Deficiency Syndrome (AIDS); AIDS (Acquired Immunodeficiency Syndrome); American Social Health Association; Chlamydia; Condyloma; Epididymitis; Gonorrhea; HIV; Hepatitis B; Herpes Symplex Virus 1; Herpes, Genital; Human Papilloma Virus; Sexually Transmitted Diseases; STDs; Syphilis, Acquired; Syphilis, Congenital

1241 American Sudden Infant Death Syndrome Institute

509 Augusta Drive
Marietta, GA 30067

Phone: (770) 426-8746
Fax: (770) 426-1369
Toll Free: (800) 232-7437
E-mail: prevent@sids.org
http://www.sids.org

The American Sudden Infant Death Syndrome Institute is a not-for-profit organization dedicated to preventing sudden infant death syndrome (SIDS) and to ensuring that the medical and corporate communities, government agencies, and general public share the sense of urgency in preventing SIDS. Sudden infant death syndrome is characterized by the sudden death of any infant or young child that is unexpected by history and for which no adequate cause of death can be found. The institute was founded to develop a comprehensive national program of research, clinical care, and education and to focus national attention and resources on the problem of SIDS. Established in 1983, the organization provides support groups, promotes research, engages in-patient and professional education, and offers clinical services.

President: Alfred Steinschneider, M.D., Ph.D.
Executive Director: Betty McEntire, Ph.D.
Year Established: 1983
Acronym: American SIDS Institute

Keywords
American Sudden Infant Death Syndrome Institute; Crib Death; SIDS; Sudden Infant Death Syndrome

1242 American Syringomyelia Alliance Project, Inc.

300 N Green Street
Suite 412
PO Box 1586
Longview, TX 75606-1586

Phone: (903) 236-7079
Fax: (903) 757-7456
Toll Free: (800) 272-7282
E-mail: info@asap.org
http://www.asap.org

The American Syringomyelia Alliance Project (ASAP), which was established in 1988, is a national nonprofit organization that functions as a clearinghouse for information on syringomyelia, a rare progressive condition characterized by the presence of abnormal fluid-filled cavities within the spinal cord and Chiari malformation. The organization provides information to people with syringomyelia and Chiari malformation, and seeks to increase public awareness of the disorders. The project also encourages medical research and seeks to raise funds for the investigation into the possible causes of, and the development of new treatments for, the disorder. The American Syringomyelia Alliance Project publishes a newsletter and produces informational materials and videotapes. It also hosts an annual conference and has a self-help network project.

President: Mark S. Kane (2002-Present)
Executive Director: Patricia (Williams) Maxwell
Year Established: 1988
Acronym: ASAP

Keywords
American Syringomyelia Alliance Project, Inc.; Arachnoiditis; Arnold Chiari Malformation; ASAP; Chiari I; Chiari II; Syringobulbia; Syringomyelia

1243 American Tinnitus Association

P.O. Box 5
Portland, OR 97207

Phone: (503) 248-9985
Fax: (503) 248-0024
Toll Free: (800) 634-8978
E-mail: tinnitus@ata.org
http://www.ata.org

The American Tinnitus Association is a national, not-for-profit, self-help organization dedicated to helping people with tinnitus and their healthcare providers. Tinnitus is a condition characterized by sensation of sound for which there is no external source. Such perceived sounds are often described as a buzzing, ringing, whistling, or clicking sensation. The association's activities include research for a cure and management of the condition; production and distribution of public awareness materials; educational programs for the professional and lay communities; establishment of, and guidance for, self-help groups and their leaders; promotion of community hearing-protection programs; and financial assistance to people who are unable to afford healthcare services for their tinnitus. Founded in 1979, the organization maintains a bibliographic service and publishes a variety of informational brochures and a quarterly journal, "Tinnitus Today."

President: W.F.S. Hopmeier, BC-HIS
Executive Director: Cheryl D. McGinnis, MBA, CAE
Year Established: 1979
Acronym: ATA

Keywords
Acoustic Neuroma; American Tinnitus Association; ATA; Financial Assistance; Meniere's Disease; Research; Ringing in the Ears; Tinnitus

1244   American Vitiligo Research Foundation, Inc.

PO Box 7540
Clearwater, FL 33758

Phone: (727) 461-3899
Fax: (727) 461-4796
E-mail: vitiligo@avrf.org
www.avrf.org

American Vitiligo Research Foundation, Inc. (AVRF), a voluntary 501(c)3 organization, provides public awareness about vitiligo through dedicated work, education and counseling. AVRF seeks to make a difference to those afflicted by this disease, focusing on children and families affected by vitiligo. Vitiligo is a dermatological condition characterized by the appearance of white patches on the skin on different parts of the body as a result of the destruction of the cells that make pigment. AVRF works toward its mission through services such as patient networking and referrals.

President: Stella Pavides (1995-) Present
Executive Director: Stella Pavlides Dir.
Year Established: 1995
Acronym: AVRF

Keywords
American Vitiligo Research Foundation, Inc.; AVRF Calendar; Embracing Diversity; Networking; Physician Referral; Seminars; Vitiligo

1245   amfAR (American Foundation for AIDS Research)

120 Wall Street
Thirteenth Floor
New York, NY 10005-3902

Phone: (212) 806-1600
Fax: (212) 806-1601
Toll Free: (800) 392-6327
E-mail: webmaster@amfar.org
http://www.amfar.org

The American Foundation for AIDS Research (amfAR) is the largest U.S. nonprofit dedicated to AIDS research, AIDS prevention, treatment education, and the advocacy of sound AIDS-related public policy. Educational materials include the amfAR Global Link and amfAR Treatment Insider.

President: Mathilde Krim, Ph.D. (Chairman of the Board)
Executive Director: Jerome Radwin
Year Established: 1985
Acronym: amfAR

Keywords
AIDS (Acquired Immunodeficiency Syndrome); AIDS Dysmorphic Syndrome; amfAR (American Foundation for AIDS Research); ARC; Dysmorphic AIDS; Dysmorphic Acquired Immune Deficiency Syndrome

1246   Amyloidosis Australia, Inc.

17 Victoria Street
Ferntree Gully
Victoria, 3156, Australia

Phone: +61 (0) 3-9758-2172
Fax: +61 (0) 3-9758-2172
E-mail: ellen@amyloidosisaustralia.org
http://www.amyloidosisaustralia.org

President: Ellen Reid (President)
Executive Director: Jean Reid (Secretary)
Year Established: 2005
Acronym: AmyOz

Keywords
AA; Advocacy; AmyOz; AL; Amyloidosis; Amyloidosis Australia, Inc.; Apolipoprotein Amyloidosis;

Beta 2 Microglobulin Amyloidosis; Cerebral Amyloid Angiopathy; Cutaneous Amyloidosis; Familial Amyloidosis; Familial Mediterranean Fever; Gelsolin Amyloidosis; Localized Amyloidosis; Lyzosyme Amyloidosis; Multiple Myeloma; Networking; Primary Amyloidosis; Research; Secondary Amyloidosis; Support Groups; Transthyretin Amyloidosis

1247 Amyloidosis Network International

7118 Cole Creek Drive
Houston, TX 77092

Phone: (713) 466-4351
Toll Free: (888) 269-5643

Amyloidosis Network International is a not-for-profit support organization dedicated to providing information, mutual support, and resources to individuals and families affected by amyloidosis. This is a chronic disorder in which an abnormal starch-like protein complex (amyloid) accumulates in certain tissues and organs of the body. Amyloidosis may occur as a primary disorder for unknown reasons (idiopathic) or secondary to underlying disorders such as rheumatoid arthritis, familial Mediterranean fever, cancer of the bone marrow (i.e., multiple myeloma), or tuberculosis. In addition, some forms of amyloidosis may be inherited. Amyloidosis Network International serves as a support group for individuals and families affected by the various forms of amyloidosis. It is affiliated with the Amyloidosis Support Network, which provides information online.

President: Jim Lang
Executive Director: Same as above.

Keywords
Abercrombie Syndrome; Amyloid Arthropathy of Chronic Hemodialysis Amyloidosis; Amyloidosis; Amyloidosis Network International; Amyloidosis of Familial Mediterranean Fever; Atypical Amyloidosis; Cardiopathic Amyloidosis; Hereditary Nephropathic Amyloidosis; Lichen Amyloidosis; Macular Amyloidosis; Neuropathic Amyloidosis; Paramyeloidosis; Pericollagen Amyloidosis; Primary Cutaneous Amyloidosis; Primary Nonhereditary Amyloidosis; Secondary Generalized Amyloidosis; Waxy Disease

1248 Amyloidosis Research Foundation

4174 Meyers Avenue
Waterford, MI 48329

Phone: (248) 884-0156
Fax: (248) 673-1477
E-mail: info@amyloidosisresearchfoundation.org
http://www.amyloidosisresearchfoundation.org

President: Mary O'Donnell (President)
Year Established: 2003
Acronym: ARF

Keywords
Amyloidosis; Amyloidosis Research Foundation; ARF; Research

1249 Amyloidosis Support Groups, Inc.

232 Orchard Drive
Wood Dale, IL 60191

Phone: (630) 350-7539
Fax: (847) 350-0577
Toll Free: (866) 404-7539
E-mail: muriel@amyloidosissupport.com
http://www.amyloidosissupport.com

Amyloidosis Support Groups, Inc., is a not-for-profit, rare disorder organization whose aim is to offer support to patients, families, and caregivers affected by amyloidosis, a group of disorders caused by abnormal folding, clumping, and/or accumulation of particular proteins within the tissues of various organs of the body. The organization exists to establish self-sufficient amyloidosis support groups. It sponsors annual retreats to train the facilitators of these groups. In addition, Amyloidosis Support Groups, Inc., provide referrals, information and patient advocacy, and support for research on this disease.

President: Muriel Finkel (President)
Executive Director: Elinda Lado (Secretary)
Acronym: ASG

Keywords
Advocacy; Amyloidosis; Amyloidosis Support Groups, Inc; ASG; Networking; Research; Support Groups

1250 Amyloidosis Support Network, Inc.

1490 Herndon Lane
Marietta, GA 30062

Phone: (770) 977-1500
Fax: (678) 560-7280
Toll Free: (800) 689-1238
E-mail: info@amyloidosis.org
http://www.amyloidosis.org

Then Amlyoidosis Support Network (ASN) is a not-for profit, patient advocacy organization committed to increasing the rate of early detection of amyloidosis, thereby improving survivability and quality of life. Amyloidosis is a group of diseases in which one or more organ systems in the body accumulate deposits of abnormal proteins in amounts sufficient to impair normal function. The Amyloidosis Support Network's primary function is to "link those affected by amyloidosis to further support resources" and increase public and professional awareness so that the disease can be detected earlier and properly treated.

President: Dennis Krysmalski
Year Established: 2000
Acronym: ASN

Keywords
Amyloid; Amyloidosis; Amyloidosis Support Network, Inc.

1251 Amyotrophic Lateral Sclerosis Association

27001 Agoura Road
Suite 150
Calabasas Hills, CA 91301-5104

Phone: (818) 880-9007
Fax: (818) 880-9006
Toll Free: (800) 782-4747
TDD: (818) 593-3540
E-mail: als@alsa-national.org
http://www.alsa.org

The Amyotrophic Lateral Sclerosis Association (ALSA) is a national, not-for-profit, voluntary health organization dedicated to the fight against amyotrophic lateral sclerosis (ALS). ALS, also known as "Lou Gehrig's disease," is a rapidly progressive neuromuscular disease characterized by degeneration of the motor neurons responsible for transmitting electrical impulses from the brain to the voluntary muscles throughout the body. ALSA consists of a growing network of over 135 local volunteer chapters and support groups across the United States. The association seeks to encourage, identify, fund, and monitor cutting-edge research into the cause, prevention, and possible cure of ALS. The organization also offers support on how to cope with the disease, provides referrals, and serves as the national information resource on ALS for medical professionals, affected individuals, and family members. ALSA also makes referrals to physicians, clinics, extended care facilities, home health agencies, visiting nurse agencies, transportation assistance, and medical equipment supplies. In addition, it has a patient registry and distributes information on the latest research and clinical trials.

President: Gary Leo
Year Established: 1985
Acronym: ALSA

Keywords
Amyotrophic Lateral Sclerosis Association; ALS; ALSA; Amyotrophic Lateral Sclerosis; Amyotrophic Lateral Sclerosis Association (ALSA); Lou Gehrig's Disease; Motor Neuron Disease; Polyglucosan Body Disease, Adult; Primary Lateral Sclerosis

1252 Anaphylaxis Campaign

P.O. Box 275
Farnsborough
Hants, GU14 6SX, United Kingdom

Phone: +44 (0) 1252-54-2029
Fax: +44 (0) 1252-37-7140
E-mail: info@anaphylaxis.org.uk
http://www.anaphylaxis.org.uk/

The Anaphylaxis Campaign is a health organization in the United Kingdom dedicated to providing information, support, and guidance concerning anaphylaxis. Established in 1994, the campaign is committed to raising awareness in the food industry and within the healthcare communities to ensure optimum provision of information to, and treatment of, affected individuals. Anaphylaxis is a severe allergic reaction upon exposure to certain foods, drugs, chemicals, or insect stings. The condition occurs due to an over-reaction of the body's immune system in response to a previously encountered allergen. Within minutes, in some cases seconds, affected individuals may experience flushing of the skin; hives; swelling of the mouth and throat; difficulty speaking, swallowing, and/or breathing; nausea and vomiting; low blood pressure (hypotension); irregular heart beat (arrhythmia); and/or collapse and unconsciousness. The Anaphylaxis Campaign promotes research, provides a variety of educational materials, and has a web site.

President: Dr. William Frankland
Executive Director: David Reading
Year Established: 1994

Keywords
Anaphylaxis; Anaphylaxis Campaign

1253 ANDO (Apoyo al Nino Down)

Dept. of Medical Genetics, Children's Hospital
111 Michigan Avenue
Washington, DC 20010

Phone: (202) 884-2187
Fax: (202) 884-2390
E-mail: curuburo@cnmc.org

ANDO (Apoyo al Nino Down) is a not-for-profit organization that provides information on Down syndrome to Hispanic families. Down syndrome is a chromosomal disorder in which all, or a portion of, chromosome 21 appears three times rather than twice in cells of the body. ANDO provides support groups, genetic counseling, patient networking, and educational materials to patients, family members, and the general public. It is based in the Department of Medical Genetics at the Children's National Medical Center at Washington, DC.

President: Cynthia J. Tippt
Executive Director: Catherine Uruburo
Year Established: 1997
Acronym: ANDO

Keywords
ANDO; ANDO (Apoyo al Nino Down); Apoyo al Nino Down; Down Syndrome; Support Groups

1254 Androgen Insensitivity Syndrome Support Group (AISSG)

P.O. Box 2148
Duncan, OK 73534-2148

E-mail: aissgusa@hotmail.com
http://www.aissgusa.org

The AISSG-USA provides information and support to people affected by the complete and partial forms of androgen insensitivity syndrome (AIS), and a variety of similar conditions. It provides services for adults with the condition, parents of affected children, and medical professionals. These services include information and referrals, phone support, advocacy, regional meetings, conferences and publications.

President: Kathryn Gallagher
Year Established: 1996
Acronym: AISSG-USA

Keywords
5 Alpha Reductase Deficiency; AIS; AISSG; AISSG-USA; Ambiguous Genitalia; Androgen Insensitivity Syndrome; Androgen Insensitivity Syndrome Support Group (AISSG); Androgen Insensitivity Syndrome, Partial; Mixed Gonadal Dysgenesis; Morris Syndrome; MRKH; PAIS; Primary Ammenorhea; Pure Gonadal Dygenesis; Reifenstein Syndrome; Swyer's Syndrome; Vaginal Hypoplasia

1255 Anemia Institute for Research and Education

151 Bloor Street West
Suite 600
Toronto, Ontario, M5S 1S4, Canada

Phone: (416) -96-9-74
Fax: (416) -96-9-74
Toll Free: (877) -99-2-63
E-mail: info@anemiainstitute.org
http://www.anemiainstitute.org

Anemia Institute for Research and Education (AIRE) is a not for profit advocacy organization founded in 2000. The mission of AIRE is to promote education, research, and advocacy about anemia. Anemia is any condition in which the number of red blood cells, the amount of hemoglobin, and the volume of packed red blood cells in the blood are lower than normal levels. AIRE hopes to achieve a better quality of life and health outcome for those at risk. AIRE offers patient networking and advocacy as services, which are helping them, work towards their goals.

President: Margery Konan (Program Director)
Executive Director: Durhane Wong-Rieger, PhD (President & CEO)
Year Established: 2000
Acronym: AIRE

Keywords
Acquired Aplastic Anemia; Acquired Immune Deficiency Syndrome; Advocacy; Anemia; AIDS; AIRE; Anemia Institute for Research and Education; Aplastic Anemia; French; Hepatitis C; HIV; Iron Deficiency Anemia; Kidney Disease; Myelodysplasia; Networking; Research; Sickle Cell Disease; Thalassemia Major; Thalassemia Minor

1256 Anencephaly Support Foundation

30827 Sifton
Spring, TX 77386

Phone: (281) 364-9222
Toll Free: (888) 206-7526
E-mail: info@asfhelp.com
http://www.asfhelp.com/asf/home

The Anencephaly Support Foundation is a national not-for-profit organization dedicated to providing support, information, and assistance to parents and professionals who are dealing with anencephaly. The foundation collects medical articles dealing with causation and prevention; provides phone and mail support; provides other necessary resources; offers lectures to the medical community about issues concerning anencephaly; and is involved in ongoing legislation designed to initiate national birth defect monitoring. Established in 1992, the foundation provides additional educational materials including support-group information and personal testimonies.

President: David Andis (1992 to Present)
Executive Director: Anne Andis
Year Established: 1992
Acronym: ASF

Keywords
Anencephaly; Anencephaly Support Foundation; ASF

1257 Angelman Syndrome Foundation, Inc.

3015 E. New York Street
Suite A2265
Aurora, IL 60504

Phone: (630) 978-4245
Fax: (630) 978-7408
Toll Free: (800) 432-6435
E-mail: info@angelman.org
http://www.angelman.org

The Angelman Syndrome Foundation, Inc. (ASF) is a not-for-profit organization. Its mission is to advance the awareness and treatment of Angelman syndrome through education and information, research, and support for individuals with Angelman syndrome, their families, and other concerned parties. Angelman syndrome is a rare genetic disorder characterized by mental and motor retardation, absence of speech, muscular abnormalities, unprovoked laughter, and characteristic facial abnormalities. Established in 1992, the Angelman Syndrome Foundation offers national, regional, and local support systems for affected individuals and their families. It also promotes and supports research on the diagnosis, treatment, management, and prevention of Angelman syndrome. The Angelman Syndrome Foundation offers a variety of educational and support materials through its web site, regular newsletter, brochures, pamphlets, and audiovisual materials.

President: Jay Vogelsang
Executive Director: Eileen Braun
Year Established: 1992
Acronym: ASF

Keywords
Angelman Syndrome; Angelman Syndrome Foundation, Inc.; AS; ASF

1258 Angelman Syndrome Support and Education Research Trust

Freepost Assert EH21 6ZX
Sittingbourne
Kent, ME10 1NE, United Kingdom

Phone: +44 (0) 1980-65-2617

The Angelman Syndrome Support and Research Trust (ASSERT) is an international nonprofit organization dedicated to providing information and support to families and caregivers of individuals who have Angelman syndrome. This rare genetic disorder is characterized by congenital mental retardation, the absence of speech, unprovoked laughter, unusual facial features, and muscular abnormalities. Established in 1986 and consisting of 450 members, ASSERT maintains a patient registry and raises funds for education of affected individuals and for ongoing research into the causes, treatment, and prevention of this disorder. ASSERT also offers a variety of educational materials including brochures and a regional newsletter.

President: Jeremy Webb
Year Established: 1986
Acronym: ASSERT

Keywords
Angelman Syndrome; Angelman Syndrome Support and Education Research Trust; Angelman Syndrome Support Group; AS

1259 Angioma Alliance

107 Quaker Meeting House Road
Williamsburg, VA 23188

Phone: (757) 258-3355
Fax: (757) 962-2923
Toll Free: (866) 432-5226
E-mail: info@angiomaalliance.org
http://www.angiomaalliance.org

The Angioma Alliance is a non-profit, charitable organization created by people affected by cavernous angioma. Cavernous angiomas are clusters of abnormal blood vessels found in the brain, spinal cord, and, rarely, other areas of the body. They can cause seizures, stroke symptoms, hemorrhages, and headache. Its goals are: 1) to ensure that everyone with cavernous angioma has access to informational materials written in layperson's terms 2) to provide support for persons affected by the illness 3) to promote research and 4) to educate the public so that those affected by the illness will receive understanding and support. Its web site provides information about the illness, networking/support opportunities, updates on research, and information about participating in ongoing research studies. The alliance distributes patient education materials through neurosurgeons, neurologists, and genetics professional nationally. Angioma Alliance sponsors national family educational conferences, exhibits at medical conventions, and offers a toll-free number for support and education.

President: Cornelia Lee
Year Established: 2002

Keywords
Angioma Alliance; Cavernomas; Cavernous Angioma; Cavernous Hemangioma; Cavernous Malformation; CCM; Cerebral Cavernous Malformation; Networking; Portuguese; Support Groups; Venous Angioma

1260   Aniridia Network
17 Sandmartin Crescent
Colchester, Essex, CO3 8WQ, United Kingdom

Phone: +44 (0) 7779-85-9624
E-mail: Hannah@aniriddia.org
http://www.aniridia.org

The Aniridia Network is an international, not-for-profit organization dedicated to supporting individuals and families affected by aniridia and to increasing awareness of aniridia around the world. Aniridia is a rare genetic vision disorder characterized by abnormal development of the eye's iris. Founded in 1998, the Aniridia Network provides education, networking and advocacy to those affected by the disorder.

President: Hannah James
Year Established: 1998

Keywords
Aniridia; Aniridia Network; Aniridia Network International; Vision Disorders

1261   Anorchidism Support Group
P.O. Box 3025
Romford, RM3 8GX, United Kingdom

Phone: +44 (0) 1708-37-2597
E-mail: asg.uk@virgin.net
http://freespace.virgin.net/asg.uk

The Anorchidism Support Group (ASG) is a voluntary organization that promotes research and provides educational materials and support to individuals who are affected by anorchia, a condition characterized by absence of one or both testes at birth. Established in 1995, ASG provides support groups for affected individuals and their families, patient networking, and educational materials including brochures and regular newsletters. The organization also provides updates concerning research into this condition.

President: Lorraine Bookless (1995 to Present)
Year Established: 1995
Acronym: ASG

Keywords
Anorchia; Anorchidism; Anorchidism Support Group; Anorchism; Testicles; Testicular Regression Syndrome; TRS; Undescended Testicles; Vanishing Testes; VTS; Syndrome

1262   Antiphospholipid Antibody Support Group
Marvin Nelson
4228 Deer Path Road
Apex, NC 27539-7282

Phone: (919) 362-8977
http://www.egroups.com/group/aplsuk

The Antiphospholipid Antibody Support Group is a not-for-profit web group providing information to the patients and families that have been affected by antiphospholipid syndrome. This is a rare autoimmune disorder characterized by recurring blood clots. It may also be associated with repeated spontaneous abortions for no apparent reason in young women. The syndrome may occur in individuals with lupus or related autoimmune diseases or as a primary syndrome in otherwise healthy individuals. In addition to providing information, the support group offers support, patient networking, and general education. In addition to its web site, APLSUK offers a chat group on Sunday night at 9 PM Eastern Time. Most of the people involved with the group are not medical professionals, but rather sufferers and their caregivers.

President: Marvin Nelson
Acronym: APLSUK

Keywords
Antiphospholipid Antibody Support Group; Antiphospholipid Syndrome; APS; Bloodclot; DVT; Heart Attack; Hughes Syndrome; Livido; Migraine; Miscarriage; Pulminary Embolism; Stroke; TIA

1263   Anxiety Disorders Association of America
8730 Georgia Avenue
Suite 600
Silver Spring, MD 20912

Phone: (240) 485-1001
Fax: (240) 485-1035
E-mail: anxdis@adaa.org
http://www.adaa.org

The mission of the Anxiety Disorders Association of America (ADAA) is to promote the prevention and cure of anxiety disorders and to improve the lives of all affected individuals. ADAA offers several materials concerning anxiety disorders including a quarterly newsletter that contains clinical information and updates, news on the latest events that ADAA is sponsoring, and personal accounts from affected individuals and members who share their experiences. ADAA also sponsors a variety of events each year including "National Anxiety Disorders Screening Day" and an annual national conference.

Executive Director: Heather Murray (Executive Coordinator)
Year Established: 1980
Acronym: ADAA

Keywords
Anxiety Disorders Association of America; Anxiety Disorders; Panic Disorders

1264 Apert Syndrome Support Group

8708 Kathy
St. Louis, MO 63126

Phone: (314) 965-3356
E-mail: N/A

The Apert Syndrome Support Group is a voluntary, not-for-profit, self-help organization dedicated to providing information and support to families of children with Apert syndrome. Apert syndrome is a rare genetic disorder characterized by premature closure of the fibrous joints between certain bones of the skull, fusion or webbing of the fingers and/or toes, and unusual facial features. Established in 1983, the Apert Syndrome Support Group enables affected families to exchange information, support, and resources through its networking program.

President: Beth Bruns, Co-Chair, (1983-Present)
Executive Director: Daniel Bruns (Co-Chair)
Year Established: 1983

Keywords
Acrocephalosyndactyly Type 1; ACS 1; Apert Syndrome; Apert Syndrome Support Group; Craniofacial Conditions; Surgery, Craniofacial; Syndactylic Oxycephaly

1265 Aphasia Hope Foundation

2436 W. 137th St
Leawood, KS 66224

Phone: (913) 402-8306
Toll Free: (866) 449-5804
E-mail: judistradinger@aphasiahope.org
http://www.aphasiahope.org

The Aphasia Hope Foundation began in 1997 as the result of a personal experience of an aphasia survivor and his caregivers. Even after consulting with professionals and researching available literature, they found very little helpful information regarding aphasia. Today, the foundation has a twofold mission: to promote research into the prevention and cure of aphasia and to ensure that all survivors of aphasia and their caregivers are aware of, and have access to, the best possible treatments. Aphasia is a speech and language difficulty that results from a stroke, head injury, or other neurological condition. Many aphasia survivors have problems reading, writing, and calculating, as well. The AHF is continually striving for the accomplishment of its mission through its three core areas: research, education, and advocacy.

President: Jim Hunt
Executive Director: Judi Stradinger
Year Established: 1997
Acronym: AHF or HOPE

Keywords
Aphasia; Aphasia Hope Foundation; Service Organization

1266 Aplastic Anemia & MDS International Foundation, Inc.

P.O. Box 613
Annapolis, MD 21404-0613

Phone: (410) 867-0242
Fax: (410) 867-0240
Toll Free: (800) 747-2820
E-mail: help@aamds.org
http://www.aamds.org

Founded in 1983, the Aplastic Anemia & MDS International Foundation, Inc., is a 501(c)(3) nonprofit organization with the following mission: to serve as a resource for patient assistance, advocacy, and support; provide educational materials and medical information; and to fund medical research to find effective treatments and cure for aplastic anemia, myelodysplastic syndromes, and related bone marrow diseases. Aplastic anemia results in decreased function of the bone marrow producing symptoms such as increasing weakness, fatigue, recurrent or persistent infections, and bleeding. In about 50 percent of cases, the exact cause is not known.

President: Dr. Robert F. Carroll
Executive Director: Marilyn M. Baker
Year Established: 1983
Acronym: AA&MDSIF

Keywords
AA & MDSIF; Acquired Aplastic Anemia; Advocacy; Aplastic Anemia & MDS International Foundation, Inc.; Aplastic Anemia Foundation of America, Inc.; Bone Marrow Failure; Chronic Myelomonocytic Leukemia; CMML; Hemoglobinuria, Paroxysmal Nocturnal; Myelodysplastic Syndromes; PNH; Paroxysmal Nocturnal Hemoglobinemia; Pure Red Cell Aplasia, Acquired; RA; RAEBT; RARS; Refractory Anemia; Refractory Anemia with Excess Blasts in Transformation; Refractory Anemia with Ringed Sideroblasts

1267 Aplastic Anemia & Myelodysplasia Association of Canada

11181 Yonge Street
Suite 321
Richmond Hill
Ontario, L4S 1L2, Canada

Phone: (905) 780-0698
Fax: (888) 840-0039
E-mail: info@aamac.ca
http://www.aamac.ca

The Aplastic Anemia & Myelodysplasia Association of Canada is a voluntary, not-for-profit organization founded in 1987 that is dedicated to the support of individuals with aplastic anemia or myelodysplasia and their family members. Aplastic anemia is a rare form of anemia in which there are abnormally low levels of red blood cells, white blood cells, and platelets in the blood. Myelodysplastic syndromes are a group of related bone marrow disorders. The association disseminates information in understandable lay terminology and has a network of volunteers with personal experience with these conditions who are able to give guidance and support during times of need. In addition, the association informs the public and healthcare professionals about aplastic anemia and myelodysplasia, and raises funds for medical research.

President: Gord Sanford
Executive Director: Silvia Marchesin
Year Established: 1987
Acronym: AAMAC

Keywords
Aplastic Anemia & Myelodysplasia Association of Canada; Aplastic Anemia Association of Canada; He-

moglobinuria; Myelodysplasia; Myelodysplastic Syndromes; Paroxysmal Nocturnal; PNH

1268 APS Foundation of America, Inc.

PO Box 801
624 North 10th Street
Suite 4
La Crosse, WI 54602-0801

Phone: (608) 782-2626
Fax: (608) 782-6569
E-mail: apsfa@apsfa.org
http://www.apsfa.org

The APS Foundation of America offers support and understanding to individuals, family members, friends, and caregivers affected by antiphospholipid antibody syndrome. This is an autoimmune disorder in which the body recognizes certain normal components of blood and/or cell membranes as foreign substances and produces antibodies against them. It causes multiple miscarriages, thrombosis, "young strokes" (ones that occur under age 45), and heart attacks. Women are more likely than men to be affected. The APS Foundation seeks to raise awareness of the syndrome. It also supports research.

President: Ms. Christina M. Pohlman (President)
Executive Director: Heidi Pongagi (Vice President)
Year Established: 2005
Acronym: APSFA

Keywords
Antiphospholipid Antibody Syndrome; APS Foundation of America, Inc; APSFA; Deep Vein Thrombosis; GI Bleeds; Heart Disease; Lupus; Migraine; Networking; Pulmonary Embolism; Stroke; Support Groups; Transient Ischemic Attack

1269 Ara Parseghian Medical Research Foundation

3530 E. Campo Abierto
Suite 105
Tucson, AZ 85718-3327

Phone: (520) 577-5106
Fax: (520) 577-5212
E-mail: victory@parseghian.org
http://www.parseghian.org

The Ara Parseghian Medical Research Foundation is an international, not-for-profit, voluntary organization dedicated to funding research projects to expedite a cure for Niemann-Pick disease type C (NP-C); promoting collaborative research efforts among experts in cholesterol metabolism; and studying parallel pediatric neurodegenerative disorders. NP-C, a rare inherited disorder of childhood, is a degenerative disease that causes progressive deterioration of the nervous system due to an inability to properly break down cholesterol. Excessive amounts of cholesterol accumulate in the brain, liver, and spleen leading to a variety of symptoms and findings. These may include abnormal enlargement of the liver and spleen (hepatosplenomegaly); difficulty walking (ataxia) and positioning the arms and legs; slurred or slow speech; difficulties performing certain eye movements (vertical supranuclear gaze palsy); and additional symptoms. During mid-adolescence, progressive neurological problems usually lead to life-threatening complications. The foundation's purpose is to speed the search for a cure by funding research and promoting worldwide interaction among scientists, research institutes, universities and pharmaceutical companies working on NP-C and related diseases.

President: Cindy K. Parseghian (1994 to present).
Executive Director: Glen A. Shepherd
Year Established: 1994
Acronym: APMRF

Keywords
Ara Parseghian Medical Research Foundation; Niemann Pick Disease Type C; NP C

1270 The Arc (A National Organization on Mental Retardation)
1010 Wayne Avenue
Suite 650
Silver Spring, MD 20910

Phone: (301) 565-3842
Fax: (301) 565-3843
Toll Free: (800) 433-5255
TDD: (817) 277-0553
E-mail: info@thearc.org
http://www.thearc.org/

The Arc is the largest organization in the United States that is solely devoted to improving the lives of all children and adults with cognitive, intellectual, and developmental disabilities including mental retardation. The organization offers support to families affected by these diabilities and fosters research and educational programs on the prevention of mental retardation. The Arc is committed to securing opportunities for all people with mental retardation. To this end, the organization emphasizes personal opportunities for choice in education, housing, employment, and entertainment.

The Arc is further committed to reducing the incidence and limiting the consequences of disabilities through research, advocacy, and mutual support. It provides a wide variety of educational materials for parents, teachers, healthcare professionals, and others. Many materials are available in Spanish, and most are free downloads online at www.thearc.org.

President: Leo Berggreen (2004-2006)
Executive Director: Sue D. Swenson
Year Established: 1950
Acronym: The ARC

Keywords
5-Oxoprolinuria; Aarskog Syndrome; Acidemia, Isovaleric; Acidemia, Methylmalonic; Acrocallosal Syndrome, Schinzel Type; Acrodysostosis; Adrenoleukodystrophy; Agenesis of the Corpus Callosum; Aicardi Syndrome; AIDS Dysmorphic Syndrome; Alagille Syndrome; Alexander's Disease; Alternating Hemiplegia of Childhood; Anemia, Pernicious; Angelman Syndrome; Aniridia Cerebellar Ataxia Mental Deficiency; Apert Syndrome; Arachnoid Cysts; The Arc (a national organization on mental retardation); Arginase Deficiency; Aspartylglycosaminuria; Attention Deficit Hyperactivity Disorder; Bardet-Biedl Syndrome; Bartter Syndrome; Beckwith-Wiedemann Syndrome; Borjeson Syndrome; C Syndrome; Cardio Facio Cutaneous Syndrome; Carnosinemia; Carpenter Syndrome; Cataract Dental Syndrome; CHARGE Syndrome; Cerebellar Agenesis; Chromosome 3 Monosomy 3p2; Chromosome 4 Monosomy 4q; Chromosome 4 Monosomy Distal 4q; Chromosome 4 Ring; Chromosome 6 Partial Trisomy 6q; Chromosome 7 Monosomy 7p2; Chromosome 8 Monosomy 8p2; Chromosome 9 Partial Monosomy 9p; Chromosome 9 Ring; Chromosome 9 Tetrasomy 9p; Chromosome 9 Trisomy 9p Multiple Variants; Chromosome 11 Monosomy 11q; Chromosome 11 Partial Trisomy 11q; Chromosome 13 Monosomy 13q; Chromosome 14 Ring; Chromosome 14 Trisomy Mosaic; Chromosome 15 Ring; Chromosome 18 Monosomy 18p; Chromosome 18 Tetrasomy 18p; Chromosome 18q Syndrome; Chromosome 22 Ring; Chromosome 22 Trisomy Mosaic; Coffin Lowry Syndrome; Coffin Siris Syndrome; Cohen Syndrome; Conradi Hunermann Syndrome; Cornelia de Lange Syndrome; Cri du Chat Syndrome; Crouzon Disease; Cutis Marmorata Telangiectatica Congenita; De Barsy Syndrome; DiGeorge Syndrome; Down Syndrome; Dubowitz Syndrome; Dyggve Melchior Clausen Syndrome; Dyskeratosis Congenita; Ectodermal Dysplasia; Ellis-van Creveld Syndrome; Encephalitis, Rasmussen's; Epidermal Nevus Syndrome; Fahr's Disease; Fetal Alcohol Syndrome; Fetal Hydantoin

Syndrome; FG Syndrome; Fiber Type Disproportion; Fibroplasia, Retrolental; Focal Dermal Hypoplasia; Fountain Syndrome; Fraser Syndrome; Froelich's Syndrome; Ganglioside Sialidase Deficiency; Gareis Mason Syndrome; Gaucher Disease; Glutaricaciduria I; Goldenhar Syndrome; Gorlin Chaudhry Moss Syndrome; Hallermann-Streiff Syndrome; Hallervorden Spatz Disease; Hartnup Disease; Histidinemia; Holoprosencephaly; Homocystinuria; Hunter Syndrome; Hurler Syndrome; Hydranencephaly; Hydrocephalus; Hyperglycinemia, Nonketotic; Hyperprolinemia Type II; Hypomelanosis of Ito; Hypothyroidism; I-Cell Disease; Ichthyosis, Sjogren Larsson Syndrome; Ivemark Syndrome; Jackson Weiss Syndrome; Joubert Syndrome; Kabuki Make Up Syndrome; Kallmann Syndrome; KBG Syndrome; Keratoconus; Kinsbourne Syndrome; Kufs Disease; Larsen Syndrome; Leigh's Disease; Lenz Microphthalmia Syndrome; Leprechaunism; Lesch Nyhan Syndrome; Leukodystrophy; Leukodystrophy, Krabbe; Lipodystrophy; Lowe's Syndrome; Mannosidosis; Maple Syrup Urine Disease; Marshall Smith Syndrome; MASA Syndrome; Meckel Syndrome; Meningitis; Meningitis, Tuberculous; Mentally Retarded; Moebius Syndrome; Moyamoya Disease; Mucopolysaccharidoses; Muscular Dystrophy, Becker; Muscular Dystrophy, Fukuyama Type; Neuropathy, Giant Axonal; Noonan Syndrome; Norrie Disease; Oculocerebral Syndrome with Hypopigmentation; Oral Facial Digital Syndrome; Pallister Hall Syndrome; Pallister Killian Mosaic Syndrome; Pallister W Syndrome; Paraplegia, Hereditary Spastic; Penta X Syndrome; Perisylvian Syndrome, Congenital Bilateral; Phenylketonuria; Phocomelia Syndrome; Phosphoglycerate Kinase Deficiency; Pseudo Hurler Polydystrophy; Pseudohypoparathyroidism; Pyruvate Dehydrogenase Deficiency; Rett Syndrome; Rickets, Vitamin D Deficiency; Rieger Syndrome; Robert's Syndrome; Rothmund Thomson Syndrome; Rubella, Congenital; Rubinstein Taybi Syndrome; Russell Silver Syndrome; Ruvalcaba Syndrome; Saethre Chotzen Syndrome; Sanfilippo Syndrome; Schindler Disease; Schinzel Giedion Syndrome; Seckel Syndrome; Septooptic Dysplasia; Sialidosis; Simpson Dysmorphia Syndrome; Sly Syndrome; Smith Lemli Opitz Syndrome; Smith Magenis Syndrome; Sotos Syndrome; Sturge Weber Syndrome; Syphilis, Congenital; Telecanthus with Associated Abnormalities; Tetrahydrobiopterin Deficiency; Toxoplasmosis; Trichorhinophalangeal Syndrome Type I; Triplo X Syndrome; Trisomy; Trisomy 4p; Trisomy 13 Syndrome; Trisomy 18 Syndrome; Tuberous Sclerosis; Tyrosinemia, Hereditary; WAGR Syndrome; West Syndrome; Wieacker Syndrome; Williams Syndrome; Wilms' Tumor; Wolf Hirschhorn Syndrome; Xeroderma Pigmentosum; Zellweger Syndrome; Zimmermann Laband Syndrome

1271 ARPKD/CHF Alliance

P.O. Box 70
Kirkwood, PA 17536

Phone: (717) 529-5555
Fax: (717) 529-5500
E-mail: info@arpkd.org
http://www.arpkd.org

The ARPKD/CHF Alliance is a non-profit, self-help organization dedicated to providing information and support to individuals and families affected by autosomal recessive polycystic kidney disease, a chronic and progressive disease that causes eventual kidney failure and liver abnormalities (congenital hepatic fibrosis). There is no cure, and life-threatening complications may develop soon after birth. Many parents receive the diagnosis before the baby is born. The alliance provides information, networking opportunities, and support for basic and clinical research.

President: Colleen Zak (Coordinator)
Executive Director: Same as above.
Year Established: 2001
Acronym: ARPKD Family Support Group

Keywords
ARPKD; ARPKD/CHF Alliance; Austosomal Reseccive Polycystic Kidney Disease; Autosomal Recessive Polycystic Kidney Disease; Caroli's Disease; Caroli's Syndrome; Childhood PKD; Childhood Polycystic Kidney Disease; Congenital Hepatic Fibrosis; Infantile Autosomal Recessive Polycystic Kidney Disease; Infantile PKD; Infantile Polycystic Kidney Disease; Juvenile Autosomal Recessive Polycystic Kidney Disease; Neonatal Autosomal Recessive Polycystic Kidney Disease; PKD; Polycystic Kidney Disease; Ductal Plate Malformation; Esophegeal Varices; Portal Hypertension

1272 Arrhythmogenic Right Ventricular Dysplasia Registry

1501 N. Campbell
Room 5153
Tucson, AZ 85724-5046

Phone: (520) 626-6262
Fax: (520) 626-4333

Toll Free: (800) 483-2662
E-mail: kgear@E-mail.arizona.edu
http://www.arvd.org/

The Arrhythmogenic Right Ventricular Dysplasia (ARVD) Registry is a not-for-profit registry that was formally established in 1997 to identify cases of ARVD. An NIH-funded five-year study of ARVD was started in September 2001, for newly diagnosed ARVD cases. The goal of the study is to find the genetic mutations causing ARVD, to determine how initial findings predict long-term prognosis and to evaluate the criteria for diagnosis of ARVD. Information about the NIH study can be found on ARVD.org and ARVD.com. Multiple enrolling centers in the United States and Canada are participating in the study. A brochure for physicians is available. A reprint of an article for patients is available.

President: Frank I. Marcus, M.D. (Co-Director) (1996 to Present).
Executive Director: Kathleen Gear, R.N. (Registry Coordinator)
Year Established: 1994
Acronym: ARVD Registry

Keywords
Arrhythmogenic Right Ventricular Dysplasia Registry; ARVD; Arrhythmogenic Right Ventricular Dysplasia Registry of the United States; ARPKD; Dysplasia, Arrhythmogenic Right Ventricular; Dysplasia, Right Ventricular

1273 Arthritis Foundation

1330 West Peachtree Street
Atlanta, GA 30309

Phone: (404) 872-7100
Fax: (404) 872-0457
Toll Free: (800) 568-4045
E-mail: help@arthritis.org
http://www.arthritis.org

The Arthritis Foundation is a not-for-profit voluntary health organization dedicated to supporting research into the prevention and cure of arthritis and providing services to improve the quality of life for affected individuals. Arthritis, an inflammatory condition of the joints that may result in swelling and pain, is a joint disease that may be due to a number of different underlying causes. Established in 1948, the Arthritis Foundation disseminates information worldwide on how arthritis is diagnosed, how it is inherited, how it affects pregnancy, its potential symptoms, and treatments. The organiza-

tion works for all people affected by any of the more than 100 forms of arthritis or related diseases. In nationwide chapters, the foundation helps support research, offers professional and community education programs, provides referral services, engages in government advocacy, and conducts fund-raising activities.

President: John H. Klippel, MD
Year Established: 1948

Keywords
Ankylosing Spondylitis; Arthritis; Arthritis Foundation; Fibromyalgia; Gout; Lupus; Osteoarthritis; Polymyalgia Rheumatica; Pseudoxanthoma Elasticum; PXE; Rheumatoid; Scleroderma

1274 Arthritis Foundation of Australia

GPO Box 121
Sydney
New South Wales, 2001, Australia

Phone: +61 (0) 2-9552-6085
Fax: +61 (0) 2-9552-6078
E-mail: info@arthritisaustralia.com.au
http://www.arthritisaustralia.com.au

The Arthritis Foundation of Australia is a not-for-profit organization that is committed to providing care, education, and research for people affected by arthritis and other musculoskeletal disorders. The term arthritis, meaning inflammation of the joints, may encompass several conditions or disease states, such as osteoarthritis, rheumatoid arthritis, ankylosing spondylitis, gout, and others. The Arthritis Foundation of Australia, which was founded in 1949, is dedicated to promoting research into the causes, control, and cure of arthritis; supporting the professional education and training of physicians and allied health professionals; and enhancing community awareness of the needs of those affected by arthritis. The foundation's additional objectives include representing people with arthritis nationally and internationally, serving as national secretariat of affiliated state and territory foundations, and assisting affiliated foundations in promoting self-management programs for people with arthritis. The Arthritis Foundation of Australia currently consists of eight state and territory affiliates.

President: Mark Franklin
Year Established: 1949

Keywords
Arthritis; Arthritis Foundation of Australia

1275 **Arthritis Society**

393 University Avenue
Suite 1700
Toronto
Ontario, M5G IE6, Canada

Phone: (416) 979-7228
Fax: (416) -97-9-83
Toll Free: (800) 321-1433
E-mail: info@arthritis.ca
http://www.arthritis.ca

The Arthritis Society is a not-for-profit organization in Canada dedicated to funding and promoting arthritis research, patient care, and public education. Arthritis, an inflammatory condition of the joints that may result in swelling and pain, is a joint disease that may be due to a number of different underlying causes. The society's mission is to search for the underlying causes and subsequent cures for arthritis, and to promote the best possible care and treatment for people with arthritis. Established in 1948, the society, which serves 10 provincial divisions of Canada, engages in patient advocacy; promotes patient and professional education; provides networking services for affected individuals and family members; and offers appropriate referrals. It also provides a variety of educational materials including a regular newsletter, brochures, and pamphlets. A toll-free number (800-321-1433) is maintained by the organization for use in Canada only.

President: John Fleming (CEO)
Executive Director: Wendy Wong
Year Established: 1948
Acronym: TAS

Keywords
Arthritis; Arthritis Society

1276 **Arthrogryposis Group**

Beak Cottage
Dunley
Stourport-on-Severn, DY13 OTZ, United Kingdom

Phone: +44 (0) 1747-82-2655
Fax: +44 (0) 1747-82-2655
E-mail: taguk@aol.com
http://tagonline.org.uk

The Arthrogryposis Group is a not-for-profit voluntary health organization dedicated to offering contact, information, and support to people with arthrogryposis and their families. Arthrogryposis is a non-progressive condition that limits range of movement in the joints and is accompanied by muscle weakness. Established in 1984, the organization provides information to professionals and other interested parties, encourages public awareness, and furthers research in the field. In addition, the organization sponsors regional events, activity camps, and annual conferences for all families, Group members, and other interested individuals. Educational materials produced and distributed by the organization include a quarterly newsletter, a documentary video, brochures, and an authoritative booklet.

President: Micky Macartney (1996 to Present).
Executive Director: Diana Piercy (Contact Person)
Year Established: 1984
Acronym: TAG

Keywords
AMC; Arthrogryposis Group; Arthrogryposis Multiplex Congenita

1277 **ASA Kids**

895 Morning Glory
Bridge City, TX 77611

Phone: (409) 735-4332
E-mail: oliphint4@peoplepc.com
http://www.asakids.org

ASA Kids is an online support forum for families dealing with argininosuccinic aciduria, one of several hereditary urea cycle disorders. These disorders are caused by a deficiency of one of the enzymes needed for the breakdown of ammonia into urea, which is normally excreted in the urine. The deficiencies cause an excess of ammonia in the blood and body tissues. If left untreated, argininosuccinic aciduria may lead to brain damage and, eventually, to coma. ASA Kids strives to connect families for support, to provide information about the disorder, and to provide links to other available information.

Year Established: 1999

Keywords
Arginino Succinic Aciduria; Arginino Succinate Lyase Deficiency; Argininosuccinic Aciduria; ASA Kids

1278 **Asbestos Disease Awareness Organization**

1525 Aviation Boulevard
Suite 318
Redondo Beach, CA 90278

Phone: (310) 480-2989
Fax: (310) 798-9235
E-mail: info@AsbestosDiseaseAwareness.org
http://www.asbestosdiseaseawareness.org

The Asbestos Disease Awareness Organization (ADAO) is a 501c3 nonprofit organization. Founded in 2004 by patients and families affected by asbestos, ADAO seeks to give patients and concerned citizens a united voice, while raising public awareness about the dangers of asbestos exposure and asbestos-related diseases. ADAO offers online support groups, patient advocacy, and education to patients and the general public.

President: Alan Reinstein (2004-present)
Executive Director: Linda Reinstein
Year Established: 2004
Acronym: ADSO

Keywords
ADAO; Asbestos; Asbestos Disease Awareness Organization; Chronic Pulmonary Respiratory Disorders; Esophageal Cancer; Kidney and Bowel Problems; Larynx Cancer; Lung Cancer; Mesothelioma; Stomach Cancer

1279 Asherman's Syndrome Online Community

Cyprus

Phone: +357 2-472-3716
Fax: +357 2-472-4150
E-mail: ashermansbook@yahoo.com
http://www.ashermans.org

Asherman's Syndrome Online Community is an international community of women from all over the world who have been diagnosed with Asherman's syndrome. The purpose of this community is for members to give support to each other by sharing information. Asherman's syndrome is an acquired uterine disease characterized by the formation of scar tissue (adhesions) in the uterus. Most patients with Asherman's have scanty or absent menstruation (amenorrhea) but some have normal menstruation. Some patients do not menstruate but feel pain each month at the time that menstruation would normally occur. Symptoms can also include recurrent miscarriage or in some cases infertility. Founded in 1999, the online community serves women in countries throughout the world.

Year Established: 1999
Acronym: ASOC

Keywords
Amenorrhea; Asherman; Asherman's Syndrome;Ashermans Syndrome Online Community; ASOC; Intra-Uterine Adhesions; Intrauterine Adhesions; Intra-Uterine Synechiae; Intrauterine Synechiae

1280 Association CMTC

Bitterschoten 15
Leusden, 3831 PC, The Netherlands

Phone: +31 (0) 33-494-6671
E-mail: afr.vd.heijden@hccnet.nl
http://www.cmtc.nl

The CMTC Association is the English name for an organization based in The Netherlands that provides information and other services to those affected with, or working on, van Lohuizen syndrome, which is also known as cutis marmorata telangiectatica congenita (CMTC). On its web site and in its print materials, the organization provides information in English and German, as well as Dutch. CMTC, first described by a Dutch pediatrician in 1922, is a skin affliction that produces a marbled skin and is sometimes associated with other conditions. The main goals of the organization are to increase the well being of those affected by the disease and stimulate research into the causes and treatment of CMTC.

President: Mr. A.F.R. van der Heijden, PMP
Year Established: 1997
Acronym: CMTC

Keywords
Association CMTC; CMTC Association; Cutis Marmorata Telangiectatica Congenita

1281 Association for Children with Down Syndrome, Inc.

4 Fern Place
Plainview, NY 11803

Phone: (516) 933-4700
Fax: (516) 933-9524
E-mail: msmith@acds.org
http://www.acds.org

The Association for Children with Down Syndrome, Inc. (ACDS) is an international, not-for-profit, voluntary organization dedicated to providing information and support to individuals affected by Down syndrome, their families, and healthcare professionals. Down syndrome is a congenital disorder resulting from abnormalities affecting chromosome 21. Established in 1966, the Association for Children with Down Syndrome offers a wide variety of programs and services. Its 5 Plus Program provides recreational and social services for individuals with Down syndrome from five years of age through adulthood, and for their families. In addition, the ACDS's association with the Child Development Center/Genetics Program at North Shore University Hospital-Cornell University Medical College helps make many essential services available to ACDS families, such as pediatric cardiology, psychology, and gastroenterology services. The ACDS also promotes research, provides families with home and hospital visitations, and has a trained parent counselor. Additional programs and services include parent advocacy training and assistance; regular conferences and workshops for parents and professionals; and a special library that offers up-to-date toys, books, and videos.

President: Stuart H. Schoenfeld (1996 to Present)
Executive Director: Michael Smith
Year Established: 1966
Acronym: ACDS

Keywords
Association for Children with Down Syndrome, Inc.; Chromosome 21 Mosaic 21 Syndrome; Chromosome 21 Translocation 21 Syndrome; Down Syndrome; Down Syndrome, Mosaic; Trisomy 21 Syndrome

1282 Association for Children with Life-Threatening or Terminal Conditions and Their Families

Orchard House
Orchard Lane
Bristol, BS1 5DT, United Kingdom

Phone: +44 (0) 117-922-1556
Fax: +44 (0) 117-930-4707
E-mail: info@act.org.uk
http://www.act.org.uk

The Association for Children with Life-Threatening or Terminal Conditions and Their Families (ACT) is a UK-based international nonprofit organization dedicated to providing resources for parents and professionals caring for children with life-threatening or terminal conditions. Its mission is to facilitate the best possible care for affected children and their families by promoting models of good practice, providing information and education, and stimulating research and informed debate. Comprised of 200 members, ACT represents the needs of affected children and their families, and campaigns for the provision of a flexible network of care and support. It also provides a UK-wide information resource for children, parents, caregivers, and professionals.

President: Professor David Baum (1995 to Present)
Executive Director: Stella Elston
Year Established: 1993
Acronym: ACT

Keywords
ACT; Association for Children with Life-Threatening or Terminal Conditions and their Families; Children's Palliative Care; Complex Needs; Life-Limiting; Life-Threatening; Life-Threatening Illnesses; Paediatric Palliative Care; Pediatric Palliative Care; Terminal Conditions; Terminal Illness

1283 Association for Glycogen Storage Disease

P.O. Box 896
Durant, IA 52747

Phone: (563) 785-6038
Fax: (563) 785-6038
E-mail: maryc@agsdus.org
http://www.agsdus.org

The Association for Glycogen Storage Disease is an international, not-for-profit organization that acts as a focus for individuals with glycogen storage diseases and their families. Glycogen storage diseases are a group of rare inborn errors of metabolism characterized by deficiencies of certain enzymes involved in the metabolism of glycogen. The association seeks to foster communication between affected individuals for the purpose of mutual support and information sharing. Other goals include increasing public awareness of these disorders and promoting medical research into the various forms of glycogen storage diseases. Funds have been used to award college grants and scholarships to students with these disorders and award research grants to medical professionals working on glycogen storage diseases. The association also fosters publicity in local newspapers to make the public more aware of these diseases and to highlight the need for more research and funding for glycogen storage disease. Educational materials include brochures, newsletters, and a parent handbook.

President: Hollie Swain (1979-Present)
Executive Director: Same as above.
Year Established: 1979
Acronym: AGSD

Keywords
Acid Maltase Deficiency; Andersen Disease; Association for Glycogen Storage Disease; Forbes Disease;

Glycogen Storage Disease; GSD; HERS Disease; McArdle Disease; Pompe Disease; Tarui Disease; Von Gierke Disease

1284 Association for Glycogen Storage Disease (UK)

9 Lindop Road
Hale
Altricham
Cheshire, WA159DZ, United Kingdom

Phone: (161) 980-7303
Fax: (161) 226-3813
E-mail: president@agsd.org.uk
http://www.agsd.org.uk

The Association for Glycogen Storage Disease (UK) is a registered charity that acts as a contact and support group for individuals and families affected by glycogen storage disease. Glycogen storage diseases (GSD) are a group of rare inborn errors of metabolism characterized by deficiencies of certain enzymes involved in the metabolism of glycogen. ASGD (UK) was established in 1985 and acts as a focus for educational, scientific, and fund-raising activities related to the disorder. Other goals of the association include protecting and promoting the best interests of individuals affected by GSD; encouraging the improvement of facilities for treatment, study, education, and recuperation; and assisting in the organization of support groups throughout the world. The association holds an annual general meeting and offers limited scholarships for travel and accommodation to those who would otherwise not be able to afford to attend. In addition to informational brochures published in English, Urdu, Spanish and Polish, ASGD (UK) also publishes a quarterly, self-titled newsletter.

President: Ann Phillips (1989 to Present)
Executive Director: Sue Del Mar (Treasurer)
Year Established: 1985
Acronym: AGSD (UK)

Keywords
Acid Maltase Deficiency; Andersen Disease; Association for Glycogen Storage Disease (UK); Cori Disease; Forbes Disease; Glycogen; Glycogen Storage Disease I; Glycogen Storage Disease III; Glycogen Storage Disease IV; Glycogen Storage Disease VI; Glycogen Stoarage Disease VIII; Glycogen Storage Disease Type V; Glycogenosis Type II; Glycogenosis Type III; HERS Disease; Liver Affected; McArdle Disease; Metabolic; Muscle Affected; Pompe Disease; Storage; Tarui Disease; Von Gierke Disease

1285 Association for International Cancer Research

Madras House
St. Andrews
Fife, KY16 9EH, Scotland

Phone: +44 (0) 1334-47-7910
Fax: +44 (0) 1334-47-8667
E-mail: enquiries@aicr.org.uk
http://www.aicr.org.uk/

The Association for International Cancer Research (AICR) is an independent, nonprofit organization that was established in Scotland in 1984 to support fundamental research into cancer. The term "cancer" refers to a group of diseases that are characterized by uncontrolled cellular growth that may invade surrounding tissues and spread (metastasize) to other bodily tissues or organs. Different cancers may be classified based upon the organ and cell type involved, the nature of the malignancy, and the disease's clinical course. The Association for International Cancer Research is committed to funding research in areas that are relatively underfunded or unexplored. A major aspect of AICR's approach is to recognize the importance of international collaborations in studying the varying frequency of the different forms of cancer from country to country. The association funds research projects in many different countries and encourage collaboration between individual research grant recipients.

President: J.F. Matthews (Chairman)
Executive Director: Derek Napier (Chief Executive)
Year Established: 1984
Acronym: AICR

Keywords
Association for International Cancer Research; Cancer

1286 Association for Macular Diseases, Inc.

210 East 64th Street
New York, NY 10021

Phone: (212) 605-3719
Fax: (212) 605-3795
E-mail: association@retinal-research.org
http://www.macula.org/association/about.html

The Association for Macular Diseases is a national, not-for-profit, voluntary organization that seeks to inform, educate, motivate, and give practical advice and coping strategies to people with retinal degeneration due to macular disease. Age-related macular degeneration is the major cause of legal blindness in Americans over the age of 50. Established in 1978, the association has workspace, donated by the Macular Foundation, at the Manhattan Eye, Ear & Throat Hospital. The association's quarterly newsletter "Eyes Only" informs members of qualified researchers and the most current optical and electronic devices that improve sight. In addition, it offers referrals for diagnosis and treatment and arranges public seminars with professional specialists. The association also distributes educational brochures and fact sheets about macular degeneration.

President: Nikolai Stevenson
Executive Director: Same as above.
Year Established: 1978
Acronym: AMD

Keywords
Association for Macular Diseases, Inc.; Macular Degeneration (Age Related); Macular Diseases

1287   Association for Repetitive Motion Syndromes (ARMS)
PO Box 471973
Aurora, CO 80047-1973

Phone: (303) 369-0803
http://www.certifiedpst.com/arms

The Association for Repetitive Motion Syndromes (ARMS) is a not-for-profit organization committed to assisting workers at-risk or injured by repetitive motion syndromes. ARMS also provide assistance to employers, workers compensation specialists, and healthcare professionals. Assistance is available in the United States and abroad via the Internet, by telephone, and through written information packets.

President: Stephanie S. Barnes, 1992 to Present
Executive Director: Same as above.
Year Established: 1992
Acronym: ARMS

Keywords
ARMS; Association for Repetitive Motion Syndromes (ARMS); Carpal Tunnel Syndrome; Neuritis, Median; Neuropathy, Constrictive Median; CTS; Neuropathy, Median; Repetitive Motion Syndrome; Thenar Amyotrophy of Carpal Origin

1288   Association for Spina Bifida and Hydrocephalus
ASBAH House
42 Park Road
Peterborough, PE1 2UQ, United Kingdom

E-mail: postmaster@asbah.org
http://www.asbah.org

The Association for Spina Bifida and Hydrocephalus (ASBAH) is a voluntary organization dedicated to providing services to people with spina bifida and/or hydrocephalus, and their care providers. Spina bifida is characterized by malformation of the spinal column in which incomplete closure of certain vertebrae leaves a portion of the spinal cord exposed. Hydrocephalus is a condition characterized by inhibition of the normal flow of cerebrospinal fluid (CSF) and abnormal widening (dilatation) of the cerebral spaces of the brain (ventricles), causing accumulation of CSF in the skull and potentially increased pressure on brain tissue. Established in 1966, ASBAH aims to keep its clients' knowledge up-to-date, extend their choices, maximize opportunities for independence, and help their integration in society. The organization's unique network of advisers provides advice and close support at times of special need to individuals and families in England, Wales, and Northern Ireland. Specialist advisers in education, continence, mobility, and medical matters back up the service. Through nationwide and regional networks, these professionals develop and maintain expertise in spina bifida and hydrocephalus so that they may inform and assist other professionals in giving the best possible service.

Executive Director: Andrew Russell
Year Established: 1966
Acronym: ASBAH

Keywords
Association for Spina Bifida and Hydrocephalus; Hydrocephalus; Spina Bifida

1289   Association Francophone Des Glycogenoses
1, Impasse de la Grande PALU
Izon, 33450, France

Phone: +33 (0) 557-74-86-86
Fax: +33 (0) 557-74-75-99
E-mail: afg@glycogenoses.org
http://www.glycogenoses.org

The Association Francophone Des Glycogenoses (AFG) is a unique organization dedicated to assisting individuals and families affected by a rare group of genetic diseases that impair the body's ability to metabolize or break down glycogen (glycogenesis). Termed "glycogen storage diseases," these familial disorders are characterized by the abnormal accumulation of glycogen in various organs of the body. Symptoms vary greatly depending upon the specific organ systems that are affected, and may include muscle weakness without loss of muscle mass (atrophy), abnormal enlargement of the heart (cardiomegaly), liver (hepatomegaly), and/or tongue (macroglossia), as well as heart and kidney problems. These diseases include (but are not limited to) Von Gierke disease (type 1), Cori disease (type III), Andersen disease (type IV), and Pompe disease (type II). Established in 1992, the association is dedicated to identifying families affected by these diseases and providing appropriate information about the different forms of the disease. In addition, the Association Francophone Des Glycogenoses is interested in stimulating ongoing research into the treatment and potential cure of these disorders.

President: Dominique Espinasse
Year Established: 1992
Acronym: AFG

Keywords
Andersen Disease; Association Francophone Des Glycogenoses; Cori Disease; Glycogen Storage Disease; GSD; Pompe Disease; Von Gierke Disease

1290 Association Fransaise Contre l'amylose

66, rue Saint Jacques
Immeuble le Pacin II
Marseille, 13006, France

Phone: +33 (0) 442-94-90-86
Fax: +33 (0) 442-94-90-87
http://www.amylose.asso.fr

Association Fransaise Contre l'amylose, is a voluntary, not-for-profit, self-help organization that was established in 1994 in France in memory of Paulette, who was affected by a hereditary form of amyloidosis. Amyloidosis is a chronic disorder in which an abnormal starch-like protein complex (amyloid) accumulates in certain tissues and organs of the body. Amyloidosis may occur as a primary disorder for unknown reasons (idiopathic) or may occur secondary to other underlying disorders such as rheumatoid arthritis, familial Mediterranean fever, cancer of the bone marrow (i.e., multiple myeloma), or tuberculosis. In addition, some forms of amyloidosis may be inherited. The specific symptoms and findings vary greatly in range and severity, depending upon which areas of the body are affected. The association is dedicated to promoting and supporting medical research in the fight against amyloidosis; furthering the knowledge of affected individuals, family members, and healthcare professionals; working in association with other related organizations; and providing networking opportunities to individuals with amyloidosis and family members. It also provides appropriate referrals to genetic counseling and engages in patient advocacy.

President: Yves Ghiron (1994 to Present)
Executive Director: Yannick Ghiron
Year Established: 1994

Keywords
Abercrombie Syndrome; Amyloid Arthropathy of Chronic Hemodialysis; Amyloidosis; Amyloidosis, Atypical; Amyloidosis, Cardiopathic; Amyloidosis, Hereditary Nephropathic; Amyloidosis, Lichen; Amyloidosis, Macular; Amyloidosis, Neuropathic; Amyloidosis of Familial Mediterranean Fever; Amyloidosis, Pericollagen; Amyloidosis, Primary Cutaneous; Amyloidosis, Primary Nonhereditary; Amyloidosis, Secondary Generalized; Association Fransaise Contre l'amylose; Association Paulette Ghiron-Bistagne Contre L'Amylose (Amyloidosis); Paramyloidosis; Waxy Disease

1291 Association of Gastrointestinal Motility Disorders, Inc. (AGMD)

AGMD International Corporate Headquarters
11 North Street
Lexington, MA 02420

Phone: (781) 861-3874
Fax: (781) 861-7834
E-mail: gimotility@msn.com
http://www.agmd-gimotility.org

The Association of Gastrointestinal Motility Disorders, Inc. (AGMD) is an international, non-profit organization that functions as an information resource center for people affected by digestive motility disorders. The organization also serves as an integral resource for members of the medical community. AGMD was established in 1991 and was formerly known as the Association of Gastrointestinal Motility Disorders, Inc. AGMD offers three newsletters: the AGMD Beacon, AGMD Search And Research, and the AGMD Digestive Motility Forum. It also offers many other educational materials. Periodically AGMD distributes questionnaires to its members for the purpose of collecting information, which is later compiled and published in order to gain better insight into digestive motility diseases. AGMD also provides networking to its members, as well as referral lists of physicians who treat digestive motility diseases.

President: Mary-Angela De Grazia-DiTucci
Year Established: 1991
Acronym: AGMD

Keywords
Achalasia; AGMD; American Society of Adults with Pseudo-obstruction, Inc.; Association of Gastrointestinal Motility Disorders, Inc. (AGMD); CIP; Colonic Inertia; Constipation; Diffuse Esophageal Spasm; Gastroesphageal Reflux Disease; Gastroparesis; Hirschprung's Disease; Hypermotility; Hypomotility; Intestinal Pseudo-obstruction; Irritable Bowel Syndrome; Motility Disorders; Muscular Dystrophy, Oculo Gastrointestinal

1292 Association of Genetic Support of Australasia, Inc.

66 Albion Street
Surry Hills
New South Wales, 2010, Australia

Phone: +61 (0) 2-0211-1462
Fax: +61 (0) 2-9211-8077
E-mail: info@agsa-geneticsupport.org.au
http://www.agsa-geneticsupport.org.au

The Association of Genetic Support of Australasia, Inc., is a not-for-profit organization dedicated to facilitating support for those affected directly or indirectly by genetic conditions throughout Australasia. The aims of AGSA are to provide a contact point for families who are affected by genetic conditions for which there is no support group; facilitate access to support groups for families with particular genetic disorders; provide a forum for the exchange of information regarding available community services; educate medical and allied health professionals and the community about genetic disorders; and consult with government bodies, both federal and state, for appropriate funding for genetic services. Program activities include support groups, genetic counseling, patient advocacy, patient networking, and referrals.

President: Scott Brightwell
Executive Director: Dianne Petrie
Year Established: 1988
Acronym: AGSA

Keywords
Association of Genetic Support of Australasia, Inc.

1293 Associazione Internazionale Ring 14 (Ring 14 International Support Group)

Via Victor Marie Hugo nr. 34
Reggio Emilia, 42100, Italy

Phone: +39 (0) 522-32-2607
Fax: +39 (0) 522-32-4835
E-mail: info@ring14.com
http://www.ring14.com

Associazione Internazionale Ring 14 (Ring 14 International Support Group) was established in 2002 to identify and connect families with children affected by ring 14 syndrome in order to provide support; promote social, political and scientific activity for diagnosis and research of therapy; and raise funds to promote research and scholarships. Associazione Ring 14 is working to establish the first medical and scientific "Data Bank" on this syndrome; design a protocol of medical survey for Ring 14 syndrome patients to investigate the correlation between clinical manifestations and molecular genetic changes; and create a network of consultants including doctors, scientists, and healthcare workers.

President: Azzali Stefania
Year Established: 2002
Acronym: Associazione Ring 14

Keywords
Associazione Internazionale Ring 14; Associazione Internazionale Ring 14 (Ring 14 International Support Group); Chromosomal Deletions; Chromosome 14 Ring

1294 Associazione Italiana Mucopolisaccaridosi e Malattie Affini (ONLUS)

Via Savona 13
20144 Milano, Italy

Phone: +39 (0) 283-24-1292
Fax: +39 (0) 289-42-5180
E-mail: sede.milano@mucopolisaccaridosi.it
http://www.mpssociety.it

The Associazione Italiana Mucopolisaccaridosi is a not-for-profit, self-help organization dedicated to providing support and information on mucopolysaccharidosis (MPS) and related diseases to Italian families and professionals. The mucopolysaccharidoses, mucolipidoses (ML), and other related disorders are rare inherited diseases in which the body is deficient in certain enzymes. As a result, progressive damage occurs as complex sugars and/or fats accumulate in various tissues of the body. Established in 1991, the organization hosts conferences, funds research, and provides educational materials.

President: Flavio Bertoglio (2001-present)
Year Established: 1991
Acronym: A.I.MPS

Keywords
Associazione Italiana Mucopolisaccaridosi; Associazione Italiana Mucopolisaccaridosi e Malattie Affini (ONLUS); ERT; Hunter Syndrome; Hurler Syndrome; Italian; Maroteaux Lamy Syndrome; ML; Morquio Syndrome; MPS; Mucolipidoses; Mucopolysaccharidoses; ONLUS; Scheie Syndrome

1295   Asthma and Allergy Foundation of America, Inc.

1233 20th Street NW
Suite 402
Washington, DC 20036

Phone: (202) 466-7643
Fax: (202) 466-8940
Toll Free: (800) 727-8462
E-mail: info@aafa.org
http://www.aafa.org

Founded in 1953, the Asthma and Allergy Foundation of America serves patients with asthma and allergic diseases and their healthcare providers. Headquartered in Washington, DC, AAFA has a full-time professional staff and a national network of 11 chapters and more than 50 educational support groups. AAFA's mission is to provide community-based education, outreach, advocacy, and research. It offers patients and healthcare professionals a Clinical Trials Resource Center, an Asthma and Allergy Answers Library, a Brochures and Fact Sheets Clearinghouse, information and resources on the AAFA web site and in its publications.

Executive Director: Mary Worstell, M.P.H.
Year Established: 1953
Acronym: AAFA

Keywords
Allergy; Asthma; Asthma and Allergy Foundation of America, Inc.

1296   Asthma Society of Canada

425 - 130 Bridgeland Avenue
Suite 425
Toronto
Ontario, M6A 1Z4, Canada

Phone: (416) 787-4050
Fax: (416) 787-5807
Toll Free: (866) 787-4050
E-mail: info@asthma.ca
http://www.asthma.ca/adults/

The Asthma Society of Canada (ASC) is a national, not-for-profit, volunteer-based organization dedicated to enhancing the quality of life of people living with asthma and eliminating the disorder. Asthma is a chronic disease characterized by recurrent attacks of breathlessness and wheezing due to narrowing of small airways in the lungs (bronchioles). The society, which was established in 1973, offers a toll-free help line with trained health professionals to answer questions; develops and distributes print materials on asthma; facilitates support groups that enable affected individuals and family members to share information and mutual support; and runs camps for affected children. In addition, it promotes and funds asthma research, publishes a quarterly newsletter, and maintains a web site.

Executive Director: Chris Haromy (Contact Person)
Year Established: 1973
Acronym: ASC

Keywords
Asthma; Asthma Society of Canada

1297   A-T Children's Project (Ataxia Telangiectasia Children's Project)

668 South Military Trail
Deerfield Beach, FL 33442

Phone: (954) 481-6611
Fax: (954) 725-1153
Toll Free: (800) 543-5728
E-mail: info@atcp.org
http://www.atcp.org

The A-T Children's Project (Ataxia Telangiectasia Children's Project) is a national, not-for-profit organization that was established in 1993. Ataxia-telangiectasia is a rare, inherited, progressive disorder characterized by an impaired ability to control voluntary movement (ataxia); rapid, involuntary eye movements (nystagmus); permanent dilation of certain small blood vessels, resulting in small red lesions on the skin and other areas (telangiectasia); and immune deficiency, causing an increased predisposition to certain bacterial infections and malignancies. The purpose of the project is to raise funds to accelerate scientific research aimed at finding a cure or a therapy that would improve the lives of affected children. The specific goals include finding a cure or therapy; increasing awareness of the disorder; and encouraging and funding scientific research directed at specific treatments. The project's activities also include the establishment and maintenance of a cell-bank for unlimited access by research scientists. The A-T Children's Project has established a National AT Clinical Center at Johns Hopkins Hospital, Baltimore, MD.

President: Brad A. Margus (1993-Present)
Executive Director: Jennifer Thornton
Year Established: 1993
Acronym: A-TCP

Keywords
AT; A-T Children's Project (Ataxia Telangiectasia Children's Project); Ataxia Telangiectasia; Ataxia-Telangiectasia Children's Project; A-TCP

1298   A-T Medical Research Foundation
5241 Round Meadow Road
Hidden Hills, CA 91301

Phone: (818) 704-8146
Fax: (818) 703-8310
E-mail: gsmith@gspartners.com

George and Pam Smith to support the search for a cure for ataxia telangiectasia, a rare, genetic, neurological disorder with which their daughter Rebecca was diagnosed, founded the A-T Medical Research Foundation. It is characterized by progressively impaired coordination of voluntary movements and immune system deficiencies. People with A-T also are at increased risk for developing certain malignancies. The A-T Medical Research Foundation provides funding for research laboratories at UCLA and the Sackler School of Medicine in Israel, in addition to funding other research around the world. It hosts international conferences to encourage the sharing of information among researchers.

President: George Smith

Keywords
A T Medical Research Foundation; A-T Medical Research Foundation; Ataxia Telangiectasia; Ataxia Telangiectasia Research Foundation

1299   Ataxia Support Group
c/o Rose Gallant
185 Loch Lomond Road
Saint John, NB, E2J 3S3, Canada

The Ataxia Support Group is a rare disease organization that provides information and support to patients and families affected by hereditary ataxias. This is a group of neurological disorders (ataxias) of varying degrees of rarity that are inherited, in contrast to a related group of neurological disorders that are acquired through accidents, injuries, or other external agents. The Ataxia Support Group works toward its goals through education and support groups.

President: Rose M. Gallant (1979-present)

Keywords
Ataxia Support Group; Ataxia; Dominant Hereditary Ataxia; Recessive Hereditary Ataxia; Support Groups

1300   Ataxia-Telangiectasia Society (UK)
IACR-Rothamsted Research
Harpenden
Hertfordshire, AL5 2JQ, United Kingdom

Phone: +44 (0) 1582-76-0733
Fax: +44 (0) 1582-76-0162
E-mail: ATCharity@aol.com
http://www.atsociety.org.uk

The Ataxia-Telangiectasia Society is a registered charity in the United Kingdom dedicated to providing support and information to individuals and families affected by ataxia-telangiectasia. This is a rare inherited progressive disorder characterized by an impaired ability to control voluntary movements (ataxia); rapid, involuntary eye movements (nystagmus); permanent dilation of certain small blood vessels, resulting in small red lesions on the skin and other areas (telangiectasias); and primary immune deficiency, causing an increased predisposition to certain bacterial infections and malignancies. The A-T Society raises funds for research into the possible treatment and eventual cure for AT and supports a national AT clinic in Nottingham, England. It also endeavors to raise awareness of A-T in both the medical community and the general population.

President: Rev. Canon Paul Thomas (2002-Present)
Executive Director: Maureen Poupard (Honorary Secretary)
Year Established: 1989
Acronym: A-T Society

Keywords
Ataxia Telangiectasia; Ataxia Telangiectasia Society (UK); Ataxia-Telangiectasia Society (UK)

1301 Atresia/Microtia Online E-mail Support Group

E-mail: AtresiaMicrotia-owner@yahoogroups.com
http://health.groups.yahoo.com/group/AtresiaMicrotia

Founded in 1999, the Atresia/Microtia Online E-mail Support Group is a rare disorder Internet support group for patients and families affected by aural atresia and/or microtia. Aural atresia is a condition in which the external ear canal is absent or underdeveloped. Microtia is a deformity or absence of the outer ear. As an online support group, the Atresia/Microtia Online E-mail Support Group is intended as a forum for patients and their families worldwide. This forum allows patients to network with one another and also with healthcare professionals. Atresia/Microtia Online E-mail Support Group strives to educate both patients and the general public.

Year Established: 1999

Keywords
Atresia/Microtia Online E-mail Support Group; Atresia/Microtia Online E mail Support Group; Aural Atresia; BOR Syndrome; Branchio Oto Renal Syndrome; Goldenhar Syndrome; Hearing Aids; Hemifacial Microsomia; Microtia; Networking; Oculo Auriculo Vertebral Spectrum; Support Groups; Treacher Collins Syndrome

1302 Attention Deficit Disorder Association

P.O. Box 543
Pottstown, PA 19464

Phone: (484) 945-2101
Fax: (610) 970-7520
E-mail: mail@add.org
http://www.add.org

Attention Deficit Disorders Association is a non-profit organization devoted to the needs of people with attention deficit disorder (AD/HD). Its mission is to educate the public, healthcare professionals, educators, members of the media and legislators on the challenges faced by individuals with AD/HD and the benefits that derive from appropriate treatment. ADDA is focused on the particular needs of adults, young adults, and families living with AD/HD with respect to work issues, relationship and family issues, parenting, medication, organization, time management and life in the home. For its members, it provides information, support, and a connection to others with AD/HD around the world.

President: Daivd Giweec
Year Established: 1989
Acronym: ADDA

Keywords
ADD; ADHD; Attention Deficit Disorder; Attention Deficit Disorder Association; Attention Deficit Hyperactivity Disorder; National Attention Deficit Disorder Association

1303 Auditory-Verbal International, Inc.

1390 Chainbridge Road
#100
McLean, VA 22101

Phone: (703) 739-1049
Fax: (703) 739-0395
TDD: (703) 739-0874
E-mail: audiverb@aol.com
http://www.auditory-verbal.org/

Auditory-Verbal International, Inc., a voluntary, not-for-profit organization that was established in 1987, is dedicated to making the auditory verbal approach available to all children who are hearing impaired. This approach uses a set of guiding principles to help children who are deaf or hard of hearing work toward independent functioning. AVI sponsors research related to hearing impairment, encourages international communication among parents and professionals, and provides scholarships and awards to support teacher/therapist training.

President: Tom Lucchesi
Executive Director: Sara Lake
Year Established: 1987
Acronym: AVI

Keywords
Auditory-Verbal International, Inc.; Hearing Impairment; Hearing Loss; Verbal, Auditory

1304 Australian Herpes Management Forum

Marian Villa, Westmead Hospital
Grosvenor Place
Westmead
New South Wales, NSW 2145, Australia

Phone: +61 (0) 2-8230-3843
Fax: +61 (0) 2-9845-6287
E-mail: ahmf@ahmf.com.au
http://www.ahmf.com.au

The Australian Herpes Management Forum (AHMF) is a voluntary organization that serves as an independent forum for the development of recommendations and protocols for the management and control of herpes virus infections in Australia. Although such objectives are achieved independently, reference is made to International Herpes Management Forum (IHMF) recommendations where appropriate. The mission of the Australian Herpes Management Forum is to improve the awareness, understanding, management, and control of herpes virus infections in Australia. Herpes viruses cause several inflammatory skin diseases that are characterized by the formation of small, often painful blisters. Such inflammatory skin diseases include genital herpes, cold sores, chickenpox, and shingles.

Executive Director: Dr. Chris Miller (Contact Person)
Year Established: 1997
Acronym: AHMF

Keywords
Australian Herpes Management Forum; Herpesvirus

1305 Australian Leukodystrophy Support Group, Inc.
10 Mitchell Street
Mentone, Victoria, 3194, Australia

Phone: +61 (0) 3-9584-7070
Fax: +61 (0) 3-9583-4379
E-mail: leuko@vicnet.net.au
http://www.alds.org.au

The Australian Leukodystrophy Support Group, Inc, provides professional counseling to leukodystrophy sufferers and their families; increases public awareness of leukodystrophy; acts as a source of information for healthcare providers; raises funds for research; and provides educational materials for patients and families. Leukodystrophy is the name given to a group of very rare, progressive, metabolic, genetic diseases that affect the brain, spinal cord and often the peripheral nerves. The name comes from the Greek "leuko" meaning "white" and "dystrophy" meaning "imperfect growth or development." ALDS provides assistance and information to those affected by the leukodystrophies. ALDS also supports research into the disorder. ALDS offers a newsletter, and brochures on the leukodystrophies.

President: Sr. Julie Thomas (1992 - present)
Year Established: 1992
Acronym: ALDS

Keywords
Australian Leukodystrophy Support Group, Inc.; Leukodystrophies

1306 Australian Lung Foundation
P.O. Box 847
Lutwyche, Queensland, 4030, Australia

Phone: +61 (0) 7-3357-6388
Fax: +61 (0) 7-3357-6988
Toll Free: 1 (800) 654-301
E-mail: enquires@lungnet.com.au
http://www.lungnet.com.au

The Australian Lung Foundation is a not-for-profit organization that is committed to improving the quality of life of individuals affected by lung disease and promoting lung health in Australia. Established in 1990, the foundation raises funds in support of lung disease research; educates patients and the broader public on the treatment and prevention of lung disease, fosters patient support activities, and influences public and corporate policy to ensure safe living and working environments. The ALF's activities include providing annual research grants and awards; working with industries to enhance employee safety and corporate productivity; and conducting conferences that are open to all members of the medical community, government and corporate bodies, special interest groups, and patient support organizations.

President: Dr. Robert Edwards (National Chairman)
Executive Director: William Darbishire
Year Established: 1990
Acronym: ALF

Keywords
Australian Lung Foundation; Lung Disease

1307 Australian Women's Health Network
School of Health and Social Development
Deakin University, 221 Burwood Highway
Burwood, Victoria, 3125, Australia

Phone: +61 (0) 3-9244-6688
Fax: +61 (0) 3-9244-6017
http://www.awhn.org.au/

The Australian Women's Health Network (AWHN) is a not-for-profit, community-based, consultative organization that provides a national voice on women's health issues. The network, which was established in 1986, serves as a women's health advocacy, information, and lobbying organization. It has affiliated networks in all states and territories of Australia. The national, state, and territory networks frequently consult and work together with other organizations representing women to address major issues. The network's broad aims include maintaining and increasing a national focus on women's health issues, functioning as a national advocacy and information sharing organization, and serving as an umbrella organization for state and territory women's health networks.

Executive Director: Helen Keleher (Contact)
Year Established: 1986
Acronym: AWHN

Keywords
Australian Women's Health Network; Women's Health

1308 Autism Network for Hearing and Visually Impaired Persons

7510 Ocean Front Avenue
Virginia Beach, VA 23451

Phone: (757) 428-9036
Fax: (757) 428-0019

The Autism Network for Hearing and Visually Impaired Persons is a voluntary organization that was founded to serve the needs of people with autism who also have a hearing or visual impairment. Established in 1992, the network was adopted as a formal committee of the Autism Society of America. The goals of the organization include the creation and maintenance of a database of people with autism combined with a sensory disability in order to establish a network for communication, education, research, and advocacy. The network also seeks to develop centers to diagnose and evaluate individuals with these disorders. In addition, the organization works to educate physicians within the community and present educational sessions at the Autism Society of America National Annual Conference.

President: Dolores and Alan Bartel (Contact Persons)
Year Established: 1992

Keywords
Autism Network for Hearing and Visually Impaired Persons; Hearing Impairment with Autism; Visual Impairment with Autism

1309 Autism Network International

P.O. Box 448
Syracuse, NY 13235

Phone: (315) 476-2462
Fax: (315) 425-1978
E-mail: jisincla@mailbox.syr.edu
http://www.ani.ac

Autism Network International (ANI) is a self-help and advocacy organization formed by and for autistic people. Established in 1992 and consisting of approximately 340 members, ANI believes that the best advocates for autistic people are autistic people themselves. ANI provides a forum for autistic people to share information, peer support, and tips for coping and problem solving. In addition to promoting self-advocacy for verbal autistic adults, ANI also works to improve the lives of autistic people whom, whether because they are too young or because they do not have adequate communication skills, are currently unable to act independently as self-advocates. Autism Network International assists autistic people who are unable to participate directly by providing information and referrals to parents and teachers. Autism Network International has an online forum for information and support, and holds an annual retreat that is attended by autistic people and families from all over the world.

Executive Director: Jim Sinclair
Year Established: 1992
Acronym: ANI

Keywords
Advocacy; ANI; Autism; Autism, Infantile; Autism Network International; Kanner Syndrome

1310 Autism Research Institute

4182 Adams Avenue
San Diego, CA 92116

Phone: (619) 281-7165
Fax: (619) 563-6840
http://www.autismresearchinstitute.com

The Autism Research Institute (ARI) is an international voluntary organization dedicated to assisting parents and professionals concerned with autism. Autism is a non-progressive neurologic disorder characterized by language and communication deficits, withdrawal from social contacts, and extreme reactions to changes in the immediate environment. ARI was founded in 1967 to conduct and foster scientific research designed to improve the methods of diagnosing, treating, and preventing autism. ARI also disseminates research findings to parents and other interested individuals. The institute's databank contains approximately 29,000 detailed case histories of children with autism. The records were compiled from over 60 countries.

President: Rosemary King (1992 to Present)
Executive Director: Bernard Rimland, Ph.D.
Year Established: 1967
Acronym: ARI

Keywords
ARI; Asperger Syndrome; Autism; Autism Research Institute; Fragile X Syndrome; Landau Kleffner Syndrome; Pervasive Developmental Disorder; Rett Syndrome

1311 Autism Society of America

7910 Woodmont Avenue
Suite 300
Bethesda, MD 20814-3015

Phone: (301) 657-0881
Fax: (301) 657-0869
Toll Free: (800) 328-8476
http://www.autism-society.org

The Autism Society of America, a national, not-for-profit, advocacy organization established in 1965, is dedicated to providing information, assistance, support, and advocacy on behalf of individuals with autism and their families. Autism is a nonprogressive neurological disorder characterized by language and communication deficits, withdrawal from social contacts, and extreme reactions to changes in the immediate environment. The society supports ongoing medical research into the causes, prevention, and treatment of autism; promotes public awareness; and provides information and support to help affected individuals become fully participating members of their communities and advocates for legislation on Capitol Hill. In addition, the society makes referrals to appropriate sources of support and treatment. Abundant information about autism in both English and Spanish can be found on the society's web site.

President: Lee Grossman (2005-present)
Year Established: 1965
Acronym: ASA

Keywords
Advocacy; ASA; Autism; Autism Society of America

1312 Autoimmune Information Network, Inc

PO Box 4121
Brick, NJ 08723

Phone: (732) 262-0450
Fax: (732) 262-0450
E-mail: autoimmunehelp@aol.com
http://www.aininc.org (site under construction)

The Autoimmune Information Network, Inc. (AIN) is a 501c3 organization formed to help people who have autoimmune disorders. These are disorders in which the body's own immune system attacks bodies tissues, for reasons that often are not understood. Autoimmunity is a major cause of chronic disease. AIN services include support groups, referrals, networking, and advocacy.

Executive Director: Barbara Yodice
Year Established: 2005
Acronym: AIN

Keywords
Advocacy; Autoimmune Information Network, Inc; AIN; Networking; Support Groups

1313 Autoimmunity Research Foundation

3423 Hill Canyon Avenue
Thousand Oaks, CA 91360

Phone: (805) 492-3693
Fax: (877) 805-9941
E-mail: foundation@autoimmunityresearch.org
http://www.autoimmunityresearch.org/index.html

The Autoimmunity Research Foundation is a 501 (c) 3 organization that was established to support and encourage research on autoimmune diseases. These are the various diseases that occur when one's own immune system for some reason attacks itself by mistake. Most autoimmune diseases occur among women, often during the childbearing years. By conducting research on these diseases, the foundation hopes to, in its own words, "Solve the enigma of autoimmunity, one disease at a time."

President: Dr. Trevor D. Marshall (Director)
Executive Director: Ms. Belinda Fenter (Director)
Year Established: 2004
Acronym: ARF

Keywords
ARF; Autoimmune Diseases; Autoimmunity Research Foundation

1314 AVENUES

P.O. Box 5192
Sonora, CA 95370

E-mail: info@avenuesforamc.com
http://www.avenuesforamc.com

AVENUES, a voluntary, not-for-profit organization is a national support group for people with arthrogryposis multiplex congenita, a rare congenital disease characterized by the presence of multiple joint contractures. Established in 1980, AVENUES is dedicated to providing information to affected individuals, their families, and health care professionals interested in arthrogryposis, a rare disorder characterized by reduced mobility of many joints in the body. The organization provides a variety of educational and support materials on its web site including a directory of clinics and medical professionals with a special interest in arthrogryposis, an annotated bibliography on arthrogryposis, pamphlets, and links to other resources.

President: James Schmidt
Year Established: 1980
Acronym: AVENUES

Keywords
AMC; AVENUES; Arthrogryposis; Arthrogryposis Multiplex Congenita; Service Organization

1315 BackCare, the Charity for Healthier Backs

16 Elmtree Road
Teddington
Middlesex, TW11 8ST, United Kingdom

Phone: +44 (0) 181-977-5474
Fax: +44 (0) 181-943-5318
E-mail: info@backcare.org.uk
http://www.backcare.org.uk

BackCare, the Charity for Healthier Backs is a registered as National Back Pain Association and dedicated to providing information and support to people who are affected by back pain, their family members, and healthcare professionals. Established in 1968, the association strives to fulfill its mission, which is to fund patient-oriented research into the causes and treatment of back pain; educate people to use their bodies sensibly and thus reduce the incidence of back pain; and help form and support branches through which individuals affected by back pain. BackCare organizes the annual National Back Care Awareness week to raise awareness of the causes and ways of preventing back injury. Publications include a regular newsletter, educational pamphlet series, videos, and books geared both toward individuals experiencing back pain and their caregivers.

President: Stanley W. Grundy, CBE
Executive Director: Nia Taylor
Year Established: 1968
Acronym: BackCare

Keywords
Back Pain; BackCare; BackCare, the Charity for Healthier Backs; National Back Pain Association

(BackCare, the Charity for Healthier Backs); Pain, Chronic

1316 Band-Aides & Blackboards

Lehman College, CUNY
Bronx, NY 10468

Phone: (718) 960-8898
E-mail: fleitas@optonline.net
http://www.lehman.cuny.edu/bandaides

"Band-Aides & Blackboards: When Chronic Illness . . . or Some Other Medical Problem . . . Goes to School" is a web site for healthy children and those with chronic illnesses or disabilities, parents, healthcare providers, and educators. The purposes of this web site are to provide a forum for children with chronic disorders or disabilities to talk about their daily experiences and challenges; to help sensitize other children to what it is like to grow up with medical problems; to provide information and support for parents of children with such disabilities; and to provide links to age-appropriate teaching programs and other classroom activities for teaching programs. This site uses a combination of colorful graphics, music, drawings, and interactive children's activities.

President: Joan Fleitas, Ed.D., R.N.
Year Established: 1997

Keywords
Band Aides & Blackboards; Band-Aides & Blackboards; Chronic Illness and School; Networking; Teaching Programs, Age-Appropriate

1317 Barth Syndrome Foundation, Inc.

Box 974
Perry, FL 32348

Phone: (850) 223-1128
Fax: (850) 223-3911
E-mail: inquiries.rd@barthsyndrome.org
http://www.barthsyndrome.org

The Barth Syndrome Foundation, Inc., supports the needs of families affected by Barth syndrome through the exchange of information regarding this rare, life-threatening disorder. It also assists physicians by providing resources to aid in the diagnosis and treatment of Barth syndrome, an inherited neuromuscular disease characterized by neutropenia, cardiomyopathy, growth retardation, and fine or gross motor delay. The foundation provides contacts to the physicians who treat affected boys and also provides information to promote earlier diagnosis of this disease. The organizers of the foundation are creating a registry of physicians and affected children. Established in 2000, the foundation is a voluntary, not-for-profit, self-help organization. It serves families in the United States and abroad with a newsletter, reports, brochures, advocacy, and networking. It also promotes research.

President: Valerie M. Bowen "Shelley"
Year Established: 2000
Acronym: BSF

Keywords
3 Methylgluticonic Aciduria; Advocacy; BSF; Barth Syndrome; Barth Syndrome Foundation, Inc.; Cariomyopathy; Chronic Fatigue Syndrome; Networking; Neutropenia; Small Stature

1318 Basal Cell Carcinoma Nevus Syndrome Life Support Network
PO Box 321
Burton, OH 44021

Phone: (440) 635-0078
Fax: (440) 635-0267
Toll Free: (866) 842-1895
E-mail: info@bccns.org
www.bccns.org

The Basal Cell Carcinoma Nevus Syndrome Life Support Network provides healthcare, counseling, and support services to children and adults manifesting inherited, metabolic, or genetic disorders or diseases most commonly known as basal cell carcinoma nevus syndrome, with particular emphasis on diagnosis and treatment of children evidencing the initial onset of BCCNS. Individuals with this syndrome, which is also known as Gorlin syndrome, are predisposed to cancer and congenital malformations. This organization provides referrals to healthcare facilities and/or specialists, group and individual counseling, networking, and education. It has an online forum for members.

President: Bryant Bradley
Executive Director: Kristi Schmitt Burr
Year Established: 1999
Acronym: BCCNS Life Support Network

Keywords
Basal Cell Carcinoma Nevus Syndrome; Basal Cell Carcinoma Nevus Syndrome Life Support Network; Basal Cells; BCCNS; BCNS; Gorlin Goltz Syndrome; Gorlin Syndrome; NBCCS; Networking; Nevoid Basal Cell Carcinoma Syndrome; Odontogenic Keratocysts

1319 Batten Disease Support and Research Association
c/o BDSHA
11250 Road
10K
Ottawa, OH 45875

Phone: (740) 927-4298
Fax: (740) 927-4298
Toll Free: (800) 448-4570
E-mail: bdsra1@bdsra.com
http//www.dsra.org

The Batten Disease Support and Research Association is a voluntary, not-for-profit organization dedicated to promoting the civil and human rights of people with Batten disease. Batten disease, an extremely rare inherited disorder, is a progressive degenerative neuro metabolic disease characterized by gradual intellectual deterioration, seizure episodes, progressive movement (motor) impairment, and progressive visual impairment. Symptoms begin to occur at approximately five to 13 years of age. The association seeks to maximize the opportunities of affected individuals through medical, educational, vocational, rehabilitative, and financial means, and to educate lay persons and professionals concerning the special needs of people with the disease. Established in 1987, the Batten Disease Support and Research Association provides referral services to help affected families secure benefits available by law and maintains a database of individuals with Batten disease on state, national, and international levels. It functions as a national registry for researchers throughout the world who are studying Batten disease.

President: George Maxim
Executive Director: Lance W. Johnston
Year Established: 1987
Acronym: BDSRA

Keywords
Batten Disease Support and Research Association; Batten Disease; Haltia Santavuori; Jansky Bielschowski; Kufs Disease; NCL; Neuronal Ceroid Lipofuscinosis; Neuronal Ceroid Lipofuscinosis, Juvenile Type; Santavuori Disease; Spielmeyer Vogt Disease

1320 BC Neurofibromatosis Foundation
203-1001 Cloverdale
Victoria, BC, V8X 4C9, Canada

Phone: (205) -37-0-75
Fax: (205) -37-0-75
Toll Free: (800) -38-5-BC
TDD: (999) -99-9-99
E-mail: bcnf@bcnf.bc.ca
http://www.bcnf.bc.ca

The British Columbia (BC) Neurofibromatosis Foundation is a membership-driven organization that provides education and funds research to improve treatments and find a cure for neurofibromatosis, a rare, genetic disorder characterized by the development of multiple, non-cancerous tumors. The BCNF supports individuals with neurofibromatosis and their families.

President: Ms. Laura Kondzins (February 2002)
Executive Director: Mr. John Sanderson
Year Established: 1984
Acronym: BCNF

Keywords
BC Neurofibromatosis Foundation; Cafe au lait; Fibroma; Genetic Disease; NF 1; NF 2; Neurofibromatosis; Neurofibromatosis Type 1; Neurofibromatosis Type 2; Optic Glioma; Plexiform; Rare Disease; Scoliosis; Tumor

1321   Beckwith Wiedemann Support Network

2711 Colony Rd
Ann Arbor, MI 48104

Phone: (734) 973-0263
Fax: (734) 973-9721
Toll Free: (800) 837-2976
E-mail: a800bwsn@aol.com
http://www.beckwith-wiedemann.org

The Beckwith-Wiedemann Support Network (BWSN) is a voluntary, not-for-profit organization dedicated to providing peer support and information to individuals and families affected by Beckwith-Wiedemann syndrome (BWS). This syndrome, also known as exomphalos-macroglossia-gigantism syndrome, is a rare genetic disorder characterized by a wide range of growth abnormalities including an abnormally enlarged tongue (macroglossia); excessive size and height (gigantism); and/or protrusion of portions of the intestines through an abnormal opening in the abdominal wall where the umbilical cord joined the fetal abdomen (exomphalos or omphalocele). Established in 1990, the network is committed to increasing public and professional awareness of Beckwith-Wiedemann syndrome; facilitating the flow of information among affected families and healthcare professionals; and promoting and supporting research into the causes, early detection, and treatment of BWS. The Beckwith-Wiedemann Support Network shares information with other BWS groups around the world and maintains a listing of appropriate referrals. The network also maintains a toll-free helpline for parents and enables affected families to exchange information, assistance, and resources through its networking program.

President: Susan Fettes (1989-Present)
Executive Director: Susan Fettes
Year Established: 1990
Acronym: BWSN

Keywords
Beckwith Wiedemann Support Network; Beckwith-Wiedemann Syndrome; Bulldog Syndrome; BWS; DGSX Golabi Rosen Syndrome, Included; Dysplasia Gigantism Syndrome, X Linked; Exomphalos Macroglossia Gigantism Syndrome; SDYS; SGB Syndrome; Simpson Dysmorphia Syndrome; Simpson Golabi Behmel Syndrome

1322   Beckwith-Wiedemann Children's Foundation

9031 Cascadia Avenue
Everett, WA 98208

Phone: (425) 338-4610
Fax: (425) 357-8575
E-mail: BWCFcheryl@aol.com
http://www.beckwith-wiedemannsyndrome.org

Beckwith-Wiedemann Children's Foundation (BWCF) is a non-profit, voluntary organization run by family members of children affected by Beckwith-Wiedemann syndrome (BWS). This is a rare genetic disorder characterized by a wide spectrum of symptoms and findings that vary from case to case. In many affected individuals, findings associated with the syndrome include above-average weight and length at birth or increased growth after birth, an unusually large tongue, enlargement of certain abdominal organs, and/or abdominal wall defects. BWCF's mission is to provide assistance to those affected by Beckwith-Weidemann syndrome though education, conferences, and a telephone support line. BWCF offers assistance with insurance claims and travel to medical facilities for treatment.

President: Cheryl Hendrickson
Executive Director: Kathy Kruger
Year Established: 2002
Acronym: BWCF

Keywords
Beckwith; Beckwith-Wiedemann Children's Foundation; Beckwith-Wiedemann Syndrome; BWCF; BWS; EMG; Ear Pits/Creases; Macroglossia; Macrosomia; Omphalocele; Visceromegaly; Wiedemann-Beckwith Syndrome

1323 **Beckwith-Wiedemann Family Forum**
105 Yehudah Street, Apartment 2
Modi'in, 71700, Israel

Phone: +972 (0) 8-971-4544
E-mail: julie@netor.co.il
http://www.geocities.com/beckwith_wiedemann

The Beckwith-Wiedemann Family Forum was created as a way for people interested in BWS to get support and share information. Beckwith-Wiedemann syndrome is a rare genetic disorder characterized by a broad spectrum of symptoms and findings that may include enlargement of certain abdominal organs, advanced bone age, and greater than normal length and weight at birth. The major goals of the Beckwith-Wiedemann Family Forum are to provide a place where people interested in BWS can find information quickly, to provide a forum for interested people to meet on the Internet to discuss BWS related issues, and to let newly affected families of BWS know they are not alone.

President: Julie Beja (2002-present)
Year Established: 2002
Acronym: BWFF

Keywords
Beckwith-Wiedemann Family Forum; Beckwith-Wiedemann Syndrome; Hemihyperplasia; Hemihypertrophy; Hepatoblastoma; Lingual reduction; Macroglossia; Neonatal Hypoglycemia; Omphalocele; Partial Glossectomy; Wilms Tumor

1324 **Behcet's Organisation Worldwide**
PO Box 27
Watchet
Somerset, TA23 0YJ, United Kingdom

Phone: +44 (0) 7713-22-0303
E-mail: information@behcetsuk.org
http://www.behcets.org

The Behcet's Organisation Worldwide (BOW) is a voluntary, not-for-profit, self-help organization, whose aims and objectives are to assist patients and physicians by providing information about Behcet's disease and to advance public education into the causes and treatment of this disease and its associated conditions. Behcet's is a rare multisystem inflammatory disorder affecting the skin, eyes, and, in some instances, joints, blood vessels, central nervous system and/or digestive tract. The exact cause is unknown. Through its Books Into Local Libraries project, the BOW is creating an informational booklet about Behcet's, to be placed in local libraries and translated into several languages. The BOW is global in its approach, with coordinators in several countries and headquarters in the United Kingdom. It provides written material in English, Spanish, Portuguese, German, French, Italian and Arabic.

President: Alex Knight
Year Established: 1998
Acronym: B.O.W.

Keywords
Autoimmune; Behcets; Behcets Disease; Behcet's Organisation Worldwide; Behcet's Syndrome; Deep Vein Thrombosis; Glaucoma; Immune system; Inflammation; Iritis; Lupus; Medicine; Multiple Sclerosis; Rheumatism; Ulcers; Uveitis; Vasculitis

1325 **Belgian Association for Metabolic Diseases (BOKS)**
Alice Nahonlann 7
Melsele, 9120, Belgium

Phone: +32 (0) 3-775-4839
E-mail: info@boks.be
http://www.boks.be

The Belgian Association for Metabolic Diseases (BOKS) is a rare-disorder organization dedicated to improving the quality of life, and the span of life, for patients with metabolic disorders. Metabolic disorders have to do with disturbances, often inherited; in the way food is broken down and used by the body. BOKS offers reports, brochures and audio-visual aids to patients, family members, the general public, and health and other professionals. BOKS also provides services that include support groups, patient networking, and education for patients and the general public.

President: Mrs. De Baere Lutgarde (1994-present)
Executive Director: Mr. Serpentier Rik
Acronym: BOKS

Keywords
Belgian Association for Metabolic Diseases; Belgian Association for Metabolic Diseases (BOKS); BOKS; Metabolic Diseases

1326 **Benign Essential Blepharospasm Research Foundation, Inc.**
P.O. Box 12468
637 N. 7th Street
Suite 102
Beaumont, TX 77726-2468

Phone: (409) 832-0788
Fax: (409) 832-0890
E-mail: bebrf@blepharospasm.org
http://www.blepharospasm.org/

The Benign Essential Blepharospasm Research Foundation (BEBRF) is a national, voluntary health organization that was formed to promote research into the cause, treatment, and potential cure of benign essential blepharospasm (BEB) and other disorders of the facial musculature. BEB is characterized by intermittent, involuntary contractions or spasms of the muscles around the eyes. In some cases, an inability to open the eyelids due to involuntary muscle spasms may result in functional blindness. Established in 1981, BEBRF provides encouragement to affected individuals and their families through state coordinators and local support groups. District directors coordinate activities in their regions and direct affected individuals to medical centers where these conditions are treated. BEBRF also acts as a clearinghouse for information on BEB, Meige's syndrome, and hemifacial spasm and distributes materials including brochures, bimonthly newsletters, and physician reprint articles.

President: Mary Lou Thompson
Executive Director: Mary Smith
Year Established: 1981
Acronym: BEBRF

Keywords
BEB/M; BEBRF; Benign Essential Blepharospasm Research Foundation, Inc.; Blepharospasm, Benign Essential; Dystonia, Cranial; Dystonia, Focal; Hemifacial Spasm; Meige Syndrome; Support Groups

---

1327 Bernard-Soulier Syndrome Website and Registry
Royal College of Surgeons in Ireland
123 St. Stephen's Green
Dublin 2, Ireland

Phone: +353 (0) 1-402-2100
E-mail: bernard-soulier@rcsi.ie
http://www.bernardsoulier.org

The Bernard-Soulier Syndrome Website and Registry has been set up by Dr. Dermot Kenny, Director of the Clinical Research Centre at the Royal College of Surgeons in Ireland, to help physicians and patients learn more about this syndrome. Bernard-Soulier syndrome is a severe, hereditary, rare bleeding disorder. It is hoped that physicians will contribute information to the registry to build a body of valuable information

over time. The site is run on a not-for-profit basis and is supported by a number of other physicians and scientists with a particular interest in this syndrome.

Executive Director: Dermot Kenny
Year Established: 2000
Acronym: RCSI

Keywords
Bernard Soulier Syndrome; Bernard Soulier Syndrome Website and Registry; Bernard-Soulier Syndrome Website and Registry; Congenital Bleeding Disorder; Giant Platelets; Thrombocytopenia

---

1328 B*E*T*A: Behavior Education Training Associates
P.O. Box 225129
San Francisco, CA 94122

Phone: (415) 564-7830
Fax: (415) 242-1302
Toll Free: (800) 368-2382
E-mail: beta.sf@juno.com
http://www.aintmisbehavin.com

The mission of B*E*T*A (Behavior Education Training Associates) is to assist people considered disabled to maximize their participation and involvement in all areas of life.

Year Established: 1987
Acronym: B*E*T*A

Keywords
B*E*T*A; B*E*T*A: Behavior Education Training Associates

1329 Better Hearing Institute
515 King Street
Suite 420
Alexandria, VA 22314

Phone: (703) 684-3391
Fax: (703) 684-6048
Toll Free: (800) 327-9355
E-mail: mail@betterhearing.org
http://www.betterhearing.org

The Better Hearing Institute (BHI) is a not-for-profit corporation that educates the public about the neglected problem of hearing loss and what can be done about it. Founded in 1973, we are working to: Erase the stigma and end the embarrassment that prevents millions of people from seeking help for hearing loss;

show the negative consequences of untreated hearing loss for millions of Americans; and promote treatment and demonstrate that this is a national problem that can be solved.

Executive Director: Sergei Kochkin
Year Established: 1973
Acronym: BHI

Keywords
Better Hearing Institute; Deafness, Nerve; Hearing Impairment; Hearing Loss; Tinnitus

1330 Birth Defect Research for Children, Inc.
930 Woodcock Road
Suite 225
Orlando, FL 32803

Phone: (407) 895-0802
Fax: (407) 895-0824
E-mail: staff@birthdefects.org
http://www.birthdefects.org

Birth Defect Research for Children, Inc. (BDRC) formerly the Association of Birth Defect Children gives parents and expectant parents information about specific birth defects, their causes and treatments, support group referrals and parent-matching services. BDRC also provides information about environmental exposures that may be associated with birth defects. To study these exposures further, BDRC sponsors the National Birth Defect Registry, a research project designed to collect data on all kinds of birth defects and prenatal/preconceptual exposures of mothers and fathers.

Executive Director: Betty Mekdeci
Year Established: 1982
Acronym: BDRC

Keywords
Adams Oliver Syndrome; Agenesis of the Corpus Callosum; Agent Orange; Amniotic Bands; Anencephaly; Arnold Chiari Malformation; Attention Deficit Disorder; Autism; BDRC; Biliary Atresia; Birth Defect Research For Children, Inc.; Birth Defects; Bjornstad Syndrome; Bladder Exstrophy Epispadias Cloacal Exstrophy Complex; Cerebral Palsy; CHARGE Syndrome; Cleft Palate and Cleft Lip; Clubfoot; Congenital Defects; Craniosyntosis, Primary; Down Syndrome; Ear, Patella, Short Stature Syndrome; Encephalocele; Exstrophy, Bladder; Gastroschisis; Goldenhar Syndrome; Heart Defects; Holoprosencephaly; Hydrocephalus; Hypoplastic Left Heart Syndrome;

Hypospadias; Imperforate Anus; Learning Disabilities; Limb Deformities; Maffucci Syndrome; Moebius Syndrome; Neural Tube Defects; Oculo Auriculo Vertebral Spectrum; PDD; Pierre Robin Syndrome; Poland Syndrome; Polycystic Kidney Disease; Renal Agenesis, Bilateral; Spina Bifida; Tethered Spinal Cord Syndrome; Tourette Syndrome; Trisomy 18; Turner Syndrome; VACTERL Association

1331 Birth Defects Foundation
BDF Centre
Hemlock Way
Cannock
Staffordshire, WS11 7GF, England

Phone: +44 (0) 8700-70-7020
Fax: +44 (0) 1543-46-8999
E-mail: info@bdfnewlife.co.uk
http://www.birthdefects.co.uk

The Birth Defects Foundation (BDF) is a UK-registered charity whose mission is to improve child health, aid families, and create awareness of child-health challenges. BDF funds basic and clinical research into the causes, prevention and treatment of birth defects. It also operates a Here to Help Service, which is manned by qualified nurses who provide a professional and confidential service by offering support to those affected by, at risk of, or concerned about birth defects. BDF publishes information for families in free publications used in hospitals and elsewhere.

Executive Director: Mrs. Sheila Brown Obe
Year Established: 1991
Acronym: BDF

Keywords
Birth Defects Foundation; Birth Defects; Noonan Syndrome

1332 Blepharophimosis, Ptosis, Epicanthus Inversus Family Network
SE 820 Meadow Vale Drive
Pullman, WA 99163

Phone: (509) 332-6628
E-mail: Lschauble@gocougs.wsu.edu
http://freespace.virgin.net/andy.bowles/

The Blepharophimosis, Ptosis, Epicanthus Inversus Family Network is a voluntary, self-help organization dedicated to gathering and disseminating information regarding blepharophimosis, ptosis, epicanthus inversus syndrome (BPES). BPES is a rare genetic disorder characterized by abnormal narrowness of the eyelids in a horizontal direction (blepharophimosis), drooping of the upper eyelids (ptosis), vertical eyelid folds on either side of the nose (epicanthus inversus), and/or other abnormalities. The group provides a support network to affected individuals and their families, and works with medical specialists and healthcare professionals to help provide the best possible care for affected individuals. Established in 1994, the organization also distributes a variety of educational and support materials through its computer database, regular newsletter, reprinted journal articles, and pamphlets. The network also conducts an annual conference for affected individuals, families and members of the medical community, research professionals and other interested individuals.

President: Lynne Schauble (1994 to present).
Executive Director: Same as above.
Year Established: 1994
Acronym: BPEI Family Network

Keywords
Blepharophimosis, Ptosis, Epicanthus Inversus Family Network; Blepharophimosis Ptosis Epicanthus Inversus Syndrome; Blepharophimosis, Ptosis, Epicanthus Inversus Support Group; BPEI Family Network; BPES

1333 Blind Children's Fund

311 W. Broadway
Suite 1
Mt. Pleasant, MI 48858

Phone: (989) 779-9966
Fax: (989) 779-0015
E-mail: bcf@blindchildrensfund.org
http://www.blindchildrensfund.org

Blind Children's Fund is an international, nonprofit organization that was established in 1978. BCF was incorporated to respond to the special educational and emotional needs of blind, visually impaired and multi-impaired children and their families. Blind Children's Fund represents a network of parents, professionals, and volunteers throughout the United States and the world who are committed to developing, organizing, and disseminating information and materials for affected families. BCF develops and distributes educational materials and literature; publishes a quarterly newsletter; and distributes national position papers relative to advocacy and program development for affected children. BCF organizes international symposia, conducts workshops and conferences, provides

in-service and consultant services, and provides a slide and tape show for UNESCO in four languages that helps train professionals and paraprofessionals who work with blind, visually impaired or multi-impaired children.

President: Karla B. Storrer
Year Established: 1978
Acronym: BCF

Keywords
Aniridia Cerebellar Ataxia Mental Deficiency; Blind Children's Fund; Blindness; Child; Multi-impaired; Visual Impairments

1334 Blind Citizens Australia

P.O. Box 24
Sunshine, Victoria, 3020, Australia

Phone: +61 (0) 3-9372-6400
Fax: +61 (0) 3-9372-6466
Toll Free: 1 (800) 033-660
TDD: +61 (0) 3-9376-9275
E-mail: bca@bca.org.au
http://www.bca.org.au

Blind Citizens of Australia (BCA) is a national, not-for-profit organization dedicated to serving as the united voice of Australians who are affected by blindness or vision impairment. Established in 1975, BCA currently has approximately 2,500 members across all Australian states and territories. The BCA's mission is to achieve equity and equality by promoting positive community attitudes and striving for high quality and accessible services that meet the needs of those affected by vision impairment or blindness. The federation has several main objectives including encouraging self-determination for affected individuals; serving as a national assembly for meetings, communication, and interchange among blind individuals from all walks of life; and providing a forum for collective self-expression and discussion. Additional objectives include working for the progressive improvement of public policies in Australia; acting as an advocate for and representing the interests of people who are print handicapped; cooperating with and supporting other organizations for disabled individuals at the local, regional, national, and international levels; and promoting enlightened attitudes among the public at large.

President: Robert Altamore
Executive Director: Bill Jolley (Executive Officer)
Year Established: 1975
Acronym: NFBCA

Keywords
Blind Citizens Australia; Blindness

1335 Blood & Marrow Transplant Information Network

2900 Skokie Valley Road
Suite B
Highland Park, IL 60035

Phone: (847) 433-3313
Fax: (847) 433-4599
Toll Free: (888) 597-7674
E-mail: help@bmtinfonet.org
http://www.bmtinfonet.org

Blood & Marrow Transplant Information Network (BMT InfoNet), formerly BMT Newsletter, is a not-for-profit organization established in 1990. It provides patient-friendly handbooks and a quarterly newsletter about bone marrow/peripheral stem cell and cord blood transplantation (BMT/PSCT). This is a medical procedure that may be used to treat certain diseases such as cancer, aplastic anemia, immune deficiency diseases, inborn errors of metabolism, and some brain tumors. Readership includes BMT/PSCT patients and survivors, their families and friends, patient support and information groups, medical personnel at BMT cancer centers, and insurance review personnel who handle such cases. BMT InfoNet links patients with survivors who can provide emotional support, maintains an online Directory of Transplant Centers in the US and Canada, an online Directory of Drugs used during transplant, and an online Resource Directory.

President: Susan Stewart (1994-Present)
Executive Director: Same as above.
Year Established: 1990
Acronym: BMT InfoNet

Keywords
Blood and Marrow Transplant; Blood & Marrow Transplant Information Network; BMT (Bone Marrow Transplant) Newsletter; Bone Pain; Donor, Bone Marrow; Donor, Cord Blood; Donor, Stem Cell; Graft-versus-Host Disease; GVHD; Hodgkin Disease; Leukemia; Lymphoma; Non Hodgkin; Non Hodgkin Lymphoma; Transplant, Stem Cell; Transplantation, Bone Marrow; Transplantation, Cord Blood; Transplantation, Peripheral Stem Cell

1336 Bloom's Syndrome Registry

The Bloom's Syndrome Registry is a research effort dedicated to collecting clinical and genetic information about Bloom's syndrome, a rare inherited disorder characterized by short stature; a sun-sensitive redness in a "butterfly pattern" on the face; and susceptibility to infections and proness to develop cancer of many types. Established in 1960, the Bloom's Syndrome Registry meets with affected individuals and their families, compiles information concerning their pedigree history, and collects and preserves DNA and biological specimens. In addition, the registry maintains copies of affected individuals' medical records and updates these records with new clinical findings and medical progress. The registry conducts ongoing research using registry data and specimens and publishes regular reports and reviews in medical journals.

Executive Director: James L. German III, M.D. (Investigator)
Year Established: 1960

Keywords
Bloom Syndrome; Bloom's Syndrome Registry

1337 Bone Marrow Foundation (The BMF)

337 E. 88th Street
Suite 1B
New York, NY 10128

Phone: (212) 828-3029
Fax: (212) 223-0081
Toll Free: (800) 365-1336
E-mail: theBMF@bonemarrow.org
http://www.bonemarrow.org

The mission of the Bone Marrow Foundation is to improve the quality of life for bone-marrow transplant patients and their families by providing financial aid, education, and emotional support. The BMF was created in 1992 to respond to the critical gap in financial coverage for patient support services. Its Patient Aid Program assists patients with the cost of donor searches, compatibility testing, bone marrow harvesting, medications, home and childcare services, medical equipment, transportation, cord blood banking, and housing expenses associated with the transplant. The BMF currently accepts applications for aid from over seventy bone marrow transplant centers throughout the United States. To fulfill the growing need for information and support for patients and their families, the BMF established the Marie M. Reynolds Resource and Education Center. It provides information to patients, their families and their clinicians. The center also seeks to provide support and encouragement to patients and families dealing with the challenge of life-threatening diseases.

Executive Director: Christina Merrill (1993-present)
Year Established: 1993
Acronym: The BMF

Keywords
Bone Marrow Foundation; Bone Marrow Foundation (The BMF); Bone Marrow Transplant; Organization Classification/Other

1338 Bowel Group for Kids Incorporated

PO Box 40
Oakdale, NSW, 2570, Austrailia

Phone: +61 (0) 2-4659-6186
Fax: +61 (0) 2-4659-6381
E-mail: gribbins@ozE-mail.com.au

A registered charity in Australia, the Bowel Group for Kids Incorporated cares for families having children with disordered gastrointestinal motility, resulting in disorders such as Hirschprung's disease and imperforate anus. These are disorders that occur when nerves or muscles of the gastrointestinal system do not function together in a coordinated fashion. The resulting symptoms may range from mild to life threatening, and include heartburn, nausea, vomiting, and diarrhea. BGK, Inc., offers parent-to-parent networking, brochures, referrals, and a newsletter. This organization was formerly known as the Australian Pseudo-obstruction Support Association.

President: Jenny Kreuzinger (2001-present)
Executive Director: Eunice Gribbin
Year Established: 1996
Acronym: BGK Inc

Keywords
Bowel Group for Kids Incorporated; Children; Gastrointestinal Disease, Children

1339 Brachial Plexus Palsy Foundation

210 Spring Haven Circle
Royersford, PA 19468

E-mail: brachial@comcast.net
http://www.membrane.com/bpp/

The Brachial Plexus Palsy Foundation (BPPF) is a nonprofit organization dedicated to raising funds for support of families who have children with brachial plexus injuries. Affected children may have paralysis of the shoulder and upper extremity due to injury of one or more of the nerves that control shoulder and upper extremity muscles (upper brachial plexus). Such injuries, which may be called Erb's palsy or upper brachial paralysis, usually occur in newborns due to birth injury. The organization supports medical facilities that research and treat such injuries, holds fund-raising events to support further research, has support groups, and produces educational materials including a newsletter.

President: Thomas J. Cirino
Executive Director: Michael F. Cirino
Acronym: BPPF

Keywords
BPPF; Brachial Plexus Injuries; Brachial Plexus Palsy; Brachial Plexus Palsy Foundation; Erb's Palsy; Paralysis, Erb Duchenne; Paralysis, Upper Brachial Plexus; Support Groups

1340 Brain and Tissue Bank for Developmental Disorders of The National Institute of Child Health and Human Development (NICHC)

University of Miami Miller School of Medicine
PAP Building, Room 410 (R-5)
1550 North West 10th Avenue
Miami, FL 33136

Phone: (305) 243-6834
Fax: (305) 243-6970
Toll Free: (800) 592-7246
E-mail: btbcoord@med.miami.edu
http://www.miami.edu/braintissue-bank/

The Brain and Tissue Bank for Developmental Disorders of The National Institute of Child Health Human Development, (NICHD) is a not-for-profit research organization dedicated to advancing meaningful research regarding developmental disorders. Established in 1993, the facility is committed to collecting, preserving, and distributing human tissues to qualified scientific investigators dedicated to the improved understanding, care, and treatment of developmental disorders. The Brain and Tissue Bank for Developmental Disorders reaches out to individuals and organizations across the United States to encourage donor registration. All donor information remains anonymous. Educational materials include reports, brochures, and audiovisual aids. The National Institute of Child Health and Human Development fund the organization.

President: Carol K. Petito, M.D., Professor of Pathology (Director)
Executive Director: Lillian M. Rodriguez (Project Coordinator)
Year Established: 1993

Keywords
Brain and Tissue Bank for Developmental Disorders at the University of Miami; Brain and Tissue Bank for Developmental Disorders of The National Institute of Child Health and Human Development (NICHC); Developmental Disorders

1341 Brain Injury Association of America

8201 Greenboro Drive
Suite 611
McLean, VA 22102

Phone: (703) 761-0750
Fax: (703) 761-0755
Toll Free: (800) 444-6443
E-mail: PublicRelations@biausa.org
http://www.biausa.org

The Brain Injury Association of America is a national health organization dedicated to creating a better future through brain injury prevention, research, education and advocacy. Established in 1980, the Brain Injury Association provides information, assistance, and a variety of programs and services to people with brain injuries and their families, healthcare professionals, and the general public. The BIAA networks with, and provides guidance to, state associations as well as hundreds of chapters and support groups that offer a range of services, including care/case management, respite care, recreational opportunities, and, in some cases, housing, transportation and emergency financial assistance. The BIAA also lobbies before Congress and the administration; encourages state agencies to develop and fund appropriate services for people with brain injuries; offers a toll-free Family Helpline; provides emergency financial assistance through its "Thumbs Up Fund"; and offers the "Brain Injury Resource Center," an interactive multimedia computer system with comprehensive brain injury information that is available at rehabilitation facilities, trauma centers, and hospitals across the country. The BIAA publishes manuals, directories, magazines, and books.

President: Susan H. Connors
Year Established: 1980
Acronym: BIAA

Keywords
Brain Injury; Brain Injury Association, Inc.; Brain Injury Association of America; Brain Injury, Traumatic; Financial Assistance Programs; Head Injury

1342 Brain Injury Resource Center

212 Pioneer Building
Seattle, WA 98104-2221

Phone: (206) 621-8558
Fax: (206) 329-0912
E-mail: brain@headinjury.com
http://www.headinjury.com/

Brain Injury Resource Center is a nonprofit clearinghouse founded and operated by head injury activists. Visitors get information, join a discussion group and build advocacy and self-care skills. Its staff catalogue resources from diverse organizations including support groups, and rehabilitation, and research sites, as well as lay and professional journals and more.

President: Constance Miller (1985 to Present)
Year Established: 1985

Keywords
Brain Injury Resource Center; Brain Injury; Head Injury; Head Injury Hotline

1343 Brain Tumor Foundation for Children, Inc.

1835 Savoy Drive
Suite 200
Atlanta, GA 30341

Phone: (770) 458-5554
Fax: (770) 458-5467
E-mail: btfc@bellsouth.net
http://www.braintumorkids.org

The Brain Tumor Foundation for Children (BTFC), Inc., is a non-profit organization established in 1983 to assist families of children with brain and spinal cord tumors. Services include informational materials and educational conferences; social, emotional and financial assistance (limited to GA and AL); educational scholarships (GA residents); year-round get-togethers and holiday celebrations; parent support group and parent networking; a website (www.braintumorkids.org); and research funding to find a cure.

President: R. Hal Meeks, Jr.
Executive Director: Mary Campbell
Year Established: 1983
Acronym: BTFC

Keywords
Brain Tumor Foundation for Children, Inc.; Tumors, Brain; Tumors, Pediatric Brain

1344   Brain Tumor Society

124 Watertown Street
Suite 3H
Watertown, MA 02472-2500

Phone: (617) 924-9997
Fax: (617) 924-9998
Toll Free: (800) 770-8287
E-mail: info@tbts.org
http://www.tbts.org

The Brain Tumor Society (BTS) is a national, not-for-profit organization dedicated to finding a cure for brain tumors, improving affected individuals' quality of life, disseminating information on brain tumors, and providing psychosocial support to affected individuals and their families. BTS raises funds and makes grants to advance carefully selected scientific research projects, improve clinical care, and find a cure. It offers a wide range of services to help individuals cope with and manage the problems associated with brain tumors. BTS offers a variety of educational programs to raise public awareness, facilitate early diagnosis and treatment, and to educate professionals about psychosocial issues associated with rare diagnoses.

President: G. Bonnie Feldman (1989-Present)
Executive Director: Neal Levitan
Year Established: 1989
Acronym: BTS

Keywords
Astrocytoma; Brain Cancer; Brain Tumor Society; BTS; Chordoma; Choroid Plexus Papilloma; CNS Lymphoma; Craniopharyngioma; Ependymoma; Ganglioneuroma; Glioblastoma Multiforme; Gliomas; Hemangioblastoma; Medulloblastoma; Meningioma; Oligodendroglioma; Schwannoma; Tumors, Brain; Tumors, Pediatric Brain; Tumors, Pineal; Tumors, Primitive Neuroectodermal; Turcot Syndrome

1345   Brain Tumour Foundation of Canada

620 Colborne Street
Suite 301
London
Ontario, N6B 3R9, Canada

Phone: (519) 642-7755
Fax: (519) 642-7192
Toll Free: (800) 265-5106
E-mail: btfc@btfc.org
http://www.braintumour.ca

The Brain Tumour Foundation of Canada is a national, not-for-profit organization dedicated to reaching every person in Canada affected by a brain tumor with support, education and information, and to funding brain tumor research. Established in 1982, the foundation is committed to providing support through national brain tumor support groups and meeting the information needs of those affected by brain tumors with educational materials. These materials include brain tumour patient resource handbooks, available in adult and pediatric versions, in English and French; a newsletter, BrainStorm; and a children's storybook, "A Friend in Hope". Program activities include monthly support group meetings, a national toll free support line, annual patient conferences, and an online Virtual Support Centre. Each year, the foundation funds Canadian research projects and is the sole funder of the Brain Tumour Tissue Bank.

President: Phyllis Retty (Board Chairperson)
Executive Director: Susan Marshall
Year Established: 1982
Acronym: BTFC

Keywords
Brain Tumor Foundation of Canada; Brain Tumors; Brain Tumour Foundation of Canada; Chordoma; Networking; Tumors, Brain; Tumors, Pediatric Brain; Tumour; Tumours

1346   British Acoustic Neuroma Association

Oak House
Ransom Wood Business Park
Southwell Road West
Mansfield
Nottinghamshire, NG21 0HJ, United Kingdom

Phone: +44 (0) 1623-63-2143
Fax: +44 (0) 1632-63-5313
Toll Free: +44 (0) 800-652-3143
E-mail: bana@ukan.freeserve.co.uk
http://www.ukan.co.uk/bana/

The British Acoustic Neuroma Association (BANA) is an international, voluntary organization in the United Kingdom that is dedicated to promoting the exchange of mutual support and information among individuals affected by acoustic neuromas. Acoustic neuroma, a benign tumor of one or two of the eighth cranial nerves (auditory or vestibulocochlear nerves), usually develops within the auditory canal. The cranial nerves are the 12 nerve pairs that arise from the brain. Associated symptoms, which may vary depending upon the size and location of the tumor, may include progressive hearing loss, balance difficulties, a sensation of ringing in the ear, and facial numbness or pain. The British Acoustic Neuroma Association was established in 1993 and currently has approximately 17 chapters. The association is committed to providing understandable information about acoustic neuroma to affected individuals and family members, and encouraging and supporting a network of local groups. In addition, it is dedicated to promoting research and publishing the results of such research concerning medical, surgical, and other procedures that may help prevent or treat acoustic neuroma or assist in the rehabilitation of patients following treatment.

President: Colin Dawes (Chairman)
Executive Director: Janet Mercer (Editor)
Year Established: 1993
Acronym: BANA

Keywords
Acoustic Neuroma; British Acoustic Neuroma Association

1347   British Liver Trust

Portman House
44 High Street
Ringwood, BH24 1AG, United Kingdom

Phone: +44 (0) 1425-46-3080
Fax: +44 (0) 1425-47-0706
E-mail: info@britishlivertrust.org.uk
http://www.britishlivertrust.org.uk

Founded in 1988, the British Liver Trust was initially set up to provide support and education, as well as to fund medical research. More recently, following a significant review, the charity's overall strategy is to cover all liver diseases, operate strategically at a national level, and have an initial focus on three key areas of activity. These activities are Information, Research, and Service Enhancement (advocating on behalf of people with liver disease). The British Liver Trust works closely with others involved in liver disease including medical professionals, other voluntary organizations, government agencies, and suppliers of products used in the treatment of liver disease. A priority for the charity is to ensure services for liver disease are specifically commissioned in the NHS throughout the UK. This is alongside the need to raise awareness of liver disease and to promote the issue within society generally.

President: Prof. Roger Williams
Executive Director: Nigel Hughes
Year Established: 1988

Keywords
British Liver Trust; Liver Disease

1348   British Lung Foundation

73-75 Goswell Road
London, EC1V 7ER, United Kingdom

Phone: +44 (0) 8458-50-5020
E-mail: info@britishlungfoundation.com
http://www.lunguk.org

The British Lung Foundation is a voluntary, not-for-profit organization in the United Kingdom dedicated to funding medical research into the prevention, treatment, and cure of all forms of lung disease. Since the foundation was founded in 1985, it has funded over 220 clinical, non-clinical, and epidemiological research grants. The British Lung Foundation is also committed to providing information, support, and resources to individuals affected by lung disease and their family members. The foundation, which has a head office in London and six branch offices throughout the UK, offers free membership in its "Breathe Easy Club" to affected individuals, family members, and other caregivers. The club serves as a support and information network throughout the UK for individuals with any form of lung disease and those who care for them. Members of the Breathe Easy Club receive support and information through the "Keep in Touch" contact service, local support groups, and a quarterly magazine entitled "Breathe Easy." The British Lung Foundation also provides information about all aspects of good lung health and the prevention, diagnosis, and treatment of respiratory disease through its leaflet series and "The Lung Report."

President: Dame Helena Shovelton (Chief Executive)
Executive Director: Same as above.
Year Established: 1984

Keywords
British Lung Foundation; Lung Disease

1349   British Porphyria Association

14 Mollison Rise
Gravesend
Kent, DA12 4QJ, United Kingdom

Phone: +44 (0) 1474-36-9231
E-mail: BPA@bodywise.go-plus.net
http://www.porphyria.org.uk

The British Porphyria Association's aim is to reach out to as many people as possible to improve the understanding of this condition. Porphyria is a group of at least seven metabolic disorders characterized by excess accumulation of the natural chemicals "porphyrins" or "porphyrin precursors" in the body. The different types vary in their clinical presentation. Clinical findings associated with the disorders generally include skin or nervous system manifestations. The BPA was established in 1999. It provides information to patients, members of patients' families, and health professionals.

President: Karen Harris
Year Established: 1999
Acronym: The BPA

Keywords
British Porphyria Association; Porphyria; Porphyria, Acute Intermittent; Porphyria, ALA-D; Porphyria, Congenital Erythropoietic; Porphyria, Erythropoietic; Porphyria, Hereditary Coproporphyria; Porphyria, Protoporphyria; Porphyria, Variegate

1350 British Retinitis Pigmentosa Society
PO Box 350
Buckingham, MK18 1GZ, United Kingdom

Phone: +44 (0) 1280-82-1334
Fax: +44 (0) 1280-81-5900
E-mail: info@brps.org.uk
http://www.brps.org.uk

The British Retinitis Pigmentosa Society (BRPS) is a voluntary, self-help organization in the United Kingdom that was established in 1975. The society is dedicated to helping affected individuals cope with vision impairment resulting from retinitis pigmentosa (RP) and stimulating research into the causes and eventual treatment of RP. Retinitis pigmentosa is a group of eye conditions characterized by degeneration of the retina, the nerve-rich membrane at the back of the eye. Although the severity and progression of the condition may vary, associated symptoms and findings often include poor vision in dim light (night blindness), abnormal pigmentation of the retina, and progressively reduced fields of vision. In most cases, retinitis pigmentosa is a hereditary condition. The British Retinitis Pigmentosa Society offers a helpline to affected individuals and family members that provides information, advice, and assistance concerning everyday living skills, careers and employment, children and education, mobility and communication needs, benefits and pensions, and other areas. In addition, the society has several publications on a range of subjects and distributes a quarterly newsletter in bold print, in Braille, or on audiotape.

Year Established: 1975
Acronym: BRPS

Keywords
British Retinitis Pigmentosa Society; Retinitis Pigmentosa

1351 British Sjogren's Syndrome Association
P.O. Box 10867
Birmingham, B16 0ZW, United Kingdom

Phone: +44 (0) 121-455-6532
Fax: +44 (0) 121-455-6532
E-mail: kate@bssa.uk.net
http://www.bssa.uk.net

The British Sjögren's Syndrome Association (BSSA) is a registered charity dedicated to providing mutual support and information to individuals affected by Sjögren syndrome. Sjögren syndrome is an autoimmune disorder characterized by degeneration of the mucus-secreting glands, particularly the tear ducts of the eyes (lacrimal) and saliva glands of the mouth. Autoimmune disorders are caused when the body's natural defenses (antibodies, lymphocytes, etc.) against invading organisms suddenly begin to attack healthy tissue. Sjögren syndrome is also associated with inflammatory disorders such as arthritis or lupus. Founded in 1986, the BSSA disseminates current information on the treatment of Sjögren syndrome to affected individuals and medical professionals. In addition to holding regular meetings in several locations throughout England, BSSA publishes journals, informational brochures, and a quarterly newsletter.

President: Dr. Simon Bowman
Executive Director: Kate Endacott (Office Manager)
Year Established: 1986
Acronym: BSSA

Keywords
British Sjogren's Syndrome Association; Dacryosialoadenopathia Atrophicans; Gougerot Houwer Sjogren; Gougerot Sjogren; Keratoconjunctivitis Sicca; Keratoconjunctivitis Sicca Xerostomia; Secreto Inhibitor Xerodermostenosis; Sicca Syndrome; Sjogren Syndrome

1352 British Stammering Association
15 Old Ford Road
London, E2 9PJ, United Kingdom

Phone: +44 (0) 208-983-1003
Fax: +44 (0) 208-983-3591
E-mail: mail@stammering.org
http://www.stammering.org

The British Stammering Association (BSA) is a nonprofit organization dedicated to offering information, guidance, support, and resources to children, adolescents, and adults affected by stammering also known as stuttering. The mission of the BSA is to initiate and support research concerning stammering, identify and promote effective treatments, offer support to those whose lives are affected by stammering, and promote public awareness. To help fulfill its mission and objectives, the BSA is committed to improving information for professionals who work with young children to help eliminate stammering; helping teachers become more responsive to the needs of pupils affected by stammering; focusing attention on the employment difficulties of affected individuals; and providing a free, UK-wide, confidential telephone advice and counseling service. The BSA is also dedicated to coordinating mutual aid and self-help opportunities for members; campaigning for improvements in the National Health Service (NHS) stammering therapy provision; and improving public understanding of the difficulties faced by affected individuals and how they may be helped.

Executive Director: Mr. Norbert Lieckfeldt
Year Established: 1978
Acronym: BSA

Keywords
British Stammering Association; Stammering; Stuttering

1353 CADASIL—Together We Have Hope
3605 Monument Drive
Round Rock, TX 78681

Phone: (512) 255-0209
Fax: (512) 255-0209
Toll Free: (877) 467-3669
E-mail: cadasil@earthlink.net OR info@cadasilfoundation.org
http://cadasilfoundation.org

CADASIL is a hereditary disease that affects the muscle walls in the small arteries that provide blood flow to the brain. It results from a protein deficiency, and is characterized by recurrent ischemic (mini-stroke) events, migraine headache, and/or severe mood disorders. CADASIL stands for cerebral autosomal dominant arteriopathy with subcortical infarcts and leukoencephalopathy. CADASIL-Together We Have Hope is a non-profit organization that provides support, encouragement, and information to those affected and their families, as well as to the medical professionals who treat affected individuals.

President: Billie Duncan-Smith (Founder/Director)
Year Established: 1998
Acronym: CADASIL

Keywords
CADASIL; CADASIL Together We Have Hope; CADASIL—Together We Have Hope; Cerebral Autosomal Dominant Arteriopathy with Subcortical Infarcts and Leukoencephalopathy; Dementia; Migraines; Strokes; TIA; White Matter

1354 CAH Support Group
2 Windrush Close
Flitwick, Bedfordshire, MK45 1PX, United Kingdom

Phone: +44 (0) 1525-71-7536
E-mail: webmaster@cah.org.uk
http://www.cah.org.uk

The CAH Support Group was formed in 1991 in the United Kingdom as a sub-group of the organization known as CLIMB (Children Living with Inherited Metabolic Diseases). The CAH Support Group exists to give support to patients and families affected by congenital adrenal hyperplasia (CAH), a group of disorders resulting from impaired ability of the adrenal glands to produce vital steroid hormones. The CAH support group works to increase awareness of CAH and to raise funds to support research. It holds conferences and publishes a newsletter which is sent our three times a year.

President: Sue Elford
Executive Director: Gavin Blackett

Keywords
Advocacy; CAH; CAH Support Group; Congenital Adrenal Hyperplasia; Networking; Research; Support Groups

1355 Caitlin Raymond International Registry
UMASS Memorial Medical Center
55 Lake Avenue North
Worcester, MA 01655

Phone: (508) 334-8969
Fax: (508) 334-8972
Toll Free: (800) 726-2824
E-mail: info@CRIR.org
http://www.crir.org

The Caitlin Raymond International Registry (CRIR) of Bone Marrow Donor Banks is a not-for-profit organization founded in 1986 as a coordinating center for conducting national and international searches for unrelated donors for individuals with diseases that are treatable by bone marrow transplantation or placental blood transfusion. CRIR strives not only to identify potential donors, but also to facilitate and coordinate the entire search process. Daily search activities include coordinating existing donor resources and assisting in the development of new bone marrow and cord blood donor sources; developing and maintaining an information service for physicians, transplant coordinators, and affected individuals regarding all available donor sources; and maintaining communications with, and problem solving for physicians, transplant coordinators, and affected individuals. The organization also distributes information concerning all available medical, financial, and community support services; monitors search progress and assists in the identification of problems resulting from unnecessary delays, costs, and/or incomplete search results; and works directly with the physician, transplant coordinator, and affected individual to tailor the search process to meet the needs of the individual.

Executive Director: Joanne Raymond
Year Established: 1986
Acronym: CRIR

Keywords
BMT; Bone Marrow Donation; Bone Marrow Donor Bank; Caitlin Raymond International Registry; Cord Blood Donation; Graft-versus-Host Disease; Transfusion, Placental Blood; Transplantation, Bone Marrow

1356 California Lyme Disease Association

P.O.. Box 1423
Ukiah, CA 95482

Phone: (707) 468-8460
E-mail: pmerv@direcway.com
http://www.lymedisease.org

The Lyme Disease Association is a voluntary, not-for-profit, education and communication center dedicated to supporting people affected by Lyme disease, the public, physicians, and any others interested in this disorder. Established in 1990, the Lyme Disease Resource Center educates the public about Lyme disease, its risks, and preventive measures. It provides a forum for physicians and other healthcare professionals to exchange ideas and information concerning symptoms, diagnosis, and treatments for Lyme disease. It also functions as a communication center for individuals and groups who assist people with Lyme disease. The center has a network of Lyme disease support

groups, engages in patient advocacy, and provides referrals to medical professionals or support groups. It offers a variety of educational and support materials through its directory. It also offers audiovisual aids, brochures, a Spanish language brochure, and a regular newsletter.

President: Phyllis Mervine
Executive Director: Lorrian Johnson, MBA, JD
Year Established: 1990
Acronym: CALDA

Keywords
Anaplasmosis; Babesiosis; CALDA; California Lyme Disease Association; Ehrlichiosis; Lyme Disease; Lyme Times; Tick-Borne Diseases

1357 Canadian Addison Society

87 Blue Ridge Close
N.W. Calgary
Alberta, T3L 2P4, Canada

Phone: (403) -54-7-69
Toll Free: (888)550-5582
E-mail: liaisonsecretary@addisonsociety.ca
http://www.addisonsociety.ca

The Canadian Addison Society (La Societe Canadienne d'Addison) is a nonprofit, voluntary agency dedicated to providing support and educational information to individuals affected by Addison's disease and their families. All society staff members are volunteers. Addison's disease is a rare disorder characterized by chronic, usually progressive, insufficient functioning of the outer layer of the adrenal glands (adrenal cortex). Deficiencies of certain hormones manufactured by the adrenals (i.e., cortisol and aldosterone) result in abnormally low levels of sodium and chloride in the blood and body tissues as well as unusually high levels of potassium (electrolyte imbalance). Increased urinary output and abnormally low blood pressure (hypotension) can lead to extremely low levels of fluid in the body (dehydration). Other early symptoms of Addison's disease may include weakness, fatigue, loss of appetite (anorexia), and a darkened discoloration of scars, skin folds, and/or mucous membranes (hyperpigmentation). The Canadian Addison Society publishes a quarterly newsletter that includes information on national and international issues from support groups around the world; information on local support group activities is also included. In addition, the society publishes an educational brochure on Addison's disease. The society has approximately 200 members and is itself a member of The Addison and Cushing International Federation.

President: Athena Elton
Executive Director: Irene Gordon - Liaison Secretary
Year Established: 1994
Acronym: N/A

Keywords
Addison's Disease; Adrenocortical Hypofunction; Adrenocortical Insufficiency; Canadian Addison Society; Chronic Adrenocortical Insufficiency; Primary Adrenal Insufficiency; Primary Failure Arenocortical Insufficiency

1358 Canadian Angelman Syndrome Society
P.O. Box 37
Priddis
Alberta, T0L 1W0, Canada

Phone: (403) 931-2415
Fax: (403) 931-2415
E-mail: cass01@telus.net
http://www.angelmancanada.org

The Canadian Angelman Syndrome Society (CASS) was incorporated in 1993 as a nonprofit charity and established to educate concerned families, the medical and educational communities, and the general public on the diagnosis, treatment, and prevention of Angelman syndrome. Angelman syndrome is a rare genetic disorder characterized by mental and motor retardation, absence of speech, muscular abnormalities, unprovoked laughter, and characteristic facial abnormalities. CASS consists of approximately 150 members who are dedicated to educating parents and professionals about Angelman syndrome and disseminating information on this disorder. CASS provides a regular newsletter, offers networking services for affected parents, and conducts a yearly conference.

President: Rob Bromley E-Mail rob@forcefour.com
Executive Director: John Carscallen, Secretary-Treasurer
Year Established: 1993
Acronym: CASS

Keywords
Angelman Syndrome; AS; Canadian Angelman Syndrome Society

1359 Canadian Association for Community Living
4700 Keele Street
Kinsmen Building
York University
North York
Ontario, M3J 1P3, Canada

Phone: (416) 661-9611
Fax: (416) 661-5701
Toll Free: (800) 856-2207
TDD: (416) 661-2023
E-mail: info@cacl.ca
http://www.cacl.ca

The Canadian Association for Community Living (CACL) is a national, nonprofit federation dedicated to developing communities that welcome people with intellectual disabilities and promoting participation of people with intellectual disabilities in all aspects of community life. Intellectual disability is usually present from birth and involves some degree of difficulty learning, conceptualizing, and adapting to social situations. The association promotes the belief that people with intellectual disabilities have the right to participate in all decisions that affect their lives. Therefore, the association's goals include creating alternatives to institutional care for people with intellectual disabilities; ensuring that all children, regardless of their level of intellectual ability, have access to education in regular classes; ensuring that all people have the opportunity to earn a living and contribute as productive members of the community; and supporting families of people with mental handicaps. The association endeavors to bring about change in personal attitudes to acceptance of people with mental handicaps. This goal is addressed through public education and training programs. CACL works with government and service agencies, individuals, and families in order to build supportive and inclusive communities. The association is a federation of ten provincial and two territorial affiliates with more than 40,000 members and 400 local associations across Canada.

President: Ms. Cheryl Gulliver
Executive Director: Michael Bach (Executive Vice President)
Year Established: 1958
Acronym: CACL

Keywords
Canadian Association for Community Living; Developmental Disability

1360 Canadian Association for Williams Syndrome
P.O. Box 2115
Vancouver
British Columbia, V6B 3T5, Canada

Phone: (604) 853-0231
Fax: (604) 853-0232
E-mail: sev@uniserve.com
http://www.caws-can.org

The Canadian Association for Williams Syndrome (CAWS) is a voluntary, nonprofit organization dedicated to providing support and assistance to families with children affected by Williams syndrome; maintaining a network for adults with Williams syndrome; and supporting research into educational, behavioral, social, and medical aspects of this syndrome. Williams's syndrome is a rare congenital disorder characterized by heart and blood vessel abnormalities, high blood calcium levels, developmental delays, characteristic facial features, and/or additional abnormalities. Established in 1984 as a parent support group, CAWS is committed to locating affected families who are unaware of the association; becoming a visible group in the medical, scientific, educational, and professional communities to facilitate referrals of newly diagnosed individuals; and providing a variety of educational materials to affected individuals, family members, and healthcare professionals.

President: Kim Di Tomaso
Year Established: 1984
Acronym: CAWS

Keywords
Beuren Syndrome; Canadian Association for Williams Syndrome; CAWS; Elfin Facies with Hypercalcemia; Hypercalcemia Syndrome, Early with Elfin Facies; Hypercalcemia, Supravalvar Aortic Stenosis; Williams Beuren Syndrome; Williams Syndrome; WMS

1361 Canadian Cancer Society
10 Alcorn Avenue
Suite 200
Toronto
Toronto, M4V 3B1, Canada

Phone: (416) 961-7223
Fax: (416) 961-4189
Toll Free: (888) 939-3333
E-mail: ccs@cancer.ca
http://www.cancer.ca/

The Canadian Cancer Society (CCS) is a national, nonprofit, community-based organization that is dedicated to eradicating cancer and improving the quality of life of people living with cancer. Established in 1937, the society currently has 350,000 volunteers, over 600 community locations, 10 provincial divisions, and one national office. The Canadian Cancer Society works to achieve its mission by promoting and supporting cancer research, educating the public, engaging in public policy advocacy efforts, and providing patient and family services. It is committed to

funding medical research, awarding fellowships to support advanced clinical training in oncology, and funding behavioral research to help determine the best ways to promote lifestyle changes that may reduce the risk of cancer. The society's public education programs work to promote the prevention and early detection of cancer by providing information and skill development through programs, advocacy, and collaboration. In addition, the Canadian Cancer Society works with coalitions of health, medical, research, and professional organizations to lobby Parliament and provincial legislatures concerning public policies that will promote health and prevent disease. The society's patient services include a Cancer Information Service; networking programs that enable individuals with cancer to communicate with trained volunteers who have also been affected by cancer; transportation to treatment centers and other practical assistance; and educational publications for affected individuals and family members.

President: Mr. Rene Gallant
Executive Director: Dr. Barbara Whylie (Chief Executive Officer)
Year Established: 1937
Acronym: CCS

Keywords
Adenoid Cystic Carcinoma; Advocacy; Breast Cancer; Canadian Cancer Society; Cancer; Cancer Encyclopedia; CCS; Cutaneous T Cell Lymphomas; Mantle Cell Lymphoma; Mesothelioma; Networking; Tobacco

---

1362 Canadian Celiac Association
5170 Dixie Road
Suite 204
Mississauga
Ontario, L4W 1E3, Canada

Phone: (905) 50-7 62
Fax: (905) 50-7 46
Toll Free: (800) 36-3 72
E-mail: info@celiac.ca
http://www.celiac.ca

The Canadian Celiac Association is a national, not-for-profit organization dedicated to providing services and support to individuals with celiac disease and dermatitis herpetiformis through programs of awareness, advocacy, education, and research. Celiac disease is a condition in which the absorptive surface of the small intestine is damaged due to ingestion of foods containing gluten, a protein found in wheat, barley, rye, and oats. Due to impaired intestinal absorption of nutrients (malabsorption), affected individuals may experience diarrhea, vomiting, swelling (distension) of the abdomen, muscle wasting, and other symptoms and findings. In addition, in some cases, affected individuals may develop a distinctive rash (dermatitis herpetiformis) that is thought to represent an immune response to dietary gluten. The Canadian Celiac Association was established in 1972 and currently has 24 local chapters throughout Canada. The purpose of the association is to assist its affiliated chapters and to represent their members' needs at the national level. The association is committed to increasing awareness of celiac disease and dermatitis herpetiformis among healthcare professionals and the public; providing current information about these conditions and gluten-free foods; acting as an advocate for individuals with celiac disease and dermatitis herpetiformis, and encouraging and promoting research.

President: Jean Gurjar
Executive Director: Kenn Tuckey
Year Established: 1972

Keywords
Canadian Celiac Association; Celiac Disease

1363 Canadian Cystic Fibrosis Foundation

2221 Yonge Street
Suite 601
Toronto
Ontario, M1B 4G8, Canada

Phone: (416) 485-9149
Fax: (416) 485-0960
Toll Free: (800) 378-2233
E-mail: info@cysticfibrosis.ca
http://www.cysticfibrosis.ca

The Canadian Cystic Fibrosis Foundation (CCFF) is a national, not-for-profit organization dedicated to helping individuals with cystic fibrosis (CF) and their family members. Cystic fibrosis is a rare inherited disorder that affects many exocrine ("outward-secreting") glands of the body including the sweat glands, salivary glands, and those within the pancreas and respiratory system. Due to unusually thick secretions of mucus that clog and obstruct air passages of the lungs, affected individuals experience chronic coughing and an increased susceptibility to repeated lung infections. Individuals with CF also exhibit an inability to break down food and absorb fats and nutrients properly; have abnormally salty sweat containing elevated levels of chloride and sodium; and/or may demonstrate other abnormalities. Established in 1960, the Canadian

Cystic Fibrosis Foundation is committed to conducting research into improved care and treatment for CF, seeking a cure or control for the disorder, and promoting public awareness. In addition, the foundation offers support groups, engages in patient advocacy, provides referrals, and promotes patient, professional, and general education.

President: Ms. Chris Black
Executive Director: Cathleen Morrison
Year Established: 1960
Acronym: CCFF

Keywords
Canadian Cystic Fibrosis Foundation; CF; Cystic Fibrosis; Mucoviscidosis; Pancreatic Fibrosis

1364 Canadian Diabetes Association

National Life Building,
1400-522 University Avenue
Toronto
Ontario, M5C 2R5, Canada

Phone: (416) 363-3373
Fax: (416) 214-1899
Toll Free: (800) 226-8464
E-mail: info@diabetes.ca
http://www.diabetes.ca

The Canadian Diabetes Association (CDA) is a voluntary organization that was founded in 1949 to serve the needs of people with diabetes. The organization currently consists of approximately 170 branches across Canada. There are different forms of diabetes, including diabetes mellitus, which is characterized by impaired fat, protein, and carbohydrate metabolism due to deficient secretion of insulin, and diabetes insipidus, a condition in which deficient production or secretion of antidiuretic hormone results in excessive thirst (polydipsia) and excessive excretion of urine (polyuria). The Canadian Diabetes Association is committed to promoting and supporting diabetes research, education, and advocacy. The CDA has several sections, councils, and committees that work to fulfill its mission, goals, and objectives. These include the clinical and scientific section, such as health care services, employment, and health insurance coverage; and a national research council that oversees the CDA's research programs and distributes funds in the forms of grants and awards to researchers.

President: Doug Philp
Executive Director: Jim O'Brien
Year Established: 1949
Acronym: CDA

Keywords
Canadian Diabetes Association; CDA; Diabetes

1365 Canadian Ehlers-Danlos Association

88 De Rose Avenue
Bolton
Ontario, L7E 1A8, Canada

Phone: (905)951-7559
Fax: (905)761-7567
E-mail: ceda@rogers.com
http://www.ehlersdanlos.ca

The Canadian Ehlers-Danlos Association (CEDA) is a nonprofit support organization dedicated to enhancing the lives of individuals affected by Ehlers-Danlos syndrome. Ehlers-Danlos syndrome (EDS) is a group of rare inherited connective tissue disorders characterized by abnormalities of the skin, ligaments, and internal organs. Although symptoms and physical features may vary greatly depending upon the specific form of EDS present, many affected individuals have thin, fragile, hyperextensible skin that may bruise easily; abnormally loose joints that are prone to repeated dislocations; widespread tissue fragility with bleeding and poor healing of wounds; and/or other abnormalities. Established in 1996, the Canadian Ehlers-Danlos Association is committed to raising awareness of EDS among the medical and professional communities; providing accurate and timely information about EDS to affected individuals, their families, and healthcare professionals; and enabling members of the organization to exchange information, support, and resources. CEDA also encourages the establishment of self-help groups in communities across Canada.

President: Jill Douglas (1996 to Present)
Year Established: 1996
Acronym: CEDA

Keywords
Canadian Ehlers Danlos Association; Canadian Ehlers-Danlos Association; CEDA; Ehlers Danlos Syndrome

1366 Canadian Fanconi Anemia Research Fund

PO Box 38157
Castlewood Postal Outlet
Toronto
Ontario, M5N 3A9, Canada

Phone: (416) -48-9-63
Fax: (416) -48-9-63
E-mail: admin@fanconicanada.org
http://www.fanconicanada.org

The Canadian Fanconi Anemia Research Fund (Fanconi Canada) is a registered charity whose mission is to fund research in Canada into an effective treatment and ultimately a cure for Fanconi Anemia and to serve as a support network for affected Canadian families. Fanconi's anemia is an inherited condition that leads to a deficiency of certain blood cells that are produced by the bone marrow. Established in 1994, CFARF promotes and supports research on Fanconi's anemia, provides information and support to affected Canadian families, and gathers information regarding Fanconi's anemia, bone marrow failure, cancer treatment, and new medications that may assist individuals with the disorder.

President: Lorne M. Shelson
Executive Director: Same as above.
Year Established: 1994
Acronym: FANCONI CANADA

Keywords
Anemia, Aplastic with Congenital Anomalies; Anemia, Constitutional Aplastic; Anemia, Fanconi's; Canada; Canadian Fanconi Anemia Research Fund; Fanconi Panmyelopathy; Pancytopenia, Congenital

1367 Canadian Foundation for the Study of Infant Deaths

586 Eglinton Avenue East
Suite 308
Toronto
Ontario, M4P 1P2, Canada

Phone: (416) 488-3260
Fax: (416) 488-3864
Toll Free: (800) 363-7437
E-mail: sidsinfo@sidscanada.org
http://www.sidscanada.org

The Canadian Foundation for the Study of Infant Deaths is a voluntary charitable organization dedicated to responding to the needs of Canadian families affected by Sudden Infant Death Syndrome (SIDS). Sudden infant death syndrome is the sudden death of any infant or young child that is unexpected by history and for which no adequate cause for death can be found. Established in 1973, the foundation is committed to promoting and supporting research into the causes of sudden infant death syndrome, facilitating programs of public education, and offering information and emotional support to bereaved families. Informational pamphlets and articles are distributed on request to parents, health professionals, emergency services personnel, and the general public. The foundation also distributes three videos, "Sam's Story: A Story for Families Surviving Sudden Infant Death Syndrome," "When the Bough Breaks," and "SIDS—Emergency Response."

President: John Rossiter (2004 to Present)
Executive Director: Richard Kaufman
Year Established: 1973
Acronym: SIDS Foundation

Keywords
Canadian Foundation for the Study of Infant Deaths; Crib Death; SIDS; Sudden Infant Death Syndrome

1368   Canadian Hearing Society

271 Spadina Road
Toronto
Ontario, M5R 2V3, Canada

Phone: (416) 928-2525
Fax: (416) 928-2506
Toll Free: (877) 347-3427
TDD: (877) 347-3429
E-mail: info@chs.ca
http://www.chs.ca

The Canadian Hearing Society (CHS) is a not-for-profit organization providing services that enhance the independence of deaf, deafened and hard of hearing people, and that encourage prevention of hearing loss. CHS was established in 1940 and currently has 13 regional offices and 16 area offices across Ontario. CHS is committed to developing and providing five core programs in each of the 13 regional offices in Ontario. Core programs include Employment Services, General Social Services, Marketing Communications, Hearing Care Counseling and Ontario Interpreter Services. Optional programs vary from region to region and are tailored to meet local needs; they include a Hearing Aid Program, Technical Devices, CONNECT Counseling Services, Audiology, Speech-Language Pathology, Hearing Help Classes, Literacy and Basic Skills, Sign Language Services, Educational Support Services, and Technology Initiatives Department. CHS also provides home support services to seniors with hearing loss, including information on technical devices, and advocacy. On a national and international basis, CHS provides consultation, material resources, advocacy and referral.

President: Kelly Duffin
Executive Director: Stephanie Ozario
Year Established: 1940
Acronym: CHS

Keywords
Canadian Hearing Society; CHS; Deafness; Hearing Loss

1369   Canadian Hemochromatosis Society

272-7000 Minoru Boulevard
Richmond
British Columbia, V6Y 3Z5, Canada

Phone: (604) 279-7135
Fax: (604) 279-7138
Toll Free: (877) 223-4766
E-mail: office@cdnhemochromatosis.ca
http://www.cdnhemochromatosis.ca/

The Canadian Hemochromatosis Society (CHS) is a non-profit support organization dedicated to providing information and support to individuals and families affected by hereditary hemochromatosis. This is a metabolic disorder characterized by excessive absorption of iron. Without appropriate treatment, excess iron may accumulate in the liver, heart, pancreas, and other organs, resulting in possible multiple organ dysfunction and tissue damage. Established in 1982, the society is committed to increasing awareness among the Canadian public and the medical community about the importance of early screening for, and diagnosis of, hemochromatosis. The society maintains a central registry of all reported cases of hereditary hemochromatosis and provides information regarding appropriate screening and diagnostic testing. CHS also publishes a biannual newsletter that is distributed to doctors and interested individuals all over the world. Its membership questionnaire includes specific questions designed to assist researchers.

President: Charmain Cottingham (1996 to Present)
Executive Director: Susan Fleury (Office Coordinator)
Year Established: 1982
Acronym: CHS

Keywords
Canadian Hemochromatosis Society; CHS; Hereditary Hemochromatosis

1370   Canadian Hemophilia Society

625 President Kennedy
Suite 505
Montreal
Quebec, H3A 1K2, Canada

Phone: (514) 848-0503
Fax: (514) 848-9661
Toll Free: (800) 668-2686
E-mail: chs@hemophilia.ca
http://www.hemophilia.ca

The Canadian Hemophilia Society (CHS) is a registered charity dedicated to improving the quality of life for all persons with hemophilia and other inherited bleeding disorders. Hemophilia is a rare inherited blood clotting (coagulation) disorder caused by inactive or deficient blood proteins (usually factor VIII). Factor VIII is one of several proteins that enable the blood to clot. Hemophilia may be classified as mild, moderate, or severe. The level of severity is determined by the percentage of active clotting factor in the blood (normal percentage ranges from 50 to 150 percent). CHS was established in 1953 and its goals and objectives are to assure that all persons with hemophilia have ready access to the highest possible level of care; assure that the hemophilia community and public are kept informed; that research will continue to improve care and seek a cure for hemophilia, and assist that persons with hemophilia living in third world countries receive appropriate of care.

President: Eric Stolte
Executive Director: Stephane Bordeleau
Year Established: 1953
Acronym: CHS

Keywords
Acquired Hemophilia; Bleeding Disorder; Canadian Hemophilia Society; Christmas Disease; CHS; Classical Hemophilia; Factor V Leiden; Factor VII Deficiency; Factor VIII Deficiency; Factor IX Deficiency; Factor X Deficiency; Factor XI Deficiency; Factor XIII Deficiency; Hemophilia; Hemophilia A; Hemophilia B; Von Willebrand Disease

1371　Canadian Immunodeficiencies Patient Organization

362 Concession 12 East
RR #2
Hastings, Ontario, K0L 1Y0, Canada

Phone: (705) 69-6 36
Fax: (705) 69-6 13
Toll Free: (87) 7 2-62 C
E-mail: info@cipo.ca
http://www.cipo.ca

CIPO, the Canadian Immunodeficiencies Patient Organization, is a national, not-for-profit organization for individuals with primary immunodeficiencies (PIDs) and their families. It is dedicated to uniting the experience, resources, and expertise of its members to achieve nationwide improvement in the care and treatment of individuals with PIDs. Primary immunodeficiencies are inherited disorders characterized by

irregularities in the cell development and/or cell maturation process of the immune system. Affected individuals may be abnormally prone to certain infections, susceptible to particular forms of cancer, and/or have additional characteristic symptoms and findings. CIPO is committed to establishing a central database of affected individuals in Canada; creating an electronic library; and supporting and encouraging the development of support groups. It is also dedicated to creating a directory of physicians currently diagnosing and treating individuals with PIDs in Canada; providing networking opportunities to affected individuals and families; and educating the medical community, affected families, and general public about primary immunodeficiencies.

President: Tina Morgan (1997 to Present)
Year Established: 1997
Acronym: CIPO

Keywords
Agammaglobulinemia, X Linked; Bruton's Disease; CIPO; Canadian Immunodeficiencies Patient Organization; Hypogammaglobulinemia Selective IgA Deficiency; Immune Deficiency Disorders; Immunodeficiency, Common Variable; Immunodeficiency, Severe Combined; SCID

1372　Canadian Liver Foundation

2235 Sheppard Avenue
Suite 1500
Toronto, Ontario, M2J 5B5, Canada

Phone: (416) 491-3353
Fax: (416) 491-4952
Toll Free: (800) 563-5483
E-mail: clf@liver.ca
http://www.liver.ca

The Canadian Liver Foundation (CLF) is a not-for-profit health organization committed to reducing the incidence and impact of liver disease by providing support for research and education into the causes, diagnosis, prevention and treatment of more than 100 diseases of the liver. Established in 1969, the CLF has established 30 chapters across Canada and provides information in both English and French. Some of the liver diseases discussed in brochures and medical information sheets available from CLF include gallstones, hemochromatosis, primary biliary cirrhosis, several forms of hepatitis, porphyria, fatty liver and liver cancer. Further information is provided on liver transplantation, the effects of sodium and management of variceal bleeding. The foundation also maintains a web site.

President: Dr. Keyork Peltekian, CEO
Executive Director: Gary Fagan
Year Established: 1969
Acronym: CLF

Keywords
Alagille Syndrome; Alpha-1 Antitrypsin Deficiency; Biliary Atresia; Canadian Liver Foundation; Cholangitis, Primary Sclerosing; Cirrhosis of the Liver; Cirrhosis, Primary Biliary; CLF; Encephalopathy, Hepatic; Fatty Liver; Gallstones; Gilbert Syndrome; Hemochromatosis; Hepatitis A; Hepatitis B; Hepatitis C; Hepatitis, Neonatal; Liver Disease; Liver Disease in Children; Liver Transplantation; Porphyria; Reye Syndrome; Sarcoidosis; Tyrosinemia; Variceal Bleeding

1373 Canadian Marfan Association

Centre Plaza Postal Outlet
128 Queen Street South
P.O. Box 42257
Mississauga
Ontario, L5M 4Z0, Canada

Phone: (905) 826-3223
Fax: (905) 826-2125
Toll Free: (866) 722-1722
E-mail: info@marfan.ca
http://www.marfan.ca

The Canadian Marfan Association is an international, nonprofit organization dedicated to preventing disabling symptoms and life-threatening complications of Marfan syndrome and improving the quality of life for people affected by this disorder. Marfan syndrome is a rare inherited connective tissue disorder characterized by abnormalities of the heart and blood vessels (cardiovascular system), skeleton, and eyes. Affected individuals may be unusually tall and thin, have abnormally large hands and feet, have malformations of the chest and spine, and experience weakness of the joints, ligaments, and tendons. The Canadian Marfan Association is dedicated to increasing public awareness of Marfan syndrome in Canada by holding public information meetings, community support group meetings, and media interviews; to providing accurate, timely information about the disorder to affected individuals, families, and physicians; assisting people with Marfan syndrome and their families with quality of life issues and helping them form self-help groups; and to acting as a communication liaison for people with Marfan syndrome with the community. The association also seeks to support and foster research in the area of connective tissue diseases.

President: Suzanne Drouin
Executive Director: Elizabeth Matos
Year Established: 1986

Keywords
Arachnodactyly; Arachnodactyly, Contractural; Canadian Marfan Association; Dolichostenomelia; Marfan Syndrome; Marfanoid Hypermobility Syndrome

1374 Canadian Mental Health Association

8 King Street East
Suite 810
Toronto
Ontario, M5C 1B5, Canada

Phone: (416) 484-7750
Fax: (416) 484-4617
E-mail: info@cmha.ca
http://www.cmha.ca

The Canadian Mental Health Association (CMHA) is a national voluntary organization that is committed to promoting the mental health of all Canadians and addressing all aspects of mental health and mental illness. Founded in 1918, the association currently has a division office in each province and territory in Canada as well as approximately 135 local branches in communities of all sizes throughout the country. CMHA's grassroots programs are meant to ensure that people with mental illness find the necessary help to cope with crisis, regain confidence, and return to their communities, families, and jobs. The association combats mental health problems and emotional disorders by providing research and information services; sponsoring research projects; conducting workshops and seminars; and offering a variety of publications including a pamphlet series, a quarterly newsletter, and policy statements. In addition, the CMHA offers housing and employment services; sponsors public education campaigns for the community, including Canada's Mental Health Week; and provides peer support and recreation services for people affected by mental illness. The association also acts as a social advocate to encourage public action and commitment to strengthening community mental health services, legislation, and policies affecting services.

President: Tom Walters
Executive Director: Edward J. Pennington (General Director)
Year Established: 1918
Acronym: CMHA

Keywords
Canadian Mental Health Association; CMHA

1375 Canadian Multiple Endocrine Neoplasm Society, Inc.

Box 100
Meota
Saskatchewan, S0M 1X0, Canada

Phone: (306) 892-2080
Fax: (306) -89-2-25
E-mail: men.society@sasketel.net
http://www.mensociety.com

Canadian Multiple Endocrine Neoplasm Society, Inc. is an international nonprofit organization dedicated to helping others with Multiple Endocrine Neoplasia Type 1 and assisting their family members. Familial Multiple Endocrine Neoplasia Type 1 (FMEN1) is a rare genetic disorder characterized by overactivity of certain endocrine glands (e.g., pituitary, parathyroid gland, and pancreatic islet cells) and excessive production of certain hormones. A variety of symptoms and physical findings may result such as abnormally increased levels of calcium in the blood (hypercalcemia), generalized fatigue, weakness, muscle and/or bone pain, constipation and/or other digestive abnormalities, and/or additional symptoms. Established in 1996, the organization is committed to collecting and distributing current information on the disease; educating the medical community about FMEN1; and providing networking services that enable affected individuals to exchange information, resources, and support.

President: Shirley Stevens (1955 to Present)
Executive Director: Cathy Fitch
Year Established: 1995

Keywords
Acromegaly; Adenomatosis, Partial Multiple Endocrine; Advocacy; Canadian Multiple Endocrine Neoplasm Society, Inc.; Familial Multiple Endocrine Neoplasia; FMEN; Gastric Carcinoids; Gastrinoma; Hyperthryroidism; Hypothryroidism; Insulinomas; MEN; Multiple Endocrine Neoplasia Type 1; Networking; Pancreatic Ulcerogenic Tumor Syndrome; Pancreatitis; ZE Syndrome; Zollinger Ellison Syndrome

1376 Canadian Organization for Rare Disorders

P.O. Box 814
Coaldale
Alberta, T1M 1M7, Canada

Phone: (403) 345-4544
Fax: (403) 345-3948

Toll Free: (877) 302-7273
E-mail: office@cord.ca
http://www.cord.ca

The Canadian Organization for Rare Disorder's (CORD) is a not-for-profit organization dedicated to the enhancement of lives of all persons affected by rare disorders through an educational and informational support network. CORD's objectives are the dissemination of information on rare disorders to all interested parties; to encourage medical research into the causes and effects of rare disorders; and to work in harmony with the media and medical community to increase public awareness about the existence of rare disorders in Canada. Upon request, CORD will link other families and individuals with similar rare disorders through a networking system.

President: Maureen Gaetz-Faubert
Executive Director: Same as above.
Year Established: 1996
Acronym: CORD

Keywords
Birth Defects; Canadian Organization for Rare Disorders; Canadian Organization for Rare Disorders (CORD); Metabolic Disorders; Mitochondrial Disorders; Neuromuscular Disorders

1377 Canadian Osteogenesis Imperfecta Society

208 Ramona Boulevard
Markham
Ontario, L3P 2K8, Canada

Phone: (905) -29-4-53
E-mail: rkhayes@ccat.on.ca
http://www.oif.org

The Canadian Osteogenesis Imperfecta Society (COIS) is an international, nonprofit, charitable organization dedicated to assisting individuals affected by osteogenesis imperfecta (OI), a genetic disorder characterized by abnormally fragile, brittle bones. Established in 1983, the society aims to provide emotional support on a personal level for parents and people with osteogenesis imperfecta; encourage and foster Canadian medical research into the underlying causes of OI; acquaint medical personnel, hospitals, educational institutions, and social agencies with all facets of osteogenesis imperfecta; maintain an up-to-date library of literature both medical and general pertaining to OI; and promote awareness of brittle bones by the public.

President: Richard Hayes
Executive Director: Same as above.
Year Established: 1983
Acronym: COIS

Keywords
Brittle Bone Disease; Canadian Osteogenesis Imperfecta Society; Ekman Lobstein Disease; Lobstein Disease Type I; Osteogenesis Imperfecta; Osteopathyrosis; Vrolik Disease Type II

1378 **Canadian Paraplegic Association**
1101 Prince of Wales Drive
Suite 230
Ottawa
Ontario, K2C 3W7, Canada

Phone: (613) 723-1033
Fax: (613) 723-1060
E-mail: cpanational@canparaplegic.org
http://www.canparaplegic.org/

The Canadian Paraplegic Association (CPA) is a national, not-for-profit federation of provincial organizations dedicated to helping individuals with spinal cord injuries or other mobility impairments achieve independence, self-reliance, and full community participation. The Canadian Paraplegic Association was founded in 1945 by a group of World War II veterans affected by paralysis. It currently has 10 provincial divisions and 47 regional offices, and provides services to a membership of more than 30,000 Canadians affected by spinal cord injuries or other mobility impairments. The CPA's provincial offices provide a variety of programs and services including personal and family counseling; educational and vocational counseling; and employment counseling. Additional services include offering assistance with locating and adapting suitable housing, obtaining equipment and supplies necessary to support independent living, and planning for immediate and future financial needs. The association also implements community advocacy programs that assist in identifying, reducing, and eliminating barriers to affected individuals' participation in the community. In addition, the Canadian Paraplegic Association offers a variety of educational resources.

President: Ned Shillington
Executive Director: Valerie Ravary
Year Established: 1945
Acronym: CPA

Keywords
Canadian Paraplegic Association; Mobility Impairment; Paralysis; Paraplegia, Quadriplegia, Spinal Cord Injury, Spine, Disability; Paraplegic; Quadriplegic

1379 **Canadian Porphyria Foundation, Inc.**
P.O. Box 1206
Neepawa
Manitoba, R0J 1H0, Canada

Phone: (204)476-2800
Fax: (204)476-2801
Toll Free: (866) -47-6-28
E-mail: porphyria@cpf-inc.ca
http://www.cpf-inc.ca/

The Canadian Porphyria Foundation, Inc. (CPF) is a voluntary organization dedicated to improving the quality of life for Canadians affected by porphyria through programs of awareness, education, service, advocacy, and research. Porphyria is a group of rare genetic disorders characterized by disturbances of porphyrin metabolism. Established in 1988 and consisting of approximately 1,000 members, CPF is committed to promoting public and professional awareness; assembling, printing, and distributing up-to-date educational materials for physicians, healthcare personnel, members, and others affected by porphyria; and offering support programs to affected individuals and their families. The goals of the organization are to promote the social welfare of affected individuals; to educate and inform physicians so that early diagnosis and proper treatment will be realized; and to promote and provide financial assistance for research into the porphyrias. The organization is also committed to encouraging, supporting, and serving physicians and researchers in their efforts to find more effective treatments for the porphyrias.

President: Lois J. Aitken (1988 to Present)
Executive Director: Same as above.
Year Established: 1988
Acronym: CPF

Keywords
AIP; Canadian Porphyria Foundation, Inc.; CEP; Congenital Erythropoietic Porphyria; CPF; EPP; Erythropoietic Protoporphyria; HCP; Hereditary Coproporphyria; PCT; Porphyria; Porphyria, Acute Intermittent; Porphyria, ALA-D; Porphyria, Cutanea Tarda; Porphyria, Variegate; Protoporphyria

1380 **Canadian Reflex Sympathetic Dystrophy Network**
P.O. Box 367
Surrey
British Columbia, V3T 5B6, Canada

Phone: (604) 505-2934
E-mail: info@canadianrsd.com
http://www.canadianrsd.com

The Canadian Reflex Sympathetic Dystrophy Network is a nonprofit organization dedicated to offering and information to individuals affected by reflex sympathetic dystrophy syndrome (RSDS), also known as complex regional pain syndrome. This is a rare disorder of the sympathetic nervous system characterized by chronic, severe pain. CRSD Network's mission is to provide information and enhance public awareness of RSDS; offer support to individuals and families living with RSDS; engage in programs of public advocacy; and provide referrals to healthcare professionals who have expertise in treating RSDS. The network answers inquiries from all over the world. Available information includes an extensive library of reprints of medical articles, brochures, and a newsletter. CRSD network is also actively engaged in establishing support groups throughout Canada.

President: Michelle Huibers
Year Established: 1994
Acronym: CRSD Network

Keywords
Canadian Reflex Sympathetic Dystrophy Network; CRPS; Reflex Sympathetic Dystrophy Syndrome; RSD

1381 Canadian Sickle Cell Society

P.O. Box 116 1801
Eglington Avenue
West Toronto, L5J 3X0, Canada

Phone: (514) 735-5109
Fax: (514) 735-5100

The Canadian Sickle Cell Society is a not-for-profit organization dedicated to educating the at-risk and general populations, recruiting and training volunteers, providing effective lobbying for improvement of services, and identifying individuals with sickle cell disease or traits and providing them with individual and family counseling. Sickle cell disease is a rare inherited blood disorder characterized by the presence of sickle or crescent-shaped red blood cells (erythrocytes) in the blood. The Canadian Sickle Cell Society was established in 1976 by affected family members with the assistance of medical and health professionals and community members. Program activities include a young adult program, family services, education, counseling, and community involvement. The society produces a variety of educational materials including pamphlets and brochures.

President: Horace Laryea, M.D.
Executive Director: Rosetta Cadogan
Year Established: 1976

Keywords
Canadian Sickle Cell Society; Sickle Cell Anemia; Sickle Cell Disease; Sickle Cell Trait

1382 Canadian Society for Mucopolysaccharide and Related Diseases, Inc.

PO Box 64714
Unionville
Ontario, L3R OM9, Canada

Phone: (905) -47-9-87
Fax: (905) -47-9-87
Toll Free: (800) -66-7-18
E-mail: lori.mps@rogers.com
http://www.mpssociety.ca

The Canadian Society for Mucopolysaccharide and Related Diseases, Inc., is an international voluntary health organization based in Ontario. Founded in 1984, the society is dedicated to functioning as a parent support group; increasing public awareness of the mucopolysaccharidoses (MPS) and related diseases; and raising funds for further research into MPS. The mucopolysaccharidoses are a group of rare hereditary diseases of lysosomal storage. These disorders are characterized by the abnormal accumulation of mucopolysaccharides in various tissues of the body such as the central nervous system, respiratory system, cardiovascular system, liver, spleen, and/or other areas. Although symptoms and findings may vary depending upon the form of the disease present, affected children often have distinctive facial abnormalities, skeletal malformations, growth delays, and mental retardation. The Canadian Society for Mucopolysaccharide and Related Diseases works through provincial families to provide local support to families of children who have recently been diagnosed; holds conferences where families and professionals can exchange ideas and information; funds research on MPS disorders; and funds the purchase of equipment for medical research. The society publishes a regular newsletter and a variety of other educational materials.

President: Judy Byrne (2003 to Present)
Executive Director: Kirsten Harkins
Year Established: 1984
Acronym: Canadian MPS Society

Keywords
Canadian MPS Society; Canadian Society for Mucopolysaccharide and Related Diseases, Inc.; Fabry Disease; Hunter Syndrome; Hurler Syndrome; I-Cell Disease; Maroteaux Lamy Syndrome; Morquio Syn-

drome; MPS; Mucopolysaccharidoses; Pseudo Hurler Polydystrophy; Sanfilippo Syndrome; Sialidosis; Sly Syndrome; Tay Sachs Disease

1383 Canadian Stuttering Association

PO Box 444
Branch NDG
Montreal
Quebec, H9B 3P8, Canada

Toll Free: (888) 788-8837
E-mail: csa@stutter.ca
http://www.stutter.ca

The Canadian Stuttering Association (CSA) is a national nonprofit organization that provides coordination for a national network of autonomous Canadian self-help groups for individuals who stutter. Such groups, which offer support and resources to affected individuals and family members, are founded on the principle that, "as people who stutter, we have much to learn from one another, no matter what language we speak." Stuttering is a speech abnormality characterized by repeated hesitation or delay in enunciating words, abnormally prolonged pauses, and repetition of parts of words or entire words. CSA is committed to working closely with speech professionals and treatment centers, serving as an impartial forum for information sharing, functioning as advocates for affected individuals, and promoting greater acceptance of people who stutter through public education. Above all, CAPS is committed to the principle that input from each organizational member across Canada is the basis for all of its work on behalf of affected children, adolescents, and adults as well as their parents, legal guardians, spouses, significant others, and families. The association's activities include sponsoring national conferences for affected individuals and family members, publishing a quarterly newsletter, and maintaining a web site on the Internet.

President: Norm McEwen (National Director)
Executive Director: David Block (Coordinator)
Year Established: 1991
Acronym: CSA

Keywords
Canadian Stuttering Association; CSA; Stuttering

1384 Canadian Syringomyelia Network

69 Penny Crescent
Markham
Ontario, L3P 5X7, Canada

Phone: (905) 471-8278
Fax: (905) 944-4844
E-mail: barb@csn.ca
http://www.csn.ca

The Canadian Syringomyelia Network (CSN) is a non-profit organization dedicated to serving as a support network for people with syringomyelia, a rare progressive condition characterized by the presence of abnormal, fluid-filled cavities within the spinal cord. Established in 1992, CSN acts as an information and referral network; builds awareness among the community; assists those who wish to establish support groups; compiles a database of people in Canada who have shown an interest in CSN and its mission; and produces a newsletter for its members and those interested in CSN's activities. The Canadian Syringomyelia Network also organizes periodic meetings and conferences, offers patient networking services, provides referrals, and produces educational materials including brochures, reports, and a regular newsletter.

President: Barbara Forrestall (1992 to Present)
Executive Director: Same as above.
Year Established: 1992
Acronym: CSN

Keywords
Arachnoiditis; Arnold-Chiari Malformation; Canadian Syringomyelia Network; Chiari I; Chiari II; CSN; Networking; Scoliosis; Syringomyelia

1385 Canadian Women's Health Network

419 Graham Avenue
Suite 203
Winnipeg
Manitoba, R3C 0M2, Canada

Phone: (204) 942-5500
Fax: (204) 989-2355
Toll Free: (888) 818-9172
E-mail: cwhn@cwhn.ca
http://www.cwhn.ca

The Canadian Women's Health Network (CWHN) is a not-for-profit organization that was established in 1993 by women representing over 70 organizations from every province and territory of Canada. It is committed to providing easy access to women's health information, resources, and research; producing user-friendly materials and resources; promoting and developing links to information and action networks; and providing forums for critical debate. Additional objectives include acting as a "watchdog" on emerging issues and trends that may affect women's health, working to change inequitable health policies and practices, encouraging community-based participatory research models, and promoting women's involvement in health research. In addition, the CWHN works with the Health Canada's Centres of Excellence for Women's Health Program to further promote communication, information sharing, and interaction among all interested groups and individuals. The CWHN also offers additional programs and services including providing a women's health information line; publishing a quarterly newsletter; gathering and cataloging women-centered, health-related resources; and maintaining a database of organizations and other resources.

President: Abby Lippman and Marsha Forrest
Executive Director: Madeline Boscoe
Year Established: 1993
Acronym: CWHN

Keywords
Canadian Women's Health Network; Women's Health

1386 Canavan Foundation

450 West End Avenue
#10C
New York, NY 10024

Phone: (212) 873-4640
Fax: (212) 873-7892
Toll Free: (877) 422-6282
E-mail: info@canavanfoundation.org
http://www.canavanfoundation.org

The Canavan Foundation is a not-for-profit organization founded in 1992 by parents and friends of children with Canavan disease. The mission of the Canavan Foundation is to provide the latest information (including a list of testing sites) for the at-risk population, educate medical and other professional communities, and to support research. Canavan disease is a rare, inherited neurological disorder caused by an enzyme deficiency and characterized by poor muscle tone, progressive mental decline, poor head control, and/or blindness. Symptoms usually become apparent when an infant is three to nine months old. Currently there is no cure for the disease.

President: Lois Neufeld (2003-present)
Year Established: 1992

Keywords
Canavan Disease; Canavan Foundation

1387 Canavan Research Foundation

Fieldstone Plaza
88 Rt. 37
New Fairfield, CT 06812

Phone: (203) 746-2436
Fax: (203) 746-3205
E-mail: info@canavan.org
http://www.canavan.org

Canavan disease is a degenerative disease that occurs because of an inherited defective gene. This interferes with the body's production of myelin, which causes interference in the body's ability to send signals throughout the brain and spinal cord. A Canavan child, who may appear healthy at birth, may become blind, paralyzed and increasingly lost to the world around him. The Canavan Research Foundation supports research seeking treatment or a cure for Canavan disease. Current research projects include gene therapy, stem cell therapy and metabolic approaches. Clinical trials have been ongoing in gene therapy at Robert Wood Johnson Hospital in New Jersey. Family support is also provided through an active web board and educational outreach. The foundation relies principally on private funding, and virtually all funding goes directly toward research.

President: Helene R. Karlin, PhD
Year Established: 1996
Acronym: CRF

Keywords
Canavan Research Foundation; Canavan's Disease; CRF; CSN; Leukodystrophy, Canavan's

1388 Canavan Research Illinois

P.O. Box 8194
Rolling Meadows, IL 60008-8194

Phone: (847) 222-0736
Fax: (847) 222-0736
Toll Free: (800) 833-2194
E-mail: canavan@canavanresearch.org
http://www.canavanresearch.org

Canavan Research Illinois is a voluntary 501(C)3, not-for-profit organization, founded in April 2000 to fund research, raise public awareness, and offer support and networking services to families affected by this rare, genetic neurodegenerative disease. Devoted to helping Canavan children everywhere, the mission is find a treatment and cure for the disease.

President: Ilyce Randell
Executive Director: PeggyShapiro-Nyeholt
Year Established: 2000

Keywords
Canavan Research Illinois; CD; Canavan's Disease; Leukodystrophy, Canavan's; Van Bogart Bertrand Syndrome

1389 Cancer Hope Network
2 North Road
Suite A
Chester, NJ 07930

Phone: (908) 879-4039
Fax: (908) 879-6518
Toll Free: (877) 467-3638
E-mail: info@cancerhopenetwork.org
http://www.cancerhopenetwork.org

The Cancer Hope Network, a national, non-profit organization, offers free, confidential, one-on-one emotional support to adult cancer patients and their caregivers. Support is provided via telephone by over 325 trained volunteers who have all been through a cancer experience, have recovered and are again leading productive lives. By giving recently diagnosed patients the gift of hope, CHN's survivor volunteers help them successfully cope with their cancer and treatment. Cancer Hope Network's educational materials include a self-titled newsletter; brochures for patients, medical facilities, and corporations; posters; and videotapes.

President: Kenneth Siegel
Executive Director: Wanda Diak
Year Established: 1981
Acronym: CHN

Keywords
Adenoid Cystic Carcinoma; Cancer; Cancer Hope Network; Caregiver Support; Chemocare; Chemotherapy; Cutaneous T Cell Lymphomas; Encouragement; Malignancies; Mantle Cell Lymphoma; Networking; Patient Matching; Peer to Peer; Radiation; Social Services

1390 Cancer Research UK
PO Box 123
Lincoln's Inn Fields
London, WC2A 3PX, United Kingdom

Phone: +44 (0) 207-242-0200
Fax: +44 (0) 207-269-3100
http://www.imperialcancer.co.uk

Cancer Research UK is a registered charity in the United Kingdom dedicated to saving lives through research into the causes, prevention, treatment, and cure of cancer. It supports the work of more than 3,000 scientists, doctors, and nurses across the UK. Its aim is to conquer cancer through world-class research in two generations.

President: Sir Paul Nurse
Year Established: 1902
Acronym: ICRF

Keywords
Brain Tumors, Primary; Cancer; Cancer Information Service at Imperial Cancer Research Fund; Cancer, Bladder; Cancer, Bone; Cancer, Cervical; Cancer, Colon; Cancer, Colorectal; Cancer, Endometrial; Cancer, Kidney; Cancer, Liver; Cancer, Lung; Cancer, Ovarian; Cancer, Pancreatic; Cancer, Prostate; Cancer Research UK; Cancer, Skin; Cancer, Stomach; Cancer, Thyroid; Carcinoma, Renal Cell; Hodgkin's Disease; Hodgkin's Lymphoma; Leukemia, Chronic Lymphocytic; Leukemia, Chronic Myelogenous; Lymphoma, Gastric Non Hodgkins Type; Melanoma; Melanoma, Malignant; Mesothelioma; Myeloma, Multiple

1391 Candlelighters Childhood Cancer Foundation
P.O. Box 498
Kensington, MD 20895-0498

Phone: (301) 962-3520
Fax: (301) 962-3521
Toll Free: (800) 366-2223
E-mail: staff@candlelighters,org
http://www.candlelighters.org

The Candlelighters Childhood Cancer Foundation (CCCF) is a 501(c)3 nonprofit organization that provides support, information, and advocacy to children with cancer, their families, adult survivors of childhood cancer, and the professionals who care for them. Those dealing with childhood cancer and its effects, at any stage, are welcome as members. CCCF's major services include an information clearinghouse; publications, including four newsletters as well as books and reprints; and a network of support groups of childhood-cancer families, located in every state. Assistance is provided in starting and maintaining a group. Services that local groups provide often include camps, speakers, conferences, transportation, and one-to-one visitations. The foundation does not provide direct financial assistance but has a financial aid list available. CCCF is also a registered lobbyist and advocates on behalf of pediatric cancer patients and families.

President: Dr. Jacob Adams
Executive Director: Ruth Hoffman
Year Established: 1970
Acronym: CCCF

Keywords
Cancer; Cancer, Childhood; Cancer, Pediatric; Candlelighters Childhood Cancer Foundation

1392 Canine Companions for Independence

2965 Dutton Avenue
P.O. Box 446
Santa Rosa, CA 95402-0446

Phone: (707) 577-1700
Fax: (707) 577-1711
Toll Free: (800) 572-2275
TDD: (707) 577-1756
E-mail: info@cci.org
http://www.cci.org

Canine Companions for Independence (CCI) is a nonprofit organization dedicated to serving the needs of people with physical and developmental disabilities by providing trained companion assistance dogs and by providing continuing support to ensure the success of the working team. CCI's assistance dogs are trained to respond to more than 50 specialized commands and become the physical extensions of their disabled partners by performing a variety of basic tasks. There are four types of assistance dogs: service dogs that perform practical tasks for a person with a physical or developmental disability; hearing dogs that are trained to alert people who are deaf or hard-of-hearing to important sounds such as telephone, alarm clock, and smoke alarm; skilled companions that provide companionship and some physical tasks; and facility dogs that work with professional caregivers in environments where interaction with a trained dog can improve the physical, mental, or emotional health of participants.

President: Ted Rogahn (2004-Present)
Executive Director: Corey Hudson
Year Established: 1975
Acronym: CCI

Keywords
Assistance Dogs; Canine Companions for Independence; Companion Dogs; Service Dogs

1393 Carcinoid Cancer Foundation, Inc.

333 Mamaroneck Avenue
#492
White Plains, NY 10605

Phone: (914) 683-1001
Fax: (914) 683-0183
Toll Free: (888) 722-3132
E-mail: carcinoid@optonline.net
http://www.carcinoid.org

The Carcinoid Cancer Foundation, Inc. is a not-for-profit organization dedicated to encouraging and supporting research and education concerning carcinoid tumors and carcinoid syndrome. A carcinoid tumor is a rare, slow-growing form of cancer characterized by overgrowth of certain cells that secrete serotonin, a naturally occurring derivative of the amino acid tryptophan. Serotonin has many functions including regulating activity of the intestinal tract. In some cases, individuals with carcinoid tumors may experience abnormally increased secretion of serotonin, resulting in carcinoid syndrome. In individuals with carcinoid syndrome, associated symptoms may include intense flushing of the face and upper body, wheezing, weight loss, severe diarrhea, and, in some cases, ulcer-like symptoms and/or eventual heart failure. The Carcinoid Cancer Foundation was established in 1968 to support research that will improve the understanding, diagnosis, and treatment of carcinoid tumor and carcinoid syndrome. It also provides understandable information to affected individuals and family members, engages in professional education, and offers networking services to affected families.

President: David Polinger (1996 to Present)
Executive Director: Richard R.P. Warner, M.D. (Medical Director)
Year Established: 1968
Acronym: CCF

Keywords
Carcinoid; Carcinoid Cancer; Carcinoid Cancer Foundation, Inc.; Carcinoid Disease; Carcinoid Syndrome; Carcinoid Tumors; Diarrhea; Flushing; Malignant Carcincooid Syndrome; Neuroendocrine tumors

1394 Cardiac Arrhythmias Research and Education Foundation, Inc.

26425 NE Allen Street
#103
P.O. Box 369
Duvall, WA 98019

Phone: (425) 788-1987
Fax: (425) 788-1927
Toll Free: (800) 404-9500
E-mail: care@longqt.org
http://www.longqt.org/

The Cardiac Arrhythmias Research and Education Foundation, Inc. (CARE Foundation) is a national not-for-profit organization dedicated to promoting physician education and public awareness of the unexpected sudden death of children and young adults due to heart rhythm disorders. Cardiac arrhythmias are disturbances in the heart's natural rhythm. These disturbances are caused by disruptions in the normal conduction of electrical signals within the heart. Due to various reasons, electrical signals may be detoured, slowed, or blocked while traveling through certain parts of the heart. This may cause the heart's natural rhythm to speed up, slow down, or become irregular, affecting the flow of blood to the body's internal organs. The CARE Foundation was founded in 1995 by a group of electrophysiologists and individuals who have been affected by sudden cardiac death. Its primary goals are to raise funds for clinical research of cardiac arrhythmias and to educate the public and the medical community about the prevention and treatment of arrhythmias. The foundation promotes screening for at-risk families and participation in ongoing genetic research studies. Foundation activities include providing physician referrals and conducting informational meetings and national seminars for affected families and physicians throughout the country.

President: Robert J. Myerburg, M.D.
Executive Director: Mary Jo Gordon
Year Established: 1995
Acronym: CARE Foundation, Inc.

Keywords
Arrhythmias; Atrial Fibrillation; ARVD; Cardiac Arrhythmias Research and Education Foundation, Inc.; Cardiomyopathy, Dilated; Cardiomyopathy, Hypertrophic; CARE Foundation, Inc.; Dyplasia, Right Ventricular; Heart Rhythm Disorders; Long QT Syndrome; Mitral Valve Prolapse; PSVT; Sudden Cardiac Death; Syncope, Neurocardiogenic; Tachycardia, Paroxysmal Supraventricular; Wolff Parkinson White Syndrome; WPW

1395 Cardio-Facio-Cutaneous International

183 Brown Rd.
Vestal, NY 13850

Phone: (607) 772-9666
Fax: (607) 748-0409
E-mail: info@cfcsyndrome.org
http://www.cfcsyndrome.org

This is an international support group for families, doctors, teachers, therapists, and other involved individuals who are assisting with children born with the very rare cardio-facio-cutaneous syndrome. The support group acts as a clearinghouse for information on all aspects of CFC syndrome. Once families register, they are included on a mailing list for newsletters, CFC Parent's Guide, and information on current research and conferences.

President: Brenda Conger
Year Established: 1999
Acronym: CFC International

Keywords
Cardio Facio Cutaneous Syndrome; Cardio-Facio-Cutaneous International; CFC; CFC International; CFC Syndrome; Delayed Development; Eating Problems; Heart Defects; Post-natal Short Stature; Skin Involvement; Teeth Dysplasia; Vision Impairment

1396 Cardiomyopathy Association

40 The Metro Centre
Tolpits Lane
Watford
Hertfordshire, WD1 8SB, United Kingdom

Phone: +44 (0) 1923-24-9977
Fax: +44 (0) 1923-24-9987
E-mail: info@caridiomyopathy.org
http://www.cardiomyopathy.org

The Cardiomyopathy Association is an international, not-for-profit, self-help organization dedicated to providing information and support to individuals affected by cardiomyopathy, their family members, and medical professionals. Cardiomyopathy is a general diagnostic term indicating a primary noninflammatory disease of the heart muscle (myocardium) that is often due to unknown causes. Established in 1989 and consisting of 1,000 members throughout the world, the Cardiomyopathy Association publishes informational brochures on different types of cardiomyopathy. Titles include "Dilated Cardiomyopathy," "Hypertrophic Cardiomyopathy," and "Arrhythmogenic Right

Ventricular Cardiomyopathy." The association also offers videotapes on these topics. In addition to disseminating information, the association also provides counseling to affected individuals and their family members and endeavors to open the lines of communication between affected individuals and families through an international networking program.

President: Carolyn Biro (Chairperson) (1989 to Present)
Executive Director: Gordon Rae
Year Established: 1989
Acronym: CMA

Keywords
ARVC; ARVD; Cardiomyopathy Association; Cardiomyopathy, Arrhythmogenic Right Ventricular; Cardiomyopathy, Congestive; Cardiomyopathy, Hypertrophic; Cardiomyopathy, Restrictive; Cardiomyopathy, Viral; DCM; Dilated Cardiomyopathy; Dysplasia, Arrhythmogenic Right Ventricular; Stenosis, Muscular Sub Aortic

1397   CARES Foundation, Inc. (Congenital Adrenal Hyperplasia, Research, Education and Support)

189 Main Street
Millburn, NJ 07041

Phone: (973) 912-3895
Fax: (973) 912-8990
Toll Free: (866) 227-3737
E-mail: info@caresfoundation.org
http://www.caresfoundation.org

CARES Foundation, Inc. is dedicated to providing support to individuals and families affected by congenital adrenal hyperplasia. It is a voluntary, 501(c)3 organization. It serves patients, health professionals, and the public with information about congenital adrenal hyperplasia; a group of disorders that result from the impaired ability of the adrenal glands to produce hormones known as corticosteriods, resulting in various metabolic problems. Services include support groups, referrals, professional education and publications, with plans to introduce Spanish language materials soon.

President: Kelly R. Leight
Executive Director: Renata Blumberg
Year Established: 2001
Acronym: CARES Foundation

Keywords
Adrenal Hyperplasia, Congenital; Adrenal Insufficiency; CAH; CARES Foundation, Inc.; CARES

Foundation, Inc. (Congenital Adrenal Hyperplasia, Research, Education and Support)

1398   Caring for Carcinoid Foundation

One Kendall Square
PMB 180
Cambridge, MA 02139

Phone: (857) 222-5492
E-mail: info@caringforcarcinoid.org
http://www.caringforcarcinoid.org

The mission of the Caring for Carcinoid Foundation is to discover a cure for carcinoid. This is a neuroendocrine cancer that, at the present time, has no cure. The foundation raises funds for research and administers grants, with the ultimate goal of finding a cure.

President: Nancy O'Hagan

Keywords
Carcinoid Syndrome; Caring for Carcinoid Foundation; Research

1399   Carol Ann Foundation & International Morquio Organization

PO Box 64184
Tucson, AZ 85728-4184

Phone: (520) 744-2531
Fax: (520) 744-2535
E-mail: mbs85705@yahoo.com
http://www.Morquio.com

Carol Ann Foundation & International Morquio Organization (CAF & IMO) is a not-for-profit, voluntary organization dedicated to seeking out people who have Morquio syndrome in order to provide a mutual aid network, act as advocate between patients and their physicians, compile medical information into a database, and pursue funding for education, families, and research. Morquio syndrome (MPS IV) is a mucopolysaccharide storage disease that occurs in two forms, type A and type B. Both forms result in the accumulation in the body and brain of large amounts of a substance called mucopolysaccharide as a result of enzyme deficiencies. The Carol Ann Foundation and International Morquio Organization provide patient networking, education, support groups, and genetic counseling services.

President: Mary Smith
Executive Director: John Harings
Year Established: 1999
Acronym: CAF & IMO

Keywords
Advocacy/Lobbyist; Carol Ann Foundation & International Morquio Organization; Government Legislation; Morquio Syndrome; Service Organization

1400 Carter Centers for Brain Research in Holoprosencephaly and Related Malformations

Texas Scottish Rite Hospital for Children
Department of Neurology
2222 Welborn Street
Dallas, TX 75219-9842

Phone: (214) 559-8411
Fax: (214) 559-8383
Toll Free: (800) 421-1121
E-mail: hpe@tsrh.org
http://www.stanford.edu/group/hpe

The Carter Centers for Brain Research in Holoprosencephaly represent the most concentrated study of holoprosencephaly in the world. The centers were created to gather, store, organize, analyze and share information about HPE, but most importantly, to help families find hope. Holoprosencephaly (HPE) is a neurological birth defect in which the fetal brain does not grow and divide, as it should during early pregnancy. The effects of this brain malformation can range from mild to severe. Specific chromosomal abnormalities and gene mutations have been identified in some patients and there is evidence that in some families, HPE is inherited. The Carter Centers are a collaborative initiative among sponsored Centers of Excellence in the field of HPE: The Texas Scottish Rite Hospital for Children in Texas; the Kennedy Krieger Institute in Maryland; Stanford University and UCSF in California; and National Institutes of Health in Maryland.

President: Dr. Nancy J. Clegg
Year Established: 1997

Keywords
Alobar Holoprosencephaly; Arhinencephaly; Carter Centers for Brain Research in Holoprosencephaly and Related Malformations; Holoprosencephaly; HPE; Lobar Holoprosencephaly; Middle Interhemispheric Variant of Holoprosencephaly; MIH

1401 CCMS Support Group

63 Stirrup Way
Burlington, NJ 08016

Phone: (609) 239-7831
Fax: (609) 239-6916
E-mail: tmontague@home.com

The Cerebro Costo Mandibular Syndrome (CCMS) Support Group is an informal network for parents of children who have CCMS. Cerebrocostomandibular syndrome is an extremely rare inherited disorder characterized by an abnormally small jaw (micrognathia), malformations of the roof of the mouth (palate), improper positioning of the tongue (glossoptosis), and abnormal development of the ribs (rib dysplasia).

Keywords
CCMS Support Group; Cerebro Costo Mandibular Syndrome

1402 CDG Family Network

PO Box 860847
Plano, TX 75074
Toll Free: (800) 250-5273

E-mail: cdgaware@aol.com
http://www.cdgs.com

The CDG Family Network is a non-profit organization founded by parents seeking information and support for those affected by a group of disorders known as congenital disorders of glycosylation (CDG). Members of the network exchange information with families and physicians, locate new families, and raise awareness among the medical community. The CDG disorders are a group of newly discovered metabolic diseases that cause abnormal tissue and organ development affecting the entire body, especially the function of the central nervous system and the peripheral nervous system.

President: Cynthia Wren-Gray
Year Established: 1996

Keywords
Carbohydrate Deficient Glycoprotein Syndrome; CDG; CDG Family Network; CDG1; CDG2; CDG3; CDG4; CDGS; CDGS Type I; CDGS Type 1b; CDGS Type II; CDGS Type III; CDGS Type IV; Hypoglycosylation Syndrome Type I

1403 Celiac Disease Foundation

13251 Ventura Boulevard
Suite 1
Studio City, CA 91604

Phone: (818) 990-2354
Fax: (818) 990-2379
E-mail: cdf@celiac.org
http://www.celiac.org

The Celiac Disease Foundation (CDF) is a nonprofit organization dedicated to providing services and support to persons with celiac disease or dermatitis herpetiformis (CD/DH) through programs of awareness, advocacy, and research. Celiac disease is a chronic, hereditary, intestinal malabsorption disorder caused by intolerance to gluten. Dermatitis herpetiformis, also known as Duhring disease, is a rare chronic skin disorder characterized by the presence of groups of severely itchy (pruritic) blisters and raised skin lesions (papules). The exact cause of this disease is not known although it is frequently associated with the inability to digest gluten (gluten-sensitive enteropathy). Established in 1990, CDF works to assist people with CD/DH and their families to understand and cope with the disease; to distribute reliable up-to-date information about CD/DH and the gluten-free diet; to increase awareness of CD/DH among healthcare professionals, food and drug manufacturers, the food service industry, the media, and the public; and to encourage celiac disease research.

President: Marvin Berman (2001 to Present)
Executive Director: Elaine Monarch
Year Established: 1990
Acronym: CDF

Keywords
Celiac Disease; Celiac Disease Foundation; Celiac Sprue; Dermatitis, Herpetiformis; DH; Gee Herter Disease; Gluten Enteropathy; Gluten Intolerance; Gluten Sensitive Enteropathy; Huebner Herter Disease; Sprue, Nontropical; Steatorrhea, Idiopathic

1404 Celiac Sprue Association/USA, Inc.
P.O. Box 31700
Omaha, NE 68131-0700

Phone: (402) 558-0600
Fax: (402) 643-4108
Toll Free: (877) 272-4272
E-mail: celiacs@csaceliacs.org
http://www.csaceliacs.org

The Celiac Sprue Association/United States of America (CSA) is a member-based, non-profit organization dedicated to helping adults and children with celiac disease and dermatitis herpetiformis through education, information and research. It is the largest non-profit information and referral organization representing the celiac community. Celiac disease is a common genetic, immune mediated, digestive disease that damages the small intestine and interferes with absorption of nutrients from food. Celiac disease is also known as celiac sprue, nontropical sprue, and gluten-sensitive enteropathy. A gluten-free diet is the primary if not the sole management of this condition. Dermati-

tis herpetiformis is often referred to as "celiac disease of the skin." There is strong evidence that the changes in the intestinal mucosa and the immunologic findings in the majority of patients are identical with those found in celiac disease. A gluten-free diet is recommended to control the skin blisters, which occur with dermatitis herpetiformis. CSA/USA, Inc supports a network of local chapters, resource units and activities for children.

President: Tom Sullivan
Executive Director: Mary Schluckebier
Year Established: 1979
Acronym: CSA/USA

Keywords
Celiac Sprue; Celiac Sprue Association/USA, Inc.; Dermatitis, Herpetiformis

1405 Center for International Blood and Marrow Transplant Research
Medical College of Wisconsin
8701 Watertown Plank Road
Milwaukee, WI 53226

Phone: (414) 456-8325
Fax: (414) 456-6530
E-mail: mnugent@hpi.mcw.edu
http://www.ibmtr.org; http://www.cibmtr.org

The Center for International Blood and Marrow Transplant Research (CIBMTR) is a research program formed in July 2004 through an affiliation of the International Bone Marrow Transplant Registry (IBMTR) of the Medical College of Wisconsin and the research arm of the National Marrow Donor Program (NMDP). Both the IBMTR and the NMDP have broad expertise in the field of blood and marrow transplantation. The IBMTR is a voluntary organization involving more than 400 centers in 47 countries that have collaborated to share patient data and conduct scientific studies since 1972. The NMDP was established in 1987 to provide unrelated donors for patients in need of hematopoietic stem cell transplants and also to conduct research to improve the outcome of such transplants. The NMDP Network includes 156 transplant centers, 84 donor centers, 103 collection centers, 84 apheresis centers and 15 cord blood banks.

President: Mary M. Horowitz, M.D., M.S. (Scientific Director) (1985 to Present).
Executive Director: Melodee L. Nugent (Contact Person)
Year Established: 1972
Acronym: CIBMTR

Keywords
Cancer; Center for International Blood and Marrow Transplant Research; International Bone Marrow Transplant Registry (IBMTR); Transplantation, Bone Marrow

---

1406 Center for Mental Retardation

3100 East 45th Street
Suite 212
Cleveland, OH 44127

Phone: (216) 341-5488
Fax: (216) 341-5669
Toll Free: (800) 899-3039
E-mail: CMR-Clev@CMR-Cleveland.org
www.cmr-cleveland.org

The Center for Mental Retardation (Edward I. and Fannie L. Baker International Resource Center for Down Syndrome) is a not-for-profit organization dedicated to improving the quality of life for individuals with mental retardation and increasing their role as valued, contributing members of society. Down syndrome is a congenital chromosomal disorder characterized by varying degrees of mental retardation, characteristic abnormalities of the head and facial area, malformations of the hands and/or feet, congenital heart defects in approximately 25 percent of affected individuals, and/or other abnormalities. In most individuals with Down syndrome, all or a portion of chromosome 21 appears three times rather than twice in cells of the body; however, in rare cases, the disorder may occur due to a chromosomal translocation involving chromosome 21 and another chromosome. Established in 1963, the Center for Mental Retardation offers a variety of services and programs including patient advocacy services, parent counseling and support, referral services, and patient and professional education. Its educational materials include brochures, pamphlets, and a regular newsletter.

President: Charles P. Royer, Esq
Executive Director: Cynthia F. Norwood
Year Established: 1963
Acronym: CMR

Keywords
Center for Mental Retardation; Chromosome 21 Mosiac 21 Syndrome; Chromosome 21 Translocation 21 Syndrome; Down Syndrome; Trisomy 21 Syndrome; Trisomy G Syndrome

---

1407 Center for Research in Sleep Disorders

1275 East Kemper Rd.
Cincinnati, OH 45246

Phone: (513) 671-3101
Fax: (513) 671-4159
TDD: (311) 111-6111
E-mail: ggaz@tristatesleep.com

The Center for Research in Sleep Disorders is a not-for-profit organization dedicated to assisting individuals with night tremors, sleep apnea, and other sleep disorders. Established in 1970, the center seeks to educate affected individuals, physicians, and the public about sleep disorders and their effects and supports ongoing studies into the causes, prevention, and treatment of sleep disorders. In addition, the Center for Research in Sleep Disorders produces educational materials including brochures and fact sheets.

President: Martin Scharf (1970-Present)
Year Established: 1970

Keywords
Apnea, Sleep; Center for Research in Sleep Disorders; Sleep Disorders; Tremor, Night

---

1408 Center for Research on Women with Disabilities

One Baylor Plaza
Houston, TX 77030

Phone: (713) 798-5782
Fax: (713) 794-4688
Toll Free: (800) 442-7693
E-mail: crowd@bcm.tmc.edu
http://www.bcm.tmc.edu/crowd/

The Center for Research on Women with Disabilities (CROWD) is a research organization dedicated to conducting ongoing research and promoting, developing, and disseminating information to expand the life choices of women with disabilities so that they may fully participate in community life. Established in 1993, the center conducts research and training activities related to the health, independence, and community integration of people with physical disabilities. It has established a database of psychosocial behaviors of women with disabilities compared to able-bodied women. The center fulfills requests for information on its research findings and is expanding its efforts to conduct training and disseminate materials targeting a variety of audiences including medical professionals, allied health professionals, counselors, social workers, educators, policy analysts, and consumers.

Executive Director: Margaret Nosek, Ph.D.
Year Established: 1993
Acronym: CROWD

Keywords
Center for Research on Women with Disabilities

1409 Central Brain Tumor Registry of the United States

244 E. Ogden
Suite 116
Hinsdale, IL 60521

Phone: (630) 655-4786
Fax: (630) 655-1756
E-mail: cbtrus@aol.com
http://www.cbtrus.org

The Central Brain Tumor Registry of the United States (CBTRUS) is a voluntary, not-for-profit organization dedicated to collecting and disseminating statistical data on all primary benign and malignant brain tumors. Such data collection is for the purposes of accurately describing incidence rates and survival patterns, evaluating diagnosis and treatment, facilitating studies concerning causes (etiology), promoting professional and public awareness, and, ultimately, working toward the possible prevention of such brain tumors. CBTRUS was incorporated in 1992 following a two-year study by the American Brain Tumor Association to determine the feasibility of a central registry for all brain tumor cases. Previously, standard data collection in the United States had been limited to malignant brain tumor cases. The CBTRUS database summarizes collaborators' data and generates statistics that are published in the form of an annual report. The annual report is mailed free of charge to over 2,000 members of the neuroscience community as well as to affected individuals, family members, and businesses upon request. In addition to data collection and dissemination, CBTRUS is dedicated to conducting special studies aimed at broadening the scope of data concerning the incidence and prevalence of brain tumors in certain populations. CBTRUS also encourages and promotes interdisciplinary dialogue with other professional and volunteer organizations.

President: Carol Kruchko (1992 to Present)
Executive Director: Same as above.
Year Established: 1992
Acronym: CBTRUS

Keywords
Brain Tumors, Benign; Brain Tumors, Malignant; Brain Tumors, Primary; Central Brain Tumor Registry of the United States

1410 Central Nervous System Vasculitis Foundation, Inc.

5170 Nash Drive
Flint, MI 48506

Phone: (810) 736-1353
E-mail: info@cnsvfinc.org
http://www.cnsvfinc.org

The Central Nervous System Vasculitis Foundation, Inc. (CNSVFINC) provides information to patients, families, and the medical community about central nervous system vasculitis (CNSV), its effects, diagnosis, and treatment. Vasculitis refers to inflammation of the blood vessels. Central nervous system vasculitis refers to cases in which the brain or spinal cord is involved. The CNSVFINC was founded in 2004, and provides support groups, networking and educational services.

President: Daneen Eller (2004-present)
Executive Director: Tracy Latimer, Vice President
Year Established: 2004
Acronym: CNSVFINC

Keywords
Advocacy; Central Nervous System Vasculitis; Central Nervous System Vasculitis Foundation, Inc.; CNSV; German; Networking; Support Groups; Vasculitis

1411 CF Alliance

P.O. Box 9204
Bardonia, NY 10954

Phone: (845) 548-0313
Fax: (845) 792-0880
E-mail: CF_ALLIANCE@yahoo.com
http://cf-alliance.tripod.com

The CF Alliance is a free international pen pal program and support group for people affected by chronic fatigue syndrome, fibromyalgia, and related illnesses. It serves an international community, including the United Kingdom, France, Germany, Australia, and New Zealand. Chronic fatigue syndrome is characterized by fatigue severe enough to reduce daily activities by at least 50 percent. Fibromyalgia is a chronic disorder characterized by pain throughout much of the body. Other diseases addressed by this organization include multiple chemical sensitivity, myalgic encephalomyelitis, irritable bowel syndrome and Raynaud's phenomenon.

Executive Director: Lee Cohen, PhD
Year Established: 1999

Keywords
CF Alliance; Chronic Fatigue Syndrome; Fibromyalgia; Myalgic Encephalomyelitis

1412 CFIDS Association of America, Inc.
PO Box 220398
Charlotte, NC 28222-0398

Phone: (704) 364-0466
Fax: (704) 365-9755
Toll Free: (800) 442-3437
E-mail: cfids@cfids.org
http://www.cfids.org

The CFIDS Association of America, Inc. is a 501(c)3 charitable organization dedicated to conquering CFIDS, also known as chronic fatigue syndrome (CFS) and myalgic encephalomyelitis (ME). The association provides information to the public and health professionals, encourages research, and promotes early diagnosis and appropriate treatment for those affected by CFIDS. The syndrome is characterized by profound fatigue that does not respond to bed rest and by other symptoms. Its onset is usually sudden, sometimes following a flu-like illness. CFIDS was established in 1987 and has 23,000 members. Educational materials now include The CFIDS Chronicle and The CFS Research Review which helps educate the health care community about the illness.

President: K. Kimberly McCleary, CEO
Year Established: 1987
Acronym: CFIDS

Keywords
CFIDS; CFIDS Association of America, Inc.; CFS; Chronic Fatigue Syndrome; Myalgic Encephalomyelitis

1413 CHADD (Children and Adults with Attention-Deficit/Hyperactivity Disorder)
8181 Professional Place
Suite 150
Landover, MD 20785

Phone: (302) 306-7070
Fax: (301) 306-7090
Toll Free: (800) 233-4050
http://www.chadd.org or www.help4adhd.org

CHADD (Children and Adults with Attention-Deficit/Hyperactivity Disorder) is a non-profit organization working to improve the lives of individuals and families affected by attention-deficit/hyperactivity disorder (AD/HD). With over 16,000 members in 250 local chapters nationwide, CHADD achieves its mission through collaborative leadership, advocacy, research, education and support. CHADD provides a support network for parents, caregivers, and individuals with AD/HD; offers a forum for continuing education; disseminates accurate, evidence-based information about AD/HD to parents, educators, adults, professionals and the media; promotes ongoing research; and advocates on behalf of the AD/HD community. Members receive CHADD's bi-monthly magazine, Attention!, and have access to the members-only section of the CHADD web site. CHADD's CDC-funded National Resource Center on AD/HD is staffed by knowledgeable information specialists who can answer questions about AD/HD.

President: Phyllis Anne Teeter Ellison, EdD
Executive Director: E. Clarke Ross, DPA
Year Established: 1987
Acronym: CHADD

Keywords
ADD; ADHD; Adults with ADD; Attention Deficit Disorder; Attention Deficit Disorder, Undifferentiated; Attention Deficit Hyperactivity Disorder; CHADD; CHADD (Children and Adults with Attention Deficit/Hyperactivity Disorder); Children and Adults with Attention Deficit Disorder; Children with ADD; Local Support

1414 Changing Faces
The Squire Centre
33-37 University Street
London, WC1E 6JN, United Kingdom

Phone: +44 (0) 845-450-0275
Fax: +44 (0) 845-450-0276
Toll Free: +44 (0) 207-391-9270
E-mail: info@changingfaces.org.uk
http://www.changingfaces.org.uk

Changing Faces is self-help, not-for-profit organization dedicated to helping people who, for any reason, have experienced facial disfigurement. It supports and represents children, young people and adults (and their families) who have a disfigurement from any cause. Established in 1992, Changing Faces provides services that include counseling, education, advocacy, and support for research.

Year Established: 1992

Keywords
Advocacy; Birthmark; Changing Faces; Cleft Lip; Cleft Palate; Disfigurement; Research

1415 Charcot-Marie-Tooth Association

2700 Chestnut Street
Chester, PA 19013

Phone: (610) 499-9264
Fax: (610) 499-9267
Toll Free: (800) 606-2682
E-mail: CMTAssoc@aol.com
http://www.charcot-marie-tooth.org

The Charcot-Marie-Tooth Association is a national voluntary health organization that functions as an educational resource for people with Charcot-Marie-Tooth disease, their families, medical professionals, the educational community, and the general public. Charcot-Marie-Tooth disease is a genetic neurological disorder characterized by weakness and atrophy of muscles first in the legs and, later, in the arms and hands. Founded in 1983, the association acts as an advocate for people with Charcot-Marie-Tooth disease by raising awareness and encouraging public and private agencies and private industry to fund and support medical research. The association acts as a liaison between the research community and people with this disorder. It also organizes and encourages the formation of local chapters and support groups. The organization produces educational materials including brochures, a bi-monthly newsletter, a book on CMT and the CMT Facts series.

President: Patrick Torchia
Executive Director: Charles Hagins
Year Established: 1983
Acronym: CMTA

Keywords
Advocacy; Charcot-Marie-Tooth Association; Charcot-Marie-Tooth Disease; CMT; CMTA; Neuromuscular Disorders; Neuropathy, Hereditary Motor and Sensory; Peroneal Muscular Atrophy; Roussy Levy Syndrome; Support Groups

1416 CHARGE Family Support Group

Langdale
5 Botham Hall Road
West Yorkshire
Huddersfield, HD3 4RJ, United Kingdom

Phone: +44 (0) 1484-64-6828
E-mail: cajthomas@btinternet.com
http://www.widerworld.co.uk/charge/index.htm

Chatting with other parents and caregivers provides a unique and needed opportunity to share anecdotal information. It offers the chance for people to tell their own stories and give support to each other. Those are the goals of the CHARGE Family Support Group, a small voluntary organization for families with children affected by CHARGE association. This rare disorder, which results from defects that occur in early fetal development, may affect several organs and systems. The group sponsors activities, such as a Family Fun Day, and has a newsletter.

President: Carol Thomas, Chairperson
Year Established: 1998

Keywords
CHARGE Association; CHARGE Family Support Group; CHARGE Syndrome

1417 CHARGE Syndrome Foundation, Inc.

409 Vandiver Drive
Suite 5-104
Columbia, MO 65202-1563

Phone: (410) 272-3839
Fax: (410) 272-1281
Toll Free: (800) 442-7604
E-mail: marion@chargesyndrome.org
http://www.chargesyndrome.org

The CHARGE Syndrome Foundation, Inc. is a national, not-for-profit, voluntary agency that was established in 1993. Its mission is to establish, maintain, and distribute information about CHARGE syndrome and provide support to affected families. The foundation supports the dissemination of information about CHARGE syndrome, supports research into its cause and management, and works with other organizations and institutions to accomplish its mission. In addition, the CHARGE Syndrome Foundation hosts a biennial conference for affected individuals, families, physicians, and other professionals such as educators and therapists.

Executive Director: Marion A. Norbury (Executive Director)
Year Established: 1993
Acronym: CHARGE

Keywords
Atresia, Posterior Choanal; CHARGE Syndrome; CHARGE Syndrome Foundation, Inc.

1418   CHERUB—Association of Families and Friends of Children with Limb Disorders

8401 Powers Road
Batavia, NY 14020

Phone: (716) 762-9997

CHERUB—Association of Family and Friends of Children with Limb Disorders is a voluntary not-for-profit organization dedicated to providing information and support to children with limb disorders (such as congenital absence of limbs), affected families, and friends through organized activities, phone support, correspondence, and visits. CHERUB has over 200 members across the United States and in several other countries. The association conducts an annual week-long summer camp for affected children from the ages of eight to 18. In addition, CHERUB provides a variety of educational and support materials including a regular newsletter and brochures.

President: Thomas Hauser (1986-Present)
Executive Director: Sandra Richenberg (Secretary)
Year Established: 1986

Keywords
Amniotic Bands; CHERUB—Association of Families and Friends of Children with Limb Disorders; Limb Disorders; Limbs, Absence of; Limbs, Congenital Absence of

1419   CHERUBS— The Association of Congenital Diaphragmatic Hernia Research, Advocacy and Support

270 Coley Road
Henderson, NC 27537

Phone: (252) 492-6003
Fax: (815) 425-9155
E-mail: dawntorrence@cherubs-cdh.org
http://www.cherubs-cdh.org

CHERUBS — The Association of Congenital Diaphragmatic Hernia Research, Advocacy and Support is an international support group for the families and physicians of children who are born with congenital diaphragmatic hernias (CDH). Congenital diaphragmatic hernia is a rare condition, present at birth that is characterized by the protrusion of organs from the abdomen into the chest through an opening in the muscle that divides the two. Established in 1993, CHERUBS is a volunteer organization associated with the March of Dimes, the Association of Birth Defect Children, Inc., and the California Birth Defects Mon-

itoring Program. It serves people in the United States, Canada, Great Britain, and Ireland. CHERUBS offers a "Parent Reference Guide," periodic newsletters, and brochures; has a parent-to-parent match up program; and provides referrals. In addition, the organization maintains a research library and compiles data from research surveys.

President: Dawn M. Torrence (1995 to Present)
Executive Director: Same as above
Year Established: 1995
Acronym: CHERUBS

Keywords
Agenesis of the Hemidiaphragm; CHERUBS—The Association of Congenital Diaphragmatic Hernia Research, Advocacy and Support; Diaphragm, Complete Agenesis of the; Diaphragmatic Hernia; Hernia, Congenital Diaphragmatic; Hernia, Morgagni; Pentalogy of Cantrell

1420   Child and Adolescent Bipolar Foundation (CABF)

1000 Skokie Boulevard
Suite 425
Wilmette, IL 60091

Phone: (947) 920-9310
Fax: (847) 920-9498
E-mail: CABF@bpkids.org
http://www.bpkids.org

The Child and Adolescent Bipolar Foundation (CABF) is a nonprofit, parent-led organization whose mission is to educate families, professionals, and the public about pediatric bipolar disorder; connect families with resources and support; advocate for and empower affected families; and support research on pediatric bipolar disorder and its cure. CABF was established in 1999, and currently consists of more than 40,000 members.

President: Ellen Solms
Executive Director: Kate Pravera
Year Established: 1999
Acronym: CABF

Keywords
Attention Deficit Hyperactivity Disorder; Bipolar Disorder; Brain Disorders; Child and Adolescent Bipolar Foundation; Child and Adolescent Bipolar Foundation (CABF); Depression; Manic Depression, Bipolar

1421 Child Brain Injury Trust

The Radcliffe Infirmary
Woodstock Road
Oxford, OX2 6HE, United Kingdom

Phone: +44 (0) 1865-55-2467
E-mail: info@cbituk.org
http://www.cbituk.org

The Child Brain Injury Trust (CBIT) offers support and information to families with a child with an acquired brain injury (ABI) and to professionals working in this field. Founded in 2003, CBIT offers programs such as networking; support groups, research, education and telephone help lines. The trust provides small grants for children and young people with ABI and their siblings. CBIT offers videos, booklets, children's storybooks and leaflets by children to those who contact them.

President: Dr. Judith Middleton
Executive Director: Lisa Turan
Year Established: 1989
Acronym: CBIT

Keywords
Brain Tumor; CBIT; Child Brain Injury Trust; Children; French; German; Meningitis; Meningitis, Bacterial; Meningitis, Meningococcal; Meningitis, Tuberculous; Networking; Stroke; Support Groups; Welsh

1422 Child Growth Foundation

2 Mayfield Avenue
Chiswick
London, W4 1PW, United Kindom

Phone: +44 (0) 208-995-0257
Fax: +44 (0) 208-995-9075
E-mail: cgflondon@aol.com
http://www.childgrowthfoundation.org.

The Child Growth Foundation, established in 1977, is a self-help organization serving patients and members of their families, health professionals, other professionals, and the public with information and services related to disorders affecting children's growth. Children who fail to grow enough, or who grow far beyond the mean, may suffer socially and psychologically, as well as medically. The foundation encourages regular assessment of children's growth so that problems may be detected early and, when it is possible, treated. The foundation also funds research on conditions that, as yet, have no treatment.

President: Tam Fry
Year Established: 1977
Acronym: CGF

Keywords
Achondroplasia; Bone Dysplasia; Child Growth Foundation; Growth Hormone Deficiency; Growth Measurements; Hormone Deficiency; IUGR; MPHD; Multiple Pituitary; PSM; Premature Sexual Maturation; Russell Silver Syndrome; Sotos Syndrome; Turner Syndrome

1423 Childhood Apraxia of Speech Association of North America

1151 Freeport Road
#243
Pittsburgh, PA 15238

Phone: (412) 767-6589
Fax: (412) 767-0534
E-mail: helpdesk@apraxia-kids.org
http://www.apraxia-kids.org

The Childhood Apraxia of Speech Association of North America, a not-for-profit organization established in 2000, exists to strengthen the support and systems of care in the lives of children with apraxia so that each child is afforded his or her best opportunity to develop speech. The association provides support, information, referral, education, and understanding, while also supporting research. Childhood apraxia of speech is a speech disorder in which affected children have difficulty correctly putting together the precise movement patterns needed for sounds, syllables, or words. Often, a child with apraxia understands language well, but has difficulty making his mouth do what his brain wants it to do.

President: Mary Sturm, MD
Executive Director: Gary Novak
Year Established: 2000
Acronym: CASANA

Keywords
Apraxia; Childhood Apraxia of Speech Association of North America

1424 Childhood Cancer Association, Inc. (Australia)

P.O. Box 1094
North Adelaide, 5006, N. Australia

Phone: +61 (0) 8-8239-1444
Fax: +61 (0) 8-8239-2300
E-mail: kidscancer@childhoodcancer.asn.au
http://www.childhoodcancer.asn.au

The Childhood Cancer Association, Inc. (Australia), is a not-for-profit organization in Australia that was formed in 1982 by several parents of children with cancer. The association is committed to providing financial, practical, and emotional support to families of children diagnosed with cancer. It promotes and supports pediatric cancer research, conducts self-help and family support group meetings, and offers its Family Service, a program that matches specially trained support workers with affected families upon referral by their specialists or social workers. The association also offers a library of materials on pediatric cancers; provides vocational assistance for adolescents who are or were previously affected by cancer; offers free, short- or long-term accommodations for out-of-town families who have children who are undergoing treatment; and outfits treatment rooms and overnight rooms in several hospitals to enable parents to stay with their children. In addition, the Childhood Cancer Association offers ongoing reimbursement to help families employ home tutors for children who have fallen behind in their school work as a result of missing school for long periods or who have developed learning disabilities due to their illness or treatment. The association also reimburses affected families for expenses that they are unable to afford, such as traveling costs; provides funds for world searches to locate compatible bone marrow donors; and funds vocational advocacy research.

President: Christopher Powell
Executive Director: Konrad Gawlik
Year Established: 1982

Keywords
Cancer; Childhood Cancer Association, Inc. (Australia)

1425   Childhood Cancer Foundation—Candlelighters Canada

55 Eglinton Avenue East
Suite 401
Toronto, Ontario, M4P 1G8, Canada

Phone: (416) 489-6440
Fax: (416) 489-9812
Toll Free: (800) 363-1062
E-mail: staff@candlelighters.ca
http://www.childhoodcancer.ca

The Candlelighters Childhood Cancer Foundation Canada (CCCFC), a national, charitable, voluntary organization is dedicated to improving the quality of life for families experiencing the effects of childhood cancer through the provision of resources, parent support groups, and the promotion of research. Established in 1987, the foundation has a network of over 50 local support groups across Canada for parents of children with

cancer; promotes and supports the development of a long-term survivor network; offers individual and group assistance; and is developing a national financial assistance program. The foundation's advocacy efforts include communicating the results of patient/family needs surveys to all levels of government; instituting task forces on professional and family issues; and forming coalitions with other organizations to address advocacy issues. The CCCFC also serves as a liaison with professionals and treatment centers, offers a speaker's bureau, and provides a wide variety of educational materials.

President: Ian Young, Chairman of the Board
Executive Director: David Stone, CEO
Year Established: 1987
Acronym: CCFCC

Keywords
Cancer; Cancer, Childhood; Cancer, Pediatric; Childhood Cancer Foundation Candlelighters Canada

1426   Childhood Disintegrative Disorder Network

85 Maple Avenue
Alleghany, NY 14706

Phone: (716) 373-5042
E-mail: jfairthorne@hotmail.com
http://info.med.yale.edu/chldstdy/autism/cdd.html

The Childhood Disintegrative Disorder Network is a voluntary, nonprofit support organization consisting of families of children with childhood disintegrative disorder (CDD), also known as Heller syndrome. This condition is characterized by a significant loss of previously acquired skills such as expressive language, adaptive behavior, and bladder control. The group's mission is to share information relating to CDD, its causes, and treatments, and to provide support and encouragement to affected families. The CDD Network works to increase its membership to encompass a larger group of affected children whose case histories may assist researchers with an interest in CDD. The network also works to promote awareness of CDD in the public and the medical establishment.

President: Madeline Catalano
Executive Director: Jenny Fairthorne
Year Established: 1995
Acronym: CDD Network

Keywords
Childhood Disintegrative Disorder; Childhood Disintegrative Disorder Network; Childhood Disintegrative Psychosis; Heller Syndrome

1427 Childhood Disintegrative Disorder Network—Australia

56 The Avenue
Nedlands, 6009, W. Australia

Phone: +61 (0) 9-386-6693
E-mail: jfairthorne@hotmail.com

The Childhood Disintegrative Disorder (CDD) Network is a voluntary organization dedicated to sharing information relating to CDD. Childhood disintegrative disorder (CDD), also known as Heller syndrome, is characterized by a significant loss of previously acquired skills such as expressive language, adaptive behavior, and bladder control. The group's mission is to share information relating to CDD, its causes, and treatments, and to provide support and encouragement to affected families. The CDD Network works to increase its membership to encompass a larger group of affected children whose case histories may assist researchers with an interest in CDD. The network also works to promote awareness of CDD in the public and the medical establishment.

President: J. Fairthorne
Executive Director: Same as above.
Year Established: 1994
Acronym: CDC Network

Keywords
CDD; Childhood Disintegrative Disorder; Childhood Disintegrative Disorder Network—Australia; Dementia, Infantile; Disintegrative Disorder; Disintegrative Psychosis; Heller Syndrome; Pervasive Developmental Disorder

1428 Children's Brain Diseases Foundation

350 Parnassus Avenue
Suite 900
San Francisco, CA 94117

Phone: (415) 665-3003
Fax: (415) 863-3452
E-mail: Jrider6022@aol.com

The Children's Brain Diseases Foundation is a national, not-for-profit organization that raises funds for medical research into the causes and treatments of Batten disease. Batten disease, also known as neuronal ceroid lipofuscinosis, is a rare, progressive, degenerative, neuro metabolic disorder characterized by gradual intellectual deterioration, seizure episodes, progressive motor impairment, and progressive visual impairment. Symptoms may begin in infancy, very early childhood, or late child-

hood depending on the specific type. There is also an adult form called Kuf's disease. Founded in 1968, the foundation provides information on Batten disease to affected families and their physicians and promotes public understanding of the disease. Research funds are provided to investigators to help maintain the momentum of research on Batten Disease; pursue new scientific opportunities in this area of study; and promote early diagnosis, effective treatment, and prevention of Batten disease. The foundation produces educational brochures including "Help To Keep the Color In a Child's Life: Erase Batten Disease."

President: Dean Rider, M.D.
Year Established: 1968
Acronym: CBDF

Keywords
Batten Disease; Children's Brain Diseases Foundation; Hydranencephaly; Kufs Disease; Leigh's Disease; Neuronal Ceroid Lipofuscinosis, Juvenile Type; Santavuori Disease; Spielmeyer Vogt Disease

1429 Children's Brain Tumor Foundation

274 Madison Avenue
Suite 1301
New York, NY 10016

Phone: (212) 448-9494
Fax: (212) 448-1022
Toll Free: (866) 228-4673
E-mail: info@cbtf.org
http://www.cbtf.org

The Children's Brain Tumor Foundation (CBTF), founded in 1988, funds scientific research on the causes of, and improved treatments for, pediatric brain and spinal cord tumors and provides support and educational services to families and survivors. CBTF distributes "A Resource Guide for Parents of Children with Brain and Spinal Cord Tumors" at no charge to families in English and Spanish, co-sponsors educational seminars and teleconferences, and provides online information through its web site. Each year, CBTF provides information and referrals to critical services to hundreds of families from all over the world. The Parent-to-Parent Network provides support to newly diagnosed families from experienced parents who have been trained as volunteers. A newsletter, The Challenge, is published twice a year.

President: Robert Budlow
Executive Director: Judy Hurley
Year Established: 1988
Acronym: CBTF

Keywords
Atypical-Teratoid- and Rhabdoid-Tumor; Brain Tumor; CBTF;Children's Brain Tumor Foundation; Chordoma; Diencephalic Syndrome; Ependymoma; Glioma, Brain Stem; Juvenile Pilocytic Astrocytoma; Medulloblastoma; PNET; Tumors, Brain; Tumors, Pediatric Brain; Tumors, Pediatric Spinal Cord; Tumors, Spinal Cord; Turcot Syndrome

1430 Children's Brittle Bone Foundation

7701 95th Street
Pleasant Prairie, WI 53158

Phone: (866) 694-2223
Fax: (262) 947-0724
E-mail: info@cbbf.org
http://www.cbbf.org

The Children's Brittle Bone Foundation (CBBF) is a voluntary health organization dedicated to promoting research into the causes, diagnosis, treatment, prevention, and eventual cure of osteogenesis imperfecta (OI). Osteogenesis imperfecta, a rare genetic disorder, is characterized by defective development of collagen. Collagen, the body's major structural protein, forms an essential part of bones, tendons, and connective tissues. Individuals with osteogenesis imperfecta have unusually fragile bones that break or fracture easily. There are four major types of the disorder that may vary greatly in severity. Osteogenesis imperfecta may be inherited as an autosomal dominant or autosomal recessive genetic trait or may be due to a new genetic mutation. More than 50 mutations in genes that encode type I collagen have been identified. Established in 1991, the Children's Brittle Bone Foundation is committed to promoting basic and clinical scientific research and to encouraging biomedical research scientists' interest in this currently underrepresented field.

President: Jim Coleman (1998–Present)
Executive Director: Kris Glicken
Year Established: 1991
Acronym: CBBF

Keywords
Brittle Bone Disease; Children's Brittle Bone Foundation; Ekman Lobstein Disease; Lobstein Disease (Type I); Osteogenesis Imperfecta; Osteopathyrosis

1431 Children's Cardiomyopathy Foundation

PO Box 547
Tenafly, NJ 07670

Phone: (201) 227-8852
Fax: (201) 227-7016

E-mail: info@childrenscardiomyopathy.org
http://www.childrenscardiomyopathy.org

The Children's Cardiomyopathy Foundation was established in 2002 by a parent who lost two young children to cardiomyopathy, a rare and underdiagnosed heart condition. It is a non-profit, tax-exempt organization dedicated to accelerating the search for a cause and cure for pediatric cardiomyopathy. Run entirely by volunteers and guided by a medical advisory board, the foundation supports critical scientific and medical research into the genetic cause, early detection and effective treatment of this chronic disease. In addition, it promotes physician education, public awareness, patient support, and advocacy for affected children and their families. The Children's Cardiomyopathy Foundation provides a pamphlet, family directory and web site with detailed information (medical information, coping & healing tips, resource links, and discussion forum) on this group of diseases.

President: Lisa Yue
Executive Director: Same as above
Year Established: 2002
Acronym: C.C.F.

Keywords
Barth Syndrome; Cardiomyopathy; Cardiomyopathy, Arrhythmogenic Right Ventricular; Cardiomyopathy, Dilated; Cardiomyopathy, Hypertrophic; Cardiomyopathy, Lethal Infantile; Cardiomyopathy, Restrictive; Cardiovascular Disorders; Children's Cardiomyopathy Foundation; Fatty Oxidation Disorders; Heart Disease; Mitochondrial Disorders; Mitochondrial Fatty Oxidation Disorders; Noonan Syndrome; Pompe Disease

1432 Children's Craniofacial Association

13140 Coit Road
Suite 307
Dallas, TX 75240

Phone: (214) 570-9099
Fax: (214) 570-8811
Toll Free: (800) 535-3643
E-mail: csmith@ccakids.com
http://www.ccakids.com

The Children's Craniofacial Association (CCA) is a not-for-profit organization dedicated to improving the quality of life for individuals with craniofacial disorders and their families. Established in 1989, CCA is devoted to addressing the medical, financial, psychosocial, emotional, and educational concerns relating to craniofacial conditions. In addition, the association advocates on behalf of affected individuals and promotes public awareness of craniofacial disorders. Through the combined efforts of its medical and parental advisory boards, CCA provides referral services and a support network for affected children and their families. The organization also provides financial assistance; sponsors workshops to help educate parents about psychosocial, medical, and insurance issues related to their children's care. The organization also refers patients to appropriate support groups and outreach programs. The group engages in patient advocacy to ensure quality care and appropriate healthcare standards, and offers an annual weekend retreat for affected individuals and their families. The Children's Craniofacial Association also provides a variety of educational materials including a regular newsletter, brochures, and a booklet series on a variety of craniofacial conditions.

President: Tim Ayers
Executive Director: Charlene Smith
Year Established: 1989
Acronym: CCA

Keywords
Aarskog Syndrome; Ablepharon Macrostomia Syndrome; Advocacy; Antley Bixler Syndrome; Apert Syndrome; Baller Gerold Syndrome; Blepharophimosis, Ptosis, Epicanthus Inversus Syndrome; Cardiofaciocutaneous Syndrome; CCA; Cerebro Oculo Facio Skeletal Syndrome; Children's Craniofacial Association; Chromosome 3, Monosomy 3p2; Chromosome 4, Monosomy Distal 4q; Chromosome 4, Partial Trisomy Distal 4q; Chromosome 4 Ring; Chromosome 4, Trisomy 4p; Chromosome 6, Partial Trisomy 6q; Chromosome 6 Ring; Chromosome 7, Partial Monosomy 7p; Chromosome 9, Partial Monosomy 9p; Chromosome 9 Ring; Chromosome 10, Distal Trisomy 10q; Chromosome 10, Monosomy 10p; Chromosome 11, Partial Monosomy 11q; Chromosome 11, Partial Trisomy 11q; Chromosome 13, Partial Monosomy 13q; Chromosome 15, Distal Trisomy 15q; Chromosome 15 Ring; Chromosome 18, Monosomy 18p; Chromosome 18 Ring; Chromosome 18, Tetrasomy 18p; Chromosome 18q SyndromeCleft Palate and Cleft Lip; Cleidocranial Dysplasia; Cornelia de Lange Syndrome; Craniofacial Anomalies; Craniofacial Conditions; Craniofrontonasal Dysplasia; Craniometaphyseal Dysplasia; Craniosynostosis, Primary; Crouzon Syndrome; Encephalocele; Facial Difference; Fraser Syndrome; Frontofacionasal Dysplasia; Frontonasal Dysplasia; Fryns Syndrome; Goldenhar Syndrome; Goodman Syndrome; Gorlin Chaudhry Moss Syndrome; Greig Cephalopolysyndactyly Syndrome; Hallermann Streiff Syndrome; Hyperostosis Frontalis Interna; IRF6 Related Disorders; Jackson

Weiss Syndrome; KBG Syndrome; Kenny Caffey Syndrome; Larsen Syndrome; Leprechaunism; Marshall Syndrome; Maxillofacial Dysostosis; Maxillonasal Dysplasia, Binder Type; Megalocornea Mental Retardation Syndrome; Miller Syndrome; Moebius Syndrome; Nager Syndrome; Networking; Oculo Auriculo Vertebral Spectrum; Oral Facial Digital Syndrom; Orocraniodigital Syndrome; Otopalatodigital Syndrome; Pallister W Syndrome; Penta X Syndrome; Pfeiffer Syndrome; Pierre Robin Sequence; Pyknodysostosis; Roberts Syndrome; Robinow Syndrome; Rubinstein Taybi Syndrome; Saethre Chotzen Syndrome; Sakati Syndrome; Scott Craniodigital Syndrome; Seckel Syndrome; Setleis Syndrome; Simpson Dysmorphia Syndrome; Summitt Syndrome; Support Groups; Telecanthus with Associated Abnormalities; Three M Syndrome; Treacher Collins Syndrome; Tricho Dento Osseous Syndrome

---

1433 Children's European Mitochondrial Disease Network
Mayfield House
30 Heber Walk
Chester Way
Northwich, CW9 5JB, United Kingdom

Phone: +44 (0) 1606-43946
Fax: +44 (0) 1606-43946
E-mail: info_cmdn@btopenworld.com
http://www.cmdn-mitonet.co.uk

The Children's Mitochondrial Disease Network (CMDN) is an international, nonprofit organization dedicated to providing information and support to individuals, families, and medical professionals affected by, or interested in, mitochondrial disorders. CMDN was established in 1998 and its objectives include promoting research into the causes and treatment of mitochondrial disorders in children and adults; providing support and information to parents, caregivers, and medical professionals; and contributing financial assistance to healthcare professionals interested in attending professional conferences that will further understanding of causes and treatments of mitochondrial disorders. Other programs and educational services available through CMDN include information on a wide range of mitochondrial disorders written in understandable lay terminology; a 24-hour help line available to parents and professionals; and disease-specific information searches.

President: Professor Tony H.V. Schapira (1998-2003)
Executive Director: Paul Preston
Year Established: 1998
Acronym: C/EMDN

Keywords
Acidosis; Children's European Mitochondrial Disease Network; Children's Mitochondrial Disease Network; COX; Cytopathy; DNA; Genes; Lactic Acid; MELAS; MERRF; Metobolic; Mitchondrial; Myopathy; NARP

1434 Children's Fund for Glycogen Storage Disease Research, Inc.
917 Bethany Mountain Road
Cheshire, CT 06410

Phone: (203) 272-2873
Fax: (203) 272-6695
E-mail: info@cureGSD.org
http://www.cureGSD.org

The Children's Fund for Glycogen Storage Disease Research is committed to funding research so that children born with glycogen storage disease type I (GSD1) will benefit from early detection, treatment and an eventual cure. It is a public, not-for-profit, 501(c) 3 foundation established in April of 2002 to make a difference in the lives of children and families affected by GSD1. This disease, also known as Von Gierke disease, is a hereditary metabolic disorder caused by the inborn lack of the enzyme glucose-6-phosphatase. Parents, families, run the foundation and friends of children affected by this disease. All fundraising and administration is done on a voluntary basis.

President: Wendy Feldman (2002-present)
Executive Director: David Feldman
Year Established: 2002

Keywords
Children's Fund for Glycogen Storage Disease Research, Inc.; Glycogen; Glycogen Storage Disease; GSD; Type 1a

---

1435 Children's Gaucher Research Fund
8110 Warren Court
Granite Bay, CA 95746

Phone: (916) 797-3700
Fax: (916) 797-3707
E-mail: research@childrensgaucher.org
http://www.childrensgaucher.org

The Children's Gaucher Research Fund is a non-profit organization that raises money for medical research aimed at finding a cure for Gaucher disease type 2 and type 3. It also provides support to families of affected children and allows families who have lost a child to this disease to participate, in their child's honor, in fund-raising for medical research. Gaucher disease is a rare, inherited, metabolic disorder in which the body is unable to rid itself of worn-out red and white blood cells so that these cells accumulate in the liver, spleen, bone marrow, and, sometimes, heart and lungs. In Children's Gaucher disease, more commonly known as types 2 and 3 Gaucher disease, all of the above-mentioned symptoms exist, but the disease is also characterized by certain neurologic symptoms such as ocular motor apraxia, a defect of horizontal eye movements; breathing problems and, sometimes, speech or cognitive delay. Founded in 1999, the Children's Gaucher Research Fund has approximately 1900 members. It serves families in the United States and Canada.

President: Gregory S. Macres
Executive Director: Deborah Macres
Year Established: 1999

Keywords
Children's Gaucher Research Fund; Gaucher Disease

1436 Children's Glaucoma Foundation
2 Longfellow Place
Suite 201
Boston, MA 02114

Phone: (617) 227-3011
Fax: (617) 227-4352
E-mail: childglau@Worldnet.ATT.net
http://www.childrensglaucoma.com

The Children's Glaucoma Foundation has a three-fold mission: to inform parents, medical personnel, and others (such as teachers and childcare workers) about the risk of blindness secondary to childhood glaucoma; to familiarize pediatricians and family physicians with the signs and symptoms of childhood glaucoma; and to support scientific investigation related to childhood glaucoma. Glaucoma is the term used for a group of eye diseases that cause progressive damage to the optical nerve. It is a leading cause of vision loss in children and a preventable cause of childhood blindness. The foundation is a not-for-profit organization serving patients, the general public, health professionals, and other professionals. It was established in 1999.

President: Dr. David S. Walton
Executive Director: Karen Sicher
Year Established: 1999
Acronym: CGF

Keywords
CGF; Children's Glaucoma Foundation; Glaucoma, Congenital

1437 Children's Heart Society

Box 52088
Garneau Postal Outlet
Edmonton
Alberta, T6G 2T5, Canada

Phone: (780) 454-7665
Fax: (780) 454-7665
Toll Free: (888) 247-9404
E-mail: childrensheart@shaw.ca
http://www.childrensheart.org

The Children's Heart Society (CHS) is a private, non-profit organization in Canada that is dedicated to supporting families of children with heart disease. The society's goals include ensuring the best possible care for children affected by heart disease, improving the quality of life of affected children and their families, educating the public about heart disease in children and their special needs, and working toward the day when no child will die from heart disease. To help fulfill its mission and goals, the Children's Heart Society conducts regular parent support meetings, holds family activities including an annual camping trip, ski trip, and summer picnic. The Children's Heart Society also has a lending library.

President: Karen Stump (1998 to Present)
Year Established: 1982
Acronym: CHS

Keywords
Children's Heart Society

1438 Children's Leukemia Research Association

585 Stewart Avenue
Suite 536
Garden City, NY 11530

Phone: (516) 222-1944
Fax: (516) 222-0457
http://www.childrensleukemia.org/index.html

The Children's Leukemia Research Association (CLRA), also known as the National Leukemia Research Association, was founded in 1965 as a not-for-profit organization to raise funds for research into the causes of, and possible cures for, leukemia, and to provide assistance to families in need as a result of the expenses incurred during leukemia treatment. Leuke-

mia is any of several types of cancer in which there is usually an abnormal accumulation of white blood cells within the bone marrow, often resulting in decreased production of red blood cells, platelets, and normal white blood cells. Organs such as the liver, lymph nodes, and brain may fail to function properly as they are infiltrated by leukemia cells. The two key functions of the CLRA are its Research Grant Program and its Patient Aid Program.

President: Gilbert A. Schwab
Executive Director: Allan D. Weinberg
Year Established: 1965
Acronym: NLRA

Keywords
Children's Leukemia Research Association; Leukemia; National Leukemia Research Association, Inc.

1439 Children's Liver Alliance

E-mail: mail@liverkids.org.au
http://www.liverkids.org.au

The Children's Liver Alliance (formerly the Biliary Atresia & Liver Transplant Network) is an international, not-for-profit, voluntary health organization that was established in 1995. The mission of the Children's Liver Alliance (CLA) is to empower the hearts and minds of children with liver disease, their families, and the medical professionals who care for them. CLA disseminates educational information about pediatric liver diseases and transplantation via written publications, seminars, and the Internet. CLA provides a support network for families of children with liver disease (both pre- and post-liver transplantation), acts as liaison between families and healthcare professionals, offers networking services, and promotes the importance of organ donation and transplantation.

President: Lisa L. Carroccio (Chairperson)
Executive Director: Kathie DeLuca (Secretary)
Year Established: 1995
Acronym: CLA

Keywords
Alagille Syndrome; Alpha-1 Antitrypsin Deficiency; Bereavement; Biliary Atresia; Byler's Syndrome; Cancer, Pediatric Liver; Children's Liver Alliance; Crigler Najjar Syndrome; Cystic Fibrosis; Galactosemia; Glycogen Storage Diseases; Hepatitis B, Pediatric; Hepatitis C, Pediatric; Hepatitis, Neonatal; Hyperoxaluria; Hyperoxaluria, Primary; Liver Dis-

ease (Children); Organ Donor Awareness; Oxalosis; Transplantation, Liver; Tyrosinemia; Wilson's Disease; Wolman's Disease

1440 Children's Liver Association for Support Services

27033 McBean Parkway
Suite 126
Valencia, CA 91355

Phone: (661) 263-9099
Fax: (661) 263-9099
Toll Free: (877) 679-8256
E-mail: SupportSrv@aol.com
http://www.classkids.org

The Children's Liver Association for Support Services (CLASS) is an all-volunteer organization dedicated to addressing the emotional, educational, and financial needs of families with children affected with liver disease and liver transplantation. Established in 1995, CLASS distributes educational materials about pediatric liver disease; offers a support network for families of children with liver disease via a telephone hotline, newsletters, and educational seminars; provides direct financial assistance to families in need due to their child's liver disease; and funds seed grants for research into causes, diagnosis, detection, treatment, and prevention of pediatric liver diseases. In addition, the association is dedicated to sponsoring educational seminars on the medical and social issues related to liver disease in children; maintaining a database of literature related to liver disease and associated topics; increasing public awareness of the importance of organ donation; soliciting funds from private and public sources; and administering and dispersing such funds to further their mission.

President: Diane Sumner (1995 to Present)
Year Established: 1995
Acronym: CLASS

Keywords
Children's Liver Association for Support Services; Children's Liver Association for Support Services (CLASS); Liver Disease; Liver Disease (Children); Transplantation, Liver; Transplantation, Tissue

1441 Children's Liver Disease Foundation

36 Great Charles Street Queensway
Birmingham, B3 3JY, United Kingdom

Phone: +44 (0) 121-212-3839
Fax: +44 (0) 121-212-4300
E-mail: info@childliverdisease.org
http://www.childliverdisease.org

The Children's Liver Disease Foundation (CLDF) is a voluntary organization dedicated to caring for children and families around the world who are affected by liver disease. Established in 1980, CLDF is dedicated to educating the medical profession and the general public about childhood liver disease; promoting research into early diagnosis, treatments, and cure; providing new facilities and trained staffs; and giving emotional support to children and families affected by pediatric liver disease. CLDF also publishes a newsletter, reports, and brochures; offers a referral service, a database, and a directory.

President: Tom Ross
Executive Director: Catherine Arkley
Year Established: 1980
Acronym: CLDF

Keywords
Alagille Syndrome; Alpha-1 Antitrypsin Deficiency; Ascites; Children's Liver Disease Foundation; Choledochal Cyst; Gilbert Syndrome; Hepatitis A; Hepatitis B; Hepatitis C; Jaundice; Liver Disease; Liver Disease (Children); Pediatric Biliary Atresia; PFIC; Pruritus; portal hypertension

1442 Children's Neurobiological Solutions Foundation

1726 Franceschi Road
Santa Barbara, CA 93103

Phone: (805) 965-8838
Fax: (805) 963-6633
Toll Free: (866) 267-5580
E-mail: info@cnsfoundation.org
http://www.cnsfoundation.org

Children's Neurobiological Solutions Foundation is a national, non-profit, 501(c)3 organization whose mission is to orchestrate cutting-edge, collaborative research with the goal of expediting the creation of effective treatments and therapies for children with neurodevelopmental abnormalities, birth injuries to the nervous system, and related neurological problems. In addition, CNS strives to provide families and healthcare providers with user-friendly access to information and education supporting their decision-making process.

President: Fia Richmond
Year Established: 2000
Acronym: CNS Foundation

Keywords
Autism; Brain Injury; Brain Repair; Cerebral Palsy; Childhood Neurological Disorders; Children's Neuro-

biological Solutions Foundation; Down Syndrome; Neurological Disability; Neurological Disorders; Pediatric Brain Repair; Regeneration; Regenerative Medicine; Stem Cells; Therapy

1443 Children's PKU Network

3970 Via de la Valle
Suite 120 E
Del Mar, CA 92014

Phone: (858) 509-0767
Fax: (858) 509-0768
Toll Free: (800) 377-6677
E-mail: pkunetwork@aol.com
http://www.pkunetwork.org/

The Children's PKU Network (CPN) is a not-for-profit organization dedicated to providing support and services to children with phenylketonuria (PKU), their families, and all those involved in the treatment of this disorder. PKU is a metabolic disorder characterized by severe mental retardation, seizures, and/or other abnormalities that may be prevented through early restriction of dietary phenylalanine. The network serves as a central operational base to assist in the gathering and dissemination of information on PKU and other related disorders, operates a national network hotline to provide PKU families with information about PKU clinics and support groups in their area, seeks to educate legislators concerning the needs of PKU families, and establishes programs for college scholarships, crisis intervention, and research. The Children's PKU Network also provides a variety of educational and support materials through its informational database, regular newsletter, reprints of medical journal articles, pamphlets, booklets, brochures, videos, and materials specifically for affected children.

President: Rhonda Connolly
Executive Director: Cindy Neptune
Year Established: 1991
Acronym: CPN

Keywords
Children's PKU Network; Hyper PHE; Hyperphenylalaninemia; Metabolic Disorders; Phenylketonuria; PKU

1444 Children's Tumor Foundation: Ending Neurofibromatosis Through Research

95 Pine Street
16th Floor
New York, NY 10005

Phone: (212) 344-6633
Fax: (212) 747-0004
Toll Free: (800) 323-7938

TDD: (212) 344-6633
E-mail: info@ctf.org
http://www.nf.org

The Children's Tumor Foundation: Ending Neurofibromatosis Through Research formerly known as the National Neurofibromatosis Foundation, is a not-for-profit, voluntary organization dedicated to improving the well-being of individuals and families affected by neurofibromatosis type I (NF1) and type II (NF2). NF1 is a rare inherited disorder characterized by the development of multiple benign tumors on the covering of nerve fibers and the appearance of brown spots and freckles on the skin. NF2 is a rare inherited disorder characterized by the development of benign tumors on both auditory nerves and in other areas of the body. Established in 1978, the foundation is dedicated to sponsoring scientific research aimed at finding the causes and cures for the neurofibromatoses, promoting the development of clinical activities, creating public awareness, and providing patient support services. In addition, NNFF promotes education of healthcare professionals, offers patient advocacy, and provides referrals to genetic counseling and support groups. It offers information through its directory, database, pamphlets, newsletters, handbooks, and audio-visual aids. The foundation supports several languages including English, Spanish, French, Italian, Vietnamese, Turkish, Arabic, Greek and Chinese.

President: John W. Risner
Executive Director: Peggy Foner, COO
Year Established: 1978
Acronym: CTF

Keywords
Ending Neurofibromatosis Through Research; Children's Tumor Foundation; Neurofibromatosis; Neurofibromatosis Type 1; Neurofibromatosis Type 2; Neurofibromatosis, Von Recklinghausen's; Neuroma, Acoustic; NF 1; NF 2; Schwannomatosis

1445 Chordoma Support Group

E-mail: chordoma@groups.msn.com
http://groups.msn.com/chordoma

The Chordoma Support Group is an international online support group for all those affected by chordomas. These are very rare primary bone tumors that can arise at almost any point along the axis of the spine from the base of the skull to the sacrum and coccyx. Members of the Chordoma Support Group offer each other friendship, support, and information.

President: Ann Wood (Group Manager)
Executive Director: Millie West
Year Established: 2001

Keywords
Chordoma; Chordoma Support Group; Dutch; French; Networking; Support Groups

1446   Choroideremia Research Foundation, Inc.
23 East Brundreth Street
Springfield, MA 01109

Phone: (413) 781-2274
Fax: (413) 785-1830
E-mail: info@choroideremia.org
http://www.choroideremia.org

The Choroideremia Research Foundation, Inc. is an international not-for-profit organization whose membership is comprised of persons with choroideremia, their families, and concerned friends. Choroideremia is a genetic disorder of sight that usually affects males. Female carriers may have mild symptoms without loss of vision. Major symptoms include a progressive loss of the central field of vision and night blindness during childhood. Established in 2000, the foundation serves members worldwide with a newsletter and other educational materials, advocacy, networking and support groups, and by supporting research.

President: Cory MacDonald
Year Established: 2000
Acronym: CHM Foundation, CHMRF, CRF

Keywords
Choroideremia; Choroideremia Research Foundation, Inc.; Choroideremia, Choroiditis Serpiginous

1447   Christopher Reeve Paralysis Foundation
500 Morris Avenue
Springfield, NJ 07081

Phone: (973) 379-2690
Fax: (973) 912-9433
Toll Free: (800) 225-0292
E-mail: info@crof.org
http://www.crpf.org, http://www.paralysis.org

The Christopher Reeve Paralysis Foundation (CRPF) is a national not-for-profit and self-help organization. Founded as a result of the merger of the American Paralysis Association and the Christopher Reeve Foundation. Its mission is to encourage and support worldwide research and activities designed to speed the progress toward a cure for paralysis caused by spinal cord injury and various central nervous system disorders. The foundation has also provided seed money for innovative medical research studies that are largely responsible for recent breakthroughs in the prevention of spinal cord injury and its treatments. In addition, CRPF international conference on spinal injury, providing an important forum for the exchange of information among leaders in the field of spinal cord injury research. The Christopher and Dana Reeve Paralysis Resource Center (PRC) is a program of the CRPF. The PRC is a national clearinghouse of information and referrals on the subject of paralysis from any cause.

President: Kathy Lewis (2004-present)
Executive Director: Susan P. Howley
Year Established: 2002
Acronym: CRPF

Keywords
Amyotrophic Lateral Sclerosis; Ataxia, Friedreich's; Central Nervous System Disorders; Cerebral Palsy; Christopher Reeve Paralysis Foundation; Christopher and Dana Reeve Paralysis Resource Center; CRPF; Guillain Barre Syndrome; Multiple Sclerosis; Paralysis; Spina Bifida; Spinal Cord Injury; Syringomyelia; Transverse Myelitis

1448   Chromosome 9P- Network
P.O. Box 54
Stanley, ID 83278
http://www.9pminus.org

The Chromosome 9p- Network is a voluntary, not-for-profit organization dedicated to providing information and support to parents of children with 9p-syndrome and healthcare professionals who work with affected individuals. 9p-syndrome is a rare chromosomal disorder caused by a partial deletion of the short arm (p) of chromosome 9. The disorder may be characterized by abnormalities of the head and face, a short neck, widely spaced nipples, genital abnormalities, low muscle tone and/or moderate mental retardation. Established in the mid-1980s, the network is dedicated to educating affected individuals and family members, professionals, and the general public. It also supports and promotes research, provides appropriate referrals, and offers a variety of educational and support materials, including reports and brochures.

President: Stephanie Marquis
Year Established: 1984

Keywords
Alfi's Syndrome; Chromosome 9 Partial Deletion 9p; Chromosome 9 Partial Monosomy 9p; Chromosome 9 Ring; Chromosome 9p Deletion; Chromosome 9p Minus; Deletion 9p Minus Syndrome; Chromosome 9P Network; Chromosome 9P- Network; Support Groups

1449 Chromosome 18 Registry & Research Society
7155 Oakridge Drive
San Antonio, TX 78229

Phone: (210) 657-4968
Fax: (210) 657-4968
E-mail: cody@chromosome18.org
http://www.chromosome18.org

The Chromosome 18 Registry & Research Society is a not-for-profit self-help organization dedicated to maintaining a registry of individuals affected by chromosome 18 abnormalities; educating affected families and the public; and encouraging, conducting, and publishing research in areas impacting affected families. The society seeks to link affected families and their physicians to the research community. Established in 1990, the Chromosome 18 Registry & Research Society promotes patient advocacy, provides phone support to affected families, offers appropriate referrals, promotes research and offers educational and support materials. Information is found in our web site, list serves, memos, newsletter, reports, scientific research updates and brochures.

President: Jannine Cody (1989-Present)
Executive Director: Claudia Traa
Year Established: 1990

Keywords
Chromosomal Abnormalities; Chromosome 18 Abnormalities; Chromosome 18 Registry and Research Society; Chromosome 18 Ring; Chromosome 18p; Chromosome 18q; Edward's Syndrome; Monosomy 18; Tetrasomy 18; Trisomy 18 Syndrome

1450 Chromosome 22 Central
237 Kent Avenue
Timmins
Ontario, P4N 3C2, Canada

Phone: (705) 268-3099
E-mail: a815@c22c.org
http://www.c22c.org

Chromosome 22 Central is a non-profit, voluntary health organization registered in both the U.S. and Canada dedicated to networking families of individuals affected by abnormalities of chromosome 22. There are several disorders that may result due to abnormalities of chromosome 22 such as deletion (monosomy), duplication (trisomy), or translocation of chromosomal material from the 22nd chromosome. The symptoms and physical features associated with such disorders depend upon the exact length, location, and nature of the specific chromosome 22 abnormalities in question. Established in 1998, Chromosome 22 Central provides international networking opportunities that enable affected families to exchange information, resources, and mutual support; offers a registry for those affected by chromosome 22 disorders; and links affected families with researchers.

President: Stephanie St-Pierre (1998 to present)
Executive Director: Stephanie St-Pierre
Year Established: 1998
Acronym: C22C

Keywords
22Q11; 22q13 Deletion Syndrome; C22C; CES; Cat Eye Syndrome; Chromosome 22 Central; Chromosome 22, Inverted Duplication (22pter 22q11); Chromosome 22, Monosomy 22Q; Chromosome 22, Partial Tetrasomy (22pter 22q11); Chromosome 22, Partial Trisomy (22pter 22q11); Chromosome 22 Ring; Chromosome 22, Supernumerary Der 22, t(11;22); Chromosome 22, Trisomy Mosaic; DiGeorge Syndrome; Emanuel Syndrome; Phelan McDermid Syndrome; R22; Ring 22; Ring 22, Chromosome; Schmid Fraccaro Syndrome; Shprintzen Syndrome, VCF Type; Trisomy 22 Mosaic; VCF Syndrome; Velocardiofacial Syndrome

1451 Chromosome Deletion Outreach, Inc.
P.O. Box 724
Boca Raton, FL 33429-0724

Phone: (561) 395-4252
Fax: (561) 395-4252
E-mail: info@chromodisorder.org
http://www.chromodisorder.org

Chromosome Deletion Outreach, Inc. is an international, non-profit organization founded in 1992 to provide support & information to individuals affected by all rare chromosome disorders: deletions, duplications (trisomies), inversions, translocations, rings and the sex chromosome disorders (47XYY, 48 XXXX, 49 XXXXY etc). CDO publishes a newsletter quarterly, provides 3 networking programs, 2 listservs, free library to members, and access to its website and medical advisory board members. CDO also has a family help line and voice mail system available 24 hours a day.

President: Linda Sorg
Year Established: 1992
Acronym: CDO

Keywords
CDO; Chromosomal Deletions; Chromosomal Duplications; Chromosome Deletion Outreach, Inc.; Genetic Syndrome; Inversions (Chromosomal); Microdeletion; Monosomy; Rare Chomosome Disorders; Ring Chromosome Disorders; Trisomy

1452 Chronic Granulomatous Disease Association, Inc.

2616 Monterey Road
San Marino, CA 91108

Phone: (626) 441-4118
E-mail: cgda@socal.rr.com
http://www.cgdassociation.org

The Chronic Granulomatous Disease Association is an international, not-for-profit organization founded in 1982. The association provides information on current treatments and medical research related to chronic granulomatous disease (CGD), an X-linked or autosomal recessive immunodeficiency disorder characterized by frequent prolonged fungal and bacterial infections affecting the skin, lungs, genitourinary tract, and mucous membranes of the mouth and intestines. The organization emotional support to people with CGD, their families, physicians, and other organizations; coordinates networking services; has a physician referral service; and maintains a medical library containing medical articles about CGD and patient treatment funding information. The organization also distributes a variety of materials including booklets, guides, the "CGD Resource Directory," a patient questionnaire, a referral guide to medical articles on CGD, and a quarterly newsletter.

President: Mary Hurley (1982-Present)
Executive Director: Unknown
Year Established: 1982
Acronym: CGDA

Keywords
CGD; Chronic Granulomatous Disease; Chronic Granulomatous Disease Association, Inc.; Chronic Granulomatous Disease of Childhood; Database; Gene Therapy; Registry; Stem Cell Transplantation

1453 Chronic Granulomatous Disease Registry

c/o Immune Deficiency Foundation
25 West Chesapeake Avenue
Suite 308
Towson, MD 21204

Phone: (410) 321-6647
Fax: (410) 321-9165
Toll Free: (800) 296-4433
E-mail: idf@primaryimmune.org
http://www.primaryimmune.org

This registry is a project of the United States Immunodeficiency Network (USIDNET) disease registry for the primary immune deficiency disorders. Chronic granulomatous disease is a rare, inherited primary immune deficiency disorder.

Keywords
Chronic Granulomatous Disease; Chronic Granulomatous Disease Registry; Granulomatous Diseases

1454 Chronic Granulomatous Disorder Research Trust (CGD)

The CGD Office
Manor Farm
Wimborne St Giles
Dorset, BH21 5NL, United Kingdom

Phone: +44 (0) 1725-51-7977
Fax: +44 (0) 1725-51-7977
E-mail: cgdresearchtrust@dial.pipex.com
http://www.cgd.org.uk

This United Kingdom charity raises funds for research seeking improved treatment and a cure for chronic granulomatous disorder (CGD), funds the employment of a specialist nurse, supports its members through shared knowledge and experience of this rare disorder, has funded the compilation of a UK CGD Registry and also an extension to the European CGD Registry, holds annual consultants conferences for medical professionals, holds family days, and promotes awareness of CGD. The condition is genetic and is associated with the defective function of certain white blood cells produced by the bone marrow. This results in an inability to 'fight off' certain bacterial and fungal infections. The CGD Research Trust is also the founder of the Jeans for Genes Campaign.

Executive Director: Dr. Liz Nelson, OBE
Year Established: 1991
Acronym: CGD RT

Keywords
Chronic Granulomatous Disease; Chronic Granulomatous Disorder Research Trust; Chronic Granulomatous Disorder Research Trust (CGD)

1455 Churg Strauss Syndrome Association

P.O. Box 671
Southampton, MA 01073

Phone: (413) 862-3636
Fax: (413) 862-3636
E-mail: cssa@cssassociation.org
http://www.cssassociation.org

The Churg Strauss Syndrome Association (CSSA) is dedicated to the identification, treatment, and cure of Churg Strauss syndrome. This is a rare disorder characterized by blood vessel inflammation that occurs throughout the body and may affect multiple organ systems, particularly the lungs. CSSA is operated and supported by volunteer efforts and is a net of patients, friends and medical professionals. The mission of CSSA is threefold: CSSA offers support and guidance to those afflicted with Churg Strauss syndrome through patient networking; it provides education and promotes public awareness of Churg Strauss syndrome through seminars, workshops, publicity campaigns, and literature; and it promotes and supports research to improve treatment and ultimately find a cure for Churg Strauss syndrome and related vasculitic diseases.

President: Jane Dion (2004-present)
Executive Director: Carol Kavanough, MD
Year Established: 2004
Acronym: CSSA

Keywords
Advocacy; Churg Strauss Syndrome; Churg Strauss Syndrome Association; Lobbying; Networking; Research; Support Groups; Vasculitis

1456 Churg-Strauss Syndrome International Support Group

E-mail: garytodd@blackpigs.freeserve.co.uk
http://www.churg-strauss.com

The Churg-Strauss Syndrome International Support Group (CSSISG) is a voluntary organization dedicated to providing information and support to families of individuals affected by Churg-Strauss syndrome. Churg-Strauss syndrome is a lung disorder often occurring as a complication of other disorders. Allergic blood vessel inflammation (angiitis or vasculitis) is accompanied by many inflammatory nodular lesions (granulomatosis) that may be small or granular, and are made up of compactly grouped cells. The age of onset varies from 15 to 70 years of age. The organization facilitates a support network for individuals affected by Churg-Strauss syndrome and their caregivers. The organization's educational materials include reprints of medical journal articles. CSSISG also works to promote awareness of this disorder among medical professionals with the hope that awareness will lead to increased efforts in determining the cause, treatment, and eventual cure of Churg-Strauss syndrome.

President: Sue Todd
Executive Director: Same
Year Established: 1997
Acronym: CSSISG

Keywords
Allergic Angiitis and Granulomatosis; Allergic Granulomatosis and Angiitis; Allergic Granulomatous Angiitis; Churg Strauss Syndrome; Churg-Strauss Syndrome International Support Group; CSS; Vasculitis, Eosinophilic Granulomatous

1457 Cicatricial Alopecia Research Foundation

PO Box 64158
Los Angeles, CA 90064

Phone: (310) 475-2419
Fax: (310) 475-4883
E-mail: info@carfintl.org
http://www.carfintl.org

The Cicatricial Alopecia Research Fund (CARF) is a not-for-profit rare disease organization that provides funds for research to find effective treatments and a cure for cicatricial (scarring) alopecia, a diverse group of rare disorders in which the hair follicle is destroyed and replaced with scar tissue. The result is permanent hair loss. Cicatricial alopecia occurs in otherwise healthy men and women of all ages and is seen worldwide. CARF, in addition to providing funds to research, supports education and advocacy and works to raise public awareness.

President: Sheila Belkin
Year Established: 2001
Acronym: CARF

Keywords
Central Centrifugal; Chronic Cutaneous Lupus Erythematosus; Cicatricial Alopecia; Cicatricial Alopecia

Research Foundation; Dissecting Cellulitis; Folliculitis Decalvans; Folliculitis Keloidalis; Frontal Fibrosing; Lichen Planopilaris; Permanent Hair Loss; Pseudopelade (Brocq); Scarring Alopecia; Tufted Folliculitis

1458 **CJD Aware!**
2527 South Carrollton Avenue
New Orleans, LA 70118-3013

Phone: (504) 861-4627
E-mail: cjdaware@iwon.com
www.angelfire.com/md3/cjdaware

CJD Aware! is dedicated to sharing information and networking to raise awareness of this rare and devastating disease. The organization is involved in education as well as fundraising to enable researchers to continue their search for a cure. CJD (Creutzfeldt-Jakob disease) is an extremely rare degenerative brain disorder characterized by sudden development of rapidly progressive neurological and neuromuscular symptoms.

Executive Director: Christy C. Brom
Year Established: 2001

Keywords
CJD; CJD Aware!; Creutzfeldt-Jakob Disease

1459 **CJD Voice**

E-mail: tunket60@sbcglobal.com
http://www.cjdvoice.org

The CJD Voice is a self-help online support group established in 1997. With approximately 350 members, CJD Voice is aimed at providing information and support to persons dealing with CJD (Creutzfeldt-Jakob disease) in a loved one. Creutzfeldt-Jakob disease is an extremely rare degenerative brain disorder that is considered the human form of mad cow disease. CJD Voice educates the public about CJD and seeks to increase funding for research.

President: Dorothy E. Kraemer
Year Established: 1997
Acronym: CJD Voice

Keywords
CJD; CJD Voice; Creutzfeldt-Jakob Disease

1460 **Cleft Lip and Palate Association (CLAPA)**
332 Goswell Road
First Floor
Green Man Tower
London, EC1V 7LQ, United Kingdom

Phone: +44 (0) 207-833-4883
Fax: +44 (0) 207-833-5999
E-mail: info@clapa.com
http://www.clapa.com

The Cleft Lip and Palate Association (CLAPA) is a registered charity in the United Kingdom and is dedicated to providing information, resources, and support to individuals affected by cleft lip and/or cleft palate, their families, and caregivers. Cleft lip and palate are common malformations that are present at birth (congenital). A cleft is an incomplete closure of the roof of the mouth (palate), lip, or both. These birth defects occur when the pair of long bones that form the upper jaw (maxillae) do not fuse properly during the early development of the embryo. The cleft may be barely noticeable or result in severe deformities requiring surgical correction. CLAPA was established in 1979 and currently consists of 45 chapters operating throughout the United Kingdom. The purpose was to forge a partnership between parents and health professionals. Today, CLAPA's mission has evolved to include organizing local parent support groups; operating a specialist service for parents and health professionals who require help in feeding infants with cleft lip and palate; encouraging and supporting research into causes and treatment; representing the interests of patients by helping to influence national health policy; conducting educational seminars for healthcare professionals and the general public; raising funds for specific treatment and equipment; and raising public awareness of cleft lip and palate through a wide range of informational materials.

Executive Director: Gareth Davies (Chief Executive)
Year Established: 1979
Acronym: CLAPA

Keywords
Cleft Lip; Cleft Lip and Palate Association (CLAPA); Cleft Palate; Hare Lip

1461 **Cleft Palate Foundation**
1504 East Franklin Street
Suite 102
Chapel Hill, NC 27514-2820

Phone: (919) 933-9044
Fax: (919) 933-9604
Toll Free: (800) 242-5338
E-mail: info@cleftline.org
http://www.cleftline.org

The Cleft Palate Foundation was founded by its parent organization, the American Cleft Palate Craniofacial Association, as the public service arm of this professional organization. The purpose of the foundation is to educate and assist the public concerning cleft lip, cleft palate, and other related craniofacial anomalies. The foundation also seeks to encourage medical research in the field of craniofacial anomalies. It operates the CLEFTLINE, a toll-free service that provides information and referrals for parents with newborns who have cleft lip and/or cleft palate and for others affected by these abnormalities. The foundation also offers free brochures and fact sheets on various aspects of these birth defects.

Executive Director: Nancy Smythe
Year Established: 1973
Acronym: CPF

Keywords
Catel Manzke Syndrome; Cerebrocostomandibular Syndrome; Chromosome 4, Monosomy Distal 4q; Cleft Lip; Cleft Palate; Cleft Palate Foundation; CPF; Craniofacial Anomalies; Diastrophic Dysplasia; Fetal Hydantoin Syndrome; Frontofacionasal Dysplasia; Hay Wells Syndrome; IRF6 Related Disorders; Moebius Syndrome; Orocraniodigital Syndrome; Rapp Hodgkin Syndrome

1462 CLIMB (Children Living with Inherited Metabolic Diseases)

Climb Building
176 Nantwich Road
Crewe, CW2 6BG, United Kingdom

Phone: +44 (0) 870-770-0325
Fax: +44 (0) 870-770-0327
E-mail: info@climb.org.uk
http://www.CLIMB.org.uk

CLIMB (Children Living with Inherited Metabolic Diseases) is an international, voluntary health agency located in the United Kingdom and is also the National Information and Advice Centre for Metabolic Diseases. Established in 1981, it is dedicated to furthering medical research into the nature of metabolic diseases in children; encouraging the ongoing investigations of the prenatal diagnosis of these diseases;

providing information, advice and support to caregivers; providing limited financial support grants; and providing information to healthcare professionals. In addition, the organization assists in the care of affected children in hospitals, homes or institutions and educates the public about metabolic diseases. CLIMB networks parents of affected children for mutual benefit and support. It also provides a regular newsletter, brochures, videos and other educational materials.

President: Phil Collins, LVO (2000-Present)
Executive Director: Steve Hannigan
Year Established: 1981
Acronym: CLIMB

Keywords
5-Oxoprolinuria; Abetalipoproteinemia; Acanthocytosis; Achondroplasia; Acidemia, Isovaleric; Acidemia, Methylmalonic; Acidemia, Propionic; Acrodermatitis Enteropathica; Adenosine Deaminase Deficiency; Adrenal Hyperplasia; Adrenal Hyperplasia, Congenital; Adrenal Hypoplasia; Adrenoleukodystrophy; Alcaptonuria; Alexander's Disease; Alkaptonuria; Alpers Disease; Alpha Mannosidosis; Alpha-1 Antitrypsin Deficiency; Alport Syndrome; Amyloidosis; Andersen Disease; Arachidonic Acid Absence of; Arginase Deficiency; Arginino Succinic Aciduria; Argininosuccinic Aciduria; Aromatic Amino Acid Decarboxylase Deficiency; Arterial Calcification of Infancy; Arylsulphatase A Deficiency; Aspartylglycosaminuria; Ataxia Telangiectasia; Barth Syndrome; Bartter Syndrome; Batten Disease; Berardinelli Lipodystrophy Syndrome; Beta Ketothiolase Deficiency; Beta Methylcrotonylglycinuria; Biotin Deficiency; Blue Diaper Syndrome; C1 Esterase Deficiency; Carbamyl Phosphate Synthetase Deficiency; Carbohydrate Deficient Glycoprotein Syndrome; Carboxylase Deficiency, Multiple; Carnitine Deficiency Syndromes; Carnitine Palmityltransferase Deficiency; Carnosinemia; CDGS; Children Living with Inherited Metabolic Diseases; Citrullinemia; CLIMB; CLIMB (Children Living with Inherited Metabolic Diseases); Cobalamin C/G Deficiency; Cockayne Syndrome; Crigler Najjar Syndrome; Cystinosis; Cystinuria; Cytochrome C Oxidase Deficiency; Diabetes Insipidus; Disaccharide Intolerance I; Erythropoietic Protoporphyria; Fabry Disease; Familial Lipoprotein Lipase Deficiency; Farber's Disease; Forbes Disease; French; Fructose Intolerance Hereditary; Fructosuria; Fucosidosis; Galactosemia; Galactosialidosis; Ganglioside Sialidase Deficiency; Gaucher Disease; German; Gilbert Syndrome; Glucose 6 Phosphate Dehydrogenase Deficiency; Glucose Galactose Malabsorption; Glutaricaciduria I; Glutaricaciduria II; Glycogen Storage Disease Type

V; Glycogen Storage Disease VIII; Gottron's Syndrome; Hallervorden Spatz Disease; Hartnup Disease; Hermansky Pudlak Syndrome; HERS Disease; Histidinemia; Homocystinuria; Hunter Syndrome; Hurler Syndrome; Hutchinson Gilford Progeria Syndrome; Hypercalcaemia, Infantile; Hyperchylomicronemia; Hyperglycinemia, Nonketotic; Hyperoxaluria, Primary Type I; Hyperprolinemia Type I; Hyperprolinemia Type II; Hypokalemia; Hypophosphatasia; Hypophosphatemic Rickets; Hypoprothrombinemia; Hypothyroidism; I-Cell Disease; Kearns Sayre Disease; LCAD; Leigh's Disease; Leprechaunism; Lesch Nyhan Syndrome; Leukodystrophy, Canavan's; Leukodystrophy, Krabbe; Leukodystrophy, Metachromatic; Lipidosis, Juvenile Dystonic; Lipodystrophy; Long Chain Acyl CoA Dehydrogenase Deficiency; Lowe's Syndrome; Lysosomal Storage Disorders; Mannosidosis; Maple Syrup Urine Disease; Maroteaux Lamy Syndrome; McArdle Disease; Medium Chain Acyl CoA Dehydrogenase Deficiency; MELAS Syndrome; MERRF Syndrome; Metabolic Disorders; Morquio Syndrome; Multiple Sulfatase Deficiency; N Acetyl Glutamate Synthetase Deficiency; Networking; Neuroaxonal Dystrophy, Infantile; Neurodegeneration with Brain Iron Accumulation Type 1; Niemann Pick Disease; Nonketotic Hyperglycinemia; Olivopontecerebellar Atrophy; Ornithine Transcarbamylase Deficiency; Ornithinemia; Osteopetrosis; Pelizaeus Merzbacher Brain Sclerosis; PEPCK Deficiency, Mitochondrial; Peroxisomal Defects; Phenylketonuria; Phosphoglycerate Kinase Deficiency; Pompe Disease; Porphyria, ALA-D; Porphyria, Acute Intermittent; Porphyria, Congenital Erythropoietic; Porphyria, Cutanea Tarda; Porphyria, Erythropoietic; Porphyria, Hereditary Coproporphyria; Porphyria, Protoporphyria; Porphyria, Variegate; Progeria; Pseudo Hurler Polydystrophy; Pseudohypoparathyroidism; Pyruvate Carboxylase Deficiency; Pyruvate Dehydrogenase Deficiency; Pyruvate Kinase Deficiency; Refsum Disease; Research Trust for Metabolic Diseases in Children (RTMDC); Rett Syndrome; Riley Day Syndrome; Sandhoff Disease; Sanfilippo Syndrome; SCAD; Schindler Disease; Short Chain Acyl CoA Dehydrogenase Deficiency; Sialidosis; Sly Syndrome; Succinic Semialdehyde Dehydrogenase Deficiency; Sucrose Isomaltose Malabsorption, Congenital; Tarui Disease; Tay Sach's Disease; Tetrahydrobiopterin Deficiency; Trimethylaminuria; Tyrosinemia, Hereditary; Valinemia; Very Long Chain Acyl CoA Dehydrogenase Deficiency; Von Gierke Disease; Williams Syndrome; Wilson's Disease; Wiskott Aldrich Syndrome; Wolman's Disease; Xanthine Oxidase Deficiency; Xanthomatosis, Cerebrotendinous; Zellweger Syndrome

1463 C-Mac Informational Services, Inc.
120 Clinton Lane
Cookeville, TN 38501-8946

Phone: (931) 268-1201
E-mail: caregiver_cmi@hotmail.com
http://www.caregivernews.org

C-Mac Informational Services, Inc., is a not-for-profit, 501c3 organization founded in 1995 to help those who provide care for people afflicted with Alzheimer's disease and other related dementias. Alzheimer's disease is a progressive condition of the brain affecting memory, thought and language. C-Mac Informational Services, Inc., is dedicated to providing education and information to caregivers, family members, and professionals involved in the care of patients afflicted with dementia of the Alzheimer's type. It provides information relative to all aspects of Alzheimer's disease and related dementias, and care giving for someone affected by one of these diseases. The services of this organization include an introductory information packet for families of newly diagnosed patients, other informational materials for caregivers and medical professionals, a telephone help line, and resource and referral assistance.

President: Helaine B. McAlonan (Founder, President & Chief Executive Officer)

Keywords
Alzheimer's Disease; C-Mac Informational Services, Inc.; Creutzfeldt Jakob Disease; Dementia; Fahr's Disease; Pick's Disease

1464 CMPD Education Foundation
PO Box 4758
Scottsdale, AZ 85261

Phone: (480) 443-1975
Fax: (480) 443-1154
E-mail: jniblack@mpdinfo.org
http://www.mpdinfo.org

The CMPD Education Foundation provides information, educational materials and support to patients and families affected with a chronic myeloproliferative disorder. These disorders are relatively rare blood diseases that include polycythemia vera, essential thrombocythemia, idiopathic myelofibrosis, chronic myelogenous leukemia, chronic monomyelocytic leukemia, hypereosinophilic syndrome, and mastocytosis. Information about

MPD-Net, an online support group for patients and families, may be found on the CMPD web site.

President: Joyce R. Niblack
Executive Director: Robert L. Niblack
Year Established: 2004

Keywords
Agnogenic Myeloid Metaplasia; CMPD Education Foundation; Chronic Myelogenous Leukemia; Chronic Myeloproliferative Disorders; Essential Thrombocythemia; Mastocytosis; Myelofibrosis; Myelofibrosis, Idiopathic; Myeloid Metaplasia with Myelofibrosis; Myeloproliferative Disorders; Polycythemia Vera; Thrombocythemia, Essential

1465 CMT United Kingdom

P.O. Box 5089
Christchurch
Dorset, BH23 7ZX, United Kingdom

Phone: +44 (0) 870-774-4314
E-mail: secretary@cmt.org.uk
http://www.cmt.org.uk

CMT United Kingdom is a support group for people with Charcot-Marie-Tooth disease, also known as hereditary motor and sensory neuropathy or peroneal muscular atrophy. It is primarily concerned with people affected with the condition in the UK and Europe. The organization produces a quarterly newsletter for members, has an annual conference, and makes leaflets and publications available for members.

Executive Director: Mrs. Karen Butcher
Year Established: 1987
Acronym: CMT UK

Keywords
Charcot-Marie-Tooth Disease; CMT; CMT United Kingdom

1466 CNS Vasculitis Foundation

9930 Morningfield
San Antonio, TX 78250-3743

Phone: (210) 523-8234
E-mail: info@cnsvf.org
http://www.cnsvf.org

The CNS Vasculitis Foundation is a voluntary, not-for-profit rare disease organization that provides information and support to patients and families affected by central nervous system vasculitis (CNSV). CNSV is a rare autoimmune disorder characterized by inflammation of the blood vessels of the brain and spinal cord. It can affect the liver, heart, lungs, and legs, and results in progressive decline of cognitive function and motor skills. Founded in 2004, the CNS Vasculitis Foundation also works to increase awareness of CNSV in the medical community and the public. It raises funds for research, and links patients and their families to doctors and agencies that can help with specific healthcare needs.

President: Marilyn P. Cannefax (2004-present)
Year Established: 2004

Keywords
Behcet's Syndrome; Central Nervous System Vasculitis; CNS Vasculitis; CNS Vasculitis Foundation; Lupus; Networking; Patient Education; Polyarteritis Nodosa; Referrals; Research; Sjogren Syndrome; Support Groups

1467 CNSV Network

769 Cleveland Avenue
Bridgeport, CT 06604

Phone: (203) 367-6599
Fax: (203) 367-6599
E-mail: support@cnsv.net
http://www.cnsv.net

CNSV.net is an Internet resource for people with central nervous system vasculitis. It also serves the families of those affected, as well as the healthcare community. Central nervous system vasculitis (CNSV) is a rare disorder that results in cognitive impairment, fatigue, sensitivity to overstimulation, and other serious problems. Founded in 2001, CNSV.net is a patient-centered, non-commercial, volunteer support service offering support groups, patient networking, and education to patients and the general public.

President: Cheryl Conway
Year Established: 2001
Acronym: cnsv network

Keywords
Angiitis; Autoimmune; Central Nervous System Vasculitis; CNS Vasculitis; CNSV; CNSV Network; CNSV.net; Headache; Isolated Angiitis; PACNS; Primary Angiitis; Stroke; Vasculitis

1468 Coalition for Pulmonary Fibrosis

1685 Bramham Lane
Suite 227
San Jose, CA 95118

Phone: (888) 266-8541
Fax: (408) 266-3289
Toll Free: (888) 222-8541
E-mail: info@coalitionforpf.org
http://www.coalitionforpf.org

The Coalition for Pulmonary Fibrosis (CPF) is a 501 (c) (3) nonprofit organization founded in 2001 to further education, patient support and research efforts for interstitial lung disease, and, specifically pulmonary fibrosis. The CPF is governed by pulmonologists, individuals affected by pulmonary fibrosis, medical research professionals and advocacy organizations.

President: Marvin I. Schwarz, MD (2001-present)
Executive Director: Mark A. Shreve-Chief Operating Officer
Year Established: 2001
Acronym: CPF

Keywords
Coalition for Pulmonary Fibrosis; Idiopathic Pulmonary Fibrosis

1469 Cobalamin Network

P.O. Box 174
Thetford Center, VT 05075-0174

Phone: (802) 785-4029
E-mail: SueBee18@valley.net

The Cobalamin Network is an informal network of parents with children who have been diagnosed with errors in the metabolism of cobalamin (vitamin B12). The Cobalamin Network enables affected families to exchange information, support and resources through phone calls, letters, and videotapes. Some informal gatherings have also been scheduled among affected families.

President: Susan L. Rump (Contact Person)
Year Established: 1988

Keywords
Cobalamin Network; Cobalamin, Inborn Error of Metabolism; Cobalimin B12 Deficiency; Cutis Marmorata Telangiectatica Congenita; Vitamin B12 Deficiency

1470 Cochrane Cystic Fibrosis and Genetic Disorders Review Group

Institute of Child Health
Royal Liverpool Children's NHS Trust
Alder Hey Hospital, Eaton Road
Liverpool, L12 2 AP, United Kingdom

Phone: +44 (0) 151-252-5696
Fax: +44 (0) 151-252-5456
E-mail: cfgd@liv.ac.uk
http://www.liv.ac.uk/cfgd/

Cochrane Cystic Fibrosis and Genetic Disorders Review Group is an international network of healthcare professionals, researchers and consumers preparing, maintaining, and disseminating systematic reviews of randomized control trials in the treatment of cystic fibrosis and other genetic disorders. The group's aim is to help people make well-informed decisions about healthcare with the aid of these reviews. Abstracts (summaries) of these reviews are available free of charge on the group's website. The Cochrane Collaboration is a non-profit organization, established as a company, limited by guarantee, and registered as a charity in the UK.

Year Established: 1995

Keywords
Cochrane Cystic Fibrosis and Genetic Disorders Review Group; Cystic Fibrosis; Galactosemia; Gaucher Disease; Hemophilia; Inborn Errors of Metabolism; Phenylketonuria; Sickle Cell Disease; Thalassemia

1471 Coffin-Lowry Syndrome Foundation

3045 255th Avenue S.E.
Sammamish, WA 98075

Phone: (425) 427-0939
E-mail: CLSFoundation@yahoo.com
http://www.clsf.info

The Coffin-Lowry Syndrome Foundation is a national, not-for-profit, self-help organization that functions as a clearinghouse for information on Coffin-Lowry syndrome and as a general forum for exchanging experiences, advice, and information with other families affected by this rare disorder. Coffin-Lowry syndrome is a genetic disorder characterized by dysmorphic facial features, mental retardation, speech delays, and musculoskeletal abnormalities. Founded in 1991, the Coffin-Lowry Syndrome Foundation seeks to become a visible group in the medical, scientific, educational, and professional communities to facilitate referrals of newly diagnosed individuals and to encourage medical and behavioral research aimed at improving the quality of life and methods of social integration for people with Coffin-Lowry syndrome. The organization maintains a mailing list of families affected by Coffin-Lowry syndrome and publishes a parent newsletter.

President: Mary Hoffman
Executive Director: Same as above.
Year Established: 1991
Acronym: CLSF

Keywords
CLSF; Coffin Lowry Syndrome; Coffin-Lowry Syndrome Foundation

1472 Cohen Syndrome Support Group

45 Compton Way
Middelton, Manchester, M24 2BU, United Kingdom

Phone: +44 (0) 1280-70-4515

The Cohen Syndrome Support Group (CSSG) is an international nonprofit organization dedicated to providing parent to parent contact for families affected by Cohen syndrome. Cohen syndrome is a rare genetic disorder characterized by multiple facial, oral, and eye abnormalities, muscle weakness, obesity, and mental retardation. Children with Cohen syndrome usually have a low birthweight, delayed growth, and obesity of the trunk that occurs during mid-childhood. Other characteristics of this disorder may include an unusually small head (microcephaly), large ears, a high nasal bridge, an abnormally short groove in the middle of the upper lip (philtrum), and prominent lips. Established in 1994, CSSG publishes a quarterly newsletter and an informational brochure entitled "Cohen Syndrome, A Guide For Parents." Comprising about 106 families, the organization is dedicated to providing international networking opportunities for affected families.

President: Sharon Casserley
Executive Director: Cathy Burnett (Assistant Coordinator)
Year Established: 1994
Acronym: CSSG

Keywords
Cohen Syndrome; Cohen Syndrome Support Group; Mirrhosseini Holmes Walter Syndrome; Pepper Syndrome

1473 Colorectal Cancer Network

P.O. Box 182
Kensington, MD 20895

Phone: (301) 879-1500
Fax: (267) 821-7080
E-mail: ccnetwork@colorectal-cancer.net
http://www.colorectal-cancer.net

Colorectal Cancer Network (CCNetwork) is a not-for-profit organization whose main goal is to help patients and families affected by colon cancer, more commonly called colorectal cancer because it affects both parts of the digestive tract, the colon and the rectum. Founded in 2000, CCNetwork provides information, support groups, and assistance in finding resources to patients and affected families.

President: Louise Bales (2003-present)
Executive Director: Priscilla Savary
Year Established: 1999
Acronym: CCNetwork, CCN

Keywords
Advocacy; Anal; Appendiceal; Cancer, Colon; CCN; CCNetwork; Colorectal; Colorectal Cancer Network; Networking; Rectal; Support Groups

1474 Coma Recovery Association, Inc.

8300 Republic Airport
Suite 106
Farmingdale, NY 11735

Phone: (631) 756-1826
Fax: (631) 756-1827
E-mail: inquiry@comarecovery.org
http://www.comarecovery.org

The Coma Recovery Association (CRA) is a not-for-profit organization dedicated to acting as a support group for friends and families of individuals who have survived coma and head injury. Established in 1980, CRA works to provide information and referrals to affected families to offer support and enable them to make informed choices regarding treatment, rehabilitation, and socialization alternatives. CRA is also an advocate for higher quality care, education, and research for individuals and families affected by coma and/or head injury. The association also hosts conferences and offers educational materials including a regular newsletter entitled "Coma Recovery Association" and brochures entitled "Traumatic Brain Injury" and "Neurological Dysfunctions."

President: Robert Werner
Executive Director: Philip Mickulas
Year Established: 1980
Acronym: CRA

Keywords
Brain Injury, Traumatic; Coma; Coma Recovery Association, Inc.; Head Injury

1475 Congenital Adrenal Hyperplasia Trust (New Zealand)

P.O. Box 29-545
Fendalton Mall, Memorial Avenue
Christchurch, 8005, New Zealand

Phone: +64 (0) 3-358-4507
Fax: +64 (0) 3-358-4506
E-mail: CAHNZ@snap.net.nz

The Congenital Adrenal Hyperplasia Trust (New Zealand) (CAHNZ Trust) is a registered trust located in New Zealand. Founded in 1996, CAHNZ Trust provides support and information to New Zealanders affected by congenital adrenal hyperplasia (CAH). This is a group of rare disorders that result from the impaired ability of the adrenal glands to produce vital steroid hormones. CAHNZ Trust provides support groups and patient networking. It publishes a newsletter three times per year.

President: Helen Mann (Coordinator)
Executive Director: Barbara Purdie (Trustee)
Year Established: 1996
Acronym: CAHNZ Trust

Keywords
Addison's Disease; Adrenal Insufficiency; CAH; CAHNZ Trust; Congenital Adrenal Hyperplasia; Congenital Adrenal Hyperplasia Trust (New Zealand); Congenital Metabolic Disorder; Networking; Polycystic Ovarian Syndrome; Precocious Puberty; Support Groups

1476 Congenital Central Hypoventilation Syndrome (CCHS) Family Support Network

71 Maple Street
Oneonta, NY 13820

Phone: (607) 432-8872
Fax: (607) 431-4351
E-mail: VanderlaanM@Hartwick.Edu
http://www.CCHSNetwork.org

The Congenital Central Hypoventilation Syndrome (CCHS) Family Support Network is a voluntary, not-for-profit, self-help organization dedicated to providing support and information to families with children affected by congenital central hypoventilation syndrome (CCHS). Congenital central hypoventilation syndrome is a rare neurological disorder of infancy and childhood characterized by a decrease in respiratory function during sleep. Established in 1989, the CCHS Family Support Network consists of families in the United States, Canada, and across the world who have children with CCHS. The network seeks to promote ongoing medical research into the cause, course, and treatment of CCHS; promotes the continuing education of the medical community about CCHS and affected individuals' special needs; provides appropriate referrals; promotes patient advocacy; and provides members with a phone directory of affected families. The network also produces a regular newsletter and holds family conferences every few years.

President: Mary B. Vanderlaan (1989-Present)
Year Established: 1989
Acronym: CCHs Network

Keywords
CCHS; Congenital Central Hypoventilation Syndrome; Congenital Central Hypoventilation Syndrome (CCHS) Family Support Network

1477 Congenital Heart Information Network

1561 Clark Drive
Yardley, PA 19067

Phone: (215) 493-3068
Fax: (215) 493-3068
E-mail: mb@tchin.org
http://www.tchin.org

The Congenital Heart Information Network, a voluntary health organization, serves an international population, including people in Canada, Europe, the United Kingdom, Australia, Asia, and the Middle East, with educational materials, referrals, advocacy, networking, and support. Its materials and services are designed for patients and families, health professionals, other professionals such as teachers and lawyers, and the general public. It provides information and other services related to all forms of congenital heart defects and syndromes, as well as heart diseases, such as cardiomyopathy and Kawasaki disease that begins in childhood.

President: Mona C. Barmash
Year Established: 1996
Acronym: C.H.I.N.

Keywords
Atrial Septal Defects; Cardiomyopathy; Congenital Heart Defects; Congenital Heart Information Network; Cor Triatriatum; Heart; Heart Block, Congenital; Heart Defects; Heart Disease; Hypoplastic Left Heart Syndrome; Kawasaki Disease; Patent Ductus Arteriosus

1478 CongenitalAdrenalHyperplasia.org

19724 East Pine
Room 149
Catossa, OK 74015

Phone: (918) 604-4039
E-mail: info@congenitaladrenalhyperplasia.org
http://www.congenitaladrenalhyperplasia.org

CongenitalAdrenalHyperplasia.org is an education and support network for individuals and families affected by congenital adrenal hyperplasia (CAH), a group of disorders that result from the impaired ability of the adrenal glands to produce vital steroid hormones. This web-based organization provides services that include links to medical web sites, frequently asked questions and answers, a message board, and archives. Other services include networking and advocacy. This organization serves patients and members of their families, as well as medical professionals.

President: Danny Carlton
Year Established: 1999

Keywords
CongenitalAdrenalHyperplasia.org; voluntary organizations 501C3rare disorder org.

1479 Conjoined Twins International

P.O. Box 10895
Prescott, AZ 86304-0895

Phone: (520) 445-2777
Fax: (520) 445-8043
E-mail: dwdegaraty@myexcel.com
http://www.conjoinedtwinsint.com

Conjoined Twins International (CTI) is a voluntary organization dedicated to providing moral and personal support to families of conjoined twins. Established in 1996 and consisting of 30 family members, CTI has support groups, provides networking services, promotes research, and offers referrals to physicians and hospitals with expertise in working with conjoined twins. The organization also offers educational and supportive materials through its database, reports, and regular newsletter.

Executive Director: Will L. Degeraty
Year Established: 1996
Acronym: CTI

Keywords
Conjoined Twins; Conjoined Twins International

1480 Contact a Family

209-211 City Road
London, EC1V 1JN, United Kingdom

Phone: +44 (0) 207-608-8700
Fax: +44 (0) 207-608-8701
E-mail: info@cafamily.org.uk
http://www.cafamily.org.uk/

Contact a Family (CaF) is a registered charity in the United Kingdom that provides support, advice, and aid to families caring for children with any disability, illness, or special need. The organization's networking program establishes links and enables communication between families affected by the same conditions. CaF has also developed support groups for various conditions, is a non-political lobbyist for patient rights, and is affiliated with hundreds of similar government, genetic, and charitable organizations throughout the United Kingdom. Contact a Family publishes a newsletter, a directory, reports, and brochures for all interested individuals; however, the organization's direct patient/family services are only available to people living in the UK.

President: Al Aynsley Green
Executive Director: Francine Bates
Year Established: 1979
Acronym: CaF

Keywords
Chronic Disabilities; Contact a Family

1481 Continence Foundation (UK)

307 Hatton Square
16 Baldwins Gardens
London, EC1N 7RJ, United Kingdom

Phone: +44 (0) 207-404-6875
Fax: +44 (0) 207-404-6875
E-mail: continence.foundation@dial.pipex.com
http://www.continence-foundation.org.uk

The Continence Foundation is a not-for-profit organization in the United Kingdom for people with bladder or bowel weakness. The foundation provides information and advice to members of the public in the form of a help line (UK only) staffed by specialist nurses, a wide range of literature and a substantial website. Information is also produced for professionals in the field, especially those new to the subject—including a section of the website providing more detailed information. The foundation also has a major campaigning role with national and local government organisations in the UK. It maintains contacts on an international level, especially via the International Continence Society.

President: Professor Linda Cardozo
Executive Director: Dr. Judith Wardle
Year Established: 1992
Acronym: CF

Keywords
Continence Foundation (UK)

1482   Cooley's Anemia Foundation, Inc.

129-09 26th Avenue
Suite 203
Flushing, NY 11354-1131

Phone: (718) 321-2873
Fax: (718) 321-3340
Toll Free: (800) 522-7222
E-mail: info@cooleysanemia.org
http://www.cooleysanemia.org

The Cooley's Anemia Foundation, Inc. is a national, not-for-profit organization dedicated to advancing the treatment and cure of Cooley's anemia, an inherited blood disorder. Established in 1954, the foundation conducts national programs that promote medical research and provides a variety of patient services and educational programs. It has more than 16 chapters throughout the United States and supports the Thalassemia Action Group (TAG), a support group for affected individuals and their families. Services provided by the Cooley's Anemia Foundation include: information on thalassemia, referrals to local medical sources and emergency medical supplies to people in need. Informational materials available from the foundation include videotapes, brochures, and regular newsletters.

President: Frank Somma
Executive Director: Jayne Restivo
Year Established: 1954
Acronym: CAF

Keywords
Anemia, Cooley's; Beta Thalassemia; CAF; Cooley's Anemia Foundation, Inc.; Sickle Cell Disease; Sickle/Thalassemia; Thalassemia; Thalassemia Intermedia; Thalassemia Major; Thalassemia Minor

1483   Cornelia de Lange Syndrome—USA Foundation, Inc.

302 West Main Street
Suite 100
Avon, CT 06001

Phone: (860) 676-8166
Fax: (860) 676-8337
Toll Free: (800) 753-2357
E-mail: info@CdLSusa.org
http://www.CdLSusa.org

The Cornelia de Lange Syndrome—USA Foundation is a non-profit, family health organization. CdLS is a rare, congenital disorder characterized by mental retardation, low birth weight, and distinctive facial features including a small head size, thin eyebrows that meet at midline, long eyelashes, a short upturned nose, and thin down turned lips. Established in 1981, the CdLS-USA Foundation exists to ensure early and accurate diagnosis of the syndrome, and help people with CdLS and others with similar characteristics make informed decisions throughout their lifetime. For information and support purposes, the CdLS-USA Foundation publishes numerous educational materials, including a bimonthly newsletter entitled "Reaching Out," an album of photographs and stories about persons with CdLS, and a "Facing the Challenge" booklet for families new to the syndrome. The CdLS-USA Foundation enlists the support and expertise of professionals from the fields of genetics, medicine, and psychology who comprise its scientific advisory committee (SAC). The CdLS-USA Foundation also maintains a toll-free information and support line, promotes activities and media events that create public awareness of the syndrome, and coordinates a biannual conference for parents and professionals from around the world.

President: Gayle Binney
Executive Director: Julie A. Mairano, M.S.
Year Established: 1981
Acronym: CdLS-USA Foundation

Keywords
BdLS; Brachmann de Lange Syndrome; CDLS; Cornelia de Lange Syndrome; Cornelia de Lange Syn-

drome—USA Foundation, Inc.; Cornelia de Lange Syndrome Foundation, Inc.; De Lange Syndrome

1484 Craniofacial Centre

300 Longwood Avenue
Boston, MA 02115

Phone: (617) 735-6309
Fax: (617) 355-6309
Toll Free: (800) 735-6309
E-mail: elizabeth.leonard@chindrens.harvard.edu

The Craniofacial Centre is a not-for-profit organization dedicated to providing evaluation and treatment of abnormalities affecting the head and facial (craniofacial) area; conducting basic and clinical research; training qualified physicians; conducting family and patient workshops and educational forums; and increasing public awareness. Established in 1972, the Craniofacial Centre assists people with all types of craniofacial abnormalities that are present at birth (congenital) such as cleft lip and/or cleft palate or acquired. The centre also has support groups, engages in patient advocacy, offers patient networking services, and provides referrals.

Executive Director: Dr. John Mulliken
Year Established: 1972

Keywords
Cleft Lip; Cleft Palate; Craniofacial Abnormalities, Acquired; Craniofacial Abnormalities, Congenital; Craniofacial Centre

1485 Craniofacial Foundation of America

975 East Third Street
Chattanooga, TN 37403

Phone: (423) 778-9192
Fax: (423) 778-8172
Toll Free: (800) 418-3223
E-mail: farmertm@erlanger.org
http://www.craniofacialcenter.com

The Craniofacial Foundation of America (CFA) is a not-for-profit organization dedicated to improving the quality of life for individuals and families affected by head and/or facial difference(s) as a result of birth defect, tumor, or trauma-related injury. Established in 1989, the foundation provides financial assistance for food, travel, and lodging expenses to qualified families traveling to the Tennessee Craniofacial Center for evaluation and treatment. The foundation provides

support services for both affected individuals and their families including regularly scheduled support group meetings and a parent-to-parent network. CFA also maintains a toll-free hotline and offers educational materials including brochures on "The History of Craniofacial Surgery" and "Post Traumatic Deformities and Facial Reconstruction in Treacher Collins Syndrome."

President: Larry A. Sargent, MD
Executive Director: Terri Farmer
Year Established: 1989
Acronym: CFA

Keywords
Apert Syndrome; Cleft Lip; Cleft Palate; Craniofacial Foundation of America; Craniosynostosis; Ear Reconstruction; Facial Difference; Hemifacial Microsomia; Hypertelorism, Ocular; Microtia; Moebius Syndrome; Nasal Encephalocele; Orthognathic Surgery; Rigid Skeletal Fixation; Surgery, Craniofacial; Treacher Collins Syndrome

1486 Creutzfeldt-Jakob Disease Foundation, Inc.

843 N. Cleveland-Massillon Road
Suite 7A
Akron, OH 44333

Phone: (330) 665-5590
Fax: (330) 668-2474
Toll Free: (800) 659-1991
E-mail: crjakob@aol.com
http://www.cjdfoundation.org

The Creutzfeldt-Jakob Disease (CJD) Foundation, Inc., a national, voluntary, not-for-profit organization, is dedicated to promoting research into CJD, increasing awareness of the disorder, and reaching out to families with loved ones affected by CJD. Creutzfeldt-Jakob disease is an extremely rare degenerative brain disorder (i.e., spongiform encephalopathy) characterized by the sudden onset of rapidly progressive neurological and neuromuscular symptoms. Such symptoms, which may include lack of coordination, muscle weakness, impairment of vision, dementia, repeated shock-like muscle spasms (myoclonus), coma, and susceptibility to repeated respiratory infections, may result in life-threatening complications less than a year after the disorder becomes apparent. Established in 1993, the CJD Foundation collects and disseminates information on CJD, provides referrals, and offers general information on other human prion diseases such as Gerstmann-Straussler-Scheinker disease, kuru, and fatal familial insomnia as well as suspected prion disorders in animals (such as "mad cow disease").

President: Florence Kranitz
Executive Director: Mark Goldfarb, Chairman of the Board
Year Established: 1993
Acronym: CJD Foundation

Keywords
BSE; Bovine Spongiform Encephalopathy; CJD; CJD Foundation; Creutzfeldt-Jakob Disease; Creutzfeldt-Jakob Disease Foundation, Inc.; Encephalopathies, Transmissible Spongiform; Encephalopathy, Transmissible Mink; Fatal Familial Insomnia; Gerstmann Straussler Scheinker Disease; Kuru; Mad Cow Disease; Prion Diseases; Scrapie

1487 Cri Du Chat Syndrome Support Group
7 Penny Lane
Barwell
Leicester, LE9 8HJ, United Kingdom

Phone: +44 (0) 145-584-1680
Fax: +44 (0) 145-584-1680
E-mail: angie@criduchat.co.uk
http://www.personal.u-net.com/~cridchat

The Cri Du Chat Syndrome Support Group is an international, nonprofit organization located in the United Kingdom. Established in 1991 and consisting of 180 families, the group exists primarily to support parents and caregivers of individuals with Cri Du Chat syndrome and to provide appropriate information on this disorder. Cri Du Chat, a rare chromosomal disorder caused by a partial deletion of chromosomal material from the short arm of chromosome 5 (5p deletion), is characterized by a distinctive catlike cry during infancy, mild to severe mental retardation, and craniofacial abnormalities including widely spaced eyes, a broad nasal bridge, an abnormally small head (microcephaly), and round face. The Cri Du Chat syndrome Support Group is committed to providing support for families and caregivers through a network of area families; raising awareness of Cri Du Chat Syndrome among medical professionals, parents, caregivers, and the general public; raising funds to promote and support ongoing research into the treatment of this disorder; distributing information; and organizing an annual conference and family meeting for affected families and healthcare professionals.

President: Angela Stokes (Coordinator) (1994 to Present)
Executive Director: Ray Clarke (Chairman)
Year Established: 1991

Keywords
Cat's Cry Syndrome; Chromosome 5 Partial Deletion 5p; Cri du Chat Syndrome; Cri Du Chat Syndrome Support Group; Le Jeune Syndrome

1488 Crigler-Najjar Association
3134 Bayberry Street
Wichita, KS 67226

Phone: (316) 685-7477
E-mail: mauckc@msn.com
http://www.criglernajjar.com

The Crigler-Najjar Association, a groups of families who have been affected by Crigler-Najja syndrome, provides information and support to patients and families world-wide who affected by Crigler-Najjar syndrome (CNS), as well as to physicians, researchers, and hospitals involved in providing care for individuals with this or other liver disease. Crigler-Najjar syndrome is a rare metabolic disorder that is caused by a liver enzyme deficiency. There are less than 20 known patients in the United States and less than an estimated 200 worldwide. Children with CNS are unable to eliminate bilirubin from their bodies and therefore must undergo daily 12-hour exposure to special blue lights. The Crigler-Najjar Association has funds available for those in desperate need of financial assistance.

President: Katie Martin
Executive Director: Cory Mauck
Year Established: 2002
Acronym: CNA

Keywords
Arias Syndrome; Bilirubin; Crigler-Najjar; Crigler-Najjar Association; Crigler-Najjar Syndrome Type I; Jaundice; Phototherapy

1489 Crohn's and Colitis Foundation of America
386 Park Avenue South
17th Floor
New York, NY 10016-9804

Phone: (212) 685-3440
Fax: (212) 779-4098
Toll Free: (800) 932-2423
E-mail: info@ccfa.org
http://www.ccfa.org

The Crohn's and Colitis Foundation of America is a not-for-profit, voluntary health organization dedicated to raising funds for research to determine the cause of and the cure for Crohn's disease and colitis. Crohn's disease and ulcerative colitis, collectively known as inflammatory bowel disease, are chronic digestive diseases of unknown cause. While Crohn's disease may affect any part of the gastrointestinal tract and often results in swelling, soreness, and inflammation of layers of the large and/or small intestinal wall, ulcerative colitis affects only the colon (large intestine), causing inflammation of the inner lining and resulting in diarrhea, often mixed with blood, cramping abdominal pain, and other symptoms. Established in 1967, the Crohn's and Colitis Foundation of America seeks to educate affected individuals, physicians, and the public about these disorders. In addition, the foundation establishes support groups, engages in patient advocacy, plays an active role in government legislation, and provides medical referrals. Educational materials produced by the organization include a regular newsletter, reports, and informative brochures.

President: Rodger DeRose
Executive Director: Eugene Kestembaum
Year Established: 1967
Acronym: CCFA

Keywords
Colitis; Colitis, Ulcerative; Crohn's and Colitis Foundation of America; Crohn's Disease

1490 Crohn's and Colitis Foundation of Canada

600-60 St. Clair Avenue East
Toronto
Ontario, M4T 1N5, Canada

Phone: (416) 920-5035
Fax: (416) 929-0364
Toll Free: (800) 387-1479
E-mail: ccfc@ccfc.ca
http://www.ccfc.ca

The Crohn's and Colitis Foundation of Canada (CCFC) is a not-for-profit voluntary health organization dedicated to raising funds for research to determine the cause of and the cure for Crohn's disease and colitis. Crohn's disease and ulcerative colitis, known as inflammatory bowel diseases, are chronic digestive disorders of unknown cause. Crohn's disease may affect any part of the digestive tract and often results in swelling, soreness, and inflammation of layers of the large and/or small intestinal wall. Ulcerative colitis af-

fects the colon (large intestine), causing inflammation of the inner lining and resulting in diarrhea, often mixed with blood, cramping abdominal pain, and other symptoms. CCFC's mission is to help find the cure for Crohn's disease and ulcerative colitis. The foundation provides educational programs for affected individuals, their families, health professionals, and the general public. In addition, it provides educational and awareness initiatives through approximately 75 local CCFC volunteer groups and CCFC community education events, featuring leading IBD specialists. The Foundation publishes a brochure series in both French and English.

President: Nathalie Fradet (2003-2006)
Executive Director: Michael Howorth
Year Established: 1974
Acronym: CCFC

Keywords
Crohn's and Colitis Foundation of Canada

1491 Crouzon Support Network

P.O. Box 1272
Edmonds, WA 98020

Phone: (425) 672-1697
E-mail: crouzons-owner@yahoogroups.com
http://www.crouzon.org

The Crouzon Support Network is a not-for-profit support organization for individuals and family members affected by Crouzon syndrome or other rare disorders characterized by abnormalities of the head and face (craniofacial). Infants with Crouzon syndrome, a rare genetic disorder, may experience premature closure of the fibrous joints between certain bones of the skull (craniosynostosis) and, in some cases, progressive hydrocephalus, a condition in which inhibition of the normal flow of cerebrospinal fluid (CSF) and abnormal widening (dilatation) of certain cavities of the brain (ventricles) may cause accumulation of CSF in the skull and increased pressure on the brain. Affected individuals may also have additional craniofacial abnormalities including widely spaced and/or abnormally prominent eyes (ocular hypertelorism and/or exophthalmos); outward deviation of one of the eyes (divergent strabismus or exotropia); a beak shaped nose; a short upper lip; an abnormally small, underdeveloped upper jaw (hypoplastic maxilla), causing the lower jaw to protrude forward (relative mandibular prognathism); and/or overcrowding of the teeth. Individuals with Crouzon syndrome may also experience visual and/or hearing impairment; vertigo, dizziness, and/or ringing in the ears (Meniere's disease); abnormal sideways curvature of the spine (scoliosis); and/or other abnormalities. The Crouzon Support Network was established in 1997 and currently has approximately 70 members. The network is dedicated to providing understandable information on Crouzon syndrome; providing support and patient advocacy services; and offering a variety of networking opportunities to affected families, enabling them to exchange information, resources, and mutual support. In addition, the Crouzon Support Network offers a listing of craniofacial clinics throughout the United States and Canada, and provides additional referrals.

President: Penny Halverson (1997 to Present)
Executive Director: Same as above.
Year Established: 1997
Acronym: CSN

Keywords
Crouzon Support Network

1492 Cruse Bereavement Care

126 Sheen Road
Richmond
Surrey, TW9 1UR, United Kingdom

Phone: +44 (0) 1819-40-481
Fax: +44 (0) 1819-40-7638
E-mail: info@crusebereavementcare.org.uk
http://www.crusebereavementcare.org.uk

Cruse Bereavement Care is a voluntary organization based in England that offers personal and confidential help to bereaved people and those who care for them. Established in 1959, Cruse has grown to include 194 branches throughout the United Kingdom. As a nondenominational organization, Cruse provides free counseling, social support groups, and information to people of all religions and beliefs (although there is a small membership fee). All counselors are trained by the organization. In addition to speaking English, some staff members are fluent in French, Farsi, Assyrian, Urdu, Hindu, and Punjabi. Cruse also offers training courses for firms and organizations; journals, books, videos, training manuals, and brochures for those interested in participating in Cruse's work; and a newsletter for its members. Cruse also advocates on behalf of bereaved people.

Executive Director: Rosemary Pearce
Year Established: 1959
Acronym: CRUSE

Keywords
Bereavement; Cruse Bereavement Care; Dying; Grief Counseling

1493 CSID Parent Support Group

26521 SE 19th Court
Sammamish, WA 98075

Phone: (425) 394-1066
E-mail: deansl@msn.com
http://www.csidinfo.com

The CSID Parent Support Group is a self-help organization dedicated to providing information and support for children and families affected by congenital sucrase isomaltase deficiency (CSID). CSID is a rare inherited metabolic disorder characterized by the deficiency or absence of the enzymes sucrase and isomaltase. The CSID Parent Support Group was established in 1997, and consists of 343 families worldwide. This organization works with physicians who are experts in treating this disorder, so children can lead normal productive lives. This includes providing guidance related to diet, meal plans, etc. The group is involved in ongoing research for the disorder, including the development of a blood test for diagnosis instead of a small bowel biopsy. Its members supply information as well that is shared with other parents.

President: Mary Slawson, President
Year Established: 1997

Keywords
CSID; CSID Parent Support Group; Congenital Sucrase Isomaltase Deficiency; Diets; Immune Deficiency Disorders; Irritable Bowel Syndrome; Meal Plans; Sucrase Isomaltase Deficiency; Sucrose; Sugar

1494 Cushing's Support and Research Foundation, Inc.

65 East India Row
Suite 22B
Boston, MA 02110

Phone: (617) 723-3674
Fax: (617) 723-3674
E-mail: cushinfo@csrf.net
http://www.csrf.net

The Cushing's Support and Research Foundation, Inc., is a not-for-profit organization dedicated to providing information and support to individuals and family members affected by Cushing's disease and Cushing's syndrome. Cushing's syndrome is a rare endocrine disorder caused by abnormally increased secretion of adrenocortical hormones due to tumors of the adrenal cortex, a tumor in the pituitary gland or ectopic (usually lung or pancreatic) tumors. Established in 1995, the Cushing Support and Research Foundation is committed to increasing public awareness of these two disorders; serving as a source of information and support for healthcare professionals; and raising and distributing funds for Cushing's disease and Cushing's syndrome research. The foundation also enables affected individuals to exchange information, resources, and support through its networking program; provides appropriate referrals (e.g., to support groups); and offers a variety of educational materials including a newsletter, fact sheets and brochures.

President: Louise Pace
Executive Director: Karen Campbell
Year Established: 1995
Acronym: CSRF

Keywords
ACTH; Adrenal Tumor; Cortisol; CSRF; Cushing Support and Research Foundation, Inc.; Cushing's Support and Research Foundation, Inc.; Cushing's Syndrome; Networking; Pituitary Tumor; Support Groups

1495 Cutaneous Lymphoma Foundation
PO Box 374
Birmingham, MI 48012

Phone: (248) 644-9014
Fax: (248) 644-9014
E-mail: info@clfoundation.org
http://www.clfoundation.org

The Cutaneous Lymphoma Foundation, formerly known as the Mycosis Fungoides Foundation, is an independent, non-profit, patient advocacy organization dedicated to supporting patients with cutaneous lymphomas by promoting awareness and education, advancing patient care, and facilitating research. Cutaneous lymphomas are lymphomas that primarily affect the skin at the time of diagnosis. Progression to internal involvement is variable and dependent on the type of cutaneous lymphoma. There are approximately 2,500 new cases each year in the United States.

President: Judy Jones (1998-present)
Year Established: 1998
Acronym: MFF

Keywords
CTCL; Cutaneous Lymphoma Foundation; Cutaneous T-Cell Lymphoma; MFF; Mycosis Fungoides; Mycosis Fungoides Foundation; Sezary Syndrome

1496 Cutis Laxa Internationale
35 Route Des Chaignes
Sainte Marie De Re, 17740, France

Phone: +33 (0) 546-55-00-59
E-mail: MCJLBoiteux@aol.com
http://www.orpha.net/nestasso/cutislax

Cutis Laxa Internationale serves a worldwide audience with the mission of breaking the isolation of patients and families affected by cutis laxa, a rare genetic disorder of the connective tissue. Its specific activities include creating a bank of data to support research, raising funds for research, supporting patient networking, and providing information about cutis laxa to medical professionals, the media and other interested parties. Established in 2001, this organization is based in France.

President: Marie-Claude Boiteux
Year Established: 2001
Acronym: CLI

Keywords
Chalasodermia; Cutis Laxa; Cutis Laxa Internationale; Dermatomegaly; Ehlers Danlos Syndrome Type 9; Elastorrhexis

1497 Cyclic Vomiting Syndrome Association (CVSA)
3585 Cedar Hill Road NW
Canal Winchester, OH 43110

Phone: (614) 837-2586
Fax: (614) 837-2586
E-mail: waitesd@cvsaonline.org
http://www.cvsaonline.org

The Cyclic Vomiting Syndrome Association (CVSA) is a voluntary, not-for-profit, self-help organization dedicated to giving affected individuals, families, and healthcare professionals the opportunity to offer and receive support and share knowledge about cyclic vomiting syndrome (CVS). The organization also promotes ongoing medical research into CVS; increases worldwide public and professional awareness of the syndrome; and serves as a resource center for information on CVS. Established in 1993 by parents of children with CVS and healthcare professionals, the

Cyclic Vomiting Syndrome Association provides referrals, promotes patient advocacy, and enables affected families to network nationally and internationally to exchange information and provide mutual support. In addition, it offers a variety of educational materials to parents, healthcare professionals, and the general public.

President: Diane Babbitt (2003-Present)
Executive Director: Debra Waites
Year Established: 1993
Acronym: CVSA

Keywords
Advocacy; CVS; CVSA; Cyclic Vomiting Syndrome; Cyclic Vomiting Syndrome Association (CVSA); Networking

1498   Cystic Fibrosis Foundation

6931 Arlington Road
Bethesda, MD 20814

Phone: (301) 951-4422
Fax: (301) 951-6378
Toll Free: (800) 344-4823
E-mail: info@cff.org
http://www.cff.org

The Cystic Fibrosis Foundation (CFF) is a voluntary, not-for-profit organization. Its mission is to assure the development of the means to cure and control cystic fibrosis (CF) and to improve the quality of life for those with the disease. CF is a genetic disease affecting approximately 30,000 children and adults in the United States. A defective gene causes the body to produce an abnormally thick, sticky mucus that clogs the lungs and leads to life-threatening lung infections. These thick secretions also obstruct the pancreas, preventing digestive enzymes from reaching the intestines to help break down and absorb food. The mucus also can block the bile duct in the liver, eventually causing permanent liver damage in approximately six percent of people with CF. Established in 1955 and consisting of chapters and branch offices throughout the United States, the CF Foundation funds its own network of CF research centers at leading universities and medical schools.

President: Robert J. Beall, PhD
Executive Director: C. Richard Mattingly
Year Established: 1955
Acronym: CFF

Keywords
CF; CF Foundation; CFF; Cystic Fibrosis; Cystic Fibrosis Foundation; Fibrocystic Disease of Pancreas; Mucoviscidosis; Pancreatic Fibrosis; Research

1499   Cystic Fibrosis Research, Inc.

Bayside Business Plaza
2670 Bayshore Parkway
Suite 520
Mountainveiw, CA 94043

Phone: (650) 404-9975
Fax: (650) 404-9981
E-mail: cfri@cfri.org
http://www.cfri.org

Cystic Fibrosis Research, Inc. (CFRI) is an independent, not-for-profit, voluntary health organization dedicated to offering emotional and educational support to families living with cystic fibrosis (CF). Cystic fibrosis is a genetic disorder that affects many exocrine glands of the body including the sweat glands, salivary glands, and glands within the pancreas and respiratory system. Associated characteristics include susceptibility to repeated lung infections, an impaired ability to absorb fats and other nutrients from food, abnormally salty sweat containing elevated levels of chloride and sodium, and/or other abnormalities. Cystic Fibrosis Research, Inc. is committed to providing a variety of educational and support programs for affected families including mail and telephone referrals and support services, regular membership meetings, parent support groups, CF support groups for ages 13 to adult, an annual conference, and a family retreat. The organization also funds cystic fibrosis research at major research centers in the U.S., supports ongoing gene therapy research, and offers community educational programs.

President: Mike Roanhaus (1998 to Present)
Executive Director: Carroll P. Jenkins
Year Established: 1975
Acronym: CFRI

Keywords
Cystic Fibrosis Research, Inc.

1500   Cystic Fibrosis Trust

Alexandria House
11 London Road
Bromley
Kent, BR11BY, United Kingdom

Phone: +44 (0) 208-646-7
Fax: +44 (0) 208-313-0462
E-mail: enquiries@cftrust.org.uk
http://www.cftrust.org.uk

Cystic fibrosis is the United Kingdom's most common, inherited, life-threatening disease. It affects more than 7,500 people in the UK, and one person in 25 carries the defective gene (more than 2.3 million carriers in the UK). Each week, five babies are born with CF and each week three young lives are lost. At present, there is no cure. The Cystic Fibrosis Trust funds medical and scientific research aimed at understanding, treating, and curing CF. It also aims to ensure that people with cystic fibrosis receive the best possible care and support in all aspects of their lives. Established in 1964, the Cystic Fibrosis Trust has approximately 16,000 members in 300 branches throughout the UK. The Cystic Fibrosis Trust provides a network of support groups for affected individuals and family members, and offers materials including information booklets, audiotapes, books, fact sheets, and video tapes, full details of which can be found on the organization's web site.

President: Rosie Barnes (Chief Executive)
Executive Director: Rosie Barnes (Chief Executive)
Year Established: 1964
Acronym: CF Trust

Keywords
CF; Cystic Fibrosis; Cystic Fibrosis Trust; Fibrocystic Disease of Pancreas; Mucosis; Mucoviscidosis; Pancreatic Fibrosis

1501 Cystic Fibrosis Worldwide

Beukenlaan 133
5616 VD
Eindhoven, 01749, The Netherlands

Phone: +31 (0) 492-259-2760
Fax: +31 (0) 492-259-2701
E-mail: info@cfww.org, cnoke@cfww.org
http://www.cfww.org

Cystic Fibrosis Worldwide works to promote access to appropriate care and education for those people living with the disease in developing countries and to improve the knowledge of cystic fibrosis among medical professionals and governments worldwide. Cystic fibrosis is an inherited disorder that affects several "outwardly secreting" glands, including respiratory, pancreatic, salivary, and sweat glands. CFW supports the search for a cure and promotes international linkage in the sharing of information. The current organization was created in January 2003 after the merger of International Cystic Fibrosis Adults (IACFA) and International Cystic Fibrosis (Mucoviscidosis) Association (ICFMA). Its philosophy is that people whose lives are affected by cystic fibrosis must have equal opportunities to participate in their society no matter where they live.

President: Mitch Messer
Executive Director: Gina Steenkamer
Year Established: 2003
Acronym: CFW

Keywords
CFW; Cystic Fibrosis; Cystic Fibrosis Worldwide

1502 Cystic Hygroma Support Group

55 Jewel Walk
Bewbush
Crawley, RH11 8BH, United Kingdom

Phone: +44 (0) 1293-57-1545

Cystic hygromas are non-malignant malformations of lymphatic vessels, usually occurring around the head and neck region. The Cystic Hygroma Support Group, established in 1983, represents approximately 120 families in the United Kingdom and also has contact with families in Australia and the United States. It publishes a periodic newsletter.

Year Established: 1983

Keywords
Cystic Hygroma; Cystic Hygroma Support Group; Cystic Hygroma and Lymphangioma Support Group; Lymphangioma

1503 Cystinosis Foundation, Inc.

604 Vernon Street
Oakland, CA 94610

Fax: (559) 222-7997
Toll Free: (800) 392-8458
E-mail: jean.cystinosis@sbcglobal.net
http://www.cystinosisfoundation.org

The Cystinosis Foundation is a not-for-profit, self-help organization dedicated to providing information and support to individuals affected by cystinosis, a rare inherited lysosomal disorder characterized by the abnormal accumulation of cystine crystals in tissues throughout the body, which may cause certain organs to malfunction. Three main forms of cystinosis are recognized: infantile nephropathic cystinosis, adolescent cystinosis (also called intermediate or juvenile cystinosis), and adult cystinosis (also known as benign cystinosis). Established in 1983, the Cystinosis Foundation is committed to raising awareness of the disorder in the medical and research communities and the public. The foundation offers support to affected individuals and their families; provides appropriate referrals; engages in patient, family, and professional education; and promotes and supports research. The Cystinosis Foundation provides a directory and a regular newsletter, which includes medical updates, editorials, member feedback, and listings of literature concerning cystinosis.

President: Jean Hobbs-Hotz
Year Established: 1983

Keywords
Cystinosis; Cystinosis Foundation, Inc.; Cystinosis, Adolescent; Cystinosis, Adult; Cystinosis, Benign; Cystinosis, Infantile Nephropathic; Cystinosis, Intermediate; Cystinosis, Juvenile

1504 Cystinosis Research Network

10 Pine Avenue
Burlington, MA 01803

Phone: (781) 229-6182
Fax: (781) 229-6030
Toll Free: (866) 276-3669
E-mail: CRN@cystinosis.org
http://www.cystinosis.org

The Cystinosis Research Network (CRN) is a voluntary, non-profit organization dedicated to supporting and advocating research, providing family assistance and educating the public and medical communities about cystinosis. The CRN's mission is the discovery of improved treatments and, ultimately, a cure for cystinosis.

President: Jose Morales (2002-present)
Executive Director: Colleen Hammond
Year Established: 1996
Acronym: CRN

Keywords
Cystinosis; Cystinosis Research Network

1505 Cystinuria Support Network

21001 NE 36th Street
Sammamish, WA 98074

Phone: (425) 868-2996
Fax: (425) 897-0675
E-mail: cystinuria@aol.com
http://www.cystinuria.com

The Cystinuria Support Network is a national, self-help organization that functions as a mutual aid and support network for people with cystinuria and their caregivers. Cystinuria is a rare genetic disorder characterized by excessive urinary excretion of the amino

acid cystine and other amino acids and the formation of urinary cystine kidney stones. The network was developed to provide a central resource to encourage mutual support and provide practical advice to affected individuals. The organization allows people to come together with their own unique strengths, hopes and concerns to offer support and understanding to one another. Established in 1994, the Cystinuria Support Network publishes a periodic newsletter with input from group participants and medical professionals.

President: Jann P. Ledbetter (1994 to Present)
Executive Director: Same as above.
Year Established: 1994
Acronym: CSN

Keywords
CSN; Cystine Kidney Stones; Cystinuria; Cystinuria Support Network; Networking

1506 Daisy Network

P.O. Box 183
Rossendale
Buckinghamshire, BB4 6WZ, United Kingdom
http://www.daisynetwork.org.uk

The Daisy Network, a premature menopause support group, is for women who have suffered a premature menopause. It provides advice and support for affected women and their families through what can be a devastating, life-changing diagnosis. Premature menopause, also called premature ovarian failure, is defined as the onset of menopause before the age of 40. It can occur for several reasons, including a malfunctioning of the body's immune system, damage to the ovaries, and, in a few cases, an inherited genetic cause. The Daisy Network provides opportunities to share feelings, experiences, and information with others. It also provides information about treatments and research in the fields of hormone replacement therapy and assisted conception. In addition, it seeks to raise awareness of the condition among the medical community and policy-makers.

President: Ms. Susan Thomas
Year Established: 1994
Acronym: Daisy Network

Keywords
Daisy Network; Menopause

1507 Dana Alliance for Brain Initiatives

745 Fifth Avenue
Suite 900
New York, NY 10151

Phone: (212) 223-4040
Fax: (212) 593-7623
E-mail: danainfo@dana.org
http://www.dana.org

The Dana Alliance for Brain Initiatives, a nonprofit organization supported by the Charles A. Dana Foundation, was established as an alliance of neuroscientists dedicated to providing information and promoting understanding concerning the personal and public benefits of brain research. The Charles A. Dana Foundation, a private philanthropic foundation with grant programs in health and education. According to the alliance, approximately one in five Americans is affected by a brain disease or disorder. The Dana Alliance for Brain Initiatives is dedicated to answering questions concerning brain-related research and providing information concerning new developments. The alliance offers a variety of periodicals, newsletters, reports, reference works, and books.

Executive Director: Walter Donway
Year Established: 1993

Keywords
ALS; Alzheimer's Disease; Amyotrophic Lateral Sclerosis; Autism; Blindness; Brain Disorders; Cerebral Palsy; Dana Alliance for Brain Initiatives; Deafness; Depression; Epilepsy; Head Injury; Headaches; Hearing Impairment; Huntington's Disease; Learning Disabilities; Lou Gehrig's Disease; Manic Depression; Multiple Sclerosis; Pain, Chronic; Parkinson's Disease; Schizophrenia; Sleep Disorders; Spinal Cord Injury; Stroke; Tourette Syndrome; Tumors, Brain; Visual Impairments

1508 Dancing Eye Syndrome Support Trust

78 Quantock Road
Worthing
West Sussex, BN13 2HQ, United Kingdom

Phone: +44 (0) 1903-53-2383
Fax: +44 (0) 1903-53-2383
E-mail: support@dancingeyes.org.uk
http://www.dancingeyes.org.uk

Dancing Eye Syndrome Support Trust is an international, voluntary organization based in the United Kingdom that is dedicated to providing information and support to individuals and families affected by dancing eye syndrome. Dancing eye syndrome (also known as Kinsbourne syndrome or opsoclonus myoclonus) is a rare neurological disorder of unknown cause that typically becomes apparent between the ages of one and three years, although in rare cases, it

may occur at any time during childhood or early adolescence. The disorder is characterized by an unsteady gait; rhythmic, involuntary motions of certain areas during voluntary movements (intention tremor); brief, shock-like muscle spasms of the arms, legs, or entire body (myoclonus); and irregular, rapid, horizontal and vertical eye movements (opsoclonus). Formed in 1988 as a support group in the United Kingdom, the Dancing Eye Syndrome Support Trust became a trust in 1997. The trust is committed to enabling parents of affected children to exchange information, support, and resources. In addition, the Dancing Eye Syndrome Support Trust holds regular meetings for members, promotes research, and offers a variety of materials including pamphlets and a regular newsletter.

President: Jane Stanton-Roberts (Secretary) (1994 to Present)
Year Established: 1997
Acronym: DES Support Trust

Keywords
Dancing Eye Syndrome; Dancing Eye Syndrome Support Trust; Encephalopathy, Myoclonic, Kinsbourne Type; Encephalopathy, Opsoclonic; Kinsbourne Syndrome; Myoclonus, Opsoclonus

1509 Danish Apert Syndrome Association (Danmarks Apertforening)

Dronningeengen 17
Vedbaek, DK-2950, Denmark

Phone: +45 4589-0300
Fax: +45 4589-0350
E-mail: soeren@lildal.com

The Danish Apert Syndrome Association (Danmarks Apertforening) is a national, voluntary, not-for-profit organization dedicated to providing information and support to individuals and family members affected by Apert syndrome. Also known as acrocephalosyndactyly type I, Apert syndrome is a rare genetic disorder characterized by premature closure of the fibrous joints between certain bones of the skull (craniosynostosis), causing the head to appear abnormally long and narrow (acrocephaly). Additional abnormalities may typically include a prominent forehead; protruding, widely spaced eyes; and/or webbing or fusion of the fingers and/or toes (syndactyly). Established in 1991, the association is committed to establishing and supporting contacts between individuals and families affected by Apert syndrome; increasing awareness of the disorder; ensuring appropriate, effective treatments; and advocating on behalf of affected individuals with healthcare institutions and professionals. The association also establishes and maintains contacts with other international, not-for-profit organizations and offers family networking services. The association's materials include a regular Danish language newsletter.

President: Soeren Lildal (1991 to Present)
Year Established: 1991

Keywords
Acrocephalosyndactyly Type 1; ACS 1; Apert Syndrome; Danish Apert Syndrome Association (Danmarks Apertforening); Oxycephaly, Syndactylic

1510 **Danish Centre for Rare Diseases and Disabilities**

Bredgade 25
Sct. Annae Passage, Opg. F.
Copenhagen K, DK-1260, Denmark

Phone: +45 3391-4020
Fax: +45 3391-4019
E-mail: chs@chs.dk
http://www.chs.dk

The Danish Centre for Rare Diseases and Disabilities is a nonprofit government organization that is concerned primarily with severe physical or mental disabilities that affect a population of less than one person in 10,000. Most of these disorders are congenital or hereditary in nature. Founded in 1990, the center's objectives are to offer nationwide support to adults and families who have children with rare disabilities or special needs, and to ensure their access to highly qualified information and counseling services; to network affected individuals and family members with other affected families thus promoting mutual support and self-help groups; to network healthcare professionals; and to promote dialogue and research. A wide range of information and counseling services is offered to all who, either as health professionals or as private persons, need information on rare diseases. Target groups are local professionals and authorities involved in the provision and coordination of counseling, treatment, education and support for persons affected by rare diseases.

Executive Director: Elisabeth Kampmann Hansen
Year Established: 1990
Acronym: CSH

Keywords
Danish Centre for Rare Diseases and Disabilities

1511 **David G. Jagelman Inherited Colorectal Cancer Registries**

Cleveland Clinic Foundation
W24-CORS Research
9500 Euclid Avenue
Cleveland, OH 44195

Phone: (216) 444-6470
Fax: (216) 445-1133
Toll Free: (800) 223-2273
E-mail: laguarl@ccf.org or bovak@ccf.org
http://www.clevelandclinic.org/registries

Established in 1978, the David G. Jagelman Inherited Colorectal Cancer Registries is a not-for-profit academic medical center recognized as a National Referral Center and an international resource for diseases of the colon and rectum. Dedicated to identifying, educating, and serving affected individuals, the organization has an educational division, a research institute, and a hospital and outpatient clinic. The organization offers risk assessments and appropriate screening tests; maintains computerized registries of affected individuals and those who may be at risk (e.g., for familial adenomatous polyposis, hereditary nonpolyposis colorectal cancer, and familial colon cancer). It suggests surveillance protocols and reviews surgical options for affected individuals. David G. Jagelman Inherited Colorectal Cancer Registries also provides a variety of educational and support materials including brochures, pamphlets, articles, and a newsletter called "Family Matters."

President: Dr. James Church (Director)
Executive Director: Lisa LaGuardia RN, BSN & Kimberly Bova RN, BSN
Year Established: 1978

Keywords
Cancer, Colon; Cancer, Colorectal; Cancer, Familial Colon; Cancer, Hereditary Nonpolyposis (Colorectal); Cancer, Large Bowel; Cancer, Rectal; Colon Diseases; Colon Polyp; Crohn's Disease; David G. Jagelman Inherited Colorectal Cancer Registries; FAP; Gardner Syndrome; Polyp, Colorectal; Polyposis, Familial Adenomatous; Rectal Diseases; Ulcerative Colitis

1512 **DBA.UK**

71-73 Main Street
Palterton
Chesterfield, S44 6UR, United Kingdom

Phone: +44 (0) 1246-82-8194
E-mail: jayson.whitaker@diamondblackfan.org.uk
http://www.diamondblackfan.org.uk

DBA.UK is the Diamond Blackfan Anemia Support Group, established in Great Britain in 1998 to help people who have been diagnosed with Diamond Blackfan Anemia, and for those with an interest in aplastic anemias, both professionally and otherwise. The aim of the group is to raise awareness of DBA, provide information to sufferers on treatments and therapies, and provide a forum for the discussion of the impact of DBA on everyday life. As a registered charity in England and Wales, it raises funds to aid research into new therapies and cures for this rare condition. DBA is a form of anemia in which the bone marrow produces little or no red blood cells, resulting in severe deterioration of normal life-sustaining functions. The condition affects 600 to 700 children and adults worldwide.

Keywords
Anemia, Blackfan Diamond; DBA.UK; Diamond Blackfan Anemia Support Group

---

1513 DDC Clinic for Special Needs Children
P.O. Box 845
15809 Madison Rd
Middlefield, OH 44062

Phone: (440) 632-1668
Fax: (440) 632-1697
E-mail: info@ddcclinic.org
http://www.ddcclinic.org

The mission of the DDC Clinic for Special Needs Children is to enhance the quality of life for children who have special needs as a result of metabolic and inherited disorders. The clinic encourages and supports early diagnosis and treatment, research, and prevention of such disorders. Established in 1999, it provides services that include support groups, patient networking and education, and referrals.

President: Darla Klein, Board President
Executive Director: Heng Wang, MD, PhD Medical Director
Year Established: 1999

Keywords
DDC Clinic for Special Needs Children; Genetic Disorders; Inherited Disorders

---

1514 Deafness Research Foundation
8201 Greensboro Drive
Third Floor
McLean, VA 22102

Phone: (703) 610-9025
Fax: (703) 610-9005

Toll Free: (800) 829-5934
E-mail: drf@drf.org

The Deafness Research Foundation is a national, voluntary health organization that offers seed research grants to help solve the problems of deafness and other serious ear disorders. It is committed to increasing public awareness about hearing health. The four primary objectives of the Deafness Research Foundation are fostering innovative research and education into the causes, treatments, and prevention of hearing loss and other dysfunctions of the auditory and balance systems; increasing awareness of measures to prevent hearing loss and the need to support research; creating greater understanding about the effect of hearing loss on people's lives; and increasing the number of scientists who are committed to hearing health. The Deafness Research Foundation also publishes materials including brochures on deafness and a grants policy fact sheet.

President: Armand P. D'Amato
Year Established: 1958
Acronym: DRF

Keywords
Auditory Dysfunction; Balance Disorders; Deafness; Deafness Research Foundation; Hearing Impairment

---

1515 DebRA Europe
DEBRA House
13 Wellington Business Park
Dukes Ride
Crowthorne, Berkshire, RG46 6LS, United Kingdom

Phone: +44 (0) 1344-77-1961
Fax: +44 (0) 1344-76-2661
E-mail: debra@debra.org.uk
http://www.debra-international.org

DebRA Europe is an international not-for-profit organization that provides support to patient and families affected by epidermolysis bullosa (EB), a group of rare, inherited skin diseases characterized by recurring painful blisters and open sores, often in response to minor trauma, as a result of the unusually fragile nature of the skin. DebRA Europe serves the common aims of individuals and families whose lives are affected by EB and promotes the provision of services that meet the needs of these individuals and families. In order to reach their goals, DebRA Europe offers support groups, education, research information, referrals, networking, and advocacy to EB patients.

President: Guy Verdot
Executive Director: John Dart
Year Established: 1992

Keywords
DebRA Europe; Advocacy; EB; Epidermolysis Bullosa; French; German; Networking; Research; Skin Disease; South Asian; Support Groups

1516 DebRA—United Kingdom

DEBRA House
13 Wellington Business Park
Dukes Ride
Crowthorne
Berkshire, RG45 6LS, United Kingdom

Phone: +44 (0) 1344-77-1961
Fax: +44 (0) 1344-76-2661
E-mail: admin@debra.org.uk
http://www.debra.org.uk

DebRA—United Kingdom is a nonprofit voluntary organization in the UK dedicated to offering information, assistance, and support to people whose lives are affected by epidermolysis bullosa (EB). EB is a group of genetic disorders in which there is a defect causing the skin layers to separate and blister either spontaneously or at the slightest friction. Symptoms usually are apparent at, or shortly after, birth. Established in 1978 by a group of parents with children affected by EB, DebRA is committed to funding international research into the causes of and possible cures for EB; providing specialist nursing and paramedical staff to support families and professionals; and publishing an extensive range of informational materials for the medical community and the general public. DebRA is also committed to providing specialist equipment or financial support in cases of special need; organizing, where appropriate, holidays for individuals with EB and their families; coordinating and assisting in the development of EB support groups worldwide; and encouraging the development of local treatment in the regions throughout the United Kingdom. DebRA provides referrals including to genetic counseling, engages in patient advocacy and lobbying, offers networking services, and engages in-patient and professional education. The organization offers a wide range of educational materials including fact sheets, brochures, pamphlets, booklets on all aspects of EB for professionals and affected families, bibliographies of medical journal articles published on EB, and videos.

President: Philip Evans
Executive Director: John Dart
Year Established: 1978
Acronym: DebRA UK

Keywords
DebRA-United Kingdom; Acantholysis Bullosa; Acanthosis Bullosa; Bullosa Hereditaria; Dowling Meara Syndrome; Dystrophic Epidermolysis Bullosa; Dystrophic Epidermolysis Bullosa Research Association-United Kingdom; EB; Epidermolysis Bullosa; Epidermolysis Bullosa Acquisita; Epidermolysis Bullosa Hereditaria; Epidermolysis Bullosa Letalias; Epidermolysis Hereditaria Tarda; Goldscheider's Disease; Hallopeau Siemens Disease; Heinrichsbauer Syndrome; Herlitz Syndrome; Hyperplastic Epidermolysis Bullosa; Keratolysis; Kobner's Disease; Localized Epidermolysis Bullosa; Polydysplastic Epidermolysis Bullosa; Simplex Epidermolysis Bullosa; Weber Cockayne Disease

1517 Degos Patients' Support Network

53 Mill Rd Avenue
Angmering, West Sussex, BN16 4HX, United Kingdom

Phone: +44 (0) 1903-78-7737
Fax: +44 (0) 1903-85-9617
E-mail: judith@degosdisease.com
http://www.degosdisease.com

The Degos Patients' Support Network is a self-help group existing to inform and support patients with the diagnosis of Degos disease, also known as malignant atrophic papulosis or Kohlmeier-Degos disease. This is a rare systemic disorder that causes small- and medium-sized arteries to become blocked. It can manifest or progress in two forms. In the first, characteristic skin lesions appear. In the second, lesions may appear in the small intestine, central nervous system, or other organs.

President: Judith Calder
Year Established: 1998

Keywords
Arteriopathy; Atrophic Papulosis; Degos Disease; Degos Patients' Support Network; Gastro Intestinal; Kohlmeier-Degos Disease; Lesion; Neuropathy; Occlusive; Skin; Vasculopathy

1518 Depression Alliance (UK)

212 Spitfire Studios, 63-71 Collier Street, London N19BE, UK
London, N19BE, United Kingdom

Phone: +44 (0) 845-123-2320
Fax: +44 (0) 207-633-0559
E-mail: information@depressionalliance.org
http://www.depressionalliance.org

The Depression Alliance is a not-for-profit organization in the United Kingdom that is run by and for individuals affected by depression and their caregivers. Depression is characterized by persistent sadness with feelings of helplessness and hopelessness. The Depression Alliance was established in 1974 and currently consists of over 3,000 members and approximately 100 self-help groups. The alliance is dedicated to providing information about the nature of depression and how it may be overcome, offering networking opportunities to affected individuals, enabling relatives and friends to understand and cope with the problems that arise when a family member or friend is depressed, and helping members form self-help groups that provide mutual support. In addition, the Depression Alliance works to raise awareness to increase public understanding, cooperates with professionals who care for affected individuals, and promotes and encourages research into the causes and treatment of depression.

Executive Director: Alison Lawrence
Year Established: 1974

Keywords
Depression Alliance (UK)

1519 Depression and Bipolar Support Alliance (DBSA)

730 North Franklin Street
Suite 501
Chicago, IL 60610-7224

Phone: (312) 642-0049
Fax: (312) 642-7243
Toll Free: (800) 826-3632
http://www.dbsalliance.org/

The National Depressive and Manic-Depressive Association (National DMDA) represents the voices of more than 23 million American adults living with depression and an additional 2.5 million adults living with manic-depression, also known as bipolar disor-

der. It is a not-for-profit organization that educates the public concerning the nature of depression and manic-depressive illnesses as treatable medical diseases. National DMDA has a grassroots network of more than 800 patient-run support groups that hold regular meetings across the United States and Canada.

President: Lydia Lewis
Executive Director: Lydia Lewis
Year Established: 1985
Acronym: DBSA

Keywords
Bipolar Disorder; Bipolar Disorder, Mixed; BMD; Depression; Depression and Bipolar Support Alliance (DBSA); Manic Bipolar Disorder; Manic Depression; Manic Depression, Bipolar; National Depressive and Manic-Depressive Association; Unipolar Disorder

1520 Depression and Related Affective Disorders Association

2330 West Joppa Road
Suite 100
Foxleigh Building
Lutherville, MD 21093-4605

Phone: (410) 955-4647
Fax: (410) 614-3241
E-mail: drada@jhmi.edu
http://www.drada.org

The Depression and Related Affective Disorders Association (DRADA) is a nonprofit organization uniting the efforts of persons with affective disorders, family members, and mental health professionals, as well as others. The mission of the organization is to provide information, assistance, and support to those with depression and manic depression by assisting self-help groups. In addition, the association lends support to research programs. Educational materials produced by the Depression and Related Affective Disorders Association includes a variety of pamphlets, books, and videos.

President: Barbara Wolf
Executive Director: Cathy Pollock
Year Established: 1986
Acronym: DRADA

Keywords
Affective Disorder, Unipolar; Affective Disorders; Depression; Depression and Related Affective Disorders Association; Manic Depression, Bipolar

1521   Dercum's Support

P.O. Box 350
Somis, CA 93066

Phone: (805) 386-3125
E-mail: dercumdata@aol.com or dercum@dercum.
org
http://www.dercum.org

Dercum's Support, a not-for-profit, self-help organization, exists to disseminate information on Dercum's disease and support the search for a cause and, ultimately, a cure. Through its Web site, the organization shares information with patients, their families and friends, researchers, medical professionals, and the general public. Dercum's disease is a disorder partially characterized by pressure of fatty deposits on nerves, resulting in weakness and pain. It occurs in both sexes. Weight gain is caused by whatever causes the other symptoms of Dercum's disease. Often, the weight gain is very large and very rapid. "Dercum's fat" is not the same metabolically as "normal fat." The tumors are often angiolipomas, meaning they contain blood. Tumors can and do occur in ALL parts of the body. Arthritis, stiffness and joint pain are common. Many sufferers are severely incapacitated as the disease progresses.

President: Maureen Rocchi
Year Established: 1998

Keywords
Angiolipomas; Dercum's Disease; Dercum's Support; Nerve Pain; Painful Fat; Tumors; Lipomas

1522   DES Action

158 S. Stanwood Road
Columbus, OH 43209

Phone: (800) 337-9288
Fax: (800) 337-9288
Toll Free: (800) 337-9288
E-mail: desaction@columbus.rr.com
http://www.desaction.org

DES Action is a nonprofit organization offering information, physician referrals, and a quarterly newsletter to help those exposed to the synthetic hormone DES (diethylstilbestrol). DES was given to prevent miscarriages. Later, studies showed it caused health problems for the mothers who were given it and the children they were carrying. Research is underway to see if problems extend to DES grandchildren, as well. DES Action offers a toll free hotline (800 337-9288), promotes DES research and encourages public education. DES Action publishes a quarterly newsletter, the Voice, which is of particular interest to those in the DES-exposed community.

President: Patti Negri
Executive Director: Frances K. Howell
Year Established: 1979

Keywords
DES Action; DES, Fetal Effects of; Diethylstilbestrol, Fetal Effects of

1523   Diabetes Insipidus Foundation, Inc.

5203 New Prospect Court
Ellicott City, MD 21043

Phone: (410) 480-0880
E-mail: info@diabetesinsipidus.org
http://www.diabetesinsipidus.org

The Diabetes Insipidus Foundation is concerned with all forms of diabetes insipidus (DI), namely neurogenic, nephrogenic, gestagenic (gestational DI), and dipsogenic. The three major goals of the foundation include promoting research, providing information, and offering support to affected individuals and their families. In the area of research, the foundation strives to increase research dollars by educating the biomedical community about the prevalence of diabetes insipidus and its numerous extra-urinary manifestations. The foundation also strives for more accurate diagnosis, more specific therapy, and, ultimately, the prevention and cure of diabetes insipidus. In addition, the foundation strives for greater public awareness and understanding of the disease by promoting public education and offering informational material such as a quarterly newsletter.

President: Jody Vilschick
Executive Director: Same as above.
Year Established: 1988
Acronym: DiF

Keywords
DI; Diabetes Insipidus; Diabetes Insipidus Foundation, Inc.; Diabetes Insipidus, Central; Diabetes Insipidus, Dipsogenic; Diabetes Insipidus, Gestagenic; Diabetes Insipidus, Gestational; Diabetes Insipidus, Nephrogenic; Diabetes Insipidus, Neurogenic; Excessive Urination; Hypothalamic Disorders; Kidney; Langerhans Cell Histiocytosis; Nocturia; Pituitary Disorders; Polyuria; Septooptic Dysplasia; Water; Wolfram Syndrome

1524 Diabetes New Zealand

P.O. Box 12-441
Oamaru, New Zealand

Phone: +64 (0) 4-499-7145
Fax: +64 (0) 4-499-7146
E-mail: admin@diabetes.org.nz
http://www.diabetes.org.nz

Diabetes New Zealand is a nationwide, non-governmental, non-profit membership organization. Established in February 1962, it acts as a national advocate and encourages local support for people affected by diabetes, raises the level of awareness of this disease, and empowers those affected to choose healthy lifestyles. It also supports research into treatment, prevention, and cure of diabetes. The mission of this organization is to supoprt its members, 41 diabetes societies throughout New Zealand, and health professionals involved with diabetes.

President: Murray Dear
Executive Director: Sarah Thomson
Year Established: 1962

Keywords
Diabetes New Zealand

1525 Diabetes UK

10 Parkway
London, NW1 7AA, United Kingdom

Phone: +44 (0) 207-424-1000
Fax: +44 (0) 207-424-1001
E-mail: info@diabetes.org.uk
http://www.diabetes.org.uk

Diabetes UK is a voluntary organization in the United Kingdom that was founded in 1934. It is dedicated to helping and caring for individuals with diabetes and their family members, representing and campaigning for their interests, and funding research. There are different forms of diabetes, including diabetes insipidus and diabetes mellitus. Diabetes insipidus is a condition in which deficient production or secretion of antidiuretic hormone results in excessive thirst (polydipsia) and excessive excretion of urine (polyuria). Diabetes mellitus is characterized by impaired fat, protein, and carbohydrate metabolism due to deficient secretion of insulin. Diabetes UK has five regional offices across the United Kingdom and a network of over 450 local groups and branches that are run by people living with diabetes. Diabetes UK offers a confidential service that provides information and support on all aspects of diabetes to affected individuals and family members. The service handles inquiries concerning such issues as employment, pregnancy, insurance, driving, diet, and many other areas. The Youth and Family Services department provides services and support to children and young people affected by diabetes, parents, teachers, career officers, and others. The department provides Youth Packs and School Packs; distributes a quarterly newsletter; offers a wide range of holiday events in the UK for affected children and adolescents from six to 18 years of age; holds regional days and annual family weekends; and conducts the Youth Diabetes Project to provide a strong voice for affected individuals from 18 to 30 years of age. In addition, the Tadpole Club is for all children with diabetes and their siblings and friends. Diabetes UK also typically funds approximately 140 to 160 ongoing research projects to investigate the causes, prevention, and treatment of diabetes; provides educational materials for affected individuals and family members; and maintains a web site on the Internet.

President: Jimmy Tarbuck
Executive Director: Paul Streets (Chief Executive)
Year Established: 1934

Keywords
Diabetes Insipidus; Diabetes Insipidus And Related Disorders; Diabetes Insipidus, Gestational; Diabetes Insulin Dependent; Diabetes Mellitus Type I; Diabetes Mellitus, Insulin Dependent; Diabetes Type I; Diabetes Type II; Diabetes UK; Diabetes and Blindness; Diabetes, Adult Onset; Diabetes, Gestational; Diabetes, Insulin Dependent; Diabetes, Juvenile; Diabetes, Non-Insulin Dependent

1526 Diamond Blackfan Anemia Registry

Schneider Children's Hospital
Hematology/Oncology/SCT
269-01 76th Avenue
New Hyde Park, NY 11040

Phone: (718) 470-3610
Fax: (718) 343-2961
Toll Free: (888) 884-3227
E-mail: eatsidaf@lij.edu
http://www.dbar.org

The Diamond Blackfan Anemia Registry (DBAR), associated with the Department of Pediatric Hematology/Oncology at Schneider Children's Hospital, Albert Einstein College of Medicine, is a research organization dedicated to acquiring, analyzing, and disseminating information on Diamond Blackfan anemia to affected individuals, their families, and medical professionals. Diamond Blackfan anemia (DBA), or pure red cell aplasia, is a rare genetic disorder characterized by moderate to severe deficiency of red blood cells. Blood cell abnormalities may be accompanied by an unusual physical appearance, paleness, weakness, and lethargy. The registry was established in 1993 to help increase understanding of the cause(s) of this disease, leading to possible treatment and, ultimately, a cure for DBA. Affected individuals and/or their families enroll in the registry by completing a registration form. This is followed by a detailed questionnaire, which is completed by the affected individual, his or her family, and physician(s). The registry serves as a conduit through which affected families correspond and network for the purposes of mutual support and education. If the family so chooses, their name is released to the family support group and they are placed on the mailing list for DBA newsletters and other communications.

Executive Director: Adrianna Vlachos, M.D.
Year Established: 1993
Acronym: DBAR

Keywords
Anemia, Blackfan Diamond; Diamond Blackfan Anemia Registry

1527 Digestive Disease National Coalition
507 Capitol Court
Suite 200
Washington, DC 20002

Phone: (202) 544-7497
Fax: (202) 546-7105
E-mail: scott@hmcw.org
http://www.ddnc.org

The Digestive Disease National Coalition (DDNC) is a not-for-profit, voluntary organization dedicated to promoting federal investment in biomedical research, representing the digestive disease community in the public arena; and serving as a resource for consumer-directed educational information. Established in 1978, DDNC encompasses 27 patient and professional organizations concerned with diseases of the digestive tract. It provides patient networking services and has several educational materials such as brochures and pamphlets on digestive disorders.

President: Dr. Maurice Cerulli
Executive Director: Dale P. Dirks
Year Established: 1978
Acronym: DDNC

Keywords
Digestive Disease National Coalition; Digestive Diseases; Gastrointestinal Disorders; Stomach Disorders

---

1528 Disability Access 4 Me
38 Harris Avenue
Albany, NY 12208

Phone: (518) 526-2563
Fax: (518) 453-9463
E-mail: rob@access4me.org
www.access4me.org

Disability Access4Me is a web site and virtual support network built by, and for, people with disabilities, their families, friends and caregivers. It provides information, resources, and connections. Systems serving elders and people with disabilities are often complex, fragmented, and overwhelming. Access4Me provides news and information about events, simple answers to frequently asked questions, and links to regional, national and international web sites that may be of assistance. Members can use a matching service to connect with individuals, families, and organizations in their area and around the world to offer and receive support on day-to-day issues.

President: Robert J. Davies
Year Established: 2003
Acronym: Access4me

Keywords
Disability Access 4 Me; General Service Org.; Interational (Specify Areas Served); Other Professional (e.g., Teacher, Lawyers); Others; Service Organization

---

1529 Disability Information & Resource Centre, Inc., South Australia
195 Gilles Street
Adelaide, SA 5000, Australia

Phone: +61 (0) 8-8236-0555
Fax: +61 (0) 8-8236-0566
TDD: +61 (0) 8-8223-7579
E-mail: dirc@dircsa.org.au
http://www.dircsa.org.au/

The Disability Information & Resource Centre (DIRC), Inc., South Australia, was founded in 1982 to provide a centralized, independent organization capable of providing information relating to any aspect of disability. DIRC is an incorporated body funded by the state government. The Management Committee includes people with disabilities and representatives of organizations that provide services to people with disabilities. DIRC's role is to "point people in the right direction" to end the confusion concerning where to go for information about disability and to refer people to the most appropriate places to meet their special needs. The organization offers information services to affected individuals, disability organizations, professionals, government departments, and any member of the public. DIRC provides a computerized information retrieval system as well as a library of books, videos, newsletters, and journals that offer information on disabilities in easy to understand language.

Executive Director: Neil Lillecrapp
Year Established: 1982
Acronym: DIRC

Keywords
South Australia; Accommodation; Assistive Technology; Disability Benefits; Disability Information & Resource Centre, Inc., South Australia (DIRC); Disability Services; Independent Living; Mobility Disorders; Travel Assistance

1530 Disabled Peoples' International
748 Broadway
Winnipeg, Manitoba, R3G 0X3, Canada

Phone: (204) 287-8010
Fax: (204) 783-6270
Toll Free: (800) 749-7773
TDD: (204) 453-1367
E-mail: infor@dpi.org
http://www.dpi.org

Disabled Peoples' International (DPI) is an international, not-for-profit, self-help group that is dedicated to the enhancement of the rights and opportunities of all disabled people. Established in 1981, DPI is dedicated to the philosophy that disabled persons are citizens with equal rights and hence should achieve full participation and equalization of opportunity with their fellow citizens in all societies. Consisting of 114 members, the organization provides several materials including a newsletter entitled "Disability International," numerous reports, and a publications listing. DPI offers several services including networking and lobbying.

President: Venus M. Ilagan
Executive Director: Jorge Aguela, Interim Managing Director
Year Established: 1981
Acronym: DPI

Keywords
Disabled Peoples' International; Disability Information; Disability Services

1531 Disorders of Chromosome 16 Foundation
331 Haddon Circle
Vernon Hills, IL 60061

Phone: (847) 816-0627
Fax: (847) 367-4031
E-mail: Kblange1@aol.com
http://www.trisomy16.org

The Disorders of Chromosome 16 Foundation, formerly the Mosaic Trisomy 16 Registry and Resource Group, is a self-help organization dedicated to providing support and information to families of children with abnormalities of chromosome 16. The foundation, which was established in 1998, serves as a central clearinghouse of information on chromosome 16 disorders for parents and researchers, provides an informational packet consisting of peer-reviewed medical journal articles, and maintains a database on the chromosomal disorder. It is also building a network of individuals who can discuss common problems and concerns encountered by affected individuals, families, friends, and caregivers. In addition, the foundation promotes education of healthcare professionals who may work with affected individuals and families and helps arrange for affected families to assist in research on chromosome 16 abnormalities.

President: Karen Lange (Contact Person) (1998 - Present).
Executive Director: Same as above.
Year Established: 1998
Acronym: DOC 16

Keywords
Disorders of Chromosome 16 Foundation; Mosaic Trisomy 16

1532 Distal Trisomy 10q Families

E-mail: trisomy10q@darylanderson.com
http://www.trisomy10q.darylanderson.com

Distal Trisomy 10q Families are a support web site for families of children with distal trisomy 10q. The primary objectives are: 1) Provide a registry of children and families with 10q so that families can contact each other. 2) Provide a place where families can submit information on their children and experiences.

3) Provide links to related web sites. 4) Provide links to related web sites.

President: Daryl Anderson
Year Established: 1997

Keywords
Chromosome 10; Distal Trisomy 10q Families; Trisomy 10q

1533 Down's Syndrome Association (UK)

Langdon Down Centre
2A Langdon Park
Teddington, Middlesex, TW11 9PS, United Kingdom

Phone: +44 (0) 845-230-0373
Fax: +44 (0) 845-230-0372
E-mail: info@downs-syndrome.org.uk
http://www.downs-syndrome.org.uk/

The Down's Syndrome Association (UK) is a voluntary organization in the United Kingdom dedicated to supporting parents and other caregivers of individuals with Down's syndrome and improving the lives of those with the condition. Down's syndrome is a chromosomal disorder in which all or a portion of chromosome 21 appears three times (trisomy) rather than twice in some (mosaicism) or all of the cells of the body. Although associated symptoms and findings may vary from case to case, many affected infants have abnormally diminished muscle tone (hypotonia); short, broad hands and feet; and characteristic abnormalities of the head and facial (craniofacial) area, including an unusually small, short head (microbrachycephaly), a flattened back portion of the head (occiput), low-set ears, a depressed nasal bridge, and a large, protruding tongue. Individuals with Down's syndrome may also have chronic respiratory infections, heart defects that are present at birth (congenital heart defects), and other physical malformations. The Down's Syndrome Association includes several branches that welcome and support new members, provide access to a range of resources, arrange social and fundraising events, and produce newsletters. The Down's Syndrome Association (UK) also provides literature on Down's syndrome and information and advice on all aspects of the welfare system.

President: Carol Boys (CEO)
Year Established: 1970

Keywords
Down's Syndrome Association (UK)

1534 Dubowitz Syndrome Support

c/o 106 Verndale Street
Warwick, RI 02889-3242

Phone: (401) 737-3138
E-mail: dubowitzsyndrome@netzero.net
http://www.dubowitzsyndrome.net

Dubowitz Syndrome Support helps and supports families, physicians, and other professionals understand Dubowitz syndrome, a very rare genetic and developmental disorder involving multiple anomalies that include growth failure/short stature, unusual facial features, a small head, possible mental retardation, and eczema. With contacts around the world, this support organization provides referrals, educational advocacy, information on travel and lodging near various clinics and medical facilities, funding opportunities for medical visits, advice on assistive technology, information about federal programs, and opportunities to network through its Internet mailing list.

Year Established: 1995

Keywords
Acquired Aplastic Anemia; Dubowitz Syndrome; Dubowitz Syndrome Support; Eczema; Facial Anomalies; Small Stature

1535 Dysautonomia Foundation, Inc.

315 West 39th Street
Suite 107
New York, NY 10018

Phone: (212) 279-1066
Fax: (212) 279-2066
E-mail: info@familialdysautonomia.org
http://www.familialdysautonomia.org

The Dysautonomia Foundation is a national, nonprofit organization founded in 1951 by parents of children with familial dysautonomia, a rare genetic disorder characterized by dysfunction of the autonomic nervous system (ANS). Symptoms and findings may include absence of pain sensation, defective secretion and discharge of tears, unusual fluctuations of body temperature, unstable blood pressure, skin blotching, impaired coordination, abnormally decreased reflex responses, and/or other abnormalities. The foundation has chapters located throughout the United States, Canada, the United Kingdom, and Israel. It provides informational materials and supports ongoing medical research and the clinical care of children with this disorder by maintaining the Familial Dysautonomia Treatment and Evaluation Center at New York University Medical Center in New York City and the Israeli Familial Dysautonomia Center at Hadassah Hospital in Jerusalem. In addition, the foundation is dedicated to funding medical research.

President: David Brenner
Executive Director: Lenore F. Roseman
Year Established: 1951
Acronym: FD

Keywords
Dysautonomia Foundation, Inc.; Familial Dysautonomia; FD; Hereditary Sensory Neuropathy Type III; Hereditary Sensory and Autonomic Neuropathy Type III; HSAN III; HSAN Type III; HSN III; Research; Riley Day Syndrome

1536   Dystonia Medical Research Foundation
1 East Wacker Drive
Suite 2430
Chicago, IL 60601-1905

Phone: (312) 755-0198
Fax: (312) 803-0138
Toll Free: (800) 377-3978
E-mail: dystonia@dystonia-foundation.org
http://www.dystonia-foundation.org

The Dystonia Medical Research Foundation is an international, not-for-profit, voluntary organization dedicated to serving people with all forms of dystonia. Dystonia is a neurological condition characterized by involuntary sustained muscle spasms. Dystonia may affect various parts of the body and can cause abnormal movements and postures. The mission of the Dystonia Medical Research Foundation is to advance research for more effective treatments and, ultimately, a cure, to promote awareness and education; and to support the needs and well being of affected individuals and families. Founded in 1976, the foundation distributes educational materials and informational videotapes, conducts symposia on this group of movement disorders, and sponsors more than 60 support groups for affected individuals and their families.

President: Claire Centrella (2005 to Present)
Executive Director: Janet Hieshetter
Year Established: 1976
Acronym: DMRF

Keywords
Blepharospasm; Dysphonia, Spasmodic; Dystonia; Dystonia Medical Research Foundation; Dystonia, Focal; Dystonia, Generalized; Dystonia, Idiopathic; Dystonia, Oromandibular; Dystonia, Primary; Dystonia, Secondary; Dystonia, Torsion; Torticollis, Spasmodic; Writer's Cramp

1537   Dystonia Society
The Dystonia Society
46-47 Britton Street
London, EC1M 5UJ, United Kingdom

Phone: +44 (0) 207-490-5671
Fax: +44 (0) 207-490-5672
E-mail: admin@dystonia.org.uk
http://www.dystonia.org.uk

The Dystonia Society is a voluntary, national, patient support organization dedicated to promoting greater awareness of dystonia within the medical community and the general public. Dystonia is a neurological condition characterized by involuntary sustained muscle spasms. These can affect various parts of the body and cause abnormal movements and postures. Established in 1983, the society disseminates information on available treatments to individuals affected by dystonia; provides emotional and informational support through a network of approximately 30 support groups; and helps to fund research into the causes, treatments, and eventual cure of dystonia. The society publishes a self-titled newsletter and several informational brochures including "Dystonia: Your Questions Answered," "Hemifacial Spasm: Your Questions Answered," and "Blepharospasm: Your Questions Answered." The Dystonia Society also produces audiovisual aids, offers a referral service, and maintains a database of patients, physicians, and treatment centers. The Dystonia Society is affiliated with the Dystonia Medical Research Foundation USA and the European Dystonia Federation.

President: Frank Gormley
Executive Director: Eileen Gascoigne
Year Established: 1983

Keywords
Blepharospasm; Dysphonia, Spasmodic; Dystonia; Dystonia Society; Dystonia, Focal; Dystonia, Generalized; Dystonia, Idiopathic; Dystonia, Oromandibular; Dystonia, Primary; Dystonia, Secondary; Dystonia, Torsion; Segawa's Disease; Torticollis; Torticollis, Spasmodic; Writer's Cramp

1538 Dystrophic Epidermolysis Bullosa Research Association of America, Inc. (DEBRA)

5 West 36th Street
Suite 404
New York, NY 10018

Phone: (212) 868-1573
Fax: (212) 868-9296
Toll Free: (866) 332-7276
E-mail: scohen@debra.org
http://www.debra.org

The Dystrophic Epidermolysis Bullosa Research Association of America (DEBRA) is a national voluntary health organization dedicated to achieving a cure for epidermolysis bullosa (EB) and improving the care and quality of life for people with this disorder and their families. EB is a group of genetic disorders in which there is a defect causing the skin layers to separate and blister either spontaneously or at the slightest friction. Symptoms usually are apparent at or shortly after birth. The association promotes and supports scientific research on the cause, diagnosis, treatment, and cure of this disorder. DEBRA seeks to meet the unique needs of affected individuals and their families through programs that supply information, assistance, support, and guidance. DEBRA is also committed to raising public awareness about the nature of epidermolysis bullosa and to representing the special concerns of affected individuals and their families to government officials. The organization offers a variety of educational materials.

President: Faith Daniels (1994-Present)
Executive Director: Suzanne J. Cohen
Year Established: 1980
Acronym: DEBRA of America

Keywords
Dystrophic Epidermolysis Bullosa; Dystrophic Epidermolysis Bullosa Research Association of America, Inc.; EB; Epidermolysis Bullosa

1539 Ear Anomalies Reconstructed: Atresia/Microtia Support Group

72 Durand Road
Maplewood, NJ 07040

Phone: (973) 761-5438
Fax: (973) 378-8930
E-mail: atresiamicrotia-subscribe@yahoogroups.com

Ear Anomalies Reconstructed: Atresia/Microtia Support Group is an international, not-for-profit, self-help organization dedicated to providing information and support to individuals affected by congenital ear anomalies such as aural atresia, microtia, and craniofacial microsomia. In affected infants and children, abnormally small, underdeveloped (hypoplastic), and/or malformed (dysplastic) ears (pinnae) with blind ending or absent external ear canals (microtia) may result in hearing impairment (conductive hearing loss). The organization offers networking services, conducts conferences that feature leading plastic surgeons and otolaryngologists, and offers regular support group meetings in the New York City area.

President: Jack Gross (contact)
Executive Director: Betsy Old
Year Established: 1986
Acronym: E.A.R.

Keywords
Ear Anomalies Reconstructed: Atresia/Microtia Support Group; Ear Anomalies, Congenital; Microsomia, Craniofacial; Microtia

1540 EAR (Education and Auditory Research) Foundation

P.O. Box 330867
Nashville, TN 37203

Phone: (615) 627-2724
Toll Free: (800) 545-4327
TDD: (615) 284-7849
E-mail: suzanne@earfoundation.org
http://www.earfoundation.org

The EAR (Education and Auditory Research) Foundation is a not-for-profit organization dedicated to integrating persons who have hearing impairments into the mainstream of society through public awareness and medical education. The foundation administers the Meniere's Network, a national network of patient support groups that provides people with the opportunity to share experiences and coping strategies. Meniere's disease is characterized by episodic vertigo, hearing loss, and ringing or roaring in the ear. Established in 1971, the EAR Foundation sponsors a variety of programs in addition to the Meniere's Network including a medical education program that offers continuing medical education (CME) courses to physicians; the "young ears" program, which focuses on raising the level of awareness among children, parents, and physicians regarding hearing preservation; and the "Minnie Pearl Scholarship Fund," which helps many hearing-impaired high school and college students further their education. The foundation publishes "STEADY," the Meniere's Network newsletter, and several brochures and booklets for both consumers and medical professionals.

Executive Director: Suzanne Wyatt
Year Established: 1971
Acronym: TEF

Keywords
Deafness; EAR (Education and Auditory Research) Foundation; Hearing Impairment; Jervell and Lange Nielsen Syndrome; Mal de Debarquement; Meniere's Disease; Networking; Nystagmus, Benign Paroxysmal Positional; Patulous Eustachian Tube; Support Groups

1541 Easter Seals National Headquarters
230 West Monroe Street
Suite 1800
Chicago, IL 60606-4802

Phone: (312) 726-6200
Fax: (312) 726-1494
Toll Free: (800) 221-6827
TDD: (312) 726-4258
E-mail: info@easterseals.com
http://www.easterseals.com

Easter Seals is a voluntary, nonprofit service organization established in 1919 to serve the needs of children and adults with disabilities and to help them achieve independence. It consists of a nationwide network of 105 affiliate societies that operates approximately 400 centers throughout the United States and Puerto Rico. The society provides rehabilitation services; technological assistance; and disability prevention, advocacy and public education programs. Among its programs and services are the provision of physical, occupational, and speech therapy for children and adults; screening programs to identify vision, speech, and hearing problems, scoliosis, and other disabling conditions; and daycare programs for children with disabilities and their non-disabled peers that foster early acceptance of persons with disabilities. In addition, Easter Seals operates parent resource centers with adaptive toys and play therapy programs for young children; offers educational evaluation services; offers job evaluation, training, and placement for people with disabilities; provides loans of such equipment as braces, crutches, wheelchairs, and hearing aids; provides medical treatment and prosthetic care; and offers head trauma programs for children and adults.

President: James E. Williams, Jr. (CEO)

Executive Director: Don E. Jackson (Chief Operations Officer)
Year Established: 1919

Keywords
Adaptive Toys; Assistive Technology; Cerebral Palsy; Easter Seals National Headquarters; Equipment Loans; Head Trauma Programs; Hearing Impairment; Infants (Stimulation Program); National Easter Seal Society, Inc.; Occupational Therapy; Prostheses; Prosthetic Care; Scoliosis; Speech Impairment; Speech Therapy; Spina Bifida; Summer Camp Adapted For Disabilities

1542 EA/TEF Child and Family Support Connection, Inc.
111 West Jackson Boulevard
Suite 1145
Chicago, IL 60604-3502

Phone: (312) 987-9085
Fax: (312) 987-9086
E-mail: info@eatef.org
http://www.eatef.org

The EA/TEF (Esophageal Atresia and Tracheoesophageal Fistula) Child and Family Support Connection is a nonprofit organization dedicated to providing educational resources as well as emotional and practical support to aid in the daily care of children affected by esophageal atresia or tracheoesophageal fistula. Esophageal atresia (EA) is a congenital birth defect characterized by lack of continuity of the esophagus (which is normally a single passage extending from the throat to the stomach). Tracheoesophageal fistula (TEF) is a birth defect characterized by the presence of an abnormal passage between the esophagus and the windpipe. It was in 1992, when eight families in the Chicago area joined forces to create a support network of parents of children born with EA/TEF. Their shared experiences were made easier with the support of others who faced similar situations and had similar questions. The network of information and support that they created was the seed for the EA/TEF Child and Family Support Connection. The organization, which currently consists of 1,200 members and 10 chapters, has become a national clearinghouse for information on these birth defects. EA/TEF provides a variety of materials through its Family Orientation Packet, a Lending Library of books and videos, educational brochures and flyers, and a regular newsletter. The organization has a national database that provides important information to parents as well as healthcare professionals.

President: Bruce Davis (1997-2000)
Executive Director: Jane Hershoff
Year Established: 1993
Acronym: EA/TEF

Keywords
EA/TEF; EA/TEF Child and Family Support Connection, Inc.; Esophageal; Fistula, TEF; Tracheoesophageal; Tracheoesophageal Fistula with or without Esophageal Atresia; VATER

1543 Eating Disorders Association

103 Prince of Wales Road
Norwich, NR1 1DW, United Kingdom

Phone: +44 (0) 1603-61-9090
Fax: +44 (0) 1603-66-4915
E-mail: info@edauk.com
http://www.edauk.com

The Eating Disorders Association (EDA) is a not-for-profit charity located in the United Kingdom that provides information, help, and support for people affected by eating disorders, particularly anorexia nervosa and bulimia. Anorexia nervosa is an illness of self-starvation; however, bulimia is a psychiatric disorder consisting of binge eating, often followed by self-induced vomiting or purges by the use of laxatives and diuretics. EDA offers support groups, education and advocacy to patients, and family members.

Acronym: EDA

Keywords
Advocacy; Anorexia Nervosa; Atypical Eating Disroders; BED; Binge Eating Disorder; Bulimia; Compulsive Overeating; Eating Disorders Association; Eating Disorders Not Otherwise Specified (EDNOS); EDA; Networking; Research; Support Groups; Welsh

1544 Eating Disorders Association (Australia)

225 Logan Road
Woollongabba, Qld, Australia

Phone: +61 (0) 7-3891-3660
Fax: +61 (0) 7-3891-3662
E-mail: admin@eda.org.au

The Eating Disorders Association of Queensland, Australia, is a non-profit organization funded by the Statewide Health and Non-Governmental Services Unit of Queensland Health. It provides information, support, and referral services for the state of Queensland. Its purpose is to improve intervention, education, and support for people affected by eating disorders, raise community awareness about the prevalence and seriousness of the disorders, and work toward the prevention of eating disorders in our society.

Keywords
Bulimia; Eating Disorders; Eating Disorders Association (Australia); Anorexia;

1545 EB Medical Research Foundation

130 Sandringham Road
Piedmont, CA 94611

Phone: (510) 530-9600
Fax: (510) 530-6100
E-mail: ebmrf@comcast.net
http://www. ebkids.org

The mission of the EB Medical Research Foundation is to relieve the suffering of children with epidermolysis bullosa, a group of diseases characterized by recurrent blister formation as the result of the presence of inherently mechanically fragile skin. The foundation provides funds for medical research and, ultimately, will fund gene therapy for EB children without adequate financial resources. Established in 1991, the foundation also provides advocacy, networking, and educational services.

President: Lynn F. Anderson
Executive Director: Lynn F. Anderson
Year Established: 1991
Acronym: EBMRF

Keywords
EB Medical Research Foundation; Epidermolysis Bullosa

1546 EDS Today

P.O. Box 88814
Seattle, WA 98138-2814

Phone: (253) 835-1735
Fax: (253) 835-1735
E-mail: info@edstoday.org
http://www.edstoday.org

EDS Today is a voluntary, 501(c)3 organization founded in 2000. Its goal is to provide information and support to patients and families living with Ehlers-Danlos syndrome, a group of genetic connective tissue disorders characterized by defects of the major structural protein in the body (collagen). Symptoms and findings include abnormally loose, flexible joints;

thin, stretchy skin; and fragility of the skin, blood vessels, and other body tissues. EDS Today is staffed 100 percent by volunteers. All donations are used to support its mission of providing information and support to people affected by EDS and to members of the medical community working to help them.

President: Christine Phillips (2000-present)
Executive Director: Barbara Uggen-Davis
Year Established: 2000
Acronym: EDS

Keywords
EDS Today

1547 Ehlers Danlos Foundation of New Zealand

Craggy Range Rd
R.D. 12
Havelock North
Hawkes Bay, New Zealand

Phone: +64 (0) 6-874-7799
Fax: +64 (0) 6-874-7799
E-mail: flopsy@ihug.co.nz
http://www.edfnz.org.nz

The Ehlers Danlos Foundation of New Zealand provides support and information to the families and sufferers of Ehlers Danlos syndrome. This is a group of hereditary connective tissue disorders characterized by defects of the major structural protein in the body. Symptoms and findings may include abnormally loose, flexible joints that may easily become dislocated; loose, thin, stretchy skin; and unusual fragility of the skin, blood vessels, and membranes. The foundation provides information to the public and the medical community about Ehlers Danlos syndrome and other related connective tissue disorders.

Executive Director: Jen Longshaw
Year Established: 1995
Acronym: EDFNZ

Keywords
Ehlers Danlos Foundation of New Zealand

1548 Ehlers-Danlos National Foundation (EDNF)

3200 Wilshire Boulevard.
Suite 1601
South Tower
Los Angeles, CA 90010

Phone: (213) 368-3800
Fax: (213) 427-0057
Toll Free: (800) 956-2902
E-mail: staff@ednf.org
http://www.ednf.org

Ehlers-Danlos National Foundation is a voluntary, self-help, not-for-profit organization that is dedicated to creating resources for the Ehlers-Danlos syndrome (EDS) community. Ehlers-Danlos syndrome is a group of inherited connective tissue disorders characterized by abnormalities of the skin, ligaments, and internal organs. Although symptoms and physical features may vary greatly depending upon the specific form of EDS present, many affected individuals may have thin, fragile, hyperextensible skin that may bruise easily; abnormally loose joints that are prone to dislocation; and widespread tissue fragility with bleeding and poor healing of wounds. Established in 1985, the foundation serves as an informational link to the medical and research community on behalf of people who have been personally affected EDS. EDNF supports medical research, produces educational and support materials and a quarterly newsletter, holds annual conference, and has 44 local groups which provide support for the EDS community throughout the country.

President: Andrew McCluskey
Year Established: 1985
Acronym: EDNF

Keywords
Cutis Laxa; EDS; Ehlers-Danlos National Foundation (EDNF); Ehlers Danlos Syndrome; Ehlers Danlos Syndrome Type I Gravis; Ehlers Danlos Syndrome Type II Mitis; Ehlers Danlos Syndrome Type V (X-Linked); Ehlers Danlos Syndrome Type VI Ocular Scoliotic; Ehlers Danlos Syndrome Type VIII Periodontal; Ehlers Danlos Syndrome Type IX Occipital Horn; Ehlers Danlos Syndrome Type X Fibronectic Platelet Defect; Ehlers Danlos Syndrome-Type III Benign Hypermobility; Ehlers Danlos Syndrome-Type IV Ecchymotic; Ehlers Danlos Syndrome-Type VII Arthrochalasis Multiplex Congenita; Ehlers Danlos Syndrome-Type Arthrochalsia; Ehlers Danlos Syndrome-Type Classical; Ehlers Danlos Syndrome-Type Dermatosparaxis; Ehlers Danlos Syndrome-Type Hypermobility; Ehlers Danlos Syndrome-Type Kyphoscliosis; Ehlers Danlos Syndrome-Type Vascular; Ehlers-Danlos National Foundation; Fibronectic Platelet Defect; Joint Hypermobility Syndrome; Service Organization

1549 Ehlers-Danlos Syndrome UK Support Group

P.O. Box 337
Aldershot, GU12 6WZ, United Kingdom

Phone: +44 (0) 1252-69-0940
E-mail: director@ehlers-danlos.org
http://www.ehlers-danlos.org

The Ehlers-Danlos Syndrome UK Support Group provides worldwide help and advice to patients and physicians alike. Information and publications are available online, as well as links to other web sites. Ehlers-Danlos syndrome is a group of hereditary connective tissue disorders characterized by defects of the major structural protein in the body (collagen). Established in 1990, the support group is a voluntary organization providing information and encouragement.

President: Tony Vause
Year Established: 1990
Acronym: EDS Worldwide Support Group

Keywords
Collagen Disease; EDS; Ehlers Danlos Syndrome; Ehlers Danlos Syndrome UK Support Group; Hypermobility

1550 Ellis Van Creveld Support Group

17 Bridlewood Trail
Honeoye Falls, NY 14472

Phone: (585) 624-8277
E-mail: olesikj@yahoo.com

The Ellis Van Creveld Support Group (EVCSG) is an international, self-help organization dedicated to providing information, support, and resources to individuals with Ellis Van Creveld syndrome and their families. Ellis Van Creveld syndrome is a rare genetic disorder characterized by short stature due to abnormal shortness of the arms and legs (short limb dwarfism); a deformity in which the legs are abnormally curved inward and the ankles are widely separated (genu valgum); the presence of extra fingers and/or toes (polydactyly); underdeveloped (dysplastic) fingernails; and/or, in some cases, heart abnormalities (congenital heart defects). The disorder is inherited as an autosomal recessive trait. The Ellis Van Creveld Support Group was established in 1997 and currently has approximately 12 members. The group is committed to providing support to parents of children with Ellis Van Creveld syndrome, particularly those with newly diagnosed infants or children; searching for and supporting other affected families;

obtaining and disseminating information on the disorder; and providing appropriate referrals. The Ellis Van Creveld Support Group also offers networking opportunities including e-mail discussion groups that enable affected families to exchange information and resources.

President: Joseph T. Olesik
Year Established: 1997
Acronym: EVCSG

Keywords
Ellis Van Creveld Support Group; Ellis Van Creveld Syndrome; EVCSG

1551 Ellis-van Creveld Syndrome Web Site

E-mail: evc@crydee.plus.com
http://www.ellisvancreveld.co.uk

The Ellis-van Creveld Syndrome Web Site is dedicated to providing parents of children with Ellis-van Creveld syndrome with information, links to other resources, and support. It is also associated with an online support group forum (http://groups.yahoo.com/group/EvCParents/). Ellis-Van Creveld syndrome is a rare genetic disorder characterized by short limb dwarfism, additional fingers and/or toes (polydactyly), abnormal development of fingernails and, in over half of the cases, congenital heart defects. This site may also be helpful to health professionals and other professionals who work with children who have this condition.

President: Kate Lawrence (2005-present)
Year Established: 2005

Keywords
Chondroectodermal Dysplasia; Ellis-van Creveld Syndrome; Ellis-van Creveld Syndrome Web Site; Ellis-van Creveld Website; EvC; Mesoectodermal Dysplasia; Networking; Support Groups

1552 Encephalitis Global

1638 Pierard Road
North Vancouver
British Columbia, V7J 1Y2, Canada

Phone: (604) -98-0-22
Fax: (604) 904-0809
E-mail: wendystation@shaw.ca
http://www.encephalitisglobal.com

Encephalitis Global offers information and support to survivors of encephalitis, which refers to inflammation of the brain, loved ones and caregivers. This organization also welcomes inquiries from people who simply wish to understand more about encephalitis.

President: Wendy Station
Year Established: 2000

Keywords
ADEM; Encephalitis; Encephalitis Global; Herpes Simplex Encephalitis; LaCrosse Mosquito-borne Encephalitis; Ramussens Seizure; St. Louis Viral Encephalitis; West Nile Virus

1553 Encephalitis Society

7B Saville Street
Malton, North Yorkshire, YO17 7LL, United Kingdom

Phone: +44 (0) 1652-62-5583
E-mail: mail@encephalitis.info
http://www.encephalitis.info

The aim of the Encephalitis Society is to improve the quality of life of those affected by encephalitis by providing support and encouragement, promoting a high quality of services, supporting research, and raising general awareness of this disease and its subsequent problems. In general, "encephalitis" means inflammation of the brain, but the term often is used to refer specifically to inflammation caused by a virus and resulting in severe, possibly life-threatening disease.

Executive Director: Elaine Dowell
Year Established: 1994

Keywords
ADEM; Brain Virus; Encephalitis; Encephalitis Society; Encephalitis, Japanese; Encephalitis, Rasmussen'; Herpes Simplex Encephalitis; Infectious Encephalitis; Para-infectious Encephalitis; Post-infectious Encephalitis; Subacute Sclerosing Pan-encephalitis; Viral Encephalitis; West Nile Encephalitis

1554 Endometriosis Association

International Headquarters
8585 North 76th Place
Milwaukee, WI 53223

Phone: (414) 355-2200
Fax: (414) 355-6065
Toll Free: (800) 992-3636
E-mail: endo@endometriosisassn.org
http://www.endometriosisassn.org

The Endometriosis Association is a nonprofit, self-help organization dedicated to providing education, support, and research for girls and women with endometriosis and their loved ones. Endometriosis is a hormone and immune system disease affecting approximately 5.5 million girls and women in North America. The name comes from the word endometrium, which is the lining of the uterus that builds up and sheds each month with the menstrual cycle. In endometriosis, tissue like that of the endometrium occurs outside the uterus. Endometriosis is a leading cause of infertility and disability in women. Several other immune diseases and some forms of cancers are more common in women with endometriosis. The flagship of the association's research program is the Endometriosis Association Research Program at Vanderbilt University. The association publishes books, brochures, video and audiotapes and CDs, and provides support programs including crisis call listeners and local support groups.

President: Mary Lou Ballweg (1980 to Present).
Year Established: 1980
Acronym: EA

Keywords
Endometrial Growths; Endometrial Implants; Endometriosis; Endometriosis Association

1555 Epilepsy Canada

1470 Peel Street
Suite 745
Montreal
Quebec, H3A 1T1, Canada

Phone: (514) 845-7855
Fax: (514) 845-7866
Toll Free: (877) 734-0873
E-mail: epilepsy@epilepsy.ca
http://www.epilepsy.ca

Epilepsy Canada (EC), established in 1966, is a not-for-profit organization dedicated to enhancing the quality of life for persons affected by epilepsy through promotion and support of research and facilitation of education and awareness initiatives that build understanding and acceptance of epilepsy. Consisting of 34 members, the organization produces educational materials including a newsletter entitled "Lumina," a pamphlet entitled "Your Medication for Epilepsy," and brochures entitled "Epilepsy: Answers to Your Questions," "Seizures and First Aid," "Seizures and Seniors," "Epilepsy and Children: What Parents Need To Know" and "Teens & Epilepsy."

President: Timothy Ryan
Executive Director: Denise Crepin
Year Established: 1966
Acronym: EC

Keywords
Convulsions; Epilepsy; Epilepsy Canada; Seizure Disorders; Seizures

1556 Epilepsy Foundation

4351 Garden City Drive
Landover, MD 20785

Phone: (301) 459-3700
Fax: (301) 577-2684
Toll Free: (800) 332-1000
TDD: (800) 332-2070
E-mail: postmaster@efa.org
http://www.epilepsyfoundation.org

The Epilepsy Foundation (formerly the Epilepsy Foundation of America) is a nonprofit organization with the goal of ensuring that people with seizures are able to participate in all life experiences. It has programs of research, education, advocacy and services. Established in 1968, the foundation has national offices in metropolitan Washington, DC, and a network of local affiliated foundations with offices in about 100 communities. National programs include a toll-free information service, information-rich website, research grants and fellowships, legal and legislative advocacy programs, Epilepsy Gene Discover Project, women's health initiative, and career choice and employment assistance. Local programs include outreach to schools and the community, support groups, camps, employment services, counseling, and information and referral. The foundation provides informational materials to the public and healthcare professionals. The National Epilepsy Library at (800) 332-4050 provides information to professionals and the public by means of computer access to major medical collections.

President: William E. Braunlich
Executive Director: Eric R. Hargis, President and CEO
Year Established: 1968
Acronym: EFA

Keywords
Audio-Visual Aids; Epilepsy; Epilepsy Foundation; Epilepsy Foundation of America; Seizure Disorders; Seizures

1557 Epilepsy Foundation of Victoria

818-824 Burke Road
Camberwell
Victoria, 3124, Australia

Phone: +61 (0) 3-9813-9111
Fax: +61 (0) 3-9882-7159

Toll Free: 1 (300) 852-853
E-mail: epilepsy@epilepsy.asn.au
http://www.epinet.org.au

The Epilepsy Foundation of Victoria is a voluntary organization in Australia dedicated to enhancing the quality of the lives of people living with epilepsy, a group of neurologic disorders characterized by sudden, recurrent episodes of uncontrolled electrochemical activity in the brain (seizures). The foundation was founded in 1964 and currently consists of six chapters. Its mission is to provide a comprehensive range of services and programs to meet the needs of individuals affected by epilepsy. These include public education programs, advocacy, referral services, employment programs, recreational support, and individual and group counseling. The foundation also promotes and supports medical and psychosocial research, conducts parent education workshops and support groups, and offers group forums that enable affected individuals and family members to exchange information and support. In addition, the Epilepsy Foundation of Victoria produces comprehensive brochures, manuals, and educational videos on epilepsy; publishes a quarterly newsletter entitled "Epiletter"; has a lending library containing a collection of books, journals, and videos concerning epilepsy; and maintains a web site on the Internet.

Executive Director: Russell Pollard
Year Established: 1964

Keywords
Epilepsy Foundation of Victoria

1558 Erb's Palsy Group

60 Anchorway Road
Warwickshire
Coventry, CV3 6JJ, United Kingdom

Phone: +44 (0) 247-641-3293
Fax: +44 (0) 247-641-9857
E-mail: info@erbspalsygroup.com
http://www.erbspalsygroup.co.uk

The Erb's Palsy Group is an international, non-profit, self-help organization dedicated to providing support and information to families in England and North and South Ireland who are affected by Erb's palsy. Erb's palsy is a paralysis of the shoulder and upper extremity that is most commonly seen in newborns. This disorder is characterized by an abnormal positioning (adduction) and internal turning of the shoulder with a rotation of the forearm. This type of nerve injury may be caused by abnormal stretching of the shoulder during a difficult labor, a delivery where the buttocks present first (breech), or excessive sideways movement of the neck during delivery. Founded in 1992, the Erb's Palsy Group publishes a self-titled newsletter and distributes several informational brochures and fact sheets. Titles include "Obstetrical Erb's Palsy," "Nerve Grafts," and "Shoulder Release." A series of brochures geared to educators is also available. The group also provides guidelines for starting and maintaining local support groups.

President: Karen Hillyer (2003 to Present)
Year Established: 1992

Keywords
Bernard Horner Syndrome; Brachial Plexus Paralysis; Duchenne Erb Paralysis; Duchenne Erb Syndrome; Duchenne's Paralysis; Erb Duchenne Palsy; Erb Duchenne Paralysis; Erb's Palsy; Erb's Palsy Group; Erb's Paralysis; Horner's Syndrome; Klumpke's Palsy; Palsy, Oculosympathetic; Paralysis, Upper Brachial Plexus

1559   Erythema Nodosum Yahoo Support Group

http://health.groups.yahoo.com/group/erythema_nodosum_Group/

The Erythema Nodosum Yahoo Support Group was created to provide an online location where patients and families affected by erythema nodosum can share information about their experiences. Erythema nodosum is a form of panniculitis that appears as painful, red, hot lumps, bumps, or nodules on the legs or elsewhere. This group provides educational resources in the form of links, files, case histories, photos, and polls of its members while providing a safe place to respectfully discuss treatment options.

President: Rebecca Strecker (2003-present)
Year Established: 150

Keywords
Erythema Nodosum Yahoo Support Group

1560   Erythromelalgia Association
24 Pickering Ln
Wethersfield, CT 06109-3682

Phone: (860) 529-5261
E-mail: memberservices@erythromelalgia.org
http://www.erythromelalgia.org

The Erythromelalgia Association is an international, not-for-profit organization dedicated to providing emotional

support for people with erythromelalgia (EM), funding research into the causes and treatments of EM, and increasing awareness of the rare disease EM and its symptoms among healthcare practitioners and the general public. Erythromelalgia is a rare vascular disorder characterized by episodes of sudden widening of certain blood vessels (paroxysmal vasodilatation), particularly affecting the skin of the feet and/or hands. Symptoms may include severe burning pain, redness, and/or increased skin temperature. Primary or familial erythromelalgia may be inherited as an autosomal dominant genetic trait. Erythromelalgia may also occur secondary to several other underlying disorders or due to the use of certain medications. Established in 1999 and currently consisting of approximately 500 members worldwide, the Erythromelalgia Association has several main objectives, including increasing awareness of erythromelalgia among healthcare professionals, affected individuals, family members, and the general public; providing emotional support to those diagnosed with the disorder; fostering communication among affected individuals and family members; and promoting research into the causes, effects, diagnosis, and treatment of erythromelalgia. The association is also committed to working closely with medical organizations that are currently involving in finding new treatments for erythromelalgia; stressing the need for special accommodations for affected individuals; and working to ensure the availability of information for those involved in finding treatments and potential cures for the disorder.

President: Raymond Salza, Secretary/Treasurer
Executive Director: Lennia Machen, President
Year Established: 1999
Acronym: TEA

Keywords
Erythermalgia; Erythromelalgia; Erythromelalgia Association; Gerhardt Disease; Mitchell Disease; Weir Mitchell Disease

1561   Erythropoietic Protoporphyria Research and Education Fund
Channing Lab., Harvard Med. School
Brigham & Women's Hospital
181 Longwood Avenue
Boston, MA 02115-5804

Phone: (617) 525-8249
Fax: (617) 731-1541
E-mail: mmmathroth@rics.bwh.harvard.edu
mmmathroth@rics.bwh.harvard.edu

The Erythropoietic Protoporphyria Research and Education Fund (EPPREF) is a not-for-profit organization dedicated to disseminating knowledge about erythropoietic protoporphyria (EPP) to affected individuals, physicians, and the general public; operating and maintaining a referral service for individuals with EPP; and assisting physicians in any way necessary to bring about optimal care for affected individuals. Erythropoietic protoporphyria is a rare, inherited, metabolic disorder characterized by a deficiency of the enzyme ferrochelatase (FECH). Due to abnormally low levels of FECH, excessive amounts of protoporphyrin accumulate in the plasma, red blood cells, and liver. Symptoms may include hypersensitivity of the skin to sunlight and some types of artificial light (photosensitivity); itchiness and redness of the skin and/or a burning sensation after exposure to light, particularly on the skin of the hands, arms, and face; and/or, in rare cases, complications related to liver and gallbladder function. Established in 1978, the EPPREF offers information to physicians, maintains a registry, and publishes articles concerning EPP within the peer-reviewed medical literature.

President: Micheline M. Mathews-Roth, M.D.
Executive Director: Same as above.
Year Established: 1978
Acronym: EPPREF

Keywords
EPP; Erythropoietic Protoporphyria Research and Education Fund; Erythropoietic Protoporphyria; Erythropoietic Protoporphyria Research and Education Fund (EPPREF)

1562 Esophageal Cancer Awareness Association, Inc.

P.O. Box 3842
Ithaca, NY 14850-3842

Phone: (607) 257-1141
Fax: (607) 255-0349
Toll Free: (866) 370-3222
E-mail: jgillett@ecaware.org
http://www.ecaware.org/

Esophageal Cancer Awareness Association, Inc., (ECAA) is a voluntary, not-for-profit rare disorder organization whose mission is to promote worldwide understanding and support for esophageal cancer patients and caregivers. There are two major types of esophageal cancer, squamous cell and adenocarcinoma of the esophagus. These two conditions make up between 12,000 and 18,000 cases per year in the United States. ECAA was formed in July 2002 and

conducted its first annual meeting that same year. It provides support groups, patient networking, and advocacy for patients and families. ECAA also provides education to professionals.

President: James W. Gillett (2002-2005)
Year Established: 2002
Acronym: ECAA

Keywords
Advocacy; Esophageal Adenocarcinoma; Esophageal Cancer; Esophageal Cancer Awareness Association, Inc.; Networking; Squamous Cell Carcinoma; Support Groups

1563 euro-ATAXIA

Boherboy, Dunlavin
Co Wicklow, Ireland

Phone: +353 (0) 45-40-1218/40-1478
Fax: +353 (0) 45-40-1371
E-mail: mary.kearney@euro-ataxia.org
http://www.euro-ataxia.org

euro-ATAXIA, the European Federation of Hereditary Ataxias, is a multinational federation of non-profit associations dedicated to encouraging and supporting research to identify the causes and mechanisms of the hereditary ataxias. Hereditary ataxias are a group of progressive, chronic, neurological disorders that affect voluntary movement and coordination. Established in Belgium in 1989, euro-ATAXIA is an alliance of associations representing Belgium, France, Spain, The Netherlands, Germany, Sweden, Switzerland, Ireland, Finland, Great Britain, and Italy. It endeavors to monitor and support research into hereditary ataxias; centralize and communicate information to its members; encourage collaboration of all international organizations concerned with hereditary ataxia; examine the social, political, cultural, and other issues that concern the well-being of people with hereditary ataxia; and ensure that medical research into hereditary ataxias is ongoing. Additionally, euro-ATAXIA facilitates patient networking and publishes a periodic newsletter.

President: Marco Meinders
Year Established: 1989

Keywords
Ataxia Telangiectasia; Ataxia, Friedreich's; Ataxia, Hereditary; Ataxia, Marie's; euro ATAXIA; euro-ATAXIA

1564 European Alliance of Neuromuscular Disorders Associations

MDG Malta 4,
Gzira Road
Gzira, GAR 04, Malta

Phone: +356 2134-6688
Fax: +356 2131-8024
E-mail: eamda@hotmail.com
http://www.eamda.net

The European Alliance of Neuromuscular Disorders Associations, formerly the European Alliance of Muscular Dystrophy Associations, (EAMDA) is a nonprofit organization that serves as an information network, providing advice about neuromuscular conditions and offering information, support, and resources to its member organizations and families, caregivers, and professionals throughout Europe. It includes a Youth Organization that is made up of delegates who represent the young people in their own national associations, addressing issues related to quality of life, self-image, and medical intervention. The EAMDA also offers a variety of educational materials including fact sheets on neuromuscular disorders such as muscular dystrophy, a regular newsletter, and several additional publications.

President: Boris Sustaric
Year Established: 1971
Acronym: EAMDA

Keywords
European Alliance of Neuromuscular Disorders Associations

1565 European Chromosome 11q Network

Tom and Gabi Birle
Ahornstr. 13
Hebertshausen, 85421, Germany

Phone: +49 (0) 313-1742-3345
Fax: +49 (0) 313-1742-6980
E-mail: info@11q.org
http://www.11q.org

The European Chromosome 11q Network is an international self-help organization dedicated to providing information, assistance, and support to parents of children with abnormalities of the long arm of chromosome 11 (11q). Such 11q chromosome disorders include Jacobsen syndrome, a rare chromosomal disorder also known as "partial deletion" or "partial monosomy" of chromosome 11q; duplication (or "tri-

somy") of chromosomal material on 11q; or other chromosomal abnormalities. Associated symptoms and physical features depend upon the exact length, location, and nature of the specific 11q chromosomal abnormality in question. Established in 1997, the European Chromosome 11q Network is dedicated to networking parents of affected children, collecting and disseminating information concerning 11q chromosomal disorders, following the latest scientific developments, promoting research, and organizing international conferences on 11q disorders for affected families.

President: Annet van Betuw (1996 - Present).
Executive Director: Same as above.
Year Established: 1997

Keywords
11q Chromosomal Abnormalities; Austria; Chromosome 11 Partial Monosomy 11q; Chromosome 11 Partial Trisomy 11q; Chromosome 11 Partial Trisomy 11q13 qter; Chromosome 11 Partial Trisomy 11q21 qter; Chromosome 11 Partial Trisomy 11q23 qter; Chromosome 11q; Chromosome 11q Partial Trisomy; Chromosome 11q Syndrome Partial; Deletion 11q Syndrome Partial; Distal 11q Monosomy; Distal 11q Syndrome; Distal Trisomy 11q; European Chromosome 11q Network; Jacobsen Syndrome; Monosomy 11q, Partial; Trisomy 11q Partial

1566 European Dystonia Federation

69 East King Street
Helensburgh
Argyll & Bute, G84 7RE, United Kingdom

Phone: +44 (0) 1436-67-8799
Fax: +44 (0) 1436-67-8799
E-mail: sec@dystonia-europe.org
http://www.dystonia-europe.org

The European Dystonia Federation (EDG) is a union of national dystonia patient advocacy groups in Europe. EDG is a non-profit organization that supports and, where possible, coordinates the work of its member groups to fulfill their three main objectives of providing authorative information, spreading awareness of dystonia, and promoting research. The federation is registered in Belgium and holds an annual General Assembly of member group delegates. The working language is English. The federation also works to establish relations with governmental and other agencies, and with neurological and other specialists of the international medical community.

President: Mrs. Didi Jackson (2004-2007)
Executive Director: Alistair Newton
Year Established: 1993
Acronym: EDF

Keywords
Dystonia; EDF; European Dystonia Federation

1567 European League of Stuttering Associations

31 Grosvenor Road
Jesmond
Newcastle-upon-Tyne, NE2 2RL, Great Britain

Phone: +44 (0) 191-281-8003
Fax: +44 (0) 191-281-8003
E-mail: elsa@bvss.de
http://www.stuttering.ws/

The European League of Stuttering Associations (ELSA) is an international, nonprofit organization dedicated to facilitating the exchange of information among organizations, representing the interests of Europeans who stutter. Stuttering is a speech abnormality characterized by repeated hesitation or delay in enunciating words, abnormally prolonged pauses, and repetition of parts of words or entire words. ELSA promotes the exchange of information among European national organizations by conducting and compiling surveys; maintaining a library of the European associations' educational materials; publishing a regular newsletter; and conducting seminars that bring together organizational board members, other interested delegates, and professionals in the field. ELSA also provides advocacy for the interests and needs of affected individuals before the European Council and the European Union.

Year Established: 1990
Acronym: ELSA

Keywords
European League of Stuttering Associations

1568 European Long QT Syndrome Information Center

(Web Site on the Internet)
Ronnerweg 2
Nidau, 2560, Switzerland

Phone: +41 (0) 79-474-1535
E-mail: info@qtsyndrome.ch
http://www.qtsyndrome.ch

The European Long QT Syndrome (LQTS) Information Center is a web site on the Internet created by an individual with LQTS from Switzerland. There are two forms of long QT syndrome, one without deafness (Romano Ward syndrome) and one with deafness (Jervell and Lange-Nielsen syndrome). Long QT syndrome is characterized by an abnormality in the heart's electrical system. In the lower chambers (ventricles) of the heart, the normal duration of one phase of electrical activity is referred to as the Q-T interval. In long QT syndrome, there are abnormally prolonged intervals of electrical activity in the ventricles (prolonged Q-T), resulting in seizures and a fast, uneven heartbeat (ventricular fibrillation). The main goal of the web site is to provide information about long QT syndrome to affected individuals, their families, medical professionals, and interested individuals worldwide. The site also provides information on diagnostic criteria and potential therapies and has dynamic linkage to sites with further information.

President: Jon Mettler
Executive Director: Same as above.
Year Established: 1997
Acronym: LQTS-EIC

Keywords
Cardio Auditory Syndrome; Cardioauditory Syndrome of Jervell and Lange Nielsen; Congenital Deafness and Functional Heart Disease; Deafness Functional Heart Disease; European Long QT Syndrome Information Center; Jervell and Lange-Nielsen Syndrome; Long QT Syndrome; Long QT Syndrome European Information Center; QT Prolongation with Extracellular Hypocalcinemia; QT Prolongation without Congenital Deafness; QT Prolonged with Congenital Deafness; Romano Ward Syndrome

---

1569 European Lupus Erythematosus Federation

27-43 Eastern Road
Romford
Essex, RM1 3NH, United Kingdom

Phone: +44 (0) 1708-73-1251
Fax: +44 (0) 1708-73-1252
E-mail: elef@rheumanet.org
http://www.elef.rheumanet.org/

The European Lupus Erythematosus Federation (ELEF) is an international, voluntary federation that consists of national lupus groups throughout Europe. Systemic lupus erythematosus (SLE), also known as lupus, is an autoimmune disorder characterized by chronic inflammation affecting connective tissues of the body. Different tissues and organs may be affected, and the range and severity of associated symptoms and findings may vary from case to case. In some affected individuals, symptoms may include extreme fatigue; muscle pain; joint swelling, stiffness, and pain; skin rashes; hair loss; and other abnormalities. Established in 1989, the European Lupus Erythematosus Federation currently represents 15 countries, 16 lupus organizations, and approximately 16,500 affected individuals and family members. The ELEF is committed to collecting information on all medical and psychosocial aspects of lupus; promoting awareness of the disease among individuals with lupus, the general public, and members of the health, welfare, and medical professions; and encouraging and conducting surveys and research projects related to the disease and publishing the results of such research. The federation is also dedicated to promoting awareness of lupus support groups that are available for affected individuals and family members in each member country; sponsoring or promoting European symposia on all aspects of lupus; gaining representation on any European or international body whose interests will be of benefit to members of the federation; and assisting with the establishment of support groups in other European countries where none currently exists.

President: Brian Hanner (Chairman)
Executive Director: Same as above.
Year Established: 1989
Acronym: ELEF

Keywords
European Lupus Erythematosus Federation

1570 European Multiple System Atrophy Study Group

Department of Neurology
University of Innsbruck
Acichstrasse 35, A-6020, Austria

Phone: +43 (0) 513-504-3850
E-mail: office@emsa-sg.org
http://www.emsa-sg.org

The European Multiple System Atrophy Study Group (EMSA-SG) was formed in 1999 by 20 research groups in 11 European countries (Germany, Austria, France, United Kingdom, Portugal, Spain, Italy, Sweden, Denmark, and Slovenia) and Israel. Currently, its projects include setting up a Multiple System Atrophy (MSA) Registry. MSA is a sporadic, adult-onset neurodegenerative disorder affecting the brain and spinal cord of unknown cause.

President: Coordinator: Professor Werner Powe, MD
Year Established: 2001

Keywords
European Multiple System Atrophy Study Group

1571 European Organization for Research and Treatment of Cancer

Avenue E Mounier 83 bte 11
Brussels, 1200, Belgium

Phone: +32 (0) 2-774-1611
Fax: +32 (0) 2-772-2004
E-mail: eortc@eortc.be
http://www.eortc.be

The European Organization for Research and Treatment of Cancer (EORTC) is an international, not-for-profit, research organization dedicated to conducting, developing, coordinating, and stimulating basic and clinical research on cancer and related problems. The EORTC was established in 1962 by a group of oncologists who felt that extensive, comprehensive research in such fields may often be beyond the means of individual European laboratories and hospitals, and could best be accomplished through multidisciplinary, multinational efforts. The EORTC's primary objective is to raise the standard of cancer treatment through the development of new drugs and new regimens. The EORTC consists of a pan-European network involving more than 2,500 clinical investigators and scientists in more than 350 hospitals and research institutions in over 30 countries.

President: Professor Allan van Oosterom (2000-2003)
Executive Director: Francoise Meunier (Director General)
Year Established: 1962
Acronym: EORTC

Keywords
Cancer; European Organization for Research and Treatment of Cancer

1572 EURORDIS

(Plateforme Maladies Rares)
102 rue Didot
Paris, 75014, France

Phone: +33 (0) 1-56-53-52-10
Fax: +33 (0) 1-56-53-52-15
E-mail: eurordis@eurordis.org
http://www.eurordis.org

EURORDIS, the European Organization for Rare Disorders, is a voluntary organization that is dedicated to improving the quality of life of all those affected by rare disorders. Its purpose is to encourage research and development of promising therapeutic options for the treatment of rare diseases; to insure the best possible health care throughout the European Union for those affected by rare disorders; and to improve the overall quality of life of those affected by rare diseases. Additional goals include the stimulation of coordinated research efforts at the European level to increase the knowledge of rare disorders, their causes, and new and effective treatments; the provision of a European platform to a wide variety of national patient organizations to coordinate their actions at the European level; and the provision of a patient interest-driven mediator between all the various European structures and institutions that are involved in public health responses to the needs of persons with rare disorders.

President: Terkel Andersen
Executive Director: Yann Le Cam
Year Established: 1997
Acronym: EURORDIS

Keywords
European Organization For Rare Diseases; EURORDIS; Inherited Disorders; Rare Diseases

---

1573   Evans Syndrome Support and Research Group
1376 Presidential Highway
Jefferson, NH 03583

Phone: (603) 586-7983
Fax: (603) 586-7983
E-mail: lnalou@aol.com
http://www.homebrewemporium.com/lna/evans.htm

The Evans Syndrome Support and Research Group is a not-for-profit, self-help organization dedicated to providing information and support to individuals with Evans syndrome. This is a disorder characterized by acquired hemolytic anemia, the chronic premature destruction of red blood cells and thrombocytopenia, abnormally low levels of circulating blood platelets. White blood cells are affected causing neutropenia also. Established in 1992, the group provides appropriate referrals, offers various forms of support, and provides educational materials to affected individuals, family members, and healthcare professionals.

President: Lou Addington (1992-Present)
Year Established: 1992

Keywords
Anemia, Acquired Hemolytic and Thrombocytopenia; Autoimmune; Evans Syndrome; Evans Syndrome Support and Research Group; Neutropenia; Chronic ITP

1574   Eye Cancer Network
115 East 61st St
New York, NY 10021

Phone: (212) 832-8170
Fax: (212) 888-4030
E-mail: pfinger@eyecancer.org
http://www.eyecancer.com

The Eye Cancer Network, a web-based organization, provides information for patients with eye cancer and the health professionals who care for them. Its activities include general, professional, and patient education; support for research; patient networking; genetic counseling; support group coordination; referrals and maintenance of a database. It serves an international audience. The network provides patient-to-patient and doctor-to-doctor interactive bulletin boards.

President: Paul T. Finger, MD
Executive Director: Paul T. Finger, MD
Year Established: 1998
Acronym: ECN

Keywords
Adenoid Cystic Carcinoma; Basal Cell Carcinoma; Choroidal Melanoma; Choroidal Metastasis; Conjunctiva; ECN; Eye Cancer; Eye Cancer Network; Iris Melanoma; Malignant Melanoma; Networking; Orbital Lymphoma; Retinoblastoma; Rhabdomyosarcoma; Squamous Carcinoma; Support Groups

---

1575   EyeCare Foundation
115 East 61st Street
Suite 5B
New York, NY 10021

Phone: (212) 832-7297
Fax: (212) 888-4030
E-mail: contactus@eyecarefoundation.org
http://www.eyecarefoundation.org

The EyeCare Foundation is a nonprofit charity for patients with ocular tumors, cancers, macular degeneration and related eye diseases. It promotes multicenter cooperation, as well as web-based education and support groups.

President: Mr. George Smith
Executive Director: Paul T. Finger, MD, FACS
Year Established: 1998
Acronym: ECF

Keywords
Choroideremia; ECF; Eye Cancer; EyeCare Foundation; Macular Degeneration; Retinoblastoma; Serpiginous Choroiditis

1576 Fabry Support & Information Group

108 NE 2nd Street
P.O. Box 510
Concordia, MO 64020-0510

Phone: (660) 463-1355
Fax: (660) 463-1356
E-mail: info@fabry.org
http://www.fabry.org

The Fabry Support & Information Group is a nonprofit, 501(c)3 organization. Established in 1996, it distributes information about Fabry disease to increase understanding, offers emotional support and networking services, and publishes a biannual newsletter. Fabry disease is an inherited disorder that is one of a group known as lysosomal storage disorders. It has widely varied symptoms that include burning pains in the hands and feet, hearing loss and tinnitus, angiokeratoma, impaired sweating, premature strokes, whorl-like corneal opacities, gastrointestinal distress, renal insufficiency, and cardiac involvement. Clinical onset usually occurs in childhood or adolescence, but symptoms are frequently misinterpreted or ignored. Unfortunately, accurate diagnosis is frequently established in adulthood, when the disease has progressed to key organ dysfunction or failure. Earlier diagnosis of Fabry disease may result in more effective symptom management and improved quality of life. Enhancing awareness of Fabry disease among the public and health professionals is an important function of the Fabry Support & Information Group.

President: Kathy Johnson
Executive Director: Jack Johnson
Year Established: 1996
Acronym: FSIG

Keywords
Alpha Galactosidase A Deficiency; Anderson Fabry Disease; Angiokeratoma Corporis Diffusum; Angiokeratoma Diffuse Ceramide Trihexosidase Deficiency; Fabry Disease; Fabry Support & Information Group; GLA Deficiency; Glycolipid Lipidosis; Lipidosis, Hereditary Dystopic

1577 FACES: The National Craniofacial Association

P.O. Box 11082
Chattanooga, TN 37401

Phone: (423) 266-1632
Fax: (423) 267-3124
Toll Free: (800) 332-2373
E-mail: faces@faces-cranio.org
http://www.faces-cranio.org

FACES: The National Craniofacial Association is a not-for-profit organization whose purpose is to provide families with financial assistance for travel to major medical centers for reconstructive surgery; offer information and support to affected families; and increase public awareness and understanding of facial abnormalities. Educational materials produced by FACES include brochures, a quarterly newsletter, and information packets on specific craniofacial disorders.

President: Lynne G. Mayfield
Year Established: 1969
Acronym: FACES

Keywords
Ablepharon Macrostomia Syndrome; Acrocallosal Syndrome, Schinzel Type; Antley Bixler Syndrome; Apert Syndrome; Baller Gerold Syndrome; Blepharophimosis, Ptosis, Epicanthus Inversus Syndrome; Branchio Oculo Facial Syndrome; C Syndrome; Carpenter Syndrome; Cerebro Oculo Facio Skeletal Syndrome; Chromosome 10, Distal Trisomy 10q; Chromosome 11, Partial Monosomy 11q; Chromosome 13, Partial Monosomy 13q; Chromosome 4, Monosomy Distal 4q; Chromosome 4, Partial Trisomy Distal 4q; Chromosome 7, Partial Monosomy 7p; Cleidocranial Dysplasia; Cornelia de Lange Syndrome; Craniofacial Disorders; Craniofacial Genetics; Craniofrontonasal Dysplasia; Craniometaphyseal Dysplasia; Craniosynostosis, Primary; Crouzon Syndrome; Encephalocele; FACES; FACES: The National Craniofacial Association; Facial Anomalies; Fraser Syndrome; Freeman Sheldon Syndrome; Frontofacionasal Dysplasia; Fryns Syndrome; Goodman Syndrome; Gorlin Chaudhry Moss Syndrome; Greig Cephalopolysyndactyly Syndrome; Hallermann Streiff Syndrome; Hanhart Syndrome; Hyperostosis Frontalis Interna; Jackson Weiss Syndrome; Johanson Blizzard Syndrome; KBG Syndrome; Kenny Caffey Syndrome; Larsen Syndrome; Maxillofacial Dysostosis; Maxillonasal Dysplasia, Binder Type; Miller Syndrome; Moebius Syndrome; Nager Syndrome; Oral Facial Digital Syndrome; Orocraniodigital Syndrome; Otopalatodigital Syndrome Type I and II; Pallister W Syndrome; Pfeiffer Syn-

drome Type I; Pierre Robin Sequence; Roberts Syndrome; Rubinstein Taybi Syndrome; Ruvalcaba Syndrome; Saethre Chotzen Syndrome; Sakati Syndrome; Scott Craniodigital Syndrome; Simpson Dysmorphia Syndrome; Skull disorders; Summitt Syndrome; Telecanthus with Associated Abnormalities; Treacher Collins Syndrome; Tricho Dento Osseous Syndrome; Velocardiofacial Syndrome; Waardenburg Syndrome

1578 Fair Foundation

78629 Bougainvillea Drive
Palm Desert, CA 92211

Phone: (760) 200-2766
Fax: (760) 227-9471
E-mail: fair@dc.rr.com
http://www.fairfoundation.org

The FAIR Foundation was established to change the way government research money is spent. Specifically, it is dedicated to increasing research funding for diseases that kill more Americans than AIDS does, and also for diseases that cause great suffering but have low mortality rates. FAIR is an acronym for Fair Allocations In Research.

President: Richard Darling, DDS (President & CEO)
Year Established: 1999
Acronym: FAIR

Keywords
Advocacy; FAIR; Fair Allocations in Research; Fair Foundation; Research Funding

1579 Familial Dysautonomia Hope Foundation

1170 Green Knolls Drive
Buffalo Grove, IL 60089

Phone: (847) 913-0455
Fax: (847) 913-8589
E-mail: info@fdhope.org
http://www.fdhope.org

The mission of the Familial Dysautonomia Hope Foundation (FD Hope), a voluntary, not-for-profit organization established in 2001, is to expand and accelerate scientific research to find a cure for familial dysautonomia while improving the lives of the children and adults who are challenged by the disease. Familial dysautonomia is a rare genetic disorder of the autonomic nervous system that primarily affects people of Eastern European Jewish heritage. It is characterized by diminished sensitivity to pain, lack of overflow tearing in the eyes, and unusual fluctuations of body temperature and blood pressure. Familial Dysautonomia Hope provides publications, advocacy, and patient networking services.

President: Lynn Lieberman
Year Established: 2001
Acronym: FD Hope

Keywords
Advocacy; Familial Dysautonomia; Familial Dysautonomia Hope Foundation; FD Hope; Networking; Riley Day Syndrome

1580 Familial GI Cancer Registry

Mt. Sinai Hospital
600 University Avenue
Suite 1157
ON, M5G 1X5, Canada

Phone: (416) 586-8334
Fax: (416) 586-8644
E-mail: tberk@mtsinai.on.ca
http://www.mtsinai.on.ca/familialgicancer

The Familial GI Cancer Registry is a professional and research center dedicated to providing professional services as well as emotional support to people affected by familial gastrointestinal cancer and their families. Established in 1980, the center conducts research studies and has an investigative team focused on innovative surgical techniques related to gastrointestinal cancer. The center also has a molecular diagnostic program and offers a screening service for family members who may be at risk for the hereditary form of the disease. Along with its scientific and medical departments, the center also has a genetic counseling department that offers advice and support to affected individuals and families. The Familial GI Cancer Registry maintains a database of affected individuals and produces educational and support materials including pamphlets, brochures, family guides, and a biannual newsletter. The registry relays information regarding hospital and community resources through a patient library.

Executive Director: Teri Berk, Clinical Coordinator
Year Established: 1980
Acronym: FGICR

Keywords
Cancer, Familial Gastrointestinal; Cancer, Hereditary Colon; Cancer, Hereditary Nonpolyposis (Colorectal); Familial Adenomatous Polyposis; Familial GI Cancer Registry; Polyposis, Familial; Turcot Syndrome

1581 Families of Spinal Muscular Atrophy

P.O. Box 196
Libertyville, IL 60048

Fax: (847) 367-7623
Toll Free: (800) 886-1762
E-mail: audrey@fsma.org
http://www.curesma.com

Families of Spinal Muscular Atrophy (SMA) is a volunteer-driven, not-for-profit organization dedicated solely to eradicating SMA by promoting and supporting research, helping families cope through informational programs and support, and educating the public and the medical community about SMA. Spinal muscular atrophy is a motor neuron disease. Motor neurons are nerve cells in the spinal cord, which send out nerve fibers to muscles throughout the body. The motor neurons affect the voluntary muscles that are used for activities such as crawling, walking, head and neck control, and swallowing. Established in 1984 by a group of concerned parents, Families of Spinal Muscular Atrophy now has more than 24 chapters worldwide and more than 5,000 members families and is a founding member of the International Alliance for Spinal Muscular Atrophy. FSMA continues to be at the forefront of research, funding, both basic science researches, drug testing programs (Project Cure SMA) and its own drug discovery efforts. The organization supports several languages including Spanish, Italian, German, Polish, Greek, and Yiddish.

President: Audrey Lewis
Executive Director: Audrey Lewis
Year Established: 1984
Acronym: Families of SMA

Keywords
Atrophy, Spinal Muscular; Families of Spinal Muscular Atrophy; Kugelberg Welander Syndrome; Muscular Atrophy, Aran Duchenne; Oppenheim Disease; SMA; Werdnig Hoffmann Disease

1582 Family Empowerment Network: Supporting Families Affected by FAS/FAE

Department of Family Medicine
777 South Mills Street
Madison, WI 53703

Phone: (608) 262-6590
Fax: (608) 265-3352
Toll Free: (800) 462-5254
E-mail: fen@fammed.wisc.edu

The Family Empowerment Network: Support For Families Affected by FAS/FAE (Fetal Alcohol Syndrome and Fetal Alcohol Effects) is a voluntary organization established to empower families affected by fetal alcohol syndrome and fetal alcohol effects through programs of education and support. The goals of the network are to provide support, education, and training to families affected by FAS/FAE and provide information and training to professionals involved with families affected by FAS/FAE. The organization networks families with support groups and professionals on a national level; conducts an annual family retreat; maintains a toll-free family information line; conducts an annual conference; and offers ongoing technical assistance. The network also provides a variety of materials including the quarterly newsletter "FEN Pen."

Executive Director: Georgiana Wilton, PhD
Year Established: 1992
Acronym: FEN

Keywords
Family Empowerment Network: Supporting Families Affected by FAS/FAE; FAE; FAS; Fetal Alcohol Effects; Fetal Alcohol Syndrome

1583 Fanconi Anemia Research Fund, Inc.

1801 Willamette Street
Suite 200
Eugene, OR 97401

Phone: (541) 687-4658
Fax: (541) 687-0548
Toll Free: (800) 828-4891
E-mail: info@fanconi.org
http://www.fanconi.org/

The Fanconi Anemia Research Fund is a non-profit organization that raises funds for medical research into Fanconi anemia, an inherited condition that leads to a deficiency of certain blood cells that are produced by the bone marrow. Established in 1989, the organization supports numerous investigators who are working on various approaches to gene identification and therapy. The Fanconi Anemia Research Fund sponsors an annual international Fanconi Anemia Research Symposium to stimulate scientific progress and collaborative research among scientists. Additionally, the fund develops and maintains a communication network that supplies information and support to affected families and their physicians. Educational materials include the "FA Handbook," "Standards for Clinical Care" and twice yearly Family Newsletters and a Science Letter. The fund also moderates an electronic list serve for FA patients and their parents.

President: Barry Rubenstein
Executive Director: Mary Ellen Eiler
Year Established: 1989
Acronym: FA Research Fund

Keywords
Aplastic Anemia; Bone Marrow Failure Syndrome; Fanconi Anemia Research Fund, Inc.

1584   Federacion Espanola de Enfermedades Raras (FEDER)

Av. Francisco Javier
9 Edificio Sevilla 2 Planta 10 / Mod. 24
Sevilla, 41018, Spain

Phone: +34 954-989-892
Fax: +34 954-989-893
E-mail: feder@enfermedades-raras.org
http://www.enfermedades-raras.org

The aims of FEDER are to enhance awareness and recognition of rare disorders; improve the medical, social, and financial care that patients receive; call on appropriate authorities to set up nationwide reference, diagnostic, and therapeutic centers for each disease or group of diseases; promote and support initiatives that encourage prevention, research, and collaboration; develop and implement orphan drug regulations; and defend patient rights and interests.

President: Moises Abascal Alonso (1999-present)
Executive Director: Moises Abascal Alonso
Year Established: 1999
Acronym: FEDER

Keywords
Federacion Espanol De Enfermedades Raras (FEDER); Patient Network; Patient Organization; Patient Rights; Rare Diseases; Rare Diseases Helpline

1585   Federation of Families for Children's Mental Health

1101 King Street
Suite 420
Alexandria, VA 22314

Phone: (703) 684-7710
Fax: (703) 836-1040
E-mail: ffcmh@ffcmh.org
http://www.ffcmh.org

The Federation of Families for Children's Mental Health is a not-for-profit, parent-run, advocacy organization focused on the needs of children and youth with emotional, behavioral, or mental disorders and their families. The federation's mission is to provide leadership in the field of children's mental health and develop necessary human and financial resources to meet its goals. The federation addresses the unique needs of children and youth with emotional, behavioral, or mental disorders from birth through the transition to adulthood. It works to ensure the rights to full citizenship, support, and access to community-based services for all affected children and their families. The federation also seeks to provide information and engage in advocacy regarding research, prevention, early intervention, family support, education, transition services, and other services.

President: Barbara Sample
Executive Director: Barbara Huff
Year Established: 1988
Acronym: FFCMH

Keywords
Behavioral Disorders; Disabilities (Children); Emotional Disorders; Federation of Families for Children's Mental Health; Mental Disorders

1586   FG Syndrome Family Alliance

946 NW Circle Boulevard 290
Corvallis, OR 97330

Phone: (617) 577-9050
E-mail: info@fg-syndrome.org
http://www.fg-syndrome.org

The FG Syndrome Family Alliance (FGFA) was established in 1997 as a support organization for families of children with FG syndrome, a rare genetic disorder characterized by varying degrees of mental retardation, delayed motor development, abnormally diminished muscle tone (hypotonia), characteristic abnormalities of the head and facial (craniofacial) area, respiratory problems, visual and/or hearing impairment, and/or gastrointestinal, skeletal, heart, and/or other abnormalities. Associated symptoms and findings may vary greatly in range and severity from case to case. Mental retardation is not an obligatory finding in the FG syndrome, and some individuals with the FG syndrome are gifted. Because FG syndrome is inherited as an X-linked recessive trait, it is usually fully expressed in males only. The FG Syndrome Family Alliance currently serves over 200 families around the world. The alliance is dedicated to providing information and support to families of children with FG syndrome; offering networking services including an online mailing list (listserv) and regional coordinators, enabling parents to exchange mutual support, information, and resources; and assisting researchers in the development of an international registry for FG syndrome. The alliance assists researchers by helping them access candidates for studies, including recent studies on gene mapping and behavioral phenotype. It is currently working with its medical advisors to create standards of care document for pediatricians caring for patients with the FG syndrome. The organization hosts an international medical and family conference every three years.

President: Sara Anne A. Gelser (1997 to Present)
Executive Director: Same as above.
Year Established: 1997
Acronym: FGSFA

Keywords
Agenesis of the Corpus Callosum; Autism; Chronic Constipation; FG Syndrome; FG Syndrome Family Alliance; FGSFA; Mentally Retarded; Opitz FG Syndrome; Opitz Kaveggia Syndrome; Tethered Spinal Cord; X-Linked

1587 Fibromyalgia Association UK

PO Box 206
Stourbridge
West Midlands, DY9 8YL, United Kingdom

Phone: +44 (0) 870-220-1232
Fax: +44 (0) 138-486-9467
E-mail: fmauk@hotmail.com
http://www.fibromyalgia-associationuk.org/

The Fibromyalgia Association UK is an international, voluntary organization in the United Kingdom dedicated to providing information, support, and resources to individuals affected by fibromyalgia, a chronic condition characterized by musculoskeletal pain, stiffness, and spasm and associated sleep disturbances. The exact cause of fibromyalgia is unknown. However, the condition appears to develop after certain infections or injuries, or may occur due to, or in association with, other underlying conditions or disorders, such as rheumatoid arthritis. The Fibromyalgia Association UK provides understandable information on fibromyalgia and promotes networking opportunities that enable affected individuals and family members to exchange mutual support and information. The association also has a web site on the Internet that discusses the organization's history and mission, provides information

on fibromyalgia, and offers linkage to additional support groups, newsgroups, FAQs ("frequently asked questions") on the condition, and related web sites.

President: Gerry Crossley
Executive Director: Pam Stewart
Year Established: 1992
Acronym: FM UK

Keywords
Fibromyalgia Association UK

1588 Fight ALD

P.O. Box 3318
Vista, CA 92085

E-mail: info@fightald.org
http://www.fightald.org

President: Janis Sherwood (Founder/Admin Director)
Executive Director: William Sherwood (President)

Keywords
Adrenoleukodystrophy; Adrenomyeloneuropathy; Advocacy; Fight ALD; Networking

1589 Fight for Sight, Inc.

381 Park Avenue South
Suite 809
New York, NY 10016

Phone: (212) 679-6060
Fax: (877) 679-6060
E-mail: info@fightforsight.com
http://www.fightforsight.com

Fight For Sight, Inc., once known as the National Council to Combat Blindness, is a voluntary, not-for-profit organization dedicated to the restoration and preservation of sight through eye research and treatment. Established in 1946, and consisting of approximately 500 members, Fight For Sight provides awards, grants, and fellowships to accredited medical colleges, hospitals, and eye centers throughout the nation and in foreign countries; supports eye clinics at leading institutions, enabling thousands of disadvantaged youngsters to receive quality eye care; and has support groups. The organization also offers a variety of educational materials.

President: Kenneth Barasch, M.D.
Executive Director: Mary Prudden
Year Established: 1946

Keywords
Blindness; Eye Diseases; Fight for Sight, Inc.; Visual Disorders

1590 First Candle-SIDS Alliance

1314 Bedford Avenue
Suite 210
Baltimore, MD 21208

Phone: (410) 653-8226
Fax: (410) 653-8709
Toll Free: (800) 221-7437
E-mail: info@firstcandle.org
http://www.firstcandle.org

First Candle-SIDS Alliance exists to ensure the elimination of sudden infant death syndrome through medical research and education, while providing support to those affected by an infant death. It is a national, non-profit voluntary health organization that unites families, caregivers, health professionals and scientists with government, business and community service groups. As a sponsor of the national Back to Sleep Campaign, the SIDS Alliance supplies information on SIDS to new and expectant parents and the general public via a nationwide 24-hour, toll free hotline and its web site. It works closely with the National Institute of Child Health and Human Development to advocate for a coordinated research agenda for the nation.

President: Marian Sokol
Executive Director: Deborah Boyd
Year Established: 1987
Acronym: SIDS Alliance

Keywords
Crib Death; First Candle-SIDS Alliance; Infants (Life Threatening Events); SIDS; Sudden Infant Death Syndrome

1591 Floating Harbor Syndrome Support Group

160 Guild NE
Grand Rapids, MI 49505

E-mail: floatingharbor@sbcglobal.net
http://www.hometown.aol.com/jdswanson

The Floating Harbor Syndrome Support Group is a voluntary organization that provides information and encouragement to parents of children affected by Floating Harbor syndrome. This syndrome is a rare genetic disorder that was named for the first two identified patients who were seen at Boston Floating Hospital and Harbor General Hospital in California. Its main characteristics include short stature, delayed bone growth, delay in expressive language, and distinctive facial features, such as a broad nose, wide mouth, thin lips, and deep-set eyes. The support group serves all populations and coordinates patient networking and patient education. It also provides publications that include a newsletter, brochures, pictures of children with FHS, and a membership directory.

President: Deana Swanson
Year Established: 1999
Acronym: FHSSG-NA

Keywords
Floating Harbor Syndrome; Floating Harbor Syndrome Support Group

1592 FOCUS Families—For Our Children's Unique Sight

2453 Emerald Street
San Diego, CA 92109

Phone: (858) 273-1473
Toll Free: (866) 362-8750
E-mail: support@focusfamilies.org
http://www.focusfamilies.org

FOCUS Families—For Our Children's Unique Sight is a national, not-for-profit organization dedicated to providing information, education and support to families whose children are affected by rare septo optic dysplasia and/or optic nerve hypoplasia. Headquartered in San Diego, California, the organization distributes current medical literature visual disorder ONH; provides information on community resources; conducts annual national conventions in the United States and in Europe; assists in coordinating local social events; and publishes the quarterly newsletter, "Focal Points." For those families who choose to participate, there is a registry of members for the purpose of diagnosis matching.

President: Unknown
Executive Director: Pilar V. Hari
Year Established: 1991
Acronym: FOCUS

Keywords
DeMorsier Syndrome; Demorsiers Disease/Disorder; FOCUS Families for Our Children's Unique Sight; FOCUS—for Our Children's Unique Sight; Hypoplasia, Optic Nerve; Microphthalmos; Optic Nerve Hy-

poplasia; Sclerocornea; Septooptic Dysplasia; Visual Disorders

1593 FOD (Fatty Oxidation Disorders) Family Support Group

1559 New Garden Road, 2E
Greensboro, NC 27410

Phone: (336) 547-8682
E-mail: deb@fodsupport.org
http://www.fodsupport.org

The Fatty Oxidation Disorders (FOD) Family Support Group was established in 1991 as a way of dealing with the sudden death of the founders' daughter, Kristen, in 1985 from undiagnosed medium chain acyl CoA dehydrogenase deficiency (MCAD). MCAD is a very rare metabolic disorder that results in the abnormal accumulation of fatty acids in the liver and in the brain. The mission of the FOD Family Support Group is to connect and network with FOD families and professionals across the world and to provide emotional support, share practical information, and inform families of new developments in diagnosis, research and treatment.

Executive Director: Deb Lee Gould, M.Ed. (1991 to Present)
Year Established: 1991
Acronym: FOD

Keywords
ACADM Deficiency; Acyl CoA Dehydrogenase Deficiency Long Chain; Carnitine Deficiency; Carnitine Deficiency Syndromes; Carnitine Palmitoyl Transferase II; CPTII; Dicarboxylicaciduria due to MCADH Deficiency; Electron Transfer Flavoprotein; FOD (Fatty Oxidation Disorders) Family Support Group; Fatty Oxidation Disorders; Genetic Metabolic Disorder; Glutaricaciduria II; L3 Hydroxy Acyl CoA Dehydrogenase Deficiency; LCAD Deficiency; LCADH Deficiency; Long Chain Acyl CoA Dehydrogenase Deficiency; Medium Chain Acyl CoA Dehydrogenase Deficiency; Metabolic Disorders; SCAD; Short Chain Acyl CoA Dehydrogenase Deficiency

1594 FOLKS: Friends of Landau Kleffner Syndrome

3 Stone Buildings (Ground Floor)
Lincoln's Inn
London, WC2A 3XL, United Kingdom

Phone: +44 (0) 870-847-0707
Fax: +44 (0) 130-275-2662

E-mail: RAHantusch@compuserve.com
http://www.bobjanet.demon.co.uk/lks/folks.html

FOLKS: Friends of Landau Kleffner Syndrome is a voluntary organization in the United Kingdom (UK) that was established in 1989 by parents of children with Landau Kleffner syndrome (LKS). The organization, which currently consists of approximately 100 members, is dedicated to providing information, support, and resources to families of children with LKS and related disorders. In addition, FOLKS is committed to advancing the education of the medical profession and the general public concerning LKS and its implications for affected families as well as promoting research into the disorder, publishing the results of such studies, and supporting organizations that conduct such research in the UK. Landau Kleffner syndrome is a rare disorder that becomes apparent at an average of five years of age. Children with the disorder experience regression of language skills, loss of speech, and, in some cases, behavioral problems including poor attention and irritability.

Year Established: 1989
Acronym: FOLKS

Keywords
Aphasia; Aphasia, Acquired with Convulsive Disorder; Aphasia, Infantile Epileptic; FOLKS: Friends of Landau Kleffner Syndrome; Landau Kleffner Syndrome; LKS

1595 Food Allergy & Anaphylaxis Network

11781 Lee Jackson Highway
Suite 160
Fairfax, VA 22033-3309

Phone: (703) 691-3179
Fax: (703) 691-2713
Toll Free: (800) 929-4040
E-mail: faan@foodallergy.org
http://www.foodallergy.org/

The Food Allergy & Anaphylaxis Network (FAAN) is a Virginia based not-for-profit organization representing Americans who have food allergies. Established in 1991, FAAN's mission is to raise public awareness, to provide advocacy and education, and to advance research on behalf of those affected by food allergies and anaphylaxis.

President: Anne Munoz-Furlong (1991 to Present).
Year Established: 1991
Acronym: FAAN

Keywords
Anaphylaxis; FAAN; Food Allergy; Food Allergy &
Anaphylaxis Network; Food Allergy Network; egg
allergy; fish allergy; milk allergy; peanut allergy;
seafood allergy; shellfish allergy; soy allergy; tree nut
allergy; wheat allergy

1596 Forward Face, Inc.

317 East 34th Street
Room 901
New York, NY 10016

Phone: (212) 684-5860
Fax: (212) 684-5864
Toll Free: (800) 393-3223
E-mail: info@forwardface.org
http://www.forwardface.org

Forward Face provides children and their families with
immediate support to manage the medical and social effects of facial differences. It educates, advocates, and
raises public awareness about craniofacial conditions.
Forward Face, started by parents of children with facial
differences, is a non-profit tax-exempt organization. It
began in 1978 serving families undergoing treatments
at New York University Medical Center's Institute of
Reconstructive and Plastic Surgery (IRPS). While en-
joying a close affiliation with IRPS, Forward Face has
evolved into a national organization serving the needs
of children with craniofacial conditions at clinics and
hospitals across the U.S. and worldwide. Its services include help with travel, housing, and/or living expenses
so family members can be with their children during
craniofacial surgeries; meetings and social gatherings to
network and share information; education and advocacy;
the Inner Faces support group for teens and young adults
that offers mentoring, role models, participatory theater
and workshops; trained volunteers for one-to-one hospital visits, home visits, caring phone calls and written
communications; and information on craniofacial centers around the country.

President: Barbara Robertson
Executive Director: Terri Brooks
Year Established: 1978

Keywords
Ablepharon Macrostomia Syndrome; Acrocallosal
Syndrome, Schinzel Type; Advocacy; Apert; Baller
Gerold Syndrome; Birth Defects; Blepharophimosis,
Ptosis, Epicanthus Inversus Syndrome; Cardiofacio-
cutaneous Syndrome; Carpenter Syndrome; Cerebro
Oculo Facio Skeletal Syndrome; Chromosome 4, Par-
tial Trisomy Distal 4q; Chromosome 10, Distal Tri-
somy 10q; Cleft Palate and Cleft Lip; Cornelia de
Lange Syndrome; Craniofacial Anomalies; Craniofa-
cial Conditions; Craniofrontonasal Dysplasia; Cran-
iosynostosis; Craniosynostosis, Primary; Crouzon;
Crouzon Syndrome; Encephalocele; Forward Face,
Inc.; Fraser Syndrome; Frontofacionasal Dysplasia;
Frontonasal Dysplasia; Fryns Syndrome; Goldenhar
Syndrome; Goodman Syndrome; Gorlin Chaudhry
Moss Syndromee; Hanhart Syndrome; Hemangiomas;
Hemifacial Microsomia; Hydrocephalus; IRF6 Re-
lated Disorders; Jackson Weiss Syndrome; Maxillo-
facial Dysostosis; Microtia; Moebius Syndrome;
Nager Syndrome; Networking; Oral Facial Digital
Syndrome; Orocraniodigital Syndrome; Pallister W
Syndrome; Pfeiffer Syndrome; Pierre Robin Se-
quence; Roberts Syndrome; Saethre Chotzen Syn-
drome; Sakati Syndrome; Scott Craniodigital Syn-
drome; Seckel Syndrome; Setleis Syndrome; Summitt
Syndrome; Support Groups; Telecanthus with Associated Abnormalities; Treacher Collins Syndrome

1597 Foundation ERFO-centrum

Vredehofstraat 31
Soestdijk, 3761 HA, The Netherlands

Phone: +31 (0) 35-602-7173
Fax: +31 (0) 35-602-7440
E-mail: erfocentrum@erfocentrum.nl
http://www.erfelijkheid.nl

The mission of ERFO-centrum is to promote knowledge of genetic and non-genetic congenital disorders
among the general public as well as healthcare
providers. Such information includes medical and care
aspects and physical, judicial, ethical and social concerns.

Executive Director: Mrs. D. Moerman
Year Established: 2000

Keywords
Foundation ERFO Centrum; Foundation ERFO-centrum

1598 Foundation Fighting Blindness (Canada)

60 St. Clair Avenue East
Suite 703
Toronto, Ontario, M4T 1N5, Canada

Phone: (416) -36-0-42
Fax: (416) -36-0-00
Toll Free: (800) -46-1-33
E-mail: info@ffb.ca
http://www.ffb.ca

The Foundation Fighting Blindness (Canada) is a charity that was founded in 1974 by a small group of family's intent on finding a cure for the diseases affecting the vision of their children. It works to find causes, treatments, and ultimately, cures for retinitis pigmentosa, macular degeneration and related retinal diseases. Its members do this by promoting research and developing public awareness. In addition to sponsoring support groups, the foundation offers educational materials and networking to patients, families and the healthcare community at large.

President: Donna Green, President
Executive Director: Sharon Colle
Year Established: 1974
Acronym: FFB-C

Keywords
Bardet-Biedl Syndrome; Choroideremia; Cone Rod Dystrophy; Foundation Fighting Blindness (Canada); French; Leber's Congenital Amaurosis; Macular Degeneration; Networking; Research; Retinal Disease; Retinitis Pigmentosa; Stargardt Macular Dystrophy; Support Groups; Usher Syndrome

1599 Foundation Fighting Blindness, Inc.

11435 Cronhill Drive
Owings Mills, MD 21117-2220

Phone: (410) 568-0150
Fax: (410) 363-2393
Toll Free: (800) 683-5555
TDD: (800) 683-5551
E-mail: info@blindness.org
http://www.fightblindness.org

The urgent mission of the Foundation Fighting Blindness is to drive the research that will provide preventions, treatments, and cures for people affected by retinitis pigmentosa, macular degeneration, Usher syndrome, and the entire spectrum of retinal degenerative diseases. FFB offers information and referral services for affected individuals and their families as well as for doctors and eye care professionals. The foundation also provides comprehensive information kits on retinitis pigmentosa, macular degeneration, and Usher syndrome. Its newsletter, In Focus, presents articles on coping, research updates, and foundation news, and is published three times per year. A national conference is held every other year.

President: William T. Schmidt
Executive Director: Randy Hove
Year Established: 1971
Acronym: FFB

Keywords
Foundation Fighting Blindness; Foundation Fighting Blindness, Inc.; Macular Degeneration; Refsum Disease; Retinal Degeneration Diseases; Retinitis Pigmentosa; RP; Stargardt's Disease; Usher's Syndrome; Visual Impairments

1600 Foundation for a Cure for Mitochondrial Diseases, Inc.

81 Wood Pond Road
Cheshire, CT 06410

Phone: (203) 699-0022
E-mail: mitocure@snet.net
http://www.mitocure.org

The mission of The Foundation For A Cure For Mitochondrial Diseases, Inc., is to raise money that will go directly to research seeking to cure mitochondrial diseases. The foundation pledges that 100 percent of the funds raised will go directly to research. Mitochondrial diseases are hereditary disorders that affect the ability of cells within the body to produce energy. The foundation covers several diseases, including MELAS, MERRF, and Leigh's Syndrome, among others. Established in 2000, it supports research and serves patients and their family members, health professionals and the general public.

President: William E. Cunningham
Executive Director: Sandra Cunningham
Year Established: 2000
Acronym: MITOCURE

Keywords
Foundation for a Cure for Mitochondrial Diseases, Inc.; Mitochondrial Diseases

1601 Foundation for Children with Atypical HUS

7018 Forest Oak Drive
Barnhart, MO 63012

Phone: (636) 942-4425
Fax: (314) 429-3790
E-mail: SaturnRacer1@cs.com
http://www.AtypicalHus.50megs.com

The Foundation for Children with Atypical HUS is a not-for-profit organization that provides information to families affected by this disease, provides support for families and loved ones, maintains a registry of cases in the United States, and raises funds for research. The letters "HUS" stands for "hemolytic uremic syndrome," Hemolytic refers to the blood, and uremic refers to kidney function. Regular HUS, a rare condition, is caused by a bacterium such as E. coli. Atypical HUS is a rare condition that is not caused by an external agent. Instead, a chain of events, such as blood clotting, begins that causes damage to the vascular system,red blood cells, lowering platelet counts, and ultimately, also affects kidney function.

President: Bill Biermann
Year Established: 2001
Acronym: Atypical HUS

Keywords
Atypical Hemolytic Uremic Syndrome; Foundation for Children with Atypical HUS; Hemolytic Uremic Syndrome; HUS

1602 Foundation for Ichthyosis & Related Skin Types
1601 Valley Forge Road
Lansdale, PA 19446

Phone: (215) 631-1411
Fax: (215) 631-1413
Toll Free: (800) 545-3286
E-mail: info@scalyskin.org
http://www.scalyskin.org

The Foundation for Ichthyosis & Related Skin Types (FIRST) is a voluntary organization dedicated to helping individuals and families affected by the inherited skin diseases collectively called the ichthyoses. The ichthyoses are a group of rare, inherited disorders characterized by abnormally dry, scaly, thickened skin due to abnormalities in the production of the protein keratin. FIRST provides support, information, education, and advocacy for individuals and families affected by ichthyosis. FIRST supports research into the causes, treatment, and ultimate cure for ichthyosis.

President: Laura Phillips
Executive Director: Jean Pickford
Year Established: 1981
Acronym: FIRST

Keywords
Darier Disease; Disorders of Cornification; Epidermal Nevus Syndrome; Epidermolytic Hyperkeratosis; Erythrokeratodermas; Foundation for Ichthyosis & Related Skin Types; Foundation for Ichthyosis & Related Skin Types (FIRST); Ichthyosis (General); RUD Syndrome; Sjogren Larsson Syndrome; Variable Peeling Skin Syndrome

1603 Foundation for Nager and Miller Syndromes
13210 SE 342nd Street
Auburn, WA 98092

Fax: (253) 288-7679
Toll Free: (800) 507-3667
E-mail: fnms4u@ameritech.net
http://www.fnms.net

The Foundation for Nager and Miller Syndromes is an international, not-for-profit organization that functions as a support group for people affected by two similar genetic conditions (Nager and Miller syndromes) involving severe facial and limb abnormalities. The foundation serves as an information clearinghouse that links other similarly challenged families. An extensive library of resources and medical reports is available to those with Nager and Miller syndromes and their physicians. The organization has initiated and is involved in a genetic research project that is working to locate the genes responsible for these disorders. This study is being conducted at the University of Maryland in Baltimore and John Hopkins. The foundation also provides scholarships to children between the ages of 8 and 18 years who wish to attend a summer camp program in Indiana called About Face. This camp allows children to experience independence and to meet others with similar problems. The foundation publishes a biannual newsletter entitled "All About Me." Articles from this newsletter are regularly reprinted in various other publications. Interpreters are available for written correspondence in German, Portuguese, French, Italian, Spanish, and Polish.

President: DeDe Ann Quill
Year Established: 1992
Acronym: FNMS

Keywords
Acrofacial Dysostosis, Postaxial; Foundation for Nager and Miller Syndromes; G Tube Support; Miller Syndrome; Nager Syndrome

1604 Foundation for Prader-Willi Research
6407 Bardstown Road
Suite 252
Louisville, KY 40291

Phone: (502) 384-8405
Fax: (502) 749-9388
E-mail: info@pwsresearch.org
http://www.pwsresearch.org

President: Rachel Tugon (Executive Director)
Executive Director: Theresa V. Strong, Ph.D. (Chair, Scntfc Advsry Bd)
Year Established: 2001
Acronym: FPWR

Keywords
Advocacy; FPWR; Foundation for Prader Willi Research; Foundation for Prader-Willi Research; Networking; Prader Willi Syndrome; Research

1605 Foundation for Sarcoidosis Research

2502 North Clark Street
Chicago, IL 60614

Phone: (773) 525-2510
Fax: (773) 525-2512
Toll Free: (800) 358-5477
E-mail: info@stopsarcoidosis.org
http://www.stopsarcoidosis.org

The Foundation for Sarcoidosis Research (FSR) is a non-profit organization dedicated to improving care for sarcoidosis patients and to finding a cure for this disease. Sarcoidosis (pronounced SAR-COY-DOE-SIS) is a devastating, potentially fatal, inflammatory disease that can appear in almost any organ in the body. Although the lungs are affected in more than 90% of patients, the disease often attacks the heart, eyes, central nervous system, liver and kidneys. Once thought rare, sarcoidosis is now believed to be more common, and is known to affect people worldwide.

President: Andrea Wilson
Executive Director: Debbie Durrer
Year Established: 2000
Acronym: FSR

Keywords
Fibrosis, Idiopathic Pulmonary; Foundation for Sarcoidosis Research; FSR; Granuloma; Granulomatous Diseases; Immune Disease; Inflammation; Inflammatory Disease; Interstitial Lung Diseases; K.I.S.S.; KISS; Lung Disease; Research; Sarcoidosis

1606 Foundation for the Study of Infant Deaths

Artillery House
11-19 Artillery Row
London, SW1P 1RT, United Kingdom

Phone: +44 (0) 870-787-0885
Fax: +44 (0) 870-787-0725

Toll Free: +44 (0) 870-787-0554
E-mail: fsid@sids.org.uk
http://www.sids.org.uk/fsid

This organization funds medical research into sudden infant death, and provides support and information to parents. It also provides infant health education to reduce the risk of sudden infant death. Located in the United Kingdom, the foundation provides books, leaflets, posters, videos, and other educational materials.

President: Joyce Epstein
Acronym: FSID

Keywords
Foundation for the Study of Infant Deaths; Infant Death; Sudden Infant Death Syndrome

1607 Foundation for Thymic Cancer Research

1 N. 34th Avenue
Longport, NJ 068403

Phone: (609) 823-6081
E-mail: info@thymic.org
http://www.thymic.org

The goals of the Foundation for Thymic Cancer Research include: 1) to collect and share information regarding the treatment, prognosis, and causes of thymic-related cancers and carcinomas, and make this information available at no charge; 2) to educate family physicians and oncologists to the nature of thymic-related cancers to improve diagnosis and treatments; 3) to identify the various modes of treatment and to promote research into other modes; 4) to help promote the development of support systems and a better understanding of the various forms of thymic-related cancers; 5) to collect anecdotal patient histories that may help other patients; 6) to develop a database of physicians, pathologists, and other medical personnel with experience in thymic-related cancers and carcinomas; and 7) to develop products (such as wearing apparel for radiation-sensitive skin) and services to ease the suffering of patients having radiation therapy to the head and neck area due to thymic-related cancers and carcinomas.

President: Alan Neibauer (2002 to present)
Executive Director: Alan Neibauer
Year Established: 2002

Keywords
Foundation for Thymic Cancer Research; Carcinoma

1608 Fragile X Society

Road End House
6 Stortford Road
Great Dunmow, Essex, CM6 1DA, United Kingdom

Phone: +44 (0) 1371-87-5100
Fax: +44 (0) 1371-85-9915
E-mail: info@fragilex.org.uk
http://www.fragilex.org.uk

The Fragile X Society aims to improve the quality of life of all those affected by fragile X syndrome by providing mutual support to fragile X families, providing information to families and professionals, and encouraging research into all aspects of fragile X syndrome. This syndrome is the most common known cause of inherited learning disability. It shows itself in a wide range of difficulties with learning and developmental delay, as well as social, language, attention, emotional, and behavioral problems.

President: Lynne Zwink (Chair)
Year Established: 1990

Keywords
Fragile X; Fragile X Society; Fragile X Syndrome; Learning Disability; Networking; Research; Support Groups

1609 FRAXA Research Foundation

45 Pleasant Street
Newburyport, MA 01950

Phone: (978) 462-1866
Fax: (978) 463-9985
E-mail: info@fraxa.org
http://www.fraxa.org

The FRAXA Research Foundation is a voluntary, not-for-profit organization dedicated to providing support for individuals affected by fragile X syndrome, an X-linked disorder characterized by mental retardation, a large jaw, a high forehead, enlarged testes, and/or other abnormalities in affected males and, in some cases, mild mental retardation in females (heterozygotes). The foundation is also committed to aiding the research efforts of concerned medical professionals throughout the United States. Founded in 1994 by parents of children with fragile X syndrome, the FRAXA Research Foundation is dedicated to educating public officials and the general population about fragile X and to supporting ongoing medical research. The foundation works toward these goals by awarding research grants to university-based scientists and physicians whose purpose is to find

treatments for fragile X syndrome and by encouraging the publication of articles to increase awareness of fragile X syndrome. In addition, the FRAXA Research Foundation puts families with affected children in touch with one another and welcomes questions about this disorder from concerned individuals.

President: Katie Clapp (1994 to Present)
Year Established: 1994
Acronym: FRAXA

Keywords
Fellowships; Fragile X Syndrome; FRAXA Research Foundation; FRAXA Research Foundation, Inc.; Genetic Disorders; Medical Research; Mental Impairment; Mental Retardation

1610 Freeman-Sheldon Parent Support Group

509 East Northmont Way
Salt Lake City, UT 84103

Phone: (801) 364-7060
E-mail: fspsg@mail.burgoyne.com
http://www.fspsg.org

Established in 1982, the Freeman-Sheldon Parent Support Group is an international, voluntary organization that acts as a clearinghouse for information and as a support group for families and individuals affected by Freeman-Sheldon syndrome. This rare genetic disorder is characterized by distinctive abnormalities of the head and facial area including an abnormally small mouth that has a "whistling" appearance; a flat, expressionless face; and/or deeply set, widely spaced eyes. In many cases, additional abnormalities may also be present including malformations of the fingers and/or the feet. The Parent Support Group seeks to provide emotional support, shared experiences, and current medical findings to affected individuals and families, and serves as a resource for healthcare providers, educators, and the general public. It actively encourages and participates in medical research on the cause and treatment of this disease. It also produces educational materials including brochures, a newsletter, a members-only directory, and a bibliography of current medical literature.

Executive Director: Joyce Dolcourt
Year Established: 1982
Acronym: FSPSG

Keywords
Dysplasia, Craniocarpotarsal; Dystrophy, Craniocarpotarsal; Freeman Sheldon Syndrome; Freeman-Shel-

don Parent Support Group; FSPSG; Whistling Face Syndrome

1611 Friedreich's Ataxia Research Alliance

2001 Jefferson Davis Highway
Suite 209
Arlington, VA 22202

Phone: (703) 413-4468
Fax: (703) 413-4467
E-mail: fara@FAResearchAlliance.org
http://www.FAResearchAlliance.org

The Friedreich's Ataxia Research Alliance is a not-for-profit, voluntary organization dedicated to the pursuit of education, scientific and research activities leading to treatments for Friedreich's ataxia and the related sporadic ataxias. Friedreich's ataxia is a rare genetic disorder characterized by the loss of muscle strength and coordination (ataxia), heart enlargement (hypertrophic cardiomyopathy), diabetes, scoliosis, slurred speech and impairment of vision and hearing. Established in 1998, the alliance promotes basic and clinical biomedical research into Friedreich's ataxia and the related sporadic ataxias by conducting seminars and conferences for the research community, providing peer-reviewed research grants, and collaborating with other organizations. Program activities include newsletters, brochures, and a web site.

President: Ronald J. Bartek (1998 to Present)
Year Established: 1998
Acronym: FARA

Keywords
Ataxia; FARA; Friedreich's Ataxia; Friedreich's Ataxia Research Alliance

1612 Friends of Disabled Adults and Children, Too! Inc.

4900 Lewis Road
Stone Mountain, GA 30083

Phone: (770) 491-9014
Fax: (770) 491-0026
E-mail: fodac@fodac.org
http://www.fodac.org

Friends of Disabled Adults and Children, Too! Inc. (FODAC) is a non-profit organization dedicated to providing necessary services and support to physically and mobility impaired people of all ages. Established in 1986, the organization provides free mobility impairment, rehabilitative, and home healthcare equip-

ment. FODAC also has programs for vehicle modification; ramp building on homes, and the distribution of disposable medical equipment. FODAC also provides some vocational reentry and Medicare services.

President: Ed Butchart (1986-Present)
Executive Director: Christopher Brand
Year Established: 1986
Acronym: FODAC

Keywords
Friends of Disabled Adults and Children, Too! Inc.; Friends of Disabled Adults, Inc.; Mobility Impairment; Physical Impairment

1613 FSH Society, Inc.

3 Westwood Road
Lexington, MA 02420

Phone: (781) 860-0501
Fax: (781) 860-0599
E-mail: carol.perez@fshsociety.org
http://www.fshsociety.org

The FSH (facioscapulohumeral) Society, Inc., is a voluntary, not-for-profit organization created to address issues and needs specifically related to facioscapulohumeral muscular dystrophy, commonly called FSH or FSHD. This is a rare inherited muscle disease the main effect of which is progressive weakening and loss of skeletal muscle. Established in 1989, the FSH Society is dedicated to encouraging and promoting research into the nature of this disease through solicitation of grants and contributions from private foundations, the pharmaceutical industry, and other sources. The society also seeks to develop educational programs aimed at the medical community, government bodies, and the public. It accumulates and disseminates timely information about FSHD and actively cooperates with related organizations to foster communication among all interested parties. In addition, the FSH Society promotes professional education; provides appropriate referrals including support groups; and promotes patient advocacy and legislation beneficial to individuals with FSHD. It offers a variety of educational and support materials including brochures, fact sheets, and a newsletter. The FSH Society also provides grants for research.

President: Daniel Paul Perez (1992-Present)
Executive Director: Carol A. Perez
Year Established: 1989
Acronym: FSH Society, Inc.

Keywords
Chromosome 4q35; Facioscapulohumeral Muscular Dystrophy; Facioscapulohumeral Society, Inc.; Facioscapulohumeral Syndrome; FSH Society; FSH Society, Inc.; FSHD; Muscular Dystrophy, Facioscapulohumeral

1614 FSH-Muscular Dystrophy Support Group

8 Caldecote Gardens
Bushey Heath, Hertfordshire, WD23 4GP, United Kingdom

Phone: +44 (0) 208-950-7500
Fax: +44 (0) 208-950-7300
E-mail: fshgroup@hotmail.com
http://www.fsh-group.org

The FSH-Muscular Dystrophy Support Group seeks to improve the quality of life for all those with FSH (facioscapulohumeral muscular dystrophy) and those who care for them. FSH is a muscle-wasting condition, caused by a genetic defect, which may be affecting the level of many of the different proteins in muscles. It is a type of muscular dystrophy.

President: Ms. Lorraine Jonas (Secretary)
Executive Director: Norman Jonas (Administrator)
Year Established: 1985
Acronym: FSH-MD Support Group

Keywords
Facioscapulohumeral Muscular Dystrophy; FSH; FSH Muscular Dystrophy Support Group; FSH-MD; FSH-MD Support Group; FSH-Muscular Dystrophy Support Group; Networking; Support Groups

1615 Fundacion Alfa-1 de Puerto Rico

P.O. Box 6729
Bayamon, PR 00960-9007

Phone: (787) 743-0268
Fax: (787) 743-0268
E-mail: fundacion@alfa1.org
http://www.alfa1.org

The Alpha-1 Foundation of Puerto Rico is an international, nonprofit organization dedicated to providing support to individuals and families affected by alpha-1 antitrypsin deficiency through programs of education, advocacy, and support of research. Alpha-1 antitrypsin deficiency is a rare hereditary metabolic disease characterized by low levels of the enzyme alpha-1 antitrypsin and progressive degenerative and destructive changes in the lungs. The organization's main goal is to increase awareness of alpha-1 antitrypsin deficiency among the general public and healthcare professionals. Established in 1997, the organization also encourages early detection and treatment of this disorder. It produces educational materials, including translations of brochures published by the Alpha-1 Antitrypsin Deficiency Association.

Executive Director: Elaine Alfonzo (Coordinator)
Year Established: 1997

Keywords
Bronchitis, Chronic; Chronic Inflamation; Chronic Inflamation of the Liver; Chronic Obstructive Pulmonary Disease; Cirrhosis; COPD; Emphysema; Emphysema, Chronic; Fundación Alfa 1 de Puerto Rico; Hepatitis, Neonatal; Hereditary Emphysema; Liver Cancer; Non responsive Asthma; Panniculitis

1616 Fundacion Distonia (Dystonia)

Avenida Irarrazaval 5185
Oficinia 311
Nunoa
Santiago, Chile

Phone: +56 (0) 2-226-8874
Fax: +56 (0) 2-226-7346
http://www.distonia.cl/

Fundacion Distonia (Dystonia) is a not-for-profit organization in Chile dedicated to providing information, support, and resources to individuals affected by dystonia, a group of neuromuscular disorders characterized by abnormal muscle rigidity that results in involuntary muscle spasms, abnormal movement patterns, and/or unusual fixed positioning of affected muscles. Dystonia may involve a particular area of the body (focal dystonia) or may be more generalized. Fundacion Distonia was established in 1997 and currently consists of approximately 145 members. The organization is committed to promoting awareness of dystonia among affected individuals and family members, health care professionals, and the general public; engaging in patient advocacy; and conducting support groups for individuals with dystonia and their family members. Fundacion Distonia also has a program to provide free botulinum toxin therapy to affected individuals who cannot otherwise afford such treatment. During such therapy, minute amounts of a toxin produced by the bacteria Clostridium botulinum (botulinum toxin) are injected directly into affected muscles, causing temporary muscular paralysis, thereby preventing spasms and abnormal contraction associated with dystonia. Fundacion Distonia also has informational brochures, a regular newsletter, and a web site on the Internet. The organization's materials are provided in Spanish and French.

President: Benedicte de Pauw (1997 to Present)
Executive Director: Eliana Arre
Year Established: 1997

Keywords
Fundacion Distonia (Dystonia)

1617 Galactosaemia Support Group

31 Cotysmore Road
Sutton Coldfield
West Midlands, B75 6BJ, United Kingdom

E-mail: sue@gsg1.freeserve.co.uk
http://www.gsgnews.tripod.com

The Galactosaemia Support Group (GSG) is a self-help organization that establishes contact and fosters support between patients of all ages with galactosemia, a genetic disorder resulting from defective metabolism of galactose. GSG also offers guidance on foods that are lactose-free, promotes public and professional awareness about galactosemia, and raises funds to support galactosemia research. GSG publishes a newsletter and informational leaflets. Although it is based in the United Kingdom, the group will assist those who contact them from other countries.

President: Sue Bevington
Year Established: 1988
Acronym: GSG

Keywords
Galactosaemia Support Group; Galactosemia

1618 Gambia Epilepsy Association

P.O. Box 132
Banjul, The Gambia, West Africa

Phone: +220 995-5362
Fax: +220 422-7214
E-mail: epilepsygambia@yahoo.co.uk

Gambia Epilepsy Association (GEA) is a general services organization established in 2002 to address the needs of patients who are affected by epilepsy. Epilepsy is a group of disorders characterized by recurrent seizures as a result of unusual electrical activity within the brain. GEA provides advocacy, counseling, prevention and public enlightenment programs. Specific needs are met in areas such as housing, food, clothing, and education. GEA activities also include a registry and support groups.

Executive Director: Dr. James C
Year Established: 2002
Acronym: GEA

Keywords
Epilepsy; Gambia Epilepsy Association

1619 Gastro-Intestinal Research Foundation

70 East Lake Street
Suite 1015
Chicago, IL 60601-5907

Phone: (312) 332-1350
Fax: (312) 332-4757
E-mail: girf@earthlink.net
http://www.girf.org

The Gastro-Intestinal Research Foundation (GIRF) is a not-for-profit, voluntary organization dedicated to raising funds to help promote ongoing gastroenterologic research. Gastroenterology is the study of the digestive system and the disorders that affect the digestive tract. Established in 1962, the foundation has a registry and provides information to interested individuals. The foundation also conducts two seminars on gastro-intestinal health issues each year. These seminars are free and open to the public. The foundation has a variety of educational materials including a regular newsletter and produces brochures on inflammatory bowel disease and women's health issues relating to gastro-intestinal conditions.

President: Barry S. Katz
Executive Director: Jennifer J. Wright
Year Established: 1962
Acronym: GIRF

Keywords
Digestive Diseases; Gastrointestinal Disorders; Gastro-Intestinal Research Foundation; Inflammatory Bowel Disease

1620 Gauchers Association (UK)

3 Bull Pitch
Dursley
Gloucestershire, GL11 4NG, United Kingdom

Phone: +44 (0) 1453-54-9231
E-mail: ga@gaucher.org.uk
http://www.gaucher.org.uk

The Gauchers Association is a nonprofit support group dedicated to providing information and support to families in the United Kingdom, Ireland, and elsewhere whose lives have been affected by Gaucher's disease. Gaucher's disease is the most common type of lipid storage disease (others include Tay-Sachs, Fabry's, and Neimann-Pick diseases) and is characterized by anemia, fatigue, easy bruising, and a tendency to bleed more easily than normal. Established in 1991 and currently consisting of 150 members, the Gauchers Association provides information to the general public and medical professionals about Gaucher's disease, and actively encourages ongoing medical research.

President: Jeremy Manuel (Chairman)
Executive Director: Tanya Collin-Histed
Year Established: 1991

Keywords
Acid Beta Glucosidase Deficiency; Anemia, Familial Splenic; Cerebrosidosis-Lipidosis; Gaucher Disease; Gaucher Disease (Infantile); Gaucher Disease, Acute Cerebral; Gaucher Disease, Norrbottnian; Gauchers Association (UK); Glucocerebrosidase Deficiency; Glucocerebrosidosis; Histiocytosis, Lipid Kerasin Type; Lipidosis, Glucosyl Ceramide

1621 **GBS/CIDP Foundation International**
P.O. Box 262
Wynnewood, PA 19096

Phone: (610) 667-0131
Fax: (610) 667-7036
E-mail: info@gbsfi.com
http://www.gbsfi.com

GBS/CIDP Foundation International, which was established in 1980, provides emotional support and assistance to people affected by this rare disease of the peripheral nervous system. The foundation currently consists of approximately 18,000 members in 160 chapters. It arranges personal visits to affected individuals in hospitals and rehabilitation centers; fosters research into the cause, treatment, and other aspects of the disorder; and directs affected individuals with long-term disabilities to resources for vocational, financial, and other forms of assistance. The foundation's medical advisory board includes neurologists who are active in Guillain-Barre research, physicians in rehabilitation medicine, and physicians who have had Guillain-Barre syndrome. The GBS/CIDP Foundation International also supplies informational materials such as a directory, newsletters, and other literature about the disorder, including a comprehensive 55-page booklet entitled "An Overview for the Layperson."

President: Kim Koehlinger
Executive Director: Estelle Benson
Year Established: 1980
Acronym: GBS

Keywords
Acute Motor Axonal Neuropathy; AIDP Acute Inflammatory Demyelinating Polyneuropathy; AMAN Campylobacter Jejuni; Chronic Inflammatory Demyelinating Polyneuropathy; CIDP; GBS; GBS/CIDP Foundation International; Guillain Barre Syndrome; Miller Fisher Syndrome; Multifocal Motor Neuropathy; Plasmapheresis; Polyneuritis, Acute Idiopathic; Polyneuritis, Chronic

1622 **GeneTests-GeneClinics**
University of Washington School of Medicine
Department of Pediatrics
9725 Third Avenue NE
Suite 602
Seattle, WA 98115

Phone: (206) 221-4674
Fax: (206) 221-4679
E-mail: genetests@genetests.org
http://www.genetests.org

The GeneTests-GeneClinics, a web site funded by the National Library of Medicine, is a medical genetics information resource developed for physicians, other healthcare providers, and researchers, available at no cost to all interested persons. Funding sources include the National Library of Medicine and the National Human Genome Research Institute at the National Institutes of Health, Health Resources and Services Administration, and the US Department of Energy. The site includes: GeneReviews, an online publication of expert-authored disease reviews; Laboratory Directory, an international directory of genetic testing laboratories; clinic directory, an international directory of genetics and prenatal diagnosis clinics; and educational materials including an illustrated glossary, information about genetic services and teaching tools.

President: Roberta A. Pagon, M.D. (Principal Investigator)
Executive Director: Gina McCullough-Grohs (Program Coordinator)

Keywords
GeneClinics; GeneTests; GeneTests-GeneClinics; Helix; Inherited Disorders

1623 Genetic Alliance

4301 Connecticut Avenue NW
Suite 404
Washington, DC 20008-2304

Phone: (202) 966-5557
Fax: (202) 966-8553
Toll Free: (800) 336-4363
E-mail: info@geneticalliance.org
http://www.geneticalliance.org

Genetic Alliance is an international coalition comprised of more than 600 advocacy, research and healthcare organizations that represent millions of individuals with genetic conditions and their interests. As a broad-based coalition of key stakeholders, it leverages the voices of millions of individuals living with genetic conditions. The board and staff of Genetic Alliance empower individuals and families affected by genetic conditions by promoting public participation in informed dialogue; access to quality resources essential for informed choices; leadership development within advocacy communities; involvement of consumers in public policy and healthcare discussions; and collaboration with diverse, underserved and underrepresented communities.

President: Sharon Terry, President and CEO
Executive Director: Mary Davidson
Year Established: 1986

Keywords
Advocacy; Alliance of Genetic Support Groups; Genetic Alliance; Genetic Counseling Referrals; Inherited Disorders

1624 Genetic and Rare Conditions Site

4023 Wescoe
University of Kansas Med Center
3901 Rainbow Boulevard
Medical Genetics, Mail Stop 2024
Kansas City, KS 66160-7318

Phone: (913) 588-6022
Fax: (913) 588-4060
E-mail: dcollins@kumc.edu
http://www.kumc.edu/gec/support

The Genetic and Rare Conditions Site provides information on genetic conditions and birth defects for professionals, educators, and individuals. It links to sites for lay advocacy and support groups, clinics with genetic counselors and geneticists, and sites for children and young adults.

President: Debra Collins
Executive Director: Debra Collins
Year Established: 1996
Acronym: GEC

Keywords
Counseling; GEC; Gene; Genetic and Rare Conditions Site; Hereditary; Support Groups

1625 Genetic Interest Group

Unit 4D
Leroy House
436 Essex Rd
London, N1 3QP, United Kingdom

Phone: +44 (0) 207-704-3141
Fax: +44 (0) 207-359-1447
E-mail: mail@gig.org.uk
http://www.gig.org.uk

The Genetic Interest Group (GIG) is a national alliance of organizations with a membership of more than 130 charities that support children, adults, and families affected by genetic disorders. The primary goal of GIG is to promote awareness and understanding of genetic disorders so that high-quality services for people affected by genetic conditions are developed and made available to all who need them. GIG publishes a quarterly newsletter and seeks to educate the public and raise awareness of human genetics and genetic disorders.

President: Mr. Alastair Kent
Executive Director: Tom Barclay
Year Established: 1988
Acronym: GIG

Keywords
Genetic Interest Group

1626 Genetic Support Network of Victoria

10th Floor, Royal Childrens Hospital
Flemington Road
Parkville, Victoria, 3052, Australia

Phone: +61 (0) 3-8341-6315
Fax: +61 (0) 3-8341-6390
E-mail: info@gsnv.org.au
http://www.gsnv.org.au

The Genetic Support Network of Victoria provides an information, education, support, and advocacy network to empower people to overcome the challenges presented to them by genetic conditions. It provides services, such as facilitating the exchange of information and resources, for existing genetic support groups, and it also aids in the development of new groups. It refers patients and families to support groups for their specific disease. The network was established in 1996.

President: Mr. Tony Briffa (2003-present)
Executive Director: Leah Lonsdale, Genetic Support Coordinator
Year Established: 1999
Acronym: GSNV

Keywords
Genetic Support Network of Victoria

1627   Geneva Centre for Autism
112 Merton Street
Toronto, Ontario, M4S 2 Z8, Canada

Phone: (416) -32-2-78
Fax: (416) -32-2-58
E-mail: info@autism.net
www.autism.net

Geneva Centre for Autism (GCA) is a not-for-profit, voluntary organization located in Toronto, Canada. Founded in 1974, GCA empowers individuals with autism and their families to participate fully within their communities. Autism is a lifelong, nonprogressive neurologic disorder typically appearing before the age of 30 months. It is characterized by language and communication deficits, withdrawal from social contacts and extreme reactions to changes in the immediate environment. GCA offers support groups, patient networking and education to those in need.

President: Roger Nainby (1996-present)
Executive Director: Margaret Whelan
Year Established: 1974
Acronym: GCA

Keywords
Advocacy; Asperger's Syndrome; Autism; Autism Spectrum Disorders; Chinese; Foreign Languages; French; Geneva Centre for Autism; Greek; Lobbying; Networking; Registry; Support Groups

---

1628   Gilda Radner Familial Ovarian Cancer Registry
Roswell Park Cancer Institute
Elm and Carlton Streets
Buffalo, NY 14263-0001

Phone: (716) 845-4503
Fax: (716) 845-8266

Toll Free: (800) 682-7426
E-mail: gradner@roswellpark.org
http://www.ovariancancer.com

The Gilda Radner Familial Ovarian Cancer Registry, located at the Roswell Park Cancer Institute, is dedicated to enrolling families with two or more close relatives with ovarian cancer, promoting and conducting research into the causes and treatment of familial ovarian cancer, and providing information and support to affected individuals and family members. Comedienne Gilda Radner died in 1989 after a long, courageous battle against ovarian cancer. Neither she nor her husband, Gene Wilder, knew that her family history of ovarian and breast cancer put her at a high risk for developing ovarian cancer. The registry, which was renamed in her honor, currently has over 1,700 families enrolled. Ovarian cancer refers to a group of diseases that are characterized by uncontrolled growth and division of cells of the ovary. The cells may grow to form a tumor on the ovary and may also break off from the main tumor and spread (metastasize) to other parts of the body. The Gilda Radner Familial Ovarian Cancer Registry conducts research into the causes of familial ovarian cancer in collaboration with investigators at Stanford University of Medicine and Cambridge University. Research goals include identifying new genes associated with familial ovarian cancer and characterizing lifestyle choices that may reduce ovarian cancer risk in women who may be more susceptible to the disease. The ultimate goal of the registry is to acquire information that will lead to better methods of detecting ovarian cancer and prevent the disease in future generations.

Executive Director: M.S. Piver, MD
Year Established: 1989

Keywords
Gilda Radner Familial Ovarian Cancer Registry

1629   GIST Cancer Research Fund
55 Saw Mill Road
New City, NY 10956

Phone: (845) 634-6060
E-mail: tania5kids@aol.com
http://www.gistinfo.org

The GIST Cancer Research Fund (GCRF) was established in 2001 for the purpose of supporting and encouraging research on gastrointestinal stromal tumors (GIST), which belong to a group of cancers known as soft tissue sarcomas. GCRF also provides information on GIST and helps newly diagnosed patients learn about resources available to them. The number of new cases of GIST in the United States annually is estimated to be 5,000 to 6,000. Gastrointestinal stromal tumors arise in the intestinal tract, with the most common site being the stomach. GCRF provides information on GIST to patients, family members, the general public and the medical community. It conducts fundraising activities to support research related to the diagnosis and treatment of GIST. Other services include support groups and patient networking.

President: Tania Stutman (Chairperson)
Executive Director: Robert Stutman
Year Established: 2001
Acronym: GCRF

Keywords
Gastrointestinal Stromal Tumor; GCRF; GIST; GIST Cancer Research Fund; Networking

---

1630 GIST Support International

12 Bomaca Drive
Doylestown, PA 18901

Phone: (215) 340-9374
Fax: (215) 340-1630
E-mail: gsi@gistsupport.org
http://www.gistsupport.org

GIST Support International (GSI) is a not-for-profit voluntary organization dedicated to outreach, education and support for gastrointestinal stromal tumor patients, their families, and friends. Gastrointestinal stromal tumors belong to a group of cancers known as soft-tissue sarcomas. GSI promotes and encourages ongoing research in the quest for a cure. Through its web site and open enrollment E-mail-based mailing list, GSI provides support and educational information for interested individuals.

President: Lee Ann Lamb
Executive Director: Marina Symcox
Year Established: 2003
Acronym: GSI

Keywords
Gastrointestinal Stromal Tumor; GIST; GIST Support International; Networking; Support Groups

---

1631 Glaucoma Research Foundation

490 Post Street
Suite 1427
San Francisco, CA 94102

Phone: (415) 986-3162
Fax: (415) 986-3763
Toll Free: (800) 826-6693
E-mail: info@glaucoma.org
http://www.glaucoma.org

The Glaucoma Research Foundation is a national, voluntary organization dedicated to protecting and preserving the sight and independence of people with glaucoma through research and education. Glaucoma is a condition characterized by abnormally increased pressure of the fluid of the eye, potentially resulting in partial or complete loss of vision without appropriate treatment. Established in 1978, the Glaucoma Research Foundation provides information and support concerning the various forms of glaucoma including normal tension, pigmentary, congenital, childhood, open-angle, closed-angle, exfoliative, pseudo-exfoliative, and secondary glaucoma. The foundation engages in patient and professional education and conducts and supports various glaucoma research efforts including the Glaucoma Family History Project and the Normal Tension Glaucoma Study.

President: Thomas M. Brunner
Executive Director: Rita Loskill
Year Established: 1978
Acronym: GRF

Keywords
Eye Disorders; Glaucoma; Glaucoma Research Foundation; Glaucoma, Closed Angle; Glaucoma, Congenital; Glaucoma, Exfoliative; Glaucoma, Normal Tension; Glaucoma, Open Angle; Glaucoma, Pigmentary; Glaucoma, Pseudoexfoliative; Glaucoma, Secondary

---

1632 Gluten Intolerance Group of North America

15110 10th Avenue SW
Suite A
Seattle, WA 98166-1820

Phone: (206) 246-6652
Fax: (206) 246-6531
E-mail: info@gluten.net
http://www.gluten.net

The Gluten Intolerance Group of North America is a national, non-profit organization dedicated to providing information and support to individuals with gluten intolerance diseases, Celiac disease and/or dermatitis herpetiformis, as well as to the families of those affected, healthcare professionals, and the public. Celiac disease is a chronic, immune-mediated intestinal malabsorption disorder caused by intolerance to gluten. Small itchy blisters on the skin surface characterize dermatitis herpetiformis, most commonly on body pressure points, such as elbows, knees, and feet. GIG offers a variety of program services including annual education conferences for professionals and patients; a summer Kid's Camp; a quarterly newsletter and other activities to support the patient, health professionals. It also provides public education and advocates for health changes important to persons with gluten intolerance. Materials available include patient resource guides, cookbooks, book reviews, research reports, information on specific drug therapies, brochures, videotapes for purchase or rental and a quarterly newsletter.

President: Ray Wikle
Executive Director: Cynthis Kupper, RD, CD
Year Established: 1974
Acronym: GIG

Keywords
Celiac Sprue; Dermatitis, Herpetiformis; Duhring Disease; Gluten Intolerance; Gluten Intolerance Group of North America; Gluten Sensitivity

1633 GOLD, Global Organisation for Lysosomal Diseases

P.O. Box 609
Chalfont St Giles, HP8 4WU, United Kingdom

Phone: +44 (0) 1494-87-0708
E-mail: info@goldinfo.org
http://www.goldinfo.org

The Global Organisation for Lysosomal Diseases is an international collaboration of scientific and medical associations, patient groups, and commercial concerns dedicated to improving the lives of patients with lysosomal diseases. Lysosomal storage diseases are inherited metabolic diseases characterized by a build-up of various toxic materials in the body's cells as a result of enzyme deficiencies.

President: Dr. Ann Hale

Keywords
GOLD, Global Organisation for Lysosomal Diseases

1634 Goldenhar Syndrome Support Network Society

9325 163 Street
Alberta, T5R 2P4, Canada

Phone: (780) 842-3420
E-mail: support@goldenharsyndrome.org
http://www.goldenharsyndrome.org

The Goldenhar Syndrome Support Network is a not-for-profit organization dedicated to providing support and information to families and individuals affected by Goldenhar syndrome and its associated conditions. Goldenhar syndrome, often used synonymously with oculo-auriculo-vertebral (OAV) spectrum, is a rare disorder that is apparent at birth (congenital). It is characterized by a wide spectrum of symptoms and physical features that may vary greatly in range and severity from case to case. However, such abnormalities tend to involve the cheekbones, jaws, mouth, ears, eyes, and/or bones of the spinal column (vertebrae).

President: Barb Miles (1998-Present)
Executive Director: Lynn Perlitz
Year Established: 1998
Acronym: GSSN

Keywords
Facio Auriculo Vertebral Spectrum; Goldenhar Syndrome; Goldenhar Syndrome Support Network Society; Hemifacial Microsomia; HFM; OAV Spectrum; Oculo Auriculo Vertebral Dysplasia; Oculo Auriculo Vertebral Spectrum

1635 Gorlin Syndrome Group

11 Blackberry Way
Penwortham, Preston, PR1 9LQ, United Kingdom

Phone: +44 (0) 1772-51-7624
E-mail: gorlin.group@btconnect.com
http://www.gorlingroup.co.uk

The Gorlin Syndrome Group is a rare-disorder organization located in the United Kingdom. Founded in 1992, it has three objectives. The first is to relieve sickness, and to protect and preserve the health of people affected by Gorlin syndrome, a hereditary condition that can affect various organs. Individuals with this syndrome usually have the three main characteristics, which are skin cancers, cysts of the jaw, and pits on the palms and soles of the feet. In addition, other less common complaints may be linked to this syndrome. The second goal of the Gorlin Syndrome Group is to promote the advancement of education of the medical community and the general public. The third is to promote research into the causes, effects, treatments, and management of Gorlin syndrome, and to disseminate the results. The Gorlin Syndrome Group offers patient networking, and support groups among its services.

President: Mrs. Sally Webster
Year Established: 1992

Keywords
Gorlin Syndrome; Gorlin Syndrome Group; Networking; Nevoid Basal Cell Carcinoma Syndrome; Research; Support Groups

1636 Group B Strep Association

P.O. Box 16515
Chapel Hill, NC 27516

E-mail: bstrep@mindspring.com
http://www.groupbstrep.org

The Group B Strep Association (GBSA) is a voluntary not-for-profit organization dedicated to educating the public about group B streptococcus (GBS) bacterial infections during pregnancies. Established in 1990 by parents whose babies were affected by GBS infections, the Group B Strep Association works closely with its medical advisory board of researchers and physicians to help bring about guidelines for testing and treatment of GBS. The organization promotes routine screening of pregnant women for GBS and generates continuing support for vaccine research. The Group B Strep Association promotes patient advocacy, public awareness, and beneficial legislation and provides a variety of educational and support materials to patients, family members, healthcare professionals, and the general public. These include a newsletter and brochures.

President: Gina Burns (1990-Present)
Year Established: 1990
Acronym: GBSA

Keywords
Group B Strep Association; Group B Streptococcus; Infection in Newborns; Meningitis; Pre Term Labor; Sepsis

1637 Guardians of Hydrocephalus Research Foundation

2618 Avenue Z
Brooklyn, NY 11235

Phone: (718) 743-4473
Fax: (718) 743-1171
Toll Free: (800) 458-8655
E-mail: GHRF2618@aol.com

The Guardians of Hydrocephalus Research Foundation is a national, voluntary health organization dedicated to aiding and assisting children with hydrocephalus and their families. Hydrocephalus is an abnormal accumulation of cerebrospinal fluid, causing a build-up of pressure inside the head. The efforts of the foundation are directed at disseminating information to the general public so that a better understanding of hydrocephalus will be established. The foundation supports research into the causes, prevention, and cure of hydrocephalus. For example, the foundation conducts a research program at the New York University Medical Center, interacts with physicians and medical centers across the United States and Canada including the Universities of California at San Francisco and San Diego, the Texas Medical Center, and Sick Children's Hospital in Toronto, Canada. The foundation also offers networking services to parents and supports the development of Satellite Information Centers, which are designed to form a network of information, assistance, and support. The foundation's materials include pamphlets, reprints, fact sheets, and booklets.

President: Michael Fischetti Sr.
Executive Director: Unknown
Year Established: 1977
Acronym: GHRF

Keywords
Acrocallosal Syndrome, Schinzel Type; Agenesis of the Corpus Callosum; Craniosynostosis, Primary; Dandy Walker Malformation; Diencephalic Syndrome; Encephalocele; Guardians of Hydrocephalus Research Foundation; Hydranencephaly; Hydrocephalus; Walker Warburg Syndrome

1638 Guillain-Barre Syndrome Foundation of Canada, Inc.

P.O.Box 42016
2852 John Street
Markham, Ontario, L3R 5R0, Canada

Phone: (905) -64-0-00
Fax: (905) -64-0-98
E-mail: keast@sprint.ca
http://www.gbsfi.com

Guillain-Barre Syndrome Foundation of Canada, Inc., is a rare disorder support group that provides information and education to patients and families affected by Guillain-Barre syndrome (GBS). This is an inflammatory disorder characterized by the rapid onset of weakness and, often, paralysis of the legs, arms, breathing muscles, and face. Founded in 2003, the Guillain-Barre Syndrome Foundation of Canada provides support, advocacy, networking, and referrals to its patients.

President: Dr. Denise Bowes (2004-2006)
Executive Director: Ms. Susan Keast
Year Established: 2003
Acronym: GBSFCI

Keywords
Advocacy; Chronic Ideopathic Demyelinating Neuropathy; CIDP; GBS; Guillain Barre Syndrome; Guillain Barre Syndrome Foundation of Canada, Inc.; Guillain-Barre Syndrome Foundation of Canada, Inc.; Miller Fisher Syndrome; Networking; Research; Support Groups

1639 Guillain-Barre Syndrome Support Group

Lincolnshire County Council Offices
Eastgate
Sleaford
Lincolnshire, NG34 7EB, United Kingdom

Phone: +44 (0) 1529-30-4615
Toll Free: +44 (0) 800-37-4803
E-mail: admin@gbs.org.uk
http://www.gbs.org.uk

The Guillain-Barre Syndrome Support Group of the United Kingdom is a national voluntary health organization dedicated to providing information, support, and resources to affected individuals, family members, and friends. Guillain-Barre syndrome (GBS) is a rare, rapidly progressive disorder that affects nerves outside the brain and spinal cord (peripheral nervous system). GBS frequently follows an upper respiratory or gastrointestinal infection. The syndrome is characterized by nerve inflammation (polyneuritis) and associated with weakness, tingling and numbness that may rapidly progress to paralysis. Such symptoms initially affect the feet and spread to the trunk, arms, and face. The syndrome often resolves in a few weeks or months, but some residual symptoms may persist for longer periods. Although the exact cause of Guillain-Barre syndrome is unknown, it is thought to result from an abnormal autoimmune response following infection. The Guillain-Barre Syndrome Support Group of the United Kingdom was founded in 1985 and currently consists of approximately 2,000 members. The group is committed to educating affected individuals, healthcare professionals, and the public about Guillain-Barre syndrome. In addition, the group provides educational materials including a regular newsletter entitled "Reaching Out" and several guides such as "GBS: Quick Guide," "The GBS Patient in Intensive Care," and "Other Neuropathies."

President: Glennys Sanders (Honorary President) (1986 to Present)
Executive Director: Andy Leitch (Chairman)
Year Established: 1985
Acronym: GBS Support Group

Keywords
Chronic Inflammatory Demyelinating Polyradiculoneuropathy; Churg Strauss Syndrome; CIDP; Guillain Barre Syndrome; Guillain-Barre Syndrome Support Group; Neuropathy, Peripheral; Transverse Myelitis

1640 Gynecologic Cancer Foundation

230 West Monroe
Suite 2528
Chicago, IL 60638

Phone: (312) 578-1439
Fax: (312) 578-9769
Toll Free: (800) 444-4441
E-mail: info@thegcf.org
http://www.thegcf.org

The Society of Gynecologic Oncologists (SGO) as a not-for-profit charitable organization to support philanthropic programs to benefit women who have, or are at risk for developing gynecologic cancer established the Gynecologic Cancer Foundation (GCF). The mission of the Gynecologic Cancer Foundation is to ensure public awareness of gynecologic cancer prevention, early diagnosis and proper treatment. In addition, the foundation supports research and training related to gynecologic cancers. GCF advances this mission by increasing public and private funds that aid in the development and implementation of programs to meet these goals.

President: Karl C. Podratz, MD, PhD
Executive Director: Karen Carlson
Year Established: 1991
Acronym: GCF

Keywords
Cancer, Cervical; Cancer, Endometrial; Cancer, Gynecological; Cancer, Ovarian; Cancer, Uterine; Cancer, Vulvar; Gynecologic Cancer Foundation

1641 Hairy Cell Leukemia Research Foundation

2345 County Farm Lane
Schaumburg, IL 60194-4809

Phone: (847) 843-1975
Fax: (815) 425-6734

Toll Free: (800) 693-6173
E-mail: eugene.j.farrell@att.net (all lower case)
http://www.hairycellleukemia.org

The Hairy Cell Leukemia Research Foundation is an organization created and run by HCL patients, with the goal of providing support and information to individuals and families, as well as raising funds for research. It is an all-volunteer, non-profit organization. Hairy cell leukemia is a rare blood disorder that affects mostly males in middle age. However, it has been identified in both sexes and among younger adults. It is a chronic leukemia and does not develop into acute leukemia.

President: Sherwood Hanford
Executive Director: Eugene J. Farrell
Year Established: 1985

Keywords
Hairy Cell Leukemia Research Foundation; Leukemia, Hairy Cell

1642 Hallermann-Streiff Syndrome Support Group

3524 Blenheim Road
Phoenix, MD 21131

Phone: (410) 628-2326
E-mail: hmbeam@comcast.net
http://www.hallerman-streiffsupport.org

The Hallermann-Streiff Syndrome Support Group is a not-for-profit, voluntary organization whose goal is to connect families who have Hallermann-Streiff syndrome, a rare genetic syndrome that is primarily characterized by distinctive malformations of the skull and facial region, degenerative skin changes, and short stature. Many affected individuals also have abnormalities of the eyes or the lenses of the eyes. The group offers support, friendship and information to affected individuals and families. It also seeks to raise awareness among medical professionals and the general public.

Year Established: 2005

Keywords
Advocacy; Blindness; Cranio-Facial; Dwarfism; Hallermann Streiff Syndrome; Hallerman-Streiff Syndrome Support Group; Support Groups

1643 Hansen's Disease: Leonard Wood Memorial American Leprosy Foundation

11600 Nebel Street
Rockville, MD 20852, SUA

Phone: (301) 984-1336
Fax: (301) 770-0580
E-mail: lwm-alf@erols.com

The Leonard Wood Memorial American Leprosy Foundation is a not-for-profit research organization dedicated to providing information on and conducting research into the treatment and eventual cure of leprosy. Leprosy is a progressive, chronic infectious disease caused by the bacteria, Mycobacterium leprae. This disease affects the nerves that are located outside the central nervous system and the skin, mucous membranes, and eyes. The organization seeks to conduct, maintain, and support laboratory investigations, clinical studies, and related research with the goal of eradicating the disease. The foundation is also committed to the dissemination of information concerning the source, diagnosis, treatment, and prevention of leprosy. In addition, it seeks to voluntarily aid, establish, maintain, and support clinics, hospitals, and laboratories for the diagnosis and treatment of this disease. Information and reports are provided and research is being conducted on leprosy at the foundation's clinical facility in the Philippines.

Executive Director: Priscilla Reed (Admin. Director)
Year Established: 1928
Acronym: LWM or ALF

Keywords
Hansen's Disease; hello; Leonard Wood Memorial American Leprosy Foundation; Lepra; Leprosy

1644 Headlines—Craniofacial Support

128 Beesmoor Road
Bristol, BS36 2JP, United Kingdom

Phone: +44 (0) 145-485-0557
E-mail: info@headlines.org.uk
http://www.headlines.org.uk

The purpose of Headlines, The Craniofacial Support Group is to support, inform, and advise anyone having, or dealing with, craniosynostosis and associated conditions and syndromes, such as Crouzon syndrome, Saethre-Chotzen syndrome, Pfeiffer syndrome, and Apert's syndrome. These are conditions and syndromes in which abnormalities of the shape of the skull affect the appearance of the head and/or face. Based in the United Kingdom, Headlines has members in 16 countries. In addition to patient education and networking, it provides other services that include publication of a newsletter and support of health professionals. The organization was established in 1993.

President: Gillian M. Ruff—Group Administrator
Year Established: 1993
Acronym: Headlines

Keywords
Apert Syndrome; Craniofacial Disorders; Craniosynostosis; Crouzon Disease; Headlines—Craniofacial Support; Headlines, The Craniofacial Support Group; Menkes Disease; Pfeiffer Syndrome; Saethre Chotzen Syndrome

1645 Healing Exchange Brain Trust

186 Hampshire Street
Cambridge, MA 021391320

Phone: (617) 876-2002
Fax: (617) 876-2332
E-mail: info@braintrust.org
http://www.braintrust.org

The Healing Exchange Brain Trust is a nonprofit organization dedicated to providing, promoting, and improving communication opportunities for individuals who are personally affected by, or who professionally treat or study, localized neurologic disorders (e.g., brain tumors) and subsequent or related healthcare concerns. In 1993, a brain tumor survivor founded the e-mail discussion list known as the BRAINTMR mailing list. The Healing Exchange Brain Trust was later established in 1997 to expand on the purpose and objectives of the BRAINTMR mailing list, utilize new technology, and address new topics. The trust is dedicated to creating, maintaining, offering, or endorsing communication vehicles to promote national and international networking among affected individuals, family members, friends, health professionals, and researchers. In addition, the trust is committed to conveying its knowledge, experiences, and resources to the broader healthcare community and the public to foster acceptance, understanding, and aid for individuals affected by neurologic conditions; to increase public awareness; and to further develop innovative resources. The Healing Exchange Brain Trust also seeks to emphasize ways in which affected individuals, family members, and healthcare professionals may work together to achieve healing and well-being.

Executive Director: Samantha Scolamiero (Founding Director)
Year Established: 1997
Acronym: T.H.E. Brain Trust

Keywords
Healing Exchange Brain Trust

1646 Healing the Children Northeast, Inc.

P.O. Box 129
New Milford, CT 06776

Phone: (860) 355-1828
Fax: (860) 350-6634
E-mail: htcne@htcne.org
http://www.htcne.org

Healing The Children Northeast, Inc. (HTCNE) is an international, voluntary organization dedicated to providing medical and surgical treatment to children from impoverished backgrounds. Established in 1985 and currently consisting of approximately 2,000 members and 14 chapters, HTCNE assembles volunteer teams of medical and surgical health professionals to travel to host countries where children and young adults are treated free of charge. HTCNE's "Medical Missions Abroad" program serves over 3,000 children annually and provides over three million dollars in donated services. Healing The Children Northeast is committed to expanding the Medical Missions Abroad program to meet the increasing needs of children worldwide. HTCNE provides referrals to appropriate healthcare agencies, maintains a database, and offers a variety of materials including brochures, pamphlets, booklets, reports, Spanish language materials, videos, and a quarterly newsletter entitled "Healing."

President: Paul Martel
Year Established: 1985
Acronym: HTCNE

Keywords
Craniofacial Anomalies; Craniofacial Disorders; Craniofacial Surgery; Ear Nose and Throat Surgery; Healing the Children Northeast, Inc.; Heart Defects; Plastic Surgery

1647 Heart and Stroke Foundation of Canada

222 Queen Street
Suite 1402
Ottawa
Ontario, K1P 5VP, Canada

Phone: (613) 569-4361
Fax: (613) 569-3278
E-mail: itstaff@hsf.ca
http://www.heartandstroke.ca; http://www.fmcoeur.ca

The Heart and Stroke Foundation is a national, voluntary, non-profit organization whose mission is to improve the health of Canadians by preventing and reducing disability and death from heart disease and stroke through research, health promotion and advocacy. The Heart and Stroke Foundation of Canada is a federation of ten independent provincial foundations and one national office, led and supported by a force of more than 250,000 volunteers. To fulfill its mission and objectives, the foundation offers a variety of programs and services including sponsoring conferences and scientific meetings; offering scientific awards to recognize the merits of medical researchers' contributions; providing advocacy and representation for its provincial divisions; engaging in lobbying efforts; and providing position statements.

President: Carolyn Brooks
Executive Director: Heather Rourke (Contact Person)
Acronym: HSFC

Keywords
Cardiovascular Disorders; Cerebrovascular Disease; Heart Disease; Heart and Stroke Foundation of Canada; Stroke

1648   Heart Foundation of Australia
Australia

Phone: +61 (0) 2-6269-2631
Fax: +61 (0) 2-6282-5877
E-mail: julia.trevena@heartfoundation.com.au
http://www.heartfoundation.com.au/

The Heart Foundation of Australia is an independent, not-for-profit organization dedicated to reducing disability and life-threatening complications from heart and blood vessel (cardiovascular) disease and improving the cardiovascular health of Australians. Established in 1959, the foundation currently has divisional offices in every state and territory in Australia. The Heart Foundation of Australia works to fulfill its mission and objectives by supporting research concerning cardiovascular health and disease as well as offering educational and other programs directed to health professionals, patients, family members, and the general public that will help to promote cardiovascular health. The foundation supports research programs in major Australian hospitals and universities and establishes links with leading research institutions in the United States and Europe. In addition, it offers a comprehensive series of publications on the prevention and treatment of cardiovascular disease. The foundation provides such resource materials to affected individuals, family members, physicians, allied health professionals, teachers, employers, community groups, journalists, and the general public.

President: Mr. H.R. Hope, BComm, LLB
Executive Director: Dr. Lyn Roberts
Year Established: 1959
Acronym: NHFA

Keywords
Heart Foundation of Australia

1649   Helen Keller National Center for Deaf-Blind Youths and Adults
141 Middle Neck Road
Sands Point, NY 11050

Phone: (516) 944-8900
Fax: (516) 944-7302
TDD: (516) 944-8637
E-mail: hkncinfo@hknc.org
http://www.hknc.org

The mission of the Helen Keller National Center is to enable each person who is deaf-blind to live and work in his or her community of choice. The center provides comprehensive vocational rehabilitation training at its headquarters in New York, as well as assistance with job and residential placements when the training is completed. It has ten regional offices and more than 40 affiliated agencies, a National Training Team and an Older Adult Program. HKNC is a partner in the National Technical Assistance Consortium for Children and Young Adults who are deaf-blind and with DB-LINK, a clearinghouse for information on children who are deaf-blind. HKNC also maintains a national registry of individuals who are deaf-blind.

Executive Director: Joseph J. McNulty
Year Established: 1969
Acronym: HKNC

Keywords
Blindness; CHARGE Syndrome; Deaf Blind; Deafblindness; Deafness and Blindness; Deafness (Children); Helen Keller National Center for Deaf Blind Youths and Adults; Rubella, Congenital; Usher's Syndrome

1650   HELLP Syndrome Society, Inc.
P.O. Box 44
Bethany, WV 26032
http://www.hellpsyndrome.org

The HELLP Syndrome Society, Inc., is a voluntary, rare disease organization. Founded in 1995, HELLP Syndrome Society aims to educate, and inform patients, family members, health professionals, and the general public on HELLP syndrome, a complication of pregnancy that may become life threatening to both mother and baby. The HELLP Syndrome Society provides moral support and helps to raise money for research and education.

President: Stephen Bohach
Year Established: 1995

Keywords
HELLP; HELLP Syndrome; HELLP Syndrome Society, Inc.

1651 Hemangioma Support System
c/o Cynthia Schumerth
1484 Sand Acres Drive
DePere, WI 54115

Phone: (920) 336-9399

The Hemangioma Support System is a national self-help organization dedicated to providing moral support to families affected by hemangiomas. Hemangiomas are benign tumors that are caused by abnormal distribution of blood vessels. Such tumors most commonly occur in infancy or childhood. The organization provides information on capillary and cavernous hemangiomas and offers networking services to affected families, enabling them to exchange information, support, and resources.

President: Cynthia Schumerth
Executive Director: Leslie Andrisiak

Keywords
Angioma, Cavernous; Cavernomas; Cavernous Hemangioma; Hemangioma; Hemangioma Support System; Hemangioma, Capillary; Hemangioma, Familial; Nevus Cavernosus; Vascular Cavernous Malformations, Congenital; Vascular Tumor

1652 Hemimegalencephaly Support Group
18 Oak Street
Shepparton
Victoria, 3630, Australia

Phone: +61 (0) 3-5822-2797
E-mail: hmegroup@cv.quik.com.au
http://www.cv.quik.com.au/hmegroup

The Hemimegalencephaly (HME) Support Group is an international parent support group based in Australia. The HME Support Group is dedicated to of-fering help, support, and information to parents and other family members of children affected by hemimegalencephaly, a rare brain malformation characterized by enlargement of one of the cerebral hemispheres. Associated symptoms often include early, frequent seizures that are often difficult to control and variable developmental delays. The HME Support Group works to fulfill its mission through offering information and mutual support, visiting affected families when possible, and maintaining a web site on the Internet. The organization's web site provides understandable information on hemimegalencephaly, promotes networking among affected families via e-mail, and has a guest book area for online visitors.

Executive Director: Sue Cowper
Year Established: 1996
Acronym: HME Support Group

Keywords
Hemimegalencephaly Support Group

1653 Hemophilia Federation of America
1405 West Pinhook Road
Suite 101
Lafayette, LA 70503

Phone: (337) 261-9787
Fax: (337) 261-1787
Toll Free: (800) 203-9797
E-mail: s.swindle@cox-internet.com
http://www.hemophiliafed.org

The Hemophilia Federation of America exists for the sole purpose of serving its constituents as a patient advocate for, but not limited to, product safety, treatment, insurance, and quality of life issues in a positive and proactive manner. It serves all people with coagulation disorders and complications of treatment, including HIV.

President: Carl Weixler
Year Established: 1993
Acronym: HFA

Keywords
Hemophilia Federation of America; Schools

1654 Henshaws Society for Blind People
John Derby House
88/92 Talbot Road
Old Trafford, Manchester, M16 0GS, United Kingdom

Phone: +44 (0) 161-872-1234
Fax: +44 (0) 161-848-9889
E-mail: info@hsbp.co.uk
http://www.hsbp.co.uk

Henshaws Society for Blind People (HSBP) operates out of several cities in the United Kingdom, providing a range of educational, residential, daycare and community services for blind and visually impaired people of all ages. Services include patient advocacy and networking, support groups, support for research, referrals, and educational materials for patients, caregivers, and medical professionals.

President: Tim Fawcett, Chairman (2001-present)
Executive Director: Dianne Asher, Chief Executive
Year Established: 1873
Acronym: HSBP

Keywords
Blindness; Eye Conditions; Henshaws Society for Blind People; Networking; Research; Support Groups; United Kingdom; Visual Disabilities; Visual Impairments

1655 Hepatitis B Foundation

700 East Butler Avenue
Doylestown, PA 18901-2697

Phone: (215) 489-4900
Fax: (215) 489-4920
E-mail: info@hepb.org
http://www.hepb.org

The Hepatitis B Foundation is a national, non-profit organization dedicated to finding a cure and improving the quality of life for those affected by hepatitis B worldwide. Its commitment includes funding research, promoting disease awareness, supporting immunization and treatment initiatives, and serving as the primary source of information for patients and their families, the medical and scientific community and the general public. Hepatitis B is the most common serious liver infection in the world. Hepatitis B is caused by the hepatitis B virus (HBV), which attacks liver cells and can lead to liver failure, cirrhosis (scarring) or cancer of the liver. Materials provided by the Hepatitis B Foundation include the B Informed newsletter; videos in English, Chinese, Korean, and Vietnamese; brochures; and comprehensive informational packets. Interactive E-mail and a telephone HelpLine are also available.

President: Timothy Block, PhD

Executive Director: Molli C. Conti, Associate Director
Year Established: 1991
Acronym: HBF

Keywords
Hepatitis A; Hepatitis B; Hepatitis B Foundation; Hepatitis C

1656 Hepatitis C Outreach Project

P.O. Box 248
Vancouver, WA 98666

Phone: (503) 285-8712
E-mail: info@hcop.org
http://www.hcop.org

The mission of the Hepatitis C Outreach Project is to inspire, support, and enhance community efforts toward prevention, awareness, education, and treatment of hepatitis C and to promote organ donation. This voluntary organization is committed to working with organizations, agencies, and professional individuals to develop partnerships resulting in quality programming and good public decision-making, based on accurate information regarding hepatitis C. Hepatitis C is a viral infection of the liver, transmitted primarily through infected blood and blood products. It is estimated that 85 percent of those who have such an infection are not aware of it. Delayed diagnosis leaves people at risk for serious damage to the liver.

President: Virginia Lester, RN, MSN
Year Established: 1992
Acronym: HCOP

Keywords
Cirrhosis; Hepatitis C; Hepatitis C Outreach Project; Liver Transplantation

1657 Hepatitis C Society of Canada

P.O. Box 33544
50 Dundurn Street South
Hamilton
Ontario, L8P 4X4, Canada

Phone: (905) 524-0212
Fax: (905) 524-0224
Toll Free: (800) 65-2 43
E-mail: mail@hepatitiscsociety.com
http://www.hepatitiscsociety.com

The Hepatitis C Society of Canada (HeCSC) is a national, voluntary, nonprofit organization dedicated to providing comfort and support to those infected with the hepatitis C virus, their family members, and other concerned individuals; promoting public awareness of hepatitis C and its transmission, care, and prevention; seeking fair treatment of all people living with and affected by hepatitis C; and promoting research that will help to prevent, treat, and cure hepatitis C. Viral hepatitis is inflammatory liver disease caused by viral infection. There are several forms of viral hepatitis that may be caused by different viruses. The virus responsible for hepatitis C, known as HCV, travels in the blood to the liver where it invades liver cells, multiplies, and damages or destroys liver cells. The Hepatitis C Society of Canada has a network of over 20 support groups across Canada to promote mutual support among affected individuals and family members. The society also offers local counseling, support, and referral services via its 800 line; communicates on behalf of employees for fair treatment in the workplace; and assists affected individuals in obtaining benefits from the disability pension plan.

President: Sandi MacKinnon, Acting Chair
Executive Director: Tim McClemont
Year Established: 1994
Acronym: HeCSC

Keywords
Hepatitis C Society of Canada

1658   Hepatitis Foundation International
504 Blick Drive
Silver Spring, MD 20904

Phone: (301) 622-4200
Fax: (301) 622-4702
Toll Free: (800) 891-0707
E-mail: hfi@comcast.net
http://www.hepatitisfoundation.org

Hepatitis Foundation International (HFI) is a voluntary, not-for-profit membership organization dedicated to increasing awareness of the worldwide problem of viral hepatitis and educating the public and health care providers about its prevention, diagnosis, and treatment. Viral hepatitis is inflammatory liver disease caused by viral infection. There are several different forms of viral hepatitis that may be caused by different viruses. These include hepatitis A, hepatitis B, hepatitis C, hepatitis D, and hepatitis E. Depending upon the specific form of the disease and other factors, viral hepatitis may cause liver cell damage, associated scarring of the liver (cirrhosis), and, in some cases, an increased risk of liver cancer. In some cases, affected individuals may have no apparent symptoms. Hepatitis Foundation International was established in 1995 and currently consists of approximately 35,000 members. The foundation focuses exclusively on bringing viral hepatitis under control by supporting research to find cures; providing educational programs and materials to inform health professionals, affected individuals, family members, and the public concerning new diagnostic and treatment methods; and offering a support network for those who are affected by viral hepatitis. Hepatitis Foundation International also engages in patient advocacy and lobbying, provides appropriate referrals, and has a registry. The foundation offers a wide range of educational materials including brochures; posters, information sheets, booklets, and a primer for teachers concerning hepatitis B and substance abuse prevention, a coloring book for children and a regular newsletter entitled "Hepatitis Alert."

President: Thelma King Thiel (1995 - Present)
Executive Director: Phillipe Verheyen (Chief Operating Officer)
Year Established: 1995
Acronym: HFI

Keywords
Diffuse Hepatocellular Inflammatory Disease; French; HBV; Hepatitis A; Hepatitis B; Hepatitis C; Hepatitis D; Hepatitis E; Hepatitis Foundation International; Hepatitis, Non A, Non B (Hepatitis C); HFI; NANB Hepatitis; Neonatal Hepatitis

1659   Hereditary Angioedema Association, Inc.
24 Greenwood Street
Providence, RI 02909

Phone: (401) 272-1327
Fax: (401) 272-4488
http://www.haea.org

The Hereditary Angioedema Association, Inc., is a non-profit organization dedicated to serving persons with angioedema resulting from CI inhibitor deficiency by increasing awareness of the disease and providing patients and physicians with authoritative and readily accessible information about it. The association also serves as a support network for patients, as well as an advocate for research seeking effective therapies and an ultimate cure. Hereditary angioedema is a rare inherited vascular disorder characterized by an excessive accumulation of body fluids that may block the normal flow of blood or lymphatic fluid, resulting in swelling at various locations in the body. With 150 members, the association provides services that include support groups, patient networking, a newsletter, and patient/professional education.

President: Anthony Castaldo
Executive Director: Dennis DeMarinis, Jr.
Year Established: 2000
Acronym: HAE

Keywords
Angioedema, HAE; Hereditary; Hereditary Angioedema Association, Inc.

1660 Hereditary Colon Cancer Association (HCCA)

H6/S16 (5124) C.S.C
600 Highland Avenue
Madison, WI 53792

Phone: (608) 263-1017
Fax: (608) 280-7292
E-mail: cecole@wisc.edu
http://www.hereditarycc.org

The Hereditary Colon Cancer Association (HCCA) provides information and support to patients who are at risk for inherited colon cancers. It also serves as a source of information to health professionals. It seeks to raise and distribute funds for research on the prevention of inherited colon cancers. An annual March Colorectal Cancer Awareness Campaign, two issues annually of the Prevention Advocate newsmagazine, and annual conference for both patients/families and medical professionals are the major yearly projects. With approximately 1800 members, the association was established in 1999.

President: Carolyn Cole
Year Established: 1999
Acronym: HCCA

Keywords
Gardner Syndrome; Hereditary Colon Cancer Association (HCCA); Peutz Jeghers Syndrome; Polyposis, Familial Adenomatous; Polyposis, Juvenile; Turcot's Syndrome

1661 Hereditary Colorectal Cancer Registry

550 N. Broadway
Suite 108
Baltimore, MD 21205-2011

Phone: (410) 955-4041
E-mail: hccregistry@jhmi.edu
http://www.coloncancer.org

This registry is operated through the Molecular Genetics Laboratory of Johns Hopkins Oncology Center. In addition to serving as the foundation for research on hereditary colorectal cancer at Johns Hopkins, the registry provides information on hereditary colorectal cancer to patients and their families, as well as to medical professionals.

Keywords
Cancer, Colon; Familial Adenomatous Polyposis; Hereditary Colorectal Cancer Registry; Polyposis; Turcot Syndrome

1662 Hereditary Disease Foundation

3960 Broadway
6th Floor
New York, NY 10032

Phone: (212) 928-2121
Fax: (212) 928-2172
E-mail: cures@hdfoundation.org
http://www.hdfoundation.org

The Hereditary Disease Foundation is a non-profit research organization established in 1971. Focusing on Huntington's disease as a model for neurodegenerative disorders, the foundation supports an interdisciplinary workshop program that recruits scientists to develop and apply new technologies; supports basic research on genetic illness through grant and postdoctoral fellowship programs at major universities; and provides research tissue to medical investigators. The Hereditary Disease Foundation is supported and guided by a scientific advisory board and a board of trustees. Educational materials produced by the foundation include newsletters, press releases, workshop reports, and reprints.

President: Nancy S. Wexler, PhD (1983-Present)
Executive Director: Judith Lorimer
Year Established: 1971
Acronym: HDF

Keywords
Chorea, Chronic Progressive; Chorea, Degenerative; Chorea, Hereditary; Chorea, Hereditary Chronic Progressive; Chorea, Huntington's; Hereditary Disease Foundation; Huntington's Disease; Huntington's Disease, Very Early Onset; Woody Guthrie's Disease

1663 **Hereditary Multiple Exostoses Support Group**

P.O. Box 395
Headington DO
Oxford, OX3 9WF, United Kingdom

Phone: +44 (0) 1438-86-1866
E-mail: support@hmesg.co.uk
http://www.hmesg.co.uk/

The Hereditary Multiple Exostoses (HME) Support Group is a voluntary, self-help organization in the United Kingdom dedicated to providing information and support to families affected by hereditary multiple exostoses, a rare disorder characterized by multiple bony growths (multiple exostoses) on the surface of various bones of the body. Such bony growths may cause deformities, such as of the shoulder, ankles, ribs and/or wrists. The disorder may be inherited as an autosomal dominant trait. The HME Support Group was established in 1997 and currently has approximately 300 members. The group links families in similar situations and geographical areas; holds regular meetings, publishes a newsletter and has a web site.

President: Helen Small (Chairperson) (1997 to Present)
Executive Director: Dawn Searle (Contact Person)
Year Established: 1997
Acronym: HME Support Group

Keywords
Hereditary Multiple Exostoses Support Group

1664 **Hereditary Neuropathy Foundation, Inc.**

P.O. Box 287103
New York, NY 10128

Phone: (917) 648-6971
E-mail: info@hnf-cure.org
http://www.hnf-cure.org

The Hereditary Neuropathy Foundation is committed to increasing awareness of Charcot Marie Tooth disease (CMT) and funding research. CMT is an inherited neuromuscular disease that is characterized by muscle weakness and atrophy, primarily in the legs but also in the small muscles of the hands. It can impair a person's ability to walk, impede the normal use of one's hands, and even result in the loss of sensation in both hands and feet. NHF publishes educational content, including video streaming, related to CMT on its website. It is committed to expanding awareness of the genetics, diagnosis, and coping methods, both

physician and emotional, associated with CMT. HNF seeks to increase publicity and media attention to inform the public about CMT and the need for early intervention.

President: Allison T. Moore (2002-present)
Executive Director: Susan Wheeler
Year Established: 2002
Acronym: HNF

Keywords
Hereditary Neuropathy Foundation, Inc.

1665 **Hereditary Tyrosinemia Group (Groupe Aide Aux Enfants Tyrosinemiques Du Quebec)**

3162 rue Granville
Jonquiere
Quebec, G7S 2B9, Canada

Phone: (418) 54-8-15
E-mail: gerard.tremblay@sympatico.ca
http://www.cegep-chicoutimi.qc.ca/gaetq/

The Hereditary Tyrosinemia Group (Groupe Aide Aux Enfants Tyrosinemiques Du Quebec) is a not-for-profit organization in Quebec dedicated to providing information, assistance, and support to parents of children with hereditary tyrosinemia, a rare inborn error of metabolism of the amino acid tyrosine. The disorder, which is caused by deficiency of the enzyme fumarylacetoacetase, is inherited as an autosomal recessive trait. Associated symptoms and findings may become apparent soon after birth or during early childhood and may include liver and/or kidney dysfunction, neurologic abnormalities such as developmental delay and mental retardation, and/or other abnormalities. The Hereditary Tyrosinemia Group was established in 1989 and currently consists of approximately 100 members. The group provides referrals for genetic counseling, offers information on management of the disease, and promotes and supports research. In addition, the group holds regular meetings for members; provides networking services, enabling affected families to exchange mutual support, information, and resources; and offers educational materials including brochures.

President: Gerard Tremblay
Executive Director: Same as above.
Year Established: 1989
Acronym: GAETQ

Keywords
Hereditary Tyrosinemia Group (Groupe Aide Aux Enfants Tyrosinemiques Du Quebec); Tyrosinemia, Hepatorenal Type; Tyrosinemia, Hereditary; Tyrosyluria

1666 Hermansky-Pudlak Syndrome Network, Inc.

One South Road
Oyster Bay, NY 11771-1905

Phone: (516) 922-4022
Fax: (516) 624-0640
Toll Free: (800) 789-9477
E-mail: appell@worldnet.att.net or dappell@hpsnetwork.org
http://www.hermansky-pudlak.org or http://www.hpsnetwork.org

The Hermansky-Pudlak Syndrome (HPS) Network is an advocacy organization for individuals and families affected by Hermansky-Pudlak syndrome. HPS is an autosomal recessive inborn error of metabolism characterized by albinism, visual impairment, and a bleeding disorder caused by dysfunctional platelets. Presently, the genes associated with HPS1 through HPS7 have been identified, and identification of more genes is expected. HPS1 and HPS4 involve pulmonary fibrosis, which can become life threatening by middle age. Granulomatous inflammatory bowel disease similar to Crohn's disease occurs in approximately 15% of individuals across all mutations. The HPS Network, established in 1992, is dedicated to networking individuals, physicians and researchers for the purpose of education and research. The network maintains a registry and creates educational materials and newsletters. Annual conferences, international meetings and presentations are among some of the outreach priorities. A cure is the ultimate goal.

President: Donna Jean Appell, R.N. (1992-Present)
Executive Director: Same as above.
Year Established: 1992
Acronym: HPS Network, Inc.

Keywords
Albinism; Granulomatous Inflammatory Bowel Disease; Hermansky Pudlak Syndrome; Hermansky-Pudlak Syndrome Network; Hermansky-Pudlak Syndrome Network, Inc.; HPS Network, Inc.; Lung Disease, Fibrotic; Platelet Storage Pool Disorder; Pulminary Fibrosis; Renal Disease

1667 HHT Foundation International, Inc.

P.O. Box 329
Monkton, MD 21111

Phone: (410) 357-9932
Fax: (410) 357-9931
Toll Free: (800) 448-6389
E-mail: hhtinfo@hht.org
http://www.hht.org

The HHT Foundation International, Inc., is a not-for-profit organization dedicated to increasing public and professional awareness and understanding of hereditary hemorrhagic telangiectasia (HHT), also known as Osler Weber Rendu syndrome. This is an inherited vascular (blood vessel) disorder characterized by direct connections between arteries and veins with no intervening capillaries, or by the dilation of small vessels. These telangiectases occur in various organs of the body such as the lungs, brain, liver, GI tract, nose, mouth, lips, fingers and toes. The HHT Foundation supports ongoing medical research into the causes, prevention, and treatment of HHT, and offers patient education materials and referrals from a web site and through a toll-free number and an international number. Educational information for medical professionals and for patients is available by mail, via the web site and by newsletter.

President: Beth Plan (2004-2006)
Executive Director: Marianne S. Clancy, Executive Director
Year Established: 1990
Acronym: HHT Foundation

Keywords
Hereditary Hemorrhagic Telangiectasia; HHT; HHT Foundation; HHT Foundation International, Inc.; Osler Weber Rendu Syndrome; Rendu Osler Weber Syndrome

1668 Hidradenitis Suppurativa Foundation, Inc

801 West Hawthorn Street
#206
San Diego, CA 92101

Phone: (619) 255-7781
Fax: (619) 239-3271
E-mail: info@hs-foundation.org
http://www.hs-foundation.org

The Hidradenitis Suppurativa Foundation, Inc., (HSF) is a national, not-for-profit organization that was founded to fund efforts to determine the molecular and cellular causes of hidradenitis suppurativa, a chronic disease that occurs as a result of obstruction of hair follicles and secondary infection and inflammation of certain sweat glands. The features of HS include painful lesions, scarring, and recurrent discharge on the skin under the arms, around the groin and buttocks, and under the breasts. It is not contagious and is not a sexually transmitted disease. The foundation hopes to aid in the development and delivery of more effective therapies for patients with HS, and also supports education and advocacy.

President: Michelle Barlow (President)
Executive Director: Robert Howes (Vice Presidet)
Year Established: 2005
Acronym: HSF

Keywords
Advocacy; Hidradenitis Suppurativa; Hidradenitis Suppurativa Foundation, Inc; HSF; Research

1669 Histiocytosis Association of America

72 East Holly Avenue
Suite 101
Pitman, NJ 08071

Phone: (856) 589-6606
Fax: (856) 589-6614
Toll Free: (800) 548-2758
E-mail: histiocyte@aol.com
http://www.histio.org

The Histiocytosis Association of America is a national, not-for-profit organization committed to the promotion of scientific research into the histiocytoses and the development of improved control and management of these diseases. The ultimate goal is medical research leading to the prevention and cure of histiocytosis. Established in 1986, the association seeks to provide solutions to problems that are specific to people who have histiocytosis and offers support to affected individuals and their families. It promotes public education and produces educational materials. These include brochures, a networking directory, and "white papers" that are used in the evaluation of children with Langerhans cell histiocytosis (LCH) and other histiocytoses. Diseases that are represented by the association include histiocytosis X, Langerhans cell histiocytosis, Letterer-Siwe disease, Hand-Schuller-Christian syndrome, eosinophilic granuloma, pulmonary granuloma, Hashimoto-Pritzker syndrome, Langerhans cell granulomatosis, familial hemophagocytic lymphohistiocytosis, virus-associated hemophagocytic lymphohistiocytosis, xanthogranuloma, and diabetes insipidus with Langerhans cell histiocytosis.

President: Jeffrey M. Toughill (1993-Present)
Executive Director: Jeffrey M. Toughill
Year Established: 1986

Keywords
Granuloma, Eosinophilic; Granuloma, Pulmonary Eosinophilic; Granulomatosis, Langerhans Cell; Hand Schuller Christian Syndrome; Hashimoto Pritzker Syndrome; Histiocytosis; Histiocytosis Association of America; Histiocytosis Type I; Histiocytosis X; Histiocytosis, Langerhans Cell; Histiocytosis, Pure Cutaneous; Histiocytosis, Sinus; Histiocytosis, Sinus with Massive Lymphadenopathy; Letterer Siwe Disease; Lymphohistiocytosis, Familial Hemophagocytic; Lymphohistiocytosis, Virus-Associated Hemophagocytic; Reticuloendotheliosis, Non Lipid; Reticulohistiocytoma; Xanthogranuloma

1670 Histiocytosis Association of Canada

29095 Okanagan Mission RPO
Kelowan, BC, V1W 1K2, Canada

Phone: (250) -76-4-61
Fax: (250) -76-4-61
E-mail: histio.canada@shaw.ca
http://www.histio.org/ca

The Histiocytosis Association of Canada provides information to patients and families affected by Langerhans cell histiocytosis, a rare disorder that primarily affects children but may also be found among adults. Although the disease was first described more than 100 years ago, little has been known about it until recent years. In patients with this disease, too many histiocytes (a type of white blood cell) accumulate in certain areas within the body and cause a significantly long list of health problems. The Histiocytosis Association of Canada works to educate affected families and the public and encourages research and relays information to medical professionals.

President: Wendy Hazel

Keywords
Canada; Eosinophilic Granuloma; Hand Schuller Christian Syndrome; Histiocytosis Association of Canada; Histiocytosis X; Langerhans Cell Histiocytosis; Letterer Siwe Disease; Networking; Patient Education; Professional Education; Referrals

1671 HITS (UK) (Family Support Network)

C/O Terri Grant
Saskatchewan
99 Great Cambridge Road
London, N17 7LN, United Kingdom

Phone: +44 (0) 7940-11-4943
Fax: +44 (0) 208-352-1824
E-mail: tgrant@hitsuk.freeserve.co.uk
http://www.e-fervour.com/hits

The aim of HITS (UK), Family Support Network, is to enrich the lives of children and families affected by Hypomelanosis of Ito by encouraging communication, facilitating the flow of information between families and health professionals, and generally reducing the sense of isolation patients and families may experience. A voluntary, not-for-profit organization, the network publishes a quarterly newsletter, organizes an annual family event, and promotes broader understanding of hypomelanosis of Ito. This rare disorder can affect individuals in many different ways. It may produce dermatologic or neurologic symptoms, specific eye conditions, seizures, autism, and/or abnormalities of the bones, among other things. The Family Support Network operates predominantly in the U.K., where it is based, but will provide assistance in other parts of the world, if necessary.

President: Terri Grant
Year Established: 2000
Acronym: H.I.T.S.

Keywords
HITS (UK) (Family Support Network); H.I.T.S. (UK) (Family Support Network); Hypomelanosis of Ito

1672 HKPP Listserv/Periodic Paralysis Newsdesk

2235 B 36th Street SW
Calgary, Alberta, T3E 2Z3, Canada

Phone: (403) -24-4-72
E-mail: deb.greant@shaw.ca
http://www.hkpp.org

HKPP Listserv/ Periodic Paralysis Newsdesk facilitates the timely diagnosis and optimal care of individuals affected by periodic paralysis. This is accomplished by providing medical information to both patients and medical professionals, and encouraging the search for better diagnostic and treatment methods, and, ultimately, a cure. HKPP Listserv/Periodic Paralysis Newsdesk also provides day-to-day peer support for patients and families. The periodic paralyses are a group of muscle diseases characterized by muscle weakness appearing at irregular intervals.

President: Deborah Cavel-Greant/Donald Anderson
Year Established: 1997
Acronym: HKPP List

Keywords
HKPP Listserv/Periodic Paralysis Newsdesk

1673 HOPE (The Heart of Pediatric Electrophysiology)

P.O. Box 519
Park Ridge, NJ 07565

Phone: (201) 505-9383
Fax: (201) 505-0920
Toll Free: (877) 394-4673
E-mail: info@heartbeatsofhope.org,
info@timothysyndrome.org
http://www.heartbeatsofhope.org;
http://www.timothysyndrome.org

HOPE (The Heart of Pediatric Electrophysiology) is a not-for-profit organization whose mission is to provide support, awareness and research information for individuals and families affected by cardiac arrhythmias. HOPE is primarily concerned with electrical disturbances of the heart that create abnormally prolonged cardiac "repolarization" times (long QT interval). These types of heart irregularities can be life threatening, and they affect approximately 250,000 young people in the United States. Timothy syndrome, a rare genetic disorder identified in 2004, is a condition toward which HOPE devotes a high degree of attention. Children with Timothy syndrome often have heart defects, including heart rhythm disturbances, and HOPE is instrumental is providing research information about this disorder. HOPE promotes the development of support groups, conferences and camps for children and young adults. It also provides funding for research into the diagnosis and treatment of a spectrum of cardiac arrhythmias.

President: Christine Badame (1999-present)
Year Established: 1999

Keywords
Advocacy; Arrhythmogenic Right Ventricular Dysplasia; ARVD; Cardiac; Cardiac Arrhythmia; Catecholaminergic Polymorphic Ventricular Tachycardia; CPVT; Heart; HOPE; HOPE (The Heart of Pediatric Electrophysiology); Hypertropic Cardiomyopathy; Long QT Syndrome; LQTS; Networking; Registry; Research; Timothy Syndrome; Torsades de Pointe; Ventricular Fibrillation; Ventricular Tachycardia; Wolf-Parkinson-White Syndrome; WPW

1674 The Hormone Foundation

8401 Connecticut Avenue
Suite 900
Chevy Chase, MD 20815

Fax: (310) 941-0259
Toll Free: (800) 467-6663
E-mail: hormone@endo-sociey.org
http://www.hormone.org

The Hormone Foundation, the public education affiliate of The Endocrine Society, is dedicated to serving as a resource for the public by promoting the prevention, treatment and cure of hormone-related conditions through public outreach and education. Program areas include diabetes, obesity, menopause, hormone abuse, thyroid diseases, and rare endocrine conditions.

President: Lisa Fish, MD
Executive Director: Jim Straight
Year Established: 1997

Keywords
Adrenal; Adrenal Hyperplasia; Diabetes; Diabetes Insipidus; Diabetes, Insulin Dependent; Endocrine; Endocrinology; Growth Disorders; Hormone; Hormone Foundation; Hypoparathyroidism; Hypothyroidism; Menopause; Metabolic Syndrome; Obesity; Osteoporosis; PCOS; Pituitary; Polycystic Ovary Syndrome; Pseudohypoparathyroidism; Steroid Abuse; Thyroid

1675 Hospice Web

Web Site on the Internet

E-mail: hospice@hospiceweb.com
http://www.hospiceweb.com

Hospice Web, a web site on the Internet, explains the purpose of and unique services provided by hospice care. Hospice Web also provides a searchable online directory of the over 2,500 hospices in the United States, helping online users quickly locate hospices in their local areas; a "Frequently Asked Questions" (FAQ) area; dynamic links to other hospice sites on the Internet; a bulletin board area called "Hospice Talk" where online users can post, respond to, or simply read other online users' hospice-related questions; and more.

Keywords
Bereavement; Hospice Directory; Hospice Web; Hospice Web (Web Site on the Internet); Life-Threatening Illnesses; Terminal Illness

1676 HS-USA, Inc.

7362 High Hill Drive
Brighton, MI 48116-9143

Phone: (810) 231-3419
E-mail: info@hs-usa.org
http://www.hs-usa.org

HS-USA, Inc., provides emotional support to individuals in the United States affected by hidradenitis suppurativa, a chronic disease of the sweat glands that causes recurring, boil-like lesions, particularly under the arms or in the anal/genital region. HS-USA, Inc., solicits funds for research into the causes, treatments and cures of this disease. It also strives to educate the public and medical professionals about hidradenitis suppurativa and its emotional impact on those affected.

President: R. Vix Kennedy (2001-present)
Executive Director: R. Vix Kennedy
Year Established: 2001
Acronym: HS-USA

Keywords
Acne Inversa; Apocrine Disorders; Apocrine Glands; Boils; Folliculitis; Hidradenitis; Hidradenitis Suppurativa; HS-USA, Inc.; Insulin Resistance; Sweat Glands; Verneuils

1677 Human BSE Foundation

Matfen Court
Chester Le Street
County Durham, DH2 2TX, United Kingdom

Phone: +44 (0) 191-389-4157
E-mail: info@hbsef.org
http://www.hbsef.org

The Human BSE Foundation (HBSEF) is a registered charity in the UK founded in 1999. Its founders, and those who currently run the organization, are people who have lost a loved one, or are currently nursing a loved one, affected by variant Creutzfeldt-Jakob disease (vcjd), the form of mad cow disease that affects humans. HBSEF helps relatives, friends, and caregivers of people with human BSE. It provides: a help line to support patients, a rapid response system to assist in cases of hardship, information to caretakers regarding the needs of patients, an information bank to support lobbying efforts, and education for medical professionals and other care providers.

President: J. Gibbs (2003-2005
Executive Director: Frances Hall
Year Established: 1999

Keywords
Human BSE Foundation

1678 Human Growth Foundation

997 Glen Cove Avenue
Glen Head, NY 11545

Phone: (516) 671-4041
Fax: (516) 671-4055
Toll Free: (800) 451-6434
E-mail: hgf1@hgfound.org
http://www.hgfound.org/

The Human Growth Foundation is a national, voluntary, not-for-profit organization that was established in 1965. It is dedicated to expanding and accelerating medical research into growth and growth disorders. Composed of concerned parents, friends of children with growth problems, adults experiencing growth hormone deficiency, and interested health professionals, the Human Growth Foundation supports family education and service, public education, support for training of growth specialists and education of medical professionals. It conducts national education conferences, makes starter research grants to investigators, and coordinates Human Growth Month. The foundation also publishes informational pamphlets, booklets, and a monthly newsletter and serves as an information clearinghouse for families of children who have growth disorders.

President: Dr. Stephen Kemp
Executive Director: Patricia Costa
Year Established: 1965
Acronym: HGF

Keywords
Achondrogenesis; Achondroplasia; Acrodysostosis; Acromicric Dysplasia; Arthrogryposis Multiplex Congenita; Bloom Syndrome; Camptomelic Syndrome; Cardio Facio Cutaneous Syndrome; Chromosome 15 Ring; Cockayne Syndrome; Conradi Hunermann Syndrome; Costello Syndrome; Diastrophic Dysplasia; Dwarfism, Laron; Dyggve Melchior Clausen Syndrome; Dyschondrosteosis; Dystrophy, Asphyxiating Thoracic; Ear, Patella, Short Stature Syndrome; Ellis-van Creveld Syndrome; Fairbank Disease; Floating Harbor Syndrome; Froelich's Syndrome; Growth Delay, Constitutional; Growth Hormone Deficiency; Human Growth Foundation; Hypochondroplasia; ISS;

Jansen Type Metaphyseal Chondrodysplasia; Kenny Caffey Syndrome; Kniest Dysplasia; Kniest Syndrome; Laron Dwarfism; Laron Syndrome; LEOPARD Syndrome; Leprechaunism; Leri Pleonosteosis; Marshall Smith Syndrome; McKusick Type Metaphyseal Chondrodysplasia; Megalocornea Mental Retardation Syndrome; Meier Gorlin Syndrome; Metaphyseal Chondrodysplasia, McKusick Type; Metatropic Dysplasia I; Metatropic Dysplasia Type II; Mulibrey Nanism Syndrome (Perheentupa Syndrome); Multiple Epiphyseal Dysplasia; Noonan Syndrome; Perheentupa Syndrome; Robinow Syndrome; Rothmund Thomson Syndrome; RSS; Russell Silver Syndrome; Ruvalcaba Syndrome; Seckel Syndrome; Septooptic Dysplasia; SGA; Short Stature; SHORT Syndrome; Spondyloepiphyseal Dysplasia Congenital; Spondyloepiphyseal Dysplasia Tarda; Trichorhinophalangeal Syndrome Type I; Trichorhinophalangeal Syndrome Type III; Turner Syndrome; Weaver Syndrome; Weill Marchesani Syndrome; Weismann Netter Stuhl Syndrome

---

1679 Hunter's Hope Foundation, Inc.

P.O. Box 643
3859 N. Buffalo Street
Orchard Park, NY 14127

Phone: (716) 667-1200
Fax: (716) 667-1212
Toll Free: (877) 984-4673
E-mail: info@huntershope.org
http://www.huntershope.org

The mission of the Hunter's Hope Foundation, Inc., is to foster public awareness of Krabbe disease and other leukodystrophies in order to increase the likelihood of early detection, to provide information and service linkages to families of children with leukodystrophies, to fund research aimed at identifying new therapies, and, ultimately, to seek a cure. Leukodystrophy is the name given to a group of very rare, progressive, metabolic diseases that affect the brain, spinal cord and, often, the peripheral nerves. Krabbe disease is one type of leukodystrophy. A not-for-profit organization, the Hunter's Hope Foundation serves an international audience, providing educational materials for patients, families, health professionals, and the public. It also provides advocacy, referrals, and a registry.

President: Jacque Waggoner
Executive Director: Jacque Waggoner
Year Established: 1997
Acronym: Hunter's Hope

Keywords
Adrenoleukodystrophy; Alexander's Disease; Hunter's Hope Foundation, Inc.; Leukodystrophy; Leukodystrophy, Canavan's; Leukodystrophy, Globoid Cell; Leukodystrophy, Krabbe; Leukodystrophy, Metachromatic; Lysosomal Storage Diseases; Pelizaeus Merzbacher Brain Sclerosis; Refsum Disease; Zellweger Syndrome

1680 **Huntington Society of Canada**
151 Frederick Street
Suite 400
Kitchener
Ontario, N2H 2M2, Canada

Phone: (519) 749-7063
Fax: (519) 749-8965
Toll Free: (800) 998-7398
E-mail: info@hsc-ca.org
http://www.huntington society.org

The Huntington Society of Canada is a national, not-for-profit network of volunteers and professionals dedicated to finding a cure and treatment for Huntington's disease and improving the quality of life for affected individuals and family members. Huntington's disease (HD) is an inherited degenerative brain disorder characterized by irregular, involuntary movements (chorea); abnormal gait; slurred speech; and progressive disorientation and loss of intellectual function (dementia). Founded in 1973 to fight Huntington's disease through research, service, and education, the society now includes over 50 volunteer chapters and area representatives in all areas of Canada; an expanding network of professional counselors and caregivers; an international team of scientists and physicians; the National Office in Kitchener, Ontario; the Huntington Society of Quebec; and several sister organizations in other countries, forming the International Huntington Association. The Huntington Society of Canada funds basic and clinical research (including partial funding of the research that located the disease gene for HD in 1993); supports the Canadian HD DNA Bank for testing and research; provides information to affected families and professionals; and raises awareness of HD across Canada. The society also sponsors summer holiday and day activity programs for affected individuals; runs local support groups; offers crisis counseling and referral services; and provides a variety of materials on HD.

Year Established: 1973
Acronym: HSC

Keywords
Chorea, Chronic Progressive; Chorea, Degenerative; Chorea, Hereditary; Chorea, Hereditary Chronic Progressive; Chorea, Huntington's; Huntington Society of Canada; Huntington's Disease; Huntington's Disease, Very Early Onset; Woody Guthrie's Disease

1681 **Huntington's Association of South Africa**
13 Davidson Street
Rynfield, Benoni 1501
Gauteng, Republic of South Africa

Phone: +27 (0) 11-849-4984
Fax: +27 (0) 11-484-2489
E-mail: judy.christie@nhls.ac.za
http://www.huntintons.org.za.

The Huntington's United Group of Gauteng in the Republic of South Africa provides support and encouragement to individuals and families affected by Huntington's disease. This is a genetic, neurodegenerative disorder characterized by the gradual development of involuntary muscle movements affecting the hands, feet, face, and trunk, and the gradual deterioration of cognitive processes and memory.

Year Established: 2004
Acronym: HUGG

Keywords
Advocacy; HUGG; Huntington's Association of South Africa; Huntington's Disease; Huntington's United Group of Gauteng; Networking; Support Groups

1682 **Huntington's Disease Association (Christchurch) Inc.**
Box 13018
Armagh, Christchurch, New Zealand

Phone: +64 (0) 3-981-0523
E-mail: shirleyandbrian@paradise.net.nz
http://www.huntingtons.org.nz/Chch.htm

The Huntington's Disease Association (Christchurch), Inc., is an nonprofit, voluntary organization dedicated to supporting families with Huntington's disease in all ways possible. Huntington's disease is an inherited degenerative brain disorder characterized by irregular, involuntary movements (chorea); abnormal gait; slurred speech; and progressive disorientation and loss of intellectual function (dementia). Established in 1981 in New Zealand, the association is committed to educating professionals, supplying information to rest homes and hospitals, and advocating on behalf of individuals with Huntington's disease and their families. The association also hopes to set up supportive networks throughout New Zealand so that families affected by this disorder can meet with one another and have access to medical personnel who have a familiarity with Huntington's disease. The association produces a newsletter, brochures, and audio-visual aids.

President: Jaccy Creake
Executive Director: Judith Baker (Secretary/Treasurer)
Year Established: 1981

Keywords
Huntington's Disease Association (Christchurch) Inc.

1683 Huntington's Disease Society of America

505 Eighth Avenue
Suite 902
New York, NY 10018

Phone: (212) 242-1968
Fax: (212) 239-3430
Toll Free: (800) 345-4372
E-mail: info@hdsa.org
http://www.hdsa.org

The Huntington's Disease Society of America (HDSA) is a national, voluntary health organization dedicated to improving the lives of people with Huntington's disease and to finding a cure for this disease. Huntington's disease is an inherited degenerative brain disorder characterized by irregular, involuntary movements; abnormal gait; slurred speech; and progressive disorientation and loss of intellectual function (dementia). Currently consisting of 40,000 members and 32 chapters across the United States, the society supports medical research into the causes and treatment of Huntington's disease, maintains a national network of services and referrals to assist affected individuals and families and offers a variety of materials through its brochures, newsletters, reports, audiovisual aids, and directory.

President: Barbara Boyle
Executive Director: Barbara Boyle
Year Established: 1986
Acronym: HDSA

Keywords
Chorea, Chronic Progressive; Chorea, Degenerative; Chorea, Hereditary; Chorea, Hereditary Chronic Progressive; Chorea, HDSA; Huntington's; Huntington's Disease; Huntington's Disease Society of America;

Huntington's Disease, Very Early Onset; Woody Guthrie's Disease

1684 Hydrocephalus Association

870 Market Street
Suite 705
San Francisco, CA 94102

Phone: (415) 732-7040
Fax: (415) 732-7044
Toll Free: (888) 598-3789
E-mail: info@hydroassoc.org
http://www.hydroassoc.org

The Hydrocephalus Association is a national, not-for-profit organization that provides support, education and advocacy for families, individuals and professionals dealing with the complex issues of hydrocephalus, the abnormal accumulation of cerebrospinal fluid within the brain. Established in 1983, the organization provides a variety of services including an outreach program that provides one-on-one support; an annual scholarship awarded to young adults with hydrocephalus; and a biennial national conference. Educational materials include books, resource guide, directory of neurosurgeons and a quarterly newsletter.

President: Russell Fudge
Executive Director: Dory Kranz
Year Established: 1983

Keywords
Acrocallosal Syndrome, Schinzel Type; Agenesis of the Corpus Callosum; Arnold-Chiari Malformation; Chiari Malformation; Craniosynostosis, Primary; Dandy Walker Malformation; Diencephalic Syndrome; Encephalocele; Hydranencephaly; Hydrocephalus; Hydrocephalus Association; MASA Syndrome; Mulibrey Nanism Syndrome; Pallister Hall Syndrome; Perheentupa Syndrome; Spina Bifida; VACTERL with Hydrocephalus; Walker Warburg Syndrome

1685 Hydrocephalus Foundation, Inc.

910 Rear Broadway
Route 1
Saugus, MA 01906

Phone: (781) 942-1161
Fax: (781) 231-5250
E-mail: hyfii@netscape.net
http://www.hydrocephalus.org

The Hydrocephalus Foundation, Inc., is a registered 501 (c) 3 non-profit organization dedicated to providing support, educational resources and networking opportunities to patients and families affected by hydrocephalus. This is a condition in which abnormally widened (dilated) cerebral spaces in the brain (ventricles) inhibit the normal flow of cerebrospinal fluid. The foundation also promotes related research and facilitates the training of healthcare professionals to improve patient outcome.

Executive Director: Greg A. Tocco
Year Established: 1996
Acronym: HyFI

Keywords
Hydrocephalus; Hydrocephalus Foundation, Inc; Networking; Support Groups

1686 Hydrocephalus Support Group, Inc.
P.O. Box 4236
Chesterfield, MO 63006-4236

Phone: (636) 532-8228
Fax: (314) 251-5871
E-mail: hydrodb@earthlink.net

The Hydrocephalus Support Group, Inc. (HSG) is a nonprofit, self-help organization dedicated to providing information and support to individuals and families affected by hydrocephalus. Hydrocephalus is a condition characterized by inhibition of the normal flow of cerebrospinal fluid (CSF) within the brain. This fluid build-up can cause pressure, which can be damaging to the brain if not treated promptly. Hydrocephalus is treated surgically by inserting a piece of flexible tubing called a "shunt" into the ventricular system of the brain. Founded in 1986, HSG provides information, engages in patient advocacy, offers networking, promotes interaction with other hydrocephalus organizations and conducts meetings with speakers who address the many concerns of hydrocephalus and related conditions. HSG provides brochures explaining hydrocephalus, a newsletter and other helpful information.

President: Debby Buffa
Year Established: 1986
Acronym: HSG

Keywords
Brain Injury; Cerebral Palsy; Hydrocephalus; Hydrocephalus Support Group, Inc.; Hydrocephaly; Spina Bifida

1687 Hygeia Foundation, Inc.
P.O. Box 3943
New Haven, CT 06525

Phone: (203) 387-3589
E-mail: berman@hygeia.org
http://www.hygeia.org

The Hygeia Foundation, Inc. is a non-profit, 501c3 organization whose mission is to comfort those who grieve the loss of pregnancy or newborn child from causes which range from miscarriage to genetic disorders; to address disparities is healthcare services for medically and economically underserved families with respect, dignity and advocacy; to provide advocacy and resources for maternal and child health. The Hygeia Foundation is striving to improve the awareness of the impact of perinatal and infant loss on families, community, society, and supports the premise that perinatal and infant morbidity and mortality can be affected by providing all women and their families who have been experiencing losses, the availability of perinatal bereavement counseling, pre and inter-conception counseling (including an evaluation and understanding of their losses) and access to comprehensive women's healthcare services.

President: Michael R. Berman, M.D.
Year Established: 1995
Acronym: Hygeia

Keywords
Bereavement; Grieving; Hygeia Foundation, Inc.; Hygeia: An Online Journal for Pregnancy and Neonatal Loss (Web Site on the Internet); Miscarriage; Neonatal Loss; Perinatal Loss; Pregnancy Complications; Pregnancy Loss

1688 Hyperacusis Network
P.O. Box 8007
Green Bay, WI 54308

Phone: (920) 866-3377
E-mail: earhelp@yahoo.com
http://www.hyperacusis.net

The Hyperacusis Network is an international, self-help organization for individuals affected by hyperacusis, a condition characterized by painful sensitivity to normal environmental sound. Established in 1991, the network provides information on hyperacusis, tinnitus, recruitment, and hyperacute hearing. Consisting of 700 members, the organization shares ways to cope with hyperacusis; provides ongoing support; offers information and assistance in securing disability benefits; and reports on current research and treatment options through a monthly newsletter.

President: Dan Malcore (Indefinite)
Year Established: 1991

Keywords
Hearing, Hyperacute; Hyperacusis; Hyperacusis Network; Meniere's Disease; Recruitment, Acoustic; Tinnitus; Vertigo

1689   Hypermobility Syndrome Association

12 Greenacres
Hadleigh
Benfleet, Essex, SS7 2JB, United Kingdom

Phone: +44 (0) 845-345-4465
E-mail: info@hypermobility.org
http://www.hypermobility.org

This is a support group for individuals and families affected by hypermobility syndrome, a composite term referring to laxity of the joints. At one end of the spectrum, this would include diseases such as Marfan syndrome, with potentially serious complications. At the other end, it would include conditions such as benign joint hypermobility syndrome, which may result in pain or other problems but do not pose a serious threat to life and health. The association provides information and educational materials to medical practitioners, as well as to patients and families. Members are welcome from all countries.

President: Nicki Bane
Year Established: 1985
Acronym: HMSA

Keywords
Ehlers Danlos Syndrome; Hypermobility Syndrome; Hypermobility Syndrome Association

1690   Hypertrophic Cardiomyopathy Association of America

P.O. Box 306
Hibernia, NJ 07842

Phone: (973) 983-7429
Fax: (973) 983-7870
Toll Free: (877) 329-4262
E-mail: support@4hcm.org
http://www.4hcm.org

The Hypertrophic Cardiomyopathy Association of America is a national self-help organization dedicated to providing information and support to individuals with hypertrophic cardiomyopathy (HCM) and family members. HCM is a primary noninflammatory disease of the heart muscle characterized by enlargement of the lower left chamber of the heart (left ventricle) and of the fibrous partition dividing the two ventricles (interventricular septum). This results in obstruction of outflow of blood from the ventricle and reduced cardiac output. The organization provides information to the medical community; acts as a referral service for affected individuals and family members, offers networking services, promotes and supports research, and publishes a regular newsletter entitled "HCMA News."

President: Lisa Salberg
Year Established: 1996
Acronym: HCMA

Keywords
Cardiomyopathy, Hypertrophic; HCMA; Hypertrophic Cardiomyopathy Association of America

1691   Hypoparathyroidism Association, Inc.

2835 Salmon Street
Idaho Falls, ID 83406

Phone: (208) 524-3857
Fax: (208) 524-2619
E-mail: hpth@hypoparathyroidism.org, hpth@cableone.net
http://www.hypoparathyroidism.org

The Hypoparathyroidism Association is a self-help group that publishes a newsletter for the purpose of providing a support system for people with hypoparathyroidism and their families. Hypoparathyroidism is a condition characterized by abnormally decreased levels of calcium in the blood due to insufficient production of parathyroid hormones. Symptoms may include weakness; muscle cramps; abnormal sensations such as tingling, burning, and numbness (paresthesia) of the hands; excessive nervousness; uncontrollable cramping spasms of certain muscles; and/or other symptoms. The association seeks to inform healthcare professionals about this rare condition. The newsletter is intended for patients with hypoparathyroidism and their families. A typical issue includes general information about hypoparathyroidism, support group information, and personal essays and letters. Established in 1994, the group also seeks to inform healthcare professionals about this rare condition. The newsletter is intended for patients with hypoparathyroidism and their families. A typical issue includes general information about hypoparathyroidism, support group information, personal essays and letters, news and announcements about the use of the Internet in providing support to patients, and acknowledgments to community organizations who have helped patients.

President: James E. Sanders
Executive Director: Same as above.
Year Established: 1994

Keywords
Community organization; Coping; Hypoparathyroidism; Hypoparathyroidism Association, Inc.; Hypoparathyroidism Newsletter; Kenny Caffey Syndrome; Pseudohypoparathyroidism

1692 IDEAS (IsoDicentric 15 Exchange, Advocacy and Support)

c/o Paul Rivard
Box 4616
Manchester, NH 03108

Phone: (717) 225-5229
E-mail: omfp@idic15.org
http://www.idic15.org

IDEAS (IsoDicentric 15 Exchange Advocacy and Support) is a network of parents and professionals providing information and support to families of children and adults diagnosed with IsoDicentric 15 or other abnormalities of chromosome 15. It was founded in 1994 to support families of children with an IsoDicentric 15 (also called Inverted Duplication of Chromosome 15) and the healthcare professionals who work with them. IsoDicentric 15 is a rare chromosomal disorder that may result in mental retardation, seizures and neurological problems, and autistic-like behaviors. The group also functions as an advocate for children and adults affected by this chromosomal disorder. IDEAS publishes a newsletter entitled "The Mirror" that offers information on current research along with family profiles. The organization provides current information on this disorder and offers support to affected families and other interested individuals. There is also a web site, which provides current information and resources.

President: Nicole Cleary (2001-Present)
Executive Director: Donna Bennett
Year Established: 1994
Acronym: IDEA

Keywords
IDEAS; IDEAS (IsoDicentric 15 Exchange, Advocacy and Support); Inverted Duplication Exchange, Advocacy and Support (IDEAS); Iso Dicentric 15 Exchange

1693 IgA Nephropathy Support Network

89 Ashfield Road
Shelburne Falls, MA 01370

http://www.igansupport.org

The IgA Nephropathy Support Network is a national, voluntary organization dedicated to helping people with IgA nephropathy and their families. IgA nephropathy is a kidney disorder characterized by chronic inflammation of the kidney, blood in the urine (hematuria), abnormally increased levels of protein in the urine (proteinuria), deposits of IgA immunoglobulin in certain areas of the kidney, and other symptoms and physical findings. The primary goal of the IgA Nephropathy Support Network is to function as a clearinghouse for information on IgA nephropathy. To further this goal, the network has prepared pamphlets on the disease and maintains an extensive database of current medical literature related to IgA nephropathy. Patient concerns and the latest medical research are covered in the organization's newsletter. The IgA Nephropathy Support Network also promotes research into the causes, treatments, and possible cures of IgA nephropathy.

President: Dale M. Hellegers (1992 to Present)
Year Established: 1993

Keywords
IgA Nephropathy; IgA Nephropathy Support Network

1694 Ileostomy and Internal Pouch Support Group (UK)

Peverill House
1-5 Mill Road
Ballyclare
Co. Antrim, BT39 9DR, United Kingdom

Phone: +44 (0) 289-334-4043
Fax: +44 (0) 289-332-4606
Toll Free: 0800 0184 724
E-mail: info@the-ia.org.uk
http://www.the-ia.org.uk/

The Ileostomy and Internal Pouch Support Group is a registered charity in the United Kingdom dedicated to helping individuals who have undergone surgical removal of the colon (colectomy) and creation of an ileostomy or an ileo-anal pouch. In individuals who receive an ileostomy, an opening is established between the lower region of the small intestine (ileum) and the abdominal wall, and the body's waste material is collected in an externally attached bag. In individuals with an internal pouch, a reservoir is constructed from a section of the ileum. The Ileostomy and Internal Pouch Support Group was founded in 1956 by a group of people who had ileostomies and by some members of the medical profession. The organization currently includes over 60 local groups throughout Great Britain and Ireland. The group is committed to helping affected individuals return to fully active lives as soon as possible; assisting them with all aspects of their rehabilitation including social activities and relationships with family members, friends, employers, and others; and working in close cooperation with medical authorities as part of a team whose primary aim is the complete rehabilitation of every individual who has received an ileostomy or internal pouch. The Ileostomy and Internal Pouch Support Group is also dedicated to improving knowledge about the management of ileostomies or pouches; encouraging development of new ostomy equipment and skin care preparations; and promoting and coordinating research concerning the diseases that may lead to such surgical procedures and ways to improve the quality of life with an ileostomy or an internal pouch.

President: info@the-ia.org.uk
Executive Director: Same as above.
Year Established: 1956
Acronym: ia

Keywords
Ileostomy and Internal Pouch Support Group (UK)

1695 Immune Deficiency Foundation
40 West Chesapeake Avenue
Suite 308
Towson, MD 21230

Phone: (410) 321-6647
Fax: (410) 321-9165
Toll Free: (800) 296-4433
E-mail: idf@primaryimmune.org
http://www.primaryimmune.org

The Immune Deficiency Foundation is a national, not-for-profit, voluntary health organization that was founded in 1980 by a group of parents with children affected by primary immune deficiency diseases. The foundation has concentrated on creating a national focus for these disorders by supporting research, physician training, and patient and family education. Its objectives are to promote and support scientific research

into the causes, prevention, treatment, and cure of primary immune deficiency diseases; to promote training in medical research and clinical treatment; to gather, coordinate, and disseminate information concerning research and treatment of these disorders; to conduct education campaigns to increase public awareness; and to establish support systems for affected individuals and families throughout the United States. The foundation produces a variety of educational materials including general information booklets; illustrated booklets for children, and a slide set entitled "Our Immune System."

President: Marcia Boyle
Executive Director: Same as above.
Year Established: 1980
Acronym: IDF

Keywords
Agammaglobulinemias, Primary; Angioedema, Hereditary; Ataxia Telangiectasia; B Lymphocyte Disorders; C2 Deficiency; C3 Deficiency; Candidiasis, Chronic Mucocutaneous; Chromosome 10, Monosomy 10p; Chronic Granulomatous Disease; Common Variable Immunodeficiency; Complement Disorders; DiGeorge Syndrome; Goodpasture Syndrome; Granulomatous Disease; Hyper IgM Syndrome; IDF; IgA Deficiency, Selective; IgG Subclass, Deficiencies of; Immune Deficiency Disorders; Immune Deficiency Foundation; Immunodeficiency, Severe Combined; Job Syndrome; Lymphadenopathy, Angioimmunoblastic with Dysproteinemia; McKusick Type Metaphyseal Chondrodysplasia; Neutrophil Defects; Nezelof's Syndrome; Phagocytic Disorders; SCID; Severe Combined Immunodeficiency; T Lymphocyte Disorders; Wiskott Aldrich Syndrome; X Linked Lymphoproliferative Syndrome

---

1696 Immunization Action Coalition/Hepatitis B Coalition
1573 Selby Avenue
Suite 234
St. Paul, MN 55104-6328

Phone: (651) 647-9009
Fax: (651) 647-9131
E-mail: admin@immunize.org
http://www.immunize.org AND www.vaccineinformation.org

The Immunization Action Coalition (IAC) is a nonprofit organization that works to prevent disease by creating and distributing educational materials for health professionals and the public that enhance delivery of safe and effective immunization services and increase their use. The coalition also facilitates communication within the broad immunization community, including parents, concerning issues of safety, efficacy, and the use of vaccines. The Hepatitis B Coalition, a program of IAC, promotes hepatitis B vaccination for all children 0-18 years of age, HBsAg screening for all pregnant women, hepatitis B testing and vaccination for risk groups, and education and treatment for people who are chronically infected with hepatitis B.

Executive Director: Deborah L. Wexler, MD
Year Established: 1990
Acronym: IAC

Keywords
Amharic; Arabic; Armenian; Cambodian; Chickenpox; Chinese; Croatian; Diphtheria; French; German; Haitian Creole; Hepatitis A; Hepatitis B; Hindi; Hmong; IAC; Ilocano; Immunization Action Coalition/Hepatitis B Coalition; Japanese; Korean; Laotian; Measles; Mumps; Persian; Pertussis; Polish; Portuguese; Punjabi; Romanian; Rubella; Russian; Samoan; Serbo Croatian; Tetanus; Thai; Turkish; Vietnamese; Virus, Varicella Zoster

1697 In Touch Trust
10 Norman Road
Sale
Cheshire, M33 3DF, United Kingdom

Phone: +44 (0) 161-905-2440
Fax: +44 (0) 161-718-5787
E-mail: worthington@netscapeonline.co.uk

The In Touch Trust is a not-for-profit organization dedicated to bringing together parents of children with similar special needs such as learning and/or physical disabilities. The trust has a particular interest in assisting those caring for children affected by rare and complex conditions. Established in 1968 and consisting of approximately 1,400 members, In Touch enables parents to network with others whose children may have the same or similar conditions. The trust also provides information concerning a wide range of support groups for specific disorders, many of which help families to come together for the purpose of mutual support. Many of these groups have grown out of the contacts provided by In Touch and are able to offer advice to anyone wishing to set up a new group. In Touch is primarily a service for parents. All inquiries are answered personally by the organizer or her assistant and aim to provide encouragement, sup-

port, and information. Educational materials include a newsletter entitled "In Touch" and a general information sheet.

President: Ann Worthington (1968 to Present)
Year Established: 1968
Acronym: IN TOUCH

Keywords
In Touch Trust; Learning Disabilities

1698 Incontinentia Pigmenti International Foundation
30 East 72nd Street
New York, NY 10021

Phone: (212) 452-1231
Fax: (212) 452-1406
E-mail: ipif@ipif.org
http://www.imgen.bcm.tmc.edu/IPIF

The National Incontinentia Pigmenti Foundation is a national, non-profit organization that was founded in 1995. Guided by a scientific advisory council, the foundation is comprised of affected individuals, physicians, educators, parents, relatives, and volunteers, all of whom are interested in taking a leadership role in supporting research, education, and funding for incontinentia pigmenti (IP). IP is a rare genetic disorder affecting the skin, hair, and teeth. Symptoms may vary greatly in severity from person to person, even within the same family. In some cases, neurological complications, including seizures and/or mental retardation, can occur as a consequence of IP. The mission of the Incontinentia Pigmenti International Foundation is to encourage and support research on IP and to provide family support and education. The organization publishes a newsletter, maintains a national database of health professionals who are experienced with IP, provides referrals, and offers emotional support and the sharing of resources. In addition, the foundation seeks to provide the medical care community with relevant medical information on IP; create awareness of IP on a worldwide basis; and collect and catalogue medical articles on IP.

President: Susanne Bross Emmerich (1995 to Present)
Executive Director: Same.
Year Established: 1995
Acronym: NIPF

Keywords
Bloch Siemens Sulzberger Syndrome; Bloch Sulzberger Syndrome; Incontinentia Pigmenti; Incon-

tinentia Pigmenti International Foundation; IP; National Incontinentia Pigmenti Foundation

1699 Independent Holoprosencephaly Support Site
Web Site on the Internet

E-mail: hpe@att.net
http://hpe.home.att.net

The Independent Holoprosencephaly Support Site is a web site dedicated to enabling families of children with holoprosencephaly (HPE) to share information, support, common experiences, and resources. Holoprosencephaly is a birth defect that occurs early in pregnancy and results in failure of the brain to grow forward and divide in the way that it should. Many pregnancies that involve HPE end in miscarriage. The Independent Holoprosencephaly Support Site provides referrals to organizations, describes the various forms of holoprosencephaly, offers a glossary of commonly used medical terms, and discusses research that has identified the gene responsible for HPE. The site also enables online visitors to subscribe to the HPE e-mail list, enabling affected families to regularly communicate with one another to exchange information and resources via e-mail.

Keywords
Arhinencephaly; Holoprosencephaly; Holoprosencephaly Malformation Complex; Holoprosencephaly Sequence; Holoprosencephaly, Alobar; Holoprosencephaly, Familial Alobar; Holoprosencephaly, Lobar; Holoprosencephaly, Semilobar; HPE; Hydracephaly; Hydrocephaly; Independent Holoprosencephaly Support Site; Independent Holoprosencephaly Support Site (Web Site on the Internet); Microcephaly

1700 Infant Botulism Treatment and Prevention Program
850 Marina Bay Parkway
Room E361
Richmond, CA 94804

Phone: (510) 231-7600
E-mail: ibtpp@infantbotulism.org
http://www.infantbotulism.org

The Infant Botulism Treatment and Prevention Program of the California Department of Health Services provides information for parents, physicians, and others regarding infant botulism. Its services include putting parents in touch with others whose children have experienced infant botulism.

Keywords
Infant Botulism Treatment and Prevention Program

1701 Inflammatory Breast Cancer Research Foundation
321 High School Road, NE
149
Brainbridge Island, WA 98110

Fax: (801) 751-8922
Toll Free: (877) 786-7422
E-mail: info@ibcresearch.org
http://www.ibcresearch.org

The Inflammatory Breast Cancer Research Foundation (IBC Research Foundation) assists scientists and researchers in their quest to determine the definitive cause of inflammatory breast cancer (IBC) and to develop treatments and, ultimately, a cure. The organization's goals are to ignite interest in the study of IBC at every level; to increase awareness of IBC among primary care physicians, nursing professionals, and others to minimize the time from presentation to diagnosis; to increase public awareness to encourage woman to seek medical attention for common IBC symptoms soon after they appear; and to empower patients, caregivers, families and friends to pursue meaningful paths in support of diagnosis and treatment of IBC.

President: G. Owen Johnson (1999-present)
Executive Director: Ginny Mason, BSN, RN
Year Established: 1999
Acronym: IBC Research Foundation

Keywords
Breast Cancer; Cancer; Inflammatory Breast Cancer; Inflammatory Breast Cancer Research Foundation; reserach

1702 Inherited High Cholesterol Foundation
University of Utah
Cardiovascular Genetics Research
410 Chipeta Way
Room 161
Salt Lake City, UT 84108

Phone: (801) 581-8720
Fax: (801) 581-5402
Toll Free: (888) 244-2465

The Inherited High Cholesterol Foundation (IHCF) is a not-for-profit organization dedicated to promoting the early diagnosis and treatment of inherited cholesterol disorders by assisting in the identification of family members who may be predisposed to such disorders. Established in 1995 and currently consisting of approximately 5,400 members, the foundation works in association with the MEDPED (Make Early Diagnoses and Prevent Early Deaths in Medical Pedigrees) program, an international collaboration consisting of research centers around the world dedicated to developing and implementing programs to identify affected individuals and their relatives. The Inherited High Cholesterol Foundation educates members of high-risk families, healthcare providers, insurance companies, appropriate medical institutions and agencies, and the general public about inherited cholesterol disorders such as familial hypercholesterolemia, familial defective apoB, polygenic hypercholesterolemia, and familial combined hyperlipidemia. Individuals with such inherited conditions may be prone to highly elevated levels of cholesterol and an associated risk of early heart attack. The Inherited High Cholesterol Foundation also offers local support to affected individuals and family members and provides a variety of educational materials including pamphlets, brochures, leaflets, and newsletters.

Executive Director: Susan Stephenson, Pharm.D.
Year Established: 1995
Acronym: IHCF

Keywords
Familial Hypercholesterolemia; Hypercholesterolemia; IHCF; Inherited High Cholesterol Foundation

1703 Instituto de Errores Innatos del Metabolismo

Carrera 7 No 43-82
Bogota, Columbia
S.A. Edificio 53 Lab. 305A

Phone: +57 1-320-8320
Fax: +57 1-338-4548
E-mail: abarrera@javeriana.edu.co
http://www.javeriana.edu.co

Instituto de Errores Innatos del Metabolismo (IEIM) is a non-profit organization devoted to enhancing awareness and increasing understanding of inborn errors of metabolism among affected families, medical professionals, and the public. Based in Bogota, Colombia, IEIM also encourages research on these diseases, which are present at birth and represent the inability to break down (metabolize) certain substances within the body because of missing or defective enzymes. Services provided by this institute include genetic counseling, support groups, a genetics center, research, and patient/professional education. The primary language on the Web site is Spanish.

President: Luis Alejandro Barrera
Year Established: 1997
Acronym: IEIM

Keywords
Aspartylglycosaminuria; Cystinosis; Fabry Disease; Gaucher Disease; Hunter Disease; IEIM; Inborn Errors of Metabolism; Instituto de Errores Innatos del Metabolismo; Instituto de Errores Innatos del Metabolismo (IEIM); Leukodystrophy, Metachromatic; Lysosomal Storage Diseases; Morquio Disease; Mucopolysacchridoses; Niemann Pick Disease; Pompe Disease; Research; Support Groups; Tay Sach's Disease

1704 International Alliance of ALS/MND Associations

P.O. Box 246
Northampton, NN1 2PR, United Kingdom

Phone: +44 (0) 1604-61-1821
Fax: +44 (0) 1604-61-1852
E-mail: alliance@alsmndalliance.org
http://www.alsmndalliance.org

The International Alliance of ALS/MND Associations was founded in November 1992 to provide a forum for support and the exchange of information among the worldwide associations. More than 50 national patient support and advocacy groups from over 40 countries worldwide have joined together to form this international alliance. Amyotrophic lateral sclerosis, or motor neurone disease, is a muscle wasting condition, which affects individuals and those who care for them across the world. To help people with the disease, groups of people have come together to form associations.

President: Rodney Harris (Chairperson)
Executive Director: Zoe Tebbutt (Alliance Co-ordinator)
Year Established: 1992

Keywords
ALS; Amyotrophic Lateral Sclerosis; Charcot Marie Tooth; Degenerative Neurological; International Allicane of ALS/MND Associations; International Patient Organization; Lou Gehrig's Disease; MND; Motor Neuron Disease; SLA;

1705 International Bundle Branch Block Association

6631 West 83rd Street
Los Angeles, CA 90045-2875

Phone: (310) 670-9132

The International Bundle Branch Block Association (IBBBA) is a non-profit organization dedicated to providing information to the public and to medical professionals about bundle branch block, a heart dysfunction for which there is no known cure at this time. IBBBA is also concerned with heart conditions related to bundle branch block. In addition to providing information through its publications and a speaker's bureau, it provides support and encouragement to patients and families and assists medical professionals with a bank of information to show trends and aid in medical research.

President: Unknown.
Executive Director: Rita Kurtz Lewis
Year Established: 1979
Acronym: IBBBA

Keywords
International Bundle Branch Block Association

1706 International Cancer Alliance for Research and Education

4853 Cordell Avenue
Suite 14
Bethesda, MD 20814

Phone: (301) 656-3461
Fax: (301) 654-8684
Toll Free: (800) 422-7361
E-mail: info@icare.org
http://www.icare.org

The International Cancer Alliance for Research and Education (ICARE) is a non-profit organization that provides focused information to individuals affected by cancer and their physicians on an ongoing, person-to-person basis. Cancer is a general term referring to a group of diseases characterized by uncontrolled cellular growth that may invade surrounding tissues and spread (metastasize) to other bodily tissues or organs. The different cancers may be classified based upon the organ and cell type involved, the nature of the malignancy, and the disease's clinical course. ICARE has developed several patient-centered programs through a process of collection, evaluation, and dissemination of information, bringing affected individuals into contact with physicians and scientists from around the world. The alliance is operated by a network of scientists, clinicians, staff members, and lay volunteers, many of who are affected by cancer themselves. The alliance maintains the ICARE Registry; a confidential membership listing that permits ongoing dialogue between ICARE and its network members.

Acronym: ICARE

Keywords
Cancer; Cancer, Bladder; Cancer, Bone; Cancer, Bowel; Cancer, Breast; Cancer, Cervical; Cancer, Childhood; Cancer, Colon; Cancer, Colorectal; Cancer, Familial Colon; Cancer, Gynecologic; Cancer, Hereditary Colon; Cancer, Kidney; Cancer, Liver; Cancer, Lung; Cancer, Medullary; Cancer, Ovarian; Cancer, Pancreatic; Cancer, Prostate; Cancer, Rectal; Cancer, Renal Cell; Cancer, Skin; Cancer, Thyroid; Cancer, Uterine; Hodgkin's Disease; International Cancer Alliance for Research and Education; Lymphoma; Melanoma

1707 International Center for Fabry Disease

Department of Human Genetics
Mt. Sinai School of Medicine
Box 1498
New York, NY 10029

Phone: (212) 659-6779
Fax: (212) 659-6780
Toll Free: (800) 322-7963
E-mail: fabry.disease@mssm.edu
http://www.mssm.edu/genetics/fabry

The International Center for Fabry Disease is a voluntary, not-for-profit organization dedicated to aiding in the diagnosis, treatment, and management of Fabry disease, a rare inherited disorder of lipid metabolism characterized by the abnormal accumulation of certain fatty substances in various organs of the body. Symptoms may include clusters of discolorations on the skin (angiokeratomas), abdominal pain, pain in the hands and feet, as well as intolerance to heat due to a lack of sweating. Later in the course of the disease, kidney failure, heart problems, and/or neurological symptoms may cause serious complications. Established in 1974, the International Center for Fabry Disease promotes and supports ongoing research on Fabry disease and engages in patient and professional education. The center also makes referrals and provides educational and support information to affected individuals, family members, healthcare professionals, and the general public through its database, reports, and brochures.

President: Robert Desnick, M.D., Ph.D.
Year Established: 1974

Keywords
Alpha Galactosidase A Deficiency; Anderson Fabry Disease; Angiokeratoma Corporis Diffusum; Fabry Disease; GLA Deficiency; International Center for Fabry Disease; Lipidosis, Glycolipid; Rehabilitation Facilities (Various)

1708 International Children's Anophthalmia Network (ican)

5501 Old York Road
Albert Einstein Medical Center
Levy 2 West
(ican) C/O Genetics
Philadelphia, PA 19141

Phone: (215) 456-8722
Fax: (215) 456-2356
Toll Free: (800) 580-4226
E-mail: bardakjiant@einstein.edu
http://www.anophthalmia.org

The International Children's Anophthalmia Network (ICAN), a voluntary, not-for-profit organization, is a group of families and professionals dedicated to lending support to individuals who want to learn more about microphthalmia and anophthalmia (eyes that are abnormally small, completely absent, or consist only of vestigial portions). Members of this network are offered the opportunity to enroll in the Anophthalmia/Microphthalmia Registry, which was established to identify all syndromes associated with anophthalmia/ microphthalmia, describe the spectrum of associated anomalies, and investigate whether any teratogens are involved in the etiology of anophthalmia/microphthalmia. The network also enables parents with affected children to share personal experiences, information, and support; take advantage of its database of physicians and educational resources; and learn about ongoing research and medical issues. It provides referrals to genetic counseling, support groups, and other services and promotes professional and patient education, as well as a variety of educational and support materials. A program of screening for eye development gene mutations was initiated in 1999 and is ongoing with the participation of eight labs worldwide. It is coordinated through the Genetics Division at Albert Einstein Medical Center in Philadelphia and supported by the members of ICAN.

President: Sherry Salatto
Year Established: 1993
Acronym: ICAN

Keywords
Anophthalmia; ican (International Children's Anophthalmia Network); International Children's Anophthalmia Network (ican); International Children's Anophthalmia Network (ICAN); Microphthalmia

1709 International Costello Syndrome Support Group (UK)

90 Parkfield Road North
New Moston
Manchester, M40 3RQ, United Kingdom

Phone: +44 (0) 161-682-2479
E-mail: c.stone8@ntlworld.com
http://www.costellokids.org.uk

The International Costello Syndrome Support Group is a voluntary, non-profit organization dedicated to providing support and information to individuals and families affected by Costello Syndrome. Costello Syndrome is a rare disorder characterized by growth delay after birth (postnatal), leading to short stature; excessive, redundant loose skin on the neck, palms of the hands, fingers, and soles of the feet; development of benign (non-cancerous) growths (papillomata) around the mouth (perioral) and nostrils (nares); mild mental retardation; and/or characteristic facial appearance. Established in 1996, the group publishes a newsletter approximately every four months. It serves as a source of information for affected families as well as a forum for information exchange and the sharing of personal stories.

President: Colin & Cath Stone (Contact Persons)
Year Established: 1996
Acronym: ICSSG

Keywords
Costello Syndrome; International Costello Syndrome Support Group (UK)

1710 International Diabetes Federation

19 Aveune Emile de Mot
Brussels, B-1000, Belgium

Phone: +32 (0) 2-538-5511
Fax: +32 (0) 2-538-51144
E-mail: idf@idf.org
http://www.idf.org/

The International Diabetes Federation (IDF) is a federation dedicated to working with its member associations to enhance the lives of people affected by diabetes mellitus, a condition characterized by impaired carbohydrate, fat, and protein metabolism due to deficient production or action of insulin. In type I diabetes, little or no insulin is produced, resulting in an abrupt onset of such symptoms as abnormal thirst, excessive urination, extreme fatigue, constant hunger, blurred vision, irritability, and additional symptoms and findings. This condition, which usually becomes apparent during childhood or adolescence, requires administration of insulin. Type II diabetes, is characterized by insufficient production of insulin, causing a gradual onset of fatigue, blurred vision, unusual thirst, frequent urination, and other abnormalities. This condition typically becomes apparent during adulthood and may often be controlled through diet, routine exercise, and oral medications. The International Diabetes Federation was established in 1950 and has evolved into an umbrella organization consisting of 185 national associations in 145 countries.

President: Prof. Pierre Lefäbvre
Executive Director: Luc Hendrickx
Year Established: 1950
Acronym: IDF

Keywords
International Diabetes Federation

1711 International Dyslexia Association

Chester Building
Suite 382
8600 LaSalle Road
Baltimore, MD 21286-2044

Phone: (410) 296-0232
Fax: (410) 321-5069
Toll Free: (800) 222-3123
E-mail: info@interdys.org
http://www.interdys.org

The International Dyslexia Association (IDA) is a voluntary, not-for-profit, international organization concerned with the complex issues of dyslexia. IDA membership consists of a variety of professionals in partnership with people with dyslexia and their families. Established in 1949, IDA is committed to helping affected individuals achieve their personal potential, strengthening their learning abilities, and removing educational, social, and cultural barriers to language acquisition and use. In addition, the IDA actively promotes effective teaching approaches and related clinical educational intervention strategies for affected people. The association supports and encourages interdisciplinary study and research; facilitates the exploration of causes and early identification of

dyslexia; and is committed to the wide dissemination of research-based knowledge on the condition. IDA provides a bibliography of published materials on dyslexia and a variety of educational brochures and referral services.

President: Nancy L Henessy
Executive Director: Megan Cohen
Year Established: 1949
Acronym: IDA

Keywords
Dyslexia; International Dyslexia Association; Language Disabilities; Orton Dyslexia Society

1712 International Essential Tremor Foundation

11111 West 95th Street
Suite 260
Overland Park, KS 66214-1824

Phone: (913) 341-3880
Fax: (913) 341-1296
Toll Free: (888) 387-3667
E-mail: Staff@essentialtremor.org
http://www.essentialtremor.org

The International Essential Tremor Foundation (IETF) is a source of information on essential tremor for patients, families, and healthcare professionals worldwide. The IETF was created to provide information, services, and support to individuals and families affected by essential tremor (ET). The organization encourages and promotes research in an effort to determine the cause(s), treatment(s), and ultimately the cure(s) for ET. The IETF is the only worldwide organization dedicated to meeting the needs of those whose daily lives are challenged by ET. The IETF maintains an extensive international referral service composed of knowledgeable movement disorder neurologists who assist patients and families in receiving correct diagnoses and treatment. These referrals are available upon request or online at www.essentialtremor.org/seeking_help.

President: Shari Finsilver
Executive Director: Catherine S. Rice
Year Established: 1988
Acronym: IETF

Keywords
Essential Tremor; International Essential Tremor Foundation; International Tremor Foundation; Parkinson's Disease; Tremor; Tremor, Benign; Tremor, Be-

nign Essential; Tremor, Essential; Tremor, Familial; Tremor, Senile

1713 International Fanconi Anemia Registry

c/o Arleen Auerbach, Ph.D.
Rockefeller University
1230 York Avenue
Box 77
New York, NY 10021

Phone: (212) 327-8862
Fax: (212) 327-8262
E-mail: auerbac@mail.rockefeller.edu
http://www.rockefeller.edu/labheads/auerbach/auerbach.html

The goal is to obtain clinical and genetic information on patients with Fanconi anemia, in order to learn how to optimize growth and development of affected children and to increase understanding of this rare syndrome. Fanconi anemia is an autosomal recessive syndrome associated with chromosomal instability, variable skeletal and other congenital abnormalities, bone-marrow failure, and predisposition to malignancy, particularly acute myelogenous leukemia and squamous cell carcinomas.

Keywords
Anemia, Fanconi's; International Fanconi Registry

1714 International Federation for Spina Bifida and Hydrocephalus

Attn. Els De Clercq
Cellebroersstraat 16
B-1000
Brussels, B1000, Brussels

E-mail: info@ifglobal.org
http://www.ifglobal.org

The International Federation for Spina Bifida and Hydrocephalus is a worldwide organization created in 1979 by members of national organizations serving families affected by hydrocephalus and spina bifida. Its membership consists of national organizations for spina bifida and hydrocephalus in more than 40 countries. Its mission is to improve the quality of life for people affected by spina bifida and hydrocephalus, and to provide information and expertise aimed at decreasing the prevalence of these conditions.

President: Pierre Mertens

Keywords
Hydrocephalus; International Federation for Hydrocephalus and Spina Bifida; International Federation

for Spina Bifida and Hydrocephalus; Schwartz Jampel Syndrome; Spina Bifida; Tethered Spinal Cord Syndrome

1715 International Fibrodysplasia Ossificans Progressiva Association

P.O.Box 196217
Winter Springs, FL 32719-6217

Phone: (407) 365-4194
Fax: (407) 365-3213
E-mail: together@ifopa.org
http://www.ifopa.org

The International Fibrodysplasia Ossificans Progressiva Association (IFOPA) is a voluntary, not-for-profit organization for men, women, and children with FOP, an extremely rare connective tissue disorder in which the body produces bone in abnormal locations. Established in 1988, the association is dedicated to promoting and funding research on FOP and making medical resources available to affected individuals. It assists individuals with FOP in any manner reasonably related to their medical concerns including making adaptive equipment and transportation available. The association seeks to educate affected individuals, family members, healthcare and other professionals, and the public about this disorder and foster relationships and the sharing of information between people with FOP. It also engages in patient advocacy, provides appropriate referrals, and offers a variety of educational materials including a quarterly newsletter, reports, brochures, and a directory of articles and videos.

President: Jeannie L. Peeper (1988-Present)
Executive Director: Marilyn Hair (Vice President)
Year Established: 1988
Acronym: IFOPA

Keywords
Fibrodysplasia Ossificans Progressiva (FOP); International Fibrodysplasia Ossificans Progressiva Association; Myositis Ossificans

1716 International Foundation for Functional Gastrointestinal Disorders

P.O. Box 170864
Milwaukee, WI 53217

Phone: (414) 964-1799
Fax: (414) 964-7176
Toll Free: (888) 964-2001
E-mail: iffgd@iffgd.org
http://www.iffgd.org

The International Foundation for Functional Gastrointestinal Disorders (IFFGD) is a non-profit, educational and research organization dedicated to addressing the issues affecting individuals with functional gastrointestinal (GI) disorders. These disorders include irritable bowel syndrome (IBS), incontinence, diarrhea, constipation, pelvic floor pain, anorectal pain, abdominal bloating or pain, esophageal disorders, gastroduodenal disorders, and biliary disorders. Founded in 1990, IFFGD offers support to affected individuals and their families. The foundation also works with the medical, healthcare, and research communities to increase awareness of these disorders and to promote research efforts to improve diagnosis and treatment. Educational materials include a quarterly newsletter entitled "Digestive Health Matters: Participate in Your Health" and several fact sheets on various gastrointestinal disorders and their treatment alternatives. IFFGD also distributes a "Personal Daily Diary" that is designed to help individuals with gastrointestinal disorders gain a more complete understanding of their condition through the regular recording of important details.

President: Nancy J. Norton (1991 to Present)
Executive Director: Same as above.
Year Established: 1991
Acronym: IFFGD

Keywords
Bowel Dysfunction; Constipation; Diarrhea; Esophageal Disorders; Gastroesophageal Reflux; Gastrointestinal Disorders, Functional; GER/GERD; Hirschsprung's Disease; IBS; Incontinence; International Foundation for Functional Gastrointestinal Disorders; Intestinal Pseudoobstruction; Irritable Bowel Syndrome; Megacolon, Congenital; Pain, Anorectal; Pelvic Floor Pain

---

1717 International Foundation for Optic Nerve Disease (IFOND)
P.O. Box 777
Cornwall, NY 12518

Phone: (845) 534-7250
Fax: (845) 534-7250
E-mail: IFOND@AOL.COM
http://www.IFOND.ORG

The International Foundation for Optic Nerve Disease (IFOND) is a voluntary organization that promotes research into the causes, prevention, and treatment of optic nerve disease. It also disseminates information about optic nerve disease to patients, their families, and healthcare providers. Optic nerve disease includes diseases such as ischemic optic neuropathy, which is

the most common cause of vision loss in persons over age 50; Leber's hereditary optic neuropathy, an inherited disease that occurs most often in young men in their 20s; toxic optic nerve disease, in which nerve damage and blindness may result from certain medications, alcohol, and other substances; and glaucomatous optic nerve disease. Established in 1995, IFOND provides educational materials for patients, families, health professionals and the general public. It also helps patients network with others affected by the same diseases.

President: Ivan Bodis-Wollner, M.D.
Executive Director: Fred Diehl
Year Established: 1995
Acronym: IFOND

Keywords
AION; Anterior; Anterior Ischemic Opic Neuropathy; Antioxidant; IFOND; International Foundation for Optic Nerve Disease (IFOND); ION; Leber Hereditary Optic Neuropathy; Leber Optic Atrophy; Leber's Optic Atrophy; LOA; Mitochondrial Disease; Optic Nerve Disease; Optic Neuritis; Optic Neuropathy; Regeneration; Toxic Optic Neuropathy

---

1718 International Glaucoma Association
108 C Warner Road
London, SE5 9HQ, United Kingdom

Phone: +44 (0) 207-7377-3265
Fax: +44 (0) 207-7346-5929
E-mail: info@iga.org.uk
http://www.iga.org.uk

The International Glaucoma Association (IGA) is an international voluntary organization in the United Kingdom dedicated to offering advice and support to individuals with glaucoma, increasing public awareness, campaigning for improved services for affected individuals, and supporting clinical research. The association's aim is to prevent the loss of sight from glaucoma throughout the world through establishment of an international membership and cooperation with similar societies that have the same objectives. Glaucoma is a group of eye disorders in which abnormally increased pressure of the fluid of the eye damages the optic nerve, resulting in visual impairment. The optic nerve transmits visual impulses from the nerve-rich, light-sensitive membrane lining the eyes (retinas) to the brain. The International Glaucoma Association was established in 1974 and currently has over 15,000 members in approximately 60 countries. The association campaigns for improved detection methods for those at risk for glaucoma; responds to thousands of information requests each year via phone, fax, mail, and e-mail; provides networking opportunities for affected individuals and family members; and conducts regular discussion forums.

President: Mr. R. Pitts (Chief Executive) (1974 to Present).
Executive Director: Mr. D. Wright, M.S.A.E.
Year Established: 1974
Acronym: IGA

Keywords
International Glaucoma Association

1719   International Huntington Association

Callunahof 8
Harfsen, 7217 ST, The Netherlands

Phone: +31 (0) 57-343-1595
Fax: +31 (0) 57-343-1719
E-mail: iha@huntington-assoc.com
http://www.huntington-disease.org

The International Huntington Association (IHA) is a multinational federation of 32 member agencies that share common concern for individuals diagnosed with Huntington's disease and their families. Member agencies promote health consumer and medical professional educational initiatives; individual and family support; psychosocial, clinical, and biomedical research; and ethical and legal considerations related to Huntington's disease in their respective countries. Huntington's disease (HD) is an inherited degenerative brain disorder characterized by irregular, involuntary movements (chorea); abnormal gait (ataxia); slurred speech (dysarthria); and progressive disorientation and loss of intellectual function (dementia). Established in 1974, the organization's primary goals include promoting international collaboration in the search for a cure for HD; maintaining close liaison with research scientists who form the Research Group on Huntington's Disease of the World Federation of Neurology; developing new educational materials and resources as well as sharing these resources with member countries; assisting in the organization of new national HD groups and development of existing organizations; and publishing an international newsletter that is distributed to all members and to representatives in those countries where no HD group is yet organized. Educational materials are provided in a variety of languages including German, Dutch, French, Spanish, Norwegian, Danish, and Portuguese.

President: Ms. Christiane Lohkamp
Executive Director: Gerrit R Dommerholt
Year Established: 1979
Acronym: IHA

Keywords
International Huntington Association

1720   International Institute of Reconstructive Microsurgery

330 West Brambleton Avenue
Norfolk, VA 23510

Phone: (757) 625-6347
Fax: (757) 625-2131
E-mail: mrc1@erols.com

The International Institute of Reconstructive Microsurgery (IIRM) is a voluntary organization dedicated to research and education in the area of reconstructive microsurgery. Established in 1992, IIRM has a fellowship program that trains three to five fellows each year in microsurgery; supports clinical research on procedures to correct facial paralysis, infant injuries at birth, nerve damage, etc.; and offers patient care programs that provide necessary surgery for children who are medically needy. The organization produces a regular newsletter entitled "International Institute of Reconstructive Microsurgery."

President: Julia K. Terzis, M.D., Ph.D. (1992 to Present)
Executive Director: Frank J. Wolf (Treasurer)
Year Established: 1992
Acronym: IIRM

Keywords
Brachial Plexus Paralysis; Erb's Palsy; International Institute of Reconstructive Microsurgery; Microsurgery; Nerve Injuries; Paralysis, Facial

1721   International Interstitial Cystitis Patient Network Foundation

Burgemeester Le Fevre de Montignylaan 73
Rotterdam, 3055 NA, The Netherlands

Phone: +31 (0) 10-461-3330
Fax: +31 (0) 10-285-7158
E-mail: info@painful-bladder.org
http://www.painful-bladder.org

The International Interstitial Cystitis Patient Network (IICPN) Foundation promotes the interests of patients throughout the world with interstitial cystitis. Interstitial cystitis is a chronic, painful inflammatory condition of the bladder wall characterized by pressure and pain above the pubic area along with increased frequency and urgency of urination. The IICPN Foundation provides information through its newsletter and web site. It also assists patients by referring them to local interstitial cystitis support groups and providing them with up-to-date information and contacts. The foundation stimulates global research, and promotes international cooperation and collaboration in the interstitial cystitis patient community.

President: Jane Meijlink, Chairman (jane-m@dds.nl)
Executive Director: Toby Meijlink
Year Established: 2004
Acronym: IICPN Foundation

Keywords
Cystitis; IICPN; International Interstitial Cystitis Patient Network Foundation; Interstitial Cystitis; Painful Bladder Syndrome

1722 International Joseph Disease Foundation, Inc.

P.O. Box 994268
Redding, CA 96099

Phone: (530) 246-4722
Fax: (530) 232-2773
E-mail: MJD@ijdf.net
http://www.ijdf.net

International Joseph Disease Foundation, Inc. is a not-for-profit, voluntary organization that was established in 1977. The foundation is dedicated to assisting individuals who are affected by, or may be at risk for, Machado Joseph disease by providing information on the disorder, supporting and promoting clinical research, and helping affected individuals locate medical, social, and genetic counseling services. Joseph disease is a rare inherited disorder of the central nervous system characterized by the slow degeneration of certain areas of the brain. The foundation also engages in public education and offers a variety of materials including fact sheets, a flier on the history of the disease, and a newsletter.

President: Rebecca Kendall (2002-Present)
Executive Director: Sheri Bashor
Year Established: 1977
Acronym: IJDF

Keywords
International Joseph Disease Foundation, Inc.; Joseph's Disease; Machado-Joseph Disease; MJD; Spinocerebellar Ataxia Type III

1723 International Lesch-Nyhan Disease Association

11402 Ferndale Street
Philadelphia, PA 19116

Phone: (215) 677-4206

The International Lesch-Nyhan Disease Association is a not-for-profit, self-help organization dedicated to providing information and support to families of children diagnosed with Lesch-Nyhan disease. Lesch-Nyhan disease is a rare inborn error of purine metabolism characterized by the absence of the enzyme HPRT. Symptoms include impaired kidney function, joint pain, muscle weakness, neurological impairment, and self-mutilating behavior such as lip and finger biting and/or head banging. Established in 1994, the International Lesch-Nyhan Disease Association promotes awareness of the disease among healthcare professionals and the general public, and engages in patient advocacy. It also enables affected families to exchange information, support, and resources and offers a variety of informational and support information through its database, directory, article reprints, and brochures.

President: Leslie Cornely (1994-Present)
Executive Director: Unknown
Year Established: 1994

Keywords
International Lesch-Nyhan Disease Association; Lesch Nyhan Syndrome

1724 International Long QT Syndrome Registry

P.O. Box 653
University of Rochester Medical Center
Rochester, NY 14642-8653

Phone: (585) 276-0016
Fax: (585) 273-5283

The International Long QT Syndrome Registry is a research organization that maintains an international database on long QT syndrome. The aim of the registry is to improve understanding of the genetics and natural history of this rare heart disorder. It also seeks to improve treatments for affected individuals. Families with the disorder and physicians who participate in this worldwide registry program aid efforts toward improved treatments. The registry also publishes in the peer-reviewed medical literature.

Executive Director: Jennifer Robinson, MS
Year Established: 1975

Keywords
International Long QT Syndrome Registry; Jervell and Lange-Nielsen Syndrome; Long QT Syndrome; Romano Ward Syndrome

---

1725 International Mosaic Down Syndrome Association

P.O. Box 1052
Franklin, TX 77856

Phone: (979) 828-1868
Fax: (775) 295-9373
E-mail: mosaicdownsydrome@yahoo.com
http://www.imdsa.com

The International Mosaic Down Syndrome Association (IMDSA) is a non-profit organization that is designed to assist any individual whose life has been affected by mosaic down syndrome. IMDSA provides information and support, assists in research, and strives to increase awareness in medical, educational, and public communities throughout the world. Because of the rarity of mosaic down syndrome, the organization is mostly Internet-based. It does have country representatives in many countries to contact new parents of children with MDS. Its web site, www.imdsa.com, offers an online translator through Babel Fish.

President: Kristy Colvin (2001-present)
Year Established: 1999
Acronym: IMDSA

Keywords
Down Syndrome; International Mosaic Down Syndrome Association

---

1726 International Myeloma Foundation

12650 Riverside Drive
Suite 206
North Hollywood, CA 91607

Phone: (818) 487-7455
Fax: (818) 487-7454
Toll Free: (800) 452-2873
E-mail: TheIMF@myeloma.org
http://www.myeloma.org

The International Myeloma Foundation (IMF) is a non-profit foundation dedicated to improving the lives of people affected by myeloma (a bone marrow cancer) while working toward prevention and a cure. The IMF provides programs and services to aid in the research, diagnosis, treatment and management of myeloma. These include: An in-depth information package, a comprehensive website (www.myeloma.org), a free weekly E-mail newsletter, a free quarterly print newsletter, a hotline staffed by NCI-trained specialists (800-452-CURE), national and international patient and family seminars, a worldwide network of support groups, and a Bank On A Cure genetic data research project.

President: Susan Lavitt Novis
Executive Director: Brian G.M. Durie, M.D. (Chairman of the Board)
Year Established: 1990
Acronym: IMF

Keywords
International Myeloma Foundation; Myeloma, Multiple; Myelomas

---

1727 International Myotonic Dystrophy Organization

P.O. Box 1121
Sunland, CA 91041-1121

Phone: (818) 951-2311
Fax: (818) 352-0096
Toll Free: (866) 679-7954
E-mail: info@myotonicdystrophy.org & myotonicorg@aol.com
http://www.myotonicdystrophy.org

The International Myotonic Dystrophy Organization, Inc. (IMDO) functions on an international basis, supporting patients with information and services worldwide. The organization assists patients and their families with their problems via the toll-free help line and/or e-mail and mail. IMDO has a web site, publishes a monthly e-newsletter, offers Medical Alert cards and some educational materials, and facilitates support groups as well as Pen Pals via e-mail. The organization provides referrals and reference information to the public and professionals, promotes collaborative research and disseminates research information. The International Myotonic Dystrophy Organization is a 501(c) organization.

President: Richard Weston
Executive Director: Anny Slazik
Year Established: 2000
Acronym: IMDO

Keywords

Apathy; Depression; Dystrophy; Encopresis; International Myotonic Dystrophy Organization; Learning Disabilities; Muscle Weakness; Myotonia; Myotonic; Myotonic Dystrophy; Sleep Disorder; Swallowing Problems

1728 International Network of Ataxia Friends

2141 Palerme
Laval
Quebec, H7K 3R7, Canada

Phone: (450) 663-3664
E-mail: internaf-owner@yahoogroups.com
http://internaf.org

International Network of Ataxia Friends (INTERNAF) is a web site and a mailing list for ataxia patients, family and friends that serves as a support group and information exchange vehicle. There are currently over 580 subscribers from more than 40 countries worldwide. Subscription is free. Ataxia is an impaired ability to coordinate certain voluntary movements. The condition may occur due to, or in association with, several different underlying disorders or conditions. Those who don't wish to receive 20 or more separate E-mails per day from the regular subscription option may choose to receive a summary E-mail. There is also a list for professionals.

Executive Director: Michel Beaudet
Year Established: 1996
Acronym: INTERNAF

Keywords

INTERNAF; International Network of Ataxia Friends; MJD; MSA; SCA

1729 International Oral Lichen Planus Support Group

Baylor College Of Dentristy
3302 Gaston Avenue
Attn: The Stomaology Center
Dallas, TX 75246

Phone: (214) 828-8100
Fax: (214) 874-4532
E-mail: nburkhart@tambcd,edu
http://www.tambcd.edu/lichen

The International Oral Lichen Planus Support Group addresses concerns with and offers emotional support to individuals and families, serves as a central resource for information, and provides a worldwide referral system for university-based dental schools and treatment facilities where there are professionals knowledgeable about the treatment of oral lichen planus. It serves as a resource for patients, family members, researchers, and practitioners. Oral lichen planus is a disease of unknown origin that occurs more often in women than in men. It is characterized by the appearance of lesions or ulcers on the skin or genitalia or in the mouth. It may be related to an allergic reaction in some cases, and stress may also sometimes play a role in its appearance.

Executive Director: Nancy Burkhart and Terry Rees (Co-Directors)
Year Established: 1997
Acronym: IOLPSG

Keywords

International Oral Lichen Planus Support Group; IOLPSG; Lichen Planus

1730 International Organization of Glutaric Acidemia

Rd #4, Box 299-A
Blairsville, PA 15717

Phone: (724) 459-0179
E-mail: mmetil@helicon.net
http://www.glutaricacidemia.org

The International Organization of Glutaric Acidemia (IOGA) is an international, voluntary, nonprofit organization dedicated to promoting early detection of, preventing neurological damage from, and assisting in the treatment of, those affected by glutaric acidemia type I (GA1) and other neurological diseases. GA1 is an inborn error of metabolism in which deficiency of the enzyme glutaryl-CoA dehydrogenase results in abnormal accumulation and excretion of glutaric acid. Symptoms and physical findings may include motor delays; mental retardation; diminished muscle tone; progressive involuntary irregular muscle movements and impairment or distortion of voluntary movements. Established in 1995, IOGA engages in patient advocacy and education, offers family networking services, promotes research, and provides referrals.

President: Michael Metil (1996 to Present)
Executive Director: Cay Welch (Co-Founder and Contact Person)
Year Established: 1995
Acronym: IOGA

Keywords
Dicarboxylic Aminoaciduria; GA1; Glutaric Aciduria I; Glutaric Aciduria Type I; Glutaricacidemia I; Glutaricaciduria I; Glutaryl CoA Dehydrogenase Deficiency; International Organization of Glutaric Aciduria

---

1731 International Ostomy Association
102 Allingham Gardens
Toronto, Ontario, M3H 1Y2, Canada

Phone: (416) 63-3 67
Fax: (416) 63-3 67
http://www.ostomyinternational.org

The International Ostomy Association (IOA) is a not-for-profit federation of over 60 ostomy associations committed to improving the quality of life of individuals with ostomies and other related surgeries. An ostomy is a surgical procedure (e.g., colostomy, ileostomy, urostomy) in which an artificial opening (stoma) is formed in the abdominal wall to allow the passage of urine or intestinal contents. Ostomies are required when individuals have lost normal functioning of the bladder or bowel due to birth defects, disease, or injury. The International Ostomy Association is committed to encouraging the highest possible standards of surgery, medical attention, and patient after-care and assisting member organizations in helping affected individuals achieve the quality of life they seek after such surgical procedures. The aims of the association include providing information and management guidelines to member associations, helping to form new ostomy associations, and representing the interests of all individuals who receive ostomies and related surgeries.

Year Established: 1993
Acronym: IOA

Keywords
International Ostomy Association

1732 International Paruresis Association
P.O. Box 65111
Baltimore, MD 21209

Phone: (410) 601-0027
Fax: (410) 601-0035
Toll Free: (800) 247-3864
E-mail: info@paruresis.org
http://www.shybladder.org

The International Paruresis Association was formed in 1996 to raise public awareness, provide support, and give out the latest information about paruresis, also known as shy bladder syndrome. Paruresis is an anxiety disorder that makes it difficult for people to urinate in certain situations, such as when they must use a public restroom. The association serves as an information clearinghouse and resource center, sponsors workshops to help those affected overcome this phobia, and promotes research to help identify the cause and effective treatments.

President: Tom Achatz (2003-present)
Year Established: 1997
Acronym: IPA

Keywords
Advocacy; Bladder Dysenergia; Chronic Pelvic Floor Dysfunction; Functional Bladder Disorder; International Paruresis Association; Micturophobia; Pee Shy; Psychogenic Urinary Retention; Shy Bladder; Shy Kidneys; Urophobia

---

1733 International Patient Organization for Primary Immunodeficiencies
Firside
Main Road
Downderry
Cornwall, PL11 3LE, United Kingdom

Phone: +44 (0) 1503-25-0668
Fax: +44 (0) 1503-25-0668
E-mail: info@ipopi.org
http://www.ipopi.org/

The members of the International Patient Organization for Primary Immunodeficiencies (IPOPI) are national patient organizations for the primary immunodeficiencies (PIDs). These are inherited disorders in which part of the body's immune system is missing or doesn't function properly. IPOPI's purpose is to unite the experience, expertise, resources, and influence of its members in order to achieve worldwide improvement in the care and treatment of individuals with primary immunodeficiency disorders. It strives to be responsive on an international level to the issues of greatest concern to its members. These issues include blood product safety, improving patient diagnosis, gene therapy, immunoglobulin therapy, patient organization development, patient and professional education, and prospects from mapping the human genome.

President: Bob LeBein
Executive Director: David Watters
Year Established: 1990
Acronym: IPOPI

Keywords

Agammaglobulinemia, X-linked; Agammaglobulinemias, Primary; Blood Product Safety; Bruton's Disease; DiGeorge Syndrome; Gene therapy for Primary Immunodeficiency Disorders; Granulomatous Disease, Chronic; Hypogammaglobulinemia Selective IgA Deficiency; Immunodeficiencies, Primary; Immunodeficiency, Common Variable; Immunodeficiency, Severe Combined; International Patient Organization for Primary Immunodeficiencies; Job Syndrome; Lymphadenopathy, Angioimmunoblastic with Dysproteinemia; Lymphoproliferative Syndrome, X-linked; Mapping the Human Genome; Nezelof's Syndrome; SCID; Transplantation, Bone Marrow; Wiskott Aldrich Syndrome

1734 International Pemphigus Foundation

1540 River Park Drive
Suite 208
Albany, CA 94706

Phone: (916) 922-1298
Fax: (916) 922-1458
E-mail: pemphigus@pemphigus.org
http://www.pemphigus.org

The International Pemphigus Foundation is a nonprofit, voluntary organization formed to increase awareness of pemphigus among the general public and the medical community and to function as an information clearinghouse on autoimmune blistering diseases. Pemphigus is a group of rare autoimmune skin disorders characterized by the development of blisters in the outer layer of the skin and/or on mucous membranes that line the mouth, eyes, and rectum. Founded in 1994, the foundation seeks to provide emotional and informational support to individuals who have been diagnosed with pemphigus, their families, and friends. A quarterly newsletter disseminates information on the disease and current treatments to all interested parties. With the assistance of medical specialists and researchers from Johns Hopkins Medical Center and New York University Medical Center, the foundation works toward one of its principal goals: to raise funds for more extensive research into finding a cure for this disease.

President: Sonia Tramel
Executive Director: Janet D. Segall (1994-present)
Year Established: 1994
Acronym: IPF

Keywords

Bullous Pemphigoid; Cicatricial; Cicatricial Pemphigoid; Foliaceus Fogo Selvagem; Hailey Hailey Disease; International Pemphigus Foundation; Mucous Membrane Pemphigoid; National Pemphigus Vulgaris Foundation; Pemphigoid; Pemphigus; Pemphigus Brazilian; Pemphigus Erythematosus; Pemphigus Foliaceus; Pemphigus Herpetiformis; Pemphigus Vegetans; Pemphigus Vulgaris; Pemphigus, Benign Chronic Familial; Pemphigus, Benign Familial; Pemphigus, Brazilian; Pemphigus, Drug Induced; Skin Disorders

1735 International Pleuropulmonary Blastoma Registry

345 Smith Avenue North
Mail Stop 70-301
Children's Hospitals & Clinic
St. Paul, MN 55102

Phone: (651) 220-6772
Fax: (651) 220-6005
E-mail: info@ppbregistry.org
http://www.ppbregistry.org

The International Pleuropulmonary Blastoma Registry is a not-for-profit organization of physicians, scientists, and data analysts from many institutions who, with the cooperation of families and physicians all over the world, collect and evaluate cases of pleuropulmonary blastoma (PPB). PPB has occurred for years, but because of its rarity, it has become widely recognized only since the mid-1980s. The goals of the International Registry are: to provide pathologic review and to confirm the diagnosis of this rare cancer, to dispense as much information as possible to all interested parties including families, to make treatment recommendations, to continue to collect clinical data on this disease, to facilitate basic scientific research on PPB, and to publish its observations.

President: Yoav Messinger, MD
Executive Director: Jack Priest, MD
Year Established: 1988
Acronym: International PPB Registry

Keywords

Blastoma Pleuropulmonar; BPP; International PPB Registry; International Pleuropulmonary Blastoma Registry; Pleuropulmonales Blastom; Pleuropulmonary Blastoma; Pleuropulmonary Blastoma Registry; Pneumoblastome; PPB; PPB Registry

1736 International Registry of Werner Syndrome

University of Washington
Department of Pathology
Box 357470
Health Science Building K543
Seattle, WA 98195

Phone: (206) 543-5088
Fax: (206) 685-8356
E-mail: nbhanson@u.washington.edu
http://www.wernersyndrome.org

The International Registry of Werner Syndrome (IRWS), associated with the Department of Pathology of the University of Washington, is a not-for-profit research organization dedicated to providing clinical and genetic information on Werner syndrome to healthcare professionals and researchers. Werner syndrome, a rare autosomal recessive disorder, is characterized by abnormally short stature in childhood and premature aging beginning in adolescence or early adulthood. Established in 1986, IRWS works to ascertain and genotype individuals with Werner syndrome from around the world and to establish and cryopreserve cell lines from affected individuals.

President: George M. Martin, M.D. (Principal Investigator) (1986 to Present)
Executive Director: Junko Oshima, M.D., Ph.D.
Year Established: 1986
Acronym: IRWS

Keywords
International Registry of Werner Syndrome; Progeria of Adulthood; Progeroid Syndromes; Werner Syndrome; WNS; WS

1737 International Rett Syndrome Association

9121 Piscataway Road
Suite 2-B
Clinton, MD 20735

Phone: (301) 856-3334
Fax: (301) 856-3336
Toll Free: (800) 818-7388
E-mail: irsa@rettsyndrome.org
http://www.rettsyndrome.org

Established in 1984, the International Rett Syndrome Association is a not-for-profit, voluntary organization dedicated to three missions: research, advocacy and family support. Rett syndrome, a rare genetic neurological disorder that affects primarily females, is characterized by normal early development in the first year of life followed by a regression, which leads to severe handicaps by the age of three years. Clinical symptoms include loss of purposeful hand use, stereotyped hand movements, decelerated head growth, dyspraxia, irregular breathing and seizures. IRSA funds biomedical, clinical and therapeutic research; engages in patient advocacy; promotes family and professional education; provides referrals to support groups, genetic counseling, and other services; and promotes legislation beneficial to affected individuals and families. The association's mission includes supporting and promoting research into the prevention, control, and cure of the disorder; increase public awareness; and providing emotional support for affected families. The International Rett Syndrome Association engages in patient advocacy; promotes family and professional education; provides referrals to support groups, genetic counseling, and other services; and promotes legislation beneficial to affected individuals and families. The association also provides a variety of educational and support information through its directory, quarterly newsletters, books, audiovisual materials, brochures, and fliers.

President: Kathy Hunter (1984-Present)
Executive Director: Barry Rinehart
Year Established: 1984
Acronym: IRSA

Keywords
Dyspraxia; Hand Use; International Rett Syndrome Association; MECP2; Methylation; Rett Syndrome; Rett's; RS; RTT; Zoghbi

1738 International Scleroderma Network

7455 France Avenue South
Suite 266
Edina, MN 55435

Phone: (952) 831-3091
Toll Free: (800) 564-7099
E-mail: site-inquiries@sclero.org
http://www.sclero.org

The International Scleroderma Network (ISN) is a rare disorder organization whose main goal is to provide medical information, public awareness, and support services for people affected by scleroderma and related illnesses. The network also supports international peer-reviewed research on scleroderma. This is a rare progressive disease that leads to hardening and tightening of the skin and connective tissues. In some cases, it also affects the blood vessels and internal organs. Scleroderma is more common in women than in men.

Acronym: ISN

Keywords
Acrokeratoelastoidosis; Advocacy; Antiphospholipid Syndrome; Arthritis; Atrophoderma of Pierini and Pasini; Autoimmune; Autoimmune Anemia of Chronic Disease; Autoimmune Ear Disease; Autoimmune Eye Disease; Behcet's; Bone Marrow Cancer; Cancer; Chemotherapy-Induced Schleroderma; Chronic Fatigue Syndrome (CFS); CREST Syndrome; Depression; Dermatitis Artefacta; Dermatology; Dermatomyositis; Diabetes; Diffuse Scleroderma; Endometriosis; Eosinophilic Fasciitis; Fatigue; Fibromyalgia (FMS); Glaucoma/Retinal; Graft-Versus-Host-Disease; GVHD; Idiopathic Thromocytopenic Purpura; International Scleroderma Network; Interstitial Cystitis; ISN; Keloidal Scleroderma; Leukemia; Lichen Sclerosus; Limited Systemic Scleroderma; Linear Scleroderma; Lupus; Mandibuloacral Dysplasia; MCTD; MG; Microscopic Polyangitis; Morphea Scleroderma; MS; Multiple Sclerosis; Myasthenia Gravis; Myeloma; Nephrogenic Fibrosing Dermopathy; Networking; Neuromuscular Diseases; Overlap Syndrome; PAN; Pancytopenia; Parry Rombergs Syndrome; POEMS; Polyarteritis Nodosa; Polymyositis; Progeria; PsA; Pseudoscleroderma; Psoriatic Sacroiliitis; RA; Radiation Port Scleroderma; Research; Rheumatoid Arthritis; SLE; Sarcoidosis; Scleredema Adultorum Buschke; Scleroderma; Scleroderma Like; Scleromyxedema; Skin Diseases; Stiff Skin Syndrome; Support Groups; Systemic Lupus Erythematosus; Thyroid Disease; Tuberculous Fasciitis; UCTD; UCTD/MCTD; Vasculitis; Vitiligo; Vulvodynia; Werner's Syndrome

1739 International Society for Mannosidosis & Related Diseases, Inc.

1030 Saxon Hill Drive
Cockeysville, MD 21030

Phone: (410) 628-9991
E-mail: pres@mannosidosis.org
http://www/mannosidosis.org

The International Society for Mannosidosis & Related Diseases, Inc. (ISMRD) is a 501(c)(3) organization based in the United States and a leading advocate for families worldwide affected by glycoprotein and related storage diseases. Through partnerships built with medicine, science and industry, it seeks to detect and

cure these diseases, and to provide a network of support and information. Its mission is to advocate for people whose lives are affected by diseases that include alpha and beta mannosidosis, aspartylglucosaminuria, fucosidosis, galactosialidosis, Schindler disease, and mucolipidosis I and II.

President: Paul Murphy
Year Established: 1999
Acronym: ISMRD

Keywords
Alpha Mannosidosis; Aspartylglucosaminuria; Beta Mannosidosis; Fucosidosis; Galactosialidosis; Glycoprotein Storage Diseases; I Cell Disease; International Society for Mannosidosis & Related Diseases, Inc.; Lysosomal Storage Diseases; Mannosidosis; Mucolipidosis; Pseudo Hurler Polydystrophy; Schindler Disease; Sialidosis

1740 International Ventilator Users Network (IVUN) (Affiliate of Post-Polio Health International)

4207 Lindell Boulevard
Suite 110
St. Louis, MO 63108-2915

Phone: (314) 534-0475
Fax: (314) 534-5070
E-mail: ventinfo@post-polio.org
http://www.post-polio.org/ivun

International Ventilator Users Network (IVUN) is an international, non-profit organization dedicated to supporting the independent living, self-direction, dignity, and personal achievement of ventilator users. Established in 1987, IVUN endeavors to network ventilator users and their families with other affected families and with healthcare professionals committed to home mechanical ventilation. The organization also compiles and disseminates information including a quarterly newsletter entitled "Ventilator-Assisted Living" and the annually updated "Resource Directory for Ventilator-Assisted Living." IVUN is an affiliate of Post-Polio Health International, formerly Gazette International Networking Institute, which was founded in 1960 as a source of information about polio and its late effects.

President: Frederick M. Maynard, M.D.
Executive Director: Joan L. Headley, MS
Year Established: 1987
Acronym: IVUN

Keywords
International Ventilator Users Network; International Ventilator Users Network (IVUN) (Affiliate of Post Polio Health International); Ventilation, Home Mechanical

---

1741 International WAGR Syndrome Association

2063 Regina
Lincoln Park, MI 48146

Phone: (313) 381-4302
Fax: (775) 295-3693
E-mail: ReachingOut@wagr.org
http://www.wagr.org

International WAGR Syndrome Association is a support and information group for families affected by WAGR syndrome and/or aniridia, as well as the medical and educational professionals who work with these families. WAGR is an acronym, which stands for Wilm's tumor, aniridia, genito-urinary abnormalities, and mental retardation. A combination of two of these conditions may indicate WAGR syndrome. WAGR syndrome is caused by a deletion in the short arm of chromosome 11 (11p13-). International WAGR Syndrome Association was established in 1998, and encourages its members to share information on the management of symptoms and related topics. Its services include an Internet support group, an informative website, patient networking, and a quarterly newsletter. All services are free, and available to anyone in the world.

President: Kelly Trout, RN, BSN
Year Established: 1998

Keywords
Aniridia; International WAGR Syndrome Association; Patient Education; WAGR Syndrome

---

1742 International Waldenstrom's Macroglobulinemia Foundation

3932D Swift Road
Sarasota, FL 34231

Phone: (941) 927-4963
Fax: (941) 927-4467
E-mail: info@iwmf.com
http://www.iwmf.com

The International Waldenstrom's Macroglobulinemia Foundation (IWMF) is a non-profit support and information organization for individuals with Waldenstrom's macroglobulinemia (WM), a malignant lymph and blood cell disorder characterized by one or more of the following symptoms: abnormal enlargement of the liver and spleen (hepatosplenomegaly), weakness, anemia, fatigue, and excessive bleeding. Established in 1994, IWMF publishes a monthly newsletter that provides information on current therapies and clinical evaluations. Comprised of more than 2,300 members throughout the world, the organization also offers a telephone support networking service and provides support and understanding to individuals and families affected by WM. IWMF also maintains a database containing information regarding WM, medications that may be used to treat the disorder, and updates on ongoing clinical research studies. The organization sponsors an Internet discussion group.

President: Judith May
Executive Director: Sara McKinnie
Year Established: 1994
Acronym: IWMF

Keywords
International Waldenstrom's Macroglobulinemia Foundation; Macroglobulinemia; Macroglobulinemia, Waldenstrom's; Purpura, Hyperglobulinemic; Purpura, Waldenstrom's; Waldenstrom's Macroglobulinemia Support Group; Waldenstrom's Syndrome; WM

1743 Intersex Society of North America

979 Golf Course Drive
Suite 282
Rohnert Park, CA 94928

Fax: (801) 348-5350
E-mail: info@isna.org
http://www.isna.org

The Intersex Society of North America works through public education and advocacy for medical reform to create a world free of shame, secrecy, and unwanted genital surgery for people born with atypical anatomy. Founded in 1993, the society is a voluntary organization providing patient advocacy, networking, informational materials, and audio-visual aids. It serves patients and family members, health professionals, and the general public.

President: Thea Hillman
Executive Director: Cheryl Chase
Year Established: 1993
Acronym: ISNA

Keywords
Adrenal Hyperplasia, Congenital; Gonadal Dysgenesis (45X); Gonadal Dysgenesis (XO); Hermaphroditism; Hermaphroditism, True; Hypospadias; Intersex Society of North America; Klinefelter Syndrome

1744 Interstitial Cystitis Association

110 North Washington Street
Suite 340
Rockville, MD 20850

Phone: (301) 610-5300
Fax: (301) 610-5308
Toll Free: (800) 435-7422
E-mail: ICAmail@ichelp.org
http://www.ichelp.org

The Interstitial Cystitis Association of America (ICA) is a voluntary, not-for-profit organization working on behalf of all individuals with interstitial cystitis (IC), an inflammatory disease of the bladder in which chronic inflammation of the lining of the bladder and swelling of the bladder's interior walls result in pressure and pain above the pubic area and frequency and urgency of urination. Established in 1984 by individuals with interstitial cystitis, the association is dedicated to providing affected individuals with the most current information on the disease; offering a support network to affected individuals and their families; increasing awareness of the disease among the medical community and the general public; and establishing a national database to compile and study data concerning interstitial cystitis and promote research to find an effective treatment and cure for IC. The Interstitial Cystitis Association of America also promotes patient advocacy; testifies before Congress to support legislation beneficial to people with IC; funds several research projects for interstitial cystitis including its own Pilot Research Project Program; and conducts ICA national meetings and scientific workshops for interstitial cystitis researchers. It offers a variety of materials to affected individuals and the medical community including a regular newsletter, reports, journal article reprints, transcripts of workshops, brochures, videos, and audio tapes.

President: Vicki Ratner, MD
Year Established: 1984
Acronym: ICA

Keywords
Cystitis, Submucosal; Ellis Van Creveld Support Group; Fibrosis, Panmural; Hunner's Ulcer or Syndrome; IC; Interstitial Cystitis; Interstitial Cystitis Association; Interstitial Cystitis Association of America, Inc.; Ulcer, Submucosal of the Bladder

1745 Intestinal Multiple Polyposis and Colorectal Cancer Registry

P.O. Box 11
Conyngham, PA 18219

Phone: (717) 788-3712
Fax: (717) 788-4046
E-mail: user291524@aol.com

The Intestinal Multiple Polyposis and Colorectal Cancer Registry, also known as IMPACC, is a not-for-profit, self-help, service organization that was established in 1986. The purpose of the group is to provide information and support to people affected by multiple polyposis or hereditary colorectal cancer, their families, and their physicians. Multiple familial polyposis is a group of rare inherited conditions of the gastrointestinal system characterized by benign growths (adenomatous polyps) lining the mucous membrane of the intestine. Because such growths have high malignant potential, affected individuals may potentially develop cancer of the colon and/or rectum. The registry promotes ongoing medical research into the causes, treatment, and prevention of these disorders. IMPACC also offers a variety of services including genetic counseling, referrals to appropriate avenues of treatment, and a quarterly newsletter.

President: Ann Fagan
Executive Director: Unknown
Year Established: 1986
Acronym: IMPACC

Keywords
Cancer, Colorectal; Cronkhite Canada Disease; Gardner Syndrome; Intestinal Multiple Polyposis and Colorectal Cancer Registry; Peutz Jeghers Syndrome; Polyposis, Familial; Polyposis, Intestinal Multiple; Polyposis, Multiple Familial; Turcot's Syndrome

1746 Intracranial Hypertension Research Foundation (IHRF)

6517 Buena Vista Drive
Vancouver, WA 98661

Phone: (360) 693-4473
Fax: (360) 694-7062
E-mail: info@ihrfoundation.org
http://www.ihrfoundation.org

The Intracranial Hypertension Research Foundation (IHRF) is a non-profit foundation involved in promoting, encouraging and facilitating progress through research in the understanding and management of chronic primary and secondary intracranial hypertension (IH). Chronic IH is a general name for the disorder in which the cerebrospinal fluid within the skull is too high. It often leads to loss of vision, several disabling headaches, and significant neurological difficulties. For patients, IHRF provides a support system, educational programs and communication tools. For physicians and scientists, IHRF sponsor research in basic and clinical sciences, education, training and patient care programs in the US and worldwide.

President: Emanuel Tanne, M.D.
Year Established: 2001
Acronym: IHRF

Keywords
Benign Intracranial Hypertension; Chronic Intracranial Hypertension; Idiopathic Intracranial Hypertension; Intracranial Hypertension Research Foundation (IHRF); Primary Intracranial Hypertension; Pseudotumor Cerebri; Secondary Intracranial Hypertension

1747 Irish Chronic Pain Association
Carmichael Centre for Voluntary Groups
Coleraine House, Coleraine St.
Dublin, 7, Ireland

Phone: +353 (0) 1-804-7567
E-mail: info@chronicpainireland.org
http://www.chronicpainireland.org

The Irish Chronic Pain Association is the principal support group in Ireland for the 600,000 people with chronic pain. The ICPA is a registered charity, run by volunteers. Monthly support meetings are held in Dublin, and a quarterly newsletter is produced. The ICPA is a member of the Neurological Alliance of Ireland and the European Pain Network. The ICPA runs a series of self-help workshops in addition to an outreach program of regional lectures and support.

President: Frances Whelan (Chairperson)
Year Established: 1992
Acronym: ICPA

Keywords
Arthritis; Chronic Benign Pain; Chronic Low Back Pain; Chronic Non-Organic Pain; Chronic Pain; Complex Regional Pain Syndrome; Fibromyalgia; ICPA; Irish Chronic Pain Association; Migraine; Neuro-

pathic Pain; Nociceptive Pain; Reflex Sympathetic Dystrophy Syndrome; Support Groups

1748 Irish Haemophilia Society
Iceland House
Arran Court, Arran Quay
Dublin, 7, Ireland

Phone: +353 (0) 1-872-4466
Fax: +353 (0) 1-872-4494
E-mail: haemophiliasociety@eircom.net
http://www.haemophilia-society.ie

President: Margaret Dunne
Executive Director: Nina Storey (Office Manager)
Year Established: 1968
Acronym: IHS

Keywords
Advocacy; Bleeding Disorder; Hemophilia; IHS; Irish Haemophilia Society; Support Groups; Von Willebrand Disease

1749 Irish Heart Foundation
4 Clyde Road
Ballsbridge, Dublin, 4, Ireland

Phone: +353 (0) 1-668-5001
Fax: +353 (0) 1-668-5896
E-mail: info@irishheart.ie
http://www.irishheart.ie

The Irish Heart Foundation (IHF) was established in 1966 to help reduce premature death and disability from cardiovascular disease and stroke. IHF works toward achieving this goal through research, education, and community service. Located in Ireland, IHF is a general health organization offering services that include support groups, patient networking, and advocacy for patients and their families.

President: Mr. Michael O'Shea (CEO)
Year Established: 1966
Acronym: IHF

Keywords
Advocacy; Cardiomyopathy; Cardiovascular Disease; IHF; Irish Heart Foundation; Networking; Pediatric Cardiomyopathy; Research; Stroke; Support Groups

1750 Iron Disorders Institute

P.O. Box 675
Taylors, SC 29687

Phone: (864) 292-1175
Fax: (864) 292-1878
Toll Free: (888) 565-4766
E-mail: comments@irondisorders.org
http://www.irondisorders.org

The Iron Disorders Institute (IDI) is a voluntary, not-for-profit resource center providing information and educational materials about iron-related disorders and diseases. Serving a worldwide audience, it strives to maintain cooperative relationships with governmental health agencies and other professional organizations. It encourages research on iron-related health problems to improve the quality of life for patients and reduce health-care costs. Established in 1996, it publishes a magazine on iron disorders and coordinates a broad range of other services, includes support groups, networking, educational materials, and patient advocacy.

President: Aran Gordon
Executive Director: Cheryl Garrison
Year Established: 1996
Acronym: IDI

Keywords
African Siderosis; Anemia of Chronic Disease; Anemias, Sideroblastic; Cirrhosis; Diabetes; Heart Attack; Hemochromatosis; IDI; Iron Deficiency Anemia; Iron Disorders Institute; Iron Overload; Juvenile Hemochromatosis; Liver Disease

1751 Iron Overload Diseases Association, Inc.

433 Westwind Drive
North Palm Beach, Fl 33408-5123

Phone: (561) 840-8512
Fax: (561) 842-9881
E-mail: iod@ironoverload.org
http://ironoverload.org

Iron Overload Diseases Association, Inc. is a voluntary, not-for-profit organization dedicated to leading the search for individuals who have undiagnosed hemochromatosis and preventing the health problems that may result. Hereditary hemochromatosis is a metabolic disorder characterized by increased absorption of dietary iron. Without appropriate treatment, excessive iron may accumulate in the liver, heart, pancreas, and other organs, causing organ dysfunction and tissue damage. Established in 1981, the association is also committed to providing information and support to affected individuals and their families; educating the general public; promoting and supporting research; and pressing for earlier diagnosis and more effective treatment for hemochromatosis. The association acts as an international clearinghouse for affected individuals, family members, and physicians; provides telephone consultations; offers referrals to genetic counseling and support groups; promotes patient advocacy; and conducts an annual medical symposium as well as conference meetings between patients and health-care professionals.

President: Roberta Crawford
Executive Director: Steve Barfield, VP
Year Established: 1981
Acronym: IOD

Keywords
Hemochromatosis, Hereditary; Iron Overload Disease; Iron Overload Diseases Association, Inc.; Porphyria; Thalassemia

1752 Irritable Bowel Information & Support Association of Australia, Inc.

P.O. Box 7092
Sippy Downs
Queensland, 5456, Australia

Fax: +61 (0) 7-3396 -4436
Toll Free: +61 (0) 1 300-651-131
E-mail: contact@ibis-australia.org
http://www.ibis-australia.org

The Irritable Bowel Information & Support Association of Australia, Inc. (IBIS) is a support group consisting of individuals affected by irritable bowel syndrome (IBS) and their family members. IBS is a chronic, non-inflammatory condition characterized by abdominal pain and irregular bowel movements including constipation, diarrhea, or both, in the absence of any demonstrable disease. The Irritable Bowel Information & Support Association of Australia includes members from throughout Australia and New Zealand, many of whom belong to IBIS regional support groups that conduct regular meetings with guest speakers. The association is also dedicated to cooperating with the medical profession when appropriate to supply information necessary for IBS research and disseminating information to members and the general public. IBIS members receive regularly updated listings of publications on IBS and a quarterly newsletter that includes articles on the care and control of IBS, meeting listings, and research updates.

Executive Director: Roger Fewster (Contact Person)
Acronym: IBIS

Keywords
Irritable Bowel Information & Support Association of Australia, Inc.

1753 Israeli Huntington Disease Support Group

3 Lubezky Street
Gedera, 70700, Israel

Phone: +972 8 8598573
Fax: +972 (0) 8-859-8573
E-mail: niradn@012.net.il

The Israeli Huntington Disease Support Group is a self-help organization in Israel dedicated to providing information, support, and resources to individuals with Huntington's disease, a rare genetic disorder. Huntington's disease is characterized by the progressive development of rapid, jerking involuntary movements (chorea) and mental deterioration that leads to confusion and disorientation, impaired control of judgment and impulses, and progressive deterioration of memory and intellectual function (dementia). Although the age at onset may vary from case to case, most affected individuals initially experience symptoms during the fourth decade of life. The Israeli Huntington Disease Support Group currently consists of approximately 60 members. The group offers support and counseling for individuals with Huntington's disease and their family members; promotes professional and public awareness concerning the needs of affected individuals and families; and is dedicated to enhancing services for those affected by the disorder. In addition, the group provides patient advocacy services, engages in lobbying efforts, and offers educational materials including brochures.

President: Dr. Nira Dangoor (Contact Person)

Keywords
Israeli Huntington Disease Support Group

1754 Italian Registry of Myelofibrosis with Myeloid Metaplasia

Laboratoria Di Informatica Medica
IRCCS Policlinico San Matteo
Viale Golgi 19
Pavia, 27100, Italy

Phone: 800-279-656
Fax: +39 (0) 382-503-393
E-mail: marchettim@smatteo.pv.it
http://www.myelofibrosis.net

The Italian Registry of Myelofibrosis with Myeloid Dysplasia (Registro Italiano Della Mielofibrosi Con Metaplasia Mieloide or RIMM) is a not-for-profit registry of patients with myeloid metaplasia, a rare chronic disorder of the bone marrow that tends to affect older people. It is believed that there are approximately 300 new cases of this disorder each year in Italy. By maintaining records on enrolled patients, RIMM studies the epidemiology of the disease, its natural history, clinical research results, and treatment outcomes. Another goal is to enhance quality and continuity of care through cooperation and sharing of guidelines between research/treatment centers. RIMM was established in 1998.

President: Giovanni Barosi
Executive Director: Monia Marchetti
Year Established: 1998
Acronym: RIMM

Keywords
Italian Registry of Myelofibrosis with Myeloid Metaplasia; Myeloproliferative Diseases; Neoangiogenesis; Network

1755 ITP Foundation

381 Post Road
Darien, CT 06820

Phone: (203) 655-6954
Fax: (203) 655-7997
E-mail: info@itpfoundation.org
http://www.itpfoundation.org

The ITP Foundation was established in 2003 to raise awareness of immune thrombocytopenic purpura (ITP), a rare bleeding disorder characterized by the abnormal decrease of the blood cells known as platelets. Since platelets help to prevent and stop bleeding, a common symptom of ITP is abnormal bleeding into the skin. There are both acute and chronic forms of this disease. The ITP Foundation helps families with affected children and adolescents who need financial assistance to manage and treat the disorder. It also raises funds to further ITP research. The ITP Foundation takes an active role in raising awareness through outreach efforts on both local and national levels. This is done through sporting, social, and educational events.

President: Michael E. McGuire, Jr. (2003-present)
Year Established: 2003
Acronym: ITPF

Keywords
Immune Thrombocytopenic Purpura; ITP; ITP Foundation; Platelets; Purpura, Idiopathic Thrombocytopenic

1756 ITP People Place

P.O. Box 61533
Potomac, MD 20859

Phone: (301) 770-6636
Fax: (301) 770-6638
Toll Free: (877) 528-3538
E-mail: pdsa@pdsa.org
http://www.itppeople.com

ITP People Place is a web site on the Internet dedicated to providing information, support, resources, and online networking opportunities to individuals with idiopathic thrombocytopenic purpura (ITP). ITP is characterized by abnormally low levels of circulating blood platelets (thrombocytopenia) without a readily apparent cause or underlying disease (idiopathic). The disorder may be characterized by small areas of abnormal bleeding (minor hemorrhages) within skin (dermal) layers or layers below the mucous membranes (submucosal), causing the appearance of small purplish spots on the skin (petechia); bleeding from mucous membranes that may be manifested by nose bleeds, for example; increased susceptibility to bruising; and/or other symptoms. In some cases, affected individuals may exhibit fever, slight enlargement of the spleen (splenomegaly), and/or other characteristics. The ITP People Place site offers understandable information about the potential underlying causes of ITP, symptoms and findings associated with the disorder, current treatments, and research conducted on ITP.

President: Joan Young

Keywords
ITP People Place; ITP; Purpura, Idiopathic Thrombocytopenia; Purpura, Idiopathic Thrombocytopenic; Purpura, Immune Thrombocytopenic; Thrombocytopenic Purpura, Idiopathic; Thrombocytopenic Purpura, Immune; Werlhof Disease

1757 ITP Society of the Children's Blood Foundation

Children's Blood Foundation
333 East 38th Street
Suite 830
New York, NY 10016

Phone: (212) 297-4336
Fax: (212) 297-4340
Toll Free: (800) 487-7010
http://www.childrensbloodfoundation.org/

The ITP Society of the Children's Blood Foundation is a not-for-profit organization dedicated to promoting the welfare of and addressing the issues that affect people with immune or idiopathic thrombocytopenic purpura (ITP), a condition characterized by deficiency of circulating blood platelets resulting in bleeding into the skin and other organs. The ITP Society was founded in 1994 under the auspices of The Children's Blood Foundation. The society's goals are to provide patient support and give appropriate referrals; support ongoing medical research to advance the knowledge and treatment of ITP; and educate the public and medical communities about the disorder. The ITP Society provides educational and support materials including fact sheets, brochures, and booklets.

Executive Director: Susan R. Byrne
Year Established: 1994

Keywords
ITP; ITP Society; ITP Society of the Children's Blood Foundation; Purpura, Idiopathic Thrombocytopenia; Purpura, Idiopathic Thrombocytopenic; Purpura, Immune Thrombocytopenic; Thrombocytopenic Purpura, Idiopathic; Thrombocytopenic Purpura, Immune; Werlhof Disease

1758 ITP Support Association

Synehurst, Kimbolton Road
Bolnhurst, Beds, MK44 2EW, United Kingdom

Phone: +44 (0) 870-777-0559
Fax: 01144 +44 (0) 870-777-0559
E-mail: shirley@itpsupport.org.uk
http://www.itpsupport.org.uk

The ITP Support Association is a not-for-profit registered charity founded in 1995. Its aims are to promote the welfare of ITP (idiopathic thrombocytopenic purpura) patients, fund research, and collaborate with the medical profession in collecting and disseminating clinical data. Idiopathic thrombocytopenic purpura is a rare autoimmune bleeding disorder characterized by the abnormally low levels of certain blood cells called platelets, creating a condition known as thrombocytopenia. The association provides patient support and a contact network, organizes annual conventions, and publishes numerous booklets and fact-sheets on ITP and related subjects. It also publishes a quarterly newsletter, The Platelet.

President: Shirley Watson (1995-present)
Year Established: 1995

Keywords
ITP Support Association

1759 Ivemark Syndrome Association
71 Milton Rd
Taunton, TA1 2JQ, United Kingdom

Phone: +44 (0) 1823-25-7430
E-mail: ingridgladki@aol.com

The Ivemark Syndrome Association is a voluntary, not-for-profit organization dedicated to providing information and support to families affected by Ivemark syndrome. Ivemark syndrome, a rare disorder that is usually apparent at birth. The symptoms are, absence of the spleen, malformations of the cardiovascular system and abnormal displacement of the abdomen and intestines. Founded in 1996, the association aims to offer support to other familes affected by Ivemark syndrome; to raise awareness of the disorder within the medical community and among other interested individuals; and to network families in similar situations. Educational materials include a regular newsletter.

President: Liz Fisher
Executive Director: Ingrid Gladki
Year Established: 1996

Keywords
Asplenia Syndrome; Ivemark Syndrome; Ivemark Syndrome Association

1760 James Stewardson Research and Welfare Trust for Children with TPI (Triose Phosphate Isomerase) Deficiency
3 Duncombe Close
Bramhall
Stockport
Cheshire, SK7 3DD, United Kingdom

Phone: +44 (0) 161-439-3146
E-mail: tpi.trust@tpitrust.com
http://www.tpitrust.com

The James Stewardson Research and Welfare Trust for Children with TPI (Triose Phosphate Isomerase) Deficiency is a charity in the United Kingdom that was established in 1994 by the family of a young boy with triose phosphate isomerase deficiency. TPI deficiency is an extremely rare inborn error of metabolism characterized by deficiency of the enzyme triose phosphate isomerase. Associated symptoms and findings, which typically become apparent between six months and two years of age, include premature destruction of red blood cells (hemolytic anemia); increased susceptibility to infections; progressive impairment of certain brain functions, although intellect is typically unaffected; and progressive neuromuscular dysfunction including loss of previously acquired motor skills, impaired muscle control, muscle rigidity, fixed postures, and muscle spasms. TPI deficiency is inherited as an autosomal recessive genetic trait. The James Stewardson TPI Trust is dedicated to locating and making contact with affected families across the globe; working with researchers who are dedicated to locating and characterizing the gene responsible for TPI deficiency; and promoting additional, ongoing research to learn more about the disorder, its effects, and possible treatments such as enzyme replacement or gene therapy.

Year Established: 1994

Keywords
James Stewardson Research and Welfare Trust for Children with TPI (Triose Phosphate Isomerase) Deficiency; Triose Phosphate Isomerase Deficiency;

1761 JDF—Juvenile Diabetes Research Foundation Canada
7100 Woodbine Avenue
Markham
Ontario, L3R 5J2, Canada

Phone: (905) 944-8700
Fax: (905) 944-0800
Toll Free: (877) 287-2533
E-mail: general@jdfc.ca
http://www.jdfc.ca

JDF-Juvenile Diabetes Research Foundation Canada is an international, not-for-profit organization dedicated to raising funds to support and promote diabetes research. Diabetes is a chronic metabolic disorder that affects the body's ability to properly manufacture or utilize insulin, a hormone necessary for the body to transport food glucose into cells for energy. There are several types of diabetes including insulin-dependent diabetes mellitus, IDDM (also known as juvenile diabetes); non-insulin dependent (type II, also known as adult-onset diabetes); and gestational diabetes. Established in 1974 and consisting of 14 chapters, JDF supports research advances in therapies to reduce the risk of diabetes-caused blindness, decrease the number of amputations due to diabetes, and control high blood pressure associated with diabetes; disease management practices that help maintain tight control of glucose levels to prevent or delay complications of diabetes; and practices that afford women with diabetes the opportunity for safe pregnancies and healthy children.

President: Ron Forbes
Year Established: 1974
Acronym: JDF

Keywords
Diabetes; Diabetes, Adult Onset; Diabetes, Gestational; Diabetes, Juvenile; Diabetes Mellitus, Insulin Dependent; Diabetes, Non-Insulin Dependent; Diabetes Research Foundation Canada; Diabetes Type I; Diabetes Type II; IDDM; JDF—The Diabetes Research Foundation; Juvenile

1762 Jeffrey Modell Foundation

747 Third Avenue
34th Floor
New York, NY 10017

Phone: (212) 819-0200
Fax: (212) 764-4180
Toll Free: (866) 469-6474
E-mail: info@jmfworld.org
http://www.info4pi.org

The Jeffrey Modell Foundation (JMF) is an international, not-for-profit, organization dedicated to helping individuals and family members affected by primary immunodeficiency disorders. The foundation is active in four main areas: research, physician and patient education, patient support, and public awareness of primary immune deficiency. The foundation provides funding of research fellowships and laboratory facilities; sponsors physician symposia in the United States, Canada, and Europe as well as grand rounds, seminars, and other educational activities for physicians; offers publications for both the lay and medical communities; and provides affected individuals with access to leading medical centers with departments of clinical immunology. The JMF also sponsors K.I.D.'s (Kids with Immunodeficiency) Days for affected children and their families; is engaged in ongoing education campaigns to promote awareness of primary immune deficiency (PI) in the general public; conducts advocacy on behalf of affected individuals; and is committed to ongoing biomedical research into primary immune deficiency. The JMF also publishes a regular newsletter for affected individuals and family members, physicians, and researchers; offers general materials on the primary immune deficiency disorders as well as materials on specific PID disorders for lay and medical audiences; and has a 24-hour JMF Hotline at (800) Jeff-844.

President: Frederick & Vicki Modell Co-Founders
Executive Director: Venessa Tenembaum
Year Established: 1987
Acronym: JMF

Keywords
Adenosine Deaminase Deficiency; Agammaglobulinemia, X-linked; Bare Lymphocyte Syndrome; CGD; Chediak Higashi Syndrome; Granulomatous Disease, Chronic; Hyper IgM Syndrome; Hypogammaglobulinemia, Common Variable; IgA Deficiency; Immune Deficiency Disorders, Primary; Immunodeficiency, Severe Combined; Jeffrey Modell Foundation; Nezelof's Syndrome; Nucleoside Phosphorylase Deficiency; PID; SCID; WAS; Wiskott Aldrich Syndrome

1763 Jennifer Trust for Spinal Muscular Atrophy

Elta House
Birmingham Road
Stratford-upon-Avon
Warwickshire, CV37 0AQ, United Kingdom

Phone: +44 (0) 870-774-3651
Fax: +44 (0) 870-774-3652
E-mail: jennifer@jtsma.org.uk
http://www.jtsma.org.uk

The Jennifer Trust is a national support group for spinal muscular atrophy (SMA). It provides information, support and advice, welfare grants for specialist equipment, information for families and healthcare professionals, bereavement support and research into both practical management and potential treatments. SMA is a genetically inherited condition causing muscle wasting. The severity of the condition depends on the type and age of onset. The severest form is often fatal during the first year of life. The main purpose of the group is to provide support, information, understanding, and friendship to those whose lives are affected by SMA. Established in 1985 and currently consisting of 1,500 members, JTSMA conducts an annual weekend conference, has an area contact network of people who provide local support to affected individuals and family members, and offers a variety of educational materials including informational leaflets, booklets, a JTSMA Library Book List, a JTSMA Toy List, and a regular newsletter entitled Holding Hands.

President: Victor Hassan
Executive Director: Anita Macaulay
Year Established: 1985
Acronym: JTSMA

Keywords
Atrophy, Spinal Muscular; Jennifer Trust for Spinal Muscular Atrophy; Kugelberg Welander Syndrome; SMA; Werdnig Hoffmann Disease

1764 John Douglas French Alzheimer's Foundation
11620 Wilshire Boulevard
Suite 270
Los Angeles, CA 90025

Phone: (310) 445-4650
Fax: (310) 479-0516
E-mail: jdfaf@earthlink.net
http://www.jdfaf.org

The John Douglas French Alzheimer's Foundation (JDFAF) is a voluntary, research organization founded in 1983 to help patient and families affected by Alzheimer's disease, a progressive condition of the brain affecting memory, thought and language. The mission of JDFAF is to provide seed money for promising research and scientists who might not otherwise be funded. It is their objective to support cutting edge research, individually or in a collaborative effort, which can expedite the day when we might delay the onset and advancement, and find a cure for Alzheimer's.

President: Michael M. Minchin, Jr (President)
Executive Director: Gwen Waggoner (Drctr of Research Administration)
Year Established: 1983
Acronym: JDFAF

Keywords
Alzheimer's Disease; JDFAF; John Douglas French Alzheimer's Foundation; Research

1765 Johns Hopkins Hereditary Colorectal Cancer Registry
550 North Broadway
Suite 108
Baltimore, MD 21205-2011

Phone: (410) 955-3875
Fax: (410) 614-9544
Toll Free: (888) 772-6566
E-mail: hccregistry@jhmi.edu
http://www.hopkins-gi.org

The Johns Hopkins Hereditary Colorectal Cancer Registry is a research organization that maintains a registry of families affected by different forms of hereditary colorectal cancer including hereditary colon cancer, familial adenomatous polyposis, hereditary nonpolyposis colorectal cancer, juvenile polyposis, and Peutz-Jeghers syndrome. Established in 1973, the registry currently includes hundreds of families affected by these disorders. Interested individuals are offered the opportunity to participate in ongoing research studies. The registry also offers educational materials to people affected by hereditary forms of colon cancer, their families, and physicians.

President: Kathy Romas (Program Coordinator)
Executive Director: Francis M. Giardiello, M.D.
Year Established: 1973

Keywords
Cancer, Colon; Cancer, Familial Colon; Cancer, Hereditary Colorectal; Cancer, Hereditary Nonpolyposis (Colorectal); FAP; Johns Hopkins Colorectal Cancer Registry; Johns Hopkins Hereditary Colorectal Cancer Registry; Peutz Jeghers Syndrome; Polyposis, Familial Adenomatous; Polyposis, Juvenile

1766 Joubert Syndrome Foundation and Related Cerebellar Disorders
6931 South Carlinda Avenue
Columbia, MD 21046

Phone: (410) 997-8084
Fax: (410) 992-9184
E-mail: joubertduquette@comcast.net
http://www.joubertsyndrome.org

The Joubert Syndrome Foundation and Related Cerebellar Disorders is an international network of parents who share emotional support, knowledge, and experiences about Joubert syndrome, a rare genetic disorder characterized by partial or complete absence of a certain area of the brain (cerebellar vermis), diminished muscle tone (hypotonia), mental retardation, psychomotor retardation, abnormal eye movements, and respiratory abnormalities including episodes of abnormally rapid breathing. Established in 1992, the organization maintains a networking list, produces a regular newsletter, conducts biannual conferences, promotes public awareness, and seeks to educate physicians and their support teams about this rare disorder.

President: Cheryl Duquette (1994-Present)
Executive Director: Unknown.
Year Established: 1992
Acronym: JSF

Keywords
Joubert Syndrome; Joubert Syndrome Foundation; Joubert Syndrome Foundation and Related Cerebellar Disorders; Joubert Syndrome Parents-In-Touch Network

1767 Justin Gordon and Menkes Syndrome Network

932 Tatumville Highway
Gilbertsville, KY 42044

Phone: (270) 362-0778
E-mail: danigordon72@hotmail.com
http://www.menkessyndrome.com

The Menkes Syndrome Foundation provides networking for parents with, or who have had, children with Menkes syndrome or disease. This syndrome is a genetic disorder of copper metabolism beginning before birth. Copper cannot be transported through the body to the brain. Structural changes occur in the hair, brain, bones, and arteries with death usually occurring by age 2-3. Through the web site and message board this network provides information and support to people worldwide who are and have been touched by Menkes syndrome.

President: Danielle Gordon
Year Established: 2000
Acronym: TMSF

Keywords
Copper; Justin Gordon; Justin Gordon and Menkes Syndrome Network; Kinky Hair; Menkes; Menkes Disease; Network; Seizures

1768 Juvenile Diabetes Foundation Australia

Level 4
80-84 Chandos Street
St. Leonards
New South Wales, 2065, Australia

Phone: +61 (0) 2-9966-0400
Fax: +61 (0) 2-9966-0172
E-mail: info@jdrf.org.au
http://www.jdfa.org.au

The Juvenile Diabetes Research Foundation Australia is a not-for-profit organization affiliated with the Juvenile Diabetes Research Foundation International in the United States. Established in 1982, the foundation is dedicated to funding basic and applied medical research to help discover a cure for diabetes and prevent its complications. Juvenile diabetes, also known as insulin-dependent diabetes or type I diabetes mellitus, is characterized by impaired carbohydrate, fat, and protein metabolism due to deficient production of insulin. This form of diabetes is an autoimmune disease in which insulin-secreting cells of the pancreas are destroyed due to an abnormal immune response. Associated symptoms have an abrupt onset and typically include excessive thirst and urination, weight loss and blurred vision. The Juvenile Diabetes Re-

search Foundation Australia is committed to promoting and supporting scientific research; providing educational resources that are specific to the needs of children, young adults, and family members affected by juvenile diabetes; engaging in advocacy and lobbying efforts; and providing networking opportunities that enable those affected by juvenile diabetes to exchange information, resources, and mutual support.

President: Sheila Royles (Chief Executive Officer)
Executive Director: Sue Alberti (President)
Year Established: 1982
Acronym: JDFA

Keywords
Juvenile Diabetes Foundation Australia

1769 Juvenile Diabetes Research Foundation International

120 Wall Street, 19th Floor
New York, NY 10005-4001

Phone: (212) 785-9500
Fax: (212) 785-2873
Toll Free: (800) 533-2873
E-mail: info@jdrf@org
http://www.jdrf.org

The Juvenile Diabetes Research Foundation International (JDRF) is the leading charitable founder and advocate of juvenile (type I) diabetes research worldwide. The mission of JDRF is to find a cure for diabetes and its complications through the support of research.

President: Peter Van Etten
Year Established: 1970
Acronym: JDRF

Keywords
Advocacy; Diabetes, Insulin Dependent; JDRF; Juvenile Diabetes Research Foundation International; Research; Retinopathy, Diabetic

1770 Juvenile Scleroderma Network, Inc.

1204 W. 13th Street
San Pedro, CA 90731

Phone: (310) 519-9511
Fax: (310) 519-9511
Toll Free: (866) 338-5892
E-mail: jsdinfo@jsdn.org
http://www.jsdn.org

The Juvenile Scleroderma Network (JSDN), a voluntary organization, invites family's world-wide to become involved and help provide support and friendship to families who have a child with juvenile scleroderma. It also serves families in Canada, South America, Europe, the United Kingdom, and Australia. Scleroderma is a connective tissue disease involving skin, blood vessels, and the immune system. Children who have juvenile scleroderma may experience confusion about their illness, anger about changes in their appearance, and fear of the unknown. For parents to be able to help their children deal with such feelings, it is important for them to have a support network to exchange information and find emotional reassurance. The network's services include advocacy, support groups for parents and children, networking, publications, and research. Spanish language materials are available.

President: Kathy Gaither
Year Established: 1999
Acronym: JSDN

Keywords
CREST Syndrome; Juvenile Scleroderma Network, Inc.; Morphea; Scleroderma, Diffuse; Scleroderma, Linear; Scleroderma, Localized; Scleroderma, Systemic

---

1771   Kabuki Syndrome Network

8060 Struthers Crescent
Regina
Saskatchewan, S4Y 1J3, Canada

Phone: (306) 543-8715
E-mail: margot@kabukisyndrome.com
http://www.kabukisyndrome.com

The Kabuki Syndrome Network is a voluntary network dedicated to providing information and mutual support to parents with children affected by Kabuki syndrome. Kabuki syndrome is a rare disorder characterized by a wide spectrum of physical findings and symptoms including characteristic facial features, mild to moderate intellectual impairment, diminished muscle tone (hypotonia), skeletal abnormalities, and/or congenital heart defects. Physical findings and symptoms vary greatly from case to case. KSN provides a bi-annual newsletter to its members. The network compiles and maintains a family directory of those affected by Kabuki syndrome. It also provides information on Kabuki syndrome, a list of references for further information, and a list that defines the various medical terminology associated with Kabuki syndrome. A newsletter (The Kabuki Journal) is mailed to KSN's members twice a year.

President: Margot Schmiedge (1999-present)
Executive Director: Same as above.
Year Established: 1997

Keywords
Kabuki Syndrome Network

1772   KDWB-Variety Family Center

200 Oak St, SE
Suite 260
Minneapolis, MN 55455-2002

Phone: (612) 626-3087
Fax: (612) 624-0997
TDD: (612) 626-3939
E-mail: kdwb-var@umn.edu
promise.umn.edu

The Center for Children with Chronic Illness and Disability (C3ID) is a pediatric research, training, and rehabilitation center that is committed to fostering the physical, physiological, and social development and well being of infants, children, and adolescents with chronic illness and disabilities. Founded in 1989, C3ID is supported by the National Institute on Disability and Rehabilitation Research. The center works to provide opportunities, assistance, improved services and delivery systems, and useful materials and information to children with chronic illnesses and their families through local resources and federal programs. C3ID serves the United States, Canada, Australia, South America, and Western Europe. A periodic newsletter entitled "Children's Health Issues" and various reports and research findings are available in both English and Spanish.

Executive Director: Robert W. Blum, M.D., Ph.D.
Year Established: 1989

Keywords
Center for Children with Chronic Illness and Disability (C3ID); Disabilities, Chronic; Illnesses, Chronic; KDWB Variety Family Center; KDWB-Variety Family Center

---

1773   Kennedy's Disease Association

P.O. Box 1105
Coarsegold, CA 93614-1105

Phone: (559) 658-5950
E-mail: info@kennedysdisease.org
http://www.kennedysdisease.org

The Kennedy's Disease Association is a non-profit corporation established in 2000 that is staffed entirely by volunteers, all of whom are Kennedy's disease patients, carriers, spouses, caregivers, family members or friends. The goals of the association include sharing information about Kennedy's disease with those who seek it, creating a support system for those living with Kennedy's disease, increasing public awareness of this disease and its effects upon families, raising funds for research, and increasing awareness of Kennedy's disease in the medical community. Kennedy's disease is a genetic disorder that causes the death of nerve cells in the spinal cord and brainstem. It usually first appears between the ages of 30 and 50, mostly among men.

President: Bruce Gaughran
Executive Director: Terry Waite
Year Established: 2000
Acronym: KDA

Keywords
KDA; Kennedy Disease; Kennedy's Disease; Kennedy's Disease Association; Kennedy's Syndrome; SBMA; Spinal Bulbar Muscular Atrophy

1774 Kharkov Renaissance Foundation for Children with Spinal Muscular Atrophy

Gogol Street, 7
Kharkov, 61057, Ukraine

Phone: +380 57-731-31-21
Fax: +380 50-364-06-73
E-mail: info@csma.org.ua
http://www.csma.org.ua

The Kharkov Renaissance Foundation for Children with Spinal Muscular Atrophy (CSMA) is a not-for-profit, rare disorder organization located in the Ukraine. The primary goal of CSMA is to protect the rights of patients affected by spinal muscular atrophy (SMA). This is a slowly progressive, inherited muscle-weakness and muscle-wasting disease. CSMA is one of several organizations working collaboratively through the International Alliance for Spinal Muscular Atrophy. It encourages the exchange of information related to SMA around the globe. CSMA works to educate patients and their families through support groups and genetic counseling.

President: Vitaliy Matyusjenko
Year Established: 2004
Acronym: CSMA

Keywords
Advocacy; Kharkov's Renaissance Foundation (Children with spinal muscular atrophy); Kharkov Renais-

sance Foundation for Children with Spinal Muscular Atrophy; Registry; Russian; SMA; Spinal Muscular Atrophy; Support Groups; Ukranian

1775 Kidneeds Greater Cedar Rapids Foundation

Greater Cedar Rapids Foundation
200 First Street SW
Cedar Rapids, IA 52404

E-mail: kidneedsMPGN@yahoo.com
http://www.medicine.uiowa.edu/kidneeds

Kidneeds is a not-for-profit organization dedicated to finding a treatment or cure for membranoproliferative glomerulonephritis type 2 (MPGN type II). Also called dense deposit disease, MPGN type II is a kidney disease most commonly affecting children. Its cause is unknown, and there is currently no cure. Through a great variety of fundraising activities, Kidneeds raises funds for the sole purpose of supporting MPGN type II research. Established in 1997, it produces a newsletter and brochures for patients, families and caregivers.

President: Lynne Lanning
Executive Director: Dan Baldwin
Year Established: 1997
Acronym: Kidsneeds

Keywords
Glomerulonephritis, Membranoproliferative; Kidneeds; Kidneeds Greater Cedar Rapids Foundation

1776 Kidney Cancer Association

1234 Sherman Avenue
Suite 203
Evanston, IL 60202-1375

Phone: (847) 332-1051
Fax: (847) 332-2978
Toll Free: (800) 850-9132
E-mail: office@curekidneycancer.org
http://www.curekidneycancer.org

The Kidney Cancer Association is a national, nonprofit organization comprised of people who have been affected by kidney cancer, their families and friends, physicians, and researchers. The association is dedicated to improving the quality of care and increasing survival of individuals affected by kidney cancer. Established in 1990, the association works toward three primary goals: to provide information to affected individuals and physicians; to sponsor and conduct research on kidney cancer; and to act as an advocate on a federal level and with insurance companies and employers on behalf of affected individuals and their families. Comprised of more than 15,000 constituents, the organization publishes "Kidney Cancer News," an electronic newsletter, as well as several informational brochures including "We Have Kidney Cancer," "Interleukin-2 Therapy: What You Should Know," and "Kidney Cancer: Emotional vs. Rational." The association holds support group meetings several times a year in various cities so that individuals who have kidney cancer can learn how others have dealt with their disease. In addition, it conducts a yearly national convention that brings individuals together with leading physicians and researchers in the field of kidney cancer.

President: Donna Yesner
Executive Director: William P. Bro
Year Established: 1990
Acronym: KCA

Keywords
Cancer; Cancer, Kidney; Carcinoma, Renal Cell; KCA; Kidney Cancer Association

1777 Kids with Heart National Association for Children's Heart Disorders, Inc.
1578 Careful Drive
Green Bay, WI 54304-2941

Phone: (920) 498-0058
Fax: (920) 498-0058
Toll Free: (800) 538-5390
E-mail: kidswithheart@greenbaynet.com
http://www.kidswithheart.org

The Kids with Heart National Association for Children's Heart Disorders, Inc. is a not-for-profit corporation organized to provide support, education, and informational materials to families of children who have heart disorders, both congenital and acquired, to assist them in making decisions regarding their child's care. More than 25,000 infants are born with heart defects each year in the United States. Heart defects are among the most common birth defects, and are the leading cause of birth defect-related deaths. The association maintains a national database of families affected by congenital heart defects, and families who have lost a child to congenital heart defects, as well as a national database of local support groups who have registered with Kids with Heart NACHD. NACHD also carries a line of books on congenital heart defects and related issues.

President: Michelle L. Rintamaki
Year Established: 1991
Acronym: Kids with Heart NACHD

Keywords
Atrial Septal Defects; Atrioventricular Septal Defects; Cardiomyopathy; Cardiomyopathy, Arrhythmogenic Right Ventricular; Cardiomyopathy, Congestive; Cardiomyopathy, Dilated; Cardiomyopathy, Hypertrophic; Cardiomyopathy, Viral; Congenital Heart Defects; Cor Triatriatum; Hypoplastic Left Heart Syndrome; Kawasaki Disease; Kids with Heart National Association for Children's Heart Disorders, Inc.; Ventricular Septal Defects

1778 Kleine-Levin Syndrome Foundation
P.O. Box 5382
San Jose, CA 95150-5382

Phone: (408) 265-1099
Fax: (408) 269-2131
E-mail: facts@klsfoundation.org
http://www.klsfoundation.org

The Kleine-Levin Syndrome Foundation (KLS Foundation) provides information and support to patients and families affected by Kleine-Levin syndrome (KLS); a rare disorder characterized by episodes of excessive need for sleep, excessive food intake, and altered behavior. The KLS Foundation exchanges information among patients, their families, and the medical community to help in the diagnosis and care of those affected by KLS. The goals of the KLS foundation are to raise awareness, support research, and find effective treatment and a cure for KLS. The foundation offers patient networking, education, and referrals to KLS patients and their families.

President: Stephan Meier & Neal Farber (2004-present)
Executive Director: Cindy Maier
Year Established: 1998
Acronym: KLS Foundation

Keywords
French; Kleine-Levin Syndrome; Kleine-Levin Syndrome Foundation; KLS; KLS Foundation; Networking; Registry; Research

1779 Klinefelter Syndrome & Associates
11 Keats Court
Coto de Caza, CA 92679

Phone: (949) 858-9428
Fax: (949) 858-3443

Toll Free: (888) 999-9428
E-mail: help1@genetic.org
http://www.genetic.org

Klinefelter Syndrome & Associates is a national, voluntary organization dedicated to supporting individuals and families whose lives have been affected by Klinefelter syndrome, a rare chromosomal disorder. Males normally have one X and one Y chromosome; however, those with Klinefelter's syndrome carry at least one extra X chromosome in cells of the body (somatic). Associated symptoms and physical features may not become apparent until puberty. Such abnormalities may include abnormal smallness of the testes, infertility due to impaired function of the testes, breast enlargement (gynecomastia), unusually long legs, and/or other symptoms and physical features. Established in 1990 and currently consisting of approximately 1,500 members, the organization has national and regional support groups; offers confidential networking services; has an outreach program to the medical community to help ensure earlier diagnosis of the disorder; and offers patient pamphlets and a regular newsletter entitled "The Even Exchange."

Executive Director: Mary Davidson
Year Established: 1990
Acronym: KS&A

Keywords
Chromosome 46, XY/47,XXY (Mosiac); Chromosome 47 XXY; Chromosome 48 XXXY; Chromosome 48 XXYY; Chromosome 49 XXXXY; Chromosome XXY; Dysgenesis, Seminiferous Tubule; Hypogonadism, Hypergonadotropic; Hypogonadism, Primary; Klinefelter Syndrome; Klinefelter Syndrome and Associates

1780 Klinefelter Syndrome Association of Canada

1001 Queen Street West
Unit 3
2nd Floor
Toronto
Ontario, M6J 1H4, Canada

Phone: (416) 535-8501
E-mail: drabinovitch@hotmail.com

The Klinefelter Syndrome Association of Canada (KSAC) is a voluntary, not-for-profit, self-help organization dedicated to providing services that improve and enhance the quality of life for children and adolescents with Klinefelter syndrome, a rare chromoso-

mal disorder. Males normally have one X and one Y chromosome; however, individuals with Klinefelter syndrome have one or more extra X chromosomes in cells of the body. Associated symptoms and physical findings may not become apparent until puberty. Such abnormalities may include abnormal smallness of the testes, infertility due to absence of sperm production (azoospermia), enlargement of the breasts (gynecomastia), long legs and unusually tall stature, and/or other symptoms and findings. Established in 1987, the Klinefelter Syndrome Association of Canada is committed to promoting the early detection and treatment of Klinefelter syndrome, providing support to affected individuals and family members, promoting professional and public awareness of the disorder, and functioning as a resource service on Klinefelter syndrome.

Executive Director: David Jonathan Rabinovitch
Year Established: 1987
Acronym: KSAC

Keywords
Klinefelter Syndrome; Klinefelter Syndrome Association of Canada

1781 Klippel-Trenaunay Support Group

5404 Dundee Road
Edina, MN 55436

Phone: (952) 925-2596
Fax: (952) 925-2596
E-mail: j.vessey@att.net
http://www.k-t.org

The Klippel-Trenaunay Support Group is a voluntary, self-help organization dedicated to providing support for individuals affected with Klippel-Trenaunay syndrome and their families. Klippel-Trenaunay syndrome is a rare congenital disorder characterized by the presence of a port-wine stain on the skin, excessive growth of the soft tissues and/or bones, venous malformations, and lymphatic abnormalities. Established in 1986, the organization conducts biannual meetings for affected individuals and their families to enable them to exchange information, experiences, and support; makes medical advisors available during these meetings; and provides phone support to members. In addition, the group maintains a confidential group roster so that members may correspond with one another and raises awareness of the disease among the medical community and the general public. The Klippel-Trenaunay Support Group provides a variety of educational materials including a periodic newsletter, brochures, and a list of current medical articles on K-T syndrome.

Executive Director: Judy Vessey
Year Established: 1986
Acronym: K-T Support Group

Keywords
Klippel Trenaunay Syndrome; Klippel Trenaunay Weber Syndrome; Klippel-Trenaunay Support Group; KT Syndrome; Parkes Weber Syndrome

---

1782 Kniest SED Group

E-mail: support@ksginfo.org
http://www.ksginfo.org

The Kniest SED Group (KSG) provides educational, and social support to people with Kniest syndrome, spondyloepiphyseal dysplasia (SED), and spondylometaphyseal dysplasia (SMD) and their families. Kniest syndrome is a type of skeletal dysplasia that is characterized by short torso, round face with hollow or depressed areas, swelling and stiffness of the joints, and a stiff drawing up (contractures) of the fingers. SED is a rare genetic disorder characterized by growth deficiency before birth, spinal malformations, and/or abnormalities affecting the eyes. SMD is a rare condition characterized by a short torso and changes in metaphyseal layer of long bones. KSG offers services via its web site including patient networking, patient and professional education, and support groups. KSG offers lists of scholarships, adaptive equipment resources, anti-bullying links, advocacy information, research, stories by and about people with dwarfism, and help for parents of newly diagnosed children.

Acronym: KSG

Keywords
Advocacy; Alternative Therapies; Bullying; Kniest; Kniest SED Group; Kniest Syndrome; Pain Management; Physician Referral; Scholarships; Short Trunk Dwarfism; Spondyloepiphyseal Dysplasia; Spondyloepiphyseal Dysplasia Tarda; Spondyloepiphyseal Dysplasia, Congenital; Spondylometaphyseal Dysplasia

---

1783 La Chainette
9, rue des Ecrenauxe
Sainte Luce sur Loire, 44980, France

Phone: +33 (0) 240-25-88-63
E-mail: lachainette@aol.com
http://www.networkchain.org

La Chainette is a not-for-profit rare disease organization based in France. Founded in 2002, La Chainette is a network that uses mainly the Internet as a point of contact for individuals or isolated groups of people directly or indirectly affected by the same rare disease. The goal of this organization is to provide a link, through the web, to patients and families who are isolated or when no organization exists for their disorder.

President: Yves Martin (2005-2005)
Year Established: 2002
Acronym: LA Chainette

Keywords
La Chainette; Networking; Rare Diseases

1784 Lactic Acidosis Support Trust
1A Whitley Close
Middlewich
Cheshire, CW10 0NQ, United Kingdom

Phone: +44 (0) 1606-83-719
Fax: +44 (0) 1606-83-7198

The Lactic Acidosis Support Trust is a not-for-profit voluntary health organization located in the United Kingdom. Established in 1993, the trust works toward its goal of promoting research into the cause, treatment, and prenatal diagnosis of lactic acidosis and mitochondrial cytopathies. It provides counseling, advice, and support to parents and caregivers of children with these rare conditions; and encourages healthcare professionals to become specialists in this field of medicine. The trust seeks to provide information to parents or other relatives on a 24-hour basis and to provide physicians with financial support and grants to further their research. Fund-raising events include dances, coffee mornings, and other sponsored activities. The Lactic Acidosis Support Trust produces several educational materials including pamphlets, brochures, and a newsletter.

President: Paul Preston
Executive Director: Unknown.
Year Established: 1993
Acronym: LAST

Keywords
Alpers Disease; Barth Syndrome; Cardiomyopathy, Hypertrophic; Carnitine Deficiency Syndromes; Complex 1 NADH Deficiency; Complex II; Complex III; Complex IV; Complex V; COX Deficiency; Cytochrome C Oxidase Deficiency; Disease, Lethal Infantile Mitochondrial; Encephalomyopathy, Mitochondrial; Encephalomyopathy, Mitochondrial (adult);

Encephalomyopathy, Mitochondrial (childhood); Epilepsy, Myoclonic; Glutaricaciduria I; Glutaricaciduria II; Kearns Sayre Disease; LCAD Deficiency; Lactic Acidosis; Lactic Acidosis Support Trust; Leber's Optic Atrophy; Leigh's Disease; Leigh's Disease, Adult; Leigh's Disease, Childhood; Luft Disease; MCAD; Medium Chain Acyl CoA Dehydrogenase Deficiency; MELAS Syndrome; MERRF Syndrome; Mitochondrial Diseases, Undiagnosed; Mitochondrial Disorders; Mitochondrial Fatty Oxidation Disorders; Mitochondrial MtDNA Mutations; Mitochondrial Respiratory Chain Complex I; Mitochondrial Respiratory Chain Complex II; Mitochondrial Respiratory Chain Complex III; Mitochondrial Respiratory Chain Complex IV; Mitochondrial Respiratory Chain Complex V; MNGIE; Myoneurogastrointestinal Disorder and Encephalopathy; Myopathy, Adult, Late Onset; Myopathy, Congenital; Myopathy, Congenital of Childhood; Myopathy, Infantile; Myopathy, Mitochondrial; NARP; Neuropathy Ataxia and Retinitis Pigmentosa; Ophthalmoplegia, Progressive External; Oxidative Phosphorylation Diseases; PEPCK Deficiency; Phosphoenolpyruvate Carboxykinase Deficiency; Pyruvate Carboxylase Deficiency; Pyruvate Dehydrogenase Deficiency, Adult; Pyruvate Dehydrogenase Deficiency, Childhood; Respiratory Chain Disorders; SCAD

1785 LAM Foundation

10105 Beacon Hills Drive
Cincinnati, OH 45241

Phone: (513) 777-6889
Fax: (513) 777-4109
E-mail: lam@one.net
http://www.lam.uc.edu

The LAM Foundation is an international, non-profit organization dedicated to finding a cure for lymphangioleiomyomatosis (LAM). LAM is a rare progressive lung disease that affects females, usually of childbearing age. The disease is characterized by the abnormal growth of smooth muscle, leading to airway obstruction and cystic lesions (blebs) in the lungs. The symptoms of lymphangioleiomyomatosis may include shortness of breath, coughing, and/or difficulty breathing (dyspnea), especially following periods of exercise or exertion. Affected individuals may experience repeated episodes of chest pain due to fluid accumulations around the lungs (pleural effusions), potentially resulting in collapse of a lung (pneumothorax). The exact cause of lymphangioleiomyomatosis is not known. Founded in 1995, the organization believes that the cause of the disease will be uncovered by sci-entific research. The LAM Foundation's main objectives are to support efforts by the scientific community to develop better methods of prevention, diagnosis, and treatment; to undertake activities that will increase the amount of funding nationwide to support research on LAM; and to serve as an information resource to women affected by LAM and their families.

President: Sue Byrnes (1995 to Present) (Founder)
Year Established: 1995

Keywords
LAM; LAM Foundation; Lymphangioleiomatosis; Lymphangioleiomyomatosis; Lymphangiomyomatosis, Pulmonary

1786 Learning Disabilities Association of America

4156 Library Road
Pittsburgh, PA 15234-1349

Phone: (412) 341-1515
Fax: (412) 344-0224
Toll Free: (888) 300-6710
E-mail: info@ldaamerica.org
http://www.ldaamerica.org

The Learning Disabilities Association of America (LDA) is a national, not-for-profit, voluntary and advocacy organization that was established in 1964 by a group of concerned parents. It is dedicated to defining and finding solutions for the broad spectrum of learning disabilities (e.g., visual, auditory, motor, communication, and logical thinking problems). The association has 50 state affiliates and more than 550 local chapters. Members include parents, professionals from many different disciplines, and other concerned citizens. The association works directly with school systems in planning and implementing programs for the early identification and diagnosis of children with learning disabilities. The Learning Disabilities Association's Public Policy Committee provides information and recommends action on pending legislation that may affect children with learning disabilities and/or their families.

President: Suzanne Fornaro
Year Established: 1964
Acronym: LDA

Keywords
Attention Deficit Hyperactivity Disorder; Dubowitz Syndrome; Dyslexia; Gerstmann Syndrome; LDA; Learning Disabilities; Learning Disabilities Association of America; Triplo X Syndrome

1787 Learning Disabilities Association of Canada

323 Chapel Street
Suite 200
Ottawa
Ontario, K1N 7Z2, Canada

Phone: (613) 23-8 57
Fax: (613) 23-5 53
E-mail: information@ldac-taac.ca
http://www.ldac-taac.ca

The Learning Disabilities Association of Canada (LDAC) is a national, non-profit, voluntary organization established in 1963 and incorporated in 1971. The organization's mission is to provide a national voice for persons with learning diabilities and those who support them in Canada. There is a Learning Disabilities Association in each province and two territories of Canada, and from these extend a network of chapters in more than 75 communities across the country. LDAC activities include the collection and dissemination of information on learning disabilities in the areas of prevention, early identification, assessment, education, intervention, social interaction, health, coping skills, family support, advocacy, transitions, and employment, among others. LDAC has published a number of manuals, guides, self-help and reference books to meet the needs of persons with learning disabilities.

President: Fraser Green
Executive Director: Pauline Mantha
Year Established: 1963
Acronym: LDAC

Keywords
Dyslexia; LDAC; Learning Disabilities; Learning Disabilities Association of Canada; Special Education

1788 Learning Disabilities Worldwide

P.O. Box 142
Weston, MA 02493

Phone: (781) 890-5399
Fax: (781) 890-5555
E-mail: info@ldwworldwide.org
http://www.ldworldwide.org

Learning Disabilities Worldwide (LDW) is an international organization dedicated to improving the lives of individuals with learning disabilities. Founded in 2002, LDW strives to increase awareness and understanding through multilingual media productions and publications that serve populations across cultures and nations. Its educational enrichment programs are designed to serve individuals with learning disabilities, their families, and the professionals in their lives. It publishes a peer-reviewed journal on the topic, "Learning Disabilities: A Contemporary Journal," and the "Yellow Pages International Service Directory." LDW also presents the annual "World Congress on Learning Disabilities."

President: David Bradburn
Executive Director: Teresa Allissa Citro
Year Established: 1965
Acronym: LDW

Keywords
Dyslexia; LDW; Learning Disabilities; Learning Disabilities Worldwide

1789 Les Turner Amyotrophic Lateral Sclerosis Foundation, Ltd.

8142 Lawndale Avenue
Skokie, IL 60076

Phone: (847) 679-3311
Fax: (847) 679-9109
Toll Free: (888) 257-1107
E-mail: info@lesturnerals.org
http://www.lesturnerals.org

The Les Turner Amyotrophic Lateral Sclerosis Foundation is a voluntary health organization dedicated to raising funds for ALS research, patient services, and public awareness. Amyotrophic lateral sclerosis (ALS), also known as Lou Gehrig's disease, is a progressive neurological disease that causes impaired breathing, speaking, and swallowing, as well as muscle weakness and eventually total paralysis. Intellectual function remains unaffected and there is no known cure. The Les Turner ALS Foundation was established in 1977 and provides educational materials for affected individuals and family members, healthcare professionals, and the general public. Program services include referrals and counseling, audio-visual aids, and a periodic newsletter, "ALS Today." Consisting of over 1,000 members, the organization offers support groups and patient networking to affected individuals, family members, and caregivers.

President: Harvey Gaffen (1979 to Present)
Executive Director: Wendy Abrams
Year Established: 1977
Acronym: Les Turner ALS Fdt

Keywords
ALS; Amyotrophic Lateral Sclerosis; Aran Duchenne Muscular Atrophy; Gehrig's Disease; Les Turner ALS Fdt; Les Turner Amyotrophic Lateral Sclerosis Foundation, Ltd.; Lou Gehrig's Disease; Motor System Disease (Focal and Slow); Primary Lateral Sclerosis

1790 Lesch-Nyhan Syndrome Registry

School of Medicine
Department of Psychiatry
18 East 13th Street
Bellevue Hospital
New York, NY 10016

Phone: (212) 263-6458
Fax: (212) 629-9523
E-mail: lta1@nyu.edu
http://www.lndinfo.org

The registry is operated through a multipurpose web site for parents, patients, teachers, doctors, researchers, and students. Parents can get information on genetic testing and medical care. They can learn about adaptive equipment and exchange handyman suggestions. Parents are encouraged to register, and get help with networking. Doctors can find medical information and other areas of interest. Researchers can make contact with research subjects and participate in the research forum and essay. Students can get help with basic information and research projects. There is a glossary, a bibliography, and help finding Internet library sites. Everyone can participate in the forum. Topics include "Favorite Medicines," "Diet for Behavior and Health," "Research Ideas," "Politics and LND," and others. A patient "refrigerator door" is provided where patients can submit artwork, photos and written material. There is also an E-mail "pen pal" service that helps patients meet other patients with Lesch-Nyhan disease. Comments, suggestions and submissions are encouraged.

Executive Director: Lowell T. Anderson, M.D.
Year Established: 1990

Keywords
HGPRT, Absence of; HPRT, Absence of; Hereditary Hyperuricemia and Choreoathetosis Syndrome; Hyperuricemia Oligophrenia; Hyperuricemia, Choreoathetosis, Self Mutilation Syndrome; Hypoxanthine Guanine Phosphoribosyltranferase Deficiency (Complete Absense of); Juvenile Gout, Choreoathetosis, and Mental Retardation Syndrome; Lesch Nyhan Syndrome; Lesch Nyhan Syndrome Registry; Nyhan Syndrome

1791 Let Them Hear Foundation

1900 University Avenue
#101
East Palo Alto, CA 94303

Phone: (650) 462-3143
Fax: (650) 462-3143
Toll Free: (877) 735-2929
E-mail: info@letthemhear.org
http://www.letthemhear.org

The Let Them Hear Foundation is a not-for-profit organization providing information, support groups, genetic counseling and other services for individuals and families affected by congenital and acquired hearing impairments. It also seeks to educate medical professionals and the general public regarding hearing healthcare issues and practices.

Executive Director: Rob McCleland
Year Established: 1994
Acronym: LTHF

Keywords
5p-Minus Syndrome; Advocacy; Albers-Schonberg Disease of Osteopetrosis; Alexander Disease; Alport Syndrome; Anderson-Warburg Syndrome; Anemia, Fanconi's; Ataxia, Friedreich's; Atresia; Auditory Neuropathy; Branchio Oto Renal Syndrome; Cerebral Palsy; Charcot-Marie-Tooth Disease; CHARGE Syndrome; Chromosome 6 Ring; Cleidocranial Dysostosis; Cockayne Syndrome; Connexin 26; Connexin 30; Cornelia de Lange Syndrome; Cri du Chat Syndrome; Crouzon Syndrome; Cytomegalic Inclusion Disease; Duane Syndrome; Ectodermal Dysplasia; Enlarged Vestibular Aquaduct Syndrome; Epstein Syndrome; Fechtner Syndrome; Fehr's Corneal Dystrophy; Fragile X Syndrome; GJB2 Gene; GJB6; Goldenhar Syndrome; Hallgren's Syndrome; Hearing Impairment; Hemifacial Microsomia; Hereditary Arthro-Ophthalmopathy; Hunter Syndrome; Hurler's Syndrome; Jervell and Lange-Nielsen Syndrome; Klippel-Feil Syndrome; Lange-Nielsen Syndrome; Leber's Syndrome; Let Them Hear Foundation; Lobster-Claw Syndrome; Long QT Syndrome; LTHF; Macrothrombocytopathia; Marfan Syndrome; Marshall/Stickler Syndrome; Micrognatha; Microtia; Moebius Syndrome; Mohr's Syndrome; Mosaic Syndrome; Muckle Wells Syndrome; Mucopolysaccharidoses; Mucopolysaccharidosis Type I; Muscular Dystrophy; Neurofibromatosis; Neurofibromatosis Type 1 (NF 1); Neurofibromatosis Type 2 (NF 2); Norrie Disease; Norrie Warburg Syndrome; Oculo Auriculo Vertebral Spectrum; Osteogenesis Imperfecta; Osteopetrosis; Otopalatodigital Syndrome; Paget's Disease; Pendred

Syndrome; Pierre Robin Sequence; Pyle's Disease; Refsum Disease; Research; Ring 6 Disorder; Saddle-Nose Syndrome; Schiebe Aplasia; Stickler Syndrome; Support Groups; Surcardiac Syndrome; Tay Sach's Disease; Townes-Brocks Syndrome; Treacher Collins Syndrome; Trisomy 13 Syndrome; Trisomy 13-15; Trisomy 18 Syndrome; Trisomy 21 Syndrome; Turner Syndrome; Usher Syndrome; Van Buchem's Syndrome; Van Der Hoeve's Syndrome; Von Recklinghausen's Neurofibromatosis; Waardenburg Syndrome; Wildervanck Syndrome

1792 Let's Face It (USA)

P.O. Box 29972
Bellingham, WA 98228-1972

Phone: (360) 676-7325
E-mail: letsfaceit@faceit.org
http://www.faceit.org

Let's Face It (USA) is the United States branch of an international, voluntary, nonprofit support and information network for people with facial differences, their families, and healthcare professionals. Established in the United Kingdom in 1984 and in the United States in 1987, Let's Face It is committed to networking affected individuals, family members, friends, and healthcare professionals, and educating the public about facial differences. It also seeks to enable people who are facially different to share their experiences through a mutual help network and provide continuing education to medical, nursing, and allied health professionals. Let's Face It provides a variety of educational and support materials, including an every-other-year resource directory that can be downloaded from its web site.

President: Betsy Wilson (1987 to Present)
Executive Director: Same as above.
Year Established: 1987

Keywords
Apert Syndrome; Branchio Oculo Facial Syndrome; Carpenter Syndrome; Cleft Palate and Cleft Lip; Craniofacial Disorders; Crouzon Disease; Goldenhar Syndrome; Goodman Syndrome; Greig Cephalopolysyndactyly Syndrome; Let's Face It (USA); Marshall Syndrome; Maxillofacial Dysostosis; Nager Syndrome; Oral Facial Digital Syndrome; Oto Palato Digital Syndrome Types I and II; Pallister W Syndrome; Pfeiffer Syndrome; Saethre Chotzen Syndrome; Sakati Syndrome; Summitt Syndrome; Treacher Collins Syndrome

1793 Leukaemia CARE

2 Shrubbery Avenue
Worcester, WR1 1QH, United Kingdom

Phone: +44 (0) 1905-33-0003
Fax: +44 (0) 1905-33-0090
E-mail: info@leukaemiaCARE.org.uk
http://www.leukaemiacare.org.uk

Leukaemia CARE is a national charity that provides care and support to patients, their families and caregivers during the difficult journey through the diagnosis and treatment of leukemia or an allied blood disorder. Leukaemia CARE provides the only dedicated free phone CARE Line for patients and their families that enables people to discuss their feelings, concerns and emotions at such a difficult period of time. (The number for the CARE line is: 0800 169 6680.) In addition, it provides information, holidays, limited financial support and operates CARE Teams throughout the United Kingdom to ensure that there is local support wherever a patient and his family live.

Executive Director: Marc Stowell
Year Established: 1967

Keywords
Leukaemia CARE

1794 Leukemia & Lymphoma Society

1311 Mamaroneck Avenue
3rd Floor
White Plains, NY 10605

Phone: (914) 949-5213
Fax: (914) 949-6691
Toll Free: (800) 955-4572
E-mail: infocenter@LLS.org
http://www.LLS.org

The Leukemia & Lymphoma Society is a national, voluntary health agency dedicated to curing leukemia, lymphoma, Hodgkin's disease and myeloma, and to improving the quality of life of patients and their families. The society was established in 1949 as the de Villiers Foundation. In 2000, the society changed its name from The Leukemia Society of America to The Leukemia & Lymphoma Society to emphasize its commitment to fighting all blood-related cancers. Today, the society supports the following major programs: research, patient services, public and professional education, advocacy and community services. With headquarters in White Plains, NY, the society has chapter offices across the United States.

President: Dwayne Howell
Year Established: 1949
Acronym: LSA

Keywords
Advocacy; Anemia, Sideroblastic; Cancer, Blood-Related; Cutaneous T Cell Lymphomas; Hodgkin's Disease; Leukemia; Leukemia & Lymphoma Society; Leukemia Society of America, Inc.; Leukemia, Chronic Lymphocytic; LSA; Leukemia, Chronic Myelogenous; Leukemia, Hairy Cell; Lymphoma; Lymphoma, Gastric Non Hodgkins Type; Mantle Cell Lymphoma; Myelodysplastic Syndromes; Myeloma, Multiple; Radiation Syndromes; Support Groups

1795 Lewy Body Dementia Association, Inc.

P.O. Box 451429
Atlanta, GA 31145-9429

Phone: (404) 935-6444
Fax: (480) 422-5434
Toll Free: (800) 539-9767
E-mail: office@lbda.org
http://www.lewybodydementia.org

The Lewy Body Dementia Association (LBDA) is a not-for-profit, voluntary, general service organization founded in 2003. It is dedicated to improving the quality of life for those who suffer from lewy body dementia, a progressive brain disease with no known cure. Although symptoms vary, hallucinations and fluctuating cognition are usually present, along with features of Alzheimer's disease and/or Parkinson's disease. The association helps patients, as well as their families and caregivers, by providing information and offering support and advice. In addition, it promotes awareness of this disorder among medical professionals and encourages research.

President: Angela Taylor
Year Established: 2003
Acronym: LBDA

Keywords
LBDA; Lewy Body Dementia; Lewy Body Dementia Association, Inc.

1796 Life Raft Group

40 Galesi Drive
Wayne, NJ 07470

Phone: (972) 837-9092
Fax: (973) 837-9095
E-mail: LifeRaft@liferaftgroup.org
http://www.LifeRaftGroup.org

The Life Raft Group is an international, Internet-based, non-profit organization providing support, through education and innovative research, to patients with a rare cancer called gastrointestinal stromal tumor (GIST), most of whom are being treated with a new oral cancer drug called Gleevec (Glivec outside the United States). The Life Raft Group provides information to patients, medical professionals, and researchers, and supports research related to treatment of, and ultimately a cure for, GIST.

President: Stan Bunn (January 2003-December 2005)
Executive Director: Norman Scherzer
Year Established: 2002
Acronym: LRG

Keywords
Gastrointestinal Stromal Tumor; GIST; Gist Cancer; Gist Tumor; Gleevec; Life Raft Group; Patient Support

1797 Li-Fraumeni Syndrome International Registry

Dana Farber Cancer Institute
44 Binney Street
Mayer 3A
Boston, MA 02115

Phone: (617) 632-2510
Fax: (617) 632-3161
Toll Free: (800) 828-6622
TDD: (617) 632-5330
E-mail: Dana-FarberContactUs@dfci.harvard.edu
http://www.dfci.harvard.edu

The Li-Fraumeni Syndrome International Registry is a not-for-profit health organization dedicated to compiling data concerning families with Li-Fraumeni syndrome and providing them with information regarding surveillance and intervention options. Li-Fraumeni syndrome is a familial disorder consisting of the appearance of early breast cancer. Established in 1969, the registry provides referrals to genetic counseling and other services and works to educate affected families and healthcare professionals. It provides a variety of educational and support materials, including a regular newsletter, videotapes concerning genetic testing, brochures, and fliers.

President: David Nathan
Executive Director: Fred Li
Year Established: 1969

Keywords
Li Fraumeni Syndrome; Li-Fraumeni Syndrome International Registry

1798 Lightning Strike & Electric Shock Survivors International, Inc.
P.O. Box 1156
Jacksonville, NC 28541-1156

Phone: (910) 346-4708
Fax: (910) 346-4708
E-mail: lightning1@ec.rr.com (OR) smarshburns@yahoo.com
http://www.lightning-strike.org

Lightning Strike & Electric Shock Survivors, Inc., is an international group for those who have been struck by lightning or have received a damaging electrical shock. Its mission is to communicate with other members by acting as a resource for information and encouraging family members to better understand the physical, emotional, and psychological symptoms associated with lightning strikes and damaging electrical shocks. The organization supports survivors by listening to their health issues and concerns, and providing an avenue for members to express their feelings, fears, and emotions. The group also supports the study of long-term physical and emotional consequences of exposure to lightning strikes and damaging electrical shock.

President: Steve Marshburn, Sr. President/Founder
Executive Director: Joyce A. Marshburn
Year Established: 1989
Acronym: LS&ESSI, INC.

Keywords
Lightning; Lightning Strike; Lightning Strike & Electric Shock Survivors International, Inc; LS & ESSI, Inc.

1799 Lissencephaly Contact Group
209-211 City Road
London, EC1V 1JN, United Kingdom

Phone: +44 (0) 207-608-8700
Toll Free: +44 (0) 808-808-3555
E-mail: info@lissencephaly.org.uk
http://www.lissencephaly.org.uk

The Lissencephaly Contact Group is an international self-help organization in the United Kingdom dedicated to networking affected families and promoting awareness of lissencephaly and other rare, related brain conditions. Lissencephaly is a rare birth defect in which the folds of the brain are incompletely formed; as a result, the brain has a smooth surface instead of the normal folds and grooves. In some cases, affected individuals may exhibit additional abnormalities, such as a small head (microcephaly), episodes of uncontrolled electrical disturbances in the brain (seizures), and/or other physical abnormalities. Severe mental retardation may also be present. Lissencephaly may be due to a spontaneous (de novo) genetic change that occurs for unknown reasons (sporadic), be inherited as an autosomal recessive genetic trait, or occur in association with various underlying disorders. The Lissencephaly Contact Group is committed to enabling affected families to share information and experiences; helping interested families meet and/or correspond; and obtaining and disseminating current information on lissencephaly for the benefit of affected families and interested professionals. It also provides referrals and offers a variety of educational materials including brochures, pamphlets, and a regular newsletter.

President: Kathleen Wood (Contact Person)
Year Established: 1988

Keywords
Agyria; Lissencephaly; Lissencephaly Contact Group; Miller Dieker Syndrome; Neuronal Migration Disorders; Pachygyria; Polymicrogyria; Schizencephaly; Walker Warburg Syndrome

1800 Lissencephaly Network, Inc.
10408 Bitterroot Court
Fort Wayne, IN 46804

Phone: (219) 432-4310
Fax: (219) 432-4310
E-mail: lissencephalyOne@aol.com
http://www.lissencephaly.org/

The Lissencephaly Network is a non-profit organization that serves children with lissencephaly and their families throughout the United States and 22 other countries around the world. Lissencephaly is a rare birth defect in which the folds of the brain are incompletely formed; as a result, the brain has a smooth surface instead of the normal folds and grooves. In some cases, affected individuals may exhibit additional abnormalities, such as a small head (microcephaly), episodes of uncontrolled electrical disturbances in the brain (seizures), and/or other physical abnormalities. Established in 1991, the Lissencephaly Network offers updated medical information, referrals to genetic counseling, equipment sharing, and parent-to-parent talks. It publishes a newsletter three times a year and has a directory that lists members. A comprehensive database is maintained on medical and developmental histories of affected children. A variety of informational materials is produced and distributed by the Lissencephaly Network.

President: Dianna Fitzgerald (1991-Present)
Executive Director: Dianna Fitzgerald
Year Established: 1991

Keywords
Agyria; Cortical Dysplasia; Lissencephaly; Lissencephaly Network, Inc.; Lissencephaly, Frontal; Lissencephaly, Partial; Lissencephaly, Posterior; Lissencephaly, X-linked; MEB; Miller Dieker Syndrome; Neuronal Migration Disorders; Pachygyria; Perisylvian Syndrome, Congenital Bilateral; Polymicrogyria; Schizencephaly; Walker Warburg Syndrome

1801 Lithium Information Center/Obsessive Compulsive Information Center

Madison Institute of Medicine
7617 Mineral Point Road
Suite 300
Madison, WI 53717

Phone: (608) 827-2470
Fax: (608) 827-2479
E-mail: mim@miminc.org
http://www.miminc.org

The Lithium Information Center and Obsessive Compulsive Information Center are affiliated with the Madison Institute of Medicine; a not-for-profit organization committed to conceptualizing, developing, and disseminating innovative approaches to the education of professionals, consumers, and the general public about psychiatric disorders and their treatment. An additional focus of the institute is clinical research as a vehicle to advance the frontiers of medicine and improve quality of life. At the core of the institute's educational efforts are the Lithium Information Center (LIC) and the Obsessive Compulsive Information Center (OCIC). The LIC acquires, catalogs, and disseminates information on the biomedical uses of lithium and other medications for the treatment of bipolar (manic-depressive) disorder, a psychiatric disorder in which affected individuals experience recurrent mood swings. The OCIC distributes biomedical information concerning obsessive-compulsive disorder (OCD) and related disorders. OCD is an anxiety disorder characterized by repetitive actions or rituals (compulsions) performed in response to recurrent obsessive thoughts.

President: Margaret Baudhuin (Coordinator)
Executive Director: James Jefferson, MD & John Greist MD (Co-Directors)
Year Established: 1975

Keywords
Lithium Information Center/Obsessive Compulsive Information Center

1802 Little Hearts, Inc.

P.O. Box 171
Cromwell, CT 06416

Phone: (860) 635-0006
Fax: (860) 635-0006
Toll Free: (866) 435-4673
E-mail: lh@littlehearts.net
http://www.littlehearts.org

Little Hearts, Inc. is a non-profit organization that provides support, resources, networking and hope to families affected by congenital heart defects (CHD). Membership consists of parents who have or are expecting a child with a CHD, adults with a CHD and parents whose child lost his or her battle with CHD. Established in 1998, this organization offers one-to-one phone contact, monthly support group meetings, networking, newsletters, annual picnics and projects (yearly and monthly photo calendars). It sponsors two online E-mail support groups, one for all members and one for parents who have a lost a child to CHD.

President: Lenore M. Cameron
Year Established: 1998

Keywords
Atresia, Tricuspid; Atrial Septal Defects; Coarctation of the Aorta; Congenital Heart Defects; Double Outlet Right Ventricle; Eisenmenger Syndrome; Hypoplastic Left Heart Syndrome; Little Hearts, Inc.; Patent Ductus Arteriosus; Tetralogy of Fallot; Total Anomalous Pulmonary Venous Return; Transposition of the Great Arteries; Ventricular Septal Defects

1803 Little People of America, Inc.

5289 Northeast Elam Young Parkway
Suite F100
Hillsboro, OR 97124

Phone: (503) 846-1562
Fax: (503) 846-1590
Toll Free: (888) 572-2001
E-mail: info@lpaonline.org
http://www.lpaonline.org

Little People of America (LPA) is a voluntary, not-for-profit, self-help organization dedicated to providing support and information to people of short stature, their families, and healthcare professionals. Short stature is generally caused by one of the more than 200 medical conditions known as dwarfism. Established in 1957, the organization provides support and guidance to affected individuals of all ages; offers medical, environmental, educational, vocational, and parental guidance; and networks with national and international growth-related and genetic support groups. The organization's Parents Group gives parents of short-stature individuals the opportunity to exchange ideas about healthcare, home and school adaptation, laws that affect their children, and everyday community experiences. Little People of America also offers information on employment, education, disability rights, adoption of short-stature children, medical issues, clothing, adaptive devices, and parenting tips. In addition, the organization conducts seminars and provides educational scholarships and medical assistance grants. Little People of America provides appropriate referrals, offers information to local physicians who are working with short-stature individuals for the first time, and provides a variety of educational and support materials such as brochures and regular newsletters.

Year Established: 1957
Acronym: LPA

Keywords
Achondrogenesis; Achondroplasia; Acrodysostosis; Alstrom's Disease; Camptomelic Syndrome; Conradi Hunermann Syndrome; Dwarfism; Dyschondrosteosis; Growth Delay, Constitutional; Growth Hormone Deficiency; Hypochondroplasia; Kenny Caffey Syndrome; Kniest Dysplasia; Kniest Syndrome; Laron Dwarfism; Little People of America; Little People of America, Inc.; Marshall Smith Syndrome; Meier Gorlin Syndrome; Metaphyseal Chondrodysplasia, McKusick Type; Metatropic Dysplasia I; Metatropic Dysplasia Type II; Mulibrey Nanism; Mulibrey Nanism Syndrome (Perheentupa Syndrome); Russell Silver Syndrome; Seckel Syndrome; Short Stature; SHORT Syndrome; Spondyloepiphyseal Dysplasia Congenital; Spondyloepiphyseal Dysplasia Tarda; Weaver Syndrome; Weill Marchesani Syndrome; Weismann Netter Stuhl Syndrome

1804   Little People's Research Fund, Inc.

616 Old Edmondson Avenue
2nd Floor
Catonsville, MD 21228-3305

Phone: (410) 747-1100
Fax: (410) 747-1374
Toll Free: (800) 232-5773
E-mail: lprf@lprf.org
http://www.lprf.org

The Little People's Research Fund was established in 1980 as a not-for-profit health organization dedicated to raising funds for patient care, medical research, and education of the medical community and the general public about dwarfism. The organization's goals include funding research on orthopedic disabilities associated with dwarfism; providing funds for direct patient care/services; working to establish a training program for medical professionals; and supporting the Pierre House for families affected by dwarfism. In addition to raising funds, the organization sponsors clinics throughout the country, works to educate the community about dwarfism, and assists indigent families with medical expenses, transportation, and housing while in Baltimore for treatment. The Little People's Research Fund produces educational materials that include brochures, pamphlets, audio-visual aids, and a newsletter.

President: Charles E. McElwee (1980-Present)
Executive Director: Charles E. McElwee
Year Established: 1980
Acronym: LPRF

Keywords
Achondrogenesis; Achondroplasia; Acrodysostosis; Conradi Hunermann Syndrome; Dwarfism; Dyschondrosteosis; Dysplasia, Diastrophic; Dysplasia, Skeletal; Growth Delay, Constitutional; Growth Hormone Deficiency; Hypochondroplasia; Kenny Caffey Syndrome; Kniest Dysplasia; Kniest Syndrome; Laron Dwarfism; Little People's Research Fund, Inc.; Marshall Smith Syndrome; Metaphyseal Chondrodysplasia, McKusick Type; Metatropic Dysplasia I; Metatropic Dysplasia Type II; Mulibrey Nanism Syndrome (Perheentupa Syndrome); Rehabilitation Facilities (Various); Russell Silver Syndrome; Seckel Syndrome; SHORT Syndrome; Spondyloepiphyseal Dysplasia Congenital; Weaver Syndrome; Weill Marchesani Syndrome; Weismann Netter Stuhl Syndrome

1805   Living with Trisomy 13

E-mail: info@livingwithtrisomy13.org
http://www.livingwithtrisomy13.org

Living with Trisomy 13 is a web-based support group that focuses on bringing families of trisomy 13 patients together. Trisomy 13 syndrome is a rare chromosomal disorder in which all or a portion of chromosome 13 appears three times (trisomy) rather than twice in cells of the body. The presence of an extra chromosome 13 is also sometimes called Patau syndrome. It is characterized by low birth weight, heart defects, and defects of the eyes, spine, and abdomen, among other characteristics. Sometimes trisomy 13 is present in a mosaic pattern, in which the extra chromosome is only present in some cells of the body. Living with Trisomy 13 provides information sharing, referrals, and support for affected families.

President: ThereseAnn Siegle (therese@livingwithtrisomy13.org)
Year Established: 2005

Keywords
Advocacy; Living with Trisomy 13; Networking; Patau Syndrome; Research; Support Groups; Trisomy 13 Syndrome

1806 Locks of Love
2925 10th Avenue North
Suite 102
Lake Worth, FL 33461

Phone: (561) 963-1677
Fax: (561) 963-9914
Toll Free: (888) 896-1588
TDD: (561) 963-1677
E-mail: info@locksoflove.org
http://www.locksoflove.org

Locks of Love is a voluntary, not-for-profit organization whose main goal is to return a sense of self-confidence and normalcy to children suffering from hair loss by providing high quality hair prostheses to financially disadvantaged children. Locks of Love helps children with such rare diseases as alopecia areata, ectodermal dysplasia, loose anagen syndrome, and trichotillomania, among others. Founded in 1997, Locks of Love provides educational services and networking to patients, families, healthcare professionals, and the general community.

President: Madonna W. Coffman
Executive Director: Susan Stone

Keywords
Alopecia Areata; Cancer Treatment Hair Loss; Cartilage Hair Hypoplasia; Congenital Hair Growth Abnormality; Ectodermal Dysplasia; Graft-Versus-Host-Disease; Hair Loss, Children; Hair Prosthesis; Locks of Love; Loose Anagen Syndrome; Monilethrix; Networking; Trichotillomania; Wig

1807 Lowe Syndrome Association
18919 Voss Road
Dallas, TX 75287

Phone: (612) 869-5693
Fax: (612) 866-3222
E-mail: info@lowesyndrome.org
http://www.lowesyndrome.org

The Lowe Syndrome Association is an international, voluntary health organization composed of parents, healthcare professionals, and other interested individuals. Established in 1983, its primary purposes are to foster communication among families, promote a better understanding of the syndrome, provide medical and educational information, and encourage and support research. Activities include publishing and disseminating printed materials, maintaining a web site, sponsoring international conferences, and sponsoring medical research grants.

President: Mary Tietz (2003-Present)
Year Established: 1983
Acronym: LSA

Keywords
Lowe Syndrome Association; Lowe's Disease; Lowe's Syndrome; Oculocerebrorenal Syndrome

1808 Lung Association
3 Raymond Street
Suite 300
Ottawa
Ontario, K1R 1A3, Canada

Phone: (613) 569-6411
Fax: (613) 569-8860
E-mail: info@lung.ca
http://www.lung.ca/

The Lung Association is a national, non-profit organization in Canada dedicated to improving respiratory health, and combatting respiratory disease. The association works to fulfill its mission by promoting research, increasing public awareness, and providing patient support programs. Established in 1900, the association is an umbrella organization that currently consists of ten provincial and one territorial association. Each provincial association maintains a professional staff that includes health educators who work with volunteers to develop and conduct community program services. One of the association's primary objectives is to reduce tobacco use. In addition, the Lung Association is committed to supporting respiratory health and disease research. Nationally, the association provides research funding that is administered by the Canadian Thoracic Society, the Canadian Nurses Respiratory Society, and the Physiotherapy Cardio-

Respiratory Society. Each member association also supports research at the provincial level. The Lung Association also provides a variety of educational materials and has a web site on the Internet.

President: Deirdre Freiheit, President and CEO
Year Established: 1900
Acronym: CLA

Keywords
Lung Association

1809 Lupus Canada

590 Alden Road
Suite 211
Markham
Ontario, L3R 8N2, Canada

Phone: (905) 513-0004
Fax: (905) 513-9516
Toll Free: (800) 661-1468
E-mail: lupuscanada@bellnet.ca
http://www.lupuscanada.org

Lupus Canada is a national association of regional lupus support groups and their various branches. These groups of volunteers are dedicated to providing support and information to people who have lupus, their families, and friends. Lupus is a chronic autoimmune disorder that can affect any organ of the body. In lupus, the body's immune system malfunctions and attacks the bodies own tissue. Established in 1987, Lupus Canada produces educational materials, promotes research, and provides advocacy on behalf of the lupus community.

President: Mae Boa (2004 to Present)
Executive Director: Judi Farrell
Year Established: 1987

Keywords
Disseminated Lupus Erythematosus; DLE; Drug-induced Lupus; Lupus; Lupus Canada; Neonatal Lupus; SLE; Subacute Cutaneous Lupus Erythematosus; Systemic Lupus Erythematosus

---

1810 Lupus Foundation of America, Inc.

2000 L Street NW
Suite 710
Washington, DC 20036

Phone: (202) 349-1155
Fax: (202) 349-1156
Toll Free: (800) 558-0121
E-mail: info@lupus.org
http://www.lupus.org

Established in 1977, the Lupus Foundation of America is a non-profit, voluntary health organization dedicated to improving the diagnosis and treatment of lupus, supporting individuals and families affected by the disease, increasing awareness of lupus among health professionals and the public, and finding the cure. The LFA seeks to increase public and private sector funding of lupus research, and provides direct financial support to lupus researchers; educates the public, physicians and other health professionals about lupus symptoms, diagnosis and treatment; advocates for public policies that increase government funding for lupus research, education programs, and support services; and collaborates with support groups and other interested partners to serve the needs of individuals with lupus, their families and caregivers.

President: Sandra Raymond
Executive Director: V. Terry Bell (Chairman)
Year Established: 1977
Acronym: LFA

Keywords
Antiphospholipid Syndrome; LFA; Lupus; Lupus Foundation of America, Inc.; MCTD; Mixed Connective Tissue Disease; Neonatal Lupus; SLE; Systemic Lupus Erythematosus

---

1811 Lupus Society of Alberta

1301 - 8 Street SW
Suite 200
Calgary, Alberta, T2R 1B7, Canada

Phone: (403) -22-8-79
Fax: (403) -22-8-78
Toll Free: (888) -24-2-91
E-mail: lupuslsa@shaw.ca
www.lupus.ab.ca

Lupus Society of Alberta (LSA) is a not-for-profit rare disorder organization located in Calgary, Alberta, Canada. Founded in 1973, LSA provides information on lupus and encourages research to find a cure. Lupus is a chronic, inflammatory autoimmune disorder affecting the connective tissue. LSA services include support groups, advocacy, networking, and education to patients, family members, the general public, and healthcare professionals.

President: Marlee Winston (2004-present)
Executive Director: Rosemary E. Church
Year Established: 1973
Acronym: LSA

Keywords
Arthritis; Canada; Lupus; Lupus Nephritis; Lupus Society of Alberta; Networking; Research; Scleroderma; Sjogren Syndrome; Support Groups; Systemic Lupus Erythematosus

1812 Lupus UK

St. James House
Eastern Road
Romford
Essex, RM1 3NH, United Kingdom

Phone: +44 (0) 1708-73-1251
Fax: +44 (0) 1708-73-1252
E-mail: Headoffice@lupusuk.org.uk
http://www.geocities.com/HotSprings/2911/

Lupus UK is a voluntary organization in the United Kingdom dedicated to providing information and support to individuals affected by systemic lupus erythematosus (SLE), an autoimmune disorder that is characterized by chronic inflammation affecting the skin, joints, or other connective tissues of the body. Different tissues and organs may be involved, and the range and severity of associated symptoms and findings may vary greatly from case to case. In some individuals with the disorder, symptoms may include weakness and fatigue; persistent flu-like symptoms; joint inflammation, swelling, stiffness, and pain; skin rashes, such as the appearance of a rash across the bridge of the nose and the cheeks ("butterfly" rash); abnormal sensitivity of the skin to light; hair loss; and other abnormalities. Lupus UK was established in 1978 and currently consists of 27 regional groups throughout Great Britain and Northern Ireland. The organization, which is a self-help group run by volunteers, is committed to providing support and assistance to all affected individuals; promoting communication between members and the medical professionals involved in their care; and offering practical assistance. Lupus UK is also dedicated to promoting professional and public awareness of lupus.

President: Graham RV Hughes, M.D.
Executive Director: Chris Maker
Year Established: 1978

Keywords
Lupus UK

1813 Lyme Disease Foundation

P.O. Box 332
Tolland, CT 06084

Phone: (860) 525-2000
Fax: (860) 525-8425
Toll Free: (800) 886-5963
E-mail: lymefnd@aol.com
http://www.lyme.org

The Lyme Disease Foundation, Inc. (LDF) is a voluntary, not-for-profit organization dedicated to finding the solutions to Lyme disease (LD) and other tick-borne disorders. Established in 1988, it funds research on LD, conducts international scientific conferences, and publishes a peer-reviewed scientific journal. It has successfully lobbied Congress for federal funds dedicated to Lyme disease education and research. In addition, the Lyme Disease Foundation provides appropriate referrals, promotes patient advocacy, and supports the development of educational programs for affected individuals, family members, the medical and scientific communities, and the public. The Lyme Disease Foundation's many educational and support materials include a monthly self-help newsletter and a Lyme Disease Awareness Pack. A Lyme Disease Scientific Pack includes reprints of medical articles, scientific slide show information, and guidelines for establishing and conducting a self-help group. In addition, the foundation distributes educational program materials for students, workplace and community education program materials, poster sets, brochures, and videotapes.

President: Karen Vanderhoof-Forschner (1988-Present)
Executive Director: Thomas E. Forschner
Year Established: 1988
Acronym: LDF

Keywords
Lyme Disease; Lyme Disease Foundation; Spirochetosis; Tick-borne Disease

1814 Lymphatic Research Foundation

100 Forest Avenue
East Hills, NY 11548

Phone: (516) 625-9675
Fax: (516) 625-9410
E-mail: lrf@lymphaticresearch.org
http://www.lymphaticresearch.org

The Lymphatic Research Foundation's mission is to promote and support biomedical research to find improved treatment options and cures for lymphatic disease, including lymphedema and related lymphatic disorders. The lymphatic system is a circulatory network of vessels, ducts, and nodes that filter and distribute certain fluid (lymph) and blood cells throughout the body. The primary symptom of hereditary lymphedema is swelling or puffiness in various parts of the body due to the accumulation of lymphatic fluid in the soft layers of tissue under the skin. The program goals of the LRF include increasing public and private funding for lymphatic research, fostering collaboration and the exchange of information and resources among researchers, providing research grants and awards, and promoting a national tissue bank and patient registry.

President: Wendy Chaite, Esq.
Year Established: 1998

Keywords
Audio-Visual Aids; Lymphatic Research Foundation

1815 Lymphoedema (Lymphedema) Association of Australia
94 Cambridge Terrace
Malvern
South Australia, 5061, Australia

Phone: +61 (0) 8-8271-2198
Fax: +61 (0) 8-8271-8776
E-mail: casley@internode.on.net
http://www.lymphoedema.org.au

The Lymphoedema (Lymphedema) Association of Australia (LAA) is a not-for-profit, international organization that was founded in 1982 to encourage research into lymphedema and its treatment. It disseminates information among physicians, therapists, affected individuals, and family members. Lymphedema is a condition characterized by the abnormal accumulation of lymph fluid, the associated swelling of certain body tissues due to lymphatic system abnormalities that cause obstruction of normal lymph flow into the bloodstream. Lymph is a bodily fluid that contains certain white blood cells (lymphocytes), fats, and proteins, and functions as an essential part of the immune system. Individuals with lymphedema may experience swelling that increases over time; a feeling of heaviness, tightness, and discomfort in the affected area; tenderness or pain; susceptibility to infection; and, in some severe cases, loss of mobility. The Lymphoedema Association of Australia currently has approximately 2,000 members throughout the world.

President: Dr. Judith R. Casley-Smith (Chairman)
Year Established: 1982
Acronym: LAA

Keywords
Lymphoedema (Lymphedema) Association of Australia

1816 Lymphoma Association (UK)
P.O. Box 386
Haddenham
Aylesbury
Bucks, HP20 2GA, United Kingdom

Phone: +44 (0) 1296-61-9400
E-mail: lymphoma.org.uk
http://www.lymphoma.org.uk

The Lymphoma Association is a voluntary organization in the United Kingdom that was established in 1986 to provide information and emotional support to anyone whose life has been affected by cancer of the lymphatic system (lymphoma). Lymphoma may be classified into two major categories that are distinguished by cell type: Hodgkin's disease and non-Hodgkin's lymphoma. Both may be characterized by similar symptoms including painless swelling of lymph nodes, night sweats, fever, fatigue, itching, and weight loss. The Lymphoma Association offers a variety of programs and services including providing information about lymphomas, their treatments, and related topics; offering a listening service for affected individuals and family members; and providing telephone links to volunteers who have direct experience with lymphoma. The association also has a lending library service of books, videotapes, and audio tapes; publishes a regular newsletter; and has a network of support groups across the United Kingdom that are open to anyone with an interest in lymphoma. The support groups provide affected individuals and family members with the opportunity to meet other people affected by lymphoma and to find support, friendship, information, and resources. Many groups also invite speakers and organize social activities.

President: Dr. David Lynch
Executive Director: David Cash (Chief Executive)
Year Established: 1986

Keywords
Lymphoma Association (UK)

1817 Lymphoma Foundation Canada
16-1375 Southdown Road
Suite 236
Mississauga
Ontario, L5J 2Z1, Canada

Phone: (905) 822-5135
Fax: (905) 278-1524
Toll Free: (866) 6-59-5
E-mail: info@lymphoma.ca
http://www.lymphoma.ca

The Lymphoma Research Foundation Canada (LRFC) is a not-for-profit organization that was founded in 1998 to provide support for those affected by lymphoma and for individuals who conduct research in the diagnosis, treatment, and cure of these diseases. Lymphoma is a group of cancers affecting the lymphatic system, which is a network of glands and vessels that collect the thin, watery fluid known as lymph from different areas of the body and drain it into the bloodstream. The lymphatic system also functions as an essential part of the immune system. Lymphoma may be classified into two major categories that are distinguished by cell type: Hodgkin's disease and non-Hodgkin's lymphoma. Both may be characterized by similar symptoms including night sweats, painless swelling of lymph nodes, fever, fatigue, itching, and weight loss. The focus of the LRCF is on lymphoma issues and treatment in Canada. The LRCF provides information on research currently being conducted in Canada; offers understandable reports on the lymphatic system that include the incidence, classification, causes, diagnosis, staging, and treatment of lymphomas; and has a web site.

Executive Director: Karen Van Rassel
Year Established: 1998
Acronym: LFC

Keywords
Blood Disorder; Cancer; CLL; Cutaneous T Cell Lymphomas; Hodgkin's Lymphoma.; LFC; Lymphoma; Lymphoma Foundation Canada; Mantle Cell Lymphoma; NHL; Non Hodgkin's Lymphoma

1818 Lymphoma Research Foundation

111 Broadway
19th Floor
New York, NY 10006

Phone: (212) 349-2910
Fax: (212) 349-2886
Toll Free: (800) 235-6848
E-mail: LRF@lymphoma.org
http://www.lymphoma.org

The Lymphoma Research Foundation of America (LRFA) and Cure for Lymphoma Foundation merged to become the Lymphoma Research Foundation. This is a national, voluntary, nonprofit organization dedicated to funding lymphoma research and providing comprehensive educational and support programs to increase awareness and knowledge of lymphoma nationwide. Lymphoma refers to cancer of the lymphatic system, which is a network of glands and vessels that circulate a thin, watery fluid known as lymph throughout the body. Lymphoma is classified into two major categories that are distinguished by cell type: Hodgkin's disease and non-Hodgkin's lymphoma. Both may be characterized by similar symptoms including night sweats, painless swelling of lymph nodes, fever, fatigue, itching, and weight loss. The foundation's primary mission is to fund lymphoma research at universities and cancer centers across the nation through annual research grants and fellowship awards. In addition, the LRFA provides a one-on-one "phone buddy support program" that matches affected individuals by cell type, stage and grade, or treatment plan; offers a lymphoma helpline that directs affected individuals and family members to cancer resources and clinical trial information; and conducts free support groups.

President: Jerry Freundlich
Executive Director: Suzanne Bliss
Year Established: 1991
Acronym: LRF

Keywords
Cutaneous T Cell Lymphomas; Hodgkin's Disease; LRF; Lymphoma; Lymphoma Research Foundation; Lymphoma, Gastric, Non Hodgkins Type; Mantle Cell Lymphoma; Monocytoid B Cell Lymphoma

1819 Lymphovenous Association of Ontario

PM Postal, Box 55241
1800 Sheppard Avenue East
Toronto, Ontario, M2J 5A0, Canada

Phone: (416) 410-2250
Toll Free: (877) 723-0033
E-mail: lymphontario@yahoo.com
www.lymphontario.org

The Lymphovenous Association of Ontario is a voluntary, not-for-profit health organization that was established in 1996 to develop a networking group for affected individuals, family members and healthcare professionals in Ontario with an interest in lymphovenous disorders. The lymphatic system includes a complex network of vessels that drain lymph from various areas of the body into the bloodstream. (Lymph is a bodily fluid that contains certain white blood cells [lymphocytes], fats, and proteins and functions as an essential part of the immune system.) In some cases, lymphatic malformations may be present at birth; in other cases, obstruction of normal lymph flow may occur secondary to certain inflammatory conditions, infectious diseases, benign or malignant growths, surgical procedures, radiation therapy, and/or other factors. The Lymphovenous Association of Ontario is committed to providing information and support to affected individuals and family members; raising public and professional awareness of lymphovenous disorders, their causes, and treatments; and supporting research toward improved treatment methods and possible cures. The association is also dedicated to providing networking opportunities for affected individuals and families, enabling the exchange of mutual support, information, and resources. In addition, the association engages in patient advocacy, has a directory, provides appropriate referrals, and conducts an annual general meeting and conference.

President: Joanne Young
Year Established: 1996
Acronym: LAO

Keywords
Breast Cancer; Cancer; Edema; LAO; Lymphedema; Lymphovenous Association of Ontario; Post Cancer Swelling; Primary Lymphedema; Secondary Lymphedema

1820 Lymphovenous Canada
8 Silver Avenue
Toronto
Ontario, M6R 1X8, Canada

Phone: (416) -53-3-24
Fax: (416) -53-9-83
TDD: (999) -99-9-99
E-mail: info@lymphovenous-canada.ca
http://www.lymphovenous-canada.ca

Lymphovenous Canada is an e-networking of organizations, groups, and researcher across Canada interested in promoting research, public awareness, and support serviced to help those with lymphatic disorders, such as lymphedema, Klippel-Trenaunay (KT) syndrome, lymphangioma, hemangioma, and vascular malformations. Established in 1996, Lymphovenous Canada is a supporter of the goals of the Canadian Lymphedema Foundation.

President: Cathy McPherson (Administrator)
Year Established: 1996
Acronym: CLF

Keywords
Canadian Lymphedema Foundation/Lymphovenous Canada; Cancer Related; Hemangioma; Klippel Trenaunay Syndrome; Klippel Trenaunay Weber Syndrome; Lymphangioma; Lymphangiomas; Lymphatic Malformations; Lymphedema, Hereditary; Lymphovenous Canada; Medical Education; Scientific Research; Vascular Malformations

1821 Lysosomal Diseases New Zealand
125 Cuba Street
Petone
Lower Hutt City, 6008, New Zealand

Phone: +64 (0) 4-566-7707
Fax: +64 (0) 4-566-7717
E-mail: john.forman@xtra.co.nz
http://www.ldnz.org.nz

Lysosomal Diseases New Zealand provides support and advocacy for patients/families affected by lysosomal storage diseases. These diseases occur as a result of inherited genetic defects that lead to an enzyme deficiency. LDNZ works in partnership with patients and their families, clinicians, researchers and industry to promote advances related to the diagnosis, treatment and, ultimately, cure of these diseases.

President: John Forman
Year Established: 1999
Acronym: LDNZ

Keywords
Batten Disease; Fabry Disease; Gaucher Disease; Glycoprotein Storage Diseases; Lysosomal Diseases New Zealand; Lysosomal Storage Diseases; MPS; Mucolipidosis; Mucopolysaccharide Disease; Oligosaccharide Disease; Tay Sach's Disease

1822 MAAP Services for Autism and Asperger Syndrome
P.O. Box 524
Crown Point, IN 46308

Phone: (219) 662-1311
Fax: (219) 662-0638
E-mail: chart@netnitco.net
http://www.maapservices.org

MAAP Services, Inc., is a non-profit organization dedicated to assisting family members of individuals with advanced forms of autism by offering information and advice on autism, and by providing the opportunity to network with others in similar circumstances. In addition, MAAP Services works to inform professionals and the general public about autism and the needs of those affected. Autism is a syndrome characterized by difficulty in verbal and/or nonverbal communication, ranging from not speaking at all to being unable to interpret body language or participate comfortably in two-way conversation. Established in 1984, MAAP Services, Inc., supports professionals and families of individuals with autism by responding to phone calls and letters from family members, professionals, and individuals with autism who need support and advice. The organization also produces educational materials.

President: Susan J. Moreno (1991 to Present)
Executive Director: Mary Anne Neiner, Assistant Director
Year Established: 1984
Acronym: MAAP

Keywords
Autism; MAAP Services for Autism and Asperger Syndrome; MAAP Services, Inc.

1823 Macular Degeneration Support, Inc.
3600 Blue Ridge
Grandview, MO 64030

Phone: (816) 761-7080
Fax: (816) 761-7080
E-mail: director@mdsupport.org
http://www.mdsupport.org

Macular Degeneration Support, Inc. (MD Support) is an all-volunteer, Internet-based community with an extensive web site, a large e-mail discussion group, and a message board for patients and families affected by macular degeneration, a hereditary eye (retinal) disorder. The Internet services of MD Support were developed for the purpose of offering people the information and support they need to deal with loss of central vision. A 12-member professional advisory board of doctors, social workers, and rehabilitation specialists backs MD Support.

President: Dan Roberts
Year Established: 1998
Acronym: MD Support

Keywords
Blind; Degeneration; Disease; Eye; Impaired; Macula; Macular; Macular Degeneration Support, Inc.; Retina; Visual

1824 Macular Disease Society
Darwin House
13a Bridge Street
Andover, Hampshire, SP10 1BE, United Kingdom

Phone: +44 (0) 1264-35-0551
Fax: +44 (0) 1264-35-0558

The Macular Disease Society (MDS) is a not-for-profit charity that offers support groups to patients and family members affected by macular degeneration. This is a degenerative disease affecting the macula or center of the retina of the eye. It results in progressive loss of central vision. The goal of MDS is to provide information, help, support, and advice to patients, their families, and healthcare professionals. MDS also supports, sponsors, and monitors research into the cause of, and treatments for, macular degeneration.

Year Established: 1987
Acronym: MDS

Keywords
Macular Degeneration; Macular Disease Society; Support Groups

1825 Madisons Foundation
P.O. Box 241956
Los Angeles, CA 90024

Phone: (310) 264-0826
Fax: (310) 264-4766
E-mail: getinfo@madisonsfoundation.org
http://www.madisonsfoundation.org

Madisons Foundation is dedicated to helping doctors and parents deal with children who have rare diseases through research, education, and support. It raises funds to support pediatric research at the Jonsson Comprehensive Cancer Center and the Mattel Children's Hospital at the University of California at Los Angeles; provides internships to medical students to learn effective and compassionate communication with parents and children; and provides informational and networking services for parents.

Executive Director: Mary Wallace
Year Established: 2001

Keywords
Children; Madisons Foundation; Networking; Rare Diseases; Rare Disorders; Research; Support Groups

1826 MAGIC Foundation for Children's Growth

6645 W. North Avenue
Oak Park, IL 60302

Phone: (708) 383-0808
Fax: (708) 383-0899
Toll Free: (800) 362-4423
E-mail: mary@magicfoundation.org
http://www.magicfoundation.org

The MAGIC Foundation is a national, non-profit organization dedicated to helping children and adults with growth-related disorders. Established in 1989, it provides services that include public education and awareness, quarterly newsletters, national networking, an annual convention, disorder specific brochures, and a Kids Program. Its current divisions include growth hormone deficiency, Russell Silver syndrome, McCune Albright syndrome, congenital adrenal hyperplasia, precocious puberty, Turner syndrome, septo optic dysplasia, panhypopituitarism, adult growth hormone deficiency, genital and reproductive anomalies in children and rare disorders. Educational materials produced by the foundation include general brochures, a networking form, disorder specific brochures, and a video entitled Just Say Yes to growth hormone.

President: Mary Andrews, Chairman
Executive Director: Dianne Tamburrino
Year Established: 1989
Acronym: MAGIC

Keywords
Achondrogenesis; Achondroplasia; Acrodysostosis; Adrenal Hyperplasia, Congenital; Arthrogryposis Multiplex Congenita; CAH; Cardio Facio Cutaneous Syndrome; Cockayne Syndrome; Conradi Hunermann Syndrome; CPP; Down Syndrome with Growth Hormone Deficiency; DS; Dyggve Melchior Clausen Syndrome; Dyschondrosteosis; Dysplasia, Diastrophic; Dystrophy, Asphyxiating Thoracic; Ellis-van Creveld Syndrome; Fairbank Disease; Froelich's Syndrome; Growth Delay, Constitutional; Growth Disorders; Growth Hormone Deficiency; Growth Retardation In Down Syndrome; Hypochondroplasia; Hypothyroidism, Congenital; Kniest Dysplasia; Kniest Syndrome; Laron Dwarfism; MAGIC Foundation for Children's Growth; Marshall Smith Syndrome; McCune Albright Syndrome; Metaphyseal Chondrodysplasia, McKusick Type; Metatropic Dysplasia I; Metatropic Dysplasia Type II; Noonan Syndrome; Puberty, Precocious; Robinow Syndrome; Russell Silver Syndrome; Seckel Syndrome; SHORT Syndrome; Spondyloepiphyseal Dysplasia Congenital; Spondy-

loepiphyseal Dysplasia Tarda; Turner Syndrome; Weaver Syndrome; Weill Marchesani Syndrome

1827 Malignant Hyperthermia Association of the United States (MHAUS)

11 East State Street
P.O. Box 1069
Sherburne, NY 13460-1069

Phone: (607) 674-7901
Fax: (607) 674-7910
E-mail: info@mhaus.org
http://www.mhaus.org

The Malignant Hyperthermia Association of the United States (MHAUS) is a nonprofit, voluntary organization dedicated to reducing morbidity and mortality related from malignant hyperthermia (MH). It seeks to improve the medical care of people susceptible to malignant hyperthermia and provide support information for people with this uncommon disorder. It also seeks to improve scientific understanding of MH and promote ongoing medical research on this disorder and related ones. Educational materials produced by MHAUS include brochures; a booklet, "Understanding MH"; an in-service video; a quarterly newsletter; MH procedure manuals for hospital and office-based surgeries; and a directory of MH muscle biopsy and molecular genetic testing locations in North America.

President: Henry Rosenberg, MD, CPE
Executive Director: Dianne Daughtery
Year Established: 1981
Acronym: MHAUS

Keywords
Anesthesia; Anesthetics; Central Core Disease; Dantrolene; Freeman Sheldon Syndrome; General Anesthesia; Malignant Hyperthermia; Malignant Hyperthermia Association of the United States; Malignant Hyperthermia Association of the United States (MHAUS); MH; MHAUS; Myotonia Congenita; Neuroleptic Malignant Syndrome; Schwartz Jampel Syndrome

1828 Malignant Hyperthermia Investigation Unit

Toronto General Hospital
200 Elizabeth Street
CCRW-2, Room ES3-403A
Toronto
Ontario, M5G 2C4, Canada

Phone: (416) 340-3128
Fax: (416) 340-4960
E-mail: info@mhacanada.org
http://www.mhacanada.org

The Malignant Hyperthermia Association is dedicated to studying and reducing complications associated with malignant hyperthermia. This is a hereditary disorder in which a person does not react appropriately to certain drugs (e.g., anesthetics) due to a genetic abnormality. Founded in 1976, the association has three main objectives: education, communication, and research. It provides financial support to current test standardization and genetic and lymphocyte research. In addition, the organization also produces educational materials of interest to the general public and medical professionals.

President: Morris Altman, M.D. (1996 to Present)
Executive Director: Carole Elliott
Year Established: 1979
Acronym: MHIU

Keywords
Canadian Malignant Hyperthermia Association; Hyperpyrexia, Fulminating; Hyperthermia of Anesthesia; Malignant Fever; Malignant Hyperpyrexia; Malignant Hyperthermia; Malignant Hyperthermia Investigation Unit; MH; Myopathy, Pharmacogenic

1829   MAME, Inc. (Mothers Against Myalgic Encephalomyelitis)

1 Orne Square
Salem, MA 01970

Phone: (978) 744-8293
Fax: (978) 744-2027
E-mail: MAME@mame-net.org
http://www.mame-net.org

Mothers Against Myalgic Encephalomyelitis, a voluntary organization, provides information to patients, family members, healthcare professionals, and the general public about myalgic encephalomyelitis, a disorder affecting the central, peripheral, and autonomic nervous systems and the muscles. Although its exact cause is not known, it is thought to be caused by a viral infection in association with an immune system abnormality. In addition to serving an educational function, Mothers Against Myalgic Encephalomyelitis has advocacy and fund-raising activities. Although it serves the nation as a whole, its membership is currently focused in Massachusetts and Texas.

President: Jean Harrison
Year Established: 1999
Acronym: M.A.M.E

Keywords
Advocacy; Chronic Fatigue Syndrome; M.A.M.E; MAME, Inc. (Mothers Against Myalgic Encephalomyelitis); Myalgic Encephalomyelitis

1830   Maple Syrup Urine Disease Family Support Group

82 Ravine Road
Powell, OH 43065

Phone: (740) 548-4475
E-mail: dbulcher@aol.com
http://www.msud-support.org/

The Maple Syrup Urine Disease Family Support Group (MSUD) is a non-profit organization dedicated to providing opportunities for support to affected individuals and their families, encouraging research, and disseminating educational materials. Maple syrup urine disease is a rare, inherited metabolic disorder that, if left untreated, can result in mental retardation, physical disabilities, and life-threatening complications. In infants with MSUD, three branched chain amino acids (leucine, isoleucine, and valine) abnormally accumulate in the blood causing harmful effects that interfere with brain functions. Established in 1982, MSUD publishes a periodic newsletter entitled, "Maple Syrup Urine Disease Newsletter." The support group produces and distributes educational materials such as brochures on maple syrup urine disease and organizes an international education conference for families and professionals held every two years.

President: Sandy Bulcher
Year Established: 1982
Acronym: MSUD Family Support Group

Keywords
BCKD Deficiency; Branched Chain Alpha Ketoacid Dehydrogenase Deficiency; Branched Chain Ketonuria I; Ketoacid Decarboxylase Deficiency; Maple Syrup Urine Disease; Maple Syrup Urine Disease Family Support Group; MSUD

1831   March of Dimes Birth Defects Foundation

1275 Mamaroneck Avenue
White Plains, NY 10605

Phone: (914) 428-7100
Fax: (914) 997-4763
Toll Free: (888) 663-4637
E-mail: Askus@marchofdimes.com
http://www.marchofdimes.com

The March of Dimes Birth Defects Foundation is a national, not-for-profit organization that was established in 1938. The mission of the foundation is to improve the health of babies by preventing birth defects, premature birth and infant mortality. The March of

Dimes funds programs of research, community services, education, and advocacy. Educational programs that seek to prevent birth defects are important to the foundation and, to that end, it also produces a wide variety of printed informational materials and videos. The Pregnancy & Newborn Health Education Center is staffed by trained health information specialists who provide researched information on pregnancy issues, complications and risks, newborn care, birth defects, genetic diseases and related topics as well as referrals to relevant organizations and support groups. The March of Dimes Birth Defects Foundation has added an E-mail and web site for Spanish speaking individuals.

President: Jennifer L. Howse, PhD
Year Established: 1938

Keywords
5-Oxoprolinuria; AIDS (Acquired Immunodeficiency Syndrome); AIDS, Perinatal; Aarskog Syndrome; Aase Syndrome; Abetalipoproteinemia; Acanthocytosis; Acanthosis Nigricans; Achalasia; Achondrogenesis; Achondroplasia; Acidemia, Isovaleric; Acidemia, Methylmalonic; Acidemia, Propionic; Acrocallosal Syndrome, Schinzel Type; Acrodermatitis Enteropathica; Acrodysostosis; Adams Oliver Syndrome; Adie Syndrome; Adrenal Hyperplasia, Congenital; Adrenoleukodystrophy; Afibrinogenemia, Congenital; Agammaglobulinemias, Primary; Agenesis of the Corpus Callosum; Aicardi Syndrome; Alagille Syndrome; Albinism; Alexander's Disease; Alkaptonuria; Alpha-1 Antitrypsin Deficiency; Alport Syndrome; Alstrom's Disease; Alternating Hemiplegia of Childhood; Alzheimer's Disease; Amelogenesis Imperfecta; Amniotic Bands; Amyloidosis; Andersen Disease; Anemia, Blackfan Diamond; Anemia, Fanconi's; Anemia, Hemolytic, Acquired Autoimmune; Anemia, Hemolytic, Cold Antibody; Anemia, Hemolytic, Warm Antibody; Anemia, Hereditary Nonspherocytic Hemolytic; Anemia, Hereditary Spherocytic Hemolytic; Anemia, Pernicious; Anemia, Sideroblastic; Anencephaly; Angelman Syndrome; Angioedema, Hereditary; Aniridia; Ankylosing Spondylitis; Anodontia; Antithrombin III Deficiency; Antley Bixler Syndrome; APECED Syndrome; Aplasia Cutis Congenita; Apraxia, Ocular Motor, Cogan Type; Arginase Deficiency; Arginino Succinic Aciduria; Arnold Chiari Syndrome; Arthrogryposis Multiplex Congenita; Asherman's Syndrome; Ataxia Telangiectasia; Ataxia with Vitamin E Deficiency; Ataxia, Friedreich's; Ataxia, Hereditary; Ataxia, Marie's; Atresia, Duodenal; Atresia, Jejunal; Atrial Septal Defects; Atrophy, Olivopontocerebellar; Autism; Autoimmune Thyroiditis; Baller Gerold Syndrome; Bannayan Riley Ruvalcaba Syndrome; Bardet-Biedl Syndrome;

Barth Syndrome; Bartter Syndrome; Beals Syndrome; Beckwith-Wiedemann Syndrome; Benign Essential Tremor; Bernard Soulier Syndrome; Biliary Atresia; Birth Defects; Bjornstad Syndrome; Blepharophimosis Ptosis Epicanthus Inversus Syndrome; Bloom Syndrome; Blue Diaper Syndrome; Blue Rubber Bleb Nevus; Borjeson Syndrome; Bowen Hutterite Syndrome; Branchio Oculo Facial Syndrome; Branchio Oto Renal Syndrome; Broad Beta Disease; C Syndrome; Camptomelic Syndrome; Canavan Disease; Carbamyl Phosphate Synthetase Deficiency; Carboxylase Deficiency, Multiple; Cardio Auditory Syndrome; Cardio Facio Cutaneous Syndrome; Carnitine Deficiency Syndromes; Carnitine Palmityltransferase Deficiency; Carnosinemia; Caroli Disease; Carpenter Syndrome; Cataract Dental Syndrome; Cataracts; Catel Manzke Syndrome; Caudal Regression Syndrome; Cavernous Hemangioma; Cayler Syndrome; Celiac Sprue; Central Core Disease; Cerebellar Agenesis; Cerebellar Degeneration, Subacute; Cerebellum, Parenchymatous Cortical Degeneration of; Cerebral Palsy; Cerebro Costo Mandibular Syndrome; Cerebro Oculo Facio Skeletal Syndrome; Charcot-Marie-Tooth Disease; CHARGE Syndrome; Chediak Higashi Syndrome; Cholestasis; Chondrocalcinosis, Familial Articular; Choroideremia; Chromosome 3 Monosomy 3p2; Chromosome 3 Trisomy 3q2; Chromosome 4 Monosomy 4q; Chromosome 4 Monosomy Distal 4q; Chromosome 4 Partial Trisomy Distal 4q; Chromosome 4 Ring; Chromosome 4, Trisomy 4p; Chromosome 5 Trisomy 5p; Chromosome 6 Partial Trisomy 6q; Chromosome 6 Ring; Chromosome 7 Monosomy 7p2; Chromosome 7, Partial Monosomy 7p; Chromosome 8, Monosomy 8p2; Chromosome 9 Partial Monosomy 9p; Chromosome 9 Ring; Chromosome 9 Tetrasomy 9p; Chromosome 9 Trisomy 9p Multiple Variants; Chromosome 9 Trisomy Mosaic; Chromosome 10 Monosomy 10p; Chromosome 11 Monosomy 11q; Chromosome 11 Partial Trisomy 11q; Chromosome 13 Monosomy 13q; Chromosome 13, Partial Monosomy 13q; Chromosome 14 Ring; Chromosome 14 Trisomy Mosaic; Chromosome 15 Ring; Chromosome 18 Monosomy 18p; Chromosome 18 Ring; Chromosome 18 Tetrasomy 18p; Chromosome 18q Syndrome; Chromosome 21 Ring; Chromosome 22 Ring; Chromosome 22 Trisomy Mosaic; Citrullinemia; Cleft Palate and Cleft Lip; Cleidocranial Dysplasia; Clubfoot; Cockayne Syndrome; Coffin Lowry Syndrome; Coffin Siris Syndrome; Cohen Syndrome; Common Variable Immunodeficiency; Cone Dystrophy; Congenital Fibrosis of the Extraocular Muscles; Congenital Heart Defects; Conjunctivitis Ligneous; Conradi Hunermann Syndrome; Corneal Dystrophy; Cornelia de Lange Syndrome; Costello Syndrome; Craniofrontonasal Dysplasia; Craniometaphyseal Dysplasia; Craniosynostosis, Primary; Cri du Chat Syndrome;

Crohn's Disease; Crouzon Disease; Cutis Laxa; Cutis Marmorata Telangiectatica Congenita; Cystic Fibrosis; Cystic Hygroma; Cystinosis; Cystinuria; Dandy Walker Malformation; Darier Disease; De Barsy Syndrome; De Santis Cacchione Syndrome; Dejerine Sottas Disease; Dentin Dysplasia, Coronal; Dentin Dysplasia, Radicular; Dentinogenesis Imperfecta Type III; Dextrocardia with Situs Inversus; DiGeorge Syndrome; Diabetes Insipidus; Diabetes Insulin Dependent; Diastrophic Dysplasia; Disaccharide Intolerance I; Down Syndrome; Drash Syndrome; Duane Syndrome; Dubin Johnson Syndrome; Dubowitz Syndrome; Dupuytren's Contracture; Dyggve Melchior Clausen Syndrome; Dysautonomia, Familial; Dyschondrosteosis; Dyskeratosis Congenita; Dyslexia; Dysplasia, Diastrophic; Dysplasia, Oculo Dento Digital; Dysplastic Nevus Syndrome; Dystonia, Torsion; Dystrophy, Asphyxiating Thoracic; Dystrophy, Myotonic; Ectodermal Dysplasia; Ectrodactyly Ectodermal Dysplasia Cleft Lip/Palate; Eisenmenger Syndrome; Ellis-van Creveld Syndrome; Emphysema, Congenital Lobar; Empty Sella Syndrome; Encephalocele; Endocardial Fibroelastosis; Engelmann Disease; Epidermal Nevus Syndrome; Epidermolysis Bullosa; Epidermolytic Hyperkeratosis; Epilepsy; Erythroderma desquamativa of Leiner; Erythromelalgia; Erythropoietic Protoporphyria; Esophageal Atresia and/or Tracheoesophageal Fistula; Ewing's Sarcoma; Exostoses, Multiple; Exstrophy of the Bladder; Fabry Disease; Facioscapulohumeral Muscular Dystrophy; Factor IX Deficiency; Factor XIII Deficiency; Fahr's Disease; Fairbank Disease; Familial Adenomatous Polyposis; Familial Juvenile Hyperuricemic Nephropathy; FAP; Farber's Disease; Femoral Facial Syndrome; Fetal Hydantoin Syndrome; Fetal Valproate Syndrome; FG Syndrome; Fiber Type Disproportion, Congenital; Fibrodysplasia Ossificans Progressiva (FOP); Fibromatosis, Congenital Generalized; Fibroplasia, Retrolental; Filippi Syndrome; Floating Harbor Syndrome; Focal Dermal Hypoplasia; Forbes Disease; Fountain Syndrome; Fragile X Syndrome; Fraser Syndrome; Freeman Sheldon Syndrome; Frontofacionasal Dysplasia; Frontonasal Dysplasia; Fructose Intolerance Hereditary; Fructosuria; Fryns Syndrome; Galactosemia; Galloway Mowat Syndrome; Ganglioside Sialidase Deficiency; Gardner Syndrome; Gastroschisis; Gaucher Disease; Gilbert Syndrome; Giroux Barbeau Syndrome; Glanzmann Thrombasthenia; Glucose 6 Phosphate Dehydrogenase Deficiency; Glucose Galactose Malabsorption; Glutaricaciduria I; Glutaricaciduria II; Glycogen Storage Disease VIII; Glycosuria, Renal; Goldenhar Syndrome; Goodman Syndrome; Gordon Syndrome; Gorlin Chaudhry Moss Syndrome; Gottron's Syndrome; Granulomatous Disease, Chronic; Graves' Disease; Greig Cephalopolysyndactyly Syndrome; Growth

Hormone Deficiency; Hageman Factor Deficiency; Hajdu Cheney Syndrome; Hallermann-Streiff Syndrome; Hallervorden Spatz Disease; Hanhart Syndrome; Hartnup Disease; Hashimoto's Syndrome; Hay Well's Syndrome; Heart Block, Congenital; Hemangioma Thrombocytopenia Syndrome; Hematuria, Benign Familial; Hemochromatosis, Hereditary; Hemophilia; Hemorrhagic Telangiectasia, Hereditary; Hepatic Fibrosis, Congenital; Hermansky Pudlak Syndrome; Hermaphroditism, True; Herpes, Neonatal; Hirschsprung's Disease; Histidinemia; Holoprosencephaly; Holt Oram Syndrome; Homocystinuria; Horner's Syndrome; Hunter Syndrome; Huntington's Disease; Hurler Syndrome; Hydranencephaly; Hydrocephalus; Hyper IgM Syndrome; Hypercholesterolemia; Hyperchylomicronemia; Hyperexplexia; Hyperglycinemia, Nonketotic; Hyperlipoproteinemia Type III; Hyperlipoproteinemia Type IV; Hyperostosis Frontalis Interna; Hyperoxaluria, Primary Type I; Hyperprolinemia Type II; Hypochondroplasia; Hypohidrotic Ectodermal Dysplasia; Hypomelanosis of Ito; Hypoparathyroidism; Hypophosphatasia; Hypophosphatemia, Familial; Hypoplastic Left Heart Syndrome; Hypothyroidism; Hypotonia, Benign Congenital; I-Cell Disease; Ichthyosis (General); Ichthyosis Congenita; Ichthyosis Hystrix, Curth Macklin Type; Ichthyosis Vulgaris; Ichthyosis, X-linked; Ichthyosis, Chanarin Dorfman Syndrome; Ichthyosis, CHILD Syndrome; Ichthyosis, Erythrokeratodermia Progressiva Symmetrica; Ichthyosis, Erythrokeratodermia Variabilis; Ichthyosis, Erythrokeratolysis Hiemalis; Ichhyosis, Harlequin Type; Ichthyosis, Keratosis Follicularis Spinulosa Decalvans; Ichthyosis, Lamellar Recessive; Ichthyosis, Netherton Syndrome; Ichthyosis, Peeling Skin Syndrome; Ichthyosis, Sjogren Larsson Syndrome; Ichthyosis, Tay Syndrome; Immunodeficiency, Severe Combined; Imperforate Anus; Incontinentia Pigmenti; Infantile Neuroaxonal Dystrophy; Intestinal Pseudoobstruction; Isaacs' Syndrome; Ivemark Syndrome; Jackson Weiss Syndrome; Jarcho Levin Syndrome; Job Syndrome; Joseph's Disease; Joubert Syndrome; Kabuki Make Up Syndrome; Kallmann Syndrome; Kartagener Syndrome; KBG Syndrome; Kearns Sayre Syndrome; Kenny Caffey Syndrome; Keratitis, Ichthyosis Deafness Syndrome; Keratoconus; Keratosis Follicularis; Keratosis, Seborrheic; Kernicterus; Klinefelter Syndrome; Klippel Trenaunay Syndrome; Klippel-Feil Syndrome; Kniest Syndrome; Kufs Disease; Kugelberg Welander Syndrome; Lactose Intolerance; LADD Syndrome; Lambert Eaton Myasthenic Syndrome; Langerhans Cell Histiocytosis; Laron Dwarfism; Larsen Syndrome; Laurence Moon Syndrome; Leber's Congenital Amaurosis; Leber's Optic Atrophy; Legg Calve Perthes Syndrome; Leigh's Disease; Leiner Disease; Lenz Microphthalmia Syndrome; LEOPARD Syndrome; Leprechaunism; Lesch Nyhan Syndrome; Leukemia, Chronic Lymphocytic; Leukodystrophy; Leukodystrophy, Canavan's; Leukodystrophy, Krabbe; Leukodystrophy, Metachromatic; Lipodystrophy; Lissencephaly; Loken Senior Syndrome; Long Chain Acyl CoA Dehydrogenase Deficiency; Lowe's Syndrome; Lymphatic Malformations; Lymphedema, Hereditary; Lynch Syndromes; Lysosomal Storage Disorders; Machado Joseph Disease; Maffucci Syndrome; Malignant Hyperthermia; Manic Depression, Bipolar; Mannosidosis; Maple Syrup Urine Disease; March of Dimes Birth Defects Foundation; Marcus Gunn Phenomenon; Marden Walker Syndrome; Marfan Syndrome; Maroteaux Lamy Syndrome; Marshall Syndrome; Maxillofacial Dysostosis; Maxillonasal Dysplasia, Binder Type; May Hegglin Anomaly; McArdle Disease; McCune Albright Syndrome; Meckel Syndrome; Mediterranean Fever, Familial; Medium Chain Acyl CoA Dehydrogenase Deficiency; Medullary Cystic Disease; Medullary Sponge Kidney; Melanoma, Malignant; Meleda Disease; Melkersson Rosenthal Syndrome; Melnick Needles Syndrome; Menkes Disease; Metaphyseal Chondrodysplasia, McKusick Type; Metaphyseal Chondrodysplasia, Schmid Type; Metatropic Dysplasia I; Metatropic Dysplasia Type II; Microvillus Inclusion Disease; Miller Syndrome; Mitral Valve Prolapse Syndrome; Moebius Syndrome; Motor Neuron Disease; Moyamoya Disease; Mucopolysaccharidoses; Mulibrey Nanism Syndrome (Perheentupa Syndrome); Mullerian Aplasia; Multiple Sulfatase Deficiency; MURCS Association; Muscular Dystrophy, Becker; Muscular Dystrophy, Duchenne; Muscular Dystrophy, Emery Dreifuss; Muscular Dystrophy, Fukuyama Type; Muscular Dystrophy, Landouzy Dejerine; Muscular Dystrophy, Limb Girdle; Muscular Dystrophy, Oculo Gastrointestinal; Myoclonic Progressive Familial; Myoclonus; Myopathy, Congenital, Batten Turner Type; Myopathy, Desmin Storage; Myopathy, Myotubular; Myopathy, Nemaline; Myopathy, Scapuloperoneal; N Acetyl Glutamate Synthetase Deficiency; Nager Syndrome; Nail Patella Syndrome; Nemaline Myopathy; Neonatal Lupus; Nephronophthisis; Neu Laxova Syndrome; Neuroacanthocytosis; Neurofibromatosis Type 1; Neurofibromatosis Type 2; Neuropathy, Congenital Hypomyelination; Neuropathy, Giant Axonal; Neuropathy, Hereditary Sensory Type I; Neuropathy, Hereditary Sensory Type II; Neutropenia, Chronic; Neutropenia, Cyclic; Nevoid Basal Cell Carcinoma Syndrome; Nezelof's Syndrome; NF 2; Niemann Pick Disease; Noonan Syndrome; Norrie Disease; Oculo Auriculo Vertebral Spectrum; Oculocerebral Syndrome with Hypopigmentation; Oculocerebrocutaneous Syndrome; Olivopontocerebellar Atrophy, Hereditary; Ollier Disease; Opitz Syndrome; Oral Facial Digital Syndrome; Or-nithine Transcarbamylase Deficiency; Orocraniodigital Syndrome; Osteogenesis Imperfecta; Osteopetrosis; Oto Palato Digital Syndrome Types I and II; Pachydermoperiostosis; Paget's Disease; Pallister Hall Syndrome; Pallister Killian Mosaic Syndrome; Pallister W Syndrome; Pancreatic Islet Cell Tumor; Papillon Lefevre Syndrome; Paramyotonia Congenita; Paraplegia, Hereditary Spastic; Parry Romberg Syndrome; Pelizaeus Merzbacher Brain Sclerosis; Pemphigus; Penta X Syndrome; Pentalogy of Cantrell; PEPCK Deficiency; Peutz Jeghers Syndrome; Pfeiffer Syndrome; Phenylketonuria; Pheochromocytoma; Phocomelia Syndrome; Phosphoglycerate Kinase Deficiency; Pierre Robin Syndrome; Pityriasis Rubra Pilaris; Poland Syndrome; Polycystic Kidney Disease; Polycystic Liver Disease; Polyglucosan Body Disease, Adult; Polyposis, Familial; Pompe Disease; Popliteal Pterygium Syndrome; Porphyria; Porphyria, Acute Intermittent; Porphyria, ALA-D; Porphyria, Congenital Erythropoietic; Porphyria, Cutanea Tarda; Porphyria, Hereditary Coproporphyria; Porphyria, Variegate; Prader Willi Syndrome; Precocious Puberty; Progressive Osseous Heteroplasia (POH); Proteus Syndrome; Prune Belly Syndrome; Pseudo Hurler Polydystrophy; Pseudoachondroplastic Dysplasia; Pseudocholinesterase Deficiency; Pseudohypoparathyroidism; Pseudoxanthoma Elasticum; Psoriasis; Pterygium Syndrome, Multiple; Puberty, Precocious; Pulmonary Hypertension, Primary; Purpura; Pyruvate Carboxylase Deficiency; Pyruvate Kinase Deficiency; Rabson-Mendenhall Syndrome; Rapp Hodgkin Ectodermal Dysplasia; Refsum Disease; Reifenstein Syndrome; Renal Agenesis, Bilateral; Restless Legs Syndrome; Retinitis Pigmentosa; Retinoblastoma; Retinoschisis; Retinoschisis, X-linked Juvenile; Rett Syndrome; Rh Disease; Rickets, Hypophosphatemic; Rieger Syndrome; Robert's Syndrome; Robinow Syndrome; Romano Ward Syndrome; Rosenberg Chutorian Syndrome; Rothmund Thomson Syndrome; Roussy Levy Syndrome; Rubella, Congenital; Rubinstein Taybi Syndrome; Russell Silver Syndrome; Ruvalcaba Syndrome; Saethre Chotzen Syndrome; Sakati Syndrome; Sandhoff Disease; Sanfilippo Syndrome; Sarcoma, Ewing's; Schindler Disease; Schinzel Giedion Syndrome; Schmidt Syndrome; Schwartz Jampel Syndrome; Seckel Syndrome; Seitelberger Disease; Septooptic Dysplasia; Severe Combined Immunodeficiency; Short Chain Acyl CoA Dehydrogenase Deficiency; SHORT Syndrome; Shprintzen VCF Syndrome; Shwachman Syndrome; Sialidosis; Sickle Cell Disease; Simpson Dysmorphia Syndrome; Sirenomelia Sequence; Sly Syndrome; Smith Lemli Opitz Syndrome; Smith Magenis Syndrome; Sneddon Syndrome; Sotos Syndrome; Spina Bifida; Spinal Muscular Atrophy; Split Hand Deformity; Spondyloepiphyseal Dysplasia Congenital; Spondyloepiphyseal Dysplasia Tarda; Sprengel Deformity; Stenosis, Spinal; Stickler Syndrome; Sturge Weber Syndrome; Succinic Semialdehyde Dehydrogenase Deficiency; Sucrose Isomaltose Malabsorption, Congenital; Summitt Syndrome; Tangier Disease; Tarui Disease; Tay Sach's Disease; Telecanthus with Associated Abnormalities; Tetrahydrobiopterin Deficiency; Tetralogy of Fallot; Thalassemia; Thalassemia Major; Thalassemia Minor; Thomsen Disease; Three M Syndrome; Thrombasthenia of Glanzmann and Naegeli; Thrombocythemia, Essential; Thrombocytopenia Absent Radius Syndrome; Thrombocytopenia, Essential; Tongue, Fissured; Tooth and Nail Syndrome; TORCH Syndrome; Tourette Syndrome; Townes-Brocks Syndrome; Treacher Collins Syndrome; Tricho Dento Osseous Syndrome; Trichorhinophalangeal Syndrome Type I; Trichorhinophalangeal Syndrome Type II; Trichorhinophalangeal Syndrome Type III; Trimethylaminuria; Triplo X Syndrome; Triploid Syndrome; Trismus Pseudocamptodactyly Syndrome; Trisomy; Trisomy 4p; Trisomy 13 Syndrome; Trisomy 18 Syndrome; True Hermaphroditism; Truncus Arteriosus, Persistent; Tuberous Sclerosis; Turcot Syndrome; Turner Syndrome; Twin to Twin Transfusion Syndrome; Tyrosinemia, Hereditary; Urticaria, Cold; Usher's Syndrome; VACTERL Association; VACTERL with Hydrocephalus; Valinemia; Vascular Malformations of the Brain; Ventricular Septal Defects; Von Gierke Disease; Von Hippel Lindau Disease; Waardenburg Syndrome; WAGR Syndrome; Waldmann Disease; Walker Warburg Syndrome; Wandering Spleen; Weaver Syndrome; Weill Marchesani Syndrome; Weismann Netter Stuhl Syndrome; Werdnig Hoffman Disease; Werner Syndrome; West Syndrome; Wieacker Syndrome; Wildervanck Syndrome; Williams Syndrome; Wilms' Tumor; Wilson's Disease; Winchester Syndrome; Wiskott Aldrich Syndrome; Wolf Hirschhorn Syndrome; Wolff Parkinson White Syndrome; Wolfram Syndrome; Wyburn Mason Syndrome; X Linked Lymphoproliferative Syndrome; Xeroderma Pigmentosum; XYY Syndrome; Zellweger Syndrome; Zimmermann Laband Syndrome; Zollinger Ellison Syndrome

1832 Marfan Association UK

Rochester House
5 Aldershot Road
Fleet
Hampshire, GU51 3NG, United Kingdom

Phone: +44 (0) 1252-81-0472
Fax: +44 (0) 1252-81-0473
E-mail: marfan@tinyonline.co.uk
http://www.marfan.org.uk

The Marfan Association UK is a service, research, and advocacy organization dedicated to supporting, educating, and researching Marfan syndrome. Marfan syndrome is an inherited disorder that affects the connective tissues of the heart and blood vessels (cardiovascular system). Established in 1984, the Marfan Association works with affected individuals, family members, specialists, researchers, general practitioners, and other medical specialists in the support role. Consisting of 1,600 members and 70 support groups, the organization produces educational materials including a self-titled newsletter, reports, brochures, fact sheets, and a directory. Program activities sponsored by the organization include awareness meetings, which are underway nationally on a continuing basis (a Marfan text is provided as appropriate) and support meetings, which are planned in its offices. The organization works to improve the effectiveness of the Marfan Support Network and provides translations of some materials in Spanish, Greek, and Russian.

President: Diane Rust (Chairman/Support Coordinator) (1984 to present).
Executive Director: Same as above.
Year Established: 1984

Keywords
Arachnodactyly; Arachnodactyly, Contractural; Connective Tissue Disorders; Dolichostenomelia; Joint Hypermobility Syndrome; Marfan Association UK; Marfan Syndrome; Marfanoid Hypermobility Syndrome

1833 Marinesco-Sjogren Syndrome Support Group

1640 Crystal View Circle
Newbury Park, CA 91320

Phone: (805) 499-7410
E-mail: mss@marinesco-sjogren.org
http://www.marinesco-sjogren.org

The Marinesco-Sjogren Syndrome Support Group, established in 2000, provides support to families affected by Marinesco-Sjogren syndrome (MSS) and encourages communication between physicians and researchers. Marinesco-Sjogren syndrome is a hereditary disorder characterized by a loss of muscle coordination, loss of clearness in the eyes' lenses, very small stature, progressive muscle weakness, hypergonadotropic hypogonadism, and mental retardation.

President: Colleen Yinger
Year Established: 2000
Acronym: MSS Support Group

Keywords
Ataxia; Cataracts; Hypergonadotropic Hypogo-nadism; Marinesco Sjogren Syndrome; Marinesco Sjogren Syndrome Support Group; Marinesco-Sjogren Syndrome Support Group; Mental Retardation; Small Stature

1834 Mario Negri Institute for Pharmacological Research

Clinical Research Center for Rare Diseases "Aldo e Cele Dacco"
Mario Negri Institute for Pharmacological Research
Via G.B. Camozzi
Ranica
Bergamo, 3-24020, Italy

Phone: +39 (0) 35-453-5304
Fax: +39 (0) 35-453-5373
E-mail: raredis@marionegri.it
http://www.marionegri.it

The Instituto di Ricerche Farmacologiche Mario Ne-gri (Mario Negri Institute for Pharmacological Re-search) in Ranica, Italy, is a not-for-profit foundation established in 1963. The center operates on three lev-els: the Clinical Research Center, the Information Center for Rare Diseases, and the European School for Rare Diseases. The Clinical Research Center is a fully equipped hospital devoted entirely to clinical re-search. The aim is to develop research projects with special emphasis on rare diseases and innovative di-agnostic and therapeutic procedures. The Information Center for Rare Diseases is a service to the public that provides up-to-date information on rare disorders with emphasis on causes, genetics, prevention, and inves-tigational treatments of these disorders. The goal of the center is to create a computerized rare disease data-base containing updated information on rare disorders and a directory of specialized physicians and clinical research centers in Europe that are familiar with a va-riety of rare diseases. The European School for Rare Diseases functions as a forum for cultural activities aimed at specialists and health professionals. Work-shops and conferences are scheduled throughout the year. Clinical training includes short "basic" courses, intensive courses, and clinical research studies.

President: Prof. Silvio Garattini
Executive Director: Giuseppe Remuzzi, M.D.
Year Established: 1992

Keywords
Mario Negri Institute for Pharmacological Research; Rare Disease Information Center (Italy)

1835 Mastocytosis Society, Inc.

P.O. Box 511
Plainville, CT 06062

Phone: (860) 284-0186
E-mail: jbar5@verizon.net
http://www.tmsforacure.org

The Mastocytosis Society is a voluntary, not-for-profit, self-help organization dedicated to providing information and support to individuals with mastocy-tosis and their caregivers, as well as those affected by idiopathic mast cell activation disorder and urticaria pigmentosa. The society seeks to work collaboratively towards a cure for mastocytosis, idiopathic mast cell activation, and urticaria pigmentosa. Mastocytosis is a rare disorder characterized by abnormal accumula-tions of specific cells (mast cells) normally found in connective tissue. The liver, spleen, lungs, bone, skin, and sometimes the membrane surrounding the brain and spine (meninges) may be affected. Established in 1994, the Mastocytosis Society produces a periodic newsletter entitled "The Mastocytosis Chronicles." It is distributed to more than 200 subscribers across the United States and throughout the world. In addition, a medical questionnaire has been developed by the so-ciety for the purposes of data collection to identify similarities in those diagnosed with mastocytosis, id-iopathic mast cell activation, and urticaria pigmentosa.

President: Rita Barlow (Chairman)
Executive Director: Valerie Slee
Year Established: 1995
Acronym: TMS

Keywords
Idiopathic Mast Cell Activation; Mast Cell Disease; Mastocystosis, Systemic; Mastocytosis; Mastocytosis Society, Inc.; Urticaria Pigmentosa

1836 Mathew Forbes Romer Foundation, Inc.

9858 Glades Road
Suite 191
Boca Raton, FL 33434

Phone: (561) 477-0337
Fax: (561) 477-0077
E-mail: MFRF@aol.com
http://www.mfrfoundation.org

The mission of the Mathew Forbes Romer Founda-tion, Inc., is to promote and lead critical programs and services addressing awareness, testing, counseling, and research initiatives that hold promise for the prevention and eventual cure of fatal children's genetic diseases of the brain. Its services include advocacy, networking, patient and professional education, and genetic counseling.

President: Kevin Romer (1998-present)
Year Established: 1998
Acronym: MFRF

Keywords
Advocacy; Brain; Children's; Genetic Diseases; Lysosomal Storage Diseases; Mathew Forbes Romer Foundation, Inc; Networking; Tay Sachs

1837 MdDS Balance Disorder Foundation, a National Heritage Foundation

255 Copper Beech Drive
Blue Bell, PA 19422

Phone: (215) 542-9167
E-mail: mddsfoundation@yahoo.com
http://www.nhffoundations.net/mdds

MdDS Balance Disorder Foundation, A National Heritage Foundation (MdDS Foundation) is a not-for-profit, rare disorder organization founded in 2003. Its mission is to promote awareness, seek a cure, and assist patients who have been affected by Mal de Debarquement Syndrome (MdDS). MdDS is characterized by a persistent sense of motion, which may cause loss of balance, most commonly brought on by a cruise or other motion experience. Funds acquired by the organization will be used to inform medical professionals, as well as the public, and support research toward treatments and a cure for this little-understood disorder.

President: Roger Josselyn (2003-present)
Executive Director: Susan Barnes
Year Established: 2003
Acronym: MdDS Foundation

Keywords
MdDS Balance Disorder Foundation, National Heritage Foundation

1838 ME Association

4 Top Angel
Buckingham, MK18 1TH, United Kingdom

Phone: +44 (0) 1280-82-1602
E-mail: meconnection@meassociation.org.uk
http://www.meassociation.org.uk

The ME Association is a not-for-profit health organization that supports patients and families in the UK affected by myalgic encephalomyelitis/chronic fatigue syndrome. This syndrome is characterized by excessive fatigue that does not respond to bedrest. The fatigue is severe enough to reduce the average daily activities of the affected individual by at least 50 percent. Founded in 1976, the ME Association offers services that include networking, education, and advocacy for those affected by this syndrome.

President: Christine Llewellyn (2003-present)
Executive Director: Gill Saving (Operations Manager)
Year Established: 1976
Acronym: MEA

Keywords
Chronic Fatigue Syndrome/Myalgic Encephalomyelitis; Lobbying; ME Association; Networking; Research; Support Groups; United Kingdom

1839 Melnick-Needles Syndrome Support Group

4 Kivner Lane
Bexhill-On-Sea
East Sussex, TN40 2ST, United Kingdom

Phone: +44 (0) 142-42-1779
E-mail: gill@melnickneedlesyndrome.com
http://www.melnickneedlesyndrome.com

The Melnick-Needles Syndrome Support Group is a voluntary, self-help organization dedicated to helping families of children with Melnick-Needles syndrome (MNS). This is a rare hereditary disorder characterized by abnormal bone development and characteristic abnormalities of the head and face (craniofacial) area. Established in 1994 as an affiliate of Contact a Family, the Melnick-Needles Syndrome Support Group is committed to providing information, assistance, and moral support to member families as well as those whose children have just been diagnosed. The support group also works to raise awareness among professionals and disseminates information concerning treatment options. It enables affected families to share their experiences and resources with one another and works to make contact with other affected families. The Melnick-Needles Support Group provides members with fact sheets on MNS.

President: Gill Carter
Executive Director: Same as above.
Year Established: 1994
Acronym: MNS Support Group

Keywords
Melnick Needles Osteodysplasty; Melnick Needles Syndrome; Melnick-Needles Syndrome Support Group; Osteodysplasty of Melnick and Needles

1840 Melorheostosis Association

6611 Clayton Road
Suite 209
St. Louis, MO 63117

Phone: (314) 727-0887
E-mail: lynbpickel@earthlink.net; Lyn@melorheostosis.org
http://www.melorheostosis.org

The Melorheostosis Association is a not-for-profit organization dedicated to finding the cause, treatments and cure for melorheostosis. This is a rare condition that affects both bone and soft tissue. It can result in severe functional limitation, pain and deformity. The Melorheostosis Association hosts an annual conference for patients, physicians, and researchers, and also publishes a newsletter. Its web site provides information for patients and families, as well as for treating physicians, researchers and other professionals.

President: Lyn B. Pickel
Executive Director: Kathleen D. Harpet (Primary Conact)
Year Established: 2003

Keywords
Advocacy; Hyperostosis of Corticol Bone; Melorheostosis; Melorheostosis Association; Networking; Research

1841 Meningitis Foundation of America

6610 North Shadeland Avenue
Suite 220
Indianapolis, IN 46220

Phone: (317) 595-6383
Fax: (317) 595-6370
Toll Free: (800) 668-1129
E-mail: support@musa.org
http://www.musa.org

The Meningitis Foundation of America (MFA) is a voluntary, not-for-profit organization dedicated to providing information and support to individuals who have had personal experience with meningitis, their families, healthcare professionals, and the general public. Established in 1997, the foundation is committed to alerting the public and the medical communities about the initial symptoms of meningitis and the need for early diagnosis and immediate treatment. Meningitis is an inflammation of the protective membranes surrounding the brain and/or spinal cord (meninges). In most cases, meningitis results from viral or bacterial infection. Viral meningitis is more common than bacterial meningitis and may often be mild. Bacterial meningitis may be extremely serious, rapidly causing potentially life-threatening complications. The foundation offers a 24-hour hotline, provides networking services for affected individuals and families, and engages in advocacy.

President: David Spilker (1997 to Present)
Executive Director: Same as above.
Year Established: 1997
Acronym: MFA

Keywords
Meningitis; Meningitis Foundation of America; Spinal Meningitis

1842 Meningitis Research Foundation (UK)

Midland Way
Thornbury
Bristol, BS35 2BS, United Kingdom

Phone: +44 (0) 1454-28-1811
Fax: +44 (0) 1454-28-1094
Toll Free: 808-8800-3344
E-mail: info@meningitis.org
http://www.meningitis.org

Meningitis Research Foundation is a not-for-profit organization in the United Kingdom and Republic of Ireland that fights death and disability from meningitis and septicemia, and supports people affected by these diseases. Meningitis is characterized by inflammation of the protective membranes (meninges) surrounding the brain and spinal cord. The condition is usually due to infection with certain bacteria or viruses. Septicemia is systemic disease characterized by the presence of invading microorganisms or their toxins in the bloodstream. Meningitis Research Foundation, which was founded in 1989, funds vital research into the prevention, detection and treatment of meningitis and septicemia, raises awareness of the diseases, and offers support through in-depth information.

President: Howard Bell (Chairman of Trustees)
Executive Director: Denise Vaughn (Chief Executive)
Year Established: 1989

Keywords
Meningitis; Meningitis Research Foundation (UK); Meningococcal Disease; Pneumococcal Disease; Septicaemia

1843 Mental Health Foundation (UK)

9th Floor, Sea Containers House
20 Upper Gound
London, SE1 9QB, United Kingdom

Phone: +44 (0) 207-803-1100
Fax: +44 (0) 207-803-1111
E-mail: mhf@mhf.org.uk
http://www.mentalhealth.org.uk

The Mental Health Foundation is a not-for-profit organization in the United Kingdom that is concerned with all aspects of mental health, including mental illness and learning disabilities. Established in 1949, the foundation is committed to pioneering new approaches to delivering services, treatment, and care that will help meet the needs of affected individuals and increase understanding of mental illness and learning disabilities. It works closely with health, housing, and social services agencies across the UK, professional bodies, research centers, the voluntary sector, and the government. Current programs include providing biomedical research grants that focus on bridging research knowledge of effective intervention and its use in practice, funding projects to work with parents affected by depression, and working in partnership with schools to promote a whole school approach to the mental health of children and young people. The Mental Health Foundation has also established the Foundation for People with Learning Disabilities. This foundation provides the "Choice Initiative," which is dedicated to providing assistance to people affected by severe, profound, and multiple learning disabilities.

President: Sir William Utting CBE
Executive Director: Dr. Andrew McCulloch
Year Established: 1949
Acronym: MHF

Keywords
Mental Health Foundation (UK)

1844 Meralgia Paresthetica Foundation

702 Pierce Street NE
Minneapolis, MN 55413

Phone: (612) 362-8988
E-mail: macew001@umn.edu
http://www.umn.edu/~macew001/meralgia

The Meralgia Paresthetica Foundation is a general service organization dedicated to providing information, assistance, and support to individuals with meralgia paresthetica (MP) and their families. Also known as lateral femoral cutaneous neuropathy (LFCN), meralgia paresthetica is an uncommon condition in which direct mechanical pressure or traction on the lateral femoral cutaneous nerve of the thigh may cause burning, tingling, and numbness. Such mechanical pressure may result from a number of factors such as obesity, swelling of the abdomen due to abnormal accumulation of fluid, or pregnancy; in addition, tight garments (e.g., belts, jeans, backpack straps), prolonged standing, and/or other factors may exacerbate symptoms. Although the course of MP tends to be benign in most cases, symptoms may continue periodically for several years. Established in 1995, the Meralgia Paresthetica Foundation promotes research, offers understandable information on MP, and has a web site on the Internet.

President: Karen E. MacEwan (1995 to Present).
Executive Director: Same as above.
Year Established: 1995
Acronym: MPF

Keywords
Meralgia Paresthetica; Meralgia Paresthetica Foundation; MP; Neuropathy, Lateral Femoral Cutaneous

1845 Mesothelioma Applied Research Foundation, Inc.

1123 Chapala Street
#200
P.O. Box 91840
Santa Barbara, CA 93190-1840

Phone: (805) 560-8942
Fax: (805) 560-8962
E-mail: j-wayne@marf.org
http://www.marf.org

The mission of the Mesothelioma Applied Research Foundation (MARF) is to eradicate mesothelioma as a life-ending disease. Malignant mesothelioma is a rare form of cancer in which cancer cells invade the linings of the chest or abdomen. Most people who have it have worked on jobs where they inhaled asbestos. MARF solicits and rigorously reviews applications, and then awards significant grants, for research on the prevention, early detection, and treatment of mesothelioma. Through its web site and literature, its direct communications, and its volunteer Family Advocacy Board, MARF provides patients, family members and physicians with hope, encouragement, and information. In addition, MARF works to enhance awareness of this disease and to encourage federal funding for research.

President: Roger G. Worthington
Executive Director: Christopher E. Hahn
Year Established: 1999
Acronym: MARF

Keywords
Asbestos; MARF; Mesothelioma; Mesothelioma Applied Research Foundation, Inc.

1846 Metatropic Dysplasia Dwarf Registry
3393 Geneva Drive
Santa Clara, CA 95051

Phone: (408) 244-6354
Fax: (408) 296-6317
E-mail: figone@netgate.net
http://www.lpbayarea.org/metatrophic

The Metatropic Dysplasia Dwarf Registry is a group comprised of parents and adults with metatropic dwarfism who have united to form a self-help group for the purpose of mutual support. The registry collects and exchanges information about metatropic dwarfism, which is a very rare form of dwarfism. The registry seeks to gather information that will help affected individuals, their families, and physicians. Established in 1980, the Metatropic Dysplasia Dwarf Registry was formed to collect data and case histories from families with metatropic dwarfism. To this end, the registry distributes a detailed registry questionnaire for the purposes of gathering information, networking, and mutual support. A list of physicians who are specialists in care and treatment of people with dwarfism is also available from the registry.

President: Shirley Figone (1980-Present)
Year Established: 1980

Keywords
Dwarfism, Metatropic; Kniest Dysplasia; Kniest Syndrome; Metatropic Dysplasia I; Metatropic Dysplasia Dwarf Registry; Metatropic Dysplasia Type II

1847 MHE and Me—A Support Group for Kids with Multiple Hereditary Exostoses
14 Stony Brook Drive
Pine Island, NY 10969

Phone: (845) 258-6058
Fax: (845) 258-6058
E-mail: mheandme@yahoo.com
http://www.geocities.com/mheandme

MHE and Me is a support group for children with multiple hereditary exostoses (MHE). Besides providing peers and creating a supportive community for children with MHE, the organization provides families with educational materials and resources to best help the children affected by this rare genetic disorder. MHE is characterized by multiple bony growths or tumors (exostoses) that are covered by cartilage. These growths vary in size, location and number, depending on the individual. MHE and Me is a member of the MHE Coalition.

Executive Director: Susan Wynn
Year Established: 1999
Acronym: MHE and Me

Keywords
MHE; MHE and Me a Support Group for Kids with Multiple Hereditary Exostoses; MO; Multiple Hereditary Exostosis; Multiple Osteochondromas; Osteochondroma

---

1848 MHE (Multiple Hereditary Exostoses) Family Support Group
8838 Holly Lane
Olmsted Falls, OH 44138-2701

Phone: (440) 235-6325
E-mail: CheleZ1@aol.com
http://www.geocities.com/mhecoalition

The MHE (Multiple Hereditary Exostoses) Family Support Group is a national organization dedicated to providing counseling, medical information, and a forum for individuals and families affected by MHE. MHE is a rare disorder in which bony growths or bumps (exostoses) form on the bones of affected individuals. These growths vary in size, location, and number depending upon the individual. Established in 1993, MHE consists of 40 members. Educational materials include a brochure entitled "Multiple Hereditary Exostoses, What Is It?" Program activities include a support group, genetic counseling referrals, advocacy, and education.

President: Chele Zelina
Executive Director: Susan Wynn
Year Established: 1993
Acronym: MHE

Keywords
Aclasis, Diaphyseal; Exostoses Syndrome, Multiple; Exostoses, Multiple; Exostoses, Multiple Cartilaginous; Exostoses, Multiple Hereditary; External Chondromatosis Syndrome; MHE; MHE (Multiple Hereditary Exostoses) Family Support Group; Osteochondromatosis, Multiple

---

1849 Miami Project to Cure Paralysis
University of Miami School of Medicine
P.O. Box 01690
Mail Locator R-48
Miami, FL 33101

Phone: (305) 243-6001
Fax: (305) 243-6017
Toll Free: (800) 782-6387
E-mail: mpinfo@miamiproj.med.miami.edu
http://www.themiamiproject.org

The Miami Project to Cure Paralysis of the University of Miami School of Medicine is a non-profit research center dedicated to finding more effective treatments and, ultimately, a cure for paralysis that results from spinal cord injury (SCI). Spinal cord injury results from trauma to, or disease of, the spinal cord. The primary result of SCI is paralysis. Founded in 1985, the Miami Project is a coalition of researchers, clinicians, and therapists whose expertise all relates directly to spinal cord injury and whose full-time focus is spinal cord research. Clinical and rehabilitation programs require the participation of a limited number of volunteers. In addition to basic research, the Miami Project offers the 1-800-STAND UP information line for questions regarding spinal cord injury research. It also publishes informational brochures and, two times a year, a newsletter.

President: Barth A. Green, M.D. (1986 - Present)
Executive Director: Suzie Sayfie
Year Established: 1985

Keywords
Brain Injury; Central Nervous System Disorder; Miami Project to Cure Paralysis; Paralysis; Spinal Cord Injury

---

1850 Micro & Anophthalmic Children's Society
22 Lower Park Street
Holyhead
Isle of Anglesey
North Wales, L65 1DU, United Kingdom

Phone: +44 (0) 870-600-6227
E-mail: enquiries@macs.org.uk
http://www.macs.org.uk/#

The Micro and Anophthalmic Children's Society (MACS) is a not-for-profit organization in the United Kingdom dedicated to providing information, assistance, and support to families of children with microphthalmia or anophthalmia. Microphthalmia is a developmental abnormality characterized by abnormal smallness of one or both eyes. Individuals with anophthalmia exhibit absence of rudimentary (vestigial) portions of the eyes. Established in 1993, MACS, which includes approximately 200 families, is dedicated to providing networking services; arranging yearly gatherings for affected families; raising awareness concerning the needs of visually impaired and blind children; providing a resource library containing videos, books, toys, and information materials; and acquiring computer technology for the production of large print and braille books for the benefit of affected children. MACS offer a variety of educational materials including brochures, pamphlets, and a regular newsletter.

President: John Karvaski
Executive Director: Barry Stickings
Year Established: 1993
Acronym: MACS

Keywords
Anophthalmia; Micro & Anophthalmic Children's Society; Microphthalmia

---

1851 Microcephaly Support Group
22 Auctioneers Court
Auctioneers Way
Old Cattlemarket
Northampton, NN1 1EY, United Kingdom

Phone: +44 (0) 1604-60-3743
E-mail: dorothy@microcephaly.org.uk
www.microcephaly.org.uk

The Microcephaly Support Group (MSG) is an international, voluntary health organization in the United Kingdom dedicated to providing information, support, and networking opportunities to families of children with microcephaly, a condition characterized by abnormal smallness of the head. Microcephaly may be apparent at birth or within the first months or years of life. The effects of microcephaly may vary greatly from case to case. Such effects may include mild to profound mental retardation, developmental delays, feeding difficulties, visual impairment, and episodes of uncontrolled electrical disturbances in the brain (seizures). Microcephaly may occur as an isolated condition or due to, or in association with, many underlying disorders. Established in 1992, the Microcephaly Support Group currently has over 400 members nationwide; in addition, the group has contact with many affected families overseas. It is committed to providing ongoing information and support to affected families; promoting and supporting research; and providing networking opportunities that enable affected families to exchange mutual support, information, and resources. The group also has a sibling pen pal club and provides a variety of educational materials including an information sheet and a regular newsletter.

President: Jacqui Smith (Contact Person) (1993 to Present)
Executive Director: Annie Cawthorn (Coordinator)
Year Established: 1992
Acronym: MSG

Keywords
Microcephaly Support Group

1852 Mitochondria Research Society

P.O. Box 1952
Buffalo, NY 14221

Phone: (716) 845-8017
Fax: (716) 845-1047
E-mail: mitoresearch@mitoresearch.org
http://www.mitoresearch.org

The Mitochondria Research Society (MRS) is a nonprofit, international organization of scientists and physicians. The purpose of MRS is to find a cure for mitochondrial diseases by promoting research on basic science of mitochondria, mitochondria pathogenesis, prevention, diagnosis, and treatment throughout the world. Mitochondrial diseases are hereditary disorders that affect the ability of cells within the body to produce energy. The society fosters public education and training, and provides a platform for communication and dissemination of knowledge among scientists, physicians, and others interested in mitochondria. MRS conducts regular national and international scientific meetings and publishes a professional journal, "Mitochondrion," and a newsletter, "MitoMatters."

President: Keshav K. Singh, Founder & Director
Year Established: 2000
Acronym: MRS

Keywords
Mitochondria Research Society; Mitochondrial Disease; Mitochondrial Disorders

1853 ML 4 (Mucolipidosis Type IV Foundation)

719 E 17 Street
Brooklyn, NY 11230

Phone: (718) 434-5067
E-mail: www@ml4.org
http://www.ML4.org

The Mucolipidosis Type IV Foundation is a not-for-profit voluntary organization of parents and professionals committed to raising funds for medical research into the cause and possible treatments for mucolipidosis type IV. Established in 1983, the foundation uses all donations to fund scientific research. The foundation supports areas of medical research, which includes the definition of the exact biochemical mechanism of the disorder, development of treatments and discovery of a cure. In addition, the foundation is a major support system for families affected by mucolipidosis type IV. The gene has been discovered and a carrier test is available, as well as improved diagnostic techniques. The foundation is currently supporting work at Brigham and Women's Hospital, and is working closely with a team supervised by Dr. Roscoe Brady at the NIH. Educational materials produced by the foundation include a brochure and fact sheet.

President: Randy Yudenfriend Glaser
Year Established: 1983
Acronym: ML4 Foundation

Keywords
Ganglioside Sialidase Deficiency; ML 4 (Mucolipidosis Type IV Foundation); Mucolipidosis IV

1854 Moebius Syndrome Association

c/o Marg Haalstra-Koke
10 Francis Avenue
Chatham
Ontario, N7M 6E3, Canada

Phone: (519) 354-7845
E-mail: marg@ciaccess.com
http://www.ciaccess.com/moebius/msfoc/msfoc.htm

The Moebius Syndrome Association is an international, not-for-profit organization in Canada dedicated to providing information, assistance, and support to affected families. Moebius syndrome is an extremely rare developmental disorder characterized by incomplete development of certain nerves arising from the brain (sixth and seventh cranial nerves), resulting in eye muscle and facial paralysis and/or other symptoms and findings. The disorder is thought to be genetic and is apparent at birth (congenital). The Moebius Syndrome Association was established in 1997 and currently consists of approximately 900 affected families worldwide. The association is committed to increasing public and professional awareness of Moebius syndrome, promoting research, engaging in-patient and professional education, and offering networking opportunities to affected families. In addition, the association links individuals and families to support groups throughout the world, engages in lobbying, has a directory, and provides a variety of educational materials including pamphlets, reports, and a regular newsletter and has a web site.

President: Marg Haalstra-Koke (1997 to Present)
Executive Director: Same as above.
Year Established: 1997

Keywords
Moebius Syndrome Association

1855 Moebius Syndrome Foundation

P.O. Box 147
Pilot Grove, MO 65276

Phone: (660) 834-3406
Fax: (660) 834-3407
E-mail: vickimc@iland.net
http://www.moebiussyndrome.com

The Moebius Syndrome Foundation is a national, not-for-profit, voluntary organization, which was founded in 1994. Its mission is to provide information and support to individuals with Moebius syndrome and their families, promote greater awareness and understanding of Moebius syndrome, and to advocate for scientific research to advance the diagnosis and treatment of Moebius syndrome and its associated conditions. Moebius syndrome is a rare neurological condition characterized by paralysis or paresis of the 6th and 7th cranial nerves resulting in a lack of facial expression (patients can't smile), lack of lateral eye movement and lack of blinking. In some cases other cranial nerves may be involved. The foundation provides a network of information and communication to affected individuals and their families, and seeks to educate the medical community and general public about this disorder. It works with other Moebius foundations around the world to advocate research into the condition. The foundation hosts conferences every two years for people with Moebius, their families and professionals.

President: Vicki McCarrell
Year Established: 1994

Keywords
Facial Diplegia Syndrome, Congenital; Facial Paralysis; Moebius Syndrome; Moebius Syndrome Foundation

1856 Montgomery Heart Foundation for Cardiomyopathy

1830 E. Monument Street
Suite 7300
Baltimore, MD 21205

Phone: (402) 502-2578
Fax: (443) 287-4109
E-mail: njohnso5@jhmi.edu
http://www.hopkinsmedicine.org/cardiomyopathy/

The Montgomery Heart Foundation for Cardiomyopathy is a not-for-profit organization dedicated to providing private funding to support genetic research for familial cardiomyopathy and raising awareness of the disease to help promote the advancement of a cure. Cardiomyopathy is a term used to describe a heterogeneous group of disorders causing primary heart muscle dysfunction in both men and women, often leading to heart failure or life-threatening complications. Established in 1993, the foundation provides direct financial support for research studies focusing on the cause and treatment of cardiomyopathies; creates a constituency for cardiomyopathy and makes the needs and interests of this known to researchers, clinicians, and the general public; facilitates the flow of information between researchers, clinicians, and affected individuals about new developments and breakthroughs; informs the general public about this disease; and offers up-to-date information to affected individuals and their families.

President: Robert A. Montgomery, M.D., Ph.D. (1993 to Present)
Executive Director: Meg Friske Montgomery (Administrator)
Year Established: 1993

Keywords
Arrhythmogenic Right Ventricular Cardiomyopathy; ARVCM; ARVD; Cardiomyopathy, Arrhythmogenic

Right Ventricular; Familial Dilated Cardiomyopathy; FDCM; Hypertrophic Cardiomyopathy; IDCM; Idiopathic Dilated Cardiomyopathy; Montgomery Heart Foundation for Cardiomyopathy; Peripartum Cardiomyopathy; Restrictive Cardiomyopathy

1857 Motor Neurone Disease Association

P.O. Box 246
Northampton, NN1 2PR, United Kingdom

Phone: +44 (0) 1604-25-0505
Fax: +44 (0) 1604-62-4726
E-mail: enquiries@mndassociation.org
http://www.mndassociation.org

The Motor Neurone Disease (MND) Association is a unique authority on MND. It is an independent charity and the only national organization in England, Wales and Northern Ireland dedicated to supporting people with MND. This group of diseases affects nerve cells (motor neurons) in the brain and spinal cord. The MND Association works to ensure that people affected by MND can secure the care and support they need. It also promotes and funds research into causes of, and a cure for, the disease. Other services include a national telephone help line, a network of Regional Care Advisers, a range of literature on all aspects of the disease, free loan of specialist equipment and limited financial support. The association has a national office in Northampton, and over 85 branches nationwide. The MND Association relies entirely on donations and receives no government funding.

President: Lady Halifax
Executive Director: George Levvy
Year Established: 1979
Acronym: MND Association

Keywords
ALS; Amyotrophic Lateral Sclerosis; MND; Motor Neuron Disease; Motor Neurone Disease Association; Palsy, Progressive Bulbar; PBP; PLS; Primary Lateral Sclerosis

1858 Mouth Cancer Foundation

1 Kestrel Drive
Sandal, Wakefield
West Yorkshire, WF2 6SB, United Kingdom

Phone: +44 (0) 845-126-0479
Fax: +44 (0) 845-126-0479
E-mail: info@mouthcancerfoundation.org
http://www.mouthcancerfoundation.org

The Mouth Cancer Foundation (MCF) was established in 2004 to serve as a support organization in the United Kingdom for people with mouth, throat and other head and neck cancer. Cancer can occur in any part of the mouth, tongue, lips, and throat. MCF provides information and referrals to patients and families, as well as to health professionals.

President: Dr. Vinod K. Joshi
Executive Director: Mr. Krishan L. Joshi
Year Established: 2004
Acronym: MCF

Keywords
Advocacy; Cancer; Chinese; French; German; Head and Neck Cancer; Italian; Japanese; Korean; MCF; Mouth Cancer; Mouth Cancer Foundation; Networking; Support Groups; Throat Cancer

1859 Moving Forward

2934 Glenmore Avenue
Kettering, OH 45409

Phone: (937) 293-0409

Moving Forward is a voluntary, not-for-profit, self-help organization dedicated to disseminating information about myoclonus to affected individuals and their families. Myoclonus, a syndrome with more than 75 classifications, is a neurological movement disorder characterized by sudden, shock-like, involuntary contractions of muscles. The disorder may interfere with walking, speech, and/or manual activities. Myoclonus may be caused by a chemical imbalance, a brain or spinal cord injury, a stroke, epilepsy, or another underlying disorder. Established in 1995, Moving Forward is a networking group that promotes awareness of myoclonus and its many different forms; engages in patient and professional education; and promotes and supports research. The organization offers brochures as well as a resource list of books, articles, and videos. Moving Forward also provides a listing of movement disorder clinics throughout the country as well as several organizations that can offer further information, assistance, networking services, and additional support.

President: Unknown
Executive Director: Pauline F. Dill, Ed.S
Year Established: 1995

Keywords
Moving Forward; Myoclonus

1860 Mowat Wilson Support Group

13 Barry Avenue
Ingol
Preston
Lancashire, United Kingdom

Phone: +44 (0) 1772-76-0119
E-mail: mwsupport@blueyonder.co.uk

The aim of the Mowat Wilson Support Group is to make people aware of Mowat-Wilson syndrome and to put families who have an affected member in touch with other members or professionals. The group also shares information regarding the syndrome, and provides a message/forum board and chat room. Mowat-Wilson syndrome is a rare genetic disorder characterized by distinct facial features, moderate to severe intellectual disability and various congenital anomalies that do not occur in every case.

Acronym: Mwsupport

Keywords
Behaviour Problems; Epilepsy; Heart Conditions; Hirschsprung's Disease; Learning Difficulties; Mowat Wilson Support Group; Mowat Wilson Syndrome; Mwsupport

1861 Moyamoya.com

P.O. Box 9602
Wichita, KS 67277

E-mail: admin@moyamoya.com
http://www.moyamoya.com

Moyamoya.com is an Internet-based, self-help organization. Founded in 2003, it is dedicated to providing support to patients and family members affected by Moyamoya syndrome. This is a progressive disorder that affects the blood vessels in the brain and may lead to inadequate blood supply, and therefore inadequate oxygen delivery to the brain. As a rare-disorder organization, Moyamoya.com provides information to healthcare professionals and the general public, in addition to patients and families.

President: Daren Johnson
Year Established: 2003

Keywords
Hemorrhage; Moyamoya.com; Seizure; TIA

1862 MS Ireland

80 North Cumberland Road
Dublin 4, Ireland

Phone: +353 (0) 1-678-1600
Fax: +353 (0) 1-678-1601
E-mail: info@ms-society.ie
http://www.ms-society.ie

The Multiple Sclerosis Society of Ireland is a not-for-profit organization dedicated to providing information, support, and resources to individuals affected by multiple sclerosis (MS). Multiple sclerosis is a progressive disease characterized by loss of myelin from nerve fibers within the brain and spinal cord (central nervous system). Myelin is a fatty substance that forms a protective, insulating sheath around certain nerve fibers, serving as an electrical insulator. The severity of MS may vary from case to case. Associated symptoms may include numbness, tingling, weakness, incoordination, visual abnormalities, and speech disturbances. The MS Society of Ireland was established in 1963 and currently consists of approximately six regional offices, 40 branches, and a network of community volunteers across Ireland. The society's programs and services include offering a helpl ine for any queries concerning MS, providing respite care, and conducting seminars and workshops for affected individuals, family members, and other caregivers. In addition, the society promotes and funds MS research, offers support services to its voluntary branches, and maintains a web site.

President: William Lonergan
Executive Director: Michael Dineen (General Manager)
Year Established: 1963
Acronym: MS Ireland

Keywords
MS Ireland

1863 Multiple Myeloma Research Foundation

51 Locust Avenue
Suite 201
New Canaan, CT 06840

Phone: (203) 972-1520
Fax: (203) 972-1259
E-mail: info@themmrf.org
http://www.multiplemyeloma.org

The Multiple Myeloma Research Foundation (MMRF) is driven by a single purpose: to accelerate the search for a cure for multiple myeloma. The MMRF was incorporated in 1998 and founded by twin sisters, Karen Andrews and Kathy Giusti, after Kathy was diagnosed with multiple myeloma. Since then, it has been dedicated to improving therapeutic options for people with multiple myeloma by funding myeloma research, building collaborations among researchers and industry, providing information to patients and family members, raising awareness of multiple myeloma, and advocating optimal patient care.

President: Kathy Giusti (1998-present)
Executive Director: Scott Santarella
Year Established: 1998
Acronym: MMRF

Keywords
Multiple Myeloma Research Foundation

1864 Multiple Sclerosis Association of America

706 Haddonfield Road
Cherry Hill, NJ 08002

Fax: (856) 661-9797
Toll Free: (800) 532-7667
E-mail: msaa@msaa.com
http://www.msaa.com

The Multiple Sclerosis Association of America's (MSAA) mission is to ease the day-to-day challenges of individuals with multiple sclerosis (MS) and their care partners. MSAA has a wide array of programs and services that bring ongoing support and direct services to people with MS and their families' throughout the country. MSAA also serves to promote great understanding of multiple sclerosis and the diverse needs and challenges of people with MS.

President: Douglas Franklin
Year Established: 1970
Acronym: MSAA

Keywords
Disseminating Sclerosis; MS; Multiple Sclerosis; Multiple Sclerosis Association of America; Sclerosis, Insular

1865 Multiple Sclerosis International Federation

3rd Floor Skyline House
200 Union Street
London, SE1 0LX, United Kingdom

Phone: +44 (0) 207-620-1911
Fax: +44 (0) 207-620-1922
E-mail: info@msif.org
http://www.msif.org

The Multiple Sclerosis International Federation (MSIF, formerly IFMSS) is an international not-for-profit federation of 42 national multiple sclerosis societies throughout the world. Multiple sclerosis (MS) is a progressive disease characterized by loss of myelin from nerve fibers within the brain and spinal cord (central nervous system). Myelin is a fatty substance that forms a protective, insulating sheath around certain nerve fibers, serving as an electrical insulator. The severity of MS may vary from case to case. Associated symptoms may include numbness, tingling, weakness, incoordination, visual abnormalities, and speech disturbances. Established in 1967, MSIF links the work of national MS societies worldwide. It is committed to working together and with the international research community to eliminate MS and its devastating effects. It also speaks out on a global level for those affected by MS. Its priorities are: stimulating global research; stimulating the active exchange of information; and providing support for the development of new and existing MS societies. The federation's ultimate goal is helping to eradicate multiple sclerosis. The federation also conducts international conferences, provides educational publications on various aspects of MS, and maintains a web site that offers understandable information on MS in several different languages.

President: Sarah Phillips
Executive Director: Christine Purdy (Chief Executive)
Year Established: 1967
Acronym: MSIF

Keywords
MS; Multiple Sclerosis; Multiple Sclerosis International Federation

1866 Multiple Sclerosis Society of Canada

175 Bloor Street East
Suite 700
Toronto
Ontario, M4W 3R8, Canada

Phone: (416) 922-6065
Fax: (416) 922-7538
E-mail: info@mssociety.ca
www.mssociety.ca

The Multiple Sclerosis Society of Canada is a national, not-for-profit, voluntary organization that was founded in 1948 by a small group of International Federation (MSIF) members. Multiple sclerosis (MS) is a disease that is frequently progressive characterized by loss of myelin from nerve fibers within the brain and spinal cord (central nervous system). Myelin is a fatty substance that forms a protective, insulating sheath around certain nerve fibers, serving as an electrical insulator. The severity of MS may vary from case to case. Associated symptoms may include numbness, tingling, weakness, incoordination, visual abnormalities, and speech disturbances. The mission of the MS Society of Canada is to be a leader in finding a cure for MS and enabling affected individuals to enhance their quality of life. The society funds research into the cause, prevention and cure of MS. It provides a variety of services for people with MS and their families including supportive counseling, referrals, self-help groups, and educational workshops. The society also offers an equipment program for affected individuals, conducts social and recreational activities, provides information about MS for healthcare professionals, and has a network of specialized MS clinics across Canada.

President: David Knight
Executive Director: Alistair M. Fraser
Year Established: 1948
Acronym: MS Society

Keywords
MS; MS Research; MS Society; Multiple Sclerosis; Multiple Sclerosis Society of Canada

---

1867 Multiple Sclerosis Society of Great Britain and Northern Ireland

372 Edgware Road
Staple Corner
London, NW2 6ND, United Kingdom

Phone: +44 (0) 208-438-0700
Fax: +44 (0) 208-438-0701
E-mail: info@mssociety.org.uk
http://www.mssociety.org.uk

The Multiple Sclerosis Society of Great Britain and Northern Ireland is a not-for-profit organization dedicated to offering local and national services to individuals whose lives have been affected by multiple sclerosis (MS), and promoting and funding MS research. Multiple sclerosis is a progressive disease characterized by loss of myelin from nerve fibers within the brain and spinal cord (central nervous system). Myelin is a fatty substance that forms a protective, insulating sheath around certain nerve fibers,

serving as an electrical insulator. The severity of MS may vary from case to case. Associated symptoms may include numbness, tingling, weakness, incoordination, visual abnormalities, and speech disturbances. The MS Society was established in 1953 and currently consists of approximately 350 UK branches, and 45,000 members across Great Britain and Northern Ireland. The society offers a variety of services and programs including telephone counseling, financial assistance for affected individuals, respite and holiday centers, residential and day centers, and transportation assistance. In addition, the MS Society is committed to funding biomedical research; supporting applied research to improve the lives of affected individuals; working with other charities that serve people with MS; lobbying for equitable prescribing and funding of therapies; and improving statutory services by educating professionals about MS.

President: Sarah Phillips
Executive Director: Mike O'Donovan
Year Established: 1953
Acronym: MS Society

Keywords
Multiple Sclerosis Society of Great Britain and Northern Ireland

---

1868 MUMS (Mothers United for Moral Support, Inc.) National Parent-to-Parent Network

150 Custer Court
Green Bay, WI 54301-1243

Phone: (920) 336-5333
Fax: (920) 339-0995
Toll Free: (877) 336-5333
E-mail: mums@netnet.net
http://www.netnet.net/mums/

MUMS (Mothers United for Moral Support, Inc.) is a not-for-profit support organization that matches parents with other parents whose children have the same disabilities, rare disorders, chromosomal abnormalities or health conditions. The parents can exchange medical information, as well as names of physicians, clinics, medical resources or research programs. MUMS maintains a database of over 20,000 families from 54 countries covering more than 3,400 disorders, and also networks with other organizations to increase the possibility of finding a match. MUMS puts parents in touch with support groups dealing with their child's disability and publishes a newsletter for parents and professionals. MUMS can even match parents whose children do not have a diagnosis by symptoms.

President: Julie Gordon (1979-Present)
Year Established: 1979
Acronym: MUMS

Keywords
Brain Damage; HBOT; Hyperbaric Oxygen Therapy; MUMS; MUMS (Mothers United for Moral Support, Inc) National Parent to Parent Network; Networking; Parent to Parent Matching; Rare Diseases; Rare Disorders; Support Groups; Trisomy; Undiagnosed; Vaccine Injury

1869 Muscular Dystrophy Association

3300 E. Sunrise Dr
Tucson, AZ 85718

Phone: (520) 529-2000
Fax: (520) 529-5300
Toll Free: (800) 344-4863
E-mail: mda@mdausa.org
http://www.mdausa.org

Established in 1950, the Muscular Dystrophy Association (MDA) is a non-profit, voluntary health agency dedicated to providing comprehensive medical services to individuals affected by over 40 neuromuscular diseases. MDA provides these services at some 230 hospital-affiliated clinics across the United States. The association's worldwide research program allocates more than $28 million a year, seeking cures and treatments for neuromuscular disorders. MDA funds some 400 individual scientific investigations each year at a cost of $57 a minute, around the clock. This represents the largest single initiative to advance current knowledge of neuromuscular diseases and to find cures and treatments for this group of diseases.

President: Robert Ross
Year Established: 1950
Acronym: MDA

Keywords
Amyotrophic Lateral Sclerosis; Ataxia, Friedreich's; Ataxia, Marie's; CMT; Carnitine Deficiency Syndromes; Carnitine Palmityltransferase Deficiency; Central Core Disease; Charcot-Marie-Tooth Disease; Dejerine Sottas Disease; Dermatomyositis; Eaton Lambert Syndrome; Facioscapulohumeral Muscular Dystrophy; Forbes Disease; Fukuyama Type Congenital Muscular Dystrophy; Glycogen Storage Disease Type V; Inclusion Body Myositis; Kennedy Disease; Kugelberg Welander Syndrome; Lambert Eaton Myasthenic Syndrome; McArdle Disease; MDA; MELAS Syndrome; MERRF Syndrome; Metabolic Muscle Disease; Motor Neuron Disease; Muscular Dystrophy; Muscular Dystrophy Association; Muscular Dystrophy, Becker; Muscular Dystrophy, Duchenne; Muscular Dystrophy, Emery Dreifuss; Muscular Dystrophy, Facioscapulohumeral; Muscular Dystrophy, Fukuyama Type; Muscular Dystrophy, Landouzy Dejerine; Muscular Dystrophy, Limb Girdle; Myasthenia Gravis; Myopathy; Myopathy, Nemaline; Myopathy, Scapuloperoneal; Myositis, Inclusion Body; Myotonia Congenita; Myotonic Dystrophy; Myotubular Myopathy; Neuromuscular Disorders; Paramyotonia Congenita; Phosphoglycerate Kinase Deficiency; Polymyositis; Pompe Disease; Spinal Muscular Atrophy; Tarui Disease; Thomsen Disease; Werdnig Hoffmann Disease

1870 Muscular Dystrophy Association (Australia)

GPO Box 9932
Melbourne, 3001, Australia

Phone: +61 (0) 3-9320-9555
Fax: +61 (0) 3-9320-9595
Toll Free: 1 (800) 656-632
E-mail: info@mda.org.au
http://www.mda.org.au

The Muscular Dystrophy Association (MDA) is a not-for-profit organization in Australia that was founded in the early 1970s by a group of people affected by muscular dystrophy (MD). Muscular dystrophy refers to a group of genetic disorders characterized by progressive degeneration of muscle fibers, resulting in associated weakness, disability, and deformity. The different forms of muscular dystrophy may be categorized based upon age at onset, specific muscle groups affected, rate of disease progression, and mode of inheritance. The Muscular Dystrophy Association is committed to improving the quality of life of individuals with muscular dystrophy and other neuromuscular diseases. To fulfill its mission and objectives, the association provides a variety of educational materials, conducts MDA camps for children and adults with neuromuscular disorders, and promotes and supports research. The association's materials include information sheets on different forms of muscular dystrophy, parent's guides, glossaries, and materials discussing the various aspects of these disorders. In 1985, the association established the Muscular Dystrophy Research Foundation to help ensure sufficient funding to accelerate research and to provide funds required for treatment programs. The MDA, in association with St. Vincent's Hospital and the Department of Medicine, Melbourne University, is also affiliated with the Melbourne Neuromuscular Research Centre, and sponsors scientific research seminars and conferences.

Executive Director: Boris M. Struk
Year Established: 1971
Acronym: MDA

Keywords
Amyotrophic Lateral Sclerosis; Ataxia, Friedreich's; Ataxia, Marie's; Becker Muscular Dystrophy; Benign Congenital Hypotonia; Carnitine Deficiency Syndromes; Carnitine Palmitoyltransferase Deficiency; Carnitine Palmityltransferase Deficiency; Central Core Disease; Charcot-Marie-Tooth Disease/Peroneal Muscular Atrophy Association, Inc.; CMT; Congenital Fiber Type Disproportion; Dejerine Sottas Disease; Dermatomyositis; Duchenne Muscular Dystrophy; Eaton Lambert Syndrome; Emery Dreifuss Muscular Dystrophy; Forbes Disease; Fukuyama Type Muscular Dystrophy; Inclusion Body Myositis; Kugelberg Welander Syndrome; Landouzy Dejerine Muscular Dystrophy; Limb Girdle Muscular Dystrophy; McArdle Disease; Metabolic Muscle Disease; Motor Neuron Disease; Muscular Dystrophy; Muscular Dystrophy Association (Australia); Myasthenia Gravis; Myopathy; Myotonic Dystrophy; Myotubular Myopathy; Nemaline Myopathy; Neuromuscular Disease; Oculo Gastrointestinal Muscular Dystrophy; Paramyotonia Congenita; Phosphoglycerate Kinase Deficiency; Polymyositis; Pompe Disease; Scapuloperoneal Disease; Tarui Disease; Thomsen Disease; Walker Warburg Syndrome; Werdnig Hoffmann Disease

1871 Muscular Dystrophy Association of Canada

900-2345 Yonge Street
Toronto
Ontario, M4P 2E5, Canada

Phone: (416) -48-8-00
Fax: (416) -48-8-75
Toll Free: (866)-MUSCLE-8
E-mail: info@mdac.ca
http://www.mdac.ca

The Muscular Dystrophy Association of Canada (MDAC) is a not-for-profit voluntary organization dedicated to eliminating neuromuscular disorders and alleviating the associated symptoms. Neuromuscular disorders are a group of diseases affecting the body's

ability to move, due to an underlying neurological disease. Whether the problem originates within the motor nerve cell, the nerve, or the muscle, the most commonly experienced symptoms are varying degrees of progressive muscle weakness and wasting. There are over 40 nerve and muscle disorders covered under the umbrella of the Muscular Dystrophy Association of Canada. The association's three main goals are funding research that will ultimately result in discovering the causes, treatments, and cures for muscular dystrophy and other neuromuscular disorders; providing support services that assist individuals and families affected by neuromuscular disorders; and providing information to affected individuals, their families, healthcare professionals, educators, and the general public as to the nature and management of neuromuscular disorders. Services provided by MDAC include the dissemination of information, advocacy, referrals, travel assistance, and some financial assistance with mobility equipment. MDAC also houses donated equipment for use by clients upon request.

President: James Cumming
Executive Director: Yves Savoie
Year Established: 1954
Acronym: MDAC

Keywords
Ataxia, Friedreich's; Charcot-Marie-Tooth Disease; CMT; Guillain Barre Syndrome; Muscular Dystrophy; Muscular Dystrophy Association of Canada; Muscular Dystrophy, Becker; Muscular Dystrophy, Duchenne; Muscular Dystrophy, Emery Dreifuss; Muscular Dystrophy, Fukuyama Type; Muscular Dystrophy, Landouzy Dejerine; Muscular Dystrophy, Limb Girdle; Muscular Dystrophy, Oculo Gastrointestinal; Neuromuscular Disorders; Peroneal Muscular Atrophy

1872 Muscular Dystrophy Campaign

7-11 Prescott Place
London, SW4 6BS, United Kingdom

E-mail: info@muscular-dystrophy.org
http://www.muscular-dystrophy.org

Muscular Dystrophy Campaign is a UK-based voluntary research organization dedicated to identifying the causes of muscular dystrophy and allied conditions to develop treatments while working to discover a cure. Muscular dystrophy is a group of rare, genetic, muscle-wasting diseases. In some forms of MD, muscles of the hips and shoulders are weakened, walking abnormalities (ataxia) develop, and learning difficulties may be present. Muscular Dystrophy Campaign was established in 1959 and is affiliated with two other organizations, the European Alliance of MDA and the World Alliance of MDA. It provides funding for several Muscle Centers that are designed to provide comprehensive medical care to individuals with neuromuscular conditions, and to provide researchers within and between the centers with medical data and samples that will assist research.

President: Sue Barker MBE
Executive Director: Philip Butcher
Year Established: 1959
Acronym: MDC

Keywords
Facioscapulohumeral Muscular Dystrophy; Limb Girdle Muscular Dystrophy; MDC; Muscular Dystrophy; Muscular Dystrophy Campaign; Muscular Dystrophy, Becker; Muscular Dystrophy, Duchenne; Muscular Dystrophy, Emery Dreifuss; Muscular Dystrophy, Fukuyama Type; Muscular Dystrophy, Landouzy Dejerine; Muscular Dystrophy, Oculo Gastrointestinal; Werdnig Hoffmann Disease

1873   **Muscular Dystrophy Ireland**
71/72 North Brunswich Street
Dublin 7, Ireland

Phone: +353 (0) 1-872-1501
Fax: +353 (0) 1-872-4482
E-mail: info@mdi.ie
http://www.mdi.ie/

Muscular Dystrophy Ireland (MDI) is a national, voluntary, nonprofit organization with a membership of over 500 individuals and families throughout Ireland. The organization's primary objective is to provide support to people with neuromuscular conditions and their families through the provision of a range of services, including family support, information, respite services, holidays, youth activities, transport, and independent living and training opportunities. Muscular dystrophy is a collective term referring to a variety of genetic neuromuscular disorders characterized by progressive degeneration and weakening of muscles. The different forms of muscular dystrophy may be categorized based upon age at onset, specific muscle groups affected, rate of disease progression, the genetic mutation and mode of inheritance. Muscular Dystrophy Ireland was founded in 1972 and currently has a network of offices throughout Ireland. In addition to providing supportive services, MDI is committed to promoting and supporting research, conducting annual general meetings, organizing special

youth activities for its younger members, and offering a variety of educational materials.

President: Sean MacReamoinn
Executive Director: Joe Mooney
Year Established: 1972
Acronym: MDI

Keywords
Facioscapulohumeral Muscular Dystrophy; MDI; Muscular Dystrophy Ireland; Neuromuscular Conditions

1874   **Myalgic Encephalopathy Association**
The ME Association
4 Top Angel
Buckingham Industrial Park
Buckingham
Buchinghamshire, MK18 1TH, United Kingdom

Phone: +44 (0) 871-222-7824
Fax: +44 (0) 182-082-1602
E-mail: gill.briody@meassociation.org.uk
http://www.meassociation.org.uk

The Myalgic Encephalopathy Association is a nonprofit organization in the United Kingdom dedicated to providing information, support and resources to individuals affected by myalgic encephalopathy, their family members, and healthcare professionals. Myalgic encephalopathy (ME) is a condition more commonly known by doctors as chronic fatigue syndrome in both the United States and the UK. ME is characterized by persistent, disabling fatigue and post-exertional malaise, accompanied by some combination of impaired concentration and memory, muscle pain, lower fever, sore throat and headaches, with such symptoms not being attributable to any other known underlying cause. Symptoms vary from person to person, and fluctuate in intensity from day to day. The cause of the condition is as yet unknown. The ME Association was established in 1976 and has a national office in Buckinghamshire, a regional office in Scotland, and a network of volunteers and supporters throughout the UK. The association's information and support service, ME Connect, is available by telephone every day of the year, 2-4 pm and 7-9 pm.

Executive Director: Val Hockey
Year Established: 1976
Acronym: ME Association

Keywords
Encephalomyelitis, Myalgic; Myalgic Encephalopathy Association

1875 Myasthenia Gravis Association (UK)
First Floor
Southgate Business Centre
Normanton Road
Derby, DE23 6UQ, United Kingdom

Phone: +44 (0) 1332-29-0219
Fax: +44 (0) 1332-29-3641
Toll Free: +44 (0) (800) 919-922
E-mail: mg@mgauk.org.uk
http://www.mgauk.org.uk

The Myasthenia Gravis Association (MGA) is a not-for-profit organization in the United Kingdom that is dedicated to promoting the welfare of individuals affected by myasthenia gravis, an autoimmune disorder in which the body's immune system attacks and damages nerve signal receptor areas in muscles, causing muscle weakness and fatigue. Although the disease may affect any muscle of the body, muscles of the eyes, lips, tongue, throat, and neck are often affected. The Myasthenia Gravis Association was established in 1968 and currently includes approximately 62 branches (and another five on the way) throughout the United Kingdom and the Republic of Ireland. The association is committed to offering information and support to affected individuals and their family members, promoting public and professional awareness, and raising funds for research to improve diagnosis and treatment of the disease and, ultimately, to find a cure.

President: Prof. John Newsom-Davis
Executive Director: Alasdiar Nimmo (Chief Executive)
Year Established: 1968
Acronym: MGA

Keywords
MGA; Myasthenia Gravis; Myasthenia Gravis Association (UK)

1876 Myasthenia Gravis Foundation of America
1821 University Avenue W. Suite S256
St. Paul, MN 55104

Phone: (651) 917-6256
Fax: (651) 917-1835
Toll Free: (800) 541-5454
E-mail: mgfa@myasthenia.org
http://www.myasthenia.org

The Myasthenia Gravis Foundation of America is a national, not-for-profit agency whose mission is to facilitate the timely diagnosis and optimal care of individuals affected by myasthenia gravis and closely related disorders and to improve their lives through programs of patient services, public information, medical research, professional education, advocacy and patient care. Myasthenia gravis is a rare autoimmune disease affecting the neuromuscular junction and producing weakness of voluntary muscles. The foundation produced a quarterly newsletter, brochures, newsletters, pamphlets, a Survival Guide, information cards and manuals for nurses and physicians. Founded in 1952, the Myasthenia Gravis Foundation has more than 36 chapters and 100 support groups.

President: Ester Land
Executive Director: L J Taugher
Year Established: 1952
Acronym: MGFA, Inc.

Keywords
Advocacy; Autoimmune Polyendocrine Syndrome Type II; Lambert-Eaton Myasthenic Syndrome; LEMS; MGFA; Myasthenia Gravis; Myasthenia Gravis Foundation of America; Myasthenia Gravis, Congenital; Support Groups

1877 Myasthenia Gravis Links
Web Site on the Internet

E-mail: stanley.way@prodigy.net
http://pages.prodigy.net/stanley.way/myasthenia/

Myasthenia Gravis Links Internet site contains information on myasthenia gravis for affected individuals, family members, physicians, healthcare professionals, researchers, and the general public. Myasthenia gravis is a rare autoimmune disease affecting the neuromuscular junction and producing weakness in voluntary muscles. This web site provides information on myasthenia gravis in understandable terminology, but also contains more detailed and technical medical information covering every aspect of the disorder (e.g., diagnosis, causes, treatments, etc.), a variety of online networking opportunities (including listservs, chat rooms, newsgroups, bulletin boards, etc.), and links to additional organizations within the United States and across the world that provide information and support for those affected by myasthenia gravis.

Keywords
Myasthenia Gravis; Myasthenia Gravis Links; Myasthenia Gravis Links (Web Site on the Internet); Myasthenia Gravis, Congenital

1878 Myocarditis Program at Mayo Clinic

Mayo Clinic
Attn: Leslie T Cooper, MD
200 First Street SW
Rochester, MN 55905

Phone: (507) 284-3680
Fax: (507) 266-0228
E-mail: cooper.leslie@mayo.edu
http://www.mayo.edu/research/giant_cell_myocarditis/communications.html

The Myocarditis Program at Mayo Clinic provides information to patients and professionals, and serves as a center for research into the causes and treatment of myocarditis, is with a focus on giant cell myocarditis and cardiac sarcoidosis. Giant cell myocarditis (GCM), a rare disorder that presents with inflammation of the heart muscle, typically affects young, previously healthy individuals. GCM is characterized by the progressive inability of the heart to pump blood effectively to the lungs and the rest of the body and irregularities in the rhythm of the heartbeat originating in the lower chambers of the heart, resulting in potentially life-threatening complications. Cardiac sarcoidosis is characterized by involvement of the heart in systemic sarcoidosis. Sarcoidosis, an uncommon multisystem disorder of unknown cause, is characterized by the formation of rounded, granular, inflammatory nodules (tubercles) consisting of cells resembling those that line internal and external surfaces of the body (epithelioid tissue).

President: Leslie T. Cooper, M.D.
Year Established: 1996

Keywords
GCM; Giant Cell Myocarditis; Heart Failure; Myocarditis Program at Mayo Clinic; Sarcoidosis, Cardiac

1879 Myositis Association

1233 20th Street NW
Suite 402
Washington, DC 20036

Phone: (202) 887-0088
Fax: (202) 466-8940
Toll Free: (800) 821-7356
E-mail: tma@myositis.org
http://www.myositis.org

The Myositis Association is a voluntary organization whose mission is to improve the lives of those affected by inflammatory myopathies, provide a support network, act as a resource for patients and the medical community, advocate for patients, and promote research into the cause and treatment of the diseases. Inflammatory myopathies are a group of muscle disorders characterized by inflammation and degeneration of skeletal muscle. The organization provides services worldwide, including support groups, patient networking, newsletters, research, patient and professional education, brochures, database, referrals and registry.

Executive Director: Bob Goldberg
Year Established: 1993
Acronym: TMA

Keywords
Dermatomyositis; IBM; Inclusion Body Myositis; Inflammatory Myopathies; JDM; Juvenile Dermatiomyosits; Myositis; Myositis Association; Myositis, Hereditary Inclusion Body; Myositis, Inclusion Body; Polymyositis

1880 Myositis Support Group

146 Newtown Road
Woolston, Southampton
Hampshire, S019 9HR, United Kingdom

Phone: +44 (0) 2380-44-9708
Fax: +44 (0) 2380-39-6402
E-mail: enquiries@myositis.org.uk
http://www.myositis.org.uk

The Myositis Support Group, also known as the Dermatomyositis and Polymyositis Support Group, is based in the United Kingdom. It offers support and advice for the following rare forms of myositis: dermatomyositis, polymyositis, inclusion body myositis, and juvenile dermatomyositis. The support group raises funds to support research and is now working in collaboration with the Myositis Association of America to ensure that all sufferers and their families receive good information and advice, and that research is optimized.

Executive Director: Les Oakley

Keywords
Autoimmune Diseases; Dermatomyositis; Dermatomyositis and Polymyositis Support Group; Inclusion Body Myositis; Juvenile Dermatiomyosits; Muscle Diseases; Myositis Support Group; Polymyositis

1881 Myotonic Dystrophy Support Group

35A Carlton Hill
Carlton, Nottingham, NgH 1BG, United Kingdom

Phone: +44 (0) 115-987-5869
Fax: +44 (0) 115-987-6462
E-mail: mdsg@tesco.net
http://www.mdsguk.org

The Myotonic Dystrophy Support Group is a self-help group of volunteers who work throughout the United Kingdom to promote awareness of myotonic dystrophy, a form of muscular dystrophy that affects adults, and provide information and support to patients, family members, and healthcare professionals. The Myotonic Dystrophy Support Group offers friendship to reduce the sense of isolation patients can feel after they have received a diagnosis. The group offers opportunities for affected individuals to share their concerns or needs with others who understand their feelings.

President: Mrs. Margaret Bowter (National Coordinator)

Keywords
Myotonic Dystrophy; Myotonic Dystrophy Support Group; Support Groups

1882 Myotubular Myopathy Resource Group

2602 Quaker Drive
Texas City, TX 77590

Phone: (409) 945-8569
Fax: (409) 945-2162
E-mail: info@mtmrg.org
http://www.mtmrg.org

Established in 1993, the Myotubular Myopathy Resource Group is a not-for-profit, voluntary organization dedicated to enabling affected families to exchange support, resources, and information about this rare disorder. X-linked myotubular myopathy is a rare disorder characterized by weakness of the respiratory muscles causing respiratory distress. In addition, infants with this form of myotubular myopathy are generally weak and have a loss of muscle tone causing poor sucking and an inability to swallow. Weakness of the jaw, tongue, lips, cheeks, mouth, throat, and neck muscles may also be present. The resource group is also committed to identifying affected families, educating the medical community about the disorder, working with several researchers who are attempting to locate the responsible gene, and offering educational materials including fact sheets, reports, and a regular newsletter.

President: Gary Scoggin
Executive Director: Pamela Scoggin
Year Established: 1993

Keywords
Myopathy, X-linked Centronuclear; Myotubular Myopathy Resource Group; Myotubular Myopathy, X-linked; X-Linked Myotubular Myopathy Resource Group

1883 Nail Patella Syndrome Networking/Support Group

67 Woodlake Drive
Holland, PA 18966

Phone: (215) 504-4659
Fax: (215) 504-4659
E-mail: pacali@aol.com
http://www.hometown.aol.com/pacali/npspage.html

This all-inclusive group offers a web site with medical information, photos and x-rays of typical characteristics, as well as links to NPS genetic research, a photo album and a discussion group for people with NPS and their families. The discussion group currently has over 375 members from all over the world. NPS is a rare genetic disorder causing abnormalities of the fingernails, knees, elbows, hips and other joints. Clubbed feet, kidney disease, glaucoma and a host of other anomalies may also be associated with NPS. The discussion/support group was established in 1996 for people with Nail Patella Syndrome, their families and medical professionals.

President: Carol Ferensak
Year Established: 1996
Acronym: NPS

Keywords
Bent Dislocated Elbows; Clubbed Feet; Fingernail Deformities; Fong's Disease; Iliac Horn Syndrome; Iliac Horns; Kidney Disease; Nail Patella Syndrome; Nail Patella Syndrome Networking/Support Group; NPS; Onychoosteodysplasia; Square Knees; Thumb Nails

1884 Nail Patella Syndrome Worldwide

25826 Norrington Square
South Riding, VA 20152

Phone: (703) 542-5597
Fax: (703) 542-5597
E-mail: npsw@nailpatella.org
http://www.nailpatella.org

Nail Patella Syndrome Worldwide was established to support individuals with NPS. It provides medical information, networking opportunities, and friendship. The group publishes a quarterly newspaper and has also published a medical brochure. The organization is based in California, but serves members from around the world. Nail Patella Syndrome is a rare genetic disorder that is usually apparent at birth or during early childhood. It is often misdiagnosed. Although the associated symptoms and physical characteristics may vary, characteristic abnormalities include improper development of the fingernails, toenails, kneecaps, and certain bones at the bend of the elbow. In addition, this syndrome sometimes results in abnormalities of the eyes and kidneys among other symptoms.

President: Joanne Mansour
Year Established: 2000
Acronym: NPSW

Keywords
Absent Patella; Crooked Elbows; Fong's Disease; Glaucoma; IBS; Nail Patella Syndrome; Nail Patella Syndrome Worldwide; Pointed Moons; Small Patella; Webbing; Widow's Peak

1885   Nail-Patella Syndrome (NPS) Web Site

E-mail: PACALI@aol.com
http://www.members.aol.com/PACALI/npspage.html

The Nail-Patella Syndrome Web Site is a site on the Internet created by Carol Ferensak, an individual with Nail-Patella syndrome who has traced the disorder back at least three generations in her family. Nail-Patella syndrome (NPS), an extremely rare inherited disorder, may be characterized by improper development of the fingernails and/or toenails; absence and/or underdevelopment of the knee caps (patellae); dislocation and/or webbing of the elbow(s); abnormal projections of bone from the upper portion of both sides of the hipbone (bilateral iliac horns); and/or, in some cases, eye abnormalities. Approximately 30 to 40 percent of affected individuals may also experience abnormalities in kidney function (nephropathy and/or proteinuria) that may be apparent during childhood or later in life. The NPS Web Site is dedicated to providing information on the disorder as well as enabling affected individuals and family members to locate one another, share their stories, and exchange information, support, mutual concerns, and resources.

President: Carol Ferensak (Webmaster)

Keywords
Fong Disease; Nail Patella Syndrome; Nail-Patella Syndrome (NPS) Web Site; NPS; Onychoosteo-

dysplasia; Onychoosteodysplasia, Hereditary; Turner Kieser Syndrome

1886   Narcolepsy and Cataplexy Foundation of America

445 E. 68th Street
L12
New York, NY 10021

Phone: (212) 570-5506

The Narcolepsy and Cataplexy Foundation of America (NCFA) is a voluntary, not-for-profit, self-help organization dedicated to providing information on narcolepsy and cataplexy to affected individuals, the medical community, and the general public. Information on treatment options and current research is available from the foundation. Narcolepsy is a rare disorder characterized by abnormal drowsiness during the day, sudden extreme muscle weakness (cataplexy), hallucinations, paralysis while sleeping, and disrupted sleep during the night. Established in 1976, the Narcolepsy and Cataplexy Foundation of America provides referrals to physicians and treatment centers; promotes research into narcolepsy; provides referrals to support groups; and offers educational information through brochures.

President: Dr. Helen Demitroff (1976-Present)
Executive Director: Same as above.
Year Established: 1976
Acronym: NCFA

Keywords
Apnea, Sleep; Cataplexy; Narcolepsy; Narcolepsy and Cataplexy Foundation of America; Sleep Disorders

1887   Narcolepsy Institute

Montefiore Medical Center
111 East 210th Street
Bronx, NY 10467

Phone: (718) 920-6799
Fax: (718) 654-9580
E-mail: MGoswami@NarcolepsyInstitute.org
http://www.narcolepsyinstitute.org

The Narcolepsy Institute is a not-for-profit, voluntary organization dedicated to providing comprehensive care to people with narcolepsy, a genetic disorder characterized by excessive daytime drowsiness. An individual with narcolepsy feels an irresistible urge to sleep during the day and often has disturbed nocturnal sleep as well. Established in 1985, the institute provides information, advocacy, and care to patients. It also works to enhance awareness of narcolepsy among medical professionals.

Executive Director: Meeta Goswami MPH, Ph.D. (1985 to Pesent)
Year Established: 1985

Keywords
Narcolepsy; Narcolepsy Institute

1888 Narcolepsy Network, Inc.

79 Main Street
North Kingstown, RI 02852

Phone: (401) 667-2523
Fax: (401) 633-6567
Toll Free: (888) 292-6522
E-mail: narnet@narcolepsynetwork.org
http://www.narcolepsynetwork.org

The Narcolepsy Network is a national voluntary organization that was formed to serve the needs of people with narcolepsy. Its membership composed of persons with narcolepsy, family members, friends, healthcare professionals, and other interested individuals. The network is dedicated to improving the quality of life for people with narcolepsy and finding a cure for this disorder. To this end, the organization maintains a network of local support groups and chapters. It promotes programs of communication, advocacy, research, support, and education. A booklet titled "Narcolepsy: A Guide to Understanding" provides information on narcolepsy. Topics covered within the booklet include the symptoms, causes and diagnosis of the disorder, associated sleep apnea, treatments and social implications. The organization also distributes a reading list, bibliography, and an educational materials order form.

President: Sharon D. Smith
Executive Director: Eveline Honig
Year Established: 1986
Acronym: NN

Keywords
Apnea, Sleep; Cataplexy; DQB1*0602; DRB1*1502; HLA DQB*0602; HLA DRB*1501; Hypnagogic Hallucinations; Hypocretin; Hypothalamus; Narcolepsy; Narcolepsy Network, Inc.; Orexin; REM; Sleep Paralysis

1889 National Adrenal Diseases Foundation

505 Northern Boulevard
Suite 200
Great Neck, NY 11021

Phone: (516) 487-4992
Fax: (516) 829-5710
E-mail: NADFmail@aol.com
http://www.medhelp.org/nadf

The National Adrenal Diseases Foundation (NADF) is a not-for-profit organization dedicated to providing information, education, and support to patients diagnosed with adrenal diseases such as Addison's disease, Cushing's syndrome, and congenital adrenal hyperplasia. The foundation also provides support and information to family members and to medical professional caregivers. The foundation connects patients with the 31 NADF affiliated support groups across the nation. Established in 1985, NADF provides quarterly newsletters, educational pamphlets and fact sheets.

President: Thomas LeMasters
Executive Director: Melanie Wong
Year Established: 1985
Acronym: NADF

Keywords
Achard-Thiers Syndrome; ACTH Deficiency; Addison's Disease; Adrenal Diseases; Adrenal Hyperplasia; Adrenal Hyperplasia, Congenital; Adrenal Hypoplasia; Adrenal Insufficiency; Adrenalectomy; Adrenomyeloneuropathy; Allgrove's Syndrome; Amenorrhea, Primary; APECED Syndrome; Autoimmune Polyendocrine Syndrome; Conn Syndrome; Cushing's Syndrome; Hyperaldosteronism; NADF; National Adrenal Diseases Foundation; Pheochromocytoma; Precocious Puberty; Schmidt Syndrome; Triple A Syndrome

1890 National Advisory Service to Parents of Children with a Stoma (NASPCS)—The Charity for Incontinent and Stoma Children

51 Anderson Drive
Darvel, Ayrshire Ayrshire, KA17 0DE, United Kingdom

Phone: +44 (0) 1560-32-2024
http://www.naspcs.co.uk/

The National Advisory Service to Parents of Children with a Stoma (NASPCS), also known as the Charity for Incontinent and Stoma Children, serves the parents of children who have, for any reason, undergone surgery to create an artificial opening (stoma) to the small intestine (ileostomy), the large intestine (colostomy), or one of the ureters (urostomy). Information booklets, as well as leaflets, are available to help children and their parents understand and cope with conditions that affect the bowels or bladder and require the creation of a stoma. The Charity also helps by making contact between more experienced parents and patients and those who are beginning or about to begin the experience.

President: John B. Malcolm

Keywords
Imperforate Anus; Imperforate Anus Contact Group; National Advisory Service to Parents of Children with a Stoma (NASPCS)—The Charity for Incontinent and Stoma Children

1891 National Alliance for Autism Research

Research Park
99 Wall Street
Princeton, NJ 08540

Phone: (609) 430-9160
Fax: (609) 430-9163
Toll Free: (888) 777-6227
E-mail: naar@naar.org
http://www.naar.org

The National Alliance for Autism Research (NAAR) is a voluntary organization dedicated to promoting and supporting biomedical research into the prevention, treatment, and potential cure of autism spectrum disorders. Autism is characterized by extreme withdrawal and an inability to speak or communicate, to relate to others, or to learn or understand human interaction. Autism is considered a pervasive developmental disorder since it affects fine motor, gross motor, language, communicative, emotional, cognitive, and behavioral skills. The National Alliance for Autism Research was founded in 1994 by parents who were concerned about the limited amount of biomedical research conducted into the causes, prevention, treatment, and cure of autism spectrum disorders. The organization, which now has approximately 7,000 members, promotes research in autism, conducts conferences for parents and researchers, provides assistance to brain bank sites to help strengthen research capabilities, and encourages the pharmaceutical industry to develop treatment agents beneficial to individuals with autism.

President: Glenn R. Tringali
Executive Director: David Maxson
Year Established: 1994
Acronym: NAAR

Keywords
Asperger Syndrome; Autism; NAAR; National Alliance for Autism Research; PDD/NOS; Pervasive Developmental Disorder

1892 National Alliance for Hispanic Health

1501 16th Street, NW
Washington, DC 20036

Phone: (202) 387-5000
Fax: (202) 265-8027
Toll Free: (866) 782-2645
E-mail: alliance@hispanichealth.org
http://www.hispanichealth.org

The National Alliance for Hispanic Health (NAHH) is a not-for-profit organization dedicated to serving Hispanic consumers throughout the United States. Founded in 1973, NAHH is the oldest health network for Hispanics in the country. It offers information in Spanish and English to patients, family members, health professionals, and the general public. This information is given in reports or brochures.

President: Jane L. Delgado, PhD, MS
Year Established: 1973
Acronym: NAHH

Keywords
Limited English Proficiency; National Alliance for Hispanic Health

1893 National Alliance for the Mentally Ill

Colonial Place Three
2107 Wilson Boulevard.
Suite 300
Arlington, VA 22201-3042, ISA

Phone: (703) 524-7600
Fax: (703) 524-9094
Toll Free: (800) 999-6264
TDD: (703) 516-7227
E-mail: membership@nami.org
http://www.nami.org

The National Alliance for the Mentally Ill (NAMI) is a not-for-profit, voluntary health organization dedicated to providing mutual support, education, advocacy, and research funding for people affected by mental illness, their families, and friends. The organization also serves those who have been diagnosed with schizophrenic depression and other related disorders. Established in 1979, this self-help organization refers individuals to nationwide support groups, services, and outreach programs. Educational materials produced by the organization include a database, directories, annual reports, informational brochures, pamphlets, a bimonthly newsletter entitled "The Advocate," and "The Decade of the Brain," NAMI's quarterly publication for presenting research, clinical practices and advances, and policy updates relevant to serious brain disorders.

President: Margaret Stout
Executive Director: Mike Fitzpatrick
Year Established: 1979
Acronym: NAMI

Keywords
Anorexia Nervosa; Antisocial Personality Disorder; Anxiety; Attention Deficit Hyperactivity Disorder; Autism; Bulimia; Conversion Disorder; Depersonalization Disorder; Depression; Dysthymia; Fetal Alcohol Syndrome; Manic Depression, Bipolar; Mental Illness; Mutism, Selective; NAMI; National Alliance for the Mentally Ill; Neurasthenia; Neuroleptic Malignant Syndrome; Obsessive Compulsive Disorder; Organic Mood Syndrome; Organic Personality Syndrome; Panic Anxiety Syndrome; Pica; Schizophrenia; Sleep Disorders; Tardive Dyskinesia; Tourette Syndrome; Trichotillomania; XYY Syndrome

1894 National Alliance for Thrombosis and Thrombophilia

P.O. Box 66018
Washington, DC 20035

Phone: (860) 376-3250
Fax: (614) 293-2314
E-mail: nattinfo@yahoo.com
http://www.nattinfo.org

The National Alliance for Thrombosis and Thrombophilia (NATT) is a nationwide, community-based, voluntary health organization committed to prevention and treatment of the major health problems caused by blood clots. NATT's goal is to ensure that those affected by thrombosis and thrombophilia receive early diagnosis, proper treatment, and quality support. NATT also supports research, education, and advocacy on behalf of affected individuals and their families.

President: Elizabeth Varga (Chair)
Executive Director: Tom Hogan (Secretary)
Year Established: 2003
Acronym: NATT

Keywords
Advocacy; Anticardiolipin Antibodies; Antiphospholipid Antibody Syndrome; Antithrombin Deficiency; Blood Clots; Blood Clotting Disorders; Deep Vein Thrombosis; Factor V Leiden; Hyperhomocysteinemia; Lupus Anticoagulant; MTHFR Mutations; NATT; National Alliance for Thrombosis and Thrombophilia; Networking; Protein C Deficiency; Protein S Deficiency; Prothrombin G20210A Mutations (Factor II); Pulmonary Embolism; Research; Thrombophilia; Thrombosis

1895 National Alopecia Areata Foundation

14 Mitchell Boulevard
San Rafael, CA 94903

Phone: (415) 472-3780
Fax: (415) 472-5343
E-mail: INFO@NAAF.ORG
http://www.NAAF.ORG

The National Alopecia Areata Foundation is a voluntary health organization and a primary source of funding for research on basic hair biology and alopecia areata. Established in 1981, the foundation leads medical research efforts by raising private funds and awarding grants to qualified investigators at university centers in the United States, Canada, and Europe. It also seeks to inform government officials about alopecia areata in an effort to obtain federal funding for research studies on this disorder. The foundation conducts on-going public awareness programs to increase the public's understanding of this disorder. As a worldwide center for educational materials, the foundation supplies a wide variety of information, support, and resources for people with alopecia areata and their physicians. Numerous brochures, a handbook, a foundation report, newsletters, a novel entitled "Herman," and a video called "This Weird Thing That Makes My Hair Fall Out" are available from the foundation.

Executive Director: Vicki Kalabokes (Pres. & Chief Exec. Officer)
Year Established: 1981
Acronym: NAAF

Keywords
Alopecia; Alopecia Areata; Alopecia Totalis; Alopecia Universalis; National Alopecia Areata Foundation

1896 National Amputation Foundation, Inc.

40 Church Street
Malverne, NY 11565

Phone: (516) 887-3600
Fax: (516) 887-3667
E-mail: AMPS76@aol.com
www.nationalamputation.org

The National Amputation Foundation, Inc., (NAF) is a not-for-profit organization comprised of amputee volunteers who offer their support to amputees and their families. People with amputations that were present at birth (congenital) are also served by the foundation. NAF's objective is to aid a new amputee in returning to as normal a life as possible within the sphere of his or her potential. Established in 1919, the foundation provides affected individuals with appropriate referrals to support groups, and promotes education of amputees, family members, healthcare professionals, and the general public. The foundation produces a regular newsletter as well as brochures, reprints of medical articles, and pamphlets on a variety of issues. These issues include health; psychological, and daily care concerns; questions concerning devices and prosthetics, sports and exercise, and driving; legal issues; and specific concerns regarding children or adolescents with limb loss. Used medical equipment give-a-way to any person in need (recipient responsible for pick-up).

President: Paul Bernaccio
Executive Director: Donald Sioss
Year Established: 1919
Acronym: NAF

Keywords
Amputation (Including Congenital); National Amputation Foundation, Inc.

1897 **National Ankylosing Spondylitis Society**
P.O. Box 179
Mayfield
East Sussex, TN20 6ZL, United Kingdom

Phone: +44 (0) 1435-87-3527
Fax: +44 (0) 1435-87-3027
E-mail: nass@nass.co.uk
http://www.nass.co.uk

The National Ankylosing Spondylitis Society (NASS) is a voluntary, not-for-profit, self-help organization in the United Kingdom. The society, which was established in 1976 at the Royal National Hospital for Rheumatic Diseases in Bath, has approximately 100 chapters and 9,000 members. Ankylosing spondylitis is a chronic, progressive, inflammatory disease that usually initially affects the spine and adjacent areas, eventually causing fusion of involved joints. The National Ankylosing Spondylitis Society is committed to providing information and support to affected individuals and family members; offering a forum to educate medical professionals and the general public concerning AS; and supporting and funding research. The society also engages in patient advocacy; lobbies governmental bodies and the National Health Service to ensure the provision of better facilities for treat-

ment; assists in the formation of similar societies in other countries; and forms branches across the United Kingdom that provide supervised exercise therapy sessions by physiotherapists.

President: Brian Bowman
Executive Director: Fergus T. Rogers
Year Established: 1976
Acronym: NASS

Keywords
Ankylosing Spondylitis; Marie Strumpell Disease; National Ankylosing Spondylitis Society; Spondyloarthritis; Von Bechterew Disease

---

1898 **National Aphasia Association**
7 Dey Street
Suite 600
New York, NY 10007

Phone: (212) 267-2814
Fax: (212) 267-2812
Toll Free: (800) 922-4622
E-mail: naa@aphasia.org
http://www.aphasia.org

The National Aphasia Association is a not-for-profit organization dedicated to increasing public awareness of aphasia and other communication disorders, and aiding persons with aphasia and their families. Aphasia is a neurological condition caused by damage to the left hemisphere of the brain in which communication and/or language skills (speaking, reading, writing, and comprehending others) are impaired. The Association's activities include sponsoring support groups, promoting advocacy and legislative programs, supporting ongoing medical research, and maintaining an informational web site. Other activities include support of a response center, publication of a biannual newsletter, sponsorship of biannual national gatherings, and production of fact sheets, reading lists and national listings of community-based support groups. The association also provides contact information for a national network of healthcare professionals who volunteer to respond to families in their area about local resources. A Young People's Network puts families in touch with one another for the purpose of peer support and information exchange.

President: Alan Bandler, Esq. (2001-Present)
Executive Director: Joan Peters
Year Established: 1987
Acronym: NAA

Keywords
Aphasia; Apraxia; Communication Disorders; Landau Kleffner Syndrome

1899 **National Association for Colitis & Crohn's Disease (UK)**
4 Beaumont House
Sutton Road
St. Albans
Herts, AL1 5HH, United Kingdom

Phone: +44 (0) 1727-84-4296
Fax: +44 (0) 1727-86-2550
E-mail: nacc@nacc.org.uk
http://www.nacc.org.uk/

The National Association for Colitis & Crohn's Disease (UK) is a national, voluntary association in the United Kingdom dedicated to providing information and support services to people who are living with ulcerative colitis or Crohn's disease, which are both forms of inflammatory bowel disease (IBD). The association is also committed to promoting and supporting research into the medical, healthcare, social, and psychological aspects of IBD. Ulcerative colitis is characterized by chronic inflammation and ulceration of the large intestine and the rectum. Affected individuals may experience associated pain; episodes of urgent, bloody diarrhea; fatigue; and other symptoms. Crohn's disease may affect any area of the gastrointestinal tract from the mouth to the rectum; however, in most cases, it is characterized by chronic inflammation, ulceration, and scarring of the wall of the small intestine. Associated symptoms and findings may include pain, fatigue, weight loss, episodes of urgent diarrhea, and other symptoms and findings. The National Association for Colitis & Crohn's Disease (UK) was established in 1979 and currently consists of over 27,000 members including affected individuals, their families and friends, healthcare professionals, and anyone who wishes to support the group's activities. The association conducts regular meetings; offers local support through its area groups; has a network of trained volunteer counselors who provide telephone support; and offers information and support to families with children affected by IBD through its "Smilie's People Network." In addition, the association has a fund for people in financial difficulty due to IBD and supports local hospitals through its area groups.

President: Bradley Brown (National Chairman)
Executive Director: Richard Driscoll
Year Established: 1979
Acronym: NACC

Keywords
National Association for Colitis & Crohn's Disease (UK)

1900 **National Association for Continence**
P.O. Box 1019
Charleston, SC 29402

Phone: (843) 377-0900
Fax: (342) 377-0905
Toll Free: (800) 252-3337
E-mail: memberservices@nafc.org
http://www.nafc.org

National Association for Continence (NAFC), originally known as Help for Incontinent People, is a not-for-profit, self-help organization dedicated to improving the quality of life for people with urinary incontinence. Incontinence is a condition in which one loses bladder control. Established in 1982, the organization is a source of education, advocacy, and support to the public and to healthcare professionals regarding the causes, prevention, diagnosis, treatment, and management alternatives for incontinence. NAFC's purpose is to be the leading source of education, advocacy and support to the public and to the health professional about the causes, prevention, diagnosis, treatments, and management alternatives for incontinence. The NAFC's objectives are to de stigmatize incontinence; to provide consumer information; and to provide advocacy and service for those who are affected by this problem. To achieve its objectives, NAFC offers a wide variety of publications and services.

Executive Director: Nancy Muler
Year Established: 1982
Acronym: NAFC

Keywords
Bladder Control; Consumer Education; Incontinence; National Association for Continence; Overactive Bladder; Stress Urinary Incontinence; Urge Incontinence

1901 **National Association for Parents of Children with Visual Impairments (NAPVI)**
P.O. Box 317
Watertown, MA 02472

Phone: (617) 972-7441
Fax: (617) 972-7444
Toll Free: (800) 562-6265
E-mail: napvi@perkins.org
http://www.napvi.org

Established in 1979, the National Association for Parents of Children with Visual Impairments, Inc.,

(NAPVI), is a voluntary, not-for-profit organization dedicated to providing support to the parents of children with visual impairments. The association enables parents to find information and resources for their blind or visually impaired child; helps parents to address the unique needs of visually impaired children who have additional disabilities; and provides parents with leadership, support, and training that enables them to help their children reach their fullest potential. The association also promotes outreach and networking programs; advocates the educational needs and welfare of affected children; and provides referrals to needed services. In addition, the association promotes the development of state and local organizations by and for parents of visually impaired children, and fosters communication and coordination of services among federal, state, and local agencies.

President: Mary Zabelski
Executive Director: Susan LaVenture
Year Established: 1979
Acronym: NAPVI

Keywords
Alstrom's Disease; Aniridia; Aniridia Cerebellar Ataxia Mental Deficiency; Atrophy, Essential Iris; Bardet-Biedl Syndrome; Batten's Disease; Best Vitelliform Macular Dystrophy; Blepharophimosis; Blindness; Carbohydrate Deficient Glycoprotein Syndrome Type Ia; Cat Eye Syndrome; Cataract Dental Syndrome; Cataracts; Chandler's Syndrome; CHARGE Syndrome; Choroideremia; Chromosome 6 Ring; Chromosome 18q Syndrome; Coats' Disease; Congenital Hereditary Endothelia Dystrophy; Crouzon Syndrome; DeMorsier's Syndrome; Essential Iris Atrophy; Fibroplasia, Retrolental; Goldenhar Syndrome; Hallermann-Streiff Syndrome; Hermansky Pudlak Syndrome; Laurence Moon Syndrome; Leber Hereditary Optic Neuropathy; Leber's Congenital Amaurosis; Leber's Optic Atrophy; Lenz Microphthalmia Syndrome; Megalocornea Mental Retardation Syndrome; NAPVI; National Association for Parents of Children with Visual Impairments (NAPVI); Norrie Disease; Oculo Auriculo Vertebral Spectrum; Retinitis Pigmentosa; Retinopathy of Prematurity; Retinoschisis; Rieger Syndrome; Rothmund Thomson Syndrome; Septooptic Dysplasia; Stevens-Johnson Syndrome; Stickler's Syndrome; Visually Impaired; deLange Syndrome (CdLS)

1902 National Association for Pseudoxanthoma Elasticum (NAPE)

8764 Manchester Road
Suite 200
St Louis, MO 63144-2724

Phone: (314) 962-0100
Fax: (314) 962-0100
E-mail: napestlouis@sbcglobal.net
http://www.napxe.org

The National Association for Pseudoxanthoma Elasticum (NAPE), established in 1988, is a not-for-profit organization dedicated to the support and education of patients, their families and friends, and the medical and research profession regarding pseudoxanthoma elasticum (PXE). PXE is a rare connective tissue disease that is inherited and progressive, and affects the elastic tissues of the body. NAPE promotes patient advocacy, provides an educational brochure, produces and distributes quarterly newsletters to affected individuals, families and healthcare professionals, and organize an annual conference to help those with PXE meet other with PXE and provide additional support and education. NAPE also sponsors a program to help members purchase low vision aids that they might not be able to afford otherwise.

President: Frances Benham
Year Established: 1988
Acronym: NAPE

Keywords
Groenblad Strandberg Syndrome; National Association for Pseudoxanthoma Elasticum (NAPE); Pseudoxanthoma Elasticum; PXE

1903 National Association for Visually Handicapped

22 West 21st Street
New York, NY 10010

Phone: (212) 889-3141
Fax: (212) 727-2931
E-mail: staff@navh.org
http://www.navh.org

The National Association for Visually Handicapped provides emotional support; visual aids, technology and training to visually impaired children, adults, and seniors. Founded in 1954, NAVH has helped hundreds of thousands of the "hard of seeing" resume independent, more productive, more dignified lives among their fully sighted peers. The organization also promotes the publication of educational materials and their distribution to schools, libraries, social institutions, and individuals. The association seeks to plan and assist in programs of parent and adult education relating to persons with partial seeing and to assist and encourage the partially seeing to integrate into the mainstream of society. To this end, NAVH publishes brochures, a publications listing, and other notices.

President: Dr. Lorraine H. Marchi
Executive Director: Cesar L. Gomez
Year Established: 1954
Acronym: NAVH

Keywords

Aicardi Syndrome; Alpers Disease; Alstrom's Disease; Aniridia; Aniridia Cerebellar Ataxia Mental Deficiency; Atrophy, Essential Iris; Bardet-Biedl Syndrome; Behcet's Syndrome; Best Vitelliform Macular Dystrophy; Carbohydrate Deficient Glycoprotein Syndrome Type Ia; Cataract Dental Syndrome; Cataracts; Chandler's Syndrome; Choroideremia; Choroiditis Serpiginous; Chromosome 6 Ring; Chromosome 18q Syndrome; Coats' Disease; Cogan Reese Syndrome; Corneal Dystrophy; Dandy Walker Malformation; Dysplasia, Oculo Dento Digital; Epitheliopathy, Acute Posterior Multifocal Placoid Pigment; Essential Iris Atrophy; Fibroplasia, Retrolental; Glaucoma; Hard of Seeing; Hermansky Pudlak Syndrome; Kearns Sayre Disease; Keratoconus; Keratomalacia; Laurence Moon Syndrome; Leber Hereditary Optic Neuropathy; Leber's Congenital Amaurosis; Leber's Optic Atrophy; Lenz Microphthalmia Syndrome; Loken Senior Syndrome; Lowe's Syndrome; Macular Degeneration; Macular Diseases; Maroteaux Lamy Syndrome; Megalocornea Mental Retardation Syndrome; National Association for Visually Handicapped; NAVH; Norrie Disease; Oculocerebral Syndrome with Hypopigmentation; Papillitis; Refsum Disease; Retinitis Pigmentosa; Retinopathy of Prematurity; Retinopathy, Arteriosclerotic; Retinopathy, Diabetic; Retinopathy, Hypertensive; Retinoschisis; Retinoschisis, X-linked Juvenile; Rieger Syndrome; Rosenberg Chutorian Syndrome; Rothmund Thomson Syndrome; Sandhoff Disease; Schwartz Jampel Syndrome; Septooptic Dysplasia; Tolosa Hunt Syndrome; Usher's Syndrome; Visually Impaired; Vogt Koyanagi Harada Syndrome; Waardenburg Syndrome; Weill Marchesani Syndrome; Wolfram Syndrome; X linked Juvenile Retinoschisis

1904 National Association of Anorexia Nervosa and Associated Disorders, Inc.

Box 7
Highland Park, IL 60035

Phone: (847) 831-3438
Fax: (847) 433-4632
E-mail: anad20@aol.com
http://www.anad.org

The National Association of Anorexia Nervosa and Associated Disorders, Inc., (ANAD) is a national, not-for-profit, self-help organization dedicated to increasing understanding of eating disorders and to alleviating the problems of eating disorders, especially anorexia nervosa and bulimia. The association seeks to educate the general public and professionals in the health field to become more aware of eating disorders and appropriate methods of treatment. In addition, the organization encourages and promotes research to discover the causes of eating disorders, methods of prevention, and types of treatments, and to formulate relevant statistics. The National Association of Anorexia Nervosa and Associated Disorders acts as a resource center by gathering and providing educational materials about eating disorders. Other activities sponsored by the organization include networking for mutual support, providing funds to aid those with eating disorders, and encouraging interested individuals and groups to join in seeking cures for these disorders.

President: Vivian Hanson Meehan (1976-Present)
Executive Director: Vivian Hanson Meehan
Year Established: 1976
Acronym: ANAD

Keywords

Anorexia; Anorexia Nervosa; Bulimia; Eating Disorders; National Association of Anorexia Nervosa and Associated Disorders, Inc.

1905 National Association of Laryngectomee Clubs (UK)

Lower Ground Floor
152 Buckingham Palace Road
London, SW1 W9TR, United Kingdom

Phone: +44 (0) 207-730-8585
Fax: +44 (0) 207-730-8584
E-mail: nalcuk@telinco.co.uk
http://www.nalc.ik.com

The National Association of Laryngectomee Clubs (NALC) is a national, not-for-profit organization in the United Kingdom dedicated to providing information, support, and resources to individuals who have undergone surgical removal (laryngectomy) of all or a part of the voice box (larynx) as treatment for laryngeal cancer. The association, which was established in 1976, is committed to offering assistance to clubs and groups of patients across the United Kingdom. Its programs and services include visiting patients and their families before and after surgery; providing advice and support concerning difficulties associated with laryngectomies, such as learning new ways of communicating; and offering a problem-solving and help service for affected individuals, family members and healthcare professionals. The association is also committed to increasing professional awareness concerning laryngectomies and the needs of individuals who undergo such procedures. To help fulfill this goal, association members regularly participate in lectures at nursing schools and demonstrate speech aids.

President: Mr. Ivor Smith
Executive Director: Ms. Vivien Reed (Secretary)
Year Established: 1976
Acronym: NALC

Keywords
National Association of Laryngectomee Clubs (UK)

1906 National Association of the Deaf

814 Thayer Avenue
Suite 250
Silver Spring, MD 20910-4500

Phone: (301) 587-1788
Fax: (301) 587-1791
TDD: (301) 587-1789
E-mail: NADinfo@nad.org
http://www.nad.org

The National Association of the Deaf (NAD) has been fighting for the civil rights of the deaf and hard of hearing Americans since 1880. As a national federation of state associations and affiliates, NAD offers grassroots and youth leadership development, and legal expertise across a broad spectrum of areas. These areas include, but are not limited to, accessibility, education, employment, healthcare, mental health, rehabilitation, technology, telecommunications and transportation. NAD maintains a web site where the general public can obtain information and resources.

President: Andrew Lange
Executive Director: Nancy J. Bloch
Year Established: 1880
Acronym: NAD

Keywords
Deafness; National Association of the Deaf

1907 National Association of the Physically Handicapped, Inc.

754 Staeger Street
Akron, OH 44306-2940

Phone: (330) 724-1994
Toll Free: 7435008
E-mail: trumanjm@aol.com
http://www.naph.net

The National Association of the Physically Handicapped, Inc., (NAPH) is a non-profit organization dedicated to the advancement of the social, economic, and physical welfare of the physically handicapped. NAPH's objectives are to promote public awareness of the needs of handicapped people and to push for government and legislation to meet those needs. Presently, its goals include the adjustment of buildings for handicapped people (e.g., wider doorways and proper ramps for wheelchairs, etc.); equal education and employment opportunities for the handicapped; and, in collaboration with government agencies, civic groups, and other organizations, the implementation of programs to benefit the handicapped.

President: Bernadette Travis
Executive Director: James Truman
Year Established: 1958
Acronym: NAPH

Keywords
Disability Services; National Association of the Physically Handicapped, Inc.; National Association of the Physically Handicapped, Inc. (NAPH)

1908 National Ataxia Foundation

2600 Fernbrook Lane
Suite 119
Minneapolis, MN 55447

Phone: (763) 553-0020
Fax: (763) 553-0167
E-mail: naf@ataxia.org
http://www.ataxia.org/

The National Ataxia Foundation is a national, not-for-profit organization that seeks to identify people with hereditary ataxia and to improve the physical and emotional well being of affected individuals and their families. Hereditary ataxia is a group of progressive, chronic neurological disorders that affect coordination. Established in 1957, the National Ataxia Foundation encourages and supports research to identify the causes and mechanisms of the hereditary ataxias, improve diagnosis, and develop treatment models. It also locates families affected by ataxia or at risk for ataxia in order to offer information and education;

identifies needs and services for purposes of referral; creates and makes available educational programs for ataxia families, healthcare professionals, and the general public; and increases public awareness of hereditary ataxia. In addition, the National Ataxia Foundation provides informational materials, counseling, referrals, and avenues to support groups and is responsive to the needs of its membership by achieving an acceptable balance among the funding of the various programs of education/awareness, patient services, research, administration, and fund-raising. The organization produces informational materials including brochures on hereditary ataxia, financial planning, and health insurance issues.

President: DeNiece Roach (1987-Present)
Executive Director: Donna Gruetzmacher
Year Established: 1957
Acronym: NAF

Keywords
Ataxia Telangiectasia; Ataxia with Vitamin E Deficiency; Ataxia, Friedreich's; Ataxia, Hereditary; Atrophy, Olivopontocerebellar; Kennedy Disease; Marie's Ataxia; Movement Disorders; NAF; National Ataxia Foundation; Olivopontocerebellar Atrophy, Hereditary; OPCA

1909 National Autistic Society

393 City Road
London, EC1V 1NG, United Kingdom

Phone: +44 (0) 207-833-2299
Fax: +44 (0) 207-833-9699
E-mail: nas@nas.org.uk
http://www.autism.org.uk

The National Autistic Society is a non-profit support organization, which exists to champion the rights and interests of all people with autism in the UK and to ensure that they and their families receive quality services appropriate to their needs. It has developed a range of educational and support services; runs schools and adult centers; offers families and caretakers information, advice and support; works to improve awareness of autism; offers a diagnostic and assessment service; and provides training and promotes research. Activities include: a National Autism Helpline for parents, caretakers, families and people with autism; an Information Centre for interested professionals, students, general public that draw on a research database covering all aspects of autism (including Asperger's syndrome and pervasive develop-

mental disorder); publication and distribution of a wide range of literature on autism (including the journal, "Communication").

President: Jane Asher
Executive Director: Vernon Beauchamp
Year Established: 1962
Acronym: NAS

Keywords
Asperger Syndrome; Autism; Autism, Infantile; Kanner Syndrome; National Autistic Society

1910 National Batten Disease Registry

New York Institute for Basic Research in Developmental Disabilities
1050 Forest Hill Road
Staten Island, NY 10314

Phone: (718) 494-5201
Fax: (718) 982-6346
Toll Free: (800) 952-9628
E-mail: BattenKW@aol.com

The National Batten Disease Registry was established in 1987 to identify families affected with Batten disease and provide physicians and researchers with a computerized central data bank of vital information. Batten disease is the juvenile form of a group of progressive, inherited neurological diseases known as neuronal ceroid lipofuscinoses (NCL). It occurs mostly in families of northern European Scandinavian ancestry, and is marked by rapidly progressive vision failure and neurological disturbances, which may include deterioration of intellect. Since its inception, the registry has expanded to provide additional services for both physicians and families. The information collected by the registry is available to all researchers working on Batten disease. The registry works closely with the Batten Disease Support and Research Association (BDSRA), gathering and disseminating information on Batten disease. It provides parents with the latest medical developments, names of nearby physicians, and access to a second opinion. The registry also puts parents in contact with other families.

Executive Director: Dr. Krystyna E. Wisniewski
Year Established: 1987

Keywords
Batten Disease; National Batten Disease Registry

1911 National Bone Marrow Transplant Link

20411 W. 12 Mile Road
Suite 108
Southfield, MI 48076

Phone: (248) 358-1886
Fax: (248) 358-1889
Toll Free: (800) 546-5268
E-mail: info@nbmtlink.org
http://www.nbmtlink.org

The National Bone Marrow Transplant Link (nbmtLink) is a not-for-profit, voluntary organization dedicated to helping patients, as well as their caregivers, families, and the healthcare community, meet the many challenges of bone marrow/stem cell transplants (BMT) by providing vital information and support services. Each year, thousands of patients turn to bone marrow/stem cell transplants to treat cancer and other life-threatening illnesses. While a BMT can be a very effective treatment, it is a long and demanding process for patients and their loved ones. Since its founding in 1992, the National Bone Marrow Transplant Link has helped thousands of individuals worldwide through its comprehensive web site, publications for patients and caregivers, Emmy Award winning video, volunteer peer support programs, resource referrals and educational forums. The National Bone Marrow Transplant Link is funded through private, foundation and corporate donations.

President: Myra Jacobs (Director)
Year Established: 1992
Acronym: National BMT Link/nbmtLink

Keywords
Anemia; BMT; Bone Marrow Tranplant; Cord Blood Transplant; Hyper IgM Syndrome; Leukemia; Lymphoma; Myelodysplastic Syndromes; Myelofibrosis, Idiopathic; National BMT Link; National Bone Marrow Transplant Link; NBMTLink; Non-Hodgkin's Disease; SCT; Stem Cell Transplant; Wiskott Aldrich Syndrome; X Linked Lymphoproliferative Syndrome

1912 National Brain Tumor Foundation

22 Battery Street
Suite 612
San Francisco, CA 94111-5520

Phone: (415) 834-9970
Fax: (415) 834-9980
Toll Free: (800) 934-2873
E-mail: nbtf@braintumor.org
http://www.braintumor.org

The National Brain Tumor Foundation is a national, not-for-profit, voluntary organization that serves as a comprehensive center for information regarding resources and support services for people whose lives are affected by brain tumor disease. Established in 1981, the National Brain Tumor Foundation also provides financial support for investigational studies into the causes, prevention, and treatments of brain tumors. To these ends, the National Brain Tumor Foundation has funded basic and applied laboratory research and clinical trials of new treatments at major institutions in the United States. The organization has also supported research into quality of life issues that regularly confront people with brain tumors. A comprehensive guide is available for affected individuals and their families who want to learn more about brain tumors. The National Brain Tumor Foundation also produces a variety of educational materials including a newsletter entitled, "Search." Affected individuals and family members may also receive referrals to a network of support groups throughout the United States.

President: Jan McCormack
Executive Director: Robert L. Tufel, MSW, MPH
Year Established: 1981
Acronym: NBTF

Keywords
Adenoma, Pituitary; Astrocytoma; Astrocytoma, Benign; Astrocytoma, Juvenile Piplocytic; Astrocytoma, Malignant; CNS Lymphoma; Carcinomatosis, Meningeal; Chordoma; Craniopharyngioma; Ependymoma; Ganglioneuroma; Glioblastoma Multiforme; Glioma, Brain Stem; Glioma, Mixed; Gliomas; Medulloblastoma; Meningioma; National Brain Tumor Foundation; NBTF; Networking; Neurofibromatosis; Oligodendroglioma; Pseudotumor Cerebri; Schwannoma; Support Groups; Tuberous Sclerosis; Tumors, Brain; Tumors, Pineal; Tumors, Primitive Neuroectodermal; Tumors, Vascular; Turcot Syndrome

1913 National Center for Chromosome Inversions

282 SE Anastasia Street
Lake City, FL 32025-1730

Phone: (386) 752-1548
E-mail: ncfci@msn.com

The National Center for Chromosome Inversions is a non-profit, voluntary health organization that helps support basic medical research on chromosomal inversions and functions as a point of connection for parents of affected children. Chromosome inversions are a rare defect in which two or more portions of a chromosome break off, become separated, and rejoin the chromosome in the wrong order. Established in 1992, the National Center for Chromosome Inversions has a variety of educational materials.

President: Jacqueline Barker (1995-Present)
Executive Director: Jacqueline Barker
Year Established: 1993
Acronym: NCFCI

Keywords
Cat Eye Syndrome; Chromosomal Inversions; Inversions (Chromosomal); National Center for Chromosome Inversions

1914 National Center for Learning Disabilities

381 Park Avenue South
#1401
New York, NY 10016

Phone: (212) 545-7510
Fax: (212) 545-9665
Toll Free: (888) 575-7373
E-mail: help@ncld.org
http://www.ld.org

The National Center for Learning Disabilities (NCLD) works to ensure that the nation's 15 million children, adolescents, and adults with learning disabilities have every opportunity to succeed in school, work, and life. It provides essential information to parents, professionals, and individuals with learning disabilities, promotes research and programs to foster effective learning, and advocates for policies to protect and strengthen educational rights and opportunities.

Executive Director: James H. Wendorf
Year Established: 1977
Acronym: NCLD

Keywords
Attention Deficit Hyperactivity Disorder; Dyslexia; Learning Disabilities; National Center for Learning Disabilities; NCLD; Triplo X Syndrome

1915 National Cervical Cancer Coalition (NCCC)

2625 Alcatraz Avenue
Suite 282
Berkeley, CA 94705

Phone: (818) 909-3849
Fax: (818) 780-8199

E-mail: info@nccc-online.org
http://www.nccc-online.org

The National Cervical Cancer Coalition (NCCC) is a voluntary, not-for-profit organization dedicated to educating the public and healthcare professionals about issues related to cervical cancer. (The cervix is the neck of the uterus or the lower portion of the uterus that extends into the vagina.) Prior to the development of cancer, abnormal changes occur within cells on the surface of the cervix (cervical dysplasia) that may be detected by a cervical smear test known as a "Pap smear." Abnormal cervical smears indicate the need for further investigation and possible treatment. The NCCC serves as an independent coalition of women's groups, affected individuals and family members, healthcare providers, companies, and associations. Established in 1997 and currently consisting of approximately 800 members, the coalition is dedicated to enhancing awareness of the traditional Pap smear and new technologies, treatments for cervical dysplasia and cancer, and reimbursement issues concerning cervical cancer screening.

President: Alan Kaye (1997 to Present)
Executive Director: Hollis Forster
Year Established: 1997
Acronym: NCCC

Keywords
National Cervical Cancer Coalition (NCCC)

1916 National CFIDS Foundation, Inc.

103 Aletha Road
Needham, MA 02492-3931

Phone: (781) 449-3535
Fax: (781) 449-8606
E-mail: gailronda@aol.com
http://www.ncf-net.org

The National CFIDS Foundation, Inc., is an all-volunteer group dedicated to finding the cause and subsequent treatment of myalgic encephalomyelitis, also known as chronic fatigue syndrome and chronic fatigue immune dysfunction syndrome. The goals are to serve as an advocate for those affected by chronic fatigue syndrome, fund research, and provide accurate and timely information about this disease and related disorders. Established in 1987, the National CFIDS Foundation is a voluntary, not-for-profit organization providing educational materials, patient networking, patient advocacy and other services throughout the United States.

President: Gail Kansky
Executive Director: Jill McLaughlin
Year Established: 1987
Acronym: NCF

Keywords
CFS; Chronic Fatigue Syndrome; Fibromyalgia; ME; Myalgic Encephalomyelitis; National CFIDS Foundation, Inc.

1917 **National Childhood Cancer Foundation**
P.O. Box 60012
Suite 402
Arcadia, CA 91066-6012

Phone: (626) 447-1674
Fax: (626) 447-6359
Toll Free: (800) 458-6223
E-mail: nccf-info@nccf.org
http://www.nccf.org/nccf/

The National Childhood Cancer Foundation (NCCF) is a charitable foundation that raises funds to support the research work of the Children's Oncology Group (COG) at over 235 hospitals throughout North America, and at sites in Australia and Europe. All members collaborate to standardize diagnostic, treatment and response criteria for each type of childhood cancer. Treatment and research results from all hospitals are collated in the COG Patient Data Center. Effective new treatments are shared with members of the network and physicians throughout the world who treat children with cancer. NCCF also advocates on behalf of children with cancer and their families. The vision of NCCF is for a world free of the devastating impact of cancer upon infants, children and young adults.

President: Paul T. Burke
Executive Director: Jenina Garrett (VP of Operations & Controller)
Year Established: 1990
Acronym: NCCF

Keywords
ALL; AML; Cancer; Childhood; Children's Oncology Group; CureSearch; Ewing's Sarcoma; Leukemia; Lymphoma; National Childhood Cancer Foundation; Neuroblastoma; Non Hodgkins Lymphoma; Osteogenic Sarcoma; Retinoblastoma; Rhabdomyosarcoma; Sarcoma; Wilms' Tumor

1918 **National Chronic Fatigue Syndrome & Fibromyalgia Association**
P.O. Box 18426
Kansas City, MO 64133

Phone: (816) 313-2000
Fax: (816) 524-6782
E-mail: information@ncfsfa.org
http://www.ncfsfa.org

The National Chronic Fatigue Syndrome & Fibromyalgia Association is a voluntary health organization that was incorporated in 1988. The association was formed to educate and inform the public about the nature and impact of chronic fatigue syndrome and related disorders. In 1993, fibromyalgia was added to the organization's educational efforts. The primary focus of the National Chronic Fatigue Syndrome & Fibromyalgia Association is to offer scientifically accurate information to people with chronic fatigue syndrome and fibromyalgia. Brochures, booklets, and videos are available from the organization. A periodic newsletter and fact sheet are also produced and distributed by the organization.

President: Orvalene Prewitt (1988 to Present)
Executive Director: Orvalene Prewitt
Year Established: 1988
Acronym: NCFSFA

Keywords
Fatigue Syndrome; Fibromyalgia; Granuloma, Eosinophilic; Hospice Hands; Myalgic Encephalomyelitis; National Chronic Fatigue Syndrome & Fibromyalgia Association; NCFSFA

1919 **National Coalition for Cancer Survivorship**
1010 Wayne Avenue
Suite 770
Silver Spring, MD 20910-5600

Phone: (301) 650-9127
Fax: (301) 565-9670
Toll Free: (877) 622-7937
E-mail: infor@canceradvocacy.org
http:// www.canceradvocacy.org

The National Coalition for Cancer Survivorship is a survivor-led organization, in the country and a highly respected authentic voice at the federal level, advocating for quality cancer care for all Americans and empowering cancer survivors. NCCS believes in evidence-based advocacy for systemic changes at the federal level in how the nation researches, regulates, finances and delivers quality cancer care. In 2004, NCCS launched Cancer Advocacy Now (CAN!), a legislative advocacy network that seeks to involve constituents from across the country in federal cancer-related issues. Patient education is also a priority for NCCS. NCCS offers educational materials and tools to help people advocate for their own care or that of someone they love. These materials include the award-winning Cancer Survival Toolbox®, and publications about employment rights, talking with one's doctor, maintaining hope throughout the cancer experience.

President: Ellen L. Stovall (President and CEO)
Year Established: 1986
Acronym: NCCS

Keywords
Cancer; National Coalition for Cancer Survivorship

1920 National Congenital CMV Disease Registry

Feigin Center 1102 Bates Street
Suite 1150
MC 3-2371
Houston, TX 77030-2399

Phone: (832) 824-4387
Fax: (832) 825-4347
E-mail: cmv@bcm.tmc.edu
http://www.bcm.tmc.edu/pedi/infect/cmv

The National Congenital CMV Disease Registry, based at Baylor College of Medicine in Houston, Texas, collects information on infants born after 1990 with congenital cytomegalovirus (CMV). The registry is committed to identifying disease patterns over time; describing factors that may increase a mother's risk of delivering an infant with congenital cyto-megalovirus infection; and providing the foundation for future intervention programs and collaborative research. All newborns with a confirmed diagnosis of congenital CMV are eligible to be registered. To do so, have the pediatrician obtain and complete our registry form. In addition to these activities, the Congenital CMV Disease Registry functions as a national clearinghouse for information about congenital CMV. It distributes reprints of medical articles on human cytomegalovirus infection, publishes a newsletter entitled "CMV Updates," and maintains a CMV Parent-To-Parent Support Network, and publishes an annual newsletter.

President: Gail Demmler (Prinicipal Investigator & Director)
Executive Director: Carol Griesser, RN
Year Established: 1990

Keywords
CMV; CMV, Congenital; Cytomegalovirus Infection; Cytomegalovirus, Congenital; National Congenital CMV Disease Registry

1921 National Creutzfeldt-Jakob Surveillance Unit

Bryan Matthews Building
Western General Hospital
Edinburgh, EH4 2XU, United Kingdom

Phone: +44 (0) 131-537-2128
Fax: +44 (0) 131-343-1404
E-mail: jan.mackenzie@ed.au.uk
http://www.cjd.ed.ac.uk

National Creutzfeldt-Jakob Surveillance Unit (NCJDSU) is a patient advocacy, research organization located in the United Kingdom. Founded in 1990, NCJDSU monitors Creutzfeldt-Jakob disease (CJD) in the UK in order to identify any changes in the pattern of disease that might be attributable to the emergence of bovine spongiform encephalopathy, a variant of CJD. CJD is an extremely rare degenerative brain disorder characterized by the sudden development of rapidly progressive neurological and neuromuscular symptoms. NCJDSU also identifies all cases of any form of CJD and studies the clinical features and diagnosis of these illnesses.

Executive Director: Dr. R. Knight (2005-2007)
Year Established: 1990
Acronym: NCJDSU

Keywords
Advocacy; Bovine Spongiform Encephalopathy; CJD; Creutzfeldt Jakob Disease; Jakob's Disease; Mad Cow Disease; National Creutzfeldt Jakob Surveillance Unit; National Creutzfeldt-Jakob Surveillance Unit; NCJDSU; Registry; Research

1922 National Deaf Children's Society

15 Dufferin Street
London, EC1Y 8UR, United Kingdom

Phone: +44 (0) 207-490-8656
Fax: +44 (0) 207-251-5020
E-mail: ndcs@ndcs.org.uk
http://www.ndcs.org.uk

National Deaf Children's Society (NDCS) is a voluntary organization located in the United Kingdom. Members include parents, other relatives, caregivers, and healthcare professionals working with children who have no sense of sound. NDCS supports parents in helping their children to develop their skills and abilities. The society offers support groups, research, education and referrals to assist affected children and their families in reaching their goals.

Acronym: NDCS

Keywords
Deaf Children; Deafness; National Deaf Children's Society; NDCS; Research; Support Groups

1923 National Dissemination Center for Children with Disabilities
P.O. Box 1492
Washington, D.C. 20013

Phone: (202) 884-8200
Fax: (202) 884-8441
Toll Free: (800) 695-0285
TDD: (800) 695-0285
E-mail: nichcy@aed.org
http://www.nichcy.org

The National Dissemination Center for Children with Disabilities (NICHCY) is an information clearinghouse that provides information on disabilities in children, education rights, and disability-related issues. Children up to age 22 are the special focus. NICHCY provides personal responses to questions on early intervention, special education, individualized education programs, and family and transitional issues. At NICHCY's web site, www.nichcy.org., one can access all of the center's publications, as well as an online listing of national organizations and conferences. Free and low-cost publications include resource sheets, fact sheets, briefing papers and parent guides.

Executive Director: Suzanne Ripley
Year Established: 1982
Acronym: NICHCY

Keywords
Disability Information; Disability Services; Early Intervention; National Dissemination Center for Children with Disabilities; NICHCY; Penta X Syndrome; Special Education; Students with Disabilities; Triplo X Syndrome

1924 National Down Syndrome Congress
1370 Center Drive
Suite 102
Atlanta, GA 30338

Phone: (770) 604-9500
Fax: (770) 604-9898
Toll Free: (800) 232-6372
E-mail: info@ndsccenter.org
http://www.ndsccenter.org

The National Down Syndrome Congress (NDSC), a not-for-profit organization established in 1971, is committed to building a sense of community among all those concerned with Down syndrome. The congress provides leadership through of public policy and encourages ethically responsible research in all aspects of Down syndrome. It seeks to educate professionals, parents, and the community about Down syndrome, and fosters self-advocacy, rights, and full participation in all aspects of community life. The NDSC is also dedicated to developing position statements on major issues; providing a network that links state and local groups and affiliates; and enhancing relationships within the organizations' communities and the broader disability community. The National Down Syndrome Congress provides a telephone hotline offering information on any subject related to Down syndrome. It conducts an annual convention, provides appropriate referrals, and coordinates a local parent group network and maintains directory of such groups to promote parent-to-parent and parent-to-professional networking.

President: Judy Martz
Executive Director: David C. Tolleson
Year Established: 1971
Acronym: NDSC

Keywords
Down Syndrome; National Down Syndrome Congress; Trisomy 21 Syndrome; Trisomy G Syndrome

1925 National Down Syndrome Society
666 Broadway
8th Floor
New York, NY 10012-2317

Phone: (212) 460-9330
Fax: (212) 979-2873
Toll Free: (800) 221-4602
E-mail: info@ndss.org
http://www.ndss.org/

The mission of the National Down Syndrome Society (NDSS) is to benefit people with Down syndrome and their families through leadership in education, research, and advocacy. Down syndrome is a chromosomal disorder caused by an error in cell division that results in the presence of an additional chromosome 21. It occurs in one of 800 live births, in all races and economic groups. NDSS was established in 1979 to ensure that all people with Down syndrome have the opportunity to achieve their full potential in community life.

President: Thomas J. O'Neill
Executive Director: Alan Brownstein
Year Established: 1979
Acronym: NDSS

Keywords
Down Syndrome; National Down Syndrome Society; NDSS; Trisomy 21

1926 National Dysautonomia Research Foundation

P.O. Box 301
Red Wing, MN 55066-0102

Phone: (651) 267-0525
Fax: (651) 267-0524
E-mail: ndrf@ndrf.org
http://www.ndrf.org

The National Dysautonomia Research Foundation (NDRF) is a national, not-for-profit, voluntary organization dedicated to providing information and support to individuals affected by dysfunction of the autonomic nervous system (dysautonomia). The autonomic nervous system controls involuntary (automatic or reflex) activities of the organs, blood vessels, glands, and a variety of tissues in the body. Many disorders may be associated with dysautonomia including Shy-Drager syndrome (multiple system atrophy), postural orthostatic tachycardia syndrome (POTS), familial dysautonomia, and neurocardiogenic syncope. The NDRF strives to provide contacts to additional organizations that may be of assistance to individuals with dysautonomia; advocates on behalf of affected individuals in support of ongoing research efforts; supplies news organizations with timely and accurate information on dysautonomia; and raises funds for research. The foundation provides a variety of educational materials including a regular newsletter.

President: Daniel P. Smith
Executive Director: Linda Smith
Year Established: 1997
Acronym: NDRF

Keywords
Autonomic Disorders, Central; Autonomic Disorders, Peripheral; Autonomic Failure, Pure; Catecholamine Disorders; Chagas Disease; Diabetic Autonomic Failure; Dysautonomia; Guillain Barre Syndrome; Hypotension, Orthostatic; Hypovolemia, Idiopathic; Mitral Valve Prolapse Syndrome; Multiple System Atrophy; National Dysautonomia Research Foundation; NDRF; Neuropathy, Autonomic; Orthostatic Intolerance Syndrome; Parkinson's Disease; Pheochromocytoma; Polyneuropathy, Acute Idiopathic; Postural Orthostatic Tachycardia Syndrome; POTS; Shy-Drager Syndrome; Syncope, Neurocardiogenic

1927 National Eating Disorders Association

603 Stewart Street
Suite 803
Seattle, WA 98101

Phone: (206) 382-3587
Fax: (206) 292-9890
Toll Free: (800) 931-2237
E-mail: info@NationalEatingDisorders.org
http://www.nationaleatingdisorders.org

The mission of the National Eating Disorders Association is to eliminate eating disorders and body dissatisfaction by employing comprehensive strategies that help prevent young people from developing eating disorders; insuring that those who suffer from eating disorders receive information and support; promoting research into causes, prevention, and treatment; and advocating for public policies that recognize eating disorders as serious mental illnesses, promote increased access to care, and provide funding for research, prevention, and treatment. Eating disorders include anorexia, bulimia, and binge eating.

President: Pauline Powers, MD (2005-2006)
Executive Director: Lynn Grefe, MA
Year Established: 1987
Acronym: N.E.D.A.

Keywords
Anorexia Nervosa; Binge Eating; Bulimia Nervosa; Compulsive Overeating; Eating Disorders; Eating Disorders Awareness and Prevention, Inc. (EDAP); National Eating Disorders Association

1928 National Eosinophilia Myalgia Syndrome Network

Jann Heston, President
P.O. Box 3016
155 Delaware Avenue
Lexington, OH 44904-1212

Phone: (614) 583-5720
Fax: (614) 737-7384
E-mail: NEMSN2005@aol.com
http://www.NEMSN.org

The National Eosinophilia-Myalgia Syndrome Network, Inc., (NEMSN) is a not-for-profit organization founded in 1995 to help eosinophilia myalgia syndrome (EMS) survivors and their families. EMS has been associated with the ingestion of large amounts of contaminated L-tryptophan, a dietary supplement often sold in health food stores. It is a disease of abrupt onset causing severe, disabling, chronic muscle pain, skin symptoms and other neurotoxic reactions. The NEMSN offers patient education, networking and advocacy to patients in the United States, Canada, the UK, Australia, and other areas though the Internet. NEMSN also offers information and education to health professionals.

President: Jann Heston
Year Established: 1995
Acronym: NEMSN

Keywords
National Eosinophilia Myalgia Syndrome Network; NEMSN.org

1929 National Eye Care Project

655 Beach Street
San Francisco, CA 94109-1336

Fax: (415) 561-8567
Toll Free: (800) 222-3937
E-mail: pubserv@aao.org
http://www.eyecareamerica.org

The National Eye Care Project, established in 1986, is a not-for-profit organization dedicated to providing medical and surgical eye care to the financially disadvantaged elderly population. The program is designed so that volunteer ophthalmologists can provide eye care at no out-of-pocket cost to the individual regardless of insurance coverage (or lack thereof). In order to qualify for this program, the patient must be at least 65 years of age, have citizenship or legal residency in the United States, must demonstrate a need

for financial aid, and must have no access to an ophthalmologist or an alternative method of receiving care (e.g., HMO, veteran's hospital). Program activities include patient advocacy, patient and general education, brochures, pamphlets, and referrals.

Executive Director: Betty Lucas
Year Established: 1986
Acronym: NECP

Keywords
Eye Diseases; National Eye Care Project; NECP; Visual Disorders

1930 National Federation of the Blind

1800 Johnson Street
Baltimore, MD 21230

Phone: (410) 659-9314
Fax: (410) 685-5653
E-mail: nfb@nfb.org
http://www.nfb.org

The National Federation of the Blind is a national, voluntary, not-for-profit organization dedicated to providing information and support to individuals who are blind, their families, and professionals; ensuring complete integration of the blind into society; and acting as a vehicle for collective self-expression of the blind. Established in 1940, the organization, which has over 50,000 members, has more than 700 affiliates throughout the United States and Puerto Rico. The federation engages in family advocacy; provides a talking newspaper using a touch-tone telephone; oversees America's Jobline with the Department of Labor; offers referrals and scholarships; and assists in the development and evaluation of technology for blind individuals. The federation provides support referrals and a variety of aids and devices for blind and visually impaired individuals. It promotes and supports research.

President: Marc Maurer (1986-Present)
Year Established: 1940
Acronym: NFB

Keywords
Blindness; Diabetes and Blindness; National Federation of the Blind; Retinitis Pigmentosa; Visually Impaired

1931 National Fetal AntiConvulsant Syndrome Association

P.O. Box 7416
Annan, DG12 5ET, United Kingdom

Phone: +44 (0) 1461-20-6870
Fax: +44 (0) 1461-20-6-870
E-mail: facsline3@aol.com
http://www.facsline.org

The National Fetal AntiConvulsant Syndrome Association provides advice and support to families and health workers involved with children who have been affected by anticonvulsant drugs prescribed for their mothers during pregnancy. The major problems encountered include spina bifida, cleft palate, congenital heart disease, kidney abnormalities, and limb defects. There is also an increased incidence of minor birth defects, including learning problems and speech delay. The association works to increase awareness of these various problems, to put families in touch with each other, to encourage families in their quest for a firm diagnosis, to ensure that future mothers are made aware of risks, and to promote and participate in research.

President: Rheane O'Neill
Executive Director: Same as above.
Year Established: 1996
Acronym: NFACSA

Keywords
Fetal Anticonvulsant Syndrome; Fetal Carbamezapine Syndrome; Fetal Hydantoin Syndrome; Fetal Valproate Syndrome; National Fetal AntiConvulsant Syndrome Association

1932   National Foundation for Ectodermal Dysplasias
410 East Main Street
P.O. Box 114
Mascoutah, IL 62258-0114

Phone: (618) 566-2020
Fax: (618) 566-4718
E-mail: info@nfed.org
http://www.nfed.org

The National Foundation for Ectodermal Dysplasias (NFED), which was established in 1981, is a not-for-profit service organization committed to being the authoritative resource for information on the ectodermal dysplasia (ED) syndromes; providing services that meet the physical, emotional, informational, and social needs of affected individuals and their families; and supporting research on the ED syndromes. The ED syndromes are a group of rare inherited disorders that typically affect the hair, teeth, nails, and/or skin. The foundation provides informational materials and

support for families affected by ED syndromes in the United States and around the world. It also provides medical and dental professionals with useful information on early diagnosis and treatment options. The NFED maintains a database of healthcare professionals who have experience in treating people with ED.

President: Keith Throm (2002-Present)
Executive Director: Mary Kaye Richter
Year Established: 1981
Acronym: NFED

Keywords
CHANDS; Christ SiemansTouraine Syndrome; Clouston Syndrome; ED; EEC Syndrome; Ectodermal Dysplasia; Ectodermal Dysplasia, Anhidrotic; Ectodermal Dysplasia, Hypohidrotic; Ectrodactyly Ectodermal Dysplasia Cleft Lip/Palate; Ellis-van Creveld Syndrome; Hay Well's Syndrome; IP; Incontinentia Pigmenti; Naegeli Syndrome; National Foundation for Ectodermal Dysplasias; ODD Syndrome; Oculo Dento Digital Dysplasia; Pachyonychia Congenita; Rapp Hodgkin Ectodermal Dysplasia; Rapp Hodgkin Syndrome; Schopf Schultz Passarge Syndrome; Tooth and Nail Syndrome; Tricho Dento Osseous Syndrome; Trichorhinophalangeal Syndrome Type I; Trichorhinophalangeal Syndrome Type II; Trichorhinophalangeal Syndrome Type III; Witkop Ectodermal Dysplasia

1933   National Foundation for Facial Reconstruction
317 East 34th Street
Room 901
New York, NY 10016

Phone: (212) 263-6656
Fax: (212) 263-7534
Toll Free: (800) 422-3223
E-mail: whitney@nffr.org
http://www.nffr.org

The National Foundation for Facial Reconstruction is a not-for-profit organization dedicated to helping people affected by craniofacial disorders lead productive and fulfilling lives. Established in 1951, the National Foundation for Facial Reconstruction, through its support of the Institute of Reconstructive Plastic Surgery at New York University Medical Center, provides assistance to those affected by craniofacial conditions. The foundation's broad programs include sponsorship of medical research; professional training; social, psychological, and financial assistance, and programs of public education. Educational materials produced and distributed by the foundation include a variety of informative brochures.

Executive Director: Whitney Burnett
Year Established: 1951
Acronym: NFFR

Keywords
Apert Syndrome; Branchio Oculo Facial Syndrome; Cleft Lip; Cleft Palate; Craniofacial Anomalies; Craniofacial Conditions; Craniometaphyseal Dysplasia; Facial Difference; Fraser Syndrome; Marshall Syndrome; Maxillonasal Dysplasia, Binder Type; National Foundation for Facial Reconstruction; Oral Facial Digital Syndrome; Oto Palato Digital Syndrome Types I and II; Pallister W Syndrome; Sakati Syndrome; Shprintzen VCF Syndrome; Summitt Syndrome

1934 National Foundation for Transplants
1102 Brookfield Road
Suite 200
Memphis, TN 38119

Phone: (901) 684-1697
Fax: (901) 684-1128
Toll Free: (800) 489-3863
E-mail: info@transplants.org
http://www.transplants.org

The National Foundation for Transplants (NFT) is a national, not-for-profit organization dedicated to helping individuals who are in need of organ or tissue transplants through financial assistance, advocacy, and emotional support. NFT sets up local fund-raising campaigns in honor of patients enrolled with NFT. Friends, relatives, and others in the patient's community conduct the campaign with the training, guidance and direction of NFT's professional staff. Money raised enables NFT to pay for the patient's outstanding transplant-related bills. In addition, NFT provides advocacy for the patient and his or her family concerning billing and hospital deposit issues, and provides support to patients and their families in times of stress.

President: Larry Pardue
Executive Director: Jackie Hancock, Jr.
Year Established: 1983
Acronym: NFT

Keywords
Bone Marrow; Donation; Eisenmenger Syndrome; Financial Help; Help with Transplants; National Foundation for Transplants; NFT; Organ Transplant Fund, Inc.; Patient Fundraising; Transplant Costs; Transplant Finances; Transplantation, Organ

1935 National Fragile X Foundation
P.O. Box 190488
San Francisco, CA 94119

Phone: (925) 938-9300
Fax: (925) 938-9315
Toll Free: (800) 688-8765
E-mail: NATLFX@FragileX.org
http://www.FragileX.org

The National Fragile X Foundation is a non-profit organization which unites the fragile X community to enrich lives through educational and emotional support, promote public and professional awareness, and advance research toward improved treatments and a cure for fragile X syndrome. Fragile X syndrome is an inherited defect of the X chromosome that can cause mental impairment, including retardation and autism. Established in 1984, the National Fragile X Foundation produces a variety of educational and support materials. These materials include a web site with over 1500 pages of information, a free handbook and brochure, a quarterly journal, pamphlets, and numerous books, videos and CDs. The NFXF also holds international conferences for families and professionals and provides grants for clinical and basic science research. In addition, the foundation maintains an 800 number to provide information, referrals and support. The NFXF is also the national organization for Fragile X - associated Tremor.

President: John Harrigan
Executive Director: Robert Miller
Year Established: 1984
Acronym: NFXF

Keywords
Ataxia; Autism; Early Menopause; Fragile X Syndrome; FXTAS; Marker X Syndrome; Martin Bell Syndrome; National Fragile X Foundation; PDD; Premature Ovarian Failure (POF); Tremor; X-Linked Mental Retardation and Macroorchidism

1936 National Gaucher Foundation, Inc.
61 General Early Drive
Harpers Ferry, WV 25425

Phone: (304) 725-6078
Fax: (304) 725-6429

Toll Free: (800) 428-2437
E-mail: ngf@gaucherdisease.org
http://www.gaucherdisease.org

The National Gaucher Foundation is a not-for-profit organization that supports medical research into causes of Gaucher disease. Gaucher disease is a rare metabolic disorder characterized by the accumulation of a fatty substance, a lipid called glucocerebrosidase. The most common symptoms of Gaucher disease are enlargement of the liver and spleen, anemia, reduced platelets (resulting in easy bruising and long clotting times), bone infarctions often leading to damage to the shoulder or hip joints, and a generalized demineralization of the bones (osteoporosis) that can lead to spontaneous fractures. Founded in 1984, the National Gaucher Foundation encourages scientific investigation into developing treatments for Gaucher disease. The organization hopes that this research will ultimately lead to a cure for the disease. In addition to funding vital research, the National Gaucher Foundation offers an extensive range of services to people with Gaucher disease and their families. These services include financial assistance and patient and physician education programs. The foundation also publishes a quarterly newsletter.

President: Dr. Robin Ely Berman
Executive Director: Rhonda P. Buyers
Year Established: 1984
Acronym: NGF

Keywords
Gaucher Disease; Gaucher Disease (Infantile); Gaucher Disease, Norrbottnian; National Gaucher Foundation, Inc.

1937 National Graves' Disease Foundation
P.O. Box 8387
Fleming Island, FL 32006

Phone: (904) 278-9488
E-mail: nancy@ngdf.org
http://www.ngdf.org

The National Graves' Disease Foundation (NGDF) is a national, voluntary, not-for-profit organization dedicated to providing resources, referrals, and current medical information to people with Graves' disease. Information provided by the foundation incorporates a multidisciplinary approach to the treatment of Graves' disease. The foundation also promotes professional education through lectures and forums, and public education through the distribution of literature,

lectures, and presentations in the media and the community. Established in 1990, the National Graves' Disease Foundation offers a one-on-one individual support network and assists in the development of locally based support groups. It establishes liaison relationships with major hospitals and research institutions, both nationally and internationally. The National Graves' Disease Foundation's Medical and Advisory Board consists of representatives from a variety of disciplines who play essential roles in the treatment and support of individuals with Graves' disease (e.g., endocrinology, surgery, ophthalmology, pharmacology, internal medicine, and family practice). The National Graves' Disease Foundation offers a variety of educational materials to patients, their families, healthcare professionals, and the general public through its computer database, bulletins, brochures, newsletters, videos, and audiotapes.

President: Nancy Hord Patterson
Executive Director: Same as above.
Year Established: 1990
Acronym: NGDF

Keywords
Graves' Disease; National Graves' Disease Foundation

1938 National Hansen's Disease Programs
1770 Physicians Park Drive
Baton Rouge, LA 70816

Phone: (225) 756-3763
Fax: (225) 756-3806
Toll Free: (800) 642-2477
E-mail: mtemplet@hrsa.gov
http://www.bphc.hrsa.gov/nhdp/

The National Hansen's Disease Programs (NHDP), a service of the Bureau of Primary Health Care of the U.S. Department of Health and Human Services, is primarily responsible for inpatient and outpatient care and treatment of Hansen's disease (leprosy). In addition to providing clinical inpatient programs in Baton Rouge, LA, NHDP coordinates outpatient programs throughout the United States, conducts professional education programs, and oversees a research program aimed at improving prevention, detection, and treatment of Hansen's disease.

Keywords
Hansen's Disease; Leprosy; National Hansen's Disease Programs

1939 National Headache Foundation
820 North Orleans
Suite 217
Chicago, IL 60610-3132

Fax: (312) 460-9049
Toll Free: (888) 643-5552
E-mail: info@headaches.org
http://www.headaches.org

Established in 1970, the National Headache Foundation is a not-for-profit organization dedicated to serving as resource to affected individuals, their families, and the physicians who treat them. The organization is also committed to promoting research into the causes of, and treatments for, headaches as well as increasing awareness among the public concerning the seriousness of headaches and the need for understanding and continuity of care for affected individuals. The National Headache Foundation funds ongoing medical research; sponsors public and professional education seminars across the country; and has a nationwide network of local support groups. In addition, the foundation, which functions as a clearinghouse of information on headaches, provides a bimonthly newsletter, brochures, and audiotapes and videotapes. Some materials are available in Spanish.

Executive Director: Suzanne E. Simons
Year Established: 1970
Acronym: NHF

Keywords
Cluster Headache; Headache (Cluster); Headaches; Migraine; National Headache Foundation

1940 National Hemophilia Foundation
116 West 32nd Street
11th Floor
New York, NY 10001

Phone: (212) 328-3700
Fax: (212) 328-3799
Toll Free: (800) 424-2634
E-mail: info@hemophilia.org
http://www.hemophilia.org

Founded in 1948, the National Hemophilia Foundation is a national, not-for-profit organization dedicated to the treatment and cure of hemophilia, related bleeding disorders and complications of those disorders, including HIV and HCV. NHF also strives to support people with bleeding disorders, their families and healthcare professionals. Plus increase public aware-

ness of bleeding disorders and advocate on behalf of affected individuals. NHF is also committed to disseminating current information on bleeding disorders; raising funds for medical research and promoting legislation beneficial to affected individuals and family members.

President: Glenn Pierce, PhD, MD
Executive Director: Richard Hellner
Year Established: 1948
Acronym: NHF

Keywords
AIDS (Acquired Immunodeficiency Syndrome); Afibrinogenemia, Congenital; Factor IX Deficiency; Factor XIII Deficiency; Hageman Factor Deficiency; Hemophilia; HIV; National Hemophilia Foundation; Von Willebrand Disease

1941 National Hydrocephalus Foundation
12413 Centralia
Lakewood, CA 90715-1623

Phone: (562) 924-6666
Fax: (562) 924-6666
Toll Free: (888) 857-3434
E-mail: nhf@earthlink.net
http://www.nhfonline.org

The National Hydrocephalus Foundation is a nonprofit organization incorporated in 1979. Its mission is to establish and facilitate a communication network among those affected by hydrocephalus and their families, provide information and educational materials, increase public awareness, and promote and support research related to cause, prevention, and treatment. Hydrocephalus is a condition in which cerebrospinal fluid accumulates in the skull and puts pressure on the brain tissue. It has several different forms. The foundation has a reference library, with printed materials and videos, and produces a quarterly newsletter, which includes medical articles, human interest stories, book reviews, and updates on available resources, including special education services and web sites.

President: Michael Fields
Executive Director: Debbi Fields
Year Established: 1979
Acronym: NHF

Keywords
Agenesis of the Corpus Callosum; Aqueductal Stenosis; Arnold Chiari; Dandy Walker Malformation; Encephalocele; Hydranencephaly; Hydrocephalus; Intra-

ventricular Hemorage; IVH; MASA; NPH; National Hydrocephalus Foundation; Normal Pressure Hydrocephalus; IVH; Spina Bifida

1942 National Hypertension Association, Inc.

324 East 30th Street
New York, NY 10016

Phone: (212) 889-3557
Fax: (212) 447-7032
Toll Free: (800) 575-9355
E-mail: nathypertension@aol.com
http://www.nathypertension.org

The National Hypertension Association, Inc., (NHA) is a not-for-profit organization dedicated to combating the chronic health problem of high blood pressure (hypertension) by developing, directing, and implementing effective programs to promote research, educate the public, and ensure prompt detection and effective treatment of hypertension. The NHA is committed to researching the causes of essential hypertension and enhancing the understanding of certain secondary types of hypertension through basic laboratory research studies, thereby improving treatment of these conditions; educating and alerting the public to the dangers of hypertension; informing physicians as well as medical students of the most current advances in its causes, diagnosis, treatment, and prevention; and detecting hypertension wherever it exists in the most economical and effective way. Established in 1977 by a group of concerned scientists, doctors, and philanthropists, NHA offers charitable blood pressure screening, provides work-site detection programs, and has a well-defined program of basic and clinical research to gain better insight into the causes of hypertension. Materials include brochures, pamphlets, a regular newsletter, reports, and information packets.

President: William M. Manger, M.D., Ph.D. (1977 to Present)
Executive Director: Francine R. Rowley
Year Established: 1977
Acronym: NHA

Keywords
Hypertension; Hypertension, Essential; National Hypertension Association, Inc.; Secondary Hypertension

1943 National Keratoconus Foundation

8733 Beverly Boulevard
Suite 201
Los Angeles, CA 90048

Phone: (310) 423-6455
Fax: (310) 423-0163
Toll Free: (800) 521-2524
E-mail: info@nkcf.org
http://www.nkcf.org

The National Keratoconus Foundation (NKCF) is a non-profit, 501(c) 3 organization whose mission is to disseminate educational materials to individuals affected by keratoconus (KC) and their families, as well as to eye care professionals. Keratoconus is characterized by the slow progressive thinning and protrusion of the curved transparent outer layer of fibrous tissue covering the eyeball. The disease leads to vision impairment. Established in 1985, NKCF supports research into keratoconus and its causes, treatments, and eventual cure. Informational materials include a reference guide, brochures, and a quarterly newsletter. Program activities include communication channels for affected individuals and their families through an outreach program, an e-mail support groups and a toll free information line. NKCF maintains a registry of individuals affected by keratoconus and eye care providers who have a special interest and expertise in treating people with keratoconus.

President: Jon Pynoos, Ph.D.
Executive Director: Catherine Warren, RN
Year Established: 1986
Acronym: NKCF

Keywords
Conical Cornea; Eye Disorders; Keratoconus; Keratoconus, Congenital; National Keratoconus Foundation; NKCF; Visual Disorders

1944 National Kidney Foundation

30 East 33rd Street
New York, NY 10016

Phone: (212) 889-2210
Fax: (212) 689-9261
Toll Free: (800) 622-9010
E-mail: info@kidney.org
http://www.kidney.org

Established in 1950, the National Kidney Foundation is a voluntary, not-for-profit organization dedicated to preventing kidney and urinary tract diseases, improving the health and well being of individuals and families affected by these diseases, and increasing the availability of organs for transplantation. The foundation is committed to gaining adequate support for research and research training; fostering continuing education of healthcare professionals; expanding and developing patient services and community resources; increasing public awareness of kidney diseases; monitoring health policy development; and increasing fund-raising for new programs and research. In addition, the foundation supports and promotes medical research into the causes, prevention, and treatment of kidney diseases. A wide variety of educational materials is produced and distributed by the foundation. These materials are listed in a booklet entitled Public and Professional Education Materials.

President: Brian J.G. Pereira, MD, MD, NBA
Executive Director: John Davis
Year Established: 1950
Acronym: NKF

Keywords
Alport Syndrome; Argininosuccinic Aciduria; Atypical Hemolytic Uremic Syndrome; Bartter Syndrome; Blue Diaper Syndrome; Branchio Oto Renal Syndrome; Cancer, Kidney; Cancer, Renal Cell; Carbamyl Phosphate Synthetase Deficiency; Citrullinemia; Cystinuria; Drash Syndrome; Fibrosis, Retroperitoneal; Fraser Syndrome; Galloway Mowat Syndrome; Glomerulonephritis; Glomerulosclerosis; Glycosuria, Renal; Goodpasture Syndrome; Granulomatosis, Wegener's; Hematuria, Benign Familial; Hemolytic Uremic Syndrome; Hepatic Fibrosis, Congenital; IgA Nephropathy; Interstitial Cystitis; Kidney Disease; Kidney Stones; Loken Senior Syndrome; Medullary Cystic Disease; Medullary Sponge Kidney; Mullerian Aplasia; Myeloma, Multiple; MURCS Association; N Acetyl Glutamate Synthetase Deficiency; Nail Patella Syndrome; National Kidney Foundation; Nephrotic Syndrome; NKF; Ornithine Transcarbamylase Deficiency; Polycystic Kidney Disease; Purpura, Henoch Shonlein; Renal Agenesis, Bilateral; Renal Failure, Chronic; Urinary Tract Disease; Urinary Tract Infection; WAGR Syndrome; Wilms' Tumor

1945   National Lipedema Association, Inc.

27 Freeman Street
Arlington, MA 02474

Phone: (781) 734-0367
Fax: (781) 646-2628
Toll Free: (800) 809-2503
E-mail: info@lipedema.org
http://www.lipedema.org

The National Lipedema Association, Inc., (NLA) is a voluntary, rare disease organization founded in 2004. Lipedema involves an excessive accumulation of subcutaneous fat, primarily from the waist to a distinct line just above the ankles, although it can also involve the arms and abdomen. The disease can be inherited and affects women almost exclusively. The fat presents in a typical pattern that is bilateral and symmetrical. The disease often is confused with obesity, but lipedemic fat generally is not mobilized by diet and exercise, and lipedema can appear in women of all sizes, including women who are anorexic. Although it can be diagnosed as early as age two, it usually presents first at puberty and often becomes worse during pregnancy and at menopause. Lipedema can be a factor in causing secondary lymphedema, an accumulation of lymphatic fluid that causes swelling, usually in the arms and/or legs. The NLA's mission is to educate medical providers and patients about lipedema, and to promote research that benefits lipedema patients. NLA offers patient and professional education, patient advocacy, and networking.

President: Rebecca Morris
Year Established: 2004
Acronym: NLA

Keywords
Lipedema; Lipoedema; Lymphatic disorders; Lymphedema; Lymphoedema; Metabolic Disorders; National Lipedema Association, Inc; Networking; Obesity

1946   National Lymphatic and Venous Diseases Foundation, Inc.

70 Heritage Avenue
Unit 9
Portsmouth, NH 03801

Phone: (603) 334-8600
Fax: (603) 334-6464
Toll Free: (800) 301-2103

The National Lymphatic and Venous Foundation, Inc., is a not-for-profit organization dedicated to helping individuals affected by chronic lymphedema and venous diseases. Established in 1978, the foundation has a nationwide membership. The National Lymphatic and Venous Foundation, Inc., provides appropriate referrals, including those to support groups; engages in patient advocacy; promotes legislation beneficial to affected individuals; and supports and promotes research. The foundation also offers educational and support information to affected individuals, family members, and healthcare professionals through its database, regular newsletter, brochures, and audio-visual aids.

President: Mary F. Bellini (1987-Present)
Executive Director: Ellen Fox (Co-Founder)
Year Established: 1978
Acronym: NLVF

Keywords

Cystic Hygroma; Lymphangioma, Cavernous; Lymphedema; Lymphedema, Chronic; Lymphedema, Hereditary; National Lymphatic and Venous Diseases Foundation, Inc.; Venous Disorders; Waldmann Disease

1947 National Lymphedema Network

Latham Square Building
1611 Telegraph Avenue
Suite 1111
Oakland, CA 94612-2138

Phone: (510) 208-3200
Fax: (510) 208-3110
Toll Free: (800) 541-3259
E-mail: nln@lymphnet.org
http://www.lymphnet.org

The National Lymphedema Network (NLN) is a not-for-profit organization dedicated to providing education and support to affected individuals, healthcare professionals and the general public by disseminating information on the prevention and management of primary and secondary lymphedema. Established in 1988, the National Lymphedema Network provides a toll-free Infoline that offers 24-hour recorded information. Through its direct-dial support line, the NLN offers guidance and education as well as referrals to healthcare professionals, treatment centers, and local support groups. The network is dedicated to supporting research into the causes of, and possible alternative treatments for, lymphedema and presents a large national educational conference every other year. NLN's long-term goal is to aid in the implementation of standardized quality treatment nationwide for those individuals affected by lymphedema. NLN offers a variety of educational materials, including an extensive quarterly news publication, LymphLink, and a resource guide that provides a listing of lymphedema treatment centers, therapists, diagnostic centers and suppliers across the country. Related video, audiotapes and CD ROMs are available for purchase. The network also maintains an informational research database on lymphedema.

Executive Director: Saskia R. J. Thiadens (Founder)
Year Established: 1988
Acronym: NLN

Keywords

Lymphedema; Lymphedema, Hereditary; Lymphedema, Primary; Lymphedema, Secondary; National Lymphedema Network

1948 National Marfan Foundation

22 Manhasset Avenue
Port Washington, NY 11050

Phone: (516) 883-8712
Fax: (516) 883-8040
Toll Free: (800) 862-7326
E-mail: staff@marfan.org
http://www.marfan.org

The National Marfan Foundation is a voluntary, not-for-profit organization dedicated to the support and education of people affected by Marfan syndrome and related connective tissue disorders. Families and individuals affected by Marfan syndrome, an inherited disorder of the connective tissue that may affect the skeleton, lungs, eyes, heart, blood vessels, and other areas of the body established the foundation in 1981. The National Marfan Foundation has a three-fold purpose: to support and promote research; to disseminate accurate and timely information about this condition to affected individuals, family members, and physicians; and to provide means for affected individuals and relatives to share experiences, support one another, and improve their medical care. To help meet these goals, the foundation sponsors research grants to investigators studying any or all disciplines involved in Marfan syndrome, and conducts annual conferences. It has a network of chapters, support groups, and contacts across the country and provides a variety of educational and support materials for affected individuals, family members, healthcare professionals, teachers, and other professionals. These materials include a newsletter called "Connective Issues," an annual research supplement, booklets, and a listing of thousands of articles and books on Marfan syndrome. Other informational materials include brochures, fact sheets, videos, resource manual and posters.

President: Joseph Gagliano, Jr.
Executive Director: Carolyn Levering
Year Established: 1981
Acronym: NMF

Keywords

Aneurysm; Aortic Dissection; Aortic Enlargement; Aortic Rupture; Arachnodactlyl; Arachnodactlyl, Contractural; Arachnodactyly; Arachnodactyly, Contractural; Beals Syndrome; Dislocated Lenses;

Dolichostenomelia; Flat Feet; High Arched Palate; Indented Chest Wall; Joint Hypermobility; Marfan Syndrome; Marfanoid Hypermobility Syndrome; Mitral Valve Prolapse; Myopia; National Marfan Foundation; Protruding Chest Wall; Scoliosis; Voluntary Health Organization

---

1949 National Marrow Donor Program

3001 Broadway Street NE
Suite 500
Minneapolis, MN 55413-1753

Phone: (612) 627-5800
Fax: (612) 627-8125
Toll Free: (800) 627-7692
http://www.marrow.org

The National Marrow Donor Program (NMDP) is a not-for-profit organization dedicated to establishing, maintaining, and improving a system that provides transplants of bone marrow and other hematopoietic cells from volunteer, unrelated donors for individuals with leukemia and other life-threatening blood diseases. Established in 1988, NMDP maintains a registry of 2,795,616 volunteer marrow donors; its network consists of 101 donor centers, 114 collection centers, 107 transplant centers, and 12 recruitment centers. There is a special need for volunteer marrow donors from the African American, Asian/Pacific Islander, Hispanic, and American Indian/Alaskan Native communities. To address this need, NMDP is currently conducting four specially targeted national recruitment campaigns to increase registry representation of minority volunteers. NMDP maintains a database on unrelated transplant outcomes for research, as well as an office of patient advocacy to assist affected individuals and their families regarding medical and financial concerns.

Executive Director: Craig W.S. Howe, M.D. (Chief Executive Officer)
Year Established: 1986
Acronym: NMDP

Keywords
Myelodysplastic Syndromes; National Marrow Donor Program; NMDP; Stem Cell Transplant; Transplantation, Bone Marrow

---

1950 National Meningitis Association

22910 Chestnut Road
Lexington Park, MD 20653

Phone: (866) 366-3662
Fax: (877) 703-6096
E-mail: support@nmaus.org
http://www.nmaus.org

The National Meningitis Association (NMA) is a non-profit organization founded by five parents whose children have died or suffered long-term disabilities from meningococcal meningitis. NMA's mission is to educate families, medical professionals, and others about bacterial meningitis and prevention approaches to the disease. Meningococcal meningitis is caused by bacteria that invade the lining of the brain and spinal cord (meninges). Nearly one-third of the 2,000 to 3,000 cases that occur annually in the United States result in death or severe disability, such as limb amputations and organ damage. NMA offers information and referrals to those who contact them.

Executive Director: Lynn Bozof

Keywords
Advocacy; Meningitis; Meningitis, Meningococcal; Meningococcemia; National Meningitis Association

---

1951 National Mental Health Association

2001 North Beauregard Street
12th Floor
Alexandria, VA 22311

Phone: (703) 684-7722
Fax: (703) 684-5968
Toll Free: (800) 969-6642
TDD: (800) 433-5959
E-mail: infoctr@nmha.org
http://www.nmha.org

Established in 1909, the National Mental Health Association (NMHA) is a non-profit mental health advocacy organization concerned with all aspects of mental health and mental illness. The Association's Resource Center Serves the general public by providing literature about mental illness and referrals to mental health services. In addition, the Resource Center provides technical assistance to mental health consumer and consumer supporter organizations, advocacy organizations, and NMHA's nationwide network of 340 Affiliate offices.

President: Michael Faenza (President/CEO)
Executive Director: Cynthia Folcareelli (Executive Vice President)
Year Established: 1909
Acronym: NMHA

Keywords
Advocacy; Anorexia Nervosa; Antisocial Personality Disorder; Attention Deficit Hyperactivity Disorder; Autism; Bereavement; Bulimia; Conversion Disorder; Depersonalization Disorder; Depression; Dysthymia;

Fetal Alcohol Syndrome; Kleine-Levin Syndrome; Manic Depression, Bipolar; Mental Illness; Mutism, Elective; Mutism, Selective; National Mental Health Association; Neurasthenia; Neuroleptic Malignant Syndrome; NMHA; Obsessive Compulsive Disorder; Organic Mood Syndrome; Organic Personality Syndrome; Panic Anxiety Syndrome; Pica; Schizophrenia; Support Groups; Tardive Dyskinesia; Trichotillomania; Wernicke Korsakoff Syndrome; XYY Syndrome

1952 National Mental Health Consumers' Self-Help Clearinghouse

1211 Chestnut Street
Suite 1207
Philadelphia, PA 19107-6312

Phone: (212) 751-1810
Fax: (215) 636-6312
Toll Free: (800) 553-4539
E-mail: info@mhselfhelp.org
http://www.mhselfhelp.org

The National Mental Health Consumers' Self-Help Clearinghouse is a self-help technical assistance organization that was established in 1985. The clearinghouse handles thousands of inquiries annually from people who are concerned with mental health issues. Clients include mental health care consumers, family members, professionals, and other interested people whom request information and technical assistance about starting and developing self-help projects, self-advocacy projects and consumer-run mental health services. The clearinghouse also provides on-site consultations to individuals and groups interested in self-help group and consumer-run service development. In addition, it sponsors conferences and training events and has developed a wide variety of printed pamphlets and manuals on issues related to developing self-help and self-advocacy projects. A national quarterly newsletter, "The Key," provides assistance to consumers, their families, advocates, and physicians.

President: Joseph Rogers
Year Established: 1985
Acronym: NMHCSHC

Keywords
Anorexia Nervosa; Antisocial Personality Disorder; Attention Deficit Hyperactivity Disorder; Autism; Bulimia; Conversion Disorder; Depersonalization Disorder; Dysthymia; Fetal Alcohol Syndrome; French; Kleine-Levin Syndrome; Manic Depression, Bipolar; Mental Illness; Mutism, Elective; National Mental Health Consumers' Self Help Clearinghouse; Neuras-

thenia; Neuroleptic Malignant Syndrome; NMHC-SHC; Obsessive Compulsive Disorder; Organic Mood Syndrome; Organic Personality Syndrome; Panic Anxiety Syndrome; Pica; Trichotillomania; XYY Syndrome

1953 National MPS (Mucopolysaccharidoses/Mucolipidoses) Society, Inc.

P.O. Box 736
Bangor, ME 04402-0736

Phone: (207) 947-1445
Fax: (207) 990-3074
E-mail: info@mpssociety.org
http://www.mpssociety.org

The National MPS Society is a not-for-profit organization dedicated to acting as a support group for families affected by mucopolysaccharidoses (MPS), mucolipidoses (ML) and other related disorders; increasing professional and public awareness; and raising funds to further research into such disorders. Mucopolysaccharidoses, mucolipidoses, and related disorders are rare inherited diseases in which the body is deficient in certain enzymes. As a result, progressive damage occurs as complex sugars accumulate in various tissues of the body. Established in 1974, the National MPS Society promotes patient advocacy, provides referrals to genetic counseling and other services, and has established regional contact families to assist new families and conduct local support meetings. It produces a variety of educational and support materials including a membership directory, books, reports, brochures, videos of conferences, and a quarterly newsletter entitled, "Courage." The society also has a series of booklets on MPS and ML disorders that are designed to be daily living guides for families as well as tools for professionals who work with affected individuals.

President: Steve Holland
Executive Director: Barbara Wedehase
Year Established: 1974

Keywords
Hunter Syndrome; Hurler Scheie Syndrome; Hurler Syndrome; I-Cell Disease; Maroteaux Lamy Syndrome; ML; ML I; ML II; ML III; ML IV; Morquio Syndrome; Morquio Syndrome Type A; Morquio Syndrome Type B; MPS; MPS (Mucopolysaccharidoses/Mucolipidoses) Society, Inc.; MPS I; MPS II; MPS III; MPS IV; MPS V; MPS VI; MPS VII; Mucolipidoses; Mucopolysaccharidoses; National MPS (Mucopolysaccharidoses/Mucolipidoses) Society, Inc.; Pseudo Hurler Polydystrophy; Sanfilippo A;

Sanfilippo B; Sanfilippo Syndrome; Sanfilippo Type A; Sanfilippo Type B; Sanfilippo Type D; Scheie Syndrome; Sly Syndrome

---

1954 National Multiple Sclerosis Society

1100 New York Avenue NW
Suite 660
Washington, DC 20005

Phone: (202) 408-1500
Fax: (202) 408-0696
Toll Free: (800) 344-4867
http://www.nationalmssociety.org

The National Multiple Sclerosis Society is a voluntary, not-for-profit, health organization dedicated to ending the devastating effects of MS by advancing the cure, prevention and treatment of multiple sclerosis and by improving the lives of affected individuals. Multiple sclerosis is a chronic disorder of the central nervous system that causes the destruction of the insulation (myelin sheath) surrounding the nerve fibers in the brain and spinal cord as well as the nerve fibers themselves. Established in 1946, the National MS Society funds research which offers services for people with MS and provides professional education programs. Through its home office and 50-state network of chapters, the society serves more than a million people each year. The National MS Society also produces a wide variety of educational materials including a quarterly magazine, brochures, pamphlets, and video aids.

President: Joyce Nelson
Executive Director: Susan Sanabria, Vice President, Advocacy Programs
Year Established: 1946
Acronym: NMSS

Keywords
Demyelinating Disease; MS; Multiple Sclerosis; National Multiple Sclerosis Society; NMSS

1955 National Neutropenia Network

4547 Tillman Bluff Road
Valdosta, GA 31602

E-mail: sedpjd3@msn.com

The National Neutropenia Network is a not-for-profit, professional, self-help organization dedicated to providing a support system for affected individuals and their families, coordinating nationwide efforts to promote awareness of neutropenia, and distributing educational materials. Neutropenia is an abnormal decrease in the number of circulating white blood cells (neutrophils) in the blood. Established in 1994, the network supports general and clinical research related to neutropenia; provides information to families, the medical community, and the general public concerning the needs of affected individuals; and collects and distributes the latest medical data on neutropenia. The network is also committed to helping affected individuals and family members work with hospitals, physicians, nurses, and other healthcare professionals and identifying people and families whose lives are affected by neutropenia. It also seeks to identify the psychological effects of dealing with chronic illness and encouraging families to seek appropriate support.

President: Silke Deeley
Year Established: 1994
Acronym: NNN

Keywords
National Neutropenia Network; Neutropenia; Neutropenia, Chronic; Neutropenia, Cyclic; Neutropenia, Severe Chronic

---

1956 National Niemann-Pick Disease Foundation, Inc.

P.O. Box 49
415 Madison Avenue
Fort Atkinson, WI 53538

Phone: (920) 563-0930
Fax: (920) 563-0931
Toll Free: (877) 287-3672
E-mail: nnpdf@idcnet.com
http://www.nnpdf.org

The National Niemann-Pick Disease Foundation, Inc., is an international, voluntary, not-for-profit organization made up of parents, medical professionals, friends, relatives, and others who are committed to finding a cure for Niemann-Pick disease (NPD). Niemann-Pick is a group of rare inherited diseases in which excessive amounts of a fatty substance called sphingomyelin and/or cholesterol accumulate in many organs of the body. Established in 1991, the National Niemann-Pick Disease Foundation is dedicated to promoting medical research into the cause and cure of Niemann-Pick disease; providing medical and educational information to assist in the correct diagnosis and referral of children with Niemann-Pick disease; and providing support to families of affected children. The foundation is also committed to facilitating genetic counseling for parents who are known carriers of Niemann-Pick disease; encouraging the sharing of research information among scientists; and supporting legislation that is beneficial to affected individuals and family members. The National Niemann-Pick Disease Foundation conducts a national conference and provides a variety of educational and support materials.

Executive Director: Nadine M. Hill
Year Established: 1991
Acronym: NNPDF

Keywords
National Niemann-Pick Disease Foundation, Inc.; Neville's Disease; Niemann Pick Disease; Niemann Pick Disease Type A; Niemann Pick Disease Type B; Niemann Pick Disease Type C; Niemann Pick Disease Type D; NPD

1957 National Organization for Albinism and Hypopigmentation

P.O. Box 959
East Hempstead, NH 03826-0959

Phone: (603) 887-2310
Fax: (603) 887-6049
Toll Free: (800) 473-2310
E-mail: info@albinism.org
http://www.albinism.org

The National Organization for Albinism and Hypopigmentation (NOAH) is a national, voluntary, not-for-profit organization for people with albinism, their families, and professionals who work with them. Established in 1982, NOAH provides a network of local chapters and contact persons; offers information, support, and appropriate referrals; and promotes public and professional education. The organization also provides networking for those with special interests related to albinism and promotes and supports research that will improve diagnosis and management of albinism and hypopigmentation. Through participating in the Albinism World Alliance, NOAH networks with support groups for people with albinism in other countries and promotes development of albinism support groups throughout the world. NOAH also sponsors workshops, conferences, and outreach programs and offers a variety of educational materials including a regular newsletter, information bulletins, brochures, and information packets for libraries.

President: Michael McGowan 2001-Present
Executive Director: Same as above.
Year Established: 1982
Acronym: NOAH

Keywords
Albinism; Albinism, Oculocutaneous; Albinism, X-linked Ocular; Hypopigmentation Disorders; National Organization for Albinism and Hypopigmentation; Vitiligo

1958 National Organization for Rare Disorders, Inc.

55 Kenosia Avenue
P.O. Box 1968
Danbury, CT 06813-1968

Phone: (203) 744-0100
Fax: (203) 798-2291
Toll Free: (800) 999-6673
TDD: (203) 797-9590
E-mail: orphan@rarediseases.org
http://www.rarediseases.org

The National Organization for Rare Disorders (NORD) is a not-for-profit federation of voluntary health organizations dedicated to helping people with rare orphan diseases and assisting the organizations that serve them. Established in 1983, NORD is committed to the identification, treatment, and cure of rare disorders through programs of education, advocacy, research, and service. Through its Rare Disease Database, NORD provides reports in understandable, layperson's terminology on more than 1,100 rare disorders. Through its Organizational Database, it provides referrals to more than 2,000 nonprofit organizations and government agencies that help patients and families affected by rare diseases. In addition to patient education, NORD provides educational materials for medical professionals, including a series of free booklets for physicians and a 900-page medical text entitled The NORD Guide to Rare Disorders. It administers medication assistance programs and research grants and fellowships, and it provides advocacy on legislative matters of interest to the rare disease community.

President: Abbey S. Meyers, Ph.D. (Honorary)
Year Established: 1983
Acronym: NORD

Keywords
Memberships; National Organization for Rare Disorders, Inc.; National Organization for Rare Disorders, Inc. (NORD); Networking; Rare Diseases; Rare Disorders Organization

1959 **National Organization of Disorders of the Corpus Callosum**
PMB 363 18032-C Lemon Drive
Yorba Linda, CA 92886

Phone: (714) 747-0063
Fax: (714) 693-0808
E-mail: info@nodcc.org
http://www.nodcc.org

The National Organization of Disorders of the Corpus Callosum (NODCC) is a not-for-profit organization whose primary goal is to enhance the quality of life for individuals with agenesis of the corpus callosum and related disorders. Agenesis of the corpus callosum (ACC) is a rare abnormality of the brain structure, present at birth, characterized by the partial or complete absence (agenesis) of the bridge connecting the right and left sides of the brain (corpus callosum). NODCC gathers and disseminates information regarding ACC and related disorders. Founded in 2002, it promotes research on these conditions and provides services that include both education and networking for patients and healthcare professionals.

President: Dr. Lynn Kerlin Paul, PhD
Year Established: 2002
Acronym: NODCC

Keywords
ACC; Agenesis of Corpus Callosum; Dysgenesis of Corpus Callosum; Hypoplasia of Corpus Callosum; National Organization of Disorders of the Corpus Callosum; Networking; NODCC; Partial Agenesis of Corpus Callosum

1960 **National Organization of Vascular Anomalies—NOVA**
P.O. Box 0358
Findlay, OH 45839-0358

Phone: (419) 425-1593
Fax: (419) 425-1593
E-mail: hemangnews@msn.com
http://www.novanews.org

NOVA is a not-for-profit, voluntary organization dedicated to aiding patients and their families by providing information on the diagnosis and treatment of hemangioma and vascular malformations. It also provides resource materials to medical professionals to assist them in management of patient care. Hemangioma is the most common benign tumor of infants and children. Vascular malformations are abnormally developed blood vessels. Established in 1996 and incorporated in 1997, the NOVA serves patients and family members, the general public, health professionals, and other professionals such as educators, with programs and activities that include free medical conferences, support groups, patient networking, education, referrals, audio-visual aids, brochures, web site and a newsletter. The organization also assists with insurance claims and coordinates efforts for free transportation to medical appointments. NOVA, formerly Hemangioma Newsline changed its name in August 2004.

President: John DuBiel
Executive Director: Karla L. Hall
Year Established: 1996
Acronym: NOVA

Keywords
Hemangioma; Hemangioma Newsline; Hemangioma Thrombocytopenia Syndrome; KT Syndrome; National Organization of Vascular Anomalies —NOVA; PHACES; Port Wine Stains; Vascular Anomalies; Vascular Birthmarks; Vascular Malformation

1961 **National Organization on Fetal Alcohol Syndrome**
900 17th Street NW
Suite 910
Washington, DC 20006

Phone: (202) 785-4585
Fax: (202) 466-6456
Toll Free: (800) 666-6327
E-mail: info@nofas.org
http://www.nofas.org

The National Organization on Fetal Alcohol Syndrome is a voluntary, not-for-profit, service agency dedicated to eliminating birth defects caused by alcohol consumption during pregnancy and improving the quality of life for all those affected by fetal alcohol syndrome. Established in 1990, the organization is committed to increasing public awareness of fetal alcohol syndrome (FAS) and fetal alcohol effects (FAE); assisting in community empowerment and the promotion of preventive education through media campaigns; and training healthcare professionals, educators, and community members in addressing the specialized needs of affected children. The organization is also committed to serving as a national clearinghouse for local, regional, and state fetal alcohol syndrome organizations to ensure the effective exchange of information and resources. In addition, it engages in patient advocacy; promotes and supports research; provides appropriate referrals; and offers educational and supportive information through its database, directory, regular newsletter, reports, and brochures.

Executive Director: Thomas Donaldson
Year Established: 1990
Acronym: NOFAS

Keywords
Advocacy; FAE; FAS; Fetal Alcohol Effects; Fetal Alcohol Syndrome; National Organization on Fetal Alcohol Syndrome; NOFAS

1962 National Osteonecrosis Foundation

c/o NONF
Good Samaritan Professional Building
5601 Loch Raven Boulevard
Suite 201
Baltimore, MD 21239

Phone: (410) 532-5985
Fax: (410) 532-5908
http://www.nonf.org

The goal of the National Osteonecrosis Foundation is to act as a conduit for funding for medical research and the education of patients, as well as physicians and other health professionals. To all participating physicians and patients, it offers routine informational updates. It also acts as a referral service for patients wanting to identify physicians in their state with an interest in osteonecrosis, a bone disorder that decreases the blood supply to the affected area, leading to tiny breaks within the bone. The foundation provides educational materials about osteonecrosis, the destruction of bone that may occur as a result of bone injury or in conjunction with other diseases and conditions, and its various forms, such as Leg-Calve-Perthes disease, a type of osteonecrosis of the hip that is found only in children.

President: David S. Hungerford M.D.
Executive Director: Lynne C. Jones, PhD
Year Established: 1996
Acronym: NONF

Keywords
Avascular Necrosis; Legg Calve Perthes Syndrome; National Osteonecrosis Foundation; Osteonecrosis

1963 National Ovarian Cancer Coalition

500 NE Spanish River Boulevard
Suite 8
Boca Raton, FL 33431

Phone: (561) 393-0005
Fax: (561) 393-7275
Toll Free: (888) 682-7426
E-mail: NOCC@Ovarian.org
http://www.ovarian.org

The National Ovarian Cancer Coalition, Inc., (NOCC) is a national, non-profit, support organization dedicated to raising awareness and promoting education about ovarian cancer. The coalition is committed to improving the overall quality of life for individuals with ovarian cancer. Ovarian cancer is a disease in which malignant (cancerous) cells are found in the ovary. An ovary is one of two small, almond-shaped organs located on each side of the uterus that produce female hormones and store eggs or germ cells. NOCC's other goals include advocating for improved early detection methods to periodically screen women of all ages; taking an aggressive approach to the funding of research into ovarian cancer; and establishing a national clearinghouse to ensure the dissemination of accurate and comprehensive information on ovarian cancer.

President: Julene Fabrizio
Executive Director: Janet Langridge
Year Established: 1995
Acronym: NOCC

Keywords
National Ovarian Cancer Coalition; Ovarian Cancer

1964 National Pain Foundation

300 E. Hampden Avenue
Suite 100
Englewood, CO 80113

Phone: (303) 783-8899
Fax: (303) 692-8414
Toll Free: (866) 590-7246
E-mail: npf@nationalpainfoundation.org
http://www.nationalpainfoundation.org

The National Pain Foundation (NPF), a non-profit, 501(c)(3) organization, was established in 1998 to advance functional recovery of persons in pain through information, education and support. The goal of NPF is to empower patients by helping them become actively involved in the design of their treatment plan, exploring both traditional and complementary approaches to pain management. The National Pain Foundation provides an easy-to-use source of information and support for pain patients and their families. Through education, materials and programs, the NPF works to erase the stigma associated with pain and pain treatment. Currently included on the National Pain Foundation web site and in other NPF materials is information about chronic pain conditions such as arthritis and complex regional pain syndrome (CRPS) or reflex sympathetic dystrophy (RSD).

Executive Director: Mary Pat Aardrup
Year Established: 1998
Acronym: NPF

Keywords
Advocacy; Arthritis; Back Pain; Cancer Pain; Complex Regional Pain Syndrome; CRPS; Fibromyalgia; Headache; National Pain Foundation; Neck Pain; Networking; NPF; Pain Management; Palliative Care; Pelvic Pain

1965　National Parkinson Foundation, Inc.

1501 NW 9th Avenue/Bob Hope Road
Miami, FL 33136-1494

Phone: (305) 243-6666
Fax: (305) 243-5595
Toll Free: (800) 327-4545
E-mail: contact@parkinson.org
http://www.parkinson.org

The mission of the National Parkinson Foundation is to find the cause of, and a cure for, Parkinson disease and related neurological disorders through research; to educate general medical practitioners to detect the early warning signs of Parkinson disease; to educate patients, their caregivers, and the general public; and to improve the quality of life for both patients and caregivers.

President: Sharon Metz, RN, MPH (NPF Centers Manager)
Executive Director: Maite Moro (Field Services Manager)
Year Established: 1957
Acronym: NPF

Keywords
Advocacy; Atypical Parkinsonism; MSA; Multiple System Atrophy; NPF; National Parkinson Foundation, Inc; Networking; Oliviopontocerebellar Atrophy; OPCA; Parkinson's Disease; Parkinsonism; Progressive Supranuclear Palsy; PSP; Research; SDS; Shy-Drager Syndrome; SND; Striatonigral Degeneration; Support Groups; Young Onset Parkinson Disease

1966　National Pediatric Myoclonus Center

SIU School of Medicine
Department of Neurology, Division of Pediatric Neurology
P.O. Box 19643
Springfield, IL 62794-9643

Phone: (217) 545-7635
Fax: (217) 545-1903
E-mail: oms@siumed.edu
http://www.omsusa.org

The National Pediatric Myoclonus Center (NPMC) is a non-profit organization dedicated to providing the best care possible for children with myoclonus, a neurological movement disorder characterized by sudden, involuntary contractions of skeletal muscles. Such care includes making the correct diagnosis, searching for all reversible (curable) causes, making the best drug treatments available, providing information about myoclonus, obtaining psychological and emotional support for the children and their families, and bringing them together with other similar families. Established in 1990, NPMC also wishes to increase awareness among federal, private, and pharmaceutical agencies. Experts from various disciplines perform electrical brain wave studies, tests of mental function, blood tests, eye examinations, analysis of the chemicals in spinal fluid, x-ray studies of brain structure and other studies to better understand this disorder.

President: Michael R. Pranzatelli, M.D. (Director)
mpranzatelli@siumed.edu
Executive Director: Elizabeth D. Tate, F.N.P., C., M.N. (Manager)
Year Established: 1990
Acronym: NPMC

Keywords
Dancing Eyes Dacing Feet; Epilepsy, Progressive Myoclonic; EPM1; Kinsbourne Syndrome; Lafora Disease; Myoclonus; Myoclonus, Opsoclonus; Myopathy, Mitochondrial; National Pediatric Myoclonus Center; OMS; Opsoclonus; PME; Ramsay Hunt Syndrome; Univerricht Lundborg Disease

1967　National Pesticide Information Center

Oregon State University
333 Weniger Hall
Corvallis, OR 97331-6502

Fax: (541) 737-0761
Toll Free: (800) 858-7378
TDD: (541) 737-1197

E-mail: npic@ace.orst.edu
http://www.npic.orst.edu

The National Pesticide Information Center (NPIC), known formerly as the National Pesticide Telecommunications Network, provides objective, science-based information on a wide variety of pesticide-related topics. It is a toll-free telephone service available to anyone in the United States, Puerto Rico, and the Virgin Islands. NPIC is a cooperative effort of Oregon State University and the U.S. Environmental Protection Agency. It operates from 6:30 a.m. to 4:30 p.m. Pacific Standard Time daily, including weekends.

President: Terry Miller, Director
Executive Director: Crista Chadwick, Project Coordinator
Acronym: NPIC

Keywords
National Pesticide Information Center

1968 National PKU News

6869 Woodlawn Avenue NE
#116
Seattle, WA 98115-5469

Phone: (206) 525-8140
Fax: (206) 525-5023
E-mail: schuett@pkunews.org
http://www.pkunews.org

National PKU News is a not-for-profit organization devoted to providing news and information to all persons involved in the treatment of phenylketonuria (PKU). This is a rare metabolic disorder caused by a deficiency of the liver enzyme phenylalanine hydroxylase. Phenylketonuria is a severe progressive disorder that, if not treated early, can produce mental retardation. Founded in 1989, National PKU News publishes a newsletter three times a year and has approximately 2,000 subscribers from the United States, Canada, and 30 foreign countries. National PKU News also publishes educational materials regarding treatment of PKU. Food lists and cookbooks are also distributed by the organization.

President: Virginia E. Schuett
Executive Director: Virginia E. Schuett
Year Established: 1989

Keywords
National PKU News; PKU; Phenylketonuria

1969 National Prion Disease Pathology Surveillance Center

Case Western Reserve University
Division of Neuropathology
Institute of Pathology, Room 418
2085 Adelbert Rd
Cleveland, OH 44106-4907

Phone: (216) 368-0587
Fax: (216) 368-4090
E-mail: cjdsurv@cwru.edu
http://www.cjdsurveillance.com

The National Prion Disease Pathology Surveillance Center (NPDPSC) was created in 1997 as the national center to examine tissue for human cases of suspected prion disease occurring in the United States, most notably Creutzfeldt-Jakob disease (CJD). Creutzfeldt-Jakob disease is an extremely rare degenerative brain disorder (i.e., "spongiform" encephalopathy) characterized by sudden development of rapidly progressive neurological and neuromuscular symptoms. The NPDPSC offers referrals, reports, and research information to patients, family members, health professionals, and the general public. NPDPSC works closely with the Centers for Disease Control and Prevention (CDC) to monitor the prevalence of prion diseases in the USA and to investigate possible cases in which the disease has been acquired.

Executive Director: Pierluigi Gambetti, MD
Year Established: 1997
Acronym: NPDPSC

Keywords
National Prion Disease Pathology Surveillance Center

1970 National Prune Belly Syndrome Network

P.O. Box 154
Beloit, WI 53512

http://www.prunebelly.org

The National Prune Belly Syndrome Network is a self-help organization dedicated to providing support and information concerning prune belly syndrome, a rare disorder in which partial absence of certain abdominal muscles occurs in association with intestinal, renal, and urogenital abnormalities. Established in 1986, the organization promotes the education of affected individuals, their families, and healthcare professionals by providing reprints of medical journal articles concerning all aspects of prune belly syndrome.

President: Richard Ehrlich, M.D.
Year Established: 1986

Keywords
Eagle Barrett Syndrome; National Prune Belly Syndrome Network; Prune Belly Syndrome

1971   National Psoriasis Foundation

6600 SW 92nd Avenue
Suite 300
Portland, OR 97223-7195

Phone: (503) 244-7404
Fax: (503) 245-0626
Toll Free: (800) 723-9166
E-mail: getinfo@psoriasis.org
http://www.psoriasis.org/

The National Psoriasis Foundation is a voluntary not-for-profit organization dedicated to providing support to, and improving the quality of life for, individuals with psoriasis, a chronic skin disorder; educating the public; and promoting and supporting research for psoriasis. Established in 1968, the National Psoriasis Foundation is committed to publishing the most current information on psoriasis and providing a forum for affected individuals to speak out. The organization promotes funding for psoriasis research and seeks to establish an alliance between affected people, the medical and scientific communities, and the pharmaceutical industry. The National Psoriasis Foundation promotes patient advocacy and legislation beneficial to affected individuals; provides appropriate referrals (e.g., to support groups); and offers a variety of educational materials. These materials include a regular newsletter and reports.

President: Leslie Holsinger
Executive Director: Gail M. Zimmerman
Year Established: 1968

Keywords
Advocacy; Arthritis, Psoriatic; Eczema; Lichen Planus; National Psoriasis Foundation; Pityriasis Rosea; Psoriasis; Support Groups

1972   National Registry for Ichthyosis and Related Disorders

University of Washington
Dermatology Department, Box 356524
1959 N.E. Pacific
Seattle, WA 98195-6524

Phone: (206) 616-3179
Fax: (206) 616-6793

Toll Free: (800) 595-1265
E-mail: ichreg@u.washington.edu
http://www.skinregistry.org

The mission of the National Registry for Ichthyosis and Related Disorders is to identify individuals and families in the United States with the ichthyoses and related disorders and to encourage them to participate in the registry. The ichthyoses are a group of rare, inherited disorders characterized by abnormally dry, scaly, thickened skin due to abnormalities in the production of the protein keratin. The goal of the registry is to obtain data for study by skin biologists, pharmacologists, and other scientists in order to promote research into the diagnosis and treatment of these disorders. Interested individuals will be asked to complete a "Patient Enrollment Form"; their physicians will need to complete the "Physician's Form." The National Institutes of Health, American Academy of Dermatology, The Society of Investigative Dermatology, and the Foundation support the registry for Ichthyosis and Related Skin Types (FIRST). Individuals with ichthyosis vulgaris are not included in this registry.

President: Geoffrey W. Hamil, R.N. (1995 to present) (Coordinator)
Executive Director: Philip Fleckman, M.D. (Principal Investigator)
Year Established: 1994

Keywords
BCIE; CIE; Collodion; Congenital Ichthyosiform Erythroderma; Darier Disease; Disorders of Cornification; EHK; Epidermal Nevus Syndrome; Epidermolytic Hyperkeratosis; Erythrokeratodermas; Hailey's Disease; Harlequin Ichthyosis; Hyperkeratosis; Ichthyosis; KID Syndrome; Lamellar; LI; National Registry for Ichthyosis and Related Disorders; Netherton Syndrome; Pachyonichia Congenita; Palmar-Plantar Keratoderma; Pityriasis Rubra Pilaris; Refsum Syndrome; Sjogren Larsson Syndrome; Skin Disorders; Trichothiodystrophy; Variable Peeling Skin Syndrome; X-Linked Recessive Ichthyosis; X-LRI;

1973   National Reye's Syndrome Foundation, Inc.

426 North Lewis Street
P.O. Box 829
Bryan, OH 43506-0829

Phone: (419) 636-2679
Fax: (419) 636-9897
Toll Free: (800) 233-7393
E-mail: nrsf@reyessyndrome.org
http://www.reyessyndrome.org

The National Reye's Syndrome Foundation, Inc., is a voluntary, not-for-profit service organization dedicated to providing funding for basic research, awareness programs for the general public and the medical community, and emotional support and guidance for individuals with Reye's syndrome and their families. Reye's syndrome is a rare disease that usually follows a viral infection, such as influenza or chicken pox, and is strongly associated with the use of salicylates (e.g., aspirin). It affects the liver and brain. Established in 1974, the National Reye's Syndrome Foundation promotes patient and family advocacy; provides appropriate referrals (e.g., to support groups); and offers a variety of educational and supportive information through its database, bulletins, fact sheets, brochures, audio-visual aids, and regular newsletter. Languages supported by the foundation include English, Spanish, Laotian, Cambodian, and Vietnamese.

President: John E. Freudenberger
Executive Director: Susan Landversicht
Year Established: 1974
Acronym: NRSF

Keywords
National Reye's Syndrome Foundation, Inc.; Reye Syndrome

1974 National Sarcoidosis Resource Center
P.O. Box 1593
Piscataway, NJ 08855-1593

Phone: (732) 699-0733
Fax: (732) 699-0882
E-mail: sconroy846@aol.com
http://www.nsrc-global.net

The National Sarcoidosis Resource Center is an international, not-for-profit organization dedicated to providing support and information to individuals affected by sarcoidosis, their families, and any interested individuals. Sarcoidosis, a rare multisystem disorder of unknown cause, is characterized by the abnormal formation of inflammatory masses or nodules (granulomas) consisting of certain granular white blood cells (modified macrophages or epithelioid cells) in certain organs of the body. The granulomas that are formed are thought to affect the normal structure and, potentially, functions of the affected organ(s), causing symptoms associated with the particular body system(s) in question. Such granuloma formation most commonly affects the lungs. However, in many cases, other organs may be affected. Established in 1992 by an individual with

sarcoidosis, the National Sarcoidosis Resource Center provides information to people throughout the United States, Canada, and Europe. It maintains a registry of more than 15,000 affected individuals; provides referrals to physicians; assists in the formation of self-help groups; coordinates a networking program; and holds an annual "Sarcoidosis Awareness Day Celebration." In addition, the center conducts on ongoing study of the symptoms and demographics of individuals with sarcoidosis.

President: Sandra Conroy
Year Established: 1992
Acronym: NSRC

Keywords
Heerfordt Waldenstrom Syndrome; Lofgren's Syndrome; National Sarcoidosis Resource Center; Sarcoid of Boeck; Sarcoidosis; Sarcoidosis, Acute; Sarcoidosis, Chronic; Sarcoidosis, Subacute; Schaumann's Disease

1975 National Scoliosis Foundation
5 Cabot Place
Stoughton, MA 02072

Phone: (781) 341-6333
Fax: (781) 341-8333
Toll Free: (800) 673-6922
E-mail: nsf@scoliosis.org
http://www.scoliosis.org

The National Scoliosis Foundation is a not-for-profit organization dedicated to promoting and assisting screening programs for scoliosis (a sideways curvature of the spine) and kyphosis (a front-to-back curvature of the spine) and creating and promoting co-operating networks of educational, health care, and social services professionals from public and private institutions. It acts as a clearinghouse of information about scoliosis and kyphosis. The National Scoliosis Foundation offers a variety of educational and support materials through its computer database; information packets and educational multimedia units for teachers.

President: Joseph O'Brien
Year Established: 1976
Acronym: NSF

Keywords
Ataxia, Friedreich's; Kyphosis; National Scoliosis Foundation; Scoliosis; Spinal Deformities; Stenosis, Spinal

1976 National Self-Help Clearinghouse
365 Fifth Avenue
Suite 3300
New York, NY 10016

Phone: (212) 817-1822
Fax: (212) 817-1561
E-mail: info@selfhelpweb.org
http://www.selfhelpweb.org

The National Self-Help Clearinghouse is a self-help organization dedicated to facilitating access to self-help groups and increasing the awareness of the importance of mutual support. Established in 1978, the clearinghouse conducts training for self-help group leaders and professionals about self-help and ways to work with mutual aid groups; carries out research activities; and maintains a database of information and referrals to self-help groups. Educational materials include training materials and a periodic newsletter entitled "The Self-Help Reporter."

Executive Director: Audrey Gartner
Year Established: 1978
Acronym: NSHC

Keywords
National Self-Help Clearinghouse; Self Help Clearinghouse

1977 National SIDS and Infant Death Resource Center
8280 Greensboro Drive
Suite 300
McLean, VA 22102

Phone: (703) 821-8955
Fax: (703) 821-2098
Toll Free: (866) 866-7437
E-mail: sids@circlesolutions.com
http://www.sidscenter.org

The National SIDS/Infant Death Syndrome Resource Center (NSIDRC) provides resources, referrals, and technical assistance to SIDS families, public health, other professionals, and the general public. NSIDRC produces information sheets and other publication on SIDS and related topics. NSIDRC provides references and referral services online, grief and bereavement, medical research, and risk reduction resources, and provide annotated bibliographies from NSIDRC's database.

Executive Director: Carol Kennedy, RN, MA
Year Established: 1981
Acronym: NSIDRC

Keywords
Loss of Infant; National SIDS and Infant Death Resource Center; National Sudden Infant Death Syndrome Resource Center; NSIDRC; SIDS; Sudden Infant Death Syndrome

1978 National Sleep Foundation
1522 K Street
Suite 500
Washington, D.C. 20005

Phone: (202) 347-3471
Fax: (202) 347-3472
E-mail: nsf@sleepfoundation.org
http://www.sleepfoundation.org

The National Sleep Foundation (NSF) is an independent, nonprofit organization dedicated to improving public health and safety by achieving understanding of sleep and sleep disorders, and by supporting education, sleep-related research and advocacy. The foundation offers a variety of educational and supportive information through its website, brochures and newsletters.

President: Barbara A. Phillips, MD, MSPH
Executive Director: Richard Gelula
Year Established: 1990
Acronym: NSF

Keywords
Apnea, Central; Apnea, Mixed; Apnea, Obstructive Sleep; Apnea, Sleep; Cataplexy; Insomnia; Myoclonus, Nocturnal; Narcolepsy; National Sleep Foundation; Paralysis, Sleep; Parasomnia; Periodic Limb Movement Disorder; Periodic Movements of Sleep; Restless Legs Syndrome; RLS; Sleep Deprivation; Sleep Disorders; Sleep Eating; Sleep Talking; Sleep Terrors; Sleepwalking

1979 National Society for Phenylketonuria (UK)
P.O. Box 26642
London, N14 4ZF, United Kingdom

Phone: +44 (0) 208-364-3010
E-mail: info@nspku.org
http://www.nspku.org

The National Society for Phenylketonuria (NSPKU) is a nonprofit organization in the United Kingdom that is dedicated to providing information and support to people with phenylketonuria (PKU), their families, and their caregivers. PKU is a metabolic disorder characterized by deficiency of the enzyme phenylalanine hydroxylase, which is responsible for converting the amino acid phenylalanine into tyrosine. Without early diagnosis and restricted dietary intake of phenylalanine, an abnormal accumulation of phenylalanine may affect the normal growth and development of the brain, resulting in progressive, severe mental retardation. The National Society for Phenylketonuria was established in 1973. Its membership currently consists of over 900 families and individuals as well as more than 170 medical professionals. The society is committed to offering a network of local support groups; conducting annual conferences as well as other events throughout the year; developing and distributing targeted publications, such as materials for people with PKU, parents, medical professionals, or other professionals, such as employers or teachers; and funding the analysis of foods and the provision of equipment for PKU genetic research.

President: Sara Bartlett
Executive Director: Dave Stening
Year Established: 1973
Acronym: NSPKU

Keywords
National Society for Phenylketonuria (UK); Phenylketonuria

1980 National Spasmodic Dysphonia Association

300 Park Boulevard
Suite 350
Itasca, IL 60143

Fax: (630) 250-4505
Toll Free: (800) 795-6732
E-mail: nsda@dysphonia.org
http://www.dysphonia.org/

The National Spasmodic Dysphonia Association is a not-for-profit, 501c3 organization dedicated to advancing medical research into the causes of, and treatments of spasmodic dysphonia; promoting physician awareness of the disorder through outreach; and sponsoring support activities for people with SD and their families through educational materials, annual symposiums, support groups, and online resources. The

NSDA is the only organization that is entirely dedicated to spasmodic dysphonia. This disorder, which is a form of dystonia, is a neurological voice disorder that involves involuntary spasms of the vocal cords, causing interruptions of speech and affecting the voice quality. SD can cause the voice to break up or to have a tight, strained, or strangled quality.

President: David Barton
Executive Director: Kimberly Kuman
Year Established: 1990
Acronym: NSDA

Keywords
Dysphonia, Chronic Spasmodic; Dysphonia, Spastic; Dystonia, Laryngeal; National Spasmodic Dysphonia Association; Spasmodic Dysphonia

1981 National Spasmodic Torticollis Association

9920 Talbert Avenue
Suite 233
Fountain Valley, CA 92708

Phone: (714) 378-7837
Fax: (714) 378-7830
Toll Free: (800) 487-8385
E-mail: NSTAmail@aol.com
http://www.torticollis.org

The National Spasmodic Torticollis Association is a non-profit organization dedicated to supporting spasmodic torticollis patients in any way they can. Spasmodic torticollis is a neurological disorder that affects the muscles of the neck, causing the head to turn or pull toward the shoulder. The National Spasmodic Torticollis Association's main purpose is providing an extensive support network to affected individuals. The association is also committed to helping affected individuals locate physicians with knowledge of spasmodic torticollis; engaging in patient advocacy; and supporting and promoting research into effective treatments. The association also conducts an annual symposium and offers a variety of educational materials including a quarterly newsletter, brochures, pamphlets, and videos.

President: Dr. Larry Gulick
Executive Director: Lindy Sullivan
Year Established: 1980
Acronym: NSTA

Keywords
National Spasmodic Torticollis Association; Spasmodic Torticollis

1982 National Spinal Cord Injury Association

6701 Democracy
Suite 300-9
Bethesda, MD 20817

Phone: (301) 214-4006
Fax: (301) 881-9817
Toll Free: (800) 962-9629
E-mail: info@spinalcord.org
http://www.spinalcord.org

Founded in 1948, the National Spinal Cord Injury Association is dedicated to improving the quality of life for hundreds of thousands of Americans living with the results of spinal cord injury and disease (SCI/D) and their families. This number grows by thirty newly injured people each day. NSCIA educates and empowers survivors of spinal cord injury and disease to achieve and maintain the highest levels of independence, health and personal fulfillment. It fulfills this mission by providing an innovative Peer Support Network and by raising awareness about spinal cord injury and disease through education. Its educational programs are developed to address information and issues important to its constituency, policy makers, the general public, and the media, and include injury prevention, improvements in medical, rehabilitative and supportive services, research and public policy formulation.

President: Doug Heir
Executive Director: Marcie Roth
Year Established: 1948
Acronym: NSCIA

Keywords
National Spinal Cord Injury Association; Spinal Cord Injury

1983 National Stroke Association

9707 East Easter Lane
Englewood, CO 80112-3747

Phone: (303) 649-9299
Fax: (303) 649-1328
Toll Free: (800) 787-6537
E-mail: info@stroke.org
http://www.stroke.org

The National Stroke Association (NSA) is a national, not-for-profit, voluntary health organization dedicated to reducing the incidence and impact of stroke by changing the way it is viewed and treated. During a stroke, interruption of oxygenated blood supply to the brain or leakage of blood outside of blood vessel walls may cause damage to a portion of the brain. Depending upon the exact location and duration of lack of oxygenated blood supply to brain tissue (ischemia), affected individuals may experience a variety of symptoms such as weakness, paralysis, speech impairment, sensory abnormalities, and/or life-threatening complications. Established in 1984, the National Stroke Association promotes patient, physician, and public education; engages in patient advocacy efforts; and promotes research into improved stroke prevention, treatment, and rehabilitation. The organization, which currently has 14 chapters and approximately 7,000 members, offers networking services that enable affected individuals and family members to exchange information, assistance, and support; maintains a registry; offers support groups; and makes appropriate referrals. In addition, the NSA offers a stroke information hotline and provides a variety of materials including reports, brochures, pamphlets, videos, audiovisual aids, and a quarterly newsletter.

President: James Baranski
Executive Director: James Baranski
Year Established: 1984
Acronym: NSA

Keywords
Antiphospholipid Syndrome; Brain Attack; Cerebellar Ischemia; EMS; Ischemia; National Stroke Association; NSA; Sneddon Syndrome; Stroke; Stroke Center; TIA; Transient Ischemic Attacks

1984 National Stuttering Association

119 W. 40th Street
14th Floor
New York, NY 10018

Phone: (212) 944-4050
Fax: (212) 944-8244
Toll Free: (800) 364-1677
E-mail: info@WeStutter.org
http://www.westutter.org

National Stuttering Association (NSA) is a not-for-profit organization dedicated to people affected by stuttering. Established in 1977, it provides education, support, and empowerment tools to children and adults who stutter. In addition the organization serves their families and the speech-language pathologists who work with affected individuals. Consisting of 46 chapters and 5,000 members, the NSA also serves as an advocate and raises the consciousness of the general public about stuttering. Educational materials produced by the organization include a monthly newsletter entitled "Letting Go," audio-visual aids, and informational brochures such as "A Guide for Parents of Children Who Stutter" in English and Spanish. A networking support system, including local support groups, seeks to provide emotional support and information. The NSA also operates a toll-free national support hotline.

Executive Director: Tammy Flores
Year Established: 1977
Acronym: NSA

Keywords
National Stuttering Association; National Stuttering Project; Stuttering

1985 National Tay-Sachs and Allied Diseases Association, Inc.

2001 Beacon Street
Suite 204
Boston, MA 02135

Phone: (617) 277-4463
Fax: (617) 277-0134
Toll Free: (800) 906-8723
E-mail: info@ntsad.org
http://www.NTSAD.org

National Tay-Sachs & Allied Diseases Association, Inc., (NTSAD) is a voluntary, nonprofit health organization dedicated to the prevention and treatment of Tay-Sachs, Canavan and related genetic diseases. It provides information and support services to individuals and families affected by these diseases, as well as to the public. Its main areas of operations include public and professional education, research, genetic screening, family services, and advocacy. Through the guidance and expertise of its Scientific Advisory Committee (SAC), NTSAD promotes Tay-Sachs carrier screening, sponsors an International Tay-Sachs Laboratory Quality Control Program and publishes a list of participating labs. Through its Research Initiative, NTSAD supports scientific and medical research focusing on projects most likely to generate strong preliminary data for major funding in the area of neurodegenerative disorders affecting the central nervous system. NTSAD supports affected families through its international Parent Peer Group and Grandparent and Extended Family Group. The association conducts an annual conference for families, clinicians and researchers and a Summit of the Allied Diseases for medical professionals, patient advocacy leaders, and industry.

President: John F. Crowley, MBA, JD
Executive Director: Jayne C. Gershkowitz
Year Established: 1956
Acronym: NTSAD

Keywords
Acanthocytosis; Aspartylglycosaminuria; Cholesteryl Ester Storage Disease; Fabry Disease; Fucosidosis; Gaucher Disease; Glycosphingolipidoses; GM1 Gangliosidosis; GM2 Gangliosidosis; Hunter Syndrome; Hurler Syndrome; I-Cell Disease; Kufs Disease; Landing's Disease; Leukodystrophy; Leukodystrophy, Canavan's; Leukodystrophy, Globoid Cell; Leukodystrophy, Krabbe; Leukodystrophy, Metachromatic; Lipogranulomatosis; Lysosomal Storage Diseases; Mannosidosis, Oligosaccharidoses; Maroteaux Lamy Syndrome; ML I; ML II; ML III; ML IV; Morquio Syndrome; MPS I; MPS II; Mucolipidoses; Mucopolysaccharidoses; Multiple Sulfatase Deficiency; NTSAD; National Tay-Sachs and Allied Diseases Association, Inc.; Niemann Pick Disease; Pseudo Hurler Polydystrophy; Sandhoff Disease; Sanfilippo Syndrome A, B, C; Scheie Syndrome (MPS I-S); Schindler Disease; Sialidosis; Sly Syndrome; Sphingomyelinosis; Sulfatidosis; Tangier Disease; Tay Sach's Disease; Wolman's Disease

1986 National Transplant Assistance Fund (NTAF)

Suite 230
3475 West Chester Pike
Newtown Square, PA 19073

Phone: (610) 353-9684
Fax: (610) 353-1616
Toll Free: (800) 642-8399
E-mail: NTAF@transplantfund.org
http://www.transplantfund.org

Established in 1983 by medical professionals, the National Transplant Assistance Fund (NTAF) is a nonprofit organization dedicated to assisting organ/tissue transplant patients, and more recently, catastrophic injury patients, with the social, emotional, and financial problems that develop as a result of their disorders. NTAF educates and guides families in how to organize, launch, and sustain grass roots fundraising campaigns in their own communities. Money raised is used to pay for the uninsured expenses associated with severe medical conditions. The fund also promotes public education through organ donor drives, seminars, and lectures. The National Transplant Assistance Fund produces and distributes a wide variety of educational and support materials. These materials include a patient and family support brochure, an informational brochure for transplant professionals, organ/tissue donation brochures, a biannual newsletter, videos, organ donor cards, bumper stickers, fact sheets, buttons, green ribbons, and banners.

President: Jacob Kolff, M.D. (1983-Present)
Executive Director: Lynne Coughlin Samson Esq.
Year Established: 1983
Acronym: NTAF

Keywords
National Transplant Assistance Fund (NTAF); NTAF; Transplantation, Heart; Transplantation, Heart and Lung; Transplantation, Lung

1987 National Urea Cycle Disorders Foundation
4841 Hill Street
La Canada, CA 91011

Phone: (818) 790-2460
Fax: (818) 952-2184
Toll Free: (800) 386-8233
E-mail: info@nucdf.org
http://www.nucdf.org

The National Urea Cycle Disorders Foundation is a voluntary, not-for-profit organization dedicated to providing information and guidance to families affected by urea cycle disorders; educating health care professionals concerning the diagnosis and treatment of these disorders; and increasing public awareness. Urea cycle disorders are rare genetic disorders in which an enzyme deficiency causes an excessive accumulation of ammonia in the blood. Established in 1989, the National Urea Cycle Disorders Foundation is also committed to promoting and supporting medical research; networking families to promote the exchange of mutual support, information and resources; and educating legislators on the needs of affected families. In addition, the foundation provides appropriate referrals; engages in patient, professional, and community education; and offers educational and supportive information through its national database, directory, biannual newsletter, brochures, and pamphlets. The foundation's goals include creating a national network of families who together can stimulate medical research activities and eventually find a cure for urea cycle disorders.

President: Tresa Warner
Executive Director: Cynthia Le Mons
Year Established: 1989
Acronym: NUCDF

Keywords
Arginase Deficiency; Argininosuccinase Deficiency; Argininosuccinic Acid Synthetase Deficiency; Argininosuccinic Aciduria; AS; ASA; Carbamyl Phosphate Synthetase Deficiency; Citrullinemia; CPS; Hyperammonemia, Neonatal; Metabolic Disorders; N Acetyl Glutamate Synthetase Deficiency; NAGS Deficiency; National Urea Cycle Disorders Foundation; Networking; NUCDF; Ornithine Transcarbamylase Deficiency; OTC Deficiency; SIDS; Sudden Infant Death Syndrome; Urea Cycle Disorder, Ornithine Transcarbamylase Deficiency T; Urea Cycle Disorders

1988 National Vitiligo Foundation
700 Olympic Plaza Circle
Suite 404
Tyler, TX 75701

Phone: (903) 595-3713
Fax: (903) 593-1545
E-mail: info@nvfi.org
http://www.nvfi.org

The National Vitiligo Foundation is a voluntary, not-for-profit, self-help organization dedicated to providing information and support to individuals with vitiligo, a skin disorder in which pigment cells are destroyed, resulting in irregularly shaped white patches on the skin. Established in 1985, the foundation is committed to locating, informing, and counseling affected individuals and family members; increasing public awareness and concern for affected individuals; and promoting and funding scientific and clinical research into the cause, treatment, and cure of vitiligo. The foundation is interested in broadening the concern for people with vitiligo within the medical community and establishing a central vitiligo center and local treatment facilities across the country. In addition, the National Vitiligo Foundation promotes patient advocacy and legislation beneficial to affected individuals and engages in patient, professional, and community education. The foundation provides a variety of informational materials including a bi-annual newsletter, guidelines for physicians concerning the treatment of patients with vitiligo, fact sheets, pamphlets, and handbooks for patients, physicians, and schools.

President: Ronald S. Davis, MD
Executive Director: Anna K. Hayes
Year Established: 1985
Acronym: NVFI

Keywords
National Vitiligo Foundation; Vitiligo

1989 National Vulvodynia Association
P.O. Box 4491
Silver Spring, MD 20914-4491

Phone: (301) 299-0775
Fax: (301) 299-3999
E-mail: mate@nva.org
http://www.nva.org

The National Vulvodynia Association is a non-profit organization created in 1994 to improve the lives of individuals affected by vulvodynia, a group of chronic vulvar pain disorders. The National Vulvodynia Association seeks to educate affected women about vulvodynia to enable them to make informed choices about their treatment; encourage affected individuals to develop self-help strategies to deal with the physical and emotional aspects of these disorders; provide a support network for interested members; involve and educate family members to promote a supportive family environment; and coordinate a centralized source of information on suspected causes, current treatments, and ongoing research for healthcare professionals and affected individuals. The National Vulvodynia Association works cooperatively with other health organizations to improve understanding of vulvodynia and promote public attention to these disorders. Educational materials produced by the organization include a brochure and newsletter.

President: Phyllis Mate (1996 to Present)
Executive Director: Phyllis Mate (1996 to Present)
Year Established: 1994
Acronym: NVA

Keywords
Lichen Sclerosus; National Vulvodynia Association; Vulvar Pain, Chronic; Vulvodynia; Vulvovaginitis

1990 National Women's Health Network
514 10th Street NW
Suite 400
Washington, D.C. 20004

Phone: (202) 628-7814
Fax: (202) 347-1168
E-mail: nwhn@nwhn.org
http://www.womenshealthnetwork.org

The National Women's Health Network is a not-for-profit, voluntary health organization that provides advocacy on health issues that affect women. The network also functions as a clearinghouse for information on women's health issues and lifetime wellness. The Women's Health Information Network distributes brochures on topics such as breast and ovarian cancer, fibrocystic disease, interstitial cystitis, pelvic inflammatory disease, vulvodynia, urinary tract infections, and toxic shock syndrome. The network also distributes a regular newsletter.

President: Unknown
Executive Director: Cynthia Pearson
Year Established: 1975
Acronym: NWHN

Keywords
Ahumada Del Castillo Syndrome; Amenorrhea Galactorrhea Syndrome; Amenorrhea, Primary; Asherman's Syndrome; Cancer, Breast; Cancer, Cervical; Cancer, Ovarian; Diethylstilbestrol; Endometriosis; Fibrocystic Disease; Hyperemesis Gravidarum; Interstitial Cystitis; Lichen Sclerosus; National Women's Health Network; NWHN; Paget's Disease of the Breast; Pelvic Inflammatory Disease; Polycystic Ovary Syndrome; Stein Levanthal Syndrome; Toxic Shock Syndrome; Vulvodynia; Women's Health

1991 National Women's Health Resource Center
157 Broad Street
Suite 315
Red Bank, NJ 07701

Phone: (732) 530-3425
Fax: (732) 530-3347
Toll Free: (877) 986-9472
E-mail: mchin@healthywomen.org
http://www.healthywomen.org

The National Women's Health Resource Center is a voluntary, not-for-profit organization committed to providing information that enables women and their health care providers to make informed health decisions. Established in 1988, the center, which is a subsidiary of the Columbia Hospital for Women Foundation, has a membership that consists of individual consumers, health professionals, and organizations. It collaborates with national corporations to develop women's health campaigns and disseminate information across the country. It also refers callers to women's health care providers in all regions of the United States. The center conducts conferences and work site programs, sponsors special events, serves as a women's health information resource for the media, and authors the Women's Book of Health.

President: Elizabeth Battaglino (Director Marketing & Public Affairs)
Executive Director: Amy Niles
Year Established: 1988
Acronym: NWHRC

Keywords
Ahumada Del Castillo Syndrome; Amenorrhea Galactorrhea Syndrome; Forbes Albright Syndrome; Hyperemesis Gravidarum; Lichen Sclerosus; National Women's Health Resource Center; NWHRC

1992   NBIA Disorders Association

2082 Monaco Court
El Cajon, CA 92019-4235

Phone: (619) 588-2315
Fax: (619) 588-4093
E-mail: info@nbiadisorders.org
http://www.NBIAdisorders.org

The NBIA Disorders Association (formerly Hallervorden-Spatz Syndrome Association) is a non-profit voluntary organization founded in 1996 and dedicated to families affected by neurodegeneration with brain iron accumulation and related disorders. NBIA (neurodegeneration with brain iron accumulation) is a rare genetic, neurological movement disorder characterized by the progressive degeneration of the nervous system due to iron deposits in the brain. NBIA Disorders Association has four main goals: raising funds to further research on the disease; providing emotional support to families affected by NBIA; educating the public about NBIA; and monitoring ongoing NBIA research and informing others of research findings and progress. The association publishes a self-titled periodic newsletter; maintains an NBIA Networking Program; and publishes an educational brochure on NBIA.

President: Patricia V. Wood (1996 to Present)
Year Established: 1996
Acronym: NBIA Disorders Assoc

Keywords
Hallervorden Spatz Disease; Hallervorden Spatz Syndrome; HS; Late Infantile Neuroaxonal Dystrophy; NBIA Disorders Association; Pantothenate Kinase Associated Neurodegeneration (PKAN); Pigmentary Degeneration of Globus Pallidus, Substantia Nigra and Red Nucleus; Progressive Pallid Degeneration Syndrome

1993   Nemaline Myopathy Foundation

P.O. Box 5937
Round Rock, TX 78683-5937

Phone: (512) 388-7985
Fax: (512) 388-7985
http://www.nemalinefoundation.org

The Nemaline Myopathy Foundation is a non-profit, 501(c)(3) organization committed to promoting and supporting research into the causes, treatments, and cure for nemaline myopathy. Nemaline myopathy (NM) is a rare neuromuscular disease that occurs in approximately 1 in 50,000 live births and is characterized by extreme muscle weakness. The severity of the disease is variable and unpredictable, with prognosis ranging from neonatal death to late-onset, slowly progressive impairment of motor function. There is currently no treatment or cure for nemaline myopathy.

President: Monette Clark Smith
Year Established: 2001
Acronym: NM Foundation

Keywords
Nemaline Myopathy Foundation

1994   Nemaline Myopathy Website

E-mail: davidmcd@hotmail.com
http://www.davidmcd.btinternet.co.uk/

The Nemaline Myopathy Website is dedicated to sharing information on nemaline myopathy. This is a rare, inherited, neuromuscular disease that is usually apparent at birth (congenital) and characterized by extreme muscle weakness (hypotonia). Established in 1999, the website replaces a newsletter and provides information on the disease and related resources, as well as opportunities to network and share information.

President: David McDougall
Year Established: 1991

Keywords
CNM; Congenital Nemaline Myopathy; Congential Rod Disease; Myopathy, Nemaline; Nemaline; Myopathy; Nemaline Myopathy Newsletter; Nemaline Myopathy Website; NM; Rod Myopathy

1995   Nephcure Foundation

15 Waterloo Avenue
Suite 200
Berwyn, PA 19312

Phone: (610) 540-0186
Fax: (610) 540-0190

Toll Free: (866) 637-4287
E-mail: info@nephcure.org
http://www.nephcure.org

The Nephcure Foundation is focused on research to find the cause of nephrotic syndrome and focal segmental glomerulosclerosis (FSGS), and to improve treatments and find a cure. Nephcure offers information to patients, family members, and health professionals. This rare disease organization facilitates patient networking, patient advocacy, research, and support groups for the individuals affected by these disorders.

President: Irv Smokler, PhD (2003-present)
Executive Director: Henry Brehm
Year Established: 1999
Acronym: NEPHCURE

Keywords
Advocacy; Alonzo Mourning; Dialysis; Ed Hearn; FSGS; Focal Segmental Glomerulosclerosis; Kidney; MCNS; NEPHCURE; Nephcure Foundation; Nephrologist; Nephrotic Syndrome; Networking; NS; Renal; Research; Support Groups; Trials

1996 Nephrogenic Diabetes Insipidus Foundation

P.O. Box 1390
Main Street
Eastsound, WA 98245

Fax: (888) 376-6356
Toll Free: (888) 376-6343
E-mail: info@ndif.org
http://www.ndif.org

The Nephrogenic Diabetes Insipidus Foundation is a self-help organization dedicated to providing information and support to individuals and families affected by diabetes insipidus. This rare metabolic disease is characterized by a deficiency of the hormone vasopressin (anti-diuretic hormone [ADH]), which is produced in the posterior lobe of the pituitary gland. Excessive thirst and urination are the major symptoms of this disorder. The NDI Foundation's mission is to share information among affected families. Established in 1995 and consisting of 20 members and one chapter, the group publishes two newsletters each year and expects to publish a pamphlet directed toward caregivers and schools. The organization coordinates

an active networking program and telephone support system.

President: Mary Evans-Lee (Contact Person)
Year Established: 1995

Keywords
Diabetes Insipidus, Nephrogenic; Diabetes Insipidus, Neurohypophyseal; Diabetes Insipidus, Vasopressin Resistant; Diabetes Insipidus, Vasopressin Sensitive; NDI; Nephrogenic Diabetes Insipidus Foundation; Nephrogenic Diabetes Insipidus Parent Support Group of CHOP

1997 Neuroblastoma Children's Cancer Society

P.O. Box 957672
Hoffman Estates, IL 60195

Phone: (847) 605-1245
Fax: (847) 605-0705
Toll Free: (800) 532-5162
E-mail: Info@neurblastomacancer.org
http://www.neuroblastomacancer.org

The Neuroblastoma Children's Cancer Society is a not-for-profit, voluntary organization dedicated to significantly accelerating potential cures for neuroblastoma and related children's cancers, and to improve the quality of life of affected individuals and their families. The organization is an advocate for children and their families and is dedicated to providing support in the following ways: promoting research by highly trained medical professionals; providing research grant awards to medical specialists locally and nationwide; educating healthcare professionals on early detection and the latest advances in treatments and diagnosis; maintaining updated information on current treatment and diagnosis; and providing a resource booklet that lists non-profit organizations and other resources that offer support for affected families. Consisting of 500 members, the society produces educational materials including a resource handbook and a newsletter.

President: Jim Sexton (1994 to Present)
Executive Director: Dori Sexton
Year Established: 1994

Keywords
Neuroblastoma; Neuroblastoma Children's Cancer Society

1998   Neurofibromatosis, Inc.

P.O. Box 18246
Minneapolis, MN 55418-0246

Phone: (301) 918-4600
Toll Free: (800) 942-6825
E-mail: info@nfinc.org
http://www.nfinc.org

Neurofibromatosis, Inc., is a national, voluntary, not-for-profit organization dedicated to providing information, support, and advocacy to individuals and family members affected by neurofibromatosis type I (NF1) and type II (NF2). NF1 is a genetic disorder characterized by the development of multiple benign tumors on the covering of nerve fibers and the appearance of brown spots and freckles on the skin. NF2 is a rare genetic disorder characterized by the development of benign tumors on both auditory nerves and in other areas of the body. Established in 1988, Neurofibromatosis, Inc., services the needs of affected individuals through coordinated educational, support, and clinical and research programs. The organization provides information about NF1 and NF2 to affected individuals, family members, healthcare and other professionals, and the general public; provides referrals to local medical resources; and assists in identifying community support services. Neurofibromatosis, Inc., also encourages and supports research.

President: Miguel Lessing
Year Established: 1988
Acronym: NF

Keywords
Chromosome 17; Chromosome 22; Deafness; Learning Disabilities; Neurofibromatosis; Neurofibromatosis, Inc.; Neurofibromatosis, Peripheral; Neurofibromatosis Type 1; Neurofibromatosis Type 2; Neurofibromatosis, Von Recklinghausen's; NF; NF 1; NF 2; Proteus Syndrome; Von Recklinghausen's Disease

1999   Neuropathy Association

60 East 42nd Street
Suite 942
New York, NY 10165

Phone: (212) 692-0662
Fax: (212) 692-0668
E-mail: info@neuropathy.org
http://www.neuropathy.org

The Neuropathy Association is a national, not-for-profit organization established to help people with disorders that affect the peripheral nervous system (peripheral neuropathy). The peripheral nervous system consists of all the motor and sensory nerves that connect the brain and spinal cord to the rest of the body (i.e., the nerves outside the central nervous system). The organization is dedicated to providing patient support and education to individuals affected by peripheral neuropathy; advocating for patients' interests; and promoting research into the causes and cure of peripheral neuropathy. The objectives of the association are to provide support through programs of education and the sharing of information and experiences related to peripheral neuropathy; enhance physician awareness through programs of education to help identify, evaluate, and treat peripheral neuropathy; increase public awareness of the nature and extent of peripheral neuropathy and the need for early intervention and research; encourage pharmaceutical and biotechnology companies to develop new therapies and devices for treatment of peripheral neuropathy; and encourage government support for research into the causes and treatments of peripheral neuropathy and the need for special accommodations and facilities for people with peripheral neuropathy. The organization publishes several brochures and a periodic newsletter entitled "Neuropathy News."

President: Ronnie Chalif
Executive Director: Donald G. Jacib Ed.D
Year Established: 1995

Keywords
Neuropathy Association; Neuropathy, Peripheral; POEMS Syndrome

2000   Neuropathy Trust (International)

P.O. Box 26
Nantwich
Cheshire, CW5 5FP, United Kingdom
http://www.neurocentre.com

The Neuropathy Trust is committed to a better future for all sufferers of peripheral neuropathy and neuropathic pain, regardless of the underlying cause. Through education and communication to patients and healthcare professionals, the trust works to raise awareness of neuropathic disorders and provide a lifeline to all sufferers. The Neuropathy Trust has produced a series of educational booklets entitled "Peripheral Neuropathy: Under the Spotlight," "Diabetic Neuropathy: Under the Spotlight," and "Post Herpetic Neuralgia: Under the Spotlight." The trust also publishes a regular newsletter called "Relay." The trust's web site discusses the organization's mission, goals, and services; and provides understandable information relating to peripheral neuropathy and neuropathic pain.

President: Andrew Keen

Keywords
Burning Feet; Cancer; Diabetes; Diabetic Neuropathy; HIV; Mononeuritis Multiplex; Myelin; Nerves; Neuropathic Pain; Neuropathy Trust (International); Numbness; Pain Management; Pain Relief; Peripheral Neuropathy; Pins and Needles; Polyneuropathy; Sharp; Shooting; Stabbing; Stroke; Synapse; Tingling

2001 Neutropenia Support Association, Inc.
971 Corydon Avenue
Winnepeg
Manitoba, R3M 3S7, Canada

Phone: (204) 489-8454
Toll Free: (800) 663-8876
E-mail: stevensl@neutropenia.ca
http://www.neutropenia.ca

The Neutropenia Support Association, Inc., (NSAI) is a voluntary charity dedicated to increasing the awareness and understanding of neutropenia. Cyclic neutropenia is a rare blood disorder characterized by episodes of abnormally low levels of certain white blood cells called neutrophils; recurrent infections with fever usually occur as a result of this finding. Chronic neutropenia is a blood disorder in which bone marrow does not produce sufficient numbers of neutrophils; affected individuals are typically more susceptible to recurring infections from fungus and bacteria. Chronic neutropenia may last for months or years, and it can affect both children and adults. NSAI was founded in Canada in 1989. Its services are geared for affected individuals, families, and the medical community, and include genetic counseling, support groups, public and professional education, an international disease registry, networking opportunities, and advocacy. NSAI also maintains an "Information Library," operates a toll-free hotline, produces audiovisual aids and publishes a periodic newsletter and informational brochures. Brochures include "Neutropenia: Causes, Consequences, and Care" and "Chemotherapy and Neutropenia."

President: Lorna Stevens (1989 to Present) (Founder).
Executive Director: Jim & Janis Benzelock (Volunteers).
Year Established: 1989
Acronym: NSAI

Keywords
Congenital Immunologic Deficiency Syndrome; Granulocytopenia, Autoimmune; Hematopoiesis, Cyclic; Kostmann's Neutropenia; Kostmann's Syndrome; Leukopenia, Autoimmune; Myelodysplastic Syndromes; Myelokathexis Syndrome; Neutropenia Support Association, Inc.; Neutropenia, Autoimmune; Neutropenia, Chemotherapy Induced; Neutropenia, Chronic Idiopathic; Neutropenia, Congenital; Neutropenia, Cyclic; Neutropenia, Drug Induced; Neutropenia, Idiopathic; Neutropenia, Isoimmune Neonatal; Neutropenia, Periodic; Neutropenia, Severe Chronic; Neutropenia, Viral Induced; Neutropenias, Childhood; Shwachman Syndrome

2002 Nevus Network
The Congenital Nevus Support Group
P.O. Box 305
West Salem, OH 44287

Phone: (419) 853-4525
Fax: (405) 377-3403
E-mail: info@nevusnetwork.org
http://www.nevusnetwork.org

The Nevus Network is a voluntary, not-for-profit, self-help organization dedicated to providing support and information to individuals with giant congenital nevi (large brown birthmarks or moles) and a related condition called neurocutaneous melanosis. Established in 1983, the organization provides a network of support through letters, phone calls, and personal meetings. In addition, the Nevus Network offers educational and supportive information through its web site, information sheets, and brochures. The organization also publishes a newsletter that includes research updates, letters from readers, and member medical statistics.

Year Established: 1983
Acronym: NN

Keywords
Giant Congenital Nevus; Neurocutaneous Melanosis; Nevus; Nevus Network; Nevus, Giant Congenital; United States

2003 Nevus Outreach, Inc.
1601 Madison Boulevard
Bartlesville, OK 74006

Phone: (918) 331-0595
Fax: (281) 417-4020
Toll Free: (877) 426-3887
E-mail: mark@nevus.org
http://www.nevus.org

Nevus Outreach, Inc., (NOI) is a nonprofit, 501(c)(3) organization formed in 1997 by a group of parents dedicated to improving medical knowledge and treatment for individuals with giant congenital nevi and related disorders such as neurocutaneous melanosis. Giant congenital nevi are large, darkly pigmented moles or birthmarks (nevi) that are present at birth (congenital). Although such nevi may vary in size and shape and may cover any area of the body, they are often present on the chest, the shoulders, the upper back, the area covered by bathing trunks, the lower arms and legs, and/or various areas on the face and/or scalp. Individuals with giant nevi have an abnormally increased risk of developing malignant melanoma, a form of skin cancer. In addition, the nevus cells that appear on the skin may form in the central nervous system (neurocutaneous melanosis), which may cause neurological abnormalities and potentially life-threatening complications. The Nevus Outreach is committed to providing information, assistance, and support to affected individuals and family members; promoting additional research; and increasing awareness of these conditions among dermatologists and other health care professionals.

Executive Director: Mark Beckwith
Year Established: 1997
Acronym: NOI

Keywords
Blue Rubber Bleb Nevus; Congenital Melanocytic Nevus; Giant Nevus; Hairy Nevus; Melanosis, Neurocutaneous; Neurocutaneous Melanocytosis; Neurocutaneous Melanosis; Nevus Outreach, Inc.

2004   New Zealand Organization for Rare Disorders
125 Cuba Street
Petone
Lower Hutt City, New Zealand

Phone: +64 (0) 4-566-7707
Fax: +64 (0) 4-566-7717
E-mail: john.forman@xtra.co.nz
http://www.nzord.org.nz

The mission of the New Zealand Organization for Rare Disorders is to support and improve the level of organization and information among patients and families affected by rare disorders; promote research and education that will identify rare disorders early and ensure the best clinical care for the patient and best social support for the family; and build partnerships of patients/families, clinicians, researchers, government and industry, that accelerate the research effort towards control and cure of rare disorders.

Executive Director: John Forman
Year Established: 2000
Acronym: NZORD

Keywords
New Zealand Organization for Rare Disorders; Rare Disorders

2005   New Zealand Spasmodic Dysphonia Patient Network
15 Pluto Place
Birkenhead
Auckland, 1310, New Zealand

Phone: +64 (0) 9-482-1567
Fax: +64 (0) 9-482-1284
E-mail: dsbarton@ihug.co.nz

The New Zealand Spasmodic Dysphonia Patient Network is a voluntary, not-for-profit, self-help organization dedicated to linking individuals affected by spasmodic dysphonia. Such networking opportunities enable affected individuals and family members to exchange information, resources, and mutual support. Spasmodic dysphonia is a rare disorder characterized by stuttering, momentary periods of uncontrolled vocal spasms, tightness in the throat, and/or recurrent hoarseness. The most frequent finding associated with spasmodic dysphonia is the occurrence of sudden, momentary lapses or interruptions of vocalization. Spasmodic dysphonia is a form of dystonia, a group of neuromuscular disorders characterized by involuntary muscle spasms. There are two main types of spasmodic dysphonia: "abductor" spasmodic dysphonia, in which the vocal cords draw apart (abduction), and "adductor" spasmodic dysphonia, in which the vocal cords draw together (adduction) and may become locked. The exact cause of spasmodic dysphonia is unknown. The New Zealand Spasmodic Dysphonia Patient Network was established in 1992 and currently has approximately 65 members. In addition to providing networking services to its members, the organization has a database and publishes a regular newsletter.

President: David Barton (1992 to Present)
Executive Director: Same as above.
Year Established: 1992

Keywords
New Zealand Spasmodic Dysphonia Patient Network; Spasmodic Dysphonia, New Zealand

2006 NIDCD National Temporal Bone, Hearing and Balance Pathology Resource Registry

Massachusetts Eye & Ear Infirmary
243 Charles Street
Boston, MA 02114-3096

Phone: (617) 573-3711
Fax: (617) 573-3838
Toll Free: (800) 822-1327
TDD: (617) 573-3888
E-mail: tbregistry@meei.harvard.edu
http://www.tbregistry.org

The NIDCD National Temporal Bone, Hearing and Balance Pathology Resource Registry is a not-for-profit research organization that serves as a national resource for researchers and the public to promote research into human temporal bone and balance disorders. The registry continues and expands upon the activities of the former National Temporal Bone Banks Program established by the Deafness Research Foundation in 1960. Individuals with ear disorders such as hearing loss or balance problems may make an anatomical gift of their temporal bones and associated brain structures. These donations are vital for the advancement of knowledge and understanding of hearing and balance disorders.

President: Saumil N. Merchant, M.D. (Co-Director)
Executive Director: Sharon DeRosa (Registry Coordinator)
Year Established: 1992

Keywords
Balance Disorders; DNA Program; Facial Nerve; Hearing Loss; NIDCD National Temporal Bone, Hearing and Balance Pathology Resource Registry; Otopathology; Temporal Bone Disorder

2007 Niemann-Pick Disease Group (UK)

19 Downham View
Dursley
Gloucestershire, GL11 5GB, United Kingdom

Phone: +44 (0) 1453-51-9531
Fax: +44 (0) 1453-51-9531
E-mail: niemann-pick@zetnet.co.uk
http://www.niemannpick.org.uk

The Niemann-Pick Disease Group (UK) provides information and support to families affected by Niemann-Pick disease, a group of rare, inherited and metabolic disorders. Symptoms include yellow discoloration of the skin and eyes, progressive loss of motor skills, feeding difficulties, learning disabilities, and an abnormally enlarged liver or spleen. There are several different types of Niemann-Pick disease, and the NPDG provides information and support for all.

President: Tanya Collin-Histed, National Development Manager
Year Established: 1991
Acronym: NPDG (UK)

Keywords
Lipidosis, Juvenile Dystonic; NPDG; Neville's Disease; Niemann Pick Disease; Niemann Pick Disease Group (UK); Niemann-Pick Disease Group (UK)

2008 NIH Osteoporosis and Related Bone Diseases National Resource Center

1232 22nd Street NW
Washington, DC 20037-1292

Phone: (202) 223-0344
Fax: (202) 293-2356
Toll Free: (800) 624-2663
TDD: (202) 466-4315
E-mail: niamsboneinfo@mail.nih.gov
http://www.osteo.org

The NIH Osteoporosis and Related Bone Diseases National Resource Center (NIH ORBD NRC) provides patients, health professionals, and the public with an important link to resources and information on metabolic bone diseases such as osteoporosis, Paget's disease of bone, osteogenesis imperfecta, and primary hyperparathyroidism. Specific populations include the elderly, men, women, adolescents, and minorities. The Resource Center offers materials in English, Spanish, Chinese, Korean, Lao, Cambodian, and Vietnamese. NIH ORBD NRC is supported under a contract from the National Institute of Arthritis and Musculoskeletal and Skin Diseases, NIH, with contributions from the National Institute of Child Health and Human Development, National Institute of Dental and Craniofacial Research, National Institute of Diabetes and Digestive and Kidney Diseases, NIH Office of Research on Women's Health, DHHS Office on Women's Health, and the National Institute on Aging. NIH ORBD NRC is operated by the National Osteoporosis Foundation.

Executive Director: Susan Whittier
Year Established: 1994
Acronym: NIH ORBD~NRC

Keywords
Fibrous Dysplasia; Hyperparathyroidism, Primary; Hypophosphatasia; Myeloma Bone Disease; NIH Osteoporosis and Related Bone Diseases National Resource Center; Osteogenesis Imperfecta; Osteoporosis; Osteoporosis and Related Bone Diseases National Resource Center; Osteoporosis, Juvenile; Paget's Disease of Bone; Singleton Merten Syndrome

2009   Non-Ketotic Hyperglycinemia (NKH) International Family Network
481 Camisteo Street
Hornell, NY, 14843

Phone: (727) 799-4977
Fax: (727) 441-4942
E-mail: burkenkh@communicomm.com
http://www.nkh-network.org

The Non-Ketotic Hyperglycinemia (NKH) International Family Network is a voluntary organization dedicated to providing information and support to parents with children affected by non-ketotic hyperglycinemia. A rare inherited metabolic disorder that affects infants soon after birth, non-ketotic hyperglycinemia is caused by impairment in the breakdown of the amino acid glycine. As a result, affected infants exhibit an abnormal accumulation of glycine in body fluids, primarily the blood, cerebrospinal fluid, and urine. Symptoms and physical features may include failure to gain weight and grow at the expected rate; abnormally low muscle tone; drowsiness; episodes of uncontrolled electrical disturbances in the brain; repeated, brief, shock-like muscle spasms of the arms, legs, or entire body; and mild to severe mental retardation. Established in 1995, the non-ketotic hyperglycinemia International Family Network provides networking services that enable parents and family members to exchange information, support, and resources. It has a registry, provides referrals, and offers the "NKH International Family Network Newsletter."

President: Terina Burke
Year Established: 1995
Acronym: NKH Int'l Family Network

Keywords
Glycinemia, Nonketotic; Hyperglycinemia, Nonketotic; Non-Ketotic Hyperglycinemia (NKH) International Family Network

2010   The Noonan Syndrome Support Group, Inc.
P.O. Box 145
Upperco, MD 21155

Phone: (410) 374-5245
Toll Free: (888) 686-2224
E-mail: wanda@noonansyndrome.org
http://www.noonansyndrome.org

The Noonan Syndrome Support Group, Inc., (TNSSG, Inc.) is an international, non-profit organization that is dedicated to the sharing of information and encouragement among individuals whose lives have been affected by Noonan syndrome. Noonan syndrome is a genetic disorder that is usually apparent at birth (congenital) but is frequently difficult to diagnose. The disorder may be characterized by a wide spectrum of symptoms and physical features that may vary greatly in range and severity from case to case. However, in many individuals with Noonan syndrome, such abnormalities may include a distinctive facial appearance, a broad or a webbed neck, short stature, characteristic malformations of the breastbone (sternum), and/or heart malformations of cardiac blood and lymph vessels, blood clotting and platelet deficiencies, mild learning difficulties, and/or other symptoms and findings. Established in 1996 and composed of over 600 families from around the world, the organization publishes a quarterly newsletter, "The Noonan Connection." TNSSG, Inc., maintains a Resource Center that provides its members with access to the most recent medical journal articles and studies. Support group meetings are held annually.

President: Wanda H. Robinson (Founder)
Year Established: 1996
Acronym: TNSSG

Keywords
The Noonan Syndrome Support Group, Inc.; Noonan Syndrome; Noonan Syndrome Support Group, Inc.; Pseudo Turner Syndrome, Female; Turner Phenotype with Normal Karyotype; Turner Syndrome (Male); Turner Ullrich Syndrome

2011   Norrie Disease Association
Massachusetts General Hospital
149 13th Street
Building E, No. 6217
Charlestown, MA 02129

Phone: (617) 726-5718
Fax: (617) 724-9620

E-mail: ksims@partners.org
http://www.dnalab.org

The Norrie Disease Association is a voluntary not-for-profit service organization dedicated to providing support and information to people with Norrie disease and their families. Norrie disease is a rare inherited disorder characterized by blindness in both eyes at birth; some affected children may later develop mild to profound hearing loss and varying degrees of mental retardation. Established in 1994, the Norrie Disease Association compiles and disseminates educational and research information on the disorder; maintains a patient registry; and provides referrals to medical and/or genetic services. The association also provides educational and supportive information through its database, directory, and flyers.

Executive Director: Katherine B. Sims, M.D.
Year Established: 1994
Acronym: NDA

Keywords
Norrie Disease; Norrie Disease Association; Norrie Disease Registry

2012 North American Malignant Hyperthermia Registry of MHAUS

Children's Hospital of Pittsburgh
Room #7446
3705 Fifth Avenue at DeSoto Street
Pittsburgh, PA 15213-2583

Phone: (412) 692-6390
Fax: (412) 692-8658
Toll Free: (888) 274-7899
E-mail: bwb+@pitt.edu
http://www.mhreg.org

The North American Malignant Hyperthermia Registry is a not-for-profit research organization that is dedicated to acquiring, analyzing, and disseminating patient-specific clinical and laboratory information from patients with this syndrome. Malignant hyperthermia (MH) is an inherited condition characterized by a rapid rise in carbon dioxide production due to increased metabolism in muscle. It occurs most commonly during general anesthesia. Established in 1987, the North American Malignant Hyperthermia Registry maintains a centralized database of reports from individuals with MH susceptibility and similar syndromes. The registry has pro-

vided database services to participating MH diagnostic centers for standardization and validation of MH diagnostic testing procedures. It also provides de-identified data for investigation of the diagnosis, treatment, and prevention of MH episodes.

President: Sheila M. Muldoon, M.D. (Chairperson)
Executive Director: Barbara W. Brandom, MD
Year Established: 1987
Acronym: NAMHR

Keywords
Malignant Hyperthermia; Malignant Hyperthermia Registry of MHAUS; MH; North American Malignant Hyperthermia Registry; North American Malignant Hyperthermia Registry of MHAUS

2013 North American Riding for the Handicapped Association

P.O. Box 33150
Denver, CO 80233

Phone: (303) 452-1212
Fax: (303) 457-8496
Toll Free: (800) 369-7433
E-mail: narha@narha.org
http://www.narha.org

The North American Riding for the Handicapped Association (NARHA) is a national, nonprofit equestrian organization dedicated to serving individuals with disabilities by giving them the opportunity to ride horses. NARHA establishes safety standards, provides continuing education, and offers networking opportunities for both its individuals and operating center members. Riders are encouraged to expand the limits of their abilities in environments that promote success. Established in 1969, NARHA is headquartered in Denver, with a membership of approximately 3,600 and 600 operating centers. NARHA provides educational opportunities through regional workshops, an annual conference, and regional and state networks.

Executive Director: Sheia Kemper Dietrich
Year Established: 1969
Acronym: NARHA

Keywords
Equestrian Therapy; Horseback Riding; North American Riding for the Handicapped Association

2014 Nystagmus Network (UK)
13 Tinsley Close
Claypote
Newark
Nottinghamshire, NG23 5BS, United Kingdom

Phone: +44 (0) 1392-27-2573
E-mail: info@nystagmusnet.org
http://www.nystagmusnet.org

The Nystagmus Network is an international, self-help organization in the United Kingdom dedicated to providing information, support, and resources to individuals with nystagmus, a condition characterized by involuntary movements of the eyes. In most cases, individuals with nystagmus experience associated visual impairment (e.g., moderate to severe reduction in visual acuity). Nystagmus is often apparent at birth (congenital) and may be an isolated condition or may occur due to or in association with other visual abnormalities or a variety of underlying disorders. In other cases, nystagmus may develop later in life due to certain injuries, diseases, or disorders. The Nystagmus Network was established in 1984 and currently has over 100 members in the United Kingdom and other countries. The network's activities and services include providing a telephone helpline for affected individuals and family members in the UK; conducting regular meetings and seminars throughout the United Kingdom; responding to e-mail inquiries; and promoting and supporting research concerning the treatment of nystagmus. The organization also offers audiocassette recordings of speakers at annual meetings; provides guidelines for teachers; publishes a regular newsletter entitled "FOCUS"; and offers additional publications.

President: Vivien Jones
Executive Director: Paul White
Year Established: 1984

Keywords
Nystagmus Network (UK)

2015 Obsessive Compulsive Anonymous
P.O. Box 215
New Hyde Park, NY 11040

Phone: (516) 739-0662

Obsessive Compulsive Anonymous (OCA) is a national, nonprofit, self-help organization consisting of a fellowship of individuals dedicated to sharing their experience, strength, and hope with one another to enable them to solve their common problems and help others recover from obsessive compulsive disorder (OCD). OCD is characterized by recurrent, unwanted, and unpleasant thoughts (obsessions) and/or repetitive, ritualistic behaviors that the affected individual feels driven to perform (compulsions). Established in 1988, OCA is a fellowship of people who use the Twelve Steps, as originated by Alcoholics Anonymous and adapted for OCA, to help obtain relief from obsessions and compulsions. Although OCA does not endorse any specific treatments for OCD, the organization does recommend that its members see physicians skilled in the diagnosis and treatment of OCD. Consisting of approximately 1,000 members and 50 chapters, OCA is not allied with any sect, denomination, organization, or institution. The organization provides informational pamphlets and meeting contact lists with contacts throughout the United States and Canada.

Year Established: 1988
Acronym: OCA

Keywords
Obsessive Compulsive Anonymous; Obsessive Compulsive Disorder; Obsessive Compulsive Neurosis; OCD

2016 Obsessive-Compulsive Foundation, Inc.
P.O. Box 9573
New Haven, CT 06535

Phone: (203) 401-2070
Fax: (203) 401-2076
E-mail: info@ocfoundation.org
http://www.ocfoundation.org

The Obsessive-Compulsive Foundation is a national, not-for-profit organization dedicated to giving support to individuals with obsessive-compulsive disorder (OCD), their families and friends, medical professionals, and other concerned individuals. OCD is an anxiety disorder characterized by recurrent obsessive or compulsive thoughts that may interfere with the affected individual's normal routine, occupational functioning, social activities, and personal relationships. Established in 1986, the Obsessive-Compulsive Foundation raises funds for research; compiles and disseminates the latest treatment information; and engages in patient advocacy. It also provides appropriate referrals including support groups which engages in patient, professional, and community education. Informational and supportive materials include a bimonthly newsletter, semi-annual children's newsletter and a quarterly newsletter for support group leaders, booklets and brochures.

President: Susan Duffy
Executive Director: Patricia Perkins Doyle
Year Established: 1986
Acronym: OCF

Keywords
Obsessive Compulsive Disorder; OCD

2017 Ocular Motor Apraxia Home Page

P.O. Box 999
Cambridge, CB1 4WD, United Kingdom

Phone: +44 (0) 1223-77-5664
Fax: +44 (0) 1223-77-5662
E-mail: mod.oma@wwweb.org
http://www.wwweb.org/oma/

The Ocular Motor Apraxia Home Page is a web site on the Internet dedicated to serving as an information resource on ocular motor apraxia (OMA), a rare vision disorder characterized by absence or impairment of horizontal eye movements. These symptoms may vary from child to child, and may include colic during the first several months; head jerks and blinking; and low muscle tone, possibly linked to developmental delay. The OMA Home Page serves as a medical information resource, using the Internet to reach a small and geographically dispersed international audience. The site is dedicated to providing understandable information on OMA, offering online networking opportunities to affected individuals and family members, and promoting research into OMA.

President: R. Young (OMA coordinator)
Executive Director: Same as above.
Year Established: 1997
Acronym: OMA Home Page

Keywords
Apraxia, Congenital Oculomotor; Apraxia, Ocular Motor; Apraxia, Oculomotor; Cogan's Syndrome, Type II; Ocular Motor Apraxia Home Page; OMA

2018 Oculo-Dento-Digital Dysplasia Support Group

8810 Orchard Road
Pikesville, MD 21208

Phone: (410) 580-0882
E-mail: aboutus@odddsupportgroup.com
http://www.odddsupportgroup.com

Oculo-Dento-Digital Dysplasia Support Group (ODDD) is a not-for-profit, self-help support group whose main goal is to bring together people with oculo-dento-digital dysplasia. This rare disorder may be inherited as an autosomal dominant trait or it may be caused by a new change in the genes that occurs for no apparent reason (mutation). Signs and symptoms include webbing of the fourth and fifth fingers, an abnormally small transparent part of the eye (microcornea), a slender nose with narrow nostrils, defective tooth enamel, and dry hair that grows slowly. Members of ODDD group exchange information obtained from Web sites, physicians, and their own research.

President: John Quasney
Year Established: 2004
Acronym: ODDD

Keywords
Oculo Dento Digital Dysplasia; Oculo Dento Digital Dysplasia Support Group; Oculo-Dento-Digital Dysplasia Support Group; Research; Supports Groups

2019 Ohdo Syndrome Family Network

36 Borrowdale Avenue
Gatley Cheadle
Cheshire, SK8 4QF, United Kingdom

Phone: +44 (0) 161-428-8583
E-mail: patseville@btinternet.com

Ohdo Syndrome Family Network is a voluntary health organization located in the UK providing information to patients and their families, healthcare professionals, and the public. Ohdo syndrome, also known as Ohdo blepharophimosis syndrome, is characterized by learning difficulties in conjunction with congenital heart disease, small eye openings (blepharophimosis), drooping eyelids (blepharoptosis), and small teeth. The Ohdo Syndrome Family Network provides support and networking opportunities to parents of affected children. It also seeks to enhance awareness of this syndrome among medical professionals.

President: Patricia Seville

Keywords
Networking; Ohdo Blepharophimosis Syndrome; Ohdo Syndrome; Ohdo Syndrome Family Network; Support Groups

2020 Oley Foundation

214 Hun Memorial MC-28
Albany Medical Center
Albany, NY 12208-3478

Phone: (518) 262-5079
Fax: (518) 262-5528
Toll Free: (800) 776-6539
E-mail: BishopJ@mail.amc.edu
http://www.oley.org

The Oley Foundation is a national, non-profit organization dedicated to providing educational and emotional support, outreach activities, and clinical outcome information for individuals who depend on home intravenous (parenteral) and tube (enteral) nutrition, their families, professionals, and others. Individuals who depend on such nutrition include those who cannot receive enough nutrients from the food they eat because of severe gastrointestinal disorders that may impair their swallowing or intestinal absorption. The foundation facilitates a national network of regional volunteers who provide emotional support and outreach at the local level. Comprised of individuals who are themselves users of home nutrition and their family members, the network offers services ranging from telephone support and hospital visitation to lectures and self-help get-togethers. The Oley Foundation also sponsors yearly conferences that bring together home nutrition users with experts in the field. Educational materials produced by the Oley Foundation include brochures, audio-visual aids, and information about travel, swimming, and other topics.

President: Steve Swenson
Executive Director: Joan Bishop
Year Established: 1983

Keywords
Enteral Nutrition; Home Nutrition; Hyperal (Imentation); Intravenous Nutrition; Oley Foundation; Parenteral Nutrition; TPN; Tube Feeding

2021 OncoLink: The University of Pennsylvania Cancer Center Resource

3400 Spruce Street
2 Donner
Philadelphia, PA 19104-4283

Phone: (215) 349-5445
Fax: (215) 349-5445
E-mail: editors@oncolink.upenn.edu
http://www.oncolink.upenn.edu

OncoLink is a multimedia oncology information resource on the Internet. Its objectives are: (1) dissemination of information relevant to the field of oncology; (2) education of healthcare personnel; (3) education of affected individuals, families, and other interested parties; and (4) rapid collection of information pertinent to the specialty.

Keywords
Bone Cancer, Adult; Brain Cancer, Adult; Cancer; Cancer, Adult; Cancer, Bladder; Cancer, Breast; Cancer, Cervical; Cancer, Colon; Cancer, Endocrine System; Cancer, Endometrial; Cancer, Gastrointestinal; Cancer, Genitourinary; Cancer, Gynecologic; Cancer, Head and Neck; Cancer, Kidney; Cancer, Lung; Cancer, Ovarian; Cancer, Pancreatic; Cancer, Pediatric; Cancer, Pediatric Liver; Cancer, Prostate; Cancer, Urinary Tract; Cancer, Uterine; Cancer, Vulvar; Chemotherapy; Compassionate Need Programs; Ewing's Sarcoma; Financial Assistance Programs; Grieving; Hodgkin's Disease; Hodgkin's Lymphoma; Leukemia; Leukemia, Pediatric; Lymphoma; Lymphoma, Non Hodgkin's; Lymphoma, Pediatric; Myeloma; Neuroblastoma; OncoLink: The University of Pennsylvania Cancer Center Resource; Pain Management; Retinoblastoma; Rhabdomyosarcoma; Sarcoma; Sarcoma, Osteogenic; Skin Cancer; Transportation Assistance; Tumors, Pediatric Brain; Wilms' Tumor

2022 Online Asperger Syndrome Information and Support

E-mail: bkirby@udel.edu
http://www.aspergersyndrome.org

Online Asperger Syndrome Information and Support is a web site dedicated to providing information, support, and resources to individuals affected by Asperger syndrome and their family members. Some researchers consider Asperger syndrome a high functioning form of autism. The disorder may be characterized by poor motor skills, varied sensory- or information-processing difficulties, difficulty with social interactions, social withdrawal, and strong interest and functioning in certain educational areas. By definition, individuals with Asperger syndrome have a normal I.Q.; in addition, many may have an exceptional skill or talent in a specific area. Created by the parent of a child diagnosed with Asperger syndrome, the Online Asperger Syndrome Information and Support web site offers a variety of online networking opportunities; information on Asperger syndrome; links to research papers written on the disorder; information concerning medical centers, universities, and clinics; and links to several newsletters.

President: Barbara L. Kirby (Owner & Webmaster)
Acronym: O.A.S.I.S.

Keywords
AS; Asperger Disorder; Asperger Syndrome; Autism; Hyperlexia; Online Asperger Syndrome Information and Support

2023 Opitz G/BBB Family Network, Inc.

P.O. Box 515
Grand Lake, CO 80447

Phone: (970) 627-8935
Fax: (970) 627-8818
http://www.opitznet.org

The Opitz G/BBB Family Network is a voluntary, not-for-profit, self-help organization dedicated to providing support to individuals and family members affected by Opitz G/BBB syndrome. Opitz G/BBB syndrome is a rare hereditary disorder characterized by widely set eyes, hernias, undescended testicles and abnormal placement of the urinary opening on the underside of the penis in males, partial or total absence of the thick band of nerve fibers that connects the left and right hemispheres of the brain (hypoplasia or agenesis of the corpus callosum), swallowing difficulties, and/or additional abnormalities. Established in 1994, the Opitz G/BBB Family Network provides phone support; promotes the sharing of information, resources, and support among affected families; engages in patient advocacy; and offers appropriate referrals. It also maintains a database of members, engages in professional education, and offers a variety of educational and support materials including a regular newsletter and brochures.

President: Janet Wharton
Year Established: 1994

Keywords
BBB Syndrome; Opitz C Syndrome; Opitz FG Syndrome; Opitz Frias Syndrome; Opitz G Syndrome; Opitz G/BBB Family Network, Inc.; Opitz Syndrome

2024 Opsoclonus-Myoclonus Support Network, Inc.

4616 Brookwood Street NE
Albuquerque, NM 87109

Phone: (505) 881-2285
E-mail: sandragreenberg@hotmail.com
www.geocities.com/opso-myoclonus

The Opsoclonus-Myoclonus Syndrome Network is a not-for-profit organization dedicated to providing information and support to parents of children with opsoclonus-myoclonus syndrome. Myoclonus is a neurological movement disorder characterized by sudden, involuntary contractions of a muscle or groups of muscles. Opsoclonus is a condition in which there are non-rhythmic vertical and horizontal movements of the eyes. Established in 1994, the Opsoclonus Myoclonus Syndrome Support Network, Inc., enables parents and families to exchange information, support, and resources.

President: Sandy Greenberg
Year Established: 1994
Acronym: OMS

Keywords
Kinsbourne Syndrome; Myoclonus, Opsoclonus; OMS; Opsoclonus-Myoclonus Support Network, Inc.

2025 Organic Acidaemias UK

5 Saxon Road
Ashford
Middlesex, TW15 1QL, United Kingdom

Phone: +44 (0) 1784-24-5989
E-mail: davidpriddy@bigfoot.com

Organic Acidaemias UK is a contact group for parents of children with inherited genetic diseases of protein metabolism of single or groups of amino acids. Examples of disorders are methylmalonic acidaemia, maple syrup urine disease, propionic acidaemia, isovaleric acidaemia, argininosuccinic acidaemia, gluteric acidaemia, hydroxymethylgluteric acidaemia and ethyl-malonic-adipic aciduria. The group offers telephone support.

President: David Priddy
Year Established: 1984
Acronym: OAUK

Keywords
Acidaemia; Acidemia; Argininosuccinic Acidaemia; British Organic Acidemia Association; Glutaricaciduria I; Glutaricaciduria II; Gluteric Acidaemia; Isovaleric Acidaemia; LCAD; Medium Chain Acyl CoA Dehydrogenase Deficiency; Methylmalonic Acidaemia; Nonketotic Hyperglycinemia; Organic Acidaemias UK; Ornithine Transcarbamylase Deficiency; Proprionic Acidaemia; Pyruvate Dehydrogenase Deficiency; SCAD; Short Chain Acyl CoA Dehydrogenase Deficiency (SCAD); Urea Cycle Disorders; Very Long Chain Acyl CoA Dehydrogenase Deficiency (LCAD)

2026 Organic Acidemia Association

13210 35th Avenue North
Plymouth, MN 55441

Phone: (763) 559-1797
Fax: (763) 694-0017
E-mail: OAANews@aol.com
http://www.oaanews.org

The Organic Acidemia Association is a voluntary, not-for-profit, self-help organization dedicated to providing information and support to families of children with in-born errors of metabolism. Established in the early 1980s, the Organic Acidemia Association provides information to affected families and health care professionals across the country and internationally. The association publishes newsletters three times yearly.

President: Kathy Stagni
Executive Director: Same as above.
Year Established: 1980
Acronym: OAA

Keywords
2,4-Dienoyl-CoA Reductase Deficiency; 2MBCD; 2-Methylbutyryl-CoA Dehydrogenase Deficiency; 3-Hydroxy-3-Methylglutaryl-CoA Lyase Deficiency; 3-Hydroxyisobutyric Aciduria; 3-MCC; 3-Methylcrotonyl-CoA Carboxylase Deficiency; 3-Methylglutaconic Acidemia; 3-Methylglutaconyl-CoA Hydratase Deficiency; 5-Oxoprolinemia; Acidemia; Acidemia, Isovaleric; Acidemia, Methylmalonic; Acidemia, Organic; Acidemia, Propionic; D-2 Hydroxyglutaric Aciduria; D2-HGA; Errors of Amino Acid and Fatty Acid Metabolism; Glutaricaciduria I; Glutaricaciduria II; HMG; ICBD; Isobutyryl-CoA Dehydrogenase Deficiency; L-2-Hydroxy-Glutaricaciduria; L2HGA; LCAD; Long Chain Acyl CoA Dehydrogenase Deficiency; MCAD; Medium Chain Acyl CoA Dehydrogenase Deficiency; MGA; Multiple CoA Carboxylase Deficiency; Organic Acidemia Association; SCAD; Short Chain Acyl CoA Dehydrogenase Deficiency

2027 Organization for Anti-Convulsant Syndrome

P.O. Box 772
Pilling
Preston, PR3 6WW, United Kingdom

Phone: +44 (0) 1253-79-0000
Fax: +44 (0) 1253-79-0000
E-mail: Janet.oacs@btinternet.com
http://www.oacs-uk.co.uk/

The Organization for Anti-Convulsant Syndrome provides help and support to families of children suffering with anti-convulsant syndrome. It provides advice related to special educational needs, assistance in obtaining a diagnosis, and information to increase awareness of risks related to the use of anti-convulsant medication. Anti-convulsant syndrome is caused by the use of anti-convulsant medication during pregnancy. The syndrome is known by other names, including anti-epileptic drug syndrome and fetal valproate syndrome. It may result in learning difficulties or behavioral problems or any of various movement disorders.

President: Janet Williams
Executive Director: David and Yvette Tout
Year Established: 1999
Acronym: O.A.C.S.

Keywords
Asperger Syndrome; Attention Deficit Hyperactivity Disorder; Autism; Dyspraxia; Dystonia; Epilepsy; Fetal Anticonvulsant Syndrome; Fetal Valproate Syndrome; Organization For Anti Convulsant Syndrome; Organization for Anti-Convulsant Syndrome

2028 Organization for Understanding Cluster Headaches (O.U.C.H.)

3225 Winding Way
Round Rock, TX 78664

Phone: (214) 783-1899
E-mail: dd.ouch@gmail.com
http://www.clusterheadaches.org

Organization for Understanding Cluster Headaches (O.U.C.H.) is an information and support organization for people who have cluster headaches. These are headaches that come in groups and are very severe in intensity. They can last from 30 minutes to two hours. This rare headache condition affects less than one tenth of one percent of the world's population. OUCH serves an international audience. In addition to providing information, it encourages and participates in research.

President: Donna Delacerda
Year Established: 1999
Acronym: O.U.C.H.

Keywords
Headache, Cluster; Organization for Understanding Cluster Headaches (O.U.C.H.)

2029 ORPHANET

INSERM SC11
102 rue Didot
Paris, 75014, France

Phone: +33 (0) 156-53-81-37
Fax: +33 (0) 156-53-81-38
E-mail: orphanet@orpha.net
http://www.orpha.net

ORPHANET is a database dedicated to providing information on rare diseases and orphan drugs. Its access is free of charge. It includes an encyclopedia of rare diseases covering more than 1,300 diseases which is expert-authored and peer-reviewed, and a directory of services in Europe, including information on specialized clinics, clinical laboratories, ongoing research projects, clinical trials, registries, and support groups. ORPHANET also offers to patients the possibility to register to be informed about new clinical research projects or to be put in contact with another patient or family experiencing the same disease. ORPHANET has established a sister web site at www.orphanxchange.org to allow researchers to post their projects that may be of interest to industry. This is a tool to facilitate partnerships in the area of device and drug development.

Executive Director: Dr. Segolene Ayme (1996 to Present)
Year Established: 1996
Acronym: ORPHANET

Keywords
ORPHANET; Rare Disease Support

2030 Osteogenesis Imperfecta Foundation, Inc.

804 West Diamond Avenue
Suite 210
Gaithersburg, MD 20878

Phone: (301) 947-0083
Fax: (301) 947-0456
Toll Free: (800) 981-2663
E-mail: bonelink@oif.org
http://www.oif.org

The Osteogenesis Imperfecta Foundation, Inc., is a nonprofit organization dedicated to improving the quality of life for individuals affected by osteogenesis imperfecta through research, education, awareness, and mutual support. Osteogenesis imperfecta (OI) is a genetic disorder characterized by abnormally fragile bones. Established in 1970, the foundation offers information and support to affected individuals, family members, and health professionals. It also funds and encourages research into the causes of, and treatments for, OI. In addition, the foundation provides numerous print, video, and online resources, facilitates peer contact, fosters local support groups, holds biannual conferences, engages in patient advocacy, and provides physician referrals. Fact sheets can be downloaded from the web site.

President: Jamie Kendall
Executive Director: H. Shapiro
Year Established: 1970
Acronym: OI Foundation

Keywords
Brittle Bones; Osteogenesis Imperfecta; Osteogenesis Imperfecta Foundation, Inc.

2031 Osteopetrosis Support Trust (UK)

37 Bristol Road
Winterbourne, S Glos, BS36 1RQ, United Kingdom

Phone: +44 (0) 145-485-2199
E-mail: info@ost.org.uk
http://www.ost.org.uk

The Osteopetrosis Support Trust (OST) is a voluntary, not-for-profit organization dedicated to supporting families with children who have osteopetrosis, a rare genetic disorder characterized by increased bone density and brittle bones. Established in 1994, the trust has members throughout the United Kingdom, and across the world. OST offers support to families of affected children and some (limited) financial assistance (to families in the UK). It also promotes and supports ongoing medical research. OST produces and distributes an information leaflet and a newsletter.

President: Tracy Jones
Executive Director: Margaret Wright (Family Support)
Year Established: 1994
Acronym: OST

Keywords
FROST: Friends of the Osteopetrosis Support Trust; Osteopetrosis; Osteopetrosis Support Trust (UK)

2032 OT Resources

E-mail: gloriamacnel@att.net
http://www.orthostatictremor.org

This web site provides information about, and enhances awareness of, orthostatic tremor. It also provides opportunities for those affected to share their experiences. It includes an international forum and Internet support group. Primary orthostatic tremor consists of rhythmical muscle contractions that cause discomfort or unsteadiness when an individual is in a standing upright position.

President: Gloria Nelson

Keywords
OT Resources

2033 Oto Palatal Digital Syndrome Family Resource Network

9559 Woodridge Circle
Eden Prairie, MN 55347

Phone: (952) 947-9936
E-mail: opdsyndrome@yahoo.com
http://www.geocities.com/opdsyndrome

The Oto-Palatal-Digital Syndrome Family Resource Network was formed to provide patients afflicted with this rare genetic disorder and their family members with information, resources and support. Oto-palatal-digital syndrome presents with various findings that may include cleft palate, a downward slant of the opening between the upper and lower eyelids, hearing loss, and short fingers and toes.

President: Patricia McCormick (2001-present)
Year Established: 2001
Acronym: OPD/FRN

Keywords
Oto Palatal Digital Syndrome Family Resource Network

2034 Ovacome (UK)

EGA Hospital
Huntley Street
London, WC1E 6DH, United Kingdom

Phone: +44 (0) 207-380-9589
E-mail: ovacome@ovacome.org.uk
http://www.ovacome.org.uk

Ovacome (UK), is a national, not-for-profit support group in the United Kingdom for all those concerned with ovarian cancer, including affected individuals, family members, friends, caregivers, and health care professionals. Established in 1995, Ovacome is committed to offering networking opportunities for affected individuals through its nationwide telephone network called "FoneFriends," raising awareness of ovarian cancer, and offering information on screening, research, and treatments. In addition, Ovacome publishes a quarterly newsletter and maintains a web site on the Internet. Ovacome's web site provides information on the organization's mission and services, has a guest book area for online visitors, offers access to its newsletter, and has a "Helpfinder" area that lists ovarian cancer resources. Such resources include books, newsletters, and videos; support groups, cancer centers, and research groups; and web sites that provide additional information or support.

President: Noeline Young
Executive Director: Louise Bayne
Year Established: 1996

Keywords
Ovacome (UK); Ovarian Cancer

2035 Ovarian Cancer National Alliance

910 17th Street NW
Suite 413
Washington, DC 20006

Phone: (202) 331-1332
Fax: (202) 331-2292
E-mail: ocna@ovariancancer.org
http://www.ovariancancer.org

The Ovarian Cancer National Alliance is a voluntary, not-for-profit umbrella organization uniting ovarian cancer survivors, women's health activists, and healthcare professionals in a coordinated effort to focus national attention on ovarian cancer. The symptoms of ovarian cancer are often subtle and may be easily confused with symptoms associated with other disorders. Such symptoms commonly include pressure or bloating in the abdomen, constant and progressive changes in bladder or bowel patterns, persistent digestive problems, ongoing excessive fatigue, abnormal bleeding, and pain during intercourse. The Ovarian Cancer National Alliance, which was established in 1997, works to fight ovarian cancer by focusing on four key areas: expanding women's and healthcare providers' awareness about the disease; advocating for increased funding for research, sound genetic-testing policies, and insurance coverage of therapies; furthering the scientific understanding of ovarian cancer to improve screening and detection tools and to discover a cure; and coordinating efforts in the fight against ovarian cancer by developing networks among ovarian cancer groups and activists and other health advocates. The alliance's activities include providing expert testimony before government committees, serving as consumer representatives on federal panels that set priorities for ovarian cancer research, working closely with the Society of Gynecologic Oncologists to strengthen ovarian cancer resources, and conducting national advocacy conferences for the ovarian cancer community.

President: Virginia Ackerman
Executive Director: Sherry Salway Black
Year Established: 1997

Keywords
Ovarian Cancer National Alliance

2036 Oxalosis and Hyperoxaluria Foundation
201 East 19th Street
#12E
New York, NY 10003

Phone: (212) 777-0470
Fax: (212) 777-0471
Toll Free: (800) 643-8699
E-mail: execdirector@ohf.org
http://www.ohf.org/

The Oxalosis and Hyperoxaluria Foundation is a national voluntary organization established to inform the public, especially affected individuals, families, physicians, and medical professionals about hyperoxaluria and related conditions such as oxalosis and calcium-oxalate kidney stones. The foundation endeavors to provide a support network to those affected by hyperoxaluria. Founded in 1989, it supports and encourages research to find a cure for hyperoxaluria. The organization publishes educational materials including a summer camp list, reprints of medical journal articles, a patient resource list, and brochures entitled "Understanding Oxalosis" and "Hyperoxaluria and Low Oxalate Diet List." The organization also supports a toll-free phone number (800) OHF-8699.

President: Brett Rosen
Executive Director: Kim Hollander
Year Established: 1989
Acronym: OHF

Keywords
Oxalate Kidney Stones; Hyperoxaluria; Hyperoxaluria, Acquired; Hyperoxaluria, Primary; Hyperoxaluria, Primary Type I; Hyperoxaluria, Secondary; Oxalosis; Oxalosis and Hyperoxaluria Foundation; Oxaluria

2037 Paget Foundation for Paget's Disease of Bone and Related Disorders
120 Wall Street
Suite 1602
New York, NY 10005

Phone: (212) 509-5335
Fax: (212) 509-8492
Toll Free: (800) 237-2438
E-mail: pagetfdn@aol.com
http://www.paget.org

The Paget Foundation is a voluntary health agency devoted to serving people affected by Paget's disease of bone and certain other bone disorders, including primary hyperparathyroidism, fibrous dysplasia, osteopetrosis, and the complications of certain cancers of the skeleton. Established in 1978, it continues to provide affected individuals and their families with up-to-date information about these disorders. It also provides physician referrals, information to enhance public awareness of Paget's disease of bone and related disorders, and professional education for members of the medical community.

President: Dr. Frederick R. Singer, Chairman
Executive Director: Charlene Waldman
Year Established: 1978

Keywords
Fibrous Dysplasia; Hyperparathyroidism, Primary; McCune Albright Syndrome; Osteitis Deformans; Osteopetrosis; Paget Foundation for Paget's Disease of Bone and Related Disorders; Paget's Disease; Paget's Disease of Bone

2038 Pallister-Hall Foundation (Aust.)
Post Office Box 88
Toowoomba
Queensland, 4350, Australia

Phone: +61 (0) 7-4634-0045
Fax: +61 (0) 7-4634-0045
E-mail: info@pallisterhall.com
http://www.pallisterhall.com

The Pallister-Hall Foundation in Australia is a nonprofit, charitable organization dedicated to the health, support and education of Pallister-Hall syndrome (PHS) patients, families, caregivers, healthcare providers, and the general public. Founded to meet these goals, the PHF also promotes research on this rare, genetic disorder. The mission of the PHF is to educate and provide support worldwide through the provision of information that is in everyday language.

President: George William Helon
Year Established: 2002
Acronym: PHF (Aust.)

Keywords
Chromosome 7; Genetic Disorders; Hypothalamic Disorders; Hypothalamic Harmartomas; Pallister Hall Foundation (Aust.); Pallister Hall Syndrome; Pituitary Disorders

2039 Pallister-Hall Syndrome Family Support Network
RFD Box 3000
Fairground Road
Bradford, VT 05033

Phone: (802) 222-9683
E-mail: messer@sover.net

The Pallister-Hall Syndrome Family Support Network is a voluntary, not-for-profit organization dedicated to serving individuals and families affected by Pallister-Hall syndrome. This is a rare disorder characterized by a benign tumor in a certain area of the brain (hypothalamic hamartoblastoma), extra fingers and/or toes, an absent or extremely small anal opening, and decreased pituitary function. Established in 1994 by concerned parents and health care professionals, the network provides referrals to physicians and genetic professionals, offers access to research on Pallister-Hall syndrome, and promotes the exchange of information, support, and resources through networking with other families. It also promotes awareness of Pallister-Hall syndrome among healthcare professionals and the public.

President: Felicia Johnson (1994-Present)
Executive Director: Debra Messer
Year Established: 1994

Keywords
Pallister Hall Syndrome; Pallister Hall Syndrome Family Support Network; Pallister-Hall Foundation; Pallister-Hall Syndrome Family Support Network

2040 Pancreatic Cancer Action Network, Inc. (PanCAN)
2141 Rosecrans Avenue
Suite 7000
El Segundo, CA 90245

Phone: (310) 725-0025
Fax: (310) 725-0029
Toll Free: (877) 272-6226
E-mail: info@pancan.org(do not E-mail news updates)
http://www.pancan.org

The Pancreatic Cancer Action Network, Inc., (PanCAN) is a non-profit public benefit organization that provides a strong voice in advocacy for those affected by pancreatic cancer. PanCAN is dedicated to focusing national attention on the need to find a cure for, and ultimately to eliminate, pancreatic cancer. This will be accomplished by providing public and professional education that embraces the urgent need for more research, effective treatments, and early detection and prevention programs. Pancreatic cancer is the fourth-ranked cause of cancer death in the U.S. among both men and women. Approximately 29,000 Americans are diagnosed with pancreatic cancer each year.

President: Julie Fleshman, JD, MBA
Year Established: 1999
Acronym: PanCAN

Keywords
Cancer, Pancreatic; PanCAN; Pancreatic Cancer Action Network, Inc. (PanCAN)

2041 Pancreatica.org—Confronting Pancreatic Cancer
208 Carmel Avenue
Pacific Grove, CA 93950

Phone: (831) 658-0600
Fax: (831) 658-0518
E-mail: webmaster@pancreatica.org
http://www.pancreatica.org/

Pancreatica.org is an Internet extension of the Lorenzen Cancer Foundation. The Pancreatica site offers information concerning the diagnosis and treatment of cancer of the pancreas. It serves as a gathering point for patients and physicians, as well as a focal point for news related to diagnosis and treatment.

President: Lee Lorenzen
Executive Director: Dale O'Brien, M.D. Medical Director
Year Established: 2001
Acronym: Pancreatica

Keywords
Cancer, Pancreatic; Pancreatica.org—Confronting Pancreatic Cancer

2042 Pancreatitis Supporters Network

P.O. Box 8938
Birmingham, B13 9FW, United Kingsom

Phone: +44 (0) 121-449-2923
Toll Free: (800) 424-2923
E-mail: info@pancreatitis.org.uk
http://www.naphosting.co.uk/psn/contact.htm

The Pancreatitis Supporters Network is a self-help organization in the United Kingdom providing information about pancreatitis to patients and their families, medical professionals, and the general public. Pancreatitis can be acute or chronic. It occurs when enzymes produced to digest food turn on the pancreas, which is behind the stomach, producing inflammation. Symptoms include stomach pain, food intolerance, and nausea.

President: Jim Armour (Chairman)
Acronym: PSN

Keywords
Acute Pancreatitis; Advocacy; Cancer of the Pancreas; Chronic Pancreatitis; Networking; Pancreatitis; Pancreatitis Supporters Network; PSN; Support Groups

2043 Panniculitis Support Group

100 Pleasant Acres Road
Apt.# 208
York, PA 17402

E-mail: ladypann@yahoo.com
http://www.groups.yahoo.com/group/panniculitis/

The Panniculitis Support Group is an online support group dedicated to enabling affected individuals and family members to exchange information, resources, and mutual support. Healthcare professionals are also invited to participate in this mailing list. Panniculitis is an inflammatory condition characterized by the development of single or multiple, tender or painful bumps below the surface of the skin (subcutaneous nodules) and inflammation of the subcutaneous layer of fat. Panniculitis may occur as a separate distinct disorder in some cases due to cold or trauma or for unknown reasons (idiopathic); in other cases, panniculitis may occur in association with several different underlying disorders. Members of the Panniculitis Support Group may send their questions and comments to the group's e-mail address, where the messages are distributed to all group subscribers. Members of the group may then choose to post responses or other questions for distribution or may respond directly to the original member's e-mail address. The Panniculitis Support Group shares understandable information on the condition, diagnosis, and treatment; promotes the exchange of mutual support; and offers additional resources.

President: Gail Hubbard (List Owner)
Year Established: 1997

Keywords
Archives of Messages; Chat Available; Files; International; Links; Members Database; Panniculitis; Panniculitis Support Group; Panniculitis, Idiopathic Nodular; Panniculitis, Mesenteric; Panniculitis, Nodular Nonsuppurative; Panniculitis, Relapsing Febrile Nodular Nonsuppurative; Panniculitis, Septal; Panniculitis, Weber Christian; Photos; Private Group; Weber Christian Disease

2044 PARC: Promoting Awareness of RSD/CRPS in Canada

P.O. Box 210726 St. Catherines
Ontario, L2M 7X2, Canada

Phone: (905) -93-4-02
E-mail: rsdinfo@becon.org
http://people.becon.org/~rsdinfo/english/index.html

PARC: Promoting Awareness of RSD/CRPS in Canada is an organization whose mission is to support, educate and inform people affected by reflex sympathetic dystrophy (RSD), otherwise known as complex regional pain syndrome (CRPS). RSD is a rare disorder of the sympathetic nervous system that is characterized by chronic, severe pain. A portion of PARC's mission is to educate RSD patients, their family members, the public and the healthcare community about the importance of early diagnosis and treatment of RSD. PARC's other objectives are to educate the public and healthcare community about RSD in general; to provide support, encouragement and other services to persons living with RSD; and to fund research into the causes, controls, treatments and cures for RSD.

Year Established: 2001
Acronym: PARC

Keywords
Advocacy; Canada; Causalgia; Complex Regional Pain Syndrome; CRPS; Networking; PARC; PARC: Promoting Awareness of RSD/CRPS in Canada; Research; RSD; Support Groups

2045 **Parent Project Muscular Dystrophy**
1012 N. University Boulevard
Middletown, OH 45042
and
158 Linwood Plaza
Suite 220
Fort Lee, NJ 07024

Phone: (513) 424-0696
Fax: (513) 425-9907
Toll Free: (800) 714-5437
E-mail: Pat@parentprojectmd.org
http://www.parentprojectmd.org

Parent Project Muscular Dystrophy (formerly the Parent Project for Muscular Dystrophy Research) is a not-for-profit national health organization founded in 1994 by parents of children with Duchenne and Becker muscular dystrophy. PPMD's mission is to improve the treatment, quality of life, and long-term outlook for all individuals affected by Duchenne muscular dystrophy through research, advocacy, education, and compassion. PPMD seeks to ensure that all families, caregivers, and healthcare professionals have access to current information about treatment and care options for children with DMD/BMD. It encourages health and human services policy makers to afford the same priority to DMD/BMD as to other disorders of similar incidence and prevalence. PPMD seeks to collaborate with the international community to assure that the voices of people with DMD/BMD are heard.

President: Patricia A. Furlong (1994 to Present)
Executive Director: Kimberly Galberaith, Asst. Exec. Director
Year Established: 1994
Acronym: PPMD

Keywords
Muscular Dystrophy; Muscular Dystrophy, Becker; Muscular Dystrophy, Duchenne; Parent Project Muscular Dystrophy

2046 **Parent to Parent New Zealand**
P.O. Box 234
Waikato Mail Centre
Hamilton, New Zealand

Phone: +64 (0) 7-853-8491
Fax: +64 (0) 7-853-8491
Toll Free: 0508-236-236
E-mail: national@parent2parent.org.nz
http://www.parent2parent.org.nz

Parent to Parent of New Zealand is a non-profit organization dedicated to providing support to parents who have children with special needs. Support is provided voluntarily by trained support parents who have a child with the same or similar needs. Formed in 1983, the group has built up a support network that is now nationwide. The organization is affiliated with similar groups around the world and maintains close links with other organizations and professionals who work in related fields. Parent to Parent provides contact with a support parent, community seminars, workshops, family camps, and a resource library on different conditions. In addition to resource materials, a newsletter entitled "Parent to Parent" is available. Consisting of 14 chapters and more than 500 members, the organization also offers support groups, and patient networking.

President: Christine Zander (2002 to 2005)
Executive Director: Anne Wilkinson, CEO
Year Established: 1983

Keywords
Parent to Parent New Zealand; Parent to Parent of New Zealand

2047 **Parentpals.com**
1442 East Lincoln Avenue
#363
Orange, CA 92865

Phone: (714) 283-4758
E-mail: superpal@parentpals.com
http://www.parentpals.com

Parentpals.com, a special education web site, provides a variety of services for parents of children with special needs and professionals including information on attention deficit disorder, autism, hearing impairment, emotional disturbances, learning disabilities, mental retardation, mobility impairment, speech and language impairment, stuttering, visual impairment, traumatic brain injury, and/or other health impairments. Parentpals.com provides information from therapists, teachers, physicians, nurses, and counselors on such topics as special education services, early intervention services, and individualized education programs (IEPs); a dictionary of terms used in special education; and an index of definitions concerning certain disorders. The site also provides specific educational and therapy games to enhance children's learning and language skills. These teaching ideas are organized by four levels, ranging from level 1 with preschool tasks to level 4 for gifted students. Parentpals.com also provides weekly tips, a newsletter and message board. In addition, the site offers over 1000 dynamic links to additional web sites.

President: Leslie Kirchoff-Fauquet M.A. C.C.C. (Founder)
Year Established: 1997

Keywords
ADHD; Attention Deficit Hyperactivity Disorder; Autism; CEUs; Continuing Education; Early Intervention Services; Emotional Disturbances; Gifted Education; Hearing Impairment; Individualized Education Programs; Language Impairments; Learning Disabilities; Mentally Retarded; Mobility Impairment; Online Continuing Education; Parentpals.com; Special Education; Special Education Continuing Education; Special Education Online Continuing Education; Stuttering; Traumatic Brain Injuries; Visually Impaired

2048   Parents of Galactosemic Children, Inc.

1519 Magnolia Bluff
Gautier, MS 39553

Phone: (228) 497-5886
Fax: (228) 497-5886
Toll Free: (866) 900-7421
E-mail: president@galactosemia.org
http://www.galactosemia.org

Parents of Galactosemic Children, Inc., is a nonprofit, voluntary health organization dedicated to maximizing the potential for the development of individuals with galactosemia, which is a rare genetic metabolic disorder. Galactosemia is characterized by the inability of the body to break down (metabolize) galactose, which is a normal byproduct of lactose (e.g., milk) metabolism. The affected individual is missing the enzyme that converts galactose to glucose. Serious complications can occur including abnormal enlargement of the liver, kidney failure, cataracts, and/or brain damage. The objectives of the organization are to provide support and educational information to families affected by galactosemia and interested health care professionals; facilitate communication between professionals and families with galactosemia; and support professionals in the research of the treatment of galactosemia. Parents of Galactosemic Children, Inc., provides support to parents of affected children; publishes a self-titled periodic newsletter; seeks to stimulate ongoing clinical research; distributes ed-

ucational materials on galactosemia (e.g., a brochure entitled "Parents of Galactosemic Children"); operates a parent help line; and distributes appropriate dietary information on the disease.

President: Michelle Fowler
Executive Director: Same as above.
Year Established: 1985
Acronym: PGC

Keywords
Parents of Galactosemic Children, Inc.; Galactose 1 Phosphate Uridyl Transferase Deficiency; Galactosemia; GALT Deficiency; Parents of Galactosemic Children, Inc.

2049   Parents of Infants and Children with Kernicterus

One Superior Place
Suite 2410
Chicago, IL 60610

Phone: (312) 274-9695
E-mail: karendixon@pickonline.org
http://www.PICKonline.org

The mission of Parents of Infants and Children with Kernicterus is to prevent kernicterus and trace its causes, provide information and support to families, identify effective therapies and treatment, and seek out and fund promising research. Kernicterus is a rare neurological disorder that affects newborn infants of both sexes in equal numbers. It occurs more often in premature infants, and is characterized by hyperbilirubinemia (excessive levels of bilirubin in the blood) during infancy. Bilirubin is a byproduct of the natural breakdown of hemoglobin in red blood cells. Established in 2001, this voluntary organization provides services to patients and their families, health professionals, and the general public.

President: Karen Dixon, Ph.D.
Executive Director: Mitchell Dvorak
Year Established: 2001
Acronym: P.I.C.K.

Keywords
Parents of Infants and Children with Kernicterus; Auditory Neuropathy; Bilirubin; Cerebral Palsy; Crigler Najjar Syndrome; G6PD Deficiency; Gilbert Syndrome; Hyperbilirubinemia; Jaundice; Kernicterus; Parents of Infants and Children with Kernicterus

2050 **Parkinson's Disease Foundation, Inc.**
1359 Broadway
Suite 1509
New York, NY 10018

Phone: (212) 923-4700
Fax: (212) 923-4778
Toll Free: (800) 457-6676
E-mail: info@pdf.org
http://www.pdf.org

The Parkinson's Disease Foundation (PDF) is a leading national presence in Parkinson's disease research, patient education, and advocacy for increased federal funding. PDF is working for the nearly one million people in the U.S. living with Parkinson's by funding promising scientific research and supporting people with Parkinson's, their families and caregivers through educational programs and support services. Since its founding in 1957, PDF has awarded more than $50 million worth of scientific research in Parkinson's disease, supporting the work of leading scientists throughout the world. Its services to the Parkinson's community include provision of printed and audiovisual educational materials and a support service run by trained health professionals and medical staff to answer questions from patients, caregivers, families, and the public on any aspect of Parkinson's disease.

President: Lewis P. Rowland, M.D.
Executive Director: Robin Elliott
Year Established: 1957
Acronym: PDF

Keywords
Advocacy; Deep Brain Stimulation; Dyskinesia; Dystonia; Exercise; Multiple System Atrophy; Parkinson's Disease; Parkinson's Disease Foundation, Inc.; PDF; Sinemet; Tremor; Young-Onset

2051 **Parkinson's Disease—Movement Disorders Group**
Neurological Institute
Box 57
710 W. 168th Street
New York, NY 10032

Phone: (212) 305-5779
Fax: (212) 305-1304
E-mail: deleon@movdis.cis.columbia.edu

The Parkinson's Disease—Movement Disorders Group at Columbia Presbyterian Medical Center in New York City is a research organization dedicated to the research and treatment of movement disorders. Part of the Neurological Institute, the group was founded in the 1940s and functions as the primary research arm of the Parkinson's Disease Foundation. The mission of the group is to improve the quality of life for people with movement disorders. The group believes medical research is the means to achieve this goal. Affected individuals who join the group may have an opportunity to test new therapies. The Parkinson's Disease-Movement Disorders Group conducts workshops and seminars for healthcare professionals. The group has several e-mail addresses for different members of the organization.

President: Unknown
Executive Director: Stanley Fahn, M.D.
Year Established: 1981

Keywords
Chorea; Dystonia; Movement Disorders; Neurological Movement Disorders; Parkinson's Disease; Parkinson's Disease—Movement Disorders Group Research; Research

2052 **Pathways Awareness Foundation**
150 North Michigan Avenue, Ste.2100
Chicago, IL 60601

Phone: (312) 893-6620
Fax: (312) 893-6621
Toll Free: (800) 326-8154
TDD: (800) 326-8154
E-mail: friends@pathwaysawareness.org
http://www.pathwaysawareness.org

Established in 1988, Pathways Awareness Foundation is a national, non-profit organization dedicated to raising awareness about the gift of early detection, the benefit of early therapy, and the promise of inclusion for infants and children with movement differences. PAF honors and supports parents by providing expert knowledge, information and a sense of community as they guide their children on life's journey.

President: Maggie C. Daley (1995-present)
Executive Director: Kathy M. O'Brien
Year Established: 1988
Acronym: PAF

Keywords
Benign Congenital Hypotonia; Cerebral Palsy; PAF; Pathways Awareness Foundation; Spina Bifida

2053   PC Project

2386 East Heritage Way
Suite B
Salt Lake City, UT 84109

Phone: (877) 628-7300
Fax: (877) 628-7399
Toll Free: (877) 628-7300
E-mail: mary.schwartz@pc-project.org
http://www.pachyonychia.org

The PC Project is a voluntary, not for profit 501(c)(3) organization focused on finding a cure for pachyonychia congenita, a hereditary genetic skin disorder characterized by blisters on the feet and hands, thickened fingernails and toenails, and other painful symptoms. The organization funds research grants, sponsors scientific and patient meetings, offers patient networking, as well as educational services for both patients and medical professionals.

President: Craig T. Vincent
Executive Director: Mary E. Schwartz
Year Established: 2003
Acronym: PC Project

Keywords
Ectodermal Dysplasias; Hyperkeratosis; Leukoplakia; Networking; Pachyonychia Congenita; Pachyonychia Congenita Fund, Inc.; PC Project; Registry; Research Grants

2054   PCD Foundation

4752 Park Avenue
Minneapolis, MN 55407

Phone: (612) 822-3496
Fax: (612) 822-3496
E-mail: info@pcdfoundation.org
http://www.pcdfoundation.org

The PCD (Primary Ciliary Dyskinesia) Foundation is a voluntary, not for profit organization that promotes research, increases public awareness, and provides information and support services for individuals and families affected by inherited ciliary disorders. Another name for primary ciliary dyskinesia is Kartagener syndrome. This disease results in a chronic cough, scarring of the airways, and recurrent lung infection as a result of malfunctioning cilia, the tiny, hair-like structures that normally provide protection from unwanted inhaled particles. The PCD Foundation offers information to patients, families, health professionals, and the public. Its services include patient networking, advocacy, research and general education.

President: Michele Manion (2004-2006)
Year Established: 2003
Acronym: PCD Foundation

Keywords
PCD Foundation; Primary ciliary dyskinesia, Kartagener syndrome

2055   Pediatric Brain Tumor Foundation

302 Ridgefield Court
Asheville, NC 28806

Phone: (828) 665-6891
Fax: (828) 665-6894
Toll Free: (800) 253-6530
http://www.pbtfus.org

The Pediatric Brain Tumor Foundation (PBTF) is a voluntary, not-for-profit organization founded in 1991. It is dedicated to supporting the search for the cause and cure of childhood brain tumors. Pediatric brain tumors are the leading cause of cancer deaths in children, and 75 percent of children diagnosed with a brain tumor are younger than 15. PBTF provides programs in the areas of research, patient and general population education, patient networking, and patient advocacy.

President: Dianne Traynor (Director of Research Funding and Advocacy)
Executive Director: Louise Noble (Family Support Program Manager)
Year Established: 1991
Acronym: PBTF

Keywords
Advocacy; Astrocytoma; Brain Tumors; Diencephalic Syndrome; Glioblastoma Multiforme; Medulloblastoma; Networking; PBTF; Pediatric Brain Tumor Foundation; Pediatric Brain Tumors; Research

2056   Pediatric Brain Tumors

c/o Premier Resorts
2600 SW Third Avenue, 6th. Floor
Miami, FL 33129

Phone: (809) 523-8311
Fax: (809) 523-8400
E-mail: d.edge@verizon.net.do
http://health.groups.yahoo.com/group/Pediatricbraintumors/

Pediatric Brain Tumors is an online support group for parents of children with brain tumors. Brain tumors are abnormal growths in the brain that can be either cancerous (malignant) or noncancerous (benign). The effects on the brain of malignant and benign brain tumors can be similar and may cause the same types of problems, depending upon the type of tumor and where it is located in the brain. Pediatric Brain Tumors is mostly for parents and family members. However, medical professionals are welcome, too. Pediatric Brain Tumors is a support group and a center for networking and education for those families affected by pediatric brain tumors.

President: David M. Edge (1989-present)
Year Established: 2001
Acronym: Pediatricbraintumors

Keywords
Astrocytoma; Atypical Teratoid/Rhabdoid; Ependymoma; Glioblastoma Multiforme; Medulloblastoma; Neuroblastoma; Pediatric Brain Tumors; Pineoblastoma; Pineocytoma; PNET

2057 Pediatric Crohn's & Colitis Association, Inc.
P.O. Box 188
Newton, MA 02468

Phone: (617) 489-5854
Fax: (617) 489-5854
E-mail: questions@pcca.hypermart.net
http://pcca.hypermart.net

The Pediatric Crohn's and Colitis Association, Inc., (PCCA) is an international, not-for-profit service organization dedicated to providing information and emotional support to families of children with inflammatory bowel disease (IBD) to help ensure that affected children reach their potential in today's society. Crohn's disease and ulcerative colitis, collectively known as inflammatory bowel disease, are chronic digestive diseases of unknown cause. While Crohn's disease may affect any part of the gastrointestinal tract and often results in swelling, soreness, and inflammation of layers of the large and/or small intestinal wall, ulcerative colitis affects only the colon (large intestine), causing inflammation of the inner lining and resulting in diarrhea, often mixed with blood, cramping abdominal pain, and other symptoms. The association was founded in 1988 by a group of parents with children affected by IBD to address the broad range of issues faced by the pediatric population with these disorders. Currently consisting of over 1,200 members, PCCA is dedicated to promoting pediatric research; providing educational, emotional, social, academic, and psychological support; and addressing the role of family dynamics in dealing with a chronic ill-

ness. The organization's services include a parent hotline; support groups; patient advocacy; networking services; and medical, educational, and psychological symposia. The organization also provides a variety of educational materials including brochures, pamphlets, an information packet, and a regular newsletter.

Executive Director: Harriet Kahn
Year Established: 1988
Acronym: PCCA

Keywords
CD; Colitis, Granulomatous; Colitis, Gravis; Colitis, Thromboulcerative; Crohn's Disease; Idiopathic Non-Specific Ulcerative Colitis; Idiopathic Proctocolitis; Ileitis; Inflammatory Bowel Disease; Pediatric Crohn's & Colitis Association, Inc.; Regional Enteritis; Ulcerative Colitis; Ulcerative Colitis, Chronic Non-Specific

---

2058 Pediatric Neurotransmitter Disease Association (PND Association)
6 Nathan Drive
Plainview, NY 11803

Phone: (516) 937-0049
Fax: (516) 937-0049
E-mail: PND@PNDAssoc.org
http://www.pndassoc.org

"Pediatric neurotransmitter diseases" is an umbrella term for genetic disorders that affect the synthesis, metabolism and catabolism of neurotransmitters. Presently, the PND Association represents the following diseases: succinic semialdehyde dehydrogenase deficiency, tyrosine hydroxylase deficiency, aromatic L-amino acid decarboxylase deficiency, GTP cyclohydrolase I deficiency, and sepia pterin reductase deficiency. The PND Association is a non-profit, voluntary organization dedicated to the identification and treatment of all pediatric neurotransmitter diseases through education, advocacy and research.

President: Nancy Speller
Executive Director: John W. Speller
Year Established: 1999
Acronym: PND Assocaition

Keywords
Aromatic Amino Acid Decarboxylase Deficiency; Pediatric Neurotransmitter Disease Association (PND Association); Succinic Semialdehyde Dehydrogenase Deficiency; Tetrahydrobiopterin Deficiency; Tyrosine Hydroxylase Deficiency

2059 Pediatric/Adolescent Gastroesophageal Reflux Association, Inc.

P.O. Box 486
Buckeystown, MD 21717-0486

Phone: (301) 601-9541
E-mail: gergroup@aol.com
http://www.reflux.org

Children with many disabilities and rare disorders suffer from acid reflux in addition to their primary diagnosis. Clues are sour breath, spitting up, wet burps, drooling, crying or other pain behavior, night waking, picky eating or food refusal, and characteristic tooth damage from stomach acid. The Pediatric/Adolescent Gastroesophageal Reflux Association, Inc., (PAGER) is a non-profit, parent-led organization dedicated to offering support and information to parents of children with gastroesophageal reflux and related disorders. Founded in 1992, PAGER disseminates information on pediatric gastroesophageal reflux and related disorders, provides support and education to individuals and families affected by GER, and promotes public awareness of the condition. PAGER publishes a newsletter containing stories from families, research updates, practical ideas for affected individuals and families, and a list of new members. Also available is medical literature on GER and related disorders.

President: Beth Anderson, Founder, (1992 to Present)
Executive Director: Same as above.
Year Established: 1992
Acronym: PAGER

Keywords
Acid Reflux; Barrett Esophagus; Eating Disorders; Esophageal Atresia; Esophageal Stricture; Esophagitis; Feeding Disorders; Gastroenteritis, Eosinophillic; Gastroesophageal Reflux; Gastrointestinal Motility Disorders; GER; GERD; PAGER; Pediatric/Adolescent Gastroesophageal Reflux Association, Inc.; Reflux Disorders; Ulcer, Esophageal

2060 Pelizaeus Merzbacher Disease Support Group

43 Fir Tree Close
Flitwick, Bedfordshire, MK45 1NY, United Kingdom
E-mail: pmdsupport@dsl.pipex.com
http://www.patient.co.uk/showdoc.asp?doc=267395
59

The Pelizaeus Merzbacher Disease Support Group is for families within the United Kingdom affected by Pelizaeus Merzbacher disease, sometimes called Pelizaeus Merzbacher brain sclerosis or PMD. This is a rare inherited disease that affects the central nervous system and is associated with abnormalities of the white matter of the brain. Symptoms may include impaired ability to coordinate movement, developmental delay, involuntary muscle spasms, and progressive deterioration of intellectual function. The group is a support group for families that provides a quarterly newsletter with family updates. It focuses on families rather than on professionals.

Executive Director: Peter Buckel
Acronym: PMD Support UK

Keywords
Pelizaeus Merzbacher Disease Support Group

2061 Pemphigus & Pemphigoid Society

15934 Hesperian Boulevard
#122
San Lorenzo, CA 94580

Phone: (510) 755-4266
E-mail: PPS@1clever.org
http://www.1clever.org

The Pemphigus & Pemphigoid Society (PPS) is a not-for-profit organization dedicated to pemphigus and pemphigoid patients and their caregivers. These are rare, autoimmune, blistering skin disorders. PPS provides emotional support and information about treatments and recovery strategies to patients and their families. It also works to bring a greater awareness to the medical community and the general public, and to support research into cures for these skin diseases. It is an all-volunteer foundation, so 100 percent of donations and grants go toward these goals.

President: Sal Capo (2002-present)
Year Established: 2002
Acronym: PPS

Keywords
Blistering Disease; Bullous Disease; Bullous Pemphigoid; Lesions; Pemphigoid; Pemphigus; Pemphigus & Pemphigoid Society

2062 Periodic Paralysis Association

1124 Royal Oaks Drive
Monrovia, CA 91016

Phone: (626) 303-3244
Fax: (626) 337-1966
E-mail: info@periodicparalysis.org
http://www.periodicparalysis.org

The Periodic Paralysis Association (PPA) is a nonprofit corporation dedicated to providing educational information and advocacy to individuals suffering from the class of disorders known as periodic paralysis and non-dystrophic myotonia. These disorders are characterized by episodic loss of muscle tone ranging from mild weakness to profound global flaccid paralysis, progressive permanent muscle deterioration, severe muscle stiffness and various degrees of myotonia, twitching or other involuntary muscle movement, cardiac irregularities, and difficulty breathing. These disorders are also known as channelopathies and include hyperkalemic periodic paralysis, hypokalemic periodic paralysis, other atypical forms of periodic paralysis, Anderson's syndrome, thyrotoxic periodic paralysis, various myotonias (paramyotonia congenita, Becker's and Thomsen's myotonia, and others). The PPA also addresses periodic paralyses related to sleep disorders.

President: Patrick Cochran
Year Established: 1997
Acronym: PPA

Keywords
Andersen Tawil Syndrome (ATS); ATS; Channelopathies; Hyperkalemic Periodic Paralysis; Hypokalemic Periodic Paralysis; Myopathy; Myotonia; Normokalemic Periodic Paralysis; Paramyotonia Congenita (PMC); Periodic Paralyses Resource Center; Periodic Paralysis; Periodic Paralysis Association; PMC; Sleep Paralysis; Thyrotoxic Periodic Paralysis

2063 Perspectives Network, Inc.

P. O. Box 121012
West Melbourne, FL 32912-1012

E-mail: TPN@tbi.org
http://www.tbi.org

The Perspectives Network, Inc., (TPN) is a nonprofit organization dedicated to identifying and encouraging individual potential by providing various forums and opportunities wherein affected individuals, family members and friends, professionals and community members are encouraged to discuss issues relating to treatment, recovery, and reentry as well as creating positive changes following traumatic and acquired brain injury. Dena K. Taylor, a brain injury survivor, established TPN in 1990. The Perspectives Network provides information and education, but perhaps most importantly, it provides hope to those who survived a brain injury and to those who care for them. Educational materials include a quarterly magazine with an international circulation written by survivors, family members, and professionals; fact brochures; and a lending library and file archives containing books, videos, and topical articles. Program activities include peer communication networks for survivors, spouses, offspring, parents, and siblings; brain injury awareness workshops; support groups; and education.

President: Dena K. Taylor (1990 to Present)
Executive Director: Same as above.
Year Established: 1990
Acronym: TPN, Inc.

Keywords
Brain Injury; Brain Injury, Acquired; Brain Injury, Traumatic; Closed Head Injury; Neurological Injury; Perspectives Network, Inc.

2064 Peutz Jeghers Syndrome Online Support Group

E-mail: pj4steph@aol.com
http://www.acor.org

The Peutz-Jeghers Syndrome Online Support Group is a free e-mail support group for patients, families, friends, researchers, and physicians. It provides a forum to discuss clinical and non-clinical issues and advances pertaining to Peutz-Jeghers syndrome. This is a rare, inherited disorder characterized by multiple, initially benign nodular growths of the GI tract and an increased risk of cancer throughout the body. Discussion topics include patient experiences, psychosocial issues, new research, clinical trials, and discussions of current treatment practices. The group is one of several co-sponsored by the Association of Cancer Online Resources.

President: Stephanie Sugars
Year Established: 2000

Keywords
Peutz Jeghers Syndrome; Peutz Jeghers Syndrome Online Support Group

2065   Phoenix Society for Burn Survivors, Inc.

1835 RW Berends Drive SW
Grand Rapids, MI 49519

Phone: (616) 458-2773
Fax: (616) 258-2831
Toll Free: (800) 888-2876
E-mail: info@phoenix-society.org
http://www.phoenix-society.org/

The Phoenix Society for Burn Survivors, Inc., is an international, non-profit, self-help organization whose mission is to uplift and inspire anyone affected by burns through peer support, collaboration, education and advocacy. The society's major goal is to ease the psychosocial adjustment of severely burned individuals during and after hospitalization so they may resume full and productive lives within their communities. This is achieved through a series of support programs including peer counseling, family group meetings, and re-entry programs. The Phoenix Society works mainly through volunteer area coordinators who are burn survivors themselves or parents of burned children. They provide peer support and counseling to affected individuals and their families under the guidance and approval of medical professionals. Established in 1977 and consisting of 350 chapters, the society provides services that include a newsletter, Burn Support News, SOAR Peer Support Program, annual World Burn Congress, toll free information and referral line.

President: Ronald Siarnicki
Executive Director: Amy Acton, R.N.
Year Established: 1977

Keywords
Advocacy; Burn Survivors; Burn Vicitms; Burns; Phoenix Society for Burn Survivors, Inc.; Support Groups

2066   Pick's Disease Support Group (UK)

3 Fairfield Park
Lyme Regis
Dorset, DT7 3DS, United Kingdom

Phone: +44 (0) 1297-44-5488
E-mail: info@pdsg.org.uk
http://www.pdsg.org.uk/

The Pick's Disease Support Group is a not-for-profit organization in the United Kingdom that was established by caregivers of individuals with Pick's disease and other related disorders. Pick's disease is a progressive degenerative disease that affects the frontal and temporal lobes of the brain. Affected individuals experience frontotemporal dementia, which may be characterized by gradual disintegration of personality and emotions, behavioral abnormalities, and speech impairment. The Pick's Disease Support Group meets several times each year, publishes a regular newsletter, and maintains a web site on the Internet. The organization's newsletter contains meeting reports, articles written by professionals who care for individuals with Pick's disease, and articles written by caregivers. The Pick's Disease Support Group web site provides several back issues of the organization's newsletter, offers contact information for caregivers who are interested in networking via telephone or e-mail, and includes links to additional sources of information and support on the Internet.

President: John Rendell
Executive Director: Penelope Roques (Contact Person)
Year Established: 1998
Acronym: PDSG

Keywords
Pick's Disease Support Group (UK)

2067   Pierre Robin Network

3604 Biscayne
Quincy, IL 62305

Phone: (217) 224-0698
Fax: (217) 224-2867
E-mail: help@pierrerobin.org
http://www.pierrerobin.org

Pierre Robin Network was formed in May of 1999 by the mother of a son with Pierre Robin syndrome, which is characterized by a small lower jaw, displaced tongue, and cleft soft palate. The organization is made up of parents, relatives, caregivers, adults with PRS and professionals who have an interest in PRS. The purpose is to network families and individuals with PRS and provide information to anyone who has an interest. Parents and caregivers do not need to feel alone: having a child with PRS can be overwhelming. There are many issues associated with PRS, which are unique to PRS.

President: Nancy Barry
Executive Director: Nancy Barry
Year Established: 1999
Acronym: PRN

Keywords
Glossoptosis; Micrognathia; Pierre Robin Complex; Pierre Robin Malformation Sequence; Pierre Robin Network; Pierre Robin Sequence; Pierre Robin Syndrome; PRS; Robin Sequence; Robin Syndrome

2068   Pituitary Foundation
P.O. Box 1944
Bristol, BS99 2UB, United Kingdom

Phone: +44 (0) 845-450-0376
Fax: +44 (0) 845-450-0376 ext.6
E-mail: helpline@pituitary.org.uk
http://www.pituitary.org.uk

President: Kit Ashley (Patient Support Manager)
Year Established: 1994

Keywords
Acromegaly; Advocacy; Craniopharyngioma; Cushing's Syndrome; Diabetes Insipidus; Hypogonadism; Hypopituitarism; Kallmann Syndrome; Klinefelter Syndrome; Networking; Pituitary; Pituitary Adenoma; Pituitary Foundation; Prolactinoma; Support Groups

2069   Pituitary Network Association (PNA)
P.O. Box 1958
Thousand Oaks, CA 91358

Phone: (805) 499-9973
Fax: (805) 480-0633
E-mail: pna@pituitary.org
http://www.pituitary.org, www.acromegaly.org

The Pituitary Network Association (PNA) is a support organization dedicated to promoting, supporting, and, where possible, funding research on pituitary tumors in a sustained effort to find a cure for these illnesses. Established in 1992 by four pituitary patients undergoing experimental treatment, the association is now the world's largest pituitary support network. Its members include affected individuals, physicians, and pharmaceutical companies. The association disseminates information to affected families, the medical community, and the public concerning early detection, symptoms, treatments, and resources available to pituitary patients. The Pituitary Network Association publishes a regular newsletter and a comprehensive resource guide. The guide, entitled "The Pituitary Patient Resource Guide," assists affected individuals to locate a variety of medical, surgical, insurance, occupational, lifestyle, and health maintenance services. It also helps primary-care physicians and other medical personnel to determine where to call for advice and consultation, where to send patients for specialized treatment and surgery, and what other medical specialties should be involved in treatment.

President: Robert Knutsen (Chairman)
Year Established: 1992
Acronym: PNA

Keywords
Acromegaly; Adrenal Insufficiency; Brain; Brain Disorders; Brain Surgery; Brain Tumors; Chordoma; Craniopharyngiomas; Cushings Disease; Diabetes Insipidus; Growth Hormone Deficiency; Hypogonadism; Hypopituitarism; Pituitary Disorders; Pituitary Network Association (PNA); Pituitary Surgery; Pituitary Tumor Network Association; Pituitary Tumors; PNA; Prolactinomas

2070   Pityriasis Rubra Pilaris (PRP) Support Group (on-line)
Web Site on the Internet

E-mail: rgreene@temple.edu
http://www.prp-support.org

The Pityriasis Rubra Pilaris (PRP) Support Group (on-line) is a web site on the Internet dedicated to providing information, resources, and online networking opportunities to individuals with PRP. Pityriasis rubra pilaris is a rare and chronic skin disorder that often appears suddenly. Symptoms may include reddish-orange patches on the skin, severe flaking, uncomfortable itching, and thickening of the skin. There are several different forms of the disorder. The PRP Support Group (on-line) provides a caring forum where people can share information about PRP; including their experiences, anxieties, questions and treatment options. In addition to mutual support and understanding, there is significant advice and information regarding day-to-day care and medical treatment.

Acronym: PRP Support Group

Keywords
Erythroderma; Exfoliative Dermatitis; Ichthyosis; Pityriasis Pilaris; Pityriasis Rubra Pilaris; Pityriasis Rubra Pilaris (PRP) Online Support Group; Pityriasis Rubra Pilaris (PRP) Support Group (On-line)

2071   PKD Foundation
9221 Ward Parkway
Suite 400
Kansas City, MO 64114-3367

Phone: (816) 931-2600
Fax: (816) 931-8655
Toll Free: (800) 753-2873
E-mail: pkdcure@pkdcure.org
http://www.pkdcure.org

The PKD Foundation is the only organization in the world dedicated to finding a treatment and a cure for polycystic kidney disease (PKD). The international not-for-profit was established in 1982 to fund research, raise awareness and support the millions of families worldwide affected by PKD. The PKD Foundation conducts educational seminars and conferences; provides free informational packets (shipped anywhere in the world); publishes a quarterly national magazine and helps form and sustain PKD Foundation Chapters, or support groups.

President: Dan Larson (1994-Present)
Executive Director: Same as above.
Year Established: 1982

Keywords
PKD; PKD Foundation; PKR Foundation (Polycystic Kidney Research); Polycystic Kidney Disease

2072 Platelet Disorder Support Association

P.O. Box 61533
Potomac, MD 20859

Phone: (301) 770-6636
Fax: (301) 770-6638
Toll Free: (877) 528-3538
E-mail: pdsa@pdsa.org
http://www.pdsa.org

The Platelet Disorder Support Association is dedicated to enhancing the lives of people with immune (idiopathic) thrombocytopenic purpura (ITP) and other platelet disorders. In ITP, the body mounts an immune attack against platelets resulting in a reduced platelet count. The Platelet Disorder Support Association provides a broad range of services that include a web site, quarterly newsletter, monthly e-m-news, annual conference, research collaboration, online patient support groups, and many other publications. Established in 1998, it serves health professionals and the public, as well as patients and their families.

President: Joan Young
Year Established: 1998
Acronym: PDSA

Keywords
Idiopathic Thrombocytopenic Purpura; Immune Thrombocytopenic Purpura; ITP; Platelet Disorder Support Association; Platelets.; Purpura; Purpura, Henoch Schonlein; Purpura, Idiopathic Thrombocytopenia; Purpura, Idiopathic Thrombocytopenic; Purpura, Immune Thrombocytopenic; Thrombocytopenia; Thrombocytopenic Purpura, Idiopathic; Thrombocytopenic Purpura, Immune

2073 PMD Foundation

8001 Lincoln Drive W
Suite D
Marlton, NJ 08053

Phone: (609) 443-9623

The PMD Foundation is family-driven and proactively serves those affected by Pelizaeus-Merzbacher disease by supporting programs of education, research, service and advocacy. It is dedicated to providing patients and their families with information about their disease and assistance in identifying sources of medical care, social service, and genetic counseling; establishing a communications network among families; increasing public awareness and acting as an information source for healthcare providers; and promoting research into causes, treatment, prevention and cure of PMD. Pelizaeus-Merzbacher disease is a rare genetic disorder that usually affects only males. It is a degenerative disorder of the central nervous system in which coordination, motor abilities, and intellectual function deteriorate.

Year Established: 2001

Keywords
PMD Foundation

2074 PMP Pals Network

P.O. Box 6484
Salinas, CA 93912

Phone: (831) 424-4545
Fax: (831) 424-4545
E-mail: pmppals@yahoo.com
http://www.pmppals.org

PMP (pseudomyxoma peritonei) Pals is a self-help organization dedicated to providing information, support, and resources to individuals with pseudomyxoma peritonei and their family members. Pseudomyxoma peritonei is a rare malignancy characterized by the progressive accumulation of mucus-secreting (mucinous) tumor cells within the abdomen and pelvis. PMP develops after a small growth (polyp) located within the appendix bursts through the wall of the appendix and spreads mucus-producing tumor cells throughout surrounding surfaces (e.g., the membrane lining the abdominal cavity [peritoneum]). As mucinous tumor cells accumulate, the abdominal area becomes swollen and digestive function becomes impaired. The organization provides information concerning oncologists and surgeons who are experienced in treating PMP; promotes and support research; offers information on additional services for individuals with cancer; and promotes networking opportunities, enabling affected individuals and family members to select various "PMP Pals" networking categories (e.g., Mothers with PMP, Female PMP Patients, Male PMP Patients, Seniors with PMP, Spouses of PMP Patients, etc.). PMP Pals also publishes a regular newsletter entitled "PMP Pals: Support for Pseudomyxoma Peritonei Patients."

President: Gabriella Graham
Executive Director: Same as above.
Year Established: 1998
Acronym: PMP Pals Network

Keywords
Cancer, Appendiceal Carcinoid; Cancer, Colon; Mucinous Adenocarcinoma; Mucinous Cyst Adenomacarcinoma; Mucinous Cystadenoma; Peritoneal Carcinomatosis; PMP Pals Network; Pseudomyxoma Peritonei; Signet Ring Cell

2075 PNH Support Group

www.pnhdiseases.org

The PNH Support Group is an Internet-based support group for patients and families affected by paroxysmal nocturnal hemoglobinuria (PNH), a rare, acquired (non-genetically transmitted), chronic disorder characterized by a decreased number of red blood cells (anemia) and the presence of blood in the urine (hemoglobinuria) and plasma (hemoglobinemia), which is evident after sleeping. This disorder is associated with a heightened risk for blood clots (thrombosis), most commonly in large intra-abdominal veins. Participants in this support group share information regarding medications, bone marrow transplants, and other topics related to living with this disorder.

Keywords
PNH Support Group

2076 Polio Connection of America

P.O. Box 182
Howard Beach, NY 11414

Phone: (718) 835-5536
E-mail: w1066polio@hotmail.com
http://www.geocities.com/w1066w

Polio Connection of America, also known as the New York Post-Polio Support Group, is a voluntary, not-for-profit organization dedicated to locating polio survivors and providing them with information concerning post-polio syndrome. The syndrome, which is characterized by gradual deterioration of muscle function, usually occurs from 20 to 40 years after the onset of polio. Polio Connection of America provides appropriate referrals as well as a variety of educational materials including a regular newsletter, brochures, and booklets.

President: Eleanor Berk (1995 to Present)
Executive Director: Walter Berk
Year Established: 1980
Acronym: PCA

Keywords
Polio Connection of America; Polio, Late Effects of; Post-Polio Syndrome

2077 Polio Society

4200 Wisconsin Avenue
Suite 106273
Washington, DC 20016

Phone: (301) 897-8180
Fax: (202) 466-1911
http://www.php.com/include/agency/agency_item.php?AgencyID=1823&where_keywor ds=

The Polio Society is a national, not-for-profit, voluntary organization that was established in 1984. The society was created to provide educational resources and support group services to people who had polio and are now experiencing the late effects of polio. Activities of the organization include the maintenance of a national membership database of polio survivors and healthcare professionals; sponsorship of major national UPDATE conferences about post-polio issues; and the publication of "OPTIONS," a quarterly newsletter that contains information on current medical research, available resources, support activities, and first-hand accounts from the polio community. In addition, the society provides state-of-the-art medical and psychosocial information about the late effects of polio, including audio and videotapes of conference presentations, current scientific and lay articles, and polio-related publications. The organization also promotes public awareness of the late effects of polio through poster campaigns, local and national newspapers, radio, and network television.

President: Ed Grebenstein
Executive Director: Jessica Scheer, Ph.D
Year Established: 1984

Keywords
Polio; Polio, Late Effects of; Polio Society; Poliomyelitis; Post-Polio Syndrome

2078 Polychondritis Educational Society, Ltd.

2581 W. County 18th Street
Somerton, AZ 85350

Phone: (928) 627-1979
TDD: (928) 627-1521
E-mail: Diana_R@polychondritis.com OR
Desarae@polychondritis.com
http://www.Polychondritis.com

The Polychondritis Educational Society, Ltd., (PES) is a non-profit organization that provides educational information about relapsing polychondritis (RP) and its many different manifestations. RP is a rare, degenerative disease characterized by recurrent inflammation of cartilage. It may affect any part of the body where cartilage is present. Through on-line support groups and quarterly newsletters, PES encourages the sharing of information amongst RPer's, their family members and the medical community. Our web site includes a physician's referral database.

President: Diana A. Rutledge
Year Established: 2000
Acronym: PES

Keywords
Autoimmune Rheumatic Disease; Cartilage; Connective Tissue; Inflammation of Ear; Polychondritis; Polychondritis Educational Society, Ltd.; Relapsing Polychondritis; Rheumatic Disease; RP; RPC; Tracheal Collapse

2079 Polycystic Ovarian Syndrome Association

P.O. Box 3403
Engelwood, CO 80111
E-mail: info@pcosupport.org
http://www.pcosupport.org

The Polycystic Ovarian Syndrome Association is a voluntary organization dedicated to promoting research, and awareness, and communicating the most up-to-date information concerning polycystic ovarian syndrome (PCOS) among its membership body. PCOS is a disorder characterized by the absence of menstruation or irregular and abnormal menstruation, excessive amounts of body hair, excessive body weight, and infertility. Established in 1997, the Polycystic Ovarian Syndrome Association seeks to fulfill the following objectives: to provide a central resource of information for women with PCOS; to support research on medical and/or surgical protocols to further understand the cause of PCOS and treat its associated symptoms; to promote awareness of PCOS to the public; to educate physicians and other healthcare professionals to recognize and more fully understand PCOS and the nature of its treatment; to provide a social support network for women with PCOS and their families; to bring about an understanding of the short term and long term complications of PCOS; and to encourage approval by government health organizations of drugs and procedures that have been identified as being beneficial to women with PCOS.

President: Christine Gray-DeZarn
Year Established: 1997
Acronym: PCOSupport

Keywords
Anovulation, Chronic Hyperandrogenic; Anovulation, Follicular Hyperandrogenic; Ovarian Disease, Sclerocystic; PCOS; Polycystic Ovarian Syndrome; Polycystic Ovarian Syndrome Association; Polycystic Ovarian Syndrome, Bilateral; POS; Stein Levanthal Syndrome

2080 Post-Polio Health International

4207 Lindell Boulevard
#110
St. Louis, MO 63108-2915

Phone: (314) 534-0475
Fax: (314) 534-5070
TDD: (800) 735-2966
E-mail: info@post-polio.org
http://www.post-polio.org

Established in 1960, Post-Polio Health International (PHI) — formerly International Polio Network — including International Ventilator Users Network (IVUN), is a not-for-profit organization dedicated to supporting the independent living, self-direction, and personal achievement of people with disabilities worldwide. The mission of Post-Polio Health International is to enhance the lives and independence of polio survivors and home mechanical ventilator users by promoting education, networking, and advocacy among these individuals and healthcare providers. PHI promotes patient and professional education, has a network of support groups, and conducts workshops and conferences. PHI also provides a variety of materials including directories, newsletters, booklets, and brochures.

President: Frederick M. Maynard, MD (2002-Present)
Executive Director: Joan L. Headley, MS
Year Established: 1960
Acronym: PHI

Keywords
PPS; Polio; Polio, Late Effects of; Poliomyelitis; Post Polio Health International; Post Polio Muscular Atrophy; Post-Polio Health International; Post-Polio Syndrome

2081 Prader-Willi France

10 Rue Charles Clement
Mondrepuis, F02500, France

Phone: +33 (0) 323-98-79-04
Fax: +33 (0) 323-98-79-04
E-mail: jean-yves.belliard@wanadoo.fr
http://www.perso.wanadoo.fr/pwillifr

Prader-Willi France, established in 1996, disseminates information about, and raises awareness of, Prader-Willi syndrome. Prader-Willi syndrome is a genetic disorder characterized by diminished muscle tone, feeding difficulties, and failure to grow and gain weight during infancy, short stature, genital abnormalities and mental retardation. In addition, beginning at approximately age six months to six years, affected individuals may develop excessive body weight, especially in the lower regions of the body. Prader-Willi France helps families break their isolation and provides them with information about living with this disorder. It also encourages research. Prader-Willi France serves families in France and other French-speaking parts of the world.

President: Jean-Yves Belliard
Year Established: 1996
Acronym: PWF

Keywords
Prader Willi France; Prader Willi Syndrome; Prader-Willi France; PWS

2082 Prader-Willi Syndrome Association (UK)

125A London Rd
Derby, DE1 2QQ, United Kingdom

Phone: +44 (0) 1332-36-5676
Fax: +44 (0) 1332-36-0401
E-mail: admin@pwsa-uk.demon.co.uk
http://www.pwsa.co.uk

The Prader Willi Syndrome Association (UK) is a voluntary organization located in the United Kingdom and dedicated to promoting the care, welfare, treatment, interests, education, and advancement of persons affected by Prader Willi syndrome. These goals are achieved by contacting and supporting families concerned with the disorder; raising funds; inviting and receiving contributions by way of subscriptions and donations; establishing mutual self-help groups; and fostering and supporting ongoing research. Prader Willi syndrome is a complex multisystem disorder characterized by muscular weakness during infancy (infantile hypotonia); failure to thrive; a decrease in the efficiency of the testes or ovaries (hypogonadism); short stature and impaired intellectual and behavioral functioning. Eating excessive amounts of food (hyperphagia) leads to severe obesity in early childhood and adolescence. Established in 1981, PWSA consists of 1,200 members, including people with PWS, parents and professionals from health, social services and education. The association produces various educational materials including a quarterly magazine and brochures. In addition, the association, conducts regular support group meetings and supports ongoing patient advocacy.

President: Prof. Tony Holland (1998 to Present)
Executive Director: Narinder Sharma
Year Established: 1981
Acronym: PWSA (UK)

Keywords
Hypogenital Dystrophy with Diabetic Tendency; Hypotonia Hypomentia Hypogonadism Obesity Syndrome; Labhart Willi Syndrome; Prader Labhart Willi Fancone Syndrome; Prader Willi Syndrome; Prader Willi Syndrome Association (UK); Prader-Willi Syndrome Association (UK);Willi Prader Syndrome

2083 Prader-Willi Syndrome Association (USA)

5700 Midnight Pass Road
Suite 6
Sarasota, FL 34242

Phone: (941) 312-0400
Fax: (941) 312-0142
Toll Free: (800) 926-4797
E-mail: national@pwsausa.org
http://www.pwsausa.org

The Prader-Willi Syndrome Association (USA) is a non-profit, voluntary health organization. Founded in 1975, the association provides parents and healthcare professionals with a national and international network of information, support services, and research endeavors to expressly meet the needs of children and adults with Prader-Willi syndrome and their families. The organization comprises parents, professionals and other interested individuals who are taking active roles in improving the lives of people with Prader-Willi syndrome. Goals include normalizing life for people with Prader-Willi syndrome and their families, improving communication and education, and acting as a lifetime advocate for affected individuals. The association also supports research, interdisciplinary communication, and increased professional knowledge of treatments. Educational materials include various brochures and pamphlets.

President: Carolyn Loker
Executive Director: Janalee Heinemann
Year Established: 1975
Acronym: PWSA (USA)

Keywords
Hypogenital Dystrophy with Diabetic Tendency; Hypotonia Hypomentia Hypogonadism Obesity Syndrome; Labhart Willi Syndrome; Prader Labhart Willi Fancone Syndrome; Prader Willi Syndrome; Prader-Willi Syndrome Association, National Headquarters; Prader-Willi Syndrome Association (USA); PWS

2084 Pre-Eclampsia Society
Rhianfa
Carmel
Caernarfon
Gwynedd, LL54 7RL, United Kingdom

Phone: +44 (0) 1286-88-2685
Fax: +44 (0) 1702-20-5088
E-mail: dawnjames@clara.co.uk

The Pre-Eclampsia Society (PETS), an international not-for-profit organization, was founded in 1981 in the United Kingdom by an individual who experienced pre-eclampsia during her first pregnancy. The organization is dedicated to serving as a support and information society and is operated by those who themselves have experienced pre-eclampsia during pregnancy. Pre-eclampsia is a serious condition that may occur in females during the second half of pregnancy. The condition is characterized by high blood pressure (hypertension), abnormal fluid retention and associated swelling (edema), and the passage of abnormally increased levels of protein in the urine (proteinuria). Without appropriate treatment, pre-eclampsia may lead to eclampsia, which may be characterized by seizures, coma, and potentially life-threatening complications. The Pre-Eclampsia Society currently consists of approximately 400 members including individuals who have experienced pre-eclampsia in the past, those who are currently affected by the condition, medical professionals, and lay groups who have an interest in childbirth and pregnancy. The society offers a variety of programs and services including a library lending service, regular updates on current research, and networking opportunities that promote the exchange of mutual support, information, and resources. In addition, the society offers a variety of educational materials including brochures, pamphlets, reports, and a quarterly newsletter that contains members' letters and personal stories, members' questions and physicians' responses, and understandable information on pre-eclampsia.

President: Dawn James (1981 to Present)
Executive Director: Same as above.
Year Established: 1981
Acronym: PETS

Keywords
Pre Eclampsia Society; Pre-Eclampsia Society

2085 Prescription Parents
Prescription Parent, Inc.
P.O. Box 920554
Needham, MA 02492

Phone: (617) 499-1936
E-mail: info@prescriptionparents.org
http://www.prescriptionparents.com

Prescription Parents is a not-for-profit voluntary health organization dedicated to providing information and support to parents of children born with cleft lip and cleft palate. Established in the mid-1970s, Prescription Parents conducts parent support/newborn groups and social events for affected families.

President: Barbara Seltzer
Executive Director: Same as above.
Year Established: 1975

Keywords
Cleft Lip; Cleft Palate; Prescription Parents

2086 Primary Biliary Cirrhosis Support Group

1430 Garden Road
Pearland, TX 77581

Phone: (281) 412-9161
Fax: (281) 412-9161
E-mail: PBCers@aol.com
http://www.pbcers.org

The Primary Biliary Cirrhosis Support Group (PBCers) is a source of support and education for those who suffer from primary biliary cirrhosis and other autoimmune liver diseases. Family members and friends are also encouraged to join and learn more about PBC. The organization offers various types of support and education such as the e-mail PBC daily digest, quarterly newsletter and annual PBC conference. Members discuss medical information, pain management, medications, and research; ask questions; and vent anger and fears. The PBCers was formed in 1996. Current membership is more than 2,400 worldwide.

President: Linie Moore (1996 to present)
Year Established: 1996
Acronym: PBCers

Keywords
Cirrhosis, Primary Biliary; PBC; PBC Associated Autoimmune Disease; PBCers; Primary Biliary Cirrhosis Support Group

2087 Primary Immunodeficiency Association (UK)

Alliance House
12 Caxton Street
London, SW1H OQS, United Kingdom

Phone: +44 (0) 207-976-7640
Fax: +44 (0) 207-976-7641
E-mail: info@pia.org.uk
http://www.pia.org.uk

The Primary Immunodeficiency Association (UK) is a voluntary, not-for-profit organization in the United Kingdom dedicated to promoting awareness and early diagnosis of the various primary immunodeficiency disorders; ensuring that all affected individuals have access to the best possible treatment; providing information and support to individuals with primary immunodeficiencies, family members, and other caregivers; and encouraging and supporting original research. The primary immunodeficiencies are a group of rare genetic disorders characterized by irregularities in the cell development and/or cell maturation process of the immune system. Individuals with primary immunodeficiencies may be abnormally prone to certain bacterial, viral, fungal, and/or other infections, may experience repeated "opportunistic" infections, and may be unusually susceptible to certain forms of cancer. ("Opportunistic" infections are infections caused by microorganisms that usually do not cause disease in individuals with fully functioning immune systems or widespread [systemic] overwhelming disease by microorganisms that typically cause only localized, mild infections.) The Primary Immunodeficiency Association (UK) was established in 1990 and currently consists of 12 chapters and approximately 2,500 members. The association engages in patient advocacy; puts members in touch with one another through regional contacts and the organization's national database; and offers four or five "regional days" every year at different locations where members may network and hear presentations by immunologists. The Primary Immunodeficiency Association also provides a telephone help service during and after regular office hours; provides information and assistance concerning benefits; has a youth service for young adults and adolescents with primary immunodeficiencies; and conducts annual medical student workshops to encourage specialization in immunology. The Association's educational materials include information packets for lay people and professionals, leaflets that provide understandable information on specific primary immunodeficiency disorders and other related topics, leaflets for teachers, booklets, and a quarterly newsletter entitled "INSIGHT."

President: Mrs. Clare Tritton, QC
Executive Director: David Watters
Year Established: 1990
Acronym: PiA

Keywords
Primary Immunodeficiency Association (UK)

2088 PRISMS (Parents & Researchers Interested in Smith-Magenis Syndrome)

P.O. Box 741914
Dallas, TX 75374-1914

Phone: (972) 231-0035
Fax: (413) 826-6539
E-mail: info@prisms.org
http://www.prisms.org

PRISMS (Parents & Researchers Interested in Smith-Magenis Syndrome) is dedicated to providing information and support to families of persons with Smith-Magenis syndrome (SMS) and fostering partnerships with professionals to increase awareness and understanding of SMS. Smith-Magenis syndrome is a rare chromosomal disorder characterized by a specific pattern of physical, behavioral, and developmental features. It is caused by the absence of genetic material (deletion) from a certain region on chromosome 17. Organized and incorporated in the state of Virginia on Feb. 4, 1993, PRISMS, Inc., is governed by a nine-member board of directors. Most board members have children with Smith-Magenis syndrome.

President: Randy Beall
Executive Director: Randy Beall
Year Established: 1993
Acronym: PRISMS

Keywords
ADD; ADHD; Deletion 17p11.2; Learning Disability; Nail Biting; Parents & Researchers Interested in Smith-Magenis Syndrome; PRISMS; PRISMS (Parents & Researchers Interested in Smith-Magenis Syndrome); Self Injurious Behavior; Sleep Disorder; Smith Magenis Chromosome Region; Smith Magenis Syndrome; SMS; Tantrum

2089 Progeria Research Foundation, Inc.
532 Lowell Street
Peabody, MA 01961-3453

Phone: (978) 535-2594
Fax: (978) 535-5849
E-mail: info@progeriaresearch.org
http://www.progeriaresearch.org

Established in 1999, the mission of The Progeria Research Foundation (PRF) is to discover a cure and effective treatment for Hutchinson-Gilford progeria syndrome (Progeria or HGPS) and its aging related disorders by funding medical research, providing research-related programs, and educating the families, their physicians, scientists and the general public. Progeria (a word that comes from the Greek meaning "prematurely old") is a fatal medical disorder with a life expectancy of about 13 years. Within the first 2 years of life, children afflicted with progeria fail to develop properly; they begin to display physiological characteristics typically associated with advanced age: loss of body fat and hair, joint stiffness, hip dislocation, and rapid progression of atherosclerosis. Research on progeria, particularly on its fatal outcome,

heart disease, will benefit not only these special children, but also millions of people who suffer from heart disease and other aging related conditions. PRF is a leading resource for information and resources on progeria. PRF runs its own cell & tissue bank, medical & research database, and diagnostic testing program, and provides funding for research. Additionally, PRF runs an international patient registry and holds scientific workshops jointly with the National Institutes of Health.

President: Audrey Gordon, Esq.
Year Established: 1999
Acronym: PRF

Keywords
Cell & Tissue Bank; Cockayne Syndrome; Gottron's Syndrome; HGPS; Hutchinson Gilford Progeria Syndrome; PRF; Progeria; Progeria Research Foundation, Inc.; Progeroid Syndromes; Registry; Research; Werner Syndrome; Wiedemann Rautenstrauch Syndrome

2090 Progressive Osseous Heteroplasia Association
33 Stonehearth Square
Indian Head Park, IL 60525

Phone: (708) 246-9410
Fax: (708) 246-9410
E-mail: poha@comcast.net
http://www.pohdisease.org

The Progressive Osseous Heteroplasia Association (POHA) is a non-profit, voluntary organization dedicated to raising funds for research into finding appropriate treatment and a cure for progressive osseous heteroplasia (POH). POH is an extremely rare disorder characterized by the abnormal development of bone in areas of the body where bone is not normally present (heterotopic ossification). The disorder first appears as areas of patchy bone formation (ossification) on the skin during infancy; heterotopic ossification progresses to involve superficial and deep connective tissues, areas of fat beneath the skin (subcutaneous fat), muscles, tendons, ligaments, and the bands of fibrous tissues that support muscle (fascia). In addition to serving as a patient education organization, POHA strives toward an additional goal, to raise sufficient funds to make the medical world more aware of POH. Established in 1995, the association produces educational materials including a handbook entitled "What is POH? A Guidebook for Families," reprints of scientific and medical journal articles about POH, and a videotape of a 1995 symposium on fibrodysplasia ossificans progressiva (FOP), a similar but distinct rare disorder.

President: Catherine M. Jacobs (1995 to present)
Executive Director: Fred B. Gardner (Treasurer)
Year Established: 1995
Acronym: POHA

Keywords
POH; Progressive Osseous Heteroplasia Association; Progressive Osseous Heteroplasia Association (POHA); Progressive Osseous Heteroplasia (POH)

2091 Progressive Supranuclear Palsy (PSP Europe) Association
The Old Rectory
Wappenham
Towcester
Northamptonshire, NN12 8SQ, United Kingdom

Phone: +44 (0) 1327-86-0299
Fax: +44 (0) 1327-86-1007
E-mail: psp@pspeur.org
http://www.pspeur.org

The Progressive Supranuclear Palsy (PSP Europe) Association is a registered charity dedicated to promoting research worldwide into progressive supranuclear palsy (PSP), providing information and support to PSP afflicted families across Europe and engendering awareness of PSP and the PSP Association mainly across the UK. Progressive supranuclear palsy is a comparatively rare neurologic disorder (prevalence some 6 per 100,000). It is a progressive brain disease, involving the progressive death of neurons in the mid brain immediately above the nuclei (hence supranuclear), which control balance, movement, vision—particularly upgaze and downgaze—speech and ability to swallow. It is characterized by spastic weakness of muscles affected by the cranial nerves (i.e., muscles of the face, throat, tongue). Symptoms may include falling, difficulty walking (ataxia), vision disturbances, and difficulty in speech (dysarthria) and swallowing. The exact cause of this disorder is unknown, though there is a genetic component. Founded in 1994, the PSP Association provides a telephone counseling service staffed by nurses trained in the care of individuals with PSP, runs local support groups, holds biennial international medical workshops, annual symposiums for carers and therapists and publishes newsletters or bulletins, which update readers on the progress of the charity towards its objectives, including research, support and awareness engendering three

times a year. There are currently sixteen local support groups within the United Kingdom and the PSP Association is dedicated to forming and promoting similar groups across Europe.

President: General the Lord Gutherie of Craigiebank GCB LVO OBE
Executive Director: Brigadier Michael R. Koe, OBE (Chief Executive)
Year Established: 1994
Acronym: PSP Association

Keywords
Nuchal Dystonia Dementia Syndrome; PSP; Progressive Supranuclear Palsy; Progressive Supranuclear Palsy (PSP Europe) Association; Steele Richardson Olszewski Syndrome

2092 Propionic Acidemia Foundation
1963 McCraren Road
Highland Park, IL 60035

Phone: (847) 452-7528
E-mail: paf@pafoundation.com
http://www.pafoundation.com

The Propionic Acidemia Foundation (PAF) was created to raise and provide monetary support for academic researchers engaged in studies to find better treatments and, ultimately, a cure for propionic acidemia. Propionic acidemia is a rare metabolic disorder characterized by deficiency of propionyl CoA carboxylase, an enzyme involved in the breakdown (catabolism) of the chemical "building blocks" (amino acids) of certain proteins. Founded in 2002, PAF offers information to patients, family members, and health professionals.

President: Jill Chertot Franks (2002-present)
Year Established: 2002
Acronym: PAF

Keywords
Propionic Acidemia Foundation

2093 Proteus Syndrome Foundation
4915 Dry Stone Drive
Colorado Springs, CO 80918

Phone: (719) 264-8445
E-mail: kimkhoag@adelphia.net
http://www.proteus-syndrome.org

The Proteus Syndrome Foundation is a national, voluntary, not-for-profit organization dedicated to providing information, assistance, and support to children with proteus syndrome and their families. Proteus syndrome is a rare, extremely variable disorder of unknown cause that may be characterized by partial enlargement of the hands and/or feet; overgrowth of one side of the face, body, and/or arms and legs (hemihypertrophy); and/or an abnormally large head (macrocephaly) or asymmetry of the skull. Established in 1992, the Proteus Syndrome Foundation is committed to providing networking opportunities for affected individuals and family members; compiling a family directory; and creating a database of affected families around the world to help physicians and families obtain as much information as possible before making choices concerning surgeries and therapies. The foundation also works closely with researchers to promote clinical studies into proteus syndrome; communicates ongoing research efforts to affected families; provides referrals; engages in-patient and professional education; and offers a variety of materials including brochures, pamphlets, and a regular newsletter.

Executive Director: Kim Hoag
Year Established: 1992

Keywords
Hemihypertrophy Macrocephaly; Proteus Syndrome; Proteus Syndrome Foundation

---

2094 Prune Belly Syndrome Network, Inc.

P.O. Box 154
Beloit, WI 53512-0154

E-mail: JKING@prunebelly.org
http://www.prunebelly.org

The Prune Belly Syndrome Network, Inc., is an international, not-for-profit organization dedicated to providing information and support services for individuals with prune belly syndrome, family members, and healthcare professionals. Prune-belly syndrome, also known as Eagle-Barrett syndrome, is a rare disorder characterized by partial or complete absence of the stomach (abdominal) muscles, failure of both testes to descend into the scrotum (bilateral cryptorchidism), and/or urinary tract malformations such as abnormal widening (dilation) of the tubes that bring urine to the bladder (ureters), accumulation of urine in the ureters (hydroureter) and the kidneys (hydronephrosis), and/or backflow of urine from the bladder into the ureters (vesicoureteral reflux). Complications associated with prune-belly syndrome may include underdevelopment of the lungs (pulmonary

hypoplasia) and/or chronic renal failure. The exact cause of prune-belly syndrome is not known. The Support Network has a web site on the Internet that provides general information on prune-belly syndrome, articles from healthcare professionals concerning treatment and care, dynamic linkage to additional sources of information, and several online networking opportunities through its e-mail mailing list and chat room. Information on subscribing to the Prune Belly Syndrome Support Network's online mailing list can be obtained by visiting the organization's web site at http://healthcon.com.

Year Established: 1996
Acronym: PBSN

Keywords
Abdominal Muscle Deficiency Syndrome; Abdominal Muscles, Congenital Absence of the; Eagle Barrett Syndrome; Obrinsky Syndrome; Prune Belly Syndrome; Prune Belly Syndrome Network, Inc.

2095 Pseudotumor Cerebri Support Network

3521 Westbay Drive
Columbus, OH 43231

E-mail: PCDuncan@Juno.com
http://www.pseudotumorcerebri.com

The Pseudotumor Cerebri (PTC) Support Network is an international, non-profit, support organization dedicated to educating PTC patients, families, and medical personnel. The network also advocates for more research and better treatments for all individuals diagnosed with pseudotumor cerebri/intracranial hypertension. Pseudotumor cerebri is a syndrome of increased pressure inside the skull. Symptoms can mimic those of a brain tumor. However, no tumor is involved. Established in 1992, the PTC Network provides a comprehensive website at www.pseudotumorcerebri.com, which includes a complete copy of the organization's book, "The PTC Primer," for all to access.

President: Jennifer Duncan (Indefinite)
Executive Director: Same
Year Established: 1992
Acronym: PTC Support Network

Keywords
Intracranial Hypertension; Pseudotumor Cerebri; Pseudotumor Cerebri Support Network; PTC Support Network

2096　**Psoriatic Arthropathy Alliance**

P.O. Box 111
St. Albans
Hertfordshire, AL2 3JQ, United Kingdom

Phone: +44 (0) 870-770-3212
Fax: +44 (0) 870-770-3213
E-mail: info@thePAA.org
http://www.paalliance.org

The Psoriatic Arthropathy Alliance (PAA) is a non-profit support and informational organization for individuals affected by psoriatic arthropathy (PA) and other related conditions. Psoriatic arthropathy is a rheumatoid-like arthritic condition that is associated with psoriasis of the skin or nails, and a negative rheumatoid arthritis (RA) serology laboratory test. The disorder is more common in females than males. The mission of the PAA is to provide support and information to individuals affected by PA. Established in 1993, the alliance also monitors medical and healthcare services and supports research into the causes, prevention, and management of PA and related conditions. In addition, the group acts as a lobbyist for patient rights. Consisting of 1,000 members, the alliance produces educational materials that are available to medical professionals, medical students, and the general public. PAA publishes a periodic newsletter and a journal and offers a networking service.

President: Julie and David Chandler
Executive Director: Same as above.
Year Established: 1993
Acronym: PAA

Keywords
Arthritis, Psoriatic; Arthropathy, Psoriatic; Psoriasis; Psoriasis, Arthropathic; Psoriatic Arthropathy Alliance

2097　**The Pull-Thru Network**

2312 Savoy Street
Hoover, AL 35226

Phone: (205) 978-2930
E-mail: info@pullthrough.org
http://www.pullthrough.org

The Pull-thru Network is a non-profit, self-help organization dedicated to providing mutual support to the families of children born with an anorectal malformation, colon disease, and the associated defects and to the individuals born with these disorders. Established in 1988, the network offers appropriate refer-

rals, conducts support group meetings; gives phone and E-mail support, provides a national networking service for its members, offers a chatroom for members on its website, and provides an E-mail support group (listserv). In addition, the organization provides a variety of educational and support materials including pamphlets and a quarterly magazine for members entitled "Pull-thru Network News." The PTN News features articles on research, new techniques, personal stories, bowel management, school and daycare issues, and practical advice and helpful hints pertaining to the everyday care of children with these diagnoses.

President: Bonnie McElroy
Year Established: 1988
Acronym: PTN

Keywords
Anal Malformations; Anal Stenosis; Anorectal Malformations; Cloaca; Cloacal Exstrophy; Exstrophy; Hirschspring's Disease; Ostomy, child; Tethered Spinal Cord; The Pull Thru Network; The Pull-Thru Network; VACTERL; VATER

2098　**Pulmonary Fibrosis Foundation**

1332 North Halsted
Suite 201
Chicago, IL 60622

Phone: (312) 587-9272
Fax: (312) 587-9273
E-mail: breathe@pulmonaryfibrosis.org
http://www.pulmonaryfibrosis.org

The Pulmonary Fibrosis Foundation (PFF) is a not-for-profit organization dedicated to finding a cure for, and raising awareness of, pulmonary fibrosis, an often-terminal disease. This disease occurs due to microscopic injury, leading to scarring that causes the lungs to become stiff. The foundation is devoted to improving the quality of life for those afflicted with pulmonary fibrosis. It funds and supports research seeking treatments and, ultimately, a cure for this disease. The PFF also provides educational services for patients, their families, healthcare professionals, and the public. Its services also include networking and advocacy.

President: Mike Rosezweig, PhD (2000-present)
Year Established: 2000

Keywords
Cough; Idiopathic Pulmonary Fibrosis; ILD; IPF; Networking; PF; Pulmonary Fibrosis; Pulmonary Fibrosis Foundation; Shortness of Breath; UIP; Weight Loss

2099 Pulmonary Hypertension Association

850 Sligo Avenue
Suite 800
Silver Spring, MD 20910-4683

Phone: (301) 565-3004
Fax: (301) 565-3994
Toll Free: (800) 748-7274
E-mail: pha@phassociation.org
http://www.phassociation.org

The Pulmonary Hypertension Association (PHA) is an international, not-for-profit, voluntary organization that provides educational information and fellowship to people with primary or secondary pulmonary hypertension. Pulmonary hypertension is a condition characterized by abnormally high blood pressure in the arteries that supply the lungs. Pulmonary hypertension may be an isolated condition that may occur for unknown reasons (primary pulmonary hypertension) or may occur due to or in association with other underlying disorders or conditions (secondary pulmonary hypertension). Established in 1992, the organization addresses issues pertinent to people with these disorders such as current research, early detection, orphan drug designations, organ donor awareness, and organ transplantation. It conducts international conferences; provides a networking service; offers referrals; and publishes a quarterly newsletter, "Pathlight."

President: Jack Stibbs
Executive Director: Rino Aldrighetti (President)
Year Established: 1992
Acronym: PHA

Keywords
PPH; Pulmonary Hypertension; Pulmonary Hypertension Association; Pulmonary Hypertension, Primary; Pulmonary Hypertension, Secondary; United Patients' Association for Pulmonary Hypertension, Inc.

2100 Purine Metabolic Patients' Association (PUMPA)

209-211 City Road
London, EC1V 1JN, United Kingdom

Phone: +44 (0 207-608-8700
Fax: +44 (0) 207-608-8701
Toll Free: +44 (0) 808-808-3555
E-mail: helpline@cafamily.org.uk
http://www.pumpa.org

The Purine Metabolic Patients' Association (PUMPA) is an international, not-for-profit, support organization in the United Kingdom for individuals with purine metabolic disorders and their families. Founded in 1992 by a small group of affected families and friends, the association is dedicated to advancing knowledge of purine metabolic disorders among the medical profession and the general public in its aim to improve the care and increase the support received by affected individuals. Inborn errors in the metabolism of purines, which are compounds found in many foods, medications, and other substances, result in several different disorders. There are currently over 20 known inherited disorders of purine metabolism, causing a wide range of associated symptoms and findings. Depending upon the specific disorder, affected individuals may experience such symptoms as gout, anemia, autism, episodes of uncontrolled electrical disturbances in the brain (seizures), delayed development, deafness, kidney stones and/or renal failure, impaired immunity, self-destructive behaviors such as biting or head-banging, and/or other abnormalities. The Purine Metabolic Patients' Association is committed to providing networking services to affected individuals and families, enabling them to exchange mutual support, information, and resources. The association also promotes and supports research currently being conducted by the Purine Research Laboratory at Guy's Hospital, London. In addition, the Purine Metabolic Patients' Association offers a variety of educational materials including pamphlets, booklets providing understandable information on specific purine metabolic disorders, and a regular newsletter. The association also has a web site on the Internet that provides a description of the organization's goals and services, information on purine metabolic disorders, networking opportunities including a guest book and a forum area, and dynamic linkage to additional sources of information and support on the Internet.

President: Thomas Melvin (Chairman) (1993 to Present)
Executive Director: Derek Yardley (Manager)
Year Established: 1992
Acronym: PUMPA

Keywords
Lesch Nyhan Syndrome; Purine Disorders; Purine Metabolic Patients' Association (PUMPA)

2101 Purine Research Society

5424 Beech Avenue
Bethesda, MD 20814-1730

Phone: (301) 530-0354
Fax: (301) 564-9597
E-mail: purine@erols.com
http://www.purineresearchsociety.org

The Purine Research Society is a national, nonprofit, charitable organization dedicated to funding research and treatments for purine-related metabolic diseases. Errors in the metabolism of purines (compounds commonly found in food) can lead to a variety of disorders. Established in 1986 by parents of children with purine autism (autistic children who excrete too much uric acid in their urine), the society serves people with purine metabolic disorders and their families, healthcare professionals, and the general public. The Purine Research Society provides appropriate referrals to affected individuals and offers educational pamphlets and brochures, as well as a purine restricted diet.

Executive Director: Mrs. Tahma Metz
Year Established: 1986

Keywords
5′ Nucleotidase Defect; ADA Deficiency; Adenine Phosphoribosyltransferase Deficiency; Adenosine Deaminase Deficiency; Adenylosuccinate Lyase Deficiency; Gout; Lesch Nyhan Syndrome; Myoadenylate Deaminase Deficiency; Phosphoribosyl Pyrophosphate Synthetase Defects; Purine Disorders; Purine Metabolic Disorders; Purine Nucleoside Phosphorylase Deficiency; Purine Research Society; Xanthinuria

2102 PXE International, Inc.

4301 Connecticut Avenue NW
Suite 404
Washington, DC 20008-2304

Phone: (202) 362-9599
Fax: (202) 966-8553
E-mail: pxe@pxe.org
http://www.pxe.org

PXE International, Inc., is a voluntary organization established in 1995 for the purpose of disseminating information on pseudoxanthoma elasticum (PXE) to affected individuals, families, and doctors. PXE is an inherited disorder that affects selected connective tissue in some parts of the body. Elastic tissue in the body becomes mineralized; that is, calcium and other minerals are deposited in the tissue. This can result in changes in the skin, eyes, cardiovascular system and gastrointestinal system. PXE International initiates, funds and conducts research, and publishes information for affected individuals, families, and physicians. Educational materials are written both for lay people and medical specialists, in 8 languages and include "The MemberGram," the organization's newsletter. Composed of 4000 members, the organization maintains an international registry of affected individuals, families, and helpful medical specialists. With over 52 offices worldwide, it networks throughout the world, providing written, telephone, e-mail, and meeting connections. The PXE International Blood and Tissue Bank provides tissue samples to approved PXE research projects. In addition, the organization conducts a biennial international conference.

President: Patrick Terry
Executive Director: Sharon Terry
Year Established: 1995
Acronym: PXE

Keywords
Connective Tissue Disorders; Elastosis Dystrophica Syndrome; Groenblad Strandberg Syndrome; PXE; PXE International, Inc.; Pseudoxanthoma Elasticum; Systemic Elastorrhexis

2103 Rare Cancer Alliance

1649 North Pacana Way
Green Valley, AZ 85614

Phone: (520) 625-5495
Fax: (615) 526-4921
E-mail: sharon.lane@rare-cancer.org
http://www.rare-cancer.org

The primary purpose of Rare Cancer Alliance is to disseminate information and provide support to adult and pediatric rare cancer patients. On its web site, it provides cancer information, treatment options, and rare cancer differences. Most of the organization's members are rare cancer patients, and the alliance has support forum through which members share their information gained through their own experiences with others. The web site also provides a venue for fund raising awareness of rare cancer and funding research.

Executive Director: Sharon Lane
Year Established: 2000
Acronym: RCA

Keywords

Adenocarcinoma; Carcinoid; Carcinoma; Hodgkin's Lymphoma; Leukemia; Lymphoma; Melanoma; Mesothelioma; Neoplasm; Non-Hodgkin's; Rare Cancer Alliance; Sarcoma

2104 A Rare Disease: Fibrosing Mediastinitis

P.O. Box 755
Normangee, TX 77871

E-mail: nita@fibroshingmediastinitis.com
http://www.fibrosingmediastinitis.com

A Rare Disease: Fibrosing Mediastinitis (ARDFM) was founded in 2002 as a clearinghouse for information about medical research, physician referrals, and emotional support for patients and family members affected by fibrosing mediastinitis. Fibrosing mediastinitis is a rare disorder caused by the proliferation of tissue in the area of the chest that lies between the lungs. Major blood vessels or airways may be affected. A not-for-profit organization, ARDFM offers support groups, patient networking, and a patient registry to anyone in the world who has been affected by this disease.

President: Nita Rice (2002-present)
Year Established: 2002
Acronym: ARDFM

Keywords
ARDFM; Fibrosing Mediastinitis; Networking; Support Groups; A Rare Disease: Fibrosing Mediastinitis

2105 Rasmussen's Syndrome and Hemispherectomy Support Network

8235 Lethbridge Road
Millersville, MD 21108

Phone: (410) 987-5221
E-mail: rssnlynn@aol.com

The Rasmussen's Syndrome and Hemispherectomy Support Network is a national not-for-profit organization dedicated to providing information and support to individuals affected by Rasmussen's syndrome (Rasmussen's encephalitis) and hemispherectomy. Rasmussen's syndrome is a rare central nervous system disorder characterized by chronic active inflammation of the brain (encephalitis) and epileptic seizures of varying degrees of severity. Progressive symptoms including paralysis (usually of one side of the body) and mental retardation may also occur. Although the exact cause of this disorder is not known, it is thought to result from an unidentified viral infection. Hemispherectomy is a form of surgery commonly used in the treatment of Rasmussen's syndrome and other brain disorders. Founded in 1994 and comprised of 200 members, RSHSN publishes a periodic newsletter and disseminates reprints of medical journal articles concerning Rasmussen's syndrome and its treatments. RSHSN also maintains a support network that provides encouragement and information to individuals affected by Rasmussen's syndrome and their families.

President: Al and Lynn Miller (Founders)
Executive Director: Same as above.
Year Established: 1994
Acronym: RSHSN

Keywords
Encephalitis, Chronic Localized; Encephalitis, Rasmussen's; Epilepsy Hemiplegia and Mental Retardation; Hemispherectomy; Rasmussen's Syndrome; Rasmussen's Syndrome and Hemispherectomy Support Network

2106 Raynaud's & Scleroderma Association (UK)

112 Crewe Road
Alsager
Cheshire, ST7 2JA, United Kingdom

Phone: +44 (0) 1270-87-2776
Fax: +44 (0) 1270-88-3556
E-mail: info@raynauds.org.uk
http://www.raynauds.org.uk

The Raynaud's & Scleroderma Association (UK) is a volunatary, non-for-profit organization that was established in the United Kingdom in 1982. The association is dedicated to promoting greater awareness of Raynaud's and scleroderma; offering support, information, and advice to affected individuals and family members; and assisting in the welfare of those who have disabilities resulting from or are chronically ill due to Raynaud's and scleroderma. Raynaud's is a condition characterized by sudden, episodic contraction of the blood vessels supplying the fingers and toes (digits), causing an interruption of blood flow to the digits. Episodes are usually triggered by exposure to cold temperatures. If the condition appears to occur spontaneously with no known cause, it is known as Raynaud's disease. When it occurs due to an underlying disorder, such as scleroderma or rheumatoid arthritis, the condition is referred to as Raynaud's phenomenon. Scleroderma is a rare disorder characterized by chronic thickening and hardening of the skin. The disorder may be localized, involving changes of the skin and underlying tissues or may be systemic.

President: Anne Mawdsley, M.B.E. (Founder)
Year Established: 1982

Keywords
Raynaud's & Scleroderma Association (UK); Raynaud's Disease and Phenomenon

2107 Raynaud's Association, Inc.
94 Mercer Avenue
Hartsdale, NY 10530

Phone: (800) 280-8055
Fax: (914) 946-4685
Toll Free: (800) 280-8055
E-mail: lynn@raynauds.org
http://www.raynauds.org

The Raynaud's Association is a non-profit organization dedicated to sharing information and help in coping with daily activities among individuals who are affected by Raynaud's disease and phenomenon. Raynaud's is a common vascular disorder characterized by episodes of constriction of very small blood vessels in the fingers, toes or other extremity. Symptoms may include numbness, tingling, and cold sensations in the fingers. The purpose of the association is to share information and to provide support in dealing with everyday activities, such as holding a cold glass of soda or shopping in the refrigerated section of a supermarket. Founded in 1992, the association also works to increase public awareness of Raynaud's disease and is active in patient recruitment for ongoing clinical trials and eventually funding for research. Consisting of over 1,500 members, the organization produces educational materials including the newsletter "Cold Cuts" and a brochure about the disease. In addition, the association coordinates a national networking program and holds informal support group meetings in the New York metropolitan area.

President: Lynn Wunderman (1992 to Present) (Founder)
Year Established: 1992

Keywords
Asphyxia, Symmetric; Raynaud's & Cold Sufferers Network; Raynaud's Association, Inc.; Raynaud's Disease and Phenomenon; Raynaud's Disease, Primary

2108 Reach Out for Youth with Ileitis and Colitis, Inc.
84 Northgate Circle
Melville, NY 11747

Phone: (631) 293-3102
Fax: (631) 293-3103
E-mail: reachoutforyouth@reachoutforyouth.org
http://www.reachoutforyouth.org

Reach Out for Youth with Ileitis and Colitis, Inc., is a non-profit support organization dedicated to assisting families whose children have inflammatory bowel disease (IBD) such as ileitis or colitis. Ulcerative colitis is an inflammatory disease of the large intestine and is characterized by diarrhea, abdominal pain, fever, and bleeding from the rectum. Decreased appetite and weight loss may also occur. Ileitis or Crohn's disease, also an inflammatory bowel disorder, can affect any portion of the digestive system and has symptoms that are similar to those of colitis. Established in 1979 and consisting of approximately 400 members, the organization has helped hundreds of families cope with the effects of IBD. The group's goals include providing educational materials and emotional support to affected individuals and their families and organizing fundraising efforts to promote research into the causes and treatment of IBD. Educational seminars and a quarterly newsletter entitled "Inner Circle" assist members by keeping them informed of current activities. A hotline offers interested individuals the opportunity to communicate on a one-to-one basis, especially when acute symptoms are present. Reach Out also continues to support the IBD clinical database established 13 years ago as a crucial research tool. Our educational brochure, "The Inside Story" is available upon request.

President: Irwin Maltz
Executive Director: Susan Spellman
Year Established: 1979

Keywords
CD; Colitis; Colitis, Granulomatous; Colitis, Gravis; Colitis, Thromboulcerative; Colitis, Ulcerative; Colon, Unstable; Crohn's Disease; Enteritis, Regional; IBD; IBS; Ileitis; Inflammatory Bowel Disease; Irritable Colon Syndrome; Neurosis, Colonic; Proctocolitis; Reach Out for Youth with Ileitis and Colitis, Inc.; Spastic Colon

2109 Reach: The Association for Children with Hand or Arm Deficiency
P.O. Box 54
Helston
Cornwall, TR13 8WD, United Kingdom

Phone: +44 (0) 845-130-6225
Fax: +44 (0) 845-130-0262
E-mail: reach@reach.org.uk
http://www.reach.org.uk

Reach: The Association for Children with Hand or Limb Deficiency is a registered charity dedicated to providing information and support to families of children who have any form of upper limb deficiency. Such deficiencies may be present at birth (congenital) or acquired through accident or necessary surgery. Established in 1978, Reach provides networking opportunities that enable affected families to share information and encourage one another. Reach also provides referrals for children requiring prosthetic limbs, adaptive equipment, or surgery, and raises funds for research into new technology for the development of improved prosthetic arms. Reach also contributes to research projects, such as the effort to discover why some children are born with an incomplete arm or hand. The association publishes information including brochures, booklets such as "A Guide to Artificial Limbs," and a quarterly newsletter entitled "Within Reach." While Reach mainly serves residents of the United Kingdom, it does answer queries from all over the world.

President: Christopher Creamer
Executive Director: Sue Stokes (National Coordinator)
Year Established: 1978

Keywords
Reach: The Association for Children with Hand or Arm Deficiency

2110   Real Hope for CDH (Congenital Diaphragmatic Hernia) Foundation

1171 Vermilion Road
Vermilion, OH 41089

Phone: (216) 533-4476
E-mail: cfirestone@centurytel.net
http://www.realhopeforcdh.com

Real Hope for CDH is a parent group dedicated to families of children born with congenital diaphragmatic hernias (CDH). This is a life-threatening birth defect in which the diaphragm does not completely form, allowing some of the contents of the abdomen to protrude into the chest and hinder the normal growth of lung tissue. Founded in 2004, Real Hope for CDH is a patient support group offering information on experiences of families involved in a CDH program at

Shands Children's Hospital at the University of Florida. Approximately one in every 3000 babies is affected by CDH. Real Hope for CDH provides patient networking and informational materials to patients, professionals, and the general public.

Year Established: 2004
Acronym: Real Hope for CDH Foundation

Keywords
Advocacy; CDH; Congenital Diaphragmatic Hernia; Networking; Real Hope for CDH (Congenital Diaphragmatic Hernia) Foundation; Research; Support Groups

2111   Recurrent Respiratory Papillomatosis Foundation

P.O. Box 6643
Lawrenceville, NJ 08648-0643

Phone: (609) 530-1443
Fax: (609) 530-1912
E-mail: bills@rrpf.org
http://www.rrpf.org

The Recurrent Respiratory Papillomatosis Foundation is a national, not-for-profit, voluntary organization created to provide support and information to people with recurrent respiratory papillomatosis and their families. Established in 1992, the foundation seeks to serve as an information resource for affected individuals and their physicians, to promote public awareness, and to aid in the prevention, cure, and treatment of recurrent respiratory papillomatosis. In addition, the foundation endeavors to educate the medical community about recurrent papillomatosis, to facilitate early diagnosis of the disease, and to implement risk reduction measures. The nucleus of the network is the RRP Newsletter. It includes support network information, statistics, individual case histories, treatment developments, and additional information that further understanding and awareness of recurrent respiratory papillomatosis.

President: Marlene Stern (1994-Present)
Executive Director: William Stern
Year Established: 1992
Acronym: RRP Foundation

Keywords
Papilloma, Juvenile Laryngeal; Papilloma, Laryngeal; Papillomatosis; Papillomatosis, Recurrent Respiratory; Recurrent Respiratory Papillomatosis Foundation

2112   Reflex Sympathetic Dystrophy Syndrome Association of America

P.O. Box 502
99 Cherry Street
Milford, CT 06460

Phone: (203) 877-3790
Fax: (203) 882-8362
Toll Free: (877) 662-7737
E-mail: info@rsds.org
http://www.rsds.org

The Reflex Sympathetic Dystrophy Syndrome Association of America (RSDSA) is a not-for-profit organization founded to promote greater public and professional awareness of complex regional pain syndrome (CRPS), formerly knows as reflex sympathetic dystrophy syndrome (RSD) and support research into the causes and cure of complex regional pain symdrome/reflex sympathetic dystrophy (CRPS/RSD). The association's mission also includes the establishment and organization of support groups for affected individuals and their families; and promotion of awareness of reflex sympathetic dystrophy syndrome among healthcare professionals and the general public. Founded in 1984, the association provides a referral service to physicians, offers a pen pal service, and promotes patient advocacy. RSDA offers a variety of educational materials and services including an information packet, a quarterly newsletter, a statistical report on reflex sympathetic dystrophy syndrome derived from member questionnaires, reference articles, brochures, booklets, and videos. The association also provides educational in-service conferences for healthcare professionals and patients and has published clinical practice guidelines for the diagnosis, treatment, and management of RSD/CRPS.

President: Paul Charlesworth
Executive Director: James W. Broatch, M.S.W.
Year Established: 1984
Acronym: RSDSA

Keywords
Atrophy, Sudeck's; Causalgia; Complex Regional Pain Syndrome; Complex Regional Pain Syndrome, Type I; Complex Regional Pain Syndrome, Type II; Dystrophy, Post Traumatic; Reflex Sympathetic Dystrophy; Reflex Sympathetic Dystrophy Syndrome; Reflex Sympathetic Dystrophy Syndrome Association of America; RSD; RSDS; Shoulder Hand Syndrome

2113   Rehabilitation Research and Training Center on Aging with Developmental Disabilities

1640 W. Roosevelt Road
Department of Disability and Human Development
University of Illinois at Chicago
Chicago, IL 60608-6904

Phone: (312) 413-1520
Fax: (312) 996-6942
Toll Free: (800) 996-8845
TDD: (312) 413-0453
E-mail: rrtcamr@uic.edu
http://www.rrtcadd.org

The Rehabilitation Research and Training Center on Aging with Developmental Disabilities (RRTCADD) promotes the successful aging of adults with intellectual (mental retardation) and developmental disabilities in response to physical, cognitive, and environmental changes. RRTCADD research priorities include improving the health and function of adults with I/DD; enhancing caregiving supports and transition planning among adults with I/DD and their families; and promoting aging- and disability-friendly environments that enable adults with I/DD to participate in community life. The RRTCADD translates its research findings into progressive interventions and policies through its coordinated training, technical assistance, and dissemination activities.

Executive Director: Tamar Heller, Ph.D.
Year Established: 1988
Acronym: RRTCADD

Keywords
Aging; Developmental Disabilities; Intellectual Disabilities; Mental Retardation; Rehabilitation Research and Training Center on Aging with Developmental Disabilities; RRTCADD

2114   Research! America

1101 King St, Suite 250
Alexandria, VA 22314

Phone: (703) 739-2577
Fax: (703) 739-2372
Toll Free: (800) 366-2873
E-mail: info@researchamerica.org
http://www.researchamerica.org

Research! America is a voluntary, not-for-profit, membership supported, public education, and advocacy alliance founded in 1989. Our nearly 500 members institutions organization and corporations represent the voices of more than 100 million Americans who want medical and health research including research to prevent disease, disability and injury and to promote health, a higher national priority.

President: Mary Woolley (1990-present)
Year Established: 1989
Acronym: R!A

Keywords
Foundation; Philanthropies; Research!America; Researchers; Scientists

2115 Restless Legs Syndrome Foundation, Inc.

819 Second Street SW
Rochester, MN 55902

Phone: (507) 287-6465
Fax: (507) 287-6312
Toll Free: (877) 463-6757
E-mail: rlsfoundation@rls.org
http://www.rls.org

The Restless Legs Syndrome Foundation is a national, not-for-profit organization dedicated to achieving universal awareness, developing effective treatments, and finding the cure for restless legs syndrome. The goals of the foundation include the development, production, and distribution of medically approved materials for educational purposes and the expansion of awareness of restless legs syndrome by using mass media to inform the general public about this disorder. In addition, the foundation provides networking services for people with restless legs syndrome, their families, and healthcare professionals to share information, assistance, and support. The Restless Legs Syndrome Foundation supports research and encourages medical and nursing schools to include information on restless legs syndrome in their curricula.

President: Robert Waterman, Jr. (Board Chairperson)
Executive Director: Georgianna Bell
Year Established: 1992
Acronym: RLS Foundation

Keywords
Myoclonus, Nocturnal; Periodic Limb Movement Disorder; Restless Legs Syndrome; Restless Legs Syndrome Foundation, Inc.; RLS

2116 Restricted Growth Association

P.O. Box 4744
Dorchester
Dorset, DT2 9FA, United Kingdom

Phone: +44 (0) 1308-89-8445
Fax: +44 (0) 1308-89-8445
http://www.restrictedgrowth.co.uk

The Restricted Growth Association (RGA) is a voluntary, not-for-profit, self-help organization that was established in the United Kingdom in 1970. The association, which currently consists of approximately 680 members and eight regional chapters, is dedicated to providing information, support, and resources to individuals affected by restricted growth and their families and reducing social barriers that may prevent affected individuals' full participation and fulfillment in society. Restricted growth or "short stature" may occur due to many different underlying disorders, syndromes, or other factors. As a result, restricted growth may take many different forms, and affected individuals' height and other potentially associated symptoms and physical features may vary greatly. The Restricted Growth Association firmly believes that, in common with all of humanity, every person of restricted growth is an individual with unique abilities, emotions, and ambitions that must be encouraged to unfold to the maximum benefit of that individual. The association is committed to enhancing the role of affected individuals in society; providing support to families with newborns affected by restricted growth; offering fellowship, mutual support, and encouragement to affected individuals and their families; and furthering affected individuals' self-fulfillment and independence. The Restricted Growth Association promotes research into restricted growth disorders and conditions, conducts social events and mutual interest groups both regionally and nationally, and maintains close links with sister organizations internationally. In addition, the association also offers peer phone support for affected individuals and family members; provides educational materials on disorders responsible for restricted growth, genetics, orthopedics, treatment, and other areas; and offers practical information and support to affected individuals and parents concerning such milestones as starting school, going to college, and entering the work force. The Restricted Growth Association also provides practical help concerning suitable children's toys, sources of clothing and shoes, clothes exchanges, adaptation and manufacture of furniture and fittings, reaching aids, car modifications and additional mobility assistance, and grants and benefits. The association's educational materials include a quarterly newsletter, pamphlets, and booklets including "The Layman's Guide to Restricted Growth" and "Coping with Restricted Growth."

Executive Director: Sandy Marshall
Year Established: 1970
Acronym: RGA

Keywords
Achondrogenesis; Achondroplasia; Acrodysothosis; Bonnevie Ulrich Syndrome; Caudal Regression Syndrome; Chondrodysplasia Punctata, Rhizomelic; Conradi Hunermann Syndrome; Dyschondrosteosis; Dysplasia, Acromesomelic; Dysplasia, Cranioectodermal; Dysplasia, Diastrophic; Dysplasia, Metatrophic; Dysplasia, Multiple Ephphyseal; Ellis-van Creveld Syndrome; Fairbank Disease; Hypochondroplasia; Jarcho Levin Syndrome; Jeune Syndrome; Kaufman Syndrome; Kniest Syndrome; Leri Weill Syndrome; Madelung's Deformity; Marshall Stickler Syndrome; Pseudoachondroplasia; Restricted Growth Association; Robinow Syndrome; Russell Silver Syndrome; Seckel Syndrome; Sotos Syndrome; Spondylocostal Dyplasia; Three M Syndrome; Turner Syndrome

2117 Retinitis Pigmentosa International

P.O. Box 900
Woodland Hills, CA 91365

Phone: (818) 992-0500
Fax: (818) 992-3265
Toll Free: (800) 344-4877
E-mail: info@international.org
http://www.rpinternational.org

Retinitis Pigmentosa International (RPI) is a not-for-profit organization dedicated to promoting and supporting research to find effective treatments and cures for retinitis pigmentosa, macular degeneration, and other degenerative eye diseases. The organization promotes the education of family members, friends, physicians, and educators about the special needs of people who are visually impaired. It maintains an ongoing public awareness campaign and supports its human service programs, including its school for the blind, audio vision talking greeting cards, and TheatreVision (accessible movies for blind individuals). Established in 1972, Retinitis Pigmentosa International offers facilities that demonstrate visual aids for people who are partially-sighted and provides personal counseling, psychological counseling, and mobility training. The organization provides referrals to genetic counselors and support groups and offers a variety of educational materials including a regular newsletter and brochures.

President: Helen Harris (1972-Present)
Executive Director: Same as above.
Year Established: 1972
Acronym: RPI

Keywords
Acanthocytosis; Alstrom's Disease; Bardet-Biedl Syndrome; Coats' Disease; Cone Dystrophy; Leber's Congenital Amaurosis; Loken Senior Syndrome; Macular Degeneration; Norrie Disease; Refsum Disease; Retinal Degeneration Diseases; Retinitis Pigmentosa; Retinitis Pigmentosa International; Retinoschisis; RP; Usher's Syndrome

2118 Rett Syndrome Research Foundation (RSRF)

4600 Devitt Drive
Cincinnati, OH 45246

Phone: (513) 874-3020
Fax: (513) 874-2520
E-mail: mgriffin@rsrf.org
http://www.rsrf.org

The Rett Syndrome Research Foundation (RSRF) is the world's only organization devoted exclusively to funding biomedical research for Rett syndrome. Their mandate is clear: to find treatments and a cure for this devastating neurological disorder. Rett syndrome is a rare, neurodevelopmental disorder that is diagnosed almost exclusively in females. Affected infants and children typically develop normally until about seven to 18 months of age, when they begin to lose previously acquired skills, such as purposeful hand movements and the ability to communicate. The foundation provides a newsletter, web site and electronic newsletter for both families and researchers/clinicians.

President: Stephen Gallucci
Year Established: 1999
Acronym: RSRF

Keywords
Rett Syndrome; Rett Syndrome Research Foundation (RSRF); RSRF

2119 Ring Chromosome 20 Foundation

c/o Mercantile Safe-Deposit & Trust Company
Foundation Administration
Attn: Joe Ferlise
Hopkins Plz. P.O. Box 2257
Balitmore, MD 21201-2930

Phone: (718) 230-8042
Fax: (877) 207-4720
Toll Free: (877) 207-5520
E-mail: info@ring-chromosome-20.org
http://www.ring-chromosome-20.org

The Ring Chromosome 20 Foundation hopes to promote awareness of ring chromosome 20 and the importance to chromosomal testing in children. Ring chromosome 20 occurs when the arms of one of the pair of chromosome 20s, that are present in each cell, fuse to form a ring during pre-natal development. The mission of the Ring Chromosome 20 Foundation is to help individuals affected by ring chromosome 20 syndrome overcome the obstacle they face so they can lead happy, healthy and productive lives. The Ring Chromosome 20 Foundation works toward achieving its mission by offering, online support groups, education, and patient networking.

President: Pierra Roberts (Managing Director)
Executive Director: Stewart Ford
Acronym: R20

Keywords
Chromosomal Testing; Epilepsy; French; Networking; Refractory Epilepsy; Research; Ring Chromosome 20 Foundation; Ring Chromosome 20 Syndrome; Seizures; Support Groups

2120 Robinow Syndrome Foundation
P.O. Box 1072
Anoka, MN 55303

Phone: (763) 434-1152
Fax: (763) 434-1152
E-mail: kmkruger@comcast.net
http://www.robinow.org/

The Robinow Syndrome Foundation is a not-for-profit; self help organization dedicated to providing information and support to individuals and family members affected by Robinow syndrome. Robinow syndrome is an extremely rare inherited disorder characterized by mild to moderate short stature (dwarfism) due to growth delays after birth; distinctive abnormalities of the head and facial (craniofacial) area; additional skeletal malformations; and/or genital

abnormalities. The disorder may be inherited as an autosomal dominant or recessive genetic trait. Established in 1996, the foundation engages in-patient and professional education, provides referrals, has bi-annual conventions for members, and maintains a database. The foundation is also committed to collecting data from original case studies and including new and recent information. The Robinow Syndrome Foundation offers include a variety of educational materials including brochures, pamphlets, reports, some audiovisuals, personal and online support and a regular newsletter.

President: Karla M. Kruger (1991 to Present)
Year Established: 1996

Keywords
Covesdem Syndrome; Fetal Face Syndrome; Robinow Dwarfism; Robinow Syndrome; Robinow Syndrome Foundation

2121 R.O.C.K. (Raising Our Celiac Kids)
3527 Fortuna Ranch Rd
Encinitas, CA 92024

Phone: (858) 395-5421
Fax: (858) 756-0431
E-mail: info@celiackids.com
http://www.celiackids.com

R.O.C.K. (Raising Our Celiac Kids) provides support for families of children who are on a wheat-free/gluten-free diet, due to celiac disease, autism, allergies, or other reasons. Celiac disease is a digestive disorder in which consumption of gluten, a protein found in wheat, rye and barley, causes changes in the mucous membrane lining the small intestine, impairing its ability to absorb fats and other nutrients during digestion. Although its exact cause is unknown, genetic, immunologic, and environmental factors are thought to play some role. R.O.C.K., a voluntary 501(c)3 organization, provides services that include information, support groups, and advocacy on a national level.

President: Danna Korn (1991-present)
Year Established: 1991
Acronym: ROCK

Keywords
R.O.C.K. (Raising Our Celiac Kids)

2122   Roeher Institute
Kinsmen Building
York University
4700 Keele Street
Toronto
Ontario, M3J 1P3, Canada

Phone: (416) 661-9611
Fax: (416) 661-5701
Toll Free: (800) 856-2207
TDD: (416) 661-2023
E-mail: info@roeher.ca
http://www.roeher.ca

The Roeher Institute, located in Ontario, Canada, is a nonprofit organization dedicated to the study of public policy affecting people with intellectual impairments and other disabilities. Established in 1957, the institute has an extensive national and international network and acts as a clearinghouse for information about disability issues around the world. The institute's services include reference and referral information; customized responses to information requests; a generation of bibliographies on specific topics; and the development of customized information packages. The Roeher Institute's goals are to examine and understand issues that affect individuals with an intellectual impairment and other disabilities; to act as a center for the exchange of ideas and to encourage new ways of thinking about persons with an intellectual impairment and other disabilities; and to provide insight into the social policy, programs, laws, and other features of Canadian society that affect the capacity of people with an intellectual impairment and other disabilities to exercise their rights and fully participate in society. Educational materials include a pamphlet entitled "An International Information Centre of Disability at The Roeher Institute," a catalog that lists resource books, and a booklet entitled "Issues and Resources." The institute supports research, encourages educational activities, and provides appropriate referrals.

President: Marcia H. Rioux, Ph.D.
Executive Director: Cameron Crawford (Vice President)
Year Established: 1957

Keywords
Autism; Cerebral Palsy; Disability Services; Down Syndrome; Learning Disabilities; Mentally Retarded; Prader Willi Syndrome; Roeher Institute; Spina Bifida

2123   Romberg's Connection
10622 S. Parkside
Chicago Ridge, IL 60415

Phone: (708) 425-3496
E-mail: rombergs@hotmail.com
http://www.geocities.com/HotSprings/1018/index.html

The Romberg's Connection is an online support group dedicated to locating individuals and families whose lives are affected by Parry-Romberg syndrome and offering appropriate support. This is accomplished primarily through the mutual exchange of e-mail and regular mail correspondence, online networking through the Romberg's Connection web site, and phone contacts. Parry-Romberg syndrome is a rare disorder characterized by slowly progressive wasting (atrophy) of the soft tissues of half of the face (hemifacial atrophy). Symptoms can include distinctive changes of the eyes and hair; and sometimes neurological abnormalities including episodes of uncontrolled electrical disturbances in the brain (seizures) and episodes of severe pain in tissues supplied by the fifth cranial nerve (trigeminal nerve) including the mouth, cheek, nose, and/or other facial tissues (trigeminal neuralgia). Established in 1997, the Romberg's Connection has a membership of 350+ members, worldwide. Many of the members have met in various locations throughout the world.

President: Theresa Hildebrand (1997 to Present)
Executive Director: Steven Hildebrand
Year Established: 1997

Keywords
HFA; Parry Romberg Syndrome; Progressive Facial Hemiatrophy; Progressive Hemifacial Atrophy; PRS; Romberg Syndrome; Romberg's Connection

2124   ROPARD: The Association for Retinopathy of Prematurity and Related Diseases
P.O.Box 250425
Franklin, MI 48025

Phone: (248) 549-2671
Fax: (248) 788-4589
Toll Free: (800) 788-2020
E-mail: ropard@yahoo.com
http://www.ropard.org

The Association for Retinopathy of Prematurity and Related Diseases (ROPARD) is a not-for-profit research organization that funds basic science and clinical research to eliminate retinopathy of prematurity and associated retinal diseases. Retinopathy of prematurity is a potentially blinding disease affecting the retinas of premature infants. ROPARD also funds innovative work leading to the development of new low vision devices, teaching techniques and services for children who are visually impaired and their families.

Executive Director: Michael Trese, M.D.
Year Established: 1990
Acronym: ROPARD

Keywords
Educational Materials; ROPARD:The Association for Retinopathy of Prematurity and Related Diseases; Retinitis Pigmentosa; Retinopathy of Prematurity; Retinoschisis; X linked Juvenile Retinoschisis

2125 Rothberg Institute, Inc.
530 Whitfield Street
Guilford, CT 06437

Phone: (203) 458-7100
Fax: (203) 458-2514
E-mail: jfverney@childhooddiseases.org
http://www.childhooddiseases.org

The Rothberg Institute for Childhood Diseases is a nonprofit research institution devoted to discovering, developing and commercializing novel chemical and biological entities for the treatment of tuberous sclerosis and other orphan childhood diseases. It applies innovative drug discovery strategies, operating at the intersection of modern biology, computer science, and chemistry.

President: Dr. Jonathan M. Rothberg
Executive Director: Janet E. Verney
Year Established: 2001
Acronym: TRI

Keywords
Academia/Pharmacutical Industries; Rothberg Institute, Inc; TSC; Tuberous Sclerosis; Tuberous Sclerosis Complex

2126 Rubinstein-Taybi Parent Group USA
P.O. Box 146
Smith Center, KS 66967-0146

Phone: (785) 697-2989
Toll Free: (888) 447-2989
E-mail: lbaxter@ruraltel.net
http://www.rubinstein-taybi.org   AND   http://www. rubinsteintaybi.com

The Rubinstein-Taybi Parent Group USA is a voluntary, not-for-profit, self-help organization that is dedicated to providing information, assistance, and support to parents, healthcare professionals, and others who care for children with Rubinstein-Taybi syndrome (RTS). Established in 1984, the Rubinstein-Taybi Parent Group provides a list of families affected by this disorder for the purpose of mutual support and information exchange. In addition, the group works with individuals, families, and various organizations around the world to help them start RTS support groups; and promotes and supports research on RTS. The organization provides a variety of educational and support materials, including a directory, a periodic newsletter, brochures, and pamphlets. The group also informs members about research being conducted on Rubinstein-Taybi syndrome and timely journal articles published in the peer-evaluated medical literature.

Executive Director: Lorrie Baxter (Coordinator)
Year Established: 1984
Acronym: RTS Parent Group USA

Keywords
RTS Parent Group USA; Rubinstein Syndrome; Rubinstein Taybi Parent Group USA; Rubinstein Taybi (RTS) Broad Thumb Hallux Syndrome; Rubinstein Taybi Syndrome; Rubinstein-Taybi Parent Group

2127 Rubinstein-Taybi Syndrome UK Support Group
c/o Rosemary Robertson
Appledore Cottage
Knapton
Dilwyn
Herefordshire, HR4 8EU, United Kingdom

Phone: +44 (0) 1568-72-0350
E-mail: johnkath@tinyworld.co.uk
http://www.rtsuk.org

The Rubinstein-Taybi Syndrome UK Support Group has been offering support for a number of years to parents with children affected by Rubinstein-Taybi syndrome. Characteristic features of this syndrome include short stature, broad thumbs and/or great toes, facial abnormalities, and learning disabilities. Initially, one mother who kept in touch with everyone by telephone or letter gave support. In 1986, a few families organized the support group by producing a newsletter and arranging annual get-togethers. Since then, the group has grown from 45 to 142 families, and it offers support to a number of families in other countries where there is no support group.

Executive Director: John Peat

Keywords
Rubinstein Taybi Syndrome; Rubinstein Taybi Syndrome UK Support Group; Rubinstein-Taybi Support Group; Rubinstein-Taybi Syndrome UK Support Group

2128 SADS UK, the Ashley Jolly SAD Trust

22 Rowhedge, Brentwood
Essex, CM13 2TS, United Kingdom

Phone: +44 (0) 1277-23-0642
E-mail: info@sadsuk.org
http://www.sadsuk.org

SADS UK, The Ashley Jolly Sad Trust, is a voluntary organization that exists to help prevent the early loss of life by raising awareness of heart conditions that can cause a sudden adult/arrhythmia death (SAD). It is also dedicated to improving the lives of those adversely impacted by cardiac arrhythmia. The trust promotes heart monitoring and donates heart-monitoring equipment to doctors' surgeries for this purpose. SADS UK works to initiate government legislation (in the UK) to safeguard those who may be at risk from a fatal cardiac arrhythmia and raises awareness about the possible hereditary nature of cardiac conditions. SADS UK and its members across the UK raise funds to purchase 24-hour heart monitoring equipment and donate it to medical facilities throughout the UK. Awareness and heart monitoring are important since, in one-third of cases, there are no symptoms prior to a sudden adult/arrhythmic death.

President: Anne Jolly (Chair)
Year Established: 2000

Keywords
Advocacy; The Ashley Jolly SAD Trust; Brugada Syndrome; Cardiac Arrhythmia; Cardiomyopathy; Heart Rhythm Abnormalities; Long QT Syndrome; LQTS; Networking; Research; SADS UK, The Ashley Jolly SAD Trust; Support Groups; Wolff Parkinson White Syndrome; WPW

2129 SANE Australia

P.O. Box 226
South Melbourne
Victoria, 3065, Australia

Phone: +61 (0) 3-9682-5933
Fax: +61 (0) 3-9682-5944
Toll Free: 1 (800) 688-382
E-mail: helpline@sane.org
http://www.sane.org

SANE Australia is a national, voluntary organization dedicated to improving the well being of Australians affected by mental illness. Established in 1986, the organization is committed to promoting and conducting research, developing innovative resources for affected individuals and families, and campaigning for improved awareness, attitudes, and services. SANE Australia works to fulfill its mission and objectives by offering an information and referral help line for Australian callers who are concerned about mental illness; conducting research into the effects of mental illness; promoting public awareness through media campaigns, sponsorships, and other activities; and having an informational network of over 100 community organizations across Australia that are dedicated to working with people affected by mental illness. The organization also develops a wide range of print and multimedia resources that explain mental illness and related issues in understandable language, including fact sheets, booklets, educational software, videotapes, audio tapes, a magazine entitled "SANE News," and a series entitled "SANE Blueprints" that focuses on helping individuals affected by mental illness live in the community.

President: Professor John Funder, AO (Chairman)
Executive Director: Barbara Hocking
Year Established: 1986

Keywords
Bipolar Disorder; Mental Illness; SANE Australia; Schizophrenia

2130 Sarcoid Networking Association

6424 151st Avenue East
Sumner, WA 98390-2601

Phone: (253) 826-7737
Fax: (253) 826-7737
E-mail: sarcoidosis_network@prodigy.net
http://www.sarcoidosisnetwork.org

The Sarcoid Networking Association (SNA) is a national, not-for-profit, self-help organization dedicated to providing information and support to individuals and family members affected by sarcoidosis. Sarcoidosis, a rare multisystem disorder of unknown cause, is characterized by the abnormal formation of inflammatory masses or nodules (granulomas) consisting of certain granular white blood cells (modified macrophages or epithelioid cells) in certain organs of the body. The granulomas that are formed are thought to affect the normal structure of and, potentially, the normal functions of the affected organ(s), causing symptoms associated with the particular body system(s) in question. In individuals with sarcoidosis, such granuloma formation most commonly affects the lungs. However, in many cases, other organs may be affected. The range and severity of symptoms associated with sarcoidosis vary greatly, depending upon the specific organ(s) involved and the degree of such involvement. Established in 1992, the Sarcoid Networking Association promotes research, works to increase professional and public awareness of sarcoidosis, and provides networking services that enable affected individuals and family members to exchange information, support, and resources. The association also engages in-patient advocacy, has a directory, makes appropriate referrals, and offers a variety of materials including pamphlets, brochures, audiovisual aids, and a regular newsletter entitled "Sarcoidosis Networking."

President: Joe Ornowski
Executive Director: Dolores O'Leary
Year Established: 1992
Acronym: SNA

Keywords
Besnier Boeck Schaumann Disease; Boeck Sarcoid; Hutchinson Boeck Syndrome; Lupus Pernio; Lymphogranulomatosis, Benign; Sarcoid Networking Association; Sarcoidosis; Schaumann Syndrome; Uveoparotid Fever

---

2131   Sarcoidosis Center
6005 Park Avenue
Suite 501
Memphis, TN 38119

Phone: (901) 761-5877
Fax: (901) 761-2280
Toll Free: (877) 727-2643
E-mail: sarcoid@sarcoidcenter.com
http://www.sarcoidcenter.com

The Sarcoidosis Center provides a broad range of services for sarcoidosis patients. Sarcoidosis is a multisystem disorder that most often affects individuals between 20 and 40 years of age and is characterized by the abnormal formation of inflammatory masses or nodules of white blood cells in certain organs of the body. Organs or systems that may be affected include the lungs, liver, bone marrow, spleen, musculoskeletal system, heart, salivary glands, and/or nervous system. The center exists as a "virtual entity" on the Internet and as a real establishment in Memphis, Tenn. Areas to be addressed by the center include coordinating the exchange of information internationally. The center provides disability advice, innovative ed-

ucational materials, and a toll-free number for support and information. It also hosts workshops and Internet discussions. Although the major focus is on providing services for patients and their families, funding for research will be provided depending on the availability of funds.

President: Norman T. Soskel, MD,FACP,FCCP
Year Established: 1999

Keywords
Dyspnea; Granuloma; Lung Disease; Neurosarcoidosis; Pneumonia, Interstitial; Pulmonary; Pulmonary Function; Respiratory; Sarcoid; Sarcoidosis; Sarcoidosis Center

---

2132   Sarcoidosis Online Sites: A Comprehensive Source for Sarcoidosis Information on the Internet

E-mail: webmaster@sarcoidosisonlinesites.com
http://www.sarcoidosisonlinesites.com

Sarcoidosis Online Sites: A Comprehensive Source for Sarcoidosis Information on the Internet is a web site dedicated to educating individuals with sarcoidosis, family members, and friends; helping in the search for treatments and cure for sarcoidosis; providing online networking opportunities for those affected by the disorder; and increasing awareness of sarcoidosis and bringing the disorder to the forefront of the medical, research, and general communities. Sarcoidosis, a rare multisystem disorder of unknown cause, is characterized by the abnormal formation of inflammatory masses or nodules (granulomas) consisting of certain granular white blood cells (modified macrophages or epithelioid cells) in certain organs of the body. The granulomas that are formed are thought to affect the normal structure of and, potentially, the normal functions of the affected organ(s), causing symptoms associated with the particular body system(s) in question. In individuals with sarcoidosis, such granuloma formation most commonly affects the lungs. However, in many cases, other organs may be affected. The range and severity of symptoms associated with sarcoidosis vary greatly, depending upon the specific organ(s) involved and the degree of such involvement. Sarcoidosis Online Sites (S.O.S.) provides descriptions of and dynamic linkage to sarcoidosis related web pages under several categories including What is Sarcoidosis?, diagnostic testing, medication information, hospital resources, organizations, university resources, and chronic pain. The site also provides online networking opportunities through its guest book and produces and maintains the "NSRC Sarcoidosis Community Newsletter," a monthly online newsletter.

President: J. Lloyd
Year Established: 1997
Acronym: S.O.S.

Keywords
Autoimmune; Emphysema; Epithelioid; Erythematosus; Fibrosis; Glomerulonephritis; Granulomatous Diseases; Heerfordt Waldenstrom Syndrome; Hypothyroidism; Lofgren's Syndrome; Lymphoma; Porphyria; Sarcoid of Boeck; Sarcoidosis, Acute; Sarcoidosis, Chronic; Sarcoidosis; Sarcoidosis Online Sites: A Comprehensive Source for Sarcoidosis Information on the Internet; Sarcoidosis, Subacute; Schaumann's Disease; Sclerosis; Tuberculosis

2133   Sarcoidosis Research Institute
3475 Central Avenue
Memphis, TN 38111

Phone: (901) 219-6883
E-mail: paula@sarcoidosisresearch.org
http://www.sarcoidosisresearch.org/

The Sarcoidosis Research Institute is a national, not-for-profit organization established in 1991. The institute is dedicated to providing up-to-date information to individuals with sarcoidosis and conducting forums for affected individuals and their families. Sarcoidosis, a rare multisystem disorder of unknown cause, is characterized by the abnormal formation of inflammatory masses or nodules (granulomas) consisting of certain granular white blood cells (modified macrophages or epithelioid cells) in certain organs of the body. The granulomas that are formed are thought to affect the normal structure of and, potentially, the normal functions of the affected organ(s), causing symptoms associated with the particular body system(s) in question. In individuals with sarcoidosis, such granuloma formation most commonly affects the lungs. However, in many cases, other organs may be affected. The range and severity of symptoms associated with sarcoidosis vary greatly, depending upon the specific organ(s) involved and the degree of such involvement. The Sarcoidosis Research Institute is also dedicated to increasing public awareness of sarcoidosis and channeling appropriate information to the medical community. Educational materials produced by the Sarcoidosis Research Institute include a brochure entitled "Answers to Your Questions about Sarcoidosis" and a video called "Sarcoidosis: An Overview."

President: Paula Yette Polite (1994-Present)
Year Established: 1991
Acronym: SRI

Keywords
Heerfordt Waldenstrom Syndrome; Lofgren's Syndrome; Sarcoid of Boeck; Sarcoidosis; Sarcoidosis Research Institute; Sarcoidosis, Acute; Sarcoidosis, Chronic; Sarcoidosis, Subacute; Schaumann's Disease

2134   Sarcoma Alliance
775 E. Blithedale
#334
Mill Valley, CA 94941

Phone: (415) 381-7236
Fax: (415) 381-7235
E-mail: info@sarcomaalliance.org
http://www.sarcomaalliance.org

The Sarcoma Alliance was founded by sarcoma survivors to help guide, educate and support people with sarcomas. It also provides information and support to the families, friends, and caregivers of people with sarcomas. These rare, cancerous tumors originate in the body's connective tissues, which include fat, muscle, blood vessels, deep skin tissues, nerves, bones, and cartilage. Because sarcomas are rare, with only approximately 10,000 patients each year in the United States, and because there are many different types of sarcomas, it is difficult for patients to find understandable information about them. The Sarcoma Alliance provides such information, serving patients and health professionals in the U.S., Canada, and throughout the world.

President: Philip Leider
Executive Director: Arthur Beckert
Year Established: 1999

Keywords
Sarcoma; Sarcoma Alliance

2135   Sarcoma Foundation of America
P.O. Box 458
9884 Main Street
Damascus, MD 20872

Phone: (301) 253-8690
Fax: (301) 253-8690
E-mail: info@curesarcoma.org
http://www.curesarcoma.org

The mission of the Sarcoma Foundation of America is to act as an advocate for sarcoma medical research. Sarcoma is a cancer of the connective tissue (nerves, muscle, bone, and tendons) that is diagnosed in approximately 9,000 Americans each year. In the adult population, sarcoma represents one percent of all new cancers diagnosed. Established in 2000, the foundation provides services that include patient networking, advocacy and support for research, patient education, and promotion of general awareness of sarcoma among the public.

President: Mark Thornton, M.D.
Executive Director: Jody L. Cummings, MPH
Year Established: 2000
Acronym: SFA

Keywords
Sarcoma; Sarcoma Advocacy; Sarcoma Foundation of America; Sarcoma Research

2136 Save Babies Through Screening Foundation
4 Manor View Circle
Malvern, PA 19355

Phone: (610) 251-9876
Fax: (610) 647-5757
Toll Free: (888) 454-3383
E-mail: E-mail@savebabies.org
http://www.savebabies.org

The mission of Save Babies Through Screening Foundation is to prevent mental retardation, health complications and death that may be caused by disorders detectable through existing routine newborn screening programs.

President: Robin Haygood (2002-present)
Year Established: 1999
Acronym: SBTS

Keywords
Save Babies Through Screening Foundation; Service Organization

2137 Schepens Eye Research Institute
20 Staniford Street
Boston, MA 02114-2500

Phone: (617) 912-0100
Fax: (617) 912-0101
E-mail: geninfo@vision.eri.harvard.edu
http://www.theschepens.org/

The Schepens Eye Research Institute, a not-for-profit organization, is a prominent center for research on the eye, vision, and blinding diseases. Established in 1950 and an affiliate of the Department of Ophthalmology at Harvard Medical School, the Schepens Eye Research Institute is dedicated to research that improves the understanding, management, and prevention of eye diseases and visual deficiencies; fosters collaboration among its faculty members; trains young scientists and clinicians from around the world; promotes communication with scientists in allied fields; and is a leader in the worldwide dispersion of basic scientific knowledge of vision. The Schepens Eye Research Institute's research program focuses on eye studies and the search for causes of disease in several core areas, including retinal and macular diseases (macular degeneration and diabetic retinopathy), corneal and ocular surface diseases (dry eye syndrome and corneal infection and injury), anterior segment diseases (glaucoma), ocular immunology (ocular cancer, inflammation, viral infections), transplantation (retinal and corneal transplants), and low vision aids and diagnostic technologies. The Schepens Eye Research Institute provides a variety of materials including brochures, reports and a magazine.

President: Michael S. Gilmore, PhD
Executive Director: Same as above.
Year Established: 1950

Keywords
Anterior Segment Diseases; Cancer, Ocular; Chalazion; Chandler's Syndrome; Corneal Diseases; Corneal Infection; Corneal Injury; Dry Eye Syndrome; Duane Syndrome; Eales Disease; Eye Research; Glaucoma; Harvard Medical School; Macular Degeneration; Macular Diseases; Ocular Surface Diseases; Retinal Disorders; Retinal Transplantation; Retinopathy of Prematurity; Retinopathy, Arteriosclerotic; Retinopathy, Diabetic; Retinopathy, Hypertensive; Transplantation, Corneal

2138 Schiz Kidz Buddies Online Support Group for Schizencephaly
Web Site on the Internet

E-mail: rwjw@gte.net
http://www.geocities.com/Heartland/Meadows/7384/

Schiz Kidz Buddies Online Support Group for Schizencephaly is a web site for parents, other family members, physicians, therapists, and friends of children born with schizencephaly. Schizencephaly is a rare brain malformation due to improper development of the cerebral hemispheres of the brain during embryonic growth (neuronal dysmigration). Affected infants and children may have variable symptoms that may include seizure disorders, developmental delays, mental retardation, visual impairment, eating difficulties, and/or other symptoms. The Schizencephaly Online Support Group's web site provides general information on the condition, a variety of online networking opportunities, and dynamic links to additional sources of helpful information on the Internet.

President: Judi Wright and Lynn Niedzwiecki (Co-founders)
Year Established: 1997

Keywords
Kidz Buddies Online Support Group for Schizencephaly; Schiz Kidz Buddies Online Support Group for Schizencephaly; Schiz Kidz Buddies Online Support Group for Schizencephaly (Web Site on the Internet); Schizencephaly

2139   Schizophrenia Society of Canada

50 Acadia Avenue
Suite 205
Markham, Ontario, L3R 0B3, Canada

Phone: (905) 415-2007
Fax: (905) 415-2337
Toll Free: (888) 772-4673
E-mail: info@schizophrenia.ca
http://www.schizophrenia.ca

Founded in 1979, the Schizophrenia Society of Canada (SSC) is a national registered charity whose mission is to alleviate the suffering caused by schizophrenia and related mental disorders. SSC works with 10 provincial societies and their more than 100 chapters and branches to help affected individuals and their families have a better quality of life, while also searching for a cure. SSC is committed to: raising awareness and educating the public to help reduce stigma and discrimination; supporting families and individuals with formation and educational materials; advocating for legislative change and improved treatment and services; and supporting research through the SSC Foundation and other independent efforts.

President: John Gray
Year Established: 1979
Acronym: SSC

Keywords
Schizophrenia Society of Canada

2140   Scleroderma Foundation

12 Kent Way
Suite 101
Byfield, MA 01922

Phone: (978) 463-5843
Fax: (978) 463-5809
Toll Free: (800) 722-4673
E-mail: sfinfo@scleroderma.org
http://www.scleroderma.org

The Scleroderma Foundation (SF) is a non-profit, 501(c)3 organization dedicated to serving those affected by scleroderma. Its mission is three-fold: to help patients and their families cope with scleroderma by offering support groups, physician referrals, and educational information; to promote public awareness and education through patient and health professional seminars, informational brochures and publicity campaigns; to stimulate and support research to improve treatment options for patients and to ultimately find the cause of and cure for scleroderma and related disorders. Scleroderma is a rare connective tissue disorder characterized by abnormal thickening of the skin.

Year Established: 1998
Acronym: SF

Keywords
Alveolitis; ANA; CREST Syndrome; Diffuse; Inflammation; Limited; Mixed Connective Tissue Disease; Morphea; MCTD; Pruritus; Pulmonary Arterial Hypertension; Pulmonary Fibrosis; Pulmonary Hypertension; Raynaud's; Scleroderma; Scleroderma Foundation; Scleroderma, Linear; Sclerosis, Systemic

2141   Scleroderma Research Foundation

220 Montgomery Street
Suite 1411
San Francisco, CA 94104

Phone: (415) 834-9444
Fax: (415) 834-9177
Toll Free: (800) 441-2873
E-mail: info@sclerodermaRESEARCH.org
http://www.srfcure.org

The Scleroderma Research Foundation is a voluntary, research, non-profit organization dedicated to finding a cure for scleroderma by funding and facilitating ongoing medical research. The foundation also seeks to increase public awareness and understanding of this disorder. Established in 1987, the Scleroderma Research Foundation created a team of scientific and biomedical advisors to identify and address key issues that may lead to a cure. The efforts of the foundation and its advisory team have led to the opening of the Bay Area Scleroderma Research Center in San Francisco and the East Coast Scleroderma Research Center in Baltimore, both cross-institutional, multi-disciplinary research facilities. With participation of the National Institutes of Health (NIH) and several institutes and universities, the foundation has also assisted in the creation of clinical laboratory tests that provide for the early diagnosis of several forms of scleroderma. The provides a variety of educational materials to affected individuals, family members, healthcare and research professionals, and the general public.

President: Deann Wright
Year Established: 1987
Acronym: SRF

Keywords
CREST Syndrome; Morphea; Raynaud's Disease and Phenomenon; Scleroderma; Scleroderma Research Foundation; Scleroderma, Linear; Sclerosis, Systemic

2142 Scoliosis Association, Inc.
P.O. Box 811705
Boca Raton, FL 33481-1705

Phone: (561) 994-4435
Fax: (561) 994-2455
Toll Free: (800) 800-0669
E-mail: scolioassn.aol.com
http://www.scoliosis-assoc.org

The Scoliosis Association, Inc., is a nonprofit information and support network that was founded by scoliosis patients in 1974. Scoliosis is a sideways curvature of the spine that may appear in more than one member of a family in the same or different generations. It usually appears during adolescence, although it may appear in younger children as well. The Scoliosis Association's mission includes sponsoring support groups; education of the general public and medical professionals regarding scoliosis and related spinal problems; fostering school screening to assist in early detection; and raising funds through research. The association sponsors chapters throughout the nation that provide information and act as support groups. Affected individuals and their family members attend chapter meetings to share and discuss common problems and assist each other with the physical, emotional, and social aspects of scoliosis and related spinal deformities. Often professional speakers will attend these meetings and respond to questions. The association sponsors spine conferences, which help to update and inform patients, their families, and medical professionals about the current status of the management

and treatment of scoliosis. Videos, books, special articles, bibliographies, fact sheets, scoliometers, and posters are all available through the association.

President: Stanley Sacks (1988 - 2000) Chair and CEO
Year Established: 1974

Keywords
Kyphosis; Lordosis; Scoliosis; Scoliosis Association, Inc.

2143 Scottish Motor Neurone Disease Association
76 Firhill Rd
Glasgow, G20 7BA, Scotland

Phone: +44 (0) 141-945-1077
Fax: +44 (0) 141-945-2578
E-mail: info@scotmnd.co.uk
http://www.scotmnd.org.uk

The Scottish Motor Neurone Disease Association offers care and support to anyone living anywhere in Scotland who is diagnosed with motor neurone disease, also known as amyotrophic lateral sclerosis (ALS) or Lou Gehrig's disease. This is a serious and progressively disabling muscle-wasting condition for which there is currently no cure. The Scottish MND Association provides information on the disorder and promotes and funds research. It was established in 1981.

Executive Director: Craig Stockton
Year Established: 1981

Keywords
ALS; Amyotrophic Lateral Sclerosis; Lou Gehrig's Disease; Motor Neuron Disease; Palliative Care; Scottish Motor Neurone Disease Association

2144 Scottish Society for Autism
Hilton House
Alloa Business Park
Whins Road
Alloa, FK10 3SA, Scotland

Phone: +44 (0) 1259-72-0044
Fax: +44 (0) 1259-72-0051
E-mail: ssac@autism-in-scotland.org.uk
http://www.autism-in-scotland.org.uk

The Scottish Society for Autism is a not-for-profit, voluntary organization dedicated to providing the best possible care, support, and education for people of all ages with autism throughout Scotland. The society also works to raise the awareness of autism among the general public and professionals working in this field. Autism is a genetic disorder characterized by difficulties in relating to, or understanding, other people and social situations; difficulties in acquiring any form of communication; and a lack of imaginative ability, often substituted by obsessive, repetitive behavior and a strong resistance to change. Established in 1976, the society has programs that provide residential and day services for people with autism from all over Scotland.

President: Donald Liddel
Executive Director: Isobel Sutherland
Year Established: 1976

Keywords
Asperger Syndrome; Autism; Pervasive Developmental Disorder; Scottish Society for Autism

---

2145   **Second Wind Lung Transplant Association, Inc.**
P.O. Box 1915
Largo, FL 33779

Phone: (727) 397-3497
Fax: (727) 397-3609
Toll Free: (888) 855-9463
E-mail: heering@2ndwind.org
http://www.2ndwind.org

Second Wind Lung Transplant Association, Inc., is a not-for-profit organization dedicated to improving the quality of life for lung transplant recipients, lung surgery candidates, people with related pulmonary concerns, and their families. The association provides support, advocacy, education, information, and guidance through a spirit of service, "adding years to their lives and life to their years." Established in 1995 by a group of lung transplant recipients, candidates, and their families, Second Wind has quarterly support group meetings to provide educational programs (e.g., on nutrition, effects of medications and exercise, physical therapy) for both lung transplant candidates and recipients; to share experiences; and to enjoy social activities. In addition, the organization provides educational programs; seeks to increase organ donor awareness; and provides a quarterly newsletter entitled "AirWays" to its members.

President: Tom Archer
Year Established: 1995

Keywords
Alpha-1 Antitrypsin Deficiency; Asthma; Bronchiectasis; Bronchiolitis Obliterans; CF; Cystic Fibrosis; Emphysema; Fibrosis, Idiopathic Pulmonary; LAM; Lung Diseases; Lymphangioleiomyomatosis; Pulmonary Hypertension, Primary; Sarcoidosis; Second Wind Lung Transplant Association, Inc.

2146   **Selective Mutism Foundation, Inc.**
P.O. Box 13133
Sissonville, WV 25360

E-mail: consultsn@aol.com
http://www.selectivemutismfoundation.org

Selective Mutism Foundation, Inc., is a national, non-profit, voluntary health organization dedicated to developing and disseminating educational materials on selective mutism (SM) to affected individuals, families, professionals, and the general public; increasing the knowledge and sensitivity of professionals who treat individuals experiencing selective mutism; finding the cause and cure for this condition; improving treatments and medications for selective mutism; and developing and implementing interventions in public schools. In addition, the foundation promotes ongoing research and develops educational testing materials. Selective mutism (SM), formerly known as elective mutism, is a psychiatric disorder most commonly found in children. It is characterized by a persistent failure (for more than one month) to speak in select settings. Affected children understand spoken language and have the ability to speak. In most cases, affected children speak to their parents and a few selected others. In some cases, they do not speak to certain individuals in their household. The exact cause of this disorder is not known.

President: Sue Newman (Co-Founder/Drctr) (1991 to Present)
Executive Director: Carolyn Miller (Co-Founder/Drctr) (1991-Present)
Year Established: 1991
Acronym: SMF, Inc.

Keywords
Adult Anxiety; Anxiety Disorder; Childhood Anxiety; Mutism, Elective (Selective); Mutism, Selective; Selective Mutism Foundation, Inc.; Shyness; Social Anxiety; Social Phobia

2147 Selective Mutism Group Web Site

1130 Herkness Drive
Meadowbrook, PA 19046

Phone: (215) 887-5748
E-mail: sminfo@selectivemutism.org
http://www.selectivemutism.org

The Selective Mutism Group Web Site (SMG~CAN) is a resource, providing thousands of pages of information to read and print out to educate others. Membership in our SMG~CAN community also offers lots of opportunities for support and interaction with experts and experienced parents and teachers. The SMG~CAN is a nonprofit organization dedicated to furthering research and offering information and support to affected individuals.

Year Established: 1999
Acronym: CAN, SMG-CAN

Keywords
Anxiety Disorder; Mutism, Elective (Obsolete); Childhood Anxiety Disorder; Mutism, Selective; Selective Mutism; Selective Mutism Group Childhood Anxiety Network; Selective Mutism Group Web Site; Social Anxiety; Social Phobia

2148 Self Help for Hard of Hearing People

7910 Woodmont Avenue
Suite 1200
Bethesda, MD 20814

Phone: (301) 657-2248
Fax: (301) 913-9413
TDD: (301) 657-2249
E-mail: info@hearingloss.org
http://www.hearingloss.org

Self-Help for Hard of Hearing People (SHHH), is an international, non-profit, self-help organization dedicated to the well-being of people of all ages and communication skills who do not hear well. The aims of SHHH are to educate affected individuals, their families, hearing healthcare providers, educators, industry, and government about hearing loss and those options available to help deal with hearing loss. Established in 1979 and consisting of 240 chapters, SHHH provides information on several aspects of hearing loss, from technological and medical advances to coping and parenting strategies. The organization also advocates for improved communication access for people with hearing loss in the workplace, hotels, schools, court systems, medical, and entertainment fa-

cilities. SHHH also encourages and supports research to improve hearing aids, assistive listening devices, and other technology needs of people with hearing loss, as well as research into understanding the causes of hearing loss and for development of new treatments. Self-Help for Hard of Hearing People provides support in setting up local support groups and publishes "Hearing Loss," a bi-monthly magazine.

President: Richard Meyer
Executive Director: Terry Portis
Year Established: 1979
Acronym: SHHH

Keywords
Hearing Impairment; Hearing Loss; Self Help for Hard of Hearing People; SHHH

2149 Severe Chronic Neutropenia International Registry

Plaza 600 Building
600 Stewart Street
Suite 1503
Seattle, WA 98101

Phone: (206) 543-9749
Fax: (206) 543-3668
Toll Free: (800) 726-4463
E-mail: Registry@u.washington.edu
http://www.depts.washington.edu/registry/

Established in March of 1994, the Severe Chronic Neutropenia International Registry is a research organization supported by the NIH and directed by an advisory board of physicians who treat individuals with severe chronic neutropenia (SCN). Chronic neutropenia is a blood disorder in which the bone marrow produces a decreased number of certain white blood cells known as neutrophils. Abnormally low levels of neutrophils can cause affected individuals to become more susceptible to certain bacterial infections. The mission of the registry is to establish a worldwide database of treatment and disease related outcomes for individuals diagnosed with SCN. It is hoped that the information collected will lead to improved medical care and a focus for future medical research. The registry is international, serving patients and healthcare practitioners located in the United States, Canada, Europe, Australia, South America, Asia, and the Middle East.

President: Dale C. Dale, M.D. (Co-Director)
Executive Director: Professor Karl Welte (Co-Director)
Year Established: 1994
Acronym: SCN International Registy

Keywords
Neutropenia; Neutropenia, Chronic; Neutropenia, Congenital; Neutropenia, Cyclic; Neutropenia, Idiopathic; Neutropenia, SCN International Registy; Severe Chronic; Severe Chronic Neutropenia International Registry

2150 Severe Chronic Neutropenia International Registry Australia

2nd Floor Marian House
St. John of God Hospital
1002 Mair Street
Ballarat, 3350, Australia

Phone: +61 (0) 3-5333-4811
Fax: +61 (0) 3-5333-4813
E-mail: scnirau@ballarat.edu.au
http://www.freyja.ballarat.edu.au:8080/~scnirau/

The Severe Chronic Neutropenia International Registry Australia (SCNIRAU) is the Australian division of the Severe Chronic Neutropenia International Registry. The Australian division, which registered its first patient in 1994, currently has over 30 patients registered, while over 400 patients are registered internationally. Chronic neutropenia is a blood disorder characterized by abnormally low levels of certain white blood cells known as neutrophils that are produced by the bone marrow and play an essential role in fighting infection. Individuals with chronic neutropenia may be abnormally susceptible to certain bacterial infections and may experience other associated symptoms and/or findings. The International Registry is committed to documenting the clinical course of severe chronic neutropenia (SCN); monitoring and assessing long-term safety of primary treatments in individuals with SCN in the United States, Canada, Europe, and Australia; and studying the incidence and outcome of certain previously identified adverse events including osteoporosis, splenomegaly, cytogenetic abnormalities, myeloplastic syndrome, and leukemia.

President: George Kannourakis, MD
Executive Director: Unknown.
Year Established: 1994
Acronym: SCNIRAU

Keywords
Neutropenia, Chronic; Neutropenia, Congenital; Neutropenia, Cyclic; Neutropenia, Idiopathic; Neutropenia, Severe Chronic; Severe Chronic Neutropenia International Registry Australia

2151 Sexuality Information and Education Council of the U.S.

130 West 42nd Street
Suite 350
New York, NY 10036-7802

Phone: (212) 819-9770
Fax: (212) 819-9776
E-mail: siecus@siecus.org
http://www.siecus.org

The Sexuality Information and Education Council of the U.S. (SIECUS) is a nonprofit organization dedicated to developing, collecting, and disseminating information; promoting comprehensive education about sexuality; and advocating for the rights of individuals to make responsible sexual choices. Established in 1964, SIECUS has many different programs developed by health, education, and sexuality experts. Educational materials include a booklet entitled "How to Talk to Your Children About AIDS," a pamphlet entitled "SIECUS Publications Catalog," and a bi-monthly journal entitled the "SIECUS Report." The organization provides appropriate referrals, encourages lobbying efforts, and supports education. SIECUS maintains the Mary S. Calderone Library, with more than 5,000 books, 2,000 journals and newsletters, and 500 sexuality and AIDS curricula. The library also has a computerized database with more than 10,000 citations.

President: Joseph DiNorcia
Year Established: 1964
Acronym: SIECUS

Keywords
AIDS (Acquired Immunodeficiency Syndrome); Acquired Immune Deficiency Syndrome; Bowenoid Papulosis; Condyloma; Fitz Hugh Curtis Syndrome; Proctitis; Reiter's Syndrome; Sexual Dysfunction; Sexuality Information and Education Council of the U.S.; SIECUS—Sexuality Information and Education Council of the U.S.; Syphilis, Acquired

2152 Shaken Baby Alliance

4516 Boat Club Road
#114
Fort Worth, TX 76135

Phone: (817) 882-8686
Fax: (817) 882-8687
Toll Free: (877) 636-3727
E-mail: info@shakenbaby.com
http://www.ShakenBaby.com

The Shaken Baby Alliance is a voluntary, not-for-profit, service and advocacy organization serving victim family members and professionals concerned about shaken baby syndrome (SBS). This syndrome occurs when a child is shaken back and forth in a "whiplash" motion so that delicate veins over the brain tear and bleed, causing pressure on the brain. The damaged brain begins to swell, and vital functions, such as heart rate and breathing, are affected. Many people do not realize the harm that can result from shaking an infant or young child. The goal of the alliance is to provide information and support to affected families, serve as advocates for victims, and provide educational services as a preventive measure. The alliance is international in scope, and provides brochures in English and Spanish.

President: Bonnie Armstrong
Year Established: 1997
Acronym: SBA

Keywords
Shaken Baby Alliance; Shaken Baby Syndrome

2153 Share and Care Cockayne Syndrome Network, Inc.

P.O. Box 570618
Dallas, TX 75357

Phone: (214) 660-8353
Fax: (214) 660-8353
E-mail: J93082@aol.com
http://www.cockayne-syndrome.org

The Share and Care Cockayne Syndrome Network, Inc., is a support group providing information to families and professionals with an interest in Cockayne syndrome (CS). Cockayne syndrome is a rare form of dwarfism. It is genetic in that a recessive gene from each parent is necessary for a child to have CS. Other characteristics along with dwarfism include sun sensitivity, microcephaly, neurodevelopmental delay, mental deficiency (progressive), and loss of subcutaneous fat, premature aging, and shortened lifespan. A quarterly newsletter provides a forum for the exchange on information and a pamphlet is available in English, Spanish, Japanese, and German. The sharing of information helps people make informed decisions regarding the care of children with this rare disorder.

President: Shirley Rodriquez (Coordinator)
Executive Director: Thaddeus E. Kelly, M.D., Ph.D.
Year Established: 1993

Keywords
Classical CS; Cockayne Syndrome; CS Type I; German; Japanese; Neill Dingwall Syndrome; Share and Care Cockayne Syndrome Network; Share and Care Cockayne Syndrome Network, Inc.; Xeroderma Pigmentosum

2154 Shwachman-Diamond Syndrome Foundation

710 Brassie Drive
Grand Junction, CO 81506

Fax: (970) 255-8293
Toll Free: (877) 737-4685
E-mail: 4sskids@shwachman-diamond.org
http://www.shwachman-diamond.org

The Shwachman-Diamond Syndrome Foundation is a non-profit, voluntary support organization that functions as an international support system for people with Shwachman-Diamond syndrome and their families. Shwachman-Diamond syndrome is an extremely rare inherited disorder with multiple and varied manifestations. In most cases, the disorder may be characterized by signs of insufficient absorption (malabsorption) of fats and other nutrients due to abnormal development of the pancreas (pancreatic insufficiency); and improper functioning of the bone marrow (bone marrow dysfunction), resulting in low levels of circulating blood cells (hematologic abnormalities such as neutropenia, anemia, thrombocytopenia, hypocellularity), abnormal bone development affecting the rib cage and/or bones in the arms and/or legs (metaphyseal dysostosis); short stature. The organization maintains a central registry and medical profiles of individuals with this disorder. The registry also contains the names of medical professionals who have experience in treating people with Shwachman-Diamond syndrome or who have expressed a desire to treat people with this disorder. Established in 1994, the support group publishes a periodic newsletter and seeks to increase awareness of this disorder among the medical community and the public. Other goals of Shwachman-Diamond Syndrome International are to stimulate interest in ongoing medical research, improve treatments, and develop informational brochures and pamphlets.

President: Debbie Kadel
Executive Director: Blair Van Brunt
Year Established: 1994
Acronym: SDSF

Keywords
Anemia; Hypocellularity; Lipomatosis of Pancreas, Congenital; Malabsorption; Neutropenia; Pancreatic

Insufficiency and Bone Marrow Dysfunction; Pancytopenia; Shwachman Bodian Syndrome; Shwachman Diamond Syndrome; Shwachman Syndrome; Shwachman Syndrome Support; Shwachman-Diamond Syndrome Foundation; Thrombocytopenia

2155 Shy-Drager Syndrome/Multiple System Atrophy Support Group
P.O. Box 279
Coupland, TX 78615

Toll Free: (866) 737-4999
E-mail: don.summers@shy-drager.org
http://www.shy-drager.org/

The mission of the Shy-Drager Syndrome/Multiple System Atrophy (SDS/MSA) Support Group is to gather information from each group of people involved (patients, caregivers, family members, and physicians) and disseminate that information to all. The SDS/MSA Support Group is an information center and a "helping hand" for affected people. Through various programs, including regional patient/caregiver support group meetings, support of local groups, a toll free help line and a Web site, the SDS/MSA Support Group can reach many more people in need. The support group also works closely with physicians who are newly involved with the disease as well as those who are involved in the essential research to discover a cause, modes of treatment, and, hopefully, a cure. Information about the disease is provided on the group's Web site and through educational meetings. By sharing information, resources, and support, the SDS/MSA Support Group hopes to create a "circle of hope" for those affected by SDS/MSA. On the West Coast, those seeking MSA support may call Vera James, a member of the group, at 1-866-737-5999.

President: Don Summers

Keywords
Multiple System Atrophy; SDS/MSA; Shy-Drager Syndrome/Multiple System Atrophy Support Group; Shy Drager Syndrome/Multiple System Atrophy Support Group (SDS/MSA); Shy-Drager Syndrome; Support Groups

2156 Sickle Cell Disease Association of America, Inc.
16 S. Calvert Street
Suite 600
Baltimore, MD 21202

Phone: (410) 528-1555
Fax: (410) 528-1495

Toll Free: (800) 421-8453
E-mail: scdaa@sicklecelldisease.org
http://www.sicklecelldisease.org

The Sickle Cell Disease Association of America (SCDAA) is a voluntary service organization dedicated to educating the public and providing support to people affected by sickle cell disease. The association was founded in 1971 as the umbrella organization for community-based groups providing support and services to persons affected by sickle cell conditions. The association seeks to educate the public about sickle cell disease and the sickle cell trait and develop educational materials on these conditions for extensive circulation. It also educates legislators on issues regarding sickle cell disease and other genetic disorders and fosters ongoing medical research to improve the well being of those affected by sickle cell disease. In addition, the association supports research, advocates on behalf of all individuals affected by sickle cell diseases, and provides appropriate referrals to medical professionals. The association is the only national community-based voluntary health agency working full-time to resolve issues surrounding sickle cell conditions. The Sickle Cell Disease Association provides an extensive supply of resources. These include guidebooks, brochures, pamphlets, audio and visual tapes, fact sheets, and a periodic newsletter entitled "Sickle Cell News."

President: Dorothy C. Moore, MD (Chief Medical Officer)
Executive Director: Lynda K. Anderson (President/Chief Op. Officer)
Year Established: 1971
Acronym: SCDAA

Keywords
Anemia, Sickle Cell; Sickle Cell Disease; Sickle Cell Disease Association of America, Inc.; Sickle Cell Trait; Thalassemia Major; Thalassemia Minor

2157 SIDS and Kids, National SIDS Council of Australia Ltd
98 Morang Road
Suite 3
Hawthorn
Victoria, 3122, Australia

Phone: +61 (0) 3-9819-4595
Fax: +61 (0) 3-9818-4596
E-mail: national@sidsandkids.org
http://www.sidsandkids.org

SIDS and Kids is a national, not-for-profit organization dedicated to providing services to parents and other family members of infants who have died suddenly and unexpectedly from 20 weeks gestation to two years of age, regardless of cause. The organization was initially founded to support infant deaths from sudden infant death syndrome (SIDS). SIDS is the sudden, unexpected death of an apparently healthy infant that is not explained by previous patient history or by thorough postmortem studies. SIDS and Kids, which has a national office and nine state/territory SIDS branches, provides a 24-hour crisis outreach service to the immediate and extended families of children who have died suddenly and unexpectedly. In addition, SIDS and Kids offers ongoing support to family members, provides current information about SIDS to the public, and works to promote a greater awareness of SIDS and other infant mortality issues and their social impact. SIDS and Kids is also committed to stimulating and funding research that may help to isolate the causes of SIDS, predict at-risk populations, and develop preventive programs; providing a central bank of information to help researchers and health professionals; and disseminating information concerning SIDS research. SIDS and Kids' has a range of educational resources and a major health promotion campaign entitled "Safe Sleeping." The council also has a web site that discusses the organization's mission, goals, and services; provides information on its state/territory offices; and offers fact sheets on SIDS.

President: Ian Gittus
Executive Director: Marne Fechner, BDM
Year Established: 1986
Acronym: SIDS and KIDS

Keywords
SIDS and Kids, National SIDS Council of Australia Ltd

2158 SIDS Educational Services, Inc.
P.O. Box 2426
Cheverly, MD 20784

Phone: (301) 322-2620
Fax: (301) 322-9822
E-mail: SIDSES@aol.com
http://www.sidssurvivalguide.org

SIDS Educational Services, Inc. (SIDS-ES) is a voluntary, self-help organization that assists those who have lost children to sudden infant death syndrome (SIDS) to deal with their grief. Sudden infant death syndrome (SIDS) is the sudden death of any infant or young child that is unexpected by history and in which no adequate cause for death can be found. The orga-

nization publishes a book entitled "The SIDS Survival Guide" that is written by parents who have been affected by SIDS and experts for bereaved families and professionals. Also available is a brochure "Empathetic Support to Newly-Bereaved Families and Those Who Care About Them." SIDS-ES provides free peer contact assistance to newly bereaved families and has a book sponsorship program whereby companies, individuals, and groups donate books to newly bereaved families (often via SIDS support groups) as well as to public libraries, hospitals, doctors, police officials, and emergency responders.

President: Kee Schuth Marshall (1995 to Present)
Executive Director: Joani Nelson Horchler
Year Established: 1994
Acronym: SIDS-ES

Keywords
Crib Death; SIDS; SIDS Educational Services, Inc.; Sudden Infant Death Syndrome

---

2159 Simon Foundation for Continence
P.O. Box 815
Wilmette, IL 60091

Phone: (847) 864-3913
Fax: (847) 864-9758
Toll Free: (800) 237-4666
http://www.simonfoundation.org

The Simon Foundation for Continence is a not-for-profit, voluntary organization dedicated to removing the social stigma of this condition and to educating both medical professionals and affected individuals about cure, treatment, and management techniques. Incontinence is a condition in which one loses bladder control. Established in 1982, the foundation has worked to raise public awareness and educate people that incontinence can be cured or managed satisfactorily. Much of its work goes on behind the scenes by foundation staff, attending different programs to educate physicians and nurses about the need of people affected by incontinence. The foundation meets with manufacturers to help develop better incontinence products at lower prices for consumers. Educational materials include a quarterly newsletter entitled "The Informer" and a book entitled "Managing Incontinence: A Guide to Living With the Loss of Bladder Control." The foundation coordinates regular support group meetings, encourages constant patient advocacy, and supports patient, professional, and general education programs.

President: Cheryle B. Gartley
Executive Director: Same as above.
Year Established: 1982

Keywords
Continence; Incontinence; Leaking; OAB; Overactive
Bladder; Simon; Stress Urinary Incontinence; SUI;
Urine

**2160 Sjældne Diagnoser / Rare Disorders
Denmark**
Frederiksholms Kanal 2, 3rd Floor
Copenhagen K, 1220, Denmark

Phone: +45 3314-0010
Fax: +45 3314-5509
E-mail: mail@sjaeldnediagnoser
http://www.raredisorders.dk

The Sjældne Diagnoser / Rare Disorders Denmark is
an umbrella organization embracing 32 small organizations whose aim is to organize people with serious
rare diseases. Some of these organizations have hundreds of members. Others have only a few. Founded
in 1985, KMS advocates on behalf of people with rare
disorders, working to make sure they have access to
relevant care, resources and information.

President: Mr. Torben Groennebaek (1994-present)
Executive Director: Mrs. Dorthe Lysgaard
Year Established: 1985
Acronym: KMS

Keywords
Rare Disorders; Sjældne Diagnoser/Rare Disorders
Denmark

**2161 Sjogren's Syndrome Association, Inc. /
Association du Syndrome de Sjogren Inc.**
1650 de Maisonneuve West
Suite 401
Montreal
Quebec, H3H 2P3, Canada

Phone: (514) 934-3666
Fax: (514) 934-1241

Sjögren's Syndrome Association, Inc., (Association du
Syndrome de Sjögren, Inc.) is a voluntary, not-for-profit
health organization in Montreal, Canada, dedicated to
providing support and education to individuals affected
by Sjögren's syndrome, an immunologic disorder characterized by deficient moisture production of the tear
duct (lacrimal), salivary, and/or other glands. Associated

symptoms typically include abnormal dryness of the
eyes (keratoconjunctivitis sicca), the mouth (xerostomia), and other affected glands. The disorder most commonly affects females over the age of 40 and often occurs in association with certain autoimmune, connective
tissue disorders (e.g., rheumatoid arthritis, systemic lupus erythematosus, or scleroderma). The Sjögren's Syndrome Association was formed in 1994 to provide affected individuals and family members with practical
information and coping strategies for living with Sjögren's syndrome. The organization currently has approximately 160 members and a chapter in Ontario,
Canada. It gathers and disseminates medical information relating to Sjögren's syndrome, promotes research,
and represents the interests all individuals with the disease. In addition, the Sjögren's Syndrome Association
conducts regular group meetings and physician conferences, promotes public awareness of the disorder, and
offers a variety of educational materials including
brochures and a regular newsletter that contains medical
news, information on current research, and helpful tips
for daily living.

President: Gaetan Raymond (1998 to Present)
Executive Director: Ginette Texier
Year Established: 1994

Keywords
Sjogren's Syndrome Association, Inc. / Association du
Syndrome de Sjogren Inc.

2162 Sjogren's Syndrome Foundation, Inc.
8120 Woodmont Avenue
Suite 530
Bethesda, MD 20814

Phone: (301) 718-0300
Fax: (301) 718-0322
Toll Free: (800) 475-6473
http://www.sjogrens.org

The Sjögren's Syndrome Foundation is an international, not-for-profit organization founded in 1983 to
serve the needs of people affected by Sjögren's syndrome. Sjögren's syndrome, a disorder of unknown
cause, is characterized by deficient moisture production of the mucous-secreting glands, particularly the
tear ducts of the eyes (lacrimal) and the salivary glands
of the mouth. Primarily affecting middle-aged women,
it is thought to be due to an abnormal autoimmune response. The mission of the foundation is to support
and educate individuals affected by Sjögren's syndrome and their families; educate healthcare professionals and the general public about the disorder; and

stimulate interest in research toward improved treatments and an eventual cure. In addition, the Sjögren's Syndrome Foundation provides referrals to physicians, local chapters, and to support groups. The foundation offers postgraduate and student fellowships, and conducts comprehensive symposia on Sjögren's syndrome. Regional chapters and support groups conduct smaller regional and local gatherings. The Sjögren's Syndrome Foundation produces an extensive array of educational and support materials.

President: Ann Race
Executive Director: Phillip C. Fox, Katherine M. Hammitt
Year Established: 1983
Acronym: SSF

Keywords
Keratoconjunctivitis Sicca; Keratoconjunctivitis Sicca Xerostomia; Sicca Syndrome; Sjogren Syndrome; Sjogren's Syndrome Foundation, Inc.

2163 Skin Cancer Foundation

245 Fifth Avenue
Suite 1403
New York, NY 10016

Fax: (212) 725-5751
Toll Free: (800) 754-6490
E-mail: info@skincancer.org
http://www.skincancer.org

The Skin Cancer Foundation is a not-for-profit, international, educational, health organization dedicated to providing information on detection and prevention of skin cancer and support to those affected. The foundation seeks to educate the public about the different forms of skin cancer, and promotes and supports ongoing medical research into causes and treatment. The foundation provides support for medical research and training; functions as a major resource center for the media; and works to educate the public. Programs include screening clinics, health fairs, and corporate and community wellness programs. Educational materials produced by the organization include a wide variety of brochures, posters, books, newsletters, and audio-visual materials.

President: Perry Robins (1977-Present)
Executive Director: Mary Stine
Year Established: 1977

Keywords
Bowen's Disease; Cancer, Skin; Cancer, Squamous Cell; De Santis Cacchione Syndrome; Dysplastic

Nevus Syndrome; Melanoma; Melanoma, Malignant; Mycosis Fungoides; Nevoid Basal Cell Carcinoma Syndrome; Paget's Disease of the Breast; Skin Cancer; Skin Cancer Foundation; Xeroderma Pigmentosum

2164 Sleep/Wake Disorders Canada

3080 Bathurst Street
Suite 304
Toronto
Ontario, M6A 2A4, Canada

Phone: (416) 787-5374
Fax: (416) 787-4431
Toll Free: (800)387-9253
E-mail: swdc@globalserve.net
http://www.geocities.com/~sleepwake/

Sleep/Wake Disorders Canada (SWDC) is a national, not-for-profit, self-help organization of volunteers dedicated to providing information, practical support, and resources to Canadians with sleep/wake disorders. Such disorders include difficulties falling or staying asleep (insomnia); sleep apnea, a disorder in which breathing periodically ceases during sleep; narcolepsy, which is characterized by excessive daytime sleepiness, recurrent episodes of sleep during the day, and, in some cases, sudden loss of muscle tone (hypotonia) without loss of consciousness (cataplexy); and restless legs syndrome, a disorder characterized by unusual, unpleasant sensations deep in the legs, an overwhelming desire to move the legs to relieve such sensations, motor restlessness, and occurrence of such symptoms most frequently during the evening or early part of the night and while at rest. Established in 1981 and currently consisting of approximately 1,000 members, Sleep/Wake Disorders Canada has self-help chapters and contact representatives across Canada to provide local access for affected individuals and family members who seek information and peer support. The organization is committed to providing accurate and timely information on sleep/wake disorders to affected individuals and healthcare professionals; promoting awareness among affected families, medical professionals, and the general public; and promoting and supporting research on the underlying causes of such disorders.

President: Dr. Edward Gibson (1996 to Present)
Executive Director: Bev Devins
Year Established: 1981
Acronym: SWDC

Keywords
Sleep/Wake Disorders Canada

2165 Smith-Lemli-Opitz/RSH Advocacy and Exchange
2650 Valley Forge Drive
Boothwyn, PA 19061

Phone: (610) 485-9663
E-mail: bhook@erols.com
http://www.members.aol.com/slo97/index.html

The Smith-Lemli-Opitz/RSH Advocacy & Exchange is a voluntary, not-for-profit organization dedicated to educating the medical community, parents of affected children, educators, and the public about Smith-Lemli-Opitz/RSH syndrome. Established in 1988, the organization was created by 37 families with children affected by this rare disorder. The organization's purpose is to enable members to exchange information and experiences in an atmosphere of mutual support. In addition to informal networking, it sponsors regular national meetings where physicians, scientists, and parents can meet to learn more from each other. The organization now includes families from the United States, Canada, and throughout the world. It is devoted to patient advocacy, an ongoing exchange of information and support, and promoting and funding research on SLO/RSH. The organization produces educational materials including brochures and a regular newsletter.

President: Barbara Hook (1988-Present)
Executive Director: Unknown.
Year Established: 1988
Acronym: SLO or RSH

Keywords
RSH Syndrome; Smith Lemli Opitz Syndrome; Smith Lemli-Opitz/RSH Advocacy and Exchange

2166 Smith-Magenis Syndrome Foundation
P.O. Box 1490
BT71 4YE, United Kingsom

E-mail: info@smith-magenis.co.uk
http://www.smith-magenis.co.uk

Located in the United Kingdom, the Smith-Magenis Syndrome Contact Group is an international, self-help organization dedicated to providing information and support to individuals with Smith-Magenis syndrome and their families. Smith-Magenis syndrome is an extremely rare congenital disorder in which chromosomal material is absent from a certain portion of the short arm (p) of chromosome 17

(interstitial deletion 17p11.2) due to a spontaneous (de novo) genetic change early in embryonic development. Affected individuals may have a variety of associated symptoms and physical abnormalities including characteristic malformations of the head and facial area; abnormalities of the fingers and hands; speech delays and an unusually deep, hoarse voice; hearing loss; and/or moderate to severe mental retardation. In addition, many affected children may demonstrate self-destructive behavior. Established in 1992, the Smith-Magenis Syndrome Foundation UK is committed to disseminating information concerning Smith-Magenis syndrome to affected families and healthcare professionals; promoting awareness of the disorder in the United Kingdom; and providing networking opportunities to affected families to enable them to exchange information, support, and resources.

Year Established: 1992

Keywords
Chromosome 17 Interstitial Deletion 17p; Deletion 17p11.2; SMCR; Smith Magenis Chromosome Region; Smith Magenis Syndrome; Smith Magenis Syndrome Foundation; Smith-Magenis Syndrome Contact Group; Smith-Magenis Syndrome Foundation; SMS

2167 Sneddon Foundation (Stichting Sneddon)
Kesselloop 17
4813 NS
Breda, The Netherlands

Phone: +31 (0) 76-542-3861
E-mail: info@sneddon.nl
http://www.sneddon.nl

The Sneddon Foundation (Stichting Sneddon) was established because of the fact that people with Sneddon syndrome, as well as those with any other rare disease, face the same problem: many questions, few answers. The foundation educates and informations patients, their families, and the public about Sneddon syndrome, which is a rare progressive disorder characterized by the association of a skin disorder and neurological abnormalities. The foundation provides referrals to specialized hospitals, publishes a newsletter, and informs patients in English or Dutch about resources and developments related to Sneddon syndrome.

President: A.H.M. (Jos) Gilsing, josgilsing@sneddon.nl

Keywords

Dutch; Sneddon Foundation; Sneddon Foundation (Stichting Sneddon); Sneddon Syndrome; Stichting Sneddon; Support Groups

2168 Society for Mucopolysaccharide Diseases

46 Woodside Road
Amersham
Buckinghamshire, HP6 6AJ, United Kingdom

Phone: +44 (0) 1494-43-4156
Fax: +44 (0) 1494-43-4252
E-mail: mps@mpssociety.co.uk
http://www.mpssociety.co.uk

The Society for Mucopolysaccharide Diseases is a voluntary, international organization in the United Kingdom dedicated to providing information, support, and advocacy services to individuals and families affected by mucopolysaccharide and related diseases. The society was founded in 1982 by a group of parents with children affected by MPS disorders. The mucopolysaccharide diseases (mucopolysaccharidoses) belong to a group of rare metabolic disorders known as lysosomal storage disorders. Lysosomes are particles bound in membranes within cells that break down fats and carbohydrates. The mucopolysaccharidoses are characterized by an abnormal occurrence of certain fatty substances (mucolipids) and/or complex carbohydrates (mucopolysaccharides) within cells of particular tissues of the body. The different forms of MPS disease, such as Hurler syndrome (MPS I), Hunter syndrome (MPS II) etc. are often characterized by multiple abnormalities of the skull and face, growth delays, mental retardation, and/or additional symptoms and findings that may vary in range and severity. In many of these disorders, life-threatening complications may result during childhood. The MPS Society is committed to promoting and supporting research to further the understanding and improve the treatment of MPS disorders, offering networking services to affected families, and providing practical assistance in areas of health, welfare, education, adaptations, and respite care. It has a help line, holds regular national and regional conferences, and provides a variety of educational materials.

President: Barry Wilson (2000 to Present)
Executive Director: Christine Lavery
Year Established: 1982
Acronym: MPS Society

Keywords

Fabry; Fucosidosis; Gangliosidosis; Hunter Syndrome; Hurler Scheie; Hurler Syndrome; I-Cell Disease; Mannosidosis; Maroteaux Lamy Syndrome; MLIII; Morquio Syndrome; MPS; Mucopolysaccharidoses; Pseudo Hurler Polydystrophy; Sanfilippo; Scheie; Sialidosis; Sly Syndrome; Society for Mucopolysaccharide Diseases

2169 Society for Muscular Dystrophy Information International

P.O. Box 4790
Bridgewater
Nova Scotia, B4V 2X6, Canada

Phone: (902) -68-5-39
Fax: (902) -68-5-39
E-mail: smdi@auracom.com
http://users.auracom.com/smdi

The Society for Muscular Dystrophy Information International (SMDI) is a not-for-profit registered Canadian charity dedicated to assisting people in helping themselves by reducing the national and international isolation of individuals and organizations concerned with neuromuscular disorders/disabilities. In general, "neuromuscular disorder" is a term used to describe a group of over 50 diseases affecting the body's motor neurons (nerves and muscles). Symptoms may include varying degrees of progressive muscle weakness and loss of muscle mass (wasting). SMDI was established in 1983 to provide a non-technical information link for individuals with neuromuscular disorders and for organizations around the world; to link people with other people and organizations concerned with their disorder; to share information to assist people in helping themselves; and to create increased public awareness of this group of disorders.

President: James Dobson (1983 to Present)
Executive Director: Linda Dobson
Year Established: 1983
Acronym: SMDI International

Keywords

Muscular Dystrophy; Muscular Dystrophy, Becker; Muscular Dystrophy, Duchenne; Muscular Dystrophy, Emery Dreifuss; Muscular Dystrophy, Fukuyama Type; Muscular Dystrophy, Landouzy Dejerine; Muscular Dystrophy, Limb Girdle; Muscular Dystrophy, Oculo Gastrointestinal; Neuromuscular Disorders; Society for Muscular Dystrophy Information International

2170   Society for Progressive Supranuclear Palsy

Executive Plaza III
11350 McCormick Road
Suite 906
Hunt Valley, MD 21031

Phone: (410) 785-7004
Fax: (410) 785-7009
Toll Free: (800) 457-4777
E-mail: spsp@psp.org
http://www.psp.org

The Society for Progressive Supranuclear Palsy is dedicated to increasing awareness of this under-recognized disease, advancing research toward a cure, educating health professionals and providing hope, support and education for persons with PSP and their families. The society serves as an advocate for those affected with PSP and their caregivers. Established in 1990, it supports and promotes research into the causes, treatment, and potential cure for PSP. It publishes the PSP Advocate, which reports findings in PSP research and includes editorials and strategies for managing the disease. In addition, the society hosts research symposia and regional family conferences, and has a research program.

President: Stephen Hamer
Executive Director: Dr. Richard Gordon Zyne
Year Established: 1990
Acronym: SPSP

Keywords
Advocacy; Progressive Supranuclear Palsy; Research; PSP; Society for Progressive Supranuclear Palsy; SPSP; Steele Richardson Olszewski Syndrome

2171   SOFTWA (Support Organisation for Trisomy and Related Disorders)

E-mail: softwa@arach.net.au
http://www.trisomy9.org

SOFTWA is a non-profit organization that helps families of children affected by trisomy 9 and other rare chromosomal conditions. "Trisomy" refers to the presence of an extra chromosome. Those affected are born with a whole or partial third chromosome rather than the expected two. Trisomy 9 refers to the ninth chromosome. SOFTWA provides information and other support services for families with an affected child.

Keywords
Genetic Disorder Org.; National Chronic Fatigue Syndrome & Fibromyalgia Association; SOFTWA (Support Organisation for Trisomy and Related Disorders)

2172   Sotos Syndrome Support Association

P.O. Box 4626
Wheaton, IL 60189-4626

Toll Free: (888) 246-7772
E-mail: sssa@well.com
http://www.well.com/user/sssa/

The Sotos Syndrome Support Association (SSSA) is a voluntary, not-for-profit organization dedicated to providing information and support to individuals affected by Sotos syndrome, their families, and health-care professionals. Sotos syndrome is a rare genetic disorder characterized by excessive growth that occurs prior to and after birth (prenatally and postnatally). At birth, affected infants have unusually increased body length that is abnormal in proportion to weight, which may also be above average; in addition, newborns typically demonstrate advanced bone growth, abnormally large hands and/or feet, and characteristic facial features. The purpose of the association is to establish a social support environment for professionals and families of individuals affected by Sotos syndrome so that they can meet to exchange ideas and help one another cope; enhance the understanding of Sotos syndrome through education; coordinate an annual meeting; and provide an opportunity for professionals working with individuals affected by Sotos syndrome to collect data for research and to meet colleagues.

President: Debra Shively (1994-Present)
Year Established: 1988
Acronym: SSSA

Keywords
Gigantism, Cerebral; Growth Disorders; Sotos Syndrome; Sotos Syndrome Support Association

2173   Sotos Syndrome Support Association of Canada/Association Canadienne d'entraide du Syndrome de Sotos

1944 Dumfries
Montreal, Quebec, H3P 2R9, Canada

Fax: (514) 731-1255
E-mail: info@sssac.com
http://www.sssac.com

The mandate of SSSAC/ACESS is to provide support to persons with Sotos syndrome and their families. Since a diagnosis of Sotos syndrome is typically made in the first few years of life, it can be trying for families as they try to deal with the diagnosis, determine what they can expect for their child, and learn what they can do to best support their child's development. SSSAC/ACESS endeavors to support families by providing them with information by way of handbooks, pamphlets, Internet, public lectures, and discussions, and with emotional support by facilitating discussions with other parents who have been through similar experiences. SSSAC/ACESS also promotes public awareness of Sotos syndrome in each province in Canada, among educators, families and members of the medical community.

President: Carolyn Gregory (2002-present)
Year Established: 2002

Keywords
Sotos Syndrome Support Association of Canada/ Association Canadienne d'entraide du Syndrome de Sotos

---

2174 Southeastern Hereditary Colorectal Cancer Registry
University Hospital
1350 Walton Way
Augusta, GA 30910-3599

Phone: (706) 774-8900
Fax: (706) 774-8915
E-mail: cwheeler@uh.org

The Southeastern Hereditary Colorectal Cancer Registry is a part of University Health Care System in Augusta, Georgia. It was established to provide a mechanism for the systematic identification of individuals at risk for both familial polyposis and hereditary colorectal cancers, and to provide education to physicians, medical personnel, patients, and patients' families. Genetic testing and counseling are also provided.

Executive Director: Vendie H. Hooks, III, MD, FACS
Year Established: 1987

Keywords
Familial Adenomatous Polyposis; FAP; Hereditary Colorectal Cancer; Polyposis, Familial; Southeastern Hereditary Colorectal Cancer Registry; Turcot Syndrome

---

2175 Spasmodic Dysphonia Support Group
8 Corona Avenue
Roseville
New South Wales, 2069, Australia

Phone: +61 (0) 2-9411-2424
Fax: +61 (0) 2-9411-2424
E-mail: dennist@agsm.unsw.edu.au

The Spasmodic Dysphonia Support Group in Australia is a voluntary, not-for-profit organization dedicated to providing information, support, and resources to individuals and families affected by spasmodic dysphonia. Spasmodic dysphonia is a rare voice disorder that is a form of dystonia, a group of neuromuscular disorders characterized by involuntary muscle spasms. Spasmodic dysphonia is characterized by episodes of uncontrolled vocal spasms, difficulty speaking, tightness in the throat, and/or recurrent hoarseness. There are two types of spasmodic dysphonia: abductor spasmodic dysphonia, in which the vocal cords draw apart, and adductor spasmodic dysphonia, in which the vocal cords draw together and may become locked. Although the exact cause of spasmodic dysphonia is not known, some researchers believe that the disorder may result from abnormalities of the basal ganglia, an area of the brain that plays an essential role in coordinating movements. The Spasmodic Dysphonia Support Group (Australia) was established in 1991 and currently has approximately 120 members. The group conducts regular meetings with visiting speakers, has a database of individuals with spasmodic dysphonia, supports research, conducts surveys of affected individuals, and publishes a regular newsletter.

President: Cynthia Turner (1991-Present)
Executive Director: Helen Brake (Contact Person)
Year Established: 1991
Acronym: SD Support Group/Australia

Keywords
CSD; Dysphonia Spastica; Dysphonia, Chronic Spasmodic; Laryngeal Dystonia; Spasmodic Dysphonia; Spasmodic Dysphonia Support Group; Spastic Dysphonia

---

2176 Spasmodic Torticollis Dystonia, Inc
P.O. Box 28
Mukwonago, WI 53149

Phone: (262) 560-9534
Fax: (262) 560-9535
Toll Free: (888) 445-4588
E-mail: info@spasmodictorticollis.org
http://www.spasmodictorticollis.org

Spasmodic Torticollis Dystonia, Inc., is a not-for-profit rare-disorder organization founded in 1989. Its mission is to assist patients in finding a faster diagnosis and more effective treatment for spasmodic torticollis. Spasmodic torticollis, also known as cervical dystonia, is a form of dystonia characterized by intermittent spasms of the neck muscles resulting in involuntary rotation and tilting of the head. Once a diagnosis and treatment are known, this empowers the patients and/or family to achieve a higher quality of life. Spasmodic Torticollis Dystonia, Inc., offers education and advocacy to affected individuals and family members.

President: Howard Thiel
Executive Director: Joan Nager (Secratary)
Year Established: 1989

Keywords
Advocacy; Cervical Dystonia; Dystonia; Spasmodic Torticollis; Spasmodic Torticollis Dystonia, Inc.; ST/Dystonia. Inc.

2177 Spastic Paraplegia Foundation
11 Douglas Green
Woburn, MA 01801

Phone: (703) 495-9261
E-mail: info@sp-foundation.org
http://sp-foundation.org

The Spastic Paraplegia Foundation is committed to funding research to find cures for hereditary spastic paraplegia (HSP) and primary lateral sclerosis (PLS) so that all patients can be diagnosed, treated and cured. The foundation provides information about these disorders to patients, caregivers, physicians, and the general public, as well as support to patients who are coping with these disorders.

President: Annette Lockwood
Year Established: 2002
Acronym: SPF

Keywords
Amyotrophic Lateral Sclerosis; Multiple Sclerosis; Primary Lateral Sclerosis; Spastic Paraparesis; Spastic Paraplegia Foundation

2178 Spina Bifida and Hydrocephalus Association of Canada
977-167 Lombard Avenue
Winnipeg, Manitoba, R3B 0V3, Canada

Phone: (204) -92-5-36
Fax: (204) -92-5-36
Toll Free: (800) -56-5-94
E-mail: spinab@mts.net
http://www.sbhac.ca

The Spina Bifida and Hydrocephalus Association of Canada (SBHAC) is a not-for-profit support organiza-

tion dedicated to improving the quality of life of individuals with spina bifida and/or hydrocephalus and their families through awareness, education, and research. Spina bifida is a neural tube defect occurring early during fetal development, in which part of one or more of the bones of the spine (vertebrae) fail to develop completely, leaving a portion of the spinal cord exposed and resulting in damage to exposed nerve tissue. Hydrocephalus is a condition in which there is abnormal accumulation of cerebrospinal fluid in the skull, causing increased pressure on the brain. Established in 1981, the SBHAC currently has approximately 2,400 members in 11 chapters throughout Canada. The association provides a variety of programs and services including an 800 Help Line, support networking, educational workshops and seminars, and annual educational conference, research grants, scholarship programs for students with spina bifida and/or hydrocephalus, and public awareness programs. The association also offers a variety of educational guides and materials for schools, professionals, parents, and the general public including fact sheets; articles; a lending library of materials including books, guides, handbooks, and videos; and a regular newsletter entitled "Podium."

President: Lorelei Fletcher (2004 to Present)
Executive Director: Andrea Salmon
Year Established: 1981
Acronym: SBHAC

Keywords
Folic Acid; Hydrocephalus; Meningocele; Myelomeningocele; Spina Bifida; Spina Bifida Occulta; Spina Bifida and Hydrocephalus Association of Canada; Tethered Spinal Cord Syndrome

2179 Spina Bifida and Hydrocephalus Association of Ontario
55 Richmond Street W
P.O. Box 103
Ste 1006
Toronto, Ontario, M5V 3B1, Canada

Phone: (416) -21-4-10
Fax: (416) -21-4144
E-mail: provinivial@sbhao.on.ca
http://www.sbhao.on.ca

The Spina Bifida and Hydrocephalus Association of Ontario (SB&H) is a not-for-profit, general health organization located in Toronto. Founded in 1973, the association has as its mission to build awareness and drive education, research, support, care and advocacy for individuals and families affected by spina bifida and/or hydrocephalus. Spina bifida is a neural tube birth defect that occurs within the first four weeks of pregnancy. The spinal column fails to develop properly, resulting in damage to the spinal cord and nervous system. Hydrocephalus may be present at birth or develop later in life. It is the excessive accumulation of cerebrospinal fluid within the brain. SB&H seeks to help find a cure for these conditions, while also working to improve the quality of life for those affected. Its services include support groups, patient networking, research and advocacy.

President: Derryn V. Gill, Chairman of the Board (2001-present)
Executive Director: Joan Booth
Year Established: 1973
Acronym: SB&H

Keywords
Advocacy; French; Hydrocephalus; Networking; Normal Pressure Hydrocephalus; NPH; Research; Spina Bifida; Spina Bifida and Hydrocephalus Association of Ontario; Support Groups

2180 Spina Bifida Association of America

4590 MacArthur Boulevard NW
Suite 250
Washington, DC 20007-4226

Phone: (202) 944-3285
Fax: (202) 944-3295
Toll Free: (800) 621-3141
E-mail: sbaa@sbaa.org
http://www.sbaa.org

The Spina Bifida Association of America (SBAA) is a not-for-profit association dedicated to promoting the rights and well being of individuals with spina bifida. The association supports research into the causes, treatment, and prevention of the disease and seeks to increase public awareness of spina bifida and its prevention. Educational advancement, social and vocational development, and mainstreaming of individuals with disabilities are also goals of the association. Established in 1973 it addresses the specific needs of affected individuals, family members, healthcare professionals, and health institutions. The association promotes the continuing education of healthcare professionals involved in the treatment of spina bifida. It maintains a toll-free information and referral service, provides direct program services for its members and chapters, conducts public awareness campaigns, and holds an annual national conference addressing spina bifida issues. The Spina Bifida Association of America publishes a bimonthly newsletter, produces and distributes publica-

tions on the entire spectrum of spina bifida issues, and provides a variety of brochures and fact sheets.

Executive Director: Cindy Brownstein
Year Established: 1973
Acronym: SBAA

Keywords
Neural Tube Defects; Spina Bifida; Spina Bifida Association of America; Tethered Spinal Cord Syndrome

2181 Spina Bifida Hydrocephalus Queensland

P.O. Box 8022
Woolloongabba, Queensland, 4120, Australia

Phone: +61 (0) 7-3844-4600
Fax: +61 (0) 7-3844-4601
E-mail: info@sbhqueensland.org.au
http://www.spinabifida.org

Spina Bifida Hydrocephalus Queensland is a connecting point for information and services specific to spina bifida and hydrocephalus in Queensland, Australia. Spina bifida is a disabling birth defect that affects the development of the spine and spinal cord. Hydrocephalus results from blockage of the flow of cerebrospinal fluid through its natural pathways. The blockage causes an increase in pressure on the brain that may result in nerve damage.

President: Bill Shead (Information Officer)
Executive Director: Leslie Hughes (Administration Officer)
Year Established: 1969

Keywords
Facioscapulohumeral Muscular Dystrophy; Hydrocephalus; Networking; Sacral Agenesis; Spina Bifida; Spina Bifida Hydrocephalus Queensland; Spina Bifida Occulta; Support Groups

2182 Spinal Cord Injury Network International

3911 Princeton Drive
Santa Rosa, CA 95405-7013

Phone: (707) 577-8796
Fax: (707) 577-0605
Toll Free: (800) 548-2673
E-mail: library@spinalcordinjury.org
http://www.spinalcordinjury.org

Spinal Cord Injury Network International (SCINI) is a not-for-profit organization dedicated to responding to the needs of individuals who have experienced spinal cord injuries. Every year, approximately 10,000 individuals receive spinal cord injuries (SCI), resulting in varying degrees of paralysis (e.g., paraplegia or quadriplegia). The leading causes of spinal cord injury include motor vehicle accidents, acts of violence, falls, and sporting activities. Established in 1986, Spinal Cord Injury Network International provides affected individuals and family members with a clear understanding of the options available for leading a healthy, active life following paralysis. The network also provides links to healthcare services, organizations, agencies, specialists, and hospitals. In addition, Spinal Cord Injury Network International has a lending program of informational videos that address a variety of topics, including accessibility, autonomic dysreflexia, bladder and bowel management, brain injury, exercise, living with a disability, pressure sores, and sexuality. The network also maintains a resource library and provides materials for travelers with disabilities.

Executive Director: Lennice Ambrose
Year Established: 1986
Acronym: SCINI

Keywords
Spinal Cord Injury Network International

2183 Spinal Cord Society

19051 County Hwy. 1
Fergus Falls, MN 56537

Phone: (218) 739-5252
Fax: (218) 739-5262
http://users.aol.com/scsweb

The Spinal Cord Society is a not-for-profit organization whose members include individuals with spinal cord injuries, their families and friends, and scientists and physicians who are dedicated to finding a cure for spinal cord paralysis through improved treatment and research. Established in 1978, the society is a grassroots organization linked by over 200 chapters and more than 4,000 members throughout the United States and around the world. It society raises funds for medical research, promotes citizen advocacy, and provides appropriate referrals to treatment and support. The Spinal Cord Society has been instrumental in establishing civilian research conferences and research/treatment centers for spinal cord injury. Other projects include pioneering computerized walking technology for such injuries; artificial bone substitutes; autologous cell transplants (transplants to the

spinal cord of cells cultured from the patient's own body); and regeneration research. The Spinal Cord Society also publishes a monthly newsletter.

President: Dr. Charles E. Carson
Year Established: 1978
Acronym: SCS

Keywords
Arachnoiditis; Bone Substitutes, Artifical; FES; Paralysis, Spinal Cord; Spinal Cord Injury; Spinal Cord Society; Transplants, Autologous Cell

2184 Spinal Cord Tumor Association, Inc.

P.O. Box 461
Jay, FL 32565

Phone: (850) 675-6663
Fax: (850) 675-4934
E-mail: sctassociation@yahoo.com
http://www.spinalcordtumor.org

The Spinal Cord Tumor Association, Inc., (SCTA) is a not-for-profit, rare disorder organization formed by spinal cord tumor survivors for the purpose of supporting patients and their families. Founded in 2003, SCTA also seeks to educate the public and raise awareness of this illness, and to work with the medical community and others to improve survivors' quality of life. SCTA supports research dedicated toward the future prevention and cure of spinal cord tumors.

President: Linda Stophel
Executive Director: Robert Green
Year Established: 2003
Acronym: SCTA

Keywords
Research; SCTA; Spinal Cord Tumor; Spinal Cord Tumor Association, Inc.

2185 Spondylitis Association of America

P.O. Box 5872
Sherman Oaks, CA 91413

Phone: (818) 981-1616
Fax: (818) 981-9826
Toll Free: (800) 777-8189
E-mail: info@spondylitis.org
http://www.spondylitis.org

The Spondylitis Association of America (SAA) is a national, member-directed, non-profit organization dedicated to empowering persons living with ankylosing spondylitis (AS) through education, advocacy and support for patients, families and health professionals. Spondylitis is the most overlooked cause of persistent back pain in young adults and can affect over one million adults nationally. Established in 1983, the SAA takes a proactive, leadership role in promoting, funding and conducting research into the causes of AS. In 1988, in collaboration with National Institute of Arthritis and Musculoskeletal and Skin Diseases (NIAMS) and ten major medical centers and universities in North America, the SAA co-founded the North American Spondylitis Consortium (NASC) to lead the North American fight in uncovering the genetic causes of spondylitis and related diseases. Among other educational activities, the SAA produces a bi-monthly newsletter and other publications.

President: Tom West
Executive Director: Jane Bruckel, RN, BSN
Year Established: 1983
Acronym: SAA

Keywords
Ankylosing Spondylitis; Ankylosing Spondylitis International Federation; Arthritis, Psoriatic; ASIF; NASC; North American Spondylitis Coonsortium; Reiter's Syndrome; Spondylitis; Spondylitis Association of America

2186   Spotlight 6
2617 Ted Toad Road
Rising Sun, MD 21911

Phone: (410) 658-6264

Spotlight 6 is a not-for-profit, self-help organization dedicated to gathering and sharing information on abnormalities of chromosome 6 in children. Established in 1993, this parent-run organization provides support and information to affected families, caregivers, and concerned healthcare professionals. Spotlight 6 publishes a newsletter for members, that includes medical journal abstracts, article reprints, research updates, and more.

President: Ted Wiggins
Executive Director: Valeria Wiggins

Keywords
Chromosomal Abnormalities; Chromosome 6 Abnormalities; Chromosome 6 Deletion; Chromosome 6 Duplication; Chromosome 6 Inversion; Chromosome 6 Monosomy; Chromosome 6 Partial Deletion; Chromosome 6 Partial Duplication; Chromosome 6 Partial

Monosomy; Chromosome 6 Partial Trisomy; Chromosome 6 Ring; Chromosome 6 Translocations; Chromosome 6 Trisomy; Spotlight 6

2187   Stevens Johnson Syndrome Foundation and Support Group
P.O. Box 350333
Westminster, CO 80035-0333

Phone: (303) 635-1241
Fax: (303) 635-1241
E-mail: sjsupport@aol.com
http://www.sjsupport.org

The Stevens Johnson Syndrome (SJS) Foundation and Support Group is a national, non-profit support group organization providing emotional support to individuals affected by SJS and their families. Stevens-Johnson syndrome is a severe form of erythema multiforme characterized by blistery lesions on the mucous membranes of the mouth, throat, anogenital region, eyelids and corneal lining. Established in 1995, the group provides current information on SJS, its causes and treatments, and distributes this information through a nationwide networking system. Educational materials include reprints of current medical information on SJS.

President: Jean Farrell McCawley
Year Established: 1995
Acronym: SJS Support Group

Keywords
Dermatostomatitis, Stevens Johnson Type; Ectodermosis Erosiva Pluriorificialis; Erythema Multiforme Exudativum; Erythema Polymorphe, Stevens Johnson Type; Febrile Mucocutaneous Syndrome, Stevens Johnson Type; Herpes Iris, Stevens Johnson Type; Johnson Stevens Disease; Lyells Syndrome; SJS; Stevens Johnson Syndrome Foundation and Support Group; Stevens Johnson Syndrome Support Group; Stevens-Johnson Syndrome; TEN; Toxic Epidermal Necrolysis

2188   Stichting ERFO-centrum
Vredehofstaat 31
Soestdijk, 3761 HA, The Netherlands

Phone: +31 (0) 35-603-4040
Fax: +31 (0) 35-602-7440
E-mail: erfocentrum@erfocentrum.nl
http://www.erfelijkheid.nl

The mission of the foundation ERFO-centrum is to inform, guide, and promote knowledge among relevant target groups in health care and society about genetic and non-genetic congenital disorders. The foundation is concerned with medical and care giving needs, as well as with legal, ethical, and social concerns. It serves patients and members of their families, health professionals, other professionals, students, industry, and the general public.

President: Bernard Reuser
Executive Director: Cor Oosterwijk
Year Established: 2000
Acronym: ERFOCENTRUM

Keywords
Congenital Disorders; ERFOCENTRUM; Stichting ERFO-centrum

2189   Stickler Involved People

15 Angelina
Augusta, KS 67010

Phone: (316) 775-2993
E-mail: sip@sticklers.org
http://www.sticklers.org

The Stickler Involved People (SIP) is a voluntary organization dedicated to educating and giving support to those affected by Stickler syndrome. Stickler syndrome is a rare genetic disorder that affects connective tissue, including the joints, eyes, palate, heart, and hearing. The disorder is characterized by possible vision problems, hearing loss, early arthritis, cleft palate, and heart murmurs. It is extremely variable from case to case. Established in 1995, the organization focuses on patient networking and communication as the most effective and personal means of helping people who have this condition. In addition, the group utilizes its newsletter and on-line correspondence to further develop interpatient contact. SIP publishes informational brochures, a quarterly newsletter, and physician updates, and offers a networking service and a database of information for affected individuals. SIP also has an annual conference. New in 2003 is a college scholarship for a high school graduate diagnosed with Stickler syndrome.

President: Pat Houchin (Coordinator) (1995 to Present).
Year Established: 1995
Acronym: SIP

Keywords
Arthro Ophthalmopathy; Detached Retina; Epiphyseal Changes and High Myopia; Ophthalmarthropathy;

Pierre Robin; Stickler Involved People; Stickler Syndrome; Weissenbacher Zweymuller Syndrome

2190   Stickler Syndrome Support Group

P.O. Box 371
Walton-on-the-Thames
Surrey, KT12 2YS, United Kingdom

Phone: +44 (0) 1932-26-7635
Fax: +44 (0) 1932-26-7635
E-mail: wendy@stickler.org.uk
http://www.stickler.org.uk

The Stickler Syndrome Support Group is a voluntary health organization located in the United Kingdom. The group is dedicated to raising awareness among the general public and medical professionals. Stickler syndrome is a genetic disorder that affects the body's collagen (connective tissue), particularly the joints, eyes, palate, heart, and hearing. The disorder is extremely variable from case to case. It is characterized by possible vision problems, hearing loss, early arthritis, cleft palate, and heart murmurs. The support group offers information and support to affected individuals and families and to professionals with an interest in Stickler syndrome, and produces a range of publications on different aspects of the disorder. Through the group's quarterly newsletter, members can share experiences and keep abreast of advances in medical research.

President: Wendy Hughes (Honorary President & Founder)
Year Established: 1989
Acronym: SSSG

Keywords
Ophthalmopathy, Hereditary Progressive Arthropathy; Stickler Syndrome; Stickler Syndrome Support Group

2191   Strang-Cornell Hereditary Colon Cancer Program

428 East 72nd Street
New York, NY 10021

Phone: (212) 794-4900
Fax: (212) 794-4958
E-mail: mbertagnolli@partners.org
http://www.strang.org

The Strang-Cornell Hereditary Colon Cancer Program (SCPC) is a not-for-profit organization dedicated to providing individuals with familial adenomatous polyposis (FAP) and hereditary nonpolyposis colorectal cancer (HNPCC) clinical and educational services, as well as to foster participation in research. Colorectal cancer is a common disease in the United States. While most cases of colorectal cancer are sporadic, up to ten percent are hereditary. Hereditary colorectal cancer includes the polyposis syndromes, of which familial adenomatious polyposis is the most common, and the nonpolyposis syndromes, broadly referred to as hereditary nonpolyposis colorectal cancer. Established in 1934, this program is a collaboration between the Strang Cancer Prevention Center and the New York Hospital-Cornell Medical Center. SCPC includes three divisions: registries for FAP and HNPCC, clinical and pre-clinical research, and clinical services.

President: Monica M. Bertagnolli, M.D. (1996 to Present)
Executive Director: Andrew J. Dannenburg, M.D.
Year Established: 1934
Acronym: SCPC

Keywords
Cancer, Hereditary Non Polyposis of the Colon; FAP; Peutz Jeghers Syndrome; Polyposis, Familial Adenomatous; Polyposis, Juvenile; Strang-Cornell Hereditary Colon Cancer Program; Turcot's Syndrome

2192   Sturge Weber Foundation (UK)

Burleigh
348 Pinhoe Road
Exeter
Devon, EX4 8AF, United Kingdom

Phone: +44 (0) 1392-46-4675
Fax: +44 (0) 1392-46-4675
E-mail: support@sturgeweber.org.uk
http://www.sturgeweber.org.uk

The Sturge Weber Foundation (UK) offers support to individuals affected by Sturge Weber syndrome and to their families. It raises both public and professional awareness of this syndrome, which is usually indicated by a port wine stain around the area of the eye and forehead, with similar blood vessels on the brain (angioma). People affected by the syndrome may also have epilepsy, increased pressure in the eye (glaucoma), and some children may have learning difficulties. Some may have a weakness or stiffness affecting one side of the body, similar in appearance to that of a stroke (hemiplegia). The foundation encourages and funds research at the Sturge Weber Clinic at Great Ormond Street Hospital in London. It hosts an annual family weekend conference.

President: Mrs. Jenny Denham
Year Established: 1990
Acronym: SWF (UK)

Keywords
Sturge Weber Foundation (UK); Sturge Weber Syndrome

2193   The Sturge-Weber Foundation

1240 Sussex Turnpike
Suite A
Randolph, NJ 07869

Phone: (973) 895-4445
Fax: (973) 895-4846
Toll Free: (800) 627-5482
E-mail: swf@sturge-weber.com
http://www.sturge-weber.com

The Sturge-Weber Foundation (SWF) is a not-for-profit, 501(c)3 organization for parents, professionals, and others concerned with Port Wine stains, Sturge-Weber syndrome (SWS), and Klippel-Trenaunay (KT). A congenital disorder of unknown cause, SWS is characterized by facial discoloration and neurological abnormalities. Established in 1987, the Sturge-Weber Foundation is dedicated to acting as a clearinghouse of information on all aspects of port wine stain conditions and Sturge-Weber syndrome and offering support to all interested parties. The group seeks to educate the medical community, government agencies, and the general public; promote the funding of ongoing medical research; and establish a registry of affected individuals. The Sturge-Weber Foundation provides appropriate referrals and offers a variety of educational and support materials. These include a resource guide, medical articles, and brochures on all aspects of Sturge-Weber syndrome. Other educational resources available from the foundation include booklets, physical recommendation papers, a newsletter, and monthly e-news.

President: Karen L. Ball
Year Established: 1987
Acronym: SWF

Keywords
Birthmarks; Capillary Malformation; Cavernous Hemangioma; Glaucoma; Klippel Trenaunay Syndrome; Port Wine Stain; The Sturge-Weber Foundation; Sturge Weber Syndrome

2194   Stuttering Foundation
3100 Walnut Grove Road
Suite 603
Memphis, TN 38111-0749

Phone: (901) 452-7343
Fax: (901) 452-3931
Toll Free: (800) 992-9392
E-mail: info@stutteringhelp.org
http://www.stutteringhelp.org (and) www.tratamudez.
org (Spanish site)

The Stuttering Foundation of America (SFA) is a not-for-profit organization founded in 1947 dedicated to the improved treatment and the prevention of stuttering. The foundation publishes 28 books, 39 DVD's and videotapes, a periodic newsletter, and 19 informational brochures on stuttering. Several publications are directed toward medical professionals. The foundation maintains a toll-free hotline on stuttering and a nationwide resource list for individuals seeking a speech-language pathologist who specializes in stuttering. In addition, the foundation in collaboration with Northwestern University co-sponsors an annual "Workshop for Specialists: Stuttering Therapy," an in-depth two week training program. The foundation also co-sponsors a 4 five-day workshop for professionals who focus on working with school-age children who stutter. It maintains two web sites, one in English, the other in Spanish.

President: Jane Fraser (1982 to Present)
Year Established: 1947
Acronym: SFA

Keywords
Childhood Stuttering; Language Disorders; Speech Disorders; Stuttering; Stuttering Foundation; Stuttering Foundation of America

2195   Sudden Arrhythmia Death Syndromes Foundation
508 E South Temple
#20
Salt Lake City, UT 84102

Phone: (801) 531-0937
Fax: (801) 531-0945
Toll Free: (800) 786-7723
E-mail: sads@sads.org
http://www.sads.org

The Sudden Arrhythmia Death Syndromes (SADS) Foundation is a national, not-for-profit organization that was established in 1991. Its mission is to save the lives of children and young adults who are genetically predisposed to sudden death due to heart rhythm abnormalities. The foundation is dedicated to increasing the general publics knowledge of the warning signs of heart rhythm abnormalities that can cause sudden death in the young. SADS provides information, resources, and support to assist patients and families to make informed medical decisions and to live with the challenges of these conditions. SADS serves as a physician referral resource center and facilitates several family support groups and a person-to-person networking program. The foundation also seeks to provides advice to physicians who care for people with long qt syndrome. In addition, the foundation is interested in the identification of individuals and families at risk for these diseases and in assisting families of those affected. SADS facilitates several family support groups and a person-to-person networking program.

President: G. Michael Vincet, M.D. (1992-Present)
Executive Director: Alice Lara
Year Established: 1991
Acronym: SADS

Keywords
Anderson's Syndrome; Brugada Syndrome; CUPT; Epilepsy; Fainting; Jervell and Lange-Nielsen Syndrome; Long QT Syndrome; Romano Ward Syndrome; Sudden Arrhythmia Death Syndromes Foundation; Sudden Arrythmia Death Syndrome; Sudden Cardiac Death; Sudden Death; Syncope; Timothy's Syndrome

2196   Support for People with Oral and Head and Neck Cancer, Inc.
P.O. Box 53
Locust Valley, NY 11560-0053

Phone: (516) 759-5333
Fax: (516) 671-8794
E-mail: info@spohnc.org
http://www.spohnc.org

Support for People with Oral and Head and Neck Cancer (SPOHNC) is a patient-directed, not-for-profit organization dedicated to addressing the broad emotional, physical, and humanistic needs of oral, head, and neck cancer patients. Founded in 1991 by an oral cancer survivor, the organization produces educational materials including "News from SPOHNC," a newsletter that is published nine times each year. SPOHNC encourages and promotes increased scientific clinical research and development in the improvement of quality of life for individuals affected by oral and head and neck cancer. There are currently 37 chapters throughout the United States of SPOHNC.

President: Nancy E. Leupold (1991 to Present)
Executive Director: Same as above.
Year Established: 1991
Acronym: SPOHNC

Keywords
Adenoid Cystic Carcinoma; Cancer, Head; Cancer, Neck; Cancer, Oral; Dry Mouth; Polymorphous Low Grade Adenocarcinoma; Sinonasal Undifferentiated Carcinoma; SPOHNC; Support for People with Oral and Head and Neck Cancer, Inc.; Swallowing; Tongue Carcinoma; Xerostomia

2197 Support Organization for Trisomy 13/18 and Related Disorders, UK

7 Orwell Road
Petersfield
Hampshire, GU31 4LQ, United Kingdom

Phone: +44 (0) 121-351-3122
E-mail: enquiries@soft.org.uk
http://www.soft.org.uk

Support Organisation for Trisomy 13/18 and Related Disorders is an international, UK-based organization that serves families affected by trisomy 13/18, related disorders, and rare conditions for whom no other organization exists. SOFT provides support, assistance, and information for families in many different situations and stages of diagnosis, caregiving, and for some, grief. SOFT offers informational packets, booklets, a "link list" networking service, a newsletter, support groups, patient education, advocacy, a journal, a database, and a variety of audio-visual aids. SOFT serves the UK, the USA (in conjunction with SOFT USA), Scandinavia, Europe, New Zealand, and Australia; and through member resources, SOFT supports the English, Italian, French, German, Danish, and Swedish languages.

President: Jenny Robbins
Executive Director: Christine Rose
Year Established: 1990
Acronym: SOFT UK

Keywords
Chromosomal Abnormalities; Chromosomal Additions; Support Organization for Trisomy 13/18 and Related Disorders, UK; Trisomy; Trisomy 13 Syndrome; Trisomy 18 Syndrome

2198 Support Organization for Trisomy 18, 13, and Related Disorders

2982 South Union Street
Rochester, NY 14624-1926

Fax: (585) 594-1957
Toll Free: (800) 716-7638
E-mail: barbv@trisomy.org
http://www.trisomy.org

The Support Organization for Trisomy 18, 13, and Related Disorders (SOFT) is a voluntary, not-for-profit network consisting of affected families and professionals who are involved in the care of individuals with trisomy 18, trisomy 13, and other related disorders (e.g., other chromosomal abnormalities involving the duplication of genetic material). Established in 1979, SOFT was created to provide affected families and professionals with the additional information and support they often need when confronted with a diagnosis of trisomy 18, 13, or related chromosomal disorders. The organization enables parents to share information and support; promotes education of healthcare professionals; provides appropriate referrals to affected families; holds local chapter gatherings for interested members; and conducts an annual international conference with seminars and cost-free consultations with doctors and other professionals.

President: Barbara Van Herrewegle
Year Established: 1979
Acronym: SOFT

Keywords
Chromosomal Abnormalities; Chromosome 4 Partial Trisomy Distal 4q; Chromosome 5 Trisomy 5p; Chromosome 6 Partial Trisomy 6q; Chromosome 7 Monosomy 7p2; Chromosome 9 Tetrasomy 9p; Chromosome 9 Trisomy 9p Multiple Variants; Chromosome 9 Trisomy Mosaic; Penta X Syndrome; Support Organization for Trisomy 18, 13, and Related Disorders; Trisomy; Trisomy 4p ; Trisomy 13 Syndrome; Trisomy 18 Syndrome

2199 SWAN (Syndromes without a Name)

P.O. Box 3302
Norwood, South Australia, 5067, Australia

Phone: +61 (0) 4-3990-0272
E-mail: swanaus@optusnet.com.au
http://members.optusnet.com.au~swanaus/

An Australian group, based in South Australia, providing information, support and resources for families where a child has multiple disabilities and/or conditions and there is no unifying diagnosis. Have support meetings, the 4th Monday of month in South Australia. Promoting awareness of the difficulties children and their families face, established a database to assist children and families to link up to each other. Advocated to the Federal Government to establish a National Registrar of the children in hope that diagnosis will be attained, and now has a verbal commitment for this to occur. A syndrome is a collection of characteristics, which reflect a pattern, however for these children there is no pattern, and children and their families have a difficult path and need to connect with others of similarities.

President: Jewels Smith (2003-present)
Year Established: 2003
Acronym: SWAN

Keywords
SWAN (Syndromes without A Name); Undiagnosed; Service Organization

2200   Swedish Association of Rare Disorders

Box 1386
SE-172 27
Sundbyberg, Sweden

Phone: +46 (0) 8764-4999
Fax: +46 (0) 85464-0494
E-mail: info@sallsyntadiagnoser.nu
http://www.sallsyntadiagnoser.nu

The Swedish Association of Rare Disorders was founded in 1998 and has about 7,000 members, representing approximately 50 rare disorders. Its main mission is to help people with rare disorders make their voices heard and improve their situation by cooperating with others. The association is involved in advocacy, promoting centers of excellence for treatment, and raising the level of awareness of specific problems encountered during daily life by individuals and families affected by rare disorders. This includes, for instance, improving the understanding of the needs of children with rare disorders in their schools.

President: Elizabeth Wallenius (1998-present)
Executive Director: Raoul Dammert
Year Established: 1998

Keywords
Advocacy; Rare Diseases; Swedish; Swedish Association of Rare Disorders

2201   Swedish CDG Society

Sönnarslövsvägen 130-7
Tollarp, SE-290 10, Sweden

Phone: +46 (0) 4431-0873
E-mail: Rolf.Odselius@cdgs.info
http://www.cdgs.info/indexeng.shtml

The Swedish CDG Society provides a web site for healthcare professionals, researchers, school or assistance personnel, and families with children diagnosed with carbohydrate-deficient glycoprotein (CDG) syndromes, which are also known as congenital disorders of glycosylation. CDG syndromes are a group of extremely rare inherited metabolic disorders. Several variants have been identified. It is suspected that several more variants exist. These disorders affect most systems of the body, particularly the central nervous system (i.e., the brain and spinal cord) and the peripheral nervous system (i.e., motor and sensory nerves outside the central nervous system). The most common form of CDG syndrome is carbohydrate-deficient glycoprotein syndrome type I (CDG1). Symptoms may vary among individuals, but include impaired coordination and balance; severe muscle thinning and weakness in the legs (peripheral neuropathy); skeletal malformations; vision and/or hearing impairment; mild to severe mental retardation; and severe delays in the acquisition of skills that require the coordination of mental and muscular activity (psychomotor retardation). The society provides current information on CDGS, nternational parent contacts through e-mail, and links to other patient organizations, specialist laboratories, and clinics.

President: Jörgen Johansson
Executive Director: Eva Rubin, Treasurer and Secretary

Keywords
Carbohydrate Deficient Glycoprotein Syndrome; CDG; CDG1; CDG2; CDG3; CDG4; CDGS; CDGS Type I; CDGS Type II; CDGS Type III; CDGS Type IV; Hypoglycosylation Syndrome Type I; Swedish CDG Society

2202   Swedish Hemophilia Society

Box 1386 172 27 Sundbyberg
Stockholm, SE-102 04, Sweden

Phone: +46 (0) 8546-40510
Fax: +46 (0) 8661-9465
http://www.fbis.se/

The Swedish Hemophilia Society (FBIS) is a nonprofit organization for individuals affected by hemophilia in Sweden. Hemophilia is a group of hereditary bleeding disorders characterized by deficiency of one of the blood factors necessary for blood clotting (coagulation). Affected individuals may experience bleeding episodes that occur for no apparent reason or due to surgery, dental extractions, or injuries. Recurrent bleeding into the joints and muscles may cause painful inflammation of the joints (arthritis) and associated deformities. The Swedish Hemophilia Society, which was established in 1964, currently serves as an umbrella organization consisting of eight local societies. The FBIS disseminates information and provides assistance to these local societies. The Swedish Hemophilia Society has several primary objectives, including informing the general public, the community, and governmental institutions about hemophilia disease and improving the quality of life of affected individuals by arranging conferences and meetings where current issues are discussed. The society offers several programs and services, including providing summer and winter camps for affected children and youths, and recreation trips that provide physical training opportunities.

Executive Director: Anders Molander (Contact Person)
Year Established: 1964
Acronym: FBIS

Keywords
Swedish Hemophilia Society

2203 Swedish Sjogren's Syndrome Association

Box 359
Malmo, 20123, Sweden

Phone: +46 (0) 40-97-7955
Fax: +46 (0) 4630-7353
E-mail: inger@sjogrensyndrom.se
http://www.sjogrensyndrom.se

The Swedish Sjogren's Syndrome Association is an international, not-for-profit organization dedicated to providing information and support to individuals with Sjogren's syndrome, family members, and healthcare professionals. Sjogren's syndrome, a disorder of unknown cause, is characterized by deficient moisture production of the mucous-secreting glands, particularly the tear ducts of the eyes (lacrimal) and the salivary glands of the mouth. Associated symptoms and physical abnormalities may include abnormal dryness, itching, and burning of the eyes (keratoconjunctivitis

sicca); abnormal dryness of the mouth, resulting in cavities, other dental disorders, and loss of odor and taste sensations; and, when the lungs are affected, increased susceptibility to repeated respiratory infections. Many affected individuals also experience rheumatoid arthritis. Sjogren's syndrome, which primarily affects middle-aged women, is thought to be due to an abnormal autoimmune response. Established in 1989, the Swedish Sjogren's Syndrome Association provides networking opportunities, engages in patient education, and offers a variety of materials including reports and a regular newsletter. It has a web site in both English and Swedish that explains the history of Sjogren's syndrome, discusses current research in Sweden and around the world, and offers dynamic linkage to other helpful sources of information on the Internet.

President: Inger Siwersson
Year Established: 1989

Keywords
Gougerot Houwer Sjogren; Gougerot Sjogren; Keratoconjunctivitis Sicca; Keratoconjunctivitis Sicca Xerostomia; Sicca Syndrome; Sjogren Syndrome; Swedish Sjogren's Syndrome Association; Xerodermostenosis, Secreto-inhibitor

2204 Syncope Trust & Reflex Anoxic Seizures

P.O. Box 175
Stratford-upon-Avon
Warwickshire, CV37 8YD, United Kingdom

Phone: +44 (0) 1789-45-0564
Fax: +44 (0) 1789-45-0682
Toll Free: 0 (800) 028-6362
E-mail: trudie@stars.org.uk
http://www.stars.org.uk

Syncope Trust & Reflex Anoxic Seizures is an information and support group that exists to bring about public and professional awareness of reflex anoxic seizures (RAS). These are seizures that can occur at any age, but are most common in young children and tend to be clustered in "batches" of attacks. In an RAS episode, an unexpected stimulus, such as pain, shock, or fright, causes the heart to stop, the eyes to roll up into the head, the complexion to become deathly white, and the body to stiffen. After several seconds, the body relaxes and the heart starts beating, but the sufferer loses consciousness and may remain unconscious for an hour or longer. Established in 1993, this organization provides educational materials for patients and health professionals, gathers information to aid research into RAS, and provides support groups and other services for families. It offers information on all types of syncopes including reflex anoxic seizures, for adults and children.

President: Trudie Lobban
Year Established: 1993
Acronym: STARS

Keywords
Neurally Mediated Syncope; Neurocardiogenic Syncope; Pallid Infantile Syncope; Reflex Anoxia Seizures; Reflex Asystolic Syncope; Syncope; Syncope Trust & Reflex Anoxic Seizures; Vasovagal Syncope

2205 Syndromes without a Name (S.W.A.N.)

6 Acorn Close
Great Wyrley
Walsall
West Midlands, WS6 6JW, United Kingdom

Phone: +44 (0) 1922-70-1234
Fax: +44 (0) 1922-70-1234
E-mail: info@undiagnosed.org.uk
http://www.undiagnosed.org.uk

This not-for-profit, self-help organization, a registered charity, promotes awareness of challenges faced by children and families affected by undiagnosed diseases. It campaigns for equal rights and recognition, is building a database to help with future research, links families to others when possible, and facilitates the exchange of information and stories through its newsletter. Knowing that something is wrong with their child but lacking a diagnosis leaves parents in the difficult position of knowing that their child is different from others but not knowing why or what to do about it. The search for a diagnosis can be anguishing for both children and parents.

President: Lis Swingwood
Year Established: 1998
Acronym: S.W.A.N.

Keywords
Syndromes without a Name (S.W.A.N.); Undiagnosed

2206 Taiwan Foundation for Rare Disorders

10F, No. 52, Sec. 2
Jungshan N. Rd
Taipei City, 104, Taiwan

Phone: +886 2-2521-0717
Fax: +886 2-2567-3560
E-mail: tfrd@tfrd.org.tw
http://www.tfrd.org.tw

Taiwan Foundation for Rare Disorders was founded to provide support for rare disorder patients, who are the minority among minorities of Taiwan society. They need the support of the government and the general public in order to protect and enhance their rights. Their quality of life will be improved through encouraging medical research and establishing formal procedures in the referral, diagnosis, treatment and care of rare disorder patients. Most of the rare disorder patients known to date in Taiwan have hereditary metabolic problems. Due to the lack of medications and diagnostic equipment, the patients may not receive early and timely diagnosis, depriving them of their chance of survival, or causing impairments to major organs, which may further lead to serious complications or even death. Those who are fortunate enough to survive are struggling because either they cannot afford life-sustaining medications or such medications are not imported. There is no formal channel to obtain medications and special diets in Taiwan.

Executive Director: Joe Tyau-Chang Tseng
Year Established: 1999
Acronym: TFRD

Keywords
Taiwan Foundation for Rare Disorders

2207 Taking Action Against Language Disorders for Kids, Inc.

22980 Donna Lane
Bend, OR 97701

Phone: (503) 389-0004
Fax: (503) 389-0004

Taking Action Against Language Disorders for Kids, Inc., (TALK) is a service organization dedicated to educating the medical and educational communities and the public on the importance of early recognition of speech and language disorders in children. Established in 1992, the organization promotes the exchange of current information on speech and language disorders or impairments and other topics such as parental issues, research, behavior modification approaches, and speech/language and occupational therapy techniques. This is accomplished through an established nationwide network that is available to the public and educational and medical communities. The organization also offers parental support to affected families, providing such families with resources, articles, and other materials. It is hoped that this support will enable parents to become advocates for their children to help ensure their rights under the law. The organization also offers support to the siblings of affected children through informational literature and other resources. TALK also exchanges current information and resources with organizations and agencies locally, nationally, and worldwide and makes a library of relevant materials available to the public and medical and educational communities. In addition, the organization provides a directory and a regular newsletter.

President: Linda Newland (1992-Present)
Executive Director: Linda Newland
Year Established: 1992
Acronym: TALK

Keywords
Acidemia, Methylmalonic; Language Disorders; Siblings of Children with Disabilities; Speech Impairment; Taking Action Against Language Disorders for Kids, Inc.

2208   Tasmanian Lymphoedema (Lymphedema) Support Group

58 Doyle Avenue
Lenah Valley
Hobart
Tasmania, 7008, Australia

Phone: +61 (0) 2-2837-08

The Tasmanian Lymphoedema (Lymphedema) Support Group is a voluntary, self-help organization in Australia dedicated to providing information and support to individuals affected by lymphedema, educating and supporting family members, and promoting professional and public awareness. Lymphedema is characterized by an abnormal accumulation of lymph fluid, in and associated swelling of, certain body tissues due to lymphatic system abnormalities that cause obstruction of normal lymph flow into the bloodstream. Lymph is a bodily fluid that contains certain white blood cells (lymphocytes), fats, and proteins, and functions as an essential part of the immune system. It accumulates outside blood vessels in spaces between cells in tissues and flows back into the bloodstream via lymph vessels. Individuals with lymphedema may experience swelling that increases over time, a feeling of heaviness and discomfort in the affected area, pain, susceptibility to infection, and, in some severe cases, loss of mobility. The Tasmanian Lymphoedema Support Group was established in 1994 and currently has approximately 80 members. The group engages in patient advocacy and lobbying efforts, promotes research, and provides referrals. The Tasmanian Lymphoedema Support Group also provides a variety of educational materials including brochures and publishes a regular newsletter.

President: Patricia Gillon (1994 to Present)
Executive Director: Jill Wood
Year Established: 1994
Acronym: TLSG

Keywords
Tasmanian Lymphoedema (Lymphedema) Support Group

2209   TEF/VATER/VACTRL National Support Network

15301 Grey Fox Road
Upper Marlboro, MD 20772

Phone: (301) 952-6837
Fax: (301) 952-9152
E-mail: tefvater@ix.netcom.com
http://www.tefvater.org

The TEF/VATER/VACTRL National Support Network is a voluntary, not-for-profit, self-help organization dedicated to providing information and support to adults and families of children with narrowing of the esophageal atresia, tracheoesophageal fistula, and VATER/VACTRL association. Esophageal atresia is a condition in which the tube that carries food from the mouth to the stomach (esophagus) ends in a pouch instead of connecting to the stomach. Tracheoesophageal fistula is an abnormal connection between the esophagus and the windpipe (trachea) that may result in food being aspirated into the lungs. VATER association is a rare disorder that affects several organ systems of the body. VATER/VACTERL is an acronym that stands for (V)ertebral defects, (A)nal atresia/imperforate anus, (C)ardiac defects, (T)racheo (E)sophageal defects, (R)enal defects, or (R)adial (L)imbs defects. Established in 1992, the TEF/VATER/VACTRL National Support Network is committed to promoting and supporting research, engaging in patient advocacy, ensuring the appropriate treatment of affected individuals, and promoting patient and professional education. The network also provides appropriate referrals, such as to genetic counseling; promotes legislation beneficial to affected individuals; and offers a variety of educational and support materials through its database, directory, brochures, and a regular newsletter.

President: Unknown
Executive Director: Greg Burke, P.A.
Year Established: 1992

Keywords
Esophageal Atresia; TEF; TEF/VATER/VACTRL National Support Network; Tracheoesophageal Fistula; VACTERL; VACTRL Association; VATER; VATER Association

---

2210 Telecommunications for the Deaf, Inc.
8630 Fenton Street
Suite 604
Silver Spring, MD 20910-3803

Phone: (301) 589-3786
Fax: (301) 589-3797
TDD: (301) 589-3006
E-mail: info@tdi-online.org
http://www.tdi-online.org

Telecommunications for the Deaf, Inc., (TDI) is a non-profit advocacy organization dedicated to promoting full visual access to information and telecommunications through consumer education and involvement; technical assistance and consulting; application of existing and emerging technologies; networking and collaboration; uniformity of standards; and national policy development and advocacy. The organization serves people who are deaf, hear of hearing, deaf/blind, and/or speech-impaired. TDI's main objectives are promoting text telephone compatibility with existing communication devices; increasing toll-free services for TTY users; improving emergency access; and improving communications between TTY and other telephone users through comprehensive telecommunications relay services training. Telecommunications for the Deaf, Inc., also develops, implements, and evaluates new strategies for improving the quality and availability of visual telecommunications; encourages progress in key technologies such as television captioning; creates improved specifications and standards for equipment, telecommunications relay, and emergency services; educates the public about and supports legislation to improve telecommunications services; and builds coalitions of consumers and service providers to meet the needs of the deaf, heard of hearing, and speech-impaired. In addition, TDI provides training to industry groups and service providers who need assistance in service implementation. TDI provides a comprehensive overview of deafness and deaf culture; explains the influence of American Sign Language on TTY communication; trains personnel in telecommunications relay and emergency services;

and conducts needs assessment studies, manages focus groups, and designs surveys to guide service-improvement projects.

President: Roy Miller
Executive Director: Claude Stout
Year Established: 1968
Acronym: TDI

Keywords
Deafness; Deafness, Telecommunications for; Patient Avocacy for the Deaf; Speech Impairment; Telecommunications for the Deaf, Inc; TTY Equipment

---

2211 Tetrasomy/Pentasomy X Support Group
P.O. Box 270064
West Allis, WI 53227

E-mail: tetra-x-list-subscribe@yahoogroups.com
http://www.tetrasomy.com

The Tetrasomy/Pentasomy X Support Group provides information on rare chromosomal disorders in which females are born with extra X chromosomes. Presenting signs and symptoms may include, among other things, skeletal abnormalities and mental retardation. The group provides networking, advocacy, support, and patient education, as well as information for health professionals and other professionals, such as teachers.

President: Cynthia Bradley
Year Established: 2000
Acronym: Tetra/Penta X

Keywords
48, XXXX; 49, XXXXX; Pentasomy X; Tetrasomy X; Tetrasomy/Pentasomy X Support Group

---

2212 Thalassemia Action Group
c/o Cooley's Anemia Foundation
129-09 26th Avenue
Suite 203
Flushing, NY 11354

Phone: (718) 321-2873
Fax: (718) 321-3340
Toll Free: (800) 522-7222
E-mail: info@cooleysanemia.org
http://www.cooleysanemia.org

The Thalassemia Action Group (TAG), a nonprofit organization, is the official patient support group of the Cooley's Anemia Foundation (CAF). Thalassemia major is a rare blood disorder characterized by a marked increase in F hemoglobin and a decrease in the production of certain oxygen-carrying proteins in red blood cells (beta polypeptide chains in the hemoglobin molecule). Thalassemia major is the most severe form of chronic familial anemias that result from the premature destruction of red blood cells (hemolytic). This disease was originally described in people living near the Mediterranean Sea. Individuals with this disorder also have a reduced number of circulating red blood cells (erythrocytes). Thalassemia minor is a rare inherited blood disorder characterized by a moderately low level of hemoglobin (anemia) in red blood cells. People with thalassemia minor have one of a pair (heterozygous) of the thalassemia gene. People with two copies of the disease gene, will have thalassemia major, which is a more serious disease. In most affected individuals, the only symptom of thalassemia minor may be persistent fatigue. TAG's mission is providing affected individuals and their family members with a channel of communication and information. It hosts an annual patient and parent conference, engages in advocacy and organizes special events and opportunities for affected individuals to network.

President: Frank Somma
Executive Director: Jayne Restivo
Year Established: 1954
Acronym: TAG

Keywords
Thalassemia; Thalassemia Action Group

2213 Think First, National Injury Prevention Foundation

5550 Meadowbrook Drive
Suite 10
Rolling Meadows, IL 60008

Phone: (847) 290-8600
Fax: (847) 290-9005
Toll Free: (800) 844-6556
E-mail: thinkfirst@thinkfirst.org
http://www.thinkfirst.org

The Think First, National Injury Prevention Foundation (TFF) is a not-for-profit, voluntary organization dedicated to preventing brain and spinal cord injuries through education of individuals, community leaders, and creators of public policy. Established in 1986, TFF was founded by the American Association of Neurological Surgeons and the Congress of Neurological Surgeons. Consisting of more than 200 chapters, TFF

produces educational materials including a catalog entitled "1997 Catalog, Think First," the "Think First Fact Sheet," and brochures. The foundation conducts high school presentations, develops local programs engaging in public policy initiatives, supports public and community awareness projects, and has the "Think First For Kids" program which is implemented in elementary schools by local teachers. TFF includes more than 200 active local programs throughout the United States, Chile, Canada, Mexico, and Brazil. Each program includes sponsoring licensed physician and program coordinator who participate in the Think First high school program. More than five million students have attended Think First program presentations.

President: Michael Turner, MD (Chairperson)
Executive Director: Dorothy Zirkle (CEO)
Year Established: 1986
Acronym: TFF

Keywords
Brain Injury; Spinal Cord Injury; Think First Foundation; Think First, National Injury Prevention Foundation; Traumatic Brain Injuries

2214 Thrombocytopenia Absent Radius Syndrome Association

212 Sherwood Drive
RD 1
Linwood, NJ 08221-9745

Phone: (609) 927-0418
E-mail: tarsa@aol.com

The TAR Syndrome Association, also known as TARSA, is an international, not-for-profit, self-help organization that was established in 1981. The group functions as a support system and educational resource for families affected by thrombocytopenia absent radius (TAR) syndrome. TAR syndrome is a rare hereditary disorder characterized by abnormally low levels of circulating blood platelets and underdevelopment or absence of the radius, one of the bones of the forearm. In some cases, symptoms may include kidney abnormalities and congenital heart disease. Educational materials produced by the TAR Syndrome Association include informational brochures and an annual newsletter.

President: Sandra Puriton (1981-Present)
Executive Director: Unknown
Year Established: 1981
Acronym: TARSA

Keywords
TAR Syndrome; TAR Syndrome Association; Thrombocytopenia Absent Radius Syndrome; Thrombocytopenia Absent Radius Syndrome Association; Thrombocytopenia, Essential

2215   Thrombophilia Support Page

E-mail: debsmith@fvleiden.org
http://www.fvleiden.org

The Thrombophilia Support Page is an online resource for individuals and families affected by factor V leiden, a hereditary blood coagulation disorder. Factor V leiden may be associated with blood clots in the veins, blood clot in the lung, and other potentially serious health risks. The web site provides information for affected individuals and families on how to join the mailing list, a description of the factor V leiden mutation, and dynamic linkage to additional sources of information on such hereditary blood coagulation disorders.

President: Deb Smith (List Owner)

Keywords
Factor V Leiden Genetic Mutation; Thrombophilia Support Page

2216   ThyCa: Thyroid Cancer Survivors' Association, Inc.
P.O. Box 1545
New York, NY 10159-1545

Phone: (877) 588-7904
Fax: (630) 604-6078
Toll Free: (877) 855-7904
E-mail: thyca@thyca.org
http://www.thyca.org

ThyCa: Thyroid Cancer Survivors' Association, Inc., is a national, not-for-profit organization that educates and supports patients and families affected by thyroid cancer, a tumor or growth located within the thyroid gland. ThyCa conducts awareness and outreach programs, sponsors Thyroid Cancer Awareness Month, and sponsors thyroid cancer research funds, and research grants. Services of ThyCa includes a website, support groups, newsletters, and free online cookbook.

President: Cherry Wunderlich (Outreach Coordinator and Corresponding Secretary)
Executive Director: Gary Bloom (Board Chair)
Year Established: 1995

Keywords
Advocacy; Anaplastic Thyroid Cancer; Follicular Thyroid Cancer; Hurthle Cell Thyroid Cancer; Medullary Thyroid Cancer; Networking; Papillary Thyroid Cancer; Research; Support Groups; Tall Cell Thyroid Cancer; ThyCa; ThyCa: Thyroid Cancer Survivors' Association, Inc.; Thyroid Cancer

2217   Thyroid Foundation of America, Inc.
One Longfellow Place
Suite 1518
Boston, MA 02116

Phone: (617) 534-1500
Fax: (617) 534-1515
Toll Free: (800) 832-8321
E-mail: info@allthyroid.org
http://www.allthyroid.org

The Thyroid Foundation of America, Inc., (TFA) was established in 1985 as a national not-for-profit organization dedicated to providing support and information to affected individuals and healthcare professionals on all types of thyroid diseases. Thyroid diseases are a group of disorders of the thyroid gland typically involving overactivity of the thyroid (hyperthyroidism) or underactivity of the thyroid (hypothyroidism). TFA currently consists of three chapters and interest groups and approximately 2,000 members. The goals of the foundation include increasing public awareness of thyroid diseases and lending moral support to affected individuals and their families. TFA produces a variety of educational materials including a quarterly newsletter, "The Bridge," brochures, and reprints of medical articles.

President: Lawrence C. Wood, M.D. (1985 to Present)
Executive Director: Judy Pate
Year Established: 1985
Acronym: TFA

Keywords
Autoimmune Polyendocrine Syndrome Type II; Autoimmune Thyroiditis; Graves' Disease; Hashimoto's Syndrome; Hyperthyroidism; Hypoparathyroidism; Hypothyroidism; Nodules; Sheehan Syndrome; TFA; Thyroid Cancer, Follicular; Thyroid Cancer, Papillary; Thyroid Diseases; Thyroid Foundation of America, Inc.; Thyroiditis; Thyroiditis, Postpartum

2218 Thyroid Foundation of Canada
797 Princess Street
Kingston
Ontario, K7L 5J7, Canada

Phone: (613) 544-8364
Fax: (613) 544-9731
Toll Free: ((8) 00)-267
E-mail: thyroid@kos.net
http://www.thyroid.ca

The Thyroid Foundation of Canada (TFC) was founded in 1980 as a not-for-profit organization in response to the needs of affected individuals and their families for more information and support on all forms of thyroid diseases. Thyroid diseases are a group of disorders of the thyroid gland typically involving overactivity of the thyroid (hyperthyroidism) or underactivity of the thyroid (hypothyroidism). TFC has 22 chapters and 4,200 members. The aims of the foundation are to increase public interest in, and awareness of, thyroid diseases; lend moral support to individuals and families affected by thyroid disease; and assist in fundraising for thyroid disease research. TFC publishes a quarterly newsletter entitled "Thyrobulletin" and other patient-directed educational material. In addition, it conducts public education meetings with medical experts, and raises funds for thyroid disease research.

President: Ted Hawkins
Executive Director: Katherine Keen
Year Established: 1980

Keywords
Cancer, Anaplastic; Cancer, Follicular; Cancer, Medullary; Cancer, Papillary; Goiter; Goiter, Multinodular; Graves Hyperthyroidism; Graves Ophthalmopathy; Hyperparathyroidism; Hyperthyroidism; Hypothyroidism; Hypothyroidism, Congenital; Lymphoma; Parathyroidism; Thyroid Cancer; Thyroid Foundation of Canada; Thyroiditis; Thyroiditis, Hashimoto's; Thyroiditis, Postpartum; Thyroiditis, Silent; Thyroiditis, Subacute; de Quervain's Disease

2219 TMJ Association, Ltd.
P.O. Box 26770
Milwaukee, WI 53226-0770

Phone: (414) 259-3223
Fax: (414) 259-8112
E-mail: info@tmj.org
http://www.tmj.org

The TMJ (Temporomandibular Joint) Association, Ltd., is a national, not-for-profit, voluntary organization that promotes awareness of temporomandibular joint disorders and provides information and support for people with TMJ disorders and their families through the development of a national network of members. The mission of the TMJ Association is to improve the care and treatment of those affected by TMJ diseases/disorders through fostering research and education, with the ultimate aim of preventing these craniofacial problems. In addition, the association promotes research into the causes of TMJ and the development of safe and effective treatments. Established in 1986, the association has provided testimony to a special National Institute of Dental Research panel and played an instrumental role in NIH's utilization of a multi-institute approach to basic research of temporomandibular joint disorders. Additional testimony before the Senate Appropriations Committee played a vital role in the creation of an intensive educational program for medical professionals and the public, and the stimulation of controlled scientific research into the nature of the disorder. In addition, the association was instrumental in notifying the national media about the Vitek implant recall and creating a TMJ implant registry. The association publishes a quarterly newsletter that keeps readers updated on current research and medical, legal, legislative, and insurance issues; the newsletter also provides a forum for sharing ideas and asking questions. In addition, the TMJ Association provides informational brochures and pamphlets.

President: Terrie Cowley (1991-Present)
Year Established: 1986
Acronym: TMJA

Keywords
Jaw Pain; Temporomandibular Joint Disorder; Temporomandibular Joint Dysfunction; TMD; TMJ; TMJ Association, Ltd.

2220 Tom Wahlig Foundation—JENA
Veghestrasse 22
Muenster, 48149, Germany

Phone: +49 (0) 251-2007-9120
Fax: +49 (0) 251-2007-9122
E-mail: info@fsp-info.de
http://www.fsp-info.de

The Tom Wahlig Foundation is an independent welfare foundation whose aim is to support research in the field of familial spastic spinal paralysis as well as provide support for patients and families affected by this disease. Familial spastic spinal paralysis refers to a group of rare inherited neurological spinal cord disorders characterized by progressive weakness (paraplegia) and increased muscle tone and stiffness (spasticity) of leg muscles. Serving people in Germany, the UK, France and Austria, the foundation will sponsor symposiums to support researchers.

President: Dr. Tom Wahlig
Executive Director: Christel Meier
Year Established: 1998

Keywords
Paraparesis, Familial Spastic; Paraparesis, Hereditary Spasmodic; Paraplegia; Spastic Paraparesis; Spasticity; Strumpell's Familial Paraplegia; Tom Wahlig Foundation— JENA

2221   Tourette Syndrome Association, Inc.

42-40 Bell Boulevard
Suite 205
Bayside, NY 11361-2820

Phone: (718) 224-2999
Fax: (718) 279-9596
Toll Free: (888) 486-8738
E-mail: ts@tsa-usa.org
http://www.tsa-usa.org

The Tourette Syndrome Association, Inc. (TSA) is a national, nonprofit organization dedicated to serving the needs of individuals affected by Tourette syndrome and their families. Tourette syndrome (TS) is a hereditary neurologic movement disorder characterized by repetitive motor and vocal tics. Symptoms may include involuntary movement of the extremities, shoulders, and face accompanied by uncontrollable sounds and/or inappropriate words. Symptoms tend to be variable and follow a chronic waxing and waning course. TSA's mission is to identify the cause, find a cure, and control the effects of Tourette syndrome. To this end, TSA facilitates a research grant award program and is guided by both a volunteer national medical advisory board and a scientific advisory board. The association produces a variety of educational materials including brochures, a quarterly newsletter, and videotapes. In addition, TSA maintains a crisis hotline, provides physician referral listings, and engages in patient advocacy.

President: Judit Ungar (2003)
Executive Director: Monte N. Redman, Chairman
Year Established: 1972
Acronym: TSA

Keywords
Advocacy; Chronic Tics; Giles de la Tourette Disease; Obsessive Compulsive Disorder; TS; TSA; Tourette Syndrome; Tourette Syndrome Association, Inc.

2222   Tourette Syndrome Foundation of Canada

206-194 Jervis Street
Toronto, Ontario, M5B 2B7, Canada

Phone: (416) 861-8398
Fax: (416) 861-2472
Toll Free: (800) 361-3120
E-mail: tsfc@tourette.ca
http://www.tourette.ca

The Tourette Syndrome Foundation of Canada (TSFC) is a national, voluntary health organization dedicated to providing support and information to Canadian families affected by Tourette syndrome. Tourette syndrome (TS) is a hereditary neurologic movement disorder characterized by repetitive motor and vocal tics. Symptoms may include involuntary movements of the extremities, shoulders, and face accompanied by uncontrollable sounds and/or inappropriate words. Symptoms tend to be variable and follow a chronic waxing and waning course. TSFC's mission is to help families affected by Tourette syndrome by gathering and distributing information about the disorder; promoting local self-help and professional services; and stimulating and funding research into the cause, treatment, and potential cure of TS. TSFC organizes workshops and symposiums for healthcare professionals; develops and maintains lists of physicians who diagnose and treat TS; and supports the Brain Bank Program and collaborates with other agencies dealing with neurological disorders. The foundation publishes a tri-annual newsletter entitled "The Green Leaflet" and provides brochures, pamphlets, reports, and audiovisual aids.

President: William Radford (2001-present)
Executive Director: Rosie Wartecker
Year Established: 1976
Acronym: TSFC

Keywords
ADD; ADHD; Attention Deficit Disorder; Attention Deficit Hyperactivity Disorder; Brissaud's II; Chronic Motor Tic; Chronic Multiple Tics; Coprolalia Generalized Tic Disorder; Giles de la Tourette Disease; Giles de la Tourette Syndrome; Habit Spasms; Maladie de Tics; Obsessive Compulsive Disorder; OCD;

Passing Tics of Childhood; Tics; Tourette Disorder; Tourette Syndrome; Tourette Syndrome Foundation of Canada; Transient Tics of Childhood; TS

2223 Tracheo Oesophageal Fistula Support Group (TOFS)

St. George's Centre
91 Victory Road
Netherfield
Nottingham, NG4 2NN, United Kingdom

Phone: +44 (0) 115-961-3092
Fax: +44 (0) 115-961-3097
E-mail: office@tofs.org.uk
http://www.tofs.org.uk

The Tracheo Oesophageal Fistula Support Group (TOFS) is an international, voluntary organization dedicated to providing information and support to parents who have a child born with tracheo-esophogeal fistula (TOF). In TOF, a section of the baby's throat is abnormally joined to the windpipe (esophagus) making it difficult for food and saliva to pass into the stomach. Established in 1982, TOFS consists of a family membership and a national network of volunteers, all of whom are parents of children with TOF. The support group receives calls from affected families and professionals; maintains contact with sister organizations in other countries; and maintains a databank of information on matters such as feeding problems, tube feeding, and financial assistance. A video has been produced that explains the condition and the problems affecting children with TOF. In addition, TOFS raises funds to support its own work, to purchase equipment for hospitals and individuals, and to finance research. Support groups for affected individuals, family members, and healthcare professionals are provided along with educational materials. A national conference for members and professionals is organized every two years. Fund-raising is undertaken to assist hospitals to purchase specialized equipment.

President: Gren Shepherd
Executive Director: Christine Sherterd (Secretary)
Year Established: 1982
Acronym: TOFS

Keywords
Down Syndrome; Esophageal Stricture; Gastro-esophageal Reflux; TOFS; Tracheo Oesophageal Fistula Support Group (TOFS); VATER Association

2224 Transverse Myelitis Association

1787 Sutter Parkway
Powell, OH 43065-8806

Phone: (614) 766-1806
E-mail: ssiegel@myelitis.org
http://www.myelitis.org

The Transverse Myelitis Association (TMA) is a not-for-profit, self-help organization dedicated to providing mutual support to persons affected by transverse myelitis. Transverse myelitis is an acute spinal cord inflammation involving both sides of the spinal cord. Transverse myelitis is part of a spectrum of neuroimmunologic diseases of the central nervous system. Other disorders in this spectrum include acute disseminated encephalomyelitis (ADEM), optic neuritis and neuromyelitis Optica (Devic's disease). The TMA was established in 1994 as an organization dedicated to advocacy for those who have these rare neuroimmunologic diseases. The TMA facilitates support and networking opportunities among families, supports and conducts workshops involving both professionals and patients for the exchange of information regarding research and treatment strategies. The association also offers appropriate referrals; engages in patient and professional education; and serves as a clearinghouse of information on transverse myelitis, offering a variety of reports and brochures. TMA has members in over 80 countries around the world. A member directory is available to find members to offer information and support to patients.

President: Sanford J. Siegel (President)
Year Established: 1994
Acronym: TMA

Keywords
Acute Disseminated Encephalomyelitis; ADEM; Devic's Disease; Neuromyelitis Optica; NMO; Optic Neuritis; Transverse Myelitis; Transverse Myelitis Association

2225 TransWeb

Northern Brewery Building
1327 Jones Drive
Suite 201
Ann Arbor, MI 48105

Phone: (734) 998-7314
Fax: (734) 998-8333
E-mail: transweb@umich.edu
http://www.transweb.org

TransWeb (www.transweb.org) is a free educational resource on the internet dedicated to providing information concerning organ transplantation and donation. Its goals include providing a resource for transplant patients and families worldwide with information specifically dealing with transplant issues and problems; providing an index of sources for transplant-related information; available through the Internet and otherwise; and providing information about organ donation and transplantation to the general public in order to improve organ and tissue procurement efforts worldwide.

Executive Director: Eleanor Jones (Editor)
Year Established: 1995
Acronym: TransWeb

Keywords
Antirejection Medications; Barth Syndrome; Organ Donation; Transplant Games; Transplantation Centers, Organ; Transplantation, Organ; TransWeb; TransWeb: All About Transplantation and Donation; Webcast

2226 Treacher Collins Foundation

P.O. Box 683
Norwich, VT 05055-0683

Phone: (802) 649-3050
Toll Free: (800) 823-2055
E-mail: tcnet@geocities.com
http://www.treachercollinsfnd.org

The Treacher Collins Foundation is an organization of families, individuals, and medical professionals who are interested in developing and sharing knowledge and experiences about Treacher Collins syndrome and related conditions. A national voluntary health organization, the foundation seeks to support, inform and network families and individuals with these conditions and to serve as a resource for current information about Treacher Collins syndrome. Established in 1988, the Treacher Collins Foundation provides medical referrals, educational materials and information on other service providers who are familiar with Treacher Collins syndrome. Recognizing the value of mutual peer support, the foundation cites networking as a primary goal and promotes medical research.

President: David Drazin, Ph.D.
Executive Director: Hope Charkins M.S.W.
Year Established: 1988
Acronym: TCF

Keywords
Francheschetti Klein Syndrome; Mandibulofacial Dysostosis; Networking; TCF; Treacher Collins Foundation; Treacher Collins Francheschetti Syndrome 1; Treacher Collins Syndrome

2227 Trichotillomania Learning Center

303 Potrero Street
Suite 51
Santa Cruz, CA 95060

Phone: (831) 457-1004
Fax: (831) 426-4383
E-mail: info@trich.org
http://www.trich.org/home/default.asp

The Trichotillomania Learning Center (TLC) is a national, nonprofit organization designed to provide information, support and referrals regarding the experience and treatment of trichotillomania (compulsive hair pulling). TLC's educational resources are available to people with TTM, their friends and families, therapeutic professionals, educators, and anyone with an interest in the subject. TLC's mission is to raise public awareness, maintain a support network and referral base, and raise funds for research to find a cure for trichotillomania.

Executive Director: Christina Pearson (1990 - Present)
Year Established: 1990
Acronym: TLC

Keywords
Body Dysmorphic Disorder; Hair Pulling Syndrome; Obsessive Compulsive Disorder; OCD; Trichotillomania; Trichotillomania Learning Center

2228 Trigeminal Neuralgia Association (TNA)

2801 SW Archer Road
Gainesville, FL 32608

Phone: (352) 376-9955
Fax: (352) 376-8688
Toll Free: (800) 923-3608
E-mail: tnanational@tna-support.org
http://www.tna-support.org

The Trigeminal Neuralgia Association (TNA) is a national, not-for-profit organization dedicated to providing information, mutual aid, support, and encouragement to people with trigeminal neuralgia (TN) and their families. Trigeminal neuralgia (or tic douloureux) is a disorder of the trigeminal (fifth) cranial nerve that causes intense, episodic pain in facial areas connected to the trigeminal nerve. Founded in 1990, TNA is also committed to increasing public and professional awareness of the disorder and reducing the isolation of those affected. The organization serves as a resource and information clearinghouse for data and medical efforts on behalf of treatment for TN. It also encourages medical research into the causes and treatments for this disorder. The association's Medical Advisory Board consists of key specialists in the medical and surgical treatment of TN, dentistry, and pain management. TNA also has a network of local support groups that enable affected individuals to share experiences, receive encouragement, and obtain current information on the disorder's treatment. In addition, the association promotes patient advocacy and conducts an educational outreach program to medical and dental practitioners, and in addition, to the general public.

President: Michael G. Pasternak PhD (2003)
Executive Director: Jane Boles
Year Established: 1990
Acronym: TNA

Keywords
Advocacy; Fothergill Disease; Networking; Parry Romberg Syndrome; Support Groups; Tic Douloureux; TN; TNA; Trigeminal Neuralgia; Trigeminal Neuralgia Association; Trigeminal Neuralgia Association (TNA)

2229 Triple X Support Group

32 Francemary Road
Brockley
London, SE4 1JS, United Kingdom

Phone: +44 (0) 208-690-9445
E-mail: helenclements@hotmail.com
http://www.triplo-x.org

The Triple X Support Group is a voluntary, self-help organization dedicated to providing support, resources, and informational materials to parents of children with triple X syndrome. Also known as trisomy X or 47, XXX syndrome, triple X syndrome is a chromosomal disorder that affects females. Females normally have two X chromosomes; however, females with triple X syndrome carry three X chromosomes in cells of the body. Associated symptoms and findings may vary greatly from case to case. Whereas some affected females have very few associated symptoms, others may have physical abnormalities, delayed speech and motor skills, learning disabilities, and/or behavioral abnormalities. The Triple X Support Group was established in 1997 and currently consists of 290 families. The group provides reprints from the medical literature concerning triple X syndrome as well as brochures that describe the chromosomal disorder in lay terminology. The organization also puts affected families in touch with one another, promoting the exchange of mutual support, experiences, information, and resources.

President: Helen Clements (Contact Person)
Executive Director: Same as above.
Year Established: 1997

Keywords
Triple X Support Group; Triplo; Trisomy X

2230 Trisomy 9 International Parent Support (9TIPS)

Alice Todd
4027 E. Piedmont Drive
Highland, CA 92346

Phone: (909) 862-4470
E-mail: atoddna@sprynet.com

Trisomy 9 International Parent Support (9TIPS) is a not-for-profit group of parents dedicated to assisting families who have children with trisomy 9. Chromosomal disorders included are trisomy 9p, trisomy 9 mosaic, trisomy 9q, partial trisomy 9, and other complex chromosomal abnormalities involving extra chromosomal material from chromosome 9. The organization offers an international mutual parent support network for the purposes of information exchange and emotional support. The network also informs parents of any medical professionals who are familiar with these rare chromosomal disorders. Members may participate in the 9TIPS Listserv E-mail list. The contact for that list is blrosenfeld@gmx.net.

President: Alice Todd
Year Established: 1992
Acronym: 9-Tips

Keywords
9TIPS; Chromosome 9, Tetrasomy 9p; Chromosome 9, Trisomy 9p (Multiple Variants); Chromosome 9, Trisomy Mosaic; Trisomy; Trisomy 9 International Parent Support (9TIPS)

2231   Trisomy 12p Parent Support Organization

175 Lawndale Road
Mansfield, MA 02048

Phone: (508) 339-1680
Fax: (508) 339-0504
E-mail: maguirecb@comcast.net

The Trisomy 12p Parent Support Organization is an international, not-for-profit, self-help organization dedicated to providing information, assistance, and support to families of individuals with trisomies of the short arm (p) of chromosome 12 or other abnormalities involving the 12th chromosome. Chromosome 12, trisomy 12p, is an extremely rare chromosomal disorder in which a portion of the short arm of the 12th chromosome (12p) appears three times (trisomy) rather than twice in cells of the body. The disorder may be characterized by abnormal growth delays after birth (postnatal growth retardation); delays in the acquisition of skills requiring the coordination of mental and muscular activity (psychomotor retardation); mental retardation; abnormally diminished muscle tone (hypotonia); characteristic malformations of the head and facial (craniofacial) area; abnormally short, wide hands; and/or other abnormalities. Associated symptoms and physical findings may vary from case to case, depending upon the exact length and location of the duplicated portion of chromosome 12p. Established in 1997, the Trisomy 12p Parent Support Organization provides networking opportunities that enable affected families to exchange information, support, and helpful resources.

President: Carole Maguire
Year Established: 1997

Keywords
Chromosome 12p+; Duplication Chromosome 12p; Trisomy 12p; Trisomy 12p Parent Support Organization

2232   Tuberous Sclerosis Alliance

801 Roeder Rd
Suite 750
Silver Spring, MD 20910-4467, US

Phone: (301) 562-9890
Fax: (301) 562-9870
Toll Free: (800) 225-6872
E-mail: info@tsalliance.org
http://www.tsalliance.org

Tuberous Sclerosis Alliance, formerly the National Tuberous Sclerosis Association, is a voluntary not-for-profit organization dedicated to finding a cure for tuberous sclerosis complex (TSC) while improving the lives of those afflicted. TSC (tuberous sclerosis complex) is a genetic disorder that causes tumors to form in various organs, primarily the brain, heart, kidney, liver, skin and lungs. People with TSC often develop epilepsy, autism and learning and behavioral problems. The TS Alliance is committed to promoting and sponsoring medical research related to the diagnosis, cause, management, and cure of TS, and ensuring that affected individuals and families have access to appropriate medical services, support services, and resource information. It is involved in the development of public and professional educational programs aimed at increasing awareness of TS and prompting early diagnosis and effective treatment.

Executive Director: Nancy Taylor (CEO)
Year Established: 1974
Acronym: TS Alliance

Keywords
National Tuberous Sclerosis Association; TS; TS Alliance; TSC; Tuberous Sclerosis; Tuberous Sclerosis Alliance; Tuberous Sclerosis Complex

2233   Tuberous Sclerosis Association (UK)

P.O. Box 9644
Bromsgrove, B61 0FP, United Kingdom

Phone: +44 (0) 1527-87-1898
Fax: +44 (0) 1527-57-9452
E-mail: support@tuberous-sclerosis.org
http://www.tuberous-sclerosis.org

The Tuberous Sclerosis Association (TSA), an international, self-help organization located in the United Kingdom, was established in 1977 by a group of parents and interested physicians dedicated to providing support to individuals with tuberous sclerosis (TS) and their families, increasing awareness of the disorder, and promoting fundraising to support research. Tuberous sclerosis, a rare genetic disorder that affects the skin and nervous system, may be characterized by the development of white skin patches, red or brown birthmarks, and/or a characteristic facial rash across the cheeks and nose; developmental delays; episodes of uncontrolled electrical disturbances in the brain that cause convulsive seizures (epilepsy); mental retardation in some cases; and/or the development of benign tumors, particularly of the brain, retina, kidney, heart, and skin. The Tuberous Sclerosis Association has helped to establish specialist, multidisciplinary TS clinics in Leeds, Bath, Cambridge, Northern Ireland (Craigavon), and Scotland (Edinburgh). The TSA also supports and promotes research into the causes and management of TS through its Education and Research Fund; is in touch with over 1,000 affected families worldwide; and offers networking opportunities to affected families that enable them to exchange information, support, and resources.

President: Janet Medcalf (Head of Support Services)
Executive Director: Same as above.
Year Established: 1977
Acronym: TSA

Keywords
Bourneville Pringle Syndrome; Epiloia; Phakomatosis TS; TSC1; TSC2; Tuberous Sclerosis; Tuberous Sclerosis Association; Tuberous Sclerosis Association (UK); Tuberous Sclerosis Complex

2234 Tuberous Sclerosis Canada (Sclerose Tubereuse)

140 Green Briar Road
Alliston
Ontario, L9R 1Y1, Canada

Toll Free: (800) 347-0252
E-mail: keepsinging@sympatico.ca
http://www.tscst.org

Tuberous Sclerosis Canada or Sclerose Tubereuse (TSCST) is a not-for-profit organization dedicated to raising public awareness of tuberous sclerosis complex (TSC); encouraging mutual support between families affected by TSC; and promoting research and education. TSC is a congenital disease characterized by certain skin abnormalities and birthmarks, tuber-like growths in the eyes, the brain, heart, kidneys, and other internal organs, and varying severity of epilepsy and mental retardation. Established in 1990, TSCST facilitates a self-help network in which families affected by tuberous sclerosis support one another by telephone and share information about local services that may be available. Educational materials are available in French and English.

President: Bud Renshaw
Year Established: 1990
Acronym: TSCST

Keywords
Bourneville Pringle Syndrome; Epiloia; Phakomatosis TS; TSC1; TSC2; Tuberous Sclerosis; Tuberous Sclerosis Canada; Tuberous Sclerosis Canada (Sclerose Tubereuse); Tuberous Sclerosis Complex

2235 Turner Syndrome Society of the United States

14450 TC Jester
Suite 260
Houston, TX 77014

Phone: (832) 249-9988
Fax: (832) 249-9987
Toll Free: (800) 365-9944
E-mail: tssus@turner-syndrome-us.org
http://www.turner-syndrome-us.org

Established in 1988, the Turner Syndrome Society of the United States is a national not-for-profit self-help organization dedicated to increasing awareness and understanding of Turner syndrome and providing an active networking program for affected individuals. Turner syndrome is a rare chromosomal disorder in females that is characterized by the absence or abnormalities of one X chromosome. Symptoms may include short stature, lack of sexual development at puberty, a webbed neck, heart defects, and/or other abnormalities. The society makes referrals to appropriate support and treatment centers, and promotes the continuing education of physicians and other healthcare professionals. In addition, the organization supports ongoing medical research and enables individuals with Turner syndrome to exchange information, support, and resources through its networking program. The Turner Syndrome Society also offers a variety of educational materials including a regular newsletter, audiovisual aids and brochures.

President: Andy Rickman
Executive Director: Merriott Terry
Year Established: 1988

Keywords
45 X Syndrome; Bonnevie Ulrich Syndrome; Morgagni Turner Albright Syndrome; Turner Syndrome; Turner Syndrome Society of the United States; Turner Varny Syndrome; Turner's Syndrome Society of the United States; XO Syndrome

2236 Turner Syndrome Support Society (UK)

12 Irving Quandrant
Hardgate, Clydebank, G81 6AZ, Scotland

Phone: +44 (0) 1389-38-0385
Fax: +44 (0) 1389-38-0384
E-mail: Turner.Syndrome@tss.org.uk
http://www.tss.org.uk

The Turner Syndrome Support Society, based in the United Kingdom, offers support and information to patients, families and friends who have been affected by Turner syndrome. Turner syndrome is a rare chromosomal disorder of females characterized by short stature and the lack of sexual development at puberty. The society works with relevant specialists to promote education and understanding of the management of Turner syndrome. It encourages research into all aspects of this syndrome, including medical, psychological and educational.

President: Mrs Lynne Morris-Chairman (2002-present)
Executive Director: Arlene Smyth
Year Established: 1999
Acronym: TSSS

Keywords
Syndrome Support Society (UK); Reserach

2237 Turner's Syndrome Society

21 Blackthorn Avenue
Toronto
Ontario, M6N 3H4, Canada

Phone: (416) 781-2086
Fax: (416) 781-7245
Toll Free: (800) 465-6744
E-mail: tssincan@web.net
http:// www.turnersyndrome.ca

The Turner's Syndrome Society is a non-profit charitable organization dedicated to improving the quality of life for individuals and families affected by Turner's syndrome. Turner's syndrome is a rare chromosomal disorder that affects 1 in approximately 2,500 females. Females normally have two X chromosomes. However, in those with Turner's syndrome, one X chromosome is absent or is damaged. Affected females may exhibit short stature, webbing of the neck, absence of secondary sexual development, infertility, and/or other abnormalities. Established in 1981, the Turner's Syndrome Society provides support services and disseminates up-to-date medical information to affected families, physicians and other healthcare professionals, and the general public.

President: Pamela McKane
Executive Director: Sandi Hofbauer
Year Established: 1981
Acronym: TSS

Keywords
45 X Syndrome; Bonnevie Ulrich Syndrome; Chromosome X Monosomy X; Gonadal Dysgenesis (45X); Gonadal Dysgenesis (XO); Monosomy X; Morgagni Turner Albright Syndrome; Ovarian Dwarfism,

Turner Type; Ovary Aplasia, Turner Type; Schereshevkii Turner Syndrome; Turner Syndrome; Turner Varny Syndrome; Turner's Syndrome Society

2238 Twin to Twin Transfusion Syndrome Foundation

National Office
411 Longbeach Parkway
Bay Village, OH 44140

Phone: (440) 899-8887
Fax: (440) 899-1184
Toll Free: (800) 815-9211
E-mail: info@tttsfoundation.org
http://www.tttsfoundation.com

The Twin to Twin Transfusion Syndrome Foundation is a national, voluntary, not-for-profit organization dedicated to providing educational, emotional, and financial support to families, caregivers, and medical professionals before, during, and after pregnancies diagnosed with twin to twin transfusion syndrome (TTTS). Twin to twin transfusion syndrome is a rare disorder that affects identical twins during pregnancy when blood passes unequally from one fetus to the other through connecting blood vessels in their shared placenta. Established in 1989, the foundation is dedicated to educating families, health care professionals, and the general public about TTTS and the latest available treatments. It supports medical research on TTTS and related complications, is working to develop a national registry of all TTTS pregnancies, promotes patient and family advocacy; offers financial assistance through corporate sponsors to affected families who require treatment; and provides a referral network.

President: Mary Slaman-Forsythe (1992-Present)
Executive Director: Linda DeAngelis
Year Established: 1989

Keywords
Twin to Twin Transfusion Syndrome; Twin to Twin Transfusion Syndrome Foundation

2239 UCP (United Cerebral Palsy Associations, Inc.)

1660 L Street NW
Suite 700
Washington, D.C. 20036-5602

Phone: (202) 776-0406
Fax: (202) 776-0414
Toll Free: (800) 872-5827
TDD: (202) 973-7197
E-mail: national@ucp.org
http://www.ucp.org

UCP (United Cerebral Palsy Associations, Inc.) provides information on cerebral palsy and advocacy for the rights of persons with any disability. UCP's mission is to advance the independence, productivity and full citizenship of people with cerebral palsy and other disabilities. Cerebral palsy is a neurological movement disorder characterized by lack of muscle control and impairment in the coordination of movement. Located in Washington, DC, UCP's national office provides key services for its affiliates and also serves people with disabilities through an information and referral service, legislative advocacy, technology initiatives, and research. Direct service provision for people with disabilities and their families is offered through UCP affiliates, who serve more than 30,000 children and adults with disabilities and their families every day through programs such as therapy, assistive technology training, early intervention programs, individual and family support, social and recreation programs, community living, state and local referrals, employment assistance and advocacy. Each affiliate offers a range of services tailored to its community's needs.

President: Stephen Bennett
Year Established: 1949
Acronym: UCP

Keywords
Cerebral Palsy; Disabled; CP; Special Education; UCP; UCP National; UCP (United Cerebral Palsy Associations, Inc.); UCPA; United Cerebral Palsy; United Cerebral Palsy Association

2240   UNIQUE—Rare Chromosome Disorder Support Group
P.O. Box 2189
Caterham
Surrey, CR3 5GN, United Kingdom

Phone: +44 (0) 1883-33-0766
Fax: +44 (0) 1883-33-0766
E-mail: info@rarechromo.org
http://www.rarechromo.org

UNIQUE—The Rare Chromosome Disorder Support Group is a not-for-profit, voluntary organization dedicated to promoting awareness of rare chromosomal abnormalities. The organization was founded in 1984 and served as a source of support and information for anyone affected by any rare chromosome abnormality. UNIQUE acts as an international support group; produces a newsletter for registered members; and promotes awareness of rare chromosomal abnormalities, both among the public and relevant professionals. It main-

tains a database holding the karyotypes, phenotypes and natural histories of all affected members.

Executive Director: Beverly Searle, Ph.D. (Development Officer)
Year Established: 1984
Acronym: UNIQUE

Keywords
Aneuploidy; Balanced translocations; Chromosomal Abnormalities; Chromosomal Inversions; Duplications; Insertions; Monosomy; Rare Chromosome Abnormalities; Rare sex chromosome aneuploidy; Ring chromosomes; Robertsonian translocations; Trisomy; Unbalanced translocations; UNIQUE—Rare Chromosome Disorder Support Group

2241   United Brachial Plexus Network (UBPN)
1610 Kent Street
Kent, OH 44240

Fax: (866) 877-7004
Toll Free: (866) 877-7004
E-mail: info@ubpn.org
http://www.ubpn.org

The United Brachial Plexus Network is a registered non-profit 501 3 organization devoted to providing information, support and leadership for families and those concerned with brachial plexus injuries worldwide. Available resources include a website, online registry, Resource Directory, Prevention Program, and various outreach and awareness programs. UBPN works toward the prevention of brachial plexus injuries, and to educate medical and legal personnel, public officials, and the general public on issues surrounding these injuries. The brachial plexus refers to a bundle of nerves that conduct impulses from the spinal cord to the muscles of the arm and hand. This injury most often occurs at birth. Approximately 2-3 of every 1,000 newborns are affected by brachial plexus birth injuries. Other frequent causes include automobile, motorcycle, and boating accidents; sports injuries; animal bites; and gunshot or puncture wounds.

President: Nancy Birk
Year Established: 1999
Acronym: UBPN

Keywords
Brachial Plexus Palsy; Erb's Palsy; Klumpke's Palsy; UBPN; United Brachial Plexus Network; United Brachial Plexus Network (UBPN)

2242 United Leukodystrophy Foundation

2304 Highland Drive
Sycamore, IL 60178

Phone: (815) 895-3211
Fax: (815) 895-2432
Toll Free: (800) 728-5483
E-mail: office@ulf.org
http://www.ulf.org/

The United Leukodystrophy Foundation (ULF) is a voluntary, not-for-profit organization dedicated to helping children and adults with leukodystrophy and assisting the family members, caregivers, and professionals who serve them. Leukodystrophy is a group of rare, progressive diseases that affect the white matter of the brain. Established in 1982, the United Leukodystrophy Foundation is committed to the identification, treatment, and cure of all leukodystrophies through programs of education, advocacy, research, and service. The foundation also provides appropriate referrals, including support groups; promotes professional and patient education; and offers a variety of educational and support materials. These include a regular newsletter, brochures, and audiovisual aids.

President: Paula Brazeal (1984-Present)
Executive Director: Ron Brazeal
Year Established: 1982
Acronym: ULF

Keywords
Adrenoleukodystrophy; Adrenoleukodystrophy, Neonatal; Adrenomyeloneuropathy; Advocacy; Aicardi Goutieres Syndrome; Alexander's Disease; ARSA; Arylsulfatase A Deficiency; Axialis Extracorticales Congenita; Balo Disease; Bowen Syndrome; CACH; CADASIL; Canavan's Disease; Carbohydrate Deficient Glycoprotein Syndrome Type Ia; Cerebral Autosomal Dominant Arteriopathy with Subcortical Infarcts and Leukoencephalopathy; Cerebrohepatorenal Syndrome; Childhood Ataxia and Central Hypomeylination; Galactocerebrosidase Deficiency; Galactosialidosis; Gangliosidosis; Glycoprotein, Carbohydrate Deficient; Greenfield Disease; Hallervorden Spatz Disease; Infantile Neuroaxonal Dystrophy; Leukodystrophy; Leuko-dystrophy, Globoid; Leukodystrophy, Krabbe; Leukodystrophy, Megalencephalic; Leukodystrophy, Metachromatic; Leukodystrophy, Neuroaxonal; Leukodystrophy, Sudanophilic; Leukoencephalopathy; Lipidosis, Sulfatide; Lysosomal Storage Diseases; Mitochondrial Disease; Mucolipidosis; Mucopolysaccharidosis; Multiple Sulfatase Deficiency; Ovarioleukodystrophy; Pelizaeus Merzbacher Brain Sclerosis; Peroxisomal Disorders;

Refsum Disease; Refsum Disease, Infantile; Schindler's Disease; Sclerosis, Diffusa Family Brain; Sclerosis, Diffuse Cerebral; Seitelberger Disease; Spastic Paraparesis; Sphingolipidosis; Sulfatidosis; Support Groups; ULF; United Leukodystrophy Foundation; Van Bogart Bertrand Syndrome; Van Der Knaap Singh Disease; Vanishing White Matter Disorder; White Matter Disorders of Unknown Origin; Xanthomatosis, Cerebrotendinous; Zellweger Syndrome

2243 United Mitochondrial Disease Foundation

8085 Saltsburg Road
Suite 201
Pittsburgh, PA 15239

Phone: (412) 793-8077
Fax: (412) 793-6477
E-mail: info@umdf.org
http://www.umdf.org

The United Mitochondrial Disease Foundation (UMDF) is a voluntary, not-for-profit organization dedicated to providing education and support to individuals diagnosed with, or suspected of having, mitochondrial diseases. Established in 1995, the UMDF is dedicated to promoting research for cures and treatments of mitochondrial disorders and to providing support to affected families. In addition, the foundation networks with research professionals and alerts affected individuals and family members to upcoming clinical studies and their required protocols. The United Mitochondrial Disease Foundation provides educational and support materials to affected individuals, family members, and medical professionals through its computer database, directory, pamphlets, and regular newsletter. For education and support information, please contact UMDF, 8085 Saltsburg Road, Suite 201, Pittsburgh, PA 15239.

President: Charles A. Mohan, Jr.
Executive Director: Chris Rice
Year Established: 1995
Acronym: UMDF

Keywords
Alpers Syndrome; ATP Synthease Deficiency; Barth Syndrome; Beta Oxidation Defects; Cardiomyopathy Neutropenia Syndrome; Cardiomyopathy, Lethal Infantile; Carnitine Deficiency Syndromes; COX Deficiency; CPEO; Cytochrome C Oxidase Deficiency; Encephalomyelopathy, Subacute Necrotizing; Encephalopathy, Mitochondrial; Epilepsy, Myoclonic, and Ragged Red Fibers; Kearns Sayre Disease; Kreb

Cycle Defects; Lactic Acidosis; LCAD Deficiency; Leber's Hereditary Optic Neuropathy; Leigh's Disease; Long Chain Acyl CoA Dehydrogenase Deficiency; Luft Disease; MCAD; MELAS Syndrome; MERRF Syndrome; Mitochondrial Disorders; MNGIE; Medium Chain Acyl CoA Dehydrogenase Deficiency; Myoneurogastrointestinal Disorder and Encephalopathy; Myopathy, Mitochondrial; NADH CoQ Reductase Deficiency; NADH Dehydrogenase Deficiency; NARP; Neuropathy Ataxia and Retinitis Pigmentosa; Ophthalmoplegia, Chronic Progressive External; Pearson Syndrome; PEPCK Deficiency; PHD; Poliodystrophy, Progressive Infantile; Pyruvate Carboxylase Deficiency; Pyruvate Dehydrogenase Deficiency; Respiratory Chain Disorders; SCAD; Short Chain Acyl CoA Dehydrogenase Deficiency; Succinate Dehydrogenase Deficiency; Ubiquinone Cytochrome C Oxidoreductase Deficiency; United Mitochondrial Disease Foundation; Wolfram Syndrome

2244 United Ostomy Association of Canada

P.O. Box 825
50 Charles Street East
Toronto
Ontario, M4Y 2N7, Canada

Phone: (416) 595-5452
Fax: (416) 595-9924
Toll Free: (888) 969-9698
E-mail: info@ostomycanada.ca
http://www.ostomycanada.ca/

The United Ostomy Association (UOA) of Canada is a not-for-profit, volunteer-based organization dedicated to providing supportive and educational services to individuals who have or will have ostomies and engaging in advocacy efforts. An ostomy is a surgical procedure (e.g., colostomy, ileostomy, urostomy) in which an artificial opening (stoma) is formed in the abdominal wall to allow the passage of urine or intestinal contents. To fulfill its mission and objectives, the UOA engages in advocacy efforts on a national, provincial, community, and individual level; offers a variety of publications in English and French, including booklets, newsletters, and reference guides; and maintains a web site.

President: Patricia Cimmeck
Year Established: 1962
Acronym: UOA of Canada

Keywords
United Ostomy Association of Canada

2245 United States Costello Syndrome Family Network

244 Taos Road
Altadena, CA 91001-3953

Phone: (626) 569-6086
Fax: (626) 572-2380
E-mail: Ischoyer@adhs.org
www.costellokids.org.uk

United States Costello Syndrome Family Network (USCSFN), formerly the North American Costello Syndrome Family Network, is a voluntary rare disorder organization the mission of which is to raise awareness of Costello syndrome. This extremely rare disorder affects multiple organ systems of the body and is characterized by growth delays after birth, excessive loose skin on the neck and elsewhere, and other distinctive physical features. In addition to raising awareness, USCSFN is also dedicated to providing information, support and advocacy to families affected by this disorder. USCSFN supports and advocates for research on Costello syndrome.

President: Lisa Schoyer (2003-2005)
Year Established: 2001
Acronym: USCSFN

Keywords
United States Costello Syndrome Family Network

2146 University of Connecticut A.J. Pappanikou Center for Developmental Disabilities

263 Farmington Avenue
MC 6222
Farmington, CT 06030

Phone: (860) 679-1500
Fax: (860) 679-1571
Toll Free: (866) 623-1315
TDD: (860) 679-1502
E-mail: bruder@nso1.uchc.edu
http://www.uconnucedd.org

The University of Connecticut A.J. Pappanikou Center for Developmental Disabilities' mission is to work collaboratively to promote evidence-based practice and system change, and to provide information and support to benefit persons with disabilities and their families.

Executive Director: Mary Beth Bruder, PhD
Year Established: 1991

Keywords
Developmental Disabilities; Families Referral; University of Connecticut A.J. Pappanikou Center for Developmental Disabilities

2147   University Students with Autism and Asperger's Syndrome Web Site

E-mail: cns@dircon.co.uk
http://www.users.dircon.co.uk/~cns/index.html

The University Students with Autism and Asperger's Syndrome Web Site is dedicated to providing information, assistance, support, and resources to students with autism spectrum disorders such as Asperger's syndrome who are interested in, or are already obtaining, higher education. Asperger's syndrome, a neuropsychiatric disorder that usually is not recognized until early childhood, or, in some cases, later in life, is considered by some researchers a high functioning form of autism. The disorder may be characterized by poor motor skills, sensory- or information-processing difficulties in some areas, difficulty with social interactions, social withdrawal, and strong interest and functioning in certain educational areas. The University Students with Autism and Asperger's Syndrome Web Site provides a private online mailing list (ListServ) for students in higher education with high-functioning autism or Asperger's syndrome, parents, professionals, and others who are connected with students with HFA/AS. The site also provides listings of helpful books and articles.

Keywords
AS; Asperger Syndrome; Autism Spectrum Disorders; Autism, Asperger's Type; Autism, High Functioning; Dyspraxia; Financial Aid; HFA/AS; Hyperlexia; University Students with Autism and Asperger's Syndrome Web Site

2148   Ureterosigmoidostomy Association
690 Pleasant Hill Road
P.O. Box 392
Brunswick, ME 04011

Phone: (207) 725-2753
Fax: (320) 213-0729
E-mail: kascar@yahoo.com
http://www.theusa.org

The Ureterosigmoidostomy Association, a not-for-profit organization, provides a variety of services to raise awareness and the level of understanding of issues related to bladder extrophy (turning inside out) and bladder cancer. These services include patient advocacy; networking; support groups; a newsletter; support for research; education of patients, professionals, and the general public; and a registry.

President: Kitt A. Scarponi
Year Established: 1998
Acronym: The USA

Keywords
Bladder; Colon Cancer; Exstrophy; Ureterosigmoidostomy Association

2249   Vaincre Les Maladies Lysosomales
2 ter Avenue de Fance
Massy, 91300, France

Phone: +33 (0) 169-75-40-30
Fax: +33 (0) 160-11-15-83
E-mail: accueil@vml-asso.org
http://www.vml-asso.org

Vaincre Les Maladies Lysosomales is a voluntary, not-for-profit organization in France dedicated to providing information and support to individuals with lysosomal disorders and their families; improving the quality of life of affected individuals; and promoting and supporting research for these disorders (e.g., Pompe disease, the lipidoses, mucolipidoses, mucopolysaccharidoses, and glycoproteinoses). Established in 1990, Vaincre Les Maladies Lysosomales provides referrals to appropriate support groups; promotes public awareness campaigns; and offers informational conferences and weekend retreats for affected individuals, families, and healthcare professionals. Vaincre Les Maladies Lysosomales also offers a variety of educational materials to affected individuals, family members, and health care professionals including regular newsletters, brochures, books, and videos.

President: Jean Guy Duranceau
Executive Director: Eric Waroquet
Year Established: 1990
Acronym: Association VML

Keywords
Aspartylglucosaminidase Deficiency; Ceroid Lipofuscinosis; Cystinosis; Fabry Disease; Farber's Disease; Fucosidosis; Gaucher Disease; Glycoproteinoses; Hunter Syndrome; Hurler Syndrome; Hyperglycinemia, Nonketotic; I-Cell Disease; Landing's Disease; Leukodystrophy, Krabbe; Leukodystrophy, Metachromatic; Lipidosis; Lysosomal Storage Diseases; Man-

nosidosis; Maroteaux Lamy Syndrome; McArdle Disease; Morquio Syndrome; Mucolipidoses; Mucolipidosis II (I-Cell Disease); Mucolipidosis IV; Mucopolysaccharidoses; Multiple Sulfatase Deficiency; Niemann Pick Disease; Pompe Disease; Pseudo Hurler Polydystrophy; Sandhoff Disease; Sanfilippo Syndrome; Scheie Syndrome; Schindler Disease; Sialidase Deficiency; Sialidosis; Sly Syndrome; Tarui Disease; Tay Sach's Disease; Vaincre Les Maladies Lysosomales; Wolman's Disease

2250 Vascular Birthmarks Foundation

P.O. Box 106
Latham, NY 12110

Toll Free: (877) 823-4646
E-mail: hvbf@aol.com
http://www.birthmark.org

The Hemangioma and Vascular Birthmarks Foundation is a nonprofit organization of parents and professionals dedicated to providing information, assistance, and support to those affected by hemangiomas or other vascular birthmarks or tumors. Hemangiomas, the most common benign tumor affecting infants, are bluish or reddish flat or raised areas that are usually apparent at or within weeks after birth. Hemangiomas typically continue to grow for approximately one to two years and then begin a slow regression cycle. Vascular malformations are benign vascular lesions that are present at birth; however, in some cases, they may not become apparent for days, weeks, or even years after birth. Vascular malformations typically grow slowly and steadily throughout life with no regression cycle. The Hemangioma and Vascular Birthmarks Foundation is dedicated to educating physicians and other healthcare providers in the diagnosis and management of all vascular birthmarks; providing support, information, and referrals for all affected individuals; developing research projects concerning vascular birthmarks; and working toward the establishment of a uniform protocol for the diagnosis and treatment of vascular birthmarks.

Executive Director: Linda Rozell Shannon, M.S.
Year Established: 1994
Acronym: VBF

Keywords
Arteriovenous Malformations; Cardiofaciocutaneous Syndrome; Cavernous Hemangioma; Cutis Marmorata Telangiectatica Congenita; Hemangioma; Klippel Trenaunay Syndrome; Lymphatic Malformations; Port Wine Stain; Sturge Weber Syndrome; Vas-

cular Birthmarks; Vascular Birthmarks Foundation; Vascular Malformations; VBF

2251 Vascular Disease Foundation

1075 S. Yukon Street
Suite 320
Lakewood, CO 80226

Phone: (303) 898-0500
Fax: (303) 898-0200
Toll Free: (866) 723-4636
E-mail: info@vdf.org
http://www.vdf.org

The Vascular Disease Foundation was formed in 1998 to improve public recognition of the prevalence and seriousness of vascular disease, with an initial focus on increasing public awareness to improve prevention, diagnosis, and comprehensive treatment of peripheral arterial disease (PAD). The foundation disseminates educational information to the public, fosters vascular disease patient advocacy initiatives, and provides information to patients and to those at risk for development of common vascular disorders. PAD occurs because of blockages in the arteries in the legs, but it may also indicate that blockages are occurring in the arteries to the heart or brain. The Vascular Disease Foundation is increasing awareness and understanding of PAD and other vascular diseases for which early diagnosis and treatment may be very important.

President: Peter Gloviczki, MD
Executive Director: Sheryl Benjamin
Year Established: 1998
Acronym: VDF

Keywords
Aneurysm; Buerger's Disease; Claudication; Vascular Disease Foundation; Vascular Disease, Peripheral; Vascular Disorders

2252 VATER Connection, Inc.

1722 Yucca Lane
Emporia, KS 66801

Phone: (620) 342-6954
Fax: (620) 342-6954
E-mail: angie@vaterconnection.org
http://www.vaterconnection.org

The VATER Connection is a nonprofit organization founded by two mothers of children with VATER Association, a rare disorder that affects several organ systems of the body. "VATER," an acronym for the characteristic abnormalities associated with the disorder, stands for (V)ertebral defects, abnormalities of certain bones of the spinal column; (A)nal atresia/imperforate anus, absence or abnormal blockage of the anal opening; (T)racheo (E)sophageal defects, the presence of an abnormal connection (fistula) between the esophagus and the windpipe (trachea) and/or other malformations; and (R)enal and/or radial limb defects, malformation of the kidneys and/or abnormalities affecting the thumb side of the arm. In most cases, the disorder occurs randomly for unknown reasons (sporadically); however, some familial cases have been identified. The VATER Connection is dedicated to providing networking opportunities that enable affected families to exchange information, resources, and mutual support.

President: Angie Schreiber (Co-founder)
Year Established: 1998

Keywords
VACTEL Association; VACTERL Association; VACTERL Syndrome; VATER Association; VATER Connection, Inc.

2253 **Velo-Cardio-Facial Syndrome Educational Foundation**
P.O. Box 874
Milltown, NJ 08850

Phone: (866) 823-7335
E-mail: info@vcfsef.org
http://www.vcfsef.org

The Velo-Cardio-Facial Syndrome Educational Foundation is a national, not-for-profit, self-help organization dedicated to providing information and support to individuals affected by velo-cardio-facial syndrome, their families, physicians and other caregivers. VCFS — also known as the Shprintzen syndrome, and DiGeorge sequence — is caused by the deletion of a small segment of the long arm of chromosome 22 (specified as 22q11.2 deletion), and is one of the most common genetic disorders in humans. Velo-cardio-facial syndrome is characterized by cleft palate, heart abnormalities, learning disabilities, and over 180 other clinical findings. The foundation is committed to offering family programs, providing parent-to-parent networking, distributing educational materials about velo-cardio-facial syndrome, publishing a periodic information newsletter, and hosting an annual conference for the lay and professional members.

President: Nancy Robbins
Executive Director: Karen J. Golding-Kushner
Year Established: 1993
Acronym: VCFSEF, Inc

Keywords
22Q11; Chromosome 22; Cleft Palate; DiGeorge Syndrome; Shprintzen Syndrome; VCF; VCF Syndrome; VCFS; VCFSEF; Velo-Cardio-Facial; Velo-Cardio-Facial Syndrome Educational Foundation; Velocardiofacial Syndrome

---

2254 **Vestibular Disorders Association (VEDA)**
P.O. Box 13305
Portland, OR 97213

Phone: (503) 229-7705
Fax: (503) 229-8064
Toll Free: (800) 837-8428
E-mail: veda@vestibular.org
http://www.vestibular.org

The Vestibular Disorders Association is a national, not-for-profit organization dedicated to providing informational services and support to people with dizziness, balance disorders and related hearing problems. Established in 1983, the association provides educational materials about vestibular disorders and related topics, supports a network for people with dizziness and balance disorders, and engages in public and professional education. The association's quarterly newsletter provides current information about medical diagnosis, treatment, and research as well as tips on diet, exercise, safety, stress, and other issues that are important to people with vestibular disorders. Educational materials are available as short and longer documents (including books), videotapes and some Spanish documents. Lists of specialists for each state of the U.S. are also available.

President: Ann Katz, PT
Executive Director: Lisa Haven, PhD
Year Established: 1983
Acronym: VEDA

Keywords
Balance Disorders; Dizziness; Hearing Disorders; Inner Ear Disorders; Mal de Debarquement; Meniere Disease; Nystagmus, Benign Paroxysmal Positional; Tinnitus; VEDA; Vestibular Disorders; Vestibular Disorders Association; Vestibular Disorders Association (VEDA)

2255   VHL Family Alliance

171 Clinton Road
Brookline, MA 02445-5815

Phone: (617) 277-5667
Fax: (858) 712-8712
Toll Free: (800) 767-4845
E-mail: info@vhl.org
http://www.vhl.org

The VHL Family Alliance is a voluntary, not-for-profit organization dedicated to improving diagnosis, treatment, and quality of life for individuals and families affected by von Hippel-Lindau disease (VHL). VHL is an inherited multisystem disorder characterized by the abnormal growth of blood vessels (angiomatosis) in certain areas of the body, such as the retinas, the brain, the spinal cord, and/or the adrenal glands. Established in 1993, the alliance is committed to distributing current information about VHL to affected individuals, family members, and physicians; promoting research studies and providing research grants; maintaining a VHL tissue bank; and enabling affected individuals to exchange information, resources, and mutual support through its networking programs. The alliance also helps establish standards for clinics that specialize in the diagnosis and treatment of VHL and provides referrals to designated clinical care centers in the United States and around the world. In addition, it offers telephone support, engages in patient and family advocacy, and assists in the development of local chapters. The organization provides a variety of educational materials in several languages.

President: Joyce Wilcox Graff
Year Established: 1993
Acronym: VHLFA

Keywords
Adrenal Glands; Advocacy; Angioma; Arabic; Brain; Cancer; Carcinoma, Renal Cell; Chinese; Croatian; Danish; Dutch; Endolymphatic Sac Tumor ELST; Epididymal Cysts; French; German; Hemangioblastoma; Italian; Japanese; Networking; Norwegian; Pancreatic Cancer; Pancreatic Cysts; Pheochromcytoma; Polish; Portuguese; Spinal Cord; Tissue Bank; Tumors; VHL; VHL Family Alliance; VHLFA; Von Hippel Lindau Disease

2256   VHL Family Alliance, UK

c/o VHL Family Alliance (US)
171 Clinton Road
Brookline, MA 02445-5815

Phone: +44 (0) 1204-886112
or +44 (0) 20 7681-1796
E-mail: uk@vhl.org
http://www.vhl.cg.co.uk *or*
http://www.vhl-europa.org (and click on British Flag)

The VHL Family Alliance provides information for families and physicians about Von Hippel-Lindau (VHL), and local self-help support groups for families affected with VHL. Von Hippel-Lindau, is a genetic condition involving the abnormal growth of blood vessels in some parts of the body, which are particularly rich in blood vessels. They are in touch with more than 14,000 affected people in 72 countries, with growth currently in Spanish-speaking countries.

President: Mary Weetman, Chairman
Executive Director: Joyce Graff
Year Established: 1993
Acronym: VHLCG or VHLFA

Keywords
UK; VHL; VHL Family Alliance, UK; Von Hippel Lindau Disease

2257   Vision World Wide, Inc.

5707 Brockton Drive
#302
Indianapolis, IN 46220-5481

Phone: (317) 254-1332
Fax: (317) 251-6588
E-mail: visionworldwide@yahoo.com
http://www.visionww.org

Vision World Wide, Inc., is an international, nonprofit organization dedicated to helping address the needs of individuals who are visually impaired. Special emphasis is given to the aging population. Established in 1995, Vision World Wide accomplishes its mission through operating an information and referral toll-free telephone number, disseminating fact sheets and brochures, and working closely with rehabilitation agency administrators, counselors, educators, researchers, and radio information services with the aim of providing a variety of services and assistance to affected individuals. The organization's materials are available in large print, on audiocassette, and on PC and Macintosh computer disks. All materials are furnished at no cost or at a substantially reduced price. The organization also provides individuals with the opportunity to network with medical professionals including optometrists, and ophthalmologists.

President: Patricia L. Price (1995 to Present)
Year Established: 1995

Keywords
Cataract Dental Syndrome; Cataracts; Glaucoma; Keratitis; Macular Degeneration; RP; Retinitis Pigmentosa; Retinopathy, Diabetic; Snow Blindness; Stargardt's Disease; Uveitis; Vision World Wide, Inc.

2258 Voice of the Retarded

5005 Newport Drive
Suite 108
Rolling Meadows, IL 60008

Phone: (847) 253-6020
Fax: (847) 253-6054
E-mail: vor@compuserve.com
http://www.vor.net

Voice of the Retarded (VOR) is a national, not-for-profit, voluntary organization that was founded in 1983. The organization provides information, support, and advocacy services to individuals and family members affected by mental retardation and seeks to keep public officials, legislators, and the public informed about issues that affect people with mental retardation. VOR supports alternatives in residential living and rehabilitation systems that serve the individual needs of affected individuals and their families. The organization's activities include testimony before federal, state, and local governmental officials on issues of importance to people with mental retardation; advocacy on behalf of groups and individuals in residential, community, or home settings; education on issues of concern to those with mental retardation, and cooperation and interaction with other parent organizations that share the same concerns as VOR. The Voice of the Retarded has members in all 50 states including parents, families, providers, professionals, friends, and affiliated groups. VOR's educational materials include a weekly E-mail update, a video, brochures and a quarterly newsletter.

President: Mary McTernon
Executive Director: Tamie Hopp
Year Established: 1983
Acronym: VOR

Keywords
Developmental Disability; Mentally Retarded; Residential Options; Voice of the Retarded

2259 Vulvar Pain Foundation

203 1/2 North Main Street
Suite 203
Graham, NC 27253

Phone: (336) 226-0704
Fax: (336) 226-8518
http://www.vulvarpainfoundation.org

The Vulvar Pain Foundation (VPF) is a nonprofit organization dedicated to ending the isolation of women affected by vulvar pain and related disorders. The foundation's purposes are to give hope, support, and reliable information to affected women and their families, to advance the standard of medical practice in treating vulvar pain, and to promote scientific research. Vulvar pain is characterized by persistent burning or sensitivity of vulvar skin that is not caused by identifiable infection. Women with vulvar pain may experience various physical symptoms ranging from itching, stinging, burning, and shooting pains to hypersensitivity and sensations of dryness or swelling anywhere in the vulvar skin. Established in 1992, the Vulvar Pain Foundation currently consists of approximately 5,700 members including affected individuals and family members as well as physicians, nurses, physical therapists, researchers, biofeedback therapists, psychologists, psychiatrists, social workers, registered dietitians, health educators, and other professionals.

Executive Director: Joanne Yount
Year Established: 1992
Acronym: VPF

Keywords
Vulvar Pain; Vulvar Pain Foundation; Vulvodynia

2260 VZV Research Foundation

24 East 64th Street
Floor 5
New York, NY 10021

Phone: (212) 371-7280
Fax: (212) 838-0380
Toll Free: (800) 472-8478
E-mail: vzv@vzvfoundation.org
http://www.vzvfoundation.org

This non-profit public charity, formed in 1991, disseminates information and raises funds for research on the varicella-zoster virus, which causes chickenpox, shingles and post-herpetic neuralgia (PHN). The varicella-zoster virus first strikes individuals as chickenpox or varicella, a highly contagious disease affecting 95 percent of Americans by age 18. Later, the virus may lie dormant in nerve tissues but, in an estimated one of seven people, may reappear as shingles or herpes zoster. Complications resulting from shingles, a painful outbreak of a rash or blisters on the skin, include post-herpetic neuralgia, which can cause debilitating pain long after the shingles rash has healed. The VZV Research Foundation serves as an information resource to thousands of VZV sufferers, their families, and their physicians. It also sponsors international scientific conferences on VZV and awards research grants to study various aspects of the disease.

President: Louis R. Gary
Year Established: 1991
Acronym: VZV Research Foundation

Keywords
Chickenpox; Herpes Zoster; Neuralgia, Post Herpetic; Neuralgia, Postherpetic; Shingles; Varicella Zoster; VZV Research Foundation

2261 WE MOVE (Worldwide Education and Awareness for Movement Disorders)
204 West 84th Street
New York, NY 10024

Phone: (212) 875-8312
Fax: (212) 875-8389
E-mail: wemove@wemove.org
http://www.wemove.org

WE MOVE (Worldwide Education and Awareness for Movement Disorders) is an international, not-for-profit, organization dedicated to promoting awareness of neurological movement disorders for the purpose of early diagnosis, appropriate treatment, and patient support. As a continuing education provider, one of WE MOVE's primary focuses is to educate healthcare professionals about movement disorders and to provide accurate, up-to-date information for patients. To that end, the organization maintains a web site with both patient-directed and physician-directed information. It also creates educational programs and produces practice tools and teaching materials designed for neurologists, family practitioners, physical therapists, physiatrists, pediatricians and other healthcare workers. With web chats, printed materials, a research newsletter, online continuing medical education, support group listings, and meeting calendars, WE MOVE provides a range of services for members of the movement disorder community.

Executive Director: Judith Blazer, M.S.
Year Established: 1991

Keywords
Ataxia Telangiectasia; Ataxia, Friedreich's; Ataxia, Hereditary; Ataxia, Marie's; Atrophy, Multiple System; Blepharospasm, Benign Essential; Cerebral Palsy; Chorea; Chorea, Sydenham's; Dysphonia, Chronic Spasmodic; Dystonia; Dystonia, Torsion; Huntington's Disease; Myoclonus; Neurological Movement Disorders; Parkinson's Disease; Progressive Supranuclear Palsy; Restless Legs Syndrome; Shy-Drager Syndrome; Spasmodic Dysphonia; Spasmodic Torticollis; Spasticity; Tardive Dyskinesia; Tardive Dystonia; Tics; Torticollis; Tourette Syndrome; Tremor; WE MOVE; WE MOVE (Worldwide Education and Awareness for Movement Disorders); Wilson's Disease; Worldwide Education and Awareness for Movement Disorders

2262 Weaver Syndrome Network
4357 153rd Avenue SE
Belluvue, WA 98006

Phone: (425) 747-5382
Fax: (425) 235-6225
E-mail: dpmayer@msn.com

The Weaver Syndrome Network is a voluntary advocacy organization dedicated to providing support and information to families and caregivers of individuals with Weaver syndrome. This is a rare disorder characterized by faster than normal physical growth and bone development, distinct facial abnormalities, and developmental delays. Established in 1995, as support for families with children having Weaver syndrome, the Weaver Syndrome Network is a grassroots organization committed to establishing a network for affected individuals and developing comprehensive information on treatment options. The group also makes recommendations for optimal education and physical and social development are also made by the group. The organization supports ongoing medical research to determine the underlying cause of Weaver syndrome.

President: Patty Mayer and Jane Croteau
Year Established: 1995

Keywords
Support for Families with Children Having Weaver Syndrome; Weaver Smith Syndrome; Weaver Syndrome; Weaver Syndrome Network

2263 Wegener's Granulomatosis Association

P.O. Box 28660
Kansas City, MO 64188-8660

Phone: (816) 436-8211
Fax: (816) 436-8211
Toll Free: (800) 277-9474
E-mail: wga@wgassociation.org
http://www.wgassociation.org

The Wegener's Granulomatosis Association (formerly Wegener's Granulomatosis Support Group, Inc. International) is a voluntary, not-for-profit, self-help organization dedicated to providing information on Wegener's granulomatosis; helping affected families understand the nature of the disease; and raising public awareness. Wegener's granulomatosis is a rare multisystem disorder characterized by inflammation of the walls of blood vessels, the formation of tumor-like masses or nodules in air passages, generalized inflammation of the kidney (glomerulonephritis), and associated symptoms and findings. Established in 1986, the group has several chapters and approximately 5,000 members. The organization engages in patient and family advocacy; operates a toll-free hotline; conducts national seminars; and provides a variety of informational materials including a bimonthly newsletter, a clinical information packet, videotapes, and DVD's. The WGA also funds research into the cause, cure and treatment of Wegener's.

President: Dianne Shaw
Executive Director: Joyce A. Kullman
Year Established: 1986
Acronym: WGA

Keywords
Granulomatosis, Wegener's; Wegener's Granulomatosis Association; Wegener's Granulomatosis Support Group, Inc. (International)

2264 Wheelchairnet

5044 Forbes Tower
University of Pittsburgh
Pittsburgh, PA 15260

Phone: (412) 383-6596
Fax: (412) 383-6597
TDD: (412) 383-6598
E-mail: wheelchairnet@shrs.pitt.edu
http://www.wheelchairnet.org

The WheelchairNet web site is a project of the Rehabilitation Engineering Research Center on Wheeled Mobility of the University of Pittsburgh. It was created with a grant from the National Institute on Disability and Rehabilitation Research of the U.S. Department of Education. The site is intended for people who use wheelchairs, members of their families, clinicians who prescribe or provide wheelchairs, researchers who are interested in improving wheelchair technology, health insurers who provide payment for wheelchair products, and all others who have an interest in wheelchair design.

President: Mary Ellen Buning, PhD, OTR/L, ATP
Year Established: 1997

Keywords
Rehabilitation Facilities (Various); Wheelchairnet

2265 Wide Smiles

P.O. Box 5153
Stockton, CA 95205-0153

Phone: (209) 942-2812
Fax: (209) 464-1497
E-mail: JoSmiles@yahoo.com
http://www.widesmiles.org

Wide Smiles is a not-for-profit organization dedicated to providing support, networking, and information for families and individuals dealing with issues of cleft lip and palate. Incomplete closure of the roof of the mouth (cleft palate) and/or the presence of an abnormal groove in the upper lip (cleft lip) are considered among the most common facial birth defects. Approximately one child in 700 is born with a cleft. Wide Smiles offers networking services to affected family members; provides referrals to physicians and clinics that specialize in clefting; has a cleft lip and cleft palate research registry; offers a variety of educational materials on all aspects of clefting; provides supportive materials; and has a regular magazine entitled "Wide Smiles Quarterly."

President: Joanne Green (Director) (1991 to Present)
Executive Director: Same as above.
Year Established: 1991
Acronym: WS

Keywords
Amniotic Banding Syndrome; Catel Manzke Syndrome; Cerebrocostomandibular Syndrome; Chromosome 4, Monosomy Distal 4q; Cleft; Cleft Charms; Cleft Lip; Cleft Palate; Cleft Strong; Cleft Talk; Clefting Syndromes; Craniofacial Anomalies; Diastrophic Dysplasia; Frontofacionasal Dysplasia; IRF6 Related

Disorders; Lippy; Networking; Orocraniodigital Syndrome; Pierre Robin Sequence; Pierre Robin Syndrome; Registry; Wide Smiles; WS

2266 Williams Syndrome Association

570 Kirts Boulevard
Troy, MI 48084

Phone: (248) 244-2229
Fax: (248) 244-2230
Toll Free: (800) 806-1871
E-mail: info@williams-syndrome.org
http://www.williams-syndrome.org

The Williams Syndrome Association is a national, voluntary, not-for-profit organization dedicated to improving the lives of individuals with Williams syndrome, a rare congenital disorder characterized by heart and blood vessel abnormalities, developmental delays, characteristic facial features, and/or additional abnormalities. Established in 1983, the association is committed to locating affected individuals and their families, and disseminating current medical and educational information to families, professionals, and the public. In addition, it seeks to increase professional awareness of, and interest in, Williams syndrome and supports ongoing research into the educational, behavioral, social, and medical aspects of the disorder. The Williams Syndrome Association engages in patient and family advocacy; provides appropriate referrals including support groups; and holds annual regional conferences, social gatherings, and biennial conventions.

President: William Palmer (Since 2004)
Executive Director: Terry Monkaba
Year Established: 1983
Acronym: WSA

Keywords
Advocacy; Beuren Syndrome; Chromosome 7 Abnormalities; Elastin Deletion; Hypercalcemia Syndrome, Early with Elfin Facies; Hypercalcemia, Supravalvar Aortic Stenosis; Williams Beuren Syndrome; Williams Syndrome; Williams Syndrome Association; WMS; WSA

2267 Williams Syndrome Foundation

161 High Street
Tonbridge, TN9 1BX, United Kingdom

Phone: +44 (0) 1732-36-5152
Fax: +44 (0) 1732-36-0178
E-mail: John.nelson-wsfoundation@btinternet.com
http://www.williams-syndrome.org.uk

The Williams Syndrome Foundation is a national registered charity in the United Kingdom. It offers networking and support to families affected by Williams syndrome, a rare genetic disorder characterized by growth delays before and after birth, varying levels of mental deficiency, and distinctive facial abnormalities. The foundation provides educational materials, including a newsletter published twice a year.

Year Established: 1980

Keywords
Hypercalcaemia, Infantile; Infantile Hypercalcaemia Foundation; Williams Syndrome; Williams Syndrome Foundation

2268 Wilson's Disease Association International

1802 Brookside Drive
Wooster, OH 44691

Fax: (330) 264-0974
Toll Free: (800) 264-1450
TDD: (540) 743-1415
E-mail: info@wilsondisease.org
http://www.wilsonsdisease.org

The Wilson's Disease Association is a voluntary, self-help, not-for-profit organization dedicated to providing information and support to people with Wilson's disease, a rare inherited disorder of copper metabolism in which copper abnormally accumulates in the liver and is slowly released into other tissues and organs of the body. As this disorder progresses, abnormal copper accumulation may cause liver disease such as inflammation of the liver (hepatitis) and cirrhosis; diminished kidney function; and abnormalities of brain function resulting in muscle rigidity, tremors, speech difficulties, impaired memory and judgment, multiple psychiatric symptoms which often include aggressiveness, hostility, inappropriate behavior, poor school and work performance and distinct personality changes (dementia). The Wilson's Disease Association makes referrals to physicians for appropriate diagnosis and treatment, to genetic counseling, and to support groups. The association also engages in patient and professional education; promotes public awareness of Wilson's disease; conducts annual conferences; and offers educational and support information through its database, directory, regular newsletter, and brochures.

President: Mary Graper
Executive Director: Kimberly Symonds
Year Established: 1982

Keywords
Wilson's Disease; Wilson's Disease Association; Wilson's Disease Association International

2269 Wolf-Hirschhorn Syndrome Support Group

1 Hawthorne Villas
Holmes Chapel
Crewe, CW4 7AR, United Kingdom

Phone: +44 (0) 1477-54-9465
E-mail: whs@webk.co.uk
http://www.whs.webk.co.uk/

The Wolf-Hirschhorn Syndrome Support Group is a not-for-profit, self-help organization in the United Kingdom dedicated to gathering and disseminating information about Wolf-Hirschhorn syndrome and enabling parents of affected children to exchange information, support, and resources through its parent networking program. Wolf-Hirschhorn syndrome, a rare chromosomal disorder caused by a partial deletion of the short arm (p) of chromosome 4, is characterized by widely set eyes, an abnormally small head, cleft palate, low-set ears, undescended testicles in affected males, and/or mental and/or psychomotor retardation. Established in 1986, the group coordinates fund-raising activities; acts as a contact point for physicians and other healthcare professionals who are conducting research into the disorder; and provides information on the disorder to affected families, healthcare professionals, and other interested individuals. The group provides a variety of educational and support materials through its database, directory, regular newsletter, reports, and brochures.

President: Christine Violet Hilder (1986-Present)
Executive Director: Christine Voilet Hilder
Year Established: 1986

Keywords
Chromosome 4p Minus Syndrome; WHS; Wolf Hirschhorn Syndrome; Wolf Syndrome; Wolf-Hirschhorn Syndrome Support Group

2270 World Arnold Chiari Malformation Association

31 Newtown Woods Road
Newtown Square, PA 19073

Phone: (610) 353-4737
E-mail: internautbhm2@comcast.net
http://www.wacma.com

The World Arnold Chiari Malformation Association (WACMA) is committed to providing support, current information, and understanding to those affected by the Arnold Chiari malformation and syringomyelia. Arnold-Chiari malformation is a rare malformation of the brain that is present at birth and results in a broad range of symptoms. Syringomyelia is a neurological disorder characterized by a fluid-filled cavity within the spinal cord that, for unknown reasons, often expands during adolescence or the young adult years. Established in 1996, the WACMA seeks to raise awareness of these disorders, and their impact on the lives of those who are affected, among the medical community. With help from its members, the WACMA hopes to be able to further research into the symptoms, diagnosis, treatment, and outcomes related to Arnold Chiari malformation and syringomyelia.

President: Bernard H. Mayer
Executive Director: Chip Vierow (Webmaster)
Year Established: 1996
Acronym: WACMA

Keywords
World Arnold Chiari Malformation Association; World Arnold Chiari Malformation Association (WACMA)

2271 World Federation for Mental Health

2001 N. Beauregard
Suite 950
Alexandria, VA 22311

Phone: (703) 838-7525
Fax: (703) 519-7648
E-mail: info@wfmh.com
http://www.wfmh.org

The World Federation for Mental Health (WFMH) is an international, not-for-profit advocacy organization founded in 1948 to advance, the prevention of mental and emotional disorders, the proper treatment and care of those with such disorders, and the promotion of mental health. The federation's objectives include improving the quality of mental health services, reducing the stigma associated with mental and emotional disorders, and protecting the human rights of individuals defined as mentally ill. The Federation works to achieve its mission and goals through research conducted at collaborating centers associated with major universities, public education programs such as World Mental Health Day, consultation to the United Nations (UN) and its specialized agencies, and development of a regional structure for organization project work at the community level.

President: Mrs. Shona Sturgeon
Executive Director: Preston J. Garrison (Secretary General/CEO
Year Established: 1948
Acronym: WFMH

Keywords
World Federation for Mental Health

2272   World Federation of Hemophilia

1425 Rene Levesque Boulevard West
Suite 1010
Montreal
Quebec, H3G 1T7, Canada

Phone: (514) -87-5-79
Fax: (514) -87-5-89
E-mail: wfh@wfh.org
http://www.wfh.org

The World Federation of Hemophilia is an international, not-for-profit organization in Canada that was founded in 1963 to promote the care of individuals with hemophilia throughout the world. Hemophilia is a group of hereditary bleeding disorders characterized by deficiency of one of the blood factors necessary for blood clotting (coagulation). Affected individuals may experience bleeding episodes that occur for no apparent reason or due to surgery, dental extractions, or injuries. Recurring bleeding into the joints and muscles may cause painful inflammation of the joints (arthritis) and associated deformities. The WFH focuses its activities in healthcare development programs, humanitarian aid, data collection, public affairs, international congresses, and publications.

President: Mark Skinner
Executive Director: Miklos Fulop
Year Established: 1963
Acronym: WFH

Keywords
Articular Bleeding; Bleeding Disorders; Centre Twinning Programme; Cryoprecipitate; DDAVP; Desmo-

pressin; Factor IX Deficiency; Factor XIII Deficiency; Hemarthrosis; Hemophilia; Hemophilia Carriers; Inhibitors; Plasma Derived; Recombinant Concentrates; Von Willebrand Disease; World Federation of Hemophilia

2273   World Life Foundation

P.O. Box 571
Bedford, TX 76095

Phone: (800) 289-5433
Fax: (817) 285-0216
Toll Free: (800) 289-5433

The World Life Foundation is a voluntary, not-for-profit, domestic and international information network dedicated to supporting the study of rare metabolic disorders. Established in 1992, the foundation believes that networking among physicians, researchers, and affected individuals and families is critical to improving clinical care and the understanding of rare metabolic diseases. The foundation disseminates information to affected individuals and/or family members; assists in fulfilling the needs of affected families related to ground/air transportation to treatment centers; and publishes a regular newsletter.

President: Louis F. Baum
Executive Director: Vicki Baum (Vice President)
Year Established: 1992
Acronym: WLF

Keywords
Metabolic Disorders; World Life Foundation

2274   Worster-Drought Syndrome Support Group

10 St. Vincent Chase, Braintree, Essex CM7 9UJ UK
209-211 City Road
London, EC1V 1JN, United Kingdom

Phone: +44 (0) 207-608-8700
E-mail: national.contact@wdssg.org.uk
http://www.wdssg.org.uk

The Worster-Drought Syndrome Support Group offers support to families affected by Worster-Drought syndrome; raises awareness of this disease among health professionals and other interested individuals; and supports and promotes research. Worster-Drought syndrome is a form of cerebral palsy sometimes also known as congenital supra bulbar paresis. It is associated with a range of problems that include difficulties with chewing and swallowing, speech, and coordination. Because of the varying nature of symptoms, diagnosis is often made quite late. The syndrome is named for a physician who studied this disease in the early 1950s. Formed in 1994, the support group is based in the United Kingdom but sends information, including a newsletter, around the world.

President: Mrs. Vanessa Butt
Year Established: 1994
Acronym: WDS Support Group

Keywords
Worster-Drought Syndrome Support Group

2275 www.gcminfo.org

http://www.gcminfo.org

The Giant Cell Myocarditis Web Site (www.gcminfo.org) is dedicated to providing information on giant cell myocarditis, a rare disease that usually affects young, otherwise healthy, people. It is a rare and aggressive form of myocarditis, or inflammation of the heart muscle, with a high mortality rate. This web site provides a Frequently Asked Questions page, and encourages communication on this rare disorder, about which little has been written.

Keywords
GCM; Gcminfo; Giant Cell Myocarditis; www.gcminfo.org

2276 XLH Network Inc.
4562 Stoneledge Lane
Manlius, NY 13104

Phone: (315) 682-2659
E-mail: info@xlhnetwork.org
http://www.xlhnetwork.org

X-linked hypophosphatemia or XLH (also known as X-linked hypophosphatemic rickets, familial hypophosphatemia, familial hypophosphatemic rickets and Vitamin D-resistant rickets) is an extremely rare genetic disorder in which a child's bones do not grow and develop normally, even if normal amounts of Vitamin D are present in the diet. The XLH Network, Inc. is an emerging non-profit organization, springing from an international voluntary organization whose members are affected by, or interested in, XLH and other associated diseases. The XLH Network is dedicated to providing support, networking, and edu-

cational services to XLH patients, friends, family members, clinical practitioners, and researchers. Established in 1996, the organization maintains a web site and an associated E-mail group forum. Other services include online support, brochures and other information, and patient networking. There are approximately 500 subscribers to the mailing list. A general brochure is available in Portuguese and Spanish.

President: Joan Reed
Year Established: 1996
Acronym: XLH Network

Keywords
Familial Hypophosphatemia; Hypophosphatemic Rickets; PHEX; Rickets, Hypophosphatemic; Rickets, Vitamin D Deficiency; Vitamin D Resistant; X Linked Hypophosphatemia; XLH Network Inc.

2277 XLH Network (UK)
Elpha Green Cottage
Sparty Lea, Allendale
Northumberland, NE47 9UT, United Kingdom

Phone: 44+ (0) 1434-68-5047
Fax: +44 (0) 1434-68-5179
E-mail: Larry@XLHNetwork.org
http://www.xlhnetwork.org

The XLH Network, formed in November 1996, is an international, voluntary health organization whose members are people affected by, or interested in, X-linked hypophosphatemia (XLH). This is a genetic disease characterized by low phosphorus in the blood and bone disease (rickets) that does not get better, even when there is adequate Vitamin D in the diet and exposure to sunshine. Other names for this disorder include X-linked hypophosphatemia, X-linked hypophosphatemic rickets, familial hypophosphatemia, Vitamin D-resistant rickets (VDRR) and even genetic rickets. Its notable characteristics are bowed legs, short stature, poor teeth formation and low blood phosphorus levels. The XLH Network provides members with up-to-date information on diagnosis, treatment and research. It helps connect patients with clinicians and researchers, as well as with each other.

President: Larry Winger, Colin Steeksma
Year Established: 1996

Keywords
XLH Network (UK)

2278 X-Linked Alpha Thalassemia Family Support Network
1437 Cool Springs Drive
Mesquite, TX 75181

Phone: (972) 222-0050
E-mail: ATR-X@raredisorders.com
http://www.angelfire.com/biz2/atrx/

The X-linked Alpha Thalassemia Family Support Network is a national, self-help organization dedicated to providing information and support to individuals and families affected by X-linked alpha thalassemia mental retardation syndrome (ATR-X). This extremely rare disorder, that is fully expressed in males only, is characterized by alpha thalassemia, severe mental retardation, severe delays in the acquisition of skills requiring coordination of mental and muscular activities (psychomotor retardation), genital abnormalities, and characteristic facial abnormalities. The network engages in patient advocacy, promotes patient and general education and offers networking services.

President: David and Dayna Hughes (Contact Persons)
Executive Director: Same as above.
Year Established: 1996

Keywords
Alpha Thalassemia Mental Retardation Syndrome; Alpha Thalassemia with Hemoglobin H Inclusion; ATRX; X-Linked Alpha Thalassemia Family Support Network

2279 XP Support Group
2 Strawberry Close
Prestwood
Great Missenden, HP16 0SG, United Kingdom

Phone: +44 (0) 1494-89-0981
Fax: +44 (0) 1494-86-4439
E-mail: info@xpsupportgroup.org.uk
http://www.xpsupportgroup.org.uk

The XP Support Group provides support and encouragement to patients and families affected by xeroderma pigmentosum, a rare genetic disorder that causes extreme sensitivity to the sun's ultraviolet rays. Unless patients with XP are protected from sunlight, their skin and eyes may be severely damaged. This damage may lead to cancers of the skin and eye. The XP Support Group raises funds for XP research, gives grants for UV protective products, provides public education on the topic, and assists families to attend

Camp Sundown, a camp in New York State and it has it's own annual night time camp in February called the Owl Patrol.

President: Christopher Jardine - Chairman
Executive Director: Sandra Webb
Year Established: 1998

Keywords
Xeroderma Pigmentosum; XP; XP Support Group

2280 XP (Xeroderma Pigmentosum) Society, Inc.
437 Snydertown Road
Craryville, NY 12521

Phone: (518) 851-2612
Fax: (518) 851-2612
E-mail: xps@xps.org
http://www.xps.org

Xeroderma Pigmentosum (XP) Society, Inc., is a national, not-for-profit organization dedicated to increasing public awareness of XP and related conditions; providing direct support to individuals affected by XP and their families through information exchange and financial support; and promoting increased medical research to achieve a cure for XP. Founded in 1995, the XP Society currently has approximately 2,000 members. Xeroderma pigmentosum is a group of rare inherited skin disorders that is characterized by a heightened reaction to sunlight (photosensitivity) with skin blistering occurring after exposure to the sun. In some cases, pain and blistering may occur immediately after contact with sunlight. Acute sunburn and persistent redness or inflammation of the skin (erythema) are also early symptoms of xeroderma pigmentosum.

President: Daniel Mahar (1995 to Present)
Executive Director: Caren Mahar
Year Established: 1995
Acronym: XP Society

Keywords
Albinism; Anemia, Fanconi's; Ataxia Telangiectasia; Cockayne Syndrome; Kaposi Disease (not Kaposi Sarcoma); Lupus; Porphyria; Urticaria, Solar; Vitiligo; Xeroderma Pigmentosa; Xeroderma Pigmentosum; Xeroderma Pigmentosum Type A, I, XPA, Classical Form; Xeroderma Pigmentosum Type B, II, XPB; Xeroderma Pigmentosum Type C, III, XPC; Xeroderma Pigmentosum Type D, IV, XPD; Xeroderma Pigmen-

tosum Type F, VI, XPF; Xeroderma Pigmentosum Type G, VII, Xeroderma Pigmentosum, Dominant Type; XP; XP (Xeroderma Pigmentosum) Society, Inc.; XPG

2281   XXYY Project

P.O. Box 460265
Aurora, CO 80046-0628

Phone: (303) 400-3456
Toll Free: (888) 503-3456
E-mail: info@xxyysyndrome.org
http://www.xxyysyndrome.org

The XXYY Project is a non-profit, 501(c)3 organization founded in 1999. Its mission is to build the capacity of parents and service providers to assist males with XXYY syndrome in leading purposeful, productive lives. XXYY syndrome, also known as Klinefelter syndrome, is a genetic disorder in which the function of the testes is impaired as a result of the presence of an extra X chromosome in males. The XXYY Project offers support groups, patient networking, and patient advocacy to affected individuals and families.

President: Renee Beauregard (2003-present)
Year Established: 1999

Keywords
Children; XXYY Project

Index